ECONOMIC REPORT

OF THE
PRESIDENT

TRANSMITTED TO THE CONGRESS

MARCH 2013

TOGETHER WITH

THE ANNUAL REPORT
OF THE
COUNCIL OF ECONOMIC ADVISERS

UNITED STATES GOVERNMENT PRINTING OFFICE

WASHINGTON : 2013

For sale by the Superintendent of Documents, U.S. Government Printing Office
Internet: bookstore.gpo.gov Phone: toll free (866) 512-1800; DC area (202) 512-1800
Fax: (202) 512-2104 Mail: Stop IDCC, Washington, DC 20402-0001

ISBN 978-0-16-091737-0

C O N T E N T S

---

*For a detailed table of contents of the Council's Report, see page 11.

ECONOMIC REPORT
OF THE
PRESIDENT

ECONOMIC REPORT OF THE PRESIDENT

To the Congress of the United States:

This year's *Economic Report of the President* describes the progress we have made recovering from the worst economic crisis since the Great Depression. After years of grueling recession, our businesses have created over six million new jobs. As a nation, we now buy more American cars than we have in 5 years, and less foreign oil than we have in 20 years. Our housing market is healing, and consumers, patients, and homeowners enjoy stronger protections than ever before.

But there are still millions of Americans whose hard work and dedication have not yet been rewarded. Our economy is adding jobs, but too many of our fellow citizens still can't find full-time employment. Corporate profits have reached all-time highs, but for more than a decade, wages and incomes for working Americans have barely budged.

Our top priority must be to do everything we can to grow our economy and create good, middle-class jobs. That has to be our North Star. That has to drive every decision we make in Washington. Every day, we should ask ourselves three questions: How do we attract more jobs to our shores? How do we equip our people with the skills needed to do those jobs? And how do we make sure that hard work leads to a decent living?

We can begin by making America a magnet for new jobs and manufacturing. After shedding jobs for more than a decade, our manufacturers have added about half a million new jobs over the past 3 years. We need to accelerate that trend, by launching more manufacturing hubs that transform hard-hit regions of the country into global centers of high-tech jobs and manufacturing. We need to make our tax code more competitive, by ending tax breaks for companies that ship jobs overseas, and rewarding companies that create jobs here at home. And we need to invest in the research and technology that will allow us to harness more of our own energy and put more people back to work repairing our crumbling roads and bridges.

These steps will help entrepreneurs and small business owners expand and create new jobs. But we also need to provide every American with the skills and training they need to fill those jobs. We should start in the earliest years by offering high-quality preschool to every child in America, because we know kids in programs like these do better throughout their academic lives. We should redesign America's high schools to better prepare our students with skills that employers are looking for right now. And because taxpayers can't continue subsidizing the soaring cost of higher education, we should take affordability and value into account when determining which colleges receive certain types of Federal aid.

We also need to reward hard work and declare that no one who works full-time should have to live in poverty by raising the minimum wage so that it's a wage you can live on. And it's time to harness the talents and ingenuity of hardworking immigrants by finally passing common-sense immigration reform—continuing to strengthen border security, holding employers accountable, establishing a responsible path to earned citizenship, reuniting families, and attracting the highly-skilled entrepreneurs, engineers, and scientists that will help create jobs.

As we continue to grow our economy, we must also take further action to shrink our deficits. We don't have to choose between these two important priorities—we just have to make smart choices.

Over the last few years, both parties have worked together to reduce the deficit by more than $2.5 trillion, which puts us more than halfway towards the goal of $4 trillion in deficit reduction that economists say we need to stabilize our finances. Now we need to finish the job. But we shouldn't do it by making harsh and arbitrary cuts that jeopardize our military readiness, devastate priorities like education and energy, and cost jobs. That's not how you grow the economy. We shouldn't ask senior citizens and working families to pay down the rest of our deficit while the wealthiest are asked for nothing more. That doesn't grow our middle class.

Most Americans—Democrats, Republicans, and Independents—understand that we can't just cut our way to prosperity. That's why I have put forward a balanced approach to deficit reduction that makes responsible reforms to bring down the cost of health care for an aging generation—the single biggest driver of our long-term debt—and saves hundreds of billions of dollars by getting rid of tax loopholes and deductions for the well-off and well-connected. And we should finally pursue bipartisan, comprehensive tax reform that encourages job creation and helps bring down the deficit.

The American people don't expect their government to solve every problem. They don't expect those of us in Washington to agree on every issue. But they do expect us to put the Nation's interests before party interests. They do expect us to forge reasonable compromise where we can. Our work will not be easy. But America only moves forward when we do so together—when we accept certain obligations to one another and to future generations. That's the American story. And that's how we will write the next great chapter—together.

THE WHITE HOUSE
MARCH 2013

THE ANNUAL REPORT
OF THE
COUNCIL OF ECONOMIC ADVISERS

LETTER OF TRANSMITTAL

CouncilOfEconomicAdvisers

COUNCIL OF ECONOMIC ADVISERS

Washington, D.C., March 15, 2013

MR. PRESIDENT:

The Council of Economic Advisers herewith submits its 2013 Annual Report in accordance of the Employment Act of 1946 as amended by the Full Employment and Balanced Growth Act of 1978.

Sincerely yours,

Alan B. Krueger
Chairman

Katharine G. Abraham
Member

James H. Stock
Member

C O N T E N T S

DATA WATCH

ECONOMICS APPLICATION

CHAPTER 1

RECOVERING FROM THE PAST AND PREPARING FOR THE FUTURE

Although economics has long been called "the dismal science," it is more appropriately viewed as a "hopeful science." The right mix of economic policies and leadership can help a country to recover from a deep recession and point to the investments and reforms that will build a stronger, more stable, and more prosperous economy that works for the middle class. Conversely, government dysfunction or misguided fiscal policy can cause self-inflicted wounds to the economy. This year's *Economic Report of the President* highlights the progress that has been made in recovering from the deepest recession since the Great Depression, together with the policies that the Obama Administration is advancing to address the fundamental imbalances and threats that have built up for decades and that have created severe stress on the middle class and those striving to get into the middle class.

As President Obama embarks on a second term, the U.S. economy unquestionably stands on firmer ground than when he first took office, but more work remains to be done. Our Nation's economic recovery continued to make progress in 2012: payroll employment rose by more than 2 million, the unemployment rate fell to its lowest level in four years, new cars sold at the fastest rate since 2007, and the housing sector showed clear signs of turning a corner for the first time in more than five years. In the near term, sustaining and building upon this progress must be a priority. At the same time, the Obama Administration also remains focused on addressing a number of underlying, structural problems, many of which developed over the course of decades. Some of these problems—like stagnant middle-class incomes and excessive risk-taking in the financial sector—played a role in bringing our economy to the brink of collapse in late 2008 and early 2009. Other challenges—like the dangers of climate change and rising health care costs—could jeopardize our prosperity and security in the years ahead. Another theme that runs throughout this *Report* is that demographic changes associated with an aging population are having a profound effect on economic performance in a number of domains, from labor force participation to household consumption, as well as placing increasing pressure on the Federal budget. The Obama Administration is committed to addressing these issues, while also supporting the ongoing recovery, and in turn building an economy that is stronger, fairer and more resilient.

This *Report* reviews the progress of the ongoing economic recovery during 2012 and highlights the main goals of the President's economic agenda. These goals include strengthening the foundations of economic growth by investing in education, research, and infrastructure, and by fixing a broken immigration system through commonsense immigration reform; ensuring fairness for the middle class by reforming the tax code and health insurance system; and bolstering the economy's resilience to future challenges by addressing the dangers of climate change, moving toward energy independence, pursuing a balanced approach to deficit reduction, adding safeguards to the financial system, opening up new markets for U.S. exports, and equipping American workers to compete in the global economy.

TRACKING THE PROGRESS OF THE RECOVERY

When President Obama first entered office on January 20, 2009, the U.S. economy was in the midst of the worst downturn since the Great Depression. Real gross domestic product (GDP), the total amount of goods and services produced in the country adjusted for inflation, had just contracted at the sharpest rate in any quarter in more than 50 years, shrinking by 8.9 percent at an annual rate. This severe decline in economic output was accompanied by devastating job losses. In the year before President Obama's first inauguration, the U.S. economy lost 4.6 million private sector jobs, including 821,000 in January 2009. As bad as things were at the time, a dark cloud of uncertainty hovered over the economy, and the risk of even further deterioration was still very real. At the end of 2008, the financial system teetered on the brink of collapse and credit for businesses and households had seized up. Home prices were steadily declining, with no bottom in sight, and the fate of the American auto industry hung in the balance, as auto sales in early 2009 plunged to their lowest level in 27 years. A total of $16 trillion in wealth was erased by the financial and housing crisis, causing families to pull back on spending plans, reduce personal debt and increase savings, in turn leading companies to cut back hiring, lay off valued employees, and halt investment plans. In short, the economy was caught in a downward spiral, where consumers were pulling back because they had less income and feared job loss, businesses pulled back and reduced employment even further, and around this vicious cycle went.

Against this backdrop, the Obama Administration acted quickly and decisively to raise aggregate demand, stem the job losses, restore the flow of credit, and put the economy in a position to begin growing once again. The American Recovery and Reinvestment Act of 2009 (the Recovery Act) was the boldest measure of countercyclical fiscal stimulus in U.S. history. The Recovery Act's mix of tax cuts for individuals and businesses, aid to State and local governments, and infrastructure investment was designed to provide the economy with an immediate boost. In addition to the Recovery Act, the Obama Administration worked to stabilize the financial sector through a series of measures including stress tests for banks and rigorous requirements for banks to raise private capital and repay the government for assistance from the Troubled Asset Relief Program. The Making Home Affordable program put in place a number of initiatives that have helped millions of Americans modify or refinance their mortgages and stay in their homes. The Administration also rescued and reformed the auto industry by guiding the successful restructuring of two of America's largest automakers and preserving the critical supply network.

Soon after these steps were taken, the economy reversed course. The contraction in economic output eased in 2009 and GDP began to grow again in the third quarter of that year. The economy has now expanded for 14 consecutive quarters. Similarly, the pace of job losses slowed over the course of 2009, and the monthly change in private employment turned positive in March 2010. In recent recoveries following the end of recessions, job growth has lagged economic growth, as employers either managed to implement ways to raise labor productivity to meet demand or delayed hiring out of caution that demand would not recover. During the current recovery, sustained job growth started 9 months after GDP growth resumed, which is sooner than in the 1991 and 2001 recoveries. As shown in Figure 1-1, private employers have now increased payrolls for 35 consecutive months. The 6.1 million jobs added over this time constitute the best 35-month period of job creation since 1998–2001, more than a decade ago. In addition, some $13.5 trillion of the $16 trillion in lost wealth has been restored due to the rebounding of the equity markets and firming of house prices, although the gains in wealth have not been uniformly shared.

In 2012, the recovery continued to make progress, and the economy and American people showed their resilience in the face of several headwinds. Total nonfarm payroll employment grew by 2.2 million during the year, or roughly 181,000 jobs per month, a bit above the forecast of 167,000

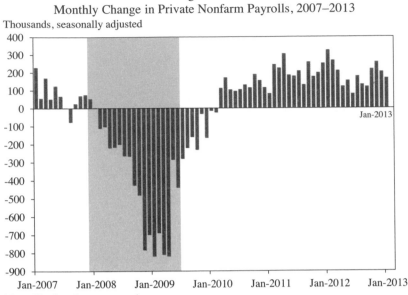

Figure 1-1
Monthly Change in Private Nonfarm Payrolls, 2007–2013

Thousands, seasonally adjusted

Jan-2013

Jan-2007   Jan-2008   Jan-2009   Jan-2010   Jan-2011   Jan-2012   Jan-2013

Note: Shading denotes recession.
Source: Bureau of Labor Statistics, Current Employment Statistics.

jobs per month that appeared in last year's *Economic Report of the President.*
The unemployment rate fell 0.7 percentage point over the course of the year
and reached its lowest level since January 2009. Almost the entire drop in the
unemployment rate resulted from increased employment rather than labor
force withdrawal. GDP expanded by 1.6 percent during the four quarters of
2012.

Although 2012 was a year of progress, it was not without challenges.
A severe drought in the Midwest subtracted from GDP growth in the second
and third quarters. Hurricane Sandy struck in late October, and based on
the latest estimates of private property damage, it was the second costliest
natural disaster in the United States during the last 40 years, behind only
Hurricane Katrina. In addition, the euro area slipped back into recession,
reflecting continued uncertainty in financial markets, further deleveraging
by households and companies, and sizable fiscal austerity measures undertaken by many European governments. The slowdown among our trading
partners in Europe and also in Asia reduced overseas demand for U.S. goods
and services. And here in the United States, the threat of scheduled tax
increases and automatic spending cuts known as the "fiscal cliff" lingered for
most of the year. The economy's performance in 2012 is reviewed in greater
detail in Chapter 2. Despite the economy's resilience during the past year,
the unemployment rate remains elevated, and more work remains to be

Figure 1-2

Real Gross Domestic Product and Trends, 1960–2012

Trillions of chained 2005 dollars, log scale

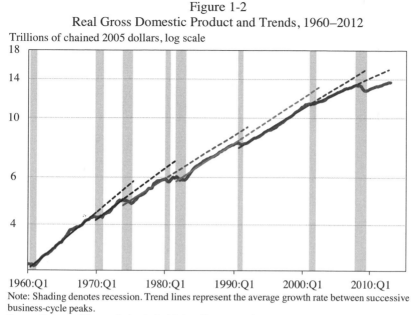

Note: Shading denotes recession. Trend lines represent the average growth rate between successive business-cycle peaks.
Source: Bureau of Economic Analysis, National Income and Product Accounts; National Bureau of Economic Research; CEA calculations.

done to boost growth and job creation. In 2013, the Administration remains focused on the need to keep moving forward, while once again avoiding the threat of self-inflicted wounds.

Placing the Recovery in Historical Context

Chapter 2 also places the recovery in broader historical context. The pattern in recoveries over the last 50 years has been that more recent recoveries tend to be marked by slower growth than the recoveries that preceded them. This tendency is documented in Figure 1-2, which shows real GDP along with trend lines based on the average growth rate between successive business-cycle peaks. The current recovery, so far, is no exception to this pattern. The single largest cause of slower trend GDP growth in recent years is changing demographics, as the rate of overall population growth moderates, the baby boomers move into retirement, and the share of the population that is of prime working age begins to decline. Productivity growth also appears to have slowed down after the 1990s, although it is unclear if the slowdown will continue.

At the same time, however, several of the factors that have restrained growth in recent years are temporary constraints that are unique to the current situation and will likely subside in the years ahead. For instance,

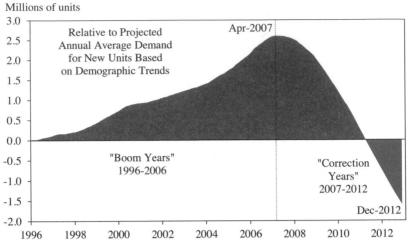

Figure 1-3
Cumulative Over- and Under-Building of Residential
and Manufactured Homes, 1996–2012

Note: The 1998 *Economic Report of the President* projected that 1.6 million new housing units per year would be needed from 1996–2006 to keep pace with demographics. Cumulative over- and under-building is measured relative to this projection.
Source: Census Bureau, New Residential Construction (completions) and Manufactured Homes Survey (placements); CEA (1998); CEA calculations.

a growing body of research has shown that recoveries following financial crises tend to be slower, because of delays in the reemergence of credit and reductions in consumer spending as households pay down debt or rebuild their savings. The Administration expects growth to quicken after households repair their balance sheets and consumers have more money to spend on goods and services. In addition, the housing sector is just now emerging from several depressed years, and much of the overbuilding that took place during the boom years has been offset by underbuilding since 2007. As Figure 1-3 shows, by the Council of Economic Advisers' (CEA) calculations, the U.S housing market has likely worked off the nationwide cumulative total of excess building that took place in the housing boom years. Consequently, activity in the housing sector is likely to return to more normal levels in the years ahead, although some regions are further ahead in this process than others.

Furthermore, despite the Administration's efforts to support State and local governments through the Recovery Act and other measures, employment in this sector has undergone an unprecedented decline. The Obama Administration will continue to look for ways to boost the hiring of teachers, police officers and firefighters, and these efforts should be helped by a broadly improving economy that eases the strain on State and local government finances. Thus, while some of the slower growth experienced in recent years is likely the unavoidable consequence of changing demography, there are still strong reasons to believe that the pace of economic growth will nonetheless pick up.

Making Progress Toward a Sustainable Fiscal Path

During 2012, the Obama Administration continued to pursue a balanced approach to fiscal policy that supports the recovery in the near term while looking to reduce the deficit and stabilize the debt over the medium and long term. The Recovery Act provided substantial support for growth in 2009 and 2010, and the economy benefited in 2011 and 2012 from extended unemployment insurance benefits and a 2 percentage point reduction in the employee contribution to the payroll tax, among other measures. At the same time, the Administration agreed to and Congress enacted $1.4 trillion in discretionary spending cuts, spread over the next decade to ease the impact on an economy that is still healing. Together with the additional revenue from the American Taxpayer Relief Act (ATRA) and interest savings, the deficit has been reduced by more than $2.5 trillion over the next 10 years. Thanks to these actions and steady economic growth, the Federal budget deficit has declined from 10.1 percent of GDP in 2009 to 7.0 percent of GDP in 2012, the largest three-year drop since 1949. The Congressional Budget Office (CBO 2013) projects that the deficit will fall to 5.3 percent of GDP in 2013. The Obama Administration has repeatedly proposed policies to bring the deficit down to below 3 percent of GDP and stabilize the national debt relative to the size of the economy in the 10-year budget window. A further discussion of the Federal budget outlook can be found in Chapter 3.

A comparison of recent economic performance in the United States with that of countries undertaking more abrupt fiscal consolidation underscores the importance of a balanced and responsible approach to return over time to a sustainable Federal budget. Figure 1-4 shows that while GDP in the United States has expanded for 14 consecutive quarters and surpassed its pre-recession peak, the recovery has faltered in places where austerity has been implemented more rapidly. President Obama has put it succinctly: "We cannot just cut our way to prosperity."

The American Taxpayer Relief Act, enacted January 2, 2013, represents an important component of the Obama Administration's approach to reducing the deficit and returning more fairness to the tax code. Before the enactment of ATRA, the Congressional Budget Office (CBO 2012a, 2012b) estimated that if the massive tax hikes and spending cuts originally scheduled to take place in 2013 had been allowed to occur, the full force of

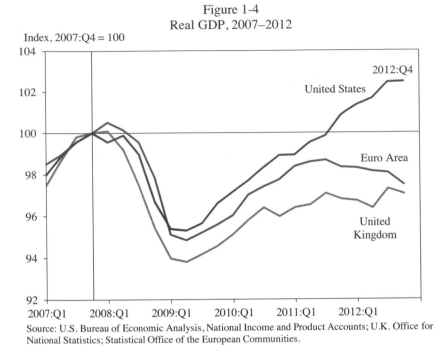

Figure 1-4
Real GDP, 2007–2012

Index, 2007:Q4 = 100

2012:Q4

United States

Euro Area

United
Kingdom

2007:Q1   2008:Q1   2009:Q1   2010:Q1   2011:Q1   2012:Q1

Source: U.S. Bureau of Economic Analysis, National Income and Product Accounts; U.K. Office for
National Statistics; Statistical Office of the European Communities.

these austerity measures, equivalent in dollar terms to roughly 4 percent of GDP, would have caused the unemployment rate to rise by more than one percentage point and likely driven the economy into another recession. The Council of Economic Advisers (CEA 2012) projected that if tax rates rose for middle-class families earning less than $250,000 a year as was planned under then-current law, U.S. consumers would have reined in their spending by nearly $200 billion in 2013. To put this in perspective, this reduction of $200 billion is approximately four times larger than the total amount that 226 million shoppers spent on the post-Thanksgiving "Black Friday" weekend in 2011, or roughly the same amount Americans spent on all the new cars and trucks sold in the United States that year. This would have been a deeply damaging self-inflicted wound to the economy.

ATRA avoided this massive fiscal retrenchment, securing permanent income tax relief for 98 percent of Americans and 97 percent of small businesses, while also asking wealthier Americans to contribute a bit more to deficit reduction. ATRA reduces the deficit by more than $700 billion over the next 10 years, largely by restoring the top marginal tax rate on upper-income households to the levels that prevailed in the 1990s and taxing these households' capital income at a 20 percent rate instead of 15 percent. At the same time, it locks in lower tax rates for the middle class permanently and extends President Obama's expansions of key tax credits that help working families pay the bills and send their children to college. Other tax credits for business investment and R&D were also extended, as was unemployment insurance for 2 million Americans who are still searching for a job. By avoiding the bulk of the tax increases that would have jeopardized the recovery while also making substantial progress on reducing the deficit, ATRA was a positive step that is representative of the balanced approach that the Administration will continue to pursue.

As this *Report* goes to press, the U.S. economy is once again confronted with the risk of a self-inflicted wound, in the form of automatic, across-the-board spending cuts known as the sequester. When originally put into place with the Budget Control Act of 2011 (BCA), these cuts were never intended to be policy, but rather to force Congress to reach agreement on a broad, long-term deficit reduction package. In the absence of such an agreement, the cuts went into effect on March 1, 2013, and threaten to slow the economy and cause hundreds of thousands of job losses if not replaced. Private economists suggest the cuts could reduce GDP growth in 2013 by around half a percentage point. This potential reduction in output is sizable, considering that most analysts expect the economy to grow around 2 to 3 percent during the year. Moreover, in the weeks and months ahead, sequestration will begin to disrupt basic functions of government on which Americans depend, from education to emergency first-response to airport security. Already, the Navy has been forced to delay the deployment of an aircraft carrier to the Persian Gulf because of the threat of the cuts. The Administration will continue to call on Congress to replace the across-the-board, indiscriminate BCA sequester with a balanced alternative that closes unfair tax loopholes, reforms entitlements, and cuts unnecessary spending. This type of approach is the best way to support the recovery in the short run, while also making progress toward returning to a sustainable budget in the long run.

While the immediate budgetary concern in 2013 is the need to replace the sequester, it is also important to remain focused on the main driver of our long-term budget challenge: the cost of health care for an aging population. One positive development, with significant implications for the economy and Federal budget if it persists, is the recent slowdown in the growth of health care spending. The rate of growth in nationwide real per capita health care expenditures has been on a downward trend since 2002, with a particularly marked slowdown over the past three years. Since 2010, health care expenditures per capita grew at essentially the same rate as GDP per capita. As shown in Figure 1-5, this development is unusual, because growth in health spending has tended to outpace overall economic growth

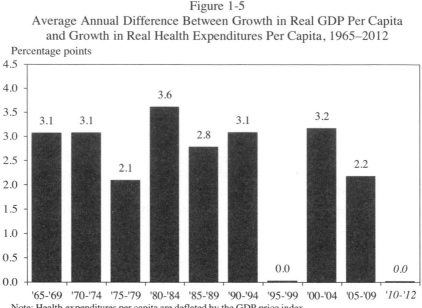

Figure 1-5
Average Annual Difference Between Growth in Real GDP Per Capita
and Growth in Real Health Expenditures Per Capita, 1965–2012

Percentage points

Note: Health expenditures per capita are deflated by the GDP price index.
Source: Bureau of Economic Analysis, National Income and Product Accounts; Centers for Medicare
and Medicaid Services, National Health Expenditure Accounts; CEA calculations.

for most of the last five decades. Although some of the narrowing of this gap
can be attributed to the effects of the recession, Chapter 5 presents evidence
that structural shifts in the health care sector are underway, spurred on in
part by the 2010 Patient Protection and Affordable Care Act (Affordable
Care Act). If the recent trends can be sustained, the resulting lower health
care costs will have a tremendously positive impact on employers, middle-
class families, and importantly, the Federal budget. Indeed, if the growth rate
of Medicare spending per beneficiary over the last five years persists into the
future, then after 75 years Medicare spending would account for only 3.8
percent of GDP, little changed from its share today, and substantially less
than what the Medicare Trustees estimate. This should not be interpreted as
a forecast but rather an indication of how sensitive long-term projections are
to the assumed rate of growth of Medicare spending per beneficiary.

In sum, the U.S. economy has come a long way over the last four
years, though more work remains. A staggering total of 8.8 million private
sector jobs were destroyed as a result of the Great Recession, but 6.1 million
jobs have been gained back. Similarly, $16 trillion in household wealth was
lost when the housing bubble burst and the economy went into recession,
but now more than $13 trillion—over 80 percent—has been regained. And
of the estimated $4 trillion in deficit reduction that many budget experts

agree is needed over the next 10 years to place the economy on a sustainable fiscal path, more than $2.5 trillion has been achieved. House prices and residential construction are on the rise, the domestic manufacturing sector is showing signs of resurgence after a decade of shedding jobs, and the U.S. auto industry is back on track, selling new cars at an increasing rate. More work remains to be done, but our Nation has come too far now to turn back.

BUILDING A STRONGER, FAIRER, MORE RESILIENT ECONOMY

While continuing to build on the progress in recovering from the recession and increasing job creation in the near term, the Obama Administration has also kept a careful focus on preparing the U.S. economy for a stronger, fairer, more resilient future. Many of the problems that caused the financial crisis and recession built up over decades, and our Nation will not have a durable economy that works for the middle class until these underlying, fundamental issues are addressed. For instance, middle-class incomes stagnated in the 2000s, and many economists have argued that households turned to credit to make up for this weak income growth. Lightly regulated—or unregulated—financial companies were all too willing to provide easy credit at nontransparent terms to meet this demand. The borrowing was unsustainable, as evidenced by the bursting of the housing bubble and the fact that outstanding household debt burdens have restrained consumer spending during the course of the recovery.

Part of the weak income growth for middle-class families can be traced to rising health care costs. By one estimate, if health care costs during the 2000s had risen at the same rate as general consumer price inflation—rather than exceeding it—the median family of four would have had an additional $5,400 in 2009 to spend on other expenses (Auerbach and Kellermann 2011). Slowing the rise in health care costs is therefore a critical part of ensuring that middle-class families can see their take-home pay start to grow consistently again.

This mix of underlying problems—stagnant middle-class incomes, excessive reliance on borrowing, and rising health care costs—motivated two of the Administration's key initiatives during the first term: the Affordable Care Act and the Dodd-Frank Wall Street Reform and Consumer Protection Act. The Affordable Care Act expands insurance coverage and puts in place meaningful reforms that will reduce the cost of medical care, ensuring that families will not be forced into bankruptcy because of an unexpected illness. The Dodd-Frank law puts an end to taxpayer-financed bailouts for big banks, restricts many of the riskiest financial practices that developed in the run-up to the crisis, and creates a new consumer watchdog to increase transparency and fairness for American families.

Strengthening the Foundations of Growth

The economy's long-run growth potential fundamentally depends on the number of workers and the productivity of those workers, which, of course, depends on the productivity of American businesses and the creativity and risk-taking of American entrepreneurs. During the second half of the 20th century, the U.S. economy benefited substantially from favorable demographics. The baby boomers were in their prime working years, and women entered the labor force in record numbers. As the size of the labor force grew more quickly during these years, so too did the economy's potential output. However, as discussed previously, population growth is expected to slow in the years ahead, and the United States is expected to undergo a dramatic demographic transition. Figure 1-6 displays the latest projections from the Census Bureau, showing that overall population growth is estimated to decline from an average of 1.2 percent per year since 1950, to just 0.7 percent per year over the next three decades. Notably, as the baby boomers move into retirement, the only major age group that will grow faster over the next 30 years than it did during the last 60 is persons aged 65 and up. As a result, the share of the population that is of prime working age will fall steadily, and the number of retirees per worker will rise. Consequently, one of the major challenges facing the U.S. economy in the decades ahead is the slowdown in potential output growth that will result from a more slowly growing population and labor force.[1]

Although the recession caused a decline in the labor force participation rate, it is important to recall that even well before the recession, the labor force participation rate showed signs that it had reached its peak in the late 1990s. This fact largely reflected the aging of the population discussed above and the plateauing of female labor force participation following four decades during which American society was transformed by an increasing number of women in the workforce. So while some discouraged workers are likely to reenter the labor force in the near term as the economy continues to heal, the long-term trend for the labor force participation rate is still likely

---

[1] Although the changing demographics of the United States are likely to have a large effect on the economy and the Federal budget in the years ahead, the challenges are even greater in other advanced countries. According to United Nations projections (UN 2011), in 2040, the ratio of persons aged 65 and older to persons aged 20–64 will be even higher in Canada, France, Germany, Italy, Japan, Korea, and the United Kingdom than it will be in the United States. The Organisation for Economic Co-operation and Development (OECD 2012) has said that the aging of populations across developed countries will be the main contributor to slower potential output growth in OECD countries in the decades ahead.

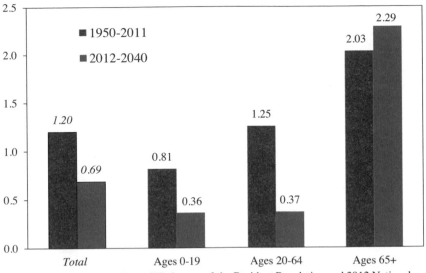

Figure 1-6
Population Growth by Age Group, 1950–2040

Average annual percent change

- 1950-2011
- 2012-2040

2.29
2.03
1.25
1.20
0.81
0.69
0.37
0.36

Total   Ages 0-19   Ages 20-64   Ages 65+

Source: Census Bureau, Annual Estimates of the Resident Population and 2012 National Population Projections; CEA calculations.

to be downward. This likelihood was acknowledged in the 2004 *Economic Report of the President*, which noted, "the long-term trend of rising participation appears to have come to an end. . . . The decline [in the labor force participation rate] may be greater, however, after 2008, which is the year that the first baby boomers (those born in 1946) reach the early-retirement age of 62."

In the face of the demographic challenges of an aging population and a more slowly growing workforce, the Administration believes it is imperative to boost the productivity of American workers by investing in education, innovation, research, and infrastructure. One way in particular to enhance the productivity of the workforce is to have a more educated workforce. As discussed in Chapter 4, the value of a college degree—as measured by the premium paid to college-educated workers—is significant. Shortly after taking office in 2009, President Obama set the goal that America would once again have the highest proportion of college-educated young people in the world by 2020. Chapter 4 details the steps the Obama Administration has taken to meet that goal, including expanding Pell Grants, establishing the American Opportunity Tax Credit, and reforming the student loan system to help make repayment more manageable for 1.6 million responsible borrowers. More recently, President Obama has called for a new Federal-State partnership that would provide all low- and moderate-income four-year-olds with high-quality preschool.

Commonsense immigration reform is another key aspect of the Administration's efforts to enhance the productivity of the American workforce, create more jobs for workers and more customers for businesses, and ease the looming demographic challenges. With a more slowly growing population and more retirees to support, the time is ripe for America to once again renew its long tradition of welcoming immigrants to our shores. Chapter 4 summarizes the economic case for reforming our immigration system to make the American economy more dynamic. Indeed, immigrants founded more than one in four new businesses in the United States in 2011 (Fairlie 2012). Moreover, commonsense immigration reform that gives undocumented immigrants a pathway to earned citizenship is needed to bring these workers out of the shadows and ensure that employers who hire only legally authorized workers and pay a decent wage are not put at a disadvantage. This type of commonsense reform strengthens the economy as a whole by maintaining competition on a level playing field. Immigrants own more than 2 million American businesses of all sizes and were critical to the creation of many of our largest companies like Yahoo! and Google. To make sure that America has a dynamic, competitive workforce and is the home of the next major innovation, it is essential to move toward an immigration system that is geared to help us grow our economy and strengthen the middle class.

Ensuring Fairness for the Middle Class

As discussed above, the American Taxpayer Relief Act was significant not just because it averted the massive tax increases and automatic spending cuts that were slated to occur at the beginning of 2013, but also because it reversed a decades-long trend of declining tax rates for the wealthiest American households. Figure 1-7 shows the average Federal (individual income plus payroll) tax rate for the top 0.1 percent of earners, as well as for the top 1 percent and the middle 20 percent. Since the mid-1990s, the average tax rate on income earned by the wealthiest Americans has trended down and was close to its historical low for most of the 2000s. Beginning in 2013, however, top earners will contribute a bit more to deficit reduction, reducing pressure to cut key investments in education, research, and infrastructure. Even with the tax changes beginning this year, the average tax rate on these high earners is still well within the lower end of its historical range.

The move toward greater fairness in the tax code is motivated by President Obama's belief that the best way to grow an economy is from the middle out, not from the top down. Over the last 30 years, the wealthiest

Figure 1-7
Average Tax Rates for Selected Income Groups
Under a Fixed Income Distribution, 1960–2013

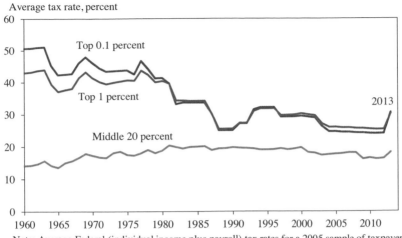

Average tax rate, percent

Note: Average Federal (individual income plus payroll) tax rates for a 2005 sample of taxpayers after adjusting for growth in the National Average Wage Index.
Source: Internal Revenue Service, Statistics of Income Public Use File; National Bureau of Economic Research, TAXSIM (preliminary for 2012 and 2013); CEA calculations.

Americans have seen their share of the nation's income increase substantially. America celebrates success, but Americans also recognize that when the middle class is squeezed and working families struggle to afford the goods and services that businesses are selling, the prosperity of the nation as a whole is jeopardized. ATRA rolls back some of the inequality that has built up since the 1980s and marks the beginning of the return to a tax code that reflects basic principles of fairness and the critical importance of the middle class to the nation's overall economic health. The Administration has proposed to raise additional revenue by closing loopholes for investment fund managers and cutting tax preferences that benefit only high-income households, as well as by making changes to the corporate tax code that would eliminate special breaks for oil and gas companies and corporate jet owners. Chapter 3 provides further detail on how the President's tax and budget policies are informed by the goal of ensuring fairness for the middle class.

In his 2013 State of the Union Address, President Obama emphasized that "our economy is stronger when we reward an honest day's work with honest wages. But today, a full-time worker making the minimum wage earns $14,500 a year. Even with the tax relief we've put in place, a family with two kids that earns the minimum wage still lives below the poverty line." For these reasons, the President proposed raising the Federal minimum wage to $9.00 an hour and indexing it to inflation thereafter. While economists have long debated the effects of the minimum wage on employment, the available evidence suggests that modest increases in the minimum wage raise the incomes of low-wage workers as a group and have little, if any, effect on employment. Doucouliagos and Stanley's (2009) careful meta-analysis of the literature concludes, "with 64 studies containing approximately 1,500 estimates, we have reason to believe that if there is some adverse employment effect from minimum-wage raises, it must be of a small and policy-irrelevant magnitude." Similarly, another literature review by Schmitt (2013) considered the most recent research published since 2000 and found, "The weight of that evidence points to little or no employment response to modest increases in the minimum wage."

In addition to being paid a wage they can live on, working families should also have some protection from the tremendous hardship that could arise in the event of an unforeseen illness or medical condition. There is a fundamental economic rationale for providing this sort of protection. As President Obama said in his second inaugural address, "The commitments we make to each other through Medicare and Medicaid and Social Security, these things do not sap our initiative, they strengthen us. They do not make us a nation of takers; they free us to take the risks that make this country great." The insurance coverage expansion and cost reduction measures contained in the Affordable Care Act are the next major steps toward ensuring that American workers have a fair shot at realizing their full potential. Already, the number of uninsured young people is falling, due to the law's requirement that health insurance plans offer dependent children coverage until age 26. In addition, millions of Americans are now receiving rebates from their health insurers as a result of the law's requirement that insurers use no more than 20 percent of premiums for profits, administrative costs, and marketing. Chapter 5 details these and other important steps that are being taken to improve our Nation's health care system, as well as the major benefits that will result for middle-class workers and families.

The President's top priority remains to make America a magnet for jobs and manufacturing in order to strengthen the middle class and promote economic growth. As discussed in Chapter 7, manufacturing has historically provided Americans with a path to the middle class, especially for less educated Americans. But as foreign competition from companies in China and elsewhere began to emerge, manufacturing work increasingly moved overseas, and millions of American jobs were lost. Manufacturing employment in the United States had been fairly stable at around 18 million jobs from 1965 to 2000, but from 2000 to 2007—before the Great Recession— manufacturing employment dropped precipitously, falling by 3.5 million jobs. Another 2.3 million manufacturing jobs were lost in the recession and its aftermath. Chapter 7 details the Administration's efforts to reverse this trend and bring manufacturing jobs back to the United States. These efforts include supporting new skills training programs for workers, investing in advanced manufacturing R&D to replenish the technology pipeline and strengthen engineering capabilities, providing tax credits for manufacturers that hire more employees in the United States, and encouraging fair trade by expanding America's global market access and leveling the playing field across nations. Many of these initiatives began during President Obama's first term and contributed to the nearly 500,000 manufacturing jobs that have been added over the last 3 years, the best period of job creation in manufacturing since the 1990s. This turnaround in manufacturing would have been inconceivable even just a few years ago, and sustaining this momentum is a key part of the Obama Administration's second-term agenda for the middle class.

Making the Economy More Resilient to Future Challenges

While the Administration works to repair the damage of the Great Recession and build an economy that works for middle-class families, it is critical that we also take steps to ensure that the economy is resilient in the face of gathering challenges. For example, although much progress has been made in moving America toward a clean energy future that does not depend on foreign oil, more work remains to be done. Chapter 6 details the scientific consensus around climate change and the dangerous consequences that could result if greenhouse gas emissions are not reduced. In addition, Chapter 6 discusses the preparatory steps being taken to avoid these harmful outcomes and ensure the economy's resiliency in the face of these risks. The Administration has increased fuel efficiency standards, launched an array of programs to encourage more efficient household energy use, and provided tax credits to companies developing renewable energy sources—all actions that will reduce greenhouse gas emissions. In 2012, net imports of petroleum products were at a 20-year low, domestic natural gas production was at an all-time high, and the use of renewable sources like wind and solar had more than doubled from 2008. These are positive steps in the right direction, and the Administration aims to continue this progress in the second term.

Chapter 8 presents the challenges and opportunities in the U.S. agricultural sector, as well as the lessons learned from the rapid productivity advances in agriculture that can be built on to raise job creation and output in other areas of the economy. In 2012, America's farmers faced the most severe drought since the 1950s but showed their resilience as net farm income for the year as a whole is estimated to have fallen just 4 percent from the record high level reached in 2011. In the years ahead, America's farmers have an especially important role to play in helping to feed a growing global population. From 2010 to 2050, the world's population is projected to rise by more than 2 billion people, and most of this increase is expected to occur in developing countries. A growing, increasingly urbanized world population will present unique challenges to the agricultural sector, as urban areas rely heavily on a stable and efficient worldwide food chain to provide nutrient-dense and diverse foods. At the same time, trade in agricultural commodities will continue to be a global endeavor in which prices respond to supply and demand conditions around the world. Chapter 8 outlines the steps the Administration is taking to build on our Nation's trade surplus in agricultural products and help farmers manage the risk of volatile prices.

Conclusion

As President Obama begins his second term, the U.S. economy is undoubtedly in a far stronger position and headed in a much better direction than it was when he first took office in January 2009, but more work remains to be done. 2012 was a year of progress, with private employers adding more than 2 million jobs and the unemployment rate falling to its lowest level in four years. While the worst of the recession is now behind us, many of its aftereffects still linger, as do a number of underlying, structural issues that built up for decades and could threaten our economy's prosperity in the years ahead. As such, the Administration's efforts in the second term will proceed along two critically important and related tracks: recovering from the past and preparing for the future.

The goals of the President's economic agenda described above—strengthening the foundations of growth, ensuring fairness for the middle class, and making the economy more resilient to future challenges—are all mutually reinforcing. America built the most prosperous economy on Earth because we recognized that investments in our individual success were inextricably linked to our success as a nation. Today, investments in research and innovation can lead to new technologies that allow for more effective, less expensive health care or cleaner sources of energy. To facilitate these new technological innovations, it is critical to have a vibrant manufacturing sector with advanced engineering capabilities. A growing manufacturing sector can also provide a path to the middle class for many American workers. And when middle-class families see their incomes rise, their increased spending on goods and services supports broad-based, sustainable economic growth—in other words, an economy that is built to last. This is just one set of examples of the synergies across the various aspects of the President's economic agenda—many more can be found in the chapters of this *Report*.

These synergies underlie the economic recovery that began during President Obama's first term and will drive the Administration's work during his second term to continue moving our economy forward.

CHAPTER 2

THE YEAR IN REVIEW AND
THE YEARS AHEAD

Following the recession that began in December 2007, the most severe since the Great Depression, the economy is healing and moving in the right direction. By the fourth quarter of 2012, real output was 2.5 percent above the level at its previous business-cycle peak in the fourth quarter of 2007. The economy has added 6.1 million private sector jobs, and 5.5 million jobs overall, since the level of employment hit bottom in February 2010. During the four quarters of 2012, real gross domestic product (GDP) increased at a moderate 1.6 percent rate. Over the 12 months of the year, 2.2 million jobs were added, and the unemployment rate, while still elevated, dropped 0.7 percentage point to 7.8 percent.

The near-term outlook is for further expansion. Consumer spending is rising moderately, as the gradual healing in the labor market lifts income and as households continue to pay off debt and rebuild wealth. A wide array of indicators suggests the housing sector is finally recovering, and the long contraction in the State and local sector appears to be coming to an end. Financial conditions continue to become more supportive; for example, senior loan officers report that banks have become more willing to lend to both small and large businesses.

Although many of the headwinds that have buffeted growth are receding, some remain. Long-term fiscal sustainability requires a path of declining government spending and rising revenue that will exert fiscal drag on the economy. In addition, ongoing congressional deliberations over the appropriate means through which long-term fiscal sustainability will be achieved foster uncertainty that could weigh on consumer and business confidence. Moreover, tepid growth across the global economy—particularly in Europe and Asia—may reduce growth in U.S. exports and slow the rebound in domestic manufacturing activity.

This chapter provides an overview of the economic recovery so far, beginning with a review of notable macroeconomic events of 2012. The chapter then turns to a broader discussion of the recovery in historical context. Although the recovery has been slow by historical standards, much—perhaps two-thirds, according to a recent study by the Congressional Budget Office (CBO 2012d)—of the slower growth relative to previous postwar recoveries reflects the long-term demographic shifts discussed in Chapter 4 as well as other long-term structural factors. The remaining one-third reflects unique cyclical factors largely related to the financial crisis, including limitations on the ability of households and small businesses to borrow, which led to associated reductions in consumption and investment; the slow recovery of the housing sector as it works off excess inventories of foreclosed and distressed properties; the contraction of State and local government budgets arising, in part, from the drop in assessed house values and property taxes; softening export demand resulting from slower growth in Asia and Europe; and limitations on conventional monetary policy due to the Federal Reserve's lowering of its main policy rate to zero percent (the "zero lower bound").

As severe as the recent recession was, the drop in real GDP in the United States as a result of the financial crisis of 2007–08 was smaller than both the average decline in other global financial crises over the past 40 years and the contraction in the aftermath of the 1929 stock market crash here in the United States. Furthermore, the recovery since June 2009 has been stronger than in most other developed economies. Active government policies helped the economy avoid an even deeper recession and have played an important role in supporting the recovery. These active policies include the American Recovery and Reinvestment Act (the Recovery Act), the temporary payroll tax cut, the extension of unemployment insurance benefits, and both standard and nonstandard monetary policy conducted by the Federal Reserve.

An Economy in Recovery: Key Events of 2012

The past year was another challenging one for an economy in the midst of a recovery from a global financial crisis. Concern over European sovereign debt and the ongoing fiscal consolidation in Europe contributed to a contraction in the European economy during the year, and growth among several of our Asian trading partners also slowed. Natural disasters such as the severe drought in the Midwest and Hurricane Sandy in the Northeast impaired economic output over much of the year. Although the economic sanctions against Iran do not appear responsible (Box 2-1), retail gasoline prices fluctuated widely over the course of 2012, which may have intermittently dampened economic activity. The possibility of tax increases and mandatory spending cuts that had been scheduled to take place at the beginning of 2013 loomed large as the year closed and may have hampered consumer and business sentiment.

Real GDP rose 1.6 percent over the four quarters of 2012, a bit below the pace in 2011 (quarterly figures are shown in Figure 2-1). Growth was uneven (but no more than usual) throughout the course of the year, reflecting, in part, the impact of the drought and Hurricane Sandy, as well as outsized swings in Federal defense outlays and inventory investment. Outside of these factors, business fixed investment and exports slowed notably from 2011. In contrast, personal consumption spending continued to post moderate gains, rising 1.9 percent over the four quarters of 2012, matching the rate of growth recorded in 2011. The fiscal contraction among State and local governments appears to be easing somewhat, and the residential construction sector, which turned a corner in 2011, strengthened further in 2012, growing for seven consecutive quarters for the first time since 2004–05.

The recovery in payroll employment, like that in real output, was uneven. Payrolls expanded briskly at the beginning of the year, but job growth slowed in the spring and early summer before picking up again in the late summer and fall. The fact that the worst months of the crisis occurred during the winter raises the question of whether normal seasonal adjustment procedures contributed volatility to higher frequency indicators, but that

Figure 2-1
Real GDP Growth, 2007–2012

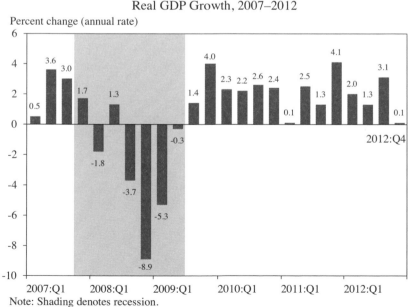

Percent change (annual rate)

Note: Shading denotes recession.
Source: Bureau of Economic Analysis, National Income and Product Accounts.

Box 2-1: Effectiveness of Iran Sanctions

In cooperation with an international coalition, the United States has established strict economic sanctions against the Islamic Republic of Iran, sanctions described by this Administration and others as "comprehensive and biting." The goal of these sanctions is to persuade the Iranian government to abandon its nuclear weapons program. Since President Obama took office, he has steadily increased unilateral and multilateral pressure on Iran because of its inability to meet its international obligations. As a part of that effort, Congress passed and the President signed the Comprehensive Iran Sanctions, Accountability, and Divestment Act of 2010, the National Defense Authorization Act for Fiscal Year 2012, and the Iran Threat Reduction and Syria Human Rights Act of 2012. These laws increased our ability to target the Iranian Central Bank, private banks supporting the Iranian regime, and—importantly— the Iranian petroleum sector. In addition to these efforts with Congress, the President has signed Executive Orders imposing additional sanctions against the Iranian energy and petrochemical sectors. These actions received support from members of the international community, including the European Union and our allies in the Middle East. The United States has also worked to establish multilateral sanctions. For example, the United States collaborated with other members of the United Nations Security Council to adopt Resolution 1929, which called on Iran to end its nuclear program and imposed the broadest multilateral sanctions ever faced by the regime.

For Iran, the consequences of the sanctions have been severe. Iranian President Mahmoud Ahmadinejad called these sanctions "the most severe and strictest sanctions ever imposed on a country." The value of Iran's currency, the rial, has dropped substantially in 2012. Governments and private firms from around the world have ended business with, and divested from, Iran, as these actions now carry a heavy price. And perhaps most importantly, oil production in Iran has nosedived (see the figure below). According to the U.S. Energy Information Administration (EIA), Iran's crude oil production, which averaged 3.7 million barrels a day in 2011, dropped to approximately 2.7 million barrels a day by the end of 2012, a decline of about 30 percent. That amounts to billions of dollars in lost revenues for the regime.

The effect of these sanctions on the U.S. economy has been minimal. The sanctions do not appear to have increased the price of oil. As shown in the figure above, while Iranian oil production has dropped, world supply has not. The effects of the sanctions are reviewed regularly; for example, Federal agencies, such as the EIA, watch closely for developments in international energy markets. The President and Congress have structured the implementation of the sanctions to minimize any impact on global energy markets and, by extension, the U.S. economy, and the authorities granted to the executive branch allow us to continue to monitor those effects going forward.

Sanctions do not always prevent or replace war. Indeed, sanctions have sometimes led to war, as shown by Lektzian and Sprecher (2007). Moreover, the fact that Iran's currency has depreciated, its oil production and exports have plunged, and its economy has slowed does not, by itself, fully answer the question: "Are the sanctions working?" The sanctions will have succeeded if and when Iran ends its nuclear program.

Evidence on the effectiveness of sanctions in other settings is mixed. In a widely-cited study, Hufbauer, Shott, and Elliott (1990) find that the rate of success of economic sanctions is low—about 35 percent. Some argue that even 35 percent is an overestimate (Pape 1997). However, Morgan, Bapat, and Krustev (2009) find that adjusting the sample of sanctions to include threats of sanctions in addition to sanctions actually imposed, and limiting the focus to more recent events, increases the success rate from 35 percent to 45 percent. The success rate is even higher when costs borne by the target are severe or when sanctions are multilateral, both of which are the case with Iran. Moreover, Marinov (2005) finds economic sanctions do tend to destabilize the governments they target, that is, they increase the probability of leadership or regime change.

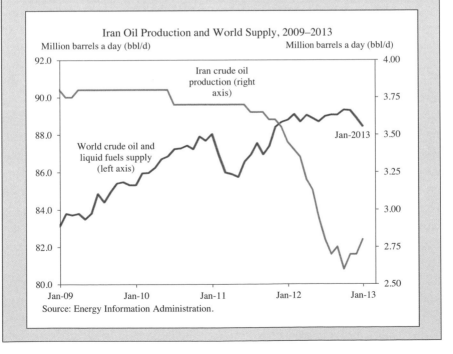

Iran Oil Production and World Supply, 2009–2013

Source: Energy Information Administration.

does not seem to be the case, as discussed in Data Watch 2-1. The unemployment rate, which fell 0.8 percentage point during 2011, fell another 0.7 percentage point during 2012, reaching 7.8 percent by the end of the year. The drop in the jobless rate during 2012 was concentrated in the first and third quarters of the year, with most—roughly 90 percent—of this decline accounted for by employment growth rather than withdrawal from the labor force.

European Crisis and the Slowdown in Global Growth

In 2012, the consequences of the European debt crisis continued to affect the world economy. In many advanced economies, fiscal consolidation, vulnerable financial systems, and market uncertainty have suppressed demand, and world economic growth has suffered as a consequence. While these adverse shocks are, for the most part, external to the United States, the globalized nature of world trade and financial markets means that the United States cannot escape their impact. Likewise, the turmoil in European financial markets led U.S. branches of foreign banks to tighten credit standards for commercial and industrial loans.

Hurricane Sandy and the Drought

Natural disasters cause human suffering and physical destruction. From the perspective of economic activity, their widespread disruptions also lead to lost work and output. Historical experience suggests, however, that over time much of this lost production is recouped. After storms, some of the missed work is made up and sizable additional expenditures are required for cleanup, repairs, and rebuilding. Thus, while hurricanes can have a major impact on regional economies, national trends in economic activity typically have not been affected by calamities such as hurricanes and droughts.

Hurricane Sandy is now estimated to have resulted in $35.8 billion in damages to private fixed assets according to the Commerce Department, which would rank it as the second costliest natural disaster in recent U.S. history after adjusting for inflation, though still well behind Hurricane Katrina in 2005. In addition, power outages that affected 8.2 million customers on October 30, and left 930,000 without power a week later, rendered many workers unable to perform their jobs. The storm also disrupted transportation centers such as seaports, airports, and rail lines, as well as refineries and factories, many of which were restored only gradually.

All told, analysts currently estimate that Hurricane Sandy lowered real GDP growth in the fourth quarter by around 0.2 to 0.5 percentage point at an annual rate. Although indicators such as industrial production, vehicle sales, and jobless claims were adversely affected in October or early

November, they subsequently improved and rebuilding activity is likely to provide some support to economic growth going forward. The region hit by Sandy has ample spare capacity available to be mobilized for storm recovery efforts: in October 2012, just before the storm hit, the unemployment rate was 0.6 percentage point higher in the five states most directly affected by Hurricane Sandy than in the rest of the country. Construction employment, in particular, had declined in the first 10 months of 2012 across these five states while seeming to have stabilized or expanded elsewhere. Supplemental Federal relief for reconstruction after Sandy, which was enacted in January 2013, should provide needed repairs and reconstruction and thereby support short-term economic growth in the region.

As a result of the severe drought in the Midwest that damaged corn and soybean harvests, farm inventory investment subtracted an average of one-fourth of a percentage point from real GDP growth in the second and third quarters of 2012 (for additional discussion, see Chapter 8). In 2013, the initial estimates of quarterly farm output will be based on the Agriculture Department's initial projection of annual farm output, which in turn will be based on an assumption of normal growing conditions. As a result, farm production, as measured in the National Income and Product Accounts, will probably jump up beginning in first quarter of 2013, bringing with it an associated bump up in estimated GDP growth.

Monetary Policy

In 2012, the Federal Open Market Committee (FOMC) continued to provide substantial policy accommodation and announced several new steps, including for the first time linking its forward guidance for the main policy interest rate to a specific level of the unemployment rate.

Between September 2011 and June 2012, the FOMC conducted the first installment of its Maturity Extension Program, widely known as Operation Twist. As first announced, the Fed said it would purchase "by the end of June 2012, $400 billion of Treasury securities with remaining maturities of 6 years to 30 years and…sell an equal amount of Treasury securities with remaining maturities of 3 years or less." According to the FOMC, the objective of this program was to "put downward pressure on longer-term interest rates" and thus provide an additional stimulus for the overall economy. In June 2012, the Committee decided to continue this program at a pace of approximately $45 billion a month, which corresponded to an additional "face value of about $267 billion by the end of December 2012," according to the minutes of the June meeting. Then, in September 2012, the FOMC announced it would further "increase policy accommodation by

Data Watch 2-1: Seasonal Adjustment in Light of the Great Recession

For the purposes of economic analysis, researchers are primarily interested in the longer-term direction of a time series and any deviations from that trend. Seasonal fluctuations in the data arising from summer holidays, seasonal shopping, and so forth can obscure these trends and deviations. As a result, most public sources of economic data endeavor to remove normal seasonal patterns from their high-frequency indicators. Unfortunately, this process of seasonally adjusting economic data is fraught with complexity. Seasonal factors cannot be directly observed and must be estimated using various statistical techniques. Moreover, the seasonal patterns for a particular series may not be constant over time. Thus, the accurate estimation of seasonal patterns is a challenge of great importance to the economics community and policymakers.

A number of analysts have argued that the severity of the Great Recession may have distorted several high-frequency economic indicators. The Great Recession, which lasted from December 2007 through June 2009, was particularly acute during the fall of 2008 and the winter of 2009. Real GDP fell more than 7 percent at an annual rate over the fourth quarter of 2008 and the first quarter of 2009, and total nonfarm payroll employment plunged by more than 4 million jobs from September 2008 to March 2009. Given the severity of the downturn during this period, some commentators have hypothesized that the outsized decline in economic activity may have been inadvertently incorporated into the seasonal factors for several key economic indicators. And as a consequence of this statistical bias in the seasonal adjustment process, these observers have raised concerns that the pace of the current recovery has exhibited an abnormal seasonal pattern in which economic activity has appeared not only substantially stronger than it really is during the fall and winter but also correspondingly weaker during the spring and summer.

A few providers of economic data have acknowledged this concern and noted that unusually sharp swings in certain indicators may not be properly accounted for by standard seasonal adjustment techniques. The Federal Reserve reported that the application of default seasonal adjustment procedures to its monthly industrial production data would have artificially raised output in many industries during the first halves of the years 2008 through 2010, if these distortions not been identified in advance and corrected (Federal Reserve Board of Governors 2011). And the Institute for Supply Management concluded that its typical seasonal adjustment procedures did not adequately identify outlier observations during the recent recession. As a result, it introduced more precise criteria for the detection of outliers as part of the seasonal adjustment of its purchasing manager survey data (Institute for Supply Management

2012). Nevertheless, it is important to emphasize that these particular issues pertain to the use of default seasonal adjustment techniques. In general, statistical agencies approach the seasonal adjustment of economic data idiosyncratically based upon the unique characteristics of each individual time series.

Indeed, detailed studies of a wide range of principal economic indicators suggest that the seasonal adjustment techniques that had already been employed by the Bureau of Labor Statistics (BLS) adequately accounted for the effects of the Great Recession. BLS analysts calculated alternative seasonal factors for total nonfarm payroll employment after manually excluding the sharp declines that were recorded during the downturn (Kropf and Hudson 2012). This counterfactual experiment failed to generate meaningful revisions to the actual published estimates of total nonfarm payroll employment since January 2010. In fact, the BLS analysts concluded that the implementation of these counterfactual seasonal factors would have revised total nonfarm payroll employment upward by a mere 24,000 jobs over the second and third quarters of 2011 (in other words, an average of 4,000 jobs a month) and downward by just 19,000 jobs over the fourth quarter of 2011 and the first quarter of 2012 (or an average of roughly 3,000 jobs a month). BLS analysts also thoroughly investigated the seasonal adjustment of the Current Population Survey data over the course of the recovery (Evans and Tiller 2012). This inquiry showed that alternative assumptions regarding seasonal adjustment did not meaningfully affect estimates of the unemployment rate since 2007.

Macroeconomic Advisers (2012) tested the stability of seasonally adjusted nominal GDP by comparing the official estimates to a proxy series that had been constructed using the source data for the national accounts. Contrary to the hypothesis that inaccuracies in the seasonal adjustment process have been artificially suppressing economic activity during the spring and summer months of the current recovery, this analysis found that seasonal factors had not been subtracting as much from GDP growth during the second and third quarters of each calendar year as they had before the downturn. All told, these analyses provide little evidence to support serious concerns over the soundness of seasonally adjusted high-frequency economic variables.

purchasing additional agency mortgage-backed securities at a pace of $40 billion per month."

The September and June actions together, the Committee said, were intended to increase the Federal Reserve's "holdings of longer-term securities by about $85 billion each month through the end of the year." In December

2012, the Committee announced that it would replace the expiring Maturity Extension Program with a program of purchases of longer-dated Treasuries at a pace of $45 billion a month, thereby further expanding its balance sheet, rather than funding these purchases with the sale of shorter-dated securities, as was the practice under Operation Twist. These purchases, combined with its September 2012 decision to purchase $40 billion a month in agency mortgage-backed securities, kept total purchases of longer-term securities at $85 billion a month.

The nature of the Fed's forward guidance also evolved over the year. The FOMC announced in September 2012 that it would explicitly condition future policy decisions on progress in the labor market and issued additional forward guidance that the Fed's main policy interest rate would likely remain low through mid-2015, an extension from late 2014 as previously announced. In December 2012, the Committee went a step further and announced that it would maintain the "exceptionally low range for the federal funds rate...at least as long as the unemployment rate remains above 6½ percent, inflation between one and two years ahead is projected to be no more than a half percentage point above the Committee's 2 percent longer-run goal, and longer-term inflation expectations continue to be well anchored." The explicit link to numerical values of economic variables replaced the previous reference to a "mid-2015" reference date that had been introduced in September.

In August 2012, during a speech at the annual Federal Reserve Bank of Kansas City Economic Symposium, Federal Reserve Chairman Ben Bernanke assessed the effectiveness of the balance sheet and forward guidance policies that had been implemented in response to the recession. Bernanke (2012a) surveyed research finding that large-scale asset purchases (LSAPs) had significantly lowered yields on long-term Treasury notes, corporate bonds, and mortgage-backed securities; reduced retail mortgage rates; and also boosted stock prices (see for example, Krishnamurthy and Vissing-Jorgenson 2011). One study by Chung and others (2012) used the Federal Reserve Board's FRB/US model of the economy and found that the early phase of the Fed's LSAPs may have raised the level of real GDP by almost 3 percent and increased private payroll employment by more than 2 million jobs, relative to what otherwise would have occurred. Although Chairman Bernanke cautioned against putting too much weight on the estimates of any particular study, he concluded that "a balanced reading of the evidence supports the conclusion that central bank securities purchases have provided meaningful support to the economic recovery while mitigating deflationary risks."

Fiscal Policy

After months of negotiations, in February 2012 Congress extended both the 2 percentage point cut in the payroll tax and the Emergency Unemployment Compensation program through the end of the year. These temporary measures, which were among the Administration's key economic priorities for 2012, had originally been put in place with the passage of the 2010 Tax Relief, Unemployment Insurance Reauthorization, and Job Creation Act. The extension through December 2012 provided critical support to American families trying to weather the various headwinds that threatened the recovery over the course of the year.

The economy faced great uncertainty as the end of calendar year 2012 approached. As a result of the confluence of various policies that had been passed in previous years, the economy faced a "fiscal cliff" of across-the-board tax hikes as the Bush-era tax cuts expired, a sharp reduction of the Alternative Minimum Tax (AMT) exemption amounts to the levels that had been in effect in 2001, the imposition of substantial spending cuts through budget sequestration, and the expiration of a number of other tax provisions. In addition, temporary measures to support the economy, including the extension of unemployment insurance benefits and the payroll tax reduction, were also set to expire. As the end-of-year deadline approached, uncertainty in financial markets ticked up, although not as much as during the August 2011 debt ceiling debate. This uncertainty was partly resolved by the passage of the American Taxpayer Relief Act by the House on January 1, 2013, averting what could have been sharply contractionary policies.[1]

Looking ahead, the American Taxpayer Relief Act—which permanently extends the middle-class tax cuts, indexes the AMT to inflation, and raises rates on the highest-income taxpayers in order to reduce the deficit relative to the previous policy baseline (see Chapter 3)—has removed much of the uncertainty about taxes facing the economy.

---

[1] Several studies suggested that going over the full fiscal cliff would likely result in a recession and substantial job losses; see for example CBO (2012a). These studies, including the CBO report, focused on cash flow effects of the fiscal cliff (revenues and spending). A growing body of literature suggests that the uncertainty created by going over the cliff would have further hurt economic activity and employment, although those channels are more difficult to quantify; see for example Bloom (2009).

Developments in 2012 and the Near-Term Outlook

Labor Market Trends

The labor market continued to heal in 2012. The private sector added 2.2 million jobs, although State and local government employment fell by 32,000, after falling by 286,000 in 2011. Private sector payroll employment has grown in each month since February 2010. Focusing on 12-month changes to abstract from monthly and seasonal volatility, the 12-month change in total nonfarm payroll employment excluding Census hiring has been smooth, hovering around 2 million jobs since the fall of 2011, as shown in Figure 2-2.

Private-sector job growth during the current recovery has been roughly comparable with that in the 1991 recovery and noticeably faster than in the 2001 recovery, as illustrated in Figure 2-3. As is typical, the recovery in hiring since 2009 lagged the recovery in output. Private nonfarm payrolls in the current recovery began growing 9 months after the business-cycle trough. By comparison, payrolls first began expanding consistently 12 months into the 1990–91 recovery, and sustained private-sector job growth in the 2001 recovery did not begin until 21 months after the official end date of the recession. Thus, although the 2007–09 recession lasted longer and led

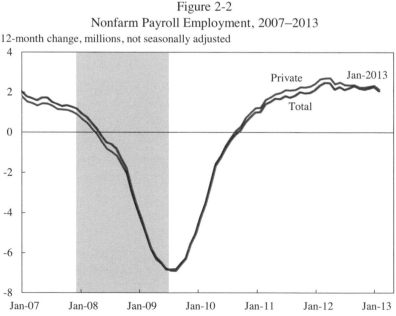

Figure 2-2
Nonfarm Payroll Employment, 2007–2013

Note: Shading denotes recession. Total excludes temporary decennial Census workers.
Source: Bureau of Labor Statistics, Current Employment Statistics.

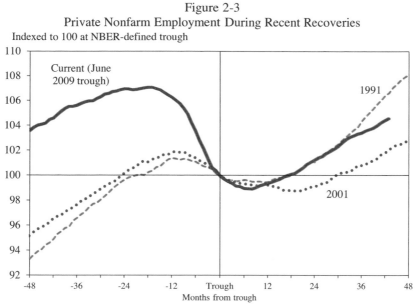

Figure 2-3
Private Nonfarm Employment During Recent Recoveries
Indexed to 100 at NBER-defined trough

Source: Bureau of Labor Statistics, Current Employment Statistics; National Bureau of Economic Research; CEA calculations.

to deeper job losses than did the recessions of 1990–91 and 2001, recovery in the labor market began somewhat sooner.

Despite continuing improvements in hiring, the unemployment rate remains elevated, reflecting both the deep losses during the recession and the steady but moderate pace of hiring during the recovery. The unemployment rate has receded from its peak of 10.0 percent in October 2009 to 7.8 percent in December 2012, with 0.7 percentage point of that decline during the 12 months of 2012 (Figure 2-4). Layoffs—as measured by the four-week average of initial claims for unemployment insurance—fell in 2012 (Figure 2-5), and other indicators of labor market adjustment such as the workweek continued to show improvement. By December 2012, the workweek had increased to 34.4 hours, recovering most of the 0.8 hour lost during the recession.[2]

Almost all of the decline in the unemployment rate in 2012 reflects growth in employment rather than labor force withdrawal.[3] Nevertheless, the recession coincided with a sharp drop in the labor force participation

[2] A lengthening of the workweek by 0.1 hour is roughly equivalent, in terms of labor input, to an increase in employment of more than 300,000 jobs.
[3] This calculation reflects an adjustment for updated Census Bureau population estimates that were incorporated into the January 2012 Current Population Survey by the Bureau of Labor Statistics (BLS). In accordance with usual practice, the BLS does not revise the official Current Population Survey estimates for earlier months to reflect the updated population values.

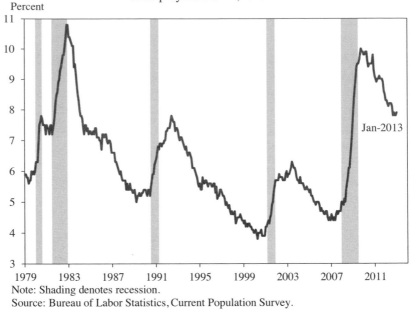

Figure 2-4
Unemployment Rate, 1979–2013

Percent

Jan-2013

Note: Shading denotes recession.
Source: Bureau of Labor Statistics, Current Population Survey.

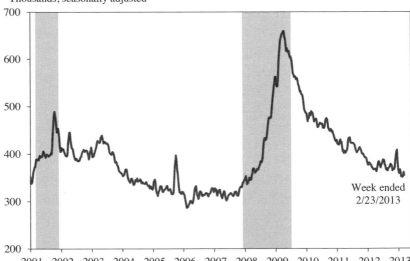

Figure 2-5
Initial Unemployment Insurance Claims, 2004–2013

Thousands, seasonally adjusted

Week ended
2/23/2013

Note: Shading denotes recession. Four-week moving average.
Source: Department of Labor, Employment and Training Administration.

rate, which fell from 66.0 percent in December 2007 to 64.9 percent in February 2010—a period when the economy shed jobs at an average rate of 320,000 a month. Since then, labor force participation has continued to decline, reaching 63.6 percent by December 2012.

To what extent can this sharp drop in the labor force participation rate be attributed to the prolonged slack in the labor market? Answering this question requires distinguishing between cyclical movements arising from the prolonged downturn and the demographic trends of an aging, and thus retiring, workforce. To this end, Table 2-1 provides a decomposition of the labor force participation rate into a trend component and a cyclical component over the current business cycle. The trend, or demographic, component from 2007–12 is estimated by extrapolating a linear trend in the labor force participation rate from the 10 years preceding 2007,[4] and the cyclical component is computed as the difference between the actual labor force participation rate and this trend.

As can be seen in the bottom half of Table 2-1, the labor force participation rate fell by 2.2 percentage points from 2007–12. Of that drop, 1.2 percentage points are attributed to a declining trend caused primarily by the aging of the workforce, while 1.0 percentage point is cyclical. An analogous calculation for 1980–85—the only other postwar period that includes a double-digit unemployment rate—shows that the labor force participation rate rose by 1.0 percentage point over the twin recessions of the early 1980s. But at that time, trend labor force participation was rising by 2.0 percentage points—a consequence primarily of the rising participation of women during that period—so the cyclical component during the early 1980s declined by 0.9 percentage point. Thus, the cyclical component of the change in the labor force participation rate during 2007–12 is close to its value over 1980–85, and so, by this measure, the recession-induced rate of labor force decline differs little from the early 1980s.

Consumption and Saving

Consumer spending, which accounts for approximately 70 percent of GDP, rose moderately in 2012, as credit conditions continued to ease, household liabilities fell relative to income, and the labor market improved. Real household consumption grew 1.9 percent during the four quarters of the year and was supported by an extension of the payroll tax cut, which first went into effect in January 2011 as part of the Tax Relief, Unemployment Insurance Reauthorization, and Job Creation Act.

---

[4] Specifically, for each gender and age group, labor force participation rates are projected using the previous 10-year trend, and the trend in the overall participation rate over the subsequent period is computed using actual population weights for each group.

Table 2-1
Labor Force Participation Rates, 1980–1985 and 2007–2012

Years	Labor Force Participation Rate, Percent		
	Year of cycle peak (actual)	Projection for five years ahead	After five years (actual)
1980–1985	63.8	65.7	64.8
2007–2012	65.9	64.6	63.7
	Decomposition of Five-Year Change, Percentage Points		
	Total	Trend	Cycle
1980–1985	1.0	2.0	-0.9
2007–2012	-2.2	-1.2	-1.0

Note: Numbers may not sum due to rounding. Based on annual averages and historically adjusted by the CEA for population controls. The projections for five years ahead are estimated by extrapolating a linear trend in age/gender-specific labor force participation rates from the 10 years preceding 1980 and 2007, respectively.
Source: Bureau of Labor Statistics, Current Population Survey; CEA calculations.

Several key developments in 2012 shaped the contours of consumer spending.

Household Income in 2012. Nominal personal income grew 5.0 percent during the four quarters of 2012, a somewhat faster pace of growth than in 2011. Growth in nominal personal income over the course of the year was largely attributable to gains in employee wages, salaries, and benefits. Real disposable personal income, which is personal income less personal taxes and adjusted for price inflation, rose 3.2 percent over the four quarters of 2012, a substantial improvement over the 2011 increase of 0.3 percent. The pattern partly reflects a moderation in inflation mostly due to a drop in energy price inflation. The expiration of the temporary payroll tax cut will subtract about $120 billion from disposable income in 2013.

Household Wealth and Saving in 2012. Households continued to rebuild their balance sheets in the aftermath of the worst economic downturn since the Great Depression. On balance, the wealth-to-income ratio, depicted in Figure 2-6, rose over the first three quarters of 2012 and has improved considerably since the beginning of 2009. Consumption as a share of disposable income tends to fluctuate with the wealth-to-income ratio. As a rule of thumb, a one dollar drop in wealth reduces annual consumer spending by two to five cents. The decline in the wealth-to-income ratio from the first quarter of 2007 to its low point in the first quarter of 2009 was equivalent to roughly 1.7 years of disposable income. Through the third quarter of 2012, this measure regained the equivalent of nearly 0.7 year of disposable income. This simple framework suggests that the household wealth lost during the recession has not yet been recovered and that this loss of wealth has left the level of consumption roughly 2 to 6 percent below

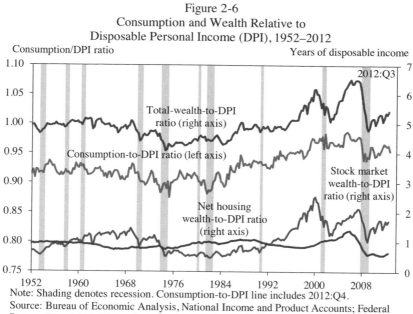

Figure 2-6
Consumption and Wealth Relative to
Disposable Personal Income (DPI), 1952–2012

Note: Shading denotes recession. Consumption-to-DPI line includes 2012:Q4.
Source: Bureau of Economic Analysis, National Income and Product Accounts; Federal
Reserve Board, Z.1; CEA calculations.

what it would have been otherwise. Much of that loss of wealth resulted from the bursting of the housing bubble, and the wealth-to-income ratio now is where it was in the mid-1990s (before the information technology stock price bubble) and early 2000s (before the housing bubble).

The personal saving rate—expressed in the National Income and Product Accounts as personal saving as a share of disposable personal income—averaged 3.9 percent in 2012, a bit lower than the rate observed in 2011. The rate of personal saving jumped during the recession as households sharply curtailed spending in response to the crisis, but overall, the saving rate fell modestly over the course of the recovery and is now at the level it was in the early 2000s.

Household Credit and Deleveraging in 2012. Lending standards for consumers, as reported in the Federal Reserve's Senior Loan Officer Opinion Survey, eased for the third consecutive year. Moreover, driven by a surge in nonrevolving lending categories (such as auto and student loans), consumer credit expanded 5.7 percent at an annual rate over the four quarters of 2012. However, because mortgage credit continued to decline, the overall level of household debt decreased 0.6 percent at an annual rate over the first three quarters of 2012. Household debt has declined every year since 2007, as households continue to deleverage.

Although household debt increased in the period before the financial crisis, the extent to which household leverage has restrained consumer spending during the recovery remains unsettled. Traditional models of consumption imply that, absent borrowing constraints, households consume a fraction of their expected lifetime wealth, which implies that the consumption-wealth ratio fluctuates around its mean (Campbell 1987; Lettau and Ludvigson 2003). This theory and its extensions imply that consumption and saving will adjust to maintain appropriate lifetime savings, so for example a loss in housing wealth will cause consumers to increase saving, as they did during and shortly after the recession, to pay down debts and rebuild retirement savings. But consumers, of course, face borrowing constraints and can be locked into mortgage or debt payment streams that might impose additional, direct limitations on consumption. Dynan (2012) and Mian, Rao, and Sufi (2012) provide evidence that these additional effects of the so-called debt overhang from the collapse in housing have further suppressed consumption during the recovery.

Whether one looks at wealth or leverage, household finances have improved substantially in recent years. From the third quarter of 2007 to the first quarter of 2009, household net worth fell by an estimated $16.1 trillion. By the third quarter of 2012, however, households had added $13.5 trillion, recovering more than 80 percent of wealth lost. Households have also made progress in reducing debt burdens. Total household debt stood at 81.4 percent of GDP in the third quarter of 2012, the lowest since 2003 and down from a peak of nearly 98 percent in 2009. Moreover, payments on mortgage and consumer debt took up about 10.6 percent of household disposable income in the third quarter of 2012, the lowest household debt service ratio since 1993.

Effect of Rising Inequality on Consumption. Some of the recent patterns in aggregate consumption behavior—including the sluggish growth in consumer spending relative to previous recoveries—may reflect the sharp rise in income inequality over the past 30 years. According to CBO (2012c), after-tax incomes of the top 1 percent of households rose by more than 155 percent from 1979 to 2009, while those of median households increased by less than 33 percent. About one-fifth of this increase in inequality is due to the declining share of income that goes to labor (Box 2-2). As discussed in the 2012 *Economic Report of the President*, some research suggests that this rise in inequality may have reduced aggregate demand, because the highest income earners typically spend a lower share of their income—at least over intermediate time horizons—than do other income groups.

Business Fixed Investment

Real business fixed investment grew 4.6 percent during the four quarters of 2012, after rising 10.2 percent in the four quarters of 2011. Both of its principal components—equipment and software investment and nonresidential structures investment—contributed to this slower growth. Investment in equipment and software slowed to 4.6 percent over the four quarters of 2012, down from robust growth of 11.4 percent in 2011. Investment in nonresidential structures increased 4.7 percent, following a 6.9 percent increase in 2011.

Within equipment and software investment, major components such as industrial equipment, transportation equipment, and information-processing equipment all posted notably slower growth in 2012 than in 2011. The relatively stable pace of GDP growth during 2011 and 2012 provided little overall stimulus to equipment investment. The slowing pattern of equipment investment growth may also partially reflect the reduced pace of bonus depreciation, which had been available at a 100 percent rate during 2011 but fell to 50 percent in 2012. (Bonus depreciation encourages investment by allowing firms to write-off equipment purchases immediately, rather than over an extended period). The American Taxpayer Relief Act (ATRA) extended the 50 percent rate through 2013.

Real investment in nonresidential structures grew 4.7 percent during the four quarters of 2012, down from 6.9 percent during 2011. Solid growth in office buildings and electric power plants was partially offset by a decline in petroleum and natural gas drilling, which followed strong growth during the preceding two years.

Despite the slower growth of business investment in 2012, the sector is poised to grow rapidly if demand accelerates because corporations have ample internal funds (Figure 2-7). Corporate profits continued to rise through the first three quarters of 2012, exceeding their pre-recession level, even as a percent of GDP, while corporate dividends remained at roughly pre-recession levels through the first three quarters of the year before spiking in the fourth quarter, before ATRA was passed. As a consequence, corporate cash flow, the sum of undistributed profits and depreciation that represents the internal funds that corporations have available for investment, has remained elevated during the recovery. Cash flow now exceeds investment, an unusual situation insofar as corporations usually have to borrow funds to finance their capital spending plans. A large portion of these investable funds has been channeled to financial investments rather than to new physical capital, as can be seen by the rising level of liquid assets held by nonfinancial corporations. Indeed, as of the third quarter of 2012, nonfinancial corporations held $1.7 trillion of liquid financial assets.

Box 2-2: Why Is the Labor Share Declining?

The "labor share" is the fraction of income that is paid to workers in wages, bonuses, and other compensation. Income of self-employed workers is also included in some definitions of labor income, as it is in the figure below. The labor share in the United States was remarkably stable in the post-war period until the early 2000s. Since then, it has dropped 5 percentage points. Because capital income is distributed more unequally than labor income, the decline in the labor share accounts for some, but not all, of the rise in inequality. CBO (2011) has estimated that 21 percent of the increase in inequality from 1979 to 2007 was accounted for by shifts between labor and other sources of income, with the remaining 79 percent accounted for by rising inequality within capital, business, or labor income. Nevertheless, the decline in the labor share has adverse implications for government revenues because wages and salaries are taxed at a higher rate than other major income sources.

The decline in the labor share is widespread across industries and across countries. An examination of the United States shows that the labor share has declined since 2000 in every major private industry except construction, although about half of the decline is attributable to manufacturing. Moreover, for 22 other developed economies (weighted by their GDP converted to dollars at current exchange rates), the labor share fell from 72 percent in 1980 to 60 percent in 2005.

Proposed explanations for the declining labor share in the United States and abroad include changes in technology, increasing globalization, changes in market structure, and the declining negotiating power of labor. Changes in technology can affect the share of income going to labor by changing the nature of the labor needed for production. More specifically, much of the investment made by firms over the past two decades has been in information technology, and some economists have suggested that information technology reduces the need for traditional types of skilled labor (Bound and Johnson 1992; Autor, Katz, and Krueger 1998). According to this argument, the labor share has fallen because traditional middle-skill work is being supplanted by computers, and the marginal product of labor has declined.

Increasing globalization also puts pressure on wages, especially wages in the production of tradable goods that can be produced in emerging market countries and some less-developed countries. These pressures on wages can lead to reductions in the labor share. Changes in market structure and in the negotiating power of labor could also lead to a declining labor share. One such change is the decline in unions and collective bargaining agreements in the United States.

These explanations are neither exhaustive nor mutually exclusive (OECD 2012). Overall, these changes have moved the distribution of income towards a winner-take-all society.

Labor Share of Nonfarm Business Income, 1947–2012

Note: "Other Developed Countries" refers to the OECD member states. The U.S. labor share includes imputed proprietor's income. The OECD labor share excludes the farm, mining, fuel, and real estate sectors, and is aggregated by the CEA on an annual basis for 22 countries using GDP weights at current exchange rates.
Source: Bureau of Labor Statistics, Productivity and Costs; OECD, Annual Indicators.

Business Inventories

Inventory investment—measured as the change in inventories from one quarter to the next—is typically an important contributor to the changes in real GDP during recessions and the early stages of recoveries. During the recession, inventories fell but by less than sales, so the ratio of inventories to sales rose; through the first two years of the recovery, inventories rose less rapidly than sales, and by the end of 2011, the inventory-sales ratio had returned to its level of the mid-2000s. With this inventory cycle behind us, real private nonfarm inventory accumulation in 2012 made only a small, slightly positive contribution to real GDP growth. Looking ahead, inventory investment is expected to make only a minor contribution to growth during 2013.

Government Outlays, Consumption, and Investment

The Federal budget deficit during fiscal year (FY) 2012—which ended on September 30, 2012—was $1.1 trillion, about $200 billion less than the

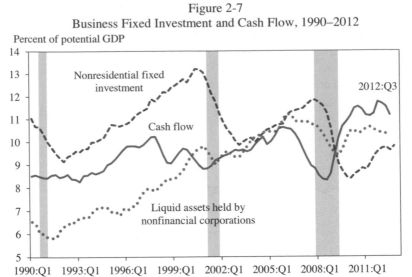

Figure 2-7
Business Fixed Investment and Cash Flow, 1990–2012

Percent of potential GDP

Note: Shading denotes recession. Potential GDP is a CBO estimate. Cash flow, from the National Income and Product Accounts, and liquid assets held by nonfinancial corporations are plotted using three-quarter moving averages. Nonresidential fixed investment line includes 2012:Q4.
Source: Bureau of Economic Analysis, National Income and Product Accounts; Federal Reserve Board, Z.1; Congressional Budget Office.

preceding year. As a share of GDP, the deficit fell to 7.0 percent in FY 2012, down from 8.7 percent in FY 2011.

As measured in the Federal unified budget, Federal receipts rose 6.4 percent in FY 2012 compared with the previous year, reflecting a 3.7 percent increase in individual income tax receipts, a 33.8 percent increase in corporate tax receipts, and a 3.2 percent increase in receipts for social insurance. The $61 billion increase in corporate tax receipts accounted for 42 percent of the rise in overall revenues. Current dollar values of individual income taxes and social insurance and retirement receipts have each risen to 97 percent of their FY 2007 levels, while corporate tax receipts were just 65 percent of their previous high.

Federal outlays declined 1.7 percent in nominal dollars in FY 2012 from FY 2011, falling from 24.1 percent of GDP to 22.8 percent of GDP. The decline in spending during the fiscal year reflected several factors, including reduced outlays on unemployment insurance, Medicaid, and defense. Specifically, fewer individuals received unemployment benefits, a temporary increase in Federal aid to states for Medicaid expired, and the number of U.S. Army personnel stationed in Afghanistan and Iraq was reduced.

During the four quarters of calendar year 2012, the National Income and Product Accounts measure of real Federal expenditures on consumption and gross investment (which does not include Federal transfers to

States and individuals) declined 2.8 percent, as a 4.9 percent decline in real defense spending more than offset a 1.5 percent increase in real nondefense spending.

The Federal deficit as a share of GDP fell for the third consecutive fiscal year in 2012. The change in this ratio is one measure of the drag on the economy imposed by fiscal consolidation, and in FY 2012, this drag was 1.7 percentage points (the difference between the deficit-GDP ratio of 8.7 percent in FY 2011 and 7.0 percent in FY 2012). Moreover, the drop in the deficit-to-GDP ratio from 10.1 percent in 2009 to 7.0 percent in 2012 is the largest 3-year decrease since 1949. Looking further ahead, policy changes to be recommended in the FY 2014 Budget will put debt as a share of the economy on a stable path and place the budget in a fiscally sustainable position in the 10-year budget window.

State and Local Governments

Although State and local governments continued to experience fiscal pressure in 2012, the long contraction in the sector finally appears to be coming to an end. State and local consumption and investment (purchases) have shown unprecedented weakness compared with previous recoveries (Figure 2-8). From the end of the recession in mid-2009 to the fourth quarter of 2012, real State and local purchases declined 6.8 percent. By contrast, during the comparable period of each of the six previous recoveries, real State

Figure 2-8
Real State and Local Government Purchases During Recoveries

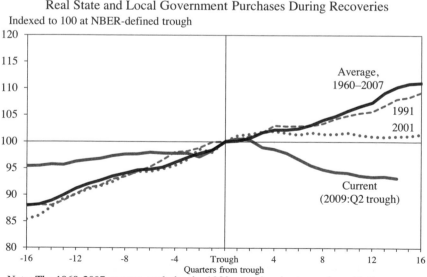

Note: The 1960-2007 average excludes the 1980 recession due to overlap with the 1981-82 recession.
Source: Bureau of Economic Analysis, National Income and Product Accounts; National Bureau of Economic Research; CEA calculations.

and local purchases posted positive growth, averaging an increase of 10.3 percent over the first three and a half years of the recovery. Nominal State and local government tax receipts increased during the first three quarters of 2012. Federal support from the Recovery Act—which helped support State and local governments during 2009 and 2010—phased out during 2011 and 2012. And while the pace of State and local government job losses eased in 2012, employment in this sector remained 724,000 jobs below its previous peak as of the end of the year, with more than 40 percent of the loss in educational services jobs.

On the revenue side, State and local tax receipts rose at an annual rate of 2.6 percent during the first three quarters of 2012, a bit below the pace during 2011. The slow recovery in State and local tax revenue reflects in part the effect of lower house prices on property tax collections. Historically, property taxes have accounted for about 30 percent of State and local government tax receipts and are critical to local governments, but property tax receipts have edged up slowly in the years after the housing bubble burst. Nationwide, property tax receipts have grown just 11.4 percent over the past five years, only slightly faster than inflation, compared with 36.0 percent growth during the preceding five year period from 2002–07. Moreover, State and local governments are still feeling the effect of the drop in house prices: because property value assessments lag behind market valuations, the effect of house prices on property tax receipts operates with a delay of about three years (Lutz 2008). Although policymakers in some states have increased the tax rate on assessed property values to partially offset declines in those values (Lutz, Molloy, and Shan 2011), local governments have still needed to adjust spending to make up for the lost revenue. Despite these difficulties, the recent upturn in house prices suggests that improvement in State and local government finances is on the horizon. In addition, revenues from sales and income taxes—which make up about 50 to 60 percent of State and local tax receipts—have also continued to recover, with income tax collections up 7.6 percent during the four quarters of 2012, and sales taxes growing 2.2 percent.

Another factor weighing on State and local government revenues has been the phase-out of the Recovery Act. After rising notably in 2009 and 2010, Federal grants-in-aid to State and local governments plunged $82.1 billion in 2011 before stabilizing during 2012. Both the earlier increase and the recent return to a lower level were largely attributable to the Recovery Act, which was designed to offer temporary support to State and local governments. The portion of Federal grants-in-aid to the States from Recovery Act programs stood at just $17.9 billion in 2012, down from a peak of more than $100 billion in 2010.

Current State and local government expenditures—which include transfers to individuals as well as government consumption—rose 2.8 percent over the four quarters of 2012, following a 0.2 percent increase in the previous year. A recent CBO report (CBO 2012b) noted that the weakness in State and local government spending relative to previous recoveries could be attributed roughly equally to three different areas: hiring of employees, purchases of goods and services, and construction spending. Despite continued spending restraint across these major components, the operating position of State and local governments deteriorated to an aggregate deficit of $140 billion by the third quarter of 2012, on pace for a fifth consecutive year of operating deficits for the sector.

State and local government employment fell 32,000 during the 12 months of 2012, a much shallower decline than the 286,000 jobs lost in 2011. Nevertheless, employment in the sector remains well below its peak in 2008. To date, the Administration has taken important steps to help State and local governments maintain critical services in public safety and education. In addition to the grants-in-aid components of the Recovery Act, the Administration established a new fund to support teaching jobs and extended the enhanced Federal matching formula for certain social services and medical insurance expenditures. In 2011, the President proposed additional resources for the teacher job fund as part of the American Jobs Act, which also would have supported the modernization of more than 35,000 schools. Although Congress did not enact this proposal, the President remains committed to supporting educators and first responders in his second term.

Real Exports and Imports

Compared with previous recessions, real exports experienced a sharper-than-usual contraction and rebound during 2007–10. This sharp cyclical decline was partly attributable to the synchronized nature of the 2007–09 contraction and recovery across nearly all countries, a collapse and rebound in commodity prices, and foreign consumers' postponement of purchases of U.S. durable goods, which account for a large share of tradable goods (Baldwin 2009). Now, with the recent slowing of world growth, real exports appear to be reverting to their historical trend (Figure 2-9), growing 1.8 percent during the four quarters of 2012, after rising 4.3 percent in 2011 and 8.8 percent in 2010. As discussed in Chapter 7, the recent slowing in export growth appears to have restrained the pace of U.S. manufacturing activity. Continued export growth will depend, in part, on healthy growth of the world economy and on exchange rates. The value of the dollar has been generally increasing since July 2011, in part reflecting increased

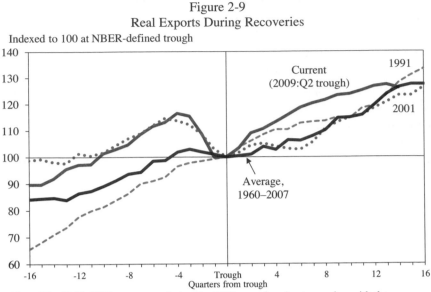

Figure 2-9
Real Exports During Recoveries

Note: The 1960-2007 average excludes the 1980 recession due to overlap with the
1981-82 recession.
Source: Bureau of Economic Analysis, National Income and Product Accounts; National
Bureau of Economic Research; CEA calculations.

international demand for U.S. Treasury bonds in a time of global financial turmoil and rapidly deteriorating global growth. Changes in the terms of trade have contributed to the weakening demand for U.S. goods abroad.

Real imports grew 0.1 percent during the four quarters of 2012, down from 10.9 percent and 3.5 percent in 2010 and 2011, respectively. A decline in imports of petroleum products offset a moderate rise in imports of nonpetroleum goods. Consistent with Houthakker and Magee (1969), the pattern in real imports parallels, but is sharper than, the general shape of the contraction and rebound in overall U.S. personal consumption spending. Because imports tend to be concentrated more in goods than is overall consumer spending, real imports move more closely with goods consumption—which is cyclically sensitive—than with total consumption. In addition, because business equipment investment includes imported capital goods, real imports track this cyclical series as well.

Shrinking exports subtracted from real GDP growth in each quarter of the worst period of the recession from the third quarter of 2008 to the first quarter of 2009, but real exports have added to real GDP in every quarter since, except for in the fourth quarter of 2012.

Housing Markets

Housing activity firmed markedly in 2012 and, although the level of activity remains low by historical standards, the recovery in the sector finally appears to be gaining momentum. On the production side, new housing starts increased to an annual rate of 900,000 units by the fourth quarter of 2012, up from an annual low of 550,000 units in 2009, and 610,000 units in 2011 (Figure 2-10). Demand for housing has also increased, with new and existing home sales reaching their highest levels of the recovery period during 2012. Similarly, inventories of unsold new homes have fallen to their lowest ever recorded level.

Following large declines from 2007 through 2011, housing prices bottomed out in early 2012, and rose 8.3 percent over the 12 months of the year, according to the CoreLogic home price index. Private sector housing experts expect house prices to appreciate at a 3.0 to 3.5 percent annual pace for the next several years. Because households have a choice between renting and owning a home, the price of new homes should increase in tandem with rental costs, at least over long periods of time. As seen in Figure 2-11, house prices increased to a level above parity with rents during the mid-2000s but descended to a level consistent with rents by the end of 2011.

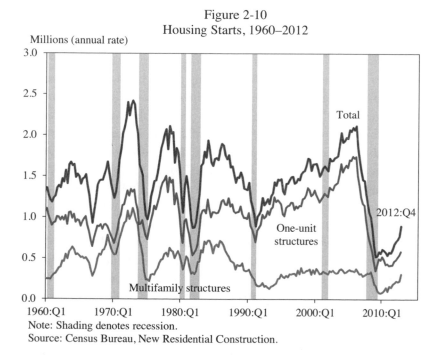

Figure 2-10
Housing Starts, 1960–2012

Note: Shading denotes recession.
Source: Census Bureau, New Residential Construction.

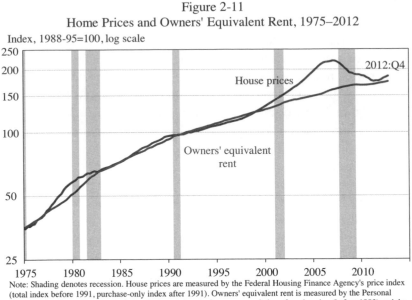

Figure 2-11
Home Prices and Owners' Equivalent Rent, 1975–2012

Index, 1988-95=100, log scale

Note: Shading denotes recession. House prices are measured by the Federal Housing Finance Agency's price index (total index before 1991, purchase-only index after 1991). Owners' equivalent rent is measured by the Personal Consumption Expenditures price index for imputed rent of owner-occupied nonfarm housing (before 1983) and the Consumer Price Index for owners' equivalent rent of residence (1983-present).
Source: Federal Housing Finance Agency, House Price Index; Bureau of Economic Analysis, National Income and Product Accounts; Bureau of Labor Statistics, Consumer Price Index; CEA calculations.

In 1998, the Council of Economic Advisers estimated that the pace of construction of new housing units and mobile homes that would be consistent with projected rates of population and household formation would be 1.64 million units a year over the 10 years from 1996 to 2006. Relative to this 1996 estimate, the subsequent 10 years through 2006 saw a period of tremendous overbuilding that led to an excess supply of 2.6 million housing units by 2007 (Figure 2-12). Since then, the very low levels of new construction effectively allowed the underlying demographics of household formation to catch up to the supply of constructed and manufactured homes nationwide by 2011, with some possible overshooting in 2012.

Although construction, sales, and prices are finally rising, progress has been impaired by the substantial stock of vacant homes and homes still in the foreclosure process; therefore, a recovery in housing starts to the annual pace of roughly 1.76 million units suggested by the demographics of household formation will likely still take several years to achieve (Masnick, McCue, and Belsky 2010). Nevertheless, sustained increases in homebuilding should provide a major impetus to economic growth over the medium term.

Several other factors also appear to be restraining the housing recovery. First, although mortgage rates are at historically low levels, approximately 22 percent of current mortgage holders were underwater (that is, the

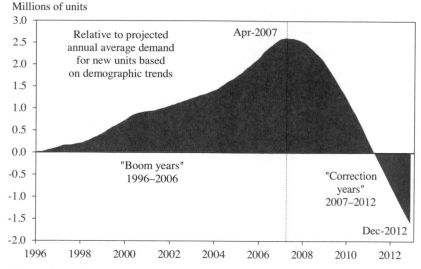

Figure 2-12
Cumulative Over- and Under-Building of Residential
and Manufactured Homes, 1996–2012

Source: Census Bureau, New Residential Construction (completions) and Manufactured
Homes Survey (placements); CEA (1998); CEA calculations.

amount owed on their mortgage exceeded the market value of their home) through the third quarter of 2012, impeding their ability to refinance or sell.

Second, although some tightening of lending standards was inevitable in the aftermath of the financial crisis, these standards have not eased by as much as expected this far into the recovery. According to the Federal Reserve Senior Loan Officer Opinion Survey, the net percentage of responding banks that have eased their standards for approving prime residential mortgage loans has been flat since the beginning of 2011, even though demand for prime residential mortgages has increased sharply. According to the April 2012 survey, which included special questions on real estate lending, more than half the lenders reported they were less likely to originate a mortgage to a borrower with a credit score of 680 today than in 2006. All told, the origination of first-lien mortgages to homebuyers now stands at its lowest level since 1995.

As the President emphasized in the State of the Union, moving forward with programs to help homeowners with strong payment histories refinance their homes will provide them with additional liquidity and will spur consumption. In addition, streamlining regulations associated with issuing new mortgages will provide creditworthy potential borrowers the opportunity to purchase homes and will further the recovery of the housing sector.

Financial Markets

Financial market conditions in the United States continued to improve, on net, in 2012, reflecting the ongoing economic recovery and the highly accommodative monetary policies undertaken by the Federal Reserve. The broad, overall improvement in financial conditions is consistent with the performance of the Standard and Poor's (S&P) 500 Composite Index, a measure of U.S. equity prices, which rose 14.4 percent over the 12 months of 2012. Measures of market volatility, such as the Chicago Board Options Exchange Market Volatility Index (also known as the VIX), were also more subdued in 2012 than they were in 2011.

Yields on 10-year Treasury notes averaged 1.7 percent in December 2012, down slightly from 2.0 percent in December 2011. For the year as a whole, the 10-year yield averaged 1.8 percent, the lowest since at least 1953 when the Federal Reserve's constant-maturity series began. Long-term interest rates in the United States were driven even lower than in 2011 by the relative safety of U.S. issues in the presence of concern over sovereign debt issues abroad and by the Federal Reserve System's program to lengthen the maturity of its holdings of U.S. government securities. With these nominal yields falling to historic lows, long-term real interest rates (that is, the nominal yield less expected inflation) also fell. Yields on Treasury Inflation-Protected Securities, an indicator of real rates, averaged negative 0.5 percent in 2012 (Figure 2-13).

Credit standards for commercial and industrial loans, as measured by the Federal Reserve Board's Senior Loan Officer Opinion Survey, have eased since the financial crisis for firms of all sizes, including small firms. Data from the Federal Deposit Insurance Corporation also suggest that the number of loans to small businesses increased in 2012, after having remained depressed through 2011. Nevertheless, the value of small-business commercial and industrial loans remains below its pre-recession level.

Wage and Price Inflation

Core consumer price inflation (the consumer price index excluding the volatile components of food and energy) was stable from 2011 to 2012, rising 1.9 percent in 2012, and down slightly from a 2.2 percent year-earlier increase (Figure 2-14). Twelve-month increases in core consumer prices have fluctuated in the fairly narrow range of 0.6 to 2.3 percent during the past three years. This relative stability is striking, given that standard Phillips curve models of inflation would predict sustained disinflationary pressure over this period because of the considerable slack in labor and product markets.

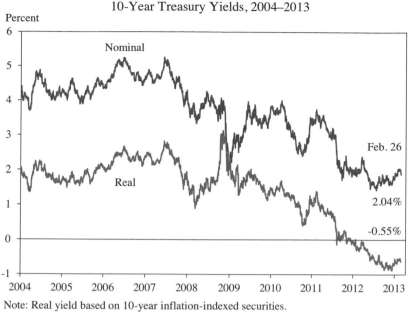

Figure 2-13
10-Year Treasury Yields, 2004–2013

Note: Real yield based on 10-year inflation-indexed securities.
Source: Federal Reserve Board, H.15.

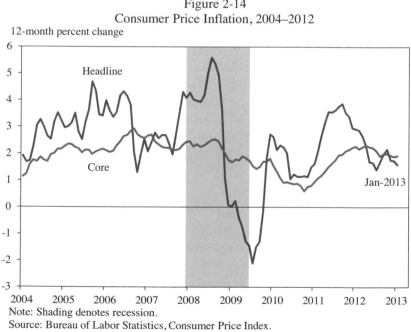

Figure 2-14
Consumer Price Inflation, 2004–2012

Note: Shading denotes recession.
Source: Bureau of Labor Statistics, Consumer Price Index.

As is usually the case, the overall, or headline, consumer price index, including food and energy prices, fluctuated more in 2012 than did core inflation. Inflation as measured by the overall consumer price index fell from 3.0 percent during the 12 months of 2011 to 1.7 percent in 2012, with the decline stemming from lower rates of food and energy inflation. Energy prices edged up only 0.5 percent during 2012, more than 6 percentage points below their 2011 pace, and food price inflation dropped 2.9 percentage points. Data Watch 2-2 discusses one of the challenges faced by statistical agencies when constructing price indexes based on statistical samples.

THE RECOVERY IN HISTORICAL PERSPECTIVE

Following the worst recession since the Great Depression, the recovery that began in the third quarter of 2009 has been a long and difficult one for many Americans. During the recession, 7.5 million jobs were lost, and real GDP fell by 4.7 percent. To date during the subsequent recovery, 4.2 million jobs have been added since June 2009, and real GDP has grown by 7.5 percent. Since the trough in employment in February 2010, the private sector has grown for 35 straight months and added over 6.1 million jobs. Real GDP growth in the United States has exceeded the cumulative growth in the euro area and the United Kingdom (Figure 1-4) as well as in Japan since the fourth quarter of 2007. Nevertheless, U.S. real GDP growth since the end of the recession has been less than the average increase in previous postwar recoveries.

From 1960 to 2007, the U.S. economy had seven recessions, and the average annual rate of growth of real GDP during the 12 quarters following those recessions was 4.2 percent. In contrast, during the 12 quarters following the trough in the second quarter of 2009, the average annual rate of growth of real GDP was 2.2 percent. After three years of recovery, the cumulative growth of real GDP was 6.3 percentage points lower than its average value for the earlier post-1960 recessions. This shortfall is depicted in Figure 2-15, which shows the paths of real GDP for the three most recent business cycles (with cyclical troughs in the first quarter of 1991, the fourth quarter of 2001, and the second quarter of 2009), along with the average path for U.S. business-cycle recoveries from 1960 through 2007. For each of the three most recent cycles, the recovery in real GDP has been slower than the 1960–2007 average. It is worth noting that the most recent recovery has been stronger than the post-2001 recovery if only private demand is considered (that is, excluding government purchases). Still, the fact remains that these three recoveries have been slower than the pre-2007 average.

Figure 2-15
Real GDP During Recoveries

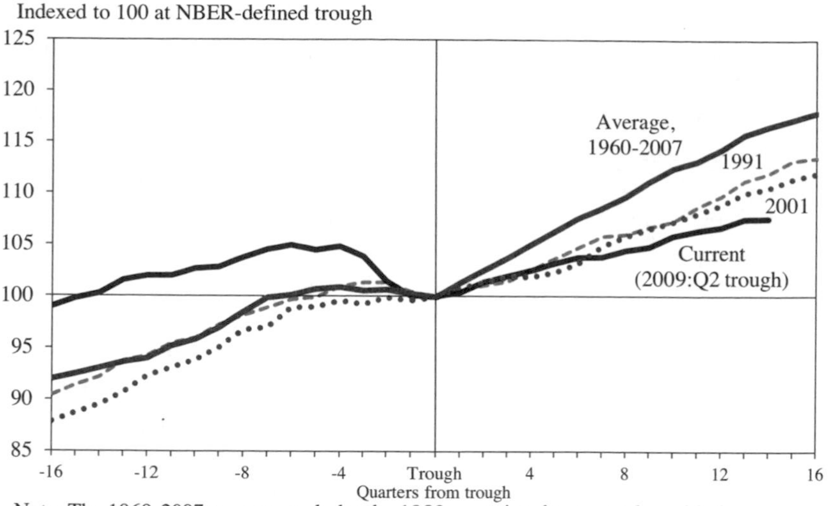

Indexed to 100 at NBER-defined trough

Note: The 1960-2007 average excludes the 1980 recession due to overlap with the 1981-82 recession.
Source: Bureau of Economic Analysis, National Income and Product Accounts; National Bureau of Economic Research; CEA calculations.

The reasons underlying the relatively slow pace of the current recovery have been the subject of considerable research. This research, discussed in more detail below, reaches three main conclusions. First, most—perhaps two-thirds, using a central estimate across studies—of the gap between the 12-quarter growth of GDP after the second quarter of 2009 and the average 12-quarter growth following previous troughs is accounted for primarily by changes in the long-term dynamics of the U.S. labor force and economy, mainly long-term demographic shifts. These demographic changes also help explain why the 1991 and 2001 recoveries were slower than the post-1960 average. Second, much of the remaining one-third of the gap can be attributed to the financial crisis dynamics discussed by Reinhart and Rogoff (2009), Reinhart and Reinhart (2010), Hall (2010), Woodford (2010), and others. This research finds that recoveries following financial crises tend to be slow because of delays in the reemergence of credit and reductions in consumer spending as households pay down debt or rebuild their savings, a process referred to as "deleveraging." Third, some unique factors proved to be particularly important impediments to this recovery, as discussed previously: the limited effectiveness of standard monetary policy caused by the zero lower bound on nominal interest rates; the presence of millions of underwater and foreclosed properties, which has impaired the recovery of the housing market; and the contraction in State and local government

Data Watch 2-2: The Effect of Statistical
Sampling on Laspeyres Indexes

The purpose of a price index is to provide a single measure of the overall rate of change in prices for some set of goods and services, for example, all purchases made by consumers. If data on all prices were readily available, the true rate of price increase could be calculated by weighting the relative increases in the prices for every item in the bundle using weights that reflect spending on the items, then combining those weighted price increases to form a price index. Because it is not possible to collect all prices, however, statistical agencies collect a sample of prices and use the sample to construct the price index.

The consequences of using a sample of prices, instead of all prices, can be significant. To be concrete, consider a Laspeyres price index, in which inflation is measured as an arithmetic weighted average of price increases for individual categories of items and the weights are spending shares measured at the beginning of the interval. In practice, each item (for example, apples or a haircut) is sold in an area (such as the Seattle metropolitan region), so the price increase of interest is an item-area price (the increase in the price of apples in Seattle from one month to the next). In reality, there are many item-area prices (one can purchase apples or haircuts at many shops in Seattle), so a sample of item-area prices is taken, and the sampled price increases (the increase in the price of apples at a given store, relative to last month's price at that store) are averaged. Since 1999, the Bureau of Labor Statistics (BLS) has computed this average of the sample of price increases within an item-area using the geometric mean.[1]

If the number of sampled prices for an item-area is large, the geometric mean of sample price changes will be close to the true item-area price. But collecting many item-area prices is expensive, so in many cases only a small number of item-area prices are collected. When computed using a small sample, the sample geometric mean tends to overstate the true geometric mean. The extent of this overstatement—the statistical bias arising from using a small sample—decreases as the number of prices sampled for an item-area increases.

How large is this finite sample bias? As an example, consider a

---

[1] The geometric mean of two numbers is the square root of their product. Suppose apple prices are sampled at two stores, one of which held prices constant and the other increased apple prices by 20 percent. Then the arithmetic mean relative price is $(1 + 1.2)/2 = 1.10$ (an increase of 10 percent), and the geometric mean is $(1 \times 1.2)^{1/2} = 1.095$ (an increase of 9.5 percent). The BLS adopted the geometric mean in part because its slightly lower increase captures the effect of shoppers migrating to the store at which apple prices remain constant, so that from the shopper's perspective the overall price increase is in fact less than 10 percent.

Laspeyres price index constructed using equal weights (that is, an index for which all item-areas have the same consumption shares), with many item-areas and with 10 prices randomly sampled per item-area. Suppose that the true item-area price increase is zero and the standard deviation of the price changes (a measure of the dispersion of the price changes) for sampled goods within each item-area is 10 percentage points. Then the bias is small: The geometric mean index for each item-area overstates the price change by only 0.05 percentage point per period, and under the assumptions made here, this translates into an upward bias of 0.05 percentage point in the overall Laspeyres index. But if only 5 items are sampled per item-area, and the standard deviation of the price changes across stores is a bit larger, say, 15 percentage points, then the bias is larger, and the price change is overstated by 0.23 percentage point per period. If this bias can be calculated (as has been done in the simple example laid out here), a technical correction can be made to the Laspeyres index to eliminate the bias. At a technical level, this bias arises because the Laspeyres index is an arithmetic weighted average of the item-area geometric means. Interestingly, if the geometric means for each item-area are aggregated to a national index using a weighted geometric mean, as with a Törnqvist price index, rather than a weighted arithmetic mean, as with the Laspeyres, the small-sample bias is eliminated, and there is no need for a technical bias correction. For further reading on small-sample bias in index numbers, see McClelland and Reinsdorf (1999) and Bradley (2005).

hiring due to sharply eroded property and sales tax bases. Given the deep and prolonged effects of financial crises, the cyclical component of the current recovery would have lagged even further behind the postwar average were it not for Federal fiscal stimulus—notably through the Recovery Act (Box 2-3), the temporary payroll tax cut, and extended unemployment insurance benefits—and for the nonstandard monetary stimulus provided by the Federal Reserve.

Demographics, Productivity, and Long-Term Economic Growth

A useful starting point for analyzing long-term trends in output is to note that GDP is the product of two terms: real GDP per worker times the number of workers. In turn, GDP per worker is the product of real GDP per hour of labor input—that is, labor productivity—times average hours per worker. Although average hours per worker have been declining, the rate of this decline since the mid-1980s has been relatively small. Thus, variation in the long-run growth rate of GDP is, to a first approximation, determined by

Box 2-3: Economic Impacts of the American Recovery and Reinvestment Act

To counter the contraction of aggregate demand in the Great Recession, Congress passed and President Obama signed into law the American Recovery and Reinvestment Act (the Recovery Act) in February 2009. The Recovery Act was a major part of the Federal government's efforts to reinvigorate the economy through direct fiscal stimulus. The Recovery Act authorized an estimated $787 billion for purchases of goods and services by the Federal government, transfers to State and local governments, payments to individuals, and temporary tax reductions for individuals and businesses (based on actual outcomes, the final total exceeded $800 billion).

Numerous studies have examined the success of the Recovery Act in raising employment and stimulating growth. As is the case with policy evaluation generally, the methodological challenge is to compare outcomes from an event that actually happened (implementation of the Recovery Act) to outcomes from a counterfactual event that did not (no Recovery Act). One approach is to use a large macroeconometric model or other statistical techniques to estimate a baseline, non-stimulus forecast that excludes Recovery Act provisions and a stimulus forecast that includes them, and then either compare the two forecasts or compare the actual data to the non-stimulus forecast. Of the studies employing this method, most estimate that the Recovery Act stimulated growth. A Congressional Budget Office study (CBO 2012b) estimated that the Recovery Act boosted the level of GDP by 0.4–1.8 percent in 2009, 0.7–4.1 percent in 2010, 0.4–2.3 percent in 2011, and 0.1–0.8 percent in 2012, with more than 90 percent of the Recovery Act's budgetary impact realized by the end of September 2012. The most recent review by the Council of Economic Advisers (CEA 2013) estimated that the Recovery Act raised the level of GDP as of the third quarter of 2010 by 2.7 percent, which is roughly in the same range estimated by CBO. A report by Blinder and Zandi (2010) estimated that the stimulus raised GDP in 2010 by 3.4 percent. Additional reports by IHS Global Insight and Macroeconomic Advisers provide estimates consistent with these ranges (as reported in CEA 2013). Estimates based on macroeconometric models typically do not include the additional benefits of avoiding very high levels of unemployment, which could be particularly persistent and exhibit so-called hysteresis; see DeLong and Summers (2012) for additional discussion.

A different approach to evaluating the Recovery Act is to use cross-state variation in Recovery Act spending levels to estimate the effects of the spending, and then to extrapolate these effects to the full economy.

Wilson (2012) studied state-level variation in Recovery Act spending to determine its employment effect; he estimated that Recovery Act spending created 2 million jobs in its first year and 3.4 million by March 2011, with substantial gains in the construction, manufacturing, education, and health industries. Conley and Dupor (2012) estimated that the spending components of the Act created between 82,000 and 1.5 million jobs. Other papers that use state-level variation to estimate Recovery Act effects on employment include Chodorow-Reich and others (2012), who investigated the employment effects of the Recovery Act's aid to states through increased Federal Medicaid matching funds, and Feyrer and Sacerdote (2011), who considered both total spending and type of spending; both papers found positive employment effects.

The range of estimates of the effect of the Recovery Act is large, and research on this topic is ongoing. Surveying the literature, however, the evidence suggests that the Recovery Act substantially lessened the impact of the Great Recession by increasing employment and output in the years immediately following the crisis.

the long-run growth rate of both productivity and the number of workers.[5] The discussion here focuses on the growth of productivity for nonfarm businesses and the growth of overall payroll employment.

Figure 2-16 shows quarterly growth of nonfarm business productivity and its cyclically adjusted long-term mean at an annual rate.[6] According to this mean, annual trend productivity growth fell from 2.6 percent in 1965 to 1.5 percent in 1985, recovered to 2.3 percent in 2005, and then fell to 2.0 percent as of 2010. Despite the considerable uncertainty and difficulty in distinguishing the trend from cyclical components given the severity of the recent recession, this pattern is in line with others in the academic literature. Gordon (2010) found that trend productivity growth declined from 2.75 percent in 1962 to 1.25 percent in 1979, then rebounded to 2.45 percent by 2002. Fernald (2012) divided the period since 1973 into three regimes of average labor productivity growth: 1.5 percent from 1973 to 1997, 3.6 percent from 1997 to 2003, and 1.6 percent from 2003 to 2012. The very strong

---

[5] Because labor productivity is conventionally measured for the nonfarm business sector, there are additional terms that account for the difference between the growth of GDP per hour and nonfarm business output per hour and between nonfarm business hours and total hours.

[6] The cyclically adjusted long-term mean, or trend, is estimated using regression methods with a cyclical component, specifically two leads and lags of the CBO's unemployment gap, and a flexible trend component. The flexible trend component is estimated by a smooth weighted average using a two-sided 15-year moving window, which is truncated at the ends of the sample.

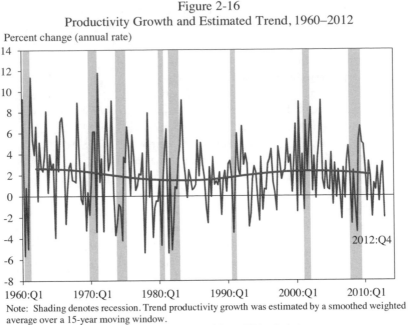

Figure 2-16
Productivity Growth and Estimated Trend, 1960–2012

Percent change (annual rate)

Note: Shading denotes recession. Trend productivity growth was estimated by a smoothed weighted average over a 15-year moving window.
Source: Bureau of Labor Statistics, Productivity and Costs; CEA calculations.

productivity growth of the late 1990s and early 2000s evident in Figure 2-16 appears, in part, to have been transitory.

Figure 2-17 plots the quarterly growth of total payroll employment and its cyclically adjusted long-term mean at an annual rate, and Figure 2-18 plots the quarterly change in employment, measured by the number of jobs; the method for computing the trends in both figures is the same as that used to calculate the trend shown in Figure 2-16. The smoothed mean growth of employment rose from 2.2 percent annually in 1965 to 2.4 percent in 1975 but then declined steadily to 2.0 percent in 1985 and just 0.8 percent in 2005. The trend in the number of jobs added remained high through the 1990s, and in fact more jobs were added in the 1990s than in the 1980s.

The high growth rate of employment in the 1970s reflected the historic surge of women into the U.S. labor force. The trend decline in employment growth since the late 1990s has been largely associated with demographics, in particular the plateauing of female labor force participation during the late-1990s, the steady multi-decade trend decline in male labor force participation, the downward trend in youth labor force participation, and, starting in the 2000s, the entry of the baby-boom generation into retirement. Demographic trends are discussed in more detail in Chapter 4. Indeed, the implications of demographic trends extend beyond the labor

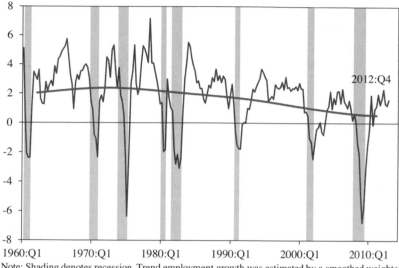

Figure 2-17
Employment Percent Growth and Estimated Trend, 1960–2012

Note: Shading denotes recession. Trend employment growth was estimated by a smoothed weighted average over a 15-year moving window.
Source: Bureau of Labor Statistics, Current Employment Statistics; CEA calculations.

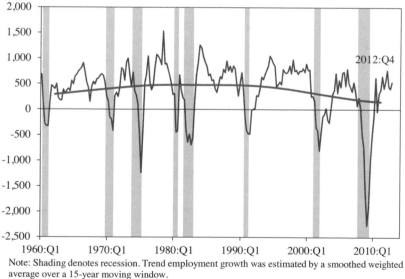

Figure 2-18
Quarterly Change in Employment and Estimated Trend, 1960–2012

Note: Shading denotes recession. Trend employment growth was estimated by a smoothed weighted average over a 15-year moving window.
Source: Bureau of Labor Statistics, Current Employment Statistics; CEA calculations.

force to include, for example, changes in the patterns of consumption as the population ages (Box 2-4).

The net effect of the declines in the long-term trends for productivity and employment has been a fairly steady decline in the long-run mean growth rate of GDP over the past 50 years. Indeed, the cyclically adjusted long-term mean growth rate of real GDP fell from 3.7 percent in 1965 to 2.9 percent in 1985 and 2.4 percent in 2005. This steady slowdown is evident in Figure 2-19, in which real GDP is plotted along with trend lines estimated using the quarterly data spanning a full business cycle as dated by the National Bureau of Economic Research (NBER), measured from one business-cycle peak to the next.[7] The slopes of these trend lines are less steep over time; in other words, the trend growth of real GDP has been slowing over this period. Indeed, trend growth has slowed enough that, after every post-1960 recession, real GDP has never attained the previous trend growth line that is implied using data from the preceding business cycle. From this perspective, the slower pace of the current recovery is not unusual or unexpected.

In a November 2012 study of the current recovery, CBO decomposed the growth of real GDP in the 12 quarters following a NBER-dated trough into trend growth plus a cyclical component. It attributed about two-thirds of the difference between the growth in real GDP in the current recovery and the average for other recoveries to slow growth in potential GDP. The CBO study estimated potential real GDP growth—that is, the maximum sustainable rate of growth of real GDP—using a presumed economy-wide production function in which potential GDP varied with the capital stock.

For comparison purposes, the long-term mean growth rate of GDP is computed here using the methodology of Figures 2-16 and 2-17. The results from this analysis are summarized in Table 2-2. As reported earlier, during the first 12 quarters of recoveries from 1960 through 2007, real GDP grew, on average, at an annual rate of 4.2 percent, whereas during the 12 quarters following the trough in the second quarter of 2009, the annual rate of GDP growth was 2.2 percent, or 2.1 percentage points below the 1960–2007 average. The estimated trend growth rate of real GDP since the second quarter of 2009, however, was 2.1 percent, or 1.1 percentage points below the average trend growth during the 1960-2007 recoveries (3.2 percent). Thus, of the 2.1 percentage points of slower-than-average growth in this recovery, fully

---

[7] The cycle starting with the peak in the first quarter of 1980 lasted only six quarters. Because it is not meaningful to estimate trends using only six quarterly observations, the cycles for the first quarter of 1980 and the third quarter of 1981 are merged for the trend estimates in Figure 2-19.

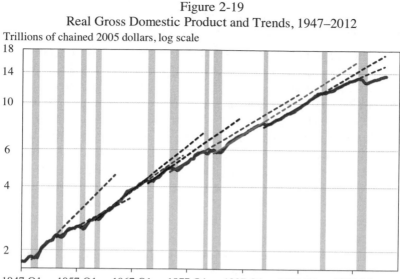

Figure 2-19
Real Gross Domestic Product and Trends, 1947–2012

Trillions of chained 2005 dollars, log scale

Note: Shading denotes recession. Trend lines represent the average growth rate between successive business-cycle peaks.
Source: Bureau of Economic Analysis, National Income and Product Accounts; National Bureau of Economic Research; CEA calculations.

1.1 percentage points, or 53 percent, can be attributed to the overall trend slowdown in real GDP growth over the past 50 years.[8]

The 1991 and 2001 recoveries also exhibited slower than average growth in real GDP (Kliesen 2003; Berger 2011; Bachmann 2011). As can be seen in Table 2-2, the slowdown in trend growth accounted for less than one-fifth of the relatively slower growth in real GDP following the 1991 recession (-0.2 percentage point of the gap of -1.1 percentage points). In contrast, slightly more than one-third of the relatively slower growth following the 2001 recession was attributable to the slowing of long-term real GDP growth (-0.5 percentage point of the gap of -1.3 percentage points).

Stock and Watson (2012) also examined reasons why the current expansion has been slower than previous postwar recoveries. They focused on the first eight quarters of the recovery and estimated that 80 percent of the slower growth in real GDP, relative to the post-1960 average for recoveries, reflected a slowdown in the long-term trend growth rate rather than cyclical factors.

---

[8] This calculation includes the 12 quarters after all troughs, so that the 1980 and 1982 recoveries overlap. Alternatively, if the 12 quarters following the trough in the fourth quarter of 1982 are dropped, 63 percent of the slower than average growth in real GDP is attributable to a slowdown in trend growth. If instead the 12 quarters following the trough in the third quarter of 1980 are dropped, 47 percent of the slower growth in real GDP is attributable to a slowdown in trend growth.

Box 2-4: Implications of Demographic Trends for Household Consumption

The aging of the U.S. population has two implications for patterns of consumption. First, people purchase different things at different ages; for example, younger households spend more on child care services and clothing, while older households spend relatively more on health care. Second, empirical research suggests that families' total amount of spending changes over time as priorities evolve. Because the age distribution of the population will change over the coming decade as the baby boom generation moves into retirement, these changes in household-level consumption will lead to aggregate changes in the types of goods consumed and, potentially, to changes in the fraction of income spent.

One way to forecast how demographic changes will affect consumption is to use data on a sample of households today to estimate average household consumption within spending categories (clothing, health care, and so on), for each subset of the population defined by age, race, sex, and ethnicity of the household head. Then, one can aggregate these averages using the projected future population for each subset to produce an overall estimate for all households. The Council of Economic Advisers undertook this exercise using consumption data from the Consumer Expenditure Survey and demographic projections from the Census Bureau. As the figure below indicates, demographic changes suggest that a greater share of household income will be spent on health care and housing, and a reduced share on education. In percentage terms, however, these changes are likely to be small.

Households' total consumption also varies over their lifetime. In Milton Friedman's (1957) permanent income hypothesis model of consumption, individuals smooth consumption to match their lifetime income, but doing so requires the ability to borrow against future income, as well as considerable planning and discipline. As an empirical matter, on average, household consumption rises as children grow up and then declines as parents enter into retirement (Attanasio et al 1999; Fernandez-Villaverde and Krueger 2007; Bullard and Feigenbaum 2007).[1] Consistent with this research, CEA projects that the aging population will lead average household consumption to decline over the next decade, with an implied reduction in the growth rate of consumer spending of perhaps 0.1 percentage point a year, relative to a benchmark in which demographics are held constant.

---

[1] One reason for the decline in consumption upon retirement, at least for some households, is reduced work-related spending such as commuting costs and uniforms, which are counted as consumption expenditures, but such declining work-related expenses do not fully account for this drop.

Many factors other than demographics will also influence future consumer spending. These factors include technological improvements, changes in income and wealth, and changes in the composition of households within demographic groups. In addition, changes in relative prices will affect the composition of spending. For example, if the price of health care increases relative to other areas, and if the demand for health care is insensitive to its price, then the share of spending on health care might be larger than these projections suggest.

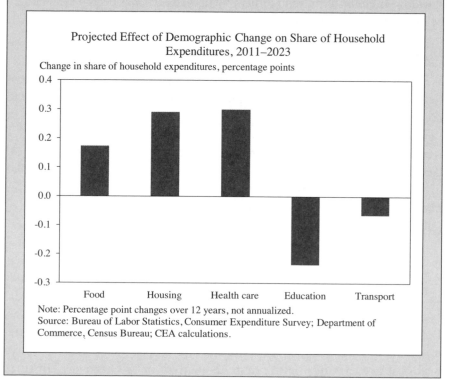

Projected Effect of Demographic Change on Share of Household Expenditures, 2011–2023

Change in share of household expenditures, percentage points

Note: Percentage point changes over 12 years, not annualized.
Source: Bureau of Labor Statistics, Consumer Expenditure Survey; Department of Commerce, Census Bureau; CEA calculations.

In summary, these estimates of the share of the relatively slower growth in real GDP during this recovery which is attributable to a slowdown in long-term trends range from 53 percent, shown in Table 2-2, to 80 percent according to Stock and Watson (2012). This fairly wide range of estimates reflects both inherent difficulties in calculating trend growth rates and conceptual differences among these approaches.[9] Taken together, however, these studies suggest that most of the relatively slower growth in real GDP during the current recovery—two-thirds, using the CBO (2012d) estimate, which is also the midpoint of these estimates—has been attributable to the slowdown in long-term trend growth, which, in turn, has been driven largely by demographic changes in the U.S. workforce.

Reasons for the Slower Cyclical Component

If two-thirds of the slower growth in real GDP during the current recovery relative to growth in previous postwar recessions is attributable to the slowdown in underlying long-term trends, then the remaining one-third can be attributed to cyclical factors that are specific to this recovery. This section summarizes four complementary attempts to quantify those cyclical factors: the 2012 CBO study discussed above, an analysis undertaken here of the sources of forecast errors during the recovery, work done on this question by the Federal Reserve as reported by Bernanke (2012b) and Yellen (2013), and the study by Stock and Watson (2012).

The CBO (2012d) study approaches the question of why the cyclical part of this recovery has been relatively slow by identifying those components of GDP that have exhibited unusually slow growth relative to their cyclical pattern. In decreasing order of importance, CBO found that the cyclical contributions to GDP of State and local government purchases, Federal government purchases (primarily defense spending), residential investment, and consumer spending were all weaker than their respective historical averages during the first 12 quarters of this recovery. In turn, CBO attributed the weakness in these components to several underlying factors. For instance, the CBO study highlighted the extraordinary weakness in housing markets during the current recovery. CBO associated the sharp

---

[9] In CBO's framework, the increase in long-term unemployment associated with the recession could result in skill deterioration and thereby a decline in potential GDP growth; this general point is also made by Federal Reserve Chairman Ben Bernanke (Bernanke 2012b). Because such declines in potential GDP are an indirect result of the recession, they may be better understood as cyclical rather than long-term trends. The trend estimates in Table 2-2 and in Stock and Watson (2012) are instead based on long-term weighted moving averages; because the resulting estimates are comparable with CBO's, one can infer that this further distinction of a cyclical change in the growth rate of potential GDP is secondary to the long-term demographic and technological trends that drive the growth slowdown.

Table 2-2
Real GDP Growth During Three Years Following Business Cycle Trough

Business Cycle Trough	(percent change at an annual rate)		
	Total	Trend	Cycle
1991:Q1	3.2	3.0	0.2
2001:Q4	2.9	2.7	0.2
2009:Q2	2.2	2.1	0.1
Average of 7 recoveries, 1960-2007	4.2	3.2	1.1
Difference from Average	Total	Trend	Cycle
1991:Q1	-1.1	-0.2	-0.9
2001:Q4	-1.3	-0.5	-0.8
2009:Q2	-2.1	-1.1	-1.0

Note: Trend growth is based on the 15-year moving average smoothed cyclically adjusted growth rate of real GDP.
Source: Bureau of Economic Analysis, National Income and Product Accounts; National Bureau of Economic Research; CEA calculations.

fall in house prices with reductions in State and local property tax revenues and the persistent glut of vacant and foreclosed homes with the weakness in residential construction. Similarly, CBO noted that, in contrast to previous postwar recoveries, the ability of monetary policy to spur economic activity has been constrained by the zero lower bound on the Federal Reserve's main policy interest rate during this expansion. The CBO analysis also pointed to low consumer confidence and heightened uncertainty as additional factors that have restrained aggregate demand since the second quarter of 2009.

A second approach to the question of why the cyclical component of this recovery has been slower than that of the postwar average is to examine whether the expansion has been hindered by unexpected events and forces. Specifically, this approach contrasts the actual, realized values for each component of GDP from the corresponding estimates that were forecast at the start of the recovery. Whereas CBO's approach identifies which components of GDP grew more slowly than their historical average, the approach used here is to identify the components that grew either more slowly or more rapidly than was forecast, thereby identifying the unexpected, or unforecast, sources of the slow growth.

Implementing this method of forecast error analysis requires a quantitative model of the U.S. economy. The one used here is developed and maintained by Macroeconomic Advisers (MA). This model is used to decompose the Administration's economic forecast for the FY 2011 Budget, which was made in November 2009. The MA model uses quarterly data to forecast hundreds of macroeconomic variables. By partitioning the variables into groups, it is possible to see how the forecast errors for each group contributed to the forecast errors for GDP. The variables were divided into five categories: international (foreign GDP, exchange rates, oil prices), fiscal (both Federal and State and local), financial and monetary (financial prices, house prices, monetary indicators, credit flows), housing activity, and other.

That Administration forecast overpredicted output growth by a small amount in 2010 and by larger amounts in 2011 and the first half of 2012; in this sense, the recovery was slower than expected. The forecast error decomposition sheds light on the sources of this unexpectedly slow recovery. During the first part of the recovery, the housing sector was weaker than anticipated, and this unexpected weakness more than accounts for the total GDP forecast error in 2010. Early in the recovery, financial and monetary factors buoyed economic activity relative to the forecast, presumably because the forecast did not fully capture the stimulative effect of nonstandard monetary policy, which was unprecedented and thus difficult to incorporate quantitatively into the forecast. Moving farther out in the forecast, however, the outlook for consumption turned overly optimistic, possibly reflecting an underestimation of the degree of deleveraging as households reduced the amount of new debt they took on and paid down existing debt. This shift in the consumption outlook explains a substantial part of the overall forecast error for both 2011 as well as the first half of 2012. Finally, deteriorating international conditions, largely owing to events unfolding in Europe, added further unanticipated drag in 2011 and especially in the first half of 2012.

These results complement Chairman Bernanke's (2012b) and Vice Chair Yellen's (2013) analyses of the relatively slow growth in the cyclical component of GDP during this recovery. In particular, Chairman Bernanke pointed to unexpected headwinds from the prolonged recovery of the housing sector, the lingering effects of the financial crisis, and the fiscal and financial problems in Europe. Yellen also noted the restraint on consumer spending from the large loss of wealth during the recession. Both emphasized the unexpectedly large declines in the State and local government sector. Indeed, Yellen estimates that, once the drag from the State and local government sector is included, the net fiscal stimulus to the economy was less in the current recovery than it was on average for prior postwar recoveries.

Stock and Watson (2012) also addressed the question of why the cyclical component of the recovery has been slower than the postwar average. In contrast to the two approaches discussed above, Stock and Watson focused on the forecasts of eight-quarter GDP growth from the vantage point of the trough. They found that these forecasts predicted slower-than-average cyclical growth during this expansion. These slow growth forecasts stem from the shocks that produced the recession, which they identify as primarily financial factors (such as borrowing constraints) and uncertainty. Thus, the Stock and Watson analysis is consistent with the Reinhart and Rogoff (2009) view that recoveries following financial recessions typically exhibit slower growth than those following other kinds of recessions. In contrast to Stock and Watson's approach, Hall (2012) used a stylized macroeconomic model to distinguish between the deleveraging effect of cutting back on consumption to rebuild wealth and the liquidity effect of higher borrowing costs, which would arise from tightened lending standards. He concluded that both effects were important during the recession, but that the deleveraging effect was short-lived, whereas the liquidity effect has been more persistent and continues to restrain investment and to contribute to the slow cyclical component of GDP.

Although the CBO analysis, the forecast error decomposition, the analyses by Bernanke and by Yellen, the study by Stock and Watson, and the study by Hall produced different numerical estimates of the causes of the relatively slow recovery, these analyses point to a common understanding of why the cyclical component of the current expansion was slow relative to previous recessions: a financial crisis that led to reductions in the ability of households and small businesses to borrow, spend, and invest; a weak recovery of the housing sector as a result of the excess inventory of vacant, foreclosed, and distressed properties; a decline in State and local spending and employment; monetary policy restrained by the zero lower bound on the Federal Reserve's main policy interest rate; and in more recent stages of the recovery, the detrimental effects of a global slowdown on U.S. economic activity. Against all of these headwinds, the stimulus from Federal fiscal policy actions and aggressive unconventional monetary policy contributed positively to the cyclical component of the recovery.

OUTLOOK FOR 2013 AND BEYOND

The Administration's economic forecast was finalized in mid-November 2012, a schedule that is dictated by its role in supporting the Administration's outlook for the FY 2014 Budget, and will be released later this year in conjunction with the Budget.

Consensus-based forecasts—that is, forecasts that combine multiple, survey-based individual forecasts (e.g., the mean or median)—typically outperform the constituent individual private forecasters' forecasts of macroeconomic variables such as GDP and the unemployment rate (Clemen 1989; Aiolfi, Capistrán, and Timmerman 2011). Consensus forecasts are thus worth following. In February 2013 the Blue Chip consensus of professional forecasters projected that real GDP would increase 2.4 percent over the four quarters of 2013, faster than the 1.6 percent gain recorded in 2012. The Philadelphia Federal Reserve Bank's Survey of Professional Forecasters

(SPF) also projected a 2.4 percent increase in 2013. For 2014, the Blue Chip consensus and the SPF consensus forecast that the economy will continue to strengthen and that year-over-year real GDP growth will increase to a 2.8 percent pace.

Looking further ahead, the Survey of Professional Forecasters expects year-over-year growth will pick up to a 2.9 percent pace in 2015 and a 3.0 percent pace in 2016. With these rates of growth, the unemployment rate, which was 7.8 percent during the fourth quarter of 2012, is projected to edge down slowly to 6.3 percent in 2016.

Importantly, most private sector forecasts reflected in the consensus forecast have not incorporated an effect for the across-the-board budget cuts, known as sequestration, which took effect on March 1.[10] These cuts will severely reduce both Federal defense and nondefense discretionary spending, with ripple effects throughout the economy. The Congressional Budget Office (2013) and Macroeconomic Advisers (2013) have estimated that, if sequestration were to remain in effect for the rest of the calendar year, it would reduce real GDP growth by 0.6 percentage point during the four quarters of 2013, relative to its path without the sequester. Moody's Analytics (2013) has estimated a reduction in real GDP growth by 0.5 percentage point.

Additionally, CBO (2013) has estimated that sequestration would lead to the loss of 750,000 lost jobs due to the sequester by the end of 2013 compared with a path without sequestration.[11] From this perspective, by the end of this year sequestration would set back the recovery by four to five months at a time when the unemployment rate remains unacceptably high. As President Obama has stated, "The longer these cuts remain in place, the greater the damage to our economy—a slow grind that will intensify with every passing day."

CONCLUSION

While much work remains, the economy is healing and moving in the right direction. The permanent extension of middle-class tax cuts and the increase in rates on the highest-income taxpayers through the enactment of the American Taxpayer Relief Act resolved the uncertainty about future tax rates that overshadowed the economy in 2012 and helped move the U.S. budget toward a more sustainable course. Some of the other headwinds that have restrained the economy during the recovery are also easing, most

---

[10] In February, 77 percent of Blue Chip panelists reported that their forecasts did not reflect the effects of full sequestration.

[11] The Bipartisan Policy Center (2012) estimates that over two years the effect would be 1 million jobs lost compared with the no-sequestration alternative.

notably in the housing sector. While risks remain, these indicators suggest a continued strengthening of the recovery, which in turn provides an increasingly resilient framework for continued progress toward fiscal sustainability and a more durable economy that works for the broad middle class.

CHAPTER 3

FISCAL POLICY

The American Taxpayer Relief Act of 2012 (ATRA), which was enacted on January 2, 2013, permanently extended the 2001 and 2003 Federal income tax cuts for 98 percent of taxpayers. The tax relief act reflects the approach supported by the President to reduce the Federal budget deficit—an approach that balances responsible reductions in government spending with new revenues and increased progressivity of the tax code. The new law extended the expansions of several tax credits enacted in the American Recovery and Reinvestment Act of 2009 (the Recovery Act) that have provided economic opportunities through tax relief and college expense assistance to 25 million low- and middle-income students and working families each year. In addition, the new law prevented a substantial cut in Medicare physician payment rates, extended emergency unemployment insurance benefits to protect 2 million workers from losing their benefits in January 2013, and permanently indexed to inflation the exemption amounts for the Alternative Minimum Tax (AMT) to provide tax certainty to tens of millions of middle-class families. The permanent fix to the AMT will protect middle-class families from being subject to a tax designed to ensure that wealthy taxpayers pay their fair share in taxes.

Together with the additional Medicare and investment income taxes for high-income taxpayers in the Affordable Care Act (ACA), ATRA has made the Federal tax system more progressive. Figure 3-1 shows the trends in average Federal individual income and employment tax rates by income class. These average tax rates, defined as the share of taxpayer income paid in taxes, are measured by holding the distribution of taxpayer income constant over time (using the 2005 distribution with incomes adjusted for growth in the National Average Wage Index) to isolate the effects of tax law changes. The tax law changes in 2013 increased the average tax rate for taxpayers in the top 1 percent and the top 0.1 percent of the income distribution by 4.9 and 6.5 percentage points, respectively, while leaving individual income tax rates unchanged for 98 percent of Americans.

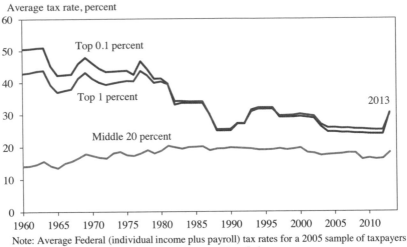

Figure 3-1
Average Tax Rates for Selected Income Groups
Under a Fixed Income Distribution, 1960–2013

Average tax rate, percent

Note: Average Federal (individual income plus payroll) tax rates for a 2005 sample of taxpayers
after adjusting for growth in the National Average Wage Index.
Source: Internal Revenue Service, Statistics of Income Public Use File; National Bureau of
Economic Research, TAXSIM (preliminary for 2012 and 2013); CEA calculations.

Another recent development in government finance is that the fiscal outlook for State and local governments has improved, although expenditures remain below pre-recession levels and State and local investment spending remains notably low. As shown in Figure 3-2, the continued decline in State and local investment is atypical. In other recoveries, State and local governments' gross real investment was typically flat for several quarters following a business-cycle trough and then increased, but, in this recovery, gross investment has failed to rebound.

This chapter highlights the declining Federal budget deficit since 2009 and the additional work needed to achieve medium- and long-term fiscal health. It then outlines the principles for Federal income tax reform set forth by President Obama in September 2011 and describes specific plans proposed by the Administration to meet these goals. The enactment of ATRA is a step toward achieving these goals, but substantial work remains to make the tax code more equitable and efficient. The chapter also reviews the State and local budget outlook and the Federal Government's role in mitigating the recent recession's effect on government finances at these levels. Finally, the chapter discusses the long-term financial challenge facing State and local governments from the underfunding of pension plans.

Figure 3-2
Real State and Local Government Gross Investment
During Recoveries

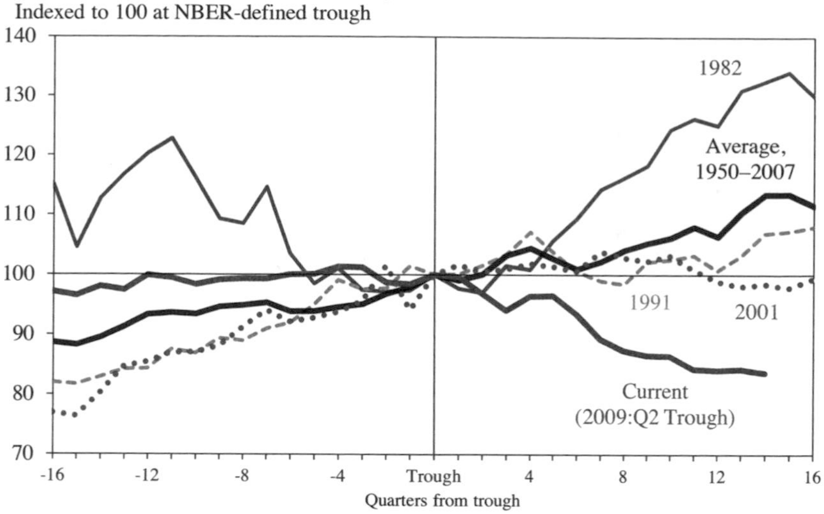
Indexed to 100 at NBER-defined trough
140
130
120
110
100
90
80
70
1982
Average,
1950–2007
1991
2001
Current
(2009:Q2 Trough)
-16
-12
-8
-4
Trough
4
8
12
16
Quarters from trough

Source: Bureau of Economic Analysis, National Income and Product Accounts; National Bureau of Economic Research; CEA calculations.

The Federal Budget Outlook

The Obama Administration has taken significant steps to restore the country's fiscal health without disrupting the continuing economic recovery. In fiscal year (FY) 2009, the Federal budget deficit was 10.1 percent of gross domestic product (GDP). This ratio fell 3.1 percentage points to 7.0 percent in 2012, the largest three-year reduction in the deficit since 1949. Under current law, the deficit is projected to fall to 5.3 percent in 2013 (CBO 2013). This decline in the deficit largely reflects the wind-down of Recovery Act spending, the reductions in spending set forth in the Budget Control Act of 2011, new revenues as a result of ATRA, and the improved performance of the economy.

The Congressional Budget Office (CBO) projects that Federal receipts will grow by 11 percent to $2.7 trillion, or 16.9 percent of GDP, in 2013 (Figure 3-3). This is the highest receipts-to-GDP ratio since 2008, but still below the average of 18.3 percent of GDP recorded between 1970 and 2000. As a percent of GDP, outlays are projected to fall from 22.2 percent in 2013 to 21.5 percent in 2017 due in large part to the spending caps put in place by the Budget Control Act as well as reductions in certain mandatory spending as the economy continues to improve. After 2017, outlays will rise, relative to GDP, as interest payments on the national debt increase and as mandatory

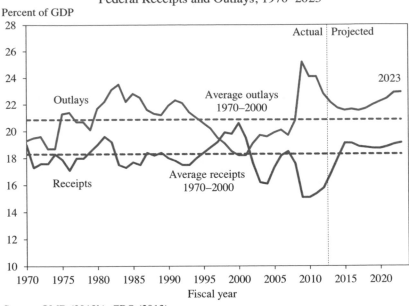

Figure 3-3
Federal Receipts and Outlays, 1970–2023

Source: OMB (2012b); CBO (2013).

health and retirement spending grows in accordance with the cost of health care and an aging population. Over the long term, these factors—rising health costs and changing demographics—are the primary drivers of fiscal imbalance (CBO 2012).

The Administration's goal of stabilizing the debt-to-GDP ratio requires reducing the deficit to 3 percent of GDP or lower. Increases in revenues and decreases in outlays in recent years have brought the Federal budget deficit—the gap between outlays and receipts—closer to that target (Figure 3-4). CBO projects that, under current law, deficits will continue to shrink over the next few years, falling below 3 percent of GDP by 2015, but will then increase steadily to 3.8 percent of GDP by 2022. Under current law, publicly held Federal debt is projected to reach 77 percent of GDP in 2023 (Figure 3-5).

Although enacted legislation and overall economic improvements will help reduce the budget deficit, other structural changes will be needed to achieve fiscal sustainability. The President has put forward a balanced deficit-reduction plan to achieve approximately $1.8 trillion in savings through a combination of reductions in discretionary spending, savings in entitlement programs, and new revenue raised by reforming tax expenditures and closing tax loopholes. When added to the more than $2.5 trillion in deficit reduction the President already signed into law, the total deficit

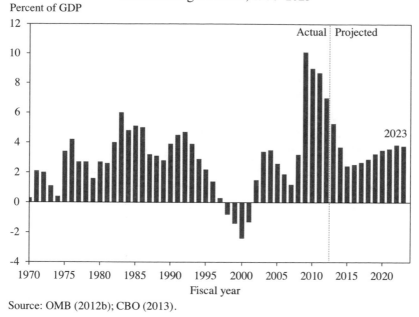

Figure 3-4
Federal Budget Deficit, 1970–2023

Percent of GDP

Source: OMB (2012b); CBO (2013).

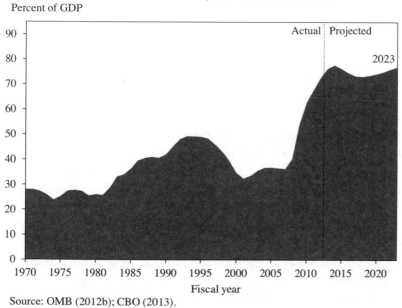

Figure 3-5
Federal Debt Held by the Public, 1970–2023

Percent of GDP

Source: OMB (2012b); CBO (2013).

reduction would amount to more than $4 trillion over ten years, a goal set by the President to stabilize the debt-to-GDP ratio and to put the country on a sustainable fiscal path over the next decade.

FEDERAL INCOME TAX REFORM

A fair, simple, and efficient tax code lays the foundation for job creation, economic growth, and an equitable society. Recognizing the crucial role tax reform can play in deficit reduction and economic growth, President Obama set forth a list of principles in September 2011 for comprehensive tax reform. These principles include lowering tax rates, cutting inefficient and unfair tax breaks, observing the "Buffett Rule" to enhance tax fairness, reducing the deficit, and increasing job creation and growth in the United States (OMB 2011).

Because revenue must be raised to finance essential services provided by the government, sound tax policy attempts to raise revenue fairly and efficiently. A number of notions of fairness can help guide tax policy: "horizontal equity" demands equal treatment of equals; the ability-to-pay principle prescribes that a taxpayer's burden should be related to her ability to pay; the benefit principle suggests that a taxpayer's burden should be related to the benefits she receives from government services. Such notions of fairness are often incomplete, and sometimes they are in conflict with each other. Still, these principles can serve as useful guides.

Fairness, however, must be balanced with efficiency. High tax rates, combined with a complex tax system and a narrow tax base (that is, with many deductions, exclusions, or exemptions), provide incentives for taxpayers to shift income between the individual and corporate tax bases, re-time income, and alter behavior in other ways to reduce tax liability (Saez, Slemrod, and Giertz 2012). In addition, although tax subsidies could encourage socially beneficial activity or correct market failures, when there are no externalities or other market failures, tax provisions that favor one activity over another can lead to an inefficient allocation of resources.

A key feature of the tax code is the schedule of statutory tax rates on marginal income. To achieve myriad tax, economic, and social policy goals, the tax code also contains a dizzying web of deductions, exemptions, exclusions, credits, and special treatment of certain income. The fact that taxpayers modify their behavior to reap the benefits of special tax provisions is bittersweet. On one hand, it means that well-thought-out tax provisions that are designed to encourage a particular activity are working. On the other hand, a taxpayer determined to avoid liability can engage in tax avoidance and thereby expend socially unproductive resources navigating the jungle of tax provisions.[1]

Tax Expenditures

The tax code contains numerous special tax provisions, referred to as "tax expenditures," which lead the tax system to deviate from taxing economic income (Box 3-1). Economic income generally follows the Haig-Simons definition of comprehensive income as consumption plus changes in net worth. Relative to a tax structure built on a comprehensive income measure, tax expenditures erode the tax base, causing the government to forgo revenue, but they provide important tax benefits to individuals and families. How such benefits are distributed over the income distribution varies widely across tax provisions. To assess the distributional effects of a given tax expenditure, the Treasury Department estimated the tax benefits of each major individual income tax expenditure under 2013 income tax law for taxpayers in different income classes.

As illustrated in Figure 3-6, the Earned Income Tax Credit (EITC) and the Child Tax Credit (including the refundable portion) provide substantial benefits to taxpayers in the lowest income quintile but have little impact on the after-tax income of taxpayers in the top three income quintiles. By contrast, the bottom two income quintiles receive almost no benefits from tax expenditures like the charitable giving deduction and deductions for State and local taxes. Almost all of those tax benefits accrue to taxpayers in the top two income quintiles. Middle and upper-middle income taxpayers benefit the most from the exclusion of employer-provided health insurance, whereas taxpayers in the bottom quintile and those in the top percentile of the income distribution receive relatively little benefit from the exclusion.

Because the tax value of deductions and exclusions increases with taxpayers' marginal tax rates, these tax expenditures provide larger benefits to high-income taxpayers than to low- and middle-income taxpayers for a given amount of deductions or exclusions. (For various measures of tax rates, see Economics Application Box 3-1.) In particular, an additional dollar of deductions or exclusions reduces taxable income by $1 and consequently reduces the liability of taxpayers in the 39.6-percent bracket and 25-percent bracket, respectively, by 39.6 cents and 25 cents. In an effort to improve tax fairness, improve efficiency, and reduce the deficit, the President has proposed to reduce the tax value of selected tax expenditures to 28 percent for high-income taxpayers, a level comparable to the tax value provided by the tax code for middle-income taxpayers.

---

[1] Behavior that reduces tax remittances without altering real investment, savings, or labor decisions is called tax avoidance when it is legal and tax evasion when it is illegal.

Box 3-1: Estimates of Tax Expenditures in the President's Budget

Tax expenditures, commonly viewed as government spending through the tax code, are defined in the Congressional Budget Act of 1974 as "revenue losses attributable to provisions of the Federal tax laws which allow a special exclusion, exemption, or deduction from gross income or which provide a special credit, a preferential rate of tax, or a deferral of tax liability."

Each year the Treasury Department estimates the value of tax expenditures in terms of the Federal income tax loss and reports the estimates in the annual Budget of the United States Government.[1] Table 17-1 of the President's fiscal year 2013 Budget lists 173 corporate and individual income tax expenditures in the tax code. Tax expenditures take many different forms:

• Exclusions and exemptions allow specific types or sources of income—such as compensation received as medical insurance or interest from municipal bonds—to be excluded or exempt from income for tax purposes.

• Deductions permit taxpayers to deduct certain types of expenses from income to calculate the taxable base. Examples include itemized deductions (which include deductions for home mortgage interest, charitable giving, State and local taxes, and medical expenses) and "above-the-line" deductions (which include deductions for student loan interest, self-employed retirement and health insurance contributions, and educators' out-of-pocket expenses).

• Tax credits reduce tax liability by the amount of the credit. When the amount of a tax credit exceeds tax liability before the credit is applied, the credit will erase the tax liability, and, if the credit is refundable, the government will pay the filer the excess amount. In the Federal Budget, the portion of a refundable credit that reduces tax liability is treated as a revenue loss, and the portion that exceeds tax liability is treated as an outlay.

• Special rates apply a lower tax rate to specific sources of income than the rate applied to ordinary income. For example, long-term capital gains and qualified dividends are taxed at lower rates than ordinary income.

• Deferrals permit taxpayers to delay including certain income in the taxable base. Such tax expenditures include accelerated depreciation

---

[1] The Joint Committee on Taxation also annually publishes a list of tax expenditures. Tax expenditure estimates do not equal the amount of revenue that would be generated if the expenditure were eliminated for two reasons: first, eliminating a tax expenditure would result in behavioral effects that could offset the revenue gain; second, removing multiple tax expenditures simultaneously creates interaction effects that depend on the particular expenditures.

or immediate expensing of business investment as well as tax incentives for retirement saving.

Table 17-3 of the FY 2013 Budget ranks tax expenditures by projected revenue effect. The 10 largest tax expenditures by the projected revenue effect for 2013–2017 are:[2]

- Exclusion of employer contributions for medical insurance premiums and medical care ($1,012 billion)
- Deductibility of mortgage interest on owner-occupied homes ($606 billion)
- 401(k)-type plans ($429 billion)
- Accelerated depreciation of machinery and equipment ($375 billion)
- Exclusion of net imputed rental income on owner-occupied housing ($337 billion)
- Special rates for capital gains ($321 billion)
- Defined benefit pension plans ($298 billion)
- Deductibility of State and local taxes other than on owner-occupied homes ($295 billion)
- Deductibility of charitable contributions, other than education and health ($239 billion)
- Exclusion of interest on public purpose State and local bonds ($228 billion).

---

[2] The estimates do not include effects on Federal outlays. Refundable tax credits, such as the Earned Income Tax Credit and the Child Tax Credit, can carry significant outlay effects.

The preferential rate on capital gains and dividends gives rise to tax benefits because these sources of income are taxed at a lower rate than ordinary income.[2] Of the selected tax expenditures in Figure 3-6, the benefits of the preferential tax rate on capital gains and dividends are most skewed to the upper end of the income distribution. The underlying tax data for Figure 3-6 suggest that taxpayers in the top 0.1 percent of the income distribution receive 41 percent of the total positive capital gains realizations and qualified dividends. Because of this unequal distribution of capital gains realizations and qualified dividends, the preferential rate provides substantially more benefit to the top 0.1 percent of taxpayers than to taxpayers in any other income class.

---

[2] One argument for the preferential rate is that corporations already pay income taxes so individual income taxes on capital gains and dividends result in double taxation. However, evidence shows that not all of the long-term capital gains are attributable to corporate stocks or mutual funds, and therefore some capital gains are never taxed at the corporate level (Wilson and Liddell 2010; Burman 2012).

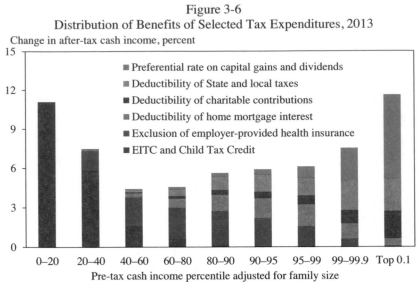

Figure 3-6
Distribution of Benefits of Selected Tax Expenditures, 2013

Change in after-tax cash income, percent

- Preferential rate on capital gains and dividends
- Deductibility of State and local taxes
- Deductibility of charitable contributions
- Deductibility of home mortgage interest
- Exclusion of employer-provided health insurance
- EITC and Child Tax Credit

Pre-tax cash income percentile adjusted for family size

Note: Estimates are the percentage reduction in after-tax cash income (2013 income levels under current law, including ATRA) from eliminating each tax expenditure. Families with negative incomes are excluded from the lowest income class.
Source: Department of the Treasury, Office of Tax Analysis calculations.

Vertical Equity

Vertical equity holds that individuals who have a greater ability to pay should contribute more in taxes than those who are less able to pay (for a discussion of tax fairness, see Economics Application Box 3-1). The President has called one specific formulation of this idea, the Buffett Rule, a basic principle of tax fairness. The Buffett Rule states that no household making over $1 million should pay a smaller share of income in taxes than middle-class families pay. Several studies have shown that the current tax system violates the Buffett Rule; many high-income families pay a smaller share of income in Federal taxes than do middle-income families (Hungerford 2011; CEA 2012; Cronin, DeFilippes, and Lin 2012). Thus, implementing the Buffett Rule, or adopting the rule as a guiding principle for tax reform, would improve tax fairness.

While the current Federal tax system is progressive, its progressivity has significantly declined since the 1960s. Figure 3-1 above shows that average tax rates for middle-income taxpayers rose slightly in the 1960s and the 1970s and then remained relatively stable since the 1980s. By contrast, Federal tax burdens for the wealthiest taxpayers have dropped dramatically since 1960 as a result of changes in tax laws. The share of income the top 0.1 percent paid in Federal individual income and employment taxes fell to 24.1 percent in 2012, about half of what this group paid in 1960.

**Economics Application Box 3-1: Marginal Tax Rates
and Average Tax Rates on Individual Income**

Marginal and average tax rates are two tax rates commonly used to describe a tax system and to measure the fraction of income people pay in taxes. A statutory marginal tax rate for an income tax is the tax rate specified by law and applied to one additional dollar of taxable income. A tax system may consist of multiple statutory rates, with each applying to a range of taxable income to form a tax bracket. A taxpayer's statutory marginal tax rate thus depends on the tax bracket in which her taxable income falls. An effective marginal tax rate is the fraction of an additional dollar of income a taxpayer actually pays to the government. The effective marginal tax rate is determined by the statutory rate as well as by other tax provisions, such as phase-ins or phase-outs of tax credits. An average, or effective, tax rate is the fraction of a taxpayer's total income that is owed as tax liability. The share of total income paid in taxes indicates the tax burden faced by a taxpayer.

One criterion for evaluating tax systems is fairness. Economics provides useful tools to help evaluate a tax system's fairness. Two important concepts are horizontal and vertical equity. Horizontal equity means equal treatment of equals, which is commonly interpreted as equal treatment of those with an equal ability to pay; vertical equity holds that those who have a greater ability to pay should contribute more in taxes than those who are less able to pay. To evaluate vertical equity, a tax can be classified as being proportional, regressive, or progressive. A tax is proportional if average tax rates are equal for taxpayers at all income levels. A tax is regressive if average tax rates fall with income, and a tax is progressive if average tax rates increase with income. Under a progressive tax system, high-income taxpayers face a larger tax burden than low-income taxpayers. This notion is long ingrained in economics. In fact, endorsing progressive taxes, Adam Smith wrote in *The Wealth of Nations* that "it is not very unreasonable that the rich should contribute to the public expense, not only in proportion to their revenue, but something more than in that proportion."

Figure 3-7 depicts the trends in effective marginal tax rates on wage income. As shown, effective marginal tax rates faced by middle-income taxpayers have been relatively constant during the past five decades, in contrast with the dramatic decline in the effective marginal tax rates faced by the top 1 percent or 0.1 percent of taxpayers. In other words, taxpayers at the top of the income distribution have always faced higher marginal tax rates on wage income than middle-income taxpayers, but the spread between their marginal tax rates has narrowed significantly since 1960. Before ATRA was

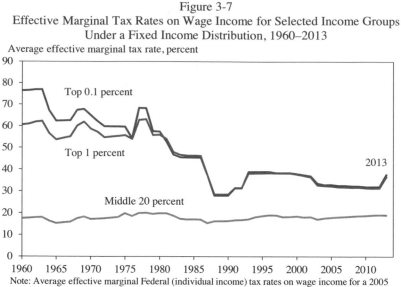

Figure 3-7
Effective Marginal Tax Rates on Wage Income for Selected Income Groups
Under a Fixed Income Distribution, 1960–2013

Average effective marginal tax rate, percent

Note: Average effective marginal Federal (individual income) tax rates on wage income for a 2005
sample of taxpayers after adjusting for growth in the National Average Wage Index.
Source: Internal Revenue Service, Statistics of Income Public Use File; National Bureau of Economic
Research, TAXSIM (preliminary for 2012 and 2013); CEA calculations.

enacted, the top effective marginal rate on wage income was close to its lowest level in the past five decades; there was only a short period in the late 1980s and early 1990s when the top effective marginal tax rate was lower than the rate in 2012.

As noted, the preferential rate on long-term capital gains is particularly regressive, and evidence suggests that capital gains realizations have become more concentrated over time. The portion of total capital gains realized by the 0.1 percent of taxpayers who reported the most capital gains income increased from 25 percent in 1987 to over 40 percent in 2010 (Lurie and Pearce 2012). Relative to the increased income concentration, the top effective marginal tax rate on long-term capital gains declined during the period (Figure 3-8). The rate ranged between 20 percent and 30 percent from the 1980s to the early 2000s, fell to 16 percent in 2003, and fell further to 15 percent in 2010 because of the scheduled elimination of the phase-out of itemized deductions under the 2001 tax cut. The rate rose to 25 percent in 2013.

In addition to individual income and employment taxes, the Federal Government collects corporate income taxes and estate taxes. Piketty and Saez (2007) examined the combined effect on vertical equity of Federal individual, employment, corporate, and estate taxes from 1960 to 2004. They argued that corporate and estate taxes substantially contributed to a

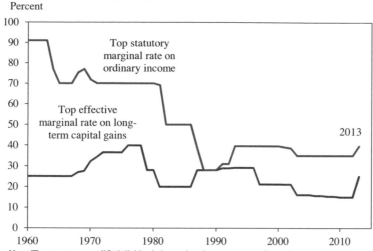

Figure 3-8
Top Marginal Tax Rates, 1960–2013

Percent

Top statutory marginal rate on ordinary income

Top effective marginal rate on long-term capital gains

2013

Note: The top rate on qualified dividends is equal to the top rate on ordinary income until 2003; thereafter, it is equal to the top rate on long-term capital gains. The top marginal rates on long-term gains calculated by Treasury include the effects of the Alternative Minimum Tax (AMT) and the phase-out of itemized deductions.
Source: Internal Revenue Service, Statistics of Income; Department of the Treasury, Office of Tax Analysis; CEA calculations.

more progressive tax system in 1960 than in 2004. Because the wealthiest taxpayers own a disproportionately large share of the nation's capital income and wealth, they bear the largest burden of the corporate income and estate taxes.[3] The Federal Government, however, has shifted away from relying on these two Federal taxes as revenue sources, leaving taxpayers at the top of the income distribution with a much lower tax burden in 2004 than in 1960. As shown in Figure 3-9, corporate tax revenues as a percent of total Federal receipts declined from 23.2 percent in 1960 to 10.1 percent in 2004. The share for estate and gift taxes declined modestly from 1.7 percent in 1960 to 1.3 percent in 2004 (OMB 2012b).

Efficiency and Simplification

From the current point of a complex tax code with many special provisions, simultaneously eliminating special provisions and lowering tax rates could make the tax code both simpler and more efficient. Cutting unfair and

---

[3] Piketty and Saez (2007) assume the burden of the corporate income tax falls on owners of capital income. Several tax policy groups, including the Treasury Department's Office of Tax Analysis, the Congressional Budget Office, and the Tax Policy Center, assume in their current tax models that the majority of the corporate tax burden—about 80 percent—is borne by capital income, whereas the remainder is borne by labor. Cronin et al. (2013) provide details of the different corporate tax incidence assumptions.

inefficient tax breaks and simplifying the tax system with lower tax rates are among the principles the President set forth for tax reform. High tax rates, coupled with a narrow tax base, cause taxpayers to adopt economically inefficient behavior. When examining the efficiency gains from tax reform, it is important to identify the behavioral margins that are in response to changes in tax policy and the resulting economic effects. In theory, lowering tax rates can lead to an increase in labor supply (or a decrease in labor supply if the income effect dominates the substitution effect), but evidence suggests that, when tax rates change, labor supply effects are small compared with tax avoidance effects (Saez, Slemrod, and Giertz 2012). One such effect occurs when investors delay realizing capital gains and hold onto assets only to avoid capital gains tax. Despite this inefficient "lock-in" effect, negative associations between top individual income tax rates on capital gains and private saving, investment, or changes in real GDP are not supported by U.S. experience (Hungerford 2012; Burman 2012).

When taxpayers make decisions in response to special provisions in the tax code, they engage in more of the tax-preferred activity than they would otherwise, thereby steering resources away from other more productive uses.[4] One major unfair and inefficient tax break is the tax treatment of partners' profits interests, also known as carried interests, in an investment partnership. Carried interests, despite being derived from performance of labor services, receive capital gains treatment. This preferential tax treatment provided for income derived from performing a specific activity induces a behavioral distortion and is economically inefficient. To improve fairness and efficiency of the tax code, the Administration has proposed to tax carried interests as ordinary income and subject that income to self-employment taxes.

In addition, the Administration has proposed to improve the tax code's efficiency by closing business loopholes and broadening the business tax base. For example, corporations currently use life insurance as a form of tax shelter because of its favorable tax treatment. Investment returns on life insurance products are allowed to accumulate tax free until policies are cashed in. As a result, businesses can take interest deductions for investment-oriented life insurance policies that cover their officers and employees before any gain is realized—and taxed—on the policies. The Administration's recent Budget would close this loophole and encourage businesses to make more efficient investment decisions by limiting the interest deductions allocable to investment in certain life insurance policies.

---

[4] If the tax-preferred activity is underconsumed or underproduced because of market failures or externalities, then a favorable treatment could increase quantity and result in more efficient allocations of resources.

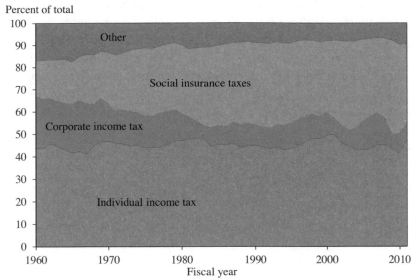

Figure 3-9
Composition of Federal Receipts, 1960–2011

Note: Other includes excise taxes, estate taxes, customs duties, and other receipts.
Source: OMB (2012b).

The President has also proposed making the Federal subsidy for State and local governments' borrowing costs more efficient by extending Build America Bonds (BABs), in which the Federal Government makes direct payments to State and local governments. Traditional tax-exempt bonds provide a Federal subsidy through a Federal tax exemption to investors for interest income received from the bonds. One study finds that as much as 20 percent of the tax revenue the Federal Government forgoes from tax-exempt bonds accrues to investors, leaving only 80 percent of the subsidy to benefit State and local governments (CBO/JCT 2009).

Complexity is another source of inefficiency in the tax code because it increases the amount of time and money taxpayers spend to comply with the law and creates opportunities for them to engage in the unproductive activity of tax avoidance. It is estimated that complying with the Federal income tax cost businesses at least $100 billion for tax year 2009 (Contos et al., forthcoming) and individuals over $50 billion for tax year 2010,[5] with the total costs amounting to approximately 1 percent of GDP. Estimating the time and monetary costs incurred by taxpayers for preparing individual income tax returns, an analysis by the Internal Revenue Service (IRS) shows

---

[5] The IRS estimates of the business and individual income tax compliance costs include out-of-pocket costs and the monetized burden associated with the time spent on preparing the returns.

sources of individual income tax compliance costs by reporting activity (Figure 3-10).[6] More than half—55 percent—of compliance costs arise from keeping track of and reporting income, and the remaining compliance costs arise mostly from calculations for tax deductions and credits. Thus, tax simplification—such as having fewer deductions and credits or streamlining income reporting—has the potential to reduce compliance burdens. Tax simplification could also enhance taxpayer compliance by reducing the opportunities for tax evasion and decreasing inadvertent taxpayer errors in calculating tax liabilities (Kopczuk 2006).[7]

Reforming the International Corporate Tax

The international provisions of the corporate tax code create opportunities for U.S. companies to reduce their taxes by locating their operations and profits abroad. The tax system is subject to gaming, as corporations manipulate complex tax rules to minimize taxes and, in some cases, shift profit that is attributable to activity performed in the United States or elsewhere to low-tax jurisdictions.

The current U.S. tax system subjects foreign subsidiaries of U.S.-based multinationals to taxes on their overseas income while allowing a tax credit for foreign taxes paid. However, corporations often do not need to pay taxes to the Federal Government on that income until they repatriate it to the United States, a rule called deferral (because it defers taxation of the income). Many companies reinvest, rather than repatriate, a significant portion of their income overseas and, as a result, may never face U.S. taxes on much of that income. The U.S. tax system is often described as "worldwide" because it taxes U.S. companies on profits earned abroad. For many companies, however, opportunities for deferral can make it effectively much closer to a territorial system—a system in which taxes are never paid on foreign income. By contrast, although most other developed countries have taken a territorial approach, some countries, including Japan and the United Kingdom, have implemented tax "triggers" that effectively apply worldwide taxation if a multinational is operating in a low-tax country.

U.S. multinational corporations have a significant opportunity to reduce overall taxes paid by shifting profits to low-tax jurisdictions—either by moving their operations and jobs there or by relying on accounting tools and transfer pricing principles to shift profits. Studies show that U.S.

---

[6] Under current law, the IRS is authorized access to Federal tax information for tax administration purposes. Certain Federal agencies have limited access to tax data for governmental statistical use. See Data Watch 3-1.

[7] For example, studies have shown that complexity may have affected EITC compliance and kept eligible taxpayers from claiming the tax credit (Holtzblatt and McCubbin 2004; Kopczuk and Pop-Eleches 2007).

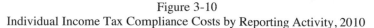

Figure 3-10
Individual Income Tax Compliance Costs by Reporting Activity, 2010

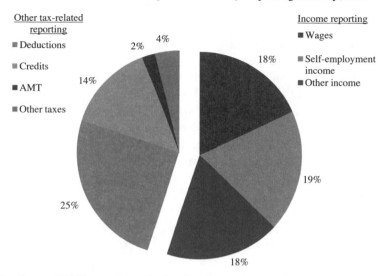

Other tax-related reporting
- Deductions
- Credits
- AMT
- Other taxes

Income reporting
- Wages
- Self-employment income
- Other income

4%
2%
14%
18%
25%
19%
18%

Note: Tax year 2010. The cost of reporting the self-employment tax deduction is included in Other taxes.
Source: Internal Revenue Service, Office of Research, Analysis, and Statistics calculations.

multinationals' decisions about the choice of where to invest are sensitive to effective tax rates in foreign jurisdictions (OECD 2008). Evidence also suggests that U.S. firms' reported profits in a foreign country increase when the country's tax rate declines relative to the U.S. rate, after taking into account other factors that would have influenced the level of income earned by U.S. firms in that foreign country (Clausing 2009; Grubert 2012).

The incentive to shift profits to low-tax jurisdictions can lead to inefficient overinvestment abroad and underinvestment in the United States. It can also erode the U.S. tax base, requiring higher tax rates on income that remains taxable in the United States to collect the same amount of revenue. Finally, the international tax system is very complex, which not only burdens companies with complicated accounting and tax requirements but also benefits companies that avoid paying taxes by manipulating intricate rules.

Business tax reform should be a foundation to maximize investment, growth, and jobs in the United States. It should properly balance the need to reduce tax incentives for U.S. companies to locate overseas with the need for them to be able to compete overseas; some overseas investments and operations are necessary to serve and expand into foreign markets in ways that benefit U.S. jobs and economic growth. The President has proposed to protect the U.S. tax base, strengthen the international corporate tax system, and encourage domestic investment by establishing a new minimum tax on

Data Watch 3-1: Federal Tax Information and Synchronization of Interagency Business Data

Each year, the Internal Revenue Service (IRS) collects tax data from hundreds of millions of taxpayers. During fiscal year 2011, more than 200 million individual income, employment, corporate income, and estate tax returns and 1.8 billion third-party information returns, such as W-2 and 1099 forms, were filed with the IRS (IRS 2012). Successful tax administration builds on taxpayers' willingness to share personal information with the tax authority and voluntarily comply with tax law (Greenia and Mazur 2006). To ensure taxpayer confidence in the tax system, the tax code contains provisions to safeguard taxpayer confidentiality by requiring each access to Federal tax information (FTI) to be authorized by law.

Under current law, access to FTI is authorized within the IRS for tax administration purposes; in other limited cases, disclosures of FTI are allowed only for specified information to specific parties for specific tasks. When considering whether to amend the law to authorize a disclosure of FTI, Congress should evaluate several factors, including the potential benefits resulting from the data usage and the risk of compromising taxpayer confidentiality or affecting their willingness to voluntarily comply with tax law.

Tax law currently authorizes disclosure of business FTI for government statistical use. It authorizes disclosure of business FTI—either for corporate or noncorporate businesses—to the Census Bureau but permits disclosure of business FTI to the Bureau of Economic Analysis (BEA) only for corporate businesses. Another Federal statistical agency, the Bureau of Labor Statistics (BLS), currently does not have access to any business FTI. The Census Bureau uses business FTI to construct its business list, and therefore many Census data products are considered to be "comingled" with tax information (Pilot 2011). Because of the access limits on BEA and BLS, the Census Bureau cannot share many of its products with these two agencies, a situation that prevents the three Federal statistical agencies from synchronizing their business data.

Business data are the fundamental elements for measuring national and local economic activity. National and local statistics on income, output, productivity, payroll, and employment are all based on business data collected by these Federal statistical agencies. Policymakers and businesses rely on these statistics to guide their decisionmaking. Thus, improving the accuracy, consistency, and reliability of national and local economic statistics can yield tremendous benefits because policy formation and business decisionmaking will be based on better quality economic statistics.

Greater synchronization of interagency business data could advance the quality of economic statistics. For example, BLS and the Census Bureau currently have different coverage and classifications in their business data. BEA's National Income and Product Accounts (NIPA) produce two measures of national economic activity: gross domestic product (GDP, which uses Census Bureau data as its primary source data) and gross domestic income (GDI, part of which uses BLS data). The two measures of national economic activity differ in part because of discrepancies in the underlying business data. Allowing Federal statistical agencies to share and coordinate business data would help to reconcile these discrepancies and thereby result in a better measurement of economic activity.

income earned by subsidiaries of U.S. corporations operating abroad (White House/Treasury 2012). That requirement would stop the tax system from rewarding companies for moving profits offshore. Thus, foreign income in a low-tax jurisdiction would be subject to immediate U.S. taxation up to the minimum tax rate, with a foreign tax credit allowed for income taxes on that income paid to the host country. At the same time, this minimum tax would be designed to keep U.S. companies on a level playing field with competitors when engaged in activities that, by necessity, must occur in a foreign country.

THE STATE AND LOCAL BUDGET OUTLOOK

State and local government expenditures have continued to rebound from the challenges created by the Great Recession, although many State and local governments have yet to return to their pre-recession spending and investment levels. State general fund spending grew by 1.6 percent in real terms in FY 2012, after a small 0.6 percent drop in FY 2011 (NASBO 2012a). In the two previous fiscal years, State general fund spending shrunk dramatically, falling by 2.6 percent in FY 2009 and 8.0 percent in FY 2010 (Figure 3-11); the real gain since 1979 has averaged 1.6 percent a year.

As local economic conditions have rebounded, fiscal distress faced by States has abated, although challenges remain. One such indicator of fiscal distress is the need to institute midyear budget cuts in response to lower-than-expected revenues or higher-than-expected outlays. In FY 2012, just 8 States made midyear budget cuts ($1.7 billion total), down from 23 States in FY 2011 ($7.8 billion), 39 States in FY 2010 ($18.3 billion), and 41 States in FY 2009 ($31.3 billion).

Figure 3-11
Real Annual Changes in State General Fund Spending, 1981–2012
Percent

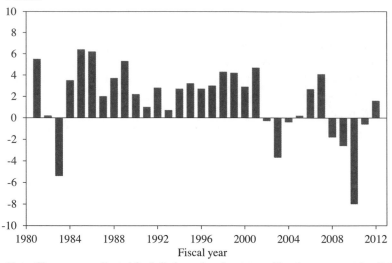

Fiscal year

Note: Changes are adjusted for inflation using the state and local government implicit price deflator.
Source: NASBO (2012a).

Like State spending, local government expenditures fell sharply during the recession. Constrained by lower revenues, cities cut back on spending more than they have in 25 years (National League of Cities 2012). General fund expenditures dropped at least 4 percent in both FY 2010 and FY 2011, almost twice as much as they did following the recession in FY 2001. Asked how they plan to change expenditures in FY 2012, local government budget officers most often said they would reduce the size of the municipal workforce, followed by delays or cancellations of capital infrastructure projects. The National League of Cities projected that expenditures will finally increase in FY 2012, but only by 0.3 percent, because local government revenues have yet to grow since the recession (National League of Cities 2012).

On the revenue side, State general fund tax revenues are poised to increase by $26.1 billion in FY 2013 after increasing by $16.6 billion in FY 2012. In nominal terms, general fund revenues are set to surpass pre-recession levels for the first time in FY 2013. The reason for this jump several years after the onset of the national recovery is that State revenues follow a cyclical pattern with macroeconomic growth but often do so with a lag.

Local government tax receipts were also decimated by the recession and have yet to rebound. A projected decrease in city general fund revenues for FY 2012 will mark the sixth consecutive year of year-over-year decreases in revenues, and city budget officers will continue to face lingering challenges. Each of the primary tax streams used by local governments—property taxes, sales taxes, and income taxes—was affected by the economic downturn. Sales tax revenues dropped sharply and first, as consumers cut back on purchases. In 2011 and 2012, however, city sales tax receipts started to rebound, with sales tax revenues increasing year-over-year in both years (Figure 3-12). Because home values fell, cities—many of which rely heavily on property taxes—faced another area of shrinking revenue. The decline in property tax collections came with a lag, however, probably because of the time needed for lower prices to translate into lower assessed values. Property tax receipts fell in 2010 and 2011 and will continue to pose challenges for strapped local governments. Home prices have started to recover, but slowly. Finally, local governments also face lower income tax receipts as unemployment challenges persist.

The Cyclicality of State and Local Government Expenditures

Particular types of State and local government spending are more sensitive to cyclical factors than others. For example, when economic conditions deteriorate, spending on "automatic stabilizers"—programs like Medicaid that provide means-tested benefits—increases. While automatic stabilizers are widely recognized as being countercyclical, less attention has

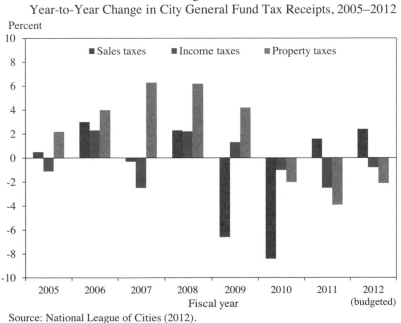

Figure 3-12
Year-to-Year Change in City General Fund Tax Receipts, 2005–2012

Source: National League of Cities (2012).

been paid to the cyclical behavior of public investment spending. One study by the Government Accountability Office (GAO 2011) examined trends in State and local government spending across the business cycle and found that capital expenditures—primarily spending on land, buildings, and equipment—are more procyclical than other types of spending (Table 3-1). The GAO found that spending on health and public welfare is countercyclical, while current expenditures on elementary and secondary education, current expenditures on highways, and capital outlays are the most procyclical categories of State and local government spending. The GAO noted that trends in capital outlays and current expenditures tend to lag the business cycle by one to two years, although there is substantial variation in the lag for current expenditures by type.

Private economists have reached similar conclusions. Echoing the GAO finding, Wang, Hou, and Duncombe (2007) studied the determinants of capital spending, noting that capital expenditures tend to be more procyclical than current expenditures. The authors cited evidence that States' and municipalities' financing decisions are affected by the business cycle, but the study did not draw conclusions about the impact of the business cycle on the level of capital spending. Similarly, McGranahan (1999) found that capital spending is more procyclical than current expenditures. On average, McGranahan found that each percentage point increase in the unemployment rate leads to a $6.94 fall in per capita capital outlays (average per capita spending is $239.85); this drop is split evenly between construction spending ($3.57) and other capital outlays ($3.37). Moreover, McGranahan found that even though State operating budgets do not include capital expenditures, States tend to reduce budgetary pressure by reducing capital spending during downturns. Hines, Hoynes, and Krueger (2001) found that all components of State and local government spending are procyclical, with capital spending (on highways, parks, and recreation, for example) generally more procyclical than current spending (on health and education, for example).

Bureau of Economic Analysis (BEA) data on State and local expenditures show that the most recent recession was somewhat atypical, with gross investment failing to rebound as in other recoveries (see Figure 3-2 above). Ideally, State and local governments would increase investment spending during recessions, both as a means of employing capital and labor, thereby helping to drive the economy out of the recession, and also as a mechanism for strengthening the economy in the future. Moreover, lower labor costs during recessions make capital projects relatively cheap, meaning that investment during recessions can provide taxpayers with a higher return on investment; historically low interest rates in recent years have further lowered the cost of capital projects. Greater investment by State and local

Table 3-1
Cyclical Behavior of State and Local Government Expenditures, 1977–2008

Expenditure function	Correlation with GDP	Cyclical behavior
General expenditures	0.34	Procyclical
Capital outlays	0.50	Procyclical
Current expenditures	0.23	Procyclical
Elementary and secondary education	0.60	Procyclical
Higher education	0.29	Procyclical
Health and hospitals	-0.36	Countercyclical
Highways	0.53	Procyclical
Police and corrections	0.38	Procyclical
Public welfare	-0.31	Countercyclical
All other current expenditures	0.40	Procyclical

Source: GAO (2011).

governments in the most recent recession would have both contributed to the recovery and built a stronger economy in future years at a relatively low cost.

Despite the downturn in investment spending relative to past recessions, the procyclical nature of State and local fiscal policy means that Federal policies can prove particularly effective at mitigating the economic effects of a downturn. State and local governments serve a vital role in providing services to their residents, and the Federal Government contributes to that role by aiding State and local governments through grants, loans, and implicit support through the tax system.

Federal grants-in-aid—which include both cash grants and grants in-kind—have been expanding over time.[8] In constant dollars (FY 2005), Federal grants to State and local governments increased from $45.3 billion in 1960 to an estimated $504.4 billion in 2012 (Figure 3-13). The composition of Federal grants to State and local governments has changed dramatically as well. In 1960, 35.3 percent of Federal grants were for payments to individuals, 47.3 percent were for physical capital, and 17.4 percent were for other uses. As projected, in 2012, the share of grants for payments to individuals grew to 60.2 percent, while the share for physical capital fell to 15.7 percent, and the share for other uses grew to 24.1 percent. Thus, over the past five decades, the share of Federal grants for physical capital has plummeted while the share devoted to individual payments has skyrocketed.

---

[8] Federal grants generally fall into one of two broad categories: categorical grants or block grants. In addition, these grants may have characteristics of one or more other types of grants: formula grants, project grants, and matching grants. Categorical grants have a narrowly defined purpose and may be awarded on a formula basis or as a project grant.

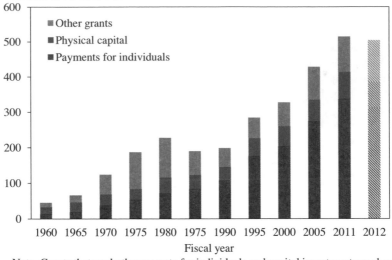

Figure 3-13
Federal Grants to State and Local Governments by Type, 1960–2012

Billions of FY 2005 dollars

Note: Grants that are both payments for individuals and capital investment are shown under capital investment. Figures for FY 2012 are estimates.
Source: OMB (2012a).

Federal Grants to States Through the Recovery Act

The Federal Government used the existing grants structure to provide swift fiscal relief during the recent recession—a time when states faced severe and unforeseen economic conditions. It did so through the Recovery Act, which provided enhanced grant funding in the areas of education, Medicaid, transportation, energy, water, and other programs.[9] Most provisions of the Recovery Act expired in 2010, but some were extended in August 2010 by Public Law 111-226, an act providing education and Medicaid assistance to the States. The temporary fiscal relief provided by the Recovery Act accounts for most of the $141.1 billion increase in Federal outlays for grants-in-aid to States from 2008 to 2010. In 2011, Federal grant outlays were $606.8 billion; this was a $1.6 billion decrease from 2010, reflecting the expiration of the temporary increase in the Federal share of State Medicaid costs and other provisions of the Recovery Act. Grant outlays for 2012 are estimated to increase by $5.7 billion to $612.4 billion.

However, outlays from grants funded through annual appropriations are estimated to decrease by $24.9 billion in 2012 from the previous year and to decrease again by $20.5 billion in 2013. These decreases reflect the

---

[9] In addition to grant funding to States, the Recovery Act created Build America Bonds, which provided State and local governments a lower-cost borrowing tool to finance public capital projects. Authority to issue Build America Bonds expired at the end of 2010.

winding down of discretionary grant spending on Recovery Act programs such as the State Fiscal Stabilization Fund as well as the enactment of caps on discretionary spending in the Budget Control Act of 2011, which constrains appropriations of new discretionary budget authority, including appropriations for grants.

By transferring aid to State and local governments, the Recovery Act helped stabilize programs that would have been cut and kept States and localities from having to institute tax increases. Had the Recovery Act not provided grants-in-aid to State and local governments, these governments would have been forced either to make deeper cuts in funding for important public programs, including critical education and health programs (and the associated jobs to support those programs), or to raise taxes to compensate for the shortfall. Either option would have been detrimental to the economic recovery. The billions of dollars provided to State and local governments were one of the reasons the Recovery Act was able to dampen the recession and put the country on a faster track to recovery.

State and Local Pensions

State and local pension plans are an important part of the nation's retirement security framework, promising future retirement benefits to 14.5 million workers employed by State and local governments in 2011 (Census Bureau 2012). About 19 percent of total employer contributions to employee retirement plans were made through State and local pension plans, and approximately 28 percent of all plan assets were accounted for by State and local pensions (CBO 2011). Pension plan contributions make up a significant component of the compensation provided to State and local government workers, including police officers, firefighters, and teachers.

Most State and local plans are defined benefit plans, which provide workers with a designated benefit based on years of service and final salary.[10] For example, a worker covered by a defined benefit plan might earn benefits equal to 2 percent of wages (often measured over the last several years of employment) multiplied by years of work and adjusted for inflation. The structure of defined benefit plans means that employer liability grows as workers earn wages and increase their tenure with State and local governments; this liability can also grow with inflation because the value of a defined benefit plan is often indexed to the cost of living. From this

---

[10] Defined benefit plans are fundamentally different from defined contribution plans, which allow workers to contribute to an individual retirement account and often offer some form of an employer match. Defined contribution plans do not provide workers with a designated retirement benefit; rather, the individual account balance grows with new contributions and investment returns.

perspective, defined benefit plans can be viewed as a form of deferred compensation, with workers reaching retirement age being owed compensation earned earlier in their career.

Defined benefit programs offer workers a steady stream of income for life, thus providing insurance against outliving assets and investment risk. One drawback to these plans, however, is the problem of underfunding, which presents a serious long-term fiscal challenge for State and local governments. Underfunding arises when the accumulated contributions in State and local government pension accounts are insufficient to cover the expected liabilities owed to public sector workers. The Pew Center on the States estimated that the public pension programs of State and local governments were underfunded by $757 billion in FY 2010, carrying $3.07 trillion in liabilities and $2.31 trillion in assets (Pew Center on the States 2012). Another study showed that the ratio of State and local pension fund assets to liabilities declined from 103 percent in 2000 to 75 percent in 2011, due in large part to market trends and the specific accounting rules adopted by most plans to value assets (Munnell et al. 2012a). While aggregate funding levels have decreased over the past decade, funding adequacy varies considerably from state to state.

Alternative approaches to calculating pension funding suggest even lower levels of funding adequacy. Unlike private pension systems, which are governed by Federal law and regulations, no Federal rules apply to State and local plans in determining plan liabilities and required contributions. Most States and local pension plans adhere to guidelines drafted by the Governmental Accounting Standards Board (GASB) to report funding adequacy, but the board does not have enforcement authority, nor can it require States and localities to adopt specific funding policies. Until June 2012, GASB standards allowed plans to use discount rates based on the expected rates of return—typically around 8 percent—to determine pension liabilities. Under this approach, pension underfunding was about $700 billion at the end of 2009 (CBO 2011), consistent with the Pew Center's estimate. In sharp contrast, CBO found that a broader measure of liabilities that uses the fair value discount rate, an approach often applied in corporate accounting, produces an underfunding estimate of $2 trillion to $3 trillion.

Low levels of funding threaten the welfare of both taxpayers and State and local government employees. One concern is that underfunded pensions will dominate State and local government budgets in upcoming decades, as an increasingly high share of revenue may be needed to provide retired government workers with promised benefits. If taxpayers must devote higher revenue to paying promised benefits to retired workers, less funding may be available for key programs like elementary education, health care, and infrastructure development. From another perspective, underfunded pensions may also pose a risk to government employees, who may see their benefits challenged as a means of achieving cuts in government spending.

Increased transparency in the budget process is a key step toward improving the adequacy of State and local pension funding. One important strategy often proposed to increase transparency is for State and local governments to adopt discount rates for liabilities that accurately portray the magnitude of their promised obligations. Critics of the old GASB discount rate argued that the high discount rate of around 8 percent ignored the role of asset risks in calculating the present value of future promised benefits. Economists often argue that pension liabilities should be discounted by the riskless rate of return because the payments to retired workers will be made with certainty (Novy-Marx and Rauh 2011).[11]

Under the new discount method approved by GASB, plans will project the portion of pension liabilities that are backed by underlying plan assets (that is, the funded portion) and the portion of liabilities that need to be covered by other resources (that is, the unfunded portion). The new standards allow States and localities to use a roughly 8 percent discount rate for funded liabilities but require the use of a riskless discount rate for pension liabilities that are unfunded (NASBO 2012b). With the new GASB standards, the estimated funding ratio of State and local pension plans would have been 57 percent in 2010, markedly lower than the 76 percent estimated under the previous method (Munnell et al. 2012b).[12] Once State and local pension underfunding is better understood through heightened reporting transparency, State and local governments might be more willing to undertake difficult financial decisions and pension reforms to shore up their pension plans.

---

[11] In a sample of 77 municipal plans, the discount rate ranged from 7.5 percent to 10.0 percent, with a median of 8.0 percent (Novy-Marx and Rauh 2011).
[12] This rate change incorporates the effects of the new discount method and other pension accounting reforms approved by GASB.

CHAPTER 4

JOBS, WORKERS AND SKILLS

The future of the American economy depends critically on our workers and their skills, especially in today's global economy. For the past three decades, American workers have faced a challenging job market. Computers and robots now perform routine tasks, reducing demand for workers in many industries and occupations. In addition, advances in communication technology and low transportation costs have enabled many production jobs to be performed in lower-wage countries abroad. The United States needs to invest in the skills of its workforce to engage effectively in the global competition for good jobs, especially in high-end manufacturing. The Nation also needs to produce and attract highly skilled workers who lead innovation, entrepreneurship, and growth.

Aside from the "skills" challenge, the United States, like many other advanced economies, also faces a "demographic" challenge. Rising longevity and lower birth rates have increased the average age of the population and reduced population growth. Even though the United States is in a relatively strong position compared to many other developed nations in this regard, the latest Census estimates project that the prime working-age population, defined as individuals aged 25–54, will continue to decline as a share of the total population, falling from 40.5 percent in 2012 to 37.9 percent by 2040. By affecting the size of the labor force as well as the ratio of retirees to the working-age population, ongoing demographic changes have a direct impact on the long-run growth of the economy.

This chapter begins by describing the demographic and labor force trends that pose challenges in the near future. It next turns to education and the steps the President has taken to ensure that all Americans have access to the education and training they need to succeed in the changing labor market. The chapter ends with an overview of immigration and its potential to help address both of the challenges ahead—the need for more workers and the need for a more skilled, innovative, and entrepreneurial workforce.

Box 4-1: Minimum Wages and Employment

In his State of the Union address, delivered on February 12, 2013, President Obama called on Congress to raise the Federal minimum wage from $7.25 to $9.00 in stages by the end of 2015 and index it to inflation thereafter. His guiding principle was that in the wealthiest nation in the world, no one who works full-time should have to live in poverty. By way of example, President Obama noted that a full-time worker making the minimum wage earns $14,500 a year. Even with the tax relief for lower-income workers that exists in current law, a family with two children and one minimum wage income still lives below the poverty line. Raising the minimum wage to $9.00 would raise the wages of approximately 15 million workers. In addition to making America a magnet for jobs and equipping workers with the skills they need, ensuring that hard work leads to a decent living is a cornerstone of the President's vision to build a stronger economy.

Economists have long studied how the minimum wage affects employment and the economy. A comprehensive survey article written in 1982 concluded that a 10 percent increase in the minimum wage lowers teen employment by 1 to 3 percent. While this reflected the opinion of most economists at the time, the consensus view among economists has since shifted as more evidence has accumulated. Indeed, by the early 1990s time-series estimates of the effect of the minimum wage on teenage employment were turning up statistically insignificant effects (Wellington 1991). The 1999 *Economic Report of the President* concluded that "modest increases in the minimum wage have had very little or no effect on employment."

The shift in consensus reflects two decades worth of studies that have made some methodological advances in the field. Since the 1990s, after the shift in the time-series evidence, economists have used differences across states in the level and timing of changes to minimum wage laws to study the effect of the minimum wage on employment of low wage workers (Card 1992). This approach arguably produces more robust estimates than the previous time-series approach of relating changes in nationwide teenage employment to movements in the federal minimum wage because it allows researchers to do a better job of controlling for other factors, such as underlying economy-wide trends, that might also affect low-wage employment. A further refinement of the state-level analysis is to focus more specifically on comparisons of adjacent states, which has the advantage that underlying economic trends are more likely to have had similar effects on nearby states (Card and Krueger 1994). A particularly compelling recent study takes this approach a step further by comparing all contiguous county-pairs in the United States that are located on the opposite side of a state border (Arindrajit Dube, T. William Lester, and Michael Reich 2011). The authors show that workers benefited in states that increased their minimum wage, such as California, Rhode Island, New York, Vermont, and Washington, relative to similar workers across the state borders. The study concluded, "For cross-state contiguous counties, we find strong earnings effects and no employment effects of minimum wage increases."

A meta-analysis by Doucouliagos and Stanley (2009) of 64 studies on the minimum wage published between 1972 and 2007, encompassing over 1,000 estimates, finds that most estimates are concentrated around zero, indicating no detectable effect (see figure). The authors conclude that the available research finds "no evidence of a meaningful adverse employment effect" of the minimum wage.

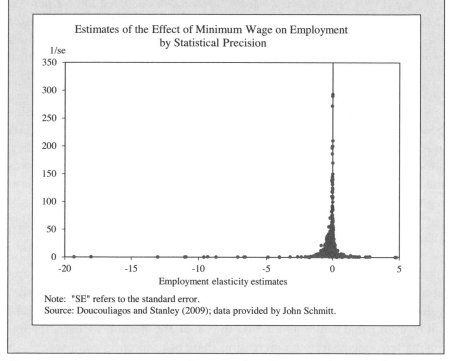

Estimates of the Effect of Minimum Wage on Employment by Statistical Precision

Note: "SE" refers to the standard error.
Source: Doucouliagos and Stanley (2009); data provided by John Schmitt.

Commonsense immigration reform can be a key contributor to future economic growth and job creation.

DEMOGRAPHIC AND LABOR FORCE TRENDS

The U.S. adult civilian non-institutional population stood at 237.8 million in 2010 and is projected to reach 263.0 million by 2020, growing at a projected annual rate of 1.0 percent, down from 1.1 percent in the 2000s and

1.2 percent in the 1990s. Further, the share of older Americans is projected to grow over the 2010–20 period, with the number of individuals aged 55 and older increasing 2.6 percent a year, while the number of 16–24 year olds remains roughly constant and the size of the working-age population grows by just 0.3 percent a year (Toossi 2012). These population projections reflect the aging of the baby-boom generation born between 1946 and 1964. Because older men and women are considerably less likely to participate in the labor force than younger individuals, these demographic trends imply that the fraction of the population in the labor force will fall. This trend has already begun.

After increasing at a steady clip for two and half decades starting in the mid-1960s, labor force participation exhibited slower growth during the 1990s and began to fall during the 2000s. The overall labor force participation rate (LFPR), which peaked at 67.1 percent in 2000, fell to 63.7 percent in 2012. Approximately half of this decline can be attributed to the aging of the population and the retirement of the oldest members of the baby-boom generation together with long-term declines in labor force participation among several of the groups shown in Figure 4-1 not related to cyclical factors (see Table 2-1 in Chapter 2).

As the figure illustrates, participation rates have fallen for all major demographic groups since 2000 with the exception of men and women aged 55 and older. The LFPR for younger men and women fell in the 2000s, although the decline for men is a continuation of a long-term trend, whereas the gradual decline for women in the 2001–07 recovery is a new development that reverses a long period of rising participation. The labor force participation rate for 16–24 year olds has dropped precipitously since 2000 after trending down since 1980.

Recent studies suggest two different explanations for the declining trend among teens and young adults. On the one hand, the increasing monetary return to educational attainment has made it more likely that young people enroll in school rather than become employed. One recent study found that while about two-thirds of the decline in participation among teens stems from an increasing share of teens enrolled in school, an additional portion is due to declining participation among those enrolled in school (Aaronson, Park, and Sullivan 2007). To the extent that young people are forgoing work for education, the decline in their labor force participation is less of a concern because they are acquiring skills that will raise their productivity when they do enter or return to work. Less optimistically, other researchers have argued that competition for low-wage jobs has been a major cause of the decline in the teen LFPR, with low-skilled adults now filling jobs that teenagers used to take (Smith 2011).

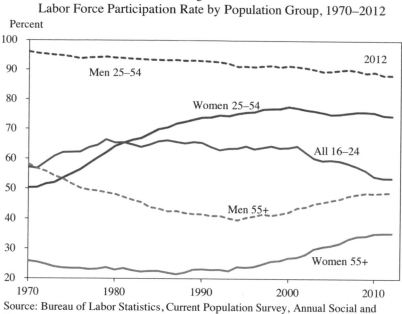

Figure 4-1
Labor Force Participation Rate by Population Group, 1970–2012

Source: Bureau of Labor Statistics, Current Population Survey, Annual Social and Economic Supplement; CEA calculations.

On the other end of the age spectrum, older workers have increased their labor force participation. Researchers have identified rising education levels and the growth of white-collar and service jobs as important explanations. Other plausible explanations that have not yet been investigated fully are improved health and reductions in the value of retirement savings (Blau and Goodstein 2010; Maestas and Zissimopoulos 2010).

The labor force participation of working-age men has declined steadily since the 1970s. One likely factor behind this trend is that real wages have declined for less skilled men. Since the early 1970s, the average real wage has fallen about 25 percent for high school dropouts and about 15 percent for high school graduates with no further education (Acemoglu and Autor 2011).

The pattern for women has been different. During the 1970s and 1980s, the economy benefited greatly as married women entered the labor force and increased potential and actual gross domestic product (GDP). As Figure 4-1 above illustrates, the growth in female labor force participation abated in the early 2000s. Different forces appear to be at work for different groups of women. Gains in employment for less educated women during the 1990s were encouraged by policy changes (for example, the Earned Income Tax Credit and welfare reform) and by strong economic growth that was not sustained in the early 2000s. Highly educated women, particularly mothers, have pulled back from the pattern of large increases in labor force participation observed in the 1970s and 1980s. Lack of hours flexibility and the challenges inherent in balancing career and family appear to be important factors for these women.

A Slowdown in Women's Participation Rates

Table 4-1 reports participation rates of working-age women in selected years that correspond to peak years of the business cycle and thus allow a focus on long-term trends. From 1969 to 1989, the labor force participation rate of working-age women increased 24.5 percentage points. The most dramatic changes in participation have occurred among married women, and more starkly, among married mothers. The LFPR among married mothers increased an astounding 31.4 percentage points from 1969 to 1999. Growth among all working-age women was slower during the 1990s, but the LFPR for working-age women increased another 4 percentage points to 77 percent in 1999. As the table shows, however, since 1999, the participation rate for these women has declined, falling to 75.6 percent by 2007.

Figure 4-2, which compares the participation rates of women born in different periods, provides insight into the rise and subsequent stagnation of participation among married mothers. Among women born between 1936 and 1945, labor force participation is moderately high at younger ages, drops during the peak child-bearing years, exhibits a subsequent reprise in mid-life, and finally declines as retirement approaches. The curve tends to rise across successive generations of women, indicating higher participation rates for each successive cohort, and the dip associated with child-bearing ages has largely disappeared. The rise in participation, however, appears to have stopped with the most recent generation. Given this pattern across birth cohorts, it is difficult to be optimistic about future increases in the labor supply of prime-age women. New birth cohorts work no more than the immediately preceding cohort at the same ages, and it is therefore unlikely they will work more at later ages. The gains during the 1970s and 1980s achieved from the increased participation of married mothers appear to have come to a standstill and perhaps even partially reversed.

What has brought about this change? One candidate explanation—that labor market prospects have declined for women in the 2000s—cannot be the whole story, since participation has fallen even among groups for whom average wages have risen. For example, according to one recent investigation, the average weekly wage of women aged 25–39 with a college degree increased 2.4 percent from 1999 to 2007, after adjusting for inflation, even as the share of this group who are employed fell 3.0 percentage points (Moffitt 2012).

Table 4-1
Labor Force Participation Rate of Women Aged 25-54, 1969–2007

	Percent				
	1969	1979	1989	1999	2007
Prime-Age Women	48.8	62.1	73.3	77.0	75.6
Marital Status					
All married	43.5	57.4	70.2	74.1	73.3
Widowed/divorced	69.6	73.4	78.4	81.6	79.0
Never married	80.5	80.8	81.8	82.6	79.9
Marital status and presence of children					
Married mothers	40.8	54.4	67.8	72.2	71.6
Widowed/divorced mothers	65.5	70.9	76.1	82.5	81.2
Never-married mothers	50.4	57.6	64.0	78.4	75.4
Race					
White	47.6	61.6	73.3	76.9	75.6
Black	58.7	66.5	74.1	79.6	77.8
Other	49.1	62.3	69.5	71.4	72.1
Education					
High school dropouts	45.0	48.7	51.3	56.1	53.2
High school graduates	49.8	62.7	73.4	75.2	73.2
Some college	48.2	66.9	78.3	80.2	79.1
College graduates	58.2	74.9	83.4	84.3	81.8

Source: Bureau of Labor Statistics, Current Population Survey; CEA calculations.

Figure 4-2
Age-Specific Labor Force Participation Rate
by Birth Cohort for Women, 1926–1992

Source: Bureau of Labor Statistics, Current Population Survey, Annual Social and
Economic Supplement; CEA calculations.

The one subgroup of women most likely to have been affected by declining labor market prospects is never-married mothers, a population that tends to have lower levels of education and correspondingly lower wages. As Table 4-1 illustrates, the labor force participation of these women rose dramatically from 64.0 percent in 1989 to 78.4 percent in 1999. One factor contributing to this increase was the 1996 welfare reform act, which replaced the welfare entitlements embodied in the old Aid for Families with Dependent Children with more temporary and conditional assistance under the Temporary Assistance to Needy Families program (Blank 2002; Moffitt 2003; Grogger 2003). Another important factor was the expansion of the Earned Income Tax Credit (EITC) in 1986, 1990, and 1993, which made work more attractive and encouraged the entry of low-wage workers into the labor force (Eissa and Liebman 1996; Meyer and Rosenbaum 2001). The impacts of these program and tax changes were amplified by the strong labor market of the second half of the 1990s, a situation that was not sustained as labor markets weakened in the 2000s. The further expansion of the EITC under the Recovery Act and the American Taxpayer Relief Act, and increasing and indexing the minimum wage as proposed by President Obama, would be expected to encourage greater labor force participation for this group in the future.

Work Schedules and Workplace Flexibility

Recent studies that examine the career trajectories of highly educated women in business and law provide some perspective on the challenges women face as they attempt to balance career and family. One study followed a cohort of University of Chicago graduates who had earned a master's in business administration (Bertrand, Goldin, and Katz 2010). While male and female graduates started their careers with similar earnings, 17 percent of the women were not working at all 10 years later, compared with only 1 percent of the men. In addition, only 62 percent of female graduates were working year-round full-time 10 years after graduation, compared with more than 92 percent of the men. The lower levels of work among these career-minded women generally were associated with motherhood, suggesting that work-family balance issues played a role.

One way that women (and others with family responsibilities) may achieve greater flexibility for juggling these competing demands is to work part time rather than full time during some periods. Traditionally, however, given that part-time jobs tended to pay lower wages, the fact that women were more likely to be in part-time work was thought to be a major impediment to women gaining equal pay (Blank and Burtless 1990; Manning and Petrongolo 2008; Bardasi and Gornick 2008). In some cases, however, offering part-time work—and greater hours flexibility more generally—may be seen by employers as a way to attract highly qualified workers, especially highly qualified women who might otherwise choose not to work.

Other advanced economies appear to be offering a different mix of work schedules and employment opportunities. Figure 4-3 shows a comparison of labor force participation rates for women, 25–54 years old, in selected advanced economies. While participation rates in France, Germany, and the United Kingdom were slightly below the U.S. rate in 1991, they were higher than the U.S. rate by 2011. Much of the rapid rise in the European participation rates for working-age women has come from increases in part-time work. In contrast, women in the United States are more likely either to work full-time—defined as 35 hours or more a week—or not to work at all. Figure 4-4 shows that, among the selected countries, U.S. women are still the most likely to work full-time.

The labor force participation rate and average hours worked among those who do participate can be used to calculate average hours worked per woman across countries. In 2005–09, women worked an average of 26.8 hours a week in the United States, more than the average of 26.4 hours per capita in France, 24.4 in the United Kingdom, 22.3 in Germany, and 20.2 in the Netherlands. The U.S. average, however, was down from 27.4 hours a week in 1995–99, while women's hours worked had risen in all the other countries.

A recent study by Blau and Kahn (2013) noted that in 1990, the United States ranked 6th among 22 developed countries in women's labor force participation, but by 2010 the United States had fallen to the 17th position. Blau and Kahn found that the increased prevalence of "family-friendly policies"—parental leave as well as part-time work entitlements—in other developed countries can account for up to 29 percent of the decline in U.S. women's LFPR relative to other countries. Among the countries shown in Figure 4-3, the greatest change in labor force participation for prime-age women occurred in the Netherlands, where the rate rose by nearly 20 percentage points between 1991 and 2011. During this period, the Netherlands instituted laws that mandate equal pay per working hour regardless of total weekly hours worked. These requirements were accompanied by other laws that establish employees' right to request changes in their weekly working hours or request parental leave on a part-time basis (OECD 2012a). As Data Watch 4-1 highlights, the United States lags behind in the availability of both paid and unpaid leave.

One question is whether rising labor force participation comes at a cost. In particular, women in other developed countries could be accepting lower wages in exchange for being able to work part-time or having access

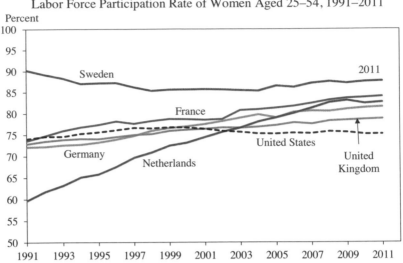

Figure 4-3
Labor Force Participation Rate of Women Aged 25–54, 1991–2011

Note: Workers on leave are considered employed. The participation rates in the KILM data are harmonized to account for differences in national data and scope of coverage, collection and tabulation methodologies, as well as for other country-specific factors such as military service requirements.
Source: International Labour Organization, Key Indicators of the Labor Market (KILM).

Figure 4-4
Percent of Women Ages 25 Years and Older Working Full-Time, 1991–2009

Note: Full-time is defined as 35 hours per week or more. Workers on leave are considered employed. The participation rates in the KILM data are harmonized to account for differences in national data and scope of coverage, collection and tabulation methodologies, as well as for other country-specific factors such as military service requirements.
Source: International Labour Organization, Key Indiciators of the Labor Market (KILM).

to other forms of workplace flexibility. Contrary to this notion, however, gender wage gaps are actually smaller in other developed countries than in the United States. For example, in 2010, the female-to-male hourly wage ratio was 77.7 percent in Germany, 78.7 percent in the United Kingdom, 81.9 percent in the Netherlands, 84.4 percent in France, and 84.4 percent in Sweden. In all of these countries, part-time work and other types of workplace flexibility, such as paid parental leave, are more available than in the United States, where the female-to-male hourly wage ratio was 75.0 percent. Part of what lies behind this phenomenon is that the wage distribution is more compressed in these other countries (Blau and Kahn 2003). Although women in the United States and France are at similar percentile positions of the overall wage distribution relative to their male counterparts, for example, wage compression translates into a much smaller gender wage gap between the average working man and woman in France compared to the United States. Comparisons across countries also suggest, however, that it is not inherently the case that greater flexibility implies lower wages.

Other recent work comparing wages and hours flexibility across occupations also challenges the notion that hours flexibility necessarily comes at a cost. Goldin and Katz (2012) provide an illustrative case study of the pharmacist occupation, where consolidation brought about by scale economies led to the rise of large retail giants. The new market structure made it possible for two part-time pharmacists to substitute for one full-time pharmacist, creating a much more flexible work environment for women. Notably, part-time pharmacists earn no less per hour than full-time pharmacists in contrast to other occupations employing female college graduates where working part-time is associated with wages as much as 20 percent lower. Among women aged 35–39 with pharmacy degrees, only 12 percent were not in the labor force, compared with 18 percent among other college graduates. The study also found that only 11 percent of women with active pharmacy licenses ever had a spell out of the workforce. Given this pattern of continuous participation, female pharmacists are likely to work more over their lifetimes than other women who start working long hours but drop out altogether mid-career as they face the often stark choice between work and family.

To be sure, not all occupations can easily accommodate flexible hours. There is some evidence, however, that even in fields such as medicine, where part-time work is rare, jobs may be evolving to accommodate more flexible schedules (Goldin and Katz 2011). More flexible schedules also seem to be gaining acceptance in the business community (CEA 2010). As more businesses adopt these practices, the cost to any one firm of their adoption will be lowered. An individual employer may be less likely to offer flexible work

Data Watch 4-1: New Evidence on Access to Paid Leave

The traditional family today is vastly different than it was decades ago. In contrast to 1975, when just 43 percent of women with children were working, nearly two-thirds of women with children were at work in 2010. The juggling of work and family is not a challenge for women alone. Among married households with children, 60 percent had two working parents. In addition, Americans are getting older. With an aging population, working families will face growing challenges in providing eldercare in the years to come. Access to paid leave and scheduling flexibility can help families deal with these challenges.

Each of the President's Budgets since FY 2011 has proposed money for a State Paid Leave Fund at the Department of Labor that would provide competitive grants to help cover start-up costs for states that choose to launch their own paid leave programs. The value to families of paid leave is illustrated by California's experience with its Paid Family Leave (PFL) program. Since 2004, employed individuals in California have been able to take up to six weeks of paid leave to spend time with a newborn or a newly adopted child or to care for a seriously ill relative. During this time, workers receive payments through the State Disability Insurance system for up to 55 percent of their earnings. A recent study found that the California program more than doubled the overall use of maternity leave, increasing it from around three to six or seven weeks for the typical new mother, with especially large growth among less advantaged mothers, while also raising the hours and wage incomes of employed mothers in the affected group by 6 to 9 percent (Rossin-Slater, Ruhm, and Waldfogel 2011).

The President's FY 2011 Budget included funding to add a module to the American Time Use Survey (ATUS) asking workers about the leave policies at their place of work. The module had questions on leave access, leave use, and unmet need for leave. Because the ATUS is linked to the Current Population Survey, rich data are available on the characteristics of people surveyed. The ATUS survey also provides much-needed information on workers' ability to adjust their schedules or location or to work from home, as well as other dimensions of workplace flexibility that can help in balancing work and family obligations.

This new survey indicates that a large fraction of American workers still lacks access to paid leave, including paid sick leave and paid family leave for the birth of a child. In addition, only 53 percent of the workers reported that they had the ability to adjust their schedule or work location. Previous studies using the National Compensation Survey have shown large disparities in access to paid leave by level of earnings. The new data confirm these findings and, in addition, document large disparities in access to paid leave and scheduling adjustments across education groups and between Hispanics and non-Hispanics (see table). Those in the top quartile of earnings are 1.7 times as likely to have access to paid leave as workers in the bottom quartile (83 percent vs. 50 percent). College-educated workers are about twice as likely to have access to paid leave as workers without a high school degree (72 percent vs. 35 percent). Only 43 percent of Hispanics have access to paid leave, compared with 61 percent of non-Hispanics. Although a large and roughly similar share of workers in most groups has access to unpaid leave, that is a poor substitute for paid leave that can be taken when the need arises.

Access to Leave by Selected Characteristics, 2011

	Percent		
	Access to paid leave	Access to unpaid leave	Access to schedule adjustment or location
Total	59.0	76.6	55.9
Gender			
Male	60.3	75.4	55.5
Female	57.5	77.9	56.3
Race/Ethnicity			
White only	58.9	76.9	56.6
Black only	60.6	76.7	49.8
Asian only	62.2	72.1	59.8
Hispanic	43.0	71.2	48.2
Non-Hispanic	61.4	77.4	57.1
Education			
Less than high school	34.9	70.4	37.6
High school	61.1	75.8	48.2
Some college	66.4	78.2	55.8
Bachelor's or higher	71.6	75.3	60.5
Weekly Earnings			
$0–$540	50.1	78.0	47.2
$541–$830	77.1	78.9	48.8
$831–$1,230	81.3	74.9	51.4
$1,230+	82.7	75.4	59.9

Notes: Education breakdown is only for individuals age 25 and over. Each earnings range represents approximately 25 percent of full-time wage and salary workers (except self-employed incorporated workers) who held only one job.
Source: Bureau of Labor Statistics, American Time Use Survey, Leave Module; CEA calculations.

schedules when other firms have not adopted the same practice out of the fear that it will attract less committed workers. This situation is similar to health insurance, where before enactment of the Affordable Care Act, a firm might not have offered health insurance in an environment where employer-provided health insurance was rare out of the fear that it would attract the least healthy workers. If all firms engage in the practice, the risk to any one firm is lowered.

Such developments may well provide a boost to the economy. Women received a majority of both bachelor's degrees (57 percent) and master's degrees (60 percent) awarded in 2010. Educational attainment commands a high return in an increasingly knowledge-based economy. It is in society's collective interest to encourage women to make full use of these educational investments by remaining in the labor market where the return to their job-related skills can be realized.

GOVERNMENT AS A PARTNER IN HUMAN CAPITAL AND SKILL FORMATION

Overwhelming evidence shows that the average return to obtaining a college education is large. In 2011, the median weekly earnings of individuals with a bachelor's degree was $1,053, compared with $638 for individuals with only a high school diploma—a 65 percent premium for the college graduate. A bachelor's degree is also the gateway to other advanced degrees that command even higher earnings premiums (Figure 4-5). The premium for college and beyond has been rising since 1980 and has continued to increase, albeit at a slower rate than in the 1980s (Acemoglu and Autor 2011). Because the number of college graduates also has been increasing over this time, the rising premium is a signal that the economy is demanding still more college graduates.

From a national perspective, an educated workforce is vital. The productivity of a nation's labor force is a key input into future economic growth, and the most direct prescription for increasing labor productivity is investment in skills. The United States has historically been a leader among developed countries in the share of its population with postsecondary education (referred to by the Organisation for Economic Co-operation and Development as "tertiary" education). That standing has fallen over the past generation, with the United States now ranked 14th among a set of 34 industrialized nations in the share of 25–34 year olds with such education (OECD 2012b). While other measures can be used to assess a nation's ability to educate its workforce—including measures of educational quality, test scores, and how well people with skills are matched to jobs that can make use

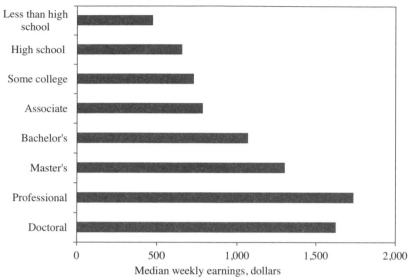

Figure 4-5
Median Weekly Earnings by Education Level, 2012

Median weekly earnings, dollars

Note: Data are for full-time wage and salary workers, 25 years and older.
Source: Bureau of Labor Statistics, Current Population Survey.

of them—the fall in the U.S. postsecondary education ranking is a reminder that we have more to do to provide America's workers with the skills to compete in today's economy.

Early learning and the quality of education from kindergarten through high school (K–12) are key determinants of successfully completing a college degree. Study after study finds that early life conditions have persistent and large effects on later life outcomes such as high school graduation rates, employment, and earnings (Cunha and Heckman 2008; Cunha, Heckman, and Schennach 2010; Almond and Currie 2011). In his State of the Union address delivered to Congress on February 12, 2013, President Obama proposed to work with states to make high-quality preschool available to every single child in America. Four years ago, the President launched the Race to the Top competition, which has proven to be successful in convincing states to develop smarter curricula and higher standards for grades K-12. In his 2013 State of the Union address, the President announced a new challenge to high schools to partner with colleges and employers to better equip students with the problem-solving and math skills that are in demand in today's high-tech economy.

President Obama wants to make the United States the leader in post-secondary attainment. In his address to Congress on February 24, 2009, he set 2020 as the year by which the Nation would once again have the highest proportion in the world of young people graduating from college. The U.S. Department of Education projects that the share of college graduates will need to increase by 50 percent to achieve this goal. That means 8 million more young adults will need to earn associate degrees, bachelor's degrees, and meaningful postsecondary certificates by 2020. To achieve this ambitious goal, the higher education system must undertake far-reaching reforms to improve college readiness, widen access, ensure quality, promote affordability and value, and accelerate completion. Colleges and universities in every state have a vital role and a unique opportunity to help America again lead the world in college attainment.

Giving America's workers the skills to compete for good jobs will require the necessary resources to educate millions of additional students. Unfortunately, State and local government support for higher education—traditionally the cornerstone of public higher education funding—has been falling for at least a decade. From 2000 to 2010, State appropriations for public four-year institutions fell from $8,029 to $6,388 per full-time student, while appropriations for public community colleges fell from $7,095 to $5,712 (in 2010 dollars).[1] This sharp drop in State support has left postsecondary institutions in need of alternative revenue sources, including additional tuition dollars. In fact, in 2010, for the first time ever, public research and master's institutions received more revenue from tuition than from State appropriations. While State appropriations fell only 0.4 percent in 2012, the effects of budget cuts stemming from the economic downturn are expected to last for some time.

Sticker tuition is the price of tuition advertised by the individual colleges. Net tuition is the price students actually pay after deducting Federal, State, and private aid, as well as various discounts offered by the institutions themselves. Between 2000 and 2012, sticker tuition increased from $4,860 to $8,370 (in 2012 dollars) per full-time student at public institutions, an increase of $3,510, and from $21,310 to $28,280 at private institutions, an increase of $6,970 (Figure 4-6). Net tuition per full-time student has increased much less than sticker tuition, going up $1,260 at public institutions and $820 at private institutions over this period. The relatively modest increase in the net cost of attending college resulted in large part from Federal policies aimed at reducing the price of education. President Obama has worked to expand these Federal programs. Expanded Pell Grants made college more affordable for 9.4 million low-income students in 2011

---

[1] States provide substantially less appropriations to private institutions on a per-student basis. State funding for private institutions was more stable over this period. For example, state appropriations per full-time student rose from $513 to $523 at private research institutions and fell from $537 to $288 at private master's institutions. (College Board 2010). See: http://chronicle.com/article/State-Spending-on-Higher/136745/

Figure 4-6
Tuition and Fees for Full-Time Undergraduate Students, 1990–2012

a. Private institutions

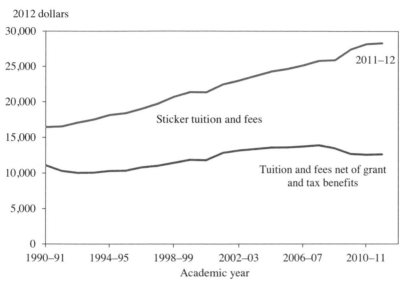

b. Public institutions

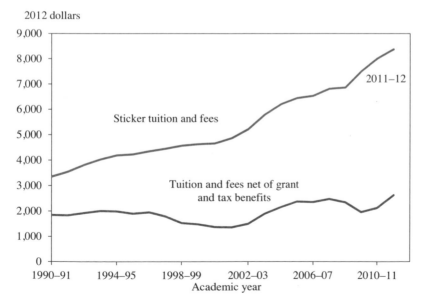

Source: The College Board, Annual Survey of Colleges, Trends in Student Aid (2012).

(2.4 million more than in 2009), and the establishment of the American Opportunity Tax Credit (AOTC) has lowered the cost of attending college for millions more.

Expanded Pell Grants

Pell Grants are the foundation of the Nation's efforts to make college affordable for students from lower- and middle-income families. Pell Grants help more than 9 million Americans a year pay for college, but the purchasing power of these grants has diminished over time. Recognizing the importance of the Pell Grant program to so many people, President Obama worked aggressively to increase the maximum award. The Health Care and Education Reconciliation Act, signed into law in 2010, raised the maximum grant from $5,550 for the 2012–13 academic year to $5,975 in 2017–18. The Act invests approximately $40 billion a year in Pell Grants to ensure that all eligible students receive an award and that these awards will be increased in future years to keep pace with inflation. These steps, together with the funding provided in the American Recovery and Reinvestment Act of 2009 (the Recovery Act) and President Obama's first two Budgets, more than doubled the total amount of funding available for Pell Grant awards.

President Obama also took steps to stabilize Pell Grant funding. In the past, the budgeting process for Pell Grants often led to funding shortfalls, as Pell Grant funding is subject to the annual appropriations process rather than financed through mandatory funding. The appropriations bill that funds Pell Grants for the upcoming academic year is passed almost a full year before the funds become available, and thus the funding is established before it can be clear what the program will cost. The recent shortfall was expected to be particularly severe because of the large number of students qualifying for the award. The Act covered the expected funding shortfall and much of the recent growth in Pell costs, putting the program on a sounder footing going forward. The Act increased investments in Pell Grants by reforming existing student loan programs to deliver loans directly to students instead of subsidizing banks through the more costly Federal Family Educational Loan program. Direct student loans are more efficient and affordable for taxpayers, and the reform allowed more than $60 billion to be reinvested in Pell Grants and other programs that support and sustain college access, while cutting billions from the national deficit (CBO 2010).

Expanded American Opportunity Tax Credit

Tax credits for higher education expenses were substantially expanded by President Obama in the Recovery Act. Before 2009, taxpayers could claim either the Lifetime Learning Credit or the Hope Scholarship Credit toward higher education expenses. The Recovery Act established the American Opportunity Tax Credit, an expanded version of the Hope Credit. The AOTC offers a larger maximum benefit, makes more middle-income taxpayers eligible, and is partially refundable. These provisions substantially enlarged both the pool of taxpayers eligible for education tax credits and the amount of money available to qualifying taxpayers.[2]

In 2010, the AOTC was one of the most widely used education tax incentives, with 11.9 million taxpayers (8.3 percent of all taxpayers) claiming the credit (Table 4-2). The AOTC benefits totaled $12.3 billion, likely making the credit more important to college affordability than all other education deductions and credits combined. The benefits of the AOTC were spread throughout the income distribution with low- and middle-income families receiving substantial benefits. Seventy-nine percent of the beneficiaries had household incomes below $100,000, and 13.1 percent of beneficiaries had household incomes below $25,000. The refundable aspect of the AOTC was particularly beneficial to low-income households. In 2010, AOTC benefits claimed as refundable credits were worth a total of $6.0 billion to American households, with those benefits flowing overwhelmingly to households with incomes under $50,000. The majority of beneficiaries of the refundable portion of the AOTC—63.6 percent—had household incomes under $25,000. In recent budget negotiations, the Administration achieved an agreement with Congress to extend the AOTC for an additional five years. If the AOTC program had been allowed to expire, 11 million college students and their families would have seen tax increases averaging $1,100. President Obama has called on Congress to make this tax credit permanent so that families can plan ahead and count on this credit for all four years of college.

Aggregate Student Loan Debt

While net tuition has risen considerably less than sticker tuition, for some low- and middle-income families, even the rise in net tuition may have put a quality education out of reach; for other students, the rise in college costs has led to substantially higher levels of borrowing. Aggregate student debt has grown steadily, from $241 billion in the first quarter of 2003 to $966 billion in the fourth quarter of 2012 (in dollars not adjusted for inflation). In contrast, after increasing earlier in the 2000s, aggregate amounts of other types of consumer debt, including mortgages, home equity loans,

---

[2] The AOTC is available to taxpayers with income below $90,000 ($180,000 if married), offering a maximum credit amount of $2,500 per student for the first four years of postsecondary education; students must be enrolled at least part-time and be pursuing a degree to be eligible. The AOTC is 40 percent refundable, meaning that taxpayers with no tax liability can claim up to $1,000 toward higher education expenses.

Table 4-2
Education Tax Incentives: The American Opportunity Tax Credit, 2010

Income Class	Returns	Amount (thousands of dollars)	Percent of income class benefitting	Percent of total benefit
$0 to $24,999	2,829,111	1,605,855	4.8	13.1
$25,000 to $49,999	3,628,972	3,579,601	10.5	29.2
$50,000 to $99,999	3,628,533	4,500,639	11.8	36.7
$100,000 to $199,999	1,776,318	2,582,592	12.4	21.0
$200,000 or more	4,122	3,385	0.1	0.0
All returns, total	11,867,055	12,272,073	8.3	100.0

Source: Internal Revenue Service, Statistics of Income.

and credit card and auto debt, have fallen since the financial crisis (Figure 4-7).[3] In fact, more student loan debt is now outstanding than either credit card debt or auto loan debt; only the mortgage debt category is larger. This rise in aggregate student loan debt, coupled with an increase in the share of student borrowers in delinquency status, has focused growing attention on student borrowing.

The rise in aggregate student debt—apparent even after adjusting the figures to account for inflation—has been driven partly by increased enrollment in postsecondary education (Figure 4-8). Between 1990 and 2012, the number of students attending college increased from 13.8 million to 21.0 million. From this perspective, the rise in aggregate student debt is partly the result of increased investment in human capital, which can be expected to lead to higher wages in the future and to a more prosperous standard of living for the cohorts who have been entering the labor market. The rise in aggregate student debt also reflects increases in the share of students who take out student loans and increases in the amount they borrow. Total borrowing has fallen in the aftermath of the financial crisis, and some of the increase in student debt may reflect families taking out student loans rather than home equity lines of credit to pay for college, but concern has been expressed about the increase in student debt.

Among students who received a bachelor's degree from a four-year public college between academic years 1999–2000 and 2010–11, the share who took out student loans rose from 54 percent to 57 percent. More importantly, the average loan amount rose by 16.1 percent, from $20,500 to $23,800 (in constant 2011 dollars). Sharply rising student loan debt not only threatens the financial stability of recent graduates but also may serve as a disincentive for younger students who are deciding whether to invest

---

[3] Aggregate mortgage debt peaked in 2008:Q3, home equity debt peaked in 2009:Q1, and auto debt, credit card debt, and other debt peaked in 2008:Q4.

Figure 4-7
Compositions of Household Debt Balance, 2003–2012

Trillions of dollars

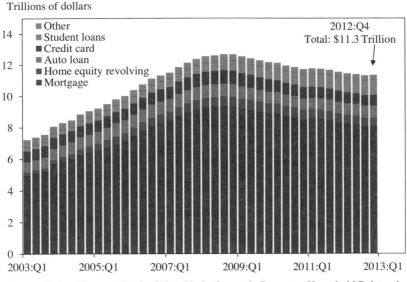

Source: Federal Reserve Bank of New York, Quarterly Report on Household Debt and Credit.

Figure 4-8
Total Postsecondary Enrollment by Type of Institution, 1990–2010

Millions of students

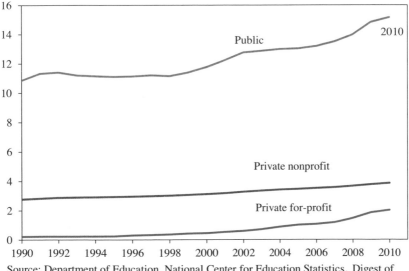

Source: Department of Education, National Center for Education Statistics, Digest of Education Statistics (2011).

in their future and obtain a college degree. To help protect taxpayers, borrowers, and the broader economy against the threat of rising student loan delinquencies, the Administration has advanced several polices designed to make it easier for students to pay back their education loans and to hold schools accountable for poor student debt outcomes after graduation.

Income-Based Repayment

Since 2009, responsible former students have been able to enroll in an Income-Based Repayment (IBR) plan to cap student loan payments. In October 2011, the Administration announced a new "Pay As You Earn" option that will reduce monthly payments for about 1.6 million current college students and borrowers; eligible borrowers include those holding any type of Federal student loan, such as Stafford, PLUS, and consolidation loans (nonfederal loans and loans in default are not eligible). Starting in 2012, the new IBR option has allowed eligible students to cap their annual loan payments at 10 percent of their discretionary income. The amount that an eligible student borrower is required to pay each month is based on adjusted gross income (AGI) and family size. Specifically, the maximum monthly payment equals 15 percent of the difference between AGI and 150 percent of the poverty threshold for a given family size, divided by 12. Eligible borrowers never have to pay more than the maximum monthly threshold; if a borrower's monthly payments are higher than this threshold, they may apply to have their monthly payments lowered. Ultimately, IBR helps responsible student loan borrowers continue to make payments on their student loans at a manageable rate. As of November 2012, the Department of Education estimated that approximately 1.37 million borrowers are participating in the IBR program.

Federal Loan Consolidation

The Administration also took important steps to allow student borrowers to better manage their debt by consolidating their Federal student loans. Starting in January 2012, an estimated 6 million current students and recent college graduates were eligible to consolidate their loans as a Direct Loan, and by so doing, reduce their interest rates. Before this policy change, approximately 5.8 million borrowers had both a Direct Loan and a Federal Family Education Loan. These loans require separate payments making borrowers more likely to default. By consolidating these loans, borrowers could achieve the convenience of a single payment to a single lender. Borrowers who took advantage of this consolidation option also received up to a 0.5 percentage point reduction in their interest rate on some of their loans, which means lower monthly payments that may save each borrower hundreds of dollars in interest over the life of the loan.

The Growth of For-Profit Colleges

Although they still account for only a small fraction of all postsecondary education students, for-profit colleges are the fastest-growing type of postsecondary school. They offer both an opportunity and a challenge for America's system of higher education. For-profit colleges have been shown to be flexible and innovative in meeting the needs of many postsecondary students, especially those who seek a nontraditional education or who require flexible arrangements for receiving their education, such as on-line and evening courses. Many for-profit colleges respond quickly to the changing needs of employers, and they can play an important role in helping more Americans earn college degrees. However, the experiences of some students at for-profit schools have been a cause for concern.

For-profit colleges have shown mixed outcomes with respect to completion rates relative to other types of institutions. For-profit completion rates in one- and two-year programs tend to be higher than completion rates for similar programs at other schools, but completion rates in for-profit bachelor programs are significantly lower. Low graduation rates not only waste taxpayer funds devoted to subsidizing the cost of education but can lead to prolonged financial hardship for students who borrow to finance their education but do not gain a college diploma to add to their earning potential.

Students at for-profit schools are about twice as likely as other students to be idle—not working or enrolled in school—six years following matriculation. In 2009, 23.6 percent of enrollees at for-profit schools were idle six years later, compared with just 10.6 percent of matriculating students at four-year public and nonprofit private schools, and 13.3 percent of matriculating students at two-year public and nonprofit private schools. As a result, the average annual earnings of for-profit graduates are about $2,000 less relative to their counterparts at other types of schools, after accounting for differences in student characteristics (Deming, Goldin, and Katz 2012). Yet another study that uses detailed data to take account of differences in student characteristics found large and significant earnings benefits from obtaining an associate degree from public and nonprofit institutions but not from for-profit institutions (Lang and Weinstein 2012).

Given the higher tuition costs at many for-profit institutions, students at these schools also leave with substantially higher debt than their counterparts at public and nonprofit schools. In 2007–08, 53 percent of bachelor's degree recipients at some for-profit four-year schools had accumulated more than $30,500 in debt, compared with 24 percent of graduates at private nonprofit schools and just 12 percent of public school graduates (Baum and Steele 2010). Default on student loans is a much more serious problem at for-profit schools. For fiscal year 2009, the three-year "cohort default rate," which measures the percentage of borrowers who enter repayment with student loans and default over a three-year period, was 22.7 percent among for-profit students, compared with just 7.5 percent for private nonprofits and 11 percent for public institutions (Department of Education 2012).

Gainful Employment

In 2010 and 2011, the Obama Administration issued a broad set of rules to strengthen occupational higher education programs at for-profit, nonprofit, and public institutions by protecting students from aggressive or misleading recruiting practices, providing consumers with better information about the effectiveness of such education and training programs, and ensuring that only eligible students or programs receive aid. One notable provision in this set of regulatory reforms was the "gainful employment" rule, which made occupational programs ineligible for Federal aid if they failed to meet a set of tests related to students' financial situations after graduation. While many occupational and for-profit institutions have pioneered new ways to reach adult students, offer online education, and meet the needs of employers, some programs have left students with large debts and poor employment prospects. Specifically, the rule stated that programs could become ineligible for financial aid if fewer than 35 percent of graduates were actively repaying their student loans; graduates were spending in excess of 30 percent of their discretionary income on student loan payments; and graduates were spending more than 12 percent of their total income on student loan payments. The gainful employment provisions were intended to align institutional incentives with the interests of students, by conditioning eligibility to receive Federal aid on student outcomes. In June 2012, a Federal judge vacated the key provisions of the gainful employment rule on the grounds that there was no factual basis for the rule's 35 percent repayment standard and that the better-grounded debt-to-income ratio standards were so intertwined with the repayment standard as to invalidate the whole rule. The Department of Education has appealed a portion of the judge's decision, asking that schools continue to be required to report information about their students' loan repayment rates and debt-to-income ratio to the Department even if this information is not used to determine eligibility for Federal funds. The Obama Administration remains committed to the principles of accountability and transparency in the use of taxpayer funds in occupational higher education programs and will continue efforts to provide students with good information about the quality and value of such programs.

What Is Driving Up Tuition Costs?

One often-posed explanation for the increase in tuition costs is that colleges require skilled labor inputs—highly educated instructors—and as education premiums rise, so do the costs of these skilled labor inputs. This explanation—an example of the Baumol's cost disease (Economics Application Box 4-1)—may be a contributing factor at private colleges but is unlikely to be the major part of the story at public institutions. Over the period 2000–10, average full-time faculty salaries increased 2 percent at public four-year colleges and actually fell at community colleges. Instructional spending as a share of total costs has been falling at public colleges as institutions seek to cut costs by substituting non-tenured and adjunct faculty for full-time tenure-track faculty. Evidence is mixed on whether this compositional shift has hurt learning outcomes with some arguing that graduation rates have suffered while others find no measurable changes. But, faculty salaries have not driven up costs.

So, what is driving up tuition costs? A recent survey article by economist Ronald Ehrenberg suggests that no single answer fits across all institutional types. Different types of institutions—private and public universities engaged in research, private and public institutions largely devoted to teaching, and public community colleges specializing in two-year instructional programs—are subject to different market forces and cost pressures (Ehrenberg 2012).

One driver of costs for many colleges is increased competition for students. The higher education market has been transformed from a state-based model where a majority of students attend local state universities to a more national—even international—market where students search over a large set of options. In this competitive environment, many institutions seek to position themselves as unique by offering an attractive mix of amenities. Published rankings likely contribute to this spending race because expenditures per student and average faculty salaries are often inputs into the rankings. Private research institutions, including the elite private universities, are in the best position to compete in this environment. These universities seek to have the most appealing facilities and the most renowned research faculty, and so at these types of institutions, the rise in tuition reflects rising average expenditure per student. At private research institutions, average spending per full-time equivalent (FTE) student on "education and related" items increased by more than $10,000, from $42,449 in 2000 to $52,710 in 2010, all measured in 2010 dollars. Spending increases have been fairly

**Economics Application Box 4-1: Baumol's Cost Disease
(or Bowen's Curse) and the Price of Education**

In the 1960s, economists William Baumol and William Bowen developed the notion, known as "Baumol's cost disease," that in certain labor-intensive industries—the example they chose was the performing arts—there is less opportunity for productivity gains to reduce labor costs. The number of musicians needed to perform Beethoven's Ninth Symphony is the same today as it was decades ago, but the number of workers needed to produce a single car has fallen considerably. Because markets dictate that wages remain comparable across industries for equally skilled workers, the relative price of products and services in sectors where productivity is stagnant will rise over time. Baumol's cost disease has been cited as a partial explanation for the long-term growth in education costs. Compensation for higher-education faculty and administrators has been rising over time, even though productivity in education has changed very little.

Whether and to what extent Baumol's cost disease plays a role in the continued rise in higher education cost is a topic of much debate. Regardless of its importance as a possible explanatory factor, improved technology and productivity growth offers a potential solution to growth in the cost of college, opening up potential new ways to deliver education. One such innovation is massive open online courses, or MOOCs, that can accommodate tens of thousands of students in a single class. Another promising innovation is courses delivered through a hybrid of online lectures and in-person tutoring. One study that used randomized trials found no significant difference in learning outcomes between traditional face-to-face statistics courses and hybrid online statistics courses, yet costs were lower in the hybrid course. Another study, also using a randomized design, found a slight advantage for live economics lectures over online lectures in the case where all ancillary materials such as web-based assignments and availability of tutors were comparable. The relatively small advantage demonstrated by live lectures, however, suggests there is room for considerable cost saving with relatively little reduction in learning outcomes (Bowen et al. 2012; Figlio, Rush, and Lin 2010).

evenly spread across categories such as instructional expenditures (faculty salaries and benefits), research (grants and contracts as well as matching funds), student services (admissions, registrar, and counseling services), and academic support (libraries and academic computing) (Figure 4-9a). While these increases may look like rising labor costs, spending on physical plant— "operation and maintenance costs"—has also increased. An important factor for private institutions is "tuition discounting," or the share of each tuition dollar that is returned to students in the form of need-based or merit grant aid. Tuition discounting at these institutions is substantial and increased from 28.6 percent in 2000 to 33.1 percent in 2008. The ability to offer tuition discounts essentially allows institutions to price discriminate in order to obtain a diverse mix of students.

In contrast, at public institutions, where most students enroll, average spending per student has not risen nearly as much, and tuition increases largely reflect institutions' attempts to compensate for declining State support (Figure 4-9b). At public community colleges, the average level of State and local appropriations per FTE student to these institutions fell from $7,095 in 2000 to $5,712 in 2010. Other public institutions lie somewhere between these two extremes, with public research institutions looking more like private research institutions, and public master's- and bachelor's-degree-granting institutions that are more oriented toward teaching looking more like community colleges. Average expenditure per FTE student at public research institutions increased from $24,178 in 2000 to $26,971 in 2010. Public research institutions shifted resources away from instructional spending by substituting non-tenured and part-time faculty for full-time, tenured faculty. Meanwhile institutional spending to support research activities increased, likely reflecting the attempt to gather new funding sources such as Federal and private research grants as State and local appropriations decreased. To compete with private universities for faculty who can attract Federal and private grants, public institutions often provide "start-up" research funds and build expensive lab facilities.

The Administration is committed to keeping college affordable for middle-class families. The Department of Education has released a College Scorecard to provide transparency for families as they evaluate their options for their higher education. The Department, along with the Consumer Financial Protection Bureau, has also designed a College Shopping Sheet to help families and students understand exactly how much money they will owe at each of the schools to which they have been accepted. President Obama has proposed a Race to the Top: College Affordability and Completion challenge to reward States that increase the number of college graduates while containing the costs of tuition. The President has also called on Congress to work with him to hold colleges accountable by considering value, affordability, and student outcomes in making determinations about which colleges and universities receive access to Federal student aid.

Figure 4-9
Average Expenditures per Full-Time-Equivalent Student
by Component, 2000–2010

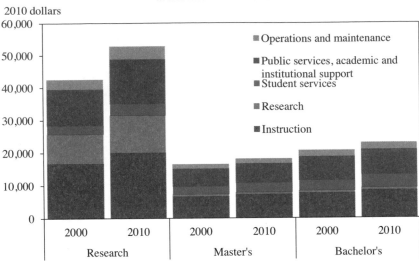

a. Private institutions

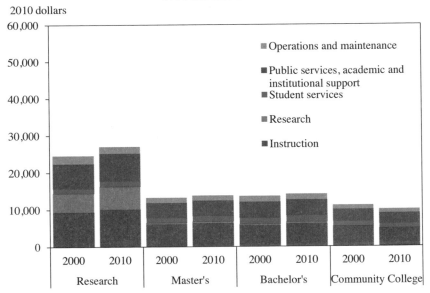

b. Public institutions

Source: Integrated Postsecondary Education Data System, Delta Cost Project.

Government as a Partner in Training

As part of the Administration's efforts to prepare workers for America's 21st century economy, meet the needs of local employers, and achieve President Obama's goal of ensuring that every American worker has the opportunity to secure at least one year of postsecondary education, the Department of Labor, along with the Department of Education, launched the Trade Adjustment Assistance Community College and Career Training (TAACCCT) grant program. This $2 billion initiative expands the capacity of community colleges to provide training and credentials to local workers needed for high-wage, high-skill employment in industries like advanced manufacturing, biotechnology, information technology, and other emerging fields. To date, the Department of Labor has awarded 45 grants to colleges across the nation to develop curricula for advanced manufacturing. For example, the Department of Labor funded the National STEM Consortium, led by Anne Arundel Community College in Maryland. This collaboration of 10 leading community colleges in nine states organized to develop nationally portable, certificate-level programs in science, technology, engineering, and mathematics and is also building a national model of multi-college cooperation in the design and delivery of high-quality, labor-market-driven occupational programs. Spokane Community College, in partnership with 11 other community colleges, worked with aerospace employers including Boeing to design an advanced curriculum in aerospace maintenance and manufacturing. The consortium known as Air Washington has been recognized by the Boeing Company for this curriculum development and for its ongoing assistance to the Boeing Academic Alignment Team. This effort includes the development of a pre-employment program to offer training in basic aerospace-related skills to adult learners, a web-based curriculum component on English as a second language, and assessments of prior learning, particularly for active military or veterans, to evaluate credit and classroom advancements based on military experiences and training. The programs funded by TAACCCT are establishing a national repository of high-quality technical curricula and related materials that can be made available at no charge to community colleges around the country.

Several existing U.S. training consortia provide successful models. Among those worth noting are Project QUEST and the Wisconsin Regional Training Partnership. Project QUEST is a training program in San Antonio aimed at the working poor with high school diplomas. The program works with firms (many of which are hospitals) in the city to identify job openings and the skills required to fill them. The firms then make a good-faith pledge to hire program graduates into jobs that meet living-wage standards and may redesign their jobs to create advancement ladders. The training is provided by local community colleges and typically lasts a year and a half. The program, which offers modest financial support and extensive counseling to the trainees, is organized and managed by a nonprofit closely linked to a community-based organization. More than 2,000 people have participated in QUEST. An evaluation found that those who completed the program saw their earnings rise by an average of $5,000 a year (Kochan, Finegold, and Osterman 2012). The Wisconsin Regional Training Partnership was established by unions and firms in Milwaukee in the 1990s and does training for manufacturing and construction. A study with random assignment of participants to treatment and control groups found significant increases in employment and incomes for program participants compared with nonparticipants (Holzer 2011).

Key features of these successful programs are the involvement of industry and worker-focused organizations, along with a commitment to continually evaluate what works and what does not, and a willingness to make adjustments. The involvement of employer groups ensures that the training is relevant; the involvement of worker-focused organizations ensures that workers share in the gains of their improved productivity. Together, the groups can work together to upgrade jobs, rather than taking current job duties and career paths as given. In some cases, as in the Wisconsin program, upgrading has meant calling on other agencies (in that case, the federally funded Manufacturing Extension Program) to help firms upgrade their management, operations, and information-technology practices so that they offer a greater return to skill (Maguire et al. 2010). The programs also have used a variety of tools (focus groups with employers, unions, and workers but also randomized controlled trials) to evaluate their programs, adjusting if necessary based on the results.

IMMIGRATION

We are a nation of immigrants and their descendants. Now, more than ever, the economic and social benefits of immigration loom large. Immigrants increase the size of the population and thus of the labor force and customer base, making an important contribution to economic growth. In 2010, there were nearly 40 million foreign-born people in the United States, representing 13 percent of the population and 16 percent of the workforce. As the United States faces the prospect of a slow-growing population, immigrants are likely to play an increasingly important role in the American economy. Immigrants work in diverse industries and occupations. While they represent 16 percent of the workforce, they account for more than 20 percent of workers in agriculture, construction, food services, and information technology. They are agricultural laborers, domestic workers, and cabdrivers as well as health care workers, computer software engineers, and medical scientists (Singer 2012). This diversity promotes economic growth as immigrants and natives often specialize in different tasks and occupations.

In addition, many highly skilled workers in the STEM fields are immigrants, and research has shown that these workers contribute importantly to innovation and growth. Many immigrants start businesses and create jobs for American workers. The United States has a distinct advantage compared with other developed nations in that flexible labor markets and robust returns to skills encourage the in-migration of these highly qualified workers. Our open society also allows immigrants to integrate better than in other countries, and we benefit from their vitality and creativity. Commonsense immigration reform can honor America's historical legacy of welcoming those willing to work hard for a better life, while also promoting its national and economic interests.

A Brief History of U.S. Immigration Policy

International migration flows from developing to developed countries are on the rise across the world. According to the latest United Nations estimates, more than 200 million people, or 3.1 percent of the world's population, live in a country that is not their original country of birth. Table 4-3 shows immigrants as a share of total population in selected advanced economies. In addition to the historical immigrant-receiving countries such as Australia, Canada, New Zealand, and the United States, the European Union, Scandinavian countries, and even Russia now have substantial foreign-born populations.[4]

Between 2001 and 2010, 10.5 million foreign-born individuals received legal-resident status (green cards) in the United States. While this is a large number, Figure 4-10 illustrates that the flow of legal immigrants is only now surpassing levels attained at the turn of the 20th century, when the population was much smaller but immigration was virtually unrestricted. The figure also shows that immigrant inflows, as a share of the total population, are far below the levels reached in the 19th century. In reaction to the large inflows in the early 1900s, particularly from Eastern and Southern Europe, Congress enacted a national quota system in 1921. The 1965 amendments to the Immigration and Nationality Act repealed the national quota system and made family reunification a priority. Under current law, immediate relatives

---

[4] The list does not include countries in the Middle East, such as Israel, Jordan, Kuwait, Qatar, and United Arab Emirates that have substantial guest-worker programs and foreign-born populations who generally make up 40 percent or more of the total population.

Table 4-3
Foreign-Born Persons in Selected Countries

Country	Percent of Total Population	
	1990	2010
New Zealand	15.5	22.4
Australia	21.0	21.9
Canada	16.2	21.3
Spain	2.1	14.1
Sweden	9.1	14.1
United States	9.1	13.5
Germany	7.5	13.1
France	10.4	10.7
United Kingdom	6.5	10.4
Russia	7.8	8.7
Japan	0.9	1.7

Source: United Nations, Department of Economic and Social Affairs, Population Division, Trends in International Migrant Stock (2008).

of U.S. citizens—spouses, minor children, and parents—are not subject to annual numerical limits. For other family members including siblings and adult children of U.S. citizens and spouses and minor children of legal permanent residents, a numerical cap of 226,000 applies. Over the 10-year period from 2002 to 2011, an average of 469,777 immediate relatives of U.S. citizens and an average of 207,927 other family members obtained permanent residency status annually (DHS 2011). As a result of numerical limits and processing backlogs, applications in the "other family member" category have long waiting times. The longest waiting periods are for applications from countries such as China, India, Mexico, and the Philippines; under the law, no more than 7 percent of total family-sponsored visas can be allotted to any single country.

Foreign workers also come to the United States through employment-based green cards. A maximum of 140,000 employment-based slots for permanent residency are available each year, although the actual cap varies since unused visas in the family program are carried over to the employment system. On average over 2002–11, 157,181 employment visas were issued annually (DHS 2011). Employment-based green cards typically require the worker to have at least a college degree or documented evidence of special skills; only 10,000 employment-based green cards are available to workers without formal education or skill requirements. Individuals can obtain employment-based green cards for making large direct investments in job-creating enterprises, although this category is limited to approximately 10,000 visas.

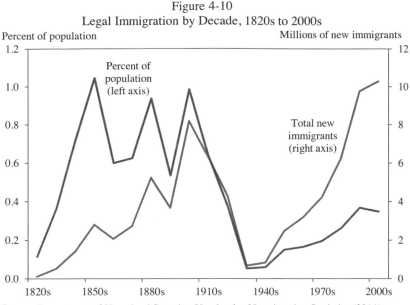

Figure 4-10
Legal Immigration by Decade, 1820s to 2000s

Source: Department of Homeland Security, Yearbook of Immigration Statistics (2011);
Department of Commerce, Census Bureau.

Foreign-born individuals are also allowed to reside and work in the United States on a temporary basis through several temporary immigrant visa programs. For example, individuals are admitted to work in the agricultural industry (H-2A visas) and other seasonal industries (H-2B visas) for short durations on specific jobs with specific employers. These visas help alleviate peak seasonal demands in certain sectors of the economy but cannot be used to employ less-skilled workers for longer durations. H-1B visas permit temporary employment for skilled professionals who are sponsored by a U.S. employer, typically in science, computer, or engineering occupations. A worker can remain in H-1B status for up to six years. Current law permits 65,000 new H-1B issuances a year, although up to 20,000 individuals who either hold advanced degrees from U.S. universities or are going to work for institutions of higher education or government research organizations are exempt from the cap. Applications for the H-1B visa are accepted starting in April for the following fiscal year. The application window closes when the annual cap is met. Demand for H-1B visas slowed during the recent recession but has picked up again, pointing to increasing demand for workers in the rapidly growing STEM occupations. One study published by the Department of Commerce found that employment in STEM occupations increased 7.9 percent from 2000 to 2010 while employment in non-STEM jobs grew just 2.6 percent over the same period. Moreover, STEM jobs are projected to grow by 17.0 percent from 2008 to 2018 (Langdon et al. 2011). In 2010, 151,710 foreign graduate students were enrolled in U.S. postsecondary institutions in STEM fields (NSF/NIH 2010). Allowing this population—already here and educated in the United States—to stay by increasing the number of visas available will ultimately position the Nation well in the global competition for new ideas, new businesses, and jobs of the future.

In part because of the limited pathways for less skilled workers to obtain legal status, an estimated 11.5 million foreign-born individuals in the United States are undocumented (Hoefer, Rytina, and Baker 2012). Bipartisan support for strengthened immigration enforcement has resulted in a well-resourced and modernized enforcement system. While effective, the fiscal burden of this system is also substantial. The Border Patrol has doubled in size over the past seven years to 21,370 agents in FY 2012. Spending for the two main immigration agencies—U.S. Customs and Border Protection and U.S. Immigration and Customs Enforcement—surpassed $17.9 billion in FY 2012, an amount that is higher than all other spending on criminal Federal law enforcement agencies (Meissner et al. 2013). Workplace enforcement, which could alleviate some of the fiscal burdens of border enforcement, has not kept pace. Effective workplace enforcement would entail enabling employers to quickly and accurately verify employees' eligibility by using an electronic employment verification system (E-Verify), and also holding those employers accountable who deliberately break the law by hiring unauthorized workers or violating labor laws.

The Department of Homeland Security estimates that of the 11.5 million unauthorized immigrant population residing in the United States in 2011, approximately 1.3 million were under 18 years of age (Hoefer, Rytina, and Baker 2012). Undocumented young people who were brought to the country as children have no clear path to future legal status that would enable them to further their education and find gainful employment outside of the shadow economy. Various versions of legislation to address the undocumented student population, often referred to as the DREAM Act, have been introduced in recent congressional sessions. The latest effort in 2010 passed the House but failed to pass the Senate. In June 2012, the Secretary of Homeland Security announced and implemented a new process, known as "Deferred Action for Childhood Arrivals," which provides work-status eligibility and relief from deportation for unauthorized immigrants who are no more than 30 years old and who arrived in the United States before age 16. While a smaller number are currently eligible to petition, up to 1.7 million young people could potentially benefit from this program once they reach the requisite age (Passel and Lopez 2012).

Foreign-born workers in the United States tend to be concentrated at both the low and the high end of the educational spectrum. Table 4-4 shows that 29.1 percent of the foreign-born have less than a high school degree. On the other hand, 10.9 percent have a master's degree or higher, a share on a par with that of the native-born. The table also shows that the foreign-born are more likely to be of working age, with 67.2 percent of the foreign-born aged 25–54 years old compared with 55.9 percent of the native population. The table also shows that foreign-born men are much more likely to be employed than native-born men.

Other countries that receive large numbers of immigrants, such as Australia and Canada, admit a majority of their immigrants based on employment skills. Australian work visas are most commonly granted to highly skilled workers. Candidates are assessed against a system that grants points for certain standards of education. In Canada, almost two-thirds of visas are issued to economic immigrants, primarily skilled workers and their dependents. Skilled workers are selected on factors such as education, English or French language abilities, and work experience. In contrast, the United States has a more "outcome"-based approach to granting visas. For example, employment visas are awarded to persons with extraordinary ability (EB-1), outstanding professors and researchers (EB-2), and skilled and unskilled workers with job offers from a U.S. employer (EB-3). While

Table 4-4
Distribution of Education, Age, and Employment
For Natives and Foreign Born Individuals, 2010–2012

	Native	Foreign Born
Education Attainment (Age 25+)		
Less than high school	9.3	29.1
High school, no college	31.7	26.0
Some college or associates	28.2	16.2
Bachelor's	19.9	17.8
Master's or higher	10.9	10.9
Age Group		
16-19	0.6	0.3
19-24	6.9	5.0
25-54	55.9	67.2
55-64	17.5	13.6
65+	19.1	13.9
Work Status		
Employed	60.3	62.4
Men	64.7	73.8
Women	56.2	51.2

Note: Sample limited to individuals 16 and over who are not enrolled in school.
Source: Bureau of Labor Statistics, Current Population Survey, Annual Social and Economic Supplement; CEA calculations.

some may argue that Canada and Australia might do a better job of attracting skilled immigrants than the United States because of their point-based systems, a recent study using detailed data compares the United States with Australia and finds that, by and large, the two countries attract similar immigrants. Skill premiums and geographic proximity, rather than the specific details of the admission criteria, play the predominant role in determining the quality of employment-based immigrants (Jasso and Rosenzweig 2008).

Since enactment of the Immigration and Nationality Act of 1965, family reunification has been a cornerstone of U.S. immigration policy. Debate continues on whether the United States should maintain this family-based system or move more toward an occupation- and skills-based system. While the question is often posed as a stark choice between two systems, in reality the two visa categories—family and employment—complement each other in important ways. In choosing a country to move to, skilled prospective immigrants envision a better life not only for themselves but for their families. Using data arranged by year of arrival and country of origin, one study found a positive correlation between the fraction of immigrants arriving on sibling preference and mean education levels of the immigrants. The data seem to support the notion that highly educated immigrants who arrive based on employment and occupational preference categories then sponsor their siblings who are also highly educated (Duleep and Regets 1996). As proposals are made to increase skill-based immigration, it is important to keep in mind that a welcoming policy toward the family is an important factor in attracting skilled workers to live and invest in the United States.

The Economic Benefits of Immigration

Conventional theory suggests that the destination country as a whole gains from immigration, though these gains may be uneven across groups. Immigrants add to the labor force and increase the economy's total output. The gains accrue to natives whose productivity is enhanced by immigrant workers—often referred to as complementary factors—as well as to capital owners. A major study published by the National Research Council in 1997 estimated the size of the "immigrant surplus" to be on the order of $14 billion in 1996 dollars, or 0.2 percent of GDP. Given the size of today's economy, this translates into $31.4 billion in 2012 dollars, even without accounting for growth in the share of the population that is foreign born.

There are additional reasons to think the above calculations may understate the full economic benefit of immigration. For one, the calculations do not take into account the fact that capital owners may boost investment in response to the increased number of workers, which may induce further economic growth. For another, the simple approach assumes a negative impact on the average wages of native workers that has been difficult to establish empirically. The same National Research Council study concluded that the body of empirical evidence pointed to a very small negative impact from immigration on wages of competing native workers—on the order of 1–2 percent and often statistically insignificant.[5] In fact, to the extent that new immigrants crowd out existing workers, research shows that those most adversely affected are recent immigrants (Lalonde and Topel 1991; Ottaviano and Peri 2012). A new immigrant with limited English skills, for example, will likely compete closely with other recent immigrants with poor English ability in jobs that do not require institutional, technical, or advanced language skills, thereby lowering the recent immigrants' wages.

Recent studies suggest, in fact, that the skills and talents that immigrants and natives bring to the labor market may not be substitutes for each other. Low-skilled immigrants may enhance the productivity of high-skilled natives. Even within skill groups, the various talents that immigrants and native workers bring to the labor market may complement each other rather than compete. The intuition behind the gains to both natives and immigrants in this case would follow from the principle of comparative advantage. For example, an immigrant worker may be an extraordinary computer programmer but have limited English skills. Rather than filling the programming job with a native worker who is not as skilled in this particular task, the employer might assign the native worker to tasks that use communication and English language skills. Some of these ideas are pursued in recent work by Giovanni Peri and co-authors (Peri and Sparber 2009; Ottaviano and Peri 2012). Other research also by Giovanni Peri compares states with differing levels of immigration and finds that immigration raises productivity by promoting efficient task specialization (Peri 2012).

Another question regards the impact of immigration on the public finances of the host country. Immigrants contribute positively to government finances by paying taxes but add to costs by using publicly provided goods and services such as roads, police, and schools. The 1997 National Research Council study estimated that, over the long run, a typical immigrant and his or her descendants would contribute about $80,000 more in taxes (in 1996 dollars) than they would receive in terms of public goods and services. This would translate into nearly $120,000 in 2012 dollars. This positive fiscal impact is attributable to several factors: most immigrants arrive at young ages; their descendants are expected to have higher incomes; immigrants help to pay for public goods such as national defense that do not entail congestion costs; and the 1996 Personal Responsibility and Work

---

[5] NRC (1997), chapter 5. Also see Card (1990), Friedberg and Hunt (1995), Card (2009), Cortes (2008). See Borjas (2003) and Borjas, Grogger, and Hanson (2011) for the opposing view.

Opportunity Reconciliation Act prohibited new immigrants from receiving public benefits for five years after arrival.

A recent Congressional Budget Office study also found that allowing undocumented immigrants a pathway to citizenship is likely to help the Federal budget. The study estimates that, had a pathway been established, Federal revenues would have increased by $48.3 billion while Federal outlays would have increased by $22.7 billion over the 2008–12 period, leading to a surplus of $25.6 billion. The revenue increase stems largely from greater receipts of Social Security payroll taxes, while the increase in outlays would be in the form of refundable income tax credits and Medicaid. This calculation does not take into account possible increases in Federal discretionary spending. There may be also additional expenditures at the State and local level on education and healthcare, which are harder to forecast (CBO 2007).

Another important economic benefit of providing a pathway to earned citizenship is that, by bringing immigrant workers out of the shadows, they will be able to obtain above-ground jobs, advance in their careers, and contribute more fully to the economy. Moreover, with a pathway to earned citizenship, immigrant workers and their employers will invest more in their skills, raising the benefit to the economy even further. Legalizing this population will also benefit U.S.-born citizens as they need no longer compete with workers who may work at below market wages due to their unauthorized status.

A Magnet for High-Skilled Immigration

A growing area of study is how high-skilled immigrants—particularly those in the STEM fields—contribute to innovation and growth. Based on the 2010 National Survey of College Graduates conducted by the National Science Foundation, immigrants represent 13.6 percent of all employed college graduates, but they account for 50 percent of PhDs working in math and computer science occupations, and 57.3 percent of PhDs in engineering occupations (Table 4-5). About two-thirds of these foreign-born PhDs hold U.S. degrees, suggesting that many of them either immigrated as children or came to attend U.S. universities and stayed.

Interestingly, one study found that 26 percent of all U.S.-based Nobel laureates over the past 50 years were foreign born. The same study also found that in the EU-12 countries, immigrants made up slightly less that 5 percent of total population and accounted for about 4 percent of those holding masters' and PhDs, in contrast to the United States (Wasmer et al. 2007).[6]

---

[6] According to the study, the data for Nobel Laureates were found at the official website of the Nobel Foundation: http://nobelprize.org/nobel/.

Table 4-5
Percentage of Foreign-Born College Graduates
by Degree and Occupation, 2010

	All	Bachelor's	Master's	Professional	Doctorate
Total	13.6	11.8	15.3	12.9	32.2
All sciences	28.6	20.3	38.1	50.7	44.2
Math/computer sciences	29.2	21.8	42.4	30.5	50.0
Life and related sciences	28.8	14.5	27.3	59.4	44.2
Physical and related sciences	23.9	12.2	21.3	49.6	38.8
Engineering	24.1	16.2	33.3	44.4	57.3

Note: Occupation refers to occupation for principal job. Sample limited to employed individuals.
Source: National Science Foundation/National Center for Science and Engineering Statistics, National Survey of College Graduates (2010).

These statistics support the view that the United States continues to be a magnet for highly skilled immigrants. Two factors likely play a role. First, the United States has flexible labor markets that are able to integrate immigrants relatively quickly. Second, the skill premium is high in the United States, and individuals with exceptional ability and willingness to work hard can thrive. These factors have enabled the Nation to benefit from large inflows of highly skilled workers.

Boosting Innovation and Entrepreneurship

In addition to the benefits already covered, recent studies have shown that immigrants promote productivity and innovation, directly and also indirectly through positive spillover effects on native researchers and scientists. Gauthier-Loiselle and Hunt (2010) found that immigrants patent at two to three times the rate of U.S.-born citizens. The study also found that immigrants further boost innovation in the economy by having positive spillovers on the native rate of innovation. Another study found that raising the number of skilled information-technology workers—as has been done by raising the cap on H-1B visas—spurs innovative activity in states that more heavily employ these workers (Kerr and Lincoln 2009).

Studies also have found that immigrants are not only exceptional workers and innovators but also highly entrepreneurial. One study found that 25 percent of venture capital companies between 1991 and 2006 were started by immigrants (Anderson and Platzer 2006). Another found that immigrants started 25 percent of engineering and technology companies founded between 1995 and 2005 (Wadhwa et al. 2007). Even outside the high-tech sector, one study found that immigrants are more likely than natives to start a company with more than 10 workers (Fairlie 2012). Immigrants are 30 percent more likely to form new businesses than U.S.-born citizens. A study by

Partnership for a New American Economy found that more than 40 percent of Fortune 500 companies were founded by immigrants or their children. The study also found that these companies are responsible for many jobs here and abroad—employing more than 10 million people worldwide—and that they generate annual revenues of $4.2 trillion.

While there is clearly room for further study, these studies generally provide little systematic evidence that increases in the supply of foreign scientists and engineers discourage natives from entering these fields or from engaging in innovative activity. For example, Gauthier-Loiselle and Hunt found that the inflow of high-skilled immigrant science and engineering workers into a state did not decrease the number of patents originated by native science and engineering workers in the state. Borjas (2007) also found that, on the whole, rising enrollment of foreign graduate students did not discourage native enrollment in science and engineering programs, although there were some disparate impacts across groups.

President Obama has supported a recent initiative to graduate 1 million more college graduates with STEM degrees. At the same time, all evidence points to the fact the United States is extraordinarily successful at attracting highly skilled workers from other countries. Sensible immigration policy would entail taking advantage of this unique situation and allowing more high-skilled immigration. The lack of clear evidence of crowding out bolsters confidence that these are not two conflicting policy goals.

Conclusion

With slowing population growth and aging of the workforce, America needs more workers. The Nation also needs to invest in the education, skills, and training of its citizens so they can fill the jobs of the future. Over the past four years, President Obama has taken an aggressive stance toward combating the rising cost of college. The expansion of the Federal Pell Grant program and the American Opportunity Tax Credit has made college more affordable for millions of students and families. Challenges still remain, including the continuing rise of tuition and levels of student debt. In his recent State of the Union address, President Obama called upon colleges to join in the effort to keep costs down. He proposed using metrics such as value, affordability, and student outcomes in distributing Federal campus-based aid. He also announced a new Race to the Top program for College Affordability and Completion, which will reward states who are willing to change their higher education policies and practices to contain tuition costs and ease students' progress toward a college degree.

With the potential to address both the need for workers and the need for skills, the gains from commonsense immigration reform loom large.

Immigration can boost the economy by adding workers and making our labor force younger and more dynamic. Offering a path to citizenship to more than 11 million currently undocumented residents will further expand the economy as this group invests in education, finds gainful employment, and pays taxes. Border enforcement has proven to be effective, but it is a drain on our public finances. Smart enforcement that balances border security with crackdowns on worksite fraud will not only have higher returns going forward, but it will also save taxpayers money. America has historically been a magnet for capable and hard-working immigrants who seek opportunities and a better life. Many of these immigrants are innovators and entrepreneurs. The smart policy ahead is to leverage America's unique advantage for future prosperity and growth.

Smart policy also involves making sure that all Americans benefit from economic growth. In his 2013 State of the Union address, President Obama reiterated his commitment that an honest day's work is rewarded with decent pay, enough to feel secure and support a family. A Federal minimum wage that keeps up with the cost of living, policies that strengthen workers' ability to bargain for decent wages and safe working conditions, and tax policies such as refundable credits that allow lower-income families to invest in their children's education, are important pieces of the foundation upon which an economy that works for the middle class is built.

↭

CHAPTER 5

REDUCING COSTS AND IMPROVING THE QUALITY OF HEALTH CARE

In March 2010, the President signed into law the Affordable Care Act. Provisions of the Act have already helped millions of young adults obtain health insurance coverage and have made preventive services more afford-able for most Americans. When fully implemented, the law will expand coverage to an estimated 27 million previously uninsured Americans and ensure the availability of affordable comprehensive coverage through tra-ditional employer-sponsored insurance and new health insurance market-places or exchanges. There are signs that the Affordable Care Act has started to slow the growth of costs and improve the quality of care through pay-for-performance programs, strengthened primary care and care coordination, and pioneering Medicare payment reforms. These provisions, as well as others in the Affordable Care Act, will help to bend the cost curve downward while laying the foundation for moving the health care system toward higher quality and more efficient care.

HEALTH CARE SPENDING

Health care spending has increased dramatically over the past half century, both in absolute terms and as a share of gross domestic product (GDP) (Figure 5-1). Spending in the U.S. health care sector totaled $2.7 tril-lion in 2011, up by a factor of 3.9 from the $698.3 billion (in 2011 dollars) spent in 1980. Health care spending in 2011 accounted for 17.9 percent of GDP—almost twice its share in 1980.

Some of the increase in health care spending is attributable to demo-graphic changes. Of the real increase in spending on prescription drugs, office-based visits, hospitalizations, and all other personal care from 1996 to 2010, for example, 11.5 percent can be accounted for by the changing

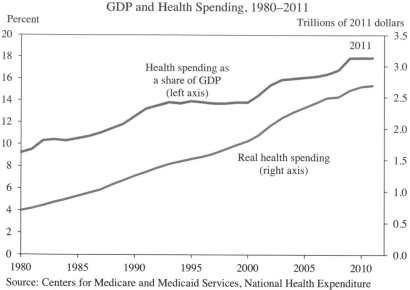

Figure 5-1
GDP and Health Spending, 1980–2011

Source: Centers for Medicare and Medicaid Services, National Health Expenditure Accounts; Bureau of Economic Analysis, National Income and Product Accounts; CEA calculations.

age structure of the population and 22.8 percent can be accounted for by increases in the size of the population (Figure 5-2).[1] The effects of population aging will become a more important driver of higher spending in coming years; by 2030, one in five Americans will be over age 65, compared with only one in eight today, and per capita medical costs in a given year are approximately three times greater for those 65 and over than for younger individuals. The majority of the increase in health care spending, historically, has come from increases in the amount spent per person over and above any effects attributable purely to population aging and population growth, reflecting increases in the use of medical services driven at least in part by the development of new technologies and increases in unit costs that exceed the overall rate of inflation.

---

[1] Total annual spending on prescription drugs, office-based visits, hospitalizations and other personal care between 1996 and 2010 was estimated using the Medical Expenditure Panel Survey (MEPS). To estimate the effect of changes in the age distribution between 1996 and 2010 on spending, age-specific spending levels and total U.S. population were held constant at 1996 levels, but the proportion of the population within each age group was allowed to reflect the 2010 age distribution. To estimate the effect of population growth between 1996 and 2010 on spending, total spending increases were calculated holding age-specific spending levels constant at 1996 levels, but allowing both the age distribution and total population to reflect their 2010 values. Then, the estimated spending increases due to changes in the age distribution were subtracted from this figure.

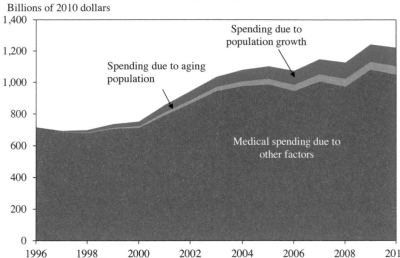

Figure 5-2
Contribution of Population Growth and Aging
to Health Care Spending, 1996–2010

Source: Department of Health and Human Services, Agency for Healthcare Research and
Quality, Medical Expenditure Panel Survey; CEA calculations.

Long-Term Spending Growth

Why has health care spending risen so much, even after taking into account changes in the size and age mix of the population? A likely piece of the story is that long-term growth in health care wages has not been accompanied by corresponding labor-saving technological progress. The theory of "cost disease" as developed by Baumol and Bowen (1966) notes that labor-saving technological progress has led to significant increases in labor productivity and hence wage growth in some important parts of the economy (such as the manufacturing sector). To compete for workers, labor-intensive sectors such as health care, education, and the performing arts also must raise their wages. According to the theory, productivity growth has been slower in these sectors. The result, the argument concludes, is an increase in the relative cost of output in these labor-intensive sectors, as higher costs are passed on to consumers in the form of higher prices.

Consistent with this theory, Nordhaus (2006) found that labor-intensive sectors generally experienced rising relative prices between 1948 and 2001. Nordhaus also found that shifts in labor from sectors that experienced labor-saving technological progress to sectors that remained relatively labor-intensive lowered overall productivity growth, as the share of labor-intensive sectors in overall output rose over the second half of the 20th century.

The cost-disease diagnosis assumes that, in labor-intensive sectors, it is difficult to reduce the amount of labor required to produce a given set of outputs. The health care sector, however, has experienced substantial technological progress, as new pharmaceutical therapies, diagnostic and medical devices, and surgical procedures have been introduced, allowing many conditions to be treated more effectively than in the past.

While some of these innovations have been labor-saving (some pharmaceuticals, for example), most others are complementary to expensive specialist labor (such as imaging and advances in surgical procedures). Consequently, technological change in medicine has caused the cost per treatment to rise, even as improvements in clinical effectiveness have led to increases in medical productivity. Technological change in medicine has contributed to long-term increases in spending. A recent study found that a quarter to a half of the rise in health care spending since 1960 can be explained by technological change in the health care system (Smith, Newhouse, and Freeland 2009). And rather than satisfying a relatively fixed demand for health care at lower cost, the development of many of these new technologies has contributed to an increase in the demand for health care services.

For some researchers, the importance of technological change for health care spending points to increases in demand as an additional explanation to the cost disease theory for why health care spending has increased disproportionately with income. If health care is a "super-normal good"—a good associated with an elasticity of consumption with respect to income that is greater than one—then as incomes rise by a certain percentage, consumption of health care rises by a greater percentage. Hall and Jones (2007) argue that this can happen if, after achieving a certain level of consumption, individuals prefer to spend additional income on life-extending health care (which allows for consumption in the extended years of life) rather than on extra consumption now. Consequently, as incomes rise, people choose to spend ever more on health care over other goods.

The disproportionate effect of income on the demand for health care may also operate through larger institutional mechanisms. Consistent with this idea, Smith, Newhouse, and Freeland (2009) find that income growth affects health care spending growth primarily through the actions of governments and employers on behalf of large insurance pools, suggesting a key role for payment reform in affecting medical spending growth.

These factors are not only a U.S. phenomenon. Indeed, while the United States has higher levels of health care spending than other members of the Organisation for Economic Co-operation and Development (OECD), the annual real rate of growth in health care spending per capita in the

United States between 1960 and 2010 was not too different from elsewhere, averaging 4.13 percent compared with 3.62 percent in the other OECD countries, adjusted for purchasing power parity. In more recent years, health care spending has continued to grow at similar annual real rates—3.10 percent in the United States and 3.30 percent in the other OECD countries between 2000 and 2010, somewhat below the long-term rates of spending growth observed since 1960.

Medical Productivity

Productivity growth in health care largely has taken the form of improvements in the quality of care, with developments in new procedures and care practices contributing to increased survival, decreased morbidity, reduction in pain, and less onerous treatment administration in many cases.

A full accounting of medical productivity growth should reflect changes not only in cost per service but also in health outcomes. However, medical productivity is often hard to measure because health outcomes are hard to measure. Recent studies comparing increases in life expectancy to increases in treatment costs over time suggest that productivity growth in the health care sector has been enormous. For example, Cutler and McClellan (2001) found that the value of increased survival rates and decreased morbidity rates as a result of improved treatment of heart attacks, low-birth-weight infants, and depression over the past few decades has far exceeded the increased spending on these conditions over the period. Using a similar methodology, Philipson et al. (2012) found that survival gains across all cancer patients in the United States between 1983 and 1999 cost on average only $8,670 per life-year gained. Estimates of the value of a statistical life-year, based on compensating wage differentials that measure the implied trade-off between wages and increased risk of fatality, are typically multiples higher (Viscusi and Aldy 2003). Therefore, even if some piece of the apparent gain in longevity results from earlier diagnosis, the introduction of these cancer therapies represents an enormous improvement in productivity. Faster growth in spending on cancer treatment in the United States than in Europe over this period is sometimes mistakenly taken to indicate the inefficiency of U.S. medical care, but it is also the case that the improvement in life expectancy for cancer patients was greater in the United States than in Europe. From 1983 to 1999, U.S. spending per cancer patient rose by $16,700 (in 2010 dollars) more than European spending per cancer patient (Figure 5-3), and U.S. cancer patient life expectancy rose by 0.4 years more than European cancer patient life expectancy (Figure 5-4), implying a cost per extra life year saved of approximately $42,000. Given the consensus

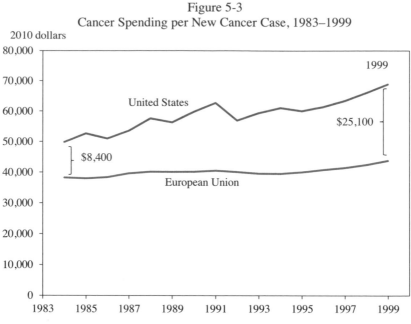

Figure 5-3
Cancer Spending per New Cancer Case, 1983–1999

Source: Philipson et al. (2012), updated data provided by the authors.

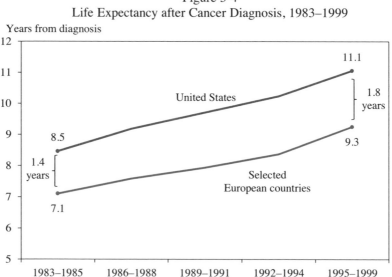

Figure 5-4
Life Expectancy after Cancer Diagnosis, 1983–1999

Note: European countries included are Finland, France, Germany, Iceland, Norway, Slovakia, Slovenia, Sweden, Scotland, and Wales.
Source: Philipson et al. (2012), updated data provided by the authors; Surveillance, Epidemiology and End Results (SEER); European Cancer Registry (EUROCARE).

in the literature that the value of additional life-years is much higher, the additional U.S. spending has been a good value.

Murphy and Topel (2006) directly estimate the aggregate monetary value of increases in longevity, finding that, if valued in the national accounts, increases in life expectancy since 1970 would have added $3.2 trillion a year to national wealth. While a different set of assumptions about the statistical value of a life year, the elasticity of intertemporal substitution, and the value individuals place on non-working hours lowers the aggregate valuation of the observed longevity increase, the order of magnitude of the estimated valuation nonetheless suggests an enormous return to the increase in health care spending over this period.

In general, estimating how much the productivity of health care has grown is a difficult task. Changes in health outcomes, morbidity rates, and patient convenience are hard to measure, hard to attribute to the use of specific technologies, and hard to value. Furthermore, limitations in available data mean that spending often cannot be disaggregated to the treatment of specific diseases or patients. Given these difficulties, it is widely agreed that aggregate measures of the output of the health care sector do a poor job of capturing the effects of productivity growth. Developing better methods to measure real output and productivity growth in health care is an important area of ongoing research (Data Watch 5-1).

Sources of Inefficiency in Health Care Spending

Although growth in overall medical productivity has been large, not all increases in medical spending are productive. Cutler and McClellan (2001) showed that improved treatment of heart attacks produced significant increases in patient longevity between 1984 and 1998. By contrast, Skinner, Staiger, and Fisher (2006) found little improvement in survival rates among heart attack patients between 1996 and 2002 despite significant growth in treatment costs. The latter study also found that the regions with the largest increases in spending also experienced the smallest gains in survival. Geographic variation in practice patterns and health outcomes implies that more than 20 percent of Medicare spending on heart attack treatment produces little health value (Skinner, Fisher, and Wennberg 2005). The case of heart attack treatment points to more general inefficiencies in the allocation of spending within the health care system.

Among the many possible sources of spending inefficiencies, several stand out as key sources of waste. First, the fragmentation of the delivery system contributes to a failure to provide patients with necessary care. That in turn can lead to complications and readmissions, particularly for the chronically ill for whom care coordination is most essential for health.

Data Watch 5-1: Toward Disease-Based Health Care Accounting

Existing national data on health expenditures generally are orga-nized by the type of medical care that individuals purchase (such as doc-tor visits or drugs). For addressing questions related to the productivity of health care, however, data on health care spending by disease would be far more useful.

Switching to disease-based accounting poses a challenge because patients often suffer from more than one disease at once, making it difficult to allocate spending to specific diseases. Three conceptual approaches to allocating spending across disease have been suggested: tracking each encounter with the health care system; tracking disease "episodes"; or identifying all conditions a person has and using regres-sion analysis to allocate spending to diseases. All three approaches have advantages and limitations, and a consensus has not yet developed on which one is preferable. Whichever approach is adopted, the universe of conditions will need to be categorized into a set of disease groups, at an appropriate level of detail, to which medical costs then can be assigned for analysis.

The Medical Expenditure Panel Survey (MEPS) is a nationally representative survey that provides information on most health spend-ing, although it fails to capture spending on behalf of institutionalized patients and active duty military. The MEPS sample is too small, however, to represent rare conditions. Although not comprehensive in their coverage, data on health care claims provide another valuable—and potentially much more detailed—source of information on health care spending. In addition to data on spending, data on health outcomes that can be linked to the disease-based spending data also are needed.

Important progress has been made toward developing disease-based health care data. The Bureau of Economic Analysis is working on a health care satellite account that will provide disease-based measures of household medical expenditures. These estimates will be based on private insurance claims data, Federal data on Medicare and Medicaid spending, and data from MEPS on the uninsured. Simultaneously, the Bureau of Labor Statistics is developing disease-based price indexes that account for shifts in treatment patterns. These indexes will be useful to the Bureau of Economic Analysis for decomposing spending into changes in prices versus changes in quantities.

The Affordable Care Act has significantly increased funding for research on patient-centered outcomes, and data will be available to qualified entities to evaluate the performance of providers and suppli-ers with respect to quality, efficiency, effectiveness, and resource use. Under the President's Open Data initiative, the Department of Health and Human Services has launched a Health Data Initiative to promote the availability of Medicare and Medicaid data, where appropriate, to researchers and entrepreneurs. Paralleling these initiatives, the Health Care Cost Institute, a nonprofit organization, has developed a claims database to be made available to researchers to foster a better understanding of what drives health care costs. These administrative data on claims hold the potential for further progress on understanding the drivers of health care spending increases and identifying high value medical care.

Second, lack of care coordination also contributes to duplicate care and overtreatment, a source of waste exacerbated by payment systems that compensate physicians based on the number of services provided (see Economic Applications Box 5-1). Overuse of expensive medical technologies is particularly costly, and some research suggests that a significant portion of coronary artery bypass graft surgery, angioplasty, hysterectomy, cataract surgery, and angiography is of questionable or low medical value (Goldman and McGlynn 2005).

Third, the failure of providers to adopt widely recognized best medical practices also contributes to waste. These failures include lack of adherence to established preventive care practices and patient safety systems, as well as widespread failure to adopt best treatment practices. In cases where the best medical practice is both clinically more effective and lower in cost—for example, the use of beta blockers in the treatment of acute myocardial infarction (Skinner and Staiger 2005, 2009)—failure to follow these practices results in worse clinical outcomes and higher readmissions and contributes to wasteful spending.

Finally, payment fraud also adds to system waste, not only through inappropriate payments but also through the administrative burden on honest providers who must adhere to the regulatory requirements of unavoidable but burdensome fraud detection systems.

Taken together, fragmentation of care, overtreatment, failures of care delivery, and payment fraud have been estimated to account for between 13 and 26 percent of national health expenditures in 2011 (Berwick and Hackbarth 2012). The magnitude of this waste offers an equally large opportunity for spending reductions and improvement in quality of care—an opportunity that underpins many of the provisions of the Affordable Care Act.

Economics Application Box 5-1: Matching in Health Care

Traditional economic analysis focuses on markets in which prices and quantities adjust so that in principle, supply equals demand. In some markets, however, prices do not exist and cannot be used to allocate resources. Gale and Shapley (1962) made early theoretical contributions to our understanding of how markets can be designed to allocate resources efficiently in the absence of prices. Taking the "marriage market" as an example, Gale and Shapley studied how, in the absence of prices, these markets can produce stable matches—matches where no alternative pairing would make both individuals in any match better off. These principles were extended by Roth, who applied them to the practical design of market institutions—for example, the market for medical students in residency programs (Roth 1984), and the assignment of students to public high schools in New York City and Boston (Abdulkadiroglu, Pathak, and Roth 2005). For these pioneering contributions, Shapley and Roth were awarded the 2012 Nobel Prize in Economic Sciences.

The market for live kidney transplants is yet another market where prices do not determine allocation. Paying for organs is a felony under the 1984 National Organ Transplant Act. Patients can receive a kidney from a compatible donor or are placed on a waiting list for a cadaveric kidney. Currently, nearly 95,000 patients in the United States are waiting for a kidney transplant. Dialysis for these patients costs approximately $60,000 a year, for a total of $30 billion a year, or 6.7 percent of total Medicare spending, the single most expensive component of Medicare. In 2011, there were about 11,000 transplants of deceased donor kidneys and only 5,770 transplants from living donors; in the same year, more than 4,700 patients died while waiting for a kidney transplant.

Many patients have willing potential donors. However, immuno-logical incompatibility greatly limits the number of transplants using live kidneys, which are preferred to cadaverous kidneys for their tissue quality and greater longevity. Patients receiving a live kidney transplant are estimated to live 10-15 years longer than they would on dialysis.

Increasing exchanges between incompatible patient-donor pairs would greatly expand the opportunity for dialysis patients to receive a living donor kidney, and increase the quality of matches. In paired kidney exchanges, a donated kidney from one (immunologically incompatible) patient-donor pair is transplanted in the patient of a second patient-donor pair, and vice versa. The potential for improving the number of live kidney transplants is greater with "chains"—exchanges involving many donor-recipient pairs. The 2007 amendment to the National Organ Transplant Act clarified that kidney paired donations

(KPD) do not constitute "valuable consideration" (that is, financial compensation), thereby paving the way for the creation of KPD exchanges.

The economic principles of stable matches developed by Shapley and Roth can be applied to KPD exchanges. Whereas the concept of stability in the medical residency setting, for example, is based on the mutual preferences of medical students and residency programs, stability in a kidney exchange is primarily based on obtaining the best matches along immunological criteria. Using these principles, transplant centers have established KPD programs, as have nonprofit organizations such as the New England Program for Kidney Exchange, founded by Roth and colleagues. Congress also established a national KPD pilot program, operated under the Organ Procurement and Transplantation Network (OPTN) as a nonprofit under Federal contract.

In 2011, the separate pilot KPD programs, including OPTN, resulted in 430 transplants—a promising start to paired kidney exchanges, but nevertheless representing only a fraction of the potential number of possible transplants.

Computer models suggest that many more transplants could be achieved each year if there were a nationwide pool of all eligible donors and recipients. A larger pool of eligible donor-recipient pairs also could potentially increase the quality of matches. A living kidney transplant (and all subsequent care) saves money over dialysis after roughly two years. On average, Medicare would save $60,000 a year for every patient who receives a living kidney transplant rather than continuing to receive dialysis, all while increasing the life expectancy of a kidney recipient by 10–15 years, again relative to dialysis treatment.

EARLY IMPLEMENTATION OF THE AFFORDABLE CARE ACT

The Affordable Care Act includes a series of provisions that will transform the Nation's health care system. By expanding coverage, the health reform law stabilizes insurance markets and makes health insurance affordable. The Affordable Care Act also includes important provisions that are aimed at reducing inefficient spending, promoting competition, and improving the quality of medical care.

Economic Benefits of Insurance

Insurance provides important economic benefits to covered households. It covers unforeseen medical expenditures, allowing individuals to receive necessary medical treatment without suffering potentially crippling financial consequences.

The 2008 Medicaid expansion in Oregon provided a unique setting in which to study the effects of health insurance on health and financial security. Because access to the Oregon Medicaid coverage expansion was offered through a lottery, the benefits of insurance could be estimated without the usual statistical concerns that purchasers of insurance differ from non-purchasers in ways related to health and financial outcomes. Finkelstein et al. (2011) found that, after one year of Medicaid coverage, previously uninsured adults in Oregon were 10 percent less likely to report having depression and 25 percent more likely to report their health as good, very good, or excellent. They also experienced lower financial strain because of medical expenses, including lower out-of-pocket expenditures, lower debt on medical bills, and lower rates of refused medical treatment because of medical debt, than individuals who were not randomly assigned to Medicaid coverage.

The benefits of having insurance coverage are large. A recent study (CBO 2012a) estimated that the insurance value of Medicaid to enrollees in the lowest quintile of income earners is equivalent to 11 percent of their before-tax income, defined by the CBO as market income plus cash transfers. As a comparison, real average before-tax incomes in the lowest quintile rose 15 percent between 1995 and 2009, while real incomes in the highest quintile rose 24 percent. Hence, the value of Medicaid is roughly comparable to the additional income that would have kept average income in the lowest quintile growing at the same rate as average income in the highest quintile.

Expanding Affordable Health Insurance Coverage

The Affordable Care Act is projected to increase the number of insured individuals in the United States by 14 million in 2014 and by 27 million in 2022 (CBO 2012b). The requirement that health insurance plans offer dependent coverage to children up to age 26 went into effect in 2010. Sommers (2012) found that this provision resulted in more than 3 million uninsured young adults gaining health insurance between September of 2010 and December of 2011.

Looking ahead to 2022, the Congressional Budget Office (CBO 2012b) projects that the Affordable Care Act will lead to an additional 12 million people being insured through Medicaid and the Children's Health Insurance Program (CHIP), with the remainder of the estimated 27 million newly insured individuals covered through employer-based insurance, the Affordable Insurance exchanges, or the Small Business Health Options Program (SHOP) exchanges (Economics Application Box 5-2). The law likely will cause some firms that currently do not offer health benefits to begin doing so, and some workers who are currently uninsured will take up employer coverage that is already offered. At the same time, the new

Economics Applications Box 5-2: Economics of Adverse Selection and the Benefits of Broad Enrollment

In health insurance markets, adverse selection occurs when relatively unhealthy individuals are more likely than healthy individuals to purchase health insurance coverage at a given price. Insurers understand this tendency and attempt to set premiums to reflect average expected expenditures in a plan. The selection of relatively unhealthy enrollees into coverage raises average expected expenditures, resulting in higher premiums and more adverse selection into coverage.

Adverse selection explains why offered premiums in the individual and small group health insurance markets often are too high for most healthy people compared with the health costs they actuarially can be expected to incur, meaning that they either pay too much for coverage or choose to go uninsured rather than pay the high premiums. In some cases, insurance markets subject to extreme adverse selection may disappear completely (Cutler and Reber 1998).

Encouraging broad participation in health insurance coverage helps tremendously to solve the market failure associated with adverse selection. For example, adverse selection is virtually nonexistent in the large group employer sponsored insurance (ESI) market. Take-up rates in this market are very high, thanks both to the tax advantages associated with ESI and to the fact that employers typically pay a portion of premiums, which makes ESI a good deal for the vast majority of employees. While employer contributions are offset by lower wages in equilibrium (Gruber 1994; Baicker and Chandra 2005), employees who decline coverage rarely recoup the employer contribution on the margin. The large enrollment in many ESI plans means that a small number of high expenditure enrollees does not dramatically affect premiums for a large risk pool. This prevents adverse selection from taking root and reinforces broad enrollment through premium stabilization and affordability.

Similarly, the Affordable Care Act encourages broad enrollment through the widespread accessibility of health insurance exchanges, the individual responsibility requirement related to the purchase of health insurance, and the financial assistance offered to lower-income earners to purchase private plans on an insurance exchange. Other provisions of the Affordable Care Act raise consumer awareness and foster consumer choice through information campaigns, standardization, and consumer search tools, similar to those implemented in the successful rollouts of the Medicare Advantage and Medicare Part D prescription drug programs. As in ESI, broad enrollment in the exchanges is expected to foster premium stability and affordability and to reduce the incidence of cost-shifting from uncompensated care to the insured.

options created by the Affordable Care Act may make employer-sponsored insurance (ESI) coverage less attractive for some employers. The net effects on the prevalence of employer-sponsored coverage, however, are likely to be small.

Based on microsimulations of firms' optimizing behavior, analysts have estimated effects of the Affordable Care Act on the number of individuals with ESI coverage ranging from a 1.8 percent decline (CBO 2012b) to a 2.9 percent increase (Eibner et al. 2011). Other estimates fall with this narrow range (Buettgens, Garrett, and Holahan 2010; Lewin Group 2010; Foster 2010) and are consistent with the small positive effects of health reform on ESI coverage observed in Massachusetts, where similar statewide health insurance reforms were legislated in 2006 (Long, Stockley, and Yemane 2009).

Consumer Protection

The Affordable Care Act also establishes numerous consumer protections related to the purchase of private health insurance, some of which are already in effect. Starting in 2014, individual and group health plans will not be allowed to deny or limit coverage on the basis of an individual's health status. And within certain limits, premiums will be allowed to vary by age, geography, family size, and smoking status, but not by individual health status, gender, or other factors.

The Affordable Care Act also requires that double-digit increases in insurance premiums be reviewed by States or the Department of Health and Human Services, with insurance companies needing to provide justification for any such premium increases. Plans may be excluded from an insurance exchange based on premium increases that are not justified. Further, since the beginning of 2011, most insurers have been allowed to retain no more than 20 percent of consumers' premiums for profits, marketing, and other administrative costs. Overhead and administrative costs in excess of this limit are to be rebated to consumers (or in the case of employer-sponsored insurance, to employers, who must pass a share of these rebates to their employees as cash, improved benefits, or lower premiums, with the share depending on the proportion of the total health plan premium paid by the employees). As of August 2012, an estimated 12.8 million Americans had received rebates totaling $1.1 billion from insurers as a result of this 80/20 medical loss ratio rule.

Health Care Spending and Quality of Care

The Affordable Care Act includes a series of provisions designed to reduce spending while improving the quality of care in the health care system. Reducing excessive payments to Medicare Advantage plans, strengthening antifraud efforts, and initiating reforms to Medicare provider payment systems, among other policies, are expected to extend the life of the Medicare Trust Fund by an additional eight years. These reforms complement numerous other provisions that improve health care quality while lowering costs.

The Hospital Value-Based Purchasing Program went into effect in October 2012. The program rewards more than 3,500 hospitals for providing high-quality care and reduces payments for hospitals demonstrating poor performance. Similar pay-for-performance programs in Medicare Advantage and the end-stage renal disease prospective payment system encourage higher-quality care and more efficient care delivery. Additionally, pay-for-reporting initiatives in which providers are rewarded for reporting procedures and outcomes have been launched in virtually every Medicare payment category, and mark the first step toward value-based purchasing.

The Partnership for Patients program is a public-private partnership that aims to reduce hospital complications and improve care transitions in more than 3,700 hospitals and partnering community-based clinical organizations. By stopping millions of preventable injuries and complications in patient care, this nationwide initiative has set as its goal saving 60,000 lives and up to $35 billion in spending, including up to $10 billion in Medicare spending, over the three years following its launch. Data provided by the Centers for Medicare and Medicaid Services (CMS) show that since the Partnership for Patients program was introduced in 2011, the hospital readmission rate within Medicare has fallen to 17.8 percent, down from an average of about 19 percent that had prevailed from 2007 through 2010 (CMS 2013) (Figure 5-5). The data also show that the declines were larger in hospitals participating in Partnership for Patients.

The Affordable Care Act builds on the investments made in the Recovery Act to encourage the use of health information technology. By making it easier for physicians, hospitals, and other providers to assess patients' medical status and provide care, electronic medical records may help eliminate redundant and costly procedures. More than 186,000 health care professionals (about one-third of eligible providers) and 3,500 hospitals (about two-thirds of eligible hospitals) have already qualified for incentive payments for the meaningful use of electronic health records authorized by the Recovery Act.

The Affordable Care Act also launched extensive efforts to prevent and detect fraudulent payments under Medicare, Medicaid, and the Children's Health Insurance Program. An important goal of the Administration's efforts has been to prevent fraudulent payments before they are made rather

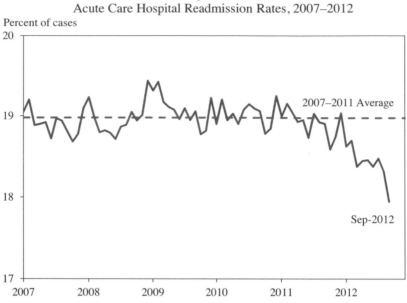

Figure 5-5
Acute Care Hospital Readmission Rates, 2007–2012

Source: Center for Medicare and Medicaid Services, Office of Enterprise Management.

than chasing them afterward, but there also are ongoing efforts to recover fraudulent payments if they occur. Antifraud efforts have recovered a record-high $14.9 billion over the last four years.

Medicare Payment Reform

Traditional fee-for-service Medicare reimburses physicians for each service provided, creating incentives for overutilization. Spending inefficiencies are exacerbated by fragmentation across providers, who historically have had few incentives to coordinate care. Likewise, the prospective payment system (PPS) for Part A hospital services, which is designed to control costs by paying hospitals a prospective amount per diagnostic-related group (DRG) episode, is not immune to waste. While the DRG-based PPS encourages more efficient care and reductions in length of stay compared with cost-based reimbursement (Sloan et al. 1988; Seshamani, et al. 2006), it also can encourage a reduction in necessary care, leading to negative short-term health effects and readmissions (Cutler 1995; Encinosa and Bernard 2005; Seshamani, et al. 2006). Further, the inpatient PPS also can be susceptible to "upcoding," whereby providers code patients as being sicker than they are to raise the risk-adjusted prospective payments (Cutler 1995; Carter et al. 2002; Dafny 2005).

To curb these inefficiencies, the Affordable Care Act has established initiatives that lay a foundation for reforming care delivery and physician payment. At their core, these initiatives are designed to foster greater coordination of care across providers, while simultaneously aligning financial incentives to encourage provider organizations to deliver higher-quality, more efficient medical care. Each initiative builds on a core of clinical and patient engagement quality measures to ensure that cost savings are derived from more efficient delivery of care and not reduced patient access or care quality.

One such initiative is the Medicare Shared Savings Program (MSSP). Under this program, providers deliver care through accountable care organizations (ACOs), contractual organizations of primary care physicians, nurses, and specialists responsible for providing care to at least 5,000 beneficiaries. The Federal Government shares any savings generated for those beneficiaries, relative to benchmarks, with ACOs that meet rigorous quality standards, giving the ACOs incentives to invest in delivery practices, infrastructure, and organizational changes that help deliver higher-quality care for lower costs. Currently, more than 4 million beneficiaries receive care from more than 250 ACOs participating in the MSSP and other CMS projects, with ACO participation and covered beneficiaries continuing to increase as the program expands.

The Affordable Care Act also created the Center for Medicare and Medicaid Innovation, which is charged with identifying, testing, and ultimately expanding new and effective systems of delivering and paying for care. The CMS Innovation Center is authorized to invest up to $10 billion in initiatives that have the potential to reduce program expenditures while preserving or enhancing quality of care furnished to individuals under Medicare, Medicaid, and the Children's Health Insurance Program. Initiatives within the CMS Innovation Center include shared savings models, as well as bundled payments to hospitals and post-acute-care providers.

The Innovation Center's Pioneer ACO program is a more aggressive version of the MSSP and is open to organizations that have had success with risk-based payment arrangements. Pioneer ACOs may keep a greater share of Medicare savings than ACOs in the MSSP but are also at greater risk for losses if spending benchmarks are not met. Successful Pioneer ACOs are also eligible to move to a population-based payment arrangement whereby they assume greater financial risks and rewards for a predetermined set of patients. This greater risk-reward profile further encourages investments in care coordination and best practice delivery reforms. Pioneer ACOs must also develop similar outcomes-based payment arrangements with other payers, extending payment innovations to the commercial market and maximizing the impact of the program's incentives.

Currently, roughly 860,000 beneficiaries are enrolled in 32 Pioneer ACOs. The Pioneer program is just entering its second year, so it is too early for any comprehensive assessment, but Pioneer ACOs do seem to be making substantial investments in infrastructure and care processes. Infrastructure investments include health information technology adoption and improved data analytic capabilities, which enable providers to identify opportunities for improvements in care processes and the quality of care. For example, the potential savings associated with early identification and treatment of patients with high propensity for developing a chronic disease have led some Pioneer ACOs to make organizational changes that place greater focus on primary care and disease management. CMS is supporting Pioneer ACOs by providing privacy-protected patient information to promote care coordination, hosting collaborative learning networks, and offering other technical assistance.

Care coordination is also central to the Comprehensive Primary Care (CPC) initiative. Primary care is critical to promoting overall health and reducing medical spending. Yet because any one insurer accounts for only a fraction of a provider's business, insurers underinvest in primary care systems that would improve care coordination. Through the CPC initiative, Medicare partners with State and commercial insurers to promote community-wide investments in the delivery of coordinated primary care. Simultaneously, through direct financial payments or shared Medicare savings, the CPC initiative rewards high-quality providers who reduce health care costs through investments in care coordination. At the end of 2012, about 500 primary care practices were participating in the CPC initiative, representing 2,343 providers serving approximately 314,000 Medicare beneficiaries.

The CMS Innovation Center has introduced bundled payments as a model for hospital payment and delivery reform. A bundled payment is a fixed payment for a comprehensive set of hospital and/or post-acute services, including services associated with readmissions. Moving from individual payments for different services to a bundled payment for a set of services across providers and care settings encourages integration and coordination of care that will raise care quality and reduce readmissions. Variants on bundled payments are being demonstrated, differing in the scope of services included in the bundle, and whether payment is retrospective (based on shared Medicare savings) or prospective, which intensifies the financial risk and return to investing in changes to the efficiency and quality of care. Currently, 467 health care organizations across 46 states are engaged in the bundled payment initiative.

Is the Cost Curve Bending?

The real rate of health expenditure growth has declined or remained constant in every year between 2002 and 2011. For each of the three years 2009, 2010 and 2011, National Health Expenditure data show the real rate of annual growth in overall health spending was between 3.0 and 3.1 percent, the lowest rates since reporting began in 1960.

Additionally, the National Health Expenditure data show that growth in Medicare spending fell from an average of 8.6 percent a year between 2000 and 2005 to an average of 6.7 percent a year between 2006 and 2010. Notably, over a third—2.5 percentage points—of the 2006–2010 growth was attributable to increases in Medicare enrollment. With the exception of a spike in 2006, the year Medicare Part D was introduced, the growth rate of Medicare spending per enrollee—a measure of health care spending intensity—has been on a downward trend since 2001, with a particularly significant slowdown over the past three years (see Figure 5-6). Projections suggest the growth rate of Medicare spending per beneficiary will decline even further. While Medicare enrollment is expected to increase 3 percent a year over the next decade (CMS 2012), the rate of growth in spending per enrollee is

Figure 5-6
Real Annual Growth Rates of National Health Expenditures Per Capita and
Medicare Spending Per Enrollee, 1990–2012

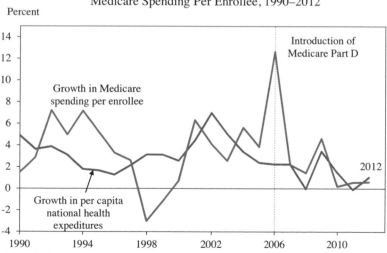

Note: Estimates for 2012 are projected.
Source: Center for Medicare and Medical Services, National Health Expenditure Accounts; CEA calculations.

projected to be approximately the same as the rate of growth in GDP per capita, according to the CBO and Office of the Actuary at CMS (Kronick and Po 2013). Similarly, the rate of growth in spending per Medicaid enrollee is projected to be near the rate of growth in GDP per capita. In the commercial health insurance market, per enrollee spending growth also has declined in recent years, the proximate cause being a slowdown in the growth rate of per-enrollee use of medical services (HCCI 2012).

There are several potential causes of the recent declines in the growth rate of spending per enrollee. One factor is the recent recession, in which job losses have caused the loss of insurance coverage. However, the recession explains only a small fraction of the declines in spending growth rates since the start of the recession. The slowdown in the growth rate of per-capita health expenditures began before the recession took hold, and has continued through the economic recovery and into 2012.

As expected, changes in real per-capita total health care spending at the state level are negatively correlated with changes in unemployment in the state between 2007 and 2009 (Figure 5-7). If the relationship in Figure 5-7 holds at the national level, then the increase in the national unemployment rate between 2007 and 2011 of 4.3 percentage points was associated with a $199 decline in spending per-capita (in 2007 dollars), or 2.6 percent of per-capita health care spending in 2007. This accounts for only 18 percent of the slowdown in spending growth since the start of the recession in 2007 and an even smaller proportion of the slowdown in spending growth since 2002, when the growth rate in real per-capita total health care spending began to decline.[2]

Structural changes in the health care market offer another explanation for the decline in per-enrollee spending growth. One possibility is that hospitals and provider groups have increasingly sought to improve efficiency—through adopting more high value medical practices and performing fewer low value procedures—in response to evidence showing their potential for cost savings and quality improvements (Fisher and Skinner, 2010). At the same time, formulary changes that encourage substitution away from branded to generic drugs, and changes in insurance design that increase patient cost sharing for both services and pharmaceuticals, also may explain a portion of the declines in spending growth per enrollee over the past decade. For example, the sharp slowdown in the growth rate of medical

---

[2] Between 2001 and 2006, real per-capital spending grew by 21.5 percent. Between 2006 and 2011, real per-capital spending grew by 7.1 percent, where the 14.4 percentage point difference in spending growth captures the slowdown in spending growth. The 2.6 percent decline in total health care spending between 2007 and 2011 attributable to the recession accounts for approximately (2.6/14.4)*100 = 18 percent of the slowdown in spending growth since the start of the recession.

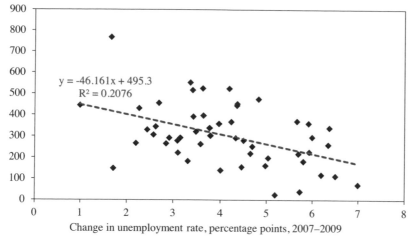

Figure 5-7
Relationship Between Change in State Unemployment Rate and Change in
Real Per-Capita Personal Health Spending, 2007–2009

Change in per capita health spending 2007–2009, 2007 dollars

$$y = -46.161x + 495.3$$
$$R^2 = 0.2076$$

Change in unemployment rate, percentage points, 2007–2009

Source: Centers for Medicare and Medicaid Services, National Health Expenditure
Accounts; Bureau of Labor Statistics, Current Population Survey; CEA calculations.

imaging since 2006 likely was due to a confluence of reforms including prior authorization, increased cost sharing and reduced reimbursements (Lee and Levy 2012). Notably, Lee and Levy found that a large fraction of the declines involved imaging identified as having unproven medical value. Similarly, payment reforms and regulations are thought to have contributed to long-run declines in Medicare spending growth rates (White 2008).

Early responses to the Affordable Care Act may have contributed to the decline in per enrollee spending since 2010 (Kronick and Po 2013). Relevant provisions of the law include provisions intended to foster coordinated care, improve primary care, reduce preventable health complications during hospitalizations, and promote the adoption of health information technology.

The decline in the hospital readmission rate, coinciding with the introduction of the Partnership for Patients program in 2011, also may point to early effects of the Affordable Care Act on spending. The Act's Medicare hospital readmissions reduction program, introduced in October 2012, should reinforce these effects. Likewise, infrastructure investments and care process changes, either funded directly by the Affordable Care Act or stimulated through the Affordable Care Act's payment reform, are other possible sources for the recent declines in spending growth.

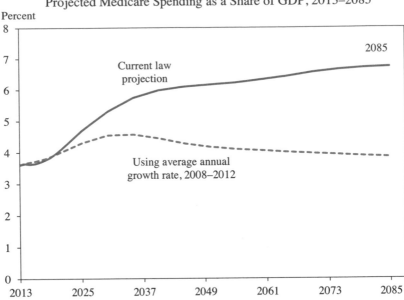

Figure 5-8
Projected Medicare Spending as a Share of GDP, 2013–2085

Percent

2085

Current law
projection

Using average annual
growth rate, 2008–2012

2013   2025   2037   2049   2061   2073   2085

Source: Medicare Trustees (2012); Social Security Trustees (2012); CEA calculations.

In addition, spending declines may reflect early changes in medical care delivery made in anticipation of impending Medicare payment reform. The Affordable Care Act moves providers towards savings-based payment models in Medicare that encourage improved coordination of care. Hospitals seeking new ways to reduce costs and increase bargaining power with suppliers and insurers may respond by consolidating their operations. Recent years have seen a continued consolidation and integration of physicians into provider networks.

The long-run growth rate of per-capita spending has significant implications for the budget. Medicare spending represented 3.7 percent of GDP in 2011 (Medicare Trustees 2012). Under current law, including cost control measures of the Affordable Care Act and the Sustainable Growth Rate-mandated physician payment cut, CMS projects that Medicare spending will rise to represent 6.7 percent of GDP in 75 years, with long-term nominal per-beneficiary spending growing at a rate on average equal to 4.3 percent per year (Medicare Trustees 2012). However, nominal growth rates of per-beneficiary Medicare spending have been declining since 2001, and over the past five years have averaged 3.6 percent. At least some of the recent decline in Medicare spending growth appears to be structural, implying that the low spending growth rates from the past few years may persist.[3] If the per-beneficiary growth rate of Medicare spending were to remain 3.6 percent per year, then after 75 years Medicare spending would account for only 3.8 percent of GDP, little changed from its share today, and substantially less than what the Medicare Trustees estimate. (Figure 5-8). This should not be interpreted as a forecast but rather an indication of how sensitive long-term projections are to the assumed rate of growth of Medicare spending per beneficiary. In this hypothetical scenario where per-beneficiary Medicare spending grows at a rate equal to the one observed over the past five years, Medicare spending as a share of GDP would be much lower than what current long-term projections suggest.

The causes for the recent and projected declines in the growth rate of medical spending and utilization, and their relationship to the major quality-improving and cost-saving provisions of the Affordable Care Act, remain an important area for future research. Enacted provisions of the health reform law appear to be having positive effects on care coordination, hospital outcomes and spending. And payment reforms that better align payment with cost and provide incentives for efficiency such as shared savings and bundled payment programs hold potential to improve to care quality and reduce medical spending.

---

[3] Regression analysis shows a flat and insignificant relationship between state-level 2007-09 changes in per-beneficiary Medicare spending and changes in unemployment, suggesting that little if any of the recent declines in per-beneficiary Medicare spending growth is related to regional cyclical factors.

CHAPTER 6

CLIMATE CHANGE AND THE PATH TOWARD SUSTAINABLE ENERGY SOURCES

The Administration is committed to a comprehensive energy strategy that supports economic and job growth, bolsters energy security, positions the United States to lead the world in clean energy, and addresses the global challenge of climate change. Finding a responsible path that balances the economic benefits of low-cost energy, the social and environmental costs associated with energy production, and our duty to future generations is a central challenge of energy and environmental policy.

The most significant long-term pollution challenge facing America and the world is the anthropogenic emissions of greenhouse gases. The scientific consensus, as reflected in the 2009 assessment by the U.S. Global Change Research Program (USGCRP) on behalf of the National Science and Technology Council, is that anthropogenic emissions of greenhouse gases are causing changes in the climate that include rising average national and global temperatures, warming oceans, rising average sea levels, more extreme heat waves and storms, and extinctions of species and loss of biodiversity. A multitude of other impacts have been observed in every region of the country and virtually all economic sectors.

As part of the United Nations Climate Change Conferences in Copenhagen and Cancún, the United States pledged to cut its carbon dioxide (CO_2) and other human-induced greenhouse gas emissions in the range of 17 percent below 2005 levels by 2020, and to meet its long-term goal of reducing emissions by 83 percent by 2050. Approximately 87 percent of U.S. anthropogenic emissions of all greenhouse gases (primarily CO_2 and methane) are energy-related, and fossil-fuel combustion accounts for approximately 94 percent of U.S. CO_2 emissions (EPA 2010a).

Climate change is often described in terms of changes in background conditions that unfold over decades, but extreme events superimposed on, and possibly amplified by, those background changes can cause severe damage. For example, storm surges superimposed on higher sea levels will cause greater flooding, heat waves superimposed on already warmer temperatures will cause greater damage to crops, and a warmer atmosphere amplifies the potential for both droughts and floods.

From an economist's perspective, greenhouse gas emissions impose costs on others who are not involved in the transaction resulting in the emissions; that is, greenhouse gas emissions generate a negative externality. Appropriate policies to address this negative externality would internalize the externality, so that the price of emissions reflects their true cost, or would seek technological solutions that would similarly reduce the externality. Such policies encourage energy efficiency and clean energy production. In addition, prudence mandates that the Nation prepare now for the consequences of climate change.

Consequences and Costs of Climate Change

The clear scientific consensus is that anthropogenic greenhouse gas emissions are causing our climate to change. These changes include increasing temperatures, rising sea levels, changing weather patterns, and increasingly severe heat waves, with negative consequences for human health, property, and ecosystems.[1]

The Changing Climate

Projections using a wide variety of climate models paint a broadly similar picture of how global temperatures can be expected to rise in response to emissions—a picture that is also consistent with observed temperature changes (Rohling et al. 2012). Likely temperature paths, from a comparison of models by the USGCRP (2009), predict that the average global temperature under a low-emissions scenario will increase by approximately 4°F by the end of this century; under the medium and high emissions scenarios, end-of-century increases are 7°F and 8°F, respectively. Some regions are projected to experience greater temperature increases than others. The Arctic has warmed by almost twice the global average in recent decades, in part because warming melts snow and ice, leading to less reflected sunlight, which causes yet more warming (Arctic Monitoring and Assessment Programme 2011).

---

[1] The scientific consensus on the effects of greenhouse gas emissions on climate is summarized in reports by the USGCRP (2009) and the International Panel on Climate Change (IPCC 2012). The draft Third National Climate Assessment report, prepared by the National Climate Assessment Development Advisory Committee, was issued for public comment in January 2013.

Warming temperatures raise sea levels because of expanding ocean water, melting mountain glaciers and ice caps, and partial melting of the Greenland and continental Antarctic ice sheets. Since 1880, the global sea level has risen about 20 centimeters, more than half of which has occurred since 1950. Projections by the National Oceanographic and Atmospheric Administration show sea levels rising over the 21st century by 19 to 200 centimeters (NOAA 2012).

Increasingly common extreme events, such as heat waves, droughts, floods, and storms, pose some of the most significant risks of climate change. In its assessment of the current scientific literature, the IPCC (2012) concluded that increases in greenhouse gases will almost certainly increase the frequency and magnitude of hot daily temperature extremes during the 21st century, while episodes of cold extremes will decrease. In addition, the length, frequency, and intensity of heat waves are very likely to increase over most land areas, and droughts may intensify (Hansen, Sato, and Ruedy 2012; Rhines and Huybers 2013). In fact, an increase in the mean temperature implies more very hot days and fewer very cold days, even if the variability of daily temperatures around the mean remains unchanged. This phenomenon—a disproportionate increase in previously extreme temperatures as the mean temperature increases—is illustrated in Figure 6-1, which displays a shift in a hypothetical distribution of possible daily temperatures. The implications of Figure 6-1 accord with observed changes over the past decades and centuries as well as with climate model simulations. For example, according to the USGCRP estimates, under a high-emissions scenario, areas of the Southeast and Southwest that currently experience an average of 60 days a year with a high temperature above 90°F will experience 150 or more such days by the end of the century.

Patterns of precipitation and storms are also likely to change, although the nature of these changes currently is more uncertain than those for temperature. Northern areas of the United States are projected to become wetter, especially in the winter and spring; southern areas, especially the Southwest, are projected to become drier. Moreover, heavy precipitation events will likely be more frequent: downpours that currently occur about once every 20 years are projected to occur every 4 to 15 years by 2100, depending on location. The strongest cold-season storms are projected to become stronger, more frequent, and more costly. For more on the costs of storms, see Box 6-1.

Figure 6 - 1
Illustrative Average Temperature Distribution

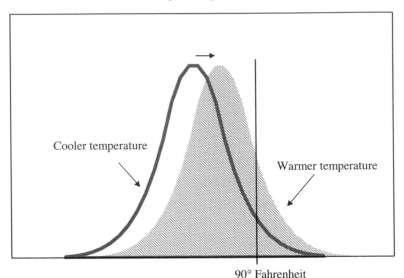

Cooler temperature

Warmer temperature

90° Fahrenheit

Source: CEA illustration.

Estimating the Economic Cost of Climate Change: The Social Cost of Carbon

Because greenhouse gas emissions cause climate change, policies to reduce climate change must focus on reducing anthropogenic greenhouse gas emissions. An important step in informing a policy response is knowing precisely where carbon emissions are coming from, and that is the purpose of the Environmental Protection Agency (EPA) Greenhouse Gas Reporting Program discussed in Data Watch 6-1.

Another critical step in formulating policy responses to climate change is to estimate the economic costs induced by emitting an additional, or marginal, ton of CO_2. This cost—which covers health, property damage, agricultural impacts, the value of ecosystem services, and other welfare costs of climate change—is often referred to as the "social cost of carbon" (SCC). Having a range for the SCC provides a benchmark that policymakers and the public can use to assess the net benefits of emissions reductions stemming from a proposed policy. Although various studies, notably Stern (2006), have estimated the cost of climate change, until recently the Federal Government did not generate its own unique set of estimates of the SCC.

In 2010, a Federal interagency working group, led by the Council of Economic Advisers and the Office of Management and Budget, produced a white paper that outlined a methodology for estimating the SCC and

Box 6-1: The Cost of Hurricanes

Hurricanes draw energy from the temperature difference between the surface ocean and mid-level atmosphere. Although no one hurricane or storm can be attributed to global warming, there is some expectation that warming surface waters will increase the maximum intensity of hurricanes, and a trend toward increasing hurricane intensity has been observed in the North Atlantic over the past three decades (Kossin et al. 2007). As the figure shows, insured losses from storms have also been increasing over the past 20 years, a trend that is driven by losses from recent large hurricanes. Because many of the losses from hurricanes are uninsured, total costs can substantially exceed insured costs.

Development near vulnerable coasts, increasing intensity of storms, and rising sea levels point toward hurricane winds, precipitation, and storm surges that are increasingly destructive. In fact, several studies project substantial increases in hurricane-related costs because of climate change.[1] It is difficult to isolate the contribution of climate change to the historical increase in hurricane costs. Nonetheless, from the perspective of social cost, the relevant facts are that the total cost is increasing, and that storm costs will increase with coastal development and could well also increase in response to greater storm severity.

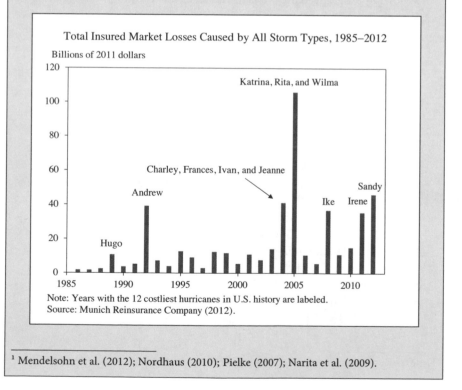

Total Insured Market Losses Caused by All Storm Types, 1985–2012

Note: Years with the 12 costliest hurricanes in U.S. history are labeled.
Source: Munich Reinsurance Company (2012).

[1] Mendelsohn et al. (2012); Nordhaus (2010); Pielke (2007); Narita et al. (2009).

Data Watch 6-1: Tracking Sources of Emissions: The Greenhouse Gas Reporting Program

In October 2009, the Environmental Protection Agency (EPA) launched its Greenhouse Gas Reporting Program, an ambitious effort to collect and make publicly available facility-level data on greenhouse gas emissions across the United States. Today, experts and non-experts alike can view, explore, and download comprehensive information on greenhouse gas emissions using the EPA's convenient online data tool. The program is a leap forward for greenhouse gas data collection and the first of its kind in its scale and "bottom-up" approach. It will be an important piece of administrative infrastructure for any future effort to regulate or price greenhouse gas emissions.

Since 1990, the EPA has reported estimates of greenhouse gas emissions in its annual Inventory of U.S. Greenhouse Gas Emissions and Sinks, in compliance with the U.S. commitment under the United Nations Framework Convention on Climate Change. These estimates, however, are mostly "top-down," in that the EPA estimates national emissions using aggregate data on fuel production, imports and exports, and inventories. In 2008, Congress instructed the agency to begin to collect facility-level data, and the EPA developed the Greenhouse Gas Reporting Program to augment the data collected through the National Greenhouse Gas Inventory. The first wave of data, which covers emissions in 2010, was made publicly available in January 2012. More than 6,000 facilities—refineries, power plants, chemical plants, landfills, and more—were required to report their emissions, which amounted to 3.2 billion tons of carbon dioxide equivalent (CO_2e) that year alone.[1] The EPA will release data on 2011 emissions in early 2013.

The EPA provides its database of facility-level greenhouse gas emissions online (http://ghgdata.epa.gov), and visitors can view data by sector or geography or both. The site's rich interface and powerful maps software permits easy spatial analysis of emissions, and built-in charts help users glean useful information from what might otherwise be an unwieldy dataset. Although the Greenhouse Gas Reporting Program is an important step forward for greenhouse gas data collection, there are a few limitations: only facilities that emit more than 25,000 tons of greenhouse gases (measured in CO_2e) a year are required to report (although some sectors are "all in," meaning even emitters below the 25,000-ton threshold report for the first three to five years), and the program does not cover emissions from agriculture or land use.

---

[1] http://www.epa.gov/ghgreporting/ghgdata/reported/index.html

provided numeric estimates (White House 2010). The SCC calculation estimates the cost of a small, or marginal, increase in global emissions. This process was the first Federal Government effort to consistently calculate the social benefits of reducing CO_2 emissions for use in policy assessment. To date, the 2010 interagency SCC values have been used to evaluate at least 17 rules at various stages in the rulemaking process by the EPA, the Department of Transportation (DOT), and the Department of Energy (DOE).

To estimate the SCC, the working group used three different peer-reviewed models from the academic literature of the economic costs of climate change and tackled some key issues in computing those costs. One issue is the choice of the discount rate used to compute the present value of future costs: because many of the costs occur in the distant future, the SCC is sensitive to the weight placed on the welfare of future generations. Another issue is how to handle some of the uncertainty surrounding climate projections. Box 6-2 explains how the working group dealt with uncertainty about the equilibrium climate sensitivity, which serves as a proxy for the climate system's response to greenhouse gas emissions.

The working group report provided four values for the social cost of emitting a ton of CO_2 in 2011: $5, $22, $36, and $67, in 2007 dollars. The first three estimates, which average the cost of carbon across various models and scenarios, differ depending on the rate at which future costs and benefits are discounted (5, 3, and 2.5 percent, respectively). The fourth value, $67, comes from focusing on the worst 5 percent of modeled outcomes, discounted at 3 percent. All four values rise over time because the marginal damages increase as atmospheric CO_2 concentrations rise.

The SCC study acknowledged that these estimates, while a substantial step forward, need refinement, for example by a more complete treatment of some damage categories. A detailed discussion of the methodology can be found in Greenstone, Kopits, and Wolverton (2013). The interagency working group has committed to update its estimates of the SCC as the literature evolves and as new scientific and economic evidence become available.

Policy Implications of Scientific and Economic Uncertainty

As a general matter, policy decisions must commonly be made in the presence of uncertainty. A standard approach for cost estimation or policy evaluation in the presence of uncertainty is to consider different scenarios and to compute a weighted average (expected value) over those scenarios. But in some cases it is difficult to quantify this uncertainty. In particular, some of the unknowns about climate change concern extreme scenarios that are far outside recorded human experience. Although such events are

Box 6-2: Handling Uncertainty About Equilibrium Climate Sensitivity

The 2010 Federal study on the social cost of carbon (SCC) used three integrated economic-geophysical models to estimate the cost of climate change: the DICE model, the PAGE5 model, and the FUND model.[1] The costs estimated by each model are sensitive to climatic, economic, and emissions parameters. A key input parameter for each model is the equilibrium climate sensitivity, defined as the increase in the long-term annual global-average surface temperature increase associated with a doubling of atmospheric carbon dioxide (CO_2) concentration relative to pre-industrial levels.

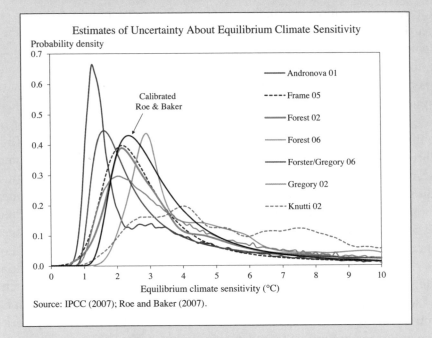

Estimates of Uncertainty About Equilibrium Climate Sensitivity

Source: IPCC (2007); Roe and Baker (2007).

The Intergovernmental Panel on Climate Change (IPCC 2012) suggests a range for the equilibrium climate sensitivity of 2–4.5°C (3.2–7.2°F), but the scientific uncertainty extends outside this range. The figure shows distributions of possible values of this parameter arising from different studies; each line in the figure corresponds to a given study, and the higher the line, the greater the chances (according to that study) of the corresponding value of the equilibrium climate sensitivity.

---

[1] The DICE model was developed by William Nordhaus, David Popp, Zili Yang, Joseph Boyer, and colleagues. The PAGE model was developed by Chris Hope with John Anderson, Paul Wenman, and Erica Plambeck. The FUND model was developed by David Anthoff and Richard Tol.

Although the distributions from different studies differ, each holds open the possibility that the value of this parameter might be very large.

This range of uncertainty over the equilibrium climate sensitivity matters for estimating the economic costs of carbon emissions: a higher value implies a more amplified response of temperature to carbon emissions, which would be associated with greater human consequences. To handle this uncertainty, the task force adopted a standard approach used by economists, which is to compute a weighted average—technically, an expected value—where the weighting reflects the uncertainty in the scientific literature. Specifically, simulations were run for many values of the equilibrium climate sensitivity drawn randomly from an assumed probability distribution and the results were averaged, producing the expected value for the SCC. The resulting SCC estimate incorporates the uncertainty in the equilibrium climate sensitivity.

therefore difficult to quantify, the possibility of very severe outcomes can and should inform policy.

One principle of policy design under uncertainty is that the policy should be able to adapt as more is learned and the uncertainty is resolved; another is that a policy should be robust to uncertainty.[2] A robust policy aims to give acceptable outcomes no matter what happens, within a given range of possible outcomes. As applied to climate change, this idea of robust policy in the face of uncertainty leads to policies that avoid worst-case outcomes. Such an approach has been advocated by Weitzman (2009, 2011), who argues that, when considering the expected damages of unmitigated global climate change, it is important to consider low probability but potentially catastrophic impacts that could occur. By focusing on avoiding the most costly climate outcomes, a climate change policy that is robust to scientific uncertainty would be more aggressive than a policy that simply focuses on quantifiable uncertainty or a consensus temperature path. If future scientific knowledge were to determine that the worst outcomes could be ruled out, then a robust policy could be adjusted. Thus, although uncertainty complicates the task of computing costs, it is not in itself a reason for inaction or delay.

---

[2] An important early paper on policymaking under uncertainty is Brainard (1967). Recent work in economics on robust policy in the face of model uncertainty includes Hansen and Sargent (2001, 2007), Giannoni (2002), Onatski and Stock (2002), and Funke and Paetz (2011).

CARBON EMISSIONS: PROGRESS AND PROJECTIONS

The past five years have seen a remarkable turnaround in U.S. emissions of carbon dioxide. As can be seen in Figure 6-2, from the early 1980s through the mid-2000s, energy-related CO_2 emissions increased from approximately 4,500 million metric tons (MMT) to a peak of just over 6,000 MMT in 2007. Since 2007, however, emissions have fallen sharply to approximately 5,500 MMT in 2011, the most recent year for which there is complete data. Indeed, as shown in the figure, this reduction in emissions makes significant progress toward achieving the Copenhagen Accord target of a 17 percent reduction in greenhouse gas emissions below 2005 levels by 2020.[3]

A natural question is what set of new events or initiatives led to the sharp reduction in emissions. There are a number of candidate explanations: reductions in the carbon content of energy, most notably the substitution of natural gas and renewables for coal; improvements in economy-wide energy efficiency; and unexpectedly low energy demand because of the recession. To estimate the contribution of these factors to the decline in emissions, one needs to posit a counterfactual path for these three variables, that is, for the carbon content of energy (CO_2 per British thermal unit, or Btu), energy use per dollar of gross domestic product (Btu/GDP), and GDP. Given a counterfactual, or baseline, path for these variables, one can decompose the decline in carbon emissions to a decline in the carbon content of energy, an accelerated improvement in energy efficiency, or a shortfall of GDP, relative to the baseline path.[4] Because the question focuses on the role of new developments, a natural approach is for the baseline to be a business-as-usual projection from a given starting point. For the purpose of this exercise, the starting point is taken to be the 2005 values of the carbon content of energy, energy efficiency, and GDP; the business-as-usual projections are made either by using historical published forecasts or by extrapolating historical trends.

The results of this decomposition estimate that actual 2012 carbon emissions are approximately 17 percent below the "business as usual" baseline. As shown in Figure 6-3, of this reduction, 52 percent was due to the recession (the shortfall of GDP, relative to trend growth), 40 percent came

---

[3] United Nations Framework Convention on Climate Change, Appendix I, http://unfccc.int/meetings/copenhagen_dec_2009/items/5264.php.

[4] Specifically, CO_2 emissions are the product of $(CO_2/Btu) \times (Btu/GDP) \times GDP$, where CO_2 represents U.S. CO_2 emissions in a given year, Btu represents energy consumption in that year, and GDP is that year's GDP. Taking logarithms of this expression, and then subtracting the baseline from the actual values, gives a decomposition of the CO_2 reduction into contributions from clean energy, energy efficiency, and the recession.

Figure 6-2
U.S. Energy-Related Carbon Dioxide Emissions, 1973–2040

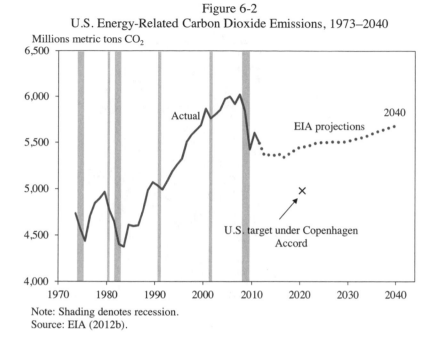

Note: Shading denotes recession.
Source: EIA (2012b).

from cleaner energy (fuel switching), and 8 percent came from accelerated improvements in energy efficiency, relative to trend. Of the cleaner energy improvements, most (approximately two-thirds) came from reductions in emissions from burning coal. Reductions in emissions from petroleum combustion also made important contributions (approximately one-third), as these high-carbon content fuels were replaced by lower carbon-content natural gas and clean renewable energy sources, notably wind and biofuels. The contribution from energy efficiency stems from efficiency improvements over the 2005–12 period that were faster than projected; in particular, the Energy Information Administration (EIA 2005) forecast a reduction in the energy content of GDP of 1.6 percent per year, but energy efficiency improved by more than this forecast.[5]

As the economy improves, GDP will rise, and the weakness of the economy in 2007–09 will no longer restrain energy consumption. Thus if the recent reductions in emissions are to be continued, a greater share will need to be borne by fuel switching into natural gas and into zero-emissions renewables, and by accelerating improvement in economy-wide energy efficiency.

---

[5] Houser and Mohan (forthcoming) undertake a similar decomposition. They use different assumptions for the baseline, including somewhat stronger post-2005 GDP growth in the "business as usual" case than is assumed here, and as a result attribute slightly more of the post-2005 reduction in CO_2 emissions to slower economic growth.

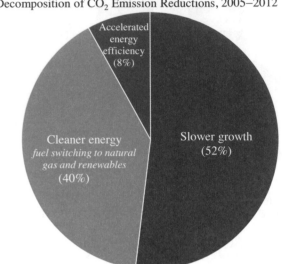

Figure 6-3
Decomposition of CO_2 Emission Reductions, 2005–2012

Accelerated energy efficiency (8%)

Cleaner energy
fuel switching to natural gas and renewables
(40%)

Slower growth (52%)

Source: Bureau of Economic Analysis, National Income and Product Accounts; EIA
(2013); CEA calculations.

POLICY RESPONSES TO THE CHALLENGE
OF CLIMATE CHANGE

As a general matter, government intervention may be warranted if an individual's action produces a negative externality; that is, if the action imposes costs on another person and those costs are not borne by the person taking the action. As with many environmental problems, the impacts of pollution are broadly shared by society, and individuals emitting pollution do not bear the full, direct costs of their individual action (or reap the full benefits individually of reducing pollution). In the case of anthropogenic emissions of greenhouse gases, the costs of climate change are borne by others, including future generations, and those costs are not reflected in the price of greenhouse gas emissions. This market failure is also present in reverse: an entrepreneur with a clever idea for reducing greenhouse gas emissions, such as a novel energy conservation technology, cannot recoup the full benefit of her innovation because there is no way she can charge those who will benefit from the abatement of those emissions.

This diagnosis of the market failure underlying climate change clarifies the need for government to protect future generations that will be affected by today's emissions. Responding to the challenge of climate change leads to a multipronged approach to policy. Four such responses are implementing market-based solutions; technology-based regulation of greenhouse gas emissions; supporting the transition of the U.S. energy sector to technologies, such as renewables and energy efficiency, that reduce our overall carbon footprint; and taking actions now to prepare for those impacts that are by now unavoidable.

Market-Based Solutions

In his 2013 State of the Union Address, President Obama urged Congress to pursue a bipartisan, market-based solution to climate change. Market-based solutions to greenhouse gas emissions provide economic incentives so that the cost of polluting reflects the economic harm caused to others by that pollution. In this sense, market-based solutions are said to "internalize" the externality caused by the pollution. Under the standard assumptions of economic theory, market-based solutions to pollution are economically efficient because those who create the externality can choose the least costly and disruptive way to reduce their emissions. Under market-based solutions, the effective price of the activity producing the negative externality is adjusted so that it reflects the cost of that externality. There are various ways that market-based solutions can be implemented, one of which is a cap-and-trade system like the one Senators McCain and Lieberman worked on.[6]

Another example of a market-based solution is a Clean Energy Standard that would require electric utilities to obtain an increasing share of delivered electricity from clean sources but would allow them to meet the standard by trading clean-energy credits. By allowing trading in credits, electric utilities that produce renewable energy at relatively low cost can sell credits to those for which renewable production would be high-cost. Thus the total cost across all utilities of meeting the standard is reduced, relative to the cost were each utility required to meet the standard without tradable credits. In this way, a market for clean energy credits harnesses private-sector incentives to minimize the cost of generating electricity from clean energy sources.[7]

Direct Regulation of Carbon Emissions and the Vehicle Greenhouse Gas / Corporate Average Fuel Economy (CAFE) Standards

Another way to address the externality of carbon emissions is by direct regulation. In 2007, the Supreme Court ruled in *Massachusetts v. EPA* that it is incumbent upon the EPA to determine whether greenhouse gases

---

[6] For a more detailed discussion of cap-and-trade, see the *2010 Economic Report of the President,* chapter 9.

[7] For further discussion of a Clean Energy Standard, see the *2012 Economic Report of the President,* chapter 6.

pose a risk to public health or welfare and, if so, to regulate greenhouse gas emissions under the Clean Air Act. In 2012, the U.S. Court of Appeals for the District of Columbia Circuit upheld the EPA's authority to regulate greenhouse gas emissions.

The Administration's corporate average fuel economy (CAFE) and greenhouse gas regulations, released in 2012 jointly by the EPA and the DOT, require automakers to increase the fuel economy of passenger cars and light trucks so that they are estimated to achieve 54.5 miles per gallon by 2025, approximately doubling the previous mileage standards.[8] The new fuel economy standards are expected to save more than 2 million barrels of oil a day by 2025—more than we import from any country other than Canada—and to reduce consumer expenditures on gasoline. The standards are projected to reduce annual CO_2 emissions by over 6 billion metric tons over the life of the program, roughly equivalent to the emissions from the United States in 2010 (White House 2011a).

The new fuel economy standards help to correct the externality that the cost of carbon emissions is not accounted for in the price of gasoline. The standards also provide a clear signal to the thousands of firms in the auto supply chain that investments in fuel-saving innovation will pay off. These innovations range from large (batteries for electric cars) to small (lighter-weight bolts), and often require suppliers to coordinate with each other. For example, use of innovative high-strength steels can reduce the overall weight of a vehicle, but only if firms making automotive parts and those making tooling for the parts each invest in new production processes (Helper, Krueger, and Wial 2012). The new standards ensure demand for fuel-saving innovations and thus provide an incentive for such investments.

Energy Efficiency

An important way to reduce greenhouse gas emissions is to use energy more efficiently, that is, to use less energy to provide a given service outcome. For example, weatherizing a home improves efficiency by requiring less energy to maintain a given inside temperature. Using less energy, in turn, reduces greenhouse gas emissions.

The Administration has made energy efficiency initiatives an important component of its energy plan.[9] These initiatives include major research

---

[8] Because the standards regulate greenhouse gas emissions, they can be met in part in ways that do not improve fuel economy. In particular, if improvements are made by reducing leakage of greenhouse gases in auto air conditioners, or by replacing refrigerants with non-greenhouse gases, then the goal of reducing greenhouse gas emissions is achieved without improving fleet fuel economy.

[9] http://www.whitehouse.gov/sites/default/files/email-files/the_blueprint_for_a_secure_energy_future_oneyear_progress_report.pdf

investments to improve the efficiency of building designs and components such as lighting, heating, and air conditioning, along with smart building controls. Other important initiatives include the weatherization of more than 1 million homes across the country, the President's Better Buildings Challenge with $2 billion in private-sector commitments to energy efficiency retrofits, new standards for residential and commercial appliances, and the Rural Energy for America Program. The Administration has also introduced a variety of programs to help consumers learn about developments in energy efficiency; one such example is the Home Energy Score, a new voluntary program from the DOE to help homeowners make cost-effective decisions about energy improvements. Additionally, as part of a broader manufacturing strategy, the Administration has partnered with manufacturing companies representing more than 1,400 plants that plan to make investments that will improve energy efficiency by 25 percent over 10 years.

An overall measure of economy-wide energy use is the amount of energy needed to generate a dollar's worth of goods and services ("energy intensity"). As is shown in Figure 6-4, the energy intensity of the U.S. economy has fallen steadily over the past quarter century, with an annual average rate of decline of 1.7 percent from 1990 through 2011. However, U.S. energy intensity is still one-third higher than that of Germany and Japan, in part because Germany and Japan have automobiles and building codes that are more energy efficient, as well as smaller homes set more densely.[10]

One reason for the decline in the energy intensity of the U.S. economy is the increasing importance of services as a share of U.S. GDP. Manufacturing is more energy-intensive than is the production of services, and for decades the share of U.S. GDP derived from services has been growing while the share derived from manufacturing has been declining. This shift from manufacturing to services therefore has reduced the energy intensity of the U.S. economy.

To control for changes in the energy-GDP ratio driven by changes in the sectoral composition of output, the DOE developed an "Economy-wide Energy Intensity Index." This index estimates the amount of energy needed to produce a basket of goods in one year, relative to the previous year. As indicated in Figure 6-5, between 1985 and 2010, the DOE Energy Intensity Index fell by 14 percent. In contrast, the energy-GDP ratio fell by 33 percent. Thus, while much of the decline in energy usage per dollar of GDP has come from improvements in energy efficiency, much of it has also come from

---

[10] In neither Germany nor Japan is the lower energy intensity due to having less manufacturing than the United States. In fact, manufacturing (an energy-intensive sector) is almost twice as high as a share of GDP in Germany as it is in the United States.

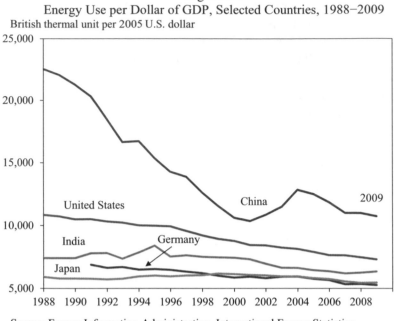

Figure 6-4
Energy Use per Dollar of GDP, Selected Countries, 1988–2009

British thermal unit per 2005 U.S. dollar

Source: Energy Information Administration, International Energy Statistics.

Figure 6-5
U.S. Energy Intensity, 1950–2010

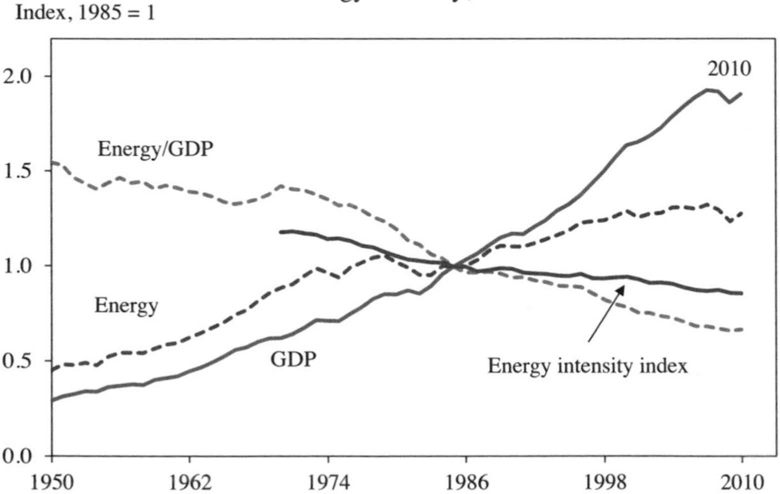

Index, 1985 = 1

Note: "Energy" is the amount of energy consumed (measured in Btu) compared to 1985 levels.
"Energy/GDP" is energy consumed divided by GDP, compared to 1985 levels. The energy intensity index is
available starting in 1970.
Source: Department of Energy, Office of Energy Efficiency and Renewable Energy, Energy Intensity
Indicators: Trend Data.

factors other than improved efficiency such as shifts in the composition of output.

The energy intensity index measures the energy footprint of U.S. production, not of U.S. consumption. This distinction arises because energy intensity includes energy used to produce exported goods and services (which are not consumed domestically) and excludes energy used to produce imports. To estimate the CO_2 intensity of consumption, as opposed to the CO_2 intensity of production, one needs to adjust U.S. CO_2 emissions for the difference of foreign emissions in the production of imports less domestic emissions in the production of exports.

Technical developments that use less energy to provide a service, such as maintaining a room at a comfortable temperature, can both reduce energy consumption and improve consumer welfare. Because technical improvements in energy efficiency reduce the energy cost of the service, consumers are better off, and because the price of the service declines, they might use more of it. For example, weatherizing a home might tempt the homeowner to bump up the thermostat a couple of degrees. This consumer response of using more of the newly efficient service is known as the rebound effect. The magnitude of the rebound effect depends on the particular service, more specifically on the elasticity of demand for the service. Viewed solely through the lens of CO_2 reduction—a lens that is appropriate because CO_2 emissions are underpriced—the rebound effect suggests that government efforts on energy efficiency should emphasize services with inelastic demand, so that price changes do not substantially alter service consumption and actual energy savings approach the technically feasible energy savings.

One such example is the services derived from automobiles. In the context of the vehicle greenhouse gas–CAFE standard discussed earlier, the EPA assumes a rebound effect of about 10 percent[11], that is, consumers will drive about 10 percent more than if the efficiency of their vehicles had not increased (EPA 2010b). In their reviews of the rebound effect, Greening, Greene, and Difiglio (2000) and Gillingham et al. (2013) suggest more generally that the rebound effect tends to range between 10 percent and 30 percent. Although much has been written on the rebound effect, the base of original research is limited, and more research is needed concerning the rebound effect (and the associated price elasticities) empirically, both in the short and long run.

---

[11] The EPA rebound estimate draws on the literature, for example, Small and Van Dender (2007).

ENERGY PRODUCTION IN TRANSITION

The United States is in a period of swift and profound change in the way that energy is produced and consumed. Thanks to recent advances in technology, more of the country's domestic oil and gas resources are now accessible. As a result, U.S. oil production has climbed to the highest level in 15 years and natural gas production reached an all-time high. This increase in domestic oil production enhances energy security, and increased natural gas production has substituted for coal, which reduces CO_2 emissions per unit of energy produced. At the same time, the Obama Administration has taken historic steps to promote greater energy efficiency and the deployment of renewable energy across the U.S. economy. In the past five years, the United States has more than doubled non-hydroelectric renewable electricity generation. The Administration is working to continue these trends through a comprehensive "all of the above" approach to energy policy that takes advantage of all domestic energy resources, while also igniting the innovation needed to lead the world in clean energy.

The transformation of the U.S. energy sector to one with a smaller carbon footprint is central to climate change policy. As Figure 6-6 shows, approximately 77 percent of U.S. energy production in 2011 came from burning fossil fuels, and the remaining 23 percent was approximately evenly split between nuclear and renewables. In broad terms, the share of natural gas (the fossil fuel with the lowest carbon content) and the share of renewables have been expanding, displacing the share of coal (the fossil fuel with the highest carbon content).

Oil and Natural Gas

New developments in exploration and production techniques and technology have made the extraction of new sources of oil and natural gas economically viable, resulting in a U.S. production boom. Figure 6-7 shows the changing consumption and production trends of natural gas in the United States, along with the U.S. share of global production since 2000. As a result of the developments in shale gas production, total U.S. natural gas production rose 27 percent, from 18.1 trillion cubic feet in 2005 to 23.0 trillion cubic feet in 2011, and wellhead prices fell 46 percent, from $7.33 per thousand cubic feet to $3.95 per thousand cubic feet. In 2011, for the first time in 30 years, energy production from dry natural gas exceeded energy production from coal.

The benefits of increased production of natural gas are observed throughout the U.S. economy. In recent years, low energy costs have become a competitive advantage to the U.S. industrial sector. Additionally, low

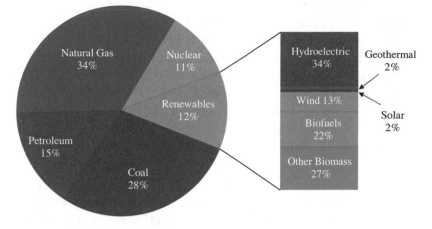

Figure 6-6
Total U.S. Primary Energy Production, 2011

Note: Natural gas includes natural gas plant liquids.
Source: EIA (2012a).

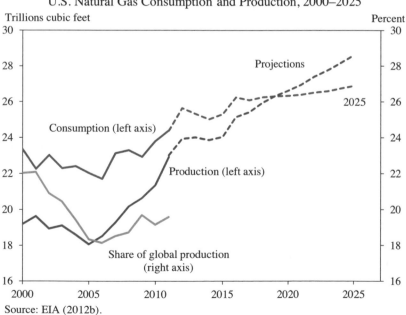

Figure 6-7
U.S. Natural Gas Consumption and Production, 2000–2025

Source: EIA (2012b).

prices for byproducts of natural gas such as methane, ethane, and propane spur growth in agriculture, petrochemical manufacturing, and other industries that use these byproducts.

In the power sector, burning natural gas produces nitrogen oxides, carbon dioxide, and other pollutants, but in lower quantities than burning coal or oil. The life-cycle emissions of greenhouse gases from a combined-cycle natural gas plant is roughly half that of a typical coal-fired power plant per kilowatt hour (Logan et al. 2012). On the other hand, methane, a primary component of natural gas and a greenhouse gas, can be emitted from natural gas systems into the atmosphere through production processes, component leaks, losses in transportation, or incomplete combustion. Measuring fugitive methane emissions from the U.S. natural gas supply chain and, more generally, understanding the potential impacts of natural gas development on water quality, air quality, ecosystems, and induced seismicity, are critical to understanding the impact on the environment of the increasing use of natural gas.

Renewable Energy

In the long run, large reductions in carbon emissions require large increases in energy production from zero-emissions sources, especially renewable energy. In the beginning of his Administration, President Obama set a goal of doubling U.S. renewable energy generation capacity from wind, solar, and geothermal sources by 2012. This ambitious goal has been achieved, thanks both to the Administration's historic investments in clean energy technologies and to decades of government-funded research and development (R&D) aimed at driving costs down to the point where renewable energy is competitive with traditional fossil-fuel energy.

Since 2008, the most significant increase in renewable energy production has been in wind energy. The dramatic increase in wind generating capacity is shown in Figure 6-8. In 2011, wind power constituted more than 30 percent of new additions to U.S. electric generating capacity: close to 6.8 gigawatts of new wind generating capacity was installed in the United States, representing an investment of $14 billion. Wind energy supplies 20 percent of electricity consumption in some states, including Iowa and South Dakota. As a nation, the United States accounts for 20 percent of total global wind power generation and 16 percent of global installed capacity. In 2012, wind power provided more than 3 percent of the nation's electricity generation (EIA 2013b).

The Administration also continues a strong commitment to the development and promotion of solar energy. An important aim is bringing the cost of solar photovoltaics down closer to grid parity with traditional,

Figure 6-8
Annual and Cumulative Growth in U.S.Wind
Power Capacity, 1998–2011

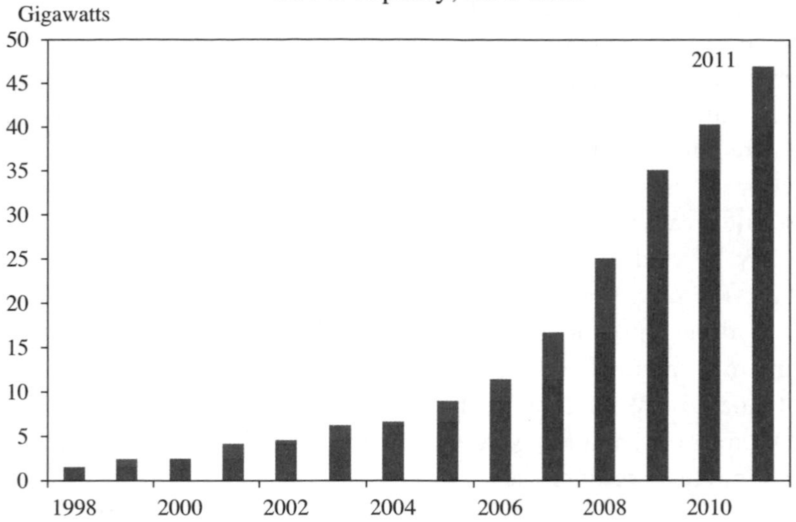

Note: Orange bars are annual additions to capacity and blue bars are total installed capacity at the outset of the year.
Source: DOE (2012b).

fossil sources of energy, including natural gas. The Administration's support for solar energy has included more than $13 billion since September 2009 through DOE programs for solar-related projects, including applied R&D, demonstrations, and the DOE clean energy loan guarantee program. In 2011, the DOE launched an ambitious new effort, the Sunshot Initiative, aimed at reducing the installed costs of solar energy systems of all sizes (residential, commercial, and utility) by an additional 75 percent by the end of the decade.

Solar photovoltaic capacity is growing rapidly, with current installed capacity estimated to be approximately 4 gigawatts.[12] The Interstate Renewable Energy Council estimates that grid-connected photovoltaic capacity increased more than tenfold between 2007 and 2011.

President Obama has set a goal of once again doubling generation from wind, solar, and geothermal sources by 2020, and has called on Congress to make the renewable energy Production Tax Credit permanent and refundable, as part of comprehensive corporate tax reform, providing incentives and certainty for investments in clean energy.[13]

---

[12] The Interstate Renewable Energy Council (IREC), the Solar Energy Industries Association (SEIA), and the National Renewable Energy Lab (NREL).
[13] http://www.whitehouse.gov/sites/default/files/uploads/sotu_2013_blueprint_embargo.pdf.

Advanced Technologies and R&D

The Federal Government also has an important role to play in R&D involving frontier fossil-fuel technologies. Notably, the Administration has invested nearly $6 billion in clean coal technology R&D—the largest such investment in U.S. history—and this strategy has attracted more than $10 billion in additional private sector capital investment. Clean coal technology involves removing CO_2 from flue gases released from burning coal, then preventing its escape into the atmosphere by injecting it underground, a process known as carbon capture and sequestration. The recovered CO_2 can potentially be used to recover hard-to-reach oil reserves, partially offsetting the carbon capture costs. Another clean coal technology in the R&D stage is hydrogen production from coal, in which the highly concentrated CO_2 stream is captured and sequestered. Advanced technologies also have the potential to make natural gas burn even cleaner by capturing and storing CO_2 emissions, and the government has a role to play in encouraging research into these technologies.

Federal research efforts on zero- and reduced-emissions energy sources extend into other domains as well, including research toward shifting cars and trucks to nonpetroleum fuels.

PREPARING FOR CLIMATE CHANGE

The policies discussed so far aim to reduce emissions of greenhouse gases and thereby to stem future costs of climate change. But the climate has not yet fully adjusted to current levels of greenhouse gases, and ongoing anthropogenic emissions will continue to increase greenhouse gas concentrations because CO_2 remains in the atmosphere for centuries. Thus, while it is important for all countries to sharply reduce CO_2 emissions to limit the extent of further climate change, even with the most concerted international efforts additional climate change is inevitable. We therefore face a world with an unavoidably changing climate for which we need to prepare.

Policies to prepare for climate change occur at many scales. At the local level, preparing for climate change can entail changing building codes to make structures more storm- and flood-resistant and investing in stronger community planning and response. More substantially, destructive effects of coastal storms can be partially dissipated by restoring natural storm barriers such as tidal wetlands, sand dunes, and coastal barrier landforms.

National policies to prepare for climate change range from providing information about likely changes in local climates and weather patterns, to supporting further research on and monitoring of climate change and its consequences, to providing proper incentives for individuals to prepare for climate change. For example, federal insurance programs, such as the Agriculture Department's crop insurance program and the Federal Emergency Management Agency's flood insurance program, provide insurance either with a subsidy or where there is no private market (that is, the price a private insurer would charge would exceed what a purchaser would be willing to pay). Revisiting federal insurance subsidies could encourage practices that could be increasingly important in the face of accelerating climate changes, such as farmers planting drought-resistant varietals or homeowners building or renovating away from flood plains.

Preparing for climate change will also entail larger-scale infrastructure investments. Some of these investments involve maintaining existing infrastructure. For example, a 2007 investigation by the American Society of Civil Engineers reported that chronic underfunding of the New Orleans hurricane protection system was one of the principal causes of the levee failures after Hurricane Katrina, a storm that inflicted over $110 billion of damages.

Other investments involve enhancing or extending existing infrastructure. For example, the electric power grid can be made more resilient to increasingly severe storms and rising sea levels by using smart grid technology, which pinpoints outage locations and helps to isolate outages, reducing the risk of widespread power shutdowns. The Recovery Act provided the single largest smart grid investment in U.S. history ($4.5 billion matched by an additional $5.5 billion from the private sector), funding both the Smart Grid Investment Grant and Smart Grid Demonstration programs, among others, to spur the Nation's transition to a smarter, stronger, more efficient, and more reliable electricity system (White House 2011b).

CONCLUSION

The scientific consensus is that the anthropogenic emission of greenhouse gases is causing climate change. The results can be seen already in higher temperatures and extreme weather, and these are but precursors of what lies ahead. Although greenhouse gas emissions and climate change are global problems, the United States is in a unique position to tackle these challenges and to provide global leadership.

The Nation has made substantial progress toward the Administration's ambitious short-term Copenhagen targets for reducing emissions of carbon dioxide, but much difficult work lies ahead. Undertaking this work, which reflects the Administration's commitment to future generations, entails many policy steps that are economically justified by the negative externalities imposed by greenhouse gas emissions. Policies to reduce emissions of greenhouse gases include market-based policies; encouraging energy efficiency; direct regulation; encouraging fuel switching to reduced-emissions fuels; and supporting the development and widespread adoption of zero-emissions energy sources such as wind and solar. And, as the country reduces emissions along this path, it also needs to prepare for the climate change that is occurring and will continue to occur. Together these policies pave the way toward a sustainable energy future.

ↄℓↄ

C H A P T E R   7

INTERNATIONAL TRADE AND COMPETITIVENESS

The United States is more closely linked with other nations through trade, investment, and financial flows than ever before. For example, total trade in goods and services as a share of gross domestic product (GDP) was approximately 31 percent in 2012, compared with 26 percent in 2000 and 11 percent in 1970. International linkages are also reaching more deeply than ever before into the organization of industries and firms. U.S. companies are increasingly part of global supply chains, in which firms buy inputs from subcontractors located in many countries. These linkages bring both challenges and opportunities for the U.S. economy and for government policy. Macroeconomic shocks and policies halfway around the world have direct effects on growth, employment, and national balance sheets here at home, just as shocks and policies in the United States affect economies across the globe.

Significant opportunities are available for U.S. firms to expand exports and create jobs, for resources to be allocated to their most productive uses, for innovation to flourish, and for consumers to enjoy higher incomes, lower prices, and expanded choice. These opportunities, however, have been accompanied by job displacement, downward wage pressures, and other adjustment costs. Government policy plays an important role in providing infrastructure and incentives that reduce these adjustment costs, promote the creation of middle-class jobs, and foster innovative ecosystems in the private sector. Administration policies in both trade and competitiveness seek to create a fair, firm foundation for the long-term prosperity of the United States and its trading partners.

THE WORLD ECONOMY AND U.S. TRADE

Fiscal consolidation, weak financial systems, and market uncertainty have adversely affected demand in many advanced economies, and world economic growth has suffered. In 2012, there were a number of shocks to global growth, including the impact of financial stresses in Europe that reached a peak in mid-summer. Given the globalized nature of world trade and finance, the United States cannot fully escape the impact of development in other nations.

Growth in World Economies

Unlike the U.S. economy, which has sustained positive economic growth for the past three years, several of the nation's major trading partners have slipped into economic contraction. In 2012, the euro area fell into recession once again, as severe austerity measures put in place to combat the region's debt crisis impeded growth. The International Monetary Fund (IMF) estimates that in 2012, the euro area economy contracted 0.4 percent, compared with growth of 2.0 percent in 2010 and 1.4 percent in 2011. While Japan was temporarily able to recover from the harsh economic slowdown resulting from the earthquake and tsunami that struck the country in early 2011, slower global demand and the phase-out of reconstruction spending brought the third largest economy in the world back into recession.

With the euro area, Japan, and the United States accounting for almost half of global GDP, slower average growth in these economies was sufficient to lower growth at the global level. Emerging market economies have relied on import demand from these large, high income economies to sustain high growth for over a decade. As import demand has weakened, particularly from Japan and Europe, economic growth in emerging markets has decelerated as well (Figure 7-1). For example, in 2012:Q2, real GDP in China grew approximately 5.65 percent at an annual rate, the lowest quarterly GDP growth China has recorded since the beginning of the global slowdown in 2008.

The Euro Crisis

After financial tensions reached a peak in mid-2012, steps were taken by both the governments of Europe and the central bank to reassure markets of the integrity of the euro area and to begin the process of reforms. In the summer of 2012, the European Central Bank announced it stood ready to stabilize the bond markets of any member state in a reform program, while governments launched the European Stability Mechanism (ESM), a joint fund to provide direct loans to governments that replaces the temporary European Financial Stability Fund (EFSF). These firewalls against financial contagion have helped restore confidence, allowing Ireland and Portugal to begin their return to financial markets. In Greece, meanwhile, European

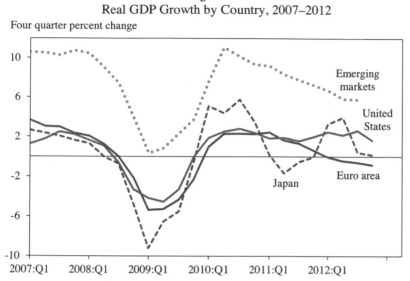

Figure 7-1
Real GDP Growth by Country, 2007–2012

Four quarter percent change

Note: Data through 2012:Q4 for all but emerging markets, for which data is available only for 2012:Q3.
Source: Country sources; U.S. Department of Commerce, Bureau of Economic Analysis; Cabinet Office of Japan; Statistical Office of the European Communities; CEA calculations.

governments made important concessions in a redesigned program that reduces Greek borrowing costs and supports continued reforms.

The combined impact of these measures produced noticeable results. Bond yields in vulnerable countries fell dramatically to more sustainable levels; in the week of the announcement of the bond buying plan, Spanish 10-year bond yields declined from 6.9 percent to 5.6 percent, and Italian 10-year bond yields fell from 5.8 percent to 5.0 percent (Figure 7-2).

Meanwhile, European authorities have taken important measures to ensure that their banks have access to liquidity and hold adequate capital. The authorities have also committed to launching a banking union with a single supervisor and a European facility to recapitalize banks in troubled countries where the governments are already facing problems managing their debts. Uncertainty remains about access to a capital backstop as well as about prospects for euro area institutions for common resolution and deposit guarantees.

Finally, while the global recovery is clearly underway, European nations are still facing challenges. The euro area reentered recession in 2012, and the IMF in January forecast a further contraction of 0.2 percent in 2013 with continuing declines in output in Italy and Spain. Unemployment in the euro area is hitting record highs, with 2012 unemployment rates in Greece

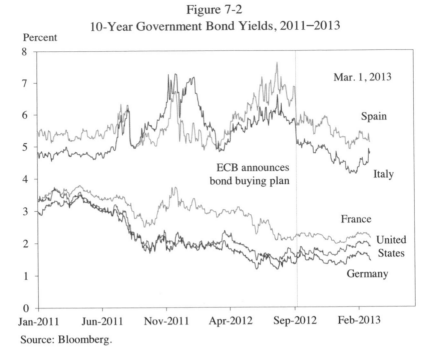

Figure 7-2
10-Year Government Bond Yields, 2011–2013

Percent

ECB announces
bond buying plan

Mar. 1, 2013

Spain

Italy

France

United
States

Germany

Source: Bloomberg.

and Spain in excess of 23 percent (Table 7-1). Sustained fiscal consolidation and the deleveraging in the banking and business sectors in the euro area continue to act as headwinds to growth. Even as European leaders continue to undertake structural reforms aimed at increasing competitiveness over the medium term, markets remain sensitive to growth and reform prospects in large economies, including countries like France, Italy and Spain. Meanwhile, a number of countries with stronger budget positions, including Germany and the Netherlands, are running significant balance of payments surpluses and thus are not an important source of demand for the European recovery. More broadly, the euro area's combined trade surplus, after adjusting for the effect of commodity prices, is rising quite rapidly, contributing to global imbalances. Weaker European economies are closing their trade deficits as imports decline with fiscal consolidation and contracting domestic demand, and Germany's current account surplus has risen back to its pre-crisis level of 6 percent thanks to the strong performance of German exports around the world.

While we are making progress on increasing U.S. exports, these also depend on expansion in overseas markets. Europe is a significant destination for American exports, accounting for more than 20 percent of U.S. goods exports and almost 40 percent of U.S. service exports. Europe is also the leading foreign source of investment in America, accounting for more

Table 7-1
Euro Area Selected Economic Indicators

	Greece		Spain		Italy		Germany	
	2009	2012	2009	2012	2009	2012	2009	2012
GDP growth (percent)	-3.3	-6.0	-3.7	-1.4	-5.5	-2.1	-5.1	0.9
Unemployment rate (percent)	9.5	23.8	18.0	25.1	7.8	10.6	7.8	5.5
Current account balance (percent of GDP)	-11.2	-2.9	-4.8	-0.8	-2.0	-1.5	5.9	6.4
Primary budget balance (percent of GDP)	-10.4	-1.7	-9.9	-4.5	-1.0	2.6	-0.9	1.4
General government debt (percent of GDP)	128.9	170.7	53.9	90.7	116.0	126.3	74.7	83.0

Source: IMF (2012); European Commission Statistical Office.

than 70 percent of all foreign direct investment in the United States in 2011. Global and U.S. economic performance will depend, in part, on continuing progress to resolve Europe's challenges.

Global Imbalances

"Global rebalancing" has been one of the Administration's major international economic policy goals for the past four years. In June 2012, the G-20 nations reiterated their support for this goal, calling upon countries with current account deficits to boost national savings, consistent with evolving economic conditions, and for countries with large current account surpluses to strengthen domestic demand and move toward greater exchange rate flexibility.

A country's current account consists predominantly of the difference between its exports and its imports of goods and services (other factors include net income on overseas assets and unilateral transfers such as foreign aid and remittances). A current account deficit occurs when a country's absorption (the sum of domestic consumption, investment and government spending) exceeds its production. In this case, it must either borrow from abroad or sell foreign assets. Current account deficits in certain countries correspond to current account surpluses in others. A current account deficit may indicate that a country offers sound investment opportunities, or it may be caused by investment bubbles or fiscal deficits. Large and persistent current account surpluses can occur when governments intervene in financial markets to prevent market-driven adjustments in interest rates and exchange rates from taking place. While large current account imbalances may not directly cause financial crises, they often indicate underlying dynamics that are unsustainable and thus have historically been important precursors to financial crises (Reinhart and Rogoff 2011).

Before the 2008 crisis, the United States was running a large current account deficit financed by surpluses from creditor nations such as China and Japan, a situation that Federal Reserve Chairman Ben Bernanke referred to as the "global saving glut" (Bernanke 2005). In China, for example, low levels of social insurance and policies designed to encourage excessive saving by firms contributed to large surpluses (Obstfeld 2012). From 2000 to 2007, the U.S. deficit ballooned to more than 5 percent of GDP, while current account surpluses in China, Germany, and Japan grew to 10, 7, and 5 percent of GDP, respectively. Current account deficits in Europe's periphery reached alarming levels. The surplus countries came to rely on unsustainable growth in net exports to drive their economies. The deficit countries relied on unsustainable growth in household consumption, construction of residential real estate, and government budget deficits for economic growth.

The crisis of 2008 brought about a distinct change in global imbalances: the U.S. current account deficit shrank to 3 percent of GDP in 2009, while current account surpluses in China and Japan dropped as well (Figure 7-3). The Administration, along with the wider international community, continues to press for a more balanced approach to growth in the world. Greater reliance on consumption, and less on exports and investment, will provide those countries with large current account surpluses with a more sustainable source of growth over the long run. The members of the G-20 have committed to moving more quickly to market-determined exchange rate systems and exchange rates that reflect underlying fundamentals.

TRADE AND THE MANUFACTURING SECTOR

Although the Nation's current account balance has improved substantially since its record deficit level of $800.6 billion in 2006, much of this improvement is due to growing surpluses of trade in services and income on investments, while the trade deficit in goods appears to have increased since the recovery from the recession began in the third quarter of 2009 (Figure 7-4). However, the increase in the goods deficit conceals the fact that from 2010 to 2012, exports of manufactures grew at a faster rate (22.0 percent) than imports (19.3 percent). The goods deficit has widened only because manufacturing imports began the period at a much higher level.

U.S. trade in manufactures, both imports and exports, has grown rapidly in recent decades primarily as a result of reductions in trade costs, the rapid growth of emerging markets, and the increasing international specialization of supply chains. Technological improvements in transportation and communication have lowered trade costs, as have reductions of tariffs and other trade barriers both at home and abroad. Emerging markets,

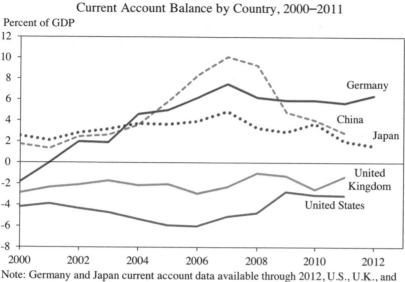

Figure 7-3
Current Account Balance by Country, 2000–2011

Note: Germany and Japan current account data available through 2012, U.S., U.K., and China data only available through 2011.
Source: Deutsche Bundesbank; Bank of Japan; United Kingdom Office for National Statistics; U.S. Department of Commerce, Bureau of Economic Analysis; Chinese State Administration of Foreign Exchange.

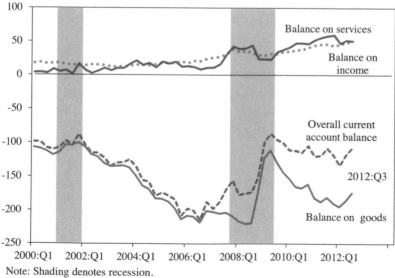

Figure 7-4
U.S. Current Account Balance and its Components, 2000–2012

Note: Shading denotes recession.
Source: U.S. Department of Commerce, Bureau of Economic Analysis.

particularly China, have grown at an impressive pace in the past decade and have moved aggressively into manufacturing. In the past 10 years, China's share of world manufacturing exports has grown from 5 percent to over 15 percent. Finally, improvements in information technology (IT) have led to the emergence of global value chains, in which tasks and components involved in production are allocated across countries to take advantage of differences in costs, skills, technology, or proximity to the market (Data Watch 7-1). As a result, trade in intermediate goods and services has grown rapidly. The effects of these forces on the U.S. economy have been profound.

Trade and Productivity

Greater openness of world markets enhances the productivity of U.S. industries and firms. Research finds that the U.S. industries experiencing the largest declines in tariffs have exhibited some of the strongest productivity gains. Bernard, Jensen, and Schott (2006) find that falling trade costs led individual U.S. manufacturing plants that already export to increase their shipments abroad, high-productivity nonexporters to become more likely to export, and low-productivity plants to become more likely to exit the domestic market. Together, these effects result in a reallocation of economic activity toward high-productivity firms, thereby raising overall industry productivity. Studies of numerous other countries show similar gains in industry productivity through trade-induced reallocation across firms.

Evidence also shows that decreases in industry-level trade costs lead to within-firm productivity growth. Lileeva and Trefler (2010), for example, found that the Canada-U.S. Free Trade Agreement caused increases in labor productivity, product innovation, and adoption rates for advanced manufacturing technologies among Canadian exporters. Pierce (2011) showed that U.S. tariffs lower the productivity of U.S. firms, in part by slowing the rate at which older, less-productive production lines are phased out in favor of new product lines. Several other studies have found that trade liberalization increases research and development (R&D) and technology upgrading.

Firm productivity and exports also can be enhanced when trade liberalization lowers the cost, and expands the variety, of imported intermediate inputs.[1] Although much of the evidence for this channel comes from studies of middle- and low-income countries, Amiti and Wei (2009) found that

---

[1] Houseman et al. (2011) concluded that the decline in input prices associated with shifts to lower-cost producers may not be fully captured by statistical agencies, and as a result the data may suggest that manufacturers are producing more goods with fewer inputs, when in fact the real value of those inputs has simply been understated. After attempting to correct for this so-called "offshoring bias," the authors concluded that average annual manufacturing productivity growth would be between 6 percent and 14 percent lower, and value-added growth would be 7 percent to 18 percent lower than official estimates between 1997 and 2007.

imports of service inputs, such as telecommunications, insurance, finance, computing, and other business services, have a significant positive effect on manufacturing productivity in the United States. In a similar vein, Francois and Woerz (2008) showed that, across advanced economies, increased import penetration in producer services results in better export performance, particularly by skill- and technology-intensive industries.

GROWTH OF TRADED SERVICES

The United States is currently the world's largest services exporter. In 2011, U.S. exports of private services exceeded $600 billion, and sales through foreign affiliates exceeded $1 trillion. Taken together, international sales of services by U.S. companies are on the order of $1.7 trillion a year, an amount equal to approximately 11 percent of U.S. GDP. Services trade accounts for approximately 30 percent of U.S. exports and 15 percent of U.S. imports. A study by the Organisation for Economic Co-operation and Development and the World Trade Organization (WTO), however, estimated that nearly 60 percent of the value of U.S. exports can be attributed to the service sector. This estimate takes into account both direct services exports, as measured in official trade statistics, and indirect services exports embodied as intermediate inputs in goods exports. The main traded service categories are "other private services" (which includes items such as business, professional, and technical services, insurance services, and financial services), royalties and license fees, and private travel.

Falling costs of travel, communication, and information technology have increased the opportunities for trade in services. Over the past 10 years, services imports and exports both almost doubled. Much of the growth was accounted for by increased trade in business services, especially digitally enabled services, defined by the Bureau of Economic Analysis (BEA) as those for which digital information and communications technologies (ICT) significantly facilitate cross-border trade. According to the BEA, from 1998 to 2010, exports of all ICT-enabled services grew at an annual rate of 9 percent to reach 61 percent of total U.S. services exports, up from 45 percent in 1998. Imports of ICT-enabled services grew at an annual rate of 10 percent, rising to 56 percent of U.S. services imports, from 34 percent. Increases in business, professional, and technical services contributed most to the overall increase in ICT-enabled services trade. The private services surplus was $162 billion in 2010; of this, $116 billion resulted from a trade surplus in ICT-enabled services.

Some estimates suggest that about 70 percent of employment in business services is in industries potentially subject to international competition

Data Watch 7-1: Implications of Global Value Chains for the Measurement of Trade Flows

While international trade and foreign direct investment have been growing rapidly for decades, recent advances in information technology along with improving industrial capabilities in emerging markets have made it profitable to segment production processes and relocate them throughout the world, creating global value chains. This shift has made it increasingly difficult to interpret international trade statistics. In the past, it was safe to assume that most if not all of the value of a traded product was created in the country that exported it. Thus, a country's industrial capabilities could be judged by the content of exports, trade rules could be tied to gross levels of trade in specific products, and exports could be directly related to domestic job creation. With the rise of global value chains, however, one can no longer be sure how much of the value of a product or service is added in the country that declares it as an export. For example, in 2009, between one-third to one-half of the total value of exports of transport parts and equipment from most major producing countries originated in a different country. Similar patterns emerge in the electronics sector: in China and Japan, the world's largest exporters of electronic goods in 2009, the foreign content of electronics exports was about 40 percent. In Mexico, the share was over 60 percent (OECD 2013).

Official trade statistics are measured in gross terms—the amount the importer pays the exporter for the good. That approach is appropriate for adding up a country's balance of payments made to, and received from, the rest of the world. To determine how much value an exporter adds to a good or service traded internationally, however, one must subtract the value of intermediate inputs supplied by other countries, including the country importing it. Removing these intermediate flows from exports gives a measure of "value-added" trade.

Measuring value-added trade reveals a number of surprising facts. For example, according to Koopman et al. (2010), in 2004 about 8 percent of total gross U.S. imports was U.S. value added in the form of U.S. intermediate inputs used in foreign production. About 25 percent of the value of U.S. gross exports was made up of imported intermediate inputs; however, about half the value of those inputs originated in the United States, so only about 13 percent of U.S. gross exports were not U.S. value added. By contrast, about 37 percent of China's exports were value added somewhere else. Johnson and Noguera (2012) estimate that, while still large, the U.S.-China imbalance is approximately 40 percent smaller when measured on a value-added basis, and the U.S.-Japan imbalance is approximately 33 percent higher. They also show that domestic value added in gross exports for the world as a whole has fallen dramatically in recent years, indicating the rise of global value chains.

The Organisation for Economic Co-operation and Development and the World Trade Organization recently released a new data set containing estimates of value-added trade for 40 countries and 18 industries for 2005, 2008, and 2009 (OECD 2013). Future releases will see an expansion in the number of countries, industries, and time periods, dating back to 1995. This effort represents a substantial improvement in the availability of information about global value chains.

(Jensen 2009). There is a widespread concern that, as business services become more tradable over time, these jobs will be lost to import competition from low-wage, labor-abundant countries. However, given the abundance of capital and highly skilled workers in the United States, the most successful U.S. export industries tend to be those that employ capital and skilled labor most intensively. In the services sector, the largest export industries—integrated record production and distribution, software publishers, web search portals, satellite telecommunications, and motion picture and video production—also pay the highest wages (Jensen 2011). The fact that the United States has consistently maintained a positive trade balance in services, and high-skill business services in particular, suggests that the world is willing to pay for the high-quality, skill-intensive services that the United States provides.

Despite America's apparent comparative advantage in tradable high-skill, high-wage business services, export activity on the part of these firms faces significant impediments. About 25 percent of manufacturing plants export; in business services, only about 5 percent of businesses export (Jensen 2009). While differences in language and culture may pose greater barriers to trade in services than in manufactures, services also are differentially affected by an array of government-imposed impediments, such as restrictions on foreign ownership and partnership arrangements; nationality, residency, or local presence requirements for service providers; licensing and accreditation requirements; and limitations on the scope of activities. Hufbauer, Schott, and Wong (2010) have estimated that the aggregate level of barriers to services imports in emerging markets such as China, India, and Indonesia is equivalent to a tariff on these imports of more than 60 percent. After decades of liberalization through trade agreements, tariffs in that range are relatively rare for goods. Recent research also has found that restrictions on foreign acquisitions, discrimination in licensing, restrictions on the repatriation of earnings, and inadequate legal recourse all have a significant negative effect on investment inflows into services sectors (Borchert, Gootiiz, and Mattoo 2012). The Administration has undertaken several important initiatives to address these impediments, discussed further below.

TRADE POLICY

World trade collapsed in 2009; the recovery, while substantial, is being held back by slow global growth. In response, in his 2010 State of the Union address, the President launched the National Export Initiative (NEI), an Administration-wide effort to double U.S. exports in support of up to 2 million additional American jobs by the end of 2014. Under the NEI, the Administration continues to focus on improving trade advocacy and export promotion efforts, removing or reducing barriers to U.S. exports of goods and services, increasing access to credit, robustly enforcing trade rules, and pursuing policies at the global level to promote strong, sustainable, and balanced growth. In 2012, U.S. exports of goods and services amounted to $2.2 trillion, an all-time record, despite challenging global economic conditions.

Longer-term trends affecting trade include the rapid growth in emerging markets and the rise of global value chains. The growth of emerging markets makes them the most likely source of future U.S. export growth. The International Monetary Fund estimates that developing countries will account for more than three-quarters of the economic growth of all U.S. trading partners in the next five years. It is vital, therefore, that the United States secure from these countries more open and transparent market access for U.S. firms. In addition, because of their growing involvement in global value chains, U.S. firms are increasingly exposed to policies and barriers behind the borders, not just at the borders, of countries around the world. Countries vary widely in their use of subsidies, export taxes, support for state-owned enterprises, financial market restrictions, ownership restrictions on foreign direct investment, government procurement, and enforcement of intellectual property rights, to name a few.

To address these challenges, the United States has pursued a robust program of enforcement of existing rules through WTO dispute settlement and a negotiating strategy for new agreements aimed at securing deep commitments with like-minded countries on a broad array of trade-related measures. The overriding goal of these latter initiatives, whether multilateral, plurilateral or bilateral, is to open markets and set standards for conduct that eventually shape the standards adopted by the global trading system. The United States continues to adhere strongly to the precept that trade liberalization at the multilateral level holds the highest potential for securing

Box 7-1: Small Businesses and the NEI

Small businesses, defined by the Small Business Administration as independent businesses having 500 or fewer employees, account for more than half of nonfarm private GDP. These 27.5 million businesses, many of them family-owned companies, are a key part of the U.S. economy. However, they are far less likely to export or to use inputs from abroad than are larger firms. In a world of imperfect financial markets, the costs of financing export operations pose an especially high barrier for smaller firms, because they are more likely to need external financing to undertake export transactions. Small businesses also can find it more difficult to learn about foreign markets and to overcome foreign trade barriers and unfair trade practices compared with larger firms.

Through the NEI, the Obama Administration is committed to helping small businesses overcome such barriers to exporting. The NEI calls for a national outreach campaign both to identify small businesses that may be able to increase their exports and to raise awareness generally among the nation's small businesses about export opportunities. The NEI provides training and other technical assistance to help small businesses prepare to become exporters, sets up pilot programs to match small businesses with export intermediaries, and outlines several measures to support small businesses once they begin to export to new markets. Thanks in part to the efforts of the NEI, a record of nearly 287,000 U.S. small and medium-size enterprises (SME) exported in 2010 (98 percent of all exporters), a total increase of more than 16,600 SMEs over 2009. The goal is to increase the national base of SME exporters by 50,000 by 2017.

wide-ranging market-opening outcomes. The United States will continue to complement its multilateral approaches with discussions at the plurilateral and bilateral levels to build consensus for, and commitments to, market-opening agreements critical to the growth of trade-supported jobs.

In 2012, market-opening trade agreements with Korea, Colombia, and Panama entered into force. The United States is currently negotiating with 10 partners in the Trans-Pacific Partnership to tackle 21st-century trade issues in the Asia-Pacific region. In January 2013, the President announced plans to negotiate toward an international services agreement with an initial group of 20 trading partners, aimed at removing impediments to global services trade. In February, the Administration announced its intention to launch negotiations for a comprehensive Transatlantic Trade and Investment Partnership with the 27-member European Union, aimed at expanding what is already the world's largest economic relationship, accounting for one-third of total goods and services trade and nearly half of global economic output.

In the WTO, the United States is advocating new approaches that can offer opportunities for agreements on issues that have been part of the Doha Development Agenda, such as trade facilitation, and in areas that are outside the Doha agenda, such as expansion of the Information Technology Agreement. The United States also welcomed Russia's membership in the WTO, a membership that will provide significant commercial opportunities for U.S. exporters.

Finally, the Administration aims to address potential disruptions that trade can cause to domestic labor markets. The Federal Government's Trade Adjustment Assistance (TAA) program is designed to assist workers whose jobs have been lost to import competition or threatened by trade-related circumstances. The program provides financial, job training, and relocation assistance to newly unemployed workers displaced by trade, with the goal of making it easier for these workers to develop new skills and then enter more vibrant sectors of the economy. In fiscal year 2012, the TAA program certified 1,131 petitions that permitted more than 81,000 workers to participate in the program.

BUILDING U.S. COMPETITIVENESS

The Nation must construct an economy based on a solid foundation of educating, innovating, and building better infrastructure, a foundation that can be strengthened in both manufacturing and in services. A hallmark of the Administration's policies is the recognition that there are many spillovers within and between economic sectors and regions. Thus, well-chosen policies reinforce each other both to increase competitiveness and to provide more middle-class jobs. For example, grants that assist workers and firms that invest in apprenticeships benefit other firms in their industry and region that can draw on a pool of skilled labor. Because of the myriad benefits that arise from having a broad base of innovative workers, economic growth and fairness go hand in hand. That is, Administration policies are built around the idea that the country does best when everyone does their fair share and plays by the same rules.

Manufacturing

While manufacturing employment has declined as a share of the workforce for the past 50 years, the absolute number of manufacturing jobs was relatively constant at about 18 million from 1965 until 2000. However, starting in 2000, manufacturing employment dropped precipitously. The

United States lost 3.5 million manufacturing jobs in the 7 years before the Great Recession and then lost another 2.3 million during the recession.

This job loss has serious implications for the economy. First, the decline in manufacturing employment significantly reduced the number of middle-class jobs, especially for less educated workers. Wages and salaries in manufacturing are 7 percent higher than in the rest of the economy, and total hourly compensation (which includes the value of benefits such as health care and pensions) is 13 percent higher. After controlling for factors such as education, age, gender, race, union status, and location, the compensation premium for manufacturing rises above 14 percent. A 2012 Department of Commerce study comparing manufacturing workers to those in other private industries finds similar results (ESA 2012). Workers of all education levels and occupations in manufacturing—from assemblers to design engineers—earn more than their peers in other industries, showing manufacturing's value in maintaining a strong American middle class. Second, growing evidence shows that manufacturing production has positive spillover impacts on other parts of the economy. Spillovers occur when one company's activities benefit other businesses even though the latter did not pay for them (Economic Application Box 7-1). As discussed below, the loss of manufacturing activity has reduced these benefits.

Spillovers Between Manufacturing Production and Innovation

The argument is sometimes made that loss of U.S. production jobs is part of an efficient global division of labor in which the United States focuses on higher-end innovative activity and cedes lower-skill production activity to other countries. However, this argument does not always hold.

First, production need not be a low-skill activity. Some of our main competitors in manufacturing employ more highly skilled production workers and pay significantly higher wages than do companies in the United States. Countries such as Germany and Denmark compete through business and government support for "high-road" production practices, in which workers participate in innovation as well as production. The higher wages paid to these highly-skilled workers are offset by their higher productivity (Helper, Krueger, and Wial 2012).

Despite its private and social benefits, however, companies do not always adopt the high-road strategy because successful implementation requires them to adopt a whole suite of interrelated practices. For example, a study of U.S. valve producers found that more-efficient firms adopted advanced information technology, while simultaneously changing their product strategy (to produce more customized valves), their operations strategy (using their new IT capability to reduce setup times, run times,

Economics Application Box 7-1: Agglomeration Economies and Spillovers Across Regions

Businesses are not spread out evenly across space but tend to clump together, or "agglomerate." As explained in Alfred Marshall's *Principles of Economics* (1890), firms group together because proximity allows them to share workers, ideas, and other inputs more easily. Numerous studies have found that establishments located near other establishments, whether in related industries (a cluster) or in diverse industries (urbanization), tend to be more productive (Rosenthal and Strange 2003).

A cluster is a geographically concentrated ecosystem of customers, suppliers, trade associations, and labor unions that do business with one another. These groups have collective capabilities. Like the common pasture in medieval English villages on which the livestock owned by many residents grazed, this "industrial commons" allows firms, particularly small firms, to nourish their technological capability using shared assets. These common resources help to accelerate innovation and commercialization. For example, firms located near each other can share equipment needed for testing, and can more easily meet face-to-face, which improves knowledge-sharing and trust-building. Service firms (such as those in the Los Angeles film industry)—not just manufacturers—benefit from agglomeration.

In some cases, both the grouping of firms and the higher productivity may be the result of a third factor. For example, several firms may each decide to locate near a natural harbor; their lower transport costs may increase their productivity, but at least initially there may be little benefit due to the proximity of other firms. Still, research suggests that the entry of a large factory to a community tends to increase the productivity of surrounding firms (Greenstone, Hornbeck, and Moretti 2010). Other research indicates that the benefits of R&D investment are primarily local, suggesting that ideas—and by extension productivity—are improved in geographically concentrated industries. Jaffe (1989) uses data from patent citations to show that inventors disproportionately build on the work of nearby scientists. Branstetter (2001) argues that the benefits of R&D appear to be primarily confined to the borders of the investing country.

Because the benefits of a shared asset spill over to help even firms that did not contribute to paying for it, and because profit-maximizing firms will not value this benefit to other firms in making their plans, market forces are unlikely to provide enough investment in shared assets. A case thus can be made for government to subsidize such activity. For example, government support for key local assets such as a university or apprenticeship program may help a cluster to develop through improved access to specialized R&D and skilled workers. Other successful clusters have emerged from a mix of firm- and government-led actions such as the cluster of computer and technology companies in Silicon Valley.

Once lost, these ecosystems can be hard to recreate. For any single firm, the decision to move production elsewhere may make economic sense. But that decision affects suppliers and the local talent pool, making it easier for the next firm to leave and harder for the next firm considering coming there to say yes. Conversely, new industries can build on foundations left by older clusters. For example, Optimus, a Pittsburgh biofuels startup, uses a 100-year-old union training program to reduce the costs of training technicians to service its innovative equipment—and to demonstrate its product. Supported by the new federal Workforce Innovation Fund, a partnership of startups, unions, and Carnegie Mellon University is creating apprenticeship programs that build on this model of shared training and product demonstration assets.

and inspection times), and human resource policies (employing workers with more problem-solving skills and using more teamwork). The success of changes in one area depended on success in other areas. For example, customizing products was not profitable without reductions in the time required to change over to making a new product, something made possible both by improved IT capabilities and the improved use of this capability by the empowered workers. Conversely, the IT and training investments often did not pay off in firms that did not customize their products (Bartel, Ichniowski, and Shaw 2007).

Second, there may be spillovers from production to innovation. Thus, while Moretti (2012) shows that the positive wage spillovers associated with innovation jobs are greater than those associated with manufacturing jobs, it may not be possible to keep the innovation jobs in the long run if production jobs are lost. For example, when production in consumer electronics migrated to Asia decades ago, the United States lost the potential to compete for follow-on innovations and subsequent production in flat-panel displays, LED lighting, and advanced batteries (Pisano and Shih 2012). Making products exposes engineers to the problems and the capabilities of existing technology, generating ideas both for improving processes and for applying a given technology to new markets. Losing this exposure makes it harder to come up with innovative ideas.[2]

---

[2] The U.S. auto industry could have ended up on this path, but as a result of the Administration's rescue of General Motors and Chrysler, and investments in innovation, the industry is growing and healthy.

Even when American firms do maintain a technological edge, their operations may be less profitable than if they were part of a vibrant industrial commons. E-ink, a Massachusetts firm now owned by its Taiwanese business partner, designed the electronic "ink" that represents the Kindle's key innovative element. Because the firm was located so far away from its Asian suppliers, its engineers were not able to interact on a daily basis with other firms in the supply chain that were inventing new products, making it hard for the firm to find new markets for its inks. The situation is similar throughout the rest of the LCD flat-panel-display industry. Harvard Business School Professor Willy Shih estimates that, because the United States has offshored much of its production capacity in this industry, U.S. firms capture only about 24 percent of the profits from U.S. Kindle sales (Pisano and Shih 2012).

Rise of Global Supply Chains

In recent decades, the structure of manufacturing has changed dramatically. Instead of vertically-integrated firms that obtain most of their inputs from within national borders, lead firms now purchase many inputs from outside suppliers around the world. Most manufacturing production today occurs in layers of specialized, smaller firms that provide components for final assembly and sale by large lead firms or original equipment manufacturers (OEMs). For example, CEA calculations estimate that in the United States in 1988, there were fewer than two employees in firms making automotive parts for every automaker employee. By 2010, parts companies had four employees for every automaker employee (Data Watch 7-2).

Because of this vertical dis-integration, almost all large U.S. manufacturers now depend on their suppliers for well over half their value-added. In most cases, these suppliers are shared with other firms. This arrangement has some advantages—for example, it may create opportunities for cross-fertilization. But shared supply chains also have a weakness in that firms' incentives to invest in their suppliers are reduced. If an OEM helps its supplier develop a new technology, the supplier's other customers—often the OEM's rivals—will enjoy these improvements without having contributed. As a result, OEMs have less incentive to make such investments and may be more inclined to shift costs and risks down the supply chain to smaller suppliers. These practices, called "free-riding" by economists, improve the larger firms' financial performance in the short run but may weaken the entire supply chain in the long run.

Data Watch 7-2: Measuring Supply Chains

The potential collapse of General Motors and Chrysler in December 2008 underscored the importance of understanding the operation of supply chains. Because the large auto manufacturers all relied on a common set of suppliers, a failure of any of the major players could have threatened the viability of the entire industry.

Measuring the size of this supply chain presents a statistical challenge. U.S. government statistical agencies assign each worksite in the United States to a single industry on the basis of its primary activity. Two North American Industrial Classification System (NAICS) codes are commonly used for reporting sales and employment in the auto industry—NAICS 3363 (motor vehicle parts manufacturing) and NAICS 3362 (motor vehicle body manufacturing)—but these codes do not capture all workplaces involved in the auto supply chain. First, many firms that make auto parts are not classified as serving the automotive market, but rather by the materials or the technology they use, such as "plastics product manufacturing" or "forging and stamping." Similarly, the NAICS codes do not link tooling producers to their customer industry. Second, the worksites that focus on nonproduction activities such as research or management are not categorized with the industry they serve; rather, they are grouped together in "Professional, Scientific, and Technical Services." In addition, contract workers in auto parts plants are assigned to the temporary help industry, rather than to motor vehicle parts production.

Using survey data for late 2010, the Council of Economic Advisers has estimated the number of jobs in the auto supply chain based on a more inclusive definition that includes all of this activity. While the conventional definition of auto parts showed employment of 553, 860 for this period, the CEA estimate was more than 1 million. The high degree of interdependence in the auto industry made the 2008 financial crisis particularly perilous, because contagion from financial troubles at one firm in the industry easily could have spread to others. The CEA's larger estimates of the size of the auto supply sector imply this risk was greater than previously realized.

Prospects for U.S. Manufacturing

The U.S. economy gained nearly 500,000 manufacturing jobs between January 2010 and January 2013, after losing more than 5 million manufacturing jobs in the previous decade (Figure 7-5). These job gains represent not just a cyclical recovery but also potentially the start of a longer-term trend toward the "in-sourcing" of manufacturing. About three-quarters of the

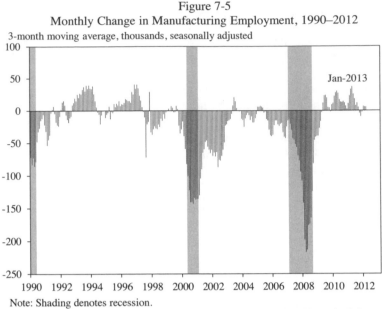

Figure 7-5
Monthly Change in Manufacturing Employment, 1990–2012
3-month moving average, thousands, seasonally adjusted

Note: Shading denotes recession.
Source: Bureau of Labor Statistics, Current Employment Statistics; CEA calculations.

increase in U.S. manufacturing shipments since the end of the recession is due to an increase in domestic demand and inventory restocking; the other quarter comes from an increase in exports. Because of the extensive spillover benefits associated with a vibrant manufacturing sector, this recovery has positive implications for long-term growth of the economy as a whole.

Since early 2012, diminished impetus from several key drivers of growth, as described in Chapter 2, has challenged the growth of U.S. manufacturing. First and most important, export growth has begun to slow, reflecting the slower pace of global growth. Second, after surging during the past few years, demand by domestic business for new capital equipment appears to have slowed. Third, firms finally appear to have replenished their inventories to levels more consistent with demand after heavily depleting stockpiles during the recession.

As noted above, "export-intensive" industries have played a large role in the recovery of manufacturing since the end of the recession. From April 2011 through February 2012, industries that export at least 20 percent of their shipments accounted for 57 percent of manufacturing output and 51 percent of manufacturing employment. During this period, manufacturing production and hiring rose faster in these industries than in others. Since February 2012, however, manufacturing production and hiring has slowed,

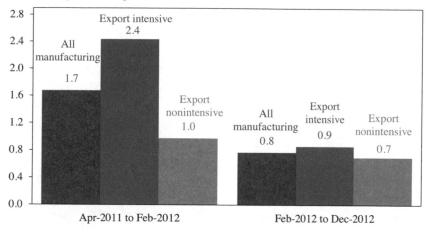

Figure 7-6
Employment in Export Intensive and Export Nonintensive
Manufacturing Industries, 2011–2012

Annualized percent change

Apr-2011 to Feb-2012   Feb-2012 to Dec-2012

Note: Export-intensive manufacturing industries are three-digit NAICS industries in which exports as a share of total shipments exceeded 19.9 percent, the average for the manufacturing sector as a whole in 2011. Export-intensive industries accounted for about 57 percent of manufacturing output in 2011.
Source: Federal Reserve Board, G.17; CEA calculations.

with nearly two-thirds of the slowdown in output and 90 percent of the slowdown in hiring occurring in export-intensive industries (Figure 7-6).

Other trends, however, suggest a brightening outlook for manufacturing. The continued recovery in the housing sector should lead to greater demand for construction supplies, and the order backlog for commercial aircraft is substantial. In addition, although production of nondurable goods like food and beverage products, plastics and rubber, and chemicals has lagged that of durable goods so far during the recovery, it should accelerate as consumer and business demand becomes more broad-based. Indeed, with capacity utilization now close to its historical average, and weekly work hours elevated above it, even a moderate rise in demand could quickly translate into a pickup in production, hiring, and investment.

Prospects for In-sourcing. Several recent reports have concluded that manufacturers increasingly view the United States as a favorable production location.[3] Factors cited for this change include trends in unit labor costs, expansion of domestic energy resources such as wind and natural gas, and greater recognition of the "hidden costs" of moving production abroad.

Over the past decade, U.S. unit labor costs—the cost of labor required to produce one unit of output—have grown much more slowly than in other

---

[3] Academic literature often refers to this phenomenon of work returning to the United States from abroad as "on-shoring."

developed nations (Figure 7-7). U.S. hourly compensation in manufacturing has grown somewhat over the past decade, but rapid productivity growth has reduced the cost of producing a unit of manufactured output in the United States. Meanwhile, when measured in U.S. dollars, the cost of manufacturing a unit of output in key trading partners has risen, in some cases substantially.

Several recent studies by management consultants argue that these trends create the potential for a "manufacturing renaissance" in the United States and estimate that the result could be 1 million or more new manufacturing jobs by 2015 (Boston Consulting Group 2012; Inch and Dutta 2012; Simchi-Levi et al. 2011). A key assumption of most of these analyses is that U.S. manufacturing wages continue to be stagnant. Thus, while these trends provide favorable tailwinds for U.S. manufacturing, they will not by themselves lead to sustainable prosperity. In contrast, the "high road" model discussed above also yields favorably low unit labor costs—but does so by increasing productivity, rather than by reducing wages.

Reassessing the Costs of Moving Production Abroad. Based on their experience during the past decade, American firms now have a greater understanding of the magnitudes of hard-to-measure costs attributable to the risks and complexities of operating far from home. Initially, "many manufacturers who had offshored their operations likely did so without a complete understanding of the 'total costs,' and thus, the total cost of offshoring was considerably higher than initially thought," according to a study of 287 manufacturers conducted by Accenture (Ferreira and Heilala 2011).

Compared with operating in the United States, setting up a supply chain in China and learning to communicate with suppliers requires many long trips and much time of top executives—time that could be spent on introducing new products or processes at home. There is also greater risk from a long supply chain, because shipping prices and delivery times can vary enormously. In addition, U.S. companies are coming to value more highly the advantages that come from having production, innovation, and design close together. For example, Intel manufactures its most advanced chips in the United States, near where they are designed (Helper, Krueger, and Wial 2012).

To take another example, Sleek Audio, a start-up manufacturer with innovative headphone technology, initially went to China for all of its production. After years of flying several times a year to China, and an incident in which millions of dollars of product had to be scrapped because of poor quality, the owners moved manufacturing to the United States. They began to work with a local manufacturer with experience in making precision products for the military, Dynamic Innovation, located within 10 minutes of Sleek Audio in Florida. In the course of redesigning the product for more

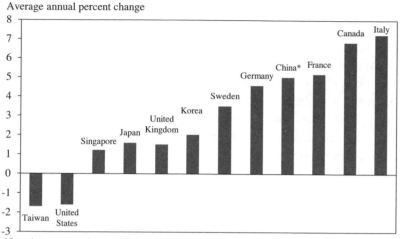

Figure 7-7
Change in Manufacturing Unit Labor Costs, 2003–2011

Average annual percent change

Note: Average annual percent change for China represents 2003–2009 data. The BLS does not track manufacturing unit labor costs for China, and many economists have expressed concern over the reliability of recent Chinese economic statistics (Wan 2013).
Source: Bureau of Labor Statistics, International Comparisons of Manufacturing Productivity and Unit Labor Costs; Ceglowski and Golub (2011).

automated U.S. production, the firms dramatically improved product quality, replacing hand-welded plastic panels with robot-welded aluminum ones that also significantly improved sound quality (winning an award from the Consumer Electronics Association). The price was higher in the United States, but the improved product features and ability to customize design more than offset this cost (Prasso 2011; Koerner 2011; Hackel 2011).

Numerous other collaborations that bring together different forms of expertise are keeping jobs in the United States. Many of these collaborations bring together shopfloor workers with a concrete understanding of plant conditions and engineers with deep technical knowledge. For example, management and members of the machinists' union at an Ashland, Kentucky chemical plant have worked together for two decades to improve both product quality and working conditions (Davidson 2013).

Productivity in Services

The service sector encompasses widely varied activities, ranging from house cleaning to data entry to investment advice. Despite this diversity, some common trends can be observed—trends similar in many respects to those seen in manufacturing.

As noted, many services are becoming increasingly globalized; as in manufacturing, there is also less vertical integration. In the hotel industry, for example, it is now common for a lead firm such as Marriott to create and advertise an overall brand, while the day-to-day oversight of the workforce is handled by a separate hotel operating company, and staffing may be organized by a temporary-services firm (Weil 2011).

As in manufacturing, there are wide variations in performance across firms within individual service industries. In retail trade, for example, in the late 1980s and 1990s, Wal-Mart's real value-added per worker was more than 40 percent higher than that of other general merchandise retailers (Johnson 2002). Trucks with on-board computers had 13 percent higher capacity utilization than trucks without them (Hubbard 2003). Much of the productivity improvement realized by high-productivity service firms has been associated with investments in information technology (Bosworth and Triplett 2007). Obtaining these performance improvements often involves investing simultaneously in information technology and in complementary organizational changes, as in the valve case described earlier. For example, retailers who can quickly integrate data on consumers' purchases with their systems for replenishing inventory are more productive than those who cannot (Wailgum 2007; Zhu 2004).

Finally, although the use of IT and other innovations in services has led to large productivity gains, the benefits of these gains have not been evenly shared. Although IT adoption has led to increased pay and autonomy for workers who interpret information, such as financial advisers, it has led to reduced employment and pay for jobs that can be described in rules that a computer can follow—jobs such as routine claims processing that require moderate skills and that once paid middle-class wages (Levy and Murnane 2005).

Creating An Economy Built To Last

A hallmark of the Administration's policies to reverse the middle-class jobs deficit is leveraging positive spillovers to raise labor demand and productivity, and to create new industries and products, while equipping American workers with the tools they need to succeed in a modern economy. The President's blueprint for creating an economy built to last aims to promote synergies within local areas and among companies that add to growth in investment and good jobs.

The following discussion uses manufacturing as an example to illustrate these policies, but their usefulness is not limited to manufacturing. For example, the U.S. Department of Agriculture has for decades helped an industry made up largely of small producers remain internationally competitive, by providing an integrated set of services with large spillover benefits to farmers and rural communities: land-grant universities for research and training; cooperative extension agents that help to diffuse practices shown by this research to be effective; access to capital (in part through the department's own credit agencies); and programs that help farmers set up cooperatives to achieve economies of scale in purchasing and marketing.

Strengthening Competitiveness: The Manufacturing Example

A competitive U.S. manufacturing sector is a key to the Administration's vision of a U.S. economy that is innovative and competitive and that provides good jobs. Rising costs abroad coupled with sustained domestic productivity gains make the United States an increasingly attractive location for investment. But good policy is also needed to fully capture the benefits of this underlying trend and encourage investment in middle-class jobs in the United States. The view that a strong "industrial commons" is important for competitiveness, but also subject to market failure, suggests that government policy should promote the creation of, and access to, these shared resources. Thus, the Administration's policies work to promote the type of manufacturing that builds innovative capability and raises living standards.

The Administration's proposals help in several ways to strengthen these types of manufacturing. First, general policies to improve productivity and wages (such as the policies to support education, health care, and a clean environment discussed in other chapters of this *Report*) are essential to building long-term economic competitiveness.

Second, the Administration has made trade policy a priority. These policies have particular importance in manufacturing. Some argue that much of the steep manufacturing employment decline in the early 2000s was caused by a sharp rise in imports from emerging nations, especially China (Autor, Dorn, and Hanson, forthcoming; Pierce and Schott 2012). In some cases, producers exporting from these nations have benefited from policies that gave them an unfair advantage relative to manufacturers in the United States. In response to these policies, the Obama Administration, in addition to pursuing the broader trade policies discussed earlier in the chapter, launched an Interagency Trade Enforcement Center charged with protecting American companies from unfair trade competition.

Third, the Administration has championed tax credits to reduce the costs of socially beneficial actions (such as R&D). These policies aim to reward firms for providing lasting social benefits. In contrast, a "smoke stack-chasing" approach tries to lure individual firms to a particular location using tax abatements and other incentives. In general, these subsidies are awarded to firms for undertaking activity that would have occurred anyway; the subsidy simply influences the location of the activity. Thus these individual incentives generally do not lead to net investment (Chirinko and Wilson 2008). State and local governments provide more than $80 billion a year on such incentives, including $25 billion to manufacturers (Story 2012).

Finally, the Administration has championed sector-specific policies that use the convening power of government to promote coordination and investment. Productive ecosystems that promote innovation and good jobs require strong partnerships among industry stakeholders, including business, government, unions, trade associations, and universities. A sectoral approach to encouraging the development of such ecosystems (in manufacturing and in other industries) can help to build simultaneously both the demand for and the supply of shared assets, such as trained workers, competent customers engaged in innovation, suppliers of components, and standards for equipment design. The supply-chain analysis above suggests that policy may be needed to address two key issues: free-rider problems that lead to underinvestment and information barriers that hinder coordination among stakeholders in a supply chain.

The Administration's flagship manufacturing initiative is a $1 billion National Network for Manufacturing Innovation fund that will create up to 15 institutes to help ensure that new technology bridges the gaps from invention to product development to manufacturing at scale. Leveraging the assets of a particular region, each institute will bring together universities, companies, and government to co-invest in the development of new technologies that spill over to provide general benefits to a region's manufacturing base, rather than just a single company. Institutes will build workforce skills and business capabilities in large and small companies. A pilot center, the National Additive Manufacturing Innovation Institute, opened last year in Youngstown, Ohio. The universities and firms participating in the institute matched the initial $30 million in federal funding with $40 million of their own.

As discussed, many firms have been slow to adopt even well-known improved practices and thus lack the capability to participate in such innovative endeavors. To help these firms upgrade their operations, the Administration has proposed increased funding for the Manufacturing Extension Partnership program, which provides a range of business services to small manufacturers.

The Administration also has proposed initiatives to replenish the technology pipeline, by increasing funding for advanced manufacturing R&D. Despite tightening budgets, the Administration has emphasized the importance of funding industrially relevant, advanced manufacturing technologies such as advanced materials, smart manufacturing, and robotics.

Conclusion

The United States economy benefits from being closely linked with other nations through trade, investment, and financial flows. The Nation's economic recovery and long-run growth prospects depend in large part on U.S. businesses being able to compete in an open, fair and growing world economy. The Federal government is determined to do its part to facilitate this outcome. Sound macroeconomic policies that aim at strong, balanced, and sustainable growth are but one element. Another is a trade policy aimed at the maintenance of open, competitive markets, compliance with WTO obligations, and leadership in the multilateral trading system. The United States pursues a policy that supports jobs through trade, enforces trade rules, bolsters international trade relationships, and partners with developing countries to fight poverty and expand opportunities.

Creating and maintaining a competitive industry or region requires continuous investment by firms, workers, and communities. These investments are often more productive if others are also investing. In a number of cases (especially in manufacturing), investments in these productive ecosystems were allowed to lapse, affecting both competitiveness and job quality. Administration policy has helped to reverse these lapses, leading to domestic economic growth and increased exports.

Many of the policies discussed in connection with manufacturing also benefit consumers and workers in the services sector, such as policies that promote access to education. In addition, sector-specific policies for services are discussed in other chapters of this *Report*. For example, as discussed in Chapter 5, the administration has convened the Partnership for Patients, which brings together hospitals and clinics in a community to work to reduce errors in patient care.

While much remains to be done, these policies have laid a foundation for competitiveness and prosperity for both the United States and its trading partners.

C H A P T E R   8

CHALLENGES AND OPPORTUNITIES IN U.S. AGRICULTURE

U.S. agriculture fared better during the Great Recession than many other sectors and remains a bright spot in the U.S. economy. Despite an extensive and severe drought in 2012, net farm income is forecast to total $112.8 billion, only 4.3 percent below the previous year's record of $117.9 billion (USDA 2013a). Strong demand for agricultural products and below-average crop yields pushed up crops prices, and along with significant crop insurance indemnity payments, helped to make the 2012 income figure the second-highest since 1974 after adjusting for inflation. (See Economics Application Box 8-1 on the 2012 drought).

The strength of the U.S. agricultural sector is due in part to the demand for American agricultural exports. The value of agricultural exports has steadily risen and now accounts for a projected 31 percent of gross farm cash income. Exports reached a near record level of $135.8 billion in 2012 and are projected to reach $142 billion in 2013 (USDA 2012a).

Increasing demand from abroad created by rising incomes and a growing middle class will present opportunities for U.S. agriculture. The world population is expected to reach more than 9.2 billion by 2050, with growth coming primarily in developing countries, most of which are net importers of food products. The convergence of population growth and rapid urbanization, especially in developing regions of the world, will likely result in growing demand for food as well as changing dietary patterns.

Trade in agricultural commodities is a global endeavor, and the U.S. agricultural sector is subject to significant price volatility at the commodity level. Because of its high degree of integration with the international marketplace, U.S. agriculture is vulnerable to price volatility induced by other countries' agricultural policies—import and export restrictions—and growing conditions. Further, while the effects of climate change on livestock and

Economics Application Box 8-1: The 2012 Drought

A drought in the summer of 2012 across much of the United States caused significant crop losses and some livestock liquidation. About 80 percent of agricultural land experienced low rainfall and high temperatures, making the 2012 drought the most extensive since 1956. A striking aspect of the 2012 drought was the rapid increase in severity in early July. While the drought eased somewhat during early September, conditions during the June to August period largely determine production for most crops. By mid-August, crops worth 50 percent of the total value of all crops were exposed to drought.

Crop losses were most substantial for corn. In the spring of 2012, the U.S. Department of Agriculture estimated an expected corn yield of 166.0 bushels an acre. By October 2012, those estimates had dropped to 122.3 bushels an acre—a reduction of 27 percent. Soybeans, somewhat more drought tolerant, experienced a 14 percent yield reduction (from 43.9 to 37.8 bushels an acre). The livestock industry, still recovering from the 2011 drought in the Southern Plains, was hit especially hard. As of late October of 2012, 54 percent of pastures and ranges in the United States were rated poor to very poor. Beef production in 2012 was projected to decline 2.3 percent from 2011 levels and to fall another 4.2 percent in 2013. Broiler and pork production were also expected to experience declines in 2013, while milk production is expected to remain stable.

The effects of the drought on food prices were reflected first in the livestock sector, with increases in the price of meat and dairy products in late 2012 and projected into 2013. The full effects of the increase in corn and other commodity prices will likely take as long as a year to be fully captured in higher retail food prices.

Despite the drought, average income for farm businesses remained steady in 2012 at $86,200, reflecting the increased prices for corn and soybeans as well as increases in crop insurance indemnities, which as of February 2013 had already paid out $12.9 billion for 2012 losses (USDA 2013). Income increases on crop farms should more than offset livestock farmers' higher feed expenses and a decline in sales of wholesale milk. Additionally, the longstanding environment of strong commodity prices and low interest rates means that farm debt-to-equity ratios are approaching historic lows, which has reduced the financial vulnerability of farms to the production shocks.

crop production systems are expected to be mixed in the next 25 years, over the long term, continued changes are expected to have generally detrimental effects on most crops and livestock.

The Agricultural Sector in 2012

In the 1920s, farm households accounted for more than 25 percent of the U.S. workforce and generated approximately 8 percent of gross domestic product (GDP). Today they account for only 1.6 percent of the work force and generate approximately 1 percent of GDP. Over the same period, the rural share of the population has fallen far less, from 49 percent to 19 percent, suggesting that rural areas are less dependent on farming's contribution to the rural economy (Table 8-1). The agricultural sector is still vital to our country, but because of growth in other sectors of the economy and rapid gains in agricultural productivity that have lowered the relative prices of agricultural products, it has become a smaller share of the U.S. economy.

The structure of farming continues to move toward fewer, but larger commercial operations producing the bulk of farm commodities, complemented by a growing number of smaller farms earning most of their income from off-farm sources. Small family farms—those with annual sales less than $250,000—make up 90 percent of U.S. farms. They also hold about 62 percent of all farm assets, including 49 percent of the land owned by farms. However, commercial farms, which make up the other 10 percent of the sector, account for 83 percent of the value of U.S. production (Table 8-2).

While most of these large farms have a positive profit margin, average profit margins for small farms are negative because of high operating costs, low sales, and lower productivity (Table 8-3). Farms are predominantly organized as sole proprietorships (86.5 percent), followed by partnerships (7.9 percent) and corporations (4.4 percent).[1]

Fifty years ago, average household income for the farm population was approximately half that of the general population. Today, however, farm households tend to be better off than other American households; in 2011, median income for farm households was about 13 percent higher than the U.S. median household income (Figure 8-1). The difference in income between farm households and the nonfarm households is due in part to the broad Department of Agriculture (USDA) definition of what constitutes a farm, which includes farms where the principal operator is retired or has a main occupation other than farming ("residence farms"). Households operating rural residence farms earn more than the U.S. median household income even though their net cash income from farming is negative. Households operating intermediate farms (farms where the principal operator is not retired and reports farming as his or her main occupation) have on average positive net cash income from their farming operations, but most household income comes from sources other than farming. The sources of

---

[1] Corporations include both Sub-chapter C and S corporations.

Table 8-1
90 Years of Structural Change in U.S. Agriculture

Year	1920	1950	1980	2000	2010
Number of farms (thousands)	6,518	5,648	2,440	2,167	2,192
Average farm size (acres)	147	213	426	436	419
Rural share of population (percent)	48.8	36.0	26.3	21.0	19.3
Farm share of workforce (percent)	25.4	12.1	3.4	1.8	1.6
Farm share of GDP (percent)	7.7	6.8	2.2	1.0	0.9

Note: 1920 data for farm share of GDP not available. Value reported is for 1930, as calculated by the Department of Agriculture, Economic Research Service.
Source: Department of Agriculture, National Agricultural Statistics Service, Farms, Land in Farms, and Livestock Operations; Bureau of Economic Analysis, GDP by Industry; Sobek (2006); CEA calculations.

Table 8-2
Farm Types

Small family farms (gross sales less than $250,000)	Rural-residence family farms:	Retirement farms. Small farms whose operators report they are retired.	
		Residential/lifestyle farms. Small farms whose operators report a major occupation other than farming.	
	Intermediate family farms	Farming-occupation farms. Small family farms whose operators report farming as their major occupation.	Low-sales farms. Gross sales less than $100,000.
			High-sales farms. Gross sales between $100,000 and $249,999.
Large-scale family farms (gross sales of $250,000 or more)	Commercial family farms:	Large family farms. Gross sales between $250,000 and $499,999.	
		Very large family farms. Gross sales of $500,000 or more	
Nonfamily farms	Any farm not classified as a family farm, that is, any farm for which the majority of the farm business is not owned by individuals related by blood, marriage, or adoption.		

Note: The National Commission on Small Farms selected $250,000 in gross sales as the cutoff between small and large-scale farms.
Source: Department of Agriculture, Economic Research Service, Farm Household Well-being

income for farm households are increasingly diversified, which means that many of them are less vulnerable to the fluctuations of farm income. In 2011, households operating commercial farms had median household incomes two and a half times the overall U.S. median household income, with most of their income from farming.

By 2000, 93 percent of farm households had income from off-farm sources, including off-farm wages, salaries, business income, investments, and Social Security. Off-farm work has played a key role in raising farm household income. In 2011, only 46 percent of principal operators of farms reported that farming was their main occupation. While farm household incomes have become more diversified, farm operations have become increasingly specialized: In 1900, a farm produced an average of about five

Table 8-3
Farm Income and Farm Operator Household Income by
USDA Farm Size Classification, 2010

	Rural residence farms	Intermediate farms	Commercial farms	All farms
Farm operator households	1,311,117	617,876	214,070	2,143,063
Average gross cash farm income (dollars)	14,974	52,790	840,315	108,320
Average gross cash farm income, by source (%)				
Crop, livestock, and other farm-related income	91.6	94.6	97.0	96.2
Government payments	8.4	5.4	3.0	3.8
Average per farm operator household (dollars)				
Total cash farm expenses	17,216	46,142	613,486	85,117
Net cash farm income	-2,242	6,648	226,829	23,203
Farm operator household income	83,738	51,054	185,098	84,440

Source: Department of Agriculture, Agricultural Resource Management Survey.

Figure 8-1
Median Income for Farm Households by Farm Type
and Income Type, 2010–2012

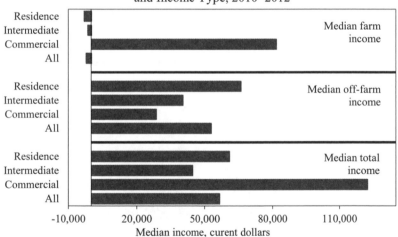

Note: 2012 forecasted values included for "all" farms. Values for farm-type breakouts are 2010–2011 averages.
Source: Department of Agriculture, Economic Research Service, Agricultural Resource Management Survey.

commodities; by 2000, the average had fallen to just over one. This change reflects not only the production and marketing efficiencies gained by concentration on fewer commodities, but also the effects of farm price and income policies that have reduced the risk of depending on returns from only one crop or just a few crops.

The average age of U.S. farmers and ranchers has been increasing over time. In 1978, 16.4 percent of principal farm operators were over age 65. By 2007, 30 percent of all farms were operated by producers over 65. In comparison, only 8 percent of self-employed workers in nonagricultural industries in 2007 were that old (Hoppe, McDonald, and Korb 2010). One reason the farming sector is relatively older is that farmers are living longer and often reside on their farms. Many established farmers never retire. Additionally, one-third of beginning farmers are over age 55, indicating that many farmers move into agriculture only after retiring from a different career. More than 20 percent of farm operators report that they are retired. Another 32 percent of all farms are operated by farmers aged 55 to 64 years. Farmers aged 55 and older account for more than half of the total value of production. Farmers under 35 contribute only 6 percent of the total value of production (Figure 8-2). This demographic transition has implications for the future of the U.S. agricultural sector.

Barriers to Entry and Succession Planning in U.S. Agriculture

Starting a farm operation can be an expensive endeavor. Startup requires access to land and capital equipment, as well as the operator's time.

Figure 8-2
Distribution of Farms by Age of Principal Operator, 2010

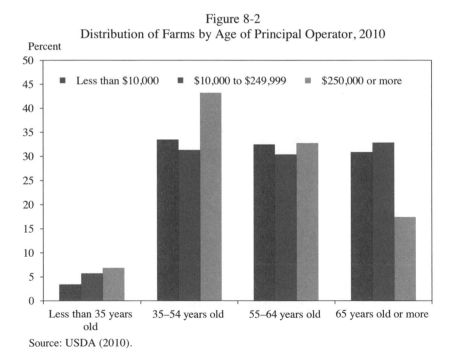

Source: USDA (2010).

In 2011, the average farm operated 415 acres and held assets worth just under $1 million, accounted for mostly by land and structures. Even for farm operators under age 35, asset values averaged $811,500, highlighting the extent to which startup costs represent a hurdle for new entrants (USDA 2011).

The Federal Government recognizes the need to support and develop new farm operators. Through the Farm Service Agency, the USDA helps beginning farmers who are unable to obtain financing from commercial lenders by targeting a portion of its direct and guaranteed loan funds to farmers and ranchers who have not operated a farm or ranch for more than 10 years and do not own a farm or ranch greater than 30 percent of the median size farm in the county, as determined by the most current Census for Agriculture.

After spending a lifetime accumulating wealth in agricultural assets, farmers often wish to pass the farm business to their heirs. Special provisions in the Federal estate tax, such as a rule that allows farm assets of an estate to be valued at their farm-use value rather than a higher market value, facilitate the transfer of farm estates from one generation to the next. (See Economics Application Box 8-2 on the Federal estate tax.)

As farmers begin to consider transitioning from active operation to retirement, questions about what will happen to their land remain. In some cases, the land is passed to an heir who continues the family business; in other cases, it is sold at auction perhaps to another farmer, but sometimes for other purposes such as residential or commercial development. As much as 2 million acres of America's farms, ranches, forests, wildlife habitat, and other open spaces are lost to fragmentation and development each year, with significant implications for water resources, outdoor recreation, wildlife, rural economies, and other resources.

Making a donation of a qualified conservation easement is one way for farmers and ranchers to maintain their current operation and conserve the amenities and natural assets of rural America for future generations. Such a donation allows the farmer to create a separate, special right on the designated land stipulating that it will be used only for certain purposes, such as agricultural production. The farmer or rancher can continue to use the land for production, knowing that in the future, it will continue to be used in the same manner. In return for placing the land into a qualified conservation easement, the landowner may deduct the value of the easement from his or her income for tax purposes.

Starting in 2006, a new law encouraged additional conservation easements by significantly expanding the tax benefits landowners may receive when they donate easements to qualified organizations, such as a land

Economics Application Box 8-2: The Federal Estate Tax and Farm Business Succession Planning

An estate—in general, a collection of assets passed down from a decedent upon his or her death—is one vehicle available to farmers to transfer agricultural property from one generation to the next. Under current law, only those returns that have a taxable estate above the exempt amount after deductions for expenses, debts, and bequests to a surviving spouse or charity are subject to the tax.

While the estate tax has been amended many times, it has never directly affected a large percentage of taxpayers, including farmers. In fact, in no year since 1916 has the percentage of adult deaths generating a taxable estate surpassed 8 percent (Jacobson, Raub, Johnson 2012). Several targeted provisions have reduced the potential impact of estate taxes on the transfer of a farm or other small business to the next generation (Durst 2009). These provisions include:

- A special provision that allows farm real estate to be valued at farm-use value rather than at its fair-market value, which is often higher because it reflects the value of the land for housing or commercial development.

- An installment payment provision that allows an estate to elect to pay the estate tax attributable to the decedent's interest in a closely held business in up to 10 equal, annual installments. The provision covers a

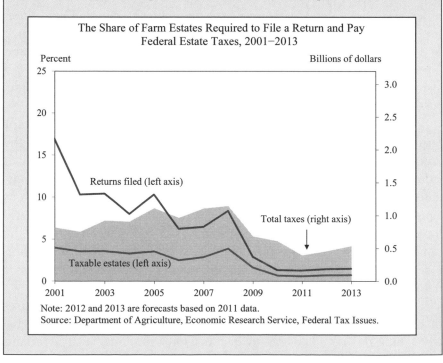

The Share of Farm Estates Required to File a Return and Pay Federal Estate Taxes, 2001–2013

Note: 2012 and 2013 are forecasts based on 2011 data.
Source: Department of Agriculture, Economic Research Service, Federal Tax Issues.

decedent whose interest in the closely held business exceeds 35 percent of the adjusted gross estate, which describes a typical farm estate.

• A provision aimed at encouraging farmers and other landowners to donate an easement or other restriction on development that has provided additional estate tax relief.

The box figure illustrates the relatively low and declining burden the Federal estate tax has placed on farm estates. In 2001, 16.9 percent of farm estates were required to file a tax return and less than 4 percent had an estate tax liability. By 2011, as a result of the generous tax-exemption amount and low tax rate, those figures had declined to 1.28 percent and 0.6 percent, respectively. Total tax liability in 2011 was also lower than it had been the prior 10 years, despite record high agricultural land value, which represents a large majority of the assets in a farm estate. The American Taxpayer Relief Act of 2012 made permanent a maximum estate tax rate of 40 percent; it also set the exclusion amount at $5 million and allowed for inflation adjustment, continuing the tax relief to most farm estates.

trust or public agency. More specifically, this enhanced incentive raises the maximum annual deduction a donor can take for the donation of a conservation easement and extends the period to claim the deduction from 5 to 15 years, from the year of the donation. In 2007 and 2008, a survey found that this incentive helped America's 1,700 local land trusts increase the pace of conservation by about 250,000 acres each year—a 36 percent increase over previous years.

The enhanced incentive provisions expired in 2009 but were renewed through December 31, 2013, by the American Taxpayer Relief Act of 2012. Making permanent the expanded tax incentives beyond 2013 would further bolster land conservation and job creation, especially on working lands, helping to keep landowners on their property and achieve a broad range of conservation outcomes.

A Mature Domestic Food Market

Americans benefit from a highly efficient agricultural sector and have higher standards of living now than at any point in the past. Of concern to producers in the U.S. food market is how much of their disposable income American consumers will spend on food in the future as well as what food products they will demand. Engel's law, which postulates that rising incomes lead to an increase in the nominal amount of income spent on food while the proportion of income spent on food falls, still holds in the United States. The share of American household budgets devoted to food fell from 15 percent in 1984 to 13 percent in 2009. However, a rise in per capita income since 1984 has counteracted the decrease in the share of household budgets devoted to food, as real per capita spending on food has increased from $3,592 in 1985 to $4,229 in 2011 (in 2011 dollars) (Figure 8-3).

As their real incomes rise, most Americans do not need larger quantities of food to satisfy their nutritional needs. They are, however, changing their food choices to include higher value foods, such as better cuts of meat, a variety of fruits and vegetables, and organic and specialty food items. A mature U.S. food market will require the agricultural sector to focus on innovations that produce value-added products for the domestic market in order to satisfy rising U.S. consumer demand for specialty goods.

New Markets in Agriculture

Organic farming has been one of the fastest-growing sectors in agriculture, and double-digit growth in sales of organic foods has provided market incentives for the U.S. agricultural sector across a broad range of products. The retail value of the organic industry grew to $31.4 billion a year in 2011, up from $21.1 billion in 2008 and $3.6 billion in 1997 (Dimitri and Oberholtzer 2009; USDA 2012a). Between 2002 and 2008, acres under organic production grew by an average of 16.5 percent a year. Organic

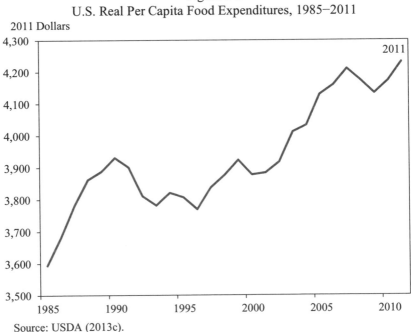

Figure 8-3
U.S. Real Per Capita Food Expenditures, 1985–2011

Source: USDA (2013c).

sales currently account for more than 3 percent of total U.S. food sales, and provide a larger share in categories such as produce and dairy. Growth has been particularly evident in the organic dairy sector, which accounted for 16 percent of organic sales in 2008. The number of organic milk cows on U.S. farms increased by annual average of 26 percent between 2000 and 2008. As demand for organic food has increased, the U.S. agricultural sector has taken steps to meet it; the number of operations certified as organic grew by 1,109—or more than 6 percent—between 2009 and 2011.

The USDA has taken steps both to promote and to regulate the growing organic food industry by establishing the National Organic Program (NOP), whose mission is to ensure the integrity of USDA-certified organic products in the United States and throughout the world. The NOP accredits nearly 50 domestic organic certifying agents who are authorized to issue an organic certificate to operations that comply with the USDA organic regulations. Between 2009 and 2011, the USDA has also supported its own scientists and university researchers with more than $117 million in funding focused on improving the productivity and success of organic agriculture. For example, USDA research on weed management for organic vegetable production has produced techniques and tools that can help control 70 percent of weeds at 15 percent of the previous cost for weed control. Spreading the USDA organic research findings to people in the field is critical, and the "eOrganic" electronic extension service funded by the USDA has become an essential tool for compiling and disseminating knowledge about organic production.

The increasing demand for organic foods has been accompanied by a growing "local" movement. The markets for organic and local food regularly overlap: organic farmers are much more likely than conventional farmers to sell their products locally (Kremen, Greene, and Hanson 2004), with about a quarter of all organic sales in 2004 made within an hour's drive of the farm (Greene et al. 2009). Similarly, 82 percent of all farmers' markets had at least one organic vendor. Sales of locally produced foods make up a small but growing part of U.S. agricultural sales, particularly for small farms. The USDA estimates that the farm-level value of local food sales totaled nearly $5 billion in 2008, or 1.6 percent of the U.S. market for agricultural products. An estimated 107,000 farms, or 5 percent of all U.S. farms, are engaged in local food systems, with small farms (those with less than $50,000 in gross annual sales) accounting for 81 percent of all farms reporting local food sales in 2008 (Low and Vogel 2011). Examples of the types of farming businesses that are engaged in local foods are direct-to-consumer marketing, farmers' markets, farm-to-school programs, community-supported agriculture, community gardens, school gardens, food hubs and market aggregators, kitchen incubators, and mobile slaughter units, among a myriad of other types of operations.

Local goods are also good for the economy. A USDA study found that produce growers selling into local and regional markets generated 13 full-time operator jobs for every $1 million in revenue earned, for a total of 61,000 jobs in 2008 (Low and Vogel 2011). Farmers that did not sell into these markets generated only three full-time operator jobs per $1 million revenue. To foster exposure to and growth in local foods, the USDA has created the Know Your Farmer, Know Your Food management and communications initiative, which helps stakeholders navigate USDA resources and efforts related to local and regional food systems. Future growth of the agricultural economy can be enhanced by growth in those sectors.

Today's Farm Structure

The current strength of the farm economy is also built on the restructuring that has taken place over time, making the most productive farms larger and more efficient. Agricultural innovations have been labor-saving, greatly reducing the amount of labor needed for specific farm tasks. Labor-saving innovations also affect farm structure, because they allow a farmer to manage more cropland or raise more livestock. In addition, innovations have led farms to contract out for specialized services. Farmers now rely extensively on private consultants, government extension agents, lenders, and supplier representatives for technical advice.

Some of these managerial innovations rely on further developments in the design of organizations and contractual relationships to effectively manage a series of complicated commercial relationships. The share of production under marketing or production contracts increased from 28 percent in 1991 to more than 38 percent by 2010. Corn, soybean, and wheat producers, for example, place about half of their production under forward contracts; many of them also invest in storage facilities to store products when anticipating future price increases, and nearly 30 percent of them use futures markets to hedge the risks from their cash sales (MacDonald and Korb 2011). Similarly, farmers have realized more intensive use of capital by leasing equipment from specialized suppliers, and they often engage additional specialized expertise and capital equipment by contracting with custom service providers for farm tasks such as spraying, field preparation, or harvesting.

Livestock operations have undergone dramatic changes in the last 30 years. Farmers now use information technology to adjust feed mixes and climate controls automatically to meet the precise needs of animals in confined feeding operations. Integrated hog operations, for example, sharply reduced the amount of feed, capital, and labor needed to produce hogs as new technologies and organizational forms swept the industry. As a result, live hog prices were nearly a third lower than they would have been without the productivity growth that occurred between 1992 and 2004, and retail pork prices were 9 percent lower (Key and McBride 2007).

The market, scientific, and technological opportunities beckoning American farmers are as great as they have ever been. Over the past three decades, a series of revolutions in the understanding of the science of living organisms and exponential growth in the processing power of information technology have raised the potential for productivity growth in American agriculture that could outstrip even the impressive record of growth it logged over the course of the 20th century. But as America's own history shows, neither revolutions in science and technology nor market signals will find practical application on America's farms and ranches without careful, effective, smart investment by public science institutions. Even America's larger farms are too small to support sophisticated basic research, and many of the most significant improvements that farms can be expected to make as they apply the fruits of this research are not patentable. The partnership between public science and the private farm must continue if these possibilities are to be realized, particularly in the face of climate change. The Obama Administration believes America's agricultural future is worth investing in and has committed to increases in scientific research that could benefit the agricultural sector for decades to come.

Investing in Agricultural Productivity

In 1950, the average dairy cow produced about 5,300 pounds of milk. Today the average cow produces about 22,000 pounds of milk, thanks to improvements in cow genetics, feed formula, and management practices. Over that time period, the number of dairy cows in America has fallen by more than half, yet U.S. milk production has nearly doubled.

Persistent gains in efficiency have defined American agriculture. Public and private investments in agricultural research and development (R&D) have helped U.S. farmers find ways to grow more with less. While growth in U.S. industrial output over the past 50 years has come primarily from increases in capital and labor, agricultural output growth mainly has come from substantial increases in total factor productivity. American farmers have continually found ways to grow more with less; new seeds are less susceptible to disease and produce higher yields, new tractors are guided by satellites and spread fertilizer optimally across the field, and animals' diets are optimally calibrated to grow larger animals with less feed. These innovations have caused improvements in farm productivity to outpace improvements in non-farm productivity over the past 25 years.

From 1948 to 2009, farm productivity nearly tripled, growing at a rate of 1.6 percent a year. In the early part of that period, increased productivity, measured as output per unit of combined inputs, combined with increased use of equipment and chemical inputs to drive the growth in agricultural output. Between 1980 and 2009, equipment stocks fell along with continued declines in labor and land inputs; chemical use continued to rise, but at a much slower rate. Despite reduced input use, agricultural output grew by 1.5 percent a year in 1980–2009, with increasing productivity accounting for almost all of the growth (Figure 8-4).

Research and Development Drives Productivity Growth

Increasing productivity on U.S. farms stems largely from the rapid and widespread adoption of a continuing series of biological, chemical, mechanical, and organizational advances. Formal research programs are carried out in universities, government labs, and private firms. Agricultural innovations building on that research are developed by input suppliers in the private sector or by public institutions.

Public support of agricultural R&D generates high payoffs for farmers and the public. Fuglie and Heisey (2007) found that every dollar invested

Figure 8-4
Farm and Nonfarm Productivity, 1948–2009

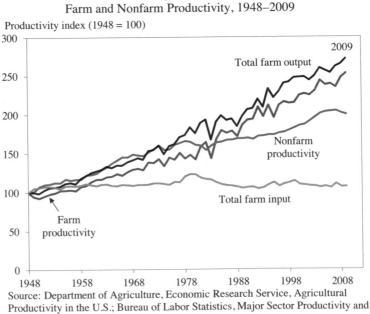

Source: Department of Agriculture, Economic Research Service, Agricultural Productivity in the U.S.; Bureau of Labor Statistics, Major Sector Productivity and Costs.

in public agricultural research generates 10 times that amount in benefits to society. Another recent study (Alston et al. 2009) found an even higher return on Federal and State agricultural research expenditures, with estimated benefits of $20 for every $1 invested. Other academic studies reached broadly similar conclusions.

Total R&D spending in agriculture reached $11 billion in 2007, or nearly 8 percent of the value added in the sector. Annual public agricultural R&D spending, through universities as well as government laboratories, rose 77 percent between 1970 and 2002 (after accounting for inflation). Public expenditures have not kept up with R&D cost inflation since, however, falling by 13 percent in real terms between 2002 and 2009. Private R&D expenditures are sensitive to the business cycle but doubled in inflation-adjusted terms between 1970 and 2007 (Figure 8-5).

Spillovers are ubiquitous in R&D in general and in agricultural R&D in particular. Ideas that are discovered by one institution may have an impact on the research productivity of another. Some of the important, and overlapping, categories of spillovers in agricultural R&D are geographical, for example, from one state or one country to another; institutional, from the private sector to the public, or vice versa, across competing institutions

Figure 8-5
Public and Private U.S. Agricultural R&D Spending, 1971–2009

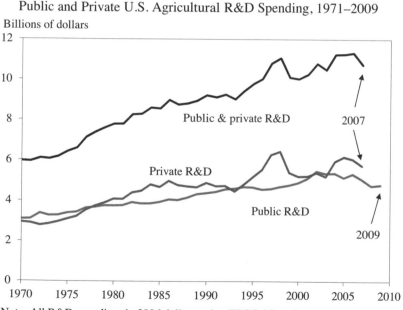

Note: All R&D spending; in 2006 dollars using ERS R&D deflator.
Source: Department of Agriculture, Economic Research Service, Agricultural Research Funding in the Public and Private Sectors.

such as universities, or from one industry to another; and across scientific areas, from "pretechnology" sciences to agricultural sciences, for example, or from biomedical science to agricultural science.

Economists have studied spillovers related to agriculture R&D (see, for example, Evenson 1988 or Griliches 1998). One of the more commonly addressed spillover areas for agricultural research is the geographical spillover from one state to another. Pardey and Alston (2011) estimated that roughly one-third of the benefits of state-level agricultural R&D are generated through spillovers to states other than those in which the research was conducted.

Conservation Practices and the Environment

The overuse of nitrogen fertilizer has widely recognized detrimental effects on the environment, especially downstream of treated fields. Particularly in the Gulf of Mexico, excess nitrogen is associated with low-oxygen environments, or "dead zones." Corn is the most widely planted crop in the United States and the largest user of nitrogen fertilizer. In 2010, more than 97 percent of planted corn acres received nitrogen fertilizer (commercial and manure), an increase of 18 percent from 2001. At the same time, farmers have improved their use of nitrogen—corn acres where nitrogen was applied in excess of agronomically necessary rates declined from 41 percent to 31 percent (Ribaudo et al. 2012).

Adoption of other conservation management practices also has the potential to reduce environmentally harmful impacts of agricultural production. Since 2000, corn, cotton, soybean, and wheat acreage under conservation tillage (mulch, ridge, and no till) has increased; conservation tillage may reduce soil erosion and water pollution but increase pest management costs (Osteen, Gottlieb, and Vasavada 2012).

The Federal Government plays an important role in encouraging conservation adoption by offering numerous conservation programs to assist private landowners in conserving the soil, water, wildlife, and other natural resources found on their property. These programs give landowners incentives to consider natural resources in their agricultural practices. Two relatively new programs, Working Lands for Wildlife and the National Water Quality Initiative, help producers stay in operation by providing financial and technical support, as well as regulatory certainty, if the landowner takes steps to restore and conserve wildlife habitat or water quality on their property.

The USDA's National Water Quality Initiative works with farmers, ranchers, and forest landowners in priority watersheds to help improve water quality and aquatic habitats in impaired streams. As of 2012, approximately

$34 million had been obligated for improvements on about 161,000 acres. Another $21 million was obligated through more than 800 contracts with private landowners for Working Lands for Wildlife, also administered by the Natural Resources Conservation Service and Fish and Wildlife Service. The contracts will restore wildlife habitat on more than 310,000 acres of range, pasture, and forest lands across the country.

Natural Capital, Conservation, and the Outdoor Economy

Agriculture, as a land use, affects a large amount of natural capital (land, water, air, and genetic resources on farms and ranches) in the United States. Based on 2002 data, private farms accounted for 41 percent of all U.S. land, including 434 million acres of cropland, 395 million acres of pasture and range, and 76 million acres of forest and woodland (Ribaudo et al. 2008). This capital can provide a host of environmental services, including water quality, air quality, flood control, wildlife, and carbon sequestration. These services can be consumed directly or combined by consumers with other goods to create final goods, such as sightseeing, fishing, wildlife viewing, or hunting, all of which support the outdoor economy.

Multisector efforts under the President's America's Great Outdoors initiative have bolstered outdoor recreation, conservation, and restoration of America's natural resources on public lands, as well as on working farms, ranches, and forests. In a 2012 study of 11 western states, economists found that national parks, monuments, and other protected Federal public lands promote more rapid job growth and are correlated with higher levels of per capita income in surrounding areas. Companies use the high quality of life provided by localities with access to healthy and protected lands and waters as a recruiting tool to attract new and talented employees who value natural beauty and outdoor recreational opportunities.

Outdoor recreation is an often overlooked but significant economic driver in the United States, with one industry study estimating that it provided 6.1 million jobs, spurred $646 billion in spending, much of it on travel and tourism, and raised $80 billion in Federal, State, and local tax revenue in 2010 (Outdoor Industry Association 2012). National parks and Federal lands and waters located across the entire United States, including in many rural areas, play a significant role in supporting the travel and tourism industry. Each year, millions of international tourists visit U.S. public lands and small towns, spending money at local businesses that provide lodging, dining, retail shopping, and entertainment. Rural America plays a particularly important role in the national tourism economy by attracting and retaining tourists for longer visits (Interior 2012).

Growing Global Demand for Food and Agricultural Commodities

The U.N. Food and Agricultural Organization (FAO) estimates that global agricultural production will need to increase by around 60 percent to meet the anticipated increase in demand in 2050, given an additional 2.3 billion people and current consumption patterns. Meeting this demand will depend largely on increases in agricultural productivity because input scarcity, particularly of natural resources and environmental services, will become more binding with population growth and climate change.

Population Growth and Urbanization

The world's population grows by more than 200,000 people each day and is expected to increase from 7 billion in 2012 to more than 9.2 billion in 2050. More than 95 percent of all population growth is expected to occur in low-income countries (Figure 8-6).

As the worldwide population increases, most of the growth will come from urbanization. More than half of the world's population was living in urban areas by 2008, compared with just 29 percent in the 1950s. Approximately 70 percent of the world population is expected to be living in urban areas by 2050 (Figure 8-7).

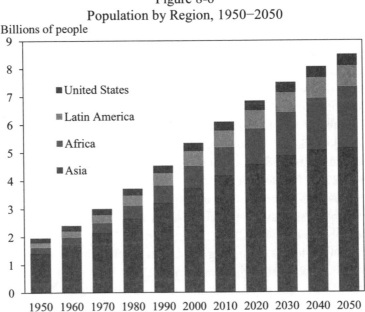

Figure 8-6
Population by Region, 1950–2050

Note: 2020–2050 data are projections.
Source: UN (2011).

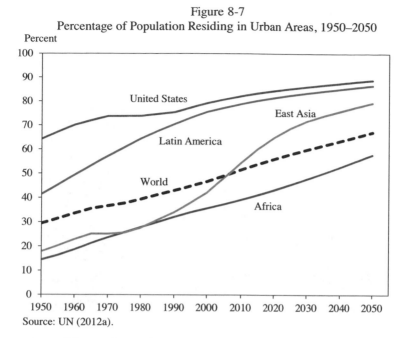

Figure 8-7
Percentage of Population Residing in Urban Areas, 1950–2050

Source: UN (2012a).

A world population living primarily in cities and towns will present unique challenges to the agricultural sector, because urban populations rely heavily on a stable and efficient worldwide food chain to provide the nutrient-dense and diverse foods they demand. The rising global population is also expected to be accompanied by falling poverty rates and increasing incomes for a large fraction of the world's population, particularly in Asia. Notably, the poverty rate in East Asia fell from nearly 80 percent in 1980 to less than 20 percent in 2005. Along with the decline in poverty, there is an emerging middle class in the Asia Pacific region that the OECD projects will increase rapidly, from 525 million in 2009, to more than 1.7 billion in 2020, and to 3.2 billion in 2030 (Figure 8-8) (Kharas 2010). The result will likely be increased consumption of food per capita and a change in diets toward a higher proportion of meat.

Rising global food demand and the expected change in dietary patterns accompanying the growth in income throughout the world, particularly in China, will lead to opportunities for growth in the U.S. agricultural sector, most notably in meat export. World meat and dairy consumption doubled between 1950 and 2009. Global meat consumption has been growing much more rapidly than consumption of grains and oilseeds, and between 1985 and 1990, production of meat (beef, pork, chicken, and turkey) rose more than 3 percent a year, well above the world's population growth rate of 1.7 percent a year.

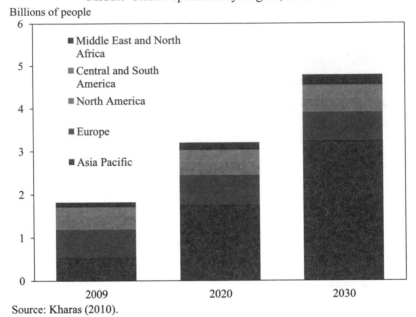

Figure 8-8
Middle-Class Population by Region, 2009–2030

Billions of people

Legend:
- Middle East and North Africa
- Central and South America
- North America
- Europe
- Asia Pacific

Source: Kharas (2010).

Pressure on Agricultural Land and the Environment

Continuing increases in the demand for agricultural products, especially resource intensive foods such as meat, are expected to have a deleterious impact on agricultural land, soil, and water, and to create broader ecosystem-level pressures (UN 2012b). According to the United Nations, global food production currently uses nearly one-quarter of all the habitable land on earth, accounts for more than 70 percent of fresh water consumption, and produces more than 30 percent of global greenhouse gas emissions. In addition, global food production accounts for 80 percent of deforestation and is the largest single cause of species and biodiversity loss.

A collaborative report on climate change prepared by the USDA and scholars from a variety of universities and other Federal and nongovernmental agencies suggests that climate change will impact both agricultural productivity and commodity price volatility (Walthall et al. 2012). The increased temperature will increase the likelihood of grain and oilseed crop failure, forest fires, insect outbreaks, and tree mortality. Further, elevated levels of carbon dioxide are expected to reduce the productivity of livestock and dairy animals and increase weed growth. Although some agricultural and forest systems may experience productivity increases in the near term, the benefits provided by these ecosystems, such as clean drinking water and natural waste decomposition, will diminish over the long term, requiring a change in management regimes. Management of water resources will become more challenging, and natural disasters such as forest fires, insect outbreaks, severe storms, and drought will occur with increased frequency and severity, placing heavy demands on management resources, such as Federal disaster assistance. (For additional discussion of climate change, see Chapter 6.)

GLOBAL COMMODITY MARKETS AND PRICE VOLATILITY

Trade in agricultural commodities is a global endeavor and prices respond to supply and demand conditions around the world. As a result, agricultural commodity markets are characterized by a high degree of volatility. Four major market fundamentals explain why that is the case. First, agricultural output is in large part at the mercy of nature. Shocks from weather, pests, and other natural phenomena have unpredictable effects on supply. With the effects of global climate change already being seen in many parts of the globe and projected to continue, the unpredictability of these impacts is likely to increase over time. Second, diets are somewhat inflexible in the short run, which means demand for certain foods remains relatively constant.[2] A third source of volatility is the natural growing cycle, which contributes to a relatively fixed short-run supply. Finally, declining stock-to-consumption ratios amplify the effects of food price shocks.

The integration of markets can also be a source of volatility. Food and energy markets in the United States and around the world have become increasingly interlinked through the use of agricultural feedstock in the production of ethanol and the use of oil and natural gas in agricultural production.[3] Growth in the use of biofuels, for example, not only increases the demand for agricultural feedstocks but may also make demand less elastic through such measures as biofuel blending requirements. As such, integration can cause shocks in one market to be transmitted to another.

Since the early 1970s, food prices have become much more volatile. In general, high food prices bring with them higher price volatility, and average real food prices in the past five years were 35 percent higher than prices in the previous decade, according to the FAO's Food Price Index. The index tracks the monthly change in the average international prices of five commodity groups, namely, meat, dairy, cereals, oils, and sugar. The index peaked in February 2011 and has since fallen 10 percent. Overall food prices

---

[2] For data on commodity and food elasticities, see USDA Economic Research Service, http://www.ers.usda.gov/data-products/commodity-and-food-elasticities.aspx.
[3] Natural gas is the primary feedstock in the production of ammonia, and ammonia is the primary input for all nitrogen fertilizers.

surged in the summer of 2012, driven by higher cereal prices. Food price spikes are not uncommon, and in most cases prices eventually fall as much as they have risen. Figure 8-9 demonstrates the increasing variability in the nominal price of corn since 1866–67.

Meeting the Challenges and Harnessing the Opportunities of Global Demand Growth

For U.S. agriculture to benefit fully from the growing food demand and changing food patterns around the world, access to the global market must be ensured. Successful efforts by the Federal Government to open foreign markets have contributed to an agricultural export boom. In FY 2012, American agricultural exports reached $135.7 billion, just short of the record high level of $137.4 billion set in FY 2011. Additionally, America runs a trade surplus in agricultural goods—a surplus that reached $32.4 billion in FY 2012 (USDA 2012b).

Open Trade and Access to Global Food Markets

The Obama Administration has made reducing trade barriers to market access overseas for U.S. farmers and ranchers a top priority, alongside

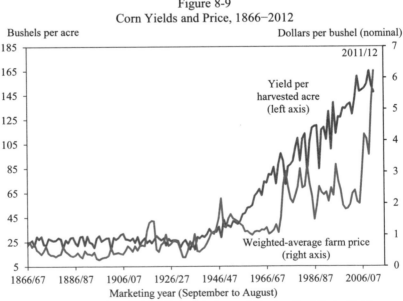

Figure 8-9
Corn Yields and Price, 1866–2012

Source: Department of Agriculture, Economic Research Service, Feed Grains Database.

efforts to ensure that America's trading partners fully honor all the commitments they have made under existing trade agreements. The President has signed several historic trade agreements that significantly expand market access for U.S. agricultural exporters. The recently implemented U.S.-Korea Free Trade Agreement (KORUS) is set to deliver substantial gains for U.S. agricultural exports in coming years. In a separate beef import protocol concluded in 2008, Korea agreed to adjust its import restrictions on U.S. beef. As a result, U.S. beef exports to Korea more than doubled in value from 2008 to 2011, to about $686 million. Under KORUS, Korea will gradually bring its tariffs on imports of U.S. beef and pork down to zero, and the U.S. meat industry will benefit from even greater gains in trade. The improved access provided by the agreement for a wide range of other products, beginning in 2012 and continuing over the agreement's phase-in period, will yield new market opportunities for U.S. exporters. The USDA estimates that, when fully implemented, KORUS will expand U.S. agricultural exports to Korea by an estimated $1.9 billion a year—gains that will benefit agricultural producers and processors across the United States. The Korean Free Trade Agreement, together with the free trade agreements with Panama and Colombia passed at the same time is expected to boost U.S. agricultural exports by $2.3 billion a year (Wainio, Gehlhar, and Dyck 2011).

The Obama Administration has worked with a number of other developing and developed countries to reopen their markets to U.S. beef products. Partly as a consequence of these steps, U.S. beef exports in 2011 exceeded 2003's historic levels for the first time, reaching $5.4 billion. Similarly, 57 countries, including many important emerging markets, have now lifted bans on U.S. poultry products. Between 2007 and 2011, the value of U.S. poultry exports increased from $4.1 billion to $5.6 billion. U.S. pork exports to the rapidly growing Chinese market soared after H1N1-related bans were lifted. Immediately before the ban, the United States exported on average about $132 million a year in pork and pork products to China. In 2010, pork exports to China totaled only $79.3 million. In 2011, pork exports to China grew by a factor of six, exceeding $477 million and quickly demonstrating the value of better access to this key emerging market. In the first quarter of 2012, roughly two years after the ban was lifted, the United States exported about $122 million in pork and pork products to China.

Hired Farm Labor Costs in a Global Economy

Hired labor is a crucial component of U.S. agricultural production. Costs associated with such labor account for 17 percent of variable production expenses for all agricultural commodities and 40 percent of expenses in the production of labor-intensive crops such as fruits, vegetables, and nursery products.

For fruits and vegetables, total agricultural production expenses are near parity between U.S. and international producers, but labor costs are often much lower for foreign growers. In response to higher labor costs, U.S. farms have already turned to mechanization of the harvesting and production processes. For example, mechanized production of raisins, including harvesting and drying of grapes, increased from 1 percent of the raisin crop to 45 percent between 2000 and 2007. Harvesting of baby leaf lettuce is currently 70–80 percent mechanized (Calvin and Martin 2010). These trends will likely increase if wages rise and could potentially lead to consolidation among growers. Some crops are not well suited for fully mechanical production, however. U.S. growers of such commodities may invest in technology that increases labor productivity, such as conveyor belts now common in Southern California strawberry fields.

Although mechanization is attractive in many cases, the costs associated with converting to mechanical processes are high, and larger farms typically stand to profit the most from mechanization. Moreover, growers may be hesitant to adopt the technology because of concerns about loss of quality. Given the difficulties associated with converting to mechanized production in the short run, the affordability of hired farm labor, and immigrant labor in particular, takes on greater importance. It is estimated that, for the past 15 years, about half of all hired laborers working in crop agriculture have lacked the proper immigration designation to work in the United States (Zahniser et al. 2012). Immigration policy, which influences the supply of and demand for labor as well as food prices ultimately paid by the consumer, is an important issue in the agricultural sector.

In their research, Zahniser et al. (2012) used a simulation to illustrate the effects different changes in immigration policy could have on the agricultural sector, including the effects of disruptions in the supply of labor on farm wages and crop production. Expanding the number of agricultural workers eligible for the H-2A Temporary Agricultural Program, which allows U.S. farms to hire temporary nonimmigrant foreign workers if not enough domestic workers are available, would increase agricultural production and exports by around 1.6 percent and 2.5 percent, respectively, in the long run for labor-intensive sectors like produce and nursery products. On the other hand, a 5.8 million decrease in the overall number of undocumented workers would reduce production and exports throughout all sectors of the economy, with agriculture and other labor-intensive sectors the hardest hit. Agricultural exports would fall by about 3.7 percent.

Improving Risk Management

Traditionally, every five years, Congress passes a bundle of legislation, commonly called the "Farm Bill" that sets national agriculture, nutrition, conservation, and forestry policy. The last Farm Bill, passed in 2008, was set to expire on September 30, 2012 but was extended through fiscal year 2013. The coming expiration of the current Farm Bill represents an opportunity to make the most significant reforms in agricultural policy in decades. The Senate Agricultural Reform, Food and Jobs Act of 2012 would end direct payments—fixed annual payments to farmers based on their farms' historical crop production, paid without regard to whether a crop is currently grown—and streamline and consolidate farm programs, as well as reduce the Federal deficit by as much as $23.6 billion over 10 years (CBO 2012). It could also strengthen priorities, such as efficient risk management, that help farmers, ranchers, and small business owners protect their investments and ensure a stable supply of needed agricultural product, while continuing to help the U.S. agricultural sector grow the economy.

Highly volatile agricultural commodity prices can create significant income risk for farmers. At the same time, the current farm safety net is inefficient and unfair, creating distortions in production and crowding out market-based risk management options. Because program commodity production is concentrated on larger farms, these farms receive the largest share of taxpayer-supported program payments, even though this group of farm households has incomes that are on average three times the average U.S. household (Figure 8-10).

Currently, those households with an average adjusted gross nonfarm income up to $500,000 are eligible to receive government payments, while those with as much as $750,000 in average adjusted farm income are eligible for direct payments. Farmers who produce fruits and vegetables do not receive any government program payments. Adding provisions that make lands that have not previously been used to grow crops ineligible for crop insurance or other Federal benefits would help protect the nation's prairies and forests from being converted into marginal cropland.

Today's agricultural commodity support programs are rooted in the landmark New Deal legislation that followed the agricultural depression of the 1920s and 1930s. These programs were designed to sustain prices and incomes for producers of cotton, milk, wheat, rice, corn, sugar, tobacco, peanuts, and other crops, at a time when a large portion of the U.S. population was engaged in farming. Today, less the 2 percent of the U.S. population is engaged in farming, and changing economic conditions and trends in agriculture since these programs began suggest that many of the original motivations for these farm programs no longer apply.

Figure 8-10
Government Commodity Payments by Farm Type

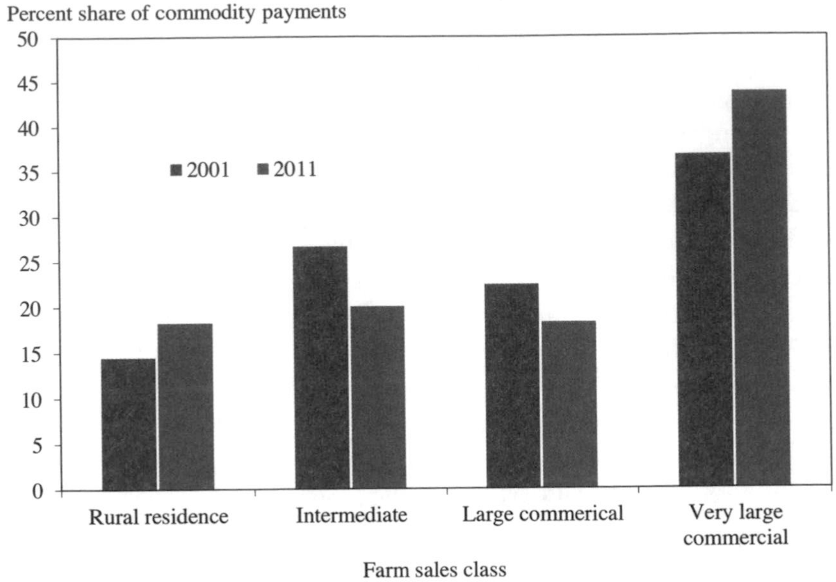

Percent share of commodity payments

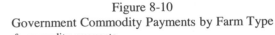

■2001 ■2011

Farm sales class

Source: USDA (2001, 2011).

For example, the increasing reliance of farm families on income earned from sources other than their farms and a shift toward market-oriented farm policies have made farms and commodity markets less vulnerable to adverse price changes than before. These changes imply that moving away from traditional commodity support programs would have a much smaller impact on farm household income than in previous decades. Nonetheless, substantial government support of agriculture remains.

Risk management involves choosing among many options for reducing the financial effects of such uncertainties. In addition to participating in government commodity programs that are available for certain commodities, farmers today have private options for managing risk that were not available when commodity price support programs were introduced. For instance, the growth of futures and options markets provides a market-based method for farmers to protect themselves against short-term price declines. Other private means to stabilize farm incomes include saving; borrowing; diversifying among different types of crops, trees, livestock and ecosystem services; contracting farm output with processors at assured prices; crop insurance and total revenue insurance; utilizing a wide range of farm management practices that reduce crop loss (such as irrigation, pesticide use); leasing out farmland; and taking advantage of expanded opportunities for earning nonfarm income.

The Dodd-Frank Wall Street Reform and Consumer Protection Act

In 2010, President Obama signed the Dodd-Frank Wall Street Reform and Consumer Protection Act, with the goal of addressing the lack of transparency, systemic risks, and interconnectedness risks in the over-the-counter (OTC) derivatives markets that, in part, precipitated the recent financial crisis. Modern farm operations—and agribusiness in general—rely greatly on services provided by the OTC derivatives market, including the swaps market. Derivatives, which are financial instruments whose value is based on the value of an underlying asset, liability, or event, perform essential economic functions of price discovery and risk management. The Act strengthens financial market regulation by requiring most standardized swaps to be centrally cleared and traded on an exchange or execution facility, with exemptions from clearing for commercial end-users; subjecting dealers and major participants that trade these derivatives to registration, business conduct, risk management, and collateral requirements; and subjecting all swaps to new recordkeeping and reporting rules.

Although the OTC derivatives market serves an important risk-management role amounting to trillions of dollars in notional value, in the past, OTC derivatives were essentially an unregulated market. The lack of market oversight allowed substantial counterparty credit risk to build up in these markets, with significant consequences for the financial system. In addition, the lack of regulation created inefficiencies by reducing information available to market participants and regulators, hampering price discovery, and facilitating opportunities for fraud. Before passage of the Act, regulators had no authority to monitor the market and prescribe rules. The new clearing and margin requirements will act as safeguards for the performance of the OTC derivatives markets, eliminating counterparty credit risk between the original traders. In addition, new real-time public reporting requirements and execution standards will improve market transparency and lower transaction costs.

The Act further seeks to protect the market for agricultural swaps, while ensuring that agricultural market participants are still able to access risk-management markets. The Act provides that derivatives on agricultural commodities may be conducted only by eligible contract participants—that is, counterparties who hold more than $10 million in assets or have a net worth of $1 million or more. Because many smaller farmers would not qualify as eligible contract participants and consequently could not engage in swap contracts that are not traded on a designated contract market (an exchange) or swap execution facility (SEF), the U.S. Commodity Futures Trading Commission granted them an exemption for physical commodity options. This exemption provides flexibility for all farmers to manage risk using agricultural derivatives contracts.

Conclusion

Although farming has become a progressively smaller share of the U.S. economy, the President believes that a vibrant U.S. agricultural sector is vital for the Nation's prosperity. U.S. agriculture has remained a bright spot in the economy during the Great Recession and its immediate aftermath and despite the most severe drought in more than a half-century. Much of the sector's success can be attributed to growth in global demand for American agricultural exports. In 2012, agricultural exports reached a near record level and are projected to continue to expand. The world's population is expected to reach more than 9.2 billion people by 2050, with most of the growth occurring in countries that are net food importers. President Obama believes that expanding overseas market access is crucial for the continued strength of American agriculture.

Persistent gains in efficiency have defined American agriculture and nearly tripled farm productivity in the second half of the twentieth century. To continue this tradition and maintain the strength of the sector, the Nation must continue to invest in agricultural R&D, helping farmers find new ways to grow more with less and to continue their stewardship of natural resources for future generations. The agricultural sector is increasingly vulnerable to price volatility because of the globalization of agricultural commodities, volatile weather conditions as a result of climate change, and changing consumption patterns. To cope with these challenges, U.S. agriculture must stay at the forefront of agricultural innovation.

REFERENCES

Chapter 1
Introduction

Auerbach, David I., and Arthur L. Kellermann. 2011. "A Decade of Health Care Cost Growth Has Wiped Out Real Income Gains for an Average U.S. Family." *Health Affairs* 30, no. 9: 1630–36.

CBO (Congressional Budget Office). 2012a. "Economic Effects of Policies Contributing to Fiscal Tightening in 2013." November.

_____. 2012b. "Economic Effects of Reducing the Fiscal Restraint That Is Scheduled to Occur in 2013." May.

_____. 2013. "The Budget and Economic Outlook: Fiscal Years 2013 to 2023." February.

CEA (Council of Economic Advisers). 1998. *Economic Report of the President.* February.

_____. 2004. *Economic Report of the President.* February.

_____. 2012. "The Middle-Class Tax Cuts' Impact on Consumer Spending & Retailers." November.

Doucouliagos, Hristos, and T.D. Stanley. 2009. "Publication Selection Bias in Minimum-Wage Research? A Meta-Regression Analysis." *British Journal of Industrial Relations* 47, no. 2: 406–28.

Fairlie, Robert W. 2012. "Open For Business: How Immigrants Are Driving Small Business Creation in the United States." The Partnership for a New American Economy. August (http://www.renewoureconomy.org/sites/all/themes/pnae/openforbusiness.pdf).

OECD (Organisation for Economic Co-operation and Development). 2012. *OECD Economic Outlook,* Issue 1. Paris. July.

Schmitt, John. 2013. "Why Does the Minimum Wage Have No Discernible Effect on Employment?" Center for Economic and Policy Research. February (http://www.cepr.net/documents/publications/min-wage-2013-02.pdf).

UN (United Nations). 2011. *World Population Prospects, The 2010 Revision.* June.

CHAPTER 2
THE YEAR IN REVIEW AND THE YEARS AHEAD

Aiolfi, Marco, Carlos Capistrán, and Allan Timmermann. 2011. "Forecast Combinations." *The Oxford Handbook of Economic Forecasting,* edited by Michael Clements and David Hendry, pp. 355-388. New York: Oxford University Press.

Attanasio, Orazio, et al. 1999. "Humps and Bumps in Lifetime Consumption." *Journal of Business Economics and Statistics* 17, no. 1: 22–35.

Autor, David H., Lawrence F. Katz, and Alan B. Krueger. 1998. "Computing Inequality: Have Computers Changed the Labor Market?" *Quarterly Journal of Economics* 113, no. 4: 1169–214.

Bachmann, Rudiger. 2011. "Understanding the Jobless Recoveries After 1991 and 2001." Working Paper. University of Michigan. September (http://www.vwlmac.rwth-aachen.de/wpcontent/uploads/bachmann_jlr_2011.pdf).

Baldwin, Richard, ed. 2009. *The Great Trade Collapse: Causes, Consequences and Prospects.* VoxEU.org eBook.

Berger, David. 2011. "Countercyclical Restructuring and Jobless Recoveries." Working Paper. Yale University. November (http://www.crei.cat/conferences/joblessrecoveries/David_Berger_JMP_Nov_16.pdf).

Bernanke, Ben S. 2012a. "Monetary Policy since the Onset of the Crisis." Speech presented at the Federal Reserve Bank of Kansas City Economic Symposium. Jackson Hole, WY. August.

_____. 2012b. "The Economic Recovery and Economic Policy." Speech presented at the New York Economic Club. New York, NY. November.

Blinder, Alan, and Mark Zandi. 2010. "How the Great Recession Was Brought to an End." July (http://www.economy.com/mark-zandi/documents/end-of-great-recession.pdf).

Bloom, Nicholas. 2009. "The Impact of Uncertainty Shocks." *Econometrica* 77, no. 3: 623–85.

Bound, John, and George Johnson. 1992. "Changes in the Structures of Wages in the 1980's: An Evaluation of Alternative Explanations." *American Economic Review* 82, no. 3: 371–92.

BPC (Bipartisan Policy Center). 2012. "Indefensible: The Sequester's Mechanics and Adverse Effects on National and Economic Security." June (http://bipartisanpolicy.org/sites/default/files/BPC%20Sequester%20Paper.pdf).

Bradley, Ralph. 2005. "Analytical Bias Reduction for Small Samples in the US Consumer Price Index." Bureau of Labor Statistics (http://www.bls.gov/osmr/pdf/st050290.pdf).

Bullard, James, and James Feigenbaum. 2007. "A Leisurely Reading of the Life-Cycle Consumption Data." *Journal of Monetary Economics* 54, no. 8: 2305–20.

Campbell, John. 1987. "Does Saving Anticipate Declining Future Labor Income? An Alternative Test of the Permanent Income Hypothesis." *Econometrica* 55, no. 6: 1249–73.

CBO (Congressional Budget Office). 2011. "Trends in the Distribution of Household Income Between 1979 and 2007." October.

_____. 2012a. "Economic Effects of Reducing the Fiscal Restraint That Is Scheduled to Occur in 2013." May.

_____. 2012b. "Estimated Impact of the American Recovery and Reinvestment Act on Employment and Economic Output from July 2012 Through September 2012." November.

_____. 2012c. "The Distribution of Household Income and Federal Taxes, 2008 and 2009." July.

_____. 2012d. "What Accounts for the Slow Growth of the Economy After the Recession?" November.

_____. 2013. "Automatic Reductions in Government Spending--aka Sequestration." February (http://www.cbo.gov/publication/43961).

CEA (Council of Economic Advisers). 1998. *Economic Report of the President.* February.

_____. 2012. *Economic Report of the President.* February.

_____. 2013. "The Economic Impact of the American Recovery and Reinvestment Act of 2009." Ninth Quarterly Report to Congress. February.

Chodorow-Reich, Gabriel, et al. 2012. "Does State Fiscal Relief During Recessions Increase Employment? Evidence from the American Recovery and Reinvestment Act." *American Economic Journal: Economic Policy* 4, no. 3: 118–45.

Chung, Hess, et al. 2012. "Have We Underestimated the Likelihood and Severity of Zero Lower Bound Events?" *Journal of Money, Credit, and Banking* 44, no. 1: 47–82.

Clemen, Robert T. 1989. "Combining Forecasts: A Review and Annotated Bibliography." *International Journal of Forecasting* 5, no. 4: 559-83.

Conley, Timothy G., and Bill Dupor. 2012. "The American Recovery and Reinvestment Act: Solely a Government Jobs Program?" Working Paper. University of Western Ontario and Ohio State University.

DeLong, Bradford J., and Lawrence H. Summers. 2012. "Fiscal Policy in a Depressed Economy." *Brookings Papers on Economic Activity* 44, no. 1. Washington: Brookings Institution.

Dynan, Karen. 2012. "Is a Household Debt Overhang Holding Back Consumption?" *Brookings Papers on Economic Activity* 44, no. 1. Washington: Brookings Institution.

Evans, Thomas D., and Richard B. Tiller. 2012. "Methodology for Seasonally Adjusting National Household Labor Force Series with Revisions for 2012." Bureau of Labor Statistics, U.S. Department of Labor. January.

Federal Reserve Board of Governors. 2011. "Industrial Production and Capacity Utilization: The 2010 Annual Revision." April.

Fernald, John. 2012. "Productivity and Potential Output Before, During and After the Great Recession." Working Paper 2012-18. Federal Reserve Bank of San Francisco. September.

Fernandez-Villaverde, Jesus, and Dirk Krueger. 2007. "Consumption over the Life Cycle: Facts from Consumer Expenditure Data." *Review of Economics and Statistics* 89, no. 3: 552–65.

Feyrer, James, and Bruce Sacerdote. 2011. "Did the Stimulus Stimulate? Real Time Estimates of the Effects of the American Recovery and Reinvestment Act." Working Paper 16759. Cambridge, MA: National Bureau of Economic Research. February.

Friedman, Milton. 1957. *A Theory of the Consumption Function.* Princeton University Press.

Gordon, Robert J. 2010. "Revisiting U.S. Productivity Growth over the Past Century with a View of the Future." Working Paper 15834. Cambridge, MA: National Bureau of Economic Research. March.

Hall, Robert E. 2010. "Why Does the Economy Fall to Pieces After a Financial Crisis?" *Journal of Economic Perspectives* 24, no. 4: 3–20.

———. 2012. "Quantifying the Forces Leading to the Collapse of GDP After the Financial Crisis." Working Paper. Hoover Institution and Stanford University. February.

Houthakker, H. S., and Stephen P. Magee. 1969. "Income and Price Elasticities in World Trade." *Review of Economics and Statistics* 51, no. 2: 111–25.

Hufbauer, Gary C., Ann Elliott, and Jeffrey Shott. 1990. *Economic Sanctions Reconsidered.* Washington, DC: Institute for International Economics.

Institute for Supply Management. 2012. "U.S. Department of Commerce Makes Annual Adjustments to Seasonal Factors for ISM Manufacturing PMI and Diffusion Indexes and ISM Non-Manufacturing NMI and Diffusion Indexes." News Release. January 31 (http://www.ism.ws/about/MediaRoom/newsreleasedetail.cfm?ItemNumber=22165).

Kliesen, Kevin L. 2003. "The 2001 Recession: How Was It Different and What Developments May Have Caused It?" *Federal Reserve Bank of St. Louis Review* 85, no. 5: 23–38.

Krishnamurthy, Arvind, and Annette Vissing-Jorgensen. 2011. "The Effects of Quantitative Easing on Interest Rates: Channels and Implications for Policy." Brookings Papers on Economic Activity 43, no. 2: 215–65. Washington: Brookings Institution.

Kropf, Jurgen, and Nicole Hudson. 2012. "Current Employment Statistics Seasonal Adjustment and the 2007–2009 Recession." *Monthly Labor Review* 135, no. 10: 42–53.

Lektzian, David J., and Christopher M. Sprecher. 2007. "Sanctions, Signals, and Militarized Conflict." *American Journal of Political Science* 51, no. 2: 415–31.

Lettau, Martin, and Sydney Ludvigson. 2003. "Understanding Trend and Cycle in Asset Values: Reevaluating the Wealth Effect on

Consumption." Working Paper 9848. Cambridge, MA: National Bureau of Economic Research. July.

Lutz, Bryon. 2008. "The Connection Between House Price Appreciation and Property Tax Revenues." *National Tax Journal* 61, no. 3: 555–72.

Lutz, Byron, Raven Molloy, and Hui Shan. 2011. "The Housing Crisis and State and Local Government Tax Revenue: Five Channels." *Journal of Regional Science and Urban Economics* 41, no. 4: 306–19.

Macroeconomic Advisers. 2012. "Seasonals, Schmeezonals!" *Macro Focus* 7, no. 1. August.

_____. 2013. "March 1 Sequestration." *Macroeconomic Advisers' Alternative Scenarios* 4, no. 1. February.

Marinov, Nikolay. 2005. "Do Economic Sanctions Destabilize Country Leaders?" *American Journal of Political Science* 49, no. 3: 564–76.

Masnick, George, Daniel McCue, and Eric Belsky. 2010. "Updated 2010–2020 Household and New Home Demand Projections." Working Paper 10-9. Joint Center for Housing Studies, Harvard University. September.

McClelland, Robert, and Marshall Reinsdorf. 1999. "Small Sample Bias in Geometric Mean and Seasoned CPI Component Indexes." Working Paper 324. Bureau of Labor Statistics, U.S. Department of Labor. August.

Mian, Atif R., Kamalesh Rao, and Amir Sufi. 2012. "Household Balance Sheets, Consumption, and the Economic Slump." Working Paper. University of Chicago Booth School.

Moody's Analytics. 2013. "U.S. Macro Outlook: Restarting the Engines." February (http://www.economy.com/dismal/article_free.asp?cid=237408&tid=5FCB4BBF-D759-422D-BD25-BFF7D505D457).

Morgan, T. Clifton, Navin Bapat, and Valentin Krustev. 2009. "The Threat and Imposition of Economic Sanctions, 1971–2000." *Conflict Management and Peace Science* 26, no. 1: 92–110.

OECD (Organisation for Economic Co-operation and Development). 2012. "Labour Losing to Capital: What Explains the Declining Labour Share?" *OECD Employment Outlook 2012*: 109–62. Paris.

Pape, Robert. 1997. "Why Economic Sanctions Do Not Work." *International Security* 22, no. 2: 90–136.

Reinhart, Carmen M., and Kenneth S. Rogoff. 2009. *This Time Is Different: Eight Centuries of Financial Folly.* Princeton University Press.

Reinhart, Carmen M., and Vincent R. Reinhart. 2010. "After the Fall." *Macroeconomic Challenges: The Decade Ahead.* Federal Reserve Bank of Kansas City. August.

Stock, James, and Mark Watson. 2012. "Disentangling the Channels of the 2007–09 Recession." *Brookings Papers on Economic Activity* 44, no. 1. Washington: Brookings Institution.

Wilson, Daniel. 2012. "Fiscal Spending Multipliers: Evidence from the 2009 American Recovery and Reinvestment Act." *American Economic Journal: Economic Policy* 4, no. 3: 251–82.

Woodford, Michael. 2010. "Financial Intermediation and Macroeconomic Analysis." *Journal of Economic Perspectives* 24, no. 4: 21–44.

Yellen, Janet L. 2013. "A Painfully Slow Recovery for America's Workers: Causes, Implications, and the Federal Reserve's Response." Speech delivered at the AFL-CIO. Washington, DC. February.

CHAPTER 3
FISCAL POLICY

Burman, Leonard E. 2012. "Tax Reform and the Tax Treatment of Capital Gains." Testimony before the House Committee on Ways and Means and the Senate Committee on Finance, September 20 (http://www.finance.senate.gov/imo/media/doc/092012%20Burman%20Testimony.pdf).

CBO (Congressional Budget Office). 2011. "The Underfunding of State and Local Pension Plans." May (http://www.cbo.gov/publication/22042).

_____. 2012. "The 2012 Long-Term Budget Outlook." June (http://www.cbo.gov/publication/43288).

_____. 2013. "The Budget and Economic Outlook: Fiscal Years 2013 to 2023." February (http://www.cbo.gov/publication/43907).

CBO/JCT (Congressional Budget Office/Joint Committee on Taxation). 2009. "Subsidizing Infrastructure Investment with Tax-Preferred Bonds." October (http://www.cbo.gov/publication/41359).

CEA (Council of Economic Advisers). 2012. *Economic Report of the President.* Washington, DC: Government Printing Office (http://www.whitehouse.gov/sites/default/files/microsites/ERP_2012_Complete.pdf).

Census Bureau. 2012. "Annual Survey of Public Pensions: State- and Locally-Administered Defined Benefit Data." November (http://www.census.gov/govs/retire/).

Clausing, Kimberly A. 2009. "Multinational Firm Tax Avoidance and Tax Policy." *National Tax Journal* 62, no. 4: 703–25.

Contos, George, et al. Forthcoming. "Tax Compliance Costs for Corporations and Partnerships: A New Look." Proceedings of the 2012 IRS-TPC Research Conference. Washington, DC.

Cronin, Julie-Anne, Portia DeFilippes, and Emily Y. Lin. 2012. "Effects of Adjusting Distribution Tables for Family Size." *National Tax Journal* 65, no. 4: 739–57.

Cronin, Julie-Anne, et al. 2013. "Distributing the Corporate Income Tax: Revised U.S. Treasury Methodology." *National Tax Journal* 66, no. 1: 239–62.

GAO (Government Accountability Office). 2011. "State and Local Governments: Knowledge of Past Recessions Can Inform Future Federal Fiscal Assistance." GAO-11-401. March (http://www.gao.gov/assets/320/317223.pdf).

Greenia, Nick, and Mark Mazur. 2006. "IRS Data, Data Users, and Data Sharing." In *Improving Business Statistics Through Interagency Data Sharing*, edited by Caryn Kuebler and Christopher Mackie, pp. 79–90. Washington, DC: National Academies Press (http://www.nap.edu/openbook.php?record_id=11738&page=79).

Grubert, Harry. 2012. "Foreign Taxes and the Growing Share of U.S. Multinational Company Income Abroad: Profits, Not Sales, Are Being Globalized." *National Tax Journal* 65, no. 2: 247–81.

Hines, James R., Jr., Hilary Hoynes, and Alan B. Krueger. 2001. "Another Look at Whether a Rising Tide Lifts All Boats." In *The Roaring Nineties: Can Full Employment Be Sustained*, edited by Alan B. Krueger and Robert Solow, pp. 493–537. New York: Russell Sage Foundation (http://www.econ.ucdavis.edu/faculty/hoynes/publications/hhk-final.pdf).

Holtzblatt, Janet, and Janet McCubbin. 2004. "Issues Affecting Low-Income Filers." In *The Crisis in Tax Administration*, edited by Henry J. Aaron and Joel Slemrod, pp. 148–200. Washington, DC: Brookings Institution Press.

Hungerford, Thomas L. 2011. "An Analysis of the 'Buffett Rule.'" Congressional Research Service. October (http://digitalcommons.ilr.cornell.edu/cgi/viewcontent.cgi?article=1870&context=key_workplace).

———. 2012. "Taxes and the Economy: An Economic Analysis of the Top Tax Rates Since 1945." Congressional Research Service. September (http://graphics8.nytimes.com/news/business/0915taxesandeconomy.pdf).

IRS (Internal Revenue Service). 2012. *Internal Revenue Service Data Book, 2012.* Washington, DC (http://www.irs.gov/uac/SOI-Tax-Stats-IRS-Data-Book#_returns).

Kopczuk, Wojciech. 2006. "Tax Simplification and Tax Compliance: An Economic Perspective." In *Bridging the Tax Gap: Addressing the Crisis in Federal Tax Administration,* edited by Max B. Sawicky, pp. 111–43. Washington, DC: Economic Policy Institute (http://www.columbia.edu/~wk2110/bin/epi.pdf).

Kopczuk, Wojciech, and Cristian Pop-Eleches. 2007. "Electronic Filing, Tax Preparers, and Participation in the Earned Income Tax Credit." *Journal of Public Economics* 91, no. 7-8: 1351–67.

Lurie, Ithai, and James Pearce. 2012. "A Markov Chain Analysis of Capital Gains Realizations: The Great Recession Versus the 2001 Recession." U.S. Department of the Treasury, Office of Tax Analysis.

McGranahan, Leslie. 1999. "State Budgets and the Business Cycle: Implications for the Federal Balanced Budget Amendment Debate." *Federal Reserve Bank of Chicago Economic Perspectives* 23, no. 3: 2–17 (http://www.chicagofed.org/digital_assets/publications/economic_perspectives/1999/ep3Q99_1.pdf).

Munnell, Alicia H., et al. 2012a. "The Funding of State and Local Pensions: 2011–2015." Issue Brief 24. Center for Retirement Research at Boston College. May (http://crr.bc.edu/wp-content/uploads/2012/05/slp_24.pdf).

Munnell, Alicia H., et al. 2012b. "How Would GASB Proposals Affect State and Local Pension Reporting?" Issue Brief 23. Center for Retirement Research at Boston College. September (http://crr.bc.edu/wp-content/uploads/2011/11/slp_23.pdf).

NASBO (National Assocation of State Budget Officers). 2012a. "The Fiscal Survey of the States." Fall (http://www.nasbo.org/sites/default/files/Fall%202012%20Fiscal%20Survey%20of%20States.pdf).

———. 2012b. "GASB Enacts Pension Accounting Reforms Regarding the Use of Discount Rates." July (http://www.nasbo.org/sites/

default/files/pdf/GASB%20Enacts%20Pension%20Accounting%20
Reforms%20Regarding%20the%20Use%20of%20Discount%20
Rates.pdf).

National League of Cities. 2012. "City Fiscal Conditions in 2012." September
(http://www.nlc.org/Documents/Find%20City%20Solutions/
Research%20Innovation/Finance/city-fiscal-conditions-research-
brief-rpt-sep12.pdf).

Novy-Marx, Robert, and Joshua D. Rauh. 2011. "The Crisis in Local Government Pensions in the United States." In *Growing Old: Paying for
Retirement and Institutional Money Management After the Financial
Crisis*, edited by Richard J. Herring, Robert E. Litan, and Yasuyuki
Fuchita, pp. 47–74. Washington, DC: Brookings Institution Press
(http://www.stanford.edu/~rauh/research/NMRLocal20101011.
pdf).

OECD (Organisation for Economic Co-operation and Development). 2008.
"Tax Effects on Foreign Direct Investment: Recent Evidence and
Policy Analysis." OECD Tax Policy Studies 17. Paris (http://www.
oecd.org/ctp/taxpolicyanalysis/taxpolicystudyno17taxeffectsonfor-
eigndirectinvestmentrecentevidenceandpolicyanalysis.htm).

OMB (Office of Management and Budget). 2011. "Living Within Our
Means and Investing in the Future: The President's Plan for
Economic Growth and Deficit Reduction." September (http://www.
whitehouse.gov/sites/default/files/omb/budget/fy2012/assets/joint-
committeereport.pdf).

_____. 2012a. "Analytical Perspectives, Budget of the United States Govern-
ment, Fiscal Year 2013" (http://www.whitehouse.gov/sites/default/
files/omb/budget/fy2013/assets/spec.pdf).

_____. 2012b. "Historical Tables, Budget of the United States Govern-
ment, Fiscal Year 2013" (http://www.whitehouse.gov/omb/budget/
Historicals).

Pew Center on the States. 2012. "The Widening Gap Update." Washington.
June (http://www.pewstates.org/uploadedFiles/PCS_Assets/2012/
Pew_Pensions_Update.pdf).

Piketty, Thomas, and Emmanuel Saez. 2007. "How Progressive Is the U.S.
Federal Tax System? A Historical and International Perspective."
Journal of Economic Perspectives 21, no. 1: 3–24.

Pilot, Adrienne. 2011. "Data Synchronization: Leveraging Existing Business Data to Better Measure the Economy." *Amstat News*,

November 1 (http://magazine.amstat.org/blog/2011/11/01/data-synchronizationscipolicy/).

Saez, Emmanuel, Joel Slemrod, and Seth H. Giertz. 2012. "The Elasticity of Taxable Income with Respect to Marginal Tax Rates: A Critical Review." *Journal of Economic Literature* 50, no. 1: 3–50 (http://elsa.berkeley.edu/~saez/saez-slemrod-giertzJEL12.pdf).

Smith, Adam. 1776. *An Inquiry into the Nature and Causes of the Wealth of Nations.* (Elecronic version: http://www2.hn.psu.edu/faculty/jmanis/adam-smith/wealth-nations.pdf).

Wang, Wen, Yilin Hou, and William D. Duncombe. 2007. "Determinants of Pay-as-You-Go Financing of Capital Projects: Evidence from the States." *Public Budgeting & Finance* 27, no. 4: 18–42.

White House/Treasury (The White House/Department of the Treasury). 2012. "The President's Framework for Business Tax Reform." February (http://www.treasury.gov/resource-center/tax-policy/Documents/The-Presidents-Framework-for-Business-Tax-Reform-02-22-2012.pdf).

Wilson, Janette, and Pearson Liddell. 2010. "Sales of Capital Assets Reported on Individual Tax Returns, 2007." *Statistics of Income Bulletin* 29, no. 3: 75–104 (http://www.irs.gov/pub/irs-soi/10winbulcapitalassets.pdf).

CHAPTER 4
JOBS, WORKERS, AND SKILLS

Aaronson, Daniel, Kyung-Hong Park, and Daniel Sullivan. 2007. "Explaining the Decline in Teen Labor Force Participation." *Chicago Fed Letter* 234. Federal Reserve Bank of Chicago.

Acemoglu, Daron, and David Autor. 2011. "Skills, Tasks, and Technologies: Implications for Employment and Earnings." In *Handbook of Labor Economics* 4B, edited by Orley Ashenfelter and David Card, pp. 1043–171. London: Elsevier.

Almond, Douglas, and Janet Currie. 2011. "Human Capital Development Before Age Five." In *Handbook of Labor Economics* 4B, edited by Orley Ashenfelter and David Card, pp. 1315–486. London: Elsevier.

Anderson, Stuart, and Michaela Platzer. 2006. "American Made: The Impact of Immigrant Entrepreneurs and Professionals on U.S. Competitiveness." Arlington, VA: National Venture Capital Association.

Bardasi, Elena, and Janet C. Gornick. 2008. "Working for Less? Women's Part-Time Wage Penalties Across Countries." *Feminist Economist* 14, no. 1: 37–72.

Baum, Sandy, and Patricia Steele. 2010. "Who Borrows Most? Bachelor's Degree Recipients with High Levels of Student Debt." New York: College Board Advocacy & Policy Center, Trends in Higher Education Series.

Bertrand, Marianne, Claudia Goldin, and Lawrence F. Katz. 2010. "Dynamics of the Gender Gap for Young Professionals in the Financial and Corporate Sectors." *American Economic Journal: Applied Economics* 2, no. 3: 228–55.

Blank, Rebecca M. 2002. "Evaluating Welfare Reform in the United States." *Journal of Economic Literature* 40, no. 4: 1105–166.

Blank, Rebecca M., and Gary T. Burtless. 1990. "Are Part-Time Jobs Bad? A Future of Lousy Jobs? The Changing Structure of U.S. Wages." Washington: Brookings Institute.

Blau, David M., and Ryan M. Goodstein. 2010. "Can Social Security Explain Trends in Labor Force Participation of Older Men in the United States." *Journal of Human Resources* 45, no. 2: 328–63.

Blau, Francine D., and Lawrence M. Kahn. 2003. "Understanding International Differences in the Gender Pay Gap." *Journal of Labor Economics* 21, no. 1: 106–44.

_____. 2013. "Female Labor Supply: Why Is the US Falling Behind." Working Paper 18702. Cambridge, MA: National Bureau of Economic Research.

BLS (Bureau of Labor Statistics). 2011. "Labor Force Statistics from the Current Population Survey: March Supplement." U.S. Department of Labor.

Borjas, George J. 2003. "The Labor Demand Curve *Is* Downward Sloping: Reexamining the Impact of Immigration on the Labor Market." *Quarterly Journal of Economics* 118, no. 4: 1335–374.

_____. 2007. "Do Foreign Students Crowd Out Native Students from Graduate Programs?" In *Science and the University*, edited by Paula E. Stephan, and Ronald G. Ehrenberg. Madison:University of Wisconsin Press.

Borjas, George J., Jeffrey Grogger, and Gordon H. Hanson. 2011. "Substitution Between Immigrants, Natives, and Skill Groups." Working

Paper 17461. Cambridge, MA: National Bureau of Economic Research.

Bowen, William G., Matthew M. Chingos, Kelly A. Lack and Thomas I. Nygren. 2012. "Interactive Learning Online at Public Universities: Evidence from Randomized Trials." New York: Ithaka S + R.

Card, David. 1990. "The Impact of the Mariel Boatlift on the Miami Labor Market." *Industrial Labor Relations Review* 43, no. 2: 245-57.

———. 1992. "Do Minimum Wages Reduce Employment? A Case Study of California, 1987-89." *Industrial and Labor Relations Review* 46, no. 1: 38–54.

———. 2009. "Immigration and Inequality." *American Economic Review* 99, no. 2: 1–21.

Card, David, and Alan B. Krueger. 1994. "Minimum Wages and Employment: A Case Study of the Fast-Food Industry in New Jersey and Pennsylvania." *American Economic Review* 84, no 4: 772–93.

CBO (Congressional Budget Office). 2007. "Cost Estimate: Senate Amendment 1150 to S. 1348, the Comprehensive Immigration Reform Act of 2007."

———. 2010. "Costs and Policy Options for Federal Student Loan Program."

CEA (Council of Economic Advisers). 2010. "Work-Life Balance and the Economics of Workplace Flexibility."

College Board. 2010. "Trends in College Pricing." Trends in Higher Education Series. New York.

Cortes, Patricia. 2008. "The Effect of Low-Skilled Immigration on U.S. Prices: Evidence from CPI Data." *Journal of Political Economy* 116, no. 3: 381–421.

Cunha, Flavio, and James J. Heckman. 2008. "Formulating, Identifying, and Estimating the Technology for the Formation of Skills." *Journal of Human Resources* 43, no. 4: 738–82.

Cunha, Flavio, James J. Heckman, and Susanne M. Schennach. 2010. "Estimating the Technology of Cognitive and Noncognitive Skill Formation." *Econometrica* 78, no. 3: 883–931.

Deming, David, Claudia Goldin, and Lawrence F. Katz. 2012. "The For-Profit Postsecondary School Sector: Nimble Critters or Agile Predators?" *Journal of Economic Perspectives* 26, no. 1: 139–64.

Department of Education. 2012. "First Official Three Year Student Loan Default Rates Published." September (http://www.ed.gov/news/press-releases/first-official-three-year-student-loan-default-rates-published).

DHS (Department of Homeland Security). 2011. "2011 Yearbook of Immigration Statistics."

Doucouliagos, Hristos, and T. D. Stanley. 2009. "Publication Selection Bias in Minimum-Wage Research? A Meta-Regression Analysis." *British Journal of Industrial Relations* 47, no. 2: 406–28.

Dube, Arindrajit, T. William Lester, and Michael Reich. 2010. "Minimum Wage Effects Across State Borders: Estimates using Contiguous Counties." *Review of Economics and Statistics* 92, no. 4: 945–64

Duleep, Harriet O., and Mark C. Regets. 1996. "Family Unification, Siblings, and Skills." In *Immigrants and Immigration Policy: Individual Skills, Family Ties, and Group Identities,* edited by Harriet Duleep and Phanindra Wunnava, pp. 219–44. Greenwich, CT: JAI Press.

Ehrenberg, Ronald G. 2012. "American Higher Education in Transition." *Journal of Economic Perspectives* 26, no. 1: 193–216.

Eissa, Nada, and Jeffrey B. Liebman. 1996. "Labor Supply to the Earned Income Tax Credit." *Quarterly Journal of Economics* 111, no. 2: 605–37.

Fairlie, Robert W. 2012. "Immigrant Entrepreneurs and Small Business Owners, and Their Access to Financial Capital." Small Business Administration, Office of Advocacy.

Figlio, David N., Mark Rush, and Lu Yin. 2010. "Is It Live or Is It Internet? Experimental Estimates of the Effect of Online Instruction on Student Learning." Working Paper 16089. Cambridge, MA: National Bureau of Economic Research.

Friedberg, Rachel M. and Jennifer Hunt. 1995. "The Impact of Immigrants on Host Country Wages, Employment and Growth." *Journal of Economic Perspectives* 9, no. 2: 23–44.

Gauthier-Loiselle, Marjolaine, and Jennifer Hunt. 2010. "How Much Does Immigration Boost Innovation?" *American Economic Journal: Macroeconomics* 2, no. 2: 31–56.

Goldin, Claudia, and Lawrence F. Katz. 2011. "The Cost of Workplace Flexibility for High-Powered Professionals." *Annals of the American Academy of Political and Social Science* 638, no. 1: 45–67.

_____. 2012. "The Most Egalitarian of All Professions: Pharmacy and the Evolution of a Family-Friendly Occupation." Working Paper 18410. Cambridge, MA: National Bureau of Economic Research.

Grogger, Jeffrey. 2003. "The Effects of Time Limits, the EITC, and Other Policy Changes on Welfare Use, Work, and Income Among Female-Headed Families." *Review of Economics and Statistics* 85, no. 2: 394–408.

Hoefer, Michael, Nancy Rytina, and Bryan Baker. 2012. "Estimates of the Unauthorized Immigrant Population Residing in the United States: January 2011." Department of Homeland Security, Office of Immigration Statistics.

Holzer, Harry J. 2011. "Raising Job Quality and Skills for American Workers: Creating More-Effective Education and Workforce Development Systems in the States." Discussion Paper 2011-10. Washington: The Hamilton Project.

Jasso, Guillermina, and Mark R. Rosenzweig. 2008. "Selection Criteria and the Skill Composition of Immigrants: A Comparative Analysis of Australian and U.S. Employment Immigration." IZA Discussion Paper. Bonn: Institute for the Study of Labor. June (http://www.iza.org/en/webcontent/publications/papers/viewAbstract?dp_id=356).

Kerr, William R., and William F. Lincoln. 2009. "The Supply Side of Innovation: H-1B Visa Reforms and US Ethnic Invention." Working Paper 09-005. Harvard Business School.

Kochan, Thomas, David Finegold, and Paul Osterman. 2012 "Who Can Fix the 'Middle-Skills' Gap?" *Harvard Business Review*. December.

Lalonde, Robert J., and Robert H. Topel. 1991. "Labor Market Adjustments to Increased Immigration." *Journal of the European Economic Association* 10, no. 1: 152–97.

Lang, Kevin, and Russell Weinstein. 2012. "Evaluating Student Outcomes at For-Profit Colleges." Working Paper 18201. Cambridge, MA: National Bureau of Economic Research.

Langdon, David, George McKittrick, David Beede, Beethika Kahn, and Mark Doms. 2011. "STEM: Good Jobs Now and for the Future." U.S. Department of Commerce, Economics and Statistics Administration.

Maestas, Nicole, and Julie Zissimopoulos. 2010. "How Longer Work Lives Ease the Crunch of Population Aging." *Journal of Economic Perspectives* 23, no. 1: 39–60.

Maguire, Sheila, Joshua Freely, Carol Clymer, Maureen Conway and Deena Schwartz. 2010. "Tuning In to Local Labor Markets." Oakland, CA: Public/Private Ventures (http://www2.oaklandnet.com/oakca/groups/ceda/documents/report/dowd021455.pdf).

Manning, Alan, and Barbara Petrongolo. 2008. "The Part-Time Pay Penalty for Women in Britain." *Economic Journal* 118, no. 526: 29–51.

Meissner, Doris, Donald M. Kerwin, Muzaffar Chishti, and Clarie Bergeron. 2013. "Immigration Enforcement in the United States: The Rise of a Formidable Machinery." Washington: Migration Policy Institute.

Meyer, Bruce D., and Dan T. Rosenbaum. 2001. "Welfare, the Earned Income Tax Credit, and the Labor Supply of Single Mothers." *Quarterly Journal of Economics* 116, no. 3: 1063–114.

Moffitt, Robert A. 2003. "The Temporary Assistance for Needy Families Program." In *Means-Tested Transfer Programs in the United States*, edited by Robert A. Moffit. pp. 291–363. Chicago: University of Chicago Press.

_____. 2012. "The U.S. Employment-Population Reversal in the 2000s: Facts and Explanations." Washington: Brookings Institute.

NRC (National Research Council). 1997. "The New Americans: Economic, Demographic, and Fiscal Effects of Immigration." Washington: National Academies Press.

NSF/NIH (National Science Foundation/National Institute of Health). 2010. "Survey of Graduate Students and Post Doctorates in Science and Engineering."

National Science Foundation/National Center for Science and Engineering Statistics. 2010. "National Survey of College Graduates."

OECD (Organisation for Economic Co-operation and Development). 2012a. "Gender Gap Report 2012." Paris (http://www3.weforum.org/docs/WEF_GenderGap_Report_2012.pdf).

_____. 2012b. "Education at a Glance 2012." Paris. (http://dx.doi.org/10.1787/eag-2012-en.)

Ottaviano, Gianmarco I.P., and Giovanni Peri. 2012 "Rethinking the Effect of Immigration on Wages." *Journal of the European Economic Association* 10, no. 1: 152–97.

Passel, Jeffrey S., and Mark Hugo Lopez. 2012. "Up to 1.7 Million Unauthorized Immigrant Youth May Benefit from New Deportation Rules." Washington: Pew Hispanic Center.

Peri, Giovanni. 2012. "The Effect of Immigration on Productivity: Evidence from U.S. States." *Review of Economics and Statistics* 94, no. 1: 348–58.

Peri, Giovanni, and Chad Sparber. 2009. "Task Specialization, Immigration and Wages." *American Economic Journal: Applied Economics* 1, no. 3: 135–69

Rossin-Slater, Maya, Christopher J. Ruhm, and Jane Waldfogel. 2011. "The Effects of California's Paid Family Leave Program on Mothers' Leave-Taking and Subsequent Labor Market Outcomes." Working Paper 17715. Cambridge, MA: National Bureau of Economic Research.

Schmitt, John. 2013. "Why Does the Minimum Wage Have No Discernible Effect on Employment?" Center for Economic and Policy Research. February (http://www.cepr.net/documents/publications/min-wage-2013-02.pdf).

Singer, Audrey. 2012. "Immigrant Workers in the U.S. Labor Force." Washington, DC: Brookings Institution.

Smith, Christopher L. 2011. "Polarization, Immigration, Education: What's Behind the Dramatic Decline in Youth Employment?" Working Paper 2011-41. Federal Reserve Board.

Toossi, Mitra. 2012. "Labor Force Projections to 2020: A More Slowly Growing Workforce." *Monthly Labor Review* 135, no: 1: 43–65.

Wadhwa, Vivek, AnnaLee Saxenian, Ben A. Rissing, and Gary Gereffi. 2007. "America's New Immigrant Entrepreneurs: Part I." Duke Science, Technology & Innovation Paper 23.

Wasmer, Etienne, Peter Fredriksson, Ana Lamo, Julián Messina, and Giovanni Peri. 2007. "The Macroeconomics of Education in Europe." In *Education and Training in Europe,* edited by G. Brunello, P. Garibaldi, and E. Wasmer, pp. 1–20. New York: Oxford University Press.

Wellington, Allison J. 1991. "Effects of the Minimum Wage on Employment Status of Youths. An Update." *Journal of Human Resources* 26, no. 1: 27–46.

Chapter 5
Reducing Costs and Improving the Quality of Health Care

Abdulkadiroglu, Atila, Parag A. Pathak, and Alvin E. Roth. 2005. "The New York City High School Match." *American Economic Review* 95, no. 2: 364–67.

Aizcorbe, Ana M., Bonnie A. Retus, and Shelly Smith. "Toward a Health Care Satellite Account." 2008. Bureau of Economic Analysis, U.S. Department of Commerce.

Aizcorbe, Ana, Eli B. Liebman, David M. Cutler, and Allison B. Rosen. 2012. "Household Consumption Expenditures for Medical Care: An Alternate Presentation." Bureau of Economic Analysis, U.S. Department of Commerce.

Baicker, Katherine, and Amitabh Chandra. 2005. "The Consequences of the Growth in Health Insurance Premiums." *American Economic Review* 95, no. 2: 214–18.

Baumol, William J., and William G. Bowen. 1966. *Performing Arts: The Economic Dilemma*. New York: Twentieth Century Fund.

BEA (Bureau of Economic Analysis). 2013. "Health Care Satellite Account." U.S. Department of Commerce (http://www.bea.gov/national/health_care_satellite_account.htm).

Berwick, Donald M., and Andrew D. Hackbarth. 2012. "Eliminating Waste in US Health Care." American Medical Association (http://www.hta.hca.wa.gov/documents/Waste_in_Healthcare_JAMA_2012.pdf).

Bradley, Ralph, et al. "Producing Disease-based Price Indexes." 2010. *Monthly Labor Review* 133, no. 2: 20–28.

Buettgens, Matthew, Bowen Garrett, and John Holahan. 2010. "America Under the Affordable Care Act." Washington: Urban Institute.

Carter, M. Grace, Melinda Beeuwkes Buntin, Orla Hayden, Susan M. Paddock, Daniel A. Relles, Greg Ridgeway, Mark E. Totten, Barbara O. Wynn. 2002. "Analyses for the Initial Implementation of the Inpatient Rehabilitation Facility Prospective Payment System." Santa Monica, CA: RAND Corporation.

CBO (Congressional Budget Office). 2012a. "The Distribution of Household Income and Federal Taxes, 2008 and 2009." July.

_____. 2012b. "Estimates for the Insurance Coverage Provisions of the Affordable Care Act Updated for the Recent Supreme Court Decision."

_____. 2013. "The Budget and Economic Outlook: Fiscal Years 2013 to 2023."

CEA (Council of Economic Advisers). 2012. *Economic Report of the President.* February.

CMS (Center for Medicare and Medicaid Services). 2012. "National Health Expenditure Projections, 2011–2012." January.

Cutler, David M. 1995. "The Incidence of Adverse Medical Outcomes Under Prospective Payment." *Econometrica* 63, no. 1: 29–50.

Cutler, David M., and Mark McClellan. 2001. "Is Technological Change in Medicine Worth It?" *Health Affairs* 20, no. 5: 11–29.

Cutler, David M., and Sarah Reber. 1998. "Paying for Health Insurance: The Tradeoff Between Competition and Adverse Selection." *Quarterly Journal of Economics* 113, no. 2: 433-66.

Dafny, Leemore. 2005. "Games Hospitals Play: Entry Deterrence in Hospital Procedure Markets." *Journal of Economics and Management Strategy* 14, no 3: 513–42.

Eibner, Christine, et al. 2011. "Employer Self-Insurance Decisions and the Implications of the Patient Protection and Affordable Care Act as Modified by the Health Care and Education Reconciliation Act of 2010 (ACA)." Santa Monica, CA: RAND Corporation.

Encinosa, William, and Didem Bernard. 2005. "Hospital Finances and Patient Safety Outcomes." *Inquiry* 42, no. 1: 60–72.

Finkelstein, Amy, et al. 2011. "The Oregon Health Insurance Experiment: Evidence from the First Year." Working Paper 17190. Cambridge, MA: National Bureau of Economic Research.

Fisher, Elliott S., and Jonathan S. Skinner. 2010. "Reflections on Geographic Variations in U.S. Health Care." Hanover, NH: Dartmouth Institute for Health Policy and Clinical Practice.

Foster, Richard S. 2010. "Estimated Financial Effects of the 'Patent Protection and Affordable Care Act." Center for Medicare & Medicare Services, Department of Health & Human Services.

Gale, David, and Lloyd Sharpley. 1962. "College Admissions and the Stability of Marriage." *American Mathematical Monthly* 69, no. 1: 9–15.

Goldman, Dana P., and Elizabeth A. McGlynn. 2005. "U.S. Health Care: Facts About Costs, Access, and Quality." Santa Monica, CA: RAND Corporation.

Gruber, Jonathan. 1994. "The Incidence of Mandated Maternity Benefits." *American Economic Review* 84, no. 3: 622-41.

Hall, Robert, and Chad Jones. 2007. "The Value of Life and the Rise in Health Spending." *Quarterly Journal of Economics* 122, no. 1: 39–72.

Healthcare.gov. 2013. "New Tools to Fight Fraud, Strengthen Federal and Private Health Programs, and Protect Consumer and Taxpayer Dollars." Department of Health and Human Services. (http://www.healthcare.gov/news/factsheets/2011/03/fraud03152011a.html).

HCCI (Health Care Cost Institute). 2012. "Health Care Cost and Utilization Report: 2011." Washington: Health Care Cost Institute.

Health Resources and Services Administration. 2011. "OPTN/SRTR 2011 Annual Data Report: Kidney" (http://srtr.transplant.hrsa.gov/annual_reports/2011/pdf/01_kidney_12.pdf).

HHS (U.S. Department of Health and Human Services). 2012. "The 80/20 Rule: Providing Value and Rebates to Millions of Consumers." June (http://www.healthcare.gov/news/reports/mlr-rebates06212012a.html).

Kronick, Richard, and Rosa Po. 2013. "Growth in Medicare Spending per Beneficiary Continues to Hit Historic Lows." Office of The Assistant Secretary for Planning and Evaluation, Department of Health and Human Services.

Lee, David, and Frank Levy. 2012 "The Sharp Slowdown in Growth of Medical Imaging: An Early Analysis Suggests Combination of Policies Was the Cause." *Health Affairs* 31, no. 8: 1-9.

Lewin Group. 2010. "Patent Protection and Affordable care Act (PPACA): Long Term Costs for Governments, Employers, Families and Providers." Staff Working Paper no. 11.

Long, Sharon K., Karen Stockley, and Alshadye Yemane. 2009. "Another Look at the Impacts of Health Reform in Massachusetts: Evidence Using New Data and a Stronger Model." *American Economic Review* 99, no. 2: 508–11.

Medicare Trustees (Board of Trustees of the Federal Hospital Insurance and Federal Supplementary Medical Insurance Trust Funds). 2012. "2012 Annual Report of the Board of Trustees of the Federal

Hospital Insurance and Federal Supplementary Medical Insurance Trust Funds." Washington, DC (http://www.cms.gov/Research-Statistics-Data-and-Systems/Statistics-Trends-and-Reports/ReportsTrustFunds/downloads/tr2012.pdf).

Murphy, Kevin M., and Robert H. Topel. 2006. "The Value of Health and Longevity." *Journal of Political Economy* 114, no. 5: 871–904.

National Kidney Registry. 2009. "Kidney Transplants Facilitated by a National Registry Can Save $100 Billion in U.S. Healthcare Costs." White Paper. Babylon, NY.

Nordhaus, William D. 2006. "Baumol's Disease: A Macroeconomic Perspective." *Contribution to Macroeconomics* 8, no. 1: 1382-382

OECD (Organisation for Economic Co-operation and Development). 2012 "How Does the United States Compare." OECD Health Data 2012. Paris (http://www.oecd.org/unitedstates/BriefingNoteUSA2012.pdf).

Philipson, Tomas, Michael Eber, Darius N. Lakdawalla, Mitra Corral, Rena Conti, and Dana P. Goldman. 2012. "An Analysis of Whether High Health Care Spending in the United States Versus Europe Is 'Worth It' in the Case of Cancer." *Health Affairs* 31, no. 4: 667-75.

Roth, Alvin E. 1984. "The Evolution of the Labor Market for Medical Interns and Residents: A Case Study in Game Theory." *Journal of Political Economy*, no. 6: 991–1016.

Seshamani, Meena, J. Sanford Schwartz, and Kevin G. Volpp. 2006. "The Effect of Cuts in Medicare Reimbursement on Hospital Mortality." *Health Services Research* 41, no. 3: 683–700.

Skinner, Jonathan, and Douglas Staiger. 2005. "Technology Adoption From Hybrid Corn to Beta Blockers," National Bureau of Economic Research Working Papers 11251.

Skinner, Jonathan, and Douglas Staiger. 2009. "Technology Diffusion and Productivity Growth in Health Care." Working Paper 14865. Cambridge, MA: National Bureau of Economic Research. April.

Skinner, Jonathan, Douglas Staiger, and Elliott Fisher. 2006. "Is Technological Change in Medicine Always Worth It? The Case Of Acute Myocardial Infarction." *Health Affairs* 25, no. 2: w34–47.

Skinner, Jonathan, Elliott Fisher, and John E. Wennberg. 2005. "The Efficiency of Medicare." In *Analyses in the Economics of Aging*, edited by D. A. Wise, pp. 129-60. Chicago, IL: University of Chicago Press.

Sloan, F., M. Morrisey, and J. Valvona. 1988. "Effects of the Medicare Prospective Payment System on Hospital Cost Containment: An Early Appraisal." *Milbank Quarterly* 66, no. 2: 191–220.

Smith, Sheila, Joseph P. Newhouse, and Mark S. Freeland. 2009. "Income, Insurance, and Technology: Why Does Health Spending Outpace Economic Growth?" *Health Affairs* 28, no. 5: 1276-284.

Social Security Trustees (Board of Trustees of the Federal Old-Age and Survivors Insurance and Federal Disability Insurance Trust Funds). 2012. "The 2012 Annual Report of the Board of Trustees of the Federal Old-Age and Survivors Insurance and Federal Disability Insurance Trust Funds." Washington, DC (http://www.ssa.gov/oact/TR/2012/tr2012.pdf).

Sommers, Benjamin D. 2012. "Number of Young Adults Gaining Insurance due to the Affordable Care Act Now Tops 3 Million." Assistant Secretary for Planning and Evaluation, U.S. Department of Health and Human Services. June (http://aspe.hhs.gov/aspe/gaininginsurance/rb.shtml).

U.S. Census Bureau. 2012. "Projections of the Population by Selected Age Groups and Sex for the United States: 2015 to 2060."

_____. 2012. "State & County QuickFacts."

USRDS (United States Renal Data System). 2011. "Costs of ESRD." Annual Data Report, ch. 11.

Viscusi, W. Kip, and Joseph E Aldy. 2003. "The Value of a Statistical Life: A Critical Review of Market Estimates Throughout the World." *Journal of Risk and Uncertainty* 27, no. 1: 5-76.

White, C. 2008. "Why Did Medicare Spending Growth Slow Down?" *Health Affairs* 27, no. 3: 793–802.

Chapter 6
Climate Change and the Path Toward Sustainable Energy Sources

Arctic Monitoring and Assessment Programme. 2011. *Snow, Water, Ice and Permafrost in the Arctic (SWIPA)*. Cambridge University Press.

BEA (Bureau of Economic Analysis). 2012. National Income and Product Accounts. U.S. Department of Commerce (http://www.bea.gov/iTable/index_nipa.cfm).

Brainard, William. 1967. "Uncertainty and the Effectiveness of Monetary Policy." American Economic Review 57, no. 2: 411–25.

DOE (U.S. Department of Energy). 2012a. "Electricity Delivery and Energy Reliability Smart Grid Investment Grant Program, Progress Report." July.

———. 2012b. "2011 Wind Technologies Market Report." August (http://www1.eere.energy.gov/wind/pdfs/2011_wind_technologies_market_report.pdf).

EIA (U.S. Energy Information Administration). 2005. "Annual Energy Outlook." February. (http://www.eia.gov/forecasts/archive/aeo05/pdf/0383(2005).pdf)

———. 2012a. "Annual Energy Review 2011." September. (http://www.eia.gov/totalenergy/data/annual/pdf/aer.pdf).

———. 2012b. "Annual Energy Outlook 2013: Early Release Overview." December. (http://www.eia.gov/forecasts/aeo/er/index.cfm).

———. 2012c. International Energy Statistics. (http://www.eia.gov/cfapps/ipdbproject/IEDIndex3.cfm#).

———. 2013a. "Monthly Energy Review January 2013" (http://www.eia.gov/totalenergy/data/monthly/pdf/mer.pdf).

———. 2013b. "Electric Power Monthly December 2012" (http://www.eia.gov/electricity/monthly/pdf/epm.pdf).

EPA (U.S. Environmental Protection Agency). 2010a. "Inventory of U.S. Greenhouse Gas Emissions and Sinks: 1990-2010." April (http://www.epa.gov/climatechange/ghgemissions/usinventoryreport.html).

———. 2010b. "Final Rulemaking to Establish Light-Duty Vehicle Greenhouse Gas Emission Standards and Corporate Average Fuel Economy Standards." April (http://www.epa.gov/otaq/climate/regulations/420r10009.pdf).

Funke, Michael, and Michael Paetz. 2011. "Environmental Policy Under Model Uncertainty: A Robust Optimal Control Approach." Climatic Change 107, no. 3: 225–39.

Giannoni, Marc P. 2002. "Does Model Uncertainty Justify Caution? Robust Optimal Monetary Policy in a Forward-Looking Model." Macroeconomic Dynamics 6, no. 1: 111–44.

Gillingham, Kenneth, et al. 2013. "The Rebound Effect Is Overplayed." Nature 493: 475–76. January.

Greening, Lorna A., David L. Greene, and Carmen Difiglio. 2000. "Energy Efficiency and Consumption—The Rebound Effect—A Survey." *Energy Policy* 28, no. 6–7: 389–401.

Greenstone, Michael, Elizabeth Kopits, and Ann Wolverton. 2013. "Developing a Social Cost of Carbon for US Regulatory Analysis: A Methodology and Interpretation." *Review of Environmental Economics and Policy* 7, no. 1: 23–46.

Hansen, James, Makiko Sato, and Reto Ruedy. 2012. "Perception of Climate Change." *Proceedings of the National Academy of Sciences* 109, no. 37: 14726-7.

Hansen, Lars P., and Thomas J. Sargent. 2001. "Robust Control and Model Uncertainty." *American Economic Review* 91, no. 2: 60–66.

_____. 2007. "Robustness". Princeton University Press.

Helper, Susan, Timothy Krueger, and Howard Wial. 2012. "Why Does Manufacturing Matter? Which Manufacturing Matters? A Policy Framework." Brookings Metropolitan Policy Program. Washington, DC: Brookings Institution.

Houser, Trevon, and Shashank Mohan. Forthcoming. "Fueling Up: The Economic and Environmental Implications of the American Oil and Gas Boom." Washington, DC: Peterson Institute for International Economics.

IPCC (Intergovernmental Panel on Climate Change). 2007. "Contribution of Working Groups I, II, and III to the Fourth Assessment Report of the Intergovernmental Panel on Climate Change," edited by R. K. Pauchari and A. Reisinger. Geneva.

_____. 2012. "Managing the Risks of Extreme Events and Disasters to Advance Climate Change Adaptation." In *Special Report of the Intergovernmental Panel on Climate Change*, edited by C. Field et al. Cambridge University Press.

Kossin, J. P., et al. 2007. "A Globally Consistent Reanalysis of Hurricane Variability and Trends." *Geophysical Research Letters* 34.

Logan, Jeffrey, et al. 2012. "Natural Gas and the Transformation of the U.S. Energy Sector: Electricity." NREL/TP-6A50-55538. Golden, CO: National Renewable Energy Laboratory for the Joint Institute for Strategic Energy Analysis.

Mendelsohn, Robert, Kerry Emanuel, Shun Chonabayashi and Laura Bakkensen. 2012. "The Impact of Climate Change on Global

Tropical Cyclone Damage." *Nature Climate Change* 2: 205-209 (doi:10.1038/nclimate1357).

Munich Reinsurance Company. 2012. "Costliest Natural Disasters: Insured Loses." NatCat Service (http://www.munichre.com/en/reinsurance/business/non-life/georisks/natcatservice/significant_natural_catastrophes.aspx).

Narita, Daiju, Richard S.J. Tol, and David Anthoff. 2009. "Damage Cost of Climate Change through Intensification of Tropical Cyclone Activities: An Application of FUND." *Climate Research* 39: 87-97.

NOAA (National Oceanic and Atmospheric Administration). 2012. "Global Sea Level Rise Scenarios for the United States National Climate Assessment." NOAA Tech Memo OAR CPO.

Nordhaus, William. 2010. "Economic Aspects of Global Warming in a Post-Copenhagen Environment." Yale University.

Onatski, Alexei, and James H. Stock. 2002. "Robust Monetary Policy Under Model Uncertainty in a Small Model of the U.S. Economy." *Macroeconomic Dynamics* 6, no. 1: 85–110.

Pielke, Roger A. 2007. "Future Economic Damage from Tropical Cyclones: Sensitivities to Societal and Climate Change." *Philosophical Transactions of the Royal Society.* doi:10.1098/rsta.2007.2086.

Rhines, A., and P. Huybers. 2013. "Frequent Summer Temperature Extremes Reflect Changes in the Mean, Not the Variance." *Proceedings of the National Academy of Sciences110, no.7: E546.* doi:10.1073/pnas.1218748110.

Roe, Gerald H., and Marcia B. Baker. 2007. "Why Is Climate Sensitivity So Unpredictable?" *Science* 318: 629–32.

Rohling, E. J., et al. 2012. "Making Sense of Palaeoclimate Sensitivity." *Nature 491: 683–91.*

Small, Kenneth A., and Kurt Van Dender. 2007. "Fuel Efficiency and Motor Vehicle Travel: The Declining Rebound Effect." *Energy Journal 28, no. 1: 25–51.*

Stern, Nicholas. 2006. *The Stern Review: The Economic Effects of Climate Change.* Cambridge University Press.

USGCRP (United States Global Change Research Program). 2009. *Global Climate Change Impacts in the United States,* edited by Thomas R. Karl, Jerry M. Melillo, and Thomas C. Peterson. Cambridge University Press.

Weitzman, Martin L. 2009. "On Modeling and Interpreting the Economics of Catastrophic Climate Change." *Review of Economics and Statistics* 91, no. 1: 1–19.

_____. 2011. "Fat-Tailed Uncertainty in the Economics of Catastrophic Climate Change." *Review of Environmental Economics and Policy* 5, no. 2: 275–92.

White House. 2010. "Technical Support Document: Social Cost of Carbon for Regulatory Impact Analysis Under Executive Order 12866." February (http://www.whitehouse.gov/sites/default/files/omb/inforeg/for-agencies/Social-Cost-of-Carbon-for-RIA.pdf).

_____. 2011a. "Driving Efficiency: Cutting Costs for Families at the Pump and Slashing Dependence on Oil." July (http://whitehouse.gov/sites/default/files/fuel_economy_report.pdf).

_____. 2011b. "A Policy Framework for the 21st Century Grid: Enabling Our Secure Energy Future." June. (http://www.whitehouse.gov/sites/default/files/microsites/ostp/nstc-smart-grid-june2011.pdf).

Chapter 7
International Trade and Competitiveness

Amiti, Mary, and Shang-Jin Wei. 2009. "Service Offshoring and Productivity: Evidence from the US." *World Economy* 20, no. 42: 203–20.

Autor, David. H., David Dorn, and Gordon H. Hanson. Forthcoming. "The China Syndrome: Local Labor Market Effects of Import Competition in the United States." *American Economic Review.*

Bartel, Ann, Casey Ichniowski, and Kathryn Shaw. 2007. "How Does Information Technology Really Affect Productivity? Plant-Level Comparisons of Product Innovation, Process Improvement and Worker Skills." *Quarterly Journal of Economics* 122, no. 4: 1721–58.

Bernanke, Ben S. 2005. "The Global Saving Glut and the U.S. Current Account Deficit." Sandridge Lecture, Virginia Association of Economists. March.

Bernard, Andrew B., J. Bradford Jensen, and Peter K. Schott. 2006. "Trade Costs, Firms and Productivity." *Journal of Monetary Economics* 53, no. 5: 917–37.

Borchert, Ingo, Batshur Gootiiz, and Aaditya Mattoo. 2012. "Policy Barriers to International Trade in Services: Evidence from a New Database."

Policy Research Working Paper 6109. Washington, DC: World Bank.

Boston Consulting Group. 2012. "Rising U.S. Exports—Plus Reshoring— Could Help Create up to 5 Million Jobs by 2020." Boston. September.

Bosworth, Barry P., and Jack E. Triplett. 2007. "The Early 21st Century U.S. Productivity Expansion Is Still in Services." *International Productivity Monitor* 14: 3–19.

Branstetter, Lee. 2001. "Are Knowledge Spillovers International or International in Scope? Microeconometric Evidence from Japan and the United States." *Journal of International Economics* 53: 53-79.

Ceglowski, Janet, and Stephen S. Golub. 2012. "Does China Still Have a Labor Cost Advantage?" *Global Economy Journal* 12, no 3.

Chirinko, Robert S., and Daniel J. Wilson. 2008. "State Investment Tax Incentives: A Zero-Sum Game?" *Journal of Public Economics* 92, no. 12: 2362–84.

Davidson, Adam. 2013. "Workers of the World, Sit Tight." *New York Times.* January 29.

ESA (Economics and Statistics Administration). 2012. *The Benefits of Manufacturing Jobs.* Department of Commerce.

Ferreira, John and Mike Heilala. 2011. "Manufacturing's Secret Shift: Gaining Competitive Advantage by Getting Closer to the Customer." Acenture. (http://www.accenture.com/sitecollectiondocuments/PDF/ Accenture_Manufacturings_Secret_Shift.pdf).

Greenstone, Michael, Richard Hornbeck,and Enrico Moretti. 2010. "Identifying Agglomeration Spillovers: Evidence from Million Dollar Plants." *Journal of Political Economy* 118, no. 3: 536–98.

Hackel, Karee. 2011. "Returning from China." *The SRQ Business Journal*: 6-7. October.

Helper, Susan, Timothy Krueger, and Howard Wial. 2012. "Why Does Manufacturing Matter? Which Manufacturing Matters? A Policy Framework." Washington, DC: Brookings Institution.

Houseman, Susan, et al. 2011. "Offshoring Bias in U.S. Manufacturing." *Journal of Economic Perspectives* 25, no. 2: 111–32.

Hubbard, Thomas N. 2003. "Information, Decisions, and Productivity: On-Board Computers and Capacity Utilization in Trucking." *American Economic Review* 93, no. 4: 1328–53.

Hufbauer, Gary Clyde, Jeffery J. Schott, and Woan Foong Wong. 2010. *Figuring Out the Doha Round.* Washington, DC: Peterson Institute for International Economics.

IMF (International Monetary Fund). 2012. "Coping with High Debt and Sluggish Growth." *World Economic Outlook: October 2012.* Washington, DC.

Inch, John, and Neil Dutta. 2012. *U.S. Manufacturing Renaissance.* New York: Bank of America Merrill Lynch. March.

Jaffe, Adam B. 1989. "Real Effects of Academic Research." *American Economic Review* 79, no. 5: 957–70.

Jensen, J. Bernard. 2009. "Globalization and Business Services: A Growth Opportunity?" Washington, DC: Georgetown University McDonough School of Business.

_____. 2011. "Global Trade in Services: Fear, Facts, and Offshoring." Washington, DC: Peterson Institute for International Economics.

Johnson, Bradford C. 2002. "Retail: The Walmart Effect." *McKinsey Quarterly.* February.

Johnson, Robert C., and Guillermo Noguera. 2012. "Fragmentation and Trade in Value Added over Four Decades." Working Paper 18186. Cambridge, MA: National Bureau for Economic Research.

Koerner, Brendan I. 2011. "Made in America: Small Businesses Buck the Offshoring Trend." *Wired.* February 28.

Koopman, Robert, et al. 2010. "Give Credit Where Credit Is Due: Tracing Value Added in Global Production Chains." Working Paper 16426. Cambridge, MA: National Bureau for Economic Research.

Levy, Frank, and Richard J. Murnane. 2005. *The New Division of Labor: How Computers Are Creating the Next Job Market.* Princeton University Press.

Lileeva, Alla, and Daniel Trefler. 2010. "Improved Access to Foreign Markets Raises Plant-Level Productivity. . .For Some Plants." *Quarterly Journal of Economics* 125, no. 3: 1051–99.

Marshall, Alfred. 1890. *Principles of Economics.* New York: Macmillan and Company.

Moretti, Enrico. 2012. *The New Geography of Jobs.* New York: Houghton Mifflin Harcourt.

Obstfeld, Maurice. 2012. "Does the Current Account Still Matter?" *American Economic Review* 102: 1–24.

OECD (Organisation for Economic Co-operation and Development). 2013. "Measuring Trade in Value-Added: An OECD-WTO Joint Initiative" (http://www.oecd.org/industry/industryandglobalisation/measuringtradeinvalue-addedanoecd-wtojointinitiative.htm).

Pierce, Justin. 2011. "Plant-level Responses to Antidumping Duties: Evidence from U.S. Manufacturers." *Journal of International Economics* 85, no. 2: 222–33.

Pierce, Justin, and Peter K. Schott. 2012. "The Surprisingly Swift Decline of U.S. Manufacturing Employment." Working Paper 18655. Cambridge, MA: National Bureau for Economic Research.

Pisano, Gregory P., and Willy C. Shih. 2012. *Producing Prosperity: Why America Needs a Manufacturing Renaissance.* Boston: Harvard Business Review Press.

Prasso, Sheridan. 2011. "Why We Left Our Factories in China." *CNN Money.* June 29.

Reinhart, Carmen M., and Kenneth S. Rogoff. 2011. "From Financial Crash to Debt Crisis." *American Economic Review* 101, no. 5: 1676–706.

Rosenthal, Stuart S., and William C. Strange. 2003. "Geography, Industrial Organization, and Agglomeration." *Review of Economics and Statistics* 85, no. 2: 377–93.

Simchi-Levi, David, James Paul Peruvankal, Narendra Mulani, and John Ferreira. 2011. "Made in America: Rethinking the Future of U.S. Manufacturing." Accenture. (http://www.accenture.com/SiteCollectionDocuments/PDF/Accenture-Made-in-America.pdf).

Story, Louise. 2012. "As Companies Seek Tax Deals, Governments Pay High Price." *New York Times,* December 1.

Wailgum, Thomas. 2007. "How Wal-Mart Lost Its Technology Edge." *CIO.* October 4.

Wan, William. 2013. "China's Economic Data Draw Sharp Scrutiny from Experts Analyzing Global Trends." *Washington Post,* February 4.

Weil, David. 2011. "Enforcing Labor Standards in Fissured Workplaces: The US Experience." *The Economic and Labor Relations Review* 22, 2: 33-54

Zhu, Kevin. 2004. "The Complementarity of Information Technology Infrastructure and E-Commerce Capability: A Resource-Based

Assessment of Their Business Value." *Journal of Management Systems* 21, no.1: 167-202.

CHAPTER 8
CHALLENGES AND OPPORTUNITIES IN U.S. AGRICULTURE

Alston, Julian M., et al. 2009. *Persistence Pays: U.S. Agricultural Productivity Growth and the Benefits from Public R&D Spending.* Natural Resource Management and Policy Series, vol. 34. Springer: New York. (http://www.card.iastate.edu/publications/synopsis.aspx?id=1155).

Calvin, Linda, and Philip Martin. 2010. "The U.S. Produce Industry and Labor: Facing the Future in a Global Economy." *Economic Research Report 106.* U.S. Department of Agriculture, Economic Research Service (http://www.ers.usda.gov/publications/err-economic-research-report/err106.aspx).

CBO (Congressional Budget Office). 2012. "Cost Estimate: S. 3240 Agriculture Reform, Food, and Jobs Act of 2012." May (http://www.cbo.gov/sites/default/files/cbofiles/attachments/s3240.pdf).

Dimitri, Carolyn, and Lydia Oberholtzer. 2009. "Marketing U.S. Organic Foods: Recent Trends from Farms to Consumers." *Economic Information Bulletin 58.* U.S. Department of Agriculture, Economic Research Service (http://www.ers.usda.gov/media/185272/eib58_1_.pdf).

Durst, Ron. 2009. "Federal Estate Taxes Affecting Fewer Farmers But the Future Is Uncertain." *Amber Waves.* U.S. Department of Agriculture, Economic Research Service (http://webarchives.cdlib.org/sw1tx36512/http:/www.ers.usda.gov/AmberWaves/June09/Features/FederalEstateTax.htm#special).

Evenson, Robert E. 1988. "Research, Extension, and U.S. Agricultural Productivity: A Statistical Decomposition Analysis." *Agricultural Productivity: Measurement and Explanation,* edited by Susan M. Capalbo and John M. Antle. Johns Hopkins University Press for Resources for the Future.

Fuglie, Keith O., and Paul W. Heisey. 2007. "Economic Returns to Public Agricultural Research." *Economic Brief 10.* U.S. Department of Agriculture, Economic Research Service (http://www.ers.usda.gov/media/195594/eb10_1_.pdf).

Greene, C., et al. 2009. "Emerging Issues in the U.S. Organic Industry." *Economic Information Bulletin* 55. U.S. Dept. of Agriculture, Economic Research Service (http://www.ers.usda.gov/media/452867/eib55fm_1_.pdf).

Griliches, Zvi. 1998. "Introduction to 'R&D: The Econometric Evidence.'" *R&D and Productivity: The Econometric Evidence*. University of Chicago Press for the National Bureau of Economic Research (http://www.nber.org/chapters/c8339.pdf).

Hoppe, Robert A., James M. MacDonald, and Penni Korb. 2010. "Small Farms in the United States: Persistence Under Pressure." *Economic Information Bulletin 63*. U.S. Department of Agriculture, Economic Research Service (http://www.ers.usda.gov/media/147007/eib63_1_.pdf).

Interior (U.S. Department of the Interior). 2012. "National Travel and Tourism Strategy." Task Force on Travel and Competiveness (http://www.doi.gov/news/pressreleases/upload/NT-TS_final051512.pdf).

Jacobson, Darien, Brian Raub, and Barry Johnson. 2012. "The Estate Tax: Ninety Years and Counting." *Compendium of Federal Estate and Personal Wealth Studies, Volume II*. Internal Revenue Service, Statistics of Income (http://www.irs.gov/uac/SOI-Tax-Stats-Compendium-of-Federal-Estate-Tax-and-Personal-Wealth-Studies,-Volume-2).

Key, Nigel, and William McBride. 2007. "The Changing Economics of U.S. Hog Production." *Economic Research Report 52*. U.S. Department of Agriculture, Economic Research Service (http://www.ers.usda.gov/media/244843/err52.pdf).

Kharas, Homi. 2010. "The Emerging Middle Class in Developing Countries." Working Paper 185. Paris: OECD Development Center (http://www.oecd.org/dev/44457738.pdf).

Kremen, Amy, Catherine Greene, and Jim Hanson. 2004. "Organic Produce, Price Premiums, and Eco-Labeling in U.S. Farmers' Markets." *Outlook*. VGS-301-01. U.S. Department of Agriculture, Economic Research Service (http://www.ers.usda.gov/media/269468/vgs30101_1_.pdf).

Low, Sarah A., and Stephen Vogel. 2011. "Direct and Intermediated Marketing of Local Foods in the United States." *Economic Research Report 128*. U.S. Department of Agriculture, Economic Research Service (http://www.ers.usda.gov/publications/err-economic-research-report/err128.aspx).

MacDonald, James M., and Penni Korb. 2011. "Agricultural Contracting Update: Contracts in 2008." *Economic Information Bulletin 72.* U.S. Department of Agriculture, Economic Research Service (http://www.ers.usda.gov/media/104365/eib72.pdf).

Osteen, Craig, Jessica Gottlieb, and Utpal Vasavade eds. 2012. "Agricultural Resources and Environmental Indicators, 2012 Edition." *Economic Information Bulletin No 98* (http://www.ers.usda.gov/media/874175/eib98.pdf).

Outdoor Industry Association. 2012. *The Outdoor Recreation Economy.* Boulder, CO (http://www.outdoorindustry.org/images/research-files/OIA_OutdoorRecEconomyReport2012.pdf?167)

Pardey, Philip G. and Julian M. Alston. 2011. "For Want of a Nail: The Case for Increased Agricultural R&D Spending." Washington, DC: American Enterprise Institute (http://www.aei.org/files/2011/11/04/-for-want-of-a-nail-the-case-for-increased-agricultural-rd-spending_152830448674.pdf).

Ribaudo, M., et al. 2008. "The Use of Markets to Increase Private Investment in Environmental Stewardship." *Economic Research Report 64,* U.S. Department of Agriculture, Economic Research Service (http://www.ers.USDA.gov/publications/err-economic-research-report/err64.aspx).

Ribaudo, M., et al. 2012. "Nitrogen Management on U.S. Corn Acres, 2001–2010." *Economic Brief No 20* (http://www.ers.usda.gov/media/947769/eb20.pdf). (http://hsus.cambridge.org/HSUSWeb/search/searchTable.do?id=Ba652-669).

UN (United Nations). 2011. "World Population Prospects: The 2010 Revision, CD-ROM Edition." Department of Economic and Social Affairs, Populations Division (http://esa.un.org/wpp/).

_____. 2012a. "World Urbanization Prospects: The 2011 Revision, CD-ROM Edition." Department of Economic and Social Affairs, Populations Division (http://esa.un.org/unup/).

_____. 2012b. "Population Distribution, Urbanization, Internal Migration and Development: An International Perspective." Department of Economic and Social Affairs.

USDA. 2001. Agricultural Resource Management Survey. Economic Research Service (http://www.ers.usda.gov/data-products/arms-farm-financial-and-crop-production-practices/tailored-reports.aspx).

_____. 2010. Agricultural Resource Management Survey. Economic Research Service (http://www.ers.usda.gov/data-products/arms-farm-financial-and-crop-production-practices/tailored-reports.aspx).

_____. 2011. Agricultural Resource Management Survey. Economic Research Service (http://www.ers.usda.gov/data-products/arms-farm-financial-and-crop-production-practices/tailored-reports.aspx).

_____. 2012a. "USDA Accomplishments 2009-2012: Organic Agriculture." (usda.gov/documents/Results-Organic-Agriculture.pdf).

_____. 2012b. "USDA Accomplishments 2009-2012: Trade." (http://www.usda.gov/documents/Results-Trade.pdf)

_____. 2013a. "U.S. and State Farm Income and Wealth Statistics." Economic Research Service.

_____. 2013b. "Summary of Business Report for 2010 thru 2013." Federal Crop Insurance Corp (http://www3.rma.usda.gov/apps/sob/current_week/sobrpt2010-2013.pdf).

_____. 2013c. "Food Expenditures." Economic Research Service (http://www.ers.usda.gov/data-products/food-expenditures.aspx).

Wainio, John, Mark Gehlhar, and John Dyck. 2011. "Selected Trade Agreements and Implications for U.S. Agriculture." *Economic Research Report 115*. U.S. Department of Agriculture, Economic Research Service (http://www.ers.usda.gov/media/128130/err115.pdf).

Walthall, C.L., et al. 2012. "Climate Change and Agriculture in the United States: Effects and Adaptation." *U.S. Department of Agriculture Technical Bulletin No 1935* (http://www.usda.gov/oce/climate_change/effects_2012/CC%20and%20Agriculture%20Report%20(02-04-2013)b.pdf).

Zahniser, Steven, et al. 2012. "The Potential Impact of Changes in Immigration Policy on U.S. Agriculture and the Market for Hired Farm Labor: A Simulation Analysis." *Economic Research Report 135*. U.S. Department of Agriculture, Economic Research Service (http://www.ers.usda.gov/publications/err-economic-research-report/err135.aspx).

COUNCIL MEMBERS AND THEIR DATES OF SERVICE

Name	Position	Oath of office date	Separation date
Murray L. Weidenbaum	Chairman	February 27, 1981	August 25, 1982
William A. Niskanen	Member	June 12, 1981	March 30, 1985
Jerry L. Jordan	Member	July 14, 1981	July 31, 1982
Martin Feldstein	Chairman	October 14, 1982	July 10, 1984
William Poole	Member	December 10, 1982	January 20, 1985
Beryl W. Sprinkel	Chairman	April 18, 1985	January 20, 1989
Thomas Gale Moore	Member	July 1, 1985	May 1, 1989
Michael L. Mussa	Member	August 18, 1986	September 19, 1988
Michael J. Boskin	Chairman	February 2, 1989	January 12, 1993
John B. Taylor	Member	June 9, 1989	August 2, 1991
Richard L. Schmalensee	Member	October 3, 1989	June 21, 1991
David F. Bradford	Member	November 13, 1991	January 20, 1993
Paul Wonnacott	Member	November 13, 1991	January 20, 1993
Laura D'Andrea Tyson	Chair	February 5, 1993	April 22, 1995
Alan S. Blinder	Member	July 27, 1993	June 26, 1994
Joseph E. Stiglitz	Member	July 27, 1993	
	Chairman	June 28, 1995	February 10, 1997
Martin N. Baily	Member	June 30, 1995	August 30, 1996
Alicia H. Munnell	Member	January 29, 1996	August 1, 1997
Janet L. Yellen	Chair	February 18, 1997	August 3, 1999
Jeffrey A. Frankel	Member	April 23, 1997	March 2, 1999
Rebecca M. Blank	Member	October 22, 1998	July 9, 1999
Martin N. Baily	Chairman	August 12, 1999	January 19, 2001
Robert Z. Lawrence	Member	August 12, 1999	January 12, 2001
Kathryn L. Shaw	Member	May 31, 2000	January 19, 2001
R. Glenn Hubbard	Chairman	May 11, 2001	February 28, 2003
Mark B. McClellan	Member	July 25, 2001	November 13, 2002
Randall S. Kroszner	Member	November 30, 2001	July 1, 2003
N. Gregory Mankiw	Chairman	May 29, 2003	February 18, 2005
Kristin J. Forbes	Member	November 21, 2003	June 3, 2005
Harvey S. Rosen	Member	November 21, 2003	
	Chairman	February 23, 2005	June 10, 2005
Ben S. Bernanke	Chairman	June 21, 2005	January 31, 2006
Katherine Baicker	Member	November 18, 2005	July 11, 2007
Matthew J. Slaughter	Member	November 18, 2005	March 1, 2007
Edward P. Lazear	Chairman	February 27, 2006	January 20, 2009
Donald B. Marron	Member	July 17, 2008	January 20, 2009
Christina D. Romer	Chair	January 29, 2009	September 3, 2010
Austan D. Goolsbee	Member	March 11, 2009	
	Chairman	September 10, 2010	August 5, 2011
Cecilia Elena Rouse	Member	March 11, 2009	February 28, 2011
Katharine G. Abraham	Member	April 19, 2011	
Carl Shapiro	Member	April 19, 2011	May 4, 2012
Alan B. Krueger	Chairman	November 7, 2011	
James H. Stock	Member	February 7, 2013	

REPORT TO THE PRESIDENT
ON THE ACTIVITIES OF THE
COUNCIL OF ECONOMIC ADVISERS
DURING 2012

The Council of Economic Advisers was established by the Employment Act of 1946 to provide the President with objective economic analysis and advice on the development and implementation of a wide range of domestic and international economic policy issues. The Council is governed by a Chairman and two Members. The Chairman is appointed by the President and confirmed by the United States Senate. The Members are appointed by the President.

THE CHAIRMAN OF THE COUNCIL

Alan B. Krueger continued to chair the Council during 2012. Dr. Krueger is on a leave of absence from Princeton University, where he is the Bendheim Professor of Economics and Public Affairs. He served as Assistant Secretary for Economic Policy at the Treasury Department from 2009 to 2010.

Chairman Krueger is a member of the President's Cabinet and is responsible for communicating the Council's views on economic matters directly to the President through personal discussions and written reports. Chairman Krueger represents the Council at Presidential economic briefings, daily White House senior staff meetings, budget meetings, Cabinet meetings, a variety of inter-agency meetings, and other formal and informal meetings with the President, the Vice President, and other senior government officials. He also meets with members of Congress well as with business, academic and labor leaders to discuss economic policy issues.

THE MEMBERS OF THE COUNCIL

Katharine G. Abraham is a Member of the Council of Economic Advisers. She is on a leave of absence from the University of Maryland, where she is a faculty associate in the Maryland Population Research Center and a professor in the Joint Program in Survey Methodology. Dr. Abraham served as the Commissioner of the Bureau of Labor Statistics from 1993 to 2001.

James H. Stock was appointed by the President on February 7, 2013. He served as Chief Economist of the Council of Economic Advisers from September 12, 2012 until then. Dr. Stock is on leave from Harvard University, where he is the Harold Hitchings Burbank Professor of Political Economy. Dr. Stock served as the Chair of the Harvard University Department of Economics from 2006 to 2009.

Carl Shapiro resigned as Member of the Council on May 4, 2012 to return to the University of California, where he is the Transamerica Professor of Business Strategy at the Haas School of Business.

AREAS OF ACTIVITIES

A central function of the Council is to advise the President on all economic issues and developments. In the past year, as in the three previous years, advising the President on policies to spur economic growth and job creation, and evaluating the effects of the policies on the economy, have been a priority.

The Council works closely with various government agencies, including the National Economic Council, the Office of Management and Budget, White House senior staff, and other officials and engages in discussions on numerous policy matters. In the area of international economic policy, the Council coordinates with other units of the White House, the Treasury Department, the State Department, the Commerce Department, and the Federal Reserve on matters related to the global financial system.

Among the specific economic policy areas that received attention in 2012 were: housing policies, including foreclosure mitigation and prevention and refinancing; implementation of the Affordable Care Act; income inequality; individual and corporate taxation; college affordability; small business lending; regional development; intellectual property and innovation; infrastructure investment; regulatory measures; trade policies; unemployment insurance; job training; and policies to promote the international competitiveness of American manufacturing companies. The Council also worked on several issues related to the quality of the data available for assessing economic conditions.

The Council prepares for the President, the Vice President, and the White House senior staff a daily economic briefing memo analyzing current economic developments, and almost-daily memos on key economic data releases. Chairman Krueger has also presented regular monthly briefings on the state of the economy to senior White House officials.

The Council, the Department of Treasury, and the Office of Management and Budget—the Administration's economic "troika"— are responsible for producing the economic forecasts that underlie the Administration's budget proposals. The Council initiates the forecasting process twice each year, consulting with a wide variety of outside sources, including leading private sector forecasters and other government agencies.

The Council was an active participant in the trade policy process, participating in the Trade Policy Staff Committee and the Trade Policy Review Group. The Council provided analysis and opinions on a range of trade-related issues involving the enforcement of existing trade agreements, reviews of current U.S. trade policies, and consideration of future policies. The Council also participated on the Trade Promotion Coordinating Committee, helping to examine the ways in which exports may support economic growth in the years to come. In the area of investment and security, the Council participated on the Committee on Foreign Investment in the United States (CFIUS), reviewing individual cases before the committee.

Council Members and staff regularly met with economists, policy officials, and government officials from other countries to discuss issues relating to the global economy. The Council's role also included policy development and planning for the G-20 Summit in Saint Petersburg, Russia, and the G-8 Summit in Northern Ireland.

The Council is a leading participant in the Organisation for Economic Co-operation and Development (OECD), an important forum for economic cooperation among high-income industrial economies. The Council coordinated and oversaw the OECD's review of the U.S. economy. Dr. Krueger is chairman of the OECD's Economic Policy Committee, and Council Members and staff participate actively in working-party meetings on macroeconomic policy and coordination and contribute to the OECD's research agenda.

The Council issued a series of reports in 2012. In February, the Council released two reports: *Supporting Retirement for American Families* and *The Economic Benefits of New Spectrum for Wireless Broadband*. In May, the Council led the preparation of a White House report on the labor market situation of America's veterans. In June, the Council was a primary contributor to a White House report on job creation in rural communities. In November, the Council led the preparation of a White House report on the impact of tax cuts on the middle class and the subsequent effect on consumer spending and retailers. The Council continued its efforts to improve the public's understanding of economic developments and of the Administration's economic policies through briefings with the economic and financial press, speeches, discussions with outside economists, presentations to outside organizations, and regular updates on major data releases on the CEA blog. The Chairman and Members also regularly met to exchange views on the economy with the Chairman and Members of the Board of Governors of the Federal Reserve System.

Public Information

The Council's annual *Economic Report of the President* is an important vehicle for presenting the Administration's domestic and international economic policies. It is available for purchase through the Government Printing Office, and is viewable on the Internet at www.gpo.gov/erp.

The Council prepared numerous reports in 2012, and the Chairman and Members gave numerous public speeches. The reports and texts of speeches are available at the Council's website, www.whitehouse.gov/cea. Finally, the Council published the monthly *Economic Indicators*, which is available on-line at www.gpo.gov/economicindicators.

The Staff of the Council of Economic Advisers

The staff of the Council consists of the senior staff, senior economists, economists, staff economists, research economists, a research assistant, and the administrative and support staff. The staff at the end of 2012 was:

Senior Staff

David P. Vandivier. . . . . Chief of Staff

Petra Smeltzer Starke. . . . . General Counsel

Steven N. Braun . . . . Director of Macroeconomic Forecasting

Adrienne Pilot . . . . Director of Statistical Office

Archana Snyder . . . . Director of Finance and Administration

Senior Economists

Bevin Ashenmiller . . . . Environment, Energy

Benjamin H. Harris . . . . Tax, Budget

Susan Helper. . . . . Manufacturing, Innovation, Small Business

Chinhui Juhn . . . . Labor

Paul Lengermann. . . . . Macroeconomics

Emily Y. Lin . . . . Tax, Budget

Rodney D. Ludema .... International
James M. Williamson .... Agriculture, Transportation, Tax
Wesley Yin .... Health, Housing

Economist
David Cho..................... Macroeconomics

Staff Economists
Nicholas Li .... Labor, Health, Housing
Ben Meiselman.................. Macroeconomics, Public Finance
Nicholas Tilipman .... Labor, Health, Immigration
Lee Tucker..................... Labor, Immigration, Housing
Jeffery Y. Zhang .... Energy, Environment,
Macroeconomics

Research Economists
Matthew L. Aks .... Macroeconomics, International
Carys Golesworthy............... International, Trade
Dina Grossman.................. Labor, Health, Immigration
Cordaye T. Ogletree............. Energy, Environment, International
Trade
Spencer Smith.................. Public Finance, Energy, Environment
Rudy Telles Jr .... Agriculture, Tax

Research Assistant
Philip K. Lambrakos .... Macroeconomics, International

Statistical Office
The Statistical Office gathers, administers, and produces statistical information for the Council. Duties include preparing the statistical appendix to the *Economic Report of the President* and the monthly publication *Economic Indicators*. The staff also creates background materials for economic analysis and verifies statistical content in Presidential memoranda. The Office serves as the Council's liaison to the statistical community.

Brian A. Amorosi................ Statistical Analyst
Sarah Murray .... Economic Statistician

Office of the Chairman

Michael P. Bourgeois. . . . . Special Assistant to the Chairman

Emily C. Berret. . . . . Special Assistant to the Members

Natasha S. Lawrence . . . . Staff Assistant

Administrative Office

The Administrative Office provides general support for the Council's activities. This includes financial management, human resource management, travel, operations of facilities, security, information technology, and telecommunications management support.

Doris T. Searles. . . . . Administrative and Information
Management Specialist

Thomas F. Hunt. . . . . Staff Assistant

Interns

Student interns provide invaluable help with research projects, day- to-day operations, and fact-checking. Interns during the year were: Norm Dannen, Laura Du, Shawn Du, Conor Foley, Scott Freitag, Rebecca Freidman, Isaac Green, Sonya Huang, Christopher Kilgore, Zachary Kleinbart, Amaze Lusompa, Nathan Mayo, John McDonough, Joel Moore, Yolanda Ngo, Robert Owens, Scott Pippin, Katharine Rodihan, Charles Rubenfeld, Rebecca Sachs, Zachary Silvis, Craig Smyser, Michael Sullivan, David Wasser, William Weber, Derek Wu, and Barr Yaron.

DEPARTURES IN 2012

Judith K. Hellerstein left her position as Chief Economist of the Council in May, and she has returned to her position as Professor of Economics at the University of Maryland, College Park.

The senior economists who resigned in 2012 (with the institutions to which they returned after leaving the Council in parentheses) were: Gene Amromin (Federal Reserve Bank of Chicago), Lee G. Branstetter (Carnegie Mellon University, Heinz College), Thomas C. Buchmueller (University of Michigan, Ross School of Business), Lisa D. Cook (Michigan State University), Robert Johansson (U.S. Department of Agriculture), Craig T. Peters (Department of Justice), Charles R. Pierret (U.S. Bureau of Labor Statistics), and Daniel J. Vine (Federal Reserve Board).

The economist who departed in 2012 was Reid Stevens (UC, Berkeley). Reid served the CEA for more than two and a half years and was the first recipient of the Robert M. Solow Award for Distinguished Service.

The staff economists who departed in 2012 were Jeffrey Borowitz, Colleen M. Carey, Judd N.L. Cramer, and Edward Zhong.

The research economists who departed in 2012 at the were Julia H. Yoo and Pedro Spivakovsky-Gonzalez.

The research assistants who departed in 2012 were Sandra M. Levy, Carter Mundell and Seth H. Werfel.

Andres Bustamante resigned from his position as Special Assistant to the Chairman and Staff Economist to pursue other endeavors. Paige Shevlin resigned from her position as Special Assistant to the Chairman. Sharon Thomas resigned from her position as Administrative Support Assistant, after serving in the Federal Government for over 25 years. Lindsay M. Kuberka completed her detail as a statistical analyst and returned to the Census Bureau.

STATISTICAL TABLES RELATING TO INCOME, EMPLOYMENT, AND PRODUCTION

C O N T E N T S

NATIONAL INCOME OR EXPENDITURE

NATIONAL INCOME OR EXPENDITURE—*Continued*

POPULATION, EMPLOYMENT, WAGES, AND PRODUCTIVITY

PRODUCTION AND BUSINESS ACTIVITY

PRICES

MONEY STOCK, CREDIT, AND FINANCE

GOVERNMENT FINANCE

CORPORATE PROFITS AND FINANCE

AGRICULTURE

AGRICULTURE—*Continued*

INTERNATIONAL STATISTICS

General Notes

Detail in these tables may not add to totals because of rounding.

Because of the formula used for calculating real gross domestic product (GDP), the chained (2005) dollar estimates for the detailed components do not add to the chained-dollar value of GDP or to any intermediate aggregate. The Department of Commerce (Bureau of Economic Analysis) no longer publishes chained-dollar estimates prior to 1995, except for selected series.

Unless otherwise noted, all dollar figures are in current dollars.

Symbols used:
 p Preliminary.
 ... Not available (also, not applicable).

Data in these tables reflect revisions made by the source agencies through January 30, 2013 with two exceptions. Current employment statistics (CES) estimates from the Department of Labor (Bureau of Labor Statistics) include revisions released February 1, 2013, and national income and product account (NIPA) estimates from the Department of Commerce (Bureau of Economic Analysis) incorporate revisions released on February 28, 2013.

TABLE B-1. Gross domestic product, 1964–2012

[Billions of dollars, except as noted; quarterly data at seasonally adjusted annual rates]

Year or quarter	Gross domestic product	Personal consumption expenditures			Gross private domestic investment						
		Total	Goods	Services	Total	Fixed investment					Change in private inventories
						Total	Nonresidential			Residential	
							Total	Structures	Equipment and software		
1964	663.6	411.5	212.3	199.2	102.1	97.2	63.0	23.7	39.2	34.3	4.8
1965	719.1	443.8	229.7	214.1	118.2	109.0	74.8	28.3	46.5	34.2	9.2
1966	787.7	480.9	249.6	231.3	131.3	117.7	85.4	31.3	54.0	32.3	13.6
1967	832.4	507.8	259.0	248.8	128.6	118.7	86.4	31.5	54.9	32.4	9.9
1968	909.8	558.0	284.6	273.4	141.2	132.1	93.4	33.6	59.9	38.7	9.1
1969	984.4	605.1	304.7	300.4	156.4	147.3	104.7	37.7	67.0	42.6	9.2
1970	1,038.3	648.3	318.8	329.5	152.4	150.4	109.0	40.3	68.7	41.4	2.0
1971	1,126.8	701.6	342.1	359.5	178.2	169.9	114.1	42.7	71.5	55.8	8.3
1972	1,237.9	770.2	373.8	396.4	207.6	198.5	128.8	47.2	81.7	69.7	9.1
1973	1,382.3	852.0	416.6	435.4	244.5	228.6	153.3	55.0	98.3	75.3	15.9
1974	1,499.5	932.9	451.5	481.4	249.4	235.4	169.5	61.2	108.2	66.0	14.0
1975	1,637.7	1,033.8	491.3	542.5	230.2	236.5	173.7	61.4	112.4	62.7	-6.3
1976	1,824.6	1,151.3	546.3	604.9	292.0	274.8	192.4	65.9	126.4	82.5	17.1
1977	2,030.1	1,277.8	600.4	677.4	361.3	339.0	228.7	74.6	154.1	110.3	22.3
1978	2,293.8	1,427.6	663.6	764.1	438.0	412.2	280.6	93.6	187.0	131.6	25.8
1979	2,562.2	1,591.2	737.9	853.2	492.9	474.9	333.9	117.7	216.2	141.0	18.0
1980	2,788.1	1,755.8	799.8	956.0	479.3	485.6	362.4	136.2	226.2	123.2	-6.3
1981	3,126.8	1,939.5	869.4	1,070.1	572.4	542.6	420.0	167.3	252.7	122.6	29.8
1982	3,253.2	2,075.5	899.3	1,176.2	517.2	532.1	426.5	177.6	248.9	105.7	-14.9
1983	3,534.6	2,288.6	973.8	1,314.8	564.3	570.1	417.2	154.3	262.9	152.9	-5.8
1984	3,930.9	2,501.1	1,063.7	1,437.4	735.6	670.2	489.6	177.4	312.2	180.6	65.4
1985	4,217.5	2,717.6	1,137.6	1,580.0	736.2	714.4	526.2	194.5	331.7	188.2	21.8
1986	4,460.1	2,896.7	1,195.6	1,701.1	746.5	739.9	519.8	176.5	343.3	220.1	6.6
1987	4,736.4	3,097.0	1,256.3	1,840.7	785.0	757.8	524.1	174.2	349.9	233.7	27.1
1988	5,100.4	3,350.1	1,337.3	2,012.7	821.6	803.1	563.8	182.8	381.0	239.3	18.5
1989	5,482.1	3,594.5	1,423.8	2,170.7	874.9	847.3	607.7	193.7	414.0	239.5	27.7
1990	5,800.5	3,835.5	1,491.3	2,344.2	861.0	846.4	622.4	202.9	419.5	224.0	14.5
1991	5,992.1	3,980.1	1,497.4	2,482.6	802.9	803.3	598.2	183.6	414.6	205.1	-.4
1992	6,342.3	4,236.9	1,563.3	2,673.6	864.8	848.5	612.1	172.6	439.6	236.3	16.3
1993	6,667.4	4,483.6	1,642.3	2,841.2	953.3	932.5	666.6	177.2	489.4	266.0	20.8
1994	7,085.2	4,750.8	1,746.6	3,004.3	1,097.3	1,033.5	731.4	186.8	544.6	302.1	63.8
1995	7,414.7	4,987.3	1,815.5	3,171.7	1,144.0	1,112.9	810.0	207.3	602.8	302.9	31.2
1996	7,838.5	5,273.6	1,917.7	3,355.9	1,240.2	1,209.4	875.4	224.6	650.8	334.1	30.8
1997	8,332.4	5,570.6	2,006.8	3,563.9	1,388.7	1,317.7	968.6	250.3	718.3	349.1	71.0
1998	8,793.5	5,918.5	2,110.0	3,808.5	1,510.8	1,447.1	1,061.1	275.1	786.0	385.9	63.7
1999	9,353.5	6,342.8	2,290.0	4,052.8	1,641.5	1,580.7	1,154.9	283.9	871.0	425.8	60.8
2000	9,951.5	6,830.4	2,459.1	4,371.2	1,772.2	1,717.7	1,268.7	318.1	950.5	449.0	54.5
2001	10,286.2	7,148.8	2,534.0	4,614.8	1,661.9	1,700.2	1,227.8	329.7	898.1	472.4	-38.3
2002	10,642.3	7,439.2	2,610.0	4,829.2	1,647.0	1,634.9	1,125.4	282.8	842.7	509.5	12.0
2003	11,142.2	7,804.1	2,728.0	5,076.1	1,729.7	1,713.3	1,135.7	281.9	853.8	577.6	16.4
2004	11,853.3	8,270.6	2,892.1	5,378.5	1,968.6	1,903.6	1,223.0	306.7	916.4	680.6	64.9
2005	12,623.0	8,803.5	3,076.7	5,726.8	2,172.3	2,122.3	1,347.3	351.8	995.6	775.0	50.0
2006	13,377.2	9,301.0	3,224.7	6,076.3	2,327.1	2,267.2	1,505.3	433.7	1,071.7	761.9	60.0
2007	14,028.7	9,772.3	3,363.9	6,408.3	2,295.2	2,266.1	1,637.5	524.9	1,112.6	628.7	29.1
2008	14,291.5	10,035.5	3,381.7	6,653.8	2,087.6	2,128.7	1,656.3	586.3	1,070.0	472.4	-41.1
2009	13,973.7	9,845.9	3,194.4	6,651.5	1,549.3	1,703.5	1,349.3	451.1	898.2	354.1	-154.2
2010	14,498.9	10,215.7	3,364.9	6,850.9	1,737.3	1,679.0	1,338.4	376.3	962.1	340.6	58.4
2011	15,075.7	10,729.0	3,624.8	7,104.2	1,854.9	1,818.3	1,479.6	404.8	1,074.7	338.7	36.6
2012 ᵖ	15,681.5	11,120.9	3,783.2	7,337.6	2,058.6	2,000.9	1,618.0	460.5	1,157.6	382.8	57.7
2009: I	13,923.4	9,768.4	3,125.5	6,642.9	1,645.8	1,812.5	1,442.9	530.5	912.4	369.6	-166.7
II	13,885.4	9,763.9	3,142.0	6,621.9	1,495.3	1,698.0	1,356.0	467.1	888.9	342.0	-202.7
III	13,952.2	9,888.8	3,244.4	6,644.4	1,465.6	1,666.1	1,312.9	421.0	891.9	353.1	-200.5
IV	14,133.6	9,962.5	3,265.5	6,697.0	1,590.4	1,637.2	1,285.4	385.6	899.8	351.9	-46.8
2010: I	14,270.3	10,069.1	3,318.2	6,750.9	1,660.4	1,627.2	1,285.8	362.7	923.1	341.3	33.2
II	14,413.5	10,148.3	3,321.7	6,826.6	1,724.7	1,683.0	1,325.2	376.6	948.6	357.8	41.7
III	14,576.0	10,243.6	3,361.0	6,882.6	1,793.3	1,683.8	1,353.8	377.1	976.8	330.0	109.5
IV	14,735.9	10,401.9	3,458.6	6,943.3	1,770.9	1,721.9	1,388.8	389.0	999.8	333.1	49.0
2011: I	14,814.9	10,566.3	3,561.4	7,004.9	1,755.9	1,722.3	1,390.8	362.4	1,028.4	331.4	33.7
II	15,003.6	10,684.9	3,604.3	7,080.6	1,819.0	1,784.2	1,448.0	397.0	1,051.0	336.2	34.8
III	15,163.2	10,791.2	3,643.6	7,147.6	1,853.8	1,857.8	1,519.4	421.8	1,097.6	338.5	-4.1
IV	15,321.0	10,873.8	3,690.0	7,183.8	1,991.1	1,909.0	1,560.1	438.2	1,122.0	348.8	82.1
2012: I	15,478.3	11,007.2	3,755.9	7,251.3	2,032.2	1,959.7	1,595.5	454.7	1,140.8	364.2	72.6
II	15,585.6	11,067.2	3,741.5	7,325.7	2,041.7	1,986.9	1,614.1	458.9	1,155.2	372.8	54.8
III	15,811.0	11,154.4	3,792.5	7,361.9	2,080.1	1,997.9	1,610.0	460.1	1,149.9	387.9	82.3
IV ᵖ	15,851.2	11,254.6	3,843.0	7,411.6	2,080.3	2,059.0	1,652.5	468.2	1,184.3	406.5	21.3

See next page for continuation of table.

Table B–1. Gross domestic product, 1964–2012—*Continued*

[Billions of dollars, except as noted; quarterly data at seasonally adjusted annual rates]

Year or quarter	Net exports of goods and services			Government consumption expenditures and gross investment					Final sales of domestic product	Gross domestic purchases [1]	Addendum: Gross national product [2]	Percent change from preceding period	
	Net exports	Exports	Imports	Total	Federal			State and local				Gross domestic product	Gross domestic purchases [1]
					Total	National defense	Non-defense						
1964	6.9	35.0	28.1	143.2	78.4	60.2	18.2	64.8	658.8	656.7	668.6	7.4	7.2
1965	5.6	37.1	31.5	151.4	80.4	60.6	19.8	71.0	709.9	713.5	724.4	8.4	8.6
1966	3.9	40.9	37.1	171.6	92.4	71.7	20.8	79.2	774.1	783.8	792.8	9.5	9.9
1967	3.6	43.5	39.9	192.5	104.6	83.4	21.2	87.9	822.6	828.9	837.8	5.7	5.7
1968	1.4	47.9	46.6	209.3	111.3	89.2	22.0	98.0	900.8	908.5	915.9	9.3	9.6
1969	1.4	51.9	50.5	221.4	113.3	89.5	23.8	108.2	975.3	983.0	990.5	8.2	8.2
1970	4.0	59.7	55.8	233.7	113.4	87.6	25.8	120.3	1,036.3	1,034.4	1,044.7	5.5	5.2
1971	.6	63.0	62.3	246.4	113.6	84.6	29.1	132.8	1,118.6	1,126.2	1,134.4	8.5	8.9
1972	-3.4	70.8	74.2	263.4	119.6	86.9	32.7	143.8	1,228.8	1,241.3	1,246.4	9.9	10.2
1973	4.1	95.3	91.2	281.7	122.5	88.1	34.3	159.2	1,366.4	1,378.2	1,394.9	11.7	11.0
1974	-.8	126.7	127.5	317.9	134.5	95.6	39.0	183.4	1,485.5	1,500.3	1,515.0	8.5	8.9
1975	16.0	138.7	122.7	357.7	149.0	103.9	45.1	208.7	1,644.0	1,621.7	1,650.7	9.2	8.1
1976	-1.6	149.5	151.1	383.0	159.7	111.1	48.6	223.3	1,807.5	1,826.2	1,841.4	11.4	12.6
1977	-23.1	159.4	182.4	414.1	175.4	120.9	54.5	238.7	2,007.8	2,053.2	2,050.4	11.3	12.4
1978	-25.4	186.9	212.3	453.6	190.9	130.5	60.4	262.7	2,268.0	2,319.1	2,315.3	13.0	13.0
1979	-22.5	230.1	252.7	500.7	210.6	145.2	65.4	290.2	2,544.2	2,584.8	2,594.2	11.7	11.5
1980	-13.1	280.8	293.8	566.1	243.7	168.0	75.8	322.4	2,794.5	2,801.2	2,822.3	8.8	8.4
1981	-12.5	305.2	317.8	627.5	280.2	196.2	83.9	347.3	3,097.0	3,139.4	3,159.8	12.1	12.1
1982	-20.0	283.2	303.2	680.4	310.8	225.9	84.9	369.7	3,268.1	3,273.2	3,289.7	4.0	4.3
1983	-51.7	277.0	328.6	733.4	342.9	250.6	92.3	390.5	3,540.4	3,586.3	3,571.7	8.7	9.6
1984	-102.7	302.4	405.1	796.9	374.3	281.5	92.7	422.6	3,865.5	4,033.6	3,967.2	11.2	12.5
1985	-115.2	302.0	417.2	878.9	412.8	311.2	101.6	466.1	4,195.6	4,332.7	4,244.0	7.3	7.4
1986	-132.5	320.3	452.9	949.3	438.4	330.8	107.6	510.9	4,453.5	4,592.6	4,477.7	5.8	6.0
1987	-145.0	363.8	508.7	999.4	459.5	350.0	109.6	539.9	4,709.2	4,881.3	4,754.0	6.2	6.3
1988	-110.1	443.9	554.0	1,038.9	461.6	354.7	106.8	577.3	5,081.9	5,210.5	5,123.8	7.7	6.7
1989	-87.9	503.1	591.0	1,100.6	481.4	362.1	119.3	619.2	5,454.5	5,570.0	5,508.1	7.5	6.9
1990	-77.6	552.1	629.7	1,181.7	507.5	373.9	133.6	674.2	5,786.0	5,878.1	5,835.0	5.8	5.5
1991	-27.0	596.6	623.5	1,236.1	526.6	383.1	143.4	709.5	5,992.5	6,019.1	6,022.0	3.3	2.4
1992	-32.8	635.0	667.8	1,273.5	532.9	376.8	156.1	740.6	6,326.0	6,375.1	6,371.4	5.8	5.9
1993	-64.4	655.6	720.0	1,294.8	525.0	363.0	162.0	769.8	6,646.5	6,731.7	6,698.5	5.1	5.6
1994	-92.7	720.7	813.4	1,329.8	518.6	353.8	164.8	811.2	7,021.4	7,177.9	7,109.2	6.3	6.6
1995	-90.7	811.9	902.6	1,374.0	518.8	348.8	170.0	855.3	7,383.5	7,505.3	7,444.3	4.7	4.6
1996	-96.3	867.7	964.0	1,421.0	527.0	354.8	172.2	894.0	7,807.7	7,934.8	7,870.1	5.7	5.7
1997	-101.4	954.4	1,055.8	1,474.4	531.0	349.8	181.1	943.5	8,261.4	8,433.7	8,355.8	6.3	6.3
1998	-161.8	953.9	1,115.7	1,526.1	531.0	346.1	184.9	995.0	8,729.8	8,955.3	8,810.8	5.5	6.2
1999	-262.1	989.3	1,251.4	1,631.3	554.9	361.1	193.8	1,076.3	9,292.7	9,615.6	9,381.3	6.4	7.4
2000	-382.1	1,093.2	1,475.3	1,731.0	576.1	371.0	205.0	1,154.9	9,896.9	10,333.5	9,989.2	6.4	7.5
2001	-371.0	1,027.7	1,398.7	1,846.4	611.7	393.0	218.7	1,234.7	10,324.5	10,657.2	10,338.1	3.4	3.1
2002	-427.2	1,003.0	1,430.2	1,983.3	680.6	437.7	242.9	1,302.7	10,630.3	11,069.5	10,691.4	3.5	3.9
2003	-504.1	1,041.0	1,545.1	2,112.6	756.5	497.9	258.5	1,356.1	11,125.8	11,646.3	11,210.0	4.7	5.2
2004	-618.7	1,180.2	1,798.9	2,232.8	824.6	550.8	273.9	1,408.2	11,788.3	12,471.9	11,944.5	6.4	7.1
2005	-722.7	1,305.1	2,027.8	2,369.9	876.3	589.0	287.3	1,493.6	12,573.0	13,345.7	12,720.1	6.5	7.0
2006	-769.3	1,471.0	2,240.3	2,518.4	931.7	624.9	306.8	1,586.7	13,317.3	14,116.5	13,449.6	6.0	6.0
2007	-713.1	1,661.7	2,374.8	2,674.2	976.3	662.3	314.0	1,697.9	13,999.6	14,741.7	14,151.9	4.9	4.2
2008	-709.7	1,846.8	2,556.5	2,878.1	1,080.1	737.8	342.3	1,798.0	14,332.7	15,001.3	14,460.7	1.9	1.8
2009	-388.7	1,587.4	1,976.2	2,967.2	1,143.6	776.0	367.6	1,823.6	14,127.9	14,362.4	14,117.2	-2.2	-4.3
2010	-511.6	1,844.4	2,356.1	3,057.5	1,223.1	817.7	405.3	1,834.4	14,440.6	15,010.6	14,708.2	3.8	4.5
2011	-568.1	2,094.2	2,662.3	3,059.8	1,222.1	820.8	401.3	1,837.7	15,039.0	15,643.7	15,327.5	4.0	4.2
2012 *p*	-560.8	2,182.6	2,743.3	3,062.9	1,214.3	809.2	405.1	1,848.6	15,623.8	16,242.3	....	4.0	3.8
2009: I	-385.4	1,523.5	1,908.9	2,894.6	1,104.9	748.0	356.9	1,789.7	14,090.2	14,308.9	14,041.7	-4.4	-9.6
II	-331.6	1,525.3	1,856.9	2,957.8	1,135.9	772.0	364.0	1,821.9	14,088.1	14,217.0	14,001.3	-1.1	-2.5
III	-398.6	1,594.7	1,993.3	2,996.4	1,157.6	788.5	369.1	1,838.8	14,152.7	14,350.8	14,115.2	1.9	3.8
IV	-439.3	1,706.3	2,145.5	3,020.0	1,175.9	795.5	380.4	1,844.1	14,180.5	14,572.9	14,310.8	5.3	6.3
2010: I	-490.2	1,751.9	2,242.0	3,030.9	1,193.7	799.3	394.3	1,837.2	14,237.0	14,760.4	14,461.7	3.9	5.2
II	-521.1	1,814.3	2,335.4	3,061.7	1,225.1	815.5	409.6	1,836.6	14,371.8	14,934.7	14,629.3	4.1	4.8
III	-533.1	1,861.2	2,394.3	3,072.3	1,239.8	831.6	408.1	1,832.5	14,466.6	15,109.2	14,793.0	4.6	4.8
IV	-502.1	1,950.4	2,452.5	3,065.2	1,233.8	824.5	409.3	1,831.4	14,686.9	15,238.0	14,948.9	4.5	3.5
2011: I	-555.4	2,030.5	2,585.9	3,048.1	1,215.2	804.9	410.3	1,832.8	14,781.2	15,370.3	15,050.1	2.2	3.5
II	-572.5	2,092.8	2,665.3	3,072.2	1,234.3	827.7	406.6	1,837.9	14,968.7	15,576.1	15,253.6	5.2	5.5
III	-549.5	2,133.3	2,682.8	3,067.7	1,227.5	837.8	389.7	1,840.2	15,167.3	15,712.7	15,421.0	4.3	3.6
IV	-594.8	2,120.3	2,715.1	3,051.0	1,211.2	812.8	398.4	1,839.7	15,238.9	15,915.9	15,585.0	4.2	5.3
2012: I	-615.8	2,157.9	2,773.7	3,054.6	1,207.7	806.4	401.3	1,846.9	15,405.7	16,094.0	15,693.2	4.2	4.6
II	-576.9	2,188.5	2,765.4	3,053.7	1,210.7	807.8	402.9	1,843.0	15,530.8	16,162.5	15,832.9	2.8	1.7
III	-516.8	2,198.7	2,715.5	3,093.3	1,241.4	834.5	406.8	1,851.9	15,728.8	16,327.8	16,054.2	5.9	4.2
IV *p*	-533.6	2,185.2	2,718.8	3,049.9	1,197.4	787.9	409.4	1,852.5	15,829.9	16,384.8	....	1.0	1.4

[1] Gross domestic product (GDP) less exports of goods and services plus imports of goods and services.
[2] GDP plus net income receipts from rest of the world.

Source: Department of Commerce (Bureau of Economic Analysis).

[Billions of chained (2005) dollars, except as noted; quarterly data at seasonally adjusted annual rates]

Year or quarter	Gross domestic product	Personal consumption expenditures			Gross private domestic investment							Change in private inventories
						Fixed investment						
		Total	Goods	Services	Total	Total	Nonresidential			Residential		
							Total	Structures	Equipment and software			
1964	3,389.4	2,107.5			382.1							
1965	3,607.0	2,240.8			435.7							
1966	3,842.1	2,367.9			474.1							
1967	3,939.2	2,438.8			452.4							
1968	4,129.9	2,579.6			478.7							
1969	4,258.2	2,676.2			506.6							
1970	4,266.3	2,738.9			473.4							
1971	4,409.5	2,843.3			527.3							
1972	4,643.8	3,018.1			589.8							
1973	4,912.8	3,167.7			658.9							
1974	4,885.7	3,141.4			610.3							
1975	4,875.4	3,212.6			502.2							
1976	5,136.9	3,391.5			603.7							
1977	5,373.1	3,534.3			694.9							
1978	5,672.8	3,690.1			778.7							
1979	5,850.1	3,777.8			803.5							
1980	5,834.0	3,764.5			715.2							
1981	5,982.1	3,821.6			779.6							
1982	5,865.9	3,874.9			670.3							
1983	6,130.9	4,096.4			732.8							
1984	6,571.5	4,313.6			948.7							
1985	6,843.4	4,538.3			939.8							
1986	7,080.5	4,722.4			933.5							
1987	7,307.0	4,868.0			962.2							
1988	7,607.4	5,064.3			984.9							
1989	7,879.2	5,207.5			1,024.4							
1990	8,027.1	5,313.7			989.9							
1991	8,008.3	5,321.7			909.4							
1992	8,280.0	5,503.2			983.1							
1993	8,516.2	5,698.6			1,070.9							
1994	8,863.1	5,916.2			1,216.4							
1995	9,086.0	6,076.2	1,896.0	4,208.5	1,254.3	1,231.2	787.9	342.0	489.4	456.1		32.1
1996	9,425.8	6,288.3	1,980.9	4,331.7	1,365.3	1,341.6	861.5	361.4	541.4	492.5		31.2
1997	9,845.9	6,520.4	2,075.3	4,465.3	1,535.2	1,465.4	965.5	387.9	615.9	501.8		77.4
1998	10,274.7	6,862.3	2,215.5	4,662.1	1,688.9	1,624.4	1,081.4	407.7	705.2	540.4		71.6
1999	10,770.7	7,237.6	2,392.0	4,853.1	1,837.6	1,775.5	1,194.3	408.2	805.0	574.2		68.5
2000	11,216.4	7,604.6	2,518.2	5,093.6	1,963.1	1,906.8	1,311.3	440.0	889.2	580.0		60.2
2001	11,337.5	7,810.3	2,597.3	5,219.1	1,825.2	1,870.7	1,274.8	433.3	860.6	583.3		–41.8
2002	11,543.1	8,018.3	2,702.9	5,318.5	1,800.4	1,791.5	1,173.7	356.6	824.2	613.8		12.8
2003	11,836.4	8,244.5	2,827.2	5,418.2	1,870.1	1,854.7	1,189.6	343.0	850.0	664.3		17.3
2004	12,246.9	8,515.8	2,953.3	5,562.7	2,058.2	1,992.5	1,263.0	346.7	917.3	729.5		66.3
2005	12,623.0	8,803.5	3,076.7	5,726.8	2,172.3	2,122.3	1,347.3	351.8	995.6	775.0		50.0
2006	12,958.5	9,054.5	3,178.9	5,875.6	2,231.8	2,172.7	1,455.5	384.0	1,071.1	718.2		59.4
2007	13,206.4	9,262.9	3,273.5	5,990.2	2,159.5	2,130.6	1,550.0	438.2	1,106.8	584.2		27.7
2008	13,161.9	9,211.7	3,192.9	6,017.0	1,939.8	1,978.6	1,537.6	466.4	1,059.4	444.4		–36.3
2009	12,757.9	9,032.6	3,098.2	5,930.6	1,458.1	1,602.2	1,259.8	368.1	885.2	344.8		–139.0
2010	13,063.0	9,196.2	3,209.1	5,987.6	1,658.0	1,598.7	1,268.5	310.6	963.9	332.2		50.9
2011	13,299.1	9,428.8	3,331.0	6,101.5	1,744.0	1,704.5	1,378.2	319.2	1,070.0	327.6		31.0
2012 ᴾ	13,591.1	9,604.9	3,433.0	6,178.0	1,911.0	1,850.1	1,484.9	351.3	1,143.5	367.1		42.7
2009: I	12,711.0	9,039.5	3,083.2	5,951.5	1,516.0	1,677.3	1,324.3	417.7	892.9	355.3		–150.2
II	12,701.0	8,999.3	3,067.0	5,926.9	1,400.7	1,593.7	1,262.0	380.1	873.2	333.7		–185.5
III	12,746.7	9,046.2	3,123.1	5,920.7	1,394.8	1,581.2	1,236.7	351.7	880.8	347.2		–181.5
IV	12,873.1	9,045.4	3,119.5	5,923.2	1,521.1	1,556.8	1,216.4	323.1	893.8	343.0		–38.8
2010: I	12,947.6	9,100.8	3,159.5	5,940.4	1,591.4	1,553.1	1,222.7	302.6	925.0	332.7		30.5
II	13,019.6	9,159.4	3,185.4	5,973.6	1,646.4	1,606.5	1,258.6	312.1	951.6	350.5		33.2
III	13,103.5	9,216.0	3,215.1	6,001.4	1,710.1	1,602.7	1,282.1	310.4	978.7	322.2		94.9
IV	13,181.2	9,308.5	3,276.5	6,034.9	1,684.3	1,632.3	1,310.5	317.4	1,000.4	323.3		45.0
2011: I	13,183.8	9,380.9	3,320.3	6,064.8	1,661.6	1,627.0	1,306.3	292.2	1,027.0	322.2		30.3
II	13,264.7	9,403.2	3,312.2	6,094.0	1,711.3	1,675.4	1,351.3	315.0	1,046.5	325.5		27.5
III	13,306.9	9,441.9	3,323.5	6,121.1	1,735.8	1,736.8	1,411.3	330.2	1,091.5	326.6		–4.3
IV	13,441.0	9,489.3	3,367.9	6,126.0	1,867.3	1,778.7	1,443.7	339.3	1,114.8	336.0		70.5
2012: I	13,506.4	9,546.8	3,406.6	6,145.9	1,895.1	1,820.6	1,470.0	349.7	1,129.6	352.1		56.9
II	13,548.5	9,582.5	3,409.4	6,178.2	1,898.4	1,840.6	1,482.9	350.2	1,142.8	359.3		41.4
III	13,652.5	9,620.1	3,439.7	6,186.7	1,928.8	1,844.8	1,476.1	350.2	1,135.4	370.9		60.3
IV ᴾ	13,656.8	9,670.0	3,476.4	6,201.3	1,921.7	1,894.4	1,510.7	355.1	1,166.3	386.1		12.0

See next page for continuation of table.

Table B–2. Real gross domestic product, 1964–2012—*Continued*

[Billions of chained (2005) dollars, except as noted; quarterly data at seasonally adjusted annual rates]

Year or quarter	Net exports	Exports	Imports	Total	Federal Total	National defense	Non-defense	State and local	Final sales of domestic product	Gross domestic purchases [1]	Addendum: Gross national product [2]	Gross domestic product	Gross domestic purchases [1]
1964		124.5	136.9	1,018.0					3,390.8	3,423.4	3,417.5	5.8	5.5
1965		128.0	151.5	1,048.7					3,587.6	3,656.1	3,636.4	6.4	6.8
1966		136.9	174.0	1,141.1					3,803.4	3,907.0	3,869.8	6.5	6.9
1967		140.0	186.7	1,228.7					3,920.0	4,014.8	3,967.7	2.5	2.8
1968		151.0	214.5	1,267.2					4,115.8	4,222.1	4,160.6	4.8	5.2
1969		158.3	226.7	1,264.3					4,245.0	4,355.0	4,288.0	3.1	3.1
1970		175.3	236.4	1,233.7					4,284.3	4,348.3	4,295.8	.2	-.2
1971		178.3	249.0	1,206.9					4,403.6	4,503.1	4,442.2	3.4	3.6
1972		191.7	277.0	1,198.1					4,636.7	4,751.8	4,678.9	5.3	5.5
1973		227.8	289.9	1,193.9					4,884.0	4,987.0	4,960.3	5.8	5.0
1974		245.8	283.3	1,224.0					4,870.0	4,922.1	4,939.8	-.6	-1.3
1975		244.3	251.8	1,251.6					4,922.1	4,867.9	4,917.2	-.2	-1.1
1976		255.0	301.1	1,257.2					5,115.9	5,184.8	5,186.8	5.4	6.5
1977		261.1	334.0	1,271.0					5,340.3	5,459.8	5,429.1	4.6	5.3
1978		288.6	362.9	1,308.4					5,634.9	5,758.4	5,728.4	5.6	5.5
1979		317.2	369.0	1,332.8					5,836.2	5,898.3	5,925.2	3.1	2.4
1980		351.4	344.5	1,358.8					5,873.6	5,784.8	5,908.3	-.3	-1.9
1981		355.7	353.5	1,371.2					5,954.4	5,939.7	6,047.3	2.5	2.7
1982		328.5	349.1	1,395.3					5,918.2	5,860.4	5,934.0	-1.9	-1.3
1983		320.1	393.1	1,446.3					6,167.6	6,203.1	6,197.1	4.5	5.8
1984		346.2	488.8	1,494.9					6,490.0	6,739.7	6,634.1	7.2	8.7
1985		356.7	520.5	1,599.0					6,833.1	7,039.4	6,888.0	4.1	4.4
1986		384.1	565.0	1,696.2					7,092.7	7,297.2	7,110.4	3.5	3.7
1987		425.4	598.4	1,737.1					7,289.9	7,512.1	7,335.9	3.2	2.9
1988		493.5	621.9	1,758.9					7,601.3	7,752.2	7,643.9	4.1	3.2
1989		550.2	649.3	1,806.8					7,860.8	7,984.2	7,917.3	3.6	3.0
1990		599.7	672.6	1,864.0					8,025.8	8,097.8	8,075.0	1.9	1.4
1991		639.5	671.6	1,884.4					8,027.9	8,027.8	8,048.8	-.2	-.9
1992		683.5	718.7	1,893.2					8,277.2	8,302.7	8,319.4	3.4	3.4
1993		705.9	780.8	1,878.2					8,508.0	8,585.7	8,556.0	2.9	3.4
1994		767.4	873.9	1,878.2					8,801.7	8,968.5	8,893.0	4.1	4.5
1995	-98.8	845.1	943.9	1,888.9	704.1	476.8	227.5	1,183.6	9,065.4	9,181.3	9,121.7	2.5	2.4
1996	-110.7	915.3	1,026.0	1,907.9	696.0	470.4	225.7	1,211.1	9,404.4	9,534.0	9,463.1	3.7	3.8
1997	-139.8	1,024.3	1,164.1	1,943.8	689.1	457.2	231.9	1,254.3	9,774.2	9,984.4	9,873.4	4.5	4.7
1998	-252.5	1,047.7	1,300.2	1,985.0	681.4	447.5	233.7	1,303.8	10,208.3	10,531.1	10,295.3	4.4	5.5
1999	-356.4	1,093.4	1,449.9	2,056.1	694.6	455.8	238.7	1,361.8	10,706.5	11,131.8	10,802.9	4.8	5.7
2000	-451.3	1,187.4	1,638.7	2,097.8	698.1	453.5	244.4	1,400.1	11,158.0	11,671.6	11,259.2	4.1	4.8
2001	-471.8	1,120.8	1,592.6	2,178.3	726.5	470.7	255.5	1,452.3	11,382.0	11,815.8	11,395.0	1.1	1.2
2002	-548.5	1,098.3	1,646.8	2,279.6	779.5	505.3	273.9	1,500.6	11,533.6	12,097.5	11,597.1	1.8	2.4
2003	-603.7	1,116.0	1,719.7	2,330.5	831.1	549.2	281.7	1,499.7	11,820.5	12,444.7	11,909.9	2.5	2.9
2004	-687.9	1,222.5	1,910.4	2,362.0	865.0	580.4	284.6	1,497.1	12,181.3	12,928.3	12,341.6	3.5	3.9
2005	-722.7	1,305.1	2,027.8	2,369.9	876.3	589.0	287.3	1,493.6	12,573.0	13,345.7	12,720.1	3.1	3.2
2006	-729.4	1,422.1	2,151.5	2,402.1	894.9	598.4	296.6	1,507.2	12,899.3	13,688.1	13,028.3	2.7	2.6
2007	-648.8	1,554.4	2,203.2	2,434.2	906.1	611.8	294.2	1,528.1	13,177.5	13,855.3	13,322.0	1.9	1.2
2008	-494.8	1,649.3	2,144.0	2,497.4	971.1	657.7	313.3	1,528.1	13,200.5	13,653.1	13,316.9	-.3	-1.5
2009	-355.2	1,498.7	1,853.8	2,589.4	1,030.6	696.9	333.7	1,561.8	12,899.7	13,102.3	12,889.0	-3.1	-4.0
2010	-419.7	1,665.6	2,085.2	2,605.8	1,076.8	717.6	359.2	1,534.1	13,010.3	13,473.0	13,253.4	2.4	2.8
2011	-408.0	1,776.9	2,184.9	2,523.9	1,047.0	699.1	347.9	1,482.0	13,265.3	13,698.8	13,522.0	1.8	1.7
2012 p	-401.5	1,836.0	2,237.6	2,481.3	1,024.1	677.3	347.0	1,461.9	13,537.5	13,984.4		2.2	2.1
2009: I	-403.5	1,452.5	1,856.0	2,531.6	995.8	670.8	325.0	1,538.3	12,870.3	13,103.7	12,819.5	-5.3	-7.3
II	-322.8	1,454.6	1,777.4	2,590.4	1,028.2	696.3	331.8	1,565.2	12,890.0	13,014.4	12,806.8	-.3	-2.7
III	-346.9	1,502.3	1,849.3	2,614.3	1,043.9	709.1	334.7	1,573.6	12,928.3	13,082.0	12,895.3	1.4	2.1
IV	-347.5	1,585.2	1,932.7	2,621.1	1,054.6	711.4	343.2	1,570.2	12,910.2	13,209.3	13,034.5	4.0	4.0
2010: I	-372.7	1,608.2	1,980.9	2,600.4	1,056.2	704.8	351.5	1,548.3	12,914.7	13,309.3	13,121.9	2.3	3.1
II	-428.7	1,645.4	2,074.2	2,618.7	1,081.0	717.3	363.7	1,542.7	12,985.4	13,436.9	13,216.5	2.2	3.9
III	-458.9	1,683.9	2,142.8	2,616.7	1,090.7	729.9	360.8	1,531.6	13,005.5	13,553.4	13,301.1	2.6	3.5
IV	-418.3	1,724.7	2,143.0	2,587.4	1,079.4	718.6	360.8	1,513.6	13,135.6	13,590.5	13,374.2	2.4	1.1
2011: I	-416.6	1,748.8	2,165.4	2,540.7	1,050.4	691.3	359.3	1,495.3	13,154.4	13,592.1	13,394.3	.1	.0
II	-399.6	1,766.4	2,166.0	2,535.4	1,057.5	705.2	352.3	1,483.4	13,234.1	13,655.2	13,486.1	2.5	1.9
III	-397.9	1,792.9	2,190.8	2,516.6	1,045.9	709.8	335.9	1,475.9	13,311.2	13,696.4	13,534.7	1.3	1.2
IV	-418.0	1,799.3	2,217.3	2,502.7	1,034.2	690.1	344.1	1,473.3	13,361.4	13,851.4	13,672.9	4.1	4.6
2012: I	-415.5	1,818.7	2,234.2	2,483.7	1,023.1	677.6	345.6	1,465.3	13,440.1	13,914.4	13,693.8	2.0	1.8
II	-407.4	1,842.1	2,249.6	2,479.4	1,022.5	677.3	345.3	1,461.6	13,497.9	13,948.5	13,763.6	1.3	1.0
III	-395.2	1,850.9	2,246.1	2,503.1	1,045.9	698.1	347.8	1,462.7	13,577.4	14,039.3	13,862.9	3.1	2.6
IV p	-387.9	1,832.5	2,220.4	2,458.9	1,005.0	656.0	349.3	1,458.0	13,634.7	14,035.5		.1	-.1

[1] Gross domestic product (GDP) less exports of goods and services plus imports of goods and services.
[2] GDP plus net income receipts from rest of the world.

Source: Department of Commerce (Bureau of Economic Analysis).

[Quarterly data are seasonally adjusted]

Year or quarter	Index numbers, 2005=100					Percent change from preceding period [1]				
	Gross domestic product (GDP)			Personal consumption expenditures (PCE)		Gross domestic product (GDP)			Personal consumption expenditures (PCE)	
	Real GDP (chain-type quantity index)	GDP chain-type price index	GDP implicit price deflator	PCE chain-type price index	PCE less food and energy price index	Real GDP (chain-type quantity index)	GDP chain-type price index	GDP implicit price deflator	PCE chain-type price index	PCE less food and energy price index
1964	26.851	19.589	19.580	19.536	20.091	5.8	1.6	1.6	1.5	1.5
1965	28.575	19.945	19.936	19.819	20.345	6.4	1.8	1.8	1.4	1.3
1966	30.437	20.511	20.502	20.322	20.805	6.5	2.8	2.8	2.5	2.3
1967	31.206	21.142	21.133	20.834	21.442	2.5	3.1	3.1	2.5	3.1
1968	32.717	22.040	22.031	21.645	22.362	4.8	4.2	4.2	3.9	4.3
1969	33.733	23.130	23.119	22.626	23.412	3.1	4.9	4.9	4.5	4.7
1970	33.798	24.349	24.338	23.685	24.510	.2	5.3	5.3	4.7	4.7
1971	34.932	25.567	25.554	24.692	25.664	3.4	5.0	5.0	4.3	4.7
1972	36.788	26.670	26.657	25.536	26.493	5.3	4.3	4.3	3.4	3.2
1973	38.920	28.148	28.136	26.913	27.505	5.8	5.5	5.5	5.4	3.8
1974	38.705	30.695	30.690	29.716	29.687	–.6	9.0	9.1	10.4	7.9
1975	38.623	33.606	33.591	32.198	32.174	–.2	9.5	9.5	8.4	8.4
1976	40.695	35.535	35.519	33.966	34.130	5.4	5.7	5.7	5.5	6.1
1977	42.566	37.796	37.783	36.171	36.320	4.6	6.4	6.4	6.5	6.4
1978	44.940	40.447	40.435	38.705	38.749	5.6	7.0	7.0	7.0	6.7
1979	46.345	43.811	43.798	42.137	41.569	3.1	8.3	8.3	8.9	7.3
1980	46.217	47.817	47.791	46.663	45.377	–.3	9.1	9.1	10.7	9.2
1981	47.390	52.326	52.270	50.833	49.342	2.5	9.4	9.4	8.9	8.7
1982	46.470	55.514	55.459	53.640	52.526	–1.9	6.1	6.1	5.5	6.5
1983	48.570	57.705	57.652	55.948	55.247	4.5	3.9	4.0	4.3	5.2
1984	52.060	59.874	59.817	58.065	57.541	7.2	3.8	3.8	3.8	4.2
1985	54.214	61.686	61.628	59.965	59.724	4.1	3.0	3.0	3.3	3.8
1986	56.092	63.057	62.991	61.427	61.974	3.5	2.2	2.2	2.4	3.8
1987	57.887	64.818	64.819	63.618	64.331	3.2	2.8	2.9	3.6	3.8
1988	60.266	67.047	67.046	66.151	67.120	4.1	3.4	3.4	4.0	4.3
1989	62.420	69.579	69.577	69.025	69.889	3.6	3.8	3.8	4.3	4.1
1990	63.591	72.274	72.262	72.180	72.872	1.9	3.9	3.9	4.6	4.3
1991	63.442	74.826	74.824	74.789	75.709	–.2	3.5	3.5	3.6	3.9
1992	65.595	76.602	76.598	76.989	78.256	3.4	2.4	2.4	2.9	3.4
1993	67.466	78.288	78.290	78.679	80.106	2.9	2.2	2.2	2.2	2.4
1994	70.214	79.935	79.940	80.302	81.875	4.1	2.1	2.1	2.1	2.2
1995	71.980	81.602	81.606	82.078	83.761	2.5	2.1	2.1	2.2	2.3
1996	74.672	83.154	83.159	83.864	85.386	3.7	1.9	1.9	2.2	1.9
1997	78.000	84.627	84.628	85.433	87.022	4.5	1.8	1.8	1.9	1.9
1998	81.397	85.580	85.584	86.246	88.284	4.4	1.1	1.1	1.0	1.5
1999	85.326	86.840	86.842	87.636	89.597	4.8	1.5	1.5	1.6	1.5
2000	88.857	88.724	88.723	89.818	91.154	4.1	2.2	2.2	2.5	1.7
2001	89.816	90.731	90.727	91.530	92.783	1.1	2.3	2.3	1.9	1.8
2002	91.445	92.192	92.196	92.778	94.390	1.8	1.6	1.6	1.4	1.7
2003	93.769	94.134	94.135	94.658	95.823	2.5	2.1	2.1	2.0	1.5
2004	97.021	96.784	96.786	97.121	97.815	3.5	2.8	2.8	2.6	2.1
2005	100.000	100.000	100.000	100.000	100.000	3.1	3.3	3.3	3.0	2.2
2006	102.658	103.237	103.231	102.723	102.265	2.7	3.2	3.2	2.7	2.3
2007	104.622	106.231	106.227	105.499	104.631	1.9	2.9	2.9	2.7	2.3
2008	104.270	108.565	108.582	108.943	107.020	–.3	2.2	2.2	3.3	2.3
2009	101.069	109.532	109.529	109.004	108.536	–3.1	.9	.9	.1	1.4
2010	103.486	111.002	110.993	111.087	110.214	2.4	1.3	1.3	1.9	1.5
2011	105.356	113.369	113.359	113.790	111.802	1.8	2.1	2.1	2.4	1.4
2012 ᵖ	107.670	115.382	115.381	115.784	113.704	2.2	1.8	1.8	1.8	1.7
2009: I	100.697	109.526	109.539	108.063	107.827	–5.3	1.0	.9	–2.1	.7
II	100.618	109.318	109.325	108.496	108.285	–.3	–.8	–.8	1.6	1.7
III	100.980	109.463	109.457	109.315	108.694	1.4	.5	.5	3.1	1.5
IV	101.981	109.820	109.793	110.142	109.339	4.0	1.3	1.2	3.1	2.4
2010: I	102.572	110.234	110.216	110.642	109.739	2.3	1.5	1.6	1.8	1.5
II	103.142	110.686	110.706	110.800	110.121	2.2	1.7	1.8	.6	1.4
III	103.807	111.248	111.238	111.154	110.395	2.6	2.0	1.9	1.3	1.0
IV	104.423	111.838	111.795	111.751	110.602	2.4	2.1	2.0	2.2	.8
2011: I	104.443	112.389	112.372	112.640	110.973	.1	2.0	2.1	3.2	1.3
II	105.084	113.109	113.109	113.633	111.599	2.5	2.6	2.6	3.6	2.3
III	105.418	113.937	113.950	114.293	112.138	1.3	3.0	3.0	2.3	1.9
IV	106.481	114.041	113.987	114.593	112.500	4.1	.4	.1	1.1	1.3
2012: I	106.999	114.608	114.599	115.300	113.122	2.0	2.0	2.2	2.5	2.2
II	107.333	115.050	115.035	115.496	113.603	1.3	1.6	1.5	.7	1.7
III	108.156	115.807	115.810	115.952	113.912	3.1	2.7	2.7	1.6	1.1
IVᵖ	108.190	116.063	116.068	116.389	114.181	.1	.9	.9	1.5	.9

[1] Quarterly percent changes are at annual rates.

Source: Department of Commerce (Bureau of Economic Analysis).

TABLE B–4. Percent changes in real gross domestic product, 1964–2012

[Percent change from preceding period; quarterly data at seasonally adjusted annual rates]

Year or quarter	Gross domestic product	Personal consumption expenditures			Gross private domestic investment				Exports and imports of goods and services		Government consumption expenditures and gross investment		
					Nonresidential fixed								
		Total	Goods	Services	Total	Structures	Equipment and software	Residential fixed	Exports	Imports	Total	Federal	State and local
1964	5.8	6.0	6.0	6.0	11.9	10.4	12.8	5.8	11.8	5.3	2.2	-1.3	6.8
1965	6.4	6.3	7.1	5.5	17.4	15.9	18.3	-2.9	2.8	10.6	3.0	.0	6.7
1966	6.5	5.7	6.3	5.0	12.5	6.8	16.0	-8.9	6.9	14.9	8.8	11.1	6.3
1967	2.5	3.0	2.0	4.1	-1.3	-2.5	-.7	-3.1	2.3	7.3	7.7	10.0	5.1
1968	4.8	5.8	6.2	5.3	4.5	1.4	6.2	13.6	7.9	14.9	3.1	.8	5.9
1969	3.1	3.7	3.1	4.5	7.6	5.4	8.8	3.0	4.8	5.7	-.2	-3.4	3.4
1970	.2	2.3	.8	3.9	-.5	.3	-1.0	-6.0	10.7	4.3	-2.4	-7.4	2.8
1971	3.4	3.8	4.2	3.5	.0	-1.6	1.0	27.4	1.7	5.3	-2.2	-7.7	3.1
1972	5.3	6.1	6.5	5.8	9.2	3.1	12.9	17.8	7.5	11.3	-.7	-4.1	2.2
1973	5.8	5.0	5.2	4.7	14.5	8.2	18.3	-.6	18.9	4.6	-.4	-4.2	2.9
1974	-.6	-.8	-3.6	1.9	.8	-2.2	2.6	-20.6	7.9	-2.3	2.5	.9	3.8
1975	-.2	2.3	.7	3.8	-9.9	-10.5	-9.5	-13.0	-.6	-11.1	2.3	.3	3.7
1976	5.4	5.6	7.0	4.3	4.9	2.4	6.3	23.5	4.4	19.6	.4	.0	.7
1977	4.6	4.2	4.3	4.1	11.3	4.1	15.1	21.5	2.4	10.9	1.1	2.1	.4
1978	5.6	4.4	4.1	4.7	15.0	14.4	15.2	6.3	10.5	8.7	2.9	2.5	3.3
1979	3.1	2.4	1.6	3.1	10.1	12.7	8.7	-3.7	9.9	1.7	1.9	2.4	1.5
1980	-.3	-.4	-2.5	1.5	-.3	5.9	-3.6	-21.2	10.8	-6.6	1.9	4.7	-.1
1981	2.5	1.5	1.2	1.8	5.7	8.0	4.3	-8.0	1.2	2.6	.9	4.8	-2.0
1982	-1.9	1.4	.7	1.9	-3.8	-1.6	-5.2	-18.2	-7.6	-1.3	1.8	3.9	.0
1983	4.5	5.7	6.4	5.2	-1.3	-10.8	5.4	41.4	-2.6	12.6	3.7	6.6	1.2
1984	7.2	5.3	7.2	3.9	17.6	13.9	19.8	14.8	8.2	24.3	3.4	3.1	3.6
1985	4.1	5.2	5.3	5.2	6.6	7.1	6.4	1.6	3.0	6.5	7.0	7.8	6.2
1986	3.5	4.1	5.6	3.0	-2.9	-11.0	1.9	12.3	7.7	8.5	6.1	5.7	6.4
1987	3.2	3.1	1.8	4.0	-.1	-2.9	1.4	2.0	10.8	5.9	2.4	3.6	1.4
1988	4.1	4.0	3.7	4.2	5.2	.7	7.5	-1.0	16.0	3.9	1.3	-1.6	3.7
1989	3.6	2.8	2.5	3.0	5.6	2.0	7.3	-3.0	11.5	4.4	2.7	1.6	3.7
1990	1.9	2.0	.6	3.0	.5	1.5	.0	-8.6	9.0	3.6	3.2	2.0	4.1
1991	-.2	.2	-2.0	1.5	-5.4	-11.1	-2.6	-9.6	6.6	-.2	1.1	-.2	2.1
1992	3.4	3.4	3.2	3.6	3.2	-6.0	7.3	13.8	6.9	7.0	.5	-1.8	2.2
1993	2.9	3.6	4.2	3.2	8.7	-.6	12.5	8.2	3.3	8.6	-.8	-3.9	1.5
1994	4.1	3.8	5.3	3.0	9.2	1.8	11.9	9.7	8.7	11.9	.0	-3.8	2.6
1995	2.5	2.7	3.0	2.5	10.5	6.4	12.0	-3.3	10.1	8.0	.6	-2.7	2.7
1996	3.7	3.5	4.5	2.9	9.3	5.7	10.6	8.0	8.3	8.7	1.0	-1.2	2.3
1997	4.5	3.7	4.8	3.1	12.1	7.3	13.8	1.9	11.9	13.5	1.9	-1.0	3.6
1998	4.4	5.2	6.8	4.4	12.0	5.1	14.5	7.7	2.3	11.7	2.1	-1.1	3.9
1999	4.8	5.5	8.0	4.1	10.4	.1	14.1	6.3	4.4	11.5	3.6	1.9	4.5
2000	4.1	5.1	5.3	5.0	9.8	7.8	10.5	1.0	8.6	13.0	2.0	.5	2.8
2001	1.1	2.7	3.1	2.5	-2.8	-1.5	-3.2	.6	-5.6	-2.8	3.8	4.1	3.7
2002	1.8	2.7	4.1	1.9	-7.9	-17.7	-4.2	5.2	-2.0	3.4	4.7	7.3	3.3
2003	2.5	2.8	4.6	1.9	1.4	-3.8	3.1	8.2	1.6	4.4	2.2	6.6	-.1
2004	3.5	3.3	4.5	2.7	6.2	1.1	7.9	9.8	9.5	11.1	1.4	4.1	-.2
2005	3.1	3.4	4.2	3.0	6.7	1.4	8.5	6.2	6.7	6.1	.3	1.3	-.2
2006	2.7	2.9	3.3	2.6	8.0	9.2	7.6	-7.3	9.0	6.1	1.4	2.1	.9
2007	1.9	2.3	3.0	1.9	6.5	14.1	3.3	-18.7	9.3	2.4	1.3	1.2	1.4
2008	-.3	-.6	-2.5	.4	-.8	6.4	-4.3	-23.9	6.1	-2.7	2.6	7.2	.0
2009	-3.1	-1.9	-3.0	-1.4	-18.1	-21.1	-16.4	-22.4	-9.1	-13.5	3.7	6.1	2.2
2010	2.4	1.8	3.6	1.0	.7	-15.6	8.9	-3.7	11.1	12.5	.6	4.5	-1.8
2011	1.8	2.5	3.8	1.9	8.6	2.7	11.0	-1.4	6.7	4.8	-3.1	-2.8	-3.4
2012 ᵖ	2.2	1.9	3.1	1.3	7.7	10.1	6.9	12.1	3.3	2.4	-1.7	-2.2	-1.4
2009: I	-5.3	-1.6	.2	-2.5	-28.9	-30.5	-27.9	-35.1	-28.7	-33.9	1.8	-3.0	4.9
II	-.3	-1.8	-2.1	-1.6	-17.5	-31.4	-8.6	-22.2	.6	-15.9	9.6	13.7	7.2
III	1.4	2.1	7.5	-.4	-7.8	-26.7	3.6	17.2	13.8	17.2	3.7	6.3	2.2
IV	4.0	.0	-.5	.2	-6.4	-28.8	6.0	-4.8	24.0	19.3	1.1	4.2	-.9
2010: I	2.3	2.5	5.2	1.2	2.1	-23.0	14.7	-11.4	5.9	10.4	-3.1	.6	-5.5
II	2.2	2.6	3.3	2.3	12.3	13.1	12.0	23.1	9.6	20.2	2.8	9.7	-1.4
III	2.6	2.5	3.8	1.9	7.7	-2.2	11.9	-28.6	9.7	13.9	-.3	3.7	-2.9
IV	2.4	4.1	7.9	2.3	9.2	9.3	9.2	1.5	10.0	.0	-4.4	-4.1	-4.6
2011: I	.1	3.1	5.4	2.0	-1.3	-28.2	11.1	-1.4	5.7	4.3	-7.0	-10.3	-4.7
II	2.5	1.0	-1.0	1.9	14.5	35.2	7.8	4.1	4.1	.1	-.8	2.8	-3.2
III	1.3	1.7	1.4	1.8	19.0	20.7	18.3	1.4	6.1	4.7	-2.9	-4.3	-2.0
IV	4.1	2.0	5.4	.3	9.5	11.5	8.8	12.1	1.4	4.9	-2.2	-4.4	-.7
2012: I	2.0	2.4	4.7	1.3	7.5	12.9	5.4	20.5	4.4	3.1	-3.0	-4.2	-2.2
II	1.3	1.5	.3	2.1	3.6	.6	4.8	8.5	5.3	2.8	-.7	-.2	-1.0
III	3.1	1.6	3.6	.6	-1.8	.0	-2.6	13.5	1.9	-.6	3.9	9.5	.3
IV ᵖ	.1	2.1	4.3	.9	9.7	5.8	11.3	17.5	-3.9	-4.5	-6.9	-14.8	-1.3

Note: Percent changes based on unrounded data.

Source: Department of Commerce (Bureau of Economic Analysis).

TABLE B–5. Contributions to percent change in real gross domestic product, 1964–2012

[Percentage points, except as noted; quarterly data at seasonally adjusted annual rates]

Year or quarter	Gross domestic product (percent change)	Personal consumption expenditures			Gross private domestic investment							
		Total	Goods	Services	Total	Fixed investment					Residential	Change in private inventories
						Total	Nonresidential					
							Total	Structures	Equipment and software			
1964	5.8	3.69	1.91	1.78	1.25	1.37	1.07	0.36	0.71	0.30	−0.13
1965	6.4	3.91	2.26	1.66	2.16	1.50	1.65	.57	1.07	−.15	.66
1966	6.5	3.50	2.02	1.48	1.44	.87	1.29	.27	1.02	−.43	.58
1967	2.5	1.82	.62	1.21	−.76	−.28	−.15	−.10	−.05	−.13	−.49
1968	4.8	3.51	1.92	1.59	.90	.99	.46	.05	.41	.53	−.10
1969	3.1	2.29	.95	1.34	.90	.90	.78	.20	.58	.13	.00
1970	.2	1.44	.24	1.19	−1.04	−.31	−.06	.01	−.07	−.26	−.73
1971	3.4	2.37	1.27	1.10	1.67	1.10	.00	−.06	.07	1.10	.58
1972	5.3	3.81	1.97	1.84	1.87	1.81	.93	.12	.81	.89	.06
1973	5.8	3.08	1.57	1.51	1.96	1.47	1.50	.31	1.19	−.04	.50
1974	−.6	−.52	−1.12	.60	−1.31	−1.04	.09	−.09	.18	−1.13	−.27
1975	−.2	1.40	.20	1.20	−2.98	−1.71	−1.14	−.43	−.70	−.57	−1.27
1976	5.4	3.51	2.08	1.43	2.84	1.42	.52	.09	.43	.90	1.41
1977	4.6	2.66	1.28	1.38	2.43	2.18	1.19	.15	1.04	.99	.25
1978	5.6	2.77	1.22	1.56	2.16	2.04	1.69	.54	1.15	.35	.12
1979	3.1	1.48	.47	1.02	.61	1.02	1.23	.53	.71	−.21	−.41
1980	−.3	−.22	−.74	.52	−2.12	−1.21	−.03	.27	−.30	−1.17	−.91
1981	2.5	.95	.34	.62	1.55	.39	.74	.40	.34	−.35	1.16
1982	−1.9	.86	.19	.67	−2.55	−1.21	−.50	−.09	−.42	−.71	−1.34
1983	4.5	3.65	1.74	1.91	1.45	1.17	−.17	−.57	.41	1.33	.29
1984	7.2	3.43	1.97	1.47	4.63	2.68	2.05	.60	1.45	.64	1.95
1985	4.1	3.32	1.41	1.90	−.17	.89	.82	.32	.50	.07	−1.06
1986	3.5	2.62	1.49	1.13	−.12	.20	−.36	−.50	.15	.55	−.32
1987	3.2	2.01	.48	1.53	.51	.09	−.01	−.11	.10	.10	.42
1988	4.1	2.64	.98	1.66	.39	.53	.58	.02	.55	−.05	−.14
1989	3.6	1.86	.66	1.20	.64	.47	.61	.07	.54	−.14	.17
1990	1.9	1.34	.16	1.18	−.53	−.32	.05	.05	.00	−.37	−.21
1991	−.2	.10	−.51	.61	−1.20	−.94	−.57	−.39	−.18	−.37	−.26
1992	3.4	2.27	.78	1.49	1.07	.79	.31	−.18	.50	.47	.29
1993	2.9	2.37	1.02	1.35	1.21	1.14	.83	−.02	.85	.31	.07
1994	4.1	2.57	1.29	1.27	1.94	1.30	.91	.05	.86	.39	.63
1995	2.5	1.81	.73	1.08	.48	.94	1.08	.17	.91	−.14	−.46
1996	3.7	2.35	1.09	1.26	1.35	1.33	1.01	.16	.85	.33	.02
1997	4.5	2.48	1.16	1.33	1.95	1.41	1.33	.21	1.12	.08	.54
1998	4.4	3.50	1.61	1.90	1.65	1.70	1.38	.16	1.22	.32	−.05
1999	4.8	3.68	1.90	1.78	1.50	1.52	1.24	.00	1.24	.28	−.02
2000	4.1	3.44	1.29	2.15	1.19	1.24	1.20	.24	.96	.05	−.05
2001	1.1	1.85	.77	1.09	−1.24	−.32	−.35	−.05	−.30	.03	−.92
2002	1.8	1.85	.99	.86	−.22	−.70	−.94	−.58	−.36	.24	.48
2003	2.5	1.97	1.12	.85	.60	.54	.14	−.10	.24	.40	.06
2004	3.5	2.30	1.09	1.22	1.57	1.15	.63	.03	.60	.52	.42
2005	3.1	2.35	1.01	1.34	.93	1.05	.69	.04	.65	.36	−.13
2006	2.7	1.98	.80	1.18	.47	.40	.86	.27	.59	−.46	.07
2007	1.9	1.60	.71	.89	−.56	−.33	.73	.46	.26	−1.05	−.23
2008	−.3	−.39	−.59	.21	−1.66	−1.15	−.09	.24	−.34	−1.05	−.51
2009	−3.1	−1.36	−.69	−.67	−3.59	−2.80	−2.08	−.85	−1.23	−.73	−.78
2010	2.4	1.28	.82	.46	1.50	−.03	.07	−.50	.56	−.09	1.52
2011	1.8	1.79	.89	.90	.62	.76	.80	.07	.72	−.03	−.14
2012 p	2.2	1.33	.74	.60	1.17	1.03	.76	.27	.49	.27	.14
2009: I	−5.3	−1.06	.06	−1.12	−7.02	−4.73	−3.54	−1.39	−2.16	−1.18	−2.29
II	−.3	−1.21	−.46	−.75	−3.52	−2.49	−1.86	−1.31	−.54	−.63	−1.03
III	1.4	1.50	1.68	−.18	−.14	−.32	−.73	−.98	.25	.40	.19
IV	4.0	−.01	−.10	.09	3.85	−.69	−.57	−.98	.40	−.12	4.55
2010: I	2.3	1.72	1.18	.54	2.13	−.10	.20	−.70	.90	−.30	2.23
II	2.2	1.81	.76	1.05	1.65	1.58	1.07	.31	.76	.51	.07
III	2.6	1.75	.86	.88	1.87	−.10	.70	−.06	.76	−.80	1.97
IV	2.4	2.84	1.78	1.06	−.75	.87	.83	.23	.60	.03	−1.61
2011: I	.1	2.22	1.27	.95	−.68	−.14	−.11	−.84	.72	−.03	−.54
II	2.5	.70	−.22	.92	1.40	1.39	1.30	.77	.53	.09	.01
III	1.3	1.18	.33	.85	.68	1.75	1.71	.51	1.20	.03	−1.07
IV	4.1	1.45	1.29	.16	3.72	1.19	.93	.31	.62	.26	2.53
2012: I	2.0	1.72	1.11	.61	.78	1.18	.74	.35	.39	.43	−.39
II	1.3	1.06	.08	.99	.09	.56	.36	.02	.35	.19	−.46
III	3.1	1.12	.85	.26	.85	.12	−.19	.00	−.19	.31	.73
IV p	.1	1.47	1.03	.44	−.20	1.36	.96	.16	.79	.40	−1.55

See next page for continuation of table.

TABLE B–5. Contributions to percent change in real gross domestic product, 1964–2012—*Continued*

[Percentage points, except as noted; quarterly data at seasonally adjusted annual rates]

Year or quarter	Net exports of goods and services							Government consumption expenditures and gross investment				
	Net exports	Exports			Imports			Total	Federal			State and local
		Total	Goods	Services	Total	Goods	Services		Total	National defense	Non-defense	
1964	0.36	0.59	0.52	0.07	−0.23	−0.19	−0.04	0.49	−0.17	−0.39	0.23	0.65
1965	−.30	.15	.02	.13	−.45	−.41	−.04	.65	−.01	−.19	.19	.66
1966	−.29	.36	.27	.09	−.65	−.49	−.16	1.87	1.24	1.21	.03	.63
1967	−.22	.12	.02	.10	−.34	−.17	−.16	1.68	1.17	1.19	−.02	.51
1968	−.30	.41	.30	.10	−.71	−.68	−.03	.73	.10	.16	−.06	.63
1969	−.04	.25	.20	.05	−.29	−.20	−.09	−.05	−.42	−.49	.06	.37
1970	.34	.56	.44	.12	−.22	−.15	−.07	−.55	−.86	−.83	−.03	.31
1971	−.19	.10	−.02	.11	−.29	−.33	.04	−.50	−.85	−.97	.12	.36
1972	−.21	.42	.43	−.01	−.63	−.57	−.06	−.16	−.42	−.60	.18	.26
1973	.82	1.12	1.01	.11	−.29	−.34	.05	−.08	−.41	−.39	−.02	.33
1974	.75	.58	.46	.12	.18	.17	.00	.52	.08	−.05	.13	.44
1975	.89	−.05	−.16	.10	.94	.87	.07	.48	.03	−.06	.09	.45
1976	−1.08	.37	.31	.05	−1.45	−1.35	−.10	.10	.00	−.02	.03	.09
1977	−.72	.20	.08	.11	−.92	−.84	−.07	.23	.19	.07	.12	.04
1978	.05	.82	.68	.15	−.78	−.67	−.11	.60	.22	.05	.16	.38
1979	.66	.82	.77	.06	−.16	−.14	−.02	.37	.20	.17	.03	.17
1980	1.68	.97	.86	.11	.71	.67	.04	.38	.39	.25	.14	−.01
1981	−.15	.12	−.09	.21	−.27	−.18	−.09	.19	.42	.38	.04	−.23
1982	−.60	−.73	−.67	−.06	.12	.20	−.08	.35	.35	.48	−.13	.01
1983	−1.35	−.22	−.19	−.03	−1.13	−1.01	−.13	.76	.63	.50	.13	.13
1984	−1.58	.63	.46	.17	−2.21	−1.83	−.39	.70	.30	.35	−.05	.40
1985	−.42	.23	.20	.02	−.65	−.52	−.13	1.41	.74	.60	.14	.67
1986	−.30	.54	.26	.28	−.84	−.82	−.02	1.27	.55	.47	.08	.71
1987	.16	.77	.56	.21	−.61	−.39	−.22	.51	.35	.35	.00	.17
1988	.82	1.24	1.04	.20	−.43	−.36	−.07	.26	−.16	−.03	−.12	.42
1989	.52	.99	.75	.24	−.48	−.38	−.09	.55	.14	−.03	.17	.41
1990	.43	.81	.56	.26	−.38	−.26	−.13	.64	.18	.00	.18	.46
1991	.64	.63	.46	.16	.02	−.04	.05	.22	−.02	−.07	.05	.24
1992	−.05	.68	.52	.16	−.72	−.78	.06	.10	−.16	−.32	.16	.26
1993	−.57	.32	.23	.10	−.90	−.85	−.05	−.16	−.33	−.31	−.02	.17
1994	−.43	.85	.67	.19	−1.28	−1.18	−.10	.00	−.30	−.27	−.04	.30
1995	.11	1.03	.85	.19	−.92	−.86	−.06	.11	−.20	−.19	−.01	.30
1996	−.15	.90	.68	.22	−1.04	−.94	−.10	.19	−.08	−.06	−.02	.27
1997	−.32	1.30	1.11	.19	−1.62	−1.44	−.17	.34	−.07	−.13	.06	.41
1998	−1.18	.26	.18	.08	−1.43	−1.21	−.22	.38	−.07	−.09	.02	.45
1999	−.99	.47	.29	.18	−1.45	−1.31	−.14	.63	.12	.07	.04	.51
2000	−.85	.91	.82	.08	−1.76	−1.52	−.24	.36	.03	−.02	.05	.33
2001	−.20	−.61	−.48	−.13	.41	.39	.02	.67	.24	.14	.09	.43
2002	−.65	−.20	−.25	.05	−.46	−.42	−.04	.84	.44	.28	.15	.40
2003	−.45	.15	.12	.03	−.60	−.56	−.04	.42	.43	.36	.07	−.01
2004	−.66	.90	.56	.34	−1.55	−1.29	−.26	.26	.28	.26	.02	−.02
2005	−.27	.67	.52	.15	−.95	−.87	−.07	.06	.09	.07	.02	−.03
2006	−.06	.93	.68	.25	−.98	−.81	−.18	.26	.15	.07	.07	.11
2007	.62	1.03	.75	.28	−.40	−.37	−.04	.25	.09	.11	−.02	.17
2008	1.21	.73	.53	.20	.47	.57	−.10	.50	.50	.36	.15	.00
2009	1.14	−1.14	−1.05	−.10	2.28	2.19	.09	.74	.46	.31	.16	.28
2010	−.52	1.29	1.11	.18	−1.81	−1.74	−.07	.14	.37	.17	.20	−.23
2011	.07	.87	.65	.22	−.80	−.72	−.08	−.67	−.23	−.15	−.09	−.43
2012 *p*	.03	.46	.41	.05	−.43	−.31	−.12	−.34	−.18	−.17	−.01	−.16
2009: I	2.45	−3.78	−3.29	−.49	6.24	5.68	.56	.37	−.23	−.37	.14	.60
II	2.47	.10	−.17	.27	2.37	2.22	.15	1.94	1.04	.83	.21	.90
III	−.70	1.48	1.46	.02	−2.18	−2.12	−.06	.79	.51	.42	.09	.28
IV	−.05	2.55	2.14	.42	−2.60	−2.55	−.05	.23	.34	.07	.27	−.12
2010: I	−.83	.70	.79	−.09	−1.53	−1.46	−.06	−.69	.04	−.22	.26	−.73
II	−1.81	1.14	.97	.17	−2.95	−2.92	−.03	.59	.78	.40	.38	−.19
III	−.95	1.18	.76	.41	−2.13	−1.79	−.34	−.06	.31	.40	−.09	−.37
IV	1.24	1.24	.96	.28	−.01	−.15	.15	−.94	−.35	−.35	.00	−.59
2011: I	.03	.75	.52	.23	−.72	−.73	.01	−1.49	−.89	−.84	−.05	−.60
II	.54	.56	.35	.21	−.02	.10	−.12	−.16	.23	.45	−.22	−.39
III	.02	.83	.59	.25	−.81	−.43	−.38	−.60	−.36	.15	−.51	−.24
IV	−.64	.21	.58	−.38	−.85	−.90	.05	−.43	−.35	−.60	.25	−.08
2012: I	.06	.60	.39	.21	−.54	−.29	−.25	−.60	−.34	−.39	.05	−.26
II	.23	.72	.67	.05	−.49	−.42	−.07	−.14	−.02	−.01	−.01	−.12
III	.38	.27	.11	.16	.11	.18	−.07	.75	.71	.64	.08	.04
IV *p*	.24	−.55	−.56	.00	.79	.60	.19	−1.38	−1.23	−1.28	.04	−.15

Source: Department of Commerce (Bureau of Economic Analysis).

TABLE B–6. Chain-type quantity indexes for gross domestic product, 1964–2012

[Index numbers, 2005=100; quarterly data seasonally adjusted]

Year or quarter	Gross domestic product	Personal consumption expenditures			Gross private domestic investment					
						Fixed investment				
								Nonresidential		
		Total	Goods	Services	Total	Total	Total	Structures	Equipment and software	Residential
1964	26.851	23.939	22.994	23.885	17.589	17.882	13.701	57.399	7.303	34.011
1965	28.575	25.453	24.623	25.204	20.058	19.708	16.088	66.553	8.641	33.017
1966	30.437	26.897	26.184	26.453	21.825	20.838	18.100	71.109	10.024	30.063
1967	31.206	27.703	26.697	27.541	20.827	20.453	17.856	69.313	9.958	29.117
1968	32.717	29.301	28.350	29.009	22.039	21.881	18.654	70.299	10.578	33.086
1969	33.733	30.399	29.216	30.303	23.323	23.242	20.070	74.096	11.513	34.063
1970	33.798	31.112	29.447	31.487	21.791	22.754	19.963	74.300	11.399	32.026
1971	34.932	32.297	30.679	32.574	24.275	24.477	19.964	73.082	11.512	40.808
1972	36.788	34.283	32.685	34.458	27.150	27.420	21.797	75.359	12.997	48.061
1973	38.920	35.982	34.378	36.091	30.331	29.926	24.968	81.520	15.381	47.752
1974	38.705	35.683	33.124	36.783	28.097	28.055	25.177	79.755	15.774	37.895
1975	38.623	36.492	33.349	38.164	23.120	25.042	22.689	71.355	14.272	32.975
1976	40.695	38.525	35.684	39.802	27.791	27.511	23.800	73.073	15.164	40.740
1977	42.566	40.146	37.215	41.447	31.989	31.465	26.486	76.079	17.449	49.486
1978	44.940	41.916	38.753	43.375	35.846	35.274	30.450	87.058	20.106	52.602
1979	46.345	42.912	39.373	44.700	36.989	37.265	33.517	98.098	21.861	50.672
1980	46.217	42.761	38.376	45.389	32.926	34.844	33.429	103.837	21.075	39.949
1981	47.390	43.410	38.830	46.203	35.886	35.623	35.333	112.161	21.971	36.747
1982	46.470	44.015	39.101	47.103	30.859	33.125	34.003	110.325	20.829	30.075
1983	48.570	46.531	41.589	49.568	33.733	35.541	33.563	98.404	21.950	42.524
1984	52.060	48.998	44.586	51.508	43.672	41.543	39.486	112.125	26.303	48.836
1985	54.214	51.551	46.931	54.173	43.266	43.729	42.103	120.095	27.974	49.608
1986	56.092	53.642	49.556	55.784	42.971	44.237	40.901	106.935	28.504	55.696
1987	57.887	55.297	50.448	58.007	44.295	44.480	40.870	103.859	28.895	56.807
1988	60.266	57.525	52.322	60.469	45.337	45.947	43.008	104.539	31.074	56.231
1989	62.420	59.152	53.643	62.301	47.156	47.328	45.409	106.616	33.351	54.524
1990	63.591	60.359	53.975	64.151	45.569	46.340	45.633	108.187	33.361	49.819
1991	63.442	60.450	52.904	65.110	41.862	43.335	43.186	96.150	32.504	45.032
1992	65.595	62.511	54.571	67.431	45.254	45.904	44.565	90.354	34.873	51.263
1993	67.466	64.731	56.838	69.589	49.299	49.839	48.456	89.768	39.226	55.450
1994	70.214	67.203	59.836	71.666	55.998	54.500	52.915	91.405	43.904	60.840
1995	71.980	69.021	61.623	73.488	57.743	58.010	58.478	97.235	49.158	58.850
1996	74.672	71.429	64.383	75.640	62.851	63.213	63.940	102.744	54.383	63.550
1997	78.000	74.066	67.453	77.973	70.672	69.045	71.658	110.280	61.861	64.751
1998	81.397	77.950	72.010	81.409	77.747	76.537	80.264	115.911	70.837	69.732
1999	85.326	82.213	77.745	84.744	84.592	83.658	88.640	116.049	80.857	74.092
2000	88.857	86.382	81.847	88.944	90.371	89.843	97.327	125.101	89.320	74.834
2001	89.816	88.718	84.417	91.134	84.023	88.142	94.614	123.191	86.438	75.258
2002	91.445	91.080	87.848	92.870	82.879	84.412	87.112	101.377	82.789	79.204
2003	93.769	93.650	91.890	94.611	86.090	87.390	88.290	97.514	85.377	85.712
2004	97.021	96.731	95.988	97.134	94.749	93.880	93.740	98.571	92.138	94.130
2005	100.000	100.000	100.000	100.000	100.000	100.000	100.000	100.000	100.000	100.000
2006	102.658	102.850	103.322	102.599	102.742	102.375	108.027	109.180	107.590	92.667
2007	104.622	105.218	106.394	104.599	99.412	100.390	115.039	124.578	111.168	75.379
2008	104.270	104.637	103.776	105.067	89.296	93.228	114.125	132.595	106.411	57.345
2009	101.069	102.602	100.697	103.558	67.124	75.494	93.507	104.659	88.911	44.489
2010	103.486	104.460	104.304	104.554	76.327	75.326	94.148	88.308	96.822	42.862
2011	105.356	107.103	108.263	106.543	80.284	80.311	102.288	90.733	107.473	42.268
2012 p	107.670	109.103	109.103	111.580	87.973	87.173	110.214	99.875	114.862	47.368
2009: I	100.697	102.681	100.211	103.924	69.786	79.032	98.291	118.743	89.688	45.843
II	100.618	102.224	99.684	103.494	64.480	75.092	93.667	108.062	87.704	43.058
III	100.980	102.757	101.506	103.385	64.208	74.501	91.786	99.980	88.474	44.799
IV	101.981	102.747	101.389	103.429	70.022	73.352	90.285	91.848	89.777	44.257
2010: I	102.572	103.377	102.691	103.729	73.259	73.180	90.749	86.033	92.913	42.934
II	103.142	104.042	103.531	104.310	75.792	75.696	93.411	88.731	95.582	45.223
III	103.807	104.685	104.499	104.795	78.722	75.515	95.162	88.245	98.309	41.570
IV	104.423	105.736	106.495	105.380	77.535	76.913	97.269	90.222	100.486	41.720
2011: I	104.443	106.559	107.915	105.903	76.492	76.660	96.954	83.055	103.161	41.577
II	105.084	106.812	107.655	106.412	78.778	78.942	100.297	89.561	105.120	41.994
III	105.418	107.251	108.021	106.886	79.906	81.835	104.746	93.866	109.637	42.139
IV	106.481	107.790	109.462	106.970	85.959	83.807	107.156	96.449	111.972	43.361
2012: I	106.999	108.443	110.722	107.318	87.241	85.785	109.108	99.421	113.460	45.433
II	107.333	108.849	110.812	107.882	87.394	86.724	110.065	99.560	114.790	46.364
III	108.156	109.276	111.796	108.031	88.793	86.923	109.557	99.558	114.049	47.855
IV p	108.190	109.843	112.992	108.286	88.463	89.258	112.124	100.962	117.148	49.819

See next page for continuation of table.

Chain-type quantity indexes for gross domestic product, 1964–2012—*Continued*

[Index numbers, 2005=100; quarterly data seasonally adjusted]

Year or quarter	Exports of goods and services			Imports of goods and services			Government consumption expenditures and gross investment				
	Total	Goods	Services	Total	Goods	Services	Total	Federal			State and local
								Total	National defense	Non-defense	
1964	9.540	9.180	10.180	6.752	5.367	15.328	42.958	59.725	69.951	40.157	32.626
1965	9.807	9.228	11.215	7.471	6.127	15.779	44.250	59.697	68.481	42.878	34.813
1966	10.487	9.870	11.986	8.581	7.093	17.783	48.149	66.303	78.306	43.320	36.998
1967	10.728	9.916	12.932	9.206	7.466	19.957	51.844	72.903	88.567	42.913	38.868
1968	11.572	10.701	13.925	10.578	9.009	20.315	53.472	73.491	90.001	41.897	41.168
1969	12.131	11.262	14.442	11.181	9.502	21.596	53.347	70.969	85.556	43.019	42.557
1970	13.435	12.546	15.729	11.658	9.874	22.722	52.059	65.738	77.800	42.567	43.738
1971	13.663	12.497	16.942	12.280	10.702	22.075	50.926	60.677	68.981	44.575	45.077
1972	14.689	13.840	16.835	13.662	12.158	23.011	50.556	58.197	63.588	47.722	46.068
1973	17.458	17.020	18.025	14.296	13.016	22.235	50.379	55.748	60.061	47.429	47.381
1974	18.837	18.371	19.432	13.972	12.654	22.210	51.648	56.243	59.595	49.891	49.164
1975	18.718	17.944	20.626	12.419	11.059	21.247	52.812	56.426	59.030	51.594	50.970
1976	19.536	18.796	21.236	14.848	13.560	22.714	53.049	56.453	58.828	52.085	51.346
1977	20.006	19.042	22.606	16.471	15.213	23.846	53.630	57.647	59.511	54.324	51.532
1978	22.115	21.170	24.496	17.898	16.577	25.546	55.210	59.092	60.019	57.700	53.216
1979	24.307	23.671	25.250	18.195	16.861	25.897	56.241	60.519	61.845	58.309	53.998
1980	26.925	26.492	26.826	16.987	15.610	25.319	57.337	63.390	64.541	61.573	53.958
1981	27.256	26.205	29.683	17.433	15.931	26.778	57.860	66.420	68.628	62.396	52.873
1982	25.173	23.837	28.860	17.214	15.531	28.205	58.876	68.989	73.814	59.402	52.898
1983	24.524	23.151	28.380	19.386	17.641	30.483	61.027	73.561	79.110	62.471	53.514
1984	26.526	24.982	30.911	24.105	21.908	38.126	63.078	75.829	82.971	61.279	55.444
1985	27.331	25.903	31.279	25.669	23.279	41.026	67.471	81.771	90.002	64.900	58.879
1986	29.429	27.233	35.820	27.863	25.665	41.488	71.573	86.407	95.766	67.130	62.669
1987	32.594	30.252	39.390	29.511	26.855	46.378	73.300	89.477	100.301	67.081	63.575
1988	37.815	35.953	42.939	30.671	27.943	47.954	74.220	88.010	99.826	63.499	65.933
1989	42.161	40.237	47.375	32.022	29.146	50.278	76.240	89.379	99.335	68.795	68.340
1990	45.954	43.623	52.372	33.168	29.995	53.564	78.655	91.185	99.305	74.465	71.112
1991	49.005	46.633	55.505	33.118	30.130	52.173	79.514	91.000	98.214	76.170	72.585
1992	52.370	50.122	58.496	35.440	32.971	50.768	79.885	89.351	93.351	81.218	74.156
1993	54.086	51.756	60.437	38.505	36.270	52.124	79.253	85.842	88.401	80.687	75.244
1994	58.802	56.790	64.275	43.098	41.114	54.901	79.245	82.555	84.072	79.525	77.197
1995	64.755	63.436	68.316	46.547	44.817	56.556	79.705	80.353	80.936	79.207	79.247
1996	70.133	69.031	73.101	50.595	49.018	59.514	80.507	79.423	79.856	78.577	81.090
1997	78.490	78.955	77.436	57.409	56.082	64.687	82.020	78.641	77.618	80.737	83.980
1998	80.281	80.717	79.303	64.119	62.727	71.721	83.759	77.758	75.978	81.374	87.291
1999	83.785	83.788	83.857	71.500	70.549	76.569	86.761	79.270	77.386	83.095	91.179
2000	90.985	93.080	86.102	80.813	80.018	84.955	88.519	79.661	76.986	85.066	93.744
2001	85.880	87.318	82.534	78.540	77.464	84.292	91.917	82.901	79.908	88.945	97.236
2002	84.160	84.176	84.115	81.213	80.341	85.837	96.192	88.953	85.782	95.357	100.473
2003	85.514	85.687	85.107	84.806	84.302	87.474	98.336	94.839	93.243	98.071	100.408
2004	93.677	92.995	95.237	94.212	93.637	97.252	99.668	98.710	98.535	99.067	100.234
2005	100.000	100.000	100.000	100.000	100.000	100.000	100.000	100.000	100.000	100.000	100.000
2006	108.969	109.425	107.935	106.099	105.920	107.059	101.359	102.127	101.588	103.237	100.910
2007	119.108	120.090	116.885	108.652	108.674	108.539	102.713	103.399	103.867	102.420	102.311
2008	126.376	127.691	123.395	105.733	104.500	112.488	105.381	110.819	111.649	109.081	102.310
2009	114.835	112.414	120.204	91.422	88.200	108.740	109.262	117.613	118.311	116.154	104.568
2010	127.623	128.479	125.805	102.832	101.309	111.507	109.955	122.883	121.829	125.049	102.711
2011	136.152	137.695	132.979	107.746	106.561	114.630	106.497	119.480	118.683	121.114	99.224
2012 ᵖ	140.687	143.462	134.517	110.345	108.779	119.335	104.701	116.871	114.977	120.804	97.877
2009: I	111.295	108.374	117.732	91.526	88.241	109.184	106.825	113.639	113.880	113.123	102.992
II	111.460	107.650	119.859	87.652	83.843	107.866	109.307	117.333	118.200	115.522	104.794
III	115.116	112.939	119.966	91.196	87.957	108.625	110.312	119.129	120.387	116.510	105.359
IV	121.467	120.692	123.258	95.312	92.760	109.284	110.602	120.352	120.776	119.460	105.128
2010: I	123.231	123.571	122.563	97.689	95.478	109.935	109.727	120.535	119.646	122.357	103.665
II	126.079	127.096	123.912	102.286	100.897	110.262	110.498	123.355	121.776	126.607	103.292
III	129.030	129.877	127.228	105.672	104.287	113.646	110.416	124.468	123.906	125.617	102.544
IV	132.151	133.371	129.517	105.680	104.571	112.185	109.179	123.172	121.987	125.614	101.342
2011: I	134.004	135.239	131.342	106.787	105.907	112.023	107.210	119.864	117.354	125.072	100.117
II	135.352	136.464	132.979	106.816	105.723	113.188	106.985	120.681	119.717	122.662	99.317
III	137.379	138.516	134.954	108.037	106.491	116.906	106.189	119.351	120.496	116.929	98.818
IV	137.871	140.559	131.896	109.345	108.122	116.402	105.604	118.024	117.163	119.792	98.643
2012: I	139.356	141.961	133.573	110.179	108.652	118.950	104.804	116.751	115.031	120.317	98.103
II	141.152	144.389	133.940	110.936	109.422	119.637	104.622	116.685	114.987	120.205	97.858
III	141.824	144.774	135.259	110.766	109.084	120.394	105.620	119.359	118.518	121.082	97.932
IV ᵖ	140.415	142.724	135.297	109.499	107.956	118.359	103.756	114.688	111.370	121.610	97.615

Source: Department of Commerce (Bureau of Economic Analysis).

[Index numbers, 2005=100, except as noted; quarterly data seasonally adjusted]

Year or quarter	Gross domestic product	Personal consumption expenditures			Gross private domestic investment					
						Fixed investment				
							Nonresidential			
		Total	Goods	Services	Total	Total	Total	Structures	Equipment and software	Residential
1964	19.589	19.536	30.013	14.572	26.710	25.640	34.142	11.801	53.952	13.003
1965	19.945	19.819	30.328	14.845	27.136	26.077	34.532	12.143	54.001	13.372
1966	20.511	20.322	30.996	15.276	27.692	26.626	35.047	12.580	54.144	13.857
1967	21.142	20.834	31.542	15.785	28.424	27.372	35.939	12.973	55.344	14.339
1968	22.040	21.645	32.642	16.467	29.485	28.472	37.203	13.621	56.831	15.100
1969	23.130	22.626	33.907	17.324	30.883	29.877	38.740	14.518	58.411	16.144
1970	24.349	23.685	35.200	18.285	32.190	31.162	40.571	15.473	60.560	16.666
1971	25.567	24.692	36.258	19.284	33.794	32.731	42.479	16.664	62.360	17.632
1972	26.670	25.536	37.186	20.102	35.206	34.135	43.914	17.863	63.112	18.703
1973	28.148	26.913	39.404	21.077	37.107	36.020	45.605	19.247	64.184	20.359
1974	30.695	29.716	44.322	22.866	40.797	39.568	50.008	21.910	68.917	22.460
1975	33.606	32.198	47.903	24.834	45.833	44.525	56.893	24.534	79.100	24.547
1976	35.535	33.966	49.777	26.556	48.366	47.106	60.048	25.741	83.754	26.124
1977	37.796	36.171	52.435	28.558	51.994	50.803	64.157	27.973	88.730	28.759
1978	40.447	38.705	55.653	30.777	56.235	55.094	68.453	30.675	93.412	32.281
1979	43.811	42.137	60.916	33.350	61.323	60.088	74.013	34.238	99.335	35.902
1980	47.817	46.663	67.737	36.802	67.080	65.710	80.541	37.421	107.819	39.789
1981	52.326	50.833	72.769	40.555	73.422	71.816	88.316	42.567	115.524	43.036
1982	55.514	53.640	74.753	43.709	77.180	75.747	93.181	45.927	120.030	45.340
1983	57.705	55.948	76.102	46.429	76.987	75.628	92.350	44.757	120.284	46.380
1984	59.874	58.065	77.541	48.846	77.538	76.070	92.127	45.147	119.234	47.713
1985	61.686	59.965	78.785	51.049	78.332	77.028	92.850	46.219	119.090	48.944
1986	63.057	61.427	78.417	53.375	80.029	78.870	94.427	47.106	120.976	50.994
1987	64.818	63.618	80.939	55.409	81.561	80.332	95.275	47.863	121.637	53.079
1988	67.047	66.151	83.072	58.123	83.424	82.415	97.392	49.895	123.155	54.913
1989	69.579	69.025	86.268	60.840	85.418	84.410	99.435	51.848	124.695	56.680
1990	72.274	72.180	89.801	63.808	87.064	86.125	101.339	53.522	126.310	58.011
1991	74.826	74.789	91.996	66.581	88.302	87.404	102.906	54.491	128.112	58.771
1992	76.602	76.989	93.106	69.236	87.993	87.152	102.048	54.502	126.605	59.486
1993	78.288	78.679	93.915	71.294	88.997	88.163	102.100	56.103	125.322	61.890
1994	79.935	80.302	94.870	73.200	90.157	89.352	102.592	58.089	124.604	64.069
1995	81.602	82.078	95.757	75.365	91.173	90.393	102.811	60.601	123.163	66.403
1996	83.154	83.864	96.809	77.473	90.786	90.149	101.612	62.141	120.199	67.828
1997	84.627	85.433	96.696	79.812	90.449	89.921	100.326	64.516	116.639	69.557
1998	85.580	86.246	95.237	81.689	89.435	89.085	98.125	67.480	111.454	71.412
1999	86.840	87.636	95.735	83.509	89.315	89.029	96.704	69.559	108.195	74.151
2000	88.724	89.818	97.655	85.818	90.283	90.083	96.750	72.298	106.893	77.415
2001	90.731	91.530	97.563	88.422	91.080	90.888	96.317	76.087	104.364	80.994
2002	92.192	92.778	96.563	90.801	91.451	91.261	95.889	79.292	102.240	83.002
2003	94.134	94.658	96.492	93.686	92.483	92.374	95.471	82.174	100.450	86.953
2004	96.784	97.121	97.929	96.688	95.633	95.543	96.837	88.441	99.900	93.297
2005	100.000	100.000	100.000	100.000	100.000	100.000	100.000	100.000	100.000	100.000
2006	103.237	102.723	102.741	101.441	103.414	104.302	104.347	103.425	112.922	100.049	106.081
2007	106.231	105.499	102.764	106.981	106.313	106.360	105.645	119.780	100.525	107.612
2008	108.565	108.943	105.912	110.584	107.501	107.587	107.717	125.706	101.000	106.296
2009	109.532	109.004	103.105	112.157	106.274	106.318	107.102	122.527	101.477	102.713
2010	111.002	111.087	104.852	114.418	104.854	105.023	105.514	121.158	99.806	102.520
2011	113.369	113.790	108.822	116.435	106.439	106.680	107.359	126.850	100.445	103.406
2012 ᵖ	115.382	115.784	110.202	118.770	107.743	108.170	108.990	131.221	101.232	104.272
2009: I	109.526	108.063	101.386	111.614	108.487	108.076	108.975	127.259	102.166	104.065
II	109.318	108.496	102.455	111.724	106.695	106.579	107.494	123.208	101.799	102.494
III	109.463	109.315	103.890	112.224	105.130	105.414	106.224	120.038	101.266	101.716
IV	109.820	110.142	104.687	113.065	104.784	105.203	105.714	119.605	100.678	102.576
2010: I	110.234	110.642	105.025	113.647	104.474	104.784	105.188	119.968	99.799	102.573
II	110.886	110.800	104.283	114.282	104.573	104.762	105.304	120.670	99.690	102.064
III	111.248	111.154	104.540	114.687	104.916	105.061	105.589	121.442	99.797	102.421
IV	111.838	111.751	105.561	115.057	105.453	105.487	105.973	122.552	99.939	103.020
2011: I	112.389	112.640	107.266	115.503	105.786	105.866	106.483	124.097	100.134	102.861
II	113.109	113.633	108.820	116.193	106.272	106.509	107.174	126.118	100.430	103.300
III	113.937	114.293	109.633	116.772	106.686	106.992	107.687	127.882	100.562	103.650
IV	114.041	114.593	109.569	117.270	107.013	107.352	108.092	129.302	100.656	103.812
2012: I	114.608	115.300	110.256	117.989	107.292	107.661	108.562	130.167	101.001	103.439
II	115.050	115.496	109.743	118.576	107.647	107.977	108.878	131.198	101.094	103.754
III	115.807	115.952	110.261	118.997	107.818	108.324	109.104	131.540	101.282	104.593
IVᵖ	116.063	116.389	110.546	119.519	108.214	108.718	109.417	131.978	101.554	105.302

See next page for continuation of table.

TABLE B–7. Chain-type price indexes for gross domestic product, 1964–2012—*Continued*

[Index numbers, 2005=100, except as noted; quarterly data seasonally adjusted]

Year or quarter	Exports and imports of goods and services		Government consumption expenditures and gross investment					Final sales of domestic product	Gross domestic purchases [1]		Percent change [2]		
	Exports	Imports	Total	Federal			State and local		Total	Less food and energy	Gross domestic product	Gross domestic purchases [1]	
				Total	National defense	Non-defense						Total	Less food and energy
1964	28.128	20.526	14.070	14.995	14.620	15.798	13.293	19.440	19.191	....	1.6	1.6	......
1965	29.023	20.812	14.444	15.379	15.024	16.104	13.662	19.798	19.524	....	1.8	1.7	......
1966	29.900	21.297	15.044	15.914	15.535	16.708	14.334	20.363	20.071	....	2.8	2.8	......
1967	31.045	21.379	15.671	16.386	15.994	17.215	15.137	20.996	20.654	....	3.1	2.9	......
1968	31.723	21.704	16.520	17.287	16.834	18.327	15.945	21.898	21.526	....	4.2	4.2	......
1969	32.796	22.270	17.517	18.226	17.757	19.284	17.013	22.988	22.582	....	4.9	4.9	......
1970	34.053	23.587	18.945	19.699	19.116	21.143	18.411	24.203	23.798	....	5.3	5.4	......
1971	35.310	25.035	20.421	21.383	20.810	22.746	19.720	25.415	25.021	....	5.0	5.1	......
1972	36.956	26.789	21.989	23.471	23.209	23.892	20.896	26.516	26.134	....	4.3	4.4	......
1973	41.816	31.446	23.594	25.080	24.911	25.231	22.495	27.992	27.647	....	5.5	5.8	......
1974	51.517	44.989	25.977	27.315	27.223	27.245	24.970	30.519	30.484	....	9.0	10.3	......
1975	56.781	48.734	28.586	30.158	29.880	30.505	27.410	33.418	33.328	....	9.5	9.3	......
1976	58.645	50.201	30.469	32.302	32.057	32.549	29.114	35.350	35.238	....	5.7	5.7	......
1977	61.033	54.624	32.583	34.742	34.486	34.993	31.005	37.614	37.617	....	6.4	6.8	......
1978	64.752	58.482	34.670	36.888	36.908	36.514	33.042	40.286	40.286	....	7.0	7.1	......
1979	72.545	68.483	37.575	39.727	39.853	39.100	35.976	43.614	43.833	....	8.3	8.8	......
1980	79.903	85.301	41.669	43.900	44.179	42.906	40.002	47.598	48.448	....	9.1	10.5	......
1981	85.810	89.886	45.768	48.165	48.542	46.917	43.975	52.074	52.909	....	9.4	9.2	......
1982	86.204	86.855	48.775	51.434	51.953	49.825	46.786	55.280	55.906	55.408	6.1	5.7	....
1983	86.544	83.601	50.717	53.218	53.775	51.501	48.857	57.464	57.865	57.569	3.9	3.5	3.9
1984	87.347	82.879	53.319	56.358	57.603	52.779	51.034	59.624	59.904	59.704	3.8	3.5	3.7
1985	84.674	80.157	54.974	57.635	58.696	54.574	53.002	61.466	61.605	61.577	3.0	2.8	3.1
1986	83.406	80.154	55.977	57.938	58.642	55.915	54.577	62.856	63.000	63.464	2.2	2.3	3.1
1987	85.516	85.008	57.541	58.642	59.236	56.953	56.849	64.607	64.978	65.506	2.8	3.1	3.2
1988	89.945	89.074	59.074	59.884	60.326	58.679	58.621	66.865	67.215	67.900	3.4	3.4	3.7
1989	91.443	91.021	60.924	61.504	61.882	60.497	60.654	69.397	69.765	70.346	3.8	3.8	3.6
1990	92.063	93.630	63.405	63.548	63.917	62.568	63.474	72.102	72.601	73.043	3.9	4.1	3.8
1991	93.283	92.848	65.606	66.070	66.222	65.672	65.443	74.655	74.980	75.539	3.5	3.3	3.4
1992	92.904	92.922	67.276	68.101	68.522	67.034	66.856	76.436	76.788	77.520	2.4	2.4	2.6
1993	92.879	92.210	68.949	69.830	69.712	70.002	68.494	78.123	78.404	79.228	2.2	2.1	2.2
1994	93.914	93.075	70.819	71.725	71.438	72.267	70.351	79.775	80.029	80.947	2.1	2.1	2.2
1995	96.070	95.625	72.753	73.717	73.161	74.830	72.252	81.449	81.743	82.722	2.1	2.1	2.2
1996	94.799	93.958	74.488	75.763	75.431	76.406	73.806	83.024	83.220	84.077	1.9	1.8	1.6
1997	93.174	90.691	75.854	77.047	76.517	78.095	75.219	84.522	84.468	85.344	1.8	1.5	1.5
1998	91.042	85.809	76.879	77.931	77.328	79.120	76.320	85.256	85.034	86.171	1.1	.7	1.0
1999	90.477	86.311	79.337	79.886	79.225	81.188	79.036	86.795	86.377	87.463	1.5	1.6	1.5
2000	92.069	90.027	82.513	82.524	81.821	83.907	82.482	88.698	88.537	89.243	2.2	2.5	2.0
2001	91.696	87.824	84.764	84.201	83.484	85.612	85.019	90.709	90.198	90.851	2.3	1.9	1.8
2002	91.322	86.846	87.003	87.318	86.624	88.689	86.810	92.168	91.498	92.384	1.6	1.4	1.7
2003	93.282	89.851	90.650	91.024	90.659	91.774	90.425	94.123	93.584	94.214	2.1	2.3	2.0
2004	96.539	94.164	94.531	95.335	94.895	96.234	94.062	96.774	96.415	96.779	2.8	3.0	2.7
2005	100.000	100.000	100.000	100.000	100.000	100.000	100.000	100.000	100.000	100.000	3.3	3.7	3.3
2006	103.440	104.131	104.842	104.107	104.421	103.468	103.276	103.240	103.354	103.127	3.2	3.4	3.1
2007	106.900	107.785	109.863	107.753	108.249	106.743	111.112	106.238	106.402	105.938	2.9	2.9	2.7
2008	111.975	119.237	115.245	111.225	112.187	109.240	117.666	108.576	109.858	108.719	2.2	3.2	2.6
2009	105.924	106.598	114.592	110.959	111.347	110.177	116.763	109.521	109.620	109.417	.9	−.2	.6
2010	110.738	112.989	117.334	113.583	113.951	112.843	119.579	110.993	111.421	110.912	1.3	1.6	1.4
2011	117.860	121.851	121.233	116.721	117.411	115.337	124.001	113.371	114.208	112.995	2.1	2.5	1.9
2012 P	118.874	122.616	123.435	118.564	119.482	116.722	126.449	115.412	116.149	114.892	1.8	1.7	1.7
2009: I	104.936	102.932	114.342	110.956	111.503	109.847	116.349	109.476	109.188	109.142	1.0	−2.4	−.4
II	104.898	104.547	114.946	110.481	110.875	109.686	116.405	109.294	109.235	109.212	−.8	.2	.3
III	106.187	107.855	114.620	110.897	111.193	110.303	116.852	109.472	109.706	109.401	.5	1.7	.7
IV	107.674	111.058	115.220	111.504	111.818	110.871	117.446	109.841	110.350	109.912	1.3	2.4	1.9
2010: I	108.972	113.200	116.555	113.016	113.420	112.206	118.694	110.242	110.920	110.403	1.5	2.1	1.8
II	110.303	112.595	116.916	113.339	113.696	112.624	119.038	110.680	111.110	110.728	1.7	.7	1.2
III	110.562	111.726	117.406	113.668	113.947	113.105	119.639	111.238	111.488	111.050	2.0	1.4	1.2
IV	113.117	114.434	118.459	114.309	114.742	113.435	120.985	111.814	112.165	111.466	2.1	2.5	1.5
2011: I	116.123	119.417	119.964	115.696	116.440	114.207	122.565	112.371	113.099	112.079	2.0	3.4	2.2
II	118.485	123.057	121.168	116.714	117.375	115.384	123.895	113.111	114.067	112.825	2.6	3.5	2.7
III	118.992	122.466	121.898	117.365	118.047	115.994	124.678	113.748	114.709	113.394	3.0	2.3	2.0
IV	117.839	122.463	121.903	117.111	117.780	115.764	124.866	114.056	114.958	113.682	.4	.9	1.0
2012: I	118.652	124.156	122.979	118.038	119.008	116.096	126.042	114.628	115.674	114.348	2.0	2.5	2.4
II	118.802	122.942	123.157	118.403	119.268	116.664	126.089	115.065	115.888	114.745	1.6	.7	1.4
III	118.792	120.907	123.574	118.679	119.541	116.948	126.605	115.849	116.298	115.077	2.7	1.4	1.2
IV P	119.249	122.458	124.031	119.135	120.111	117.182	127.061	116.104	116.734	115.399	.9	1.5	1.1

[1] Gross domestic product (GDP) less exports of goods and services plus imports of goods and services.
[2] Quarterly percent changes are at annual rates.

Source: Department of Commerce (Bureau of Economic Analysis).

TABLE B-8. Gross domestic product by major type of product, 1964-2012

[Billions of dollars; quarterly data at seasonally adjusted annual rates]

Year or quarter	Gross domestic product	Final sales of domestic product	Change in private inventories	Goods — Total: Total	Goods — Total: Final sales	Goods — Total: Change in private inventories[1]	Goods — Durable goods: Final sales	Goods — Durable goods: Change in private inventories[1]	Goods — Nondurable goods: Final sales	Goods — Nondurable goods: Change in private inventories[1]	Services[2]	Structures
1964	663.6	658.8	4.8	277.8	273.0	4.8	119.3	3.8	153.7	1.0	307.4	78.4
1965	719.1	709.9	9.2	304.3	295.1	9.2	131.6	6.2	163.5	3.0	330.1	84.7
1966	787.7	774.1	13.6	337.1	323.5	13.6	145.4	10.0	178.0	3.6	362.6	88.0
1967	832.4	822.6	9.9	345.4	335.5	9.9	150.0	4.8	185.5	5.0	397.5	89.6
1968	909.8	900.8	9.1	370.8	361.7	9.1	162.8	4.5	198.9	4.5	439.1	100.0
1969	984.4	975.3	9.2	397.6	388.4	9.2	175.7	6.0	212.7	3.2	478.6	108.3
1970	1,038.3	1,036.3	2.0	408.7	406.7	2.0	178.6	-.2	228.2	2.2	519.9	109.7
1971	1,126.8	1,118.6	8.3	432.6	424.4	8.3	186.7	2.9	237.7	5.3	565.8	128.4
1972	1,237.9	1,228.8	9.1	472.0	462.9	9.1	208.4	6.4	254.5	2.7	619.0	146.9
1973	1,382.3	1,366.4	15.9	547.1	531.2	15.9	243.6	13.0	287.6	2.9	672.2	162.9
1974	1,499.5	1,485.5	14.0	588.0	574.0	14.0	262.4	10.9	311.7	3.1	745.8	165.6
1975	1,637.7	1,644.0	-6.3	628.6	634.8	-6.3	293.2	-7.5	341.6	1.2	842.4	166.7
1976	1,824.6	1,807.5	17.1	706.6	689.5	17.1	330.9	10.8	358.6	6.3	926.8	191.2
1977	2,030.1	2,007.8	22.3	773.5	751.2	22.3	374.6	9.5	376.6	12.8	1,029.9	226.8
1978	2,293.8	2,268.0	25.8	872.6	846.8	25.8	424.9	18.2	422.0	7.6	1,147.2	273.9
1979	2,562.2	2,544.2	18.0	977.2	959.2	18.0	483.9	12.8	475.3	5.2	1,271.7	313.3
1980	2,788.1	2,794.5	-6.3	1,035.2	1,041.5	-6.3	512.3	-2.3	529.2	-4.0	1,431.6	321.3
1981	3,126.8	3,097.0	29.8	1,167.3	1,137.5	29.8	554.8	7.3	582.6	22.5	1,606.9	352.6
1982	3,253.2	3,268.1	-14.9	1,148.8	1,163.7	-14.9	552.5	-16.0	611.2	1.1	1,759.9	344.5
1983	3,534.6	3,540.4	-5.8	1,226.9	1,232.6	-5.8	592.3	2.5	640.3	-8.2	1,939.1	368.7
1984	3,930.9	3,865.5	65.4	1,402.2	1,336.8	65.4	665.9	41.4	670.9	24.0	2,102.9	425.8
1985	4,217.5	4,195.6	21.8	1,452.8	1,431.0	21.8	727.9	4.4	703.1	17.4	2,305.9	458.7
1986	4,460.1	4,453.5	6.6	1,491.2	1,484.7	6.6	758.3	-1.9	726.4	8.4	2,488.7	480.1
1987	4,736.4	4,709.2	27.1	1,570.7	1,543.6	27.1	785.3	22.9	758.3	4.2	2,668.0	497.6
1988	5,100.4	5,081.9	18.5	1,703.7	1,685.2	18.5	863.3	22.7	821.9	-4.3	2,881.7	515.0
1989	5,482.1	5,454.5	27.7	1,851.9	1,824.2	27.7	939.7	20.0	884.5	7.7	3,101.2	529.0
1990	5,800.5	5,786.0	14.5	1,923.1	1,908.5	14.5	973.2	7.7	935.3	6.8	3,343.9	533.5
1991	5,992.1	5,992.5	-.4	1,943.5	1,943.9	-.4	967.6	-13.6	976.3	13.2	3,548.6	499.9
1992	6,342.3	6,326.0	16.3	2,031.5	2,015.1	16.3	1,010.7	-3.0	1,004.4	19.3	3,788.1	522.7
1993	6,667.4	6,646.5	20.8	2,124.2	2,103.4	20.8	1,072.9	17.1	1,030.4	3.7	3,985.1	558.1
1994	7,085.2	7,021.4	63.8	2,290.7	2,226.9	63.8	1,149.8	35.7	1,077.1	28.1	4,187.2	607.3
1995	7,414.7	7,383.5	31.2	2,379.5	2,348.3	31.2	1,225.9	33.6	1,122.4	-2.4	4,396.7	638.5
1996	7,838.5	7,807.7	30.8	2,516.3	2,485.5	30.8	1,321.0	19.1	1,164.5	11.7	4,625.5	696.7
1997	8,332.4	8,261.4	71.0	2,701.2	2,630.2	71.0	1,430.7	40.0	1,199.5	31.0	4,882.5	748.6
1998	8,793.5	8,729.8	63.7	2,819.2	2,755.5	63.7	1,524.2	39.3	1,231.3	24.4	5,159.7	814.5
1999	9,353.5	9,292.7	60.8	2,990.1	2,929.3	60.8	1,633.8	37.4	1,295.5	23.4	5,485.1	878.2
2000	9,951.5	9,896.9	54.5	3,124.5	3,070.0	54.5	1,734.4	35.6	1,335.6	19.0	5,878.0	949.0
2001	10,286.2	10,324.5	-38.3	3,077.6	3,115.9	-38.3	1,731.5	-44.4	1,384.4	6.2	6,208.7	999.9
2002	10,642.3	10,630.3	12.0	3,101.2	3,089.1	12.0	1,678.9	17.7	1,410.3	-5.6	6,535.5	1,005.7
2003	11,142.2	11,125.8	16.4	3,170.7	3,154.3	16.4	1,699.3	13.0	1,455.0	3.3	6,891.2	1,080.4
2004	11,853.3	11,788.3	64.9	3,333.8	3,268.9	64.9	1,759.3	37.3	1,509.6	27.6	7,304.9	1,214.5
2005	12,623.0	12,573.0	50.0	3,475.7	3,425.8	50.0	1,873.8	35.2	1,552.0	14.7	7,783.8	1,363.4
2006	13,377.2	13,317.3	60.0	3,663.7	3,603.7	60.0	1,973.4	25.9	1,630.3	34.0	8,260.8	1,452.7
2007	14,028.7	13,999.6	29.1	3,844.1	3,815.0	29.1	2,087.3	11.2	1,727.7	17.9	8,751.8	1,432.8
2008	14,291.5	14,332.7	-41.1	3,758.6	3,799.7	-41.1	2,043.1	-23.1	1,756.6	-18.0	9,174.0	1,359.0
2009	13,973.7	14,127.9	-154.2	3,614.5	3,768.6	-154.2	1,905.3	-118.6	1,863.3	-35.6	9,245.9	1,113.3
2010	14,498.9	14,440.6	58.4	3,921.9	3,863.6	58.4	1,941.7	42.5	1,921.9	15.8	9,559.6	1,017.4
2011	15,075.7	15,039.0	36.6	4,184.7	4,148.0	36.6	2,090.7	37.6	2,057.3	-1.0	9,870.4	1,020.5
2012 ᵖ	15,681.5	15,623.8	57.7	4,458.1	4,400.3	57.7	2,212.4	66.1	2,187.9	-8.4	10,116.5	1,107.0
2009: I	13,923.4	14,090.2	-166.7	3,554.8	3,721.5	-166.7	1,907.9	-142.6	1,813.6	-24.1	9,157.7	1,211.0
II	13,885.4	14,088.1	-202.7	3,563.1	3,765.7	-202.7	1,903.4	-150.1	1,862.3	-52.6	9,200.1	1,122.2
III	13,952.2	14,152.7	-200.5	3,604.5	3,804.9	-200.5	1,919.3	-136.6	1,885.6	-63.9	9,263.8	1,083.9
IV	14,133.6	14,180.5	-46.8	3,735.5	3,782.3	-46.8	1,890.6	-45.0	1,891.7	-1.8	9,361.9	1,036.2
2010: I	14,270.3	14,237.0	33.2	3,840.1	3,806.9	33.2	1,908.3	28.2	1,898.5	5.0	9,435.2	994.9
II	14,413.5	14,371.8	41.7	3,841.3	3,799.6	41.7	1,921.4	43.7	1,878.2	-2.0	9,532.0	1,040.2
III	14,576.0	14,466.6	109.5	3,964.4	3,854.9	109.5	1,940.3	66.4	1,914.6	43.1	9,596.6	1,015.1
IV	14,735.9	14,686.9	49.0	4,041.9	3,992.9	49.0	1,996.7	31.8	1,996.2	17.2	9,674.8	1,019.2
2011: I	14,814.9	14,781.2	33.7	4,082.9	4,049.2	33.7	2,024.0	43.0	2,025.3	-9.3	9,754.3	977.6
II	15,003.6	14,968.7	34.8	4,131.2	4,096.4	34.8	2,067.1	42.5	2,029.3	-7.6	9,862.5	1,009.9
III	15,163.2	15,167.3	-4.1	4,199.2	4,203.3	-4.1	2,117.8	32.6	2,085.5	-36.7	9,930.2	1,033.8
IV	15,321.0	15,238.9	82.1	4,325.3	4,243.2	82.1	2,154.1	32.4	2,089.2	49.7	9,934.8	1,060.9
2012: I	15,478.3	15,405.7	72.6	4,373.5	4,301.0	72.6	2,180.1	59.9	2,120.9	12.7	10,021.0	1,083.7
II	15,585.6	15,530.8	54.8	4,399.3	4,344.5	54.8	2,186.7	78.8	2,157.9	-24.1	10,090.9	1,095.4
III	15,811.0	15,728.8	82.3	4,530.0	4,447.7	82.3	2,215.3	84.8	2,232.5	-2.5	10,169.3	1,111.8
IV ᵖ	15,851.2	15,829.9	21.3	4,529.4	4,508.1	21.3	2,267.7	40.8	2,240.4	-19.5	10,184.7	1,137.1

[1] Estimates for durable and nondurable goods for 1996 and earlier periods are based on the Standard Industrial Classification (SIC); later estimates are based on the North American Industry Classification System (NAICS).

[2] Includes government consumption expenditures, which are for services (such as education and national defense) produced by government. In current dollars, these services are valued at their cost of production.

Source: Department of Commerce (Bureau of Economic Analysis).

Year or quarter	Gross domestic product	Final sales of domestic product	Change in private inventories	Goods							Services[2]	Structures
				Total			Durable goods		Nondurable goods			
				Total	Final sales	Change in private inventories	Final sales	Change in private inventories[1]	Final sales	Change in private inventories[1]		
1964	3,389.4	3,390.8	17.3	718.1		17.3					2,189.6	631.5
1965	3,607.0	3,587.6	32.9	778.4		32.9					2,299.2	663.1
1966	3,842.1	3,803.4	47.1	846.0		47.1					2,441.1	663.9
1967	3,939.2	3,920.0	33.9	848.3		33.9					2,577.0	654.2
1968	4,129.9	4,115.8	30.8	882.2		30.8					2,712.9	694.5
1969	4,258.2	4,245.0	30.3	912.6		30.3					2,801.0	703.3
1970	4,266.3	4,284.3	5.6	905.0		5.6					2,858.4	673.0
1971	4,409.5	4,403.6	25.0	931.8		25.0					2,927.0	735.5
1972	4,643.8	4,636.7	25.7	995.5		25.7					3,034.9	790.2
1973	4,912.8	4,884.0	39.0	1,101.4		39.0					3,125.7	807.1
1974	4,885.7	4,870.0	29.1	1,090.8		29.1					3,194.8	723.4
1975	4,875.4	4,922.1	–12.8	1,063.5		–12.8					3,309.3	657.6
1976	5,136.9	5,115.9	34.3	1,147.0		34.3					3,400.4	719.2
1977	5,373.1	5,340.3	43.1	1,202.1		43.1					3,517.3	787.2
1978	5,672.8	5,634.9	45.6	1,282.9		45.6					3,651.8	862.8
1979	5,850.1	5,836.2	28.0	1,335.9		28.0					3,740.4	887.4
1980	5,834.0	5,873.6	–9.3	1,324.2		–9.3					3,811.4	823.0
1981	5,982.1	5,954.4	39.0	1,384.0		39.0					3,887.6	811.9
1982	5,865.9	5,918.2	–19.7	1,312.8		–19.7					3,957.1	742.6
1983	6,130.9	6,167.6	–7.7	1,369.5		–7.7					4,120.4	796.3
1984	6,571.5	6,490.0	78.3	1,539.3		78.3					4,234.4	903.9
1985	6,843.4	6,833.1	25.4	1,576.1		25.4					4,449.0	951.0
1986	7,080.5	7,092.7	8.5	1,622.2		8.5					4,635.5	965.1
1987	7,307.0	7,289.9	33.2	1,687.5		33.2					4,785.6	969.3
1988	7,607.4	7,601.3	21.9	1,792.5		21.9					4,961.7	967.6
1989	7,879.2	7,860.8	30.6	1,894.4		30.6					5,115.1	961.0
1990	8,027.1	8,025.8	16.6	1,914.2		16.6					5,269.7	941.9
1991	8,008.3	8,027.9	–1.4	1,881.9		–1.4					5,363.4	869.1
1992	8,280.0	8,277.2	17.9	1,958.7		17.9					5,522.9	902.4
1993	8,516.2	8,508.0	22.3	2,034.1		22.3					5,648.3	930.5
1994	8,863.1	8,801.7	69.3	2,177.1		69.3					5,781.5	978.4
1995	9,086.0	9,065.4	32.1	2,257.1	2,234.2	32.1	1,017.9	31.4	1,259.3	–3.3	5,902.9	988.9
1996	9,425.8	9,404.4	31.2	2,380.4	2,356.6	31.2	1,105.4	17.9	1,286.0	12.5	6,045.7	1,053.1
1997	9,845.9	9,774.2	77.4	2,566.0	2,502.1	77.4	1,216.7	40.2	1,309.2	36.1	6,208.7	1,097.8
1998	10,274.7	10,208.3	71.6	2,714.7	2,654.8	71.6	1,334.8	40.6	1,333.6	29.5	6,422.2	1,155.1
1999	10,770.7	10,706.5	68.5	2,920.1	2,847.0	68.5	1,469.2	39.5	1,384.2	27.7	6,664.0	1,202.2
2000	11,216.4	11,158.0	60.2	3,046.9	2,993.5	60.2	1,582.7	37.7	1,411.0	21.4	6,919.2	1,245.3
2001	11,337.5	11,382.0	–41.8	2,997.7	3,034.2	–41.8	1,606.7	–46.4	1,427.4	7.3	7,095.8	1,254.1
2002	11,543.1	11,533.6	12.8	3,049.9	3,038.0	12.8	1,588.8	18.1	1,451.0	–6.4	7,276.1	1,223.2
2003	11,836.4	11,820.5	17.3	3,160.3	3,142.4	17.3	1,658.0	13.5	1,485.2	3.6	7,415.9	1,263.6
2004	12,246.9	12,181.3	66.3	3,324.4	3,259.1	66.3	1,750.4	38.1	1,508.8	28.1	7,598.2	1,325.6
2005	12,623.0	12,573.0	50.0	3,475.7	3,425.8	50.0	1,873.8	35.2	1,552.0	14.7	7,783.8	1,363.4
2006	12,958.5	12,899.3	59.4	3,659.1	3,599.9	59.4	1,989.5	25.2	1,610.6	34.1	7,961.0	1,341.1
2007	13,206.4	13,177.5	27.7	3,819.6	3,792.1	27.7	2,133.1	10.8	1,660.7	16.9	8,131.5	1,267.0
2008	13,161.9	13,200.5	–36.3	3,789.7	3,834.7	–36.3	2,129.9	–21.1	1,704.8	–15.5	8,216.6	1,169.9
2009	12,757.9	12,899.7	–139.0	3,569.1	3,726.1	–139.0	1,989.3	–110.7	1,729.5	–30.9	8,221.8	974.5
2010	13,063.0	13,010.3	50.9	3,893.0	3,837.8	50.9	2,053.3	38.8	1,777.4	13.6	8,310.8	893.8
2011	13,299.1	13,265.3	31.0	4,091.4	4,057.2	31.0	2,216.3	33.2	1,839.8	.6	8,389.3	869.8
2012 ᵖ	13,591.1	13,537.5	42.7	4,312.9	4,257.0	42.7	2,346.0	57.4	1,913.4	–8.2	8,429.1	919.1
2009: I	12,711.0	12,870.3	–150.2	3,495.5	3,671.8	–150.2	1,983.3	–133.4	1,683.6	–20.4	8,179.7	1,035.6
II	12,701.0	12,890.0	–185.5	3,506.4	3,714.7	–185.5	1,981.4	–141.1	1,725.8	–47.5	8,216.9	980.6
III	12,746.7	12,928.3	–181.5	3,559.6	3,759.9	–181.5	2,011.1	–126.7	1,741.8	–57.1	8,231.6	962.7
IV	12,873.1	12,910.2	–38.8	3,715.0	3,758.1	–38.8	1,981.5	–41.7	1,766.5	1.5	8,259.2	919.0
2010: I	12,947.6	12,914.7	30.5	3,839.6	3,806.0	30.5	2,012.5	26.1	1,783.8	5.5	8,260.3	879.7
II	13,019.6	12,985.4	33.2	3,829.2	3,794.2	33.2	2,033.0	40.0	1,754.6	–4.9	8,301.5	917.4
III	13,103.5	13,005.5	94.9	3,923.4	3,818.3	94.9	2,053.3	60.0	1,759.1	36.4	8,326.5	890.6
IV	13,181.2	13,135.6	45.0	3,979.9	3,932.6	45.0	2,114.2	29.0	1,812.3	17.3	8,355.0	887.6
2011: I	13,183.8	13,154.4	30.3	4,017.0	3,987.7	30.3	2,146.2	38.1	1,835.6	–4.5	8,366.2	846.1
II	13,264.7	13,234.1	27.5	4,050.3	4,019.7	27.5	2,191.5	37.4	1,826.4	–6.1	8,396.9	864.7
III	13,306.9	13,311.2	–4.3	4,071.8	4,079.7	–4.3	2,243.2	28.6	1,837.7	–28.2	8,407.3	876.4
IV	13,441.0	13,361.4	70.5	4,226.5	4,141.5	70.5	2,284.1	28.7	1,859.7	41.3	8,386.6	891.8
2012: I	13,506.4	13,440.1	56.9	4,266.9	4,196.8	56.9	2,310.5	52.0	1,887.9	9.5	8,398.7	907.8
II	13,548.5	13,497.9	41.4	4,281.0	4,228.4	41.4	2,314.8	68.2	1,913.2	–18.6	8,423.3	911.5
III	13,652.5	13,577.4	60.3	4,345.2	4,265.4	60.3	2,349.9	73.8	1,918.5	–5.5	8,459.2	920.2
IVᵖ	13,656.8	13,634.7	12.0	4,358.3	4,337.5	12.0	2,409.8	35.5	1,933.8	–18.0	8,435.4	936.8

[1] Estimates for durable and nondurable goods for 1996 and earlier periods are based on the Standard Industrial Classification (SIC); later estimates are based on the North American Industry Classification System (NAICS).
[2] Includes government consumption expenditures, which are for services (such as education and national defense) produced by government. In current dollars, these services are valued at their cost of production.

Source: Department of Commerce (Bureau of Economic Analysis).

TABLE B–10. Gross value added by sector, 1964–2012

[Billions of dollars; quarterly data at seasonally adjusted annual rates]

Year or quarter	Gross domestic product	Business[1] Total	Nonfarm[1]	Farm	Households and institutions Total	Households	Nonprofit institutions serving households[2]	General government[3] Total	Federal	State and local	Addendum: Gross housing value added
1964	663.6	524.9	507.5	17.3	57.7	41.2	16.5	81.1	40.7	40.4	51.6
1965	719.1	570.7	550.7	19.9	61.8	43.6	18.2	86.6	42.4	44.2	54.9
1966	787.7	624.3	603.5	20.8	66.6	46.2	20.4	96.8	47.2	49.6	58.2
1967	832.4	653.6	633.5	20.1	71.8	49.1	22.7	107.0	51.5	55.5	62.1
1968	909.8	713.5	693.0	20.5	77.5	51.9	25.6	118.8	56.3	62.5	65.9
1969	984.4	769.1	746.3	22.8	85.4	56.0	29.4	130.0	59.9	70.0	71.3
1970	1,038.3	802.2	778.5	23.7	92.6	59.8	32.8	143.5	64.0	79.5	76.7
1971	1,126.8	868.3	842.9	25.4	102.2	65.5	36.7	156.4	67.7	88.6	83.9
1972	1,237.9	957.1	927.5	29.7	111.4	70.8	40.5	169.4	71.5	97.9	91.1
1973	1,382.3	1,077.4	1,030.6	46.8	121.7	76.5	45.2	183.2	73.9	109.3	98.3
1974	1,499.5	1,164.5	1,120.3	44.2	133.6	83.0	50.6	201.3	79.6	121.8	106.8
1975	1,637.7	1,265.8	1,220.1	45.6	147.5	90.8	56.7	224.5	87.3	137.2	117.2
1976	1,824.6	1,420.7	1,377.7	43.0	160.5	98.7	61.8	243.5	93.8	149.7	126.6
1977	2,030.1	1,590.0	1,546.5	43.5	175.5	107.9	67.6	264.6	102.0	162.6	140.5
1978	2,293.8	1,809.4	1,758.7	50.7	196.9	121.3	75.6	287.5	109.7	177.8	155.5
1979	2,562.2	2,028.5	1,968.4	60.1	220.8	136.0	84.8	313.0	117.6	195.4	172.9
1980	2,788.1	2,186.1	2,134.7	51.4	253.5	156.5	97.0	348.5	131.2	217.3	199.8
1981	3,126.8	2,454.0	2,389.0	65.0	287.5	177.8	109.7	385.3	147.4	237.9	228.8
1982	3,253.2	2,514.9	2,454.5	60.4	319.3	196.7	122.7	419.0	161.2	257.7	255.7
1983	3,534.6	2,741.1	2,696.2	44.9	348.2	212.5	135.6	445.4	171.2	274.1	277.7
1984	3,930.9	3,065.5	3,001.3	64.2	380.3	231.0	149.3	485.1	192.1	293.1	301.3
1985	4,217.5	3,283.9	3,220.5	63.4	410.1	250.3	159.8	523.4	205.0	318.4	333.1
1986	4,460.1	3,461.5	3,402.1	59.5	442.3	268.0	174.3	556.3	212.6	343.7	359.7
1987	4,736.4	3,662.0	3,600.5	61.5	482.8	288.0	194.8	591.5	223.3	368.2	385.5
1988	5,100.4	3,940.2	3,879.4	60.7	529.7	313.1	216.6	630.6	234.8	395.8	415.3
1989	5,482.1	4,235.7	4,162.0	73.8	574.2	337.2	237.0	672.2	246.4	425.8	443.4
1990	5,800.5	4,453.9	4,376.6	77.3	624.0	363.3	260.6	722.7	258.8	463.9	477.8
1991	5,992.1	4,558.6	4,488.0	70.6	665.9	383.7	282.2	767.6	274.8	492.8	508.1
1992	6,342.3	4,829.2	4,748.9	80.4	711.1	405.3	305.9	801.9	282.0	519.9	538.6
1993	6,667.4	5,084.1	5,012.7	71.4	752.1	428.3	323.8	831.2	285.2	546.0	562.9
1994	7,085.2	5,425.2	5,341.3	83.9	800.0	461.3	338.7	859.9	285.2	574.7	602.6
1995	7,414.7	5,677.8	5,608.7	69.1	852.1	492.2	359.9	884.8	283.6	601.2	640.7
1996	7,838.5	6,030.2	5,936.9	93.3	897.0	519.8	377.2	911.3	287.6	623.7	671.3
1997	8,332.4	6,442.8	6,354.9	87.9	949.2	550.9	398.3	940.3	290.0	650.3	708.6
1998	8,793.5	6,810.8	6,731.6	79.2	1,010.1	583.9	426.3	972.5	292.2	680.3	745.3
1999	9,353.5	7,249.0	7,177.8	71.2	1,082.9	628.4	454.5	1,021.6	300.4	721.2	798.3
2000	9,951.5	7,715.5	7,641.9	73.6	1,157.2	673.5	483.7	1,078.8	315.1	763.7	849.9
2001	10,286.2	7,913.6	7,837.4	76.2	1,232.9	719.5	513.4	1,139.6	324.9	814.7	904.4
2002	10,642.3	8,132.8	8,060.5	72.3	1,298.0	746.0	552.1	1,211.4	351.8	859.6	932.5
2003	11,142.2	8,502.8	8,410.4	92.4	1,347.2	762.7	584.5	1,292.2	382.9	909.3	938.2
2004	11,853.3	9,070.1	8,951.9	118.3	1,423.8	806.0	617.7	1,359.3	412.0	947.3	988.7
2005	12,623.0	9,680.1	9,578.0	102.0	1,506.4	864.4	642.0	1,436.5	438.7	997.7	1,054.0
2006	13,377.2	10,262.4	10,169.4	93.1	1,602.9	924.8	678.1	1,512.0	460.6	1,051.3	1,130.8
2007	14,028.7	10,738.3	10,623.4	114.9	1,685.8	968.1	717.8	1,604.6	486.0	1,118.6	1,200.6
2008	14,291.5	10,787.8	10,657.4	130.5	1,805.7	1,042.8	762.9	1,698.0	517.7	1,180.3	1,299.7
2009	13,973.7	10,367.0	10,253.7	113.2	1,844.9	1,048.3	796.5	1,761.9	553.2	1,208.6	1,322.4
2010	14,498.9	10,836.0	10,711.2	124.8	1,851.2	1,038.5	812.7	1,811.7	589.2	1,222.5	1,322.0
2011	15,075.7	11,341.2	11,202.5	138.7	1,892.1	1,055.2	836.9	1,842.4	607.0	1,235.4	1,352.0
2012 ᵖ	15,681.5	11,880.2	11,747.0	133.2	1,928.5	1,066.1	862.4	1,872.9	616.7	1,256.2	1,375.4
2009: I	13,923.4	10,341.7	10,236.6	105.1	1,836.6	1,054.1	782.6	1,745.1	543.5	1,201.6	1,323.8
II	13,885.4	10,282.6	10,171.1	111.5	1,843.4	1,047.6	795.8	1,759.4	550.9	1,208.5	1,321.1
III	13,952.2	10,339.1	10,224.9	114.2	1,846.3	1,048.0	798.3	1,766.9	556.2	1,210.7	1,323.8
IV	14,133.6	10,504.4	10,382.3	122.1	1,853.1	1,043.6	809.5	1,776.1	562.3	1,213.8	1,321.1
2010: I	14,270.3	10,619.7	10,498.8	120.9	1,852.4	1,049.1	803.3	1,798.1	581.1	1,217.0	1,331.1
II	14,413.5	10,742.3	10,618.7	123.6	1,857.3	1,047.1	810.2	1,814.0	592.1	1,221.9	1,330.8
III	14,576.0	10,912.5	10,787.5	124.9	1,849.4	1,029.4	820.0	1,814.2	590.7	1,223.6	1,312.8
IV	14,735.9	11,069.5	10,939.8	129.6	1,845.9	1,028.6	817.3	1,820.5	593.1	1,227.4	1,313.4
2011: I	14,814.9	11,108.7	10,969.4	139.3	1,874.9	1,045.9	829.0	1,831.3	601.4	1,229.9	1,337.0
II	15,003.6	11,272.8	11,137.1	135.6	1,889.5	1,055.2	834.3	1,841.3	606.0	1,235.3	1,350.9
III	15,163.2	11,417.6	11,277.5	140.1	1,896.8	1,056.9	839.9	1,848.8	610.0	1,238.7	1,355.4
IV	15,321.0	11,565.7	11,426.0	139.7	1,907.1	1,062.9	844.2	1,848.2	610.5	1,237.8	1,364.6
2012: I	15,478.3	11,693.0	11,555.7	137.3	1,923.7	1,066.4	857.4	1,861.5	613.9	1,247.6	1,371.5
II	15,585.6	11,793.3	11,662.7	130.6	1,923.7	1,065.8	858.0	1,868.5	615.7	1,252.8	1,373.1
III	15,811.0	12,006.8	11,876.7	130.1	1,926.3	1,062.9	863.4	1,878.0	617.6	1,260.3	1,373.1
IV ᵖ	15,851.2	12,027.5	11,892.9	134.6	1,940.3	1,069.5	870.8	1,883.4	619.5	1,264.0	1,383.8

[1] Gross domestic business value added equals gross domestic product excluding gross value added of households and institutions and of general government. Nonfarm value added equals gross domestic business value added excluding gross farm value added.

[2] Equals compensation of employees of nonprofit institutions, the rental value of nonresidential fixed assets owned and used by nonprofit institutions serving households, and rental income of persons for tenant-occupied housing owned by nonprofit institutions.

[3] Equals compensation of general government employees plus general government consumption of fixed capital.

Source: Department of Commerce (Bureau of Economic Analysis).

TABLE B–11. Real gross value added by sector, 1964–2012

[Billions of chained (2005) dollars; quarterly data at seasonally adjusted annual rates]

Year or quarter	Gross domestic product	Business [1]			Households and institutions			General government [3]			Addendum: Gross housing value added
		Total	Nonfarm [1]	Farm	Total	Households	Nonprofit institutions serving households [2]	Total	Federal	State and local	
1964	3,389.4	2,325.4	2,297.1	24.9	399.9	236.0	159.4	768.4	400.7	377.5	291.6
1965	3,607.0	2,489.6	2,459.8	26.5	419.7	246.9	168.6	794.2	403.4	400.5	307.1
1966	3,842.1	2,658.0	2,635.6	25.5	438.9	256.8	178.5	843.9	429.9	424.2	320.9
1967	3,939.2	2,708.9	2,681.0	27.6	457.1	267.1	186.6	888.7	457.9	442.1	335.6
1968	4,129.9	2,843.7	2,821.6	26.6	480.1	274.6	204.9	923.6	465.7	468.6	348.3
1969	4,258.2	2,930.7	2,907.6	27.5	501.2	285.9	214.9	947.2	467.1	490.0	364.6
1970	4,266.3	2,930.0	2,904.4	28.3	510.2	292.6	216.7	950.8	447.1	511.7	376.6
1971	4,409.5	3,042.6	3,014.8	29.8	531.7	305.9	224.5	952.4	426.5	532.5	393.6
1972	4,643.8	3,238.5	3,215.2	29.8	554.8	319.1	234.4	950.6	405.8	550.9	412.5
1973	4,912.8	3,465.5	3,450.9	29.5	574.6	330.6	242.7	954.9	390.7	570.2	427.8
1974	4,885.7	3,413.7	3,400.3	28.8	597.7	345.0	251.0	974.4	389.4	590.9	448.5
1975	4,875.4	3,381.8	3,344.8	34.3	617.9	354.2	262.5	990.1	387.3	608.9	462.2
1976	5,136.9	3,605.2	3,579.3	32.7	628.2	360.9	265.8	998.7	387.9	616.9	469.3
1977	5,373.1	3,805.8	3,778.7	34.5	637.5	365.0	271.3	1,009.2	389.0	626.4	481.2
1978	5,672.8	4,045.6	4,027.9	33.3	666.4	387.4	276.7	1,028.5	393.9	641.0	503.2
1979	5,850.1	4,179.9	4,155.0	36.3	695.3	405.0	287.8	1,039.5	393.5	652.4	523.0
1980	5,834.0	4,132.8	4,110.3	35.2	730.9	430.6	297.1	1,054.4	399.7	661.2	555.0
1981	5,982.1	4,247.7	4,197.8	46.5	754.1	444.1	306.8	1,060.2	405.9	660.9	576.7
1982	5,865.9	4,119.1	4,062.4	48.8	778.9	452.1	324.3	1,071.0	412.5	665.2	592.3
1983	6,130.9	4,341.0	4,323.6	31.9	801.0	460.5	338.5	1,077.9	422.0	662.5	605.4
1984	6,571.5	4,717.9	4,679.3	43.3	826.8	476.4	348.3	1,091.3	431.6	666.4	624.6
1985	6,843.4	4,937.0	4,880.9	52.9	841.2	487.4	351.2	1,122.5	443.9	685.6	649.1
1986	7,080.5	5,121.2	5,070.4	50.8	863.4	493.7	368.0	1,150.1	451.8	705.4	661.1
1987	7,307.0	5,289.8	5,239.3	51.3	895.8	506.8	388.0	1,175.3	463.6	719.0	676.8
1988	7,607.4	5,516.6	5,478.3	45.6	937.2	525.7	411.1	1,205.8	469.3	743.6	696.4
1989	7,879.2	5,720.9	5,671.7	52.3	974.8	542.0	432.9	1,234.6	475.1	766.4	712.2
1990	8,027.1	5,808.8	5,753.4	56.0	1,009.6	555.7	454.9	1,266.2	483.8	789.2	730.2
1991	8,008.3	5,757.9	5,700.5	56.9	1,038.5	572.0	467.4	1,279.4	486.7	799.4	754.6
1992	8,280.0	5,985.1	5,914.6	66.2	1,071.4	589.0	483.5	1,283.7	476.5	813.0	776.7
1993	8,516.2	6,178.1	6,121.3	57.8	1,106.9	603.5	504.9	1,286.5	467.4	824.2	789.1
1994	8,863.1	6,481.0	6,407.0	70.5	1,140.0	631.9	508.7	1,286.8	452.2	838.5	821.7
1995	9,086.0	6,663.3	6,610.4	56.4	1,175.5	651.3	524.8	1,287.7	435.1	855.1	846.9
1996	9,425.8	6,966.8	6,901.6	65.3	1,199.8	665.4	535.0	1,289.8	423.2	868.4	860.4
1997	9,845.9	7,327.5	7,253.2	72.5	1,240.5	687.6	553.5	1,299.6	415.2	885.6	885.6
1998	10,274.7	7,693.8	7,624.8	69.4	1,280.2	703.7	577.8	1,314.3	410.4	904.6	900.9
1999	10,770.7	8,123.7	8,051.5	72.8	1,325.5	740.3	585.3	1,326.3	407.1	919.5	942.3
2000	11,216.4	8,491.4	8,408.3	83.5	1,376.2	774.1	601.8	1,349.4	410.5	939.0	977.8
2001	11,337.5	8,559.5	8,482.3	77.7	1,407.0	793.1	613.4	1,373.7	412.1	961.3	997.8
2002	11,543.1	8,726.8	8,646.1	81.2	1,417.3	789.9	627.7	1,401.4	420.2	980.9	988.5
2003	11,836.4	9,001.6	8,910.5	91.6	1,417.8	787.1	631.1	1,418.2	431.5	986.7	969.3
2004	12,246.9	9,363.0	9,265.1	97.9	1,457.4	821.7	635.9	1,426.8	435.8	991.0	1,008.4
2005	12,623.0	9,680.1	9,578.0	102.0	1,506.4	864.4	642.0	1,436.5	438.7	997.7	1,054.0
2006	12,958.5	9,974.0	9,874.6	99.1	1,539.8	898.0	642.0	1,445.0	438.4	1,006.5	1,098.6
2007	13,206.4	10,172.5	10,082.1	90.3	1,571.9	914.2	657.8	1,462.5	441.8	1,020.8	1,132.4
2008	13,161.9	10,038.4	9,934.2	101.7	1,628.6	954.8	674.2	1,492.3	459.0	1,033.3	1,183.9
2009	12,757.9	9,604.7	9,484.7	117.5	1,621.5	943.0	678.6	1,522.4	486.0	1,036.7	1,181.8
2010	13,063.0	9,888.9	9,774.2	111.7	1,634.8	948.0	686.7	1,532.7	503.8	1,029.5	1,196.3
2011	13,299.1	10,123.4	10,032.3	91.9	1,647.7	948.2	698.8	1,524.7	507.8	1,017.7	1,203.5
2012 P	13,591.1	10,425.4	10,340.4	87.9	1,646.4	933.6	711.3	1,519.8	505.5	1,015.0	1,192.4
2009: I	12,711.0	9,608.5	9,496.8	108.4	1,584.2	947.8	638.0	1,511.6	475.1	1,036.7	1,182.7
II	12,701.0	9,553.4	9,436.3	114.4	1,614.2	938.8	675.2	1,523.3	485.7	1,037.9	1,176.4
III	12,746.7	9,570.8	9,442.3	127.3	1,639.9	941.7	697.6	1,525.1	489.8	1,035.7	1,182.0
IV	12,873.1	9,686.1	9,563.4	120.1	1,647.8	943.5	703.6	1,529.5	493.4	1,036.6	1,186.2
2010: I	12,947.6	9,759.3	9,641.2	115.0	1,648.3	954.2	693.9	1,531.3	498.7	1,033.2	1,201.3
II	13,019.6	9,828.9	9,707.1	118.6	1,644.1	958.2	686.2	1,538.7	507.2	1,032.1	1,206.9
III	13,103.5	9,942.0	9,827.5	111.1	1,624.7	942.1	682.4	1,531.5	504.4	1,027.7	1,190.5
IV	13,181.2	10,025.4	9,921.0	102.0	1,622.2	937.6	684.3	1,529.4	505.0	1,025.1	1,186.5
2011: I	13,183.8	10,014.0	9,917.9	95.4	1,636.8	946.9	689.6	1,528.4	507.2	1,021.9	1,199.7
II	13,264.7	10,086.5	10,000.8	87.9	1,648.5	951.3	696.7	1,525.9	507.8	1,018.8	1,207.1
III	13,306.9	10,129.3	10,040.5	90.3	1,652.1	948.4	702.8	1,522.4	507.5	1,015.6	1,204.6
IV	13,441.0	10,263.6	10,169.9	94.2	1,653.6	946.2	706.3	1,522.1	508.6	1,014.3	1,202.6
2012: I	13,506.4	10,332.0	10,237.4	95.0	1,652.4	941.5	709.7	1,521.2	507.4	1,014.6	1,199.0
II	13,548.5	10,381.4	10,290.7	92.5	1,648.1	936.5	710.2	1,518.5	505.6	1,013.7	1,194.8
III	13,652.5	10,489.8	10,409.9	84.0	1,643.5	930.4	711.5	1,520.5	504.8	1,016.4	1,189.4
IV P	13,656.8	10,498.0	10,423.5	80.2	1,641.6	926.0	713.8	1,518.8	504.2	1,015.3	1,186.2

[1] Gross domestic business value added equals gross domestic product excluding gross value added of households and institutions and of general government. Nonfarm value added equals gross domestic business value added excluding gross farm value added.
[2] Equals compensation of employees of nonprofit institutions, the rental value of nonresidential fixed assets owned and used by nonprofit institutions serving households, and rental income of persons for tenant-occupied housing owned by nonprofit institutions.
[3] Equals compensation of general government employees plus general government consumption of fixed capital.

Source: Department of Commerce (Bureau of Economic Analysis).

National Income or Expenditure | 337

Table B–12. Gross domestic product (GDP) by industry, value added, in current dollars and as a percentage of GDP, 1981–2011

[Billions of dollars; except as noted]

Year	Gross domestic product	Private industries									
		Total private industries	Agriculture, forestry, fishing, and hunting	Mining	Construction	Manufacturing			Utilities	Wholesale trade	Retail trade
						Total manufacturing	Durable goods	Non-durable goods			
						Value added					
1981	3,126.8	2,701.6	75.6	121.5	133.1	619.6	376.2	243.4	72.0	206.2	218.0
1982	3,253.2	2,791.4	71.6	118.5	131.0	606.5	359.2	247.3	83.2	206.6	226.9
1983	3,534.6	3,041.7	57.2	102.8	139.6	657.5	385.5	272.0	94.4	222.4	255.3
1984	3,930.9	3,393.0	77.0	107.2	160.7	731.8	451.0	280.7	105.7	249.8	286.8
1985	4,217.5	3,634.6	76.6	106.2	177.0	751.4	458.6	292.8	113.0	269.2	309.1
1986	4,460.1	3,840.4	73.7	70.3	197.2	777.4	468.4	308.9	117.5	279.3	331.4
1987	4,736.4	4,077.9	78.8	73.1	210.1	823.1	492.5	330.6	125.8	285.6	345.7
1988	5,100.4	4,395.3	78.1	74.1	226.5	900.2	537.9	362.2	125.1	314.3	366.8
1989	5,482.1	4,729.7	91.6	78.6	238.6	950.2	562.4	387.7	138.2	335.7	390.7
1990	5,800.5	4,994.3	95.7	88.4	243.6	968.9	558.9	410.1	145.5	347.7	400.4
1991	5,992.1	5,133.2	88.3	79.5	228.8	976.7	554.2	422.5	153.8	362.6	407.9
1992	6,342.3	5,442.0	99.3	73.6	233.2	1,016.7	574.5	442.2	159.7	380.1	430.0
1993	6,667.4	5,735.9	90.6	74.4	250.4	1,058.9	603.0	456.0	164.3	402.5	462.9
1994	7,085.2	6,119.9	105.6	75.9	277.2	1,127.3	650.2	477.1	171.2	444.5	500.5
1995	7,414.7	6,420.0	91.3	76.7	294.2	1,180.9	675.4	505.5	175.3	460.2	525.0
1996	7,838.5	6,812.6	114.2	90.0	320.9	1,208.5	705.0	503.5	173.4	492.5	556.8
1997	8,332.4	7,271.0	108.4	94.8	346.7	1,277.3	748.9	528.3	169.9	524.9	589.9
1998	8,793.5	7,694.4	100.3	81.0	383.7	1,326.7	781.2	545.6	165.1	557.3	626.9
1999	9,353.5	8,199.6	92.8	82.0	428.4	1,368.1	802.4	565.6	172.7	579.1	653.4
2000	9,951.5	8,736.1	95.6	108.9	467.3	1,415.6	839.1	576.5	173.9	617.7	686.2
2001	10,286.2	9,010.8	98.6	119.3	490.5	1,343.9	758.8	585.2	177.6	613.3	703.9
2002	10,642.3	9,289.3	94.4	109.5	494.3	1,355.5	767.8	587.8	181.0	614.9	731.2
2003	11,142.2	9,706.9	115.5	134.9	516.1	1,374.3	766.4	607.9	192.0	638.1	769.5
2004	11,853.3	10,345.6	142.7	159.3	554.2	1,482.7	822.0	660.6	208.0	684.2	795.1
2005	12,623.0	11,037.1	127.1	192.3	612.5	1,569.3	878.3	691.0	205.9	725.5	837.6
2006	13,377.2	11,709.4	122.5	229.8	651.0	1,648.4	921.3	727.1	236.0	769.7	875.8
2007	14,028.7	12,268.8	144.5	254.5	653.8	1,698.0	939.9	758.1	248.6	816.7	887.9
2008	14,291.5	12,437.1	159.4	319.2	614.2	1,628.5	904.1	724.4	257.7	824.1	848.6
2009	13,973.7	12,056.7	142.4	221.7	542.9	1,540.1	787.0	753.2	264.7	766.3	846.8
2010	14,498.9	12,532.3	157.6	251.9	523.3	1,630.5	866.7	763.8	284.5	799.0	876.0
2011	15,075.7	13,081.8	173.5	289.9	529.5	1,731.5	910.1	821.3	297.9	845.1	905.7
Percent					Industry value added as a percentage of GDP (percent)						
1981	100.0	86.4	2.4	3.9	4.3	19.8	12.0	7.8	2.3	6.6	7.0
1982	100.0	85.8	2.2	3.6	4.0	18.6	11.0	7.6	2.6	6.4	7.0
1983	100.0	86.1	1.6	2.9	3.9	18.6	10.9	7.7	2.7	6.3	7.2
1984	100.0	86.3	2.0	2.7	4.1	18.6	11.5	7.1	2.7	6.4	7.3
1985	100.0	86.2	1.8	2.5	4.2	17.8	10.9	6.9	2.7	6.4	7.3
1986	100.0	86.1	1.7	1.6	4.4	17.4	10.5	6.9	2.6	6.3	7.4
1987	100.0	86.1	1.7	1.5	4.4	17.4	10.4	7.0	2.7	6.0	7.3
1988	100.0	86.2	1.5	1.5	4.4	17.6	10.5	7.1	2.5	6.2	7.2
1989	100.0	86.3	1.7	1.4	4.4	17.3	10.3	7.1	2.5	6.1	7.1
1990	100.0	86.1	1.6	1.5	4.2	16.7	9.6	7.1	2.5	6.0	6.9
1991	100.0	85.7	1.5	1.3	3.8	16.3	9.2	7.1	2.6	6.1	6.8
1992	100.0	85.8	1.6	1.2	3.7	16.0	9.1	7.0	2.5	6.0	6.8
1993	100.0	86.0	1.4	1.1	3.8	15.9	9.0	6.8	2.5	6.0	6.9
1994	100.0	86.4	1.5	1.1	3.9	15.9	9.2	6.7	2.4	6.3	7.1
1995	100.0	86.6	1.2	1.0	4.0	15.9	9.1	6.8	2.4	6.2	7.1
1996	100.0	86.9	1.5	1.1	4.1	15.4	9.0	6.4	2.2	6.3	7.1
1997	100.0	87.3	1.3	1.1	4.2	15.3	9.0	6.3	2.0	6.3	7.1
1998	100.0	87.5	1.1	.9	4.4	15.1	8.9	6.2	1.9	6.3	7.1
1999	100.0	87.7	1.0	.9	4.6	14.6	8.6	6.0	1.8	6.2	7.0
2000	100.0	87.8	1.0	1.1	4.7	14.2	8.4	5.8	1.7	6.2	6.9
2001	100.0	87.6	1.0	1.2	4.8	13.1	7.4	5.7	1.7	6.0	6.8
2002	100.0	87.3	.9	1.0	4.6	12.7	7.2	5.5	1.7	5.8	6.9
2003	100.0	87.1	1.0	1.2	4.6	12.3	6.9	5.5	1.7	5.7	6.9
2004	100.0	87.3	1.2	1.3	4.7	12.5	6.9	5.6	1.8	5.8	6.7
2005	100.0	87.4	1.0	1.5	4.9	12.4	7.0	5.5	1.6	5.7	6.6
2006	100.0	87.5	.9	1.7	4.9	12.3	6.9	5.4	1.8	5.8	6.5
2007	100.0	87.5	1.0	1.8	4.7	12.1	6.7	5.4	1.8	5.8	6.3
2008	100.0	87.0	1.1	2.2	4.3	11.4	6.3	5.1	1.8	5.8	5.9
2009	100.0	86.3	1.0	1.6	3.9	11.0	5.6	5.4	1.9	5.5	6.1
2010	100.0	86.4	1.1	1.7	3.6	11.2	6.0	5.3	2.0	5.5	6.0
2011	100.0	86.8	1.2	1.9	3.5	11.5	6.0	5.4	2.0	5.6	6.0

[1] Consists of agriculture, forestry, fishing, and hunting; mining; construction; and manufacturing.
[2] Consists of utilities; wholesale trade; retail trade; transportation and warehousing; information; finance, insurance, real estate, rental, and leasing; professional and business services; educational services, health care, and social assistance; arts, entertainment, recreation, accommodation, and food services; and other services, except government.

Note: Data shown in Tables B–12 and B–13 are consistent with the 2012 annual revision of the industry accounts released in December 2012. For details see *Survey of Current Business*, December 2012.

See next page for continuation of table.

[Billions of dollars; except as noted]

Year	Transportation and warehousing	Information	Finance, insurance, real estate, rental, and leasing	Professional and business services	Educational services, health care, and social assistance	Arts, entertainment, recreation, accommodation, and food services	Other services, except government	Government	Private goods-producing industries [1]	Private services-producing industries [2]
					Private industries—Continued					
					Value added					
1981	110.1	123.5	502.8	197.3	152.9	92.9	76.0	425.2	949.9	1,751.7
1982	106.3	135.3	544.7	213.2	169.2	100.0	78.3	461.8	927.7	1,863.7
1983	118.0	152.5	611.6	242.4	189.7	111.5	86.8	492.9	957.1	2,084.6
1984	131.4	160.0	677.5	280.9	207.1	120.8	96.3	537.9	1,076.7	2,316.3
1985	137.1	176.4	739.4	316.3	225.4	132.0	105.3	582.9	1,111.2	2,523.4
1986	147.0	185.6	804.0	352.4	245.2	144.0	115.3	619.7	1,118.6	2,721.8
1987	152.6	197.4	850.3	384.5	277.7	152.3	121.1	658.4	1,185.0	2,892.9
1988	161.4	205.4	915.7	424.3	301.5	168.8	133.0	705.1	1,278.8	3,116.5
1989	166.3	222.4	981.0	470.4	337.4	184.0	144.8	752.4	1,358.9	3,370.8
1990	172.8	235.6	1,049.2	516.5	376.7	199.6	153.9	806.2	1,396.5	3,597.7
1991	182.3	244.3	1,109.8	524.0	413.4	205.9	155.9	858.9	1,373.2	3,760.0
1992	192.0	260.5	1,192.1	566.6	452.9	219.0	166.3	900.3	1,422.8	4,019.2
1993	206.4	279.6	1,259.3	600.9	476.4	230.9	178.3	931.4	1,474.3	4,261.6
1994	223.7	299.4	1,321.6	639.7	500.2	242.3	190.7	965.3	1,586.1	4,533.8
1995	231.7	311.5	1,405.7	687.3	523.9	255.3	200.7	994.6	1,643.1	4,776.9
1996	241.3	338.6	1,490.3	756.5	545.4	272.8	211.2	1,025.9	1,733.6	5,079.0
1997	261.8	349.4	1,610.6	842.1	571.4	300.3	223.8	1,061.3	1,827.2	5,443.8
1998	275.6	386.1	1,696.8	927.0	601.2	321.1	245.6	1,099.1	1,891.7	5,802.7
1999	287.1	438.5	1,834.0	1,010.2	638.5	355.4	259.3	1,153.9	1,971.3	6,228.3
2000	301.4	417.8	1,997.7	1,116.8	678.0	381.6	277.6	1,215.4	2,087.4	6,648.7
2001	302.6	451.1	2,154.8	1,170.7	729.2	391.2	264.2	1,275.4	2,052.3	6,958.5
2002	302.4	499.7	2,222.3	1,198.3	789.8	411.1	285.0	1,353.0	2,053.7	7,235.6
2003	319.8	506.6	2,316.5	1,260.0	847.1	427.8	288.8	1,435.3	2,140.8	7,566.1
2004	347.0	558.8	2,400.4	1,347.5	906.1	458.7	300.8	1,507.7	2,338.9	8,006.6
2005	369.5	586.5	2,598.8	1,460.2	953.5	485.4	313.0	1,585.9	2,501.2	8,535.8
2006	394.0	590.6	2,765.3	1,567.2	1,015.3	512.4	331.6	1,667.8	2,651.6	9,057.8
2007	404.9	635.5	2,857.0	1,697.6	1,076.9	549.0	343.8	1,759.9	2,750.9	9,517.9
2008	415.0	636.8	2,916.6	1,783.2	1,153.9	537.3	342.7	1,854.4	2,721.2	9,715.9
2009	396.6	604.8	2,941.8	1,693.2	1,225.6	525.4	344.4	1,917.0	2,447.1	9,609.6
2010	422.6	612.2	3,021.8	1,769.6	1,269.2	558.0	356.0	1,966.6	2,563.4	9,968.9
2011	447.9	646.6	3,058.1	1,883.9	1,311.1	591.1	369.9	1,993.8	2,724.4	10,357.4
					Industry value added as a percentage of GDP (percent)					
1981	3.5	4.0	16.1	6.3	4.9	3.0	2.4	13.6	30.4	56.0
1982	3.3	4.2	16.7	6.6	5.2	3.1	2.4	14.2	28.5	57.3
1983	3.3	4.3	17.3	6.9	5.4	3.2	2.5	13.9	27.1	59.0
1984	3.3	4.1	17.2	7.1	5.3	3.1	2.4	13.7	27.4	58.9
1985	3.3	4.2	17.5	7.5	5.3	3.1	2.5	13.8	26.3	59.8
1986	3.3	4.2	18.0	7.9	5.5	3.2	2.6	13.9	25.1	61.0
1987	3.2	4.2	18.0	8.1	5.9	3.2	2.6	13.9	25.0	61.1
1988	3.2	4.0	18.0	8.3	5.9	3.3	2.6	13.8	25.1	61.1
1989	3.0	4.1	17.9	8.6	6.2	3.4	2.6	13.7	24.8	61.5
1990	3.0	4.1	18.1	8.9	6.5	3.4	2.7	13.9	24.1	62.0
1991	3.0	4.1	18.5	8.7	6.9	3.4	2.6	14.3	22.9	62.8
1992	3.0	4.1	18.8	8.9	7.1	3.5	2.6	14.2	22.4	63.4
1993	3.1	4.2	18.9	9.0	7.1	3.5	2.7	14.0	22.1	63.9
1994	3.2	4.2	18.7	9.0	7.1	3.4	2.7	13.6	22.4	64.0
1995	3.1	4.2	19.0	9.3	7.1	3.4	2.7	13.4	22.2	64.4
1996	3.1	4.3	19.0	9.7	7.0	3.5	2.7	13.1	22.1	64.8
1997	3.1	4.2	19.3	10.1	6.9	3.6	2.7	12.7	21.9	65.3
1998	3.1	4.4	19.3	10.5	6.8	3.7	2.8	12.5	21.5	66.0
1999	3.1	4.7	19.6	10.8	6.8	3.8	2.8	12.3	21.1	66.6
2000	3.0	4.2	20.1	11.2	6.8	3.8	2.8	12.2	21.0	66.8
2001	2.9	4.4	20.9	11.4	7.1	3.8	2.6	12.4	20.0	67.6
2002	2.8	4.7	20.9	11.3	7.4	3.9	2.7	12.7	19.3	68.0
2003	2.9	4.5	20.8	11.3	7.6	3.8	2.6	12.9	19.2	67.9
2004	2.9	4.7	20.3	11.4	7.6	3.9	2.5	12.7	19.7	67.5
2005	2.9	4.6	20.6	11.6	7.6	3.8	2.5	12.6	19.8	67.6
2006	2.9	4.4	20.7	11.7	7.6	3.8	2.5	12.5	19.8	67.7
2007	2.9	4.5	20.4	12.1	7.7	3.9	2.5	12.5	19.6	67.8
2008	2.9	4.5	20.4	12.5	8.1	3.8	2.4	13.0	19.0	68.0
2009	2.8	4.3	21.1	12.1	8.8	3.8	2.5	13.7	17.5	68.8
2010	2.9	4.2	20.8	12.2	8.8	3.8	2.5	13.6	17.7	68.8
2011	3.0	4.3	20.3	12.5	8.7	3.9	2.5	13.2	18.1	68.7

Note (cont'd): Value added is the contribution of each private industry and of government to GDP. Value added is equal to an industry's gross output minus its intermediate inputs. Current-dollar value added is calculated as the sum of distributions by an industry to its labor and capital, which are derived from the components of gross domestic income.

Value added industry data shown in Tables B-12 and B-13 are based on the 2002 North American Industry Classification System (NAICS).

Source: Department of Commerce (Bureau of Economic Analysis).

National Income or Expenditure | 339

TABLE B–13. Real gross domestic product by industry, value added, and percent changes, 1981–2011

Year	Gross domestic product	Total private industries [1]	Agriculture, forestry, fishing, and hunting	Mining	Construction	Manufacturing Total manufacturing	Manufacturing Durable goods	Manufacturing Nondurable goods	Utilities	Wholesale trade	Retail trade
	Chain-type quantity indexes for value added (2005=100)										
1981	47.390	45.387	48.384	114.882	68.529	45.199	34.438	66.320	58.963	30.726	35.287
1982	46.470	44.282	51.011	109.757	60.546	41.913	31.046	64.152	57.737	30.871	35.240
1983	48.570	46.325	36.388	104.252	62.785	45.226	33.064	70.536	60.798	32.224	38.504
1984	52.060	49.753	47.087	114.545	70.655	49.545	38.389	70.782	66.262	34.845	42.183
1985	54.214	51.961	55.753	121.137	75.849	51.109	39.540	73.192	70.538	36.656	44.468
1986	56.092	53.470	54.881	116.810	77.499	51.078	39.836	72.251	74.025	40.323	47.777
1987	57.887	55.466	56.750	122.364	79.148	54.843	42.637	77.950	82.732	39.192	46.100
1988	60.266	58.098	50.675	136.911	82.976	58.683	46.870	80.123	82.022	41.306	50.726
1989	62.420	60.243	56.742	132.276	85.326	59.359	47.610	80.544	90.437	43.307	52.973
1990	63.591	61.264	60.074	130.787	84.779	58.575	46.726	80.093	95.576	42.692	53.825
1991	63.442	61.161	60.756	133.113	78.616	57.674	45.243	80.651	96.834	44.438	53.661
1992	65.595	63.537	67.964	129.022	80.403	59.597	46.187	84.672	97.689	48.490	56.467
1993	67.466	65.296	58.983	131.161	82.649	61.987	48.129	87.853	96.434	49.957	59.225
1994	70.214	68.374	70.448	142.428	87.293	66.078	51.830	92.380	99.397	53.134	63.523
1995	71.980	70.112	59.555	143.474	88.224	68.798	55.832	91.805	102.620	52.901	66.714
1996	74.672	73.146	66.286	133.682	92.982	70.997	59.253	91.157	101.716	57.783	72.881
1997	78.000	76.840	71.591	138.097	95.170	75.261	64.194	93.699	97.108	64.068	79.185
1998	81.397	80.541	69.837	148.848	98.277	79.022	70.550	92.120	95.007	74.157	84.195
1999	85.326	84.778	73.031	137.847	103.607	83.268	75.962	94.101	104.692	78.059	86.596
2000	88.857	88.667	81.603	121.027	106.961	88.584	84.443	93.958	108.309	83.510	89.942
2001	89.816	89.792	78.861	136.785	104.536	84.499	79.298	91.571	93.854	87.671	92.731
2002	91.445	91.300	82.079	138.414	100.882	86.606	82.246	92.420	97.378	88.479	95.770
2003	93.769	93.464	90.644	120.511	101.161	89.347	85.053	95.052	100.904	93.901	97.961
2004	97.021	96.945	96.510	119.237	101.134	96.658	93.004	101.453	104.815	98.912	97.982
2005	100.000	100.000	100.000	100.000	100.000	100.000	100.000	100.000	100.000	100.000	100.000
2006	102.658	102.980	100.756	108.435	96.982	104.159	106.663	101.069	100.539	102.995	102.176
2007	104.622	104.953	93.149	111.427	91.606	107.847	110.655	104.394	104.004	108.619	102.473
2008	104.270	103.909	101.279	107.236	85.547	101.545	108.932	93.038	108.818	107.416	96.613
2009	101.069	99.908	114.472	134.267	74.490	92.209	91.138	92.674	98.997	93.075	94.746
2010	103.486	102.626	111.233	121.976	73.620	98.564	103.223	93.049	109.020	96.225	101.361
2011	105.356	104.711	96.068	122.020	73.388	101.039	110.238	91.132	111.834	99.098	101.521
	Percent change from year earlier										
1981	2.5	2.6	25.8	-0.6	-8.8	4.8	2.8	7.9	-0.2	6.1	2.9
1982	-1.9	-2.4	5.4	-4.5	-11.6	-7.3	-9.8	-3.3	-2.1	.5	-.1
1983	4.5	4.6	-28.7	-5.0	3.7	7.9	6.5	10.0	5.3	4.4	9.3
1984	7.2	7.4	29.4	9.9	12.5	9.5	16.1	.3	9.0	8.1	9.6
1985	4.1	4.4	18.4	5.8	7.4	3.2	3.0	3.4	6.5	5.2	5.4
1986	3.5	2.9	-1.6	-3.6	2.2	-.1	.7	-1.3	4.9	10.0	7.4
1987	3.2	3.7	3.4	4.8	2.1	7.4	7.0	7.9	11.8	-2.8	-3.5
1988	4.1	4.7	-10.7	11.9	4.8	7.0	9.9	2.8	-.9	5.4	10.0
1989	3.6	3.7	12.0	-3.4	2.8	1.2	1.6	.5	10.3	4.8	4.4
1990	1.9	1.7	5.9	-1.1	-.6	-1.3	-1.9	-.6	5.7	-1.4	1.6
1991	-.2	-.2	1.1	1.8	-7.3	-1.5	-3.2	.7	1.3	4.1	-.3
1992	3.4	3.9	11.9	-3.1	2.3	3.3	2.1	5.0	.9	9.1	5.2
1993	2.9	2.8	-13.2	1.7	2.8	4.0	4.2	3.8	-1.3	3.0	4.9
1994	4.1	4.7	19.4	8.6	5.6	6.6	7.7	5.2	3.1	6.4	7.3
1995	2.5	2.5	-15.5	.7	1.1	4.1	7.7	-.6	3.2	-.4	5.0
1996	3.7	4.3	11.3	-6.8	5.4	3.2	6.1	-.7	-.9	9.2	9.2
1997	4.5	5.1	8.0	3.3	2.4	6.0	8.3	2.8	-4.5	10.9	8.6
1998	4.4	4.8	-2.5	7.8	3.3	5.0	9.9	-1.7	-2.2	15.7	6.3
1999	4.8	5.3	4.6	-7.4	5.4	5.4	7.7	2.2	10.2	5.3	2.9
2000	4.1	4.6	11.7	-12.2	3.2	6.4	11.2	-.2	3.5	7.0	3.9
2001	1.1	1.3	-3.4	13.0	-2.3	-4.6	-6.1	-2.5	-13.3	5.0	3.1
2002	1.8	1.7	4.1	1.2	-3.5	2.5	3.7	.9	3.8	.9	3.3
2003	2.5	2.4	10.4	-12.9	.3	3.2	3.4	2.8	3.6	6.1	2.3
2004	3.5	3.7	6.5	-1.1	.0	8.2	9.3	6.7	3.9	5.3	.0
2005	3.1	3.2	3.6	-16.1	-1.1	3.5	7.5	-1.4	-4.6	1.1	2.1
2006	2.7	3.0	.8	8.4	-3.0	4.2	6.7	1.1	.5	3.0	2.2
2007	1.9	1.9	-7.5	2.8	-5.5	3.5	3.7	3.3	3.4	5.5	.3
2008	-.3	-1.0	8.7	-3.8	-6.6	-5.8	-1.6	-10.9	4.6	-1.1	-5.7
2009	-3.1	-3.8	13.0	25.2	-12.9	-9.2	-16.3	-.4	-9.0	-13.4	-1.9
2010	2.4	2.7	-2.8	-9.2	-1.2	6.9	13.3	.4	10.1	3.4	7.0
2011	1.8	2.0	-13.6	.0	-.3	2.5	6.8	-2.1	2.6	3.0	.2

[1] Consists of agriculture, forestry, fishing, and hunting; mining; construction; and manufacturing.
[2] Consists of utilities; wholesale trade; retail trade; transportation and warehousing; information; finance, insurance, real estate, rental, and leasing; professional and business services; educational services, health care, and social assistance; arts, entertainment, recreation, accommodation, and food services; and other services, except government.

See next page for continuation of table.

TABLE B-13. Real gross domestic product by industry, value added, and percent changes, 1981–2011—*Continued*

Year	Transportation and warehousing	Information	Finance, insurance, real estate, rental, and leasing	Professional and business services	Educational services, health care, and social assistance	Arts, entertainment, recreation, accommodation, and food services	Other services, except government	Government	Private goods-producing industries [1]	Private services-producing industries [2]
	Private industries—Continued									
	Chain-type quantity indexes for value added (2005=100)									
1981	40.790	32.049	48.938	35.550	57.200	46.189	73.651	75.162	52.361	42.951
1982	38.832	31.956	49.393	35.428	57.034	47.380	70.878	75.297	48.901	42.869
1983	43.831	34.198	50.583	37.922	59.229	51.042	74.147	75.976	50.241	45.236
1984	45.938	33.874	52.452	42.010	60.919	53.218	78.074	76.794	55.880	47.804
1985	46.619	34.821	53.847	45.365	62.423	55.848	80.627	78.818	58.708	49.789
1986	46.696	34.983	54.648	48.917	63.597	59.483	82.446	80.650	58.664	51.881
1987	48.989	37.356	56.560	51.538	67.638	59.082	83.865	82.216	62.184	53.341
1988	50.432	38.579	58.607	54.138	68.238	62.454	87.958	84.340	65.702	55.673
1989	52.397	41.288	60.088	57.635	70.866	64.701	91.973	86.397	66.909	58.155
1990	55.147	42.649	61.497	60.141	73.463	66.671	93.971	88.511	66.431	59.704
1991	57.664	43.057	62.438	58.046	75.173	64.814	91.234	88.991	64.989	60.060
1992	61.325	45.429	64.388	59.787	77.453	67.092	93.331	89.513	67.163	62.511
1993	64.042	47.837	66.268	61.282	77.728	69.166	96.564	89.512	68.816	64.309
1994	69.180	50.285	67.851	63.418	78.052	71.235	101.126	89.780	73.841	66.769
1995	71.236	52.034	69.615	65.656	79.293	73.630	103.010	89.719	75.400	68.566
1996	75.138	55.321	71.251	70.179	80.204	76.742	103.940	90.120	78.077	71.717
1997	79.006	56.402	74.419	75.051	81.559	80.225	102.674	91.101	82.210	75.282
1998	78.063	62.107	76.667	79.327	82.657	82.504	108.399	92.284	85.786	79.023
1999	80.801	70.528	81.686	82.819	84.776	87.572	109.304	93.395	89.880	83.304
2000	86.201	67.832	87.064	86.923	86.688	91.104	110.957	95.142	94.368	87.019
2001	83.090	72.885	92.351	89.035	88.822	89.691	99.325	95.941	91.430	89.318
2002	81.948	80.958	92.155	89.688	92.487	91.313	102.420	97.802	92.368	90.987
2003	86.133	82.501	93.538	92.228	95.460	93.634	100.428	98.749	94.040	93.288
2004	93.911	92.679	94.519	95.440	98.332	97.751	100.685	99.445	99.161	96.307
2005	100.000	100.000	100.000	100.000	100.000	100.000	100.000	100.000	100.000	100.000
2006	104.049	101.530	104.035	103.229	103.265	102.563	101.704	100.437	102.528	103.112
2007	105.231	109.310	105.125	106.140	104.978	105.614	101.659	101.209	103.194	105.471
2008	106.182	111.156	104.357	110.288	109.833	100.271	97.388	103.008	97.973	105.673
2009	95.382	104.993	105.607	103.846	112.056	94.050	93.221	103.940	92.363	102.135
2010	101.721	108.313	106.040	106.089	113.472	100.114	93.916	104.589	95.059	104.860
2011	106.590	114.722	106.391	111.203	115.397	105.492	95.105	103.820	95.631	107.386
	Percent change from year earlier									
1981	-2.5	5.5	1.4	2.5	1.9	3.5	-3.0	0.4	3.5	2.2
1982	-4.8	-.3	.9	-.3	-.3	2.6	-3.8	.2	-6.6	-.2
1983	12.9	7.0	2.4	7.0	3.8	7.7	4.6	.9	2.7	5.5
1984	4.8	-.9	3.7	10.8	2.9	4.3	5.3	1.1	11.2	5.7
1985	1.5	2.8	2.7	8.0	2.5	4.9	3.3	2.6	5.1	4.2
1986	.2	.5	1.5	7.8	1.9	6.5	2.3	2.3	-.1	4.2
1987	4.9	6.8	3.5	5.4	6.4	-.7	1.7	1.9	6.0	2.8
1988	2.9	3.3	3.6	5.0	.9	5.7	4.9	2.6	5.7	4.4
1989	3.9	7.0	2.5	6.5	3.9	3.6	4.6	2.4	1.8	4.5
1990	5.2	3.3	2.3	4.3	3.7	3.0	2.2	2.4	-.7	2.7
1991	4.6	1.0	1.5	-3.5	2.3	-2.8	-2.9	.5	-2.2	.6
1992	6.3	5.5	3.1	3.0	3.0	3.5	2.3	.6	3.3	4.1
1993	4.4	5.3	2.9	2.5	.4	3.1	3.5	.0	2.5	2.9
1994	8.0	5.1	2.4	3.5	.4	3.0	4.7	.3	7.3	3.8
1995	3.0	3.5	2.6	3.5	1.6	3.4	1.9	-.1	2.1	2.7
1996	5.5	6.3	2.4	6.9	1.1	4.2	.9	.4	3.6	4.6
1997	5.1	2.0	4.4	6.9	1.7	4.5	-1.2	1.1	5.3	5.0
1998	-1.2	10.1	3.0	5.7	1.3	2.8	5.6	1.3	4.3	5.0
1999	3.5	13.6	6.5	4.4	2.6	6.1	.8	1.2	4.8	5.4
2000	6.7	-3.8	6.6	5.0	2.3	4.0	1.5	1.9	5.0	4.5
2001	-3.6	7.5	6.1	2.4	2.5	-1.6	-10.5	.8	-3.1	2.6
2002	-1.4	11.1	-.2	.7	4.1	1.8	3.1	1.9	1.0	1.9
2003	5.1	1.9	1.5	2.8	3.2	2.5	-1.9	1.0	1.8	2.5
2004	9.0	12.3	1.0	3.5	3.0	4.4	.3	.7	5.4	3.2
2005	6.5	7.9	5.8	4.8	1.7	2.3	-.7	.6	.8	3.8
2006	4.0	1.5	4.0	3.2	3.3	2.6	1.7	.4	2.5	3.1
2007	1.1	7.7	1.0	2.8	1.7	3.0	.0	.8	.6	2.3
2008	.9	1.7	-.7	3.9	4.6	-5.1	-4.2	1.8	-5.1	.2
2009	-10.2	-5.5	1.2	-5.8	2.0	-6.2	-4.3	.9	-5.7	-3.3
2010	6.6	3.2	.4	2.2	1.3	6.4	.7	.6	2.9	2.7
2011	4.8	5.9	.3	4.8	1.7	5.4	1.3	-.7	.6	2.4

Note: Data are based on the 2002 North American Industry Classification System (NAICS).
See Note, Table B–12.

Source: Department of Commerce (Bureau of Economic Analysis).

[Billions of dollars; quarterly data at seasonally adjusted annual rates]

Year or quarter	Gross value added of nonfinancial corporate business [1]	Consumption of fixed capital	Net value added — Total	Compensation of employees	Taxes on production and imports less subsidies	Net operating surplus — Total	Net interest and miscellaneous payments	Business current transfer payments	Corporate profits with inventory valuation and capital consumption adjustments — Total	Taxes on corporate income	Profits after tax [2]	Profits before tax	Inventory valuation adjustment	Capital consumption adjustment
1964	356.1	27.0	329.0	225.7	33.9	69.5	5.2	2.0	62.4	23.9	38.5	55.9	−0.5	7.0
1965	391.2	29.1	362.1	245.4	36.0	80.7	5.8	2.2	72.7	27.1	45.5	66.1	−1.2	7.8
1966	429.0	31.9	397.1	272.9	37.0	87.2	7.0	2.7	77.5	29.5	48.0	71.4	−2.1	8.1
1967	451.2	35.2	416.0	291.1	39.3	85.6	8.4	2.8	74.4	27.8	46.5	67.6	−1.6	8.3
1968	497.8	38.7	459.1	321.9	45.5	91.7	9.7	3.1	78.9	33.5	45.4	74.0	−3.7	8.6
1969	540.5	42.9	497.5	357.1	50.2	90.3	12.7	3.2	74.4	33.3	41.0	71.2	−5.9	9.1
1970	558.3	47.5	510.8	376.5	54.2	80.1	16.6	3.3	60.2	27.3	32.9	58.5	−6.6	8.3
1971	603.0	52.0	551.1	399.4	59.5	92.1	17.6	3.7	70.8	30.0	40.8	67.4	−4.6	8.0
1972	669.4	56.5	613.0	443.9	63.7	105.4	18.6	4.0	82.8	33.8	49.0	79.5	−6.6	9.9
1973	750.8	63.1	687.6	502.2	70.1	115.4	21.8	4.7	88.9	40.4	48.5	99.5	−19.6	9.0
1974	809.8	74.2	735.7	552.2	74.4	109.1	27.5	4.1	77.5	42.8	34.6	110.2	−38.2	5.5
1975	876.7	88.6	788.0	575.5	80.2	132.4	28.4	5.0	98.9	41.9	57.0	110.7	−10.5	−1.2
1976	989.7	97.8	892.0	651.4	86.7	153.9	26.0	7.0	121.0	53.5	67.5	138.2	−14.1	−3.2
1977	1,119.4	110.1	1,009.2	735.3	94.6	179.3	28.5	9.0	141.9	60.6	81.3	159.5	−15.7	−1.9
1978	1,272.7	125.1	1,147.5	845.1	102.7	199.7	33.4	9.5	156.8	67.6	89.2	183.7	−23.7	−3.2
1979	1,414.4	144.3	1,270.2	958.4	108.8	203.0	41.8	9.5	151.8	70.6	81.2	197.2	−40.1	−5.3
1980	1,534.5	166.7	1,367.8	1,047.2	121.5	199.1	54.2	10.2	134.7	68.2	66.5	184.1	−42.1	−7.2
1981	1,742.2	192.4	1,549.8	1,157.6	146.7	245.5	67.2	11.4	166.8	66.0	100.8	185.0	−24.6	6.5
1982	1,802.6	212.8	1,589.8	1,200.4	152.9	236.5	77.4	8.8	150.2	48.8	101.5	140.0	−7.5	17.8
1983	1,929.1	219.3	1,709.8	1,263.1	168.0	278.7	77.0	10.5	191.2	61.7	129.5	163.4	−7.4	35.2
1984	2,161.4	228.8	1,932.6	1,400.0	185.0	347.5	86.0	11.7	249.8	75.9	173.9	197.6	−4.0	56.2
1985	2,293.9	244.0	2,049.9	1,496.1	196.6	357.2	91.5	16.1	249.6	71.1	178.6	173.5	.0	76.2
1986	2,383.2	258.0	2,125.2	1,575.4	204.6	345.2	98.5	27.3	219.5	76.2	143.2	149.7	7.1	62.7
1987	2,551.0	270.0	2,280.9	1,678.4	216.8	385.6	95.9	29.9	259.9	94.2	165.7	213.5	−16.2	62.6
1988	2,765.4	287.3	2,478.1	1,804.7	233.8	439.6	107.9	27.4	304.3	104.0	200.3	264.1	−22.2	62.3
1989	2,899.2	303.9	2,595.3	1,905.7	248.2	441.5	133.9	24.0	283.5	101.2	182.3	243.1	−16.3	56.7
1990	3,035.2	321.0	2,714.2	2,005.5	263.5	445.2	143.1	25.4	276.7	98.5	178.3	243.3	−12.9	46.3
1991	3,104.1	336.1	2,768.0	2,044.8	285.7	437.5	139.6	26.6	271.3	88.6	182.7	226.8	4.9	39.6
1992	3,241.1	344.1	2,897.0	2,152.9	302.5	441.6	114.2	31.3	296.1	94.4	201.7	258.6	−2.8	40.3
1993	3,398.4	359.0	3,039.3	2,244.0	318.0	477.3	99.8	30.1	347.5	108.0	239.5	308.7	−4.0	42.9
1994	3,677.6	380.1	3,297.5	2,382.1	347.8	567.5	98.8	35.3	433.5	132.4	301.1	391.9	−12.4	54.0
1995	3,888.0	408.3	3,479.7	2,511.5	354.2	614.0	112.7	30.7	470.6	140.3	330.3	431.2	−18.3	57.6
1996	4,119.4	435.1	3,684.4	2,631.3	365.6	687.5	112.1	38.0	537.4	152.9	384.5	471.3	3.1	63.0
1997	4,412.5	466.9	3,945.6	2,814.6	381.0	750.0	124.7	39.2	586.2	161.4	424.8	506.8	14.1	65.3
1998	4,668.3	499.9	4,168.5	3,049.7	393.1	725.7	146.8	35.2	543.7	158.7	385.1	460.5	15.7	67.5
1999	4,955.5	539.3	4,416.3	3,256.5	414.6	745.1	164.5	47.1	533.5	171.4	362.1	468.6	−4.0	68.9
2000	5,279.4	590.1	4,689.4	3,541.8	439.4	708.2	192.8	47.9	467.5	170.2	297.3	432.5	−16.8	51.8
2001	5,252.5	632.0	4,620.5	3,559.4	434.5	626.7	197.7	58.9	370.1	111.2	258.8	315.1	8.0	47.0
2002	5,307.7	654.5	4,653.1	3,544.2	461.9	647.1	163.7	56.3	427.2	97.1	330.1	342.3	−2.6	87.5
2003	5,503.7	669.0	4,834.7	3,651.3	484.2	699.2	147.9	65.2	486.1	132.9	353.2	425.9	−11.3	71.5
2004	5,877.5	695.6	5,181.9	3,786.7	517.7	877.5	134.4	65.5	677.5	187.0	490.6	662.1	−34.3	49.7
2005	6,302.8	743.0	5,559.8	3,976.3	558.4	1,025.1	148.2	79.3	797.6	271.9	525.8	957.1	−30.7	−128.8
2006	6,740.3	800.9	5,939.4	4,182.3	593.3	1,163.7	164.0	75.8	923.9	307.6	616.2	1,117.9	−38.0	−156.0
2007	6,946.0	840.1	6,106.0	4,361.0	607.7	1,137.4	232.3	69.1	835.9	293.8	542.2	1,042.0	−47.2	−158.8
2008	6,991.4	864.3	6,127.1	4,441.2	615.2	1,070.8	257.7	58.1	755.0	227.4	527.7	831.2	−44.5	−31.7
2009	6,590.8	862.5	5,728.3	4,173.7	589.2	965.4	227.4	77.4	660.6	177.8	482.8	712.9	3.2	−55.4
2010	6,952.4	860.1	6,092.3	4,252.0	612.2	1,228.2	221.7	89.3	917.1	222.9	694.3	990.5	−38.7	−34.7
2011	7,366.7	893.7	6,473.0	4,472.7	645.8	1,354.5	255.9	91.5	1,007.1	246.8	760.3	1,007.0	−62.6	62.7
2012 [p]		933.6		4,659.7	657.6			84.7						−148.2
2009: I	6,633.6	874.2	5,759.4	4,209.2	584.4	965.8	257.4	76.1	632.3	167.6	464.6	612.0	81.4	−61.1
II	6,527.7	863.5	5,664.2	4,174.4	587.9	901.8	224.4	81.5	595.9	161.9	434.1	634.3	15.0	−53.4
III	6,521.4	856.6	5,664.8	4,150.5	584.4	929.9	212.9	72.6	644.4	170.0	474.4	713.3	−17.6	−51.3
IV	6,680.7	855.7	5,825.0	4,160.9	600.0	1,064.2	214.9	79.4	769.9	211.7	558.2	892.0	−66.2	−56.0
2010: I	6,828.1	855.3	5,972.8	4,176.8	605.8	1,190.1	216.2	85.3	888.6	211.9	676.7	980.5	−27.2	−64.7
II	6,894.9	857.8	6,037.1	4,235.0	609.4	1,192.6	215.1	88.2	889.4	221.1	668.3	974.1	−14.3	−70.4
III	7,033.7	860.7	6,173.0	4,288.6	614.2	1,270.3	220.7	91.9	957.6	231.5	726.1	1,020.3	−26.0	−36.7
IV	7,053.0	866.6	6,186.4	4,307.5	619.3	1,259.6	234.9	91.8	932.9	227.0	705.9	987.0	−87.2	33.1
2011: I	7,200.6	876.0	6,324.6	4,435.1	637.8	1,251.7	248.5	91.9	911.3	244.0	667.3	963.0	−121.7	70.1
II	7,367.0	888.8	6,478.2	4,465.0	646.3	1,367.0	248.9	91.7	1,026.4	253.9	772.5	1,037.8	−75.0	63.6
III	7,418.6	900.3	6,518.4	4,487.9	646.0	1,384.4	263.7	91.2	1,029.6	248.1	781.4	1,010.8	−40.6	59.3
IV	7,480.5	909.7	6,570.8	4,502.9	653.1	1,414.8	262.5	91.3	1,061.0	241.2	819.8	1,016.3	−12.9	57.6
2012: I	7,605.5	920.8	6,684.7	4,607.1	656.1	1,421.6	263.2	90.0	1,068.3	304.3	764.0	1,240.4	−23.7	−148.4
II	7,670.8	927.1	6,740.1	4,644.8	657.8	1,437.5	254.2	87.1	1,096.1	304.6	791.6	1,229.8	16.0	−149.7
III	7,693.7	937.1	6,756.5	4,673.7	656.9	1,425.9	263.4	80.5	1,082.0	307.9	774.1	1,256.5	−26.8	−147.7
IV [p]		945.7		4,713.1	659.7			81.2						−147.1

[1] Estimates for nonfinancial corporate business for 2000 and earlier periods are based on the Standard Industrial Classification (SIC); later estimates are based on the North American Industry Classification System (NAICS).

[2] With inventory valuation and capital consumption adjustments.

Source: Department of Commerce (Bureau of Economic Analysis).

TABLE B–15. Gross value added and price, costs, and profits of nonfinancial corporate business, 1964–2012

[Quarterly data at seasonally adjusted annual rates]

| Year or quarter | Gross value added of nonfinancial corporate business (billions of dollars) [1] | | Price per unit of real gross value added of nonfinancial corporate business (dollars) [1,2] | | | | | | | | |
| | Current dollars | Chained (2005) dollars | Total | Compensation of employees (unit labor cost) | Unit nonlabor cost | | | | Corporate profits with inventory valuation and capital consumption adjustments [4] | | |
					Total	Consumption of fixed capital	Taxes on production and imports [3]	Net interest and miscellaneous payments	Total	Taxes on corporate income	Profits after tax [5]
1964	356.1	1,368.1	0.260	0.165	0.050	0.020	0.026	0.004	0.046	0.017	0.028
1965	391.2	1,481.8	.264	.166	.050	.020	.026	.004	.049	.018	.031
1966	429.0	1,588.1	.270	.172	.049	.020	.025	.004	.049	.019	.030
1967	451.2	1,630.9	.277	.178	.053	.022	.026	.005	.046	.017	.029
1968	497.8	1,736.7	.287	.185	.056	.022	.028	.006	.045	.019	.026
1969	540.5	1,806.9	.299	.198	.061	.024	.030	.007	.041	.018	.023
1970	558.3	1,792.4	.311	.210	.067	.026	.032	.009	.034	.015	.018
1971	603.0	1,866.3	.323	.214	.071	.028	.034	.009	.038	.016	.022
1972	669.4	2,009.0	.333	.221	.071	.028	.034	.009	.041	.017	.024
1973	750.8	2,132.7	.352	.235	.075	.030	.035	.010	.042	.019	.023
1974	809.8	2,099.0	.386	.263	.085	.035	.037	.013	.037	.020	.016
1975	876.7	2,068.2	.424	.278	.098	.043	.041	.014	.048	.020	.028
1976	989.7	2,237.2	.442	.291	.098	.044	.042	.012	.054	.024	.030
1977	1,119.4	2,402.9	.466	.306	.101	.046	.043	.012	.059	.025	.034
1978	1,272.7	2,560.2	.497	.330	.106	.049	.044	.013	.061	.026	.035
1979	1,414.4	2,640.4	.536	.363	.116	.055	.045	.016	.057	.027	.031
1980	1,534.5	2,613.4	.587	.401	.135	.064	.050	.021	.052	.026	.025
1981	1,742.2	2,717.8	.641	.426	.154	.071	.058	.025	.061	.024	.037
1982	1,802.6	2,653.0	.679	.452	.170	.080	.061	.029	.057	.018	.038
1983	1,929.1	2,781.1	.694	.454	.171	.079	.064	.028	.069	.022	.047
1984	2,161.4	3,027.7	.714	.462	.169	.076	.065	.028	.083	.025	.057
1985	2,293.9	3,157.9	.726	.474	.173	.077	.067	.029	.079	.023	.057
1986	2,383.2	3,235.5	.737	.487	.182	.080	.072	.030	.068	.024	.044
1987	2,551.0	3,402.5	.750	.493	.180	.079	.073	.028	.076	.028	.049
1988	2,765.4	3,599.1	.768	.501	.183	.080	.073	.030	.085	.029	.056
1989	2,899.2	3,658.8	.792	.521	.194	.083	.074	.037	.077	.028	.050
1990	3,035.2	3,713.1	.817	.540	.203	.086	.078	.039	.075	.027	.048
1991	3,104.1	3,695.4	.840	.553	.214	.091	.085	.038	.073	.024	.049
1992	3,241.1	3,804.9	.852	.566	.208	.090	.088	.030	.078	.025	.053
1993	3,398.4	3,905.0	.870	.575	.207	.092	.089	.026	.089	.028	.061
1994	3,677.6	4,155.3	.885	.573	.207	.091	.092	.024	.104	.032	.072
1995	3,888.0	4,349.0	.894	.577	.209	.094	.089	.026	.108	.032	.076
1996	4,119.4	4,588.6	.898	.573	.207	.095	.088	.024	.117	.033	.084
1997	4,412.5	4,887.8	.903	.576	.208	.096	.086	.026	.120	.033	.087
1998	4,668.3	5,167.3	.903	.590	.208	.097	.083	.028	.105	.031	.075
1999	4,955.5	5,452.4	.909	.597	.214	.099	.085	.030	.098	.031	.066
2000	5,279.4	5,745.7	.919	.616	.222	.103	.085	.034	.081	.030	.052
2001	5,252.5	5,637.8	.932	.631	.235	.112	.088	.035	.066	.020	.046
2002	5,307.7	5,675.5	.935	.624	.235	.115	.091	.029	.075	.017	.058
2003	5,503.7	5,818.1	.946	.628	.234	.115	.094	.025	.084	.023	.061
2004	5,877.5	6,085.1	.966	.622	.232	.114	.096	.022	.111	.031	.081
2005	6,302.8	6,302.8	1.000	.631	.243	.118	.101	.024	.127	.043	.083
2006	6,740.3	6,543.2	1.030	.639	.249	.122	.102	.025	.141	.047	.094
2007	6,946.0	6,606.4	1.051	.660	.264	.127	.102	.035	.127	.044	.082
2008	6,991.4	6,515.9	1.073	.682	.276	.133	.103	.040	.116	.035	.081
2009	6,590.8	6,036.8	1.092	.691	.291	.143	.110	.038	.109	.029	.080
2010	6,952.4	6,369.1	1.092	.668	.280	.135	.110	.035	.144	.035	.109
2011	7,366.7	6,595.6	1.117	.678	.286	.135	.112	.039	.153	.037	.115
2009: I	6,633.6	6,028.2	1.100	.698	.298	.145	.110	.043	.105	.028	.077
II	6,527.7	5,963.9	1.095	.700	.295	.145	.112	.038	.100	.027	.073
III	6,521.4	5,992.1	1.088	.693	.289	.143	.110	.036	.108	.028	.079
IV	6,680.7	6,162.9	1.084	.675	.284	.139	.110	.035	.125	.034	.091
2010: I	6,828.1	6,312.8	1.082	.662	.278	.135	.109	.034	.141	.034	.107
II	6,894.9	6,347.1	1.086	.667	.279	.135	.110	.034	.140	.035	.105
III	7,033.7	6,421.9	1.095	.668	.278	.134	.110	.034	.149	.036	.113
IV	7,053.0	6,394.8	1.103	.674	.284	.136	.111	.037	.146	.035	.110
2011: I	7,200.6	6,499.2	1.108	.682	.285	.135	.112	.038	.140	.038	.103
II	7,367.0	6,611.2	1.114	.675	.284	.134	.112	.038	.155	.038	.117
III	7,418.6	6,586.5	1.126	.681	.289	.137	.112	.040	.156	.038	.119
IV	7,480.5	6,685.6	1.119	.674	.286	.136	.111	.039	.159	.036	.123
2012: I	7,605.5	6,768.5	1.124	.681	.285	.136	.110	.039	.158	.045	.113
II	7,670.8	6,803.6	1.127	.683	.283	.137	.109	.037	.161	.045	.116
III	7,693.7	6,738.6	1.142	.694	.287	.139	.109	.039	.161	.046	.115

[1] Estimates for nonfinancial corporate business for 2000 and earlier periods are based on the Standard Industrial Classification (SIC); later estimates are based on the North American Industry Classification System (NAICS).
[2] The implicit price deflator for gross value added of nonfinancial corporate business divided by 100.
[3] Less subsidies plus business current transfer payments.
[4] Unit profits from current production.
[5] With inventory valuation and capital consumption adjustments.

Source: Department of Commerce (Bureau of Economic Analysis).

TABLE B–16. Personal consumption expenditures, 1964–2012

[Billions of dollars; quarterly data at seasonally adjusted annual rates]

Year or quarter	Personal consumption expenditures	Goods Total	Durable Total[1]	Durable Motor vehicles and parts	Nondurable Total[1]	Nondurable Food and beverages purchased for off-premises consumption	Nondurable Gasoline and other energy goods	Services Total	Household consumption expenditures Total[1]	Housing and utilities	Health care	Financial services and insurance	Addendum: Personal consumption expenditures excluding food and energy[2]
1964	411.5	212.3	59.6	25.8	152.7	69.5	17.7	199.2	192.5	72.1	24.2	17.7	313.8
1965	443.8	229.7	66.4	29.6	163.3	74.4	19.1	214.1	206.9	76.6	26.0	19.4	339.3
1966	480.9	249.6	71.7	29.9	177.9	80.6	20.7	231.3	223.5	81.2	28.7	21.3	368.1
1967	507.8	259.0	74.0	29.6	185.0	82.6	21.9	248.8	240.4	86.3	31.9	22.8	391.1
1968	558.0	284.6	84.8	35.4	199.8	88.8	23.2	273.4	264.0	92.7	36.6	25.8	432.9
1969	605.1	304.7	90.5	37.4	214.2	95.4	25.0	300.4	290.4	101.0	42.1	28.5	470.8
1970	648.3	318.8	90.0	34.5	228.8	103.5	26.3	329.5	318.4	109.4	47.7	31.1	503.3
1971	701.6	342.1	102.4	43.2	239.7	107.1	27.6	359.5	347.2	120.0	53.7	34.1	550.1
1972	770.2	373.8	116.4	49.4	257.4	114.5	29.4	396.4	382.8	131.2	59.8	38.3	607.9
1973	852.0	416.6	130.5	54.4	286.1	126.7	34.3	435.4	420.7	143.5	67.2	41.5	670.9
1974	932.9	451.5	130.2	48.2	321.4	143.0	43.8	481.4	465.0	158.6	76.1	45.9	722.4
1975	1,033.8	491.3	142.2	52.6	349.2	156.6	48.0	542.5	524.4	176.5	89.0	54.0	800.6
1976	1,151.3	546.3	168.6	68.2	377.7	167.3	53.0	604.9	584.9	194.7	101.8	59.3	898.3
1977	1,277.8	600.4	192.0	79.8	408.4	179.8	57.8	677.4	655.6	217.8	115.7	67.8	1,002.5
1978	1,427.6	663.6	213.3	89.2	450.2	196.1	61.5	764.1	739.6	244.3	131.2	80.6	1,127.8
1979	1,591.2	737.9	226.3	90.2	511.6	218.4	80.4	853.2	825.4	273.4	148.8	87.6	1,245.4
1980	1,755.8	799.8	226.4	84.4	573.4	239.2	101.9	956.0	924.1	311.8	171.7	95.6	1,358.3
1981	1,939.5	869.4	243.9	93.0	625.4	255.3	113.4	1,070.1	1,033.9	352.0	201.9	102.0	1,507.1
1982	2,075.5	899.3	253.0	100.0	646.3	267.1	108.4	1,176.2	1,136.1	387.0	225.2	116.3	1,627.2
1983	2,288.6	973.8	295.0	122.9	678.8	277.0	106.5	1,314.8	1,271.9	421.2	253.1	145.9	1,824.2
1984	2,501.1	1,063.7	342.2	147.2	721.5	291.1	108.2	1,437.4	1,389.8	458.3	276.5	156.6	2,016.9
1985	2,717.6	1,137.6	380.4	170.1	757.2	303.0	110.5	1,580.0	1,529.7	500.7	302.2	180.5	2,215.1
1986	2,896.7	1,195.6	421.4	187.5	774.2	316.4	91.2	1,701.1	1,645.8	535.7	330.2	196.7	2,401.8
1987	3,097.0	1,256.3	442.0	188.2	814.3	324.3	96.4	1,840.7	1,782.1	571.8	366.0	207.1	2,587.3
1988	3,350.1	1,337.3	475.1	202.2	862.3	342.8	99.9	2,012.7	1,946.0	614.5	410.1	219.4	2,813.2
1989	3,594.5	1,423.8	494.3	207.8	929.5	365.4	110.4	2,170.7	2,099.0	655.6	451.2	235.7	3,019.8
1990	3,835.5	1,491.3	497.1	205.1	994.2	391.2	124.2	2,344.2	2,264.5	696.4	506.2	253.2	3,221.3
1991	3,980.1	1,497.4	477.2	185.7	1,020.3	403.0	121.1	2,482.6	2,398.4	735.5	555.8	282.0	3,351.1
1992	4,236.9	1,563.3	508.1	204.8	1,055.2	404.5	125.0	2,673.6	2,581.3	771.2	612.8	311.8	3,601.1
1993	4,483.6	1,642.3	551.5	224.7	1,090.8	413.5	126.9	2,841.2	2,746.6	814.5	648.8	341.0	3,828.2
1994	4,750.8	1,746.6	607.2	249.8	1,139.4	432.1	129.2	3,004.3	2,901.9	866.5	680.5	349.0	4,072.3
1995	4,987.3	1,815.5	635.7	255.7	1,179.8	443.7	133.4	3,171.7	3,064.6	913.8	719.9	364.7	4,291.9
1996	5,273.6	1,917.7	676.3	273.5	1,241.4	461.9	144.7	3,355.9	3,240.2	961.2	752.1	393.6	4,542.0
1997	5,570.6	2,006.8	715.5	293.1	1,291.2	474.8	147.7	3,563.9	3,451.6	1,009.9	790.9	431.3	4,821.6
1998	5,918.5	2,110.0	780.0	320.2	1,330.0	486.5	133.4	3,808.5	3,677.5	1,065.2	832.0	469.6	5,173.5
1999	6,342.8	2,290.0	857.4	350.7	1,432.6	513.6	148.8	4,052.8	3,907.4	1,125.0	863.6	514.2	5,554.6
2000	6,830.4	2,459.1	915.8	363.2	1,543.4	537.5	188.8	4,371.2	4,205.9	1,198.6	918.4	570.0	5,966.4
2001	7,148.8	2,534.0	946.3	383.3	1,587.7	559.7	183.6	4,614.8	4,428.6	1,287.7	996.6	562.8	6,255.9
2002	7,439.2	2,610.0	992.1	401.3	1,617.9	569.6	174.6	4,829.2	4,624.2	1,334.8	1,082.9	576.2	6,549.4
2003	7,804.1	2,728.0	1,019.9	401.0	1,708.1	587.5	209.5	5,076.1	4,864.8	1,393.9	1,148.2	602.5	6,846.7
2004	8,270.6	2,892.1	1,072.9	403.9	1,819.3	613.0	249.4	5,378.5	5,169.1	1,462.4	1,228.5	651.7	7,240.0
2005	8,803.5	3,076.7	1,123.4	408.2	1,953.4	644.5	303.8	5,726.8	5,515.1	1,582.6	1,308.9	698.4	7,665.3
2006	9,301.0	3,224.7	1,155.0	394.8	2,069.8	674.2	335.2	6,076.3	5,836.3	1,686.2	1,373.7	732.6	8,090.7
2007	9,772.3	3,363.9	1,188.4	399.9	2,175.5	711.2	364.8	6,408.3	6,154.4	1,756.2	1,457.7	790.3	8,485.9
2008	10,035.5	3,381.7	1,108.9	339.3	2,272.8	746.4	410.5	6,653.8	6,369.3	1,831.0	1,532.6	807.0	8,655.0
2009	9,845.9	3,194.4	1,029.6	316.0	2,164.8	742.3	299.3	6,651.5	6,372.0	1,871.6	1,601.6	741.8	8,588.9
2010	10,215.7	3,364.9	1,079.4	342.7	2,285.5	760.6	352.4	6,850.9	6,571.2	1,891.9	1,663.0	796.3	8,881.0
2011	10,729.0	3,624.8	1,146.4	373.6	2,478.4	810.2	428.3	7,104.2	6,812.3	1,929.9	1,751.6	807.1	9,271.1
2012 p	11,120.9	3,783.2	1,219.1	407.0	2,564.2	829.1	439.8	7,337.6	7,035.2	1,965.9	1,817.9	828.6	9,642.3
2009: I	9,768.4	3,125.5	1,016.3	299.2	2,109.2	739.7	261.4	6,642.9	6,360.5	1,870.2	1,573.5	746.8	8,542.4
II	9,763.9	3,142.0	1,010.4	303.6	2,131.6	739.8	275.7	6,621.9	6,345.5	1,868.8	1,595.4	733.9	8,535.9
III	9,888.8	3,244.4	1,052.7	341.3	2,191.7	741.1	321.5	6,644.4	6,366.6	1,870.1	1,613.1	735.2	8,617.0
IV	9,962.5	3,265.5	1,038.9	320.0	2,226.7	748.7	338.7	6,697.0	6,415.4	1,877.2	1,624.3	751.2	8,660.2
2010: I	10,069.1	3,318.2	1,049.1	321.1	2,269.1	758.0	357.9	6,750.9	6,472.5	1,882.5	1,626.8	779.8	8,733.6
II	10,148.3	3,321.7	1,070.2	336.5	2,251.5	753.3	335.2	6,826.6	6,546.3	1,885.6	1,648.3	804.5	8,839.5
III	10,243.6	3,361.0	1,082.6	346.3	2,278.4	757.7	344.2	6,882.6	6,603.6	1,896.8	1,674.7	800.4	8,916.5
IV	10,401.9	3,458.6	1,115.7	367.0	2,342.9	773.5	372.2	6,943.3	6,662.4	1,902.8	1,702.2	800.4	9,034.5
2011: I	10,566.3	3,561.4	1,133.9	374.5	2,427.5	791.8	419.2	7,004.9	6,722.1	1,909.7	1,726.7	800.1	9,139.0
II	10,684.9	3,604.3	1,131.8	362.2	2,472.4	807.3	431.4	7,080.6	6,790.5	1,926.0	1,749.6	800.6	9,223.8
III	10,791.2	3,643.6	1,144.8	367.4	2,498.7	817.3	435.0	7,147.6	6,848.1	1,945.2	1,754.2	815.0	9,310.3
IV	10,873.8	3,690.0	1,175.1	390.3	2,515.0	824.4	427.6	7,183.8	6,888.5	1,938.9	1,775.9	812.5	9,411.4
2012: I	11,007.2	3,755.9	1,204.6	402.1	2,551.3	827.0	440.5	7,251.3	6,956.4	1,935.2	1,800.4	827.5	9,544.2
II	11,067.2	3,741.5	1,200.3	396.0	2,541.2	827.5	428.5	7,325.7	7,019.4	1,968.3	1,803.5	830.9	9,593.0
III	11,154.4	3,792.5	1,218.9	404.5	2,573.6	829.2	443.1	7,361.9	7,060.6	1,983.5	1,825.9	825.3	9,659.9
IV p	11,254.6	3,843.0	1,252.5	425.6	2,590.5	832.6	447.1	7,411.6	7,104.5	1,976.5	1,841.9	831.0	9,772.3

[1] Includes other items not shown separately.

[2] Food consists of food and beverages purchased for off-premises consumption; food services, which include purchased meals and beverages, are not classified as food.

Source: Department of Commerce (Bureau of Economic Analysis).

TABLE B–17. Real personal consumption expenditures, 1995–2012

[Billions of chained (2005) dollars; quarterly data at seasonally adjusted annual rates]

Year or quarter	Personal consumption expenditures	Goods						Services						Addendum: Personal consumption expenditures excluding food and energy [2]
		Total	Durable		Nondurable			Total	Household consumption expenditures					
			Total [1]	Motor vehicles and parts	Total [1]	Food and beverages purchased for off-premises consumption	Gasoline and other energy goods		Total [1]	Housing and utilities	Health care	Financial services and insurance		
1995	6,076.2	1,896.0	510.5	255.6	1,437.7	548.4	264.3	4,208.5	4,068.9	1,234.8	947.6	489.9	5,123.9
1996	6,288.3	1,980.9	548.6	268.0	1,479.2	553.9	268.5	4,331.7	4,183.6	1,261.6	967.2	508.2	5,319.4
1997	6,520.4	2,075.3	593.3	286.1	1,522.7	558.8	273.9	4,465.3	4,327.6	1,290.3	997.2	525.7	5,540.7
1998	6,862.3	2,215.5	665.6	316.0	1,580.2	565.5	283.7	4,662.1	4,511.0	1,329.7	1,029.6	559.1	5,860.1
1999	7,237.6	2,392.0	752.0	345.1	1,660.7	587.3	292.4	4,853.1	4,690.8	1,371.7	1,045.7	606.2	6,199.5
2000	7,604.6	2,518.2	818.0	356.1	1,714.5	600.5	287.1	5,093.6	4,918.2	1,413.6	1,081.6	666.0	6,545.5
2001	7,810.3	2,597.3	862.4	374.3	1,745.4	607.5	289.2	5,219.1	5,029.3	1,451.4	1,135.6	661.3	6,742.5
2002	8,018.3	2,702.9	927.9	394.0	1,780.1	608.9	294.0	5,318.5	5,109.8	1,461.9	1,202.4	658.9	6,938.6
2003	8,244.5	2,827.2	989.1	404.8	1,840.7	616.5	301.9	5,418.2	5,199.4	1,480.2	1,228.3	659.2	7,145.2
2004	8,515.8	2,953.3	1,060.9	410.4	1,892.8	623.9	305.9	5,562.7	5,345.1	1,512.8	1,267.4	675.5	7,401.8
2005	8,803.5	3,076.7	1,123.4	408.2	1,953.4	644.5	303.8	5,726.8	5,515.1	1,582.6	1,308.9	698.4	7,665.3
2006	9,054.5	3,178.9	1,174.2	394.4	2,005.0	663.0	296.9	5,875.6	5,640.6	1,616.8	1,333.0	716.4	7,911.5
2007	9,262.9	3,273.5	1,232.4	401.4	2,042.9	673.2	294.4	5,990.2	5,745.2	1,626.6	1,364.0	739.8	8,110.4
2008	9,211.7	3,192.9	1,171.8	346.8	2,019.1	666.0	280.6	6,017.0	5,745.6	1,637.8	1,396.5	732.3	8,087.2
2009	9,032.6	3,098.2	1,109.1	322.6	1,982.8	654.8	282.4	5,930.6	5,656.3	1,655.2	1,420.8	680.6	7,913.4
2010	9,196.2	3,209.1	1,178.3	329.5	2,029.3	668.8	281.3	5,987.6	5,710.2	1,668.7	1,439.0	683.7	8,058.0
2011	9,428.8	3,331.0	1,262.6	347.4	2,075.2	685.3	271.5	6,101.5	5,814.3	1,677.7	1,485.5	681.8	8,292.4
2012 [p]	9,604.9	3,433.0	1,361.0	373.3	2,094.4	685.8	268.3	6,178.0	5,880.6	1,677.7	1,516.6	685.6	8,480.3
2009: I	9,039.5	3,083.2	1,091.4	312.8	1,983.7	646.4	289.0	5,951.5	5,676.1	1,652.3	1,410.4	693.3	7,922.2
II	8,999.3	3,067.0	1,085.8	313.7	1,973.3	652.3	282.9	5,926.9	5,655.8	1,653.6	1,421.0	683.1	7,882.8
III	9,046.2	3,123.1	1,138.6	347.7	1,981.4	657.0	280.0	5,920.7	5,647.9	1,655.7	1,427.2	675.0	7,927.9
IV	9,045.4	3,119.5	1,120.7	316.3	1,992.9	663.5	277.6	5,923.2	5,645.2	1,659.3	1,424.6	670.9	7,920.7
2010: I	9,100.8	3,159.5	1,135.9	312.4	2,017.7	669.4	285.9	5,940.4	5,664.3	1,662.7	1,418.3	682.2	7,958.7
II	9,159.4	3,185.4	1,164.5	324.2	2,018.3	663.2	282.2	5,973.6	5,694.5	1,665.2	1,429.1	690.0	8,027.3
III	9,216.0	3,215.1	1,184.9	331.0	2,029.4	666.1	281.5	6,001.4	5,724.2	1,672.8	1,445.1	682.2	8,077.2
IV	9,308.5	3,276.5	1,227.7	350.3	2,052.0	676.7	275.6	6,034.9	5,757.8	1,673.9	1,463.7	680.3	8,168.7
2011: I	9,380.9	3,320.3	1,249.4	355.0	2,075.3	682.8	280.2	6,064.8	5,786.1	1,672.4	1,478.8	680.8	8,235.6
II	9,403.2	3,312.2	1,242.3	336.6	2,073.5	686.0	269.9	6,094.0	5,810.1	1,679.6	1,483.3	678.3	8,265.4
III	9,441.9	3,323.5	1,258.6	338.1	2,071.4	685.9	267.9	6,121.1	5,826.6	1,686.7	1,486.2	685.8	8,302.8
IV	9,489.3	3,367.9	1,300.1	360.1	2,080.5	686.4	268.2	6,126.0	5,834.5	1,672.0	1,499.7	682.2	8,366.0
2012: I	9,546.8	3,406.6	1,336.1	371.2	2,088.9	686.4	266.5	6,145.9	5,855.1	1,662.7	1,513.3	688.6	8,437.3
II	9,582.5	3,409.4	1,335.3	361.8	2,092.0	685.4	272.0	6,178.2	5,877.6	1,685.2	1,508.4	684.4	8,444.6
III	9,620.1	3,439.7	1,364.0	370.5	2,098.2	685.9	270.0	6,186.7	5,888.8	1,690.6	1,518.4	680.0	8,480.4
IV [p]	9,670.0	3,476.4	1,408.8	389.9	2,098.7	685.7	264.8	6,201.3	5,900.8	1,672.5	1,526.5	685.3	8,558.8

[1] Includes other items not shown separately.

[2] Food consists of food and beverages purchased for off-premises consumption; food services, which include purchased meals and beverages, are not classified as food.

Note: See Table B–2 for data for total personal consumption expenditures for 1964–94.

Source: Department of Commerce (Bureau of Economic Analysis).

TABLE B–18. Private fixed investment by type, 1964–2012

[Billions of dollars; quarterly data at seasonally adjusted annual rates]

Year or quarter	Private fixed investment	Total nonresidential	Structures	Equipment and software Total	Information processing equipment and software Total	Computers and peripheral equipment	Software	Other	Industrial equipment	Transportation equipment	Other equipment	Total residential[1]	Structures Total[1]	Single family
1964	97.2	63.0	23.7	39.2	7.4	0.9	0.5	5.9	11.4	10.6	9.9	34.3	33.6	17.6
1965	109.0	74.8	28.3	46.5	8.5	1.2	.7	6.7	13.7	13.2	11.0	34.2	33.5	17.8
1966	117.7	85.4	31.3	54.0	10.7	1.7	1.0	8.0	16.2	14.5	12.7	32.3	31.6	16.6
1967	118.7	86.4	31.5	54.9	11.3	1.9	1.2	8.2	16.9	14.3	12.4	32.4	31.6	16.8
1968	132.1	93.4	33.6	59.9	11.9	1.9	1.3	8.7	17.3	17.6	13.0	38.7	37.9	19.5
1969	147.3	104.7	37.7	67.0	14.6	2.4	1.8	10.4	19.1	18.9	14.4	42.6	41.6	19.7
1970	150.4	109.0	40.3	68.7	16.6	2.7	2.3	11.6	20.3	16.2	15.6	41.4	40.2	17.5
1971	169.9	114.1	42.7	71.5	17.3	2.8	2.4	12.2	19.5	18.4	16.3	55.8	54.5	25.8
1972	198.5	128.8	47.2	81.7	19.5	3.5	2.8	13.2	21.4	21.8	19.0	69.7	68.1	32.8
1973	228.6	153.3	55.0	98.3	23.1	3.5	3.2	16.3	26.0	26.6	22.6	75.3	73.6	35.2
1974	235.4	169.5	61.2	108.2	27.0	3.9	3.9	19.2	30.7	26.3	24.3	66.0	64.1	29.7
1975	236.5	173.7	61.4	112.4	28.5	3.6	4.8	20.2	31.3	25.2	27.4	62.7	60.8	29.6
1976	274.8	192.4	65.9	126.4	32.7	4.4	5.2	23.1	34.1	30.0	29.6	82.5	80.4	43.9
1977	339.0	228.7	74.6	154.1	39.2	5.7	5.5	28.0	39.4	39.3	36.3	110.3	107.9	62.2
1978	412.2	280.6	93.6	187.0	48.7	7.6	6.3	34.8	47.7	47.3	43.2	131.6	128.9	72.8
1979	474.9	333.9	117.7	216.2	58.5	10.2	8.1	40.2	56.2	53.6	47.9	141.0	137.8	72.3
1980	485.6	362.4	136.2	226.2	68.8	12.5	9.8	46.4	60.7	48.4	48.3	123.2	119.8	52.9
1981	542.6	420.0	167.3	252.7	81.5	17.1	11.8	52.5	65.5	50.6	55.2	122.6	118.9	52.0
1982	532.1	426.5	177.6	248.9	88.3	18.9	14.0	55.3	62.7	46.8	51.2	105.7	102.0	41.5
1983	570.1	417.2	154.3	262.9	100.1	23.9	16.4	59.8	58.9	53.5	50.4	152.9	148.6	72.5
1984	670.2	489.6	177.4	312.2	121.5	31.6	20.4	69.6	68.1	64.4	58.1	180.6	175.9	86.4
1985	714.4	526.2	194.5	331.7	130.3	33.7	23.8	72.9	72.5	69.0	59.9	188.2	183.1	87.4
1986	739.9	519.8	176.5	343.3	136.8	33.4	25.6	77.7	75.4	70.5	60.7	220.1	214.6	104.1
1987	757.8	524.1	174.2	349.9	141.2	35.8	29.0	76.4	76.7	68.1	63.9	233.7	227.9	117.2
1988	803.1	563.8	182.8	381.0	154.9	38.0	34.2	82.8	84.2	72.9	69.0	239.3	233.2	120.1
1989	847.3	607.7	193.7	414.0	172.6	43.1	41.9	87.6	93.3	67.9	80.2	239.5	233.4	120.9
1990	846.4	622.4	202.9	419.5	177.2	38.6	47.6	90.9	92.1	70.0	80.2	224.0	218.0	112.9
1991	803.3	598.2	183.6	414.6	182.9	37.7	53.7	91.5	89.3	71.5	70.8	205.1	199.4	99.4
1992	848.5	612.1	172.6	439.6	199.9	44.0	57.9	98.1	93.0	74.7	72.0	236.3	230.4	122.0
1993	932.5	666.6	177.2	489.4	217.6	47.9	64.3	105.4	102.2	89.4	80.2	266.0	259.9	140.1
1994	1,033.5	731.4	186.8	544.6	235.2	52.4	68.3	114.6	113.6	107.7	88.1	302.1	295.9	162.3
1995	1,112.9	810.0	207.3	602.8	263.0	66.1	74.6	122.3	129.0	116.1	94.7	302.9	296.5	153.5
1996	1,209.4	875.4	224.6	650.8	290.1	72.8	85.5	131.9	136.5	123.2	101.0	334.1	327.7	170.8
1997	1,317.7	968.6	250.3	718.3	330.3	81.4	107.5	141.4	140.4	135.5	112.1	349.1	342.8	175.2
1998	1,447.1	1,061.1	275.1	786.0	366.1	87.9	126.0	152.2	147.4	147.1	125.4	385.9	379.2	199.4
1999	1,580.7	1,154.9	283.9	871.0	417.1	97.2	157.3	162.5	149.1	174.4	130.4	425.8	418.5	223.8
2000	1,717.7	1,268.7	318.1	950.5	478.2	103.2	184.5	190.6	162.9	170.8	138.6	449.0	441.2	236.8
2001	1,700.2	1,227.8	329.7	898.1	452.5	87.6	186.6	178.4	151.9	154.2	139.5	472.4	464.4	249.1
2002	1,634.9	1,125.4	282.8	842.7	419.8	79.7	183.0	157.0	141.7	141.6	139.6	509.5	501.3	265.9
2003	1,713.3	1,135.7	281.9	853.8	430.9	77.6	191.3	162.0	142.6	132.9	147.5	577.6	569.1	310.6
2004	1,903.6	1,223.0	306.7	916.4	455.3	80.2	205.7	169.4	142.0	161.1	157.9	680.6	671.4	377.6
2005	2,122.3	1,347.3	351.8	995.6	475.3	78.9	218.0	178.4	159.6	181.7	178.9	775.0	765.2	433.5
2006	2,267.2	1,505.3	433.7	1,071.7	505.2	84.9	229.8	190.6	178.4	198.2	189.8	761.9	751.6	416.0
2007	2,266.1	1,637.5	524.9	1,112.6	536.6	87.0	245.0	204.6	193.0	190.2	192.8	628.7	618.4	305.2
2008	2,128.7	1,656.3	586.3	1,070.0	536.4	84.9	257.2	194.3	194.5	146.9	192.2	472.4	462.7	185.8
2009	1,703.5	1,349.3	451.1	898.2	502.1	73.5	256.9	171.7	155.2	75.9	165.0	354.1	345.4	105.3
2010	1,679.0	1,338.4	376.3	962.1	517.7	72.8	260.9	183.9	155.3	123.2	165.9	340.6	331.7	112.6
2011	1,818.3	1,479.6	404.8	1,074.7	539.6	78.3	278.7	182.6	181.2	164.7	189.2	338.7	329.7	108.2
2012 ᵖ	2,000.9	1,618.0	460.5	1,157.6	555.2	79.3	293.2	182.7	197.4	196.9	208.1	382.8	373.5	128.7
2009: I	1,812.5	1,442.9	530.5	912.4	495.5	73.8	253.7	168.0	163.8	73.5	179.5	369.6	360.6	112.1
II	1,698.0	1,356.0	467.1	888.9	494.1	73.4	255.6	165.2	155.2	74.4	165.2	342.0	333.3	92.9
III	1,666.1	1,312.9	421.0	891.9	505.4	71.9	256.8	176.7	151.7	76.5	158.3	353.1	344.5	105.0
IV	1,637.2	1,285.4	385.6	899.8	513.5	75.1	261.5	177.0	149.9	79.4	156.9	351.9	343.1	111.3
2010: I	1,627.2	1,285.8	362.7	923.1	511.9	73.1	259.5	179.4	146.9	101.9	162.4	341.3	332.6	114.7
II	1,683.0	1,325.2	376.6	948.6	511.1	73.3	257.5	180.4	156.4	117.3	163.8	357.8	348.8	118.8
III	1,683.8	1,353.8	377.1	976.8	518.5	71.7	261.3	185.5	156.5	135.1	166.7	330.0	321.2	110.4
IV	1,721.9	1,388.8	389.0	999.8	529.1	73.1	265.5	190.4	161.3	138.6	170.9	333.1	324.3	106.4
2011: I	1,722.3	1,390.8	362.4	1,028.4	529.8	72.3	271.1	186.5	169.6	149.2	179.8	331.4	322.7	107.4
II	1,784.2	1,448.0	397.0	1,051.0	538.6	79.0	275.8	183.8	171.6	155.6	185.2	336.2	327.3	106.1
III	1,857.8	1,519.4	421.8	1,097.6	541.6	80.3	281.1	180.3	187.0	170.7	198.2	338.5	329.4	108.2
IV	1,909.0	1,560.1	438.2	1,122.0	548.5	81.6	286.9	180.0	196.6	183.1	193.7	348.8	339.6	111.1
2012: I	1,959.7	1,595.5	454.7	1,140.8	556.3	84.3	288.1	183.9	190.7	193.6	200.1	364.2	354.8	117.1
II	1,986.9	1,614.1	458.9	1,155.2	552.0	79.3	292.1	180.5	197.8	200.5	204.9	372.8	363.5	122.3
III	1,997.9	1,610.0	460.1	1,149.9	547.2	71.9	293.7	181.6	198.0	193.4	211.3	387.9	378.5	131.9
IV ᵖ	2,059.0	1,652.5	468.2	1,184.3	565.2	81.8	298.7	184.7	203.2	200.0	216.0	406.5	397.1	143.4

[1] Includes other items not shown separately.

Source: Department of Commerce (Bureau of Economic Analysis).

[Billions of chained (2005) dollars; quarterly data at seasonally adjusted annual rates]

Year or quarter	Private fixed investment	Nonresidential Total nonresidential	Structures	Equipment and software Total	Information processing equipment and software Total	Computers and peripheral equipment [1]	Software	Other	Industrial equipment	Transportation equipment	Other equipment	Residential Total residential [2]	Total [2]	Single family
1995	1,231.2	787.9	342.0	489.4	147.3	66.9	....	90.1	145.5	131.5	110.6	456.1	450.1	240.2
1996	1,341.6	861.5	361.4	541.4	176.5	78.5	....	98.7	150.9	136.8	114.8	492.5	486.8	262.4
1997	1,465.4	965.5	387.9	615.9	217.6	101.7	....	107.2	154.1	148.2	125.9	501.8	496.3	261.6
1998	1,624.4	1,081.4	407.7	705.2	267.1	122.8	....	120.7	160.8	162.0	138.8	540.4	534.5	290.1
1999	1,775.5	1,194.3	408.2	805.0	327.2	151.5	....	134.6	161.8	190.3	142.4	574.2	567.5	311.5
2000	1,906.8	1,311.3	440.0	889.2	386.2	172.4	....	162.0	175.8	186.2	150.4	580.0	572.6	315.0
2001	1,870.7	1,274.8	433.3	860.6	384.5	173.7	....	157.0	162.8	169.6	149.3	583.3	575.6	315.4
2002	1,791.5	1,173.7	356.6	824.2	373.9	173.4	....	142.7	151.9	154.2	148.2	613.8	605.9	327.7
2003	1,854.7	1,189.6	343.0	850.0	403.7	185.6	....	155.1	151.6	140.4	155.0	664.3	655.9	362.6
2004	1,992.5	1,263.0	346.7	917.3	443.1	204.6	....	168.1	147.4	162.3	164.4	729.5	720.1	406.1
2005	2,122.3	1,347.3	351.8	995.6	475.3	218.0	....	178.4	159.6	181.7	178.9	775.0	765.2	433.5
2006	2,172.7	1,455.5	384.0	1,071.1	516.3	227.1	....	192.8	172.9	196.5	185.5	718.2	708.1	391.1
2007	2,130.6	1,550.0	438.2	1,106.8	558.2	240.9	....	208.4	179.9	185.8	184.2	584.2	574.2	284.0
2008	1,978.6	1,537.6	466.4	1,059.4	569.7	250.8	....	202.4	172.9	142.7	177.8	444.4	434.9	178.4
2009	1,602.2	1,259.8	368.1	885.2	546.4	252.9	....	182.4	136.2	69.1	145.5	344.8	336.1	105.5
2010	1,598.7	1,268.5	310.6	963.9	571.7	259.4	....	197.6	134.6	119.6	149.9	332.2	323.0	114.5
2011	1,704.5	1,378.2	319.2	1,070.0	600.2	277.2	....	196.7	152.6	156.7	168.6	327.6	318.0	109.3
2012 p	1,850.1	1,484.9	351.3	1,143.5	622.9	292.8	....	198.4	163.3	183.6	179.6	367.1	357.2	128.9
2009: I	1,677.3	1,324.3	417.7	892.9	533.9	248.2	....	177.5	143.9	66.8	157.0	355.3	346.6	109.6
II	1,593.7	1,262.0	380.1	873.2	537.3	251.2	....	176.0	136.6	65.8	144.9	333.7	325.2	93.2
III	1,581.2	1,236.7	351.7	880.8	551.9	254.1	....	187.4	133.2	68.6	140.4	347.2	338.5	106.9
IV	1,556.8	1,216.4	323.1	893.8	562.4	258.0	....	188.7	131.2	75.0	139.6	343.0	334.1	112.1
2010: I	1,553.1	1,222.7	302.6	925.0	563.7	257.1	....	192.5	128.3	99.4	146.9	332.7	323.7	115.8
II	1,606.5	1,258.6	312.1	951.6	564.1	255.7	....	193.9	135.9	114.2	148.7	350.5	341.2	121.8
III	1,602.7	1,282.1	310.4	978.7	573.7	260.1	....	200.0	135.6	131.0	149.9	322.2	313.0	112.8
IV	1,632.3	1,310.5	317.4	1,000.4	585.1	264.5	....	204.2	138.9	133.8	154.1	323.3	314.0	107.8
2011: I	1,627.0	1,306.3	292.2	1,027.0	585.9	269.5	....	199.1	144.5	143.1	162.9	322.2	312.8	108.8
II	1,675.4	1,351.3	315.0	1,046.5	598.2	274.3	....	197.5	144.7	147.9	165.8	325.5	315.9	107.4
III	1,736.8	1,411.3	330.2	1,091.5	603.5	279.5	....	194.6	156.6	162.3	175.7	326.6	316.9	109.3
IV	1,778.7	1,443.7	339.3	1,114.8	613.4	285.4	....	195.4	164.4	173.6	169.9	336.0	326.2	111.7
2012: I	1,820.6	1,470.0	349.7	1,129.6	622.2	286.8	....	199.4	158.5	181.7	174.7	352.1	342.3	118.5
II	1,840.6	1,482.9	350.2	1,142.8	618.4	291.1	....	195.9	163.6	188.5	177.6	359.3	349.5	123.4
III	1,844.8	1,476.1	350.2	1,135.4	614.5	293.8	....	197.4	163.7	180.4	181.6	370.9	360.9	131.5
IV p	1,894.4	1,510.7	355.1	1,166.3	636.3	299.6	....	200.9	167.5	183.7	184.7	386.1	376.0	142.1

[1] Because computers exhibit rapid changes in prices relative to other prices in the economy, the chained-dollar estimates should not be used to measure the component's relative importance or its contribution to the growth rate of more aggregate series. The quantity index for computers can be used to accurately measure the real growth rate of this series. For information on this component, see *Survey of Current Business* Table 5.3.1 (for growth rates), Table 5.3.2 (for contributions), and Table 5.3.3 (for quantity indexes).
[2] Includes other items not shown separately.

Source: Department of Commerce (Bureau of Economic Analysis).

TABLE B-20. Government consumption expenditures and gross investment by type, 1964–2012

[Billions of dollars; quarterly data at seasonally adjusted annual rates]

The data columns below fall under the overall heading **Government consumption expenditures and gross investment**, divided into **Federal** (National defense; Nondefense) and **State and local**.

Year or quarter	Total	Federal: Total	National defense: Total	National defense: Consumption expenditures	National defense: Gross investment – Structures	National defense: Gross investment – Equipment and software	Nondefense: Total	Nondefense: Consumption expenditures	Nondefense: Gross investment – Structures	Nondefense: Gross investment – Equipment and software	State and local: Total	State and local: Consumption expenditures	State and local: Gross investment – Structures	State and local: Gross investment – Equipment and software
1964	143.2	78.4	60.2	48.8	1.3	10.2	18.2	14.0	2.5	1.6	64.8	45.8	17.2	1.8
1965	151.4	80.4	60.6	50.6	1.1	8.9	19.8	15.1	2.8	1.9	71.0	50.2	19.0	1.9
1966	171.6	92.4	71.7	59.9	1.3	10.5	20.8	15.9	2.8	2.1	79.2	56.1	21.0	2.1
1967	192.5	104.6	83.4	69.9	1.2	12.3	21.2	17.0	2.2	1.9	87.9	62.6	23.0	2.3
1968	209.3	111.3	89.2	77.1	1.2	10.9	22.0	18.2	2.1	1.7	98.0	70.4	25.2	2.4
1969	221.4	113.3	89.5	78.1	1.5	9.9	23.8	20.2	1.9	1.7	108.2	79.8	25.6	2.7
1970	233.7	113.4	87.6	76.5	1.3	9.8	25.8	22.1	2.1	1.7	120.3	91.5	25.8	3.0
1971	246.4	113.6	84.6	77.1	1.8	5.7	29.1	24.9	2.5	1.7	132.8	102.7	27.0	3.1
1972	263.4	119.6	86.9	79.5	1.8	5.7	32.7	28.2	2.7	1.8	143.8	113.2	27.1	3.5
1973	281.7	122.5	88.1	79.4	2.1	6.6	34.3	29.4	3.1	1.8	159.2	126.0	29.1	4.1
1974	317.9	134.5	95.6	84.5	2.2	8.9	39.0	33.4	3.4	2.2	183.4	143.7	34.7	4.9
1975	357.7	149.0	103.9	90.9	2.3	10.7	45.1	38.7	4.1	2.4	208.7	165.1	38.1	5.5
1976	383.0	159.7	111.1	95.8	2.1	13.2	48.6	41.4	4.6	2.7	223.3	179.5	38.1	5.7
1977	414.1	175.4	120.9	104.2	2.4	14.4	54.5	46.5	5.0	3.0	238.7	195.9	36.9	5.9
1978	453.6	190.9	130.5	112.7	2.5	15.3	60.4	50.6	6.1	3.7	262.7	213.2	42.8	6.6
1979	500.7	210.6	145.2	123.8	2.5	18.9	65.4	55.1	6.3	4.0	290.2	233.3	49.0	7.8
1980	566.1	243.7	168.0	143.7	3.2	21.1	75.8	63.8	7.1	4.9	322.4	258.4	55.1	8.9
1981	627.5	280.2	196.2	167.3	3.2	25.7	83.9	71.0	7.7	5.3	347.3	282.3	55.4	9.5
1982	680.4	310.8	225.9	191.1	4.0	30.8	84.9	72.1	6.8	6.0	369.7	304.9	54.2	10.6
1983	733.4	342.9	250.6	208.7	4.8	37.1	92.3	77.7	6.7	7.8	390.5	324.1	54.2	12.2
1984	796.9	374.3	281.5	232.8	4.9	43.8	92.7	77.1	7.0	8.7	422.6	347.7	60.5	14.4
1985	878.9	412.8	311.2	253.7	6.2	51.3	101.6	84.7	7.3	9.6	466.1	381.8	67.6	16.8
1986	949.3	438.4	330.8	267.9	6.8	56.1	107.6	90.1	8.0	9.5	510.9	418.1	74.2	18.6
1987	999.4	459.5	360.0	283.6	7.7	58.8	109.6	90.1	9.0	10.4	539.9	441.4	78.8	19.6
1988	1,038.9	461.6	354.7	293.5	7.4	53.9	106.8	88.3	6.8	11.7	577.3	471.0	84.8	21.5
1989	1,100.6	481.4	362.1	299.4	6.4	56.3	119.3	99.1	6.9	13.4	619.2	504.5	88.7	26.0
1990	1,181.7	507.5	373.9	308.0	6.1	59.8	133.6	111.0	8.0	14.6	674.2	547.0	98.5	28.7
1991	1,236.1	526.6	383.1	319.7	4.6	58.8	143.4	118.6	9.2	15.7	709.5	577.5	103.2	28.9
1992	1,273.5	532.9	376.8	315.2	5.2	56.3	156.1	128.9	10.3	16.9	740.6	606.2	104.2	30.1
1993	1,294.8	525.0	363.0	307.5	5.3	50.1	162.0	133.7	11.2	17.0	769.8	634.2	104.5	31.2
1994	1,329.8	518.6	353.8	300.8	5.8	47.2	164.8	139.9	10.2	14.7	811.2	668.2	108.7	34.3
1995	1,374.0	518.8	348.8	297.0	6.7	45.1	170.0	143.2	10.8	16.0	855.3	701.3	117.3	36.7
1996	1,421.0	527.0	354.8	303.2	6.3	45.4	172.2	143.4	11.3	17.5	894.0	730.2	126.8	36.9
1997	1,474.4	531.0	349.8	304.5	6.1	39.2	181.1	153.0	9.9	18.2	943.5	764.5	139.5	39.4
1998	1,526.1	531.0	346.1	300.3	5.8	39.9	184.9	154.3	10.8	19.9	995.0	808.6	143.6	42.9
1999	1,631.3	554.9	361.1	313.0	5.4	42.8	193.8	160.3	10.7	22.7	1,076.3	870.6	159.7	46.1
2000	1,731.0	576.1	371.0	321.8	5.4	43.8	205.0	174.2	8.3	22.6	1,154.9	930.6	176.0	48.3
2001	1,846.4	611.7	393.0	342.0	5.3	45.6	218.7	188.1	8.1	22.5	1,234.7	994.2	192.3	48.2
2002	1,983.3	680.6	437.7	380.7	5.8	51.2	242.9	209.8	9.9	23.2	1,302.7	1,049.4	205.8	47.5
2003	2,112.6	756.5	497.9	435.2	7.3	55.4	258.5	225.1	10.3	23.1	1,356.1	1,096.5	211.8	47.8
2004	2,232.8	824.6	550.8	481.2	7.1	62.4	273.9	240.2	9.1	24.6	1,408.2	1,139.1	220.2	48.9
2005	2,369.9	876.3	589.0	514.8	7.5	66.8	287.3	251.0	8.3	28.0	1,493.6	1,212.0	230.8	50.8
2006	2,518.4	931.7	624.9	543.9	8.1	72.9	306.8	267.1	9.5	30.2	1,586.7	1,282.3	249.9	54.5
2007	2,674.2	976.3	662.3	575.4	10.1	76.9	314.0	273.5	11.1	29.4	1,697.9	1,368.0	268.4	60.7
2008	2,878.1	1,080.1	737.8	633.3	13.7	90.9	342.3	298.5	11.4	32.4	1,798.0	1,449.2	285.0	63.8
2009	2,967.2	1,143.6	776.0	664.4	17.1	94.5	367.6	322.5	12.1	32.9	1,823.6	1,473.3	287.7	62.6
2010	3,057.5	1,223.1	817.7	702.5	16.7	98.6	405.3	353.3	16.6	35.4	1,834.4	1,496.2	276.0	62.2
2011	3,059.8	1,222.1	820.8	711.9	13.5	95.2	401.3	349.4	16.1	35.7	1,837.7	1,518.0	256.3	63.3
2012 p	3,062.9	1,214.3	809.2	703.5	8.5	97.2	405.1	355.9	12.9	36.3	1,848.6	1,530.9	251.7	66.0
2009: I	2,894.6	1,104.9	748.0	642.2	16.6	89.1	356.9	312.3	12.1	32.5	1,789.7	1,436.1	291.1	62.6
II	2,957.8	1,135.9	772.0	659.4	16.9	95.6	364.0	320.1	11.3	32.6	1,821.9	1,465.8	293.6	62.5
III	2,996.4	1,157.6	788.5	674.6	17.6	96.4	369.1	324.1	12.1	32.9	1,838.8	1,487.9	288.8	62.1
IV	3,020.0	1,175.9	795.5	681.5	17.1	96.8	380.4	333.5	13.0	33.8	1,844.1	1,503.5	277.4	63.2
2010: I	3,030.9	1,193.7	799.3	689.4	15.9	94.0	394.3	344.8	14.8	34.8	1,837.2	1,505.2	269.0	63.1
II	3,061.7	1,225.1	815.5	700.3	16.8	98.5	409.6	356.7	17.7	35.1	1,836.6	1,494.2	280.3	62.0
III	3,072.3	1,239.8	831.6	713.2	17.3	101.1	408.1	355.1	17.2	35.8	1,832.5	1,488.6	282.3	61.6
IV	3,065.2	1,233.8	824.5	707.0	16.8	100.7	409.3	356.6	16.8	35.9	1,831.4	1,496.9	272.3	62.2
2011: I	3,048.1	1,215.2	804.9	697.3	15.6	92.1	410.3	356.9	17.6	35.8	1,832.8	1,511.4	259.4	62.1
II	3,072.2	1,234.3	827.7	716.7	14.6	96.4	406.6	354.3	16.6	35.6	1,837.9	1,520.3	254.3	63.4
III	3,067.7	1,227.5	837.8	730.5	12.8	94.5	389.7	338.5	15.6	35.6	1,840.2	1,522.0	254.2	64.0
IV	3,051.0	1,211.2	812.8	704.0	11.1	97.7	398.4	348.0	14.5	35.9	1,839.7	1,518.4	257.5	63.8
2012: I	3,054.6	1,207.7	806.4	703.5	9.5	93.4	401.3	352.1	13.4	35.8	1,846.9	1,531.4	251.3	64.2
II	3,053.7	1,210.7	807.8	701.1	8.3	98.4	402.9	353.7	13.1	36.1	1,843.0	1,525.5	251.6	65.9
III	3,093.3	1,241.4	834.5	728.1	7.2	99.2	406.8	358.2	12.3	36.3	1,851.9	1,532.4	253.6	65.9
IV p	3,049.9	1,197.4	787.9	681.4	8.8	97.8	409.4	359.8	12.8	36.9	1,852.5	1,534.4	250.3	67.9

Source: Department of Commerce (Bureau of Economic Analysis).

TABLE B–21. Real government consumption expenditures and gross investment by type, 1995–2012

[Billions of chained (2005) dollars; quarterly data at seasonally adjusted annual rates]

Year or quarter	Total	Government consumption expenditures and gross investment												
		Federal									State and local			
		Total	National defense				Nondefense				Total	Consumption expenditures	Gross investment	
			Total	Consumption expenditures	Gross investment		Total	Consumption expenditures	Gross investment				Structures	Equipment and software
					Structures	Equipment and software			Structures	Equipment and software				
1995	1,888.9	704.1	476.8	424.5	10.1	43.7	227.5	201.2	15.7	13.7	1,183.6	983.0	175.4	29.1
1996	1,907.9	696.0	470.4	418.5	9.2	43.8	225.7	196.2	15.9	15.5	1,211.1	1,001.0	184.3	29.9
1997	1,943.8	689.1	457.2	412.2	8.7	38.9	231.9	203.2	13.8	16.6	1,254.3	1,027.7	196.7	33.1
1998	1,985.0	681.4	447.5	401.2	8.1	40.1	233.7	201.2	14.5	18.7	1,303.8	1,070.8	196.5	37.7
1999	2,056.1	694.6	455.8	407.6	7.2	42.4	238.7	202.9	14.0	21.7	1,361.8	1,109.5	210.9	41.8
2000	2,097.8	698.1	453.5	403.9	6.9	43.6	244.4	212.4	10.4	21.5	1,400.1	1,133.7	222.2	44.3
2001	2,178.3	726.5	470.7	418.5	6.5	46.3	255.5	224.2	9.8	21.6	1,452.3	1,172.6	234.8	45.3
2002	2,279.6	779.5	505.3	445.8	7.0	52.7	273.9	239.7	11.8	22.7	1,500.6	1,211.3	244.2	45.8
2003	2,330.5	831.1	549.2	484.1	8.5	57.0	281.7	247.1	11.9	23.0	1,499.7	1,207.5	245.5	47.2
2004	2,362.0	865.0	580.4	509.4	7.8	63.3	284.6	250.2	9.9	24.6	1,497.1	1,207.4	241.3	48.6
2005	2,369.9	876.3	589.0	514.8	7.5	66.8	287.3	251.0	8.3	28.0	1,493.6	1,212.0	230.8	50.8
2006	2,402.1	894.9	598.4	519.1	7.5	71.9	296.6	257.5	8.8	30.3	1,507.2	1,220.7	231.4	55.2
2007	2,434.2	906.1	611.8	528.0	8.8	75.1	294.2	254.7	9.8	29.7	1,528.1	1,239.8	227.6	61.6
2008	2,497.4	971.1	657.7	559.6	11.5	87.0	313.3	271.0	9.6	33.0	1,528.1	1,237.1	227.9	64.4
2009	2,589.4	1,030.6	696.9	592.1	14.4	90.7	333.7	289.8	10.1	33.7	1,561.8	1,275.9	224.8	62.6
2010	2,605.8	1,076.8	717.6	610.0	14.2	93.7	359.2	308.8	14.0	36.2	1,534.1	1,258.9	214.8	62.7
2011	2,523.9	1,047.0	699.1	599.0	11.2	89.1	347.9	298.4	13.2	36.3	1,482.0	1,229.4	192.9	63.6
2012 p	2,481.3	1,024.1	677.3	580.4	6.8	90.7	347.0	300.2	10.2	36.8	1,461.9	1,219.1	182.3	65.5
2009: I	2,531.6	995.8	670.8	571.5	13.7	85.7	325.0	281.8	9.9	33.3	1,538.3	1,253.2	224.1	62.4
II	2,590.4	1,028.2	696.3	590.4	14.2	92.0	331.8	289.2	9.4	33.3	1,565.2	1,275.5	228.5	62.4
III	2,614.3	1,043.9	709.1	601.9	14.9	92.6	334.7	290.7	10.2	33.7	1,573.6	1,285.1	227.6	62.3
IV	2,621.1	1,054.6	711.4	604.4	14.5	92.7	343.2	297.5	11.1	34.5	1,570.2	1,289.9	219.0	63.5
2010: I	2,600.4	1,056.2	704.8	601.5	13.6	89.8	351.5	303.2	12.5	35.6	1,548.3	1,276.4	211.3	63.4
II	2,618.7	1,081.0	717.3	609.5	14.3	93.7	363.7	312.4	15.0	35.9	1,542.7	1,263.6	218.8	62.4
III	2,616.7	1,090.7	729.9	619.2	14.7	96.3	360.8	309.6	14.5	36.6	1,531.6	1,252.2	212.9	62.0
IV	2,587.4	1,079.4	718.6	609.8	14.2	95.0	360.8	309.8	14.1	36.8	1,513.6	1,243.3	210.1	62.8
2011: I	2,540.7	1,050.4	691.3	591.9	13.0	86.2	359.3	307.8	14.7	36.6	1,495.3	1,237.3	198.7	62.6
II	2,535.4	1,057.5	705.2	602.9	12.2	90.2	352.3	302.4	13.7	36.2	1,483.4	1,231.0	192.6	63.7
III	2,516.6	1,045.9	709.8	611.0	10.5	88.2	335.9	287.3	12.7	36.0	1,475.9	1,225.8	190.1	64.1
IV	2,502.7	1,034.2	690.1	590.0	9.0	91.7	344.1	296.1	11.7	36.4	1,473.3	1,223.5	190.1	63.8
2012: I	2,483.7	1,023.1	677.6	582.9	7.8	87.2	345.6	298.7	10.7	36.1	1,465.3	1,221.9	184.0	64.0
II	2,479.4	1,022.5	677.3	579.8	6.7	91.5	345.3	298.6	10.4	36.6	1,461.6	1,218.7	182.5	65.5
III	2,503.1	1,045.9	698.1	600.5	5.8	92.5	347.8	301.6	9.7	36.8	1,462.7	1,219.4	183.0	65.3
IV p	2,458.9	1,005.0	656.0	558.7	7.0	91.4	349.3	302.1	10.1	37.5	1,458.0	1,216.5	179.8	67.4

Note: See Table B–2 for data for total government consumption expenditures and gross investment for 1964–94.

Source: Department of Commerce (Bureau of Economic Analysis).

TABLE B–22. Private inventories and domestic final sales by industry, 1964–2012

[Billions of dollars, except as noted; seasonally adjusted]

Quarter	Private inventories [1]								Final sales of domestic business [3]	Ratio of private inventories to final sales of domestic business	
	Total [2]	Farm	Mining, utilities, and construction [2]	Manufacturing	Wholesale trade	Retail trade	Other industries [2]	Non-farm [2]		Total	Non-farm
Fourth quarter:											
1964	154.5	42.2		58.6	20.8	25.2	7.7	112.2	40.8	3.79	2.75
1965	169.4	47.2		63.4	22.5	28.0	8.3	122.2	44.9	3.77	2.72
1966	185.6	47.3		73.0	25.8	30.6	8.9	138.3	47.4	3.92	2.92
1967	194.8	45.7		79.9	28.1	30.9	10.1	149.1	49.9	3.90	2.99
1968	208.1	48.8		85.1	29.3	34.2	10.6	159.3	55.0	3.79	2.90
1969	227.4	52.8		92.6	32.5	37.5	12.0	174.6	58.7	3.88	2.98
1970	235.7	52.4		95.5	36.4	38.5	12.9	183.3	61.9	3.81	2.96
1971	253.7	59.3		96.6	39.4	44.7	13.7	194.4	67.5	3.76	2.88
1972	283.6	73.7		102.1	43.1	49.8	14.8	209.9	75.7	3.74	2.77
1973	351.5	102.2		121.5	51.7	58.4	17.7	249.4	83.7	4.20	2.98
1974	405.6	87.6		162.6	66.9	63.9	24.7	318.1	89.8	4.52	3.54
1975	408.5	89.5		162.2	66.5	64.4	25.9	319.0	101.1	4.04	3.16
1976	439.6	85.3		178.7	74.1	73.0	28.5	354.2	111.2	3.95	3.19
1977	482.0	90.6		193.2	84.0	80.9	33.3	391.4	124.0	3.89	3.16
1978	570.9	119.3		219.8	99.0	94.1	38.8	451.7	143.6	3.98	3.15
1979	667.6	134.9		261.8	119.5	104.7	46.6	532.6	159.4	4.19	3.34
1980	739.0	140.3		293.6	139.4	111.7	54.1	598.7	174.1	4.24	3.44
1981	779.1	127.4		313.1	148.8	123.2	66.6	651.7	186.7	4.17	3.49
1982	773.9	131.3		304.6	147.9	123.2	66.8	642.6	194.8	3.97	3.30
1983	796.9	131.7		308.9	153.4	137.6	65.2	665.1	215.7	3.69	3.08
1984	869.0	131.4		344.5	169.1	157.0	66.9	737.6	233.6	3.72	3.16
1985	875.9	125.8		333.3	175.9	171.4	69.5	750.2	249.5	3.51	3.01
1986	858.0	113.0		320.6	182.0	176.2	66.3	745.1	264.2	3.25	2.82
1987	924.2	119.9		339.6	195.8	199.1	69.9	804.4	277.7	3.33	2.90
1988	999.7	130.7		372.4	213.9	213.2	69.5	869.1	304.1	3.29	2.86
1989	1,044.3	129.6		390.5	222.8	231.4	70.1	914.7	322.8	3.23	2.83
1990	1,082.0	133.1		404.5	236.8	236.6	71.0	948.9	335.9	3.22	2.82
1991	1,057.2	123.2		384.1	239.2	240.2	70.5	934.0	345.7	3.06	2.70
1992	1,082.6	133.1		377.6	248.3	249.4	74.3	949.5	370.9	2.92	2.56
1993	1,116.0	132.3		380.1	258.6	268.6	76.5	983.7	391.4	2.85	2.51
1994	1,194.5	134.5		404.3	281.5	293.6	80.6	1,060.0	413.9	2.89	2.56
1995	1,257.2	131.1		424.5	303.7	312.2	85.6	1,126.1	436.0	2.88	2.58
NAICS:											
1996	1,284.7	136.6	31.1	421.0	285.1	328.7	82.1	1,148.1	465.6	2.76	2.47
1997	1,327.3	136.9	33.0	432.0	302.5	335.9	87.1	1,190.4	492.2	2.70	2.42
1998	1,341.6	120.5	36.6	432.3	312.0	349.2	91.1	1,221.1	525.8	2.55	2.32
1999	1,432.7	124.3	38.5	457.6	334.8	377.7	99.8	1,308.4	557.2	2.57	2.35
2000	1,524.0	132.1	42.3	476.5	357.7	400.8	114.6	1,391.8	588.3	2.59	2.37
2001	1,447.3	126.2	45.3	440.9	335.8	386.0	113.0	1,321.1	603.0	2.40	2.19
2002	1,489.1	135.9	46.5	443.7	343.2	408.0	111.8	1,353.2	608.5	2.45	2.22
2003	1,545.7	151.0	54.7	447.6	352.6	425.5	114.3	1,394.7	646.2	2.39	2.16
2004	1,681.5	157.2	64.1	487.2	388.9	460.9	123.2	1,524.3	683.4	2.46	2.23
2005	1,804.6	165.2	81.7	531.5	422.8	473.7	129.8	1,639.4	727.5	2.48	2.25
2006	1,917.1	165.1	90.7	575.7	456.4	491.6	137.7	1,752.0	769.6	2.49	2.28
2007	2,077.5	188.3	95.6	635.6	497.2	511.8	148.9	1,889.2	807.0	2.57	2.34
2008	2,024.3	185.4	94.0	604.5	496.9	488.9	154.6	1,838.9	782.5	2.59	2.35
2009: I	1,950.6	180.9	89.3	586.4	472.9	471.1	150.0	1,769.6	775.3	2.52	2.28
II	1,905.7	176.0	85.9	580.9	455.9	458.9	148.1	1,729.7	768.8	2.48	2.25
III	1,866.8	171.2	85.1	578.8	438.6	445.1	148.1	1,695.6	770.2	2.42	2.20
IV	1,889.7	173.1	84.3	588.6	447.6	447.0	149.1	1,716.5	768.7	2.46	2.23
2010: I	1,930.8	182.5	86.7	603.0	455.6	452.7	150.3	1,748.3	772.1	2.50	2.26
II	1,936.9	181.3	86.9	599.5	459.1	460.3	149.7	1,755.6	781.3	2.48	2.25
III	1,998.6	191.0	88.0	613.8	485.5	470.3	149.9	1,807.6	787.4	2.54	2.30
IV	2,080.8	208.7	89.8	643.7	512.3	474.1	152.1	1,872.1	805.4	2.58	2.32
2011: I	2,180.6	232.9	92.1	681.3	535.0	482.5	156.8	1,947.7	811.0	2.69	2.40
II	2,211.1	231.3	95.0	690.7	549.7	485.6	158.9	1,979.8	823.2	2.69	2.40
III	2,225.7	235.8	95.7	690.8	554.8	489.5	159.1	1,989.8	837.2	2.66	2.38
IV	2,249.5	240.4	97.5	695.5	562.8	489.2	160.1	2,009.1	844.8	2.66	2.38
2012: I	2,286.1	242.8	99.4	711.3	574.1	498.4	160.1	2,043.3	855.6	2.67	2.39
II	2,272.5	238.3	98.6	694.8	570.2	507.9	162.7	2,034.2	865.6	2.63	2.35
III	2,320.9	236.6	98.1	710.7	594.5	517.2	163.8	2,084.3	877.7	2.64	2.37
IV p	2,337.7	236.4	103.9	710.7	597.6	522.6	166.5	2,101.3	888.2	2.63	2.37

[1] Inventories at end of quarter. Quarter-to-quarter change calculated from this table is not the current-dollar change in private inventories component of gross domestic product (GDP). The former is the difference between two inventory stocks, each valued at its respective end-of-quarter prices. The latter is the change in the physical volume of inventories valued at average prices of the quarter. In addition, changes calculated from this table are at quarterly rates, whereas change in private inventories is stated at annual rates.

[2] Inventories of construction, mining, and utilities establishments are included in other industries through 1995.

[3] Quarterly totals are at monthly rates. Final sales of domestic business equals final sales of domestic product less gross output of general government, gross value added of nonprofit institutions, compensation paid to domestic workers, and imputed rental of owner-occupied nonfarm housing. Includes a small amount of final sales by farm and by government enterprises.

Note: The industry classification of inventories is on an establishment basis. Estimates through 1995 are based on the Standard Industrial Classification (SIC). Beginning with 1996, estimates are based on the North American Industry Classification System (NAICS).

Source: Department of Commerce (Bureau of Economic Analysis).

TABLE B–23. Real private inventories and domestic final sales by industry, 1964–2012

[Billions of chained (2005) dollars, except as noted; seasonally adjusted]

Quarter	Private inventories [1]								Final sales of domestic business [3]	Ratio of private inventories to final sales of domestic business	
	Total [2]	Farm	Mining, utilities, and construction [2]	Manufacturing	Wholesale trade	Retail trade	Other industries [2]	Non-farm [2]		Total	Non-farm
Fourth quarter:											
1964	557.9	135.1		198.2	82.2	81.1	44.7	407.3	176.1	3.17	2.31
1965	590.8	137.7		212.2	87.8	89.3	46.6	437.8	191.3	3.09	2.29
1966	637.9	136.3		240.6	99.5	96.6	47.9	487.9	195.4	3.26	2.50
1967	671.8	138.8		259.6	107.7	96.6	53.5	519.5	200.3	3.35	2.59
1968	702.6	142.9		271.5	111.5	104.8	55.1	545.9	211.2	3.33	2.58
1969	732.9	142.9		284.1	119.7	112.1	57.9	576.8	215.5	3.40	2.68
1970	738.5	140.5		284.0	128.7	112.2	58.6	585.5	218.1	3.39	2.68
1971	763.5	144.6		280.6	135.5	127.4	60.7	606.1	229.3	3.33	2.64
1972	789.1	145.0		288.3	141.6	137.3	63.7	632.8	248.4	3.18	2.55
1973	828.1	146.8		309.6	145.4	148.4	67.0	673.3	257.1	3.22	2.62
1974	857.2	142.4		333.0	158.9	146.2	71.4	712.3	247.5	3.46	2.88
1975	844.4	148.2		324.6	152.1	138.8	73.3	690.9	259.3	3.26	2.66
1976	878.7	146.6		340.1	162.2	149.5	74.0	728.5	272.0	3.23	2.68
1977	921.8	153.9		349.6	175.3	158.1	79.6	764.2	286.4	3.22	2.67
1978	967.4	155.9		365.6	189.3	168.7	84.4	809.1	307.8	3.14	2.63
1979	995.4	160.2		379.7	198.7	168.6	84.3	832.8	315.0	3.16	2.64
1980	986.0	153.0		380.1	204.0	163.8	82.9	832.4	314.7	3.13	2.65
1981	1,025.0	163.1		385.2	209.8	172.8	92.3	860.6	312.4	3.28	2.75
1982	1,005.3	170.6		367.9	207.2	168.9	89.4	833.3	311.2	3.23	2.68
1983	997.7	153.1		367.5	206.3	182.7	88.3	844.0	334.7	2.98	2.52
1984	1,075.9	159.4		399.4	222.8	205.0	89.7	916.3	353.1	3.05	2.60
1985	1,101.3	166.5		392.4	229.2	220.8	94.8	934.7	369.4	2.98	2.53
1986	1,109.8	164.2		388.3	237.7	224.3	98.3	945.1	383.3	2.90	2.47
1987	1,143.0	155.1		397.6	245.4	246.1	100.8	986.2	393.8	2.90	2.50
1988	1,164.9	142.0		416.2	254.9	253.9	99.3	1,021.6	414.2	2.81	2.47
1989	1,195.6	142.0		431.8	258.5	268.8	94.8	1,052.4	426.4	2.80	2.47
1990	1,212.1	148.6		441.6	267.2	267.2	91.2	1,066.4	427.7	2.83	2.49
1991	1,210.7	146.7		434.2	271.5	267.7	94.8	1,066.8	427.4	2.83	2.50
1992	1,228.6	153.8		429.0	280.3	272.5	97.7	1,077.7	450.6	2.73	2.39
1993	1,250.8	146.3		432.9	286.5	288.3	101.2	1,107.6	466.3	2.68	2.38
1994	1,320.1	160.0		446.3	302.7	309.4	106.1	1,163.4	484.9	2.72	2.40
1995	1,352.2	147.0		461.7	316.2	321.9	108.6	1,207.7	502.7	2.69	2.40
NAICS:											
1996	1,383.4	155.3	47.6	465.7	298.0	335.3	87.6	1,230.9	528.6	2.62	2.33
1997	1,460.8	159.0	50.1	490.0	324.9	349.5	93.2	1,304.4	550.7	2.65	2.37
1998	1,532.4	160.6	59.1	507.6	348.6	364.7	99.0	1,373.9	585.4	2.62	2.35
1999	1,600.9	156.9	57.1	523.8	369.7	390.5	106.6	1,444.7	615.6	2.60	2.35
2000	1,661.1	155.2	54.3	531.9	390.4	411.1	119.3	1,505.9	638.0	2.60	2.36
2001	1,619.4	155.3	65.1	505.7	376.8	400.5	119.1	1,464.4	644.2	2.51	2.27
2002	1,632.1	152.2	61.0	500.5	376.7	424.2	118.0	1,480.0	644.8	2.53	2.30
2003	1,649.5	152.4	68.2	492.0	376.3	441.5	119.6	1,497.2	676.3	2.44	2.21
2004	1,715.8	160.3	69.6	498.0	415.0	465.2	126.0	1,555.6	696.6	2.46	2.23
2005	1,765.8	160.4	73.4	519.0	415.0	469.8	128.3	1,605.4	718.7	2.46	2.23
2006	1,825.2	156.7	90.3	536.0	428.3	480.6	132.9	1,668.6	744.4	2.45	2.24
2007	1,852.9	155.9	90.3	551.4	432.8	484.8	137.2	1,697.3	766.1	2.42	2.22
2008	1,816.6	156.9	81.8	537.3	441.7	458.3	138.8	1,659.7	730.4	2.49	2.27
2009: I	1,779.1	156.8	82.1	530.2	425.3	444.5	137.9	1,622.0	723.6	2.46	2.24
II	1,732.7	156.6	81.6	520.6	404.9	430.5	136.4	1,575.7	717.4	2.42	2.20
III	1,687.3	155.4	80.1	511.9	386.8	415.4	135.7	1,531.5	716.5	2.35	2.14
IV	1,677.6	155.5	75.5	511.7	386.1	411.5	135.0	1,521.8	713.3	2.35	2.13
2010: I	1,685.3	155.2	74.4	514.5	389.6	414.5	134.7	1,529.7	715.5	2.36	2.14
II	1,693.6	154.2	75.9	513.4	393.2	420.8	134.0	1,539.1	721.6	2.35	2.13
III	1,717.3	151.6	75.9	520.1	406.3	427.7	133.6	1,565.7	723.9	2.37	2.16
IV	1,728.5	149.3	76.9	528.8	411.8	433.6	133.2	1,579.8	736.6	2.35	2.14
2011: I	1,736.1	148.0	75.8	534.1	415.5	426.8	134.0	1,589.0	739.9	2.35	2.15
II	1,743.0	146.6	76.1	538.2	421.6	424.4	134.1	1,597.9	745.9	2.34	2.14
III	1,741.9	145.8	76.2	538.8	422.3	423.2	133.7	1,597.7	751.9	2.32	2.12
IV	1,759.6	145.5	78.1	547.7	429.8	422.3	134.2	1,616.3	758.2	2.32	2.13
2012: I	1,773.8	144.8	82.0	550.7	434.6	427.6	132.7	1,631.8	765.2	2.32	2.13
II	1,784.2	142.8	82.8	550.2	438.0	434.9	135.3	1,645.1	770.5	2.32	2.14
III	1,799.2	138.1	81.6	559.3	446.0	439.7	136.3	1,667.2	775.0	2.32	2.15
IV p	1,802.2	134.3	82.1	559.2	448.5	444.6	137.0	1,675.5	783.6	2.30	2.14

[1] Inventories at end of quarter. Quarter-to-quarter changes calculated from this table are at quarterly rates, whereas the change in private inventories component of gross domestic product (GDP) is stated at annual rates.

[2] Inventories of construction, mining, and utilities establishments are included in other industries through 1995.

[3] Quarterly totals at monthly rates. Final sales of domestic business equals final sales of domestic product less gross output of general government, gross value added of nonprofit institutions, compensation paid to domestic workers, and imputed rental of owner-occupied nonfarm housing. Includes a small amount of final sales by farm and by government enterprises.

Note: The industry classification of inventories is on an establishment basis. Estimates through 1995 are based on the Standard Industrial Classification (SIC). Beginning with 1996, estimates are based on the North American Industry Classification System (NAICS). See *Survey of Current Business*, Tables 5.7.6A and 5.7.6B, for detailed information on calculation of the chained (2005) dollar inventory series.

Source: Department of Commerce (Bureau of Economic Analysis).

National Income or Expenditure | 351

TABLE B–24. Foreign transactions in the national income and product accounts, 1964–2012

[Billions of dollars; quarterly data at seasonally adjusted annual rates]

Year or quarter	Current receipts from rest of the world					Current payments to rest of the world									Balance on current account, NIPA [2]
	Total	Exports of goods and services			Income receipts	Total	Imports of goods and services			Income payments	Current taxes and transfer payments to rest of the world (net)				
		Total	Goods [1]	Services [1]			Total	Goods [1]	Services [1]		Total	From persons (net)	From government (net)	From business (net)	
1964	42.3	35.0	26.7	8.3	7.2	34.8	28.1	19.4	8.7	2.3	4.4	0.7	3.5	0.2	7.5
1965	45.0	37.1	27.8	9.4	7.9	38.9	31.5	22.2	9.3	2.6	4.7	.8	3.8	.2	6.2
1966	49.0	40.9	30.7	10.2	8.1	45.2	37.1	26.3	10.7	3.0	5.1	.8	4.1	.2	3.8
1967	52.1	43.5	32.2	11.3	8.7	48.7	39.9	27.8	12.2	3.3	5.5	1.0	4.2	.2	3.5
1968	58.0	47.9	35.3	12.6	10.1	56.5	46.6	33.9	12.6	4.0	5.9	1.0	4.6	.3	1.5
1969	63.7	51.9	38.3	13.7	11.8	62.1	50.5	36.8	13.7	5.7	5.9	1.1	4.5	.3	1.6
1970	72.5	59.7	44.5	15.2	12.8	68.8	55.8	40.9	14.9	6.4	6.6	1.3	4.9	.4	3.7
1971	77.0	63.0	45.6	17.4	14.0	76.7	62.3	46.6	15.8	6.4	7.9	1.4	6.1	.4	.3
1972	87.1	70.8	51.8	19.0	16.3	91.2	74.2	56.9	17.3	7.7	9.2	1.4	7.4	.5	-4.0
1973	118.8	95.3	73.9	21.3	23.5	109.9	91.2	71.8	19.3	10.9	7.9	1.6	5.6	.7	8.9
1974	156.5	126.7	101.0	25.7	29.8	150.5	127.5	104.5	22.9	14.3	8.7	1.4	6.4	1.0	6.0
1975	166.7	138.7	109.6	29.1	28.0	146.9	122.7	99.0	23.7	15.0	9.1	1.3	7.1	.7	19.8
1976	181.9	149.5	117.8	31.7	32.4	174.8	151.1	124.6	26.5	15.5	8.1	1.4	5.7	1.1	7.1
1977	196.6	159.4	123.7	35.7	37.2	207.5	182.4	152.6	29.8	16.9	8.1	1.4	5.3	1.4	-10.9
1978	233.1	186.9	145.4	41.5	46.3	245.8	212.3	177.4	34.8	24.7	8.8	1.6	5.9	1.4	-12.6
1979	298.5	230.1	184.0	46.1	68.3	299.6	252.7	212.8	39.9	36.4	10.6	1.7	6.8	2.0	-1.2
1980	359.9	280.8	225.8	55.0	79.1	351.4	293.8	248.6	45.3	44.9	12.6	2.0	8.3	2.4	8.5
1981	397.3	305.2	239.1	66.1	92.0	393.9	317.8	267.8	49.9	59.1	17.0	5.6	8.3	3.2	3.4
1982	384.2	283.2	215.0	68.2	101.0	387.5	303.2	250.5	52.6	64.5	19.8	6.7	9.7	3.4	-3.3
1983	378.9	277.0	207.3	69.7	101.9	413.9	328.6	272.7	56.0	64.8	20.5	7.0	10.1	3.4	-35.1
1984	424.2	302.4	225.6	76.7	121.9	514.3	405.1	336.3	68.8	85.6	23.6	7.9	12.2	3.5	-90.1
1985	414.5	302.0	222.2	79.8	112.4	528.8	417.2	343.3	73.9	85.9	25.7	8.3	14.4	2.9	-114.3
1986	431.3	320.3	226.0	94.3	111.0	574.0	452.9	370.0	82.9	93.4	27.8	9.1	15.4	3.2	-142.7
1987	486.6	363.8	257.5	106.2	122.8	640.7	508.7	414.8	93.9	105.2	26.8	10.0	13.4	3.4	-154.1
1988	595.5	443.9	325.8	118.1	151.6	711.2	554.0	452.1	101.9	128.3	29.0	10.8	13.7	4.5	-115.7
1989	680.3	503.1	369.4	133.8	177.2	772.7	591.0	484.8	106.2	151.2	30.4	11.6	14.2	4.6	-92.4
1990	740.6	552.1	396.6	155.5	188.5	815.6	629.7	508.1	121.7	154.1	31.7	12.2	14.7	4.8	-74.9
1991	764.7	596.6	423.6	173.0	168.1	756.9	623.5	500.7	122.8	138.2	-4.9	14.1	-24.0	5.0	7.9
1992	786.8	635.0	448.0	187.0	151.8	832.4	667.8	544.9	122.9	122.7	41.9	14.5	22.0	5.4	-45.6
1993	810.8	655.6	459.9	195.7	155.2	889.4	720.0	592.8	127.2	124.0	45.4	17.1	22.9	5.4	-78.6
1994	904.8	720.7	510.1	210.6	184.1	1,019.5	813.4	676.8	136.6	160.0	46.1	18.9	21.1	6.0	-114.7
1995	1,041.1	811.9	583.3	228.6	229.3	1,146.2	902.6	757.4	145.1	199.6	44.1	20.3	15.6	8.2	-105.1
1996	1,113.5	867.7	618.3	249.3	245.8	1,227.6	964.0	807.4	156.5	214.2	49.5	22.6	20.0	6.9	-114.1
1997	1,233.9	954.4	687.7	266.7	279.5	1,363.3	1,055.8	885.7	170.1	256.1	51.4	25.7	16.7	9.1	-129.3
1998	1,240.1	953.9	680.9	273.0	286.2	1,444.6	1,115.7	930.8	184.9	268.9	60.0	29.7	17.4	13.0	-204.5
1999	1,308.8	989.3	697.2	292.1	319.5	1,600.7	1,251.4	1,047.7	203.7	291.7	57.6	32.2	18.0	7.4	-291.9
2000	1,473.7	1,093.2	784.3	308.9	380.5	1,884.1	1,475.3	1,246.5	228.8	342.8	66.1	34.6	20.0	11.4	-410.4
2001	1,350.8	1,027.7	731.2	296.5	323.0	1,742.4	1,398.7	1,171.7	227.0	271.1	72.6	38.1	16.2	18.3	-391.6
2002	1,316.5	1,003.0	700.3	302.7	313.5	1,768.1	1,430.2	1,193.9	236.3	264.4	73.5	40.6	21.6	11.3	-451.6
2003	1,394.4	1,041.0	726.8	314.2	353.3	1,910.5	1,545.1	1,289.3	255.9	284.6	80.7	41.2	25.8	13.7	-516.1
2004	1,628.8	1,180.2	817.0	363.2	448.6	2,253.4	1,798.9	1,501.7	297.3	357.4	97.1	43.6	27.2	26.3	-624.6
2005	1,878.1	1,305.1	906.1	399.0	573.0	2,618.6	2,027.8	1,708.0	319.8	475.9	115.0	48.4	35.3	31.3	-740.5
2006	2,192.1	1,471.0	1,024.4	446.6	721.1	2,990.5	2,240.3	1,884.9	355.4	648.6	101.5	51.6	28.8	21.1	-798.4
2007	2,532.7	1,661.7	1,162.0	499.7	871.0	3,248.7	2,374.8	2,000.7	374.0	747.7	126.2	59.3	36.1	30.8	-716.0
2008	2,702.9	1,846.8	1,297.5	549.3	856.1	3,381.9	2,556.5	2,146.3	410.1	686.9	138.4	66.2	37.1	35.2	-679.0
2009	2,229.9	1,587.4	1,064.7	522.7	642.4	2,612.0	1,976.2	1,587.5	388.7	498.9	137.0	66.1	49.7	21.2	-382.2
2010	2,560.9	1,844.4	1,278.5	565.9	716.5	3,009.8	2,356.1	1,947.0	409.1	507.2	146.5	73.5	51.2	21.9	-448.8
2011	2,877.9	2,094.2	1,474.5	619.7	783.7	3,343.7	2,662.3	2,229.2	433.0	531.8	149.6	73.9	55.2	20.2	-465.8
2012 ᵖ	....	2,182.6	1,542.3	640.2	....	....	2,743.3	2,291.6	451.8	....	157.1	76.4	54.3	26.4	....
2009: I	2,151.3	1,523.5	1,012.0	511.5	627.8	2,546.6	1,908.9	1,521.5	387.4	509.6	128.2	63.7	39.6	24.9	-395.4
II	2,140.3	1,525.3	1,010.6	514.7	615.0	2,494.3	1,856.9	1,475.1	381.8	499.2	138.2	65.2	53.3	19.7	-354.0
III	2,234.0	1,594.7	1,073.7	521.1	639.2	2,615.0	1,993.3	1,605.1	388.2	476.2	145.4	65.9	61.0	18.5	-381.0
IV	2,393.9	1,706.3	1,162.5	543.8	687.6	2,792.1	2,145.5	1,748.1	397.4	510.5	136.0	69.4	45.0	21.6	-398.2
2010: I	2,438.9	1,751.9	1,206.1	545.7	687.1	2,891.6	2,242.0	1,841.2	400.8	495.6	154.0	73.4	56.3	24.2	-452.7
II	2,519.3	1,814.3	1,257.3	557.0	705.1	2,966.7	2,335.4	1,932.6	402.8	489.3	142.0	73.2	46.2	22.6	-447.4
III	2,587.2	1,861.2	1,288.1	573.0	726.1	3,051.8	2,394.3	1,978.3	416.0	509.1	148.4	74.2	51.6	22.6	-464.6
IV	2,698.3	1,950.4	1,362.6	587.7	747.9	3,129.0	2,452.5	2,035.8	416.7	534.9	141.7	73.1	50.6	18.0	-430.8
2011: I	2,791.8	2,030.5	1,425.8	604.7	761.4	3,269.5	2,585.9	2,165.2	420.7	526.1	157.5	73.5	54.4	29.7	-477.7
II	2,890.2	2,092.8	1,471.8	621.0	797.4	3,364.3	2,665.3	2,234.9	430.4	547.4	151.6	73.8	63.0	14.8	-474.1
III	2,922.2	2,133.3	1,498.5	634.8	788.9	3,357.1	2,682.8	2,239.6	443.2	530.6	143.8	73.3	51.7	18.7	-434.9
IV	2,907.3	2,120.3	1,501.9	618.4	787.1	3,383.7	2,715.1	2,277.3	437.8	523.1	145.5	75.1	52.9	17.5	-476.3
2012: I	2,927.5	2,157.9	1,525.8	632.1	769.6	3,480.7	2,773.7	2,324.3	449.3	554.7	152.3	75.5	57.4	19.3	-553.2
II	2,963.6	2,188.5	1,550.5	637.9	775.1	3,448.5	2,765.4	2,312.4	453.0	527.8	155.4	76.4	54.6	24.4	-485.0
III	2,974.5	2,198.7	1,555.1	643.5	775.8	3,408.2	2,715.5	2,260.6	454.9	532.7	160.0	76.6	55.7	27.8	-433.7
IV ᵖ	....	2,185.2	1,537.8	647.5	....	....	2,718.8	2,268.9	449.9	....	160.5	77.1	49.6	33.9	....

[1] Certain goods, primarily military equipment purchased and sold by the Federal Government, are included in services. Beginning with 1986, repairs and alterations of equipment were reclassified from goods to services.

[2] National income and product accounts (NIPA).

Source: Department of Commerce (Bureau of Economic Analysis).

TABLE B–25. Real exports and imports of goods and services, 1995–2012

[Billions of chained (2005) dollars; quarterly data at seasonally adjusted annual rates]

Year or quarter	Exports of goods and services					Imports of goods and services				
	Total	Goods [1]			Services [1]	Total	Goods [1]			Services [1]
		Total	Durable goods	Non-durable goods			Total	Durable goods	Non-durable goods	
1995	845.1	574.8	363.0	216.2	272.6	943.9	765.5	422.3	360.0	180.9
1996	915.3	625.5	404.8	223.4	291.7	1,026.0	837.2	467.5	384.1	190.3
1997	1,024.3	715.4	478.0	237.9	308.9	1,164.1	957.9	544.6	424.1	206.9
1998	1,047.7	731.4	493.4	237.6	316.4	1,300.2	1,071.4	616.4	462.9	229.4
1999	1,093.4	759.2	517.0	240.8	334.6	1,449.9	1,205.0	706.2	500.2	244.9
2000	1,187.4	843.4	583.7	256.5	343.5	1,638.7	1,366.7	813.7	549.2	271.7
2001	1,120.8	791.2	535.1	255.2	329.3	1,592.6	1,323.1	763.4	564.2	269.6
2002	1,098.3	762.7	504.8	259.1	335.6	1,646.8	1,372.2	795.4	580.2	274.5
2003	1,116.0	776.4	513.7	263.8	339.6	1,719.7	1,439.9	829.7	615.2	279.8
2004	1,222.5	842.6	570.7	272.2	380.0	1,910.4	1,599.3	944.6	655.8	311.0
2005	1,305.1	906.1	624.9	281.2	399.0	2,027.8	1,708.0	1,025.4	682.6	319.8
2006	1,422.1	991.5	692.0	299.6	430.6	2,151.5	1,809.1	1,115.6	694.5	342.4
2007	1,554.4	1,088.1	756.1	331.9	466.3	2,203.2	1,856.1	1,141.2	715.7	347.1
2008	1,649.3	1,157.0	795.8	359.8	492.3	2,144.0	1,784.8	1,099.3	686.6	359.8
2009	1,498.7	1,018.6	660.4	351.1	479.6	1,853.8	1,506.4	870.9	626.4	347.8
2010	1,665.6	1,164.1	770.8	387.2	501.9	2,085.2	1,730.3	1,066.6	662.0	356.6
2011	1,776.9	1,247.6	841.1	403.0	529.8	2,184.9	1,820.0	1,161.7	666.2	366.6
2012 ᵖ	1,836.0	1,299.9	881.5	415.9	536.7	2,237.6	1,857.9	1,244.5	639.7	381.6
2009: I	1,452.5	982.0	644.0	332.1	469.7	1,856.0	1,507.1	846.1	649.8	349.2
II	1,454.6	975.4	625.7	342.4	478.2	1,777.4	1,432.0	811.3	610.4	345.0
III	1,502.3	1,023.3	660.0	355.7	478.6	1,849.3	1,502.3	874.2	619.1	347.4
IV	1,585.2	1,093.6	711.8	374.3	491.8	1,932.7	1,584.3	952.0	626.5	349.5
2010: I	1,608.2	1,119.7	730.3	381.9	489.0	1,980.9	1,630.8	984.2	641.1	351.6
II	1,645.4	1,151.6	768.0	378.3	494.4	2,074.2	1,723.3	1,057.9	662.8	352.6
III	1,683.9	1,176.8	783.0	388.1	507.6	2,142.8	1,781.2	1,101.3	678.6	363.5
IV	1,724.7	1,208.5	801.9	400.3	516.7	2,143.0	1,786.1	1,123.1	665.4	358.8
2011: I	1,748.8	1,225.4	817.8	402.2	524.0	2,165.4	1,808.9	1,145.2	668.3	358.3
II	1,766.4	1,236.5	837.3	396.6	530.5	2,166.0	1,805.7	1,141.4	668.7	362.0
III	1,792.9	1,255.1	852.9	400.3	538.4	2,190.8	1,818.8	1,165.9	662.4	373.9
IV	1,799.3	1,273.6	856.4	413.0	526.2	2,217.3	1,846.7	1,194.1	665.3	372.3
2012: I	1,818.7	1,286.3	883.2	403.4	532.9	2,234.2	1,855.8	1,238.0	642.4	380.4
II	1,842.1	1,308.3	884.6	420.6	534.4	2,249.6	1,868.9	1,253.5	642.4	382.6
III	1,850.9	1,311.8	886.0	422.4	539.6	2,246.1	1,863.1	1,243.0	645.1	385.0
IV ᵖ	1,832.5	1,293.2	872.1	417.4	539.8	2,220.4	1,843.9	1,243.6	628.8	378.5

[1] Certain goods, primarily military equipment purchased and sold by the Federal Government, are included in services. Beginning with 1986, repairs and alterations of equipment were reclassified from goods to services.

Note: See Table B–2 for data for total exports of goods and services and total imports of goods and services for 1964–94.

Source: Department of Commerce (Bureau of Economic Analysis).

TABLE B–26. Relation of gross domestic product, gross national product, net national product, and national income, 1964–2012

[Billions of dollars; quarterly data at seasonally adjusted annual rates]

Year or quarter	Gross domestic product	Plus: Income receipts from rest of the world	Less: Income payments to rest of the world	Equals: Gross national product	Less: Consumption of fixed capital			Equals: Net national product	Less: Statistical discrepancy	Equals: National income
					Total	Private	Government			
1964	663.6	7.2	2.3	668.6	66.4	48.3	18.1	602.2	0.8	601.4
1965	719.1	7.9	2.6	724.4	70.7	51.9	18.9	653.7	1.5	652.2
1966	787.7	8.1	3.0	792.8	76.5	56.5	20.0	716.3	6.2	710.1
1967	832.4	8.7	3.3	837.8	82.9	61.6	21.4	754.9	4.5	750.4
1968	909.8	10.1	4.0	915.9	90.4	67.4	23.0	825.5	4.3	821.2
1969	984.4	11.8	5.7	990.5	99.2	74.5	24.7	891.4	2.9	888.5
1970	1,038.3	12.8	6.4	1,044.7	108.3	81.7	26.6	936.4	6.9	929.5
1971	1,126.8	14.0	6.4	1,134.4	117.8	89.5	28.2	1,016.6	11.0	1,005.6
1972	1,237.9	16.3	7.7	1,246.4	127.2	97.7	29.4	1,119.3	8.9	1,110.3
1973	1,382.3	23.5	10.9	1,394.9	140.8	109.5	31.3	1,254.1	8.0	1,246.1
1974	1,499.5	29.8	14.3	1,515.0	163.7	127.8	35.9	1,351.3	9.8	1,341.5
1975	1,637.7	28.0	15.0	1,650.7	190.4	150.4	39.9	1,460.3	16.3	1,444.0
1976	1,824.6	32.4	15.5	1,841.4	208.2	165.5	42.6	1,633.3	23.5	1,609.8
1977	2,030.1	37.2	16.9	2,050.4	231.8	186.1	45.6	1,818.6	21.2	1,797.4
1978	2,293.8	46.3	24.7	2,315.3	261.4	212.0	49.5	2,053.9	26.1	2,027.9
1979	2,562.2	68.3	36.4	2,594.2	298.9	244.5	54.4	2,295.3	47.0	2,248.3
1980	2,788.1	79.1	44.9	2,822.3	344.1	282.3	61.8	2,478.2	45.3	2,433.0
1981	3,126.8	92.0	59.1	3,159.8	393.3	323.2	70.1	2,766.4	36.6	2,729.8
1982	3,253.2	101.0	64.5	3,289.7	433.5	356.4	77.1	2,856.2	4.8	2,851.4
1983	3,534.6	101.9	64.8	3,571.7	451.1	369.5	81.6	3,120.6	49.7	3,070.9
1984	3,930.9	121.9	85.6	3,967.2	474.3	387.5	86.9	3,492.8	31.5	3,461.3
1985	4,217.5	112.4	85.9	4,244.0	505.4	412.8	92.7	3,738.6	42.3	3,696.3
1986	4,460.1	111.0	93.4	4,477.7	538.5	439.1	99.4	3,939.2	67.7	3,871.5
1987	4,736.4	122.8	105.2	4,754.0	571.1	464.5	106.6	4,182.9	32.9	4,150.0
1988	5,100.4	151.6	128.3	5,123.8	611.0	497.1	113.9	4,512.8	–9.5	4,522.3
1989	5,482.1	177.2	151.2	5,508.1	651.5	529.6	121.8	4,856.6	56.1	4,800.5
1990	5,800.5	188.5	154.1	5,835.0	691.2	560.4	130.8	5,143.7	84.2	5,059.5
1991	5,992.1	168.1	138.2	6,022.0	724.4	585.4	138.9	5,297.6	79.7	5,217.9
1992	6,342.3	151.8	122.7	6,371.4	744.4	599.9	144.5	5,627.1	110.0	5,517.1
1993	6,667.4	155.2	124.0	6,698.5	778.0	626.4	151.6	5,920.5	135.8	5,784.7
1994	7,085.2	184.1	160.0	7,109.2	819.2	661.0	158.2	6,290.1	108.8	6,181.3
1995	7,414.7	229.3	199.6	7,444.3	869.5	704.6	164.8	6,574.9	52.5	6,522.3
1996	7,838.5	245.8	214.2	7,870.1	912.5	743.4	169.2	6,957.6	25.9	6,931.7
1997	8,332.4	279.5	256.1	8,355.8	963.8	789.7	174.1	7,392.0	–14.0	7,406.0
1998	8,793.5	286.2	268.9	8,810.8	1,020.5	841.6	179.0	7,790.3	–85.3	7,875.6
1999	9,353.5	319.5	291.7	9,381.3	1,094.4	907.2	187.2	8,286.9	–71.1	8,358.0
2000	9,951.5	380.5	342.8	9,989.2	1,184.3	986.8	197.5	8,804.9	–134.0	8,938.9
2001	10,286.2	323.0	271.1	10,338.1	1,256.2	1,051.6	204.6	9,081.9	–103.4	9,185.2
2002	10,642.3	313.5	264.4	10,691.4	1,305.0	1,094.0	210.9	9,386.4	–22.1	9,408.5
2003	11,142.2	353.3	284.6	11,210.9	1,354.1	1,135.9	218.1	9,856.9	16.7	9,840.2
2004	11,853.3	448.6	357.4	11,944.5	1,432.8	1,200.9	231.9	10,511.7	–22.3	10,534.0
2005	12,623.0	573.0	475.9	12,720.1	1,541.4	1,290.8	250.6	11,178.7	–95.1	11,273.8
2006	13,377.2	721.1	648.6	13,449.6	1,660.7	1,391.4	269.3	11,789.0	–242.3	12,031.2
2007	14,028.7	871.0	747.7	14,151.9	1,767.5	1,476.2	291.3	12,384.4	–12.0	12,396.4
2008	14,291.5	856.1	686.9	14,460.7	1,854.1	1,542.9	311.2	12,606.6	–2.4	12,609.1
2009	13,973.7	642.4	498.9	14,117.2	1,866.3	1,542.8	323.5	12,250.9	118.3	12,132.6
2010	14,498.9	716.5	507.2	14,708.2	1,873.4	1,539.9	333.5	12,834.8	23.3	12,811.4
2011	15,075.7	783.7	531.8	15,327.5	1,936.8	1,587.4	349.4	13,390.8	31.9	13,358.9
2012 ᵖ	15,681.5	....	....		2,011.8	1,647.8	363.9			
2009: I	13,923.4	627.8	509.6	14,041.7	1,885.5	1,562.9	322.5	12,156.2	55.5	12,100.7
II	13,885.4	615.0	499.2	14,001.3	1,867.7	1,544.7	323.0	12,133.5	132.5	12,001.0
III	13,952.2	639.2	476.2	14,115.2	1,854.4	1,531.1	323.3	12,260.7	158.6	12,102.1
IV	14,133.6	687.6	510.5	14,310.8	1,857.6	1,532.3	325.3	12,453.1	126.5	12,326.6
2010: I	14,270.3	687.1	495.6	14,461.7	1,863.1	1,534.5	328.6	12,598.6	15.6	12,583.0
II	14,413.5	705.1	489.3	14,629.3	1,867.5	1,535.4	332.1	12,761.8	39.7	12,722.1
III	14,576.0	726.1	509.1	14,793.0	1,875.5	1,540.5	335.0	12,917.5	–3.8	12,921.3
IV	14,735.9	747.9	534.9	14,948.9	1,887.7	1,549.3	338.4	13,061.2	41.8	13,019.4
2011: I	14,814.9	761.4	526.1	15,050.1	1,904.3	1,561.7	342.6	13,145.8	–50.4	13,196.3
II	15,003.6	797.4	547.4	15,253.6	1,927.4	1,580.4	347.1	13,326.2	25.1	13,301.1
III	15,163.2	788.9	530.6	15,421.5	1,948.9	1,596.5	352.4	13,472.6	82.5	13,390.1
IV	15,321.0	787.1	523.1	15,585.0	1,966.6	1,611.0	355.5	13,618.4	70.3	13,548.1
2012: I	15,478.3	769.6	554.7	15,693.2	1,984.9	1,625.9	359.0	13,708.3	1.1	13,707.2
II	15,585.6	775.1	527.8	15,832.9	2,004.8	1,642.0	362.8	13,828.1	77.7	13,750.5
III	15,811.0	775.8	532.7	16,054.2	2,019.8	1,654.2	365.6	14,034.4	138.5	13,895.9
IVᵖ	15,851.2	....	....		2,037.6	1,669.2	368.4			

Source: Department of Commerce (Bureau of Economic Analysis).

Relation of national income and personal income, 1964–2012

[Billions of dollars; quarterly data at seasonally adjusted annual rates]

Year or quarter	National income	Less: Corporate profits with inventory valuation and capital consumption adjustments	Less: Taxes on production and imports less subsidies	Less: Contributions for government social insurance, domestic	Less: Net interest and miscellaneous payments on assets	Less: Business current transfer payments (net)	Less: Current surplus of government enterprises	Less: Wage accruals less disbursements	Plus: Personal income receipts on assets	Plus: Personal current transfer receipts	Equals: Personal income
1964	601.4	75.5	54.5	22.4	17.4	3.1	1.3	0.0	53.8	33.5	514.3
1965	652.2	86.5	57.7	23.4	19.6	3.6	1.3	.0	59.4	36.2	555.5
1966	710.1	92.5	59.3	31.3	22.4	3.5	1.0	.0	64.1	39.6	603.8
1967	750.4	90.2	64.1	34.9	25.5	3.8	.9	.0	69.0	48.0	648.1
1968	821.2	97.3	72.2	38.7	27.1	4.3	1.2	.0	75.2	56.1	711.7
1969	888.5	94.5	79.3	44.1	32.7	4.9	1.0	.0	84.1	62.3	778.3
1970	929.5	82.5	86.6	46.4	39.1	4.5	.0	.0	93.5	74.7	838.6
1971	1,005.6	96.1	95.8	51.2	43.9	4.3	−.2	.6	101.0	88.1	903.1
1972	1,110.3	111.4	101.3	59.2	47.9	4.9	.5	.0	109.6	97.9	992.6
1973	1,246.1	124.5	112.0	75.5	55.2	6.0	−.4	−.1	124.7	112.6	1,110.5
1974	1,341.5	115.1	121.6	85.2	70.8	7.1	−.9	−.5	146.4	133.3	1,222.7
1975	1,444.0	133.3	130.8	89.3	81.6	9.4	−3.2	.1	162.2	170.0	1,334.9
1976	1,609.8	161.6	141.3	101.3	85.5	9.5	−1.8	.1	178.4	184.0	1,474.7
1977	1,797.4	191.8	152.6	113.1	101.1	8.5	−2.7	.1	205.3	194.2	1,632.5
1978	2,027.9	218.4	162.0	131.3	115.0	10.8	−2.2	.3	234.8	209.6	1,836.7
1979	2,248.3	225.4	171.6	152.7	138.9	13.3	−2.9	−.2	274.7	235.3	2,059.5
1980	2,433.0	201.4	190.5	166.2	181.8	14.7	−5.1	.0	338.7	279.5	2,301.5
1981	2,729.8	223.3	224.2	195.7	232.3	17.9	−5.6	.1	421.9	318.4	2,582.3
1982	2,851.4	205.7	225.9	208.9	271.1	20.6	−4.5	.0	488.4	354.8	2,766.8
1983	3,070.9	259.8	242.0	226.0	285.3	22.6	−3.2	−.4	529.6	383.7	2,952.2
1984	3,461.3	318.6	268.7	257.5	327.1	30.3	−1.9	.2	607.9	400.1	3,268.9
1985	3,696.3	332.5	286.8	281.4	341.5	35.2	.6	−.2	653.2	424.9	3,496.7
1986	3,871.5	314.1	298.5	303.4	367.1	36.9	.9	.0	694.5	451.0	3,696.0
1987	4,150.0	367.8	317.3	323.1	366.7	34.1	.2	.0	715.8	467.6	3,924.4
1988	4,522.3	426.6	345.0	361.5	385.3	33.6	2.6	.0	767.0	496.5	4,231.2
1989	4,800.5	425.6	371.4	385.2	434.1	39.2	4.9	.0	874.8	542.6	4,557.5
1990	5,059.5	434.4	398.0	410.1	444.2	40.1	1.6	.1	920.8	594.9	4,846.7
1991	5,217.9	457.3	429.6	430.2	418.2	39.9	5.7	−.1	928.6	665.9	5,031.5
1992	5,517.1	496.2	453.3	455.0	387.7	40.7	8.2	−15.8	909.7	745.8	5,347.3
1993	5,784.7	543.7	466.4	477.4	364.6	40.5	8.7	6.4	900.5	790.8	5,568.1
1994	6,181.3	628.2	512.7	508.2	362.2	41.9	9.6	17.6	947.7	826.4	5,874.8
1995	6,522.3	716.2	523.1	532.8	358.3	45.8	13.1	16.4	1,005.4	878.9	6,200.9
1996	6,931.7	801.5	545.5	555.1	371.1	53.8	14.4	3.6	1,080.7	924.1	6,591.6
1997	7,406.0	884.8	577.8	587.2	407.6	51.3	14.1	−2.9	1,165.5	949.2	7,000.7
1998	7,875.6	812.4	603.1	624.7	479.3	65.2	13.3	−.7	1,269.2	977.9	7,525.4
1999	8,358.0	856.3	628.4	661.3	481.4	69.0	14.1	5.2	1,246.8	1,021.6	7,910.8
2000	8,938.9	819.2	662.7	705.8	539.3	87.0	9.1	.0	1,360.7	1,083.0	8,559.4
2001	9,185.2	784.2	669.0	733.2	544.4	101.3	4.0	.0	1,346.0	1,188.1	8,883.3
2002	9,408.5	872.2	721.4	751.5	506.4	82.4	6.3	.0	1,309.6	1,282.1	9,060.1
2003	9,840.2	977.8	757.7	778.9	504.1	76.1	7.0	15.0	1,312.9	1,341.7	9,378.1
2004	10,534.0	1,246.9	817.0	827.3	461.6	81.7	1.2	−15.0	1,408.5	1,415.5	9,937.2
2005	11,273.8	1,456.1	869.3	872.7	543.0	95.9	−3.5	5.0	1,542.0	1,508.6	10,485.9
2006	12,031.2	1,608.3	935.5	921.8	652.2	83.0	−4.2	1.3	1,829.7	1,605.0	11,268.1
2007	12,396.4	1,510.6	972.6	959.5	731.6	103.3	−11.8	−6.3	2,057.0	1,718.5	11,912.3
2008	12,609.1	1,248.4	985.7	987.3	870.1	123.0	−16.0	−5.0	2,165.4	1,879.2	12,460.2
2009	12,132.6	1,342.3	963.5	963.1	640.5	133.4	−15.6	5.0	1,626.5	2,140.1	11,867.0
2010	12,811.4	1,702.4	998.0	983.3	567.9	140.0	−19.5	.0	1,598.3	2,284.3	12,321.9
2011	13,358.9	1,827.0	1,036.2	919.3	527.4	132.6	−26.5	.0	1,685.1	2,319.2	12,947.3
2012 ᵖ	....	....	1,069.5	948.3	503.2	127.9	−34.0	.0	1,747.3	2,375.6	13,405.9
2009: I	12,100.7	1,198.4	953.8	965.4	765.8	134.7	−16.6	20.0	1,814.8	2,033.6	11,927.5
II	12,001.0	1,243.3	959.6	965.8	633.3	140.7	−15.4	.0	1,634.4	2,171.2	11,879.3
III	12,102.1	1,403.2	959.2	960.9	582.6	123.2	−14.5	.0	1,537.8	2,169.6	11,794.9
IV	12,326.6	1,524.5	981.5	960.4	580.3	134.8	−15.8	.0	1,519.1	2,186.1	11,866.2
2010: I	12,583.0	1,648.0	987.1	974.7	586.9	138.7	−16.8	.0	1,568.6	2,256.9	12,089.8
II	12,722.1	1,625.4	994.1	983.0	568.5	139.7	−18.5	.0	1,594.4	2,266.2	12,290.6
III	12,921.3	1,747.5	1,001.9	987.1	559.6	143.9	−20.1	.0	1,598.0	2,297.9	12,397.2
IV	13,019.4	1,788.8	1,008.8	988.2	556.8	137.7	−22.5	.0	1,632.1	2,316.2	12,509.9
2011: I	13,196.3	1,723.3	1,024.8	914.5	551.4	145.7	−23.1	.0	1,674.3	2,322.5	12,856.5
II	13,301.1	1,800.9	1,037.1	919.2	513.8	127.9	−24.4	.0	1,692.4	2,319.9	12,938.9
III	13,390.1	1,830.5	1,035.7	920.8	528.4	129.5	−27.5	.0	1,689.1	2,314.7	12,976.3
IV	13,548.1	1,953.1	1,047.1	922.8	515.9	127.4	−31.1	.0	1,684.6	2,319.9	13,017.4
2012: I	13,707.2	1,900.1	1,067.7	942.6	515.6	130.5	−32.0	.0	1,696.4	2,348.0	13,227.1
II	13,750.5	1,921.9	1,069.8	944.4	489.5	127.9	−34.1	.0	1,730.8	2,365.2	13,327.0
III	13,895.9	1,967.6	1,067.8	948.7	518.2	123.8	−35.5	.0	1,712.8	2,388.0	13,406.2
IV ᵖ	....	....	1,072.7	957.6	489.6	129.3	−34.4	.0	1,849.1	2,401.3	13,663.2

Source: Department of Commerce (Bureau of Economic Analysis).

[Billions of dollars; quarterly data at seasonally adjusted annual rates]

Year or quarter	National income	Compensation of employees							Proprietors' income with inventory valuation and capital consumption adjustments			Rental income of persons with capital consumption adjustment
		Total	Wage and salary accruals			Supplements to wages and salaries			Total	Farm	Non-farm	
			Total	Government	Other	Total	Employer contributions for employee pension and insurance funds	Employer contributions for government social insurance				
1964	601.4	370.7	337.8	64.9	272.9	32.9	20.3	12.6	59.4	9.8	49.6	19.4
1965	652.2	399.5	363.8	69.9	293.8	35.7	22.7	13.1	63.9	12.0	51.9	19.9
1966	710.1	442.7	400.3	78.4	321.9	42.3	25.5	16.8	68.2	13.0	55.2	20.5
1967	750.4	475.1	429.0	86.5	342.5	46.1	28.1	18.0	69.8	11.6	58.2	20.9
1968	821.2	524.3	472.0	96.7	375.3	52.3	32.4	20.0	74.2	11.7	62.5	20.6
1969	888.5	577.6	518.3	105.6	412.7	59.3	36.5	22.8	77.5	12.8	64.7	20.9
1970	929.5	617.2	551.6	117.2	434.3	65.7	41.8	23.8	78.5	12.9	65.6	21.1
1971	1,005.6	658.9	584.5	126.8	457.8	74.4	47.9	26.4	84.7	13.4	71.3	22.2
1972	1,110.3	725.1	638.8	137.9	500.9	86.4	55.2	31.2	96.0	17.0	79.0	23.1
1973	1,246.1	811.2	708.8	148.8	560.0	102.5	62.7	39.8	113.6	29.1	84.6	23.9
1974	1,341.5	890.2	772.3	160.5	611.8	118.0	73.3	44.7	113.5	23.5	90.0	24.0
1975	1,444.0	949.1	814.8	176.2	638.6	134.3	87.6	46.7	119.6	22.0	97.6	23.4
1976	1,609.8	1,059.3	899.7	188.9	710.8	159.6	105.2	54.4	132.2	17.2	115.0	22.1
1977	1,797.4	1,180.5	994.2	202.6	791.6	186.4	125.3	61.1	146.0	16.0	130.1	19.6
1978	2,027.9	1,335.5	1,120.6	220.0	900.6	214.9	143.4	71.5	167.5	19.9	147.6	20.9
1979	2,248.3	1,498.3	1,253.3	237.1	1,016.2	245.0	162.4	82.6	181.1	22.2	159.0	22.6
1980	2,433.0	1,647.6	1,373.4	261.5	1,112.0	274.2	185.2	88.9	173.5	11.7	161.8	28.5
1981	2,729.8	1,819.7	1,511.4	285.8	1,225.5	308.3	204.7	103.6	181.6	19.0	162.6	36.5
1982	2,851.4	1,919.6	1,587.5	307.5	1,280.0	332.1	222.4	109.8	174.8	13.3	161.5	38.1
1983	3,070.9	2,035.5	1,677.5	324.8	1,352.7	358.0	238.1	119.9	190.7	6.2	184.5	38.2
1984	3,461.3	2,245.4	1,844.9	348.1	1,496.8	400.5	261.5	139.0	233.1	20.9	212.1	40.0
1985	3,696.3	2,411.7	1,982.6	373.9	1,608.7	429.2	281.5	147.7	246.1	21.0	225.1	41.9
1986	3,871.5	2,557.7	2,102.3	397.2	1,705.1	455.3	297.5	157.9	262.6	22.8	239.7	33.8
1987	4,150.0	2,735.6	2,256.3	423.1	1,833.1	479.4	313.1	166.3	294.2	28.9	265.3	34.2
1988	4,522.3	2,954.2	2,439.8	452.0	1,987.7	514.4	329.7	184.6	334.8	26.8	308.0	40.2
1989	4,800.5	3,131.3	2,583.1	481.1	2,101.9	548.3	354.6	193.7	351.6	33.0	318.6	42.4
1990	5,059.5	3,326.3	2,741.2	519.0	2,222.2	585.1	378.6	206.5	365.1	32.2	333.0	49.8
1991	5,217.9	3,438.3	2,814.5	548.8	2,265.7	623.9	408.7	215.1	367.3	27.5	339.8	61.6
1992	5,517.1	3,631.4	2,957.8	572.0	2,385.8	673.6	445.2	228.4	414.9	35.8	379.1	84.6
1993	5,784.7	3,797.1	3,083.0	589.0	2,494.0	714.1	474.4	239.7	449.6	32.0	417.6	114.1
1994	6,181.3	3,998.5	3,248.5	609.5	2,639.0	750.1	495.9	254.1	485.1	35.6	449.5	142.9
1995	6,522.3	4,195.2	3,434.4	629.0	2,805.4	760.8	496.7	264.1	516.0	23.4	492.6	154.6
1996	6,931.7	4,391.4	3,620.0	648.1	2,971.9	771.4	496.6	274.8	583.7	38.4	545.2	170.4
1997	7,406.0	4,665.6	3,873.6	671.8	3,201.8	792.0	502.4	289.6	628.2	32.6	595.6	176.5
1998	7,875.6	5,023.2	4,180.9	701.2	3,479.7	842.3	535.1	307.2	687.5	28.9	658.7	191.5
1999	8,358.0	5,353.9	4,465.2	733.7	3,731.5	888.8	565.4	323.3	746.8	28.5	718.3	208.2
2000	8,938.9	5,788.8	4,827.7	779.7	4,048.0	961.2	615.9	345.2	817.5	29.6	787.8	215.3
2001	9,185.2	5,979.3	4,952.2	821.9	4,130.3	1,027.1	669.1	358.0	870.7	30.5	840.2	232.4
2002	9,408.5	6,110.8	4,997.3	873.1	4,124.2	1,113.5	747.4	366.1	890.3	18.5	871.8	218.7
2003	9,840.2	6,382.6	5,154.6	913.3	4,241.3	1,228.0	845.6	382.4	930.6	36.5	894.1	204.2
2004	10,534.0	6,693.4	5,410.7	952.8	4,457.9	1,282.7	874.6	408.1	1,033.8	49.7	984.1	198.4
2005	11,273.8	7,065.0	5,706.0	991.5	4,714.5	1,359.1	931.6	427.5	1,069.8	43.9	1,025.9	178.2
2006	12,031.2	7,477.0	6,070.1	1,035.2	5,035.0	1,406.9	960.1	446.7	1,133.0	29.3	1,103.6	146.5
2007	12,396.4	7,855.9	6,415.5	1,089.0	5,326.4	1,440.4	980.5	459.9	1,090.4	37.8	1,052.6	143.7
2008	12,609.1	8,068.3	6,545.9	1,144.1	5,401.8	1,522.5	1,052.4	470.1	1,097.9	51.8	1,046.1	231.6
2009	12,132.6	7,799.4	6,275.3	1,175.2	5,100.1	1,524.0	1,067.2	456.9	979.4	39.9	939.5	289.7
2010	12,811.4	7,970.0	6,404.6	1,191.3	5,213.3	1,565.4	1,097.3	468.1	1,103.4	44.3	1,059.1	349.2
2011	13,358.9	8,295.2	6,661.3	1,195.3	5,466.0	1,633.9	1,139.0	494.9	1,157.3	54.6	1,102.8	409.7
2012 ᵖ	....	8,565.7	6,880.6	1,201.5	5,679.2	1,685.1	1,172.1	512.9	1,202.5	56.3	1,146.2	463.1
2009: I	12,100.7	7,824.9	6,299.1	1,167.0	5,132.1	1,525.8	1,067.6	458.2	969.5	33.7	935.8	270.2
II	12,001.0	7,801.1	6,278.2	1,176.1	5,102.1	1,523.0	1,064.5	458.5	957.0	38.5	918.5	281.5
III	12,102.1	7,773.6	6,252.2	1,177.8	5,074.4	1,521.4	1,065.7	455.7	975.8	40.6	935.2	298.9
IV	12,326.6	7,797.8	6,271.9	1,180.1	5,091.8	1,526.0	1,070.9	455.1	1,015.3	46.7	968.6	308.3
2010: I	12,583.0	7,846.6	6,298.7	1,188.0	5,110.7	1,547.9	1,082.8	465.0	1,052.4	41.5	1,010.9	340.1
II	12,722.1	7,955.4	6,394.6	1,195.8	5,198.8	1,560.8	1,092.4	468.4	1,104.8	43.6	1,061.2	352.7
III	12,921.3	8,021.4	6,449.7	1,190.1	5,259.6	1,571.7	1,102.0	469.7	1,117.1	44.6	1,072.5	350.0
IV	13,019.4	8,056.6	6,475.2	1,191.2	5,284.0	1,581.4	1,112.1	469.3	1,139.2	47.6	1,091.6	354.0
2011: I	13,196.3	8,236.3	6,618.5	1,193.8	5,424.7	1,617.8	1,125.0	492.7	1,148.0	56.0	1,092.0	390.0
II	13,301.1	8,286.4	6,656.2	1,197.4	5,458.8	1,630.2	1,135.4	494.8	1,154.7	52.6	1,102.1	404.7
III	13,390.1	8,318.1	6,678.1	1,197.7	5,480.4	1,640.0	1,144.2	495.8	1,161.4	55.3	1,106.1	413.8
IV	13,548.1	8,340.1	6,692.4	1,192.5	5,499.9	1,647.7	1,151.5	496.2	1,165.3	54.4	1,110.9	430.3
2012: I	13,707.2	8,495.7	6,825.9	1,199.1	5,626.8	1,669.8	1,159.6	510.2	1,184.3	52.3	1,132.1	445.3
II	13,750.5	8,527.7	6,849.2	1,199.8	5,649.4	1,678.5	1,167.7	510.8	1,194.9	52.5	1,142.4	452.8
III	13,895.9	8,577.6	6,888.5	1,203.3	5,685.3	1,689.1	1,176.2	512.9	1,205.4	59.4	1,146.0	471.0
IV ᵖ	....	8,661.8	6,959.0	1,203.7	5,755.3	1,702.8	1,185.0	517.8	1,225.1	61.0	1,164.1	483.5

See next page for continuation of table.

TABLE B–28. National income by type of income, 1964–2012—*Continued*

[Billions of dollars; quarterly data at seasonally adjusted annual rates]

Year or quarter	Corporate profits with inventory valuation and capital consumption adjustments									Net interest and miscellaneous payments	Taxes on production and imports	Less: Subsidies	Business current transfer payments (net)	Current surplus of government enterprises
	Total	Profits with inventory valuation adjustment and without capital consumption adjustment							Capital consumption adjustment					
		Total	Profits					Inventory valuation adjustment						
			Profits before tax	Taxes on corporate income	Profits after tax									
					Total	Net dividends	Undistributed profits							
1964	75.5	68.6	69.1	28.2	40.9	18.2	22.7	−0.5	6.9	17.4	57.3	2.7	3.1	1.3
1965	86.5	78.9	80.2	31.1	49.1	20.2	28.9	−1.2	7.6	19.6	60.7	3.0	3.6	1.3
1966	92.5	84.6	86.7	33.9	52.8	20.7	32.1	−2.1	8.0	22.4	63.2	3.9	3.5	1.0
1967	90.2	82.0	83.5	32.9	50.6	21.5	29.1	−1.6	8.2	25.5	67.9	3.8	3.8	.9
1968	97.3	88.8	92.4	39.6	52.8	23.5	29.3	−3.7	8.5	27.1	76.4	4.2	4.3	1.2
1969	94.5	85.5	91.4	40.0	51.4	24.2	27.2	−5.9	9.0	32.7	83.9	4.5	4.9	1.0
1970	82.5	74.4	81.0	34.8	46.2	24.3	21.9	−6.6	8.1	39.1	91.4	4.8	4.5	.0
1971	96.1	88.3	92.9	38.2	54.7	25.0	29.7	−4.6	7.8	43.9	100.5	4.7	4.3	−.2
1972	111.4	101.6	108.2	42.3	65.9	26.8	39.0	−6.6	9.8	47.9	107.9	6.6	4.9	.5
1973	124.5	115.4	135.0	50.0	85.0	29.9	55.1	−19.6	9.1	55.2	117.2	5.2	6.0	−.4
1974	115.1	109.6	147.8	52.8	95.0	33.2	61.8	−38.2	5.6	70.8	124.9	3.3	7.1	−.9
1975	133.3	135.0	145.5	51.6	93.9	33.0	60.9	−10.5	−1.7	81.6	135.3	4.5	9.4	−3.2
1976	161.6	165.6	179.7	65.3	114.5	39.0	75.4	−14.1	−4.0	85.5	146.4	5.1	9.5	−1.8
1977	191.8	194.8	210.5	74.4	136.1	44.8	91.3	−15.7	−3.0	101.1	159.7	7.1	8.5	−2.7
1978	218.4	222.4	246.1	84.9	161.3	50.8	110.5	−23.7	−4.0	115.0	170.9	8.9	10.8	−2.2
1979	225.4	232.0	272.1	90.0	182.1	57.5	124.6	−40.1	−6.6	138.9	180.1	8.5	13.3	−2.9
1980	201.4	211.4	253.5	87.2	166.4	64.1	102.3	−42.1	−10.0	181.8	200.3	9.8	14.7	−5.1
1981	223.3	219.1	243.7	84.3	159.4	73.8	85.6	−24.6	4.2	232.3	235.6	11.5	17.9	−5.6
1982	205.7	191.1	198.6	66.5	132.1	77.7	54.4	−7.5	14.6	271.1	240.9	15.0	20.6	−4.5
1983	259.8	226.6	234.0	80.6	153.4	83.5	69.9	−7.4	33.3	285.3	263.3	21.3	22.6	−3.2
1984	318.6	264.6	268.6	97.5	171.1	90.8	80.3	−4.0	54.0	327.1	289.8	21.1	30.3	−1.9
1985	332.5	257.5	257.5	99.4	158.1	97.6	60.5	.0	75.1	341.5	308.1	21.4	35.2	.6
1986	314.1	253.0	246.0	109.7	136.3	106.2	30.1	7.1	61.1	367.1	323.4	24.9	36.9	.9
1987	367.8	306.9	323.1	130.4	192.7	112.3	80.3	−16.2	61.0	366.7	347.5	30.3	34.1	.2
1988	426.6	367.7	389.9	141.6	248.3	129.9	118.4	−22.2	58.9	385.3	374.5	29.5	33.6	2.6
1989	425.6	374.1	390.5	146.1	244.4	158.0	86.4	−16.3	51.5	434.1	398.9	27.4	39.2	4.9
1990	434.4	398.8	411.7	145.4	266.3	169.1	97.2	−12.9	35.7	444.2	425.0	27.0	40.1	1.6
1991	457.3	430.3	425.4	138.6	286.8	180.7	106.1	4.9	27.0	418.2	457.1	27.5	39.9	5.7
1992	496.2	471.6	474.4	148.7	325.7	188.0	137.7	−2.8	24.6	387.7	483.4	30.1	40.7	8.2
1993	543.7	515.0	519.0	171.0	348.0	202.9	145.1	−4.0	28.7	364.6	503.1	36.7	40.5	8.7
1994	628.2	586.6	599.0	193.1	405.9	235.7	170.2	−12.4	41.6	362.2	545.2	32.5	41.9	9.6
1995	716.2	666.0	684.3	217.8	466.5	254.4	212.1	−18.3	50.2	358.3	557.9	34.8	45.8	13.1
1996	801.5	743.8	740.7	231.5	509.3	297.7	211.5	3.1	57.7	371.1	580.8	35.2	53.8	14.4
1997	884.8	815.9	801.8	245.4	556.3	331.2	225.1	14.1	69.0	407.6	611.6	33.8	51.3	14.1
1998	812.4	738.6	722.9	248.4	474.5	351.5	123.1	15.7	73.8	479.3	639.5	36.4	65.2	13.3
1999	856.3	776.6	780.5	258.8	521.7	337.4	184.3	−4.0	79.7	481.4	673.6	45.2	69.0	14.1
2000	819.2	755.7	772.5	265.1	507.4	377.9	129.5	−16.8	63.6	539.3	708.6	45.8	87.0	9.1
2001	784.2	720.8	712.7	203.3	509.4	370.9	138.5	8.0	63.4	544.4	727.7	58.7	101.3	4.0
2002	872.2	762.8	765.3	192.3	573.0	399.3	173.8	−2.6	109.4	506.4	762.8	41.4	82.4	6.3
2003	977.8	892.2	903.5	243.8	659.7	424.9	234.8	−11.3	85.6	504.1	806.8	49.1	76.1	7.0
2004	1,246.9	1,195.1	1,229.4	306.1	923.3	550.3	373.0	−34.3	51.8	461.6	863.4	46.4	81.7	1.2
2005	1,456.1	1,609.5	1,640.2	412.4	1,227.8	557.3	670.5	−30.7	−153.4	543.0	930.2	60.9	95.9	−3.5
2006	1,608.3	1,784.7	1,822.7	473.3	1,349.5	704.8	644.7	−38.0	−176.4	652.2	986.8	51.4	83.0	−4.2
2007	1,510.6	1,691.1	1,738.4	445.5	1,292.9	794.5	498.4	−47.2	−180.5	731.6	1,027.2	54.6	103.3	−11.8
2008	1,248.4	1,315.5	1,359.9	309.0	1,050.9	786.9	264.0	−44.5	−67.1	870.1	1,038.6	52.9	123.0	−16.0
2009	1,342.3	1,443.6	1,440.5	269.4	1,171.1	554.1	617.0	3.2	−101.3	640.5	1,023.2	59.7	133.4	−15.6
2010	1,702.4	1,777.7	1,816.3	373.3	1,443.0	600.9	842.1	−38.7	−75.2	567.9	1,055.0	57.0	140.0	−19.5
2011 ᵖ	1,827.0	1,791.6	1,854.1	379.0	1,475.1	697.2	777.9	−62.6	35.4	527.4	1,097.9	61.6	132.6	−26.5
2012 ᵖ	....	....	....	....	....	779.2	....	....	−200.6	503.2	1,130.4	60.9	127.9	−34.0
2009: I	1,198.4	1,306.6	1,225.3	214.9	1,010.3	652.4	357.9	81.4	−108.2	765.8	1,010.1	56.4	134.7	−16.6
II	1,243.3	1,342.9	1,327.9	240.5	1,087.4	548.4	538.9	15.0	−99.6	633.3	1,016.5	56.8	140.7	−15.4
III	1,403.2	1,499.3	1,516.9	285.0	1,231.9	502.4	729.5	−17.6	−96.1	582.6	1,027.7	68.5	123.2	−14.5
IV	1,524.5	1,625.7	1,691.9	337.0	1,354.9	513.3	841.6	−66.2	−101.3	580.3	1,038.4	57.0	134.8	−15.8
2010: I	1,648.0	1,758.0	1,785.2	351.1	1,434.1	554.9	879.3	−27.2	−110.0	586.9	1,043.3	56.2	138.7	−16.8
II	1,625.4	1,741.0	1,755.3	350.2	1,405.1	585.8	819.3	−14.3	−115.6	568.5	1,050.5	56.4	139.7	−18.5
III	1,747.5	1,824.6	1,850.6	385.5	1,465.1	618.1	847.0	−26.0	−77.1	559.6	1,058.6	56.7	143.9	−20.1
IV	1,788.8	1,787.0	1,874.2	406.6	1,467.6	645.0	822.6	−87.2	1.9	556.8	1,067.5	58.6	137.7	−22.5
2011: I	1,723.3	1,679.4	1,801.1	398.7	1,402.5	677.6	724.9	−121.7	43.9	551.4	1,084.5	59.6	145.7	−23.1
II	1,800.9	1,764.6	1,839.7	385.1	1,454.5	687.5	767.1	−75.0	36.3	513.8	1,099.0	61.9	127.9	−24.4
III	1,830.5	1,798.8	1,839.3	362.0	1,477.3	705.9	771.4	−40.6	31.7	528.4	1,098.2	62.4	129.5	−27.5
IV	1,953.1	1,923.5	1,936.4	370.4	1,566.1	717.9	848.2	−12.9	29.6	515.9	1,109.8	62.7	127.4	−31.1
2012: I	1,900.1	2,100.8	2,124.5	453.6	1,670.9	727.1	943.7	−23.7	−200.7	515.6	1,128.5	60.8	130.5	−32.0
II	1,921.9	2,124.3	2,108.2	443.3	1,664.9	747.5	917.4	16.0	−202.4	489.5	1,130.9	61.0	127.9	−34.1
III	1,967.6	2,167.5	2,194.4	452.4	1,742.0	760.3	981.6	−26.8	−200.0	518.2	1,128.4	60.6	123.8	−35.5
IV ᵖ	....	....	....	....	....	881.8	....	....	−199.4	489.6	1,133.7	61.0	129.3	−34.4

Source: Department of Commerce (Bureau of Economic Analysis).

National Income or Expenditure | 357

TABLE B–29. Sources of personal income, 1964–2012

[Billions of dollars; quarterly data at seasonally adjusted annual rates]

Year or quarter	Personal income	Compensation of employees, received							Proprietors' income with inventory valuation and capital consumption adjustments			Rental income of persons with capital consumption adjustment
		Total	Wage and salary disbursements			Supplements to wages and salaries			Total	Farm	Non-farm	
			Total	Private industries	Government	Total	Employer contributions for employee pension and insurance funds	Employer contributions for government social insurance				
1964	514.3	370.7	337.8	272.9	64.9	32.9	20.3	12.6	59.4	9.8	49.6	19.4
1965	555.5	399.5	363.8	293.8	69.9	35.7	22.7	13.1	63.9	12.0	51.9	19.9
1966	603.8	442.7	400.3	321.9	78.4	42.3	25.5	16.8	68.2	13.0	55.2	20.5
1967	648.1	475.1	429.0	342.5	86.5	46.1	28.1	18.0	69.8	11.6	58.2	20.9
1968	711.7	524.3	472.0	375.3	96.7	52.3	32.4	20.0	74.2	11.7	62.5	20.6
1969	778.3	577.6	518.3	412.7	105.6	59.3	36.5	22.8	77.5	12.8	64.7	20.9
1970	838.6	617.2	551.6	434.3	117.2	65.7	41.8	23.8	78.5	12.9	65.6	21.1
1971	903.1	658.3	584.0	457.4	126.6	74.4	47.9	26.4	84.7	13.4	71.3	22.2
1972	992.6	725.1	638.8	501.2	137.6	86.4	55.2	31.2	96.0	17.0	79.0	23.1
1973	1,110.5	811.3	708.8	560.0	148.8	102.5	62.7	39.8	113.6	29.1	84.6	23.9
1974	1,222.7	890.7	772.8	611.8	161.0	118.0	73.3	44.7	113.5	23.5	90.0	24.0
1975	1,334.9	949.0	814.7	638.6	176.1	134.3	87.6	46.7	119.6	22.0	97.6	23.4
1976	1,474.7	1,059.2	899.6	710.8	188.8	159.6	105.2	54.4	132.2	17.2	115.0	22.1
1977	1,632.5	1,180.4	994.1	791.6	202.5	186.4	125.3	61.1	146.0	16.0	130.1	19.6
1978	1,836.7	1,335.2	1,120.3	900.6	219.7	214.9	143.4	71.5	167.5	19.9	147.6	20.9
1979	2,059.5	1,498.5	1,253.5	1,016.2	237.3	245.0	162.4	82.6	181.1	22.2	159.0	22.6
1980	2,301.5	1,647.6	1,373.5	1,112.0	261.5	274.2	185.2	88.9	173.5	11.7	161.8	28.5
1981	2,582.3	1,819.6	1,511.3	1,225.5	285.8	308.3	204.7	103.6	181.6	19.0	162.6	36.5
1982	2,766.8	1,919.6	1,587.5	1,280.0	307.5	332.1	222.4	109.8	174.8	13.3	161.5	38.1
1983	2,952.2	2,036.0	1,678.0	1,352.7	325.2	358.0	238.1	119.9	190.7	6.2	184.5	38.2
1984	3,268.9	2,245.2	1,844.7	1,496.8	347.9	400.5	261.5	139.0	233.1	20.9	212.1	40.0
1985	3,496.7	2,412.0	1,982.8	1,608.7	374.1	429.2	281.5	147.7	246.1	21.0	225.1	41.9
1986	3,696.0	2,557.7	2,102.3	1,705.1	397.2	455.3	297.5	157.9	262.6	22.8	239.7	33.8
1987	3,924.4	2,735.6	2,256.3	1,833.1	423.1	479.4	313.1	166.3	294.2	28.9	265.3	34.2
1988	4,231.2	2,954.2	2,439.8	1,987.7	452.0	514.4	329.7	184.6	334.8	26.8	308.0	40.2
1989	4,557.5	3,131.3	2,583.1	2,101.9	481.1	548.3	354.6	193.7	351.6	33.0	318.6	42.4
1990	4,846.7	3,326.2	2,741.4	2,222.2	519.0	585.1	378.6	206.5	365.1	32.2	333.0	49.8
1991	5,031.5	3,438.4	2,814.5	2,265.7	548.8	623.9	408.7	215.1	367.3	27.5	339.8	61.6
1992	5,347.3	3,647.2	2,973.5	2,401.5	572.0	673.6	445.2	228.4	414.9	35.8	379.1	84.6
1993	5,568.1	3,790.6	3,076.6	2,487.6	589.0	714.1	474.4	239.7	449.6	32.0	417.6	114.1
1994	5,874.8	3,980.9	3,230.8	2,621.3	609.5	750.1	495.9	254.1	485.1	35.6	449.5	142.9
1995	6,200.9	4,178.8	3,418.0	2,789.0	629.0	760.8	496.7	264.1	516.0	23.4	492.6	154.6
1996	6,591.6	4,387.7	3,616.3	2,968.3	648.1	771.4	496.6	274.8	583.7	38.4	545.2	170.4
1997	7,000.7	4,668.6	3,876.6	3,204.8	671.8	792.0	502.4	289.6	628.2	32.6	595.6	176.5
1998	7,525.4	5,023.9	4,181.6	3,480.4	701.2	842.3	535.1	307.2	687.5	28.9	658.7	191.5
1999	7,910.8	5,348.8	4,460.0	3,726.3	733.7	888.8	565.4	323.3	746.8	28.5	718.3	208.2
2000	8,559.4	5,788.8	4,827.7	4,048.0	779.7	961.2	615.9	345.2	817.5	29.6	787.8	215.3
2001	8,883.3	5,979.3	4,952.2	4,130.3	821.9	1,027.1	669.1	358.0	870.7	30.5	840.2	232.4
2002	9,060.1	6,110.8	4,997.3	4,124.2	873.1	1,113.5	747.4	366.1	890.3	18.5	871.8	218.7
2003	9,378.1	6,367.6	5,139.6	4,226.3	913.3	1,228.0	845.6	382.4	930.6	36.5	894.1	204.2
2004	9,937.2	6,708.4	5,425.7	4,472.9	952.8	1,282.7	874.6	408.1	1,033.8	49.7	984.1	198.4
2005	10,485.9	7,060.0	5,701.0	4,709.5	991.5	1,359.1	931.6	427.5	1,069.8	43.9	1,025.9	178.2
2006	11,268.1	7,475.7	6,068.9	5,033.7	1,035.2	1,406.9	960.1	446.7	1,133.0	29.3	1,103.6	146.5
2007	11,912.3	7,862.2	6,421.7	5,332.7	1,089.0	1,440.4	980.5	459.9	1,090.4	37.8	1,052.6	143.7
2008	12,460.2	8,073.3	6,550.9	5,406.8	1,144.1	1,522.5	1,052.4	470.1	1,097.9	51.8	1,046.1	231.6
2009	11,867.0	7,794.4	6,270.3	5,095.1	1,175.2	1,524.0	1,067.2	456.9	979.4	39.9	939.5	289.7
2010	12,321.9	7,970.0	6,404.6	5,213.3	1,191.3	1,565.4	1,097.3	468.1	1,103.4	44.3	1,059.1	349.2
2011	12,947.3	8,295.2	6,661.3	5,466.0	1,195.3	1,633.9	1,139.0	494.9	1,157.3	54.6	1,102.8	409.7
2012 ᵖ	13,405.9	8,565.7	6,880.6	5,679.2	1,201.5	1,685.1	1,172.1	512.9	1,202.5	56.3	1,146.2	463.1
2009: I	11,927.5	7,804.9	6,279.1	5,112.1	1,167.0	1,525.8	1,067.6	458.2	969.5	33.7	935.8	270.2
II	11,879.3	7,801.1	6,278.2	5,102.1	1,176.1	1,523.0	1,064.5	458.5	957.0	38.5	918.5	281.5
III	11,794.9	7,773.6	6,252.2	5,074.4	1,177.8	1,521.4	1,065.7	455.7	975.8	40.6	935.2	298.9
IV	11,866.2	7,797.8	6,271.9	5,091.8	1,180.1	1,526.0	1,070.9	455.1	1,015.3	46.7	968.6	308.3
2010: I	12,089.8	7,846.6	6,298.7	5,110.7	1,188.0	1,547.9	1,082.8	465.0	1,052.4	41.5	1,010.9	340.1
II	12,290.6	7,955.4	6,394.6	5,198.8	1,195.8	1,560.8	1,092.4	468.4	1,104.8	43.6	1,061.2	352.7
III	12,397.2	8,021.4	6,449.7	5,259.6	1,190.1	1,571.7	1,102.0	469.7	1,117.1	44.6	1,072.5	350.0
IV	12,509.9	8,056.6	6,475.2	5,284.0	1,191.2	1,581.4	1,112.1	469.3	1,139.2	47.6	1,091.6	354.0
2011: I	12,856.5	8,236.3	6,618.5	5,424.7	1,193.8	1,617.8	1,125.0	492.7	1,148.0	56.0	1,092.0	390.0
II	12,938.9	8,286.4	6,656.2	5,458.8	1,197.4	1,630.2	1,135.4	494.8	1,154.7	52.6	1,102.1	404.7
III	12,976.3	8,318.1	6,678.1	5,480.4	1,197.7	1,640.0	1,144.2	495.8	1,161.4	55.3	1,106.1	413.8
IV	13,017.4	8,340.1	6,692.4	5,499.9	1,192.5	1,647.7	1,151.5	496.2	1,165.3	54.4	1,110.9	430.3
2012: I	13,227.1	8,495.7	6,825.9	5,626.8	1,199.1	1,669.8	1,159.6	510.2	1,184.3	52.3	1,132.1	445.3
II	13,327.0	8,527.7	6,849.2	5,649.4	1,199.8	1,678.5	1,167.7	510.8	1,194.9	52.5	1,142.4	452.8
III	13,406.2	8,577.6	6,888.5	5,685.3	1,203.3	1,689.1	1,176.2	512.9	1,205.4	59.4	1,146.0	471.0
IVᵖ	13,663.2	8,661.8	6,959.0	5,755.3	1,203.7	1,702.8	1,185.0	517.8	1,225.1	61.0	1,164.1	483.5

See next page for continuation of table.

TABLE B–29. Sources of personal income, 1964–2012—*Continued*

[Billions of dollars; quarterly data at seasonally adjusted annual rates]

Year or quarter	Personal income receipts on assets			Personal current transfer receipts								Less: Contributions for government social insurance, domestic
					Government social benefits to persons						Other current transfer receipts, from business (net)	
	Total	Personal interest income	Personal dividend income	Total	Total[1]	Social security[2]	Medicare[3]	Medicaid	Unemployment insurance	Other		
1964	53.8	35.6	18.2	33.5	31.3	16.0	....	....	2.8	7.9	2.2	22.4
1965	59.4	39.2	20.2	36.2	33.9	18.1	....	....	2.4	8.6	2.3	23.4
1966	64.1	43.4	20.7	39.6	37.5	19.8	1.0	1.9	1.9	8.1	2.1	31.3
1967	69.0	47.5	21.5	48.0	45.8	21.1	4.7	2.7	2.2	9.4	2.3	34.9
1968	75.2	51.6	23.5	56.1	53.3	24.6	5.9	4.0	2.2	10.8	2.8	38.7
1969	84.1	59.9	24.2	62.3	59.0	26.4	6.7	4.6	2.3	12.4	3.3	44.1
1970	93.5	69.2	24.3	74.7	71.7	31.4	7.3	5.5	4.2	16.0	2.9	46.4
1971	101.0	75.9	25.0	88.1	85.4	36.6	8.0	6.7	6.2	19.4	2.7	51.2
1972	109.6	82.8	26.8	97.9	94.8	40.9	8.8	8.2	6.0	21.4	3.1	59.2
1973	124.7	94.8	29.9	112.6	108.6	50.7	10.2	9.6	4.6	23.3	3.9	75.5
1974	146.4	113.2	33.2	133.3	128.6	57.6	12.7	11.2	7.0	28.4	4.7	85.2
1975	162.2	129.3	32.9	170.0	163.1	65.9	15.6	13.9	18.1	35.7	6.8	89.3
1976	178.4	139.5	39.0	184.0	177.3	74.5	18.8	15.5	16.4	38.4	6.7	101.3
1977	205.3	160.6	44.7	194.2	189.1	83.2	22.1	16.7	13.1	40.6	5.1	113.1
1978	234.8	184.0	50.7	209.6	203.2	91.4	25.5	18.6	9.4	44.6	6.5	131.3
1979	274.7	217.3	57.4	235.3	227.1	102.6	29.9	21.1	9.7	49.7	8.2	152.7
1980	338.7	274.7	64.0	279.5	270.8	118.6	36.2	23.9	16.1	61.4	8.6	166.2
1981	421.9	348.3	73.6	318.4	307.2	138.6	43.5	27.7	15.9	65.6	11.2	195.7
1982	488.4	410.8	77.6	354.8	342.4	153.7	50.9	30.2	25.2	66.1	12.4	208.9
1983	529.6	446.3	83.3	383.7	369.9	164.4	57.8	33.9	26.4	71.0	13.8	226.0
1984	607.9	517.2	90.6	400.1	380.4	173.0	64.7	36.6	16.0	73.8	19.7	257.5
1985	653.2	555.8	97.4	424.9	402.6	183.3	69.7	39.7	15.9	77.6	22.3	281.4
1986	694.5	588.4	106.0	451.0	428.0	193.6	75.3	43.6	16.5	82.4	22.9	303.4
1987	715.8	603.6	112.2	467.6	447.4	201.0	81.6	47.8	14.6	85.9	20.2	323.1
1988	767.0	637.3	129.7	496.5	475.9	213.9	86.3	53.0	13.3	92.6	20.6	361.5
1989	874.8	717.0	157.8	542.6	519.4	227.4	98.2	60.8	14.4	101.4	23.2	385.2
1990	920.8	751.9	168.8	594.9	572.7	244.1	107.6	73.1	18.2	111.9	22.2	410.1
1991	928.6	748.2	180.3	665.9	648.2	264.2	117.5	96.9	26.8	124.7	17.6	430.2
1992	909.7	722.2	187.6	745.8	729.5	281.8	132.6	116.2	39.6	140.6	16.3	455.0
1993	900.5	698.1	202.3	790.8	776.7	297.9	146.8	130.1	34.8	147.7	14.1	477.4
1994	947.7	712.7	235.0	826.4	813.1	312.2	164.4	139.4	23.9	153.5	13.3	508.2
1995	1,005.4	751.9	253.4	878.9	860.2	327.7	181.2	149.6	21.7	159.5	18.7	532.8
1996	1,080.7	784.4	296.4	924.1	901.2	342.0	194.9	158.2	22.3	162.4	22.9	555.1
1997	1,165.5	835.8	329.7	949.2	929.8	356.6	206.9	163.1	20.1	160.7	19.4	587.2
1998	1,269.2	919.3	349.8	977.9	951.9	369.2	205.6	170.2	19.7	164.0	26.0	624.7
1999	1,246.8	910.9	335.9	1,021.6	987.6	379.9	208.7	184.6	20.5	169.8	34.0	661.3
2000	1,360.7	984.2	376.5	1,083.0	1,040.6	401.4	219.1	199.5	20.7	174.8	42.4	705.8
2001	1,346.0	976.5	369.5	1,188.1	1,141.3	425.1	242.6	227.3	31.9	187.9	46.8	733.2
2002	1,309.6	911.9	397.7	1,282.1	1,247.9	446.9	259.2	250.1	53.5	208.8	34.2	751.5
2003	1,312.9	889.8	423.1	1,341.7	1,316.0	463.5	276.9	264.6	53.2	226.1	25.7	778.9
2004	1,408.5	860.2	548.3	1,415.5	1,398.6	485.5	304.7	289.7	36.4	248.3	16.9	827.3
2005	1,542.0	987.0	555.0	1,508.6	1,482.7	512.7	331.9	304.4	31.8	265.6	25.8	872.7
2006	1,829.7	1,127.5	702.2	1,605.0	1,583.6	544.1	399.2	299.0	30.4	272.1	21.4	921.8
2007	2,057.0	1,265.1	791.9	1,718.5	1,687.9	575.6	427.6	324.1	32.7	286.2	30.5	959.5
2008	2,165.4	1,382.0	783.4	1,879.2	1,842.4	605.5	461.6	338.2	50.9	341.1	36.8	987.3
2009	1,626.5	1,093.3	533.2	2,140.1	2,100.5	664.5	494.5	369.2	131.2	389.7	39.6	963.1
2010	1,598.3	1,016.6	581.7	2,284.3	2,236.9	690.2	515.3	396.6	138.9	438.1	47.4	983.3
2011	1,685.1	1,008.8	676.3	2,319.2	2,274.3	713.3	545.1	403.9	108.0	440.8	44.9	919.3
2012 ᵖ	1,747.3	990.9	756.3	2,375.6	2,329.7	762.2	562.0	415.7	80.9	436.6	45.9	948.3
2009: I	1,814.8	1,177.5	637.3	2,033.6	1,996.6	651.9	483.3	357.0	102.2	352.5	37.0	965.4
II	1,634.4	1,108.8	525.6	2,171.2	2,132.7	662.4	492.2	368.3	130.1	429.3	38.4	965.8
III	1,537.8	1,056.5	481.3	2,169.6	2,129.3	667.9	499.0	381.6	145.3	383.7	40.3	960.9
IV	1,519.1	1,030.4	488.8	2,186.1	2,143.4	675.7	503.7	369.8	147.3	393.2	42.7	960.4
2010: I	1,568.6	1,030.9	537.6	2,256.9	2,211.5	678.7	506.8	381.6	155.7	432.8	45.4	974.7
II	1,594.4	1,027.1	567.3	2,266.2	2,218.9	688.3	511.2	385.2	139.6	437.2	47.3	983.0
III	1,598.0	1,000.7	597.3	2,297.9	2,249.8	693.9	517.5	405.4	133.2	441.0	48.0	987.1
IV	1,632.1	1,007.7	624.4	2,316.2	2,267.3	699.8	525.6	414.0	126.9	441.5	49.0	988.2
2011: I	1,674.3	1,017.5	656.9	2,322.5	2,276.0	703.1	535.1	418.8	119.1	438.7	46.5	914.5
II	1,692.4	1,025.3	667.1	2,319.9	2,274.8	712.0	543.1	408.7	108.8	439.8	45.1	919.2
III	1,689.1	1,004.4	684.7	2,314.7	2,270.4	716.0	549.1	396.1	103.0	441.3	44.3	920.8
IV	1,684.6	988.0	696.6	2,319.9	2,276.0	721.9	553.1	392.0	100.9	443.5	43.9	922.8
2012: I	1,696.4	991.8	704.6	2,348.0	2,302.7	753.2	555.9	397.6	94.2	433.0	45.3	942.6
II	1,730.8	1,006.1	724.6	2,365.2	2,319.5	759.4	556.9	413.9	83.8	433.9	45.8	944.4
III	1,712.8	975.3	737.5	2,388.0	2,341.8	765.1	566.2	424.2	74.9	437.4	46.1	948.7
IV ᵖ	1,849.1	990.5	858.7	2,401.3	2,354.8	771.0	569.1	427.0	70.8	442.3	46.6	957.6

[1] Includes Veterans' benefits, not shown seperately.

[2] Includes old-age, survivors, and disability insurance benefits that are distributed from the federal old-age and survivors insurance trust fund and the disability insurance trust fund.

[3] Includes hospital and supplementary medical insurance benefits that are distributed from the federal hospital insurance trust fund and the supplementary medical insurance trust fund.

Source: Department of Commerce (Bureau of Economic Analysis).

TABLE B–30. Disposition of personal income, 1964–2012

[Billions of dollars, except as noted; quarterly data at seasonally adjusted annual rates]

Year or quarter	Personal income	Less: Personal current taxes	Equals: Disposable personal income	Less: Personal outlays Total	Personal consumption expenditures	Personal interest payments [1]	Personal current transfer payments	Equals: Personal saving	Percent of disposable personal income [2] Personal outlays Total	Personal consumption expenditures	Personal saving
1964	514.3	52.1	462.3	421.7	411.5	8.9	1.3	40.5	91.2	89.0	8.8
1965	555.5	57.7	497.8	455.1	443.8	9.9	1.4	42.7	91.4	89.2	8.6
1966	603.8	66.4	537.4	493.1	480.9	10.7	1.6	44.3	91.8	89.5	8.2
1967	648.1	73.0	575.1	520.9	507.8	11.1	2.0	54.2	90.6	88.3	9.4
1968	711.7	87.0	624.7	572.2	558.0	12.2	2.0	52.5	91.6	89.3	8.4
1969	778.3	104.5	673.8	621.4	605.1	14.0	2.2	52.5	92.2	89.8	7.8
1970	838.6	103.1	735.5	666.1	648.3	15.2	2.6	69.4	90.6	88.1	9.4
1971	903.1	101.7	801.4	721.0	701.6	16.6	2.8	80.4	90.0	87.5	10.0
1972	992.6	123.6	869.0	791.5	770.2	18.1	3.2	77.5	91.1	88.6	8.9
1973	1,110.5	132.4	978.1	875.2	852.0	19.8	3.4	102.9	89.5	87.1	10.5
1974	1,222.7	151.0	1,071.7	957.5	932.9	21.2	3.4	114.2	89.3	87.0	10.7
1975	1,334.9	147.6	1,187.3	1,061.3	1,033.8	23.7	3.8	125.9	89.4	87.1	10.6
1976	1,474.7	172.3	1,302.3	1,179.6	1,151.3	23.9	4.4	122.8	90.6	88.4	9.4
1977	1,632.5	197.5	1,435.0	1,309.7	1,277.8	27.0	4.8	125.3	91.3	89.0	8.7
1978	1,836.7	229.4	1,607.3	1,465.0	1,427.6	31.9	5.4	142.4	91.1	88.8	8.9
1979	2,059.5	268.7	1,790.9	1,633.4	1,591.2	36.2	6.0	157.5	91.2	88.8	8.8
1980	2,301.5	298.9	2,002.7	1,806.4	1,755.8	43.6	6.9	196.3	90.2	87.7	9.8
1981	2,582.3	345.2	2,237.1	2,000.4	1,939.5	49.3	11.5	236.7	89.4	86.7	10.6
1982	2,766.8	354.1	2,412.7	2,148.8	2,075.5	59.5	13.8	263.9	89.1	86.0	10.9
1983	2,952.2	352.3	2,599.8	2,372.9	2,288.6	69.2	15.1	226.9	91.3	88.0	8.7
1984	3,268.9	377.4	2,891.5	2,595.2	2,501.1	77.0	17.1	296.3	89.8	86.5	10.2
1985	3,496.7	417.3	3,079.3	2,825.7	2,717.6	89.4	18.8	253.6	91.8	88.3	8.2
1986	3,696.0	437.2	3,258.8	3,012.4	2,896.7	94.5	21.1	246.5	92.4	88.9	7.6
1987	3,924.4	489.1	3,435.3	3,211.9	3,097.0	91.7	23.2	223.4	93.5	90.2	6.5
1988	4,231.2	504.9	3,726.3	3,469.7	3,350.1	94.0	25.6	256.6	93.1	89.9	6.9
1989	4,557.5	566.1	3,991.4	3,726.4	3,594.5	103.9	28.0	265.0	93.4	90.1	6.6
1990	4,846.7	592.7	4,254.0	3,977.3	3,835.5	111.3	30.6	276.7	93.5	90.2	6.5
1991	5,031.5	586.6	4,444.9	4,131.7	3,980.1	115.0	36.7	313.2	93.0	89.5	7.0
1992	5,347.3	610.5	4,736.7	4,388.7	4,236.9	111.3	40.5	348.1	92.7	89.4	7.3
1993	5,568.1	646.5	4,921.6	4,636.2	4,483.6	107.0	45.6	285.4	94.2	91.1	5.8
1994	5,874.8	690.5	5,184.3	4,913.6	4,750.8	113.0	49.8	270.7	94.8	91.6	5.2
1995	6,200.9	743.9	5,457.0	5,170.8	4,987.3	130.6	52.9	286.3	94.8	91.4	5.2
1996	6,591.6	832.0	5,759.6	5,478.5	5,273.6	147.3	57.6	281.1	95.1	91.6	4.9
1997	7,000.7	926.2	6,074.6	5,794.2	5,570.6	159.7	63.9	280.4	95.4	91.7	4.6
1998	7,525.4	1,026.4	6,498.9	6,157.5	5,918.5	169.5	69.5	341.5	94.7	91.1	5.3
1999	7,910.8	1,107.5	6,803.3	6,595.5	6,342.8	176.5	76.2	207.8	96.9	93.2	3.1
2000	8,559.4	1,232.3	7,327.2	7,114.1	6,830.4	200.3	83.4	213.1	97.1	93.2	2.9
2001	8,883.3	1,234.8	7,648.5	7,443.5	7,148.8	203.7	91.0	204.9	97.3	93.5	2.7
2002	9,060.1	1,050.4	8,009.7	7,727.5	7,439.2	191.3	97.0	282.2	96.5	92.9	3.5
2003	9,378.1	1,000.3	8,377.8	8,088.1	7,804.1	182.7	101.3	289.6	96.5	93.2	3.5
2004	9,937.2	1,047.8	8,889.4	8,571.2	8,270.6	190.3	110.3	318.2	96.4	93.0	3.6
2005	10,485.9	1,208.6	9,277.3	9,134.1	8,803.5	210.8	119.8	143.2	98.5	94.9	1.5
2006	11,268.1	1,352.4	9,915.7	9,659.1	9,301.0	230.1	128.0	256.6	97.4	93.8	2.6
2007	11,912.3	1,488.7	10,423.6	10,174.9	9,772.3	260.9	141.7	248.7	97.6	93.8	2.4
2008	12,460.2	1,435.7	11,024.5	10,432.2	10,035.5	245.6	151.0	592.3	94.6	91.0	5.4
2009	11,867.0	1,144.6	10,722.4	10,214.3	9,845.9	217.1	151.3	508.2	95.3	91.8	4.7
2010	12,321.9	1,194.8	11,127.1	10,560.4	10,215.7	183.8	160.9	566.7	94.9	91.8	5.1
2011	12,947.3	1,398.0	11,549.3	11,059.9	10,729.0	168.0	162.8	489.4	95.8	92.9	4.2
2012 p	13,405.9	1,474.7	11,931.2	11,461.2	11,120.9	172.2	168.1	470.1	96.1	93.2	3.9
2009: I	11,927.5	1,199.7	10,727.8	10,138.1	9,768.4	221.2	148.5	589.8	94.5	91.1	5.5
II	11,879.3	1,121.3	10,758.1	10,135.4	9,763.9	221.5	150.1	622.7	94.2	90.8	5.8
III	11,794.9	1,125.6	10,669.2	10,259.6	9,888.8	219.6	151.2	409.6	96.2	92.7	3.8
IV	11,866.2	1,131.7	10,734.6	10,323.9	9,962.5	206.1	155.3	410.6	96.2	92.8	3.8
2010: I	12,089.8	1,156.9	10,932.9	10,428.2	10,069.1	199.0	160.0	504.8	95.4	92.1	4.6
II	12,290.6	1,173.0	11,117.5	10,498.4	10,148.3	189.7	160.4	619.1	94.4	91.3	5.6
III	12,397.2	1,211.8	11,185.4	10,581.5	10,243.6	176.0	161.9	603.8	94.6	91.6	5.4
IV	12,509.9	1,237.5	11,272.4	10,733.3	10,401.9	170.2	161.1	539.1	95.2	92.3	4.8
2011: I	12,856.5	1,372.5	11,484.1	10,898.1	10,566.3	170.1	161.7	585.9	94.9	92.0	5.1
II	12,938.9	1,396.6	11,542.3	11,015.1	10,684.9	167.8	162.4	527.2	95.4	92.6	4.6
III	12,976.3	1,403.8	11,572.6	11,120.9	10,791.2	167.3	162.4	451.6	96.1	93.2	3.9
IV	13,017.4	1,419.1	11,598.3	11,205.6	10,873.8	167.0	164.8	392.7	96.6	93.8	3.4
2012: I	13,227.1	1,450.8	11,776.4	11,348.7	11,007.2	175.4	166.1	427.7	96.4	93.5	3.6
II	13,327.0	1,465.2	11,861.8	11,406.1	11,067.2	171.2	167.7	455.7	96.2	93.3	3.8
III	13,406.2	1,476.5	11,929.7	11,494.7	11,154.4	171.6	168.6	435.1	96.4	93.5	3.6
IV p	13,663.2	1,506.2	12,157.0	11,595.1	11,254.6	170.7	169.8	561.9	95.4	92.6	4.6

[1] Consists of nonmortgage interest paid by households.
[2] Percents based on data in millions of dollars.

Source: Department of Commerce (Bureau of Economic Analysis).

TABLE B-31. Total and per capita disposable personal income and personal consumption expenditures, and per capita gross domestic product, in current and real dollars, 1964–2012

[Quarterly data at seasonally adjusted annual rates, except as noted]

| Year or quarter | Disposable personal income | | | | Personal consumption expenditures | | | | Gross domestic product per capita (dollars) | | Population (thousands) [1] |
| | Total (billions of dollars) | | Per capita (dollars) | | Total (billions of dollars) | | Per capita (dollars) | | | | |
	Current dollars	Chained (2005) dollars	Current dollars	Chained (2005) dollars	Current dollars	Chained (2005) dollars	Current dollars	Chained (2005) dollars	Current dollars	Chained (2005) dollars	
1964	462.3	2,367.6	2,408	12,336	411.5	2,107.5	2,144	10,980	3,458	17,660	191,927
1965	497.8	2,513.6	2,562	12,933	443.8	2,240.8	2,284	11,530	3,700	18,560	194,347
1966	537.4	2,646.1	2,733	13,460	480.9	2,367.9	2,446	12,044	4,007	19,543	196,599
1967	575.1	2,762.2	2,894	13,898	507.8	2,438.8	2,555	12,271	4,188	19,819	198,752
1968	624.7	2,887.9	3,112	14,386	558.0	2,579.6	2,780	12,850	4,532	20,573	200,745
1969	673.8	2,979.9	3,324	14,699	605.1	2,676.2	2,985	13,200	4,856	21,003	202,736
1970	735.5	3,107.3	3,586	15,151	648.3	2,738.9	3,161	13,355	5,063	20,802	205,089
1971	801.4	3,247.7	3,859	15,637	701.6	2,843.3	3,378	13,690	5,425	21,231	207,692
1972	869.0	3,405.2	4,140	16,221	770.2	3,018.1	3,669	14,377	5,897	22,121	209,924
1973	978.1	3,636.6	4,615	17,159	852.0	3,167.7	4,020	14,946	6,522	23,180	211,939
1974	1,071.7	3,608.6	5,010	16,871	932.9	3,141.4	4,362	14,686	7,010	22,841	213,898
1975	1,187.3	3,689.5	5,497	17,083	1,033.8	3,212.6	4,786	14,874	7,583	22,573	215,981
1976	1,302.3	3,836.6	5,972	17,592	1,151.3	3,391.5	5,279	15,551	8,366	23,555	218,086
1977	1,435.0	3,969.0	6,514	18,017	1,277.8	3,534.3	5,801	16,044	9,216	24,391	220,289
1978	1,607.3	4,154.6	7,220	18,662	1,427.6	3,690.1	6,413	16,575	10,303	25,481	222,629
1979	1,790.9	4,251.9	7,956	18,888	1,591.2	3,777.8	7,069	16,782	11,382	25,988	225,106
1980	2,002.7	4,293.7	8,794	18,855	1,755.8	3,764.5	7,710	16,531	12,243	25,618	227,726
1981	2,237.1	4,407.9	9,726	19,164	1,939.5	3,821.6	8,432	16,615	13,594	26,008	230,008
1982	2,412.7	4,504.4	10,390	19,397	2,075.5	3,874.9	8,938	16,686	14,009	25,260	232,218
1983	2,599.8	4,653.5	11,095	19,859	2,288.6	4,096.4	9,766	17,481	15,084	26,163	234,333
1984	2,891.5	4,986.9	12,232	21,096	2,501.1	4,313.6	10,580	18,247	16,629	27,799	236,394
1985	3,079.3	5,142.4	12,911	21,561	2,717.6	4,538.3	11,394	19,028	17,683	28,693	238,506
1986	3,258.8	5,312.6	13,540	22,073	2,896.7	4,722.4	12,036	19,621	18,531	29,418	240,683
1987	3,435.3	5,399.9	14,146	22,236	3,097.0	4,868.0	12,753	20,046	19,504	30,090	242,843
1988	3,726.3	5,633.0	15,206	22,986	3,350.1	5,064.3	13,670	20,665	20,813	31,043	245,061
1989	3,991.4	5,782.5	16,134	23,374	3,594.5	5,207.5	14,530	21,050	22,160	31,850	247,387
1990	4,254.0	5,893.6	17,004	23,557	3,835.5	5,313.7	15,331	21,240	23,185	32,085	250,181
1991	4,444.9	5,943.2	17,532	23,442	3,980.1	5,321.7	15,699	20,991	23,635	31,587	253,530
1992	4,736.7	6,152.5	18,436	23,947	4,236.9	5,503.2	16,491	21,420	24,686	32,228	256,922
1993	4,921.6	6,255.3	18,909	24,033	4,483.6	5,698.6	17,226	21,894	25,616	32,719	260,282
1994	5,184.3	6,456.0	19,678	24,505	4,750.8	5,916.2	18,033	22,456	26,893	33,642	263,455
1995	5,457.0	6,648.6	20,470	24,939	4,987.3	6,076.2	18,708	22,793	27,813	34,082	266,588
1996	5,759.6	6,867.8	21,355	25,463	5,273.6	6,288.3	19,553	23,315	29,062	34,948	269,714
1997	6,074.6	7,110.4	22,255	26,049	5,570.6	6,520.4	20,408	23,888	30,526	36,071	272,958
1998	6,498.9	7,535.4	23,534	27,287	5,918.5	6,862.3	21,432	24,850	31,843	37,207	276,154
1999	6,803.3	7,763.1	24,356	27,792	6,342.8	7,237.6	22,707	25,911	33,486	38,559	279,328
2000	7,327.2	8,157.8	25,946	28,888	6,830.4	7,604.6	24,187	26,929	35,239	39,718	282,398
2001	7,648.5	8,356.2	26,816	29,297	7,148.8	7,810.3	25,064	27,383	36,063	39,749	285,225
2002	8,009.7	8,633.2	27,816	29,981	7,439.2	8,018.3	25,835	27,846	36,958	40,087	287,955
2003	8,377.8	8,850.5	28,827	30,453	7,804.1	8,244.5	26,853	28,368	38,339	40,727	290,626
2004	8,889.4	9,152.9	30,312	31,211	8,270.6	8,515.8	28,202	29,038	40,419	41,761	293,262
2005	9,277.3	9,277.3	31,343	31,343	8,803.5	8,803.5	29,742	29,742	42,646	42,646	295,993
2006	9,915.7	9,652.8	33,183	32,303	9,301.0	9,054.5	31,126	30,301	44,767	43,366	298,818
2007	10,423.6	9,880.3	34,532	32,749	9,772.3	9,262.9	32,391	30,703	46,499	43,774	301,696
2008	11,024.5	10,119.5	36,200	33,229	10,035.5	9,211.7	32,953	30,248	46,928	43,219	304,543
2009	10,722.4	9,836.7	34,899	32,016	9,845.9	9,032.6	32,046	29,399	45,481	41,524	307,240
2010	11,127.1	10,016.5	35,920	32,335	10,215.7	9,196.2	32,978	29,686	46,805	42,169	309,776
2011	11,549.3	10,149.7	37,013	32,527	10,729.0	9,428.8	34,384	30,217	48,314	42,620	312,036
2012 p	11,931.2	10,304.8	37,964	32,789	11,120.9	9,604.9	35,385	30,562	49,897	43,245	314,278
2009: I	10,727.8	9,927.3	35,031	32,417	9,768.4	9,039.5	31,898	29,518	45,466	41,507	306,237
II	10,758.1	9,915.6	35,058	32,313	9,763.9	8,999.3	31,818	29,327	45,249	41,389	306,866
III	10,669.2	9,760.2	34,689	31,733	9,888.8	9,046.2	32,151	29,412	45,362	41,443	307,573
IV	10,734.6	9,746.4	34,820	31,615	9,962.5	9,045.4	32,316	29,341	45,846	41,757	308,285
2010: I	10,932.9	9,881.6	35,393	31,990	10,069.1	9,100.8	32,597	29,462	46,197	41,915	308,900
II	11,117.5	10,034.1	35,926	32,425	10,148.3	9,159.4	32,794	29,598	46,577	42,072	309,457
III	11,185.4	10,063.3	36,074	32,455	10,243.6	9,216.0	33,037	29,723	47,009	42,260	310,067
IV	11,272.4	10,087.4	36,283	32,469	10,401.9	9,308.5	33,481	29,962	47,431	42,427	310,679
2011: I	11,484.1	10,195.7	36,903	32,763	10,566.3	9,380.9	33,954	30,145	47,607	42,365	311,192
II	11,542.3	10,157.8	37,028	32,587	10,684.9	9,403.2	34,277	30,166	48,132	42,553	311,718
III	11,572.6	10,125.6	37,054	32,421	10,791.2	9,441.9	34,552	30,232	48,550	42,607	312,319
IV	11,598.3	10,121.5	37,065	32,346	10,873.8	9,489.3	34,750	30,325	48,962	42,954	312,917
2012: I	11,776.4	10,213.9	37,573	32,588	11,007.2	9,546.8	35,119	30,460	49,384	43,093	313,425
II	11,861.8	10,270.6	37,781	32,713	11,067.2	9,582.5	35,250	30,522	49,642	43,154	313,960
III	11,929.7	10,288.8	37,925	32,708	11,154.4	9,620.1	35,460	30,582	50,263	43,401	314,564
IV p	12,157.0	10,445.4	38,574	33,143	11,254.6	9,670.0	35,711	30,683	50,295	43,333	315,162

[1] Population of the United States including Armed Forces overseas. Annual data are averages of quarterly data. Quarterly data are averages for the period.

Source: Department of Commerce (Bureau of Economic Analysis and Bureau of the Census).

TABLE B–32. Gross saving and investment, 1964–2012

[Billions of dollars, except as noted; quarterly data at seasonally adjusted annual rates]

Year or quarter	Total gross saving	Gross saving — Net saving — Total net saving	Net private saving — Total	Personal saving	Undistributed corporate profits [1]	Wage accruals less disbursements	Net government saving — Total	Federal	State and local	Consumption of fixed capital — Total	Private	Government
1964	143.4	77.0	69.7	40.5	29.2	0.0	7.3	0.9	6.4	66.4	48.3	18.1
1965	158.5	87.7	78.0	42.7	35.3	.0	9.8	3.2	6.5	70.7	51.9	18.9
1966	168.7	92.3	82.3	44.3	38.0	.0	10.0	2.3	7.8	76.5	56.5	20.0
1967	170.6	87.6	89.9	54.2	35.8	.0	−2.3	−9.3	7.0	82.9	61.6	21.4
1968	182.0	91.6	86.6	52.5	34.1	.0	5.1	−2.4	7.5	90.4	67.4	23.0
1969	198.4	99.3	82.7	52.5	30.3	.0	16.5	8.6	8.0	99.2	74.5	24.7
1970	192.8	84.5	92.9	69.4	23.4	.0	−8.4	−15.5	7.1	108.3	81.7	26.6
1971	209.2	91.5	113.7	80.4	32.9	.4	−22.2	−28.7	6.5	117.8	89.5	28.2
1972	237.3	110.1	119.4	77.5	42.2	−.3	−9.3	−24.9	15.6	127.2	97.7	29.4
1973	292.2	151.4	147.5	102.9	44.6	.0	3.9	−11.8	15.7	140.8	109.5	31.3
1974	301.8	138.1	143.3	114.2	29.1	.0	−5.2	−14.5	9.3	163.7	127.8	35.9
1975	296.9	106.5	174.6	125.9	48.7	.0	−68.2	−70.6	2.5	190.4	150.4	39.9
1976	342.0	133.8	180.1	122.8	57.3	.0	−46.3	−53.7	7.4	208.2	165.5	42.6
1977	396.7	164.9	197.9	125.3	72.6	.0	−33.0	−46.1	13.1	231.8	186.1	45.6
1978	476.3	214.9	225.2	142.4	82.8	.0	−10.2	−28.9	18.7	261.4	212.0	49.5
1979	533.2	234.3	235.3	157.5	77.8	.0	−1.0	−14.0	13.0	298.9	244.5	54.4
1980	542.7	198.6	246.5	196.3	50.2	.0	−47.8	−56.6	8.8	344.1	282.3	61.8
1981	646.1	252.7	301.9	236.7	65.2	.0	−49.2	−56.8	7.6	393.3	323.2	70.1
1982	621.5	187.9	325.4	263.9	61.5	.0	−137.5	−135.3	−2.2	433.5	356.4	77.1
1983	602.4	151.3	322.6	226.9	95.7	.0	−171.4	−176.2	4.9	451.1	369.5	81.6
1984	753.4	279.0	426.5	296.3	130.3	.0	−147.5	−171.5	23.9	474.3	387.5	86.9
1985	738.4	232.9	389.2	253.6	135.6	.0	−156.3	−178.6	22.4	505.4	412.8	92.7
1986	709.3	170.8	344.7	246.5	98.3	.0	−173.9	−194.6	20.7	538.5	439.1	99.4
1987	782.3	211.2	348.5	223.4	125.1	.0	−137.4	−149.3	12.0	571.1	464.5	106.6
1988	901.5	290.5	411.7	256.6	155.1	.0	−121.2	−138.4	17.2	611.0	497.1	113.9
1989	924.1	272.7	386.5	265.0	121.5	.0	−113.8	−133.9	20.1	651.5	529.6	121.8
1990	917.6	226.4	396.7	276.7	120.0	.0	−170.3	−176.4	6.2	691.2	560.4	130.8
1991	951.3	227.0	451.2	313.2	138.0	.0	−224.2	−218.4	−5.8	724.4	585.4	138.9
1992	932.3	187.9	491.8	348.1	159.5	−15.8	−303.9	−302.5	−1.4	744.4	599.9	144.5
1993	958.4	180.4	461.6	285.4	169.7	6.4	−281.2	−280.2	−.9	778.0	626.4	151.6
1994	1,094.7	275.5	487.7	270.7	199.4	17.6	−212.2	−220.4	8.2	819.2	661.0	158.2
1995	1,219.0	349.6	546.6	286.3	243.9	16.4	−197.0	−206.2	9.2	869.5	704.6	164.8
1996	1,344.4	431.8	557.1	281.1	272.3	3.6	−125.3	−148.2	23.0	912.5	743.4	169.2
1997	1,525.7	561.9	585.7	280.4	308.2	−2.9	−23.8	−60.1	36.3	963.8	789.7	174.1
1998	1,654.4	633.9	553.4	341.5	212.6	−.7	80.5	33.6	46.9	1,020.5	841.6	179.0
1999	1,708.0	613.6	473.0	207.8	260.1	5.2	140.6	98.8	41.8	1,094.4	907.2	187.2
2000	1,800.1	615.8	389.4	213.1	176.3	.0	226.5	185.2	41.3	1,184.3	986.8	197.5
2001	1,695.7	439.4	414.9	204.9	210.0	.0	24.6	40.5	−15.9	1,256.2	1,051.6	204.6
2002	1,560.9	255.9	562.8	282.2	280.6	.0	−306.9	−252.8	−54.1	1,305.0	1,094.0	210.9
2003	1,552.6	198.6	613.8	289.6	309.2	15.0	−415.2	−376.4	−38.8	1,354.1	1,135.9	218.1
2004	1,738.7	305.9	693.7	318.2	390.5	−15.0	−387.8	−379.5	−8.4	1,432.8	1,200.9	231.9
2005	1,918.8	377.5	634.5	143.2	486.4	5.0	−257.1	−283.0	25.9	1,541.4	1,290.8	250.6
2006	2,196.1	535.4	688.1	256.6	430.3	1.3	−152.7	−203.8	51.0	1,660.7	1,391.4	269.3
2007	2,047.7	280.2	513.2	248.7	270.7	−6.3	−233.0	−245.2	12.2	1,767.5	1,476.2	291.3
2008	1,908.2	54.1	739.8	592.3	152.5	−5.0	−685.7	−613.5	−72.2	1,854.1	1,542.9	311.2
2009	1,555.8	−310.5	1,032.0	508.2	518.8	5.0	−1,342.6	−1,229.3	−113.2	1,866.3	1,542.8	323.5
2010	1,770.7	−102.8	1,294.9	566.7	728.2	.0	−1,397.7	−1,308.0	−89.7	1,873.4	1,539.9	333.5
2011	1,837.5	−99.3	1,240.1	489.4	750.7	.0	−1,339.4	−1,237.4	−102.0	1,936.8	1,587.4	349.4
2012 P	....	....	....	470.1	....	.0	....	....	....	2,011.8	1,647.8	363.9
2009: I	1,698.9	−186.6	940.8	589.8	331.1	20.0	−1,127.4	−1,011.8	−115.6	1,885.5	1,562.9	322.5
II	1,521.3	−346.4	1,077.0	622.7	454.3	.0	−1,423.4	−1,313.5	−109.9	1,867.7	1,544.7	323.0
III	1,435.8	−418.7	1,025.5	409.6	615.9	.0	−1,444.1	−1,318.6	−125.5	1,854.4	1,531.1	323.3
IV	1,567.1	−290.5	1,084.8	410.6	674.1	.0	−1,375.3	−1,273.5	−101.8	1,857.6	1,532.3	325.3
2010: I	1,683.7	−179.4	1,246.9	504.8	742.1	.0	−1,426.3	−1,315.2	−111.1	1,863.1	1,534.5	328.6
II	1,748.1	−119.5	1,308.5	619.1	689.4	.0	−1,427.9	−1,319.5	−108.4	1,867.5	1,535.4	332.1
III	1,847.9	−27.6	1,347.8	603.8	744.0	.0	−1,375.4	−1,303.1	−72.4	1,875.5	1,540.5	335.0
IV	1,803.0	−84.6	1,276.4	539.1	737.3	.0	−1,361.0	−1,294.4	−66.7	1,887.7	1,549.3	338.4
2011: I	1,811.2	−93.1	1,232.9	585.9	647.0	.0	−1,326.0	−1,227.3	−98.7	1,904.3	1,561.7	342.6
II	1,800.7	−126.7	1,255.6	527.2	728.4	.0	−1,382.3	−1,307.7	−74.6	1,927.4	1,580.4	347.1
III	1,813.1	−135.8	1,214.2	451.6	762.6	.0	−1,350.0	−1,232.0	−118.0	1,948.9	1,596.5	352.4
IV	1,925.0	−41.6	1,257.5	392.7	864.9	.0	−1,299.1	−1,182.6	−116.5	1,966.6	1,611.0	355.5
2012: I	1,945.6	−39.3	1,147.1	427.7	719.4	.0	−1,186.4	−1,058.7	−127.6	1,984.9	1,625.9	359.0
II	1,952.4	−52.3	1,186.7	455.7	731.0	.0	−1,239.0	−1,115.4	−123.7	2,004.8	1,642.0	362.8
III	1,982.5	−37.3	1,189.9	435.1	754.8	.0	−1,227.2	−1,087.2	−140.0	2,019.8	1,654.2	365.6
IV P	....	....	....	561.9	....	.0	....	....	....	2,037.6	1,669.2	368.4

[1] With inventory valuation and capital consumption adjustments.

See next page for continuation of table.

Year or quarter	Gross domestic investment, capital account transactions, and net lending, NIPA [2]							Addenda:						
	Gross domestic investment				Capital account transactions	Net lending or net borrowing (−), NIPA [2,5]	Statistical discrepancy	Gross private saving	Gross government saving			Net domestic investment	Gross saving as a percent of gross national income	Net saving as a percent of gross national income
	Total	Total	Gross private domestic investment	Gross government investment [3]					Total	Federal	State and local			
1964	144.2	136.7	102.1	34.6	....	7.5	0.8	118.0	25.4	13.2	12.1	70.3	21.5	11.5
1965	160.0	153.8	118.2	35.6	....	6.2	1.5	129.8	28.6	15.9	12.8	83.1	21.9	12.1
1966	174.9	171.1	131.3	39.8	....	3.8	6.2	138.7	30.0	15.3	14.6	94.6	21.5	11.7
1967	175.1	171.6	128.6	43.0	....	3.5	4.5	151.5	19.1	4.5	14.5	88.6	20.5	10.5
1968	186.4	184.8	141.2	43.6	....	1.5	4.3	154.0	28.0	12.2	15.8	94.4	20.0	10.1
1969	201.3	199.7	156.4	43.3	0.0	1.6	2.9	157.2	41.2	23.9	17.3	100.5	20.1	10.0
1970	199.7	196.0	152.4	43.6	.0	3.7	6.9	174.6	18.2	.6	17.7	87.6	18.6	8.1
1971	220.2	219.9	178.2	41.8	.0	.3	11.0	203.2	6.0	−12.2	18.3	102.2	18.6	8.1
1972	246.2	250.2	207.6	42.6	.0	−4.1	8.9	217.1	20.2	−8.3	28.5	123.1	19.2	8.9
1973	300.2	291.3	244.5	46.8	.0	8.8	8.0	257.0	35.2	5.2	30.0	150.6	21.1	10.9
1974	311.6	305.7	249.4	56.3	.0	5.9	9.8	271.1	30.7	3.7	27.0	142.0	20.1	9.2
1975	313.2	293.3	230.2	63.1	.1	19.8	16.3	325.1	−28.2	−50.9	22.7	102.9	18.2	6.5
1976	365.4	358.4	292.0	66.4	.1	7.0	23.5	345.6	−3.7	−32.3	28.6	150.2	18.8	7.4
1977	417.9	428.8	361.3	67.5	.1	−11.0	21.2	384.1	12.6	−23.1	35.7	197.1	19.6	8.1
1978	502.4	515.0	438.0	77.1	.1	−12.7	26.1	437.1	39.2	−3.9	43.2	253.6	20.8	9.4
1979	580.2	581.4	492.9	88.5	.1	−1.3	47.0	479.7	53.5	13.0	40.5	282.4	20.9	9.2
1980	588.0	579.5	479.3	100.3	.1	8.4	45.3	528.8	14.0	−26.6	40.6	235.4	19.5	7.2
1981	682.6	679.3	572.4	106.9	.1	3.2	36.6	625.2	20.9	−23.0	43.8	285.9	20.7	8.1
1982	626.2	629.5	517.2	112.3	.1	−3.4	4.8	681.9	−60.4	−97.7	37.3	196.0	18.9	5.7
1983	652.1	687.2	564.3	122.9	.1	−35.2	49.7	692.2	−89.8	−135.6	45.8	236.0	17.1	4.3
1984	784.9	875.0	735.6	139.4	.1	−90.2	31.5	814.0	−60.6	−126.9	66.3	400.6	19.1	7.1
1985	780.7	895.0	736.2	158.8	.1	−114.5	42.3	802.0	−63.6	−130.6	67.0	389.5	17.6	5.5
1986	777.1	919.7	746.5	173.2	.1	−142.8	67.7	783.8	−74.5	−143.0	68.6	381.3	16.1	3.9
1987	815.1	969.2	785.0	184.3	.1	−154.2	32.9	813.0	−30.8	−94.2	63.4	398.1	16.6	4.5
1988	892.0	1,007.7	821.6	186.1	.1	−115.9	−9.5	908.8	−7.3	−79.3	72.0	396.7	17.6	5.7
1989	980.3	1,072.6	874.9	197.7	.3	−92.7	56.1	916.1	8.0	−70.6	78.7	421.2	17.0	5.0
1990	1,001.8	1,076.7	861.0	215.7	7.4	−82.3	84.2	957.1	−39.5	−108.7	69.2	385.5	16.0	3.9
1991	1,031.0	1,023.2	802.9	220.3	5.3	2.6	79.7	1,036.6	−85.3	−146.4	61.1	298.8	16.0	3.8
1992	1,042.3	1,087.9	864.8	223.1	−1.3	−44.3	110.0	1,091.7	−159.4	−227.9	68.5	343.5	14.9	3.0
1993	1,094.2	1,172.8	953.3	219.4	.9	−79.4	135.8	1,088.0	−129.5	−202.4	72.9	394.8	14.6	2.7
1994	1,203.5	1,318.2	1,097.3	220.9	1.3	−116.0	108.8	1,148.6	−53.9	−140.3	86.4	499.0	15.6	3.9
1995	1,271.6	1,376.6	1,144.0	232.6	.4	−105.5	52.5	1,251.2	−32.2	−124.5	92.3	507.2	16.5	4.7
1996	1,370.3	1,484.4	1,240.2	244.2	.2	−114.4	25.9	1,300.5	43.9	−66.3	110.2	571.9	17.1	5.5
1997	1,511.7	1,641.0	1,388.7	252.4	.5	−129.8	−14.0	1,375.4	150.3	22.4	127.9	677.2	18.2	6.7
1998	1,569.1	1,773.6	1,510.8	262.9	.2	−204.8	−85.3	1,394.9	259.5	116.4	143.1	753.1	18.6	7.1
1999	1,637.0	1,928.9	1,641.5	287.4	4.5	−296.4	−71.1	1,380.3	327.8	183.9	143.9	834.5	18.1	6.5
2000	1,666.2	2,076.5	1,772.2	304.3	.3	−410.7	−134.0	1,376.2	424.0	273.0	151.0	892.2	17.8	6.1
2001	1,592.3	1,984.0	1,661.9	322.0	−12.9	−378.7	−103.4	1,466.5	229.2	129.1	100.1	727.7	16.2	4.2
2002	1,538.9	1,990.4	1,647.0	343.5	.5	−452.1	−22.1	1,656.8	−95.9	−163.6	67.7	685.4	14.6	2.4
2003	1,569.3	2,085.4	1,729.7	355.8	2.1	−518.2	16.7	1,749.7	−197.1	−285.5	88.4	731.4	13.9	1.8
2004	1,716.3	2,340.9	1,968.6	372.4	−2.8	−621.8	−22.3	1,894.6	−155.9	−284.6	128.7	908.2	14.5	2.6
2005	1,823.8	2,564.3	2,172.3	392.0	−12.9	−727.7	−95.1	1,925.4	−6.5	−182.6	176.1	1,022.9	15.0	2.9
2006	1,953.8	2,752.2	2,327.1	425.1	2.1	−800.5	−242.3	2,079.5	116.5	−97.2	213.8	1,091.5	16.0	3.9
2007	2,035.7	2,751.7	2,295.2	456.5	−.1	−715.9	−12.0	1,989.4	58.3	−132.6	190.9	984.2	14.5	2.0
2008	1,905.8	2,584.8	2,087.6	497.2	−5.4	−673.6	−2.4	2,282.8	−374.6	−493.5	119.0	730.7	13.2	.4
2009	1,674.1	2,056.2	1,549.3	506.9	.6	−382.7	118.3	2,574.8	−1,019.0	−1,104.6	85.5	189.9	11.1	−2.2
2010	1,794.0	2,242.9	1,737.3	505.5	.7	−449.5	23.3	2,834.8	−1,064.1	−1,177.8	113.6	369.4	12.1	−.7
2011	1,869.4	2,335.1	1,854.9	480.2	1.7	−467.4	31.9	2,827.4	−990.0	−1,100.4	110.4	398.4	12.0	−.6
2012 p	....	2,531.1	2,058.6	472.5	....	....	....	....	....	....	....	519.3	....	....
2009: I	1,754.4	2,149.7	1,645.8	503.9	.4	−395.8	55.5	2,503.8	−804.9	−888.7	83.8	264.3	12.1	−1.3
II	1,653.8	2,007.8	1,495.3	512.5	.5	−354.5	132.5	2,621.7	−1,100.4	−1,189.4	89.0	140.1	11.0	−2.5
III	1,594.4	1,975.5	1,465.6	509.9	.6	−381.6	158.6	2,556.6	−1,120.8	−1,193.4	72.6	121.0	10.3	−3.0
IV	1,693.6	2,091.8	1,590.4	501.4	.7	−398.9	126.5	2,617.1	−1,050.0	−1,146.8	96.8	234.2	11.0	−2.0
2010: I	1,699.3	2,152.0	1,660.4	491.6	.5	−453.2	15.6	2,781.4	−1,097.7	−1,187.1	89.4	288.9	11.7	−1.2
II	1,787.8	2,235.2	1,724.7	510.5	.6	−447.9	39.7	2,843.9	−1,095.8	−1,189.9	94.1	367.6	12.0	−.8
III	1,844.1	2,308.7	1,793.3	515.4	1.1	−465.7	−3.8	2,888.3	−1,040.4	−1,172.3	131.9	433.2	12.5	−.2
IV	1,844.9	2,275.6	1,770.9	504.7	.5	−431.3	41.8	2,825.7	−1,022.6	−1,161.8	139.2	387.9	12.1	−.6
2011: I	1,760.8	2,238.5	1,755.9	482.6	.6	−478.3	−50.4	2,794.6	−983.4	−1,092.6	109.3	334.2	12.0	−.6
II	1,825.8	2,300.0	1,819.0	480.9	3.8	−477.9	25.1	2,836.0	−1,035.3	−1,171.5	136.2	372.5	11.8	−.8
III	1,895.6	2,330.5	1,853.8	476.8	1.6	−436.6	82.5	2,810.7	−997.7	−1,093.5	95.9	381.7	11.8	−.9
IV	1,995.3	2,471.6	1,991.1	480.5	.7	−477.0	70.3	2,868.5	−943.6	−1,043.8	100.3	505.0	12.4	−.3
2012: I	1,946.7	2,499.9	2,032.2	467.6	.5	−553.6	1.1	2,773.0	−827.4	−919.0	91.6	515.0	12.4	−.3
II	2,030.1	2,515.1	2,041.7	473.4	.5	−485.4	77.7	2,828.7	−876.3	−974.3	98.1	510.3	12.4	−.3
III	2,121.0	2,554.7	2,080.1	474.5	.5	−434.2	138.5	2,844.1	−861.6	−945.2	83.6	534.9	12.5	−.2
IV p	....	2,554.6	2,080.3	474.3	....	....	....	....	....	....	....	517.1	....	....

[2] National income and product accounts (NIPA).

[3] For details on government investment, see Table B–20.

[4] Consists of capital transfers and the acquisition and disposal of nonproduced nonfinancial assets.

[5] Prior to 1982, equals the balance on current account, NIPA (see Table B–24).

Source: Department of Commerce (Bureau of Economic Analysis).

TABLE B–33. Median money income (in 2011 dollars) and poverty status of families and people, by race, 2002–2011

Race, Hispanic origin, and year	Families[1] Number (millions)	Families[1] Median money income (in 2011 dollars)[2]	Total Below poverty level Number (millions)	Total Below poverty level Percent	Female householder, no husband present Number (millions)	Female householder, no husband present Percent	People below poverty level Number (millions)	People below poverty level Percent	Median money income (2011 dollars) Males All people	Males Year-round full-time workers	Females All people	Females Year-round full-time workers
TOTAL (all races)[3]												
2002	75.6	$64,610	7.2	9.6	3.6	26.5	34.6	12.1	$36,553	$50,641	$21,018	$38,718
2003	76.2	64,421	7.6	10.0	3.9	28.0	35.9	12.5	36,602	50,753	21,106	38,708
2004[4]	76.9	64,370	7.8	10.2	4.0	28.3	37.0	12.7	36,335	49,613	21,036	38,241
2005	77.4	64,740	7.7	9.9	4.0	28.7	37.0	12.6	36,031	48,604	21,401	38,313
2006	78.5	65,153	7.7	9.8	4.1	28.3	36.5	12.3	35,992	50,151	22,326	39,030
2007	77.9	66,554	7.6	9.8	4.1	28.3	37.3	12.5	36,009	50,141	22,695	39,231
2008	78.9	64,264	8.1	10.3	4.2	28.7	39.8	13.2	34,640	49,910	21,798	38,324
2009[5]	78.9	63,007	8.8	11.1	4.4	29.9	43.6	14.3	33,747	51,552	21,975	39,043
2010[6]	79.6	62,136	9.4	11.8	4.8	31.7	46.3	15.1	33,221	51,733	21,430	39,651
2011	80.5	60,974	9.5	11.8	4.9	31.2	46.2	15.0	32,986	50,316	21,102	38,685
WHITE, non-Hispanic[7]												
2002	53.9	72,849	3.2	6.0	1.4	19.4	15.6	8.0	40,049	56,450	21,740	40,440
2003	54.0	73,296	3.3	6.1	1.5	20.4	15.9	8.2	39,537	56,612	22,380	41,623
2004[4]	54.3	72,626	3.5	6.5	1.5	20.8	16.9	8.7	40,100	55,941	21,951	41,583
2005	54.3	72,760	3.3	6.1	1.5	21.5	16.2	8.3	40,720	55,437	22,409	41,241
2006	54.7	73,474	3.4	6.2	1.6	22.0	16.0	8.2	40,787	56,270	23,121	41,146
2007	53.9	75,863	3.2	5.9	1.5	20.7	16.0	8.2	40,540	55,826	23,525	41,955
2008	54.5	73,195	3.4	6.2	1.5	20.7	17.0	8.6	39,077	54,680	22,719	41,230
2009[5]	54.5	70,612	3.8	7.0	1.7	23.3	18.5	9.4	38,572	55,017	23,005	42,221
2010[6]	53.8	71,076	3.9	7.2	1.7	24.1	19.3	9.9	38,326	56,377	22,400	42,636
2011	54.2	69,829	4.0	7.3	1.8	23.4	19.2	9.8	38,148	55,763	22,226	41,373
BLACK[7]												
2002	8.9	41,913	1.9	21.5	1.4	35.8	8.6	24.1	26,955	39,921	20,914	34,536
2003	8.9	42,029	2.0	22.3	1.5	36.9	8.8	24.4	26,886	40,880	20,277	33,778
2004[4]	8.9	41,851	2.0	22.8	1.5	37.6	9.0	24.7	27,017	37,769	20,669	34,703
2005	9.1	40,857	2.0	22.1	1.5	36.1	9.2	24.9	26,098	39,439	20,312	34,980
2006	9.3	42,689	2.0	21.6	1.5	36.6	9.0	24.3	27,959	39,575	21,309	34,509
2007	9.3	43,544	2.0	22.1	1.5	37.3	9.2	24.5	28,010	39,849	21,426	34,268
2008	9.4	41,657	2.1	22.0	1.5	37.2	9.4	24.7	26,380	40,334	21,098	33,621
2009[5]	9.4	40,275	2.1	22.7	1.5	36.7	9.9	25.8	24,891	41,274	20,416	34,047
2010[6]	9.6	39,811	2.3	24.1	1.7	38.7	10.7	27.4	24,031	38,914	20,266	35,117
2011	9.7	40,495	2.3	24.2	1.7	39.0	10.9	27.6	23,475	40,273	19,755	35,146
ASIAN[7]												
2002	2.8	76,242	.2	7.4	.0	14.2	1.2	10.1	38,862	53,351	22,612	40,000
2003	3.1	77,348	.3	10.2	.1	23.8	1.4	11.8	39,488	56,522	21,619	42,292
2004[4]	3.1	77,896	.2	7.4	.0	13.6	1.2	9.8	39,316	55,741	24,436	43,597
2005	3.2	79,444	.3	9.0	.1	19.7	1.4	11.1	39,418	57,290	24,932	42,411
2006	3.3	83,230	.3	7.8	.1	15.4	1.4	10.3	41,739	58,119	24,765	44,897
2007	3.3	83,668	.3	7.9	.1	16.1	1.3	10.2	40,344	55,552	26,419	44,816
2008	3.5	76,859	.3	9.8	.1	16.7	1.6	11.8	38,239	54,094	24,139	46,179
2009[5]	3.6	78,671	.3	9.4	.1	16.9	1.7	12.5	39,143	56,023	25,525	46,795
2010[6]	3.9	77,590	.4	9.3	.1	21.1	1.9	12.2	36,953	54,161	24,306	43,242
2011	4.2	72,996	.4	9.7	.1	19.1	2.0	12.3	36,334	56,283	22,039	41,411
HISPANIC (any race)[7]												
2002	9.1	42,738	1.8	19.7	.7	35.3	8.6	21.8	25,881	32,676	16,708	27,948
2003	9.3	41,911	1.9	20.8	.8	37.0	9.1	22.5	25,745	32,301	16,683	28,202
2004[4]	9.5	42,198	2.0	20.5	.9	38.9	9.1	21.9	25,667	32,027	17,208	28,928
2005	9.9	43,626	1.9	19.7	.9	38.9	9.4	21.8	25,448	31,067	17,323	28,827
2006	10.2	44,620	1.9	18.9	.9	36.0	9.2	20.6	26,161	32,986	17,578	28,662
2007	10.4	44,003	2.0	19.7	1.0	38.4	9.9	21.5	26,523	33,034	18,167	29,455
2008	10.5	41,660	2.2	21.3	1.0	39.2	11.0	23.2	25,073	32,611	17,149	28,665
2009[5]	10.4	41,660	2.4	22.7	1.1	38.8	12.4	25.3	23,337	33,175	16,997	29,237
2010[6]	11.3	40,540	2.7	24.3	1.3	42.6	13.5	26.5	23,127	32,847	16,806	30,014
2011	11.6	40,061	2.7	22.9	1.3	41.2	13.2	25.3	23,731	32,088	16,829	30,102

[1] The term "family" refers to a group of two or more persons related by birth, marriage, or adoption and residing together. Every family must include a reference person.

[2] Adjusted by consumer price index research series (CPI-U-RS).

[3] Data for American Indians and Alaska natives, native Hawaiians and other Pacific Islanders, and those reporting two or more races are included in the total but not shown separately.

[4] For 2004, figures are revised to reflect a correction to the weights in the 2005 Annual Social and Economic Supplement.

[5] Beginning with data for 2009, the upper income interval used to calculate median incomes was expanded to $250,000 or more.

[6] Reflects implementation of Census 2010-based population controls comparable to succeeding years.

[7] The Current Population Survey allows respondents to choose more than one race. Data shown are for "white alone, non-Hispanic," "black alone," and "Asian alone" race categories. ("Black" is also "black or African American.") Family race and Hispanic origin are based on the reference person.

Note: Poverty thresholds are updated each year to reflect changes in the consumer price index (CPI-U).
For details see publication Series P-60 on the Current Population Survey and Annual Social and Economic Supplements.

Source: Department of Commerce (Bureau of the Census).

TABLE B-34. Population by age group, 1940-2012

[Thousands of persons]

July 1	Total	Age (years)						
		Under 5	5-15	16-19	20-24	25-44	45-64	65 and over
1940	132,122	10,579	24,811	9,895	11,690	39,868	26,249	9,031
1941	133,402	10,850	24,516	9,840	11,807	40,383	26,718	9,288
1942	134,860	11,301	24,231	9,730	11,955	40,861	27,196	9,584
1943	136,739	12,016	24,093	9,607	12,064	41,420	27,671	9,867
1944	138,397	12,524	23,949	9,561	12,062	42,016	28,138	10,147
1945	139,928	12,979	23,907	9,361	12,036	42,521	28,630	10,494
1946	141,389	13,244	24,103	9,119	12,004	43,027	29,064	10,828
1947	144,126	14,406	24,468	9,097	11,814	43,657	29,498	11,185
1948	146,631	14,919	25,209	8,952	11,794	44,288	29,931	11,538
1949	149,188	15,607	25,852	8,788	11,700	44,916	30,405	11,921
1950	152,271	16,410	26,721	8,542	11,680	45,672	30,849	12,397
1951	154,878	17,333	27,279	8,446	11,552	46,103	31,362	12,803
1952	157,553	17,312	28,894	8,414	11,350	46,495	31,884	13,203
1953	160,184	17,638	30,227	8,460	11,062	46,786	32,394	13,617
1954	163,026	18,057	31,480	8,637	10,832	47,001	32,942	14,076
1955	165,931	18,566	32,682	8,744	10,714	47,194	33,506	14,525
1956	168,903	19,003	33,994	8,916	10,616	47,379	34,057	14,938
1957	171,984	19,494	35,272	9,195	10,603	47,440	34,591	15,388
1958	174,882	19,887	36,445	9,543	10,756	47,337	35,109	15,806
1959	177,830	20,175	37,368	10,215	10,969	47,192	35,663	16,248
1960	180,671	20,341	38,494	10,683	11,134	47,140	36,203	16,675
1961	183,691	20,522	39,765	11,025	11,483	47,084	36,722	17,089
1962	186,538	20,469	41,205	11,180	11,959	47,013	37,255	17,457
1963	189,242	20,342	41,626	12,007	12,714	46,994	37,782	17,778
1964	191,889	20,165	42,297	12,736	13,269	46,958	38,338	18,127
1965	194,303	19,824	42,938	13,516	13,746	46,912	38,916	18,451
1966	196,560	19,208	43,702	14,311	14,050	47,001	39,534	18,755
1967	198,712	18,563	44,244	14,200	15,248	47,194	40,193	19,071
1968	200,706	17,913	44,622	14,452	15,786	47,721	40,846	19,365
1969	202,677	17,376	44,840	14,800	16,480	48,064	41,437	19,680
1970	205,052	17,166	44,816	15,289	17,202	48,473	41,999	20,107
1971	207,661	17,244	44,591	15,688	18,159	48,936	42,482	20,561
1972	209,896	17,101	44,203	16,039	18,153	50,482	42,898	21,020
1973	211,909	16,851	43,582	16,446	18,521	51,749	43,235	21,525
1974	213,854	16,487	42,989	16,769	18,975	53,051	43,522	22,061
1975	215,973	16,121	42,508	17,017	19,527	54,302	43,801	22,696
1976	218,035	15,617	42,099	17,194	19,986	55,852	44,008	23,278
1977	220,239	15,564	41,298	17,276	20,499	57,561	44,150	23,892
1978	222,585	15,735	40,428	17,288	20,946	59,400	44,286	24,502
1979	225,055	16,063	39,552	17,242	21,297	61,379	44,390	25,134
1980	227,726	16,451	38,838	17,167	21,590	63,470	44,504	25,707
1981	229,966	16,893	38,144	16,812	21,869	65,528	44,500	26,221
1982	232,188	17,228	37,784	16,332	21,902	67,692	44,462	26,787
1983	234,307	17,547	37,526	15,823	21,844	69,733	44,474	27,361
1984	236,348	17,695	37,461	15,295	21,737	71,735	44,547	27,878
1985	238,466	17,842	37,450	15,005	21,478	73,673	44,602	28,416
1986	240,651	17,963	37,404	15,024	20,942	75,651	44,660	29,008
1987	242,804	18,052	37,333	15,215	20,385	77,338	44,854	29,626
1988	245,021	18,195	37,593	15,198	19,846	78,595	45,471	30,124
1989	247,342	18,508	37,972	14,913	19,442	79,943	45,882	30,682
1990	250,132	18,856	38,632	14,466	19,323	81,291	46,316	31,247
1991	253,493	19,208	39,349	13,992	19,414	82,844	46,874	31,812
1992	256,894	19,528	40,161	13,781	19,314	83,201	48,553	32,356
1993	260,255	19,729	40,904	13,953	19,101	83,766	49,899	32,902
1994	263,436	19,777	41,689	14,228	18,758	84,334	51,318	33,331
1995	266,557	19,627	42,510	14,522	18,391	84,933	52,806	33,769
1996	269,667	19,408	43,172	15,057	17,965	85,527	54,396	34,143
1997	272,912	19,233	43,833	15,433	17,992	85,737	56,283	34,402
1998	276,115	19,145	44,332	15,856	18,250	85,663	58,249	34,619
1999	279,295	19,136	44,755	16,164	18,672	85,408	60,362	34,798
2000 [1]	282,162	19,178	45,166	16,230	19,117	84,973	62,428	35,070
2001 [1]	284,969	19,298	45,236	16,372	19,757	84,523	64,492	35,290
2002 [1]	287,625	19,429	45,232	16,512	20,244	83,990	66,696	35,522
2003 [1]	290,108	19,592	45,209	16,625	20,592	83,398	68,829	35,864
2004 [1]	292,805	19,786	45,131	16,838	20,846	83,067	70,935	36,203
2005 [1]	295,517	19,917	45,059	17,029	20,960	82,764	73,137	36,650
2006 [1]	298,380	19,939	44,984	17,401	21,036	82,639	75,216	37,164
2007 [1]	301,231	20,126	44,920	17,703	21,078	82,510	77,068	37,826
2008 [1]	304,094	20,271	44,955	17,892	21,181	82,400	78,618	38,778
2009 [1]	306,772	20,245	45,103	17,933	21,384	82,211	80,273	39,623
2010 [1,2]	309,350	20,201	45,323	17,712	21,668	82,229	81,780	40,438
2011 [1,2]	311,592	20,162	45,196	17,487	22,154	82,418	82,780	41,394
2012 [1]	313,914							

[1] Data for 2000-2012 reflect the results of the 2010 Census, and do not include Armed Forces overseas.
[2] Revised total population data are available as follows: 2010, 309,326; and 2011, 311,588.

Note: Includes Armed Forces overseas beginning with 1940. Includes Alaska and Hawaii beginning with 1950.
All estimates are consistent with decennial census enumerations.

Source: Department of Commerce (Bureau of the Census).

TABLE B–35. Civilian population and labor force, 1929–2012

[Monthly data seasonally adjusted, except as noted]

Year or month	Civilian noninstitutional population [1]	Civilian labor force		Employment				Un-employ-ment	Not in labor force	Civilian labor force participa-tion rate [2]	Civilian employ-ment/population ratio [3]	Unemploy-ment rate, civilian workers [4]
		Total		Total	Agricultural	Non-agricultural						
		Thousands of persons 14 years of age and over									Percent	
1929		49,180		47,630	10,450	37,180		1,550				3.2
1933		51,590		38,760	10,090	28,670		12,830				24.9
1939		55,230		45,750	9,610	36,140		9,480				17.2
1940	99,840	55,640		47,520	9,540	37,980		8,120	44,200	55.7	47.6	14.6
1941	99,900	55,910		50,350	9,100	41,250		5,560	43,990	56.0	50.4	9.9
1942	98,640	56,410		53,750	9,250	44,500		2,660	42,230	57.2	54.5	4.7
1943	94,640	55,540		54,470	9,080	45,390		1,070	39,100	58.7	57.6	1.9
1944	93,220	54,630		53,960	8,950	45,010		670	38,590	58.6	57.9	1.2
1945	94,090	53,860		52,820	8,580	44,240		1,040	40,230	57.2	56.1	1.9
1946	103,070	57,520		55,250	8,320	46,930		2,270	45,550	55.8	53.6	3.9
1947	106,018	60,168		57,812	8,256	49,557		2,356	45,850	56.8	54.5	3.9
		Thousands of persons 16 years of age and over										
1947	101,827	59,350		57,038	7,890	49,148		2,311	42,477	58.3	56.0	3.9
1948	103,068	60,621		58,343	7,629	50,714		2,276	42,447	58.8	56.6	3.8
1949	103,994	61,286		57,651	7,658	49,993		3,637	42,708	58.9	55.4	5.9
1950	104,995	62,208		58,918	7,160	51,758		3,288	42,787	59.2	56.1	5.3
1951	104,621	62,017		59,961	6,726	53,235		2,055	42,604	59.2	57.3	3.3
1952	105,231	62,138		60,250	6,500	53,749		1,883	43,093	59.0	57.3	3.0
1953 [5]	107,056	63,015		61,179	6,260	54,919		1,834	44,041	58.9	57.1	2.9
1954	108,321	63,643		60,109	6,205	53,904		3,532	44,678	58.8	55.5	5.5
1955	109,683	65,023		62,170	6,450	55,722		2,852	44,660	59.3	56.7	4.4
1956	110,954	66,552		63,799	6,283	57,514		2,750	44,402	60.0	57.5	4.1
1957	112,265	66,929		64,071	5,947	58,123		2,859	45,336	59.6	57.1	4.3
1958	113,727	67,639		63,036	5,586	57,450		4,602	46,088	59.5	55.4	6.8
1959	115,329	68,369		64,630	5,565	59,065		3,740	46,960	59.3	56.0	5.5
1960 [5]	117,245	69,628		65,778	5,458	60,318		3,852	47,617	59.4	56.1	5.5
1961	118,771	70,459		65,746	5,200	60,546		4,714	48,312	59.3	55.4	6.7
1962 [5]	120,153	70,614		66,702	4,944	61,759		3,911	49,539	58.8	55.5	5.5
1963	122,416	71,833		67,762	4,687	63,076		4,070	50,583	58.7	55.4	5.7
1964	124,485	73,091		69,305	4,523	64,782		3,786	51,394	58.7	55.7	5.2
1965	126,513	74,455		71,088	4,361	66,726		3,366	52,058	58.9	56.2	4.5
1966	128,058	75,770		72,895	3,979	68,915		2,875	52,288	59.2	56.9	3.8
1967	129,874	77,347		74,372	3,844	70,527		2,975	52,527	59.6	57.3	3.8
1968	132,028	78,737		75,920	3,817	72,103		2,817	53,291	59.6	57.5	3.6
1969	134,335	80,734		77,902	3,606	74,296		2,832	53,602	60.1	58.0	3.5
1970	137,085	82,771		78,678	3,463	75,215		4,093	54,315	60.4	57.4	4.9
1971	140,216	84,382		79,367	3,394	75,972		5,016	55,834	60.2	56.6	5.9
1972 [5]	144,126	87,034		82,153	3,484	78,669		4,882	57,091	60.4	57.0	5.6
1973 [5]	147,096	89,429		85,064	3,470	81,594		4,365	57,667	60.8	57.8	4.9
1974	150,120	91,949		86,794	3,515	83,279		5,156	58,171	61.3	57.8	5.6
1975	153,153	93,775		85,846	3,408	82,438		7,929	59,377	61.2	56.1	8.5
1976	156,150	96,158		88,752	3,331	85,421		7,406	59,991	61.6	56.8	7.7
1977	159,033	99,009		92,017	3,283	88,734		6,991	60,025	62.3	57.9	7.1
1978 [5]	161,910	102,251		96,048	3,387	92,661		6,202	59,659	63.2	59.3	6.1
1979	164,863	104,962		98,824	3,347	95,477		6,137	59,900	63.7	59.9	5.8
1980	167,745	106,940		99,303	3,364	95,938		7,637	60,806	63.8	59.2	7.1
1981	170,130	108,670		100,397	3,368	97,030		8,273	61,460	63.9	59.0	7.6
1982	172,271	110,204		99,526	3,401	96,125		10,678	62,067	64.0	57.8	9.7
1983	174,215	111,550		100,834	3,383	97,450		10,717	62,665	64.0	57.9	9.6
1984	176,383	113,544		105,005	3,321	101,685		8,539	62,839	64.4	59.5	7.5
1985	178,206	115,461		107,150	3,179	103,971		8,312	62,744	64.8	60.1	7.2
1986 [5]	180,587	117,834		109,597	3,163	106,434		8,237	62,752	65.3	60.7	7.0
1987	182,753	119,865		112,440	3,208	109,232		7,425	62,888	65.6	61.5	6.2
1988	184,613	121,669		114,968	3,169	111,800		6,701	62,944	65.9	62.3	5.5
1989	186,393	123,869		117,342	3,199	114,142		6,528	62,523	66.5	63.0	5.3
1990 [5]	189,164	125,840		118,793	3,223	115,570		7,047	63,324	66.5	62.8	5.6
1991	190,925	126,346		117,718	3,269	114,449		8,628	64,578	66.2	61.7	6.8
1992	192,805	128,105		118,492	3,247	115,245		9,613	64,700	66.4	61.5	7.5
1993	194,838	129,200		120,259	3,115	117,144		8,940	65,638	66.3	61.7	6.9
1994 [5]	196,814	131,056		123,060	3,409	119,651		7,996	65,758	66.6	62.5	6.1
1995	198,584	132,304		124,900	3,440	121,460		7,404	66,280	66.6	62.9	5.6
1996	200,591	133,943		126,708	3,443	123,264		7,236	66,647	66.8	63.2	5.4
1997 [5]	203,133	136,297		129,558	3,399	126,159		6,739	66,837	67.1	63.8	4.9
1998 [5]	205,220	137,673		131,463	3,378	128,085		6,210	67,547	67.1	64.1	4.5
1999 [5]	207,753	139,368		133,488	3,281	130,207		5,880	68,385	67.1	64.3	4.2

[1] Not seasonally adjusted.
[2] Civilian labor force as percent of civilian noninstitutional population.
[3] Civilian employment as percent of civilian noninstitutional population.
[4] Unemployed as percent of civilian labor force.
See next page for continuation of table.

[Monthly data seasonally adjusted, except as noted]

Year or month	Civilian noninstitutional population [1]	Civilian labor force					Not in labor force	Civilian labor force participation rate [2]	Civilian employment/population ratio [3]	Unemployment rate, civilian workers [4]
		Total	Employment			Unemployment				
			Total	Agricultural	Nonagricultural					
	Thousands of persons 16 years of age and over								Percent	
2000 [5],[6]	212,577	142,583	136,891	2,464	134,427	5,692	69,994	67.1	64.4	4.0
2001	215,092	143,734	136,933	2,299	134,635	6,801	71,359	66.8	63.7	4.7
2002	217,570	144,863	136,485	2,311	134,174	8,378	72,707	66.6	62.7	5.8
2003 [5]	221,168	146,510	137,736	2,275	135,461	8,774	74,658	66.2	62.3	6.0
2004 [5]	223,357	147,401	139,252	2,232	137,020	8,149	75,956	66.0	62.3	5.5
2005 [5]	226,082	149,320	141,730	2,197	139,532	7,591	76,762	66.0	62.7	5.1
2006 [5]	228,815	151,428	144,427	2,206	142,221	7,001	77,387	66.2	63.1	4.6
2007 [5]	231,867	153,124	146,047	2,095	143,952	7,078	78,743	66.0	63.0	4.6
2008 [5]	233,788	154,287	145,362	2,168	143,194	8,924	79,501	66.0	62.2	5.8
2009 [5]	235,801	154,142	139,877	2,103	137,775	14,265	81,659	65.4	59.3	9.3
2010 [5]	237,830	153,889	139,064	2,206	136,858	14,825	83,941	64.7	58.5	9.6
2011 [5]	239,618	153,617	139,869	2,254	137,615	13,747	86,001	64.1	58.4	8.9
2012 [5]	243,284	154,975	142,469	2,186	140,283	12,506	88,310	63.7	58.6	8.1
2009: Jan [5]	234,739	154,232	142,153	2,147	140,022	12,079	80,507	65.7	60.6	7.8
Feb	234,913	154,526	141,644	2,131	139,500	12,881	80,387	65.8	60.3	8.3
Mar	235,086	154,142	140,721	2,026	138,666	13,421	80,944	65.6	59.9	8.7
Apr	235,271	154,479	140,652	2,137	138,447	13,826	80,793	65.7	59.8	9.0
May	235,452	154,742	140,250	2,144	138,044	14,492	80,710	65.7	59.6	9.4
June	235,655	154,710	140,005	2,158	137,835	14,705	80,944	65.7	59.4	9.5
July	235,870	154,505	139,898	2,126	137,822	14,607	81,365	65.5	59.3	9.5
Aug	236,087	154,300	139,481	2,098	137,360	14,819	81,787	65.4	59.1	9.6
Sept	236,322	153,815	138,810	2,036	136,728	15,005	82,507	65.1	58.7	9.8
Oct	236,550	153,804	138,421	2,044	136,453	15,382	82,746	65.0	58.5	10.0
Nov	236,743	153,887	138,665	2,102	136,645	15,223	82,855	65.0	58.6	9.9
Dec	236,924	153,120	138,025	2,091	135,925	15,095	83,804	64.6	58.3	9.9
2010: Jan [5]	236,832	153,455	138,439	2,130	136,382	15,016	83,378	64.8	58.5	9.8
Feb	236,998	153,702	138,624	2,308	136,353	15,078	83,296	64.9	58.5	9.8
Mar	237,159	153,960	138,767	2,200	136,580	15,192	83,199	64.9	58.5	9.9
Apr	237,329	154,577	139,296	2,269	136,982	15,281	82,752	65.1	58.7	9.9
May	237,499	154,110	139,255	2,196	137,024	14,856	83,389	64.9	58.6	9.6
June	237,690	153,623	139,148	2,129	136,961	14,475	84,067	64.6	58.5	9.4
July	237,890	153,709	139,167	2,175	136,935	14,542	84,180	64.6	58.5	9.5
Aug	238,099	154,078	139,405	2,183	137,158	14,673	84,022	64.7	58.5	9.5
Sept	238,322	153,966	139,388	2,168	137,208	14,577	84,356	64.6	58.5	9.5
Oct	238,530	153,681	139,097	2,347	136,829	14,584	84,849	64.4	58.3	9.5
Nov	238,715	154,140	139,046	2,194	136,882	15,094	84,575	64.6	58.2	9.8
Dec	238,889	153,649	139,295	2,195	137,110	14,354	85,241	64.3	58.3	9.3
2011: Jan [5]	238,704	153,244	139,253	2,267	137,033	13,992	85,460	64.2	58.3	9.1
Feb	238,851	153,269	139,471	2,263	137,225	13,798	85,582	64.2	58.4	9.0
Mar	239,000	153,358	139,643	2,241	137,457	13,716	85,641	64.2	58.4	8.9
Apr	239,146	153,478	139,606	2,117	137,459	13,872	85,668	64.2	58.4	9.0
May	239,313	153,552	139,681	2,228	137,435	13,871	85,761	64.2	58.4	9.0
June	239,489	153,369	139,405	2,235	137,112	13,964	86,120	64.0	58.2	9.1
July	239,671	153,325	139,509	2,232	137,214	13,817	86,345	64.0	58.2	9.0
Aug	239,871	153,707	139,870	2,378	137,410	13,837	86,165	64.1	58.3	9.0
Sept	240,071	154,074	140,164	2,245	137,904	13,910	85,997	64.2	58.4	9.0
Oct	240,269	154,010	140,314	2,225	138,182	13,696	86,260	64.1	58.4	8.9
Nov	240,441	154,096	140,771	2,251	138,525	13,325	86,345	64.1	58.5	8.6
Dec	240,584	153,945	140,896	2,380	138,508	13,049	86,640	64.0	58.6	8.5
2012: Jan [5]	242,269	154,356	141,608	2,205	139,446	12,748	87,913	63.7	58.5	8.3
Feb	242,435	154,825	142,019	2,188	139,856	12,806	87,611	63.9	58.6	8.3
Mar	242,604	154,871	142,020	2,217	139,871	12,686	87,898	63.8	58.5	8.2
Apr	242,784	154,451	141,934	2,166	139,734	12,518	88,332	63.6	58.5	8.1
May	242,966	154,998	142,302	2,274	140,033	12,695	87,968	63.8	58.6	8.2
June	243,155	155,149	142,448	2,200	140,218	12,701	88,006	63.8	58.6	8.2
July	243,354	154,995	142,250	2,224	140,013	12,745	88,359	63.7	58.5	8.2
Aug	243,566	154,647	142,164	2,146	139,918	12,483	88,919	63.5	58.4	8.1
Sept	243,772	155,056	142,974	2,198	140,767	12,082	88,716	63.6	58.7	7.8
Oct	243,983	155,576	143,328	2,195	141,245	12,248	88,407	63.8	58.7	7.9
Nov	244,174	155,319	143,277	2,121	141,149	12,042	88,855	63.6	58.7	7.8
Dec	244,350	155,511	143,305	2,088	141,190	12,206	88,839	63.6	58.6	7.8

[5] Not strictly comparable with earlier data due to population adjustments or other changes. See *Employment and Earnings* or population control adjustments to the Current Population Survey (CPS) at http://www.bls.gov/cps/documentation.htm#concepts for details on breaks in series.

[6] Beginning in 2000, data for agricultural employment are for agricultural and related industries; data for this series and for nonagricultural employment are not strictly comparable with data for earlier years. Because of independent seasonal adjustment for these two series, monthly data will not add to total civilian employment.

Note: Labor force data in Tables B–35 through B–44 are based on household interviews and relate to the calendar week including the 12th of the month. For definitions of terms, area samples used, historical comparability of the data, comparability with other series, etc., see *Employment and Earnings* or population control adjustments to the CPS at http://www.bls.gov/cps/documentation.htm#concepts.

Source: Department of Labor (Bureau of Labor Statistics).

TABLE B–36. Civilian employment and unemployment by sex and age, 1966–2012

[Thousands of persons 16 years of age and over; monthly data seasonally adjusted]

Year or month	Civilian employment							Unemployment						
	Total	Males			Females			Total	Males			Females		
		Total	16–19 years	20 years and over	Total	16–19 years	20 years and over		Total	16–19 years	20 years and over	Total	16–19 years	20 years and over
1966	72,895	46,919	3,253	43,668	25,976	2,468	23,510	2,875	1,551	432	1,120	1,324	405	921
1967	74,372	47,479	3,186	44,294	26,893	2,496	24,397	2,975	1,508	448	1,060	1,468	391	1,078
1968	75,920	48,114	3,255	44,859	27,807	2,526	25,281	2,817	1,419	426	993	1,397	412	985
1969	77,902	48,818	3,430	45,388	29,084	2,687	26,397	2,832	1,403	440	963	1,429	413	1,015
1970	78,678	48,990	3,409	45,581	29,688	2,735	26,952	4,093	2,238	599	1,638	1,855	506	1,349
1971	79,367	49,390	3,478	45,912	29,976	2,730	27,246	5,016	2,789	693	2,097	2,227	568	1,658
1972	82,153	50,896	3,765	47,130	31,257	2,980	28,276	4,882	2,659	711	1,948	2,222	598	1,625
1973	85,064	52,349	4,039	48,310	32,715	3,231	29,484	4,365	2,275	653	1,624	2,089	583	1,507
1974	86,794	53,024	4,103	48,922	33,769	3,345	30,424	5,156	2,714	757	1,957	2,441	665	1,777
1975	85,846	51,857	3,839	48,018	33,989	3,263	30,726	7,929	4,442	966	3,476	3,486	802	2,684
1976	88,752	53,138	3,947	49,190	35,615	3,389	32,226	7,406	4,036	939	3,098	3,369	780	2,588
1977	92,017	54,728	4,174	50,555	37,289	3,514	33,775	6,991	3,667	874	2,794	3,324	789	2,535
1978	96,048	56,479	4,336	52,143	39,569	3,734	35,836	6,202	3,142	813	2,328	3,061	769	2,292
1979	98,824	57,607	4,300	53,308	41,217	3,783	37,434	6,137	3,120	811	2,308	3,018	743	2,276
1980	99,303	57,186	4,085	53,101	42,117	3,625	38,492	7,637	4,267	913	3,353	3,370	755	2,615
1981	100,397	57,397	3,815	53,582	43,000	3,411	39,590	8,273	4,577	962	3,615	3,696	800	2,895
1982	99,526	56,271	3,379	52,891	43,256	3,170	40,086	10,678	6,179	1,090	5,089	4,499	886	3,613
1983	100,834	56,787	3,300	53,487	44,047	3,043	41,004	10,717	6,260	1,003	5,257	4,457	825	3,632
1984	105,005	59,091	3,322	55,769	45,915	3,122	42,793	8,539	4,744	812	3,932	3,794	687	3,107
1985	107,150	59,891	3,328	56,562	47,259	3,105	44,154	8,312	4,521	806	3,715	3,791	661	3,129
1986	109,597	60,892	3,323	57,569	48,706	3,149	45,556	8,237	4,530	779	3,751	3,707	675	3,032
1987	112,440	62,107	3,381	58,726	50,334	3,260	47,074	7,425	4,101	732	3,369	3,324	616	2,709
1988	114,968	63,273	3,492	59,781	51,696	3,313	48,383	6,701	3,655	667	2,987	3,046	558	2,487
1989	117,342	64,315	3,477	60,837	53,027	3,282	49,745	6,528	3,525	658	2,867	3,003	536	2,467
1990	118,793	65,104	3,427	61,678	53,689	3,154	50,535	7,047	3,906	667	3,239	3,140	544	2,596
1991	117,718	64,223	3,044	61,178	53,496	2,862	50,634	8,628	4,946	751	4,195	3,683	608	3,074
1992	118,492	64,440	2,944	61,496	54,052	2,724	51,328	9,613	5,523	806	4,717	4,090	621	3,469
1993	120,259	65,349	2,994	62,355	54,910	2,811	52,099	8,940	5,055	768	4,287	3,885	597	3,288
1994	123,060	66,450	3,156	63,294	56,610	3,005	53,606	7,996	4,367	740	3,627	3,629	580	3,049
1995	124,900	67,377	3,292	64,085	57,523	3,127	54,396	7,404	3,983	744	3,239	3,421	602	2,819
1996	126,708	68,207	3,310	64,897	58,501	3,190	55,311	7,236	3,880	733	3,146	3,356	573	2,783
1997	129,558	69,685	3,401	66,284	59,873	3,260	56,613	6,739	3,577	694	2,882	3,162	577	2,585
1998	131,463	70,693	3,558	67,135	60,771	3,493	57,278	6,210	3,266	686	2,580	2,944	519	2,424
1999	133,488	71,446	3,685	67,761	62,042	3,487	58,555	5,880	3,066	633	2,433	2,814	529	2,285
2000	136,891	73,305	3,671	69,634	63,586	3,519	60,067	5,692	2,975	599	2,376	2,717	483	2,235
2001	136,933	73,196	3,420	69,776	63,737	3,320	60,417	6,801	3,690	650	3,040	3,111	512	2,599
2002	136,485	72,903	3,169	69,734	63,582	3,162	60,420	8,378	4,597	700	3,896	3,781	553	3,228
2003	137,736	73,332	2,917	70,415	64,404	3,002	61,402	8,774	4,906	697	4,209	3,868	554	3,314
2004	139,252	74,524	2,952	71,572	64,728	2,955	61,773	8,149	4,456	664	3,791	3,694	543	3,150
2005	141,730	75,973	2,923	73,050	65,757	3,055	62,702	7,591	4,059	667	3,392	3,531	519	3,013
2006	144,427	77,502	3,071	74,431	66,925	3,091	63,834	7,001	3,753	622	3,131	3,247	496	2,751
2007	146,047	78,254	2,917	75,337	67,792	2,994	64,799	7,078	3,882	623	3,259	3,196	478	2,718
2008	145,362	77,486	2,736	74,750	67,876	2,837	65,039	8,924	5,033	736	4,297	3,891	549	3,342
2009	139,877	73,670	2,328	71,341	66,208	2,509	63,699	14,265	8,453	898	7,555	5,811	654	5,157
2010	139,064	73,359	2,129	71,230	65,705	2,249	63,456	14,825	8,626	863	7,763	6,199	665	5,534
2011	139,869	74,290	2,108	72,182	65,579	2,219	63,360	13,747	7,684	786	6,898	6,063	613	5,450
2012	142,469	75,555	2,152	73,403	66,914	2,274	64,640	12,506	6,771	787	5,984	5,734	609	5,125
2011: Jan	139,253	73,773	2,198	71,575	65,479	2,140	63,339	13,992	7,907	834	7,073	6,084	651	5,433
Feb	139,471	74,036	2,170	71,866	65,435	2,140	63,295	13,798	7,740	751	6,989	6,058	608	5,450
Mar	139,643	74,025	2,151	71,874	65,618	2,200	63,418	13,716	7,710	775	6,936	6,005	633	5,372
Apr	139,606	73,982	2,023	71,959	65,624	2,251	63,373	13,872	7,814	793	7,022	6,058	606	5,452
May	139,681	74,167	2,051	72,116	65,514	2,219	63,294	13,871	7,782	762	7,021	6,089	587	5,502
June	139,405	74,075	2,071	72,004	65,331	2,221	63,110	13,964	7,868	789	7,079	6,095	619	5,476
July	139,509	74,061	2,063	71,998	65,448	2,166	63,282	13,817	7,754	775	6,978	6,063	628	5,434
Aug	139,870	74,263	2,112	72,151	65,607	2,228	63,379	13,837	7,732	808	6,923	6,105	653	5,452
Sept	140,164	74,477	2,115	72,363	65,687	2,268	63,419	13,910	7,665	801	6,864	6,245	616	5,628
Oct	140,314	74,460	2,103	72,357	65,854	2,281	63,572	13,696	7,649	787	6,861	6,047	605	5,442
Nov	140,771	74,989	2,118	72,871	65,782	2,280	63,502	13,325	7,341	774	6,567	5,984	606	5,378
Dec	140,896	75,217	2,167	73,050	65,679	2,233	63,446	13,049	7,152	782	6,370	5,897	528	5,369
2012: Jan	141,608	75,257	2,119	73,138	66,351	2,272	64,080	12,748	6,794	730	6,065	5,953	612	5,341
Feb	142,019	75,271	2,092	73,179	66,748	2,291	64,457	12,806	6,885	763	6,123	5,921	603	5,318
Mar	142,020	75,344	2,106	73,238	66,676	2,254	64,422	12,686	6,844	769	6,075	5,842	684	5,158
Apr	141,934	75,301	2,156	73,145	66,632	2,178	64,454	12,518	6,762	804	5,958	5,755	629	5,126
May	142,302	75,415	2,185	73,230	66,887	2,234	64,653	12,695	6,946	803	6,143	5,749	625	5,124
June	142,448	75,522	2,223	73,299	66,926	2,311	64,616	12,701	6,936	802	6,133	5,765	604	5,161
July	142,250	75,512	2,224	73,288	66,738	2,301	64,437	12,745	6,895	806	6,089	5,850	614	5,236
Aug	142,164	75,174	2,077	73,097	66,990	2,273	64,716	12,483	6,817	829	5,988	5,666	583	5,083
Sept	142,974	75,769	2,157	73,612	67,206	2,272	64,934	12,088	6,627	802	5,825	5,455	575	4,879
Oct	143,328	76,027	2,182	73,845	67,301	2,287	65,014	12,248	6,634	800	5,834	5,614	587	5,027
Nov	143,277	75,983	2,163	73,821	67,294	2,305	64,988	12,042	6,530	783	5,747	5,512	594	4,918
Dec	143,305	76,060	2,111	73,949	67,245	2,291	64,954	12,206	6,486	739	5,746	5,721	615	5,105

Note: See footnote 5 and Note, Table B–35.

Source: Department of Labor (Bureau of Labor Statistics).

[Thousands of persons 16 years of age and over; monthly data seasonally adjusted]

Year or month	All civilian workers	White [1] Total	White [1] Males	White [1] Females	White [1] Both sexes 16–19	Black and other [1] Total	Black and other [1] Males	Black and other [1] Females	Black and other [1] Both sexes 16–19	Black or African American [1] Total	Black or African American [1] Males	Black or African American [1] Females	Black or African American [1] Both sexes 16–19
1966	72,895	65,021	42,331	22,690	5,176	7,877	4,588	3,289	545	....	....	....	....
1967	74,372	66,361	42,833	23,528	5,114	8,011	4,646	3,365	568	....	....	....	....
1968	75,920	67,750	43,411	24,339	5,195	8,169	4,702	3,467	584	....	....	....	....
1969	77,902	69,518	44,048	25,470	5,508	8,384	4,770	3,614	609	....	....	....	....
1970	78,678	70,217	44,178	26,039	5,571	8,464	4,813	3,650	574	....	....	....	....
1971	79,367	70,878	44,595	26,283	5,670	8,488	4,796	3,692	538	....	....	....	....
1972	82,153	73,370	45,944	27,426	6,173	8,783	4,952	3,832	573	7,802	4,368	3,433	509
1973	85,064	75,708	47,085	28,623	6,623	9,356	5,265	4,092	647	8,128	4,527	3,601	570
1974	86,794	77,184	47,674	29,511	6,796	9,610	5,352	4,258	652	8,203	4,527	3,677	554
1975	85,846	76,411	46,697	29,714	6,487	9,435	5,161	4,275	615	7,894	4,275	3,618	507
1976	88,752	78,853	47,775	31,078	6,724	9,899	5,363	4,536	611	8,227	4,404	3,823	508
1977	92,017	81,700	49,150	32,550	7,068	10,317	5,579	4,739	619	8,540	4,565	3,975	508
1978	96,048	84,936	50,544	34,392	7,367	11,112	5,936	5,177	703	9,102	4,796	4,307	571
1979	98,824	87,259	51,452	35,807	7,356	11,565	6,156	5,409	727	9,359	4,923	4,436	579
1980	99,303	87,715	51,127	36,587	7,021	11,588	6,059	5,529	689	9,313	4,798	4,515	547
1981	100,397	88,709	51,315	37,394	6,588	11,688	6,083	5,606	637	9,355	4,794	4,561	505
1982	99,526	87,903	50,287	37,615	5,984	11,624	5,983	5,641	565	9,189	4,637	4,552	428
1983	100,834	88,893	50,621	38,272	5,799	11,941	6,166	5,775	543	9,375	4,753	4,622	416
1984	105,005	92,120	52,462	39,659	5,836	12,885	6,629	6,256	607	10,119	5,124	4,995	474
1985	107,150	93,736	53,046	40,690	5,768	13,414	6,845	6,569	666	10,501	5,270	5,231	532
1986	109,597	95,660	53,785	41,876	5,792	13,937	7,107	6,830	681	10,814	5,428	5,386	536
1987	112,440	97,789	54,647	43,142	5,898	14,652	7,459	7,192	742	11,309	5,661	5,648	587
1988	114,968	99,812	55,550	44,262	6,030	15,156	7,722	7,434	774	11,658	5,824	5,834	601
1989	117,342	101,584	56,352	45,232	5,946	15,757	7,963	7,795	813	11,953	5,928	6,025	625
1990	118,793	102,261	56,703	45,558	5,779	16,533	8,401	8,131	801	12,175	5,995	6,180	598
1991	117,718	101,182	55,797	45,385	5,216	16,536	8,426	8,110	690	12,074	5,961	6,113	494
1992	118,492	101,669	55,959	45,710	4,985	16,823	8,482	8,342	684	12,151	5,930	6,221	492
1993	120,259	103,045	56,656	46,390	5,113	17,214	8,693	8,521	691	12,382	6,047	6,334	494
1994	123,060	105,190	57,452	47,738	5,398	17,870	8,998	8,872	763	12,835	6,241	6,595	552
1995	124,900	106,490	58,146	48,344	5,593	18,409	9,231	9,179	826	13,279	6,422	6,857	586
1996	126,708	107,808	58,888	48,920	5,667	18,900	9,319	9,580	832	13,542	6,456	7,086	613
1997	129,558	109,856	59,998	49,859	5,807	19,701	9,687	10,014	853	13,969	6,607	7,362	631
1998	131,463	110,931	60,604	50,327	6,089	20,532	10,089	10,443	962	14,556	6,871	7,685	736
1999	133,488	112,235	61,139	51,096	6,204	21,253	10,307	10,945	968	15,056	7,027	8,029	691
2000	136,891	114,424	62,289	52,136	6,160	....	....	....	....	15,156	7,082	8,073	711
2001	136,933	114,430	62,212	52,218	5,817	....	....	....	....	15,006	6,938	8,068	637
2002	136,485	114,013	61,849	52,164	5,441	....	....	....	....	14,872	6,959	7,914	611
2003	137,736	114,235	61,866	52,369	5,064	....	....	....	....	14,739	6,820	7,919	516
2004	139,252	115,239	62,712	52,527	5,039	....	....	....	....	14,909	6,912	7,997	520
2005	141,730	116,949	63,763	53,186	5,105	....	....	....	....	15,313	7,155	8,158	536
2006	144,427	118,833	64,883	53,950	5,215	....	....	....	....	15,765	7,354	8,410	618
2007	146,047	119,792	65,289	54,503	4,990	....	....	....	....	16,051	7,500	8,551	566
2008	145,362	119,126	64,624	54,501	4,697	....	....	....	....	15,953	7,398	8,554	541
2009	139,877	114,996	61,630	53,366	4,138	....	....	....	....	15,025	6,817	8,208	442
2010	139,064	114,168	61,252	52,916	3,733	....	....	....	....	15,010	6,865	8,145	386
2011	139,869	114,690	61,920	52,770	3,691	....	....	....	....	15,051	6,953	8,098	380
2012	142,469	114,769	61,990	52,779	3,665	....	....	....	....	15,856	7,302	8,553	438
2011: Jan	139,253	114,309	61,533	52,777	3,748	....	....	....	....	15,024	6,878	8,145	371
Feb	139,471	114,294	61,713	52,581	3,673	....	....	....	....	15,030	6,907	8,123	386
Mar	139,643	114,630	61,688	52,943	3,684	....	....	....	....	14,988	6,921	8,066	392
Apr	139,606	114,719	61,701	53,018	3,636	....	....	....	....	14,938	6,894	8,044	404
May	139,681	114,816	61,963	52,853	3,644	....	....	....	....	14,847	6,816	8,031	374
June	139,405	114,458	61,785	52,672	3,652	....	....	....	....	14,894	6,927	7,967	395
July	139,509	114,538	61,805	52,734	3,623	....	....	....	....	14,882	6,905	7,977	356
Aug	139,870	114,750	61,989	52,761	3,727	....	....	....	....	15,006	6,916	8,090	333
Sept	140,164	114,733	62,036	52,696	3,745	....	....	....	....	15,269	7,019	8,250	369
Oct	140,314	114,751	61,922	52,829	3,740	....	....	....	....	15,330	7,066	8,265	393
Nov	140,771	115,110	62,390	52,720	3,714	....	....	....	....	15,125	7,003	8,123	394
Dec	140,896	115,203	62,523	52,680	3,727	....	....	....	....	15,282	7,177	8,104	405
2012: Jan	141,608	114,442	61,783	52,659	3,664	....	....	....	....	15,733	7,408	8,325	418
Feb	142,019	114,687	61,949	52,738	3,626	....	....	....	....	15,761	7,252	8,509	468
Mar	142,020	114,645	61,913	52,731	3,644	....	....	....	....	15,838	7,316	8,522	405
Apr	141,934	114,438	61,857	52,582	3,607	....	....	....	....	15,910	7,257	8,653	421
May	142,302	114,817	61,894	52,923	3,665	....	....	....	....	15,808	7,294	8,514	430
June	142,448	114,730	61,906	52,824	3,771	....	....	....	....	15,879	7,348	8,530	452
July	142,250	114,428	61,921	52,507	3,702	....	....	....	....	15,833	7,285	8,549	494
Aug	142,164	114,395	61,648	52,747	3,569	....	....	....	....	15,811	7,239	8,572	429
Sept	142,974	115,002	62,086	52,916	3,625	....	....	....	....	15,891	7,264	8,626	475
Oct	143,328	115,205	62,319	52,887	3,692	....	....	....	....	16,011	7,311	8,700	444
Nov	143,277	115,124	62,200	52,924	3,718	....	....	....	....	15,952	7,361	8,591	427
Dec	143,305	115,289	62,373	52,916	3,665	....	....	....	....	15,827	7,290	8,536	387

[1] Beginning in 2003, persons who selected this race group only. Prior to 2003, persons who selected more than one race were included in the group they identified as the main race. Data for "black or African American" were for "black" prior to 2003. Data discontinued for "black and other" series. See *Employment and Earnings* or concepts and methodology of the Current Population Survey (CPS) at http://www.bls.gov/cps/documentation.htm#concepts for details.

Note: Beginning with data for 2000, detail will not sum to total because data for all race groups are not shown here.
See footnote 5 and Note, Table B–35.

Source: Department of Labor (Bureau of Labor Statistics).

[Thousands of persons 16 years of age and over; monthly data seasonally adjusted]

Year or month	All civilian workers	White[1] Total	Males	Females	Both sexes 16–19	Black and other[1] Total	Males	Females	Both sexes 16–19	Black or African American[1] Total	Males	Females	Both sexes 16–19
1966	2,875	2,255	1,241	1,014	651	622	310	312	186	....	....	....	....
1967	2,975	2,338	1,208	1,130	635	638	300	338	203	....	....	....	....
1968	2,817	2,226	1,142	1,084	644	590	277	313	194	....	....	....	....
1969	2,832	2,260	1,137	1,123	660	571	267	304	193	....	....	....	....
1970	4,093	3,339	1,857	1,482	871	754	380	374	235	....	....	....	....
1971	5,016	4,085	2,309	1,777	1,011	930	481	450	249	....	....	....	....
1972	4,882	3,906	2,173	1,733	1,021	977	486	491	288	906	448	458	279
1973	4,365	3,442	1,836	1,606	955	924	440	484	280	846	395	451	262
1974	5,156	4,097	2,169	1,927	1,104	1,058	544	514	318	965	494	470	297
1975	7,929	6,421	3,627	2,794	1,413	1,507	815	692	355	1,369	741	629	330
1976	7,406	5,914	3,258	2,656	1,364	1,492	779	713	355	1,334	698	637	330
1977	6,991	5,441	2,883	2,558	1,284	1,550	784	766	379	1,393	698	695	354
1978	6,202	4,698	2,411	2,287	1,189	1,505	731	774	394	1,330	641	690	360
1979	6,137	4,664	2,405	2,260	1,193	1,473	714	759	362	1,319	636	683	333
1980	7,637	5,884	3,345	2,540	1,291	1,752	922	830	377	1,553	815	738	343
1981	8,273	6,343	3,580	2,762	1,374	1,930	997	933	388	1,731	891	840	357
1982	10,678	8,241	4,846	3,395	1,534	2,437	1,334	1,104	443	2,142	1,167	975	396
1983	10,717	8,128	4,859	3,270	1,387	2,588	1,401	1,187	441	2,272	1,213	1,059	392
1984	8,539	6,372	3,600	2,772	1,116	2,167	1,144	1,022	384	1,914	1,003	911	353
1985	8,312	6,191	3,426	2,765	1,074	2,121	1,095	1,026	394	1,864	951	913	357
1986	8,237	6,140	3,433	2,708	1,070	2,097	1,097	999	383	1,840	946	894	347
1987	7,425	5,501	3,132	2,369	995	1,924	969	955	353	1,684	826	858	312
1988	6,701	4,944	2,766	2,177	910	1,757	888	869	316	1,547	771	776	288
1989	6,528	4,770	2,636	2,135	863	1,757	889	868	331	1,544	773	772	300
1990	7,047	5,186	2,935	2,251	903	1,860	971	889	308	1,565	806	758	268
1991	8,628	6,560	3,859	2,701	1,029	2,068	1,087	981	330	1,723	890	833	280
1992	9,613	7,169	4,209	2,959	1,037	2,444	1,314	1,130	390	2,011	1,067	944	324
1993	8,940	6,655	3,828	2,827	992	2,285	1,227	1,058	373	1,844	971	872	313
1994	7,996	5,892	3,275	2,617	960	2,104	1,092	1,011	360	1,666	848	818	300
1995	7,404	5,459	2,999	2,460	952	1,945	984	961	394	1,538	762	777	325
1996	7,236	5,300	2,896	2,404	939	1,936	984	952	367	1,592	808	784	310
1997	6,739	4,836	2,641	2,195	912	1,903	935	967	359	1,560	747	813	302
1998	6,210	4,484	2,431	2,053	876	1,726	835	891	329	1,426	671	756	281
1999	5,880	4,273	2,274	1,999	844	1,606	792	814	318	1,309	626	684	268
2000	5,692	4,121	2,177	1,944	795	....	....	....	....	1,241	620	621	230
2001	6,801	4,969	2,754	2,215	845	....	....	....	....	1,416	709	706	260
2002	8,378	6,137	3,459	2,678	925	....	....	....	....	1,693	835	858	260
2003	8,774	6,311	3,643	2,668	909	....	....	....	....	1,787	891	895	255
2004	8,149	5,847	3,282	2,565	890	....	....	....	....	1,729	860	868	241
2005	7,591	5,350	2,931	2,419	845	....	....	....	....	1,700	844	856	267
2006	7,001	5,002	2,730	2,271	794	....	....	....	....	1,549	774	775	253
2007	7,078	5,143	2,869	2,274	805	....	....	....	....	1,445	752	693	235
2008	8,924	6,509	3,727	2,782	947	....	....	....	....	1,788	949	839	246
2009	14,265	10,648	6,421	4,227	1,157	....	....	....	....	2,606	1,448	1,159	288
2010	14,825	10,916	6,476	4,440	1,128	....	....	....	....	2,852	1,550	1,302	291
2011	13,747	9,889	5,631	4,257	1,024	....	....	....	....	2,831	1,502	1,329	267
2012	12,506	8,915	4,931	3,985	1,004	....	....	....	....	2,544	1,292	1,252	272
2011: Jan	13,992	10,118	5,815	4,303	1,101	....	....	....	....	2,819	1,519	1,301	298
Feb	13,798	10,031	5,737	4,294	998	....	....	....	....	2,766	1,465	1,301	243
Mar	13,716	9,918	5,676	4,242	992	....	....	....	....	2,790	1,518	1,273	277
Apr	13,872	10,048	5,799	4,249	1,014	....	....	....	....	2,915	1,556	1,359	284
May	13,871	9,924	5,644	4,281	914	....	....	....	....	2,896	1,560	1,336	267
June	13,964	10,056	5,766	4,290	1,028	....	....	....	....	2,883	1,509	1,375	262
July	13,817	9,995	5,699	4,295	1,084	....	....	....	....	2,792	1,466	1,325	230
Aug	13,837	9,848	5,587	4,260	1,088	....	....	....	....	2,975	1,616	1,359	294
Sept	13,910	9,849	5,543	4,306	1,011	....	....	....	....	2,861	1,486	1,375	290
Oct	13,696	9,917	5,678	4,239	1,052	....	....	....	....	2,689	1,413	1,276	229
Nov	13,325	9,537	5,327	4,210	1,037	....	....	....	....	2,765	1,455	1,310	251
Dec	13,049	9,279	5,189	4,091	942	....	....	....	....	2,815	1,464	1,351	296
2012: Jan	12,748	9,174	5,050	4,124	991	....	....	....	....	2,472	1,173	1,299	255
Feb	12,806	9,131	4,994	4,137	981	....	....	....	....	2,582	1,330	1,252	244
Mar	12,686	9,058	5,006	4,052	1,056	....	....	....	....	2,573	1,278	1,295	272
Apr	12,518	9,147	4,999	4,147	1,057	....	....	....	....	2,388	1,254	1,134	257
May	12,695	9,163	5,095	4,068	1,015	....	....	....	....	2,493	1,297	1,196	246
June	12,701	9,053	5,086	3,967	994	....	....	....	....	2,670	1,314	1,356	292
July	12,745	9,151	4,992	4,159	1,010	....	....	....	....	2,590	1,371	1,219	282
Aug	12,483	8,897	5,000	3,898	1,069	....	....	....	....	2,578	1,315	1,262	265
Sept	12,082	8,635	4,816	3,819	972	....	....	....	....	2,456	1,322	1,134	280
Oct	12,248	8,588	4,793	3,796	961	....	....	....	....	2,705	1,345	1,360	307
Nov	12,042	8,416	4,652	3,765	946	....	....	....	....	2,422	1,214	1,208	277
Dec	12,206	8,485	4,609	3,876	1,011	....	....	....	....	2,577	1,288	1,289	264

[1] See footnote 1 and Note, Table B–37.

Note: See footnote 5 and Note, Table B–35.

Source: Department of Labor (Bureau of Labor Statistics).

TABLE B–39. Civilian labor force participation rate and employment/population ratio, 1966–2012

[Percent [1]; monthly data seasonally adjusted]

Year or month	Labor force participation rate							Employment/population ratio						
	All civilian workers	Males	Females	Both sexes 16–19 years	White [2]	Black and other [2]	Black or African American [2]	All civilian workers	Males	Females	Both sexes 16–19 years	White [2]	Black and other [2]	Black or African American [2]
1966	59.2	80.4	40.3	48.2	58.7	63.0	....	56.9	77.9	38.3	42.1	56.8	58.4	....
1967	59.6	80.4	41.1	48.4	59.2	62.8	....	57.3	78.0	39.0	42.2	57.2	58.2	....
1968	59.6	80.1	41.6	48.3	59.3	62.2	....	57.5	77.8	39.6	42.2	57.4	58.0	....
1969	60.1	79.8	42.7	49.4	59.9	62.1	....	58.0	77.6	40.7	43.4	58.0	58.1	....
1970	60.4	79.7	43.3	49.9	60.2	61.8	....	57.4	76.2	40.8	42.3	57.5	56.8	....
1971	60.2	79.1	43.4	49.7	60.1	60.9	....	56.6	74.9	40.4	41.3	56.8	54.9	....
1972	60.4	78.9	43.9	51.9	60.4	60.2	59.9	57.0	75.0	41.0	43.5	57.4	54.1	53.7
1973	60.8	78.8	44.7	53.7	60.8	60.5	60.2	57.8	75.5	42.0	45.9	58.2	55.0	54.5
1974	61.3	78.7	45.7	54.8	61.4	60.3	59.8	57.8	74.9	42.6	46.0	58.3	54.3	53.5
1975	61.2	77.9	46.3	54.0	61.5	59.6	58.8	56.1	71.7	42.0	43.3	56.7	51.4	50.1
1976	61.6	77.5	47.3	54.5	61.8	59.8	59.0	56.8	72.0	43.2	44.2	57.5	52.0	50.8
1977	62.3	77.7	48.4	56.0	62.5	60.4	59.8	57.9	72.8	44.5	46.1	58.6	52.5	51.4
1978	63.2	77.9	50.0	57.8	63.3	62.2	61.5	59.3	73.8	46.4	48.3	60.0	54.7	53.6
1979	63.7	77.8	50.9	57.9	63.9	62.2	61.4	59.9	73.8	47.5	48.5	60.6	55.2	53.8
1980	63.8	77.4	51.5	56.7	64.1	61.7	61.0	59.2	72.0	47.7	46.6	60.0	53.6	52.3
1981	63.9	77.0	52.1	55.4	64.3	61.3	60.8	59.0	71.3	48.0	44.6	60.0	52.6	51.3
1982	64.0	76.6	52.6	54.1	64.3	61.6	61.0	57.8	69.0	47.7	41.5	58.8	50.9	49.4
1983	64.0	76.4	52.9	53.5	64.3	62.1	61.5	57.9	68.8	48.0	41.5	58.9	51.0	49.5
1984	64.4	76.4	53.6	53.9	64.6	62.6	62.2	59.5	70.7	49.5	43.7	60.5	53.6	52.3
1985	64.8	76.3	54.5	54.5	65.0	63.3	62.9	60.1	70.9	50.4	44.4	61.0	54.7	53.4
1986	65.3	76.3	55.3	54.7	65.5	63.7	63.3	60.7	71.0	51.4	44.6	61.5	55.4	54.1
1987	65.6	76.2	56.0	54.7	65.8	64.3	63.8	61.5	71.5	52.5	45.5	62.3	56.8	55.6
1988	65.9	76.2	56.6	55.3	66.2	64.0	63.8	62.3	72.0	53.4	46.8	63.1	57.4	56.3
1989	66.5	76.4	57.4	55.9	66.7	64.7	64.2	63.0	72.5	54.3	47.5	63.8	58.2	56.9
1990	66.5	76.4	57.5	53.7	66.9	64.4	64.0	62.8	72.0	54.3	45.3	63.7	57.9	56.7
1991	66.2	75.8	57.4	51.6	66.6	63.8	63.3	61.7	70.4	53.7	42.0	62.6	56.7	55.4
1992	66.4	75.8	57.8	51.3	66.8	64.6	63.9	61.5	69.8	53.8	41.0	62.4	56.4	54.9
1993	66.3	75.4	57.9	51.5	66.8	63.8	63.2	61.7	70.0	54.1	41.7	62.7	56.3	55.0
1994	66.6	75.1	58.8	52.7	67.1	63.9	63.4	62.5	70.4	55.3	43.4	63.5	57.2	56.1
1995	66.6	75.0	58.9	53.5	67.1	64.3	63.7	62.9	70.8	55.6	44.2	63.8	58.1	57.1
1996	66.8	74.9	59.3	52.3	67.2	64.6	64.1	63.2	70.9	56.0	43.5	64.1	58.6	57.4
1997	67.1	75.0	59.8	51.6	67.5	65.2	64.7	63.8	71.3	56.8	43.4	64.6	59.4	58.2
1998	67.1	74.9	59.8	52.8	67.3	66.0	65.6	64.1	71.6	57.1	45.1	64.7	60.9	59.7
1999	67.1	74.7	60.0	52.0	67.3	65.9	65.8	64.3	71.6	57.4	44.7	64.8	61.3	60.6
2000	67.1	74.8	59.9	52.0	67.3	....	65.8	64.4	71.9	57.5	45.2	64.9	....	60.9
2001	66.8	74.4	59.8	49.6	67.0	....	65.3	63.7	70.9	57.0	42.3	64.2	....	59.7
2002	66.6	74.1	59.6	47.4	66.8	....	64.8	62.7	69.7	56.3	39.6	63.4	....	58.1
2003	66.2	73.5	59.5	44.5	66.5	....	64.3	62.3	68.9	56.1	36.8	63.0	....	57.4
2004	66.0	73.3	59.2	43.9	66.3	....	63.8	62.3	69.2	56.0	36.4	63.1	....	57.2
2005	66.0	73.3	59.3	43.7	66.3	....	64.2	62.7	69.6	56.2	36.5	63.4	....	57.7
2006	66.2	73.5	59.4	43.7	66.5	....	64.1	63.1	70.1	56.6	36.9	63.8	....	58.4
2007	66.0	73.2	59.3	41.3	66.4	....	63.7	63.0	69.8	56.6	34.8	63.6	....	58.4
2008	66.0	73.0	59.5	40.2	66.3	....	63.7	62.2	68.5	56.2	32.6	62.8	....	57.3
2009	65.4	72.0	59.2	37.5	65.8	....	62.4	59.3	64.5	54.4	28.4	60.2	....	53.2
2010	64.7	71.2	58.6	34.9	65.1	....	62.2	58.5	63.7	53.6	25.9	59.4	....	52.3
2011	64.1	70.5	58.1	34.1	64.5	....	61.4	58.4	63.9	53.2	25.8	59.4	....	51.7
2012	63.7	70.2	57.7	34.3	64.0	....	61.5	58.6	64.4	53.1	26.1	59.4	....	53.0
2011: Jan	64.2	70.5	58.2	34.5	64.6	....	61.6	58.3	63.7	53.3	25.7	59.4	....	51.9
Feb	64.2	70.6	58.2	33.7	64.6	....	61.4	58.4	63.9	53.2	25.6	59.3	....	51.9
Mar	64.2	70.5	58.2	34.2	64.6	....	61.3	58.4	63.8	53.3	25.9	59.5	....	51.7
Apr	64.2	70.5	58.2	33.7	64.7	....	61.5	58.4	63.7	53.3	25.4	59.5	....	51.4
May	64.2	70.6	58.1	33.5	64.7	....	61.0	58.4	63.9	53.2	25.4	59.5	....	51.1
June	64.0	70.5	58.0	34.0	64.5	....	61.1	58.2	63.7	53.0	25.6	59.3	....	51.2
July	64.0	70.3	58.0	33.6	64.5	....	60.7	58.2	63.7	53.1	25.2	59.3	....	51.1
Aug	64.1	70.4	58.1	34.6	64.5	....	61.7	58.3	63.8	53.2	25.9	59.4	....	51.5
Sept	64.2	70.5	58.2	34.6	64.4	....	62.1	58.4	63.9	53.2	26.2	59.3	....	52.3
Oct	64.1	70.4	58.2	34.5	64.4	....	61.7	58.4	63.8	53.3	26.2	59.3	....	52.5
Nov	64.1	70.5	58.0	34.6	64.4	....	61.1	58.5	64.2	53.2	26.3	59.5	....	51.7
Dec	64.0	70.5	57.8	34.2	64.3	....	61.8	58.6	64.4	53.1	26.4	59.5	....	52.2
2012: Jan	63.7	70.2	57.6	33.5	64.2	....	61.2	58.5	64.4	52.9	25.7	59.4	....	52.9
Feb	63.9	70.3	57.9	33.7	64.3	....	61.6	58.6	64.4	53.2	25.7	59.5	....	53.0
Mar	63.8	70.3	57.7	34.1	64.2	....	61.8	58.5	64.4	53.1	25.6	59.5	....	53.2
Apr	63.6	70.1	57.6	33.9	64.1	....	61.4	58.5	64.3	53.0	25.4	59.3	....	53.3
May	63.8	70.3	57.7	34.4	64.2	....	61.3	58.6	64.4	53.2	26.0	59.5	....	53.0
June	63.8	70.3	57.7	34.9	64.1	....	62.1	58.6	64.4	53.2	26.7	59.4	....	53.1
July	63.7	70.2	57.6	35.0	63.9	....	61.6	58.5	64.3	53.0	26.7	59.2	....	52.9
Aug	63.5	69.8	57.6	34.0	63.8	....	61.4	58.4	64.0	53.1	25.7	59.2	....	52.8
Sept	63.6	70.1	57.6	34.3	63.9	....	61.2	58.7	64.4	53.3	26.2	59.4	....	53.0
Oct	63.8	70.2	57.7	34.6	63.9	....	62.3	58.7	64.6	53.3	26.4	59.5	....	53.3
Nov	63.6	70.0	57.6	34.6	63.8	....	61.1	58.7	64.5	53.3	26.5	59.4	....	53.1
Dec	63.6	70.0	57.7	34.1	63.9	....	61.2	58.6	64.5	53.2	26.1	59.5	....	52.6

[1] Civilian labor force or civilian employment as percent of civilian noninstitutional population in group specified.
[2] See footnote 1, Table B–37.

Note: Data relate to persons 16 years of age and over.
See footnote 5 and Note, Table B–35.

Source: Department of Labor (Bureau of Labor Statistics).

Table B–40. Civilian labor force participation rate by demographic characteristic, 1972–2012

[Percent [1]; monthly data seasonally adjusted]

Year or month	All civilian workers	White [2]							Black or African American [2]						
		Total	Males			Females			Total	Males			Females		
			Total	16–19 years	20 years and over	Total	16–19 years	20 years and over		Total	16–19 years	20 years and over	Total	16–19 years	20 years and over
1972	60.4	60.4	79.6	60.1	82.0	43.2	48.1	42.7	59.9	73.6	46.3	78.5	48.7	32.2	51.2
1973	60.8	60.8	79.4	62.0	81.6	44.1	50.1	43.5	60.2	73.4	45.7	78.4	49.3	34.2	51.6
1974	61.3	61.4	79.4	62.9	81.4	45.2	51.7	44.4	59.8	72.9	46.7	77.6	49.0	33.4	51.4
1975	61.2	61.5	78.7	61.9	80.7	45.9	51.5	45.3	58.8	70.9	42.6	76.0	48.8	34.2	51.1
1976	61.6	61.8	78.4	62.3	80.3	46.9	52.8	46.2	59.0	70.0	41.3	75.4	49.8	32.9	52.5
1977	62.3	62.5	78.5	64.0	80.2	48.0	54.5	47.3	59.8	70.6	43.2	75.6	50.8	32.9	53.6
1978	63.2	63.3	78.6	65.0	80.1	49.4	56.7	48.7	61.5	71.5	44.9	76.2	53.1	37.3	55.5
1979	63.7	63.9	78.6	64.8	80.1	50.5	57.4	49.8	61.4	71.3	43.6	76.3	53.1	36.8	55.4
1980	63.8	64.1	78.2	63.7	79.8	51.2	56.2	50.6	61.0	70.3	43.2	75.1	53.1	34.9	55.6
1981	63.9	64.3	77.9	62.4	79.5	51.9	55.4	51.5	60.8	70.0	41.6	74.5	53.5	34.0	56.0
1982	64.0	64.3	77.4	60.0	79.2	52.4	55.0	52.2	61.0	70.1	39.8	74.7	53.7	33.5	56.2
1983	64.0	64.3	77.1	59.4	78.9	52.7	54.5	52.5	61.5	70.6	39.9	75.2	54.2	33.0	56.8
1984	64.4	64.6	77.1	59.0	78.7	53.3	55.4	53.1	62.2	70.8	41.7	74.8	55.2	35.0	57.6
1985	64.8	65.0	77.0	59.7	78.5	54.1	55.2	54.0	62.9	70.8	44.6	74.4	56.5	37.9	58.6
1986	65.3	65.5	76.9	59.3	78.5	55.0	56.3	54.9	63.3	71.2	43.7	74.8	56.9	39.1	58.9
1987	65.6	65.8	76.8	59.0	78.4	55.7	56.5	55.6	63.8	71.1	43.6	74.7	58.0	39.6	60.0
1988	65.9	66.2	76.9	60.0	78.3	56.4	57.2	56.3	63.8	71.0	43.8	74.6	58.0	37.9	60.1
1989	66.5	66.7	77.1	61.0	78.5	57.2	57.1	57.2	64.2	71.0	44.6	74.4	58.7	40.4	60.6
1990	66.5	66.9	77.1	59.6	78.5	57.4	55.3	57.6	64.0	71.0	40.7	75.0	58.3	36.8	60.6
1991	66.2	66.6	76.5	57.3	78.0	57.4	54.1	57.6	63.3	70.4	37.3	74.6	57.5	33.5	60.0
1992	66.4	66.8	76.5	56.9	78.0	57.7	52.5	58.1	63.9	70.7	40.6	74.3	58.5	35.2	60.8
1993	66.3	66.8	76.2	56.6	77.7	58.0	53.5	58.3	63.2	69.6	39.5	73.2	57.9	34.6	60.2
1994	66.6	67.1	75.9	57.7	77.3	58.9	55.1	59.2	63.4	69.1	40.8	72.5	58.7	36.3	60.9
1995	66.6	67.1	75.7	58.5	77.1	59.0	55.5	59.2	63.7	69.0	40.1	72.5	59.5	39.8	61.4
1996	66.8	67.2	75.8	57.1	77.3	59.1	54.7	59.4	64.1	68.7	39.5	72.3	60.4	38.9	62.6
1997	67.1	67.5	75.9	56.1	77.5	59.5	54.1	59.9	64.7	68.3	37.4	72.2	61.7	39.9	64.0
1998	67.1	67.3	75.6	56.6	77.2	59.4	55.4	59.7	65.6	69.0	40.7	72.5	62.8	42.5	64.8
1999	67.1	67.3	75.6	56.4	77.2	59.6	54.5	59.9	65.8	68.7	38.6	72.4	63.5	38.8	66.1
2000	67.1	67.3	75.5	56.5	77.1	59.5	54.5	59.9	63.1	69.2	39.2	72.8	63.1	39.6	65.4
2001	66.8	67.0	75.1	53.7	76.9	59.4	52.4	59.9	65.3	68.4	37.9	72.1	62.8	37.3	65.2
2002	66.6	66.8	74.8	50.3	76.7	59.3	50.8	60.0	64.8	68.4	37.3	72.1	61.8	34.7	64.4
2003	66.2	66.5	74.2	47.5	76.3	59.2	47.9	59.9	64.3	67.3	31.1	71.5	61.9	33.7	64.6
2004	66.0	66.3	74.1	47.4	76.2	58.9	46.7	59.7	63.8	66.7	30.0	70.9	61.5	32.8	64.2
2005	66.0	66.3	74.1	46.2	76.2	58.9	47.6	59.7	64.2	67.3	32.6	71.3	61.6	32.2	64.4
2006	66.2	66.5	74.3	46.9	76.4	59.0	46.6	59.9	64.1	67.0	32.3	71.1	61.7	35.6	64.2
2007	66.0	66.4	74.0	44.3	76.3	59.0	44.6	60.1	63.7	66.8	29.4	71.2	61.1	31.2	64.0
2008	66.0	66.3	73.7	43.0	76.1	59.2	43.3	60.3	63.7	66.7	29.1	71.1	61.3	29.7	64.3
2009	65.4	65.8	72.8	40.3	75.3	59.1	40.9	60.4	62.4	65.0	26.4	69.6	60.3	27.9	63.4
2010	64.7	65.1	72.0	37.4	74.6	58.5	38.0	59.9	62.2	65.0	25.8	69.5	59.9	25.1	63.2
2011	64.1	64.5	71.3	36.1	73.9	58.0	37.5	59.4	61.4	64.2	25.7	68.4	59.1	24.2	62.2
2012	63.7	64.0	71.0	36.7	73.5	57.4	37.1	58.7	61.5	63.6	25.6	67.7	59.8	28.2	62.6
2011: Jan	64.2	64.6	71.3	38.0	73.8	58.2	37.2	59.7	61.6	64.2	26.9	68.3	59.5	24.1	62.8
Feb	64.2	64.6	71.3	36.4	74.0	58.0	36.2	59.5	61.4	63.9	24.4	68.3	59.3	23.6	62.6
Mar	64.2	64.6	71.2	35.9	73.9	58.3	36.9	59.7	61.3	64.4	26.0	68.6	58.7	25.2	61.8
Apr	64.2	64.7	71.3	35.2	74.0	58.4	37.3	59.8	61.5	64.4	25.4	68.6	59.1	27.4	62.0
May	64.2	64.7	71.4	34.2	74.2	58.2	37.0	59.6	61.0	63.7	26.8	67.8	58.8	22.5	62.1
June	64.0	64.5	71.3	35.4	74.0	58.0	37.6	59.4	61.1	64.1	26.2	68.2	58.6	24.4	61.7
July	64.0	64.5	71.2	35.9	73.8	58.0	37.6	59.4	60.7	63.6	23.6	67.9	58.3	21.7	61.6
Aug	64.1	64.5	71.2	37.1	73.8	58.0	38.1	59.3	61.7	64.7	26.0	68.8	59.2	22.5	62.4
Sept	64.2	64.4	71.2	36.4	73.8	57.9	38.0	59.3	62.1	64.4	25.7	68.6	60.2	25.4	63.3
Oct	64.1	64.4	71.1	36.7	73.7	58.0	38.3	59.3	61.7	64.1	24.1	68.4	59.6	24.2	62.7
Nov	64.1	64.4	71.2	36.2	73.8	57.8	38.2	59.1	61.1	63.9	23.6	68.2	58.9	26.5	61.7
Dec	64.0	64.3	71.2	36.2	73.8	57.6	37.1	59.0	61.8	65.2	30.6	68.9	59.0	24.2	62.0
2012: Jan	63.7	64.2	71.1	35.7	73.8	57.6	37.4	58.9	61.2	64.0	24.4	68.4	59.0	25.8	62.0
Feb	63.9	64.3	71.2	35.4	73.9	57.6	37.0	59.0	61.6	63.9	25.2	68.2	59.8	28.0	62.6
Mar	63.8	64.2	71.2	36.3	73.8	57.5	37.7	58.8	61.8	63.9	23.6	68.3	60.1	27.1	63.0
Apr	63.6	64.1	71.1	37.0	73.6	57.4	36.5	58.8	61.4	63.2	25.9	67.3	59.8	25.0	62.9
May	63.8	64.2	71.1	37.1	73.7	57.7	36.7	59.1	61.3	63.7	23.9	68.1	59.3	27.1	62.2
June	63.8	64.1	71.1	37.9	73.6	57.4	37.4	58.8	62.1	64.2	26.0	68.3	60.3	30.2	63.0
July	63.7	63.9	71.0	37.4	73.4	57.3	37.0	58.6	61.6	64.1	28.8	67.9	59.5	30.0	62.1
Aug	63.5	63.8	70.6	37.1	73.1	57.2	36.3	58.6	61.4	63.2	24.6	67.4	59.9	28.2	62.7
Sept	63.6	63.9	70.8	36.5	73.4	57.3	36.3	58.7	61.2	63.4	28.5	67.1	59.4	29.1	62.0
Oct	63.8	63.9	71.0	37.1	73.5	57.2	36.7	58.5	62.3	63.8	27.6	67.6	61.1	29.9	63.8
Nov	63.6	63.8	70.7	36.3	73.2	57.2	37.8	58.4	61.1	63.1	26.9	66.9	59.5	27.1	62.3
Dec	63.6	63.9	70.8	36.2	73.3	57.2	38.1	58.5	61.2	63.1	21.6	67.4	59.6	28.5	62.2

[1] Civilian labor force as percent of civilian noninstitutional population in group specified.
[2] See footnote 1, Table B–37.

Note: Data relate to persons 16 years of age and over.
See footnote 5 and Note, Table B–35.

Source: Department of Labor (Bureau of Labor Statistics).

Table B–41. Civilian employment/population ratio by demographic characteristic, 1972–2012

[Percent [1]; monthly data seasonally adjusted]

Year or month	All civilian workers	White [2]							Black or African American [2]						
		Total	Males			Females			Total	Males			Females		
			Total	16–19 years	20 years and over	Total	16–19 years	20 years and over		Total	16–19 years	20 years and over	Total	16–19 years	20 years and over
1972	57.0	57.4	76.0	51.5	79.0	40.7	41.3	40.6	53.7	66.8	31.6	73.0	43.0	19.2	46.5
1973	57.8	58.2	76.5	54.3	79.2	41.8	43.6	41.6	54.5	67.5	32.8	73.7	43.8	22.0	47.2
1974	57.8	58.3	75.9	54.4	78.6	42.4	44.3	42.2	53.5	65.8	31.4	71.9	43.5	20.9	46.9
1975	56.1	56.7	73.0	50.6	75.7	42.0	42.5	41.9	50.1	60.6	26.3	66.5	41.6	20.2	44.9
1976	56.8	57.5	73.4	51.5	76.0	43.2	44.2	43.1	50.8	60.6	25.8	66.8	42.8	19.2	46.4
1977	57.9	58.6	74.1	54.4	76.5	44.5	45.9	44.4	51.4	61.4	26.4	67.5	43.3	18.5	47.0
1978	59.3	60.0	75.0	56.3	77.2	46.3	48.5	46.1	53.6	63.3	28.5	69.1	45.8	22.1	49.3
1979	59.9	60.6	75.1	55.7	77.3	47.5	49.4	47.3	53.8	63.4	28.7	69.1	46.0	22.4	49.3
1980	59.2	60.0	73.4	53.4	75.6	47.8	47.9	47.8	52.3	60.4	27.0	65.8	45.7	21.0	49.1
1981	59.0	60.0	72.8	51.3	75.1	48.3	46.2	48.5	51.3	59.1	24.6	64.5	45.1	19.7	48.5
1982	57.8	58.8	70.6	47.0	73.0	48.1	44.6	48.4	49.4	56.0	20.3	61.4	44.2	17.7	47.5
1983	57.9	58.9	70.4	47.4	72.6	48.5	44.5	48.9	49.5	56.3	20.4	61.6	44.1	17.0	47.4
1984	59.5	60.5	72.1	49.1	74.3	49.8	47.0	50.0	52.3	59.2	23.9	64.1	46.7	20.1	49.8
1985	60.1	61.0	72.3	49.9	74.3	50.7	47.1	51.0	53.4	60.0	26.3	64.6	48.1	23.1	50.9
1986	60.7	61.5	72.3	49.6	74.3	51.7	47.9	52.0	54.1	60.6	26.5	65.1	48.8	23.8	51.6
1987	61.5	62.3	72.7	49.9	74.7	52.8	49.0	53.1	55.6	62.0	28.5	66.4	50.3	25.8	53.0
1988	62.3	63.1	73.2	51.7	75.1	53.8	50.2	54.0	56.3	62.7	29.4	67.1	51.2	25.8	53.9
1989	63.0	63.8	73.7	52.6	75.4	54.6	50.5	54.9	56.9	62.8	30.4	67.0	52.0	27.1	54.6
1990	62.8	63.7	73.3	51.0	75.1	54.7	48.3	55.2	56.7	62.6	27.7	67.1	51.9	25.8	54.7
1991	61.7	62.6	71.6	47.2	73.5	54.2	45.9	54.8	55.4	61.3	23.8	65.9	50.6	21.5	53.6
1992	61.5	62.4	71.1	46.4	73.1	54.2	44.2	54.9	54.9	59.9	23.6	64.3	50.8	22.1	53.6
1993	61.7	62.7	71.4	46.6	73.3	54.6	45.7	55.2	55.0	60.0	23.6	64.3	50.9	21.6	53.8
1994	62.5	63.5	71.8	48.3	73.6	55.8	47.5	56.4	56.1	60.8	25.4	65.0	52.3	24.5	55.0
1995	62.9	63.8	72.0	49.4	73.8	56.1	48.1	56.7	57.1	61.7	25.2	66.1	53.4	26.1	56.1
1996	63.2	64.1	72.3	48.2	74.2	56.3	47.6	57.0	57.4	61.1	24.9	65.5	54.4	27.1	57.1
1997	63.8	64.6	72.7	48.1	74.7	57.0	47.2	57.8	58.2	61.4	23.7	66.1	55.6	28.5	58.4
1998	64.1	64.7	72.7	48.6	74.7	57.1	49.3	57.7	59.7	62.9	28.4	67.1	57.2	31.8	59.7
1999	64.3	64.8	72.8	49.3	74.8	57.3	48.3	58.0	60.6	63.1	26.7	67.5	58.6	29.0	61.5
2000	64.4	64.9	73.0	49.5	74.9	57.4	48.8	58.0	60.9	63.6	28.9	67.7	58.6	30.6	61.3
2001	63.7	64.2	72.0	46.2	74.0	57.0	46.5	57.7	59.7	62.1	26.4	66.3	57.8	27.0	60.7
2002	62.7	63.4	70.8	42.3	73.1	56.4	44.1	57.3	58.1	61.1	25.6	65.2	55.8	24.9	58.7
2003	62.3	63.0	70.1	39.4	72.5	56.3	41.5	57.3	57.4	59.5	19.9	64.1	55.6	23.4	58.6
2004	62.3	63.1	70.4	39.7	72.8	56.1	40.3	57.2	57.2	59.3	19.3	63.9	55.5	23.6	58.5
2005	62.7	63.4	70.8	38.8	73.3	56.3	41.8	57.4	57.7	60.2	20.8	64.7	55.7	22.4	58.9
2006	63.1	63.8	71.3	40.0	73.7	56.6	41.1	57.7	58.4	60.6	21.7	65.2	56.5	26.4	59.4
2007	63.0	63.6	70.9	37.3	73.5	56.7	39.2	57.9	58.4	60.7	19.5	65.5	56.5	23.3	59.8
2008	62.2	62.8	69.7	34.8	72.4	56.3	37.1	57.7	57.3	59.1	18.7	63.9	55.8	21.7	59.1
2009	59.3	60.2	66.0	30.2	68.7	54.8	33.4	56.3	53.2	53.7	14.3	58.2	52.8	18.6	56.1
2010	58.5	59.4	65.1	27.6	67.9	54.0	30.4	55.6	52.3	53.1	14.1	57.5	51.7	14.9	55.1
2011	58.4	59.4	65.3	27.3	68.2	53.7	30.4	55.3	51.7	52.8	14.6	56.9	50.8	14.7	54.0
2012	58.6	59.4	65.8	27.7	68.6	53.3	30.3	54.9	53.0	54.1	15.1	58.3	52.2	18.1	55.1
2011: Jan	58.3	59.4	65.1	28.8	67.9	53.8	29.4	55.5	51.9	52.6	14.0	56.8	51.3	14.3	54.7
Feb	58.4	59.3	65.3	28.0	68.1	53.6	29.1	55.3	51.9	52.8	14.5	56.9	51.1	15.0	54.4
Mar	58.4	59.5	65.2	27.5	68.1	54.0	29.8	55.6	51.7	52.8	15.5	56.9	50.7	14.5	54.0
Apr	58.4	59.5	65.2	26.5	68.1	54.0	30.2	55.4	51.4	52.5	13.7	56.8	50.6	17.2	53.6
May	58.4	59.5	65.4	26.5	68.4	53.8	30.4	55.4	51.1	51.9	14.4	55.9	50.4	14.4	53.7
June	58.2	59.3	65.2	26.6	68.1	53.6	30.5	55.2	51.2	52.7	15.3	56.7	50.0	15.1	53.1
July	58.2	59.3	65.2	26.8	68.1	53.7	29.9	55.3	51.1	52.4	14.6	56.5	50.0	12.9	53.3
Aug	58.3	59.4	65.3	27.3	68.2	53.6	31.1	55.2	51.5	52.4	14.4	56.5	50.7	11.4	54.2
Sept	58.4	59.3	65.3	27.3	68.2	53.6	31.3	55.0	52.3	53.2	14.6	57.3	51.6	14.0	54.9
Oct	58.4	59.3	65.2	27.2	68.0	53.7	31.4	55.1	52.5	53.4	15.2	57.5	51.6	15.3	54.9
Nov	58.5	59.5	65.6	27.2	68.5	53.5	31.1	55.0	51.7	52.9	13.8	57.1	50.7	16.8	53.7
Dec	58.6	59.5	65.7	27.8	68.5	53.5	30.7	55.0	52.2	54.2	15.5	58.2	50.5	16.1	53.6
2012: Jan	58.5	59.4	65.8	27.0	68.7	53.4	30.7	54.9	52.9	55.2	15.8	59.6	51.0	15.4	54.2
Feb	58.6	59.5	65.9	27.0	68.8	53.4	30.1	55.0	53.0	54.0	14.3	58.4	52.1	20.6	54.9
Mar	58.5	59.5	65.8	27.1	68.7	53.4	30.4	54.9	53.2	54.4	14.2	58.8	52.1	16.1	55.4
Apr	58.5	59.3	65.7	27.7	68.6	53.2	29.2	54.8	53.3	53.9	15.7	58.1	52.9	16.0	56.2
May	58.6	59.5	65.7	28.0	68.5	53.5	29.8	55.1	53.0	54.1	15.2	58.3	52.0	17.1	55.1
June	58.6	59.4	65.7	28.7	68.4	53.4	30.9	54.9	53.1	54.4	15.8	58.6	52.0	18.3	55.0
July	58.5	59.2	65.7	28.5	68.4	53.1	30.0	54.6	52.9	53.9	17.9	57.8	52.1	19.5	55.0
Aug	58.4	59.2	65.3	26.8	68.2	53.3	29.7	54.8	52.8	53.5	13.7	57.8	52.2	18.9	55.1
Sept	58.7	59.4	65.7	27.8	68.5	53.4	29.7	55.0	53.0	53.6	16.2	57.6	52.5	20.0	55.3
Oct	58.7	59.5	65.9	28.3	68.7	53.3	30.4	54.9	53.3	53.9	14.1	58.1	52.9	19.8	55.7
Nov	58.7	59.4	65.8	27.9	68.5	53.4	31.2	54.8	53.1	54.2	15.1	58.3	52.1	17.7	55.1
Dec	58.6	59.5	65.9	27.4	68.7	53.3	31.0	54.8	52.6	53.6	12.0	58.0	51.8	17.8	54.7

[1] Civilian employment as percent of civilian noninstitutional population in group specified.
[2] See footnote 1, Table B–37.

Note: Data relate to persons 16 years of age and over.
See footnote 5 and Note, Table B–35.

Source: Department of Labor (Bureau of Labor Statistics).

TABLE B–42. Civilian unemployment rate, 1966–2012

[Percent [1]; monthly data seasonally adjusted, except as noted]

Year or month	All civilian workers	Males			Females			Both sexes 16–19 years	By race				Hispanic or Latino ethnicity [4]	Married men, spouse present	Women who maintain families (NSA) [3]
		Total	16–19 years	20 years and over	Total	16–19 years	20 years and over		White [2]	Black and other [2]	Black or African American [2]	Asian (NSA) [2,3]			
1966	3.8	3.2	11.7	2.5	4.8	14.1	3.8	12.8	3.4	7.3	....	....	....	1.9	....
1967	3.8	3.1	12.3	2.3	5.2	13.5	4.2	12.9	3.4	7.4	....	....	....	1.8	4.9
1968	3.6	2.9	11.6	2.2	4.8	14.0	3.8	12.7	3.2	6.7	....	....	....	1.6	4.4
1969	3.5	2.8	11.4	2.1	4.7	13.3	3.7	12.2	3.1	6.4	....	....	....	1.5	4.4
1970	4.9	4.4	15.0	3.5	5.9	15.6	4.8	15.3	4.5	8.2	....	....	....	2.6	5.4
1971	5.9	5.3	16.6	4.4	6.9	17.2	5.7	16.9	5.4	9.9	....	....	....	3.2	7.3
1972	5.6	5.0	15.9	4.0	6.6	16.7	5.4	16.2	5.1	10.0	10.4	....	....	2.8	7.2
1973	4.9	4.2	13.9	3.3	6.0	15.3	4.9	14.5	4.3	9.0	9.4	....	7.5	2.3	7.1
1974	5.6	4.9	15.6	3.8	6.7	16.6	5.5	16.0	5.0	9.9	10.5	....	8.1	2.7	7.0
1975	8.5	7.9	20.1	6.8	9.3	19.7	8.0	19.9	7.8	13.8	14.8	....	12.2	5.1	10.0
1976	7.7	7.1	19.2	5.9	8.6	18.7	7.4	19.0	7.0	13.1	14.0	....	11.5	4.2	10.1
1977	7.1	6.3	17.3	5.2	8.2	18.3	7.0	17.8	6.2	13.1	14.0	....	10.1	3.6	9.4
1978	6.1	5.3	15.8	4.3	7.2	17.1	6.0	16.4	5.2	11.9	12.8	....	9.1	2.8	8.5
1979	5.8	5.1	15.9	4.2	6.8	16.4	5.7	16.1	5.1	11.3	12.3	....	8.3	2.8	8.3
1980	7.1	6.9	18.3	5.9	7.4	17.2	6.4	17.8	6.3	13.1	14.3	....	10.1	4.2	9.2
1981	7.6	7.4	20.1	6.3	7.9	19.0	6.8	19.6	6.7	14.2	15.6	....	10.4	4.3	10.4
1982	9.7	9.9	24.4	8.8	9.4	21.9	8.3	23.2	8.6	17.3	18.9	....	13.8	6.5	11.7
1983	9.6	9.9	23.3	8.9	9.2	21.3	8.1	22.4	8.4	17.8	19.5	....	13.7	6.5	12.2
1984	7.5	7.4	19.6	6.6	7.6	18.0	6.8	18.9	6.5	14.4	15.9	....	10.7	4.6	10.3
1985	7.2	7.0	19.5	6.2	7.4	17.6	6.6	18.6	6.2	13.7	15.1	....	10.5	4.3	10.4
1986	7.0	6.9	19.0	6.1	7.1	17.6	6.2	18.3	6.0	13.1	14.5	....	10.6	4.4	9.8
1987	6.2	6.2	17.8	5.4	6.2	15.9	5.4	16.9	5.3	11.6	13.0	....	8.8	3.9	9.2
1988	5.5	5.5	16.0	4.8	5.6	14.4	4.9	15.3	4.7	10.4	11.7	....	8.2	3.3	8.1
1989	5.3	5.2	15.9	4.5	5.4	14.0	4.7	15.0	4.5	10.0	11.4	....	8.0	3.0	8.1
1990	5.6	5.7	16.3	5.0	5.5	14.7	4.9	15.5	4.8	10.1	11.4	....	8.2	3.4	8.3
1991	6.8	7.2	19.8	6.4	6.4	17.5	5.7	18.7	6.1	11.1	12.5	....	10.0	4.4	9.3
1992	7.5	7.9	21.5	7.1	7.0	18.6	6.3	20.1	6.6	12.7	14.2	....	11.6	5.1	10.0
1993	6.9	7.2	20.4	6.4	6.6	17.5	5.9	19.0	6.1	11.7	13.0	....	10.8	4.4	9.7
1994	6.1	6.2	19.0	5.4	6.0	16.2	5.4	17.6	5.3	10.5	11.5	....	9.9	3.7	8.9
1995	5.6	5.6	18.4	4.8	5.6	16.1	4.9	17.3	4.9	9.6	10.4	....	9.3	3.3	8.0
1996	5.4	5.4	18.1	4.6	5.4	15.2	4.8	16.7	4.7	9.3	10.5	....	8.9	3.0	8.2
1997	4.9	4.9	16.9	4.2	5.0	15.0	4.4	16.0	4.2	8.8	10.0	....	7.7	2.7	8.1
1998	4.5	4.4	16.2	3.7	4.6	12.9	4.1	14.6	3.9	7.8	8.9	....	7.2	2.4	7.2
1999	4.2	4.1	14.7	3.5	4.3	13.2	3.8	13.9	3.7	7.0	8.0	....	6.4	2.2	6.4
2000	4.0	3.9	14.0	3.3	4.1	12.1	3.6	13.1	3.5	....	7.6	3.6	5.7	2.0	5.9
2001	4.7	4.8	16.0	4.2	4.7	13.4	4.1	14.7	4.2	....	8.6	4.5	6.6	2.7	6.6
2002	5.8	5.9	18.1	5.3	5.6	14.9	5.1	16.5	5.1	....	10.2	5.9	7.5	3.6	8.0
2003	6.0	6.3	19.3	5.6	5.7	15.6	5.1	17.5	5.2	....	10.8	6.0	7.7	3.8	8.5
2004	5.5	5.6	18.4	5.0	5.4	15.5	4.9	17.0	4.8	....	10.4	4.4	7.0	3.1	8.0
2005	5.1	5.1	18.6	4.4	5.1	14.5	4.6	16.6	4.4	....	10.0	4.0	6.0	2.8	7.8
2006	4.6	4.6	16.9	4.0	4.6	13.8	4.1	15.4	4.0	....	8.9	3.0	5.2	2.4	7.1
2007	4.6	4.7	17.6	4.1	4.5	13.8	4.0	15.7	4.1	....	8.3	3.2	5.6	2.5	6.5
2008	5.8	6.1	21.2	5.4	5.4	16.2	4.9	18.7	5.2	....	10.1	4.0	7.6	3.4	8.0
2009	9.3	10.3	27.8	9.6	8.1	20.7	7.5	24.3	8.5	....	14.8	7.3	12.1	6.6	11.5
2010	9.6	10.5	28.8	9.8	8.6	22.8	8.0	25.9	8.7	....	16.0	7.5	12.5	6.8	12.3
2011	8.9	9.4	27.2	8.7	8.5	21.7	7.9	24.4	7.9	....	15.8	7.0	11.5	5.8	12.4
2012	8.1	8.2	26.8	7.5	7.9	21.1	7.3	24.0	7.2	....	13.8	5.9	10.3	4.9	11.4
2011: Jan	9.1	9.7	27.5	9.0	8.5	23.3	7.9	25.5	8.1	....	15.8	6.9	12.1	5.9	12.7
Feb	9.0	9.5	25.7	8.9	8.5	22.1	7.9	24.0	8.1	....	15.5	6.8	11.6	5.9	13.0
Mar	8.9	9.4	26.5	8.8	8.4	22.3	7.8	24.4	8.0	....	15.7	7.1	11.4	6.0	12.3
Apr	9.0	9.6	28.1	8.9	8.5	21.2	7.9	24.7	8.1	....	16.3	6.4	11.9	6.0	11.7
May	9.0	9.5	27.1	8.9	8.5	20.9	8.0	24.0	8.0	....	16.3	7.0	11.8	5.9	12.7
June	9.1	9.6	27.6	9.0	8.5	21.8	8.0	24.7	8.1	....	16.2	6.8	11.6	6.2	12.8
July	9.0	9.5	27.3	8.8	8.5	22.5	7.9	24.9	8.0	....	15.8	7.7	11.3	6.0	12.1
Aug	9.0	9.4	27.7	8.8	8.5	22.7	7.9	25.2	7.9	....	16.5	7.1	11.2	5.7	11.9
Sept	9.0	9.3	27.5	8.7	8.7	21.4	8.2	24.4	7.9	....	15.8	7.8	11.3	5.8	12.4
Oct	8.9	9.3	27.2	8.7	8.4	21.0	7.9	24.1	8.0	....	14.9	7.3	11.4	5.8	12.3
Nov	8.6	8.9	26.8	8.3	8.3	21.0	7.8	23.9	7.7	....	15.5	6.5	11.3	5.3	12.4
Dec	8.5	8.7	26.5	8.0	8.2	19.1	7.8	22.9	7.5	....	15.6	6.8	11.0	5.2	12.9
2012: Jan	8.3	8.3	25.6	7.7	8.2	21.2	7.7	23.4	7.4	....	13.6	6.7	10.5	5.1	12.0
Feb	8.3	8.4	26.7	7.7	8.1	20.8	7.6	23.7	7.4	....	14.1	6.3	10.6	5.0	11.7
Mar	8.2	8.3	26.8	7.7	8.1	23.3	7.4	25.0	7.3	....	14.0	6.2	10.3	5.1	10.8
Apr	8.1	8.2	27.2	7.5	8.0	22.4	7.4	24.9	7.4	....	13.1	5.2	10.3	5.1	10.2
May	8.2	8.4	26.9	7.7	7.9	21.9	7.3	24.4	7.4	....	13.6	5.2	11.0	5.3	10.9
June	8.2	8.4	26.5	7.7	7.9	20.7	7.4	23.7	7.3	....	14.4	6.3	11.0	4.9	11.8
July	8.2	8.4	26.6	7.7	8.1	21.1	7.5	23.9	7.4	....	14.1	6.2	10.3	4.9	11.7
Aug	8.1	8.3	28.5	7.6	7.8	20.4	7.3	24.5	7.2	....	14.0	5.9	10.2	4.9	12.3
Sept	7.8	8.0	27.1	7.3	7.5	20.2	7.0	23.7	7.0	....	13.4	4.8	9.9	4.7	11.3
Oct	7.9	8.0	26.8	7.3	7.7	20.4	7.2	23.7	6.9	....	14.5	4.9	10.0	4.6	11.5
Nov	7.8	7.9	26.6	7.2	7.6	20.5	7.0	23.6	6.8	....	13.2	6.4	9.9	4.7	10.7
Dec	7.8	7.9	25.9	7.2	7.8	21.2	7.3	23.5	6.9	....	14.0	6.6	9.6	4.7	11.3

[1] Unemployed as percent of civilian labor force in group specified.
[2] See footnote 1, Table B–37.
[3] Not seasonally adjusted (NSA).
[4] Persons whose ethnicity is identified as Hispanic or Latino may be of any race.

Note: Data relate to persons 16 years of age and over.
See footnote 5 and Note, Table B–35.

Source: Department of Labor (Bureau of Labor Statistics).

Table B–43. Civilian unemployment rate by demographic characteristic, 1972–2012

[Percent [1]; monthly data seasonally adjusted]

Year or month	All civilian workers	White [2]							Black or African American [2]						
		Total	Males			Females			Total	Males			Females		
			Total	16–19 years	20 years and over	Total	16–19 years	20 years and over		Total	16–19 years	20 years and over	Total	16–19 years	20 years and over
1972	5.6	5.1	4.5	14.2	3.6	5.9	14.2	4.9	10.4	9.3	31.7	7.0	11.8	40.5	9.0
1973	4.9	4.3	3.8	12.3	3.0	5.3	13.0	4.3	9.4	8.0	27.8	6.0	11.1	36.1	8.6
1974	5.6	5.0	4.4	13.5	3.5	6.1	14.5	5.1	10.5	9.8	33.1	7.4	11.3	37.4	8.8
1975	8.5	7.8	7.2	18.3	6.2	8.6	17.4	7.5	14.8	14.8	38.1	12.5	14.8	41.0	12.2
1976	7.7	7.0	6.4	17.3	5.4	7.9	16.4	6.8	14.0	13.7	37.5	11.4	14.3	41.6	11.7
1977	7.1	6.2	5.5	15.0	4.7	7.3	15.9	6.2	14.0	13.3	39.2	10.7	14.9	43.4	12.3
1978	6.1	5.2	4.6	13.5	3.7	6.2	14.4	5.2	12.8	11.8	36.7	9.3	13.8	40.8	11.2
1979	5.8	5.1	4.5	13.9	3.6	5.9	14.0	5.0	12.3	11.4	34.2	9.3	13.3	39.1	10.9
1980	7.1	6.3	6.1	16.2	5.3	6.5	14.8	5.6	14.3	14.5	37.5	12.4	14.0	39.8	11.9
1981	7.6	6.7	6.5	17.9	5.6	6.9	16.6	5.9	15.6	15.7	40.7	13.5	15.6	42.2	13.4
1982	9.7	8.6	8.8	21.7	7.8	8.3	19.0	7.3	18.9	20.1	48.9	17.8	17.6	47.1	15.4
1983	9.6	8.4	8.8	20.2	7.9	7.9	18.3	6.9	19.5	20.3	48.8	18.1	18.6	48.2	16.5
1984	7.5	6.5	6.4	16.8	5.7	6.5	15.2	5.8	15.9	16.4	42.7	14.3	15.4	42.6	13.5
1985	7.2	6.2	6.1	16.5	5.4	6.4	14.8	5.7	15.1	15.3	41.0	13.2	14.9	39.2	13.1
1986	7.0	6.0	6.0	16.3	5.3	6.1	14.9	5.4	14.5	14.8	39.3	12.9	14.2	39.2	12.4
1987	6.2	5.3	5.4	15.5	4.8	5.2	13.4	4.6	13.0	12.7	34.4	11.1	13.2	34.9	11.6
1988	5.5	4.7	4.7	13.9	4.1	4.7	12.3	4.1	11.7	11.7	32.7	10.1	11.7	32.0	10.4
1989	5.3	4.5	4.5	13.7	3.9	4.5	11.5	4.0	11.4	11.5	31.9	10.0	11.4	33.0	9.8
1990	5.6	4.8	4.9	14.3	4.3	4.7	12.6	4.1	11.4	11.9	31.9	10.4	10.9	29.9	9.7
1991	6.8	6.1	6.5	17.6	5.8	5.6	15.2	5.0	12.5	13.0	36.3	11.5	12.0	36.0	10.6
1992	7.5	6.6	7.0	18.5	6.4	6.1	15.8	5.5	14.2	15.2	42.0	13.5	13.2	37.2	11.8
1993	6.9	6.1	6.3	17.7	5.7	5.7	14.7	5.2	13.0	13.8	40.1	12.1	12.1	37.4	10.7
1994	6.1	5.3	5.4	16.3	4.8	5.2	13.8	4.6	11.5	12.0	37.6	10.3	11.0	32.6	9.8
1995	5.6	4.9	4.9	15.6	4.3	4.8	13.4	4.3	10.4	10.6	37.1	8.8	10.2	34.3	8.6
1996	5.4	4.7	4.7	15.5	4.1	4.7	12.9	4.1	10.5	11.1	36.9	9.4	10.0	30.3	8.7
1997	4.9	4.2	4.2	14.3	3.6	4.2	12.8	3.7	10.0	10.2	36.5	8.5	9.9	28.7	8.8
1998	4.5	3.9	3.9	14.1	3.2	3.9	10.9	3.4	8.9	8.9	30.1	7.4	9.0	25.3	7.9
1999	4.2	3.7	3.6	12.6	3.0	3.8	11.3	3.3	8.0	8.2	30.9	6.7	7.8	25.1	6.8
2000	4.0	3.5	3.4	12.3	2.8	3.6	10.4	3.1	7.6	8.0	26.2	6.9	7.1	22.8	6.2
2001	4.7	4.2	4.2	13.9	3.7	4.1	11.4	3.6	8.6	9.3	30.4	8.0	8.1	27.5	7.0
2002	5.8	5.1	5.3	15.9	4.7	4.9	13.1	4.4	10.2	10.7	31.3	9.5	9.8	28.3	8.8
2003	6.0	5.2	5.6	17.1	5.0	4.8	13.3	4.4	10.8	11.6	36.0	10.3	10.2	30.3	9.2
2004	5.5	4.8	5.0	16.3	4.4	4.7	13.6	4.2	10.4	11.1	35.6	9.9	9.8	28.2	8.9
2005	5.1	4.4	4.4	16.1	3.8	4.4	12.3	3.9	10.0	10.5	36.3	9.2	9.5	30.3	8.5
2006	4.6	4.0	4.0	14.6	3.5	4.0	11.7	3.6	8.9	9.5	32.7	8.3	8.4	25.9	7.5
2007	4.6	4.1	4.2	15.7	3.7	4.0	12.1	3.6	8.3	9.1	33.8	7.9	7.5	25.3	6.7
2008	5.8	5.2	5.5	19.1	4.9	4.9	14.4	4.4	10.1	11.4	35.9	10.2	8.9	26.8	8.1
2009	9.3	8.5	9.4	25.2	8.8	7.3	18.4	6.8	14.8	17.5	46.0	16.3	12.4	33.4	11.5
2010	9.6	8.7	9.6	26.3	8.9	7.7	20.0	7.2	16.0	18.4	45.4	17.3	13.8	40.5	12.8
2011	8.9	7.9	8.3	24.5	7.7	7.5	18.9	7.0	15.8	17.8	43.1	16.7	14.1	39.4	13.2
2012	8.1	7.2	7.4	24.5	6.7	7.0	18.4	6.5	13.8	15.0	41.3	14.0	12.8	35.6	11.9
2011: Jan	9.1	8.1	8.6	24.2	8.0	7.5	21.1	7.0	15.8	18.1	48.2	16.8	13.8	40.6	12.8
Feb	9.0	8.1	8.5	23.1	8.0	7.5	19.5	7.1	15.5	17.5	40.7	16.6	13.8	36.4	13.0
Mar	8.9	8.0	8.4	23.2	7.9	7.4	19.2	6.9	15.7	18.0	40.3	17.1	13.6	42.7	12.6
Apr	9.0	8.1	8.6	24.7	8.0	7.4	18.9	6.9	16.3	18.4	45.8	17.3	14.5	37.1	13.5
May	9.0	8.0	8.3	22.4	7.9	7.5	17.7	7.1	16.3	18.6	46.3	17.4	14.3	36.3	13.5
June	9.1	8.1	8.5	25.0	7.9	7.5	18.9	7.0	16.2	17.9	41.8	16.9	14.7	37.9	13.9
July	9.0	8.0	8.4	25.4	7.8	7.5	20.6	7.0	15.8	17.5	38.2	16.7	14.2	40.4	13.4
Aug	9.0	7.9	8.3	26.4	7.6	7.5	18.6	7.0	16.5	18.9	44.7	17.9	14.4	49.4	13.3
Sept	9.0	7.9	8.2	24.9	7.6	7.6	17.6	7.1	15.8	17.5	42.9	16.5	14.3	45.1	13.2
Oct	8.9	8.0	8.4	25.8	7.8	7.4	18.1	7.0	14.9	16.7	36.9	15.9	13.4	36.7	12.6
Nov	8.6	7.7	7.9	25.0	7.2	7.4	18.6	6.9	15.5	17.2	41.7	16.3	13.9	36.5	13.0
Dec	8.5	7.5	7.7	23.1	7.1	7.2	17.1	6.8	15.6	16.9	49.2	15.4	14.3	33.6	13.6
2012: Jan	8.3	7.4	7.6	24.5	6.9	7.3	18.1	6.8	13.6	13.7	35.2	12.8	13.5	40.3	12.5
Feb	8.3	7.4	7.5	23.7	6.9	7.3	18.8	6.8	14.1	15.5	43.1	14.4	12.8	26.4	12.3
Mar	8.2	7.3	7.5	25.4	6.8	7.1	19.5	6.6	14.0	14.9	39.7	13.9	13.2	40.6	12.1
Apr	8.1	7.4	7.5	25.1	6.8	7.3	20.1	6.8	13.1	14.7	39.6	13.7	11.6	36.2	10.7
May	8.2	7.4	7.6	24.4	7.0	7.1	18.8	6.7	13.6	15.1	36.2	14.3	12.3	36.6	11.4
June	8.2	7.3	7.6	24.3	7.0	7.0	17.2	6.6	14.4	15.2	39.3	14.2	13.7	39.2	12.6
July	8.2	7.4	7.5	23.9	6.8	7.3	18.9	6.9	14.1	15.8	37.7	14.8	12.5	35.0	11.5
Aug	8.1	7.2	7.5	27.6	6.7	6.9	18.1	6.4	14.0	15.4	44.2	14.2	12.8	33.0	12.0
Sept	7.8	7.0	7.2	24.1	6.6	6.7	18.1	6.3	13.4	15.4	43.0	14.1	11.6	31.3	10.8
Oct	7.9	6.9	7.1	23.7	6.5	6.7	17.4	6.3	14.5	15.5	48.8	14.1	13.5	33.6	12.7
Nov	7.8	6.8	7.0	23.0	6.4	6.6	17.5	6.2	13.5	14.2	43.9	12.9	12.3	34.8	11.5
Dec	7.8	6.9	6.9	24.5	6.2	6.8	18.8	6.3	14.0	15.0	44.3	14.0	13.1	37.6	12.2

[1] Unemployed as percent of civilian labor force in group specified.
[2] See footnote 1, Table B–37.

Note: Data relate to persons 16 years of age and over.
See footnote 5 and Note, Table B–35.

Source: Department of Labor (Bureau of Labor Statistics).

TABLE B–44. Unemployment by duration and reason, 1966–2012

[Thousands of persons, except as noted; monthly data seasonally adjusted [1]]

Year or month	Un-employ-ment	Duration of unemployment						Reason for unemployment					
		Less than 5 weeks	5–14 weeks	15–26 weeks	27 weeks and over	Average (mean) duration (weeks)[3]	Median duration (weeks)	Job losers[4]			Job leavers	Re-entrants	New entrants
								Total	On layoff	Other			
1966	2,875	1,573	779	287	239	10.4	....	....	....	....	....	....	....
1967 [2]	2,975	1,634	893	271	177	8.7	2.3	1,229	394	836	438	945	396
1968	2,817	1,594	810	256	156	8.4	4.5	1,070	334	736	431	909	407
1969	2,832	1,629	827	242	133	7.8	4.4	1,017	339	678	436	965	413
1970	4,093	2,139	1,290	428	235	8.6	4.9	1,811	675	1,137	550	1,228	504
1971	5,016	2,245	1,585	668	519	11.3	6.3	2,323	735	1,588	590	1,472	630
1972	4,882	2,242	1,472	601	566	12.0	6.2	2,108	582	1,526	641	1,456	677
1973	4,365	2,224	1,314	483	343	10.0	5.2	1,694	472	1,221	683	1,340	649
1974	5,156	2,604	1,597	574	381	9.8	5.2	2,242	746	1,495	768	1,463	681
1975	7,929	2,940	2,484	1,303	1,203	14.2	8.4	4,386	1,671	2,714	827	1,892	823
1976	7,406	2,844	2,196	1,018	1,348	15.8	8.2	3,679	1,050	2,628	903	1,928	895
1977	6,991	2,919	2,132	913	1,028	14.3	7.0	3,166	865	2,300	909	1,963	953
1978	6,202	2,865	1,923	766	648	11.9	5.9	2,585	712	1,873	874	1,857	885
1979	6,137	2,950	1,946	706	535	10.8	5.4	2,635	851	1,784	880	1,806	817
1980	7,637	3,295	2,470	1,052	820	11.9	6.5	3,947	1,488	2,459	891	1,927	872
1981	8,273	3,449	2,539	1,122	1,162	13.7	6.9	4,267	1,430	2,837	923	2,102	981
1982	10,678	3,883	3,311	1,708	1,776	15.6	8.7	6,268	2,127	4,141	840	2,384	1,185
1983	10,717	3,570	2,937	1,652	2,559	20.0	10.1	6,258	1,780	4,478	830	2,412	1,216
1984	8,539	3,350	2,451	1,104	1,634	18.2	7.9	4,421	1,171	3,250	823	2,184	1,110
1985	8,312	3,498	2,509	1,025	1,280	15.6	6.8	4,139	1,157	2,982	877	2,256	1,039
1986	8,237	3,448	2,557	1,045	1,187	15.0	6.9	4,033	1,090	2,943	1,015	2,160	1,029
1987	7,425	3,246	2,196	943	1,040	14.5	6.5	3,566	943	2,623	965	1,974	920
1988	6,701	3,084	2,007	801	809	13.5	5.9	3,092	851	2,241	983	1,809	816
1989	6,528	3,174	1,978	730	646	11.9	4.8	2,983	850	2,133	1,024	1,843	677
1990	7,047	3,265	2,257	822	703	12.0	5.3	3,387	1,028	2,359	1,041	1,930	688
1991	8,628	3,480	2,791	1,246	1,111	13.7	6.8	4,694	1,292	3,402	1,004	2,139	792
1992	9,613	3,376	2,830	1,453	1,954	17.7	8.7	5,389	1,260	4,129	1,002	2,285	937
1993	8,940	3,262	2,584	1,297	1,798	18.0	8.3	4,848	1,115	3,733	976	2,198	919
1994	7,996	2,728	2,408	1,237	1,623	18.8	9.2	3,815	977	2,838	791	2,786	604
1995	7,404	2,700	2,342	1,085	1,278	16.6	8.3	3,476	1,030	2,446	824	2,525	579
1996	7,236	2,633	2,287	1,053	1,262	16.7	8.3	3,370	1,021	2,349	774	2,512	580
1997	6,739	2,538	2,138	995	1,067	15.8	8.0	3,037	931	2,106	795	2,338	569
1998	6,210	2,622	1,950	763	875	14.5	6.7	2,822	866	1,957	734	2,132	520
1999	5,880	2,568	1,832	755	725	13.4	6.4	2,622	848	1,774	783	2,005	469
2000	5,692	2,558	1,815	669	649	12.6	5.9	2,517	852	1,664	780	1,961	434
2001	6,801	2,853	2,196	951	801	13.1	6.8	3,476	1,067	2,409	835	2,031	459
2002	8,378	2,893	2,580	1,369	1,535	16.6	9.1	4,607	1,124	3,483	866	2,368	536
2003	8,774	2,785	2,612	1,442	1,936	19.2	10.1	4,838	1,121	3,717	818	2,477	641
2004	8,149	2,696	2,382	1,293	1,779	19.6	9.8	4,197	998	3,199	858	2,408	686
2005	7,591	2,667	2,304	1,130	1,490	18.4	8.9	3,667	933	2,734	872	2,386	666
2006	7,001	2,614	2,121	1,031	1,235	16.8	8.3	3,321	921	2,400	827	2,237	616
2007	7,078	2,542	2,232	1,061	1,243	16.8	8.5	3,515	976	2,539	793	2,142	627
2008	8,924	2,932	2,804	1,427	1,761	17.9	9.4	4,789	1,176	3,614	896	2,472	766
2009	14,265	3,165	3,828	2,775	4,496	24.4	15.1	9,160	1,630	7,530	882	3,187	1,035
2010	14,825	2,771	3,267	2,371	6,415	33.0	21.4	9,250	1,431	7,819	889	3,466	1,220
2011	13,747	2,677	2,993	2,061	6,016	39.3	21.4	8,106	1,230	6,876	956	3,401	1,284
2012	12,506	2,644	2,866	1,859	5,136	39.4	19.3	6,877	1,183	5,694	967	3,345	1,316
2011: Jan	13,992	2,704	3,008	2,214	6,219	37.3	21.5	8,491	1,219	7,272	911	3,355	1,352
Feb	13,798	2,437	3,098	2,199	6,006	37.4	21.3	8,384	1,278	7,106	889	3,345	1,289
Mar	13,716	2,453	2,969	1,999	6,157	39.2	21.8	8,324	1,235	7,090	894	3,298	1,308
Apr	13,872	2,749	2,965	2,150	5,834	38.6	21.0	8,304	1,291	7,013	940	3,378	1,301
May	13,871	2,696	2,899	2,051	6,153	39.5	21.8	8,262	1,237	7,025	923	3,424	1,220
June	13,964	2,999	2,996	1,868	6,213	39.6	21.8	8,166	1,219	6,947	980	3,497	1,231
July	13,817	2,643	3,026	1,992	6,143	40.4	21.5	8,119	1,226	6,894	951	3,391	1,278
Aug	13,837	2,697	3,006	2,189	6,020	40.3	22.2	8,062	1,206	6,856	980	3,510	1,260
Sept	13,910	2,758	2,889	2,023	6,261	40.4	21.9	7,981	1,188	6,794	981	3,480	1,370
Oct	13,696	2,670	3,240	1,985	5,859	38.9	20.4	7,882	1,246	6,636	1,051	3,388	1,289
Nov	13,325	2,535	2,900	2,055	5,698	40.7	21.1	7,621	1,174	6,447	1,017	3,367	1,271
Dec	13,049	2,640	2,840	1,987	5,596	40.7	20.8	7,487	1,208	6,280	943	3,359	1,286
2012: Jan	12,748	2,495	2,874	1,944	5,522	40.2	20.8	7,292	1,266	6,026	932	3,301	1,258
Feb	12,806	2,563	2,817	1,974	5,392	39.9	20.1	7,187	1,135	6,052	1,035	3,341	1,382
Mar	12,686	2,596	2,784	1,877	5,302	39.5	19.7	7,021	1,132	5,889	1,111	3,264	1,421
Apr	12,518	2,567	2,841	1,984	5,040	39.1	19.3	6,880	1,108	5,772	989	3,336	1,362
May	12,695	2,602	3,007	1,703	5,385	39.6	20.1	6,968	1,128	5,840	902	3,450	1,347
June	12,701	2,825	2,826	1,813	5,336	39.7	19.4	7,121	1,309	5,812	936	3,243	1,316
July	12,745	2,697	3,102	1,756	5,167	38.8	16.8	7,106	1,429	5,677	879	3,374	1,299
Aug	12,483	2,865	2,848	1,823	5,023	39.3	18.2	6,935	1,211	5,724	946	3,316	1,268
Sept	12,082	2,535	2,825	1,866	4,871	39.6	18.7	6,489	1,153	5,335	962	3,313	1,253
Oct	12,248	2,633	2,847	1,813	5,017	39.9	19.6	6,536	1,077	5,460	1,009	3,319	1,302
Nov	12,042	2,596	2,757	1,820	4,784	39.7	18.9	6,429	1,080	5,349	926	3,325	1,326
Dec	12,206	2,676	2,838	1,895	4,766	38.1	18.0	6,408	1,085	5,323	983	3,587	1,291

[1] Because of independent seasonal adjustment of the various series, detail will not sum to totals.
[2] For 1967, the sum of the unemployed categorized by reason for unemployment does not equal total unemployment.
[3] Beginning with January 2011, includes unemployment durations of up to 5 years; prior data are for up to 2 years.
[4] Beginning with January 1994, job losers and persons who completed temporary jobs.

Note: Data relate to persons 16 years of age and over.
See footnote 5 and Note, Table B–35.

Source: Department of Labor (Bureau of Labor Statistics).

[Thousands of persons, except as noted]

Year or month	All programs [1] Insured unemployment (weekly average) [2]	Total benefits paid (millions of dollars)	Regular State programs Covered employment [3]	Insured unemployment (weekly average) [2]	Initial claims (weekly average)	Exhaustions (weekly average) [4]	Insured unemployment as percent of covered employment	Benefits paid Total (millions of dollars)	Average weekly check (dollars) [5]
1980	3,521	16,668	86,918	3,356	488	59	3.9	14,887	99.06
1981	3,248	15,910	87,783	3,045	460	57	3.5	14,568	106.61
1982	4,836	26,649	86,148	4,059	583	80	4.7	21,769	119.34
1983	5,216	31,615	86,867	3,395	438	80	3.9	19,025	123.59
1984	3,160	18,201	91,378	2,475	377	50	2.7	13,642	123.47
1985	2,751	16,444	94,027	2,617	397	49	2.8	14,941	128.09
1986	2,667	16,325	95,946	2,621	378	52	2.7	16,188	135.65
1987	2,349	14,632	98,760	2,300	328	46	2.3	14,561	140.39
1988	2,122	13,500	101,987	2,081	310	38	2.0	13,483	144.74
1989	2,158	14,618	104,750	2,156	330	37	2.1	14,603	151.43
1990	2,527	18,452	106,325	2,522	388	45	2.4	18,413	161.20
1991	3,514	27,004	104,642	3,342	447	67	3.2	25,924	169.56
1992	4,906	39,669	105,187	3,245	408	74	3.1	26,048	173.38
1993	4,188	34,649	107,263	2,751	341	62	2.6	22,599	179.41
1994	2,941	24,261	110,526	2,670	340	57	2.4	22,338	181.91
1995	2,648	22,026	113,504	2,572	357	51	2.3	21,925	187.04
1996	2,656	22,397	116,078	2,595	356	53	2.2	22,349	189.27
1997	2,372	20,333	119,159	2,323	323	48	1.9	20,287	192.84
1998	2,264	20,091	122,427	2,222	321	44	1.8	20,017	200.58
1999	2,223	21,037	125,280	2,188	298	44	1.7	21,001	212.10
2000	2,143	21,005	128,054	2,110	301	41	1.6	20,983	221.01
2001	3,012	32,227	127,923	2,974	404	54	2.3	32,135	238.07
2002	4,453	53,350	126,545	3,585	407	85	2.8	42,266	256.79
2003	4,400	53,352	126,084	3,531	404	85	2.8	41,896	261.67
2004	3,103	36,495	127,618	2,950	345	68	2.3	35,034	262.50
2005	2,709	32,154	129,929	2,661	328	55	2.0	32,098	266.63
2006	2,521	30,917	132,177	2,476	313	51	1.9	30,852	277.20
2007	2,612	33,212	133,688	2,572	324	51	1.9	33,156	287.73
2008	3,898	51,798	133,076	3,306	424	66	2.5	43,764	297.10
2009	9,122	141,384	126,763	5,724	568	145	4.5	80,564	308.73
2010	9,723	150,047	125,816	4,487	454	122	3.6	59,771	299.31
2011	7,626	107,740	127,479	3,681	406	93	2.9	48,519	295.79
2012 p	6,035	84,115	128,825	3,293	373	81	2.6	44,156	302.44
2011: Jan	10,646	11,115.1	124,494	5,209	598	121	4.2	5,085.6	296.92
Feb	8,971	9,902.9	125,059	4,450	397	100	3.6	4,643.6	299.06
Mar	9,328	10,779.9	125,943	4,545	416	111	3.6	4,982.5	299.68
Apr	8,113	8,846.6	127,392	3,862	428	107	3.0	3,950.0	298.18
May	8,831	9,302.8	128,197	4,094	407	109	3.2	4,033.1	295.89
June	7,885	8,812.6	128,530	3,688	447	97	2.9	3,808.6	293.63
July	7,958	8,127.4	126,543	3,887	439	101	3.1	3,662.2	289.72
Aug	8,252	9,125.3	127,184	4,013	398	103	3.2	4,115.4	289.00
Sept	6,849	7,589.2	128,599	3,305	366	85	2.6	3,348.3	296.37
Oct	7,645	7,903.1	129,001	3,582	403	94	2.8	3,435.6	295.07
Nov	7,332	8,109.3	129,406	3,533	459	92	2.7	3,662.2	296.09
Dec	7,330	8,125.9	129,402	3,688	517	89	2.9	3,791.7	298.39
2012: Jan	9,048	9,585.0	126,609	4,781	548	109	3.8	4,814.2	301.26
Feb	7,567	8,424.7	127,257	4,045	375	89	3.2	4,399.6	305.37
Mar	7,174	7,979.0	128,320	3,783	354	89	2.9	4,105.7	305.30
Apr	7,454	7,811.8	129,271	3,832	387	101	3.0	3,853.5	301.67
May	6,403	7,197.3	130,469	3,282	374	92	2.5	3,587.6	304.22
June	5,844	6,243.2	131,024	3,097	388	79	2.4	3,191.6	300.47
July	6,835	7,094.9	....	3,814	422	99	....	3,764.9	296.71
Aug	5,681	6,249.1	....	3,252	356	81	....	3,422.7	297.82
Sept	5,377	5,479.8	....	3,014	311	74	....	2,964.4	303.82
Oct	5,656	6,246.0	....	3,184	391	85	....	3,338.9	303.52
Nov	5,358	5,657.8	....	3,080	470	75	....	3,137.7	304.93
Dec p	6,052	6,146.1	....	3,639	469	81	....	3,575.0	304.42

[1] Includes State Unemployment Insurance (State), Unemployment Compensation for Federal Employees (UCFE), Unemployment Compensation for Ex-service members (UCX), and Federal and State extended benefit programs. Also includes temporary Federal emergency programs: Federal Supplemental Compensation (1982-1985), Emergency Unemployment Compensation (EUC, 1991-1994), Temporary Extended Unemployment Compensation (2002-2004), EUC 2008 (2008-2012), and Federal Additional Compensation (2009-2010).
[2] The number of people continuing to receive benefits.
[3] Workers covered by regular State Unemployment Insurance programs.
[4] Individuals receiving final payments in benefit year.
[5] For total unemployment only. Excludes partial payments.

Note: Includes data for the District of Columbia, Puerto Rico, and the Virgin Islands.

Source: Department of Labor (Employment and Training Administration).

TABLE B–46. Employees on nonagricultural payrolls, by major industry, 1968–2012

[Thousands of persons; monthly data seasonally adjusted]

Year or month	Total non-agricultural employ-ment	Private industries										
		Total private	Goods-producing industries							Private service-providing industries		
			Total	Mining and logging	Con-struc-tion	Manufacturing				Total	Trade, transportation, and utilities [1]	
						Total	Durable goods	Non-durable goods			Total	Retail trade
1968	68,023	56,050	22,292	671	3,410	18,211	11,137	7,074		33,759	13,334	6,977
1969	70,512	58,181	22,893	683	3,637	18,573	11,396	7,177		35,288	13,853	7,295
1970	71,006	58,318	22,179	677	3,654	17,848	10,762	7,086		36,139	14,144	7,463
1971	71,335	58,323	21,602	658	3,770	17,174	10,229	6,944		36,721	14,318	7,657
1972	73,798	60,333	22,299	672	3,957	17,669	10,630	7,039		38,034	14,788	8,038
1973	76,912	63,050	23,450	693	4,167	18,589	11,414	7,176		39,600	15,349	8,371
1974	78,389	64,086	23,364	755	4,095	18,514	11,432	7,082		40,721	15,693	8,536
1975	77,069	62,250	21,318	802	3,608	16,909	10,266	6,643		40,932	15,606	8,600
1976	79,502	64,501	22,025	832	3,662	17,531	10,640	6,891		42,476	16,128	8,966
1977	82,593	67,334	22,972	865	3,940	18,167	11,132	7,035		44,362	16,765	9,359
1978	86,826	71,014	24,156	902	4,322	18,932	11,770	7,162		46,858	17,658	9,879
1979	89,932	73,864	24,997	1,008	4,562	19,426	12,220	7,206		48,868	18,303	10,180
1980	90,528	74,154	24,263	1,077	4,454	18,733	11,679	7,054		49,891	18,413	10,244
1981	91,289	75,109	24,118	1,180	4,304	18,634	11,611	7,023		50,991	18,604	10,364
1982	89,677	73,695	22,550	1,163	4,024	17,363	10,610	6,753		51,145	18,457	10,372
1983	90,280	74,269	22,110	997	4,065	17,048	10,326	6,722		52,160	18,668	10,635
1984	94,530	78,371	23,435	1,014	4,501	17,920	11,050	6,870		54,936	19,653	11,223
1985	97,511	80,978	23,585	974	4,793	17,819	11,034	6,784		57,393	20,379	11,733
1986	99,474	82,636	23,318	829	4,937	17,552	10,795	6,757		59,318	20,795	12,078
1987	102,088	84,932	23,470	771	5,090	17,609	10,767	6,842		61,462	21,302	12,419
1988	105,345	87,806	23,909	770	5,233	17,906	10,969	6,938		63,897	21,974	12,808
1989	108,014	90,087	24,045	750	5,309	17,985	11,004	6,981		66,042	22,510	13,108
1990	109,487	91,072	23,723	765	5,263	17,695	10,737	6,958		67,349	22,666	13,182
1991	108,377	89,832	22,588	739	4,780	17,068	10,220	6,848		67,244	22,281	12,896
1992	108,745	89,958	22,095	689	4,608	16,799	9,946	6,853		67,863	22,125	12,828
1993	110,876	91,887	22,219	666	4,779	16,774	9,901	6,872		69,668	22,378	13,021
1994	114,333	95,058	22,774	659	5,095	17,020	10,132	6,889		72,284	23,128	13,491
1995	117,336	97,904	23,156	641	5,274	17,241	10,373	6,868		74,748	23,834	13,897
1996	119,757	100,218	23,409	637	5,536	17,237	10,486	6,751		76,809	24,239	14,143
1997	122,853	103,190	23,886	654	5,813	17,419	10,705	6,714		79,304	24,700	14,389
1998	126,033	106,124	24,354	645	6,149	17,560	10,911	6,649		81,770	25,186	14,609
1999	129,098	108,791	24,465	598	6,545	17,322	10,831	6,491		84,326	25,771	14,970
2000	131,881	111,091	24,649	599	6,787	17,263	10,877	6,386		86,442	26,225	15,280
2001	131,919	110,800	23,873	606	6,826	16,441	10,336	6,105		86,927	25,983	15,239
2002	130,450	108,937	22,557	583	6,716	15,259	9,485	5,774		86,380	25,497	15,025
2003	130,100	108,517	21,816	572	6,735	14,509	8,964	5,546		86,701	25,287	14,917
2004	131,509	109,888	21,882	591	6,976	14,315	8,925	5,390		88,006	25,533	15,058
2005	133,747	111,943	22,190	628	7,336	14,227	8,956	5,271		89,753	25,959	15,280
2006	136,125	114,151	22,530	684	7,691	14,155	8,981	5,174		91,621	26,276	15,353
2007	137,645	115,427	22,233	724	7,630	13,879	8,808	5,071		93,194	26,630	15,520
2008	136,852	114,342	21,335	767	7,162	13,406	8,463	4,943		93,008	26,293	15,283
2009	130,876	108,321	18,558	694	6,016	11,847	7,284	4,564		89,764	24,906	14,522
2010	129,917	107,427	17,751	705	5,518	11,528	7,064	4,464		89,676	24,636	14,440
2011	131,497	109,411	18,047	788	5,533	11,726	7,273	4,453		91,363	25,065	14,668
2012 p	133,738	111,821	18,410	851	5,640	11,918	7,462	4,456		93,411	25,517	14,875
2011: Jan	130,464	108,208	17,797	738	5,435	11,624	7,171	4,453		90,411	24,821	14,547
Feb	130,660	108,451	17,880	740	5,478	11,662	7,199	4,463		90,571	24,868	14,557
Mar	130,865	108,674	17,923	756	5,485	11,682	7,218	4,464		90,751	24,896	14,564
Apr	131,169	108,977	17,972	768	5,497	11,707	7,238	4,469		91,005	24,990	14,634
May	131,284	109,160	18,015	776	5,524	11,715	7,257	4,458		91,145	25,013	14,639
June	131,493	109,337	18,042	788	5,530	11,724	7,274	4,450		91,295	25,076	14,676
July	131,571	109,543	18,093	799	5,547	11,747	7,290	4,457		91,450	25,116	14,710
Aug	131,703	109,672	18,109	803	5,546	11,760	7,298	4,462		91,563	25,132	14,711
Sept	131,928	109,928	18,156	811	5,583	11,762	7,307	4,455		91,772	25,166	14,733
Oct	132,094	110,102	18,165	819	5,576	11,770	7,324	4,446		91,929	25,196	14,741
Nov	132,268	110,299	18,169	823	5,577	11,769	7,334	4,435		92,130	25,246	14,769
Dec	132,498	110,548	18,242	833	5,612	11,797	7,362	4,435		92,306	25,285	14,775
2012: Jan	132,809	110,871	18,314	844	5,629	11,841	7,400	4,441		92,557	25,372	14,805
Feb	133,080	111,136	18,365	851	5,644	11,870	7,426	4,444		92,771	25,377	14,799
Mar	133,285	111,344	18,402	852	5,640	11,910	7,452	4,458		92,942	25,381	14,799
Apr	133,397	111,464	18,408	852	5,636	11,920	7,460	4,460		93,056	25,409	14,830
May	133,522	111,616	18,396	855	5,615	11,926	7,467	4,459		93,220	25,463	14,839
June	133,609	111,694	18,410	853	5,622	11,935	7,476	4,459		93,284	25,467	14,839
July	133,762	111,871	18,436	852	5,627	11,957	7,496	4,461		93,435	25,485	14,839
Aug	133,927	112,002	18,422	849	5,630	11,943	7,482	4,461		93,580	25,520	14,850
Sept	134,065	112,120	18,405	847	5,633	11,925	7,465	4,460		93,715	25,550	14,850
Oct	134,225	112,337	18,421	841	5,649	11,931	7,466	4,465		93,916	25,623	14,928
Nov	134,472	112,593	18,464	853	5,673	11,938	7,483	4,455		94,129	25,720	14,998
Dec p	134,668	112,795	18,508	859	5,703	11,946	7,491	4,455		94,287	25,781	15,009

[1] Includes wholesale trade, transportation and warehousing, and utilities, not shown separately.

Note: Data in Tables B–46 and B–47 are based on reports from employing establishments and relate to full- and part-time wage and salary workers in nonagricultural establishments who received pay for any part of the pay period that includes the 12th of the month. Not comparable with labor force data (Tables B–35 through B–44), which include proprietors, self-employed persons, unpaid family workers, and private household workers; which count persons as employed when they are not at work because of industrial disputes, bad weather, etc., even if they are not paid for the time off; which are based on a sample of the

See next page for continuation of table.

TABLE B–46. Employees on nonagricultural payrolls, by major industry, 1968–2012—*Continued*

[Thousands of persons; monthly data seasonally adjusted]

Year or month	Private industries—Continued						Government			
	Private service-providing industries—Continued									
	Information	Financial activities	Profes-sional and business services	Education and health services	Leisure and hospitality	Other services	Total	Federal	State	Local
1968	1,991	3,234	4,918	4,191	4,453	1,638	11,972	2,871	2,442	6,660
1969	2,048	3,404	5,156	4,428	4,670	1,731	12,330	2,893	2,533	6,904
1970	2,041	3,532	5,267	4,577	4,789	1,789	12,687	2,865	2,664	7,158
1971	2,009	3,651	5,328	4,675	4,914	1,827	13,012	2,828	2,747	7,437
1972	2,056	3,784	5,523	4,863	5,121	1,900	13,465	2,815	2,859	7,790
1973	2,135	3,920	5,774	5,092	5,341	1,990	13,862	2,794	2,923	8,146
1974	2,160	4,023	5,974	5,322	5,471	2,078	14,303	2,858	3,039	8,407
1975	2,061	4,047	6,034	5,497	5,544	2,144	14,820	2,882	3,179	8,758
1976	2,111	4,155	6,287	5,756	5,794	2,244	15,001	2,863	3,273	8,865
1977	2,185	4,348	6,587	6,052	6,065	2,359	15,258	2,859	3,377	9,023
1978	2,287	4,599	6,972	6,427	6,411	2,505	15,812	2,893	3,474	9,446
1979	2,375	4,843	7,312	6,767	6,631	2,637	16,068	2,894	3,541	9,633
1980	2,361	5,025	7,544	7,072	6,721	2,755	16,375	3,000	3,610	9,765
1981	2,382	5,163	7,782	7,357	6,840	2,865	16,180	2,922	3,640	9,619
1982	2,317	5,209	7,848	7,515	6,874	2,924	15,982	2,884	3,640	9,458
1983	2,253	5,334	8,039	7,766	7,078	3,021	16,011	2,915	3,662	9,434
1984	2,398	5,553	8,464	8,193	7,489	3,186	16,159	2,943	3,734	9,482
1985	2,437	5,815	8,871	8,657	7,869	3,366	16,533	3,014	3,832	9,687
1986	2,445	6,128	9,211	9,061	8,156	3,523	16,838	3,044	3,893	9,901
1987	2,507	6,385	9,608	9,515	8,446	3,699	17,156	3,089	3,967	10,100
1988	2,585	6,500	10,090	10,063	8,778	3,907	17,540	3,124	4,076	10,339
1989	2,622	6,562	10,555	10,616	9,062	4,116	17,927	3,136	4,182	10,609
1990	2,688	6,614	10,848	10,984	9,288	4,261	18,415	3,196	4,305	10,914
1991	2,677	6,561	10,714	11,506	9,256	4,249	18,545	3,110	4,355	11,081
1992	2,641	6,559	10,970	11,891	9,437	4,240	18,787	3,111	4,408	11,267
1993	2,668	6,742	11,495	12,303	9,732	4,350	18,989	3,063	4,488	11,438
1994	2,738	6,910	12,174	12,807	10,100	4,428	19,275	3,018	4,576	11,682
1995	2,843	6,866	12,844	13,289	10,501	4,572	19,432	2,949	4,635	11,849
1996	2,940	7,018	13,462	13,683	10,777	4,690	19,539	2,877	4,606	12,056
1997	3,084	7,255	14,335	14,087	11,018	4,825	19,664	2,806	4,582	12,276
1998	3,218	7,565	15,147	14,446	11,232	4,976	19,909	2,772	4,612	12,525
1999	3,419	7,753	15,957	14,798	11,543	5,087	20,307	2,769	4,709	12,829
2000	3,630	7,783	16,666	15,109	11,862	5,168	20,790	2,865	4,786	13,139
2001	3,629	7,900	16,476	15,645	12,036	5,258	21,118	2,764	4,905	13,449
2002	3,395	7,956	15,976	16,199	11,986	5,372	21,513	2,766	5,029	13,718
2003	3,188	8,078	15,987	16,588	12,173	5,401	21,583	2,761	5,002	13,820
2004	3,118	8,105	16,394	16,953	12,493	5,409	21,621	2,730	4,982	13,909
2005	3,061	8,197	16,954	17,372	12,816	5,395	21,804	2,732	5,032	14,041
2006	3,038	8,367	17,566	17,826	13,110	5,438	21,974	2,732	5,075	14,167
2007	3,032	8,348	17,942	18,322	13,427	5,494	22,218	2,734	5,122	14,362
2008	2,984	8,206	17,735	18,838	13,436	5,515	22,509	2,762	5,177	14,571
2009	2,804	7,838	16,579	19,193	13,077	5,367	22,555	2,832	5,169	14,554
2010	2,707	7,695	16,728	19,531	13,049	5,331	22,490	2,977	5,137	14,376
2011	2,674	7,697	17,332	19,883	13,353	5,360	22,086	2,859	5,078	14,150
2012 *p*	2,679	7,787	17,928	20,319	13,745	5,437	21,917	2,814	5,051	14,051
2011: Jan	2,683	7,677	17,044	19,705	13,152	5,329	22,256	2,874	5,136	14,246
Feb	2,673	7,674	17,102	19,723	13,196	5,335	22,209	2,877	5,110	14,222
Mar	2,673	7,678	17,191	19,741	13,242	5,330	22,191	2,878	5,101	14,212
Apr	2,676	7,680	17,239	19,798	13,281	5,341	22,192	2,872	5,094	14,226
May	2,676	7,701	17,298	19,816	13,293	5,348	22,124	2,872	5,084	14,168
June	2,684	7,692	17,289	19,857	13,345	5,352	22,156	2,859	5,078	14,219
July	2,678	7,697	17,319	19,900	13,382	5,358	22,028	2,859	5,054	14,115
Aug	2,633	7,704	17,384	19,936	13,399	5,375	22,031	2,851	5,077	14,103
Sept	2,675	7,702	17,451	19,988	13,410	5,380	22,000	2,846	5,076	14,078
Oct	2,677	7,710	17,485	20,028	13,459	5,382	21,992	2,846	5,058	14,088
Nov	2,677	7,721	17,528	20,052	13,515	5,391	21,969	2,841	5,052	14,076
Dec	2,682	7,728	17,588	20,080	13,541	5,402	21,950	2,841	5,042	14,067
2012: Jan	2,670	7,730	17,677	20,106	13,585	5,417	21,938	2,834	5,042	14,062
Feb	2,681	7,740	17,753	20,175	13,632	5,413	21,944	2,832	5,051	14,061
Mar	2,679	7,763	17,796	20,221	13,684	5,418	21,941	2,830	5,059	14,052
Apr	2,679	7,768	17,841	20,243	13,698	5,418	21,933	2,828	5,064	14,041
May	2,681	7,782	17,878	20,290	13,702	5,424	21,906	2,821	5,049	14,036
June	2,675	7,788	17,913	20,296	13,716	5,429	21,915	2,818	5,050	14,047
July	2,684	7,788	17,965	20,331	13,743	5,439	21,891	2,805	5,042	14,044
Aug	2,682	7,795	17,994	20,363	13,788	5,438	21,925	2,810	5,049	14,066
Sept	2,670	7,806	18,009	20,412	13,818	5,450	21,945	2,810	5,072	14,063
Oct	2,671	7,817	18,062	20,446	13,840	5,457	21,888	2,807	5,052	14,029
Nov	2,685	7,822	18,117	20,460	13,861	5,464	21,879	2,798	5,047	14,034
Dec *p*	2,682	7,831	18,119	20,510	13,894	5,470	21,873	2,796	5,044	14,033

Note (cont'd): working-age population; and which count persons only once—as employed, unemployed, or not in the labor force. In the data shown here, persons who work at more than one job are counted each time they appear on a payroll.
Establishment data for employment, hours, and earnings are classified based on the 2012 North American Industry Classification System (NAICS). For further description and details see *Employment and Earnings.*

Source: Department of Labor (Bureau of Labor Statistics).

[Monthly data seasonally adjusted]

Year or month	Average weekly hours			Average hourly earnings			Average weekly earnings, total private			
	Total private	Manufacturing		Total private		Manufacturing (current dollars)	Level		Percent change from year earlier	
		Total	Overtime	Current dollars	1982–84 dollars [2]		Current dollars	1982–84 dollars [2]	Current dollars	1982–84 dollars [2]
1966	38.5	41.4	3.9	$2.73	$8.37	$2.60	$105.23	$322.79	3.7	0.8
1967	37.9	40.6	3.3	2.85	8.48	2.71	108.07	321.64	2.7	–.4
1968	37.7	40.7	3.6	3.02	8.63	2.89	113.82	325.20	5.3	1.1
1969	37.5	40.6	3.6	3.22	8.73	3.07	120.70	327.10	6.0	.6
1970	37.0	39.8	2.9	3.40	8.72	3.24	125.79	322.54	4.2	–1.4
1971	36.7	39.9	2.9	3.63	8.92	3.45	133.22	327.32	5.9	1.5
1972	36.9	40.6	3.4	3.90	9.26	3.70	143.87	341.73	8.0	4.4
1973	36.9	40.7	3.8	4.14	9.26	3.97	152.59	341.36	6.1	–.1
1974	36.4	40.0	3.2	4.43	8.93	4.31	161.61	325.83	5.9	–4.5
1975	36.0	39.5	2.6	4.73	8.74	4.71	170.29	314.77	5.4	–3.4
1976	36.1	40.1	3.1	5.06	8.85	5.10	182.65	319.32	7.3	1.4
1977	35.9	40.3	3.4	5.44	8.93	5.55	195.58	321.15	7.1	.6
1978	35.8	40.4	3.6	5.88	8.96	6.05	210.29	320.56	7.5	–.2
1979	35.6	40.2	3.3	6.34	8.67	6.57	225.69	308.74	7.3	–3.7
1980	35.2	39.6	2.8	6.85	8.26	7.15	241.07	290.80	6.8	–5.8
1981	35.2	39.8	2.8	7.44	8.14	7.87	261.53	286.14	8.5	–1.6
1982	34.7	38.9	2.3	7.87	8.12	8.36	273.10	281.84	4.4	–1.5
1983	34.9	40.1	2.9	8.20	8.22	8.70	286.43	287.00	4.9	1.8
1984	35.1	40.6	3.4	8.49	8.22	9.05	298.26	288.73	4.1	.6
1985	34.9	40.5	3.3	8.74	8.18	9.40	304.62	284.96	2.1	–1.3
1986	34.7	40.7	3.4	8.93	8.22	9.60	309.78	285.25	1.7	.1
1987	34.7	40.9	3.7	9.14	8.12	9.77	317.39	282.12	2.5	–1.1
1988	34.6	41.0	3.8	9.44	8.07	10.05	326.48	279.04	2.9	–1.1
1989	34.5	40.9	3.8	9.80	7.99	10.35	338.34	275.97	3.6	–1.1
1990	34.3	40.5	3.9	10.20	7.91	10.78	349.72	271.10	3.4	–1.8
1991	34.1	40.4	3.8	10.52	7.83	11.13	358.51	266.95	2.5	–1.5
1992	34.2	40.7	4.0	10.77	7.79	11.40	368.25	266.46	2.7	–.2
1993	34.3	41.1	4.4	11.05	7.78	11.70	378.94	266.67	2.9	.1
1994	34.5	41.7	5.0	11.34	7.79	12.04	391.28	268.74	3.3	.8
1995	34.3	41.3	4.7	11.66	7.78	12.34	400.22	267.17	2.3	–.6
1996	34.3	41.3	4.8	12.05	7.82	12.75	413.47	268.31	3.3	.4
1997	34.5	41.7	5.1	12.51	7.94	13.14	432.05	274.14	4.5	2.2
1998	34.5	41.4	4.9	13.02	8.15	13.45	448.76	281.00	3.9	2.5
1999	34.3	41.4	4.9	13.49	8.27	13.85	463.35	283.92	3.3	1.0
2000	34.3	41.3	4.7	14.02	8.30	14.32	481.36	285.00	3.9	.4
2001	34.0	40.3	4.0	14.55	8.39	14.76	494.05	284.76	2.6	–.1
2002	33.9	40.5	4.2	14.97	8.51	15.29	507.03	288.25	2.6	1.2
2003	33.7	40.4	4.2	15.38	8.55	15.74	518.41	288.33	2.2	.0
2004	33.7	40.8	4.6	15.70	8.51	16.14	529.23	286.85	2.1	–.5
2005	33.8	40.7	4.6	16.13	8.45	16.56	544.44	285.05	2.9	–.6
2006	33.9	41.1	4.4	16.76	8.50	16.81	567.89	288.12	4.3	1.1
2007	33.9	41.2	4.2	17.44	8.60	17.26	590.24	291.09	3.9	1.0
2008	33.6	40.8	3.7	18.08	8.57	17.75	608.11	288.13	3.0	–1.0
2009	33.1	39.8	2.9	18.63	8.89	18.24	617.50	294.57	1.5	2.2
2010	33.4	41.1	3.8	19.07	8.91	18.61	637.18	297.79	3.2	1.1
2011	33.6	41.4	4.1	19.46	8.78	18.93	654.73	295.49	2.8	–.8
2012 p	33.7	41.7	4.2	19.77	8.74	19.09	666.99	294.83	1.9	–.2
2011: Jan	33.4	41.0	4.1	19.33	8.90	18.90	645.62	297.13	2.5	.7
Feb	33.5	41.3	4.2	19.34	8.86	18.90	647.89	296.70	3.0	.7
Mar	33.6	41.5	4.2	19.34	8.80	18.90	649.82	295.73	3.0	.0
Apr	33.7	41.4	4.1	19.39	8.79	18.90	653.44	296.07	3.1	–.4
May	33.6	41.5	4.1	19.44	8.78	18.93	653.18	295.11	2.5	–1.4
June	33.6	41.4	4.0	19.45	8.78	18.91	653.52	295.10	2.7	–1.3
July	33.7	41.4	4.1	19.51	8.78	18.93	657.49	295.89	2.9	–1.2
Aug	33.6	41.3	4.1	19.50	8.74	18.90	655.20	293.76	2.2	–1.9
Sept	33.7	41.4	4.1	19.52	8.72	18.92	657.82	294.00	2.5	–1.8
Oct	33.7	41.5	4.1	19.56	8.75	18.96	659.17	294.84	2.0	–1.9
Nov	33.7	41.5	4.1	19.59	8.76	18.96	660.18	295.10	2.4	–1.3
Dec	33.7	41.6	4.1	19.58	8.75	18.99	659.85	294.99	2.4	–.9
2012: Jan	33.8	41.8	4.2	19.61	8.75	19.03	662.82	295.71	2.7	–.5
Feb	33.8	41.8	4.2	19.64	8.72	19.02	663.83	294.71	2.5	–.7
Mar	33.7	41.6	4.2	19.68	8.71	19.02	663.22	293.47	2.1	–.8
Apr	33.7	41.7	4.2	19.72	8.73	19.08	664.56	294.14	1.7	–.7
May	33.7	41.6	4.2	19.70	8.75	19.03	663.89	295.03	1.6	.0
June	33.7	41.6	4.2	19.75	8.78	19.08	665.58	295.82	1.8	.2
July	33.7	41.7	4.2	19.77	8.78	19.11	666.25	295.98	1.3	.0
Aug	33.6	41.6	4.1	19.76	8.71	19.07	663.94	292.80	1.3	–.3
Sept	33.7	41.5	4.2	19.80	8.67	19.07	667.26	292.29	1.4	–.6
Oct	33.6	41.5	4.1	19.82	8.67	19.08	665.95	291.34	1.0	–1.2
Nov	33.7	41.6	4.1	19.88	8.74	19.17	669.96	294.44	1.5	–.2
Dec p	33.7	41.7	4.2	19.92	8.76	19.19	671.30	295.15	1.7	.1

[1] For production or nonsupervisory workers; total includes private industry groups shown in Table B–46.
[2] Current dollars divided by the consumer price index for urban wage earners and clerical workers on a 1982–84=100 base.

Note: See Note, Table B–46.

Source: Department of Labor (Bureau of Labor Statistics).

TABLE B–48. Employment cost index, private industry, 1997–2012

Year and month	Total private			Goods-producing			Service-providing [1]			Manufacturing		
	Total compensation	Wages and salaries	Benefits [2]	Total compensation	Wages and salaries	Benefits [2]	Total compensation	Wages and salaries	Benefits [2]	Total compensation	Wages and salaries	Benefits [2]
	Indexes on SIC basis, December 2005=100; not seasonally adjusted											
December:												
1997	74.9	77.6	68.5	74.5	78.3	67.3	75.1	77.4	69.2	74.6	78.6	67.4
1998	77.5	80.6	70.2	76.5	81.1	68.1	78.0	80.5	71.4	76.6	81.3	67.9
1999	80.2	83.5	72.6	79.1	83.8	70.5	80.6	83.4	73.8	79.2	84.1	70.3
2000	83.6	86.7	76.7	82.6	87.1	74.3	84.2	86.6	78.1	82.3	87.1	73.6
2001	87.1	90.0	80.6	85.7	90.2	77.3	87.8	89.9	82.5	85.3	90.2	76.3
	Indexes on NAICS basis, December 2005=100; not seasonally adjusted											
2001 [3]	87.3	89.9	81.3	86.0	90.0	78.5	87.8	89.8	82.4	85.5	90.2	77.2
2002	90.0	92.2	84.7	89.0	92.6	82.3	90.4	92.1	85.8	88.7	92.8	81.3
2003	93.6	95.1	90.2	92.6	94.9	88.2	94.0	95.2	91.0	92.4	95.1	87.3
2004	97.2	97.6	96.2	96.9	97.2	96.3	97.3	97.7	96.1	96.9	97.4	96.0
2005	100.0	100.0	100.0	100.0	100.0	100.0	100.0	100.0	100.0	100.0	100.0	100.0
2006	103.2	103.2	103.1	102.5	102.9	101.7	103.4	103.3	103.7	101.8	102.3	100.8
2007	106.3	106.6	105.6	105.0	106.0	103.2	106.7	106.8	106.6	103.8	104.9	101.7
2008	108.9	109.4	107.7	107.5	109.0	104.7	109.4	109.6	108.9	105.9	107.7	102.5
2009	110.2	110.8	108.7	108.6	110.0	105.8	110.8	111.1	109.9	107.0	108.9	103.6
2010	112.5	112.8	111.9	111.1	111.6	110.1	113.0	113.1	112.6	110.0	110.7	108.8
2011	115.0	114.6	115.9	113.8	113.5	114.4	115.3	114.9	116.4	113.1	112.7	113.9
2012: Mar	115.7	115.3	116.9	114.1	114.0	114.2	116.3	115.6	118.0	113.4	113.6	113.2
June	116.4	115.9	117.6	114.7	114.5	114.9	117.0	116.3	118.7	114.0	114.0	114.0
Sept	116.9	116.4	118.1	115.3	115.1	115.7	117.4	116.7	119.1	114.6	114.6	114.7
	Indexes on NAICS basis, December 2005=100; seasonally adjusted											
2011: Mar	113.3	113.2	113.5	112.0	112.1	111.6	113.8	113.5	114.3	111.2	111.4	110.8
June	114.2	113.8	115.1	112.0	112.7	113.7	114.5	114.1	115.7	112.5	112.0	113.4
Sept	114.6	114.2	115.4	113.3	113.1	113.8	115.0	114.6	116.0	112.8	112.4	113.4
Dec	115.2	114.7	116.3	114.1	113.6	115.1	115.5	115.0	116.8	113.6	113.0	114.7
2012: Mar	115.7	115.3	116.7	114.0	114.0	114.0	116.3	115.7	117.8	113.3	113.5	113.2
June	116.3	115.8	117.4	114.5	114.5	114.5	116.9	116.3	118.5	113.8	114.0	113.4
Sept	116.8	116.3	118.2	115.3	115.1	115.7	117.3	116.6	119.1	114.6	114.5	114.8
	Percent change from 12 months earlier, not seasonally adjusted											
December:												
SIC:												
1997	3.5	3.9	2.2	2.5	3.0	1.4	3.9	4.3	2.8	2.3	3.0	1.4
1998	3.5	3.9	2.5	2.7	3.6	1.2	3.9	4.0	3.2	2.7	3.4	.7
1999	3.5	3.6	3.4	3.4	3.3	3.5	3.3	3.6	3.4	3.4	3.4	3.5
2000	4.2	3.8	5.6	4.4	3.9	5.4	4.5	3.8	5.8	3.9	3.6	4.7
2001	4.2	3.8	5.1	3.8	3.6	4.0	4.3	3.8	5.6	3.6	3.6	3.7
NAICS:												
2001 [3]	4.1	3.8	5.2	3.6	3.6	3.7	4.4	3.8	5.6	3.4	3.6	3.5
2002	3.1	2.6	4.2	3.5	2.9	4.8	3.0	2.6	4.1	3.7	2.9	5.3
2003	4.0	3.1	6.5	4.0	2.5	7.2	4.0	3.4	6.1	4.2	2.5	7.4
2004	3.8	2.6	6.7	4.6	2.4	9.2	3.5	2.6	5.6	4.9	2.4	10.0
2005	2.9	2.5	4.0	3.2	2.9	3.8	2.8	2.4	4.1	3.2	2.7	4.2
2006	3.2	3.2	3.1	2.5	2.9	1.7	3.4	3.3	3.7	1.8	2.3	.8
2007	3.0	3.3	2.4	2.4	3.0	1.5	3.2	3.4	2.8	2.0	2.5	.9
2008	2.4	2.6	2.0	2.4	2.8	1.5	2.5	2.6	2.2	2.0	2.7	.8
2009	1.2	1.3	.9	1.0	.9	1.1	1.3	1.4	.9	1.0	1.1	1.1
2010	2.1	1.8	2.9	2.3	1.5	4.1	2.0	1.8	2.5	2.8	1.7	5.0
2011	2.2	1.6	3.6	2.4	1.7	3.9	2.0	1.6	3.4	2.8	1.8	4.7
2012: Mar	2.1	1.9	2.8	1.9	1.6	2.2	2.2	1.9	3.1	1.8	1.9	1.9
June	1.8	1.8	1.9	1.3	1.6	.7	2.1	1.9	2.4	1.2	1.8	.0
Sept	2.0	1.8	2.3	1.7	1.7	1.6	2.1	1.8	2.7	1.6	1.9	1.1
	Percent change from 3 months earlier, seasonally adjusted											
2011: Mar	0.5	0.4	1.1	0.6	0.4	0.9	0.6	0.3	1.2	0.6	0.5	1.1
June	.8	.5	1.4	.9	.5	1.9	.6	.5	1.2	1.2	.5	2.3
Sept	.4	.4	.3	.3	.4	.1	.4	.4	.3	.3	.4	.0
Dec	.5	.4	.8	.7	.4	1.1	.4	.3	.7	.7	.5	1.1
2012: Mar	.4	.5	.3	–.1	.4	–1.0	.7	.6	.9	–.3	.4	–1.6
June	.5	.4	.6	.4	.4	.4	.5	.5	.6	.4	.4	.4
Sept	.4	.4	.7	.7	.5	1.0	.5	.3	.5	.7	.4	1.2

[1] On Standard Industrial Classification (SIC) basis, data are for service-producing industries.
[2] Employer costs for employee benefits.
[3] Data on North American Industry Classification System (NAICS) basis available beginning with 2001; not strictly comparable with earlier data shown on SIC basis.

Note: Changes effective with the release of March 2006 data (in April 2006) include changing industry classification to NAICS from SIC and rebasing data to December 2005=100. Historical SIC data are available through December 2005.
Data exclude farm and household workers.

Source: Department of Labor (Bureau of Labor Statistics).

TABLE B–49. Productivity and related data, business and nonfarm business sectors, 1963–2012

[Index numbers, 2005=100; quarterly data seasonally adjusted]

Year or quarter	Output per hour of all persons		Output [1]		Hours of all persons [2]		Compensation per hour [3]		Real compensation per hour [4]		Unit labor costs		Implicit price deflator [5]	
	Business sector	Nonfarm business sector	Business sector	Nonfarm business sector	Business sector	Nonfarm business sector	Business sector	Nonfarm business sector	Business sector	Nonfarm business sector	Business sector	Nonfarm business sector	Business sector	Nonfarm business sector
1963	40.3	42.7	22.6	22.5	56.1	52.6	9.6	9.9	55.6	57.7	23.7	23.2	22.3	21.8
1964	41.7	44.0	24.0	24.0	57.7	54.5	9.9	10.2	57.0	58.7	23.8	23.2	22.6	22.1
1965	43.1	45.4	25.7	25.7	59.6	56.6	10.3	10.6	58.2	59.7	23.9	23.3	22.9	22.4
1966	44.9	47.0	27.5	27.5	61.2	58.6	11.0	11.2	60.4	61.5	24.5	23.8	23.5	22.9
1967	45.9	47.8	28.0	28.0	61.0	58.6	11.6	11.8	61.9	63.1	25.3	24.8	24.1	23.6
1968	47.4	49.4	29.4	29.5	61.9	59.6	12.5	12.8	64.2	65.3	26.4	25.8	25.1	24.6
1969	47.7	49.5	30.3	30.4	63.5	61.3	13.4	13.6	65.1	66.2	28.1	27.5	26.2	25.7
1970	48.6	50.2	30.3	30.3	62.2	60.4	14.5	14.6	66.3	67.1	29.7	29.1	27.4	26.8
1971	50.6	52.3	31.4	31.5	62.1	60.2	15.4	15.5	67.5	68.4	30.3	29.8	28.5	28.0
1972	52.3	54.0	33.5	33.6	64.0	62.2	16.3	16.6	69.6	70.5	31.2	30.7	29.6	28.8
1973	53.9	55.7	35.8	36.0	66.5	64.7	17.7	17.9	71.0	71.8	32.9	32.2	31.1	29.9
1974	53.0	54.8	35.3	35.5	66.6	64.8	19.4	19.7	70.1	71.0	36.6	35.9	34.1	32.9
1975	54.8	56.3	34.9	34.9	63.7	62.0	21.4	21.6	70.8	71.6	39.0	38.4	37.4	36.5
1976	56.6	58.2	37.2	37.4	65.8	64.2	23.2	23.5	72.7	73.4	41.1	40.3	39.4	38.5
1977	57.5	59.1	39.3	39.5	68.3	66.8	25.1	25.4	73.7	74.5	43.6	42.9	41.8	40.9
1978	58.2	59.9	41.8	42.1	71.8	70.3	27.3	27.6	74.9	75.8	46.9	46.1	44.7	43.7
1979	58.1	59.6	43.2	43.4	74.3	72.8	29.9	30.2	74.9	75.7	51.4	50.7	48.5	47.4
1980	58.0	59.5	42.7	42.9	73.6	72.2	33.1	33.4	74.6	75.4	57.0	56.2	52.9	51.9
1981	59.2	60.3	43.9	43.8	74.1	72.7	36.2	36.7	74.5	75.5	61.1	60.8	57.8	56.9
1982	58.7	59.7	42.6	42.4	72.5	71.1	38.8	39.3	75.4	76.3	66.1	65.8	61.1	60.4
1983	60.8	62.3	44.8	45.1	73.7	72.5	40.4	40.9	75.3	76.2	66.4	65.7	63.1	62.4
1984	62.5	63.5	48.7	48.9	78.0	76.9	42.1	42.6	75.4	76.2	67.4	67.0	65.0	64.1
1985	63.9	64.6	51.0	51.0	79.8	78.9	44.1	44.5	76.3	76.9	69.0	68.9	66.5	66.0
1986	65.7	66.6	52.9	52.9	80.5	79.5	46.4	46.8	78.8	79.5	70.5	70.3	67.6	67.1
1987	65.9	66.8	54.6	54.7	82.9	81.9	48.0	48.5	79.0	79.7	72.9	72.7	69.2	68.7
1988	66.9	67.9	57.0	57.2	85.2	84.3	50.5	50.9	80.1	80.8	75.5	75.1	71.4	70.8
1989	67.6	68.4	59.1	59.2	87.4	86.6	51.9	52.2	78.9	79.4	76.7	76.4	74.0	73.4
1990	69.0	69.6	60.0	60.1	86.9	86.3	55.2	55.5	80.0	80.3	80.0	79.7	76.7	76.1
1991	70.1	70.7	59.5	59.5	84.9	84.2	58.0	58.4	81.1	81.6	82.8	82.6	79.2	78.7
1992	73.0	73.5	61.8	61.8	84.7	84.0	61.1	61.5	83.3	83.9	83.7	83.7	80.7	80.3
1993	73.4	73.9	63.8	63.9	86.9	86.4	62.5	62.7	83.1	83.5	85.1	84.9	82.3	81.9
1994	74.1	74.7	67.0	66.9	90.4	89.6	63.4	63.9	82.6	83.2	85.6	85.5	83.7	83.4
1995	74.1	75.0	68.8	69.0	92.9	92.0	64.7	65.2	82.4	82.9	87.4	86.9	85.2	84.8
1996	76.3	76.9	72.0	72.1	94.4	93.7	66.9	67.4	82.9	83.4	87.8	87.5	86.6	86.0
1997	77.6	78.1	75.7	75.7	97.5	96.9	69.1	69.4	83.8	84.2	89.1	88.9	87.9	87.6
1998	79.9	80.4	79.5	79.6	99.4	99.0	73.3	73.6	87.7	88.0	91.7	91.5	88.5	88.3
1999	82.7	83.1	83.9	84.1	101.4	101.2	76.6	76.8	89.8	89.9	92.6	92.4	89.2	89.1
2000	85.6	85.9	87.7	87.8	102.4	102.2	82.3	82.5	93.3	93.5	96.1	96.0	90.9	90.9
2001	88.2	88.4	88.4	88.6	100.3	100.2	86.1	86.2	95.0	95.0	97.7	97.5	92.5	92.4
2002	92.2	92.4	90.2	90.3	97.8	97.6	88.8	88.9	96.4	96.5	96.4	96.2	93.2	93.2
2003	95.7	95.8	93.0	93.0	97.2	97.1	93.0	93.1	98.7	98.8	97.2	97.1	94.5	94.4
2004	98.4	98.4	96.7	96.7	98.3	98.3	96.2	96.2	99.5	99.4	97.8	97.8	96.9	96.6
2005	100.0	100.0	100.0	100.0	100.0	100.0	100.0	100.0	100.0	100.0	100.0	100.0	100.0	100.0
2006	100.9	100.9	103.0	103.1	102.1	102.2	103.8	103.8	100.5	100.5	102.8	102.8	102.9	103.0
2007	102.4	102.5	105.1	105.3	102.6	102.7	108.1	107.9	101.8	101.6	105.5	105.3	105.6	105.4
2008	103.2	103.1	103.7	103.7	100.5	100.6	111.7	111.6	101.2	101.2	108.2	108.2	107.5	107.3
2009	106.3	106.1	99.2	99.0	93.3	93.3	113.2	113.2	103.0	103.0	106.5	106.7	107.9	108.1
2010	109.5	109.4	102.2	102.0	93.3	93.3	115.4	115.5	103.3	103.4	105.4	105.6	109.6	109.6
2011	110.0	110.2	104.6	104.7	95.1	95.1	118.4	118.6	102.8	102.9	107.7	107.6	112.0	111.7
2009: I	103.9	103.9	99.3	99.2	95.5	95.5	111.5	111.5	102.5	102.5	107.3	107.4	107.6	107.6
II	105.7	105.6	98.7	98.5	93.4	93.3	113.3	113.4	103.6	103.7	107.2	107.4	107.6	107.8
III	107.2	106.9	98.9	98.6	92.2	92.2	113.9	113.9	103.3	103.3	106.3	106.5	108.0	108.3
IV	108.5	108.2	100.1	99.8	92.2	92.3	114.2	114.2	102.7	102.7	105.2	105.5	108.4	108.6
2010: I	109.1	108.9	100.8	100.7	92.4	92.4	114.5	114.6	102.8	102.9	104.9	105.2	108.8	108.9
II	108.9	108.8	101.5	101.3	93.2	93.1	115.2	115.3	103.5	103.6	105.7	106.0	109.3	109.4
III	109.8	109.7	102.7	102.6	93.5	93.5	115.8	115.9	103.7	103.7	105.4	105.6	109.8	109.8
IV	110.2	110.2	103.6	103.6	94.0	94.0	115.9	116.0	103.0	103.1	105.1	105.2	110.4	110.3
2011: I	109.5	109.7	103.5	103.5	94.5	94.4	118.4	118.5	104.0	104.2	108.1	108.1	110.9	110.6
II	109.8	110.0	104.2	104.4	94.9	94.9	118.4	118.5	103.0	103.1	107.9	107.7	111.8	111.4
III	109.9	110.1	104.6	104.8	95.2	95.2	118.3	118.5	102.1	102.3	107.6	107.6	112.7	112.3
IV	110.7	110.9	106.0	106.2	95.8	95.8	118.1	118.3	101.6	101.8	106.7	106.7	112.7	112.4
2012: I	110.5	110.7	106.7	106.9	96.6	96.5	119.8	120.0	102.4	102.6	108.4	108.3	113.2	112.9
II	111.0	111.3	107.3	107.4	96.6	96.6	120.2	120.4	102.5	102.7	108.3	108.2	113.6	113.3
III	111.7	112.0	108.2	108.5	96.9	96.9	120.4	120.6	102.2	102.4	107.9	107.7	114.5	114.1

[1] Output refers to real gross domestic product in the sector.

[2] Hours at work of all persons engaged in sector, including hours of proprietors and unpaid family workers. Estimates based primarily on establishment data.

[3] Wages and salaries of employees plus employers' contributions for social insurance and private benefit plans. Also includes an estimate of wages, salaries, and supplemental payments for the self-employed.

[4] Hourly compensation divided by the consumer price index for all urban consumers for recent quarters. The trend from 1978–2011 is based on the consumer price index research series (CPI-U-RS).

[5] Current dollar output divided by the output index.

Source: Department of Labor (Bureau of Labor Statistics).

TABLE B–50. Changes in productivity and related data, business and nonfarm business sectors, 1963–2012

[Percent change from preceding period; quarterly data at seasonally adjusted annual rates]

Year or quarter	Output per hour of all persons		Output [1]		Hours of all persons [2]		Compensation per hour [3]		Real compensation per hour [4]		Unit labor costs		Implicit price deflator [5]	
	Business sector	Nonfarm business sector	Business sector	Nonfarm business sector	Business sector	Nonfarm business sector	Business sector	Nonfarm business sector	Business sector	Nonfarm business sector	Business sector	Nonfarm business sector	Business sector	Nonfarm business sector
1963	3.9	3.5	4.6	4.7	0.7	1.1	3.6	3.4	2.2	2.1	-0.3	-0.1	0.5	0.7
1964	3.4	2.9	6.3	6.7	2.9	3.7	3.8	3.1	2.4	1.8	.4	.2	1.1	1.3
1965	3.5	3.1	7.1	7.1	3.4	3.9	3.7	3.3	2.1	1.7	.2	.2	1.6	1.3
1966	4.1	3.6	6.8	7.1	2.6	3.5	6.7	5.9	3.8	3.0	2.6	2.3	2.5	2.3
1967	2.2	1.7	1.9	1.7	-.3	.0	5.7	5.8	2.5	2.7	3.4	4.0	2.7	3.2
1968	3.4	3.4	5.0	5.2	1.5	1.8	8.1	7.8	3.7	3.5	4.5	4.3	4.0	3.9
1969	.5	.2	3.1	3.0	2.5	2.9	7.0	6.8	1.4	1.3	6.4	6.6	4.6	4.5
1970	2.0	1.5	.0	-.1	-2.0	-1.6	7.7	7.2	1.9	1.4	5.6	5.6	4.3	4.4
1971	4.1	4.0	3.8	3.8	-.3	-.2	6.3	6.4	1.8	1.9	2.1	2.3	4.2	4.3
1972	3.2	3.3	6.4	6.6	3.1	3.2	6.3	6.5	3.0	3.2	3.0	3.1	3.6	3.2
1973	3.1	3.1	7.0	7.3	3.8	4.1	8.4	8.1	2.1	1.8	5.2	4.9	5.2	3.5
1974	-1.7	-1.6	-1.5	-1.5	.2	.1	9.6	9.8	-1.3	-1.2	11.5	11.6	9.7	10.3
1975	3.5	2.8	-.9	-1.6	-4.3	-4.3	10.2	10.1	1.0	.9	6.5	7.1	9.7	10.7
1976	3.2	3.3	6.6	7.0	3.3	3.6	8.6	8.4	2.7	2.5	5.3	4.9	5.3	5.5
1977	1.7	1.6	5.6	5.6	3.8	3.9	8.0	8.1	1.4	1.5	6.2	6.5	6.0	6.3
1978	1.1	1.3	6.3	6.6	5.1	5.2	8.7	8.8	1.5	1.7	7.5	7.4	7.1	6.7
1979	-.1	-.4	3.3	3.2	3.4	3.6	9.6	9.4	.0	-.1	9.6	9.9	8.5	8.5
1980	-.2	-.3	-1.1	-1.1	-.9	-.8	10.7	10.7	-.4	-.4	10.9	11.0	9.0	9.6
1981	2.1	1.4	2.8	2.1	.7	.7	9.5	9.7	.0	.1	7.3	8.1	9.2	9.6
1982	-.8	-1.1	-3.0	-3.2	-2.3	-2.2	7.2	7.1	1.1	1.0	8.1	8.3	5.7	6.2
1983	3.6	4.4	5.4	6.4	1.8	1.9	4.1	4.2	-.1	-.1	.5	-.2	3.4	3.2
1984	2.7	2.0	8.7	8.2	5.8	6.1	4.2	4.1	.1	.0	1.5	2.0	2.9	2.9
1985	2.3	1.6	4.6	4.3	2.3	2.6	4.7	4.4	1.2	1.0	2.4	2.8	2.4	2.9
1986	2.9	3.1	3.7	3.9	.8	.8	5.1	5.2	3.3	3.4	2.2	2.1	1.6	1.7
1987	.3	.3	3.3	3.3	3.0	3.0	3.6	3.6	.2	.2	3.3	3.3	2.4	2.4
1988	1.5	1.6	4.3	4.6	2.7	2.9	5.2	5.0	1.5	1.3	3.7	3.3	3.2	3.0
1989	1.0	.8	3.7	3.5	2.6	2.7	2.7	2.6	-1.6	-1.7	1.6	1.8	3.7	3.6
1990	2.1	1.8	1.5	1.4	-.6	-.4	6.4	6.2	1.4	1.1	4.2	4.3	3.6	3.7
1991	1.5	1.5	-.9	-.9	-2.4	-2.4	5.1	5.3	1.5	1.6	3.5	3.7	3.3	3.5
1992	4.2	4.0	3.9	3.8	-.2	-.2	5.3	5.4	2.7	2.8	1.1	1.3	1.9	2.0
1993	.5	.6	3.2	3.5	2.7	2.9	2.2	2.0	-.2	-.4	1.7	1.4	2.0	2.0
1994	.9	1.0	4.9	4.7	4.0	3.6	1.5	1.8	-.6	-.3	.6	.8	1.7	1.8
1995	.0	.4	2.8	3.2	2.8	2.8	2.1	2.1	-.3	-.3	2.0	1.7	1.8	1.8
1996	2.9	2.6	4.6	4.4	1.6	1.8	3.4	3.3	.7	.6	.5	.7	1.6	1.4
1997	1.8	1.5	5.2	5.1	3.4	3.5	3.2	3.1	1.1	.9	1.5	1.6	1.6	1.9
1998	3.0	2.9	5.0	5.1	2.0	2.1	6.1	6.0	4.6	4.5	3.0	3.0	.7	.8
1999	3.5	3.3	5.6	5.6	2.0	2.2	4.5	4.3	2.4	2.2	.9	.9	.8	1.0
2000	3.5	3.4	4.5	4.4	1.0	1.0	7.4	7.4	3.9	4.0	3.7	3.9	1.8	1.9
2001	3.0	2.9	.8	.9	-2.1	-2.0	4.7	4.5	1.8	1.6	1.7	1.5	1.8	1.7
2002	4.5	4.6	2.0	1.9	-2.4	-2.5	3.1	3.2	1.5	1.5	-1.3	-1.3	.8	.9
2003	3.9	3.7	3.1	3.1	-.7	-.6	4.8	4.7	2.5	2.4	.9	1.0	1.4	1.2
2004	2.8	2.6	4.0	4.0	1.2	1.3	3.5	3.3	.7	.6	.7	.7	2.6	2.4
2005	1.7	1.6	3.4	3.4	1.7	1.7	3.9	3.9	.5	.6	2.2	2.3	3.2	3.5
2006	.9	.9	3.0	3.1	2.1	2.2	3.8	3.8	.5	.5	2.8	2.8	2.9	3.0
2007	1.5	1.5	2.0	2.1	.5	.5	4.1	4.0	1.2	1.1	2.6	2.4	2.6	2.3
2008	.7	.6	-1.3	-1.5	-2.0	-2.1	3.3	3.4	-.5	-.4	2.6	2.8	1.8	1.8
2009	3.1	2.9	-4.3	-4.5	-7.2	-7.2	1.4	1.4	1.8	1.8	-1.6	-1.5	.4	.8
2010	3.0	3.1	3.0	3.1	.0	.0	2.0	2.0	.3	.4	-1.0	-1.0	1.5	1.4
2011	.4	.7	2.4	2.6	1.9	1.9	2.6	2.7	-.5	-.5	2.2	2.0	2.2	1.9
2009: I	5.3	5.5	-5.0	-5.0	-9.8	-9.9	-3.1	-3.2	-.7	-.7	-8.0	-8.2	-1.4	-.9
II	7.1	6.8	-2.3	-2.5	-8.7	-8.7	6.5	6.7	4.5	4.7	-.5	-.2	.0	.0
III	5.8	5.2	.7	.3	-4.8	-4.7	2.3	2.0	-1.3	-1.6	-3.3	-3.1	1.5	1.9
IV	5.0	5.0	4.9	5.2	-.1	.3	.9	.9	-2.1	-2.1	-4.0	-3.9	1.6	1.0
2010: I	2.2	2.7	3.1	3.3	.9	.6	1.1	1.4	.2	.5	-1.1	-1.3	1.4	1.2
II	-.6	-.5	2.9	2.8	3.5	3.3	2.5	2.7	2.8	3.1	3.1	3.3	1.8	1.8
III	3.2	3.3	4.7	5.1	1.4	1.7	2.0	1.8	.6	.4	-1.1	-1.4	1.7	1.4
IV	1.5	1.9	3.4	3.9	1.9	1.9	.3	.5	-2.6	-2.4	-1.1	-1.4	2.4	1.8
2011: I	-2.5	-2.0	-.5	-.1	2.1	1.9	8.9	9.1	4.1	4.4	11.7	11.3	1.9	1.2
II	1.1	1.2	2.9	3.4	1.8	2.2	.2	-.2	-4.0	-4.4	-.9	-1.3	3.0	2.8
III	.5	.6	1.7	1.6	1.2	1.0	-.3	.0	-3.4	-3.1	-.8	-.6	3.5	3.5
IV	2.9	2.8	5.4	5.3	2.5	2.4	-.6	-.7	-1.9	-1.9	-3.4	-3.3	-.1	.1
2012: I	-.6	-.5	2.7	2.7	3.3	3.2	5.6	5.8	3.1	3.3	6.3	6.4	1.7	1.9
II	1.7	1.9	1.9	2.1	.2	.2	1.3	1.3	.6	.6	-.4	-.5	1.5	1.6
III	2.5	2.9	3.6	4.2	1.1	1.3	1.0	.9	-1.3	-1.4	-1.5	-1.9	3.2	2.8

[1] Output refers to real gross domestic product in the sector.
[2] Hours at work of all persons engaged in the sector. See footnote 2, Table B–49.
[3] Wages and salaries of employees plus employers' contributions for social insurance and private benefit plans. Also includes an estimate of wages, salaries, and supplemental payments for the self-employed.
[4] Hourly compensation divided by a consumer price index. See footnote 4, Table B–49.
[5] Current dollar output divided by the output index.

Note: Percent changes are calculated using index numbers to three decimal places and may differ slightly from percent changes based on indexes in Table B–49, which are rounded to one decimal place.

Source: Department of Labor (Bureau of Labor Statistics).

TABLE B–51. Industrial production indexes, major industry divisions, 1965–2012

[2007=100; monthly data seasonally adjusted]

Year or month	Total industrial production [1]	Manufacturing				Mining	Utilities
		Total [1]	Durable	Nondurable	Other (non-NAICS) [1]		
1965	31.5	28.5					
1966	34.3	31.1					
1967	35.0	31.7					
1968	37.0	33.5					
1969	38.7	34.9					
1970	37.4	33.4					
1971	37.9	33.9					
1972	41.6	37.4	25.5	57.2	75.3	106.3	46.4
1973	45.0	40.8	28.7	59.9	77.7	106.9	49.1
1974	44.9	40.7	28.5	60.1	78.2	105.4	48.9
1975	40.9	36.4	24.7	55.7	74.4	102.8	49.8
1976	44.1	39.7	27.0	60.8	76.7	103.6	52.1
1977	47.4	43.1	29.7	64.9	84.1	106.0	54.2
1978	50.1	45.8	32.1	67.3	87.0	109.3	55.6
1979	51.6	47.2	33.6	67.7	88.8	112.6	56.8
1980	50.3	45.5	32.2	65.7	91.9	114.6	57.3
1981	50.9	46.0	32.5	66.3	94.1	117.6	58.1
1982	48.3	43.5	29.7	65.3	95.1	111.8	56.2
1983	49.6	45.6	31.2	68.4	97.8	105.9	56.7
1984	54.1	50.0	35.6	71.5	102.3	112.7	60.0
1985	54.7	50.9	36.4	71.9	106.3	110.5	61.3
1986	55.3	52.0	37.0	74.0	108.4	102.5	61.8
1987	58.1	54.9	39.2	78.0	114.7	103.5	64.7
1988	61.1	57.9	42.1	80.6	114.2	106.1	68.4
1989	61.7	58.3	42.6	81.1	112.5	104.9	70.6
1990	62.3	58.8	42.8	82.4	111.2	106.4	71.9
1991	61.3	57.6	41.4	82.1	106.6	104.1	73.7
1992	63.0	59.7	43.6	84.2	104.5	101.8	73.6
1993	65.1	61.8	46.0	85.4	105.2	101.7	76.2
1994	68.5	65.5	49.9	88.4	104.3	104.1	77.7
1995	71.8	68.9	54.1	89.9	104.3	104.0	80.5
1996	75.0	72.2	58.9	90.2	103.4	105.7	82.8
1997	80.4	78.3	66.0	93.5	112.1	107.7	82.8
1998	85.1	83.5	72.9	94.9	118.8	105.7	84.9
1999	88.7	87.6	79.1	95.5	122.2	100.2	87.4
2000	92.3	91.3	84.9	95.9	121.9	102.9	89.9
2001	89.1	87.6	80.9	93.1	114.0	103.3	89.5
2002	89.3	87.8	80.9	94.2	110.2	98.4	92.3
2003	90.4	88.9	82.9	94.4	106.9	98.7	94.1
2004	92.5	91.4	86.2	95.9	107.8	98.1	95.3
2005	95.5	95.0	91.2	98.3	107.5	97.0	97.3
2006	97.6	97.4	95.4	98.8	106.2	99.4	96.7
2007	100.0	100.0	100.0	100.0	100.0	100.0	100.0
2008	96.5	95.2	96.3	94.1	93.6	101.0	99.9
2009	85.4	82.0	78.0	86.8	80.7	95.8	97.5
2010	90.1	86.7	86.0	88.7	76.5	100.7	100.9
2011	93.7	90.5	92.6	90.1	71.6	107.0	100.6
2012 *p*	97.1	94.1	99.4	91.0	69.3	112.9	98.9
2011: Jan	92.5	89.2	90.3	89.8	73.8	103.5	101.9
Feb	92.3	89.4	91.1	89.5	72.6	101.8	100.6
Mar	93.1	90.0	91.8	90.1	71.5	104.2	100.9
Apr	92.6	89.5	90.9	89.9	70.8	105.1	99.7
May	92.9	89.7	91.6	89.6	70.9	106.0	100.1
June	93.1	89.7	91.7	89.7	69.4	106.3	100.7
July	93.9	90.4	92.5	90.4	69.6	106.8	103.1
Aug	94.2	90.7	93.1	90.2	71.2	107.9	102.3
Sept	94.4	91.1	93.5	90.6	71.8	107.8	101.2
Oct	94.9	91.5	94.3	90.6	72.2	110.2	100.0
Nov	95.1	91.5	94.8	90.1	72.2	111.8	100.2
Dec	95.9	92.9	96.2	91.4	72.9	112.6	96.6
2012: Jan	96.6	93.8	98.0	91.7	72.6	113.1	94.8
Feb	97.1	94.6	99.3	92.0	72.9	111.0	95.9
Mar	96.5	94.0	99.0	91.0	71.7	110.8	95.3
Apr	97.3	94.6	100.2	91.2	71.1	111.6	97.5
May	97.3	94.0	99.7	90.5	70.1	111.4	102.7
June	97.3	94.3	100.3	90.6	69.1	111.6	99.9
July	97.9	94.6	100.6	91.0	68.6	113.0	102.8
Aug *p*	97.0	93.8	99.2	90.6	68.8	112.1	100.6
Sept *p*	97.2	93.9	98.9	91.2	68.0	113.8	99.7
Oct *p*	96.8	93.1	98.3	90.4	64.5	115.2	101.0
Nov *p*	97.8	94.3	100.4	90.7	66.3	115.5	101.2
Dec *p*	98.1	95.1	101.4	91.2	67.5	116.3	96.4

[1] Total industry and total manufacturing series include manufacturing as defined in the North American Industry Classification System (NAICS) plus those industries—logging and newspaper, periodical, book, and directory publishing—that have traditionally been considered to be manufacturing and included in the industrial sector.

Note: Data based on NAICS; see footnote 1.

Source: Board of Governors of the Federal Reserve System.

TABLE B–52. Industrial production indexes, market groupings, 1965–2012

[2007=100; monthly data seasonally adjusted]

Year or month	Total indus- trial pro- duc- tion	Final products Total	Consumer goods Total	Consumer goods Auto- motive prod- ucts	Consumer goods Other dur- able goods	Consumer goods Non- dur- able goods	Equipment Total[1]	Equipment Busi- ness	Equipment De- fense and space	Nonindustrial supplies Total	Nonindustrial supplies Con- struc- tion	Nonindustrial supplies Busi- ness	Materials Total	Materials Non- energy	Energy
1965	31.5	30.1	39.5	32.4	27.7	44.6	18.3	13.5	49.5	31.6	42.8	27.2	32.1	....	61.4
1966	34.3	33.0	41.5	32.3	30.5	46.7	21.3	15.7	58.2	33.5	44.6	29.3	35.0	....	65.3
1967	35.0	34.3	42.5	28.4	30.9	49.1	22.6	16.0	66.4	34.9	45.7	30.8	34.7	27.3	67.5
1968	37.0	35.9	45.1	33.8	33.1	51.0	23.3	16.7	66.5	36.9	48.1	32.7	37.0	29.3	70.6
1969	38.7	37.1	46.8	33.9	35.3	52.8	23.9	17.8	63.3	38.9	50.2	34.8	39.2	31.2	74.2
1970	37.4	35.7	46.2	28.6	34.2	53.7	22.2	17.1	53.6	38.3	48.4	34.9	37.8	29.3	77.9
1971	37.9	36.1	48.9	36.4	36.2	55.2	20.8	16.3	48.2	39.5	49.9	36.0	38.3	29.9	78.5
1972	41.6	39.1	52.8	39.3	41.5	58.7	22.7	18.6	46.9	44.1	56.7	39.6	42.2	33.5	81.5
1973	45.0	42.2	55.2	42.6	44.3	60.5	26.0	21.5	51.4	47.2	61.5	42.1	46.0	37.1	83.5
1974	44.9	42.1	53.6	36.9	41.7	60.6	27.3	22.7	53.1	46.7	60.0	41.9	45.9	37.0	83.2
1975	40.9	39.7	51.5	35.5	36.4	59.5	24.9	20.3	53.5	41.9	50.8	38.7	40.9	31.7	82.4
1976	44.1	42.6	55.7	40.4	40.9	63.2	26.2	21.6	51.9	44.8	54.7	41.2	44.4	35.3	84.2
1977	47.4	46.0	59.2	45.7	45.7	65.6	29.3	25.0	46.5	48.6	59.6	44.7	47.5	38.3	87.0
1978	50.1	48.8	61.0	45.4	47.8	67.9	32.6	28.2	47.4	51.3	63.0	47.1	49.9	40.8	88.0
1979	51.6	50.5	60.1	40.8	48.1	67.5	36.3	31.8	50.7	53.0	64.6	48.7	51.3	41.9	90.4
1980	50.3	50.3	57.9	31.5	44.7	67.6	38.1	32.5	60.3	50.9	59.8	47.6	49.3	39.4	91.1
1981	50.9	51.5	58.3	32.4	45.0	67.9	39.9	33.5	65.3	51.4	58.8	48.8	49.6	39.6	92.0
1982	48.3	50.3	58.1	31.5	41.8	69.1	38.0	30.6	78.0	49.6	53.4	48.2	45.8	35.6	88.0
1983	49.6	51.4	60.3	36.6	45.2	69.9	37.7	30.8	78.6	52.2	57.2	50.5	47.0	38.0	85.2
1984	54.1	55.6	63.1	40.9	50.5	71.3	43.1	35.4	90.0	56.8	62.2	54.9	51.5	42.4	90.6
1985	54.7	57.0	63.7	40.8	50.6	72.2	45.3	36.7	100.7	58.2	63.8	56.3	51.4	42.4	90.1
1986	55.3	57.9	65.9	43.9	53.5	73.9	44.6	36.2	107.0	60.2	65.9	58.1	51.3	43.3	86.6
1987	58.1	60.6	68.7	47.0	56.4	76.6	47.0	38.6	109.2	63.8	70.1	61.6	54.1	46.1	88.6
1988	61.1	63.8	71.3	49.2	59.4	79.1	50.8	42.6	110.2	66.0	71.8	63.9	57.1	49.1	91.7
1989	61.7	64.5	71.5	50.8	60.1	78.9	52.0	44.1	110.3	66.6	71.5	64.8	57.5	49.3	92.6
1990	62.3	65.2	71.9	47.8	59.9	80.2	53.1	45.6	106.4	67.6	70.9	66.3	57.9	49.4	94.5
1991	61.3	64.4	71.9	44.9	58.2	81.4	51.3	44.9	98.5	65.9	67.0	65.4	57.0	48.4	94.5
1992	63.0	65.9	74.0	52.1	60.9	82.0	52.0	46.7	91.3	67.8	69.8	66.9	58.9	50.7	93.7
1993	65.1	68.0	76.3	57.2	65.1	83.2	53.7	48.9	86.2	70.1	72.9	69.0	60.8	53.0	93.9
1994	68.5	70.9	79.4	62.8	70.4	85.2	56.0	52.2	80.9	73.5	78.1	71.8	64.7	57.2	95.4
1995	71.8	73.9	81.9	64.7	74.7	87.3	59.6	56.7	78.0	76.2	79.9	74.8	68.4	61.2	96.8
1996	75.0	76.7	83.4	65.8	78.1	88.5	64.3	62.3	76.0	79.2	83.4	77.7	71.9	65.0	98.3
1997	80.4	81.7	86.4	70.9	83.1	90.5	72.2	71.4	74.8	84.4	87.5	83.2	77.8	71.9	98.3
1998	85.1	86.4	89.6	76.2	89.7	92.5	79.1	79.0	78.0	89.1	92.1	87.9	82.4	77.3	98.5
1999	88.7	88.7	91.6	84.6	94.3	92.5	82.1	83.4	75.6	92.4	94.5	91.6	87.4	83.3	98.0
2000	92.3	91.4	93.3	86.1	98.0	93.9	86.4	89.6	67.2	95.7	96.5	95.3	91.9	88.4	99.6
2001	89.1	89.5	92.3	82.8	92.7	94.1	82.8	83.9	73.7	91.9	92.2	91.7	87.7	83.4	98.3
2002	89.3	88.9	94.1	90.9	94.9	94.6	77.4	78.2	74.5	92.0	92.2	91.9	88.7	84.7	98.0
2003	90.4	90.0	95.4	95.7	95.8	95.2	78.0	78.0	79.2	93.0	92.0	93.4	89.9	86.2	98.1
2004	92.5	91.7	96.5	95.7	98.9	96.1	81.0	81.7	77.2	94.9	94.2	95.1	92.4	89.8	97.9
2005	95.5	95.4	99.1	94.2	102.1	99.3	87.2	87.6	85.0	98.3	98.7	98.2	94.6	93.4	96.9
2006	97.6	97.9	99.6	93.0	103.5	99.9	94.3	95.7	84.1	99.8	101.1	99.2	96.5	95.7	98.1
2007	100.0	100.0	100.0	100.0	100.0	100.0	100.0	100.0	100.0	100.0	100.0	100.0	100.0	100.0	100.0
2008	96.5	96.4	95.1	84.8	92.6	97.2	99.2	97.6	107.0	94.2	90.7	95.9	97.3	95.2	100.6
2009	85.4	86.6	88.6	73.1	74.9	93.4	82.0	79.9	102.5	80.5	69.9	85.7	86.1	79.0	98.4
2010	90.1	89.4	89.6	83.5	76.5	92.7	88.9	86.5	106.7	82.6	72.6	87.6	93.3	87.7	102.5
2011	93.7	92.9	91.7	92.3	78.9	93.6	95.8	93.6	109.5	84.7	76.6	88.7	97.6	92.0	106.8
2012 p	97.1	96.3	93.0	102.6	82.2	93.1	104.0	102.9	113.4	86.9	80.1	90.3	101.5	95.6	111.1
2011: Jan	92.5	91.5	90.7	85.5	77.6	93.6	93.2	91.3	107.8	83.6	74.5	88.1	96.5	91.7	104.1
Feb	92.3	91.7	90.7	88.8	78.7	92.9	94.0	92.1	108.6	83.5	74.2	88.1	95.9	91.3	103.1
Mar	93.1	92.0	91.1	91.8	79.3	92.8	94.0	92.0	108.7	84.1	75.2	88.5	97.2	92.1	105.3
Apr	92.6	91.7	90.8	87.6	78.3	93.3	93.7	91.4	108.7	83.9	75.4	88.1	96.6	91.1	105.3
May	92.9	92.3	91.3	88.5	79.1	93.6	94.8	92.5	109.4	84.6	76.5	88.5	96.5	91.2	104.9
June	93.1	92.3	91.2	88.5	78.4	93.7	94.7	92.6	107.8	84.4	76.6	88.2	96.9	91.2	106.0
July	93.9	93.1	92.2	92.4	79.3	94.2	95.3	93.0	108.7	85.2	77.5	88.9	97.8	91.8	107.5
Aug	94.2	93.6	92.5	94.0	79.1	94.3	96.4	94.1	109.7	85.3	77.1	89.3	97.8	91.6	108.0
Sept	94.4	93.9	92.6	95.0	79.6	94.2	96.9	94.6	109.6	85.5	77.1	89.6	98.0	92.2	107.4
Oct	94.9	94.5	92.9	98.8	79.5	94.0	98.2	95.9	110.9	85.4	77.3	89.3	98.7	92.3	109.2
Nov	95.1	94.2	92.2	96.5	79.2	93.5	99.0	96.5	112.3	85.1	77.9	88.6	99.4	92.8	110.5
Dec	95.9	94.7	92.5	99.5	79.5	93.4	99.6	97.5	111.7	86.2	79.8	89.3	100.5	94.7	110.0
2012: Jan	96.6	95.4	92.9	104.2	80.8	92.9	101.3	99.5	112.0	86.5	80.2	89.6	101.2	95.8	109.9
Feb	97.1	96.2	93.3	104.6	81.5	93.2	102.9	101.0	114.8	87.6	82.0	90.3	101.2	96.4	108.5
Mar	96.5	95.5	92.3	104.5	81.0	92.0	103.0	101.2	114.7	86.8	81.1	89.6	100.8	95.4	109.3
Apr	97.3	96.2	92.9	105.8	81.8	92.6	103.9	102.6	114.0	87.6	81.7	90.4	101.6	96.3	110.0
May	97.3	96.6	93.6	103.5	82.1	93.7	103.8	102.9	111.4	87.4	80.4	90.8	101.3	95.1	111.3
June	97.3	97.0	93.4	103.8	81.9	93.5	105.3	104.8	111.0	87.2	79.7	90.8	101.1	95.3	110.4
July	97.9	97.4	93.8	102.5	83.1	94.1	105.7	105.0	113.5	87.2	79.0	91.2	102.2	96.0	112.3
Aug p	97.0	96.5	92.9	100.5	82.3	93.3	104.9	104.2	113.0	86.7	78.9	90.5	101.0	95.0	110.7
Sept p	97.2	96.8	93.3	100.6	81.6	93.9	105.0	104.0	115.4	86.7	79.3	90.3	101.2	95.0	110.9
Oct p	96.8	95.9	92.6	100.5	82.1	93.0	103.5	102.6	113.7	86.2	79.1	89.6	101.4	94.4	113.1
Nov p	97.8	96.9	93.4	104.7	84.1	93.0	105.1	104.6	113.6	87.1	80.9	90.1	102.4	95.8	113.5
Dec p	98.1	97.3	93.4	107.2	83.8	92.6	106.1	106.0	114.1	87.3	81.6	90.0	102.7	96.5	112.9

[1] Includes other items not shown separately.

Note: See footnote 1 and Note, Table B–51.

Source: Board of Governors of the Federal Reserve System.

Production and Business Activity | 385

Table B-53. Industrial production indexes, selected manufacturing industries, 1972–2012

[2007=100; monthly data seasonally adjusted]

Year or month	Durable manufacturing								Nondurable manufacturing					
	Primary metals		Fabricated metal products	Machinery	Computer and electronic products		Transportation equipment		Apparel	Paper	Printing and support	Chemicals	Plastics and rubber products	Food
	Total	Iron and steel products			Total	Selected high-technology[1]	Total	Motor vehicles and parts						
1972	110.2	114.0	60.3	56.4	0.8	0.1	47.1	43.3	276.1	68.1	49.4	41.1	34.7	55.6
1973	128.2	136.7	66.6	65.2	.9	.2	53.8	49.5	284.5	73.7	52.0	45.0	39.2	55.8
1974	131.4	146.0	65.4	68.3	1.0	.2	49.6	42.6	264.9	76.9	50.4	46.8	37.8	56.3
1975	101.9	108.3	56.5	59.5	.9	.2	45.0	37.1	259.2	66.5	47.1	41.1	31.9	55.3
1976	108.2	112.4	60.6	62.1	1.1	.3	50.3	47.3	273.7	73.4	50.5	46.0	35.2	59.7
1977	109.3	109.8	65.7	67.8	1.3	.3	54.7	53.8	291.2	76.6	54.7	50.1	41.6	60.8
1978	116.2	117.9	68.9	73.1	1.7	.4	58.2	56.1	299.6	80.1	57.9	52.6	43.5	62.7
1979	118.9	122.1	72.0	77.1	2.0	.5	58.8	51.4	284.1	81.3	59.6	53.8	42.9	62.1
1980	104.4	103.5	67.9	73.4	2.5	.7	52.1	37.9	288.3	81.1	60.0	50.9	38.4	63.2
1981	104.5	107.3	67.4	72.7	2.9	.8	50.2	36.9	286.7	82.2	61.6	51.7	40.6	64.0
1982	73.9	66.0	60.4	60.8	3.2	.9	46.2	33.3	290.6	80.8	66.2	48.4	40.0	66.5
1983	75.7	66.5	60.8	54.9	3.7	1.1	51.0	42.5	299.5	86.0	71.2	51.7	43.5	67.2
1984	83.1	73.3	66.2	64.0	4.6	1.5	57.9	50.9	304.2	90.4	77.5	54.8	50.2	68.5
1985	76.7	68.0	67.2	64.2	4.9	1.5	60.9	52.9	292.8	88.6	80.6	54.4	52.2	71.1
1986	74.9	66.4	66.7	63.2	5.1	1.6	62.3	52.8	296.7	92.3	84.7	56.8	54.4	72.1
1987	80.7	75.6	68.0	64.5	5.8	1.9	64.6	54.7	299.0	95.3	91.0	61.2	60.2	73.7
1988	90.3	88.0	71.4	71.0	6.5	2.3	66.6	58.5	294.0	99.1	93.9	64.8	62.9	75.5
1989	88.2	84.9	70.9	73.7	6.6	2.4	69.9	57.9	279.9	100.2	94.2	66.0	65.0	75.7
1990	87.1	83.9	70.0	71.9	7.2	2.7	67.7	54.4	274.6	100.1	97.8	67.5	66.8	78.1
1991	81.8	76.7	66.8	67.5	7.5	3.0	65.0	52.0	276.5	100.3	94.7	67.3	66.1	79.5
1992	83.8	80.3	68.9	67.3	8.5	3.6	67.5	59.2	282.3	102.8	99.9	68.3	71.1	81.0
1993	87.9	85.1	71.5	72.3	9.3	4.2	69.4	65.4	289.3	104.0	100.2	69.1	76.2	83.1
1994	94.6	91.8	77.7	79.2	10.9	5.3	72.6	75.1	295.4	108.5	101.3	70.9	82.5	83.6
1995	95.6	93.3	82.5	84.8	14.1	7.5	72.7	77.3	296.1	110.1	102.8	72.1	84.6	85.8
1996	97.9	95.5	85.5	87.8	18.3	10.7	74.1	77.9	288.2	106.6	103.5	73.6	87.4	84.0
1997	102.0	98.3	89.4	92.6	24.5	15.8	80.8	84.0	285.3	108.9	105.6	78.0	92.8	86.3
1998	103.8	98.2	92.3	94.9	31.5	22.0	87.9	88.4	269.8	109.8	106.8	79.2	96.1	90.1
1999	103.7	98.6	92.9	93.0	41.3	31.6	92.6	98.1	258.1	110.6	106.8	80.8	101.2	91.2
2000	100.3	97.3	96.6	97.7	53.9	44.2	88.3	97.4	246.4	107.7	107.8	81.9	102.3	92.7
2001	91.3	88.3	89.6	86.4	54.6	45.1	84.8	88.8	212.4	101.6	104.2	80.5	96.4	92.8
2002	91.3	89.2	87.6	83.3	53.1	44.6	88.6	97.6	170.4	102.9	102.1	85.1	99.8	95.0
2003	89.8	89.8	86.6	82.8	60.3	53.4	89.5	101.1	157.2	100.4	98.1	86.5	99.9	95.6
2004	97.7	101.7	86.9	86.3	68.3	60.6	89.3	101.7	134.5	101.2	98.5	90.0	101.1	95.6
2005	95.2	94.3	90.9	91.6	77.0	71.1	93.0	102.3	128.8	100.7	98.6	92.9	102.2	98.6
2006	98.0	98.4	95.9	95.9	87.4	85.0	94.2	100.8	125.2	99.6	97.8	95.2	102.8	99.5
2007	100.0	100.0	100.0	100.0	100.0	100.0	100.0	100.0	100.0	100.0	100.0	100.0	100.0	100.0
2008	100.0	106.4	96.4	97.3	106.1	112.1	89.6	80.0	77.7	95.8	93.8	92.5	90.6	98.7
2009	74.0	68.5	74.2	75.8	92.9	96.0	73.4	58.6	55.7	85.4	78.8	83.4	75.8	98.2
2010	90.8	89.0	79.3	84.5	103.0	110.2	84.7	77.7	55.6	87.2	78.9	86.3	82.5	98.0
2011	96.8	97.1	87.2	94.3	111.1	116.9	92.1	86.9	54.3	86.0	75.4	86.7	89.4	100.3
2012 _p_	99.2	100.9	93.6	100.8	115.2	114.8	104.9	102.3	52.6	83.7	74.4	86.8	92.6	102.8
2011: Jan	95.6	96.3	84.1	94.1	109.9	117.9	86.6	81.4	56.4	88.2	76.9	87.2	87.2	99.4
Feb	95.1	95.1	84.1	94.2	109.9	116.8	89.0	85.1	56.4	87.0	77.5	86.6	87.6	99.4
Mar	96.5	96.4	85.0	93.6	109.4	115.5	91.3	88.6	54.7	87.2	76.8	87.8	87.9	99.6
Apr	96.0	93.9	85.9	92.5	109.6	116.3	88.5	82.8	55.0	86.7	76.9	86.8	88.8	100.6
May	95.5	93.3	86.7	93.4	110.8	117.5	89.2	83.2	55.9	85.8	76.4	85.8	89.3	99.9
June	94.3	93.9	88.0	94.4	110.2	118.2	89.5	83.3	54.6	85.5	75.2	86.0	89.0	100.3
July	95.2	93.8	88.6	94.3	111.5	118.0	91.4	85.9	54.1	85.4	75.9	86.3	90.5	100.5
Aug	95.8	97.4	88.3	93.8	112.6	119.2	93.1	87.6	53.8	84.5	75.3	86.4	90.2	100.3
Sept	96.7	96.5	87.9	94.1	112.4	117.4	93.9	88.3	52.1	85.1	74.5	87.1	90.2	100.4
Oct	97.2	97.5	88.4	94.6	111.3	114.6	97.0	92.1	53.1	84.8	73.8	86.6	90.7	101.5
Nov	100.4	102.3	89.4	95.4	112.0	115.0	96.8	90.6	53.1	85.2	73.0	85.6	90.0	100.8
Dec	103.0	109.1	90.3	98.0	114.0	116.7	98.3	93.6	52.4	86.1	74.2	88.1	90.9	101.3
2012: Jan	103.1	107.9	91.2	99.5	114.9	115.6	101.8	99.4	54.9	85.4	75.2	88.2	91.4	102.1
Feb	103.9	108.9	92.8	101.0	115.4	115.6	103.8	100.2	54.4	86.0	75.4	87.5	92.5	102.7
Mar	100.1	105.0	92.6	102.2	114.7	115.6	104.2	101.1	53.5	84.4	74.1	87.0	91.9	102.1
Apr	102.3	106.6	93.2	102.5	116.4	116.8	105.8	104.2	53.5	85.1	74.6	87.2	92.4	102.6
May	100.2	105.2	93.7	102.1	115.4	116.6	104.8	102.9	53.8	84.6	75.0	85.9	91.4	102.0
June	96.8	96.9	94.3	104.6	116.7	116.9	106.1	104.9	52.7	82.5	75.3	86.0	92.1	102.3
July	99.1	97.2	94.7	101.1	116.5	115.4	107.6	106.4	52.4	82.3	75.4	86.3	94.0	103.7
Aug _p_	98.8	99.1	94.1	100.0	114.4	112.2	105.2	102.7	50.3	82.6	74.8	86.2	92.4	103.9
Sept _p_	93.8	89.2	94.4	100.0	114.5	112.1	105.0	101.1	51.2	82.3	73.1	86.9	92.2	104.4
Oct _p_	93.1	90.6	93.7	97.6	114.7	113.7	104.7	101.1	50.1	83.1	72.2	86.7	92.2	102.1
Nov _p_	97.4	99.6	94.3	99.2	114.4	114.0	108.1	106.9	51.8	83.4	73.3	86.5	94.3	102.7
Dec _p_	100.2	103.9	94.3	99.7	116.2	114.4	109.8	109.7	52.9	83.0	74.2	87.7	94.7	102.1

[1] Computers and peripheral equipment, communications equipment, and semiconductors and related electronic components.

Note: See footnote 1 and Note, Table B–51.

Source: Board of Governors of the Federal Reserve System.

Table B-54. Capacity utilization rates, 1965–2012

[Percent [1]; monthly data seasonally adjusted]

Year or month	Total industry [2]	Manufacturing				Mining	Utilities	Stage-of-process		
		Total [2]	Durable goods	Nondurable goods	Other (non-NAICS) [2]			Crude	Primary and semi-finished	Finished
1965	....	89.5	....	....	....	....	....	....	91.0	88.8
1966	....	91.1	....	....	....	....	....	....	91.4	91.1
1967	87.0	87.2	87.5	86.3	....	81.2	94.5	81.1	85.0	88.2
1968	87.3	87.1	87.4	86.5	....	83.6	95.1	83.4	86.8	87.1
1969	87.4	86.6	87.1	86.1	....	86.7	96.8	85.6	88.1	85.6
1970	81.3	79.4	77.8	82.1	....	89.2	96.3	85.1	81.4	78.1
1971	79.6	77.9	75.5	81.7	....	87.8	94.7	84.3	81.6	75.7
1972	84.7	83.4	82.1	85.2	85.7	90.7	95.3	88.4	88.1	79.6
1973	88.3	87.7	88.6	86.6	84.7	91.6	93.3	90.0	92.1	83.3
1974	85.1	84.4	84.7	84.2	82.7	91.0	86.9	90.9	87.3	80.3
1975	75.8	73.7	71.7	76.1	77.3	89.3	85.1	83.9	75.2	73.7
1976	79.8	78.3	76.4	81.1	77.6	89.4	85.5	86.9	80.1	76.8
1977	83.4	82.5	81.2	84.3	83.2	89.5	86.6	89.1	84.6	79.9
1978	85.1	84.4	83.8	85.1	85.0	89.7	86.9	88.7	86.3	82.1
1979	85.0	84.0	84.1	83.8	85.6	91.3	87.0	89.9	85.9	81.7
1980	80.7	78.6	77.5	79.6	86.8	91.4	85.5	89.4	78.8	79.3
1981	79.5	76.9	75.1	78.8	87.5	90.9	84.4	89.3	77.2	77.4
1982	73.6	70.8	66.4	76.3	87.3	84.2	80.2	82.3	70.5	73.0
1983	74.9	73.4	68.7	79.4	87.9	79.8	79.6	79.9	74.5	73.0
1984	80.4	79.3	76.9	82.1	89.5	85.9	82.2	85.7	81.2	77.2
1985	79.2	78.1	75.7	80.5	90.4	84.4	81.9	83.8	79.9	76.6
1986	78.7	78.4	75.4	81.8	88.8	77.6	81.1	79.1	79.8	77.1
1987	81.2	81.0	77.6	84.7	90.6	80.3	83.6	82.8	82.8	78.7
1988	84.3	84.0	82.1	86.1	88.6	84.3	86.7	86.3	85.9	81.8
1989	83.8	83.3	81.9	85.0	85.4	85.0	86.9	86.7	84.7	81.7
1990	82.5	81.7	79.6	84.2	83.7	86.6	86.5	87.7	82.7	80.7
1991	79.8	78.5	75.3	82.3	80.7	85.0	87.9	85.2	79.9	78.2
1992	80.6	79.6	77.2	82.7	80.0	84.7	86.4	85.5	81.6	78.1
1993	81.4	80.4	78.5	82.7	81.3	85.5	88.3	85.7	83.3	78.2
1994	83.6	82.8	81.6	84.5	81.4	87.0	88.4	87.9	86.4	79.2
1995	84.0	83.2	82.3	84.6	82.2	87.6	89.4	88.8	86.4	80.0
1996	83.4	82.2	81.6	83.3	80.6	90.3	90.9	89.1	85.6	79.4
1997	84.2	83.1	82.4	83.9	85.6	91.5	90.4	90.6	86.1	80.4
1998	82.8	81.6	80.6	82.4	86.9	89.0	92.7	87.2	84.2	80.2
1999	81.7	80.4	79.9	80.4	87.1	85.8	94.2	86.1	84.1	78.0
2000	81.5	79.8	79.4	79.3	87.3	90.6	93.9	88.6	84.0	76.9
2001	76.1	73.7	71.2	75.9	82.6	90.2	89.6	85.6	77.3	72.4
2002	74.9	72.9	69.9	76.1	81.4	86.1	87.6	83.0	77.1	70.7
2003	76.0	73.9	71.1	76.7	81.4	88.1	85.7	84.8	78.1	71.5
2004	77.9	76.2	73.7	78.5	82.9	88.2	84.5	86.2	80.0	73.1
2005	79.9	78.2	75.9	80.3	82.8	88.5	85.1	86.3	81.8	75.2
2006	80.3	78.5	77.1	80.0	81.3	90.2	83.2	87.7	81.4	76.0
2007	80.4	78.5	77.9	79.4	77.4	89.2	85.7	88.2	80.8	76.9
2008	77.3	74.3	74.2	74.1	77.3	89.5	84.0	86.6	76.5	73.9
2009	68.6	65.5	61.0	70.5	70.0	80.3	80.8	78.0	65.9	68.4
2010	73.7	71.2	68.4	75.1	67.2	83.9	81.1	83.6	71.5	72.4
2011	76.8	75.0	73.6	77.7	63.8	87.4	77.7	85.8	74.2	76.0
2012 P	78.7	77.2	77.4	78.3	63.2	90.2	74.6	87.9	75.7	77.9
2011: Jan	76.1	74.0	72.1	77.1	65.3	85.7	79.8	85.2	73.9	74.7
Feb	75.9	74.2	72.7	77.0	64.3	84.0	78.5	83.9	73.6	75.2
Mar	76.5	74.7	73.3	77.5	63.4	85.7	78.5	85.2	74.1	75.6
Apr	76.1	74.3	72.5	77.5	62.9	86.3	77.4	84.9	73.6	75.3
May	76.3	74.4	73.0	77.2	63.1	86.8	77.5	84.8	73.8	75.6
June	76.3	74.4	73.0	77.3	61.8	86.8	77.7	85.0	73.9	75.5
July	77.0	75.0	73.5	78.0	62.1	87.0	79.4	85.3	74.7	76.1
Aug	77.1	75.2	73.9	77.8	63.7	87.7	78.6	85.7	74.6	76.4
Sept	77.2	75.5	74.1	78.1	64.3	87.5	77.6	86.0	74.6	76.5
Oct	77.6	75.8	74.6	78.2	64.7	89.3	76.6	87.3	74.3	77.2
Nov	77.7	75.7	74.8	77.7	64.8	90.4	76.6	87.7	74.7	76.8
Dec	78.3	76.8	75.8	78.9	65.6	91.0	73.7	88.6	75.1	77.5
2012: Jan	78.7	77.5	77.0	79.0	65.4	91.2	72.2	89.0	75.1	78.4
Feb	79.0	78.0	77.9	79.3	65.8	89.4	72.9	87.3	76.0	78.7
Mar	78.4	77.4	77.5	78.4	64.9	89.1	72.3	87.1	75.4	78.1
Apr	79.0	77.8	78.3	78.5	64.5	89.5	73.8	87.5	76.0	78.6
May	78.9	77.2	77.7	77.9	63.7	89.3	77.6	86.9	76.4	78.0
June	78.8	77.4	78.0	78.0	63.0	89.2	75.4	87.0	75.9	78.3
July	79.2	77.5	78.0	78.3	62.7	90.2	77.4	87.9	76.5	78.3
Aug P	78.3	76.8	76.8	77.9	63.0	89.3	75.6	87.3	75.6	77.4
Sept P	78.4	76.7	76.4	78.4	62.4	90.5	74.8	88.2	75.2	77.5
Oct P	78.0	76.0	75.8	77.7	59.4	91.4	75.6	88.7	75.2	76.4
Nov P	78.7	76.9	77.2	77.9	61.2	91.5	75.6	88.8	76.0	77.1
Dec P	78.8	77.4	77.8	78.3	62.4	91.9	71.8	89.1	75.6	77.7

[1] Output as percent of capacity.
[2] See footnote 1 and Note, Table B-51.

Source: Board of Governors of the Federal Reserve System.

TABLE B–55. New construction activity, 1968–2012

[Value put in place, billions of dollars; monthly data at seasonally adjusted annual rates]

Year or month	Total new construction	Private construction									Public construction		
		Total	Residential buildings [1]		Nonresidential buildings and other construction						Total	Federal	State and local
			Total [2]	New housing units [3]	Total	Lodging	Office	Commercial [4]	Manufacturing	Other [5]			
1968	96.8	69.4	34.2	26.7	35.2						27.4	3.2	24.2
1969	104.9	77.2	37.2	29.2	39.9						27.8	3.2	24.6
1970	105.9	78.0	35.9	27.1	42.1						27.9	3.1	24.8
1971	122.4	92.7	48.5	38.7	44.2						29.7	3.8	25.9
1972	139.1	109.1	60.7	50.1	48.4						30.0	4.2	25.8
1973	153.8	121.4	65.1	54.6	56.3						32.3	4.7	27.6
1974	155.2	117.0	56.0	43.4	61.1						38.1	5.1	33.0
1975	152.6	109.3	51.6	36.3	57.8						43.3	6.1	37.2
1976	172.1	128.2	68.3	50.8	59.9						44.0	6.8	37.2
1977	200.5	157.4	92.0	72.2	65.4						43.1	7.1	36.0
1978	239.9	189.7	109.8	85.6	79.9						50.1	8.1	42.0
1979	272.9	216.2	116.4	89.3	99.8						56.6	8.6	48.1
1980	273.9	210.3	100.4	69.6	109.9						63.6	9.6	54.0
1981	289.1	224.4	99.2	69.4	125.1						64.7	10.4	54.3
1982	279.3	216.3	84.7	57.0	131.6						63.1	10.0	53.1
1983	311.9	248.4	125.8	95.0	122.6						63.5	10.6	52.9
1984	370.2	300.0	155.0	114.6	144.9						70.2	11.2	59.0
1985	403.4	325.6	160.5	115.9	165.1						77.8	12.0	65.8
1986	433.5	348.9	190.7	135.2	158.2						84.6	12.4	72.2
1987	446.6	356.0	199.7	142.7	156.3						90.6	14.1	76.6
1988	462.0	367.3	204.5	142.4	162.8						94.7	12.3	82.5
1989	477.5	379.3	204.3	143.2	175.1						98.2	12.2	86.0
1990	476.8	369.3	191.1	132.1	178.2						107.5	12.1	95.4
1991	432.6	322.5	166.3	114.6	156.2						110.1	12.8	97.3
1992	463.7	347.8	199.4	135.1	148.4						115.8	14.4	101.5
1993	485.5	358.2	208.2	150.9	150.0	4.6	20.0	34.4	23.4	67.7	127.4	14.4	112.9
1994	531.9	401.5	241.0	176.4	160.4	4.7	20.4	39.6	28.8	66.9	130.4	14.4	116.0
1995	548.7	408.7	228.1	171.4	180.5	7.1	23.0	44.1	35.4	70.9	140.0	15.8	124.3
1996	599.7	453.0	257.5	191.1	195.5	10.9	26.5	49.4	38.1	70.6	146.7	15.3	131.4
1997	631.9	478.4	264.7	198.1	213.7	12.9	32.8	53.1	37.6	77.3	153.4	14.1	139.4
1998	688.5	533.7	296.3	224.0	237.4	14.8	40.4	55.7	40.5	86.0	154.8	14.3	140.5
1999	744.6	575.5	326.3	251.3	249.2	16.0	45.1	59.4	35.1	93.7	169.1	14.0	155.1
2000	802.8	621.4	346.1	265.0	275.3	16.3	52.4	64.1	37.6	104.9	181.3	14.2	167.2
2001	840.2	638.3	364.4	279.4	273.9	14.5	49.7	63.6	37.8	108.2	201.9	15.1	186.8
2002	847.9	634.4	396.7	298.8	237.7	10.5	35.3	59.0	22.7	110.2	213.4	16.6	196.9
2003	891.5	675.4	446.0	345.7	229.3	9.9	30.6	57.5	21.4	109.9	216.1	17.9	198.2
2004	991.4	771.2	532.9	417.5	238.3	12.0	32.9	63.2	23.2	107.0	220.2	18.3	201.8
2005	1,104.1	870.0	611.9	480.8	258.1	12.7	37.3	66.6	28.4	113.1	234.2	17.3	216.9
2006	1,167.2	911.8	613.7	468.8	298.1	17.6	45.7	73.4	32.3	129.2	255.4	17.6	237.8
2007	1,152.4	863.3	493.2	354.1	370.0	27.5	53.8	85.9	40.2	162.7	289.1	20.6	268.5
2008	1,067.6	758.8	350.3	230.1	408.6	35.4	55.5	82.7	52.8	182.3	308.7	23.7	285.0
2009	903.2	588.3	245.9	133.9	342.4	25.4	37.3	50.5	56.3	173.0	314.9	28.4	286.5
2010	804.6	500.6	238.8	127.3	261.8	11.2	24.4	36.5	39.8	149.9	304.0	31.1	272.8
2011	778.2	495.0	237.0	123.0	258.0	8.2	22.5	40.0	40.6	146.6	283.3	30.4	252.9
2011: Jan	752.6	464.6	237.7	121.3	226.8	8.0	22.0	35.4	29.5	131.9	288.1	31.4	256.7
Feb	746.1	461.5	231.2	120.4	230.4	8.0	21.5	36.1	31.9	132.9	284.5	31.4	253.1
Mar	753.4	467.1	226.8	120.9	240.3	8.1	21.6	36.9	35.1	138.5	286.3	31.4	254.9
Apr	755.4	475.3	236.0	120.2	239.3	7.8	21.6	38.6	33.3	137.9	280.2	30.4	249.8
May	775.8	495.3	243.1	119.3	252.3	8.0	22.9	39.9	38.3	143.2	280.5	31.7	248.8
June	786.8	502.1	236.9	120.7	265.2	8.4	23.4	40.9	43.8	148.7	284.6	30.8	253.8
July	763.5	485.8	222.4	122.2	263.4	7.9	23.0	41.7	41.5	149.4	277.7	30.2	247.4
Aug	786.3	501.5	232.2	124.5	269.3	8.1	23.2	42.5	44.2	151.3	284.8	31.8	253.0
Sept	790.3	507.2	236.5	124.3	270.7	8.2	22.6	40.9	46.5	152.4	283.1	29.3	253.8
Oct	795.7	512.8	243.7	125.1	269.1	8.2	23.0	41.1	45.4	151.4	282.9	29.2	253.7
Nov	804.0	520.4	248.2	127.2	272.2	8.7	22.6	41.9	44.9	154.1	283.6	28.1	255.5
Dec	820.6	534.6	249.4	129.3	285.2	9.2	23.0	41.9	50.0	161.0	286.1	29.9	256.1
2012: Jan	824.7	547.5	249.6	132.7	297.9	9.1	23.7	43.6	44.8	176.9	277.2	26.1	251.1
Feb	820.7	544.6	252.6	135.6	291.9	9.0	23.3	42.8	46.6	170.2	276.1	26.7	249.4
Mar	817.8	544.8	249.5	135.7	295.3	10.2	24.6	43.2	46.8	170.6	273.0	27.1	245.9
Apr	825.1	552.3	254.1	139.2	298.2	10.3	24.3	43.4	47.9	172.3	272.8	25.5	247.3
May	838.8	562.1	262.6	142.4	299.5	10.4	25.3	44.2	49.4	170.2	276.6	26.9	249.8
June	845.1	566.4	271.3	147.2	295.1	10.6	25.4	43.4	48.1	167.6	278.7	25.8	252.8
July	846.6	572.4	274.7	149.6	297.7	10.8	25.7	43.3	46.6	171.2	274.2	24.8	249.4
Aug	855.9	578.0	282.4	154.0	295.5	10.9	27.1	44.4	47.0	166.1	278.0	25.3	252.6
Sept	862.2	587.5	290.5	159.0	297.0	10.6	26.8	44.6	48.2	166.8	274.7	23.7	251.0
Oct [p]	868.2	590.8	294.2	165.2	296.5	11.1	26.5	45.1	47.7	166.1	277.4	26.0	251.5
Nov [p]	866.0	589.8	295.3	167.2	294.5	11.0	26.3	44.8	47.2	165.2	276.2	24.6	251.7

[1] Includes farm residential buildings.
[2] Includes residential improvements, not shown separately.
[3] New single- and multi-family units.
[4] Including farm.
[5] Health care, educational, religious, public safety, amusement and recreation, transportation, communication, power, highway and street, sewage and waste disposal, water supply, and conservation and development.

Note: Data beginning with 1993 reflect reclassification.

Source: Department of Commerce (Bureau of the Census).

TABLE B–56. New private housing units started, authorized, and completed and houses sold, 1967–2012

[Thousands; monthly data at seasonally adjusted annual rates]

Year or month	New housing units started				New housing units authorized [1]				New housing units completed	New houses sold
	Total	Type of structure			Total	Type of structure				
		1 unit	2 to 4 units [2]	5 units or more		1 unit	2 to 4 units	5 units or more		
1967	1,291.6	843.9	71.7	376.1	1,141.0	650.6	73.0	417.5	....	487
1968	1,507.6	899.4	80.7	527.3	1,353.4	694.7	84.3	574.4	1,319.8	490
1969	1,466.8	810.6	85.1	571.2	1,322.3	624.8	85.2	612.4	1,399.0	448
1970	1,433.6	812.9	84.9	535.9	1,351.5	646.8	88.1	616.7	1,418.4	485
1971	2,052.2	1,151.0	120.5	780.9	1,924.6	906.1	132.9	885.7	1,706.1	656
1972	2,356.6	1,309.2	141.2	906.2	2,218.9	1,033.1	148.6	1,037.2	2,003.9	718
1973	2,045.3	1,132.0	118.2	795.0	1,819.5	882.1	117.0	820.5	2,100.5	634
1974	1,337.7	888.1	68.0	381.6	1,074.4	643.8	64.4	366.2	1,728.5	519
1975	1,160.4	892.2	64.0	204.3	939.2	675.5	63.8	199.8	1,317.2	549
1976	1,537.5	1,162.4	85.8	289.2	1,296.2	893.6	93.1	309.5	1,377.2	646
1977	1,987.1	1,450.9	121.7	414.4	1,690.0	1,126.1	121.3	442.7	1,657.1	819
1978	2,020.3	1,433.3	125.1	462.0	1,800.5	1,182.6	130.6	487.3	1,867.5	817
1979	1,745.1	1,194.1	122.0	429.0	1,551.8	981.5	125.4	444.8	1,870.8	709
1980	1,292.2	852.2	109.5	330.5	1,190.6	710.4	114.5	365.7	1,501.6	545
1981	1,084.2	705.4	91.2	287.7	985.5	564.3	101.8	319.4	1,265.7	436
1982	1,062.2	662.6	80.1	319.6	1,000.5	546.4	88.3	365.8	1,005.5	412
1983	1,703.0	1,067.6	113.5	522.0	1,605.2	901.5	133.7	570.1	1,390.3	623
1984	1,749.5	1,084.2	121.4	543.9	1,681.8	922.4	142.6	616.8	1,652.2	639
1985	1,741.8	1,072.4	93.5	576.0	1,733.3	956.6	120.1	656.6	1,703.3	688
1986	1,805.4	1,179.4	84.0	542.0	1,769.4	1,077.6	108.4	583.5	1,756.4	750
1987	1,620.5	1,146.4	65.1	408.7	1,534.8	1,024.4	89.3	421.1	1,668.8	671
1988	1,488.1	1,081.3	58.7	348.0	1,455.6	993.8	75.7	386.1	1,529.8	676
1989	1,376.1	1,003.3	55.3	317.6	1,338.4	931.7	66.9	339.8	1,422.8	650
1990	1,192.7	894.8	37.6	260.4	1,110.8	793.9	54.3	262.6	1,308.0	534
1991	1,013.9	840.4	35.6	137.9	948.8	753.5	43.1	152.1	1,090.8	509
1992	1,199.7	1,029.9	30.9	139.0	1,094.9	910.7	45.8	138.4	1,157.5	610
1993	1,287.6	1,125.7	29.4	132.6	1,199.1	986.5	52.4	160.2	1,192.7	666
1994	1,457.0	1,198.4	35.2	223.5	1,371.6	1,068.5	62.2	241.0	1,346.9	670
1995	1,354.1	1,076.2	33.8	244.1	1,332.5	997.3	63.8	271.5	1,312.6	667
1996	1,476.8	1,160.9	45.3	270.8	1,425.6	1,069.5	65.8	290.3	1,412.9	757
1997	1,474.0	1,133.7	44.5	295.8	1,441.1	1,062.4	68.4	310.3	1,400.5	804
1998	1,616.9	1,271.4	42.6	302.9	1,612.3	1,187.6	69.2	355.5	1,474.2	886
1999	1,640.9	1,302.4	31.9	306.6	1,663.5	1,246.7	65.8	351.1	1,604.9	880
2000	1,568.7	1,230.9	38.7	299.1	1,592.3	1,198.1	64.9	329.3	1,573.7	877
2001	1,602.7	1,273.3	36.6	292.8	1,636.7	1,235.6	66.0	335.2	1,570.8	908
2002	1,704.9	1,358.6	38.5	307.9	1,747.7	1,332.6	73.7	341.4	1,648.4	973
2003	1,847.7	1,499.0	33.5	315.2	1,889.2	1,460.9	82.5	345.8	1,678.7	1,086
2004	1,955.8	1,610.5	42.3	303.0	2,070.1	1,613.4	90.4	366.2	1,841.9	1,203
2005	2,068.3	1,715.8	41.1	311.4	2,155.3	1,682.0	84.0	389.3	1,931.4	1,283
2006	1,800.9	1,465.4	42.7	292.8	1,838.9	1,378.2	76.6	384.1	1,979.4	1,051
2007	1,355.0	1,046.0	31.7	277.3	1,398.4	979.9	59.6	359.0	1,502.8	776
2008	905.5	622.0	17.5	266.0	905.4	575.6	34.4	295.4	1,119.7	485
2009	554.0	445.1	11.6	97.3	583.0	441.1	20.7	121.1	794.4	375
2010	586.9	471.2	11.4	104.3	604.6	447.3	22.0	135.3	651.7	323
2011	608.8	430.6	10.9	167.3	624.1	418.5	21.6	184.0	584.9	306
2012 ᵖ	780.0	535.5	11.1	233.4	815.5	514.2	24.7	276.6	651.4	367
2011: Jan	632	433	....	187	566	417	21	128	523	308
Feb	518	393	....	108	536	379	16	141	621	273
Mar	600	428	....	161	590	398	16	176	589	301
Apr	552	414	....	124	578	401	22	155	542	312
May	551	409	....	136	624	412	21	191	543	308
June	615	443	....	165	633	412	23	198	580	304
July	614	429	....	176	627	417	24	186	634	297
Aug	581	422	....	152	645	429	27	189	617	292
Sept	647	422	....	219	616	428	21	167	600	306
Oct	630	439	....	175	667	444	24	199	578	314
Nov	708	460	....	239	709	451	23	235	583	327
Dec	697	520	....	153	701	454	24	223	606	339
2012: Jan	720	511	....	193	684	452	20	212	542	339
Feb	718	470	....	240	707	478	25	204	572	366
Mar	706	481	....	215	769	466	22	281	587	352
Apr	747	504	....	234	723	475	22	226	663	358
May	706	513	....	178	784	490	22	272	605	369
June	754	531	....	215	760	491	21	248	623	360
July	728	506	....	211	811	511	29	271	673	366
Aug	750	538	....	205	801	511	27	263	682	367
Sept	843	590	....	245	890	550	27	313	659	379
Oct	889	589	....	281	868	566	24	278	739	364
Nov ᵖ	851	570	....	268	900	568	28	304	675	398
Dec ᵖ	954	616	....	330	909	573	28	308	686	369

[1] Authorized by issuance of local building permits in permit-issuing places: 20,000 places beginning with 2004; 19,000 for 1994–2003; 17,000 for 1984–93; 16,000 for 1978–83; 14,000 for 1972–77; and 13,000 for 1967–71.
[2] Monthly data do not meet publication standards because tests for identifiable and stable seasonality do not meet reliability standards.

Note: One-unit estimates prior to 1999, for new housing units started and completed and for new houses sold, include an upward adjustment of 3.3 percent to account for structures in permit-issuing areas that did not have permit authorization.

Source: Department of Commerce (Bureau of the Census).

TABLE B–57. Manufacturing and trade sales and inventories, 1971–2012

[Amounts in millions of dollars; monthly data seasonally adjusted]

Year or month	Total manufacturing and trade			Manufacturing			Merchant wholesalers [1]			Retail trade			Retail and food services sales
	Sales [2]	Inventories [3]	Ratio [4]	Sales [2]	Inventories [3]	Ratio [4]	Sales [2]	Inventories [3]	Ratio [4]	Sales [2,5]	Inventories [3]	Ratio [4]	
SIC: [6]													
1971	116,895	188,991	1.62	55,906	102,567	1.83	26,492	36,568	1.38	34,497	49,856	1.45	....
1972	131,081	203,227	1.55	63,027	108,121	1.72	29,866	40,297	1.35	38,189	54,809	1.44	....
1973	153,677	234,406	1.53	72,931	124,499	1.71	38,115	46,918	1.23	42,631	62,989	1.48	....
1974	177,912	287,144	1.61	84,790	157,625	1.86	47,982	58,667	1.22	45,141	70,852	1.57	....
1975	182,198	288,992	1.59	86,589	159,708	1.84	46,634	57,774	1.24	48,975	71,510	1.46	....
1976	204,150	318,345	1.56	98,797	174,636	1.77	50,698	64,622	1.27	54,655	79,087	1.45	....
1977	229,513	350,706	1.53	113,201	188,378	1.66	56,136	73,179	1.30	60,176	89,149	1.48	....
1978	260,320	400,931	1.54	126,905	211,691	1.67	66,413	86,934	1.31	67,002	102,306	1.53	....
1979	297,701	452,640	1.52	143,936	242,157	1.68	79,051	99,679	1.26	74,713	110,804	1.48	....
1980	327,233	508,924	1.56	154,391	265,215	1.72	93,099	122,631	1.32	79,743	121,078	1.52	....
1981	355,822	545,786	1.53	168,129	283,413	1.69	101,180	129,654	1.28	86,514	132,719	1.53	....
1982	347,625	573,908	1.67	163,351	311,852	1.95	95,211	127,428	1.36	89,062	134,628	1.49	....
1983	369,286	590,287	1.56	172,547	312,379	1.78	99,225	130,075	1.28	97,514	147,833	1.44	....
1984	410,124	649,780	1.53	190,682	339,516	1.73	112,199	142,452	1.23	107,243	167,812	1.49	....
1985	422,583	664,039	1.56	194,538	334,749	1.73	113,459	147,409	1.28	114,586	181,881	1.52	....
1986	430,419	662,738	1.55	194,657	322,654	1.68	114,960	153,574	1.32	120,803	186,510	1.56	....
1987	457,735	709,848	1.50	206,326	338,109	1.59	122,968	163,903	1.29	128,442	207,836	1.55	....
1988	497,157	767,222	1.49	224,619	369,374	1.57	134,521	178,801	1.30	138,017	219,047	1.54	....
1989	527,039	815,455	1.52	236,698	391,212	1.63	143,760	187,009	1.28	146,581	237,234	1.58	....
1990	545,909	840,594	1.52	242,686	405,073	1.65	149,506	195,833	1.29	153,718	239,688	1.56	....
1991	542,815	834,609	1.53	239,847	390,950	1.65	148,306	200,448	1.33	154,661	243,211	1.54	....
1992	567,176	842,809	1.48	250,394	382,510	1.54	154,150	208,302	1.32	162,632	251,997	1.52	....
NAICS: [6]													
1992	540,199	835,900	1.53	242,002	378,710	1.57	147,261	196,914	1.31	150,936	260,276	1.67	167,841
1993	567,195	863,064	1.50	251,708	379,778	1.50	154,018	204,842	1.30	161,469	278,444	1.68	179,424
1994	609,854	926,421	1.46	269,843	399,924	1.44	164,575	221,978	1.29	175,436	304,519	1.66	194,186
1995	654,689	985,369	1.48	289,973	424,761	1.44	179,915	238,392	1.29	184,801	322,216	1.72	204,219
1996	686,923	1,004,743	1.46	299,766	430,430	1.44	190,362	241,058	1.27	196,796	333,255	1.67	216,983
1997	723,442	1,045,713	1.42	319,558	443,435	1.37	198,154	258,454	1.26	205,730	343,824	1.64	227,177
1998	742,391	1,077,665	1.43	324,984	448,853	1.39	202,260	272,297	1.32	215,147	356,515	1.62	237,746
1999	786,178	1,137,746	1.40	335,991	463,465	1.35	216,597	290,207	1.30	233,591	384,074	1.59	257,249
2000	833,868	1,196,358	1.41	350,715	481,184	1.35	234,546	309,246	1.29	248,606	405,928	1.59	273,961
2001	818,160	1,118,976	1.42	330,875	427,751	1.38	232,096	297,588	1.32	255,189	393,637	1.58	281,575
2002	823,234	1,139,378	1.36	326,227	422,924	1.29	236,294	301,436	1.26	260,713	415,018	1.55	288,256
2003	854,182	1,147,472	1.34	334,616	408,216	1.25	247,651	300,055	1.23	271,915	431,201	1.56	301,059
2004	924,912	1,240,555	1.30	359,081	440,760	1.19	276,367	339,431	1.18	289,464	460,364	1.56	320,594
2005	1,003,802	1,312,940	1.27	395,173	473,921	1.17	301,115	367,505	1.18	307,514	471,514	1.51	340,552
2006	1,066,154	1,407,372	1.28	417,963	522,568	1.20	325,351	398,586	1.18	322,840	486,218	1.49	358,073
2007	1,124,417	1,486,675	1.29	443,288	561,835	1.22	347,857	424,806	1.18	333,271	500,034	1.48	370,317
2008	1,153,856	1,461,254	1.32	455,675	541,561	1.26	369,315	442,249	1.22	328,867	477,444	1.51	366,876
2009	978,862	1,323,831	1.39	368,292	504,636	1.39	308,268	389,908	1.31	302,302	429,287	1.46	339,892
2010	1,074,209	1,433,794	1.28	409,721	549,239	1.28	344,361	429,260	1.18	320,128	455,295	1.38	358,961
2011	1,193,570	1,544,057	1.26	457,613	600,825	1.28	389,778	471,549	1.17	346,179	471,683	1.34	387,304
2011: Jan	1,154,121	1,447,106	1.25	440,892	556,808	1.26	376,856	434,085	1.15	336,373	456,213	1.36	375,739
Feb	1,154,192	1,455,471	1.26	441,022	563,565	1.28	374,427	437,988	1.17	338,743	453,918	1.34	378,934
Mar	1,181,873	1,473,392	1.25	454,480	571,115	1.26	385,965	443,400	1.15	341,428	458,877	1.34	382,115
Apr	1,185,110	1,485,294	1.25	453,257	579,290	1.28	388,422	446,698	1.15	343,431	459,306	1.34	383,810
May	1,184,326	1,499,819	1.27	453,933	584,012	1.29	387,450	454,999	1.17	342,943	460,808	1.34	383,733
June	1,193,625	1,505,090	1.26	456,833	585,643	1.28	390,895	457,671	1.17	345,897	461,776	1.34	387,045
July	1,206,331	1,510,743	1.25	467,495	588,875	1.26	391,887	460,836	1.18	346,949	461,032	1.33	388,064
Aug	1,209,034	1,520,705	1.26	464,589	591,799	1.27	397,050	462,975	1.17	347,395	465,931	1.34	388,718
Sept	1,210,232	1,518,404	1.25	463,879	591,168	1.27	396,544	459,782	1.16	349,809	467,454	1.34	391,539
Oct	1,220,243	1,531,731	1.26	466,604	597,571	1.28	399,229	466,544	1.17	354,410	467,616	1.32	396,633
Nov	1,218,633	1,537,633	1.26	466,392	600,645	1.29	397,164	466,509	1.17	355,077	470,478	1.33	397,370
Dec	1,230,038	1,544,057	1.26	470,761	600,825	1.28	404,636	471,549	1.17	354,641	471,683	1.33	396,974
2012: Jan	1,234,843	1,556,397	1.26	472,600	604,980	1.28	404,708	474,580	1.17	357,535	476,837	1.33	400,550
Feb	1,244,716	1,564,986	1.26	474,382	606,668	1.28	408,970	478,923	1.17	361,364	479,395	1.33	404,692
Mar	1,247,697	1,569,020	1.26	474,690	607,190	1.28	410,559	480,495	1.17	362,448	481,335	1.33	406,200
Apr	1,246,774	1,573,873	1.26	473,660	605,878	1.28	412,940	482,838	1.17	360,174	485,157	1.35	404,112
May	1,243,493	1,578,003	1.27	475,187	604,989	1.27	408,492	482,756	1.18	359,814	490,258	1.36	403,641
June	1,229,074	1,580,106	1.29	469,382	604,221	1.29	402,730	481,897	1.20	356,962	493,988	1.38	400,635
July	1,239,836	1,592,581	1.28	478,169	608,099	1.27	401,942	484,939	1.21	359,725	499,543	1.39	403,587
Aug	1,246,838	1,602,311	1.29	477,115	611,959	1.28	405,897	488,787	1.20	363,826	501,565	1.38	407,696
Sept	1,262,184	1,613,065	1.28	480,401	615,453	1.28	413,437	494,350	1.20	368,346	503,262	1.37	412,705
Oct	1,258,993	1,617,357	1.28	481,734	615,204	1.28	409,784	496,077	1.21	367,475	506,076	1.38	411,997
Nov [p]	1,271,580	1,621,534	1.28	483,701	615,181	1.27	419,333	498,949	1.19	368,546	507,404	1.38	413,582

[1] Excludes manufacturers' sales branches and offices.
[2] Annual data are averages of monthly not seasonally adjusted figures.
[3] Seasonally adjusted, end of period. Inventories beginning with January 1982 for manufacturing and December 1980 for wholesale and retail trade are not comparable with earlier periods.
[4] Inventory/sales ratio. Monthly inventories are inventories at the end of the month to sales for the month. Annual data beginning with 1982 are the average of monthly ratios for the year. Annual data for 1970–81 are the ratio of December inventories to monthly average sales for the year.
[5] Food services included on Standard Industrial Classification (SIC) basis and excluded on North American Industry Classification System (NAICS) basis. See last column for retail and food services sales.
[6] Effective in 2001, data classified based on NAICS. Data on NAICS basis available beginning with 1992. Earlier data based on SIC. Data on both NAICS and SIC basis include semiconductors.

Source: Department of Commerce (Bureau of the Census).

[Millions of dollars; monthly data seasonally adjusted]

Year or month	Shipments[1]			Inventories[2]								
					Durable goods industries				Nondurable goods industries			
	Total	Durable goods industries	Non-durable goods industries	Total	Total	Materials and supplies	Work in process	Finished goods	Total	Materials and supplies	Work in process	Finished goods
SIC:[3]												
1971	55,906	29,924	25,982	102,567	66,136	19,679	28,550	17,907	36,431	13,686	5,678	17,067
1972	63,027	33,987	29,040	108,121	70,067	20,807	30,713	18,547	38,054	14,677	5,998	17,379
1973	72,931	39,635	33,296	124,499	81,192	25,944	35,490	19,758	43,307	18,147	6,729	18,431
1974	84,790	44,173	40,617	157,625	101,493	35,070	42,530	23,893	56,132	23,744	8,189	24,199
1975	86,589	43,598	42,991	159,708	102,590	33,903	43,227	25,460	57,118	23,565	8,834	24,719
1976	98,797	50,623	48,174	174,636	111,988	37,457	46,074	28,457	62,648	25,847	9,929	26,872
1977	113,201	59,168	54,033	188,378	120,877	40,186	50,226	30,465	67,501	27,387	10,961	29,153
1978	126,905	67,731	59,174	211,691	138,181	45,198	58,848	34,135	73,510	29,619	12,085	31,806
1979	143,936	75,927	68,009	242,157	160,734	52,670	69,325	38,739	81,423	32,814	13,910	34,699
1980	154,391	77,419	76,972	265,215	174,788	55,173	76,945	42,670	90,427	36,606	15,884	37,937
1981	168,129	83,727	84,402	283,413	186,443	57,998	80,998	47,447	96,970	38,165	16,194	42,611
1982	163,351	79,212	84,139	311,852	200,444	59,136	86,707	54,601	111,408	44,039	18,612	48,757
1983	172,547	85,481	87,066	312,379	199,854	60,325	86,899	52,630	112,525	44,816	18,691	49,018
1984	190,682	97,940	92,742	339,516	221,330	66,031	98,251	57,048	118,186	45,692	19,328	53,166
1985	194,538	101,279	93,259	334,749	218,193	63,904	98,162	56,127	116,556	44,176	19,442	53,008
1986	194,657	103,238	91,419	322,654	211,997	61,331	97,000	53,666	110,657	42,335	18,124	50,198
1987	206,326	108,128	98,198	338,109	220,799	63,562	102,393	54,844	117,310	45,319	19,270	52,721
1988	224,619	118,458	106,161	369,374	242,468	69,611	112,958	59,899	126,906	49,396	20,559	56,951
1989	236,698	123,158	113,540	391,212	257,513	72,435	122,251	62,827	133,699	50,674	21,653	61,372
1990	242,686	123,776	118,910	405,073	263,209	73,559	124,130	65,520	141,864	52,645	22,817	66,402
1991	239,847	121,000	118,847	390,950	250,019	70,834	114,960	64,225	140,931	53,011	22,815	65,105
1992	250,394	128,489	121,905	382,510	238,105	69,459	104,424	64,222	144,405	54,007	23,532	66,866
NAICS:[3]												
1992	242,002	126,572	115,430	378,710	237,914	69,658	104,185	64,071	140,796	53,148	23,420	64,228
1993	251,708	133,712	117,996	379,778	238,766	72,637	102,034	64,095	141,012	54,206	23,404	63,402
1994	269,843	147,005	122,838	399,924	253,104	78,574	106,556	67,974	146,820	57,087	24,448	65,285
1995	289,973	158,568	131,405	424,761	267,382	85,529	106,655	75,198	157,379	60,753	25,772	70,854
1996	299,766	164,883	134,883	430,430	272,466	86,288	110,616	75,562	157,964	59,151	26,472	72,341
1997	319,558	178,949	140,610	443,435	280,961	92,290	109,906	78,765	162,474	60,157	28,516	73,801
1998	324,984	185,966	139,019	448,853	290,472	93,529	115,151	81,792	158,381	58,229	27,077	73,075
1999	335,991	193,895	142,096	463,465	296,464	97,856	114,037	84,571	167,001	61,038	28,763	77,200
2000	350,715	197,807	152,908	481,184	306,394	106,039	111,025	89,330	174,790	61,496	29,996	83,298
2001	330,875	181,201	149,674	427,751	267,633	91,261	93,845	82,527	160,118	55,754	27,053	77,311
2002	326,227	176,968	149,259	422,924	260,394	88,494	92,367	79,533	162,530	56,597	27,826	78,107
2003	334,616	178,549	156,067	408,216	246,854	82,283	88,644	75,927	161,362	56,894	27,017	77,451
2004	359,081	188,722	170,359	440,760	265,025	92,089	91,109	81,807	175,755	61,830	29,877	84,048
2005	395,173	202,070	193,103	473,921	283,742	98,470	98,738	86,534	190,179	66,948	32,828	90,403
2006	417,963	213,516	204,447	522,568	317,506	111,543	106,643	99,320	205,062	70,375	36,989	97,698
2007	443,288	223,919	219,369	561,835	334,621	116,406	117,720	100,495	227,214	75,217	44,954	107,043
2008	455,675	218,328	237,347	541,561	330,298	117,583	111,993	100,722	211,263	72,087	41,112	98,064
2009	368,292	171,886	196,406	504,636	296,449	100,596	107,264	88,589	208,187	71,403	41,928	94,856
2010	409,721	191,576	218,145	549,239	324,525	106,977	123,470	94,078	224,714	76,207	44,292	104,215
2011	457,613	209,590	248,023	600,825	358,105	116,916	138,328	102,861	242,720	81,580	46,781	114,359
2011: Jan	440,892	201,174	239,718	556,808	328,196	108,104	124,972	95,120	228,612	76,961	44,685	106,966
Feb	441,022	201,176	239,846	563,565	332,227	108,985	126,409	96,833	231,338	78,736	45,179	107,423
Mar	454,480	208,781	245,699	571,115	337,907	109,979	129,883	98,045	233,208	79,073	45,160	108,975
Apr	453,257	204,541	248,716	579,290	341,067	111,504	130,952	98,611	238,223	79,729	46,639	111,855
May	453,933	206,082	247,851	584,012	345,619	112,791	133,202	99,626	238,393	79,942	46,284	112,167
June	456,833	207,567	249,266	585,643	347,267	113,086	134,049	100,132	238,376	79,313	46,569	112,494
July	467,495	217,802	249,693	588,875	350,260	113,724	135,423	101,113	238,615	79,131	46,129	113,355
Aug	464,589	213,170	251,419	591,799	353,297	114,651	136,327	102,319	238,502	80,239	45,060	113,203
Sept	463,879	211,477	252,402	591,168	353,185	114,948	135,576	102,661	237,983	79,086	45,286	113,611
Oct	466,604	215,099	251,505	597,571	355,393	115,382	136,802	103,209	242,178	81,853	46,270	114,055
Nov	466,392	214,251	252,141	600,646	357,659	116,001	138,270	103,388	242,987	81,579	46,476	114,932
Dec	470,761	219,924	250,837	600,825	358,105	116,916	138,328	102,861	242,720	81,580	46,781	114,359
2012: Jan	472,600	220,130	252,470	604,980	360,710	118,365	139,215	103,130	244,270	81,983	47,530	114,757
Feb	474,382	219,041	255,301	606,668	361,622	118,546	140,128	102,948	245,046	81,625	47,921	115,500
Mar	474,690	221,050	253,640	607,190	362,921	119,313	140,301	103,307	244,269	82,122	47,148	114,999
Apr	473,660	222,574	251,086	605,878	363,960	119,583	140,459	103,926	241,910	82,926	45,172	113,812
May	475,187	225,096	250,091	604,989	365,566	119,651	140,764	105,151	239,423	81,513	45,809	112,101
June	469,382	225,011	244,371	604,221	366,503	119,365	141,753	105,385	237,718	81,321	45,088	111,309
July	478,169	229,046	249,123	608,099	369,847	120,210	143,370	106,267	238,252	82,241	44,261	111,750
Aug	477,115	222,397	254,718	611,959	371,952	120,817	144,197	106,938	240,007	82,541	44,734	112,732
Sept	480,401	223,480	256,921	615,453	372,820	121,273	144,375	107,172	242,633	82,818	46,339	113,476
Oct	481,734	223,498	258,236	615,204	374,011	121,383	144,569	108,059	241,193	82,154	45,498	113,541
Nov *p*	483,701	226,966	256,735	615,181	374,820	121,463	145,227	108,130	240,361	81,187	45,351	113,823

[1] Annual data are averages of monthly not seasonally adjusted figures.
[2] Seasonally adjusted, end of period. Data beginning with 1982 are not comparable with earlier data.
[3] Effective in 2001, data classified based on North American Industry Classification System (NAICS). Data on NAICS basis available beginning with 1992. Earlier data based on Standard Industrial Classification (SIC). Data on both NAICS and SIC basis include semiconductors.

Source: Department of Commerce (Bureau of the Census).

TABLE B–59. Manufacturers' new and unfilled orders, 1971–2012

[Amounts in millions of dollars; monthly data seasonally adjusted]

Year or month	New orders [1]			Unfilled orders [2]			Unfilled orders to shipments ratio [2]		
	Total	Durable goods industries		Nondurable goods industries	Total	Durable goods industries	Nondurable goods industries	Total	Durable goods industries	Nondurable goods industries
		Total	Capital goods, nondefense							
SIC: [3]										
1971	55,921	29,905	6,682	26,016	105,247	100,225	5,022	3.32	4.00	0.76
1972	64,182	35,038	7,745	29,144	119,349	113,034	6,315	3.26	3.85	.86
1973	76,003	42,627	9,926	33,376	156,561	149,204	7,357	3.80	4.51	.91
1974	87,327	46,862	11,594	40,465	187,043	181,519	5,524	4.09	4.93	.62
1975	85,139	41,957	9,886	43,181	169,546	161,664	7,882	3.69	4.45	.82
1976	99,513	51,307	11,490	48,206	178,128	169,857	8,271	3.24	3.88	.74
1977	115,109	61,035	13,681	54,073	202,024	193,323	8,701	3.24	3.85	.71
1978	131,629	72,278	17,588	59,351	259,169	248,281	10,888	3.57	4.20	.81
1979	147,604	79,483	21,154	68,121	303,593	291,321	12,272	3.89	4.62	.82
1980	156,359	79,392	21,135	76,967	327,416	315,202	12,214	3.85	4.58	.75
1981	168,025	83,654	21,806	84,371	326,547	314,707	11,840	3.87	4.68	.69
1982	162,140	78,064	19,213	84,077	311,887	300,798	11,089	3.84	4.74	.62
1983	175,451	88,140	19,624	87,311	347,273	333,114	14,159	3.53	4.29	.69
1984	192,879	100,164	23,669	92,715	373,529	359,651	13,878	3.60	4.37	.64
1985	195,706	102,356	24,545	93,351	387,196	372,097	15,099	3.67	4.47	.68
1986	195,204	103,647	23,982	91,557	393,515	376,699	16,816	3.59	4.41	.70
1987	209,389	110,809	26,094	98,579	430,426	408,688	21,738	3.63	4.43	.83
1988	228,270	122,076	31,108	106,194	474,154	452,150	22,004	3.64	4.46	.76
1989	239,572	126,055	32,988	113,516	508,849	487,098	21,751	3.96	4.85	.77
1990	244,507	125,583	33,331	118,924	531,131	509,124	22,007	4.15	5.15	.76
1991	238,805	119,849	30,471	118,957	519,199	495,802	23,397	4.08	5.07	.79
1992	248,212	126,308	31,524	121,905	492,893	469,381	23,512	3.51	4.30	.75
NAICS: [3]										
1992						451,312			5.14	
1993	246,668	128,672	40,681			425,915			4.66	
1994	266,641	143,803	45,175			435,131			4.21	
1995	285,542	154,137	51,011			447,570			3.97	
1996	297,282	162,399	54,066			488,988			4.14	
1997	314,986	174,377	60,697			513,023			4.04	
1998	317,345	178,327	62,133			496,233			3.97	
1999	329,770	187,674	64,392			505,514			3.76	
2000	346,789	193,881	69,278			549,389			3.87	
2001	322,360	172,686	57,773			509,702			4.19	
2002	318,535	169,276	52,002			478,699			4.12	
2003	331,202	175,135	53,167			504,274			4.10	
2004	357,374	187,015	57,565			556,110			4.24	
2005	397,140	204,038	68,151			653,400			4.34	
2006	424,154	219,707	74,532			797,129			4.92	
2007	449,882	230,513	80,276			947,570			5.51	
2008	453,930	216,583	73,615			996,797			6.36	
2009	347,271	150,866	46,208			802,460			7.06	
2010	409,949	191,804	63,174			879,247			6.17	
2011	458,457	210,434	71,504			969,434			6.20	
2011: Jan	442,260	202,542	64,640			887,116			6.25	
Feb	435,486	195,640	64,742			888,337			6.26	
Mar	457,096	211,397	71,772			897,489			6.09	
Apr	450,343	201,627	66,598			901,244			6.24	
May	455,513	207,662	70,328			909,446			6.23	
June	454,563	205,297	69,875			913,890			6.21	
July	469,642	219,949	72,842			922,570			6.06	
Aug	464,209	212,790	73,477			928,914			6.16	
Sept	465,368	212,966	73,056			937,149			6.23	
Oct	463,563	212,058	71,497			940,858			6.19	
Nov	471,400	219,259	75,804			952,624			6.29	
Dec	481,229	230,392	84,115			969,434			6.16	
2012: Jan	471,576	219,106	78,304			974,867			6.23	
Feb	478,879	223,578	79,777			985,934			6.36	
Mar	468,921	215,281	70,030			986,186			6.29	
Apr	465,752	214,666	69,417			984,750			6.33	
May	467,955	217,864	71,016			984,643			6.24	
June	465,739	221,368	72,741			988,660			6.28	
July	477,711	228,588	75,941			995,852			6.23	
Aug	453,411	198,693	57,756			979,304			6.28	
Sept	473,786	216,865	70,938			980,124			6.24	
Oct	477,438	219,202	72,800			983,406			6.23	
Nov [p]	477,649	220,914	70,671			984,514			6.14	

[1] Annual data are averages of monthly not seasonally adjusted figures.

[2] Unfilled orders are seasonally adjusted, end of period. Ratios are unfilled orders at end of period to shipments for period (excludes industries with no unfilled orders). Annual ratios relate to seasonally adjusted data for December.

[3] Effective in 2001, data classified based on North American Industry Classification System (NAICS). Data on NAICS basis available beginning with 1992. Earlier data based on the Standard Industrial Classification (SIC). Data on SIC basis include semiconductors. Data on NAICS basis do not include semiconductors.

Note: For NAICS basis data beginning with 1992, because there are no unfilled orders for manufacturers' nondurable goods, manufacturers' nondurable new orders and nondurable shipments are the same (see Table B–58).

Source: Department of Commerce (Bureau of the Census).

TABLE B-60. Consumer price indexes for major expenditure classes, 1969–2012

[For all urban consumers; 1982–84=100, except as noted]

Year or month	All items	Food and beverages		Apparel	Housing	Transportation	Medical care	Recreation[2]	Education and communication[2]	Other goods and services	Energy[3]
		Total[1]	Food								
1969	36.7	38.1	37.1	56.8	34.0	35.7	31.9			38.7	24.8
1970	38.8	40.1	39.2	59.2	36.4	37.5	34.0			40.9	25.5
1971	40.5	41.4	40.4	61.1	38.0	39.5	36.1			42.9	26.5
1972	41.8	43.1	42.1	62.3	39.4	39.9	37.3			44.7	27.2
1973	44.4	48.8	48.2	64.6	41.2	41.2	38.8			46.4	29.4
1974	49.3	55.5	55.1	69.4	45.8	45.8	42.4			49.8	38.1
1975	53.8	60.2	59.8	72.5	50.7	50.1	47.5			53.9	42.1
1976	56.9	62.1	61.6	75.2	53.8	55.1	52.0			57.0	45.1
1977	60.6	65.8	65.5	78.6	57.4	59.0	57.0			60.4	49.4
1978	65.2	72.2	72.0	81.4	62.4	61.7	61.8			64.3	52.5
1979	72.6	79.9	79.9	84.9	70.1	70.5	67.5			68.9	65.7
1980	82.4	86.7	86.8	90.9	81.1	83.1	74.9			75.2	86.0
1981	90.9	93.5	93.6	95.3	90.4	93.2	82.9			82.6	97.7
1982	96.5	97.3	97.4	97.8	96.9	97.0	92.5			91.1	99.2
1983	99.6	99.5	99.4	100.2	99.5	99.3	100.6			101.1	99.9
1984	103.9	103.2	103.2	102.1	103.6	103.7	106.8			107.9	100.9
1985	107.6	105.6	105.6	105.0	107.7	106.4	113.5			114.5	101.6
1986	109.6	109.1	109.0	105.9	110.9	102.3	122.0			121.4	88.2
1987	113.6	113.5	113.5	110.6	114.2	105.4	130.1			128.5	88.6
1988	118.3	118.2	118.2	115.4	118.5	108.7	138.6			137.0	89.3
1989	124.0	124.9	125.1	118.6	123.0	114.1	149.3			147.7	94.3
1990	130.7	132.1	132.4	124.1	128.5	120.5	162.8			159.0	102.1
1991	136.2	136.8	136.3	128.7	133.6	123.8	177.0			171.6	102.5
1992	140.3	138.7	137.9	131.9	137.5	126.5	190.1			183.3	103.0
1993	144.5	141.6	140.9	133.7	141.2	130.4	201.4	90.7	85.5	192.9	104.2
1994	148.2	144.9	144.3	133.4	144.8	134.3	211.0	92.7	88.8	198.5	104.6
1995	152.4	148.9	148.4	132.0	148.5	139.1	220.5	94.5	92.2	206.9	105.2
1996	156.9	153.7	153.3	131.7	152.8	143.0	228.2	97.4	95.3	215.4	110.1
1997	160.5	157.7	157.3	132.9	156.8	144.3	234.6	99.6	98.4	224.8	111.5
1998	163.0	161.1	160.7	133.0	160.4	141.6	242.1	101.1	100.3	237.7	102.9
1999	166.6	164.6	164.1	131.3	163.9	144.4	250.6	102.0	101.2	258.3	106.6
2000	172.2	168.4	167.8	129.6	169.6	153.3	260.8	103.3	102.5	271.1	124.6
2001	177.1	173.6	173.1	127.3	176.4	154.3	272.8	104.9	105.2	282.6	129.3
2002	179.9	176.8	176.2	124.0	180.3	152.9	285.6	106.2	107.9	293.2	121.7
2003	184.0	180.5	180.0	120.9	184.8	157.6	297.1	107.5	109.8	298.7	136.5
2004	188.9	186.6	186.2	120.4	189.5	163.1	310.1	108.6	111.6	304.7	151.4
2005	195.3	191.2	190.7	119.5	195.7	173.9	323.2	109.4	113.7	313.4	177.1
2006	201.6	195.7	195.2	119.5	203.2	180.9	336.2	110.9	116.8	321.7	196.9
2007	207.342	203.300	202.916	118.998	209.586	184.682	351.054	111.443	119.577	333.328	207.723
2008	215.303	214.225	214.106	118.907	216.264	195.549	364.065	113.254	123.631	345.381	236.666
2009	214.537	218.249	217.955	120.078	217.057	179.252	375.613	114.272	127.393	368.586	193.126
2010	218.056	219.984	219.625	119.503	216.256	193.396	388.436	113.313	129.919	381.291	211.449
2011	224.939	227.866	227.842	122.111	219.102	212.364	400.258	113.357	131.466	387.224	243.909
2012	229.594	233.670	233.777	126.265	222.715	217.337	414.924	114.703	133.844	394.395	246.080
2011: Jan	220.223	223.160	222.912	116.664	216.739	200.835	393.858	112.638	130.665	384.689	223.266
Feb	221.309	224.039	223.799	118.369	217.259	203.037	397.065	113.183	130.692	385.397	226.860
Mar	223.467	225.479	225.350	121.286	217.707	211.014	397.726	113.261	130.682	385.637	242.516
Apr	224.906	226.248	226.150	122.226	217.901	216.867	398.813	113.368	130.643	386.226	253.495
May	225.964	227.082	227.082	122.271	218.484	220.270	399.375	113.659	130.600	385.476	260.376
June	225.722	227.451	227.360	120.578	219.553	216.880	399.552	113.654	130.568	386.171	254.170
July	225.922	228.323	228.316	118.770	220.230	216.164	400.305	113.492	130.859	386.494	252.661
Aug	226.545	229.490	229.554	121.547	220.506	216.057	400.874	113.592	132.028	387.053	251.706
Sept	226.889	230.448	230.573	125.272	220.540	215.198	401.605	113.440	132.627	388.627	250.480
Oct	226.421	230.885	231.017	127.590	220.138	212.127	403.430	113.270	132.755	389.119	240.902
Nov	226.230	230.656	230.790	127.285	219.969	211.358	404.858	113.232	132.750	390.761	238.177
Dec	225.672	231.130	231.301	123.470	220.193	208.585	405.629	113.499	132.728	391.043	232.300
2012: Jan	226.665	232.559	232.666	122.105	220.805	210.799	408.056	114.183	133.067	391.382	236.942
Feb	227.663	232.453	232.486	123.312	221.117	214.429	410.466	114.333	133.199	391.236	242.663
Mar	229.392	232.708	232.792	127.258	221.487	220.842	411.498	114.675	133.235	392.364	253.599
Apr	230.085	233.116	233.234	128.485	221.682	223.083	412.480	114.656	133.284	393.320	255.736
May	229.815	233.257	233.339	127.688	221.971	220.768	413.655	114.689	133.470	392.859	250.306
June	229.478	233.509	233.563	125.241	223.051	216.369	415.345	115.080	133.456	393.989	244.167
July	229.104	233.557	233.630	122.300	223.316	214.294	416.759	114.944	133.546	395.418	239.972
Aug	230.379	234.017	234.156	123.568	223.699	219.110	417.123	114.929	134.039	396.161	250.306
Sept	231.407	234.172	234.298	128.630	223.901	221.745	418.039	114.963	134.639	396.155	256.332
Oct	231.317	234.718	234.878	131.359	223.708	220.232	418.359	114.774	134.767	396.337	250.523
Nov	230.221	234.742	234.896	129.573	223.814	214.525	418.653	114.763	134.736	396.702	238.946
Dec	229.601	235.230	235.390	125.656	224.032	211.853	418.654	114.442	134.694	396.814	233.473

[1] Includes alcoholic beverages, not shown separately.
[2] December 1997=100.
[3] Household energy—gas (piped), electricity, fuel oil, etc.—and motor fuel. Motor oil, coolant, etc. also included through 1982.

Note: Data beginning with 1983 incorporate a rental equivalence measure for homeowners' costs.
Series reflect changes in composition and renaming beginning in 1998, and formula and methodology changes beginning in 1999.

Source: Department of Labor (Bureau of Labor Statistics).

[For all urban consumers; 1982–84=100, except as noted]

Year or month	Food and beverages				Housing						
		Food				Shelter			Fuels and utilities		
								Owners' equivalent rent of residences [3,4]		Household energy	
	Total [1]	Total	At home	Away from home	Total [2]	Total [2]	Rent of primary residence		Total [2]	Total [2]	Energy Services
1969	38.1	37.1	38.0	34.9	34.0	32.6	44.7		28.0	22.1	24.3
1970	40.1	39.2	39.9	37.5	36.4	35.5	46.5		29.1	23.1	25.4
1971	41.4	40.4	40.9	39.4	38.0	37.0	48.7		31.1	24.7	27.1
1972	43.1	42.1	42.7	41.0	39.4	38.7	50.4		32.5	25.7	28.5
1973	48.8	48.2	49.7	44.2	41.2	40.5	52.5		34.3	27.5	29.9
1974	55.5	55.1	57.1	49.8	45.8	44.4	55.2		40.7	34.4	34.5
1975	60.2	59.8	61.8	54.5	50.7	48.8	58.0		45.4	39.4	40.1
1976	62.1	61.6	63.1	58.2	53.8	51.5	61.1		49.4	43.3	44.7
1977	65.8	65.5	66.8	62.6	57.4	54.9	64.8		54.7	49.0	50.5
1978	72.2	72.0	73.8	68.3	62.4	60.5	69.3		58.5	53.0	55.0
1979	79.9	79.9	81.8	75.9	70.1	68.9	74.3		64.8	61.3	61.0
1980	86.7	86.8	88.4	83.4	81.1	81.0	80.9		75.4	74.8	71.4
1981	93.5	93.6	94.8	90.9	90.4	90.5	87.9		86.4	87.2	81.9
1982	97.3	97.4	98.1	95.8	96.9	96.9	94.6		94.9	95.6	93.2
1983	99.5	99.4	99.1	100.0	99.5	99.1	100.1	102.5	100.2	100.5	101.5
1984	103.2	103.2	102.8	104.2	103.6	104.0	105.3	107.3	104.8	104.0	105.4
1985	105.6	105.6	104.3	108.3	107.7	109.8	111.8	113.2	106.5	104.5	107.1
1986	109.1	109.0	107.3	112.5	110.9	115.8	118.3	119.4	104.1	99.2	105.7
1987	113.5	113.5	111.9	117.0	114.2	121.3	123.1	124.8	103.0	97.3	103.8
1988	118.2	118.2	116.6	121.8	118.5	127.1	127.8	131.1	104.4	98.0	104.6
1989	124.9	125.1	124.2	127.4	123.0	132.8	132.8	137.4	107.8	100.9	107.5
1990	132.1	132.4	132.3	133.4	128.5	140.0	138.4	144.8	111.6	104.5	109.3
1991	136.8	136.3	135.8	137.9	133.6	146.3	143.3	150.4	115.3	106.7	112.6
1992	138.7	137.9	136.8	140.7	137.5	151.2	146.9	155.5	117.8	108.1	114.8
1993	141.6	140.9	140.1	143.2	141.2	155.7	150.3	160.5	121.3	111.2	118.5
1994	144.9	144.3	144.1	145.7	144.8	160.5	154.0	165.8	122.8	111.7	119.2
1995	148.9	148.4	148.8	149.0	148.5	165.7	157.8	171.3	123.7	111.5	119.2
1996	153.7	153.3	154.3	152.7	152.8	171.0	162.0	176.8	127.5	115.2	122.1
1997	157.7	157.3	158.1	157.0	156.8	176.3	166.7	181.9	130.8	117.9	125.1
1998	161.1	160.7	161.1	161.1	160.4	182.1	172.1	187.8	128.5	113.7	121.2
1999	164.6	164.1	164.2	165.1	163.9	187.3	177.5	192.9	128.8	113.5	120.9
2000	168.4	167.8	167.9	169.0	169.6	193.4	183.9	198.7	137.9	122.8	128.0
2001	173.6	173.1	173.4	173.9	176.4	200.6	192.1	206.3	150.2	135.4	142.4
2002	176.8	176.2	175.6	178.3	180.3	208.1	199.7	214.7	143.6	127.2	134.4
2003	180.5	180.0	179.4	182.1	184.8	213.1	205.5	219.9	154.5	138.2	145.0
2004	186.6	186.2	186.2	187.5	189.5	218.8	211.0	224.9	161.9	144.4	150.6
2005	191.2	190.7	189.8	193.4	195.7	224.4	217.3	230.2	179.0	161.6	166.5
2006	195.7	195.2	193.1	199.4	203.2	232.1	225.1	238.2	194.7	177.1	182.1
2007	203.300	202.916	201.245	206.659	209.586	240.611	234.679	246.235	200.632	181.744	186.262
2008	214.225	214.106	214.125	215.769	216.264	246.666	243.271	252.426	220.018	200.808	202.212
2009	218.249	217.955	215.124	223.272	217.057	249.354	248.812	256.610	210.696	188.113	193.563
2010	219.984	219.625	215.836	226.114	216.256	248.396	249.385	256.584	214.187	189.286	192.886
2011	227.866	227.842	226.201	231.401	219.102	251.646	253.638	259.570	220.367	193.648	194.386
2012	233.670	233.777	231.774	237.986	222.715	257.083	260.367	264.838	218.986	189.308	189.679
2011: Jan	223.160	222.912	220.016	228.181	216.739	249.462	251.555	257.775	214.045	187.704	189.088
Feb	224.039	223.799	221.241	228.606	217.259	249.886	251.829	258.073	215.587	189.006	189.837
Mar	225.479	225.350	223.430	229.282	217.707	250.310	252.145	258.263	216.672	190.071	190.213
Apr	226.228	226.150	224.233	230.082	217.901	250.447	252.221	258.400	217.254	190.622	190.459
May	227.082	226.976	225.356	230.501	218.484	250.745	252.393	258.587	219.956	193.498	193.698
June	227.451	227.360	225.588	231.097	219.553	251.422	252.592	259.010	225.022	199.122	200.191
July	228.323	228.316	226.891	231.580	220.230	252.155	253.085	259.573	226.643	200.587	202.002
Aug	229.490	229.554	228.354	232.513	220.506	252.546	254.003	260.178	226.493	200.144	201.564
Sept	230.448	230.573	229.739	233.032	220.540	252.647	254.628	260.459	226.409	199.814	201.270
Oct	230.885	231.017	230.196	233.459	220.138	253.101	255.651	261.034	220.450	193.058	193.843
Nov	230.656	230.790	229.380	234.046	219.969	253.312	256.367	261.503	218.199	190.444	190.572
Dec	231.130	231.301	229.982	234.435	220.193	253.716	257.189	261.797	217.674	189.711	189.891
2012: Jan	232.559	232.666	231.694	235.268	220.805	254.409	257.714	262.543	218.199	189.945	189.942
Feb	232.453	232.486	231.180	235.603	221.117	254.931	258.184	262.812	217.189	188.393	187.962
Mar	232.708	232.792	231.383	236.073	221.487	255.609	258.569	263.317	216.667	187.591	186.784
Apr	233.116	233.234	231.711	236.695	221.682	256.031	258.922	263.765	216.006	186.517	185.834
May	233.257	233.339	231.518	237.262	221.971	256.442	259.231	264.012	216.388	186.852	186.762
June	233.509	233.563	231.515	237.839	223.051	256.950	259.407	264.276	221.789	192.649	194.261
July	233.557	233.630	231.306	238.337	223.316	257.409	260.107	264.740	221.449	191.913	193.679
Aug	234.017	234.156	231.708	239.057	223.699	257.843	260.677	265.422	222.769	192.759	194.136
Sept	234.172	234.298	231.615	239.565	223.901	258.252	261.421	266.013	222.634	192.636	193.579
Oct	234.718	234.878	232.456	239.742	223.708	258.829	262.707	266.581	218.287	187.657	187.970
Nov	234.742	234.896	232.295	240.038	223.814	258.999	263.365	267.099	217.964	187.141	187.359
Dec	235.230	235.390	232.901	240.359	224.032	259.298	264.098	267.480	218.496	187.642	187.880

[1] Includes alcoholic beverages, not shown separately.
[2] Includes other items not shown separately.
[3] December 1982=100.
[4] Beginning January 2010, includes expenditure weight for second homes. Prior data are for primary residence only.

See next page for continuation of table.

[For all urban consumers; 1982-84=100, except as noted]

Year or month	Transportation							Medical care		
	Total	Private transportation					Public trans-porta-tion	Total	Medical care com-modities	Medical care services
		Total[2]	New vehicles		Used cars and trucks	Motor fuel				
			Total[2]	New cars						
1969	35.7	36.0	51.5	51.5	30.9	27.6	30.9	31.9	45.4	30.2
1970	37.5	37.5	53.1	53.0	31.2	27.9	35.2	34.0	46.5	32.3
1971	39.5	39.4	55.3	55.2	33.0	28.1	37.8	36.1	47.3	34.7
1972	39.9	39.7	54.8	54.7	33.1	28.4	39.3	37.3	47.4	35.9
1973	41.2	41.0	54.8	54.8	35.2	31.2	39.7	38.8	47.5	37.5
1974	45.8	46.2	58.0	57.9	36.7	42.2	40.6	42.4	49.2	41.4
1975	50.1	50.6	63.0	62.9	43.8	45.1	43.5	47.5	53.3	46.6
1976	55.1	55.6	67.0	66.9	50.3	47.0	47.8	52.0	56.5	51.3
1977	59.0	59.7	70.5	70.4	54.7	49.7	50.0	57.0	60.2	56.4
1978	61.7	62.5	75.9	75.8	55.8	51.8	51.5	61.8	64.4	61.2
1979	70.5	71.7	81.9	81.8	60.2	70.1	54.9	67.5	69.0	67.2
1980	83.1	84.2	88.5	88.4	62.3	97.4	69.0	74.9	75.4	74.8
1981	93.2	93.8	93.9	93.7	76.9	108.5	85.6	82.9	83.7	82.8
1982	97.0	97.1	97.5	97.4	88.8	102.8	94.9	92.5	92.3	92.6
1983	99.3	99.3	99.9	99.9	98.7	99.4	99.5	100.6	100.2	100.7
1984	103.7	103.6	102.6	102.8	112.5	97.9	105.7	106.8	107.5	106.7
1985	106.4	106.2	106.1	106.1	113.7	98.7	110.5	113.5	115.2	113.2
1986	102.3	101.2	110.6	110.6	108.8	77.1	117.0	122.0	122.8	121.9
1987	105.4	104.2	114.4	114.6	113.1	80.2	121.1	130.1	131.0	130.0
1988	108.7	107.6	116.5	116.9	118.0	80.9	123.3	138.6	139.9	138.3
1989	114.1	112.9	119.2	119.2	120.4	88.5	129.5	149.3	150.8	148.9
1990	120.5	118.8	121.4	121.0	117.6	101.2	142.6	162.8	163.4	162.7
1991	123.8	121.9	126.0	125.3	118.1	99.4	148.9	177.0	176.8	177.1
1992	126.5	124.6	129.2	128.4	123.2	99.0	151.4	190.1	188.1	190.5
1993	130.4	127.5	132.7	131.5	133.9	98.0	167.0	201.4	195.0	202.9
1994	134.3	131.4	137.6	136.0	141.7	98.5	172.0	211.0	200.7	213.4
1995	139.1	136.3	141.0	139.0	156.5	100.0	175.9	220.5	204.5	224.2
1996	143.0	140.0	143.7	141.4	157.0	106.3	181.9	228.2	210.4	232.4
1997	144.3	141.0	144.3	141.7	151.1	106.2	186.7	234.6	215.3	239.1
1998	141.6	137.9	143.4	140.7	150.6	92.2	190.3	242.1	221.8	246.8
1999	144.4	140.5	142.9	139.6	152.0	100.7	197.7	250.6	230.7	255.1
2000	153.3	149.1	142.8	139.6	155.8	129.3	209.6	260.8	238.1	266.0
2001	154.3	150.0	142.1	138.9	158.7	124.7	210.6	272.8	247.6	278.8
2002	152.9	148.8	140.0	137.3	152.0	116.6	207.4	285.6	256.4	292.9
2003	157.6	153.6	137.9	134.7	142.9	135.8	209.3	297.1	262.8	306.0
2004	163.1	159.4	137.1	133.9	133.3	160.4	209.1	310.1	269.3	321.3
2005	173.9	170.2	137.9	135.2	139.4	195.7	217.3	323.2	276.0	336.7
2006	180.9	177.0	137.6	136.4	140.0	221.0	226.6	336.2	285.9	350.6
2007	184.682	180.778	136.254	135.865	135.747	239.070	230.002	351.054	289.999	369.302
2008	195.549	191.039	134.194	135.401	133.951	279.652	250.549	364.065	296.045	384.943
2009	179.252	174.762	135.623	136.685	126.973	201.978	236.348	375.613	305.108	397.299
2010	193.396	188.747	138.005	138.094	143.128	239.178	251.351	388.436	314.717	411.208
2011	212.366	207.641	141.883	142.226	149.011	302.619	269.403	400.258	324.089	423.810
2012	217.337	212.752	144.232	144.178	150.330	312.660	271.351	414.924	333.609	440.341
2011: Jan	200.835	196.087	138.925	138.203	142.555	265.703	259.634	393.858	318.929	417.025
Feb	203.037	198.073	140.158	139.584	142.937	271.843	265.327	397.065	321.186	420.567
Mar	211.014	206.165	140.860	140.311	144.072	303.565	270.366	397.726	322.691	420.852
Apr	216.867	212.210	141.462	141.154	145.968	326.024	272.187	398.813	324.241	421.716
May	220.270	215.829	142.494	142.717	148.361	337.359	271.417	399.375	324.399	422.438
June	216.880	212.216	143.054	143.812	151.776	318.242	272.297	399.552	324.102	422.813
July	216.164	211.432	142.763	143.707	154.184	313.488	272.868	400.305	324.159	423.847
Aug	216.057	211.315	142.327	143.283	155.823	311.962	272.949	400.874	324.395	424.546
Sept	215.198	210.513	142.334	143.414	153.586	309.745	271.199	401.605	325.130	425.258
Oct	212.127	207.404	142.535	143.419	151.494	296.944	269.158	403.430	325.962	427.467
Nov	211.358	206.635	142.736	143.489	149.230	294.049	268.478	404.858	326.624	429.191
Dec	208.585	203.809	142.953	143.619	148.140	282.501	266.958	405.629	327.254	430.005
2012: Jan	210.799	206.307	143.438	143.698	147.143	292.236	263.968	408.056	329.201	432.583
Feb	214.429	210.013	144.326	144.273	147.011	306.348	265.830	410.466	331.867	434.832
Mar	220.842	216.536	144.350	144.103	148.677	330.834	269.566	411.498	333.188	435.721
Apr	223.083	218.563	144.522	144.404	151.087	336.673	275.272	412.480	333.060	437.151
May	220.768	215.978	144.401	144.477	153.565	324.589	277.929	413.655	333.131	438.766
June	216.369	211.423	144.367	144.365	155.306	304.697	276.784	415.345	333.348	441.041
July	214.294	209.458	143.953	143.924	155.815	296.502	273.033	416.759	335.048	442.305
Aug	219.110	214.763	143.749	143.704	154.851	317.798	268.755	417.123	336.004	442.410
Sept	221.745	217.530	143.725	143.535	151.118	330.923	268.791	418.039	335.721	443.812
Oct	220.232	215.832	144.011	143.787	148.293	324.131	270.681	418.359	335.768	444.242
Nov	214.525	209.745	144.762	144.701	145.862	299.777	272.244	418.653	334.285	445.278
Dec	211.853	206.874	145.181	145.163	145.234	287.408	273.364	418.654	332.684	445.955

Source: Department of Labor (Bureau of Labor Statistics).

TABLE B–62. Consumer price indexes for commodities, services, and special groups, 1969–2012

[For all urban consumers; 1982–84=100, except as noted]

| Year or month | All items (CPI-U)[1] | Commodities | | Services | Special indexes | | | | All items | | |
		All commodities	Commodities less food		All items less food	All items less energy	All items less food and energy	All items less medical care	CPI-U-X1 (Dec. 1982 = 97.6)[2]	CPI-U-RS (Dec. 1977 = 100)[3]	C-CPI-U (Dec. 1999 = 100)[4]
1969	36.7	39.9	41.7	32.4	36.8	38.0	38.4	37.0	39.4		
1970	38.8	41.7	43.4	35.0	39.0	40.3	40.8	39.2	41.3		
1971	40.5	43.2	45.1	37.0	40.8	42.0	42.7	40.8	43.1		
1972	41.8	44.5	46.1	38.4	42.0	43.4	44.0	42.1	44.4		
1973	44.4	47.8	47.7	40.1	43.7	46.1	45.6	44.8	47.2		
1974	49.3	53.5	52.8	43.8	48.0	50.6	49.4	49.8	51.9		
1975	53.8	58.2	57.6	48.0	52.5	55.1	53.9	54.3	56.2		
1976	56.9	60.7	60.5	52.0	56.0	58.2	57.4	57.2	59.4		
1977	60.6	64.2	63.8	56.0	59.6	61.9	61.0	60.8	63.2		
1978	65.2	68.8	67.5	60.8	63.9	66.7	65.5	65.4	67.5	104.4	
1979	72.6	76.6	75.3	67.5	71.2	73.4	71.9	72.9	74.0	114.4	
1980	82.4	86.0	85.7	77.9	81.5	81.9	80.8	82.8	82.3	127.1	
1981	90.9	93.2	93.1	88.1	90.4	90.1	89.2	91.4	90.1	139.2	
1982	96.5	97.0	96.9	96.0	96.3	96.1	95.8	96.8	95.6	147.6	
1983	99.6	99.8	100.0	99.4	99.7	99.6	99.6	99.6	99.6	153.9	
1984	103.9	103.2	103.1	104.6	104.0	104.3	104.6	103.7	103.9	160.2	
1985	107.6	105.4	105.2	109.9	108.0	108.4	109.1	107.2	107.6	165.7	
1986	109.6	104.4	101.7	115.4	109.8	112.6	113.5	108.8	109.6	168.7	
1987	113.6	107.7	104.3	120.2	113.6	117.2	118.2	112.6	113.6	174.4	
1988	118.3	111.5	107.7	125.7	118.3	122.3	123.4	117.0	118.3	180.8	
1989	124.0	116.7	112.0	131.9	123.7	128.1	129.0	122.4	124.0	188.6	
1990	130.7	122.8	117.4	139.2	130.3	134.7	135.5	128.8	130.7	198.0	
1991	136.2	126.6	121.3	146.3	136.1	140.9	142.1	133.8	136.2	205.1	
1992	140.3	129.1	124.2	152.0	140.8	145.4	147.3	137.5	140.3	210.3	
1993	144.5	131.5	126.3	157.9	145.1	150.0	152.2	141.2	144.5	215.5	
1994	148.2	133.8	127.9	163.1	149.0	154.1	156.5	144.7	148.2	220.1	
1995	152.4	136.4	129.8	168.7	153.1	158.7	161.2	148.6	152.4	225.4	
1996	156.9	139.9	132.6	174.1	157.5	163.1	165.6	152.8	156.9	231.4	
1997	160.5	141.8	133.4	179.4	161.1	167.1	169.5	156.3	160.5	236.4	
1998	163.0	141.9	132.0	184.2	163.4	170.9	173.4	158.6	163.0	239.7	
1999	166.6	144.4	134.0	188.8	167.0	174.4	177.0	162.0	166.6	244.7	
2000	172.2	149.2	139.2	195.3	173.0	178.6	181.3	167.3	172.2	252.9	102.0
2001	177.1	150.7	138.9	203.4	177.8	183.5	186.1	171.9	177.1	260.0	104.3
2002	179.9	149.7	136.0	209.8	180.5	187.7	190.5	174.3	179.9	264.2	105.6
2003	184.0	151.2	136.5	216.5	184.7	190.6	193.2	178.1	184.0	270.1	107.8
2004	188.9	154.7	138.8	222.8	189.4	194.4	196.6	182.7	188.9	277.4	110.5
2005	195.3	160.2	144.5	230.1	196.0	198.7	200.9	188.7	195.3	286.7	113.7
2006	201.6	164.0	148.0	238.9	202.7	203.7	205.9	194.7	201.6	296.1	117.0
2007	207.342	167.509	149.720	246.848	208.098	208.925	210.729	200.080	207.342	304.5	119.957
2008	215.303	174.764	155.310	255.498	215.528	214.751	215.572	207.777	215.303	316.2	124.433
2009	214.537	169.698	147.071	259.154	214.008	218.433	219.235	206.555	214.537	315.0	123.850
2010	218.056	174.566	152.990	261.274	217.828	220.458	221.337	209.689	218.056	320.2	125.615
2011	224.939	183.862	162.409	265.762	224.503	224.806	225.008	216.325	224.939	330.3	129.144
2012	229.594	187.577	165.264	271.374	228.962	229.717	229.755	220.553	229.594	337.2	
2011: Jan	220.223	177.480	155.682	262.701	219.820	221.666	222.177	211.714	220.223	323.4	126.700
Feb	221.309	178.874	157.221	263.480	220.937	222.506	223.011	212.709	221.309	325.0	127.286
Mar	223.467	182.728	161.804	263.956	223.192	223.315	223.690	214.907	223.467	328.2	128.353
Apr	224.906	185.311	164.964	264.256	224.731	223.798	224.118	216.346	224.906	330.3	129.062
May	225.964	186.804	166.657	264.883	225.826	224.275	224.534	217.414	225.964	331.8	129.548
June	225.722	185.266	164.461	265.928	225.485	224.635	224.891	217.158	225.722	331.5	129.531
July	225.922	184.931	163.664	266.660	225.566	225.010	225.164	217.328	225.922	331.8	129.636
Aug	226.545	185.566	164.059	267.271	226.092	225.797	225.874	217.955	226.545	332.7	129.974
Sept	226.889	186.015	164.287	267.510	226.329	226.303	226.289	218.281	226.889	333.2	130.196
Oct	226.421	185.236	163.084	267.352	225.717	226.754	226.743	217.730	226.421	332.5	129.997
Nov	226.230	184.791	162.572	267.413	225.532	226.818	226.859	217.479	226.230	332.2	129.856
Dec	225.672	183.345	160.453	267.737	224.805	226.795	226.740	216.875	225.672	331.4	129.586
2012: Jan	226.665	184.636	161.685	268.459	225.739	227.422	227.237	217.804	226.665	332.9	130.104
Feb	227.663	186.279	163.994	268.819	226.927	227.925	227.865	218.737	227.663	334.3	130.569
Mar	229.392	189.201	167.858	269.396	228.887	228.755	228.735	220.483	229.392	336.9	131.388
Apr	230.085	190.089	168.899	269.901	229.621	229.252	229.303	221.159	230.085	337.9	131.731
May	229.815	188.963	167.323	270.462	229.290	229.520	229.602	220.833	229.815	337.5	131.639
June	229.478	186.967	164.516	271.737	228.863	229.788	229.879	220.416	229.478	337.0	131.557
July	229.104	185.872	162.997	272.062	228.417	229.811	229.893	219.972	229.104	336.4	131.352
Aug	230.379	187.952	165.628	272.560	229.813	230.148	230.196	221.275	230.379	338.3	131.940
Sept	231.407	189.575	167.785	273.014	230.985	230.661	230.780	222.301	231.407	339.8	132.438
Oct	231.317	189.338	167.239	273.066	230.787	231.169	231.276	222.195	231.317	339.7	132.434
Nov	230.221	186.845	163.834	273.323	229.509	231.160	231.263	221.049	230.221	338.1	131.949
Dec	229.601	185.204	161.405	273.694	228.709	231.043	231.033	220.408	229.601	337.2	131.633

[1] Consumer price index, all urban consumers.
[2] CPI-U-X1 reflects a rental equivalence approach to homeowners' costs for the CPI-U for years prior to 1983, the first year for which the official index incorporates such a measure. CPI-U-X1 is rebased to the December 1982 value of the CPI-U (1982–84=100) and is identical with CPI-U data from December 1982 forward.
[3] Consumer price index research series (CPI-U-RS) using current methods introduced in June 1999. Data for 2012 are preliminary. All data are subject to revision annually.
[4] Chained consumer price index (C-CPI-U) introduced in August 2002. Data for 2011 and 2012 are subject to revision.

Source: Department of Labor (Bureau of Labor Statistics).

TABLE B–63. Changes in special consumer price indexes, 1969–2012

[For all urban consumers; percent change]

Year or month	All items Dec. to Dec.[1]	All items Year to year	All items less food Dec. to Dec.[1]	All items less food Year to year	All items less energy Dec. to Dec.[1]	All items less energy Year to year	All items less food and energy Dec. to Dec.[1]	All items less food and energy Year to year	All items less medical care Dec. to Dec.[1]	All items less medical care Year to year
1969	6.2	5.5	5.6	5.4	6.5	5.8	6.2	5.8	6.1	5.4
1970	5.6	5.7	6.6	6.0	5.4	6.1	6.6	6.3	5.2	5.9
1971	3.3	4.4	3.0	4.6	3.4	4.2	3.1	4.7	3.2	4.1
1972	3.4	3.2	2.9	2.9	3.5	3.3	3.0	3.0	3.4	3.2
1973	8.7	6.2	5.6	4.0	8.2	6.2	4.7	3.6	9.1	6.4
1974	12.3	11.0	12.2	9.8	11.7	9.8	11.1	8.3	12.2	11.2
1975	6.9	9.1	7.3	9.4	6.6	8.9	6.7	9.1	6.7	9.0
1976	4.9	5.8	6.1	6.7	4.8	5.6	6.1	6.5	4.5	5.3
1977	6.7	6.5	6.4	6.4	6.7	6.4	6.5	6.3	6.7	6.3
1978	9.0	7.6	8.3	7.2	9.1	7.8	8.5	7.4	9.1	7.6
1979	13.3	11.3	14.0	11.4	11.1	10.0	11.3	9.8	13.4	11.5
1980	12.5	13.5	13.0	14.5	11.7	11.6	12.2	12.4	12.5	13.6
1981	8.9	10.3	9.8	10.9	8.5	10.0	9.5	10.4	8.8	10.4
1982	3.8	6.2	4.1	6.5	4.2	6.7	4.5	7.4	3.6	5.9
1983	3.8	3.2	4.1	3.5	4.5	3.6	4.8	4.0	3.6	2.9
1984	3.9	4.3	3.9	4.3	4.4	4.7	4.7	5.0	3.9	4.1
1985	3.8	3.6	4.1	3.8	4.0	3.9	4.3	4.3	3.5	3.4
1986	1.1	1.9	.5	1.7	3.8	3.9	3.8	4.0	.7	1.5
1987	4.4	3.6	4.6	3.5	4.1	4.1	4.2	4.1	4.3	3.5
1988	4.4	4.1	4.2	4.1	4.7	4.4	4.7	4.4	4.2	3.9
1989	4.6	4.8	4.5	4.6	4.6	4.7	4.4	4.5	4.5	4.6
1990	6.1	5.4	6.3	5.3	5.2	5.2	5.2	5.0	5.9	5.2
1991	3.1	4.2	3.3	4.5	3.9	4.6	4.4	4.9	2.7	3.9
1992	2.9	3.0	3.2	3.5	3.0	3.2	3.3	3.7	2.7	2.8
1993	2.7	3.0	2.7	3.1	3.1	3.2	3.2	3.3	2.6	2.7
1994	2.7	2.6	2.6	2.7	2.6	2.7	2.6	2.8	2.5	2.5
1995	2.5	2.8	2.7	2.8	2.9	3.0	3.0	3.0	2.5	2.7
1996	3.3	3.0	3.1	2.9	2.9	2.8	2.6	2.7	3.3	2.8
1997	1.7	2.3	1.8	2.3	2.1	2.5	2.2	2.4	1.6	2.3
1998	1.6	1.6	1.5	1.4	2.4	2.3	2.4	2.3	1.5	1.5
1999	2.7	2.2	2.8	2.2	2.0	2.0	1.9	2.1	2.6	2.1
2000	3.4	3.4	3.5	3.6	2.6	2.4	2.6	2.4	3.3	3.3
2001	1.6	2.8	1.3	2.8	2.8	2.7	2.7	2.6	1.4	2.7
2002	2.4	1.6	2.6	1.5	1.8	2.3	1.9	2.4	2.2	1.4
2003	1.9	2.3	1.5	2.3	1.5	1.5	1.1	1.4	1.8	2.2
2004	3.3	2.7	3.4	2.5	2.2	2.0	2.2	1.8	3.2	2.6
2005	3.4	3.4	3.6	3.5	2.2	2.2	2.2	2.2	3.3	3.3
2006	2.5	3.2	2.6	3.4	2.5	2.5	2.6	2.5	2.5	3.2
2007	4.1	2.8	4.0	2.7	2.8	2.6	2.4	2.3	4.0	2.8
2008	.1	3.8	-.8	3.6	2.4	2.8	1.8	2.3	-.1	3.8
2009	2.7	-.4	3.3	-.7	1.4	1.7	1.8	1.7	2.7	-.6
2010	1.5	1.6	1.5	1.8	.9	.9	.8	1.0	1.4	1.5
2011	3.0	3.2	2.7	3.1	2.6	2.0	2.2	1.7	2.9	3.2
2012	1.7	2.1	1.7	2.0	1.9	2.2	1.9	2.1	1.6	2.0

Percent change from preceding month

Year or month	Unadjusted	Seasonally adjusted	Unadjusted	Seasonally adjusted	Unadjusted	Seasonally adjusted	Unadjusted	Seasonally adjusted	Unadjusted	Seasonally adjusted
2011: Jan	0.5	0.3	0.4	0.2	0.3	0.2	0.2	0.2	0.5	0.3
Feb	.5	.4	.5	.4	.4	.2	.4	.2	.5	.4
Mar	1.0	.5	1.0	.5	.4	.2	.3	.2	1.0	.6
Apr	.6	.4	.7	.4	.2	.2	.2	.2	.7	.4
May	.5	.3	.5	.3	.2	.3	.2	.3	.5	.3
June	-.1	.1	-.2	.1	.2	.2	.2	.2	-.1	.1
July	.1	.3	.0	.3	.2	.2	.1	.2	.1	.3
Aug	.3	.3	.2	.3	.3	.3	.3	.2	.3	.3
Sept	.2	.3	.1	.2	.2	.1	.2	.1	.1	.3
Oct	-.2	.0	-.3	-.1	.2	.2	.2	.2	-.3	-.1
Nov	-.1	.1	-.1	.1	.0	.2	.1	.2	-.1	.1
Dec	-.2	.0	-.3	.0	.0	.2	-.1	.1	-.3	.0
2012: Jan	.4	.2	.4	.2	.3	.2	.2	.2	.4	.2
Feb	.4	.4	.5	.5	.2	.1	.3	.1	.4	.4
Mar	.8	.3	.9	.3	.3	.2	.4	.2	.8	.3
Apr	.3	.0	.3	.0	.2	.2	.2	.2	.3	.0
May	-.1	-.3	-.1	-.3	.1	.2	.1	.2	-.1	-.3
June	-.1	.0	-.2	.0	.1	.2	.1	.2	-.2	.0
July	-.2	.0	-.2	.0	.0	.1	.0	.1	-.2	.0
Aug	.6	.6	.6	.7	.1	.1	.1	.1	.6	.6
Sept	.4	.6	.5	.7	.2	.1	.3	.1	.5	.6
Oct	.0	.1	-.1	.1	.2	.2	.2	.1	.0	.2
Nov	-.5	-.3	-.6	-.4	.0	.1	.0	.1	-.5	-.3
Dec	-.3	.0	-.3	-.1	-.1	.1	-.1	.1	-.3	.0

[1] Changes from December to December are based on unadjusted indexes.

Source: Department of Labor (Bureau of Labor Statistics).

TABLE B–64. Changes in consumer price indexes for commodities and services, 1941–2012

[For all urban consumers: percent change]

Year	All items		Commodities				Services				Medical care [2]		Energy [3]	
			Total		Food		Total		Medical care					
	Dec. to Dec. [1]	Year to year	Dec. to Dec. [1]	Year to year	Dec. to Dec. [1]	Year to year	Dec. to Dec. [1]	Year to year	Dec. to Dec. [1]	Year to year	Dec. to Dec. [1]	Year to year	Dec. to Dec. [1]	Year to year
1941	9.9	5.0	13.3	6.7	15.7	9.2	2.4	0.8	1.2	0.0	1.0	0.0	....	....
1942	9.0	10.9	12.9	14.5	17.9	17.6	2.3	3.1	3.5	3.5	3.8	2.9	....	....
1943	3.0	6.1	4.2	9.3	3.0	11.0	2.3	2.3	5.6	4.5	4.6	4.7	....	....
1944	2.3	1.7	2.0	1.0	.0	-1.2	2.2	2.2	3.2	4.3	2.6	3.6	....	....
1945	2.2	2.3	2.9	3.0	3.5	2.4	.7	1.5	3.1	3.1	2.6	2.6	....	....
1946	18.1	8.3	24.8	10.6	31.3	14.5	3.6	1.4	9.0	5.1	8.3	5.0	....	....
1947	8.8	14.4	10.3	20.5	11.3	21.7	5.6	4.3	6.4	8.7	6.9	8.0	....	....
1948	3.0	8.1	1.7	7.2	-.8	8.3	5.9	6.1	6.9	7.1	5.8	6.7	....	....
1949	-2.1	-1.2	-4.1	-2.7	-3.9	-4.2	3.7	5.1	1.6	3.3	1.4	2.8	....	....
1950	5.9	1.3	7.8	.7	9.8	1.6	3.6	3.0	4.0	2.4	3.4	2.0	....	....
1951	6.0	7.9	5.9	9.0	7.1	11.0	5.2	5.3	5.3	4.7	5.8	5.3	....	....
1952	.8	1.9	-.9	1.3	-1.0	1.8	4.4	4.5	5.8	6.7	4.3	5.0	....	....
1953	.7	.8	-.3	-.3	-1.1	-1.4	4.2	4.3	3.4	3.5	3.5	3.6	....	....
1954	-.7	.7	-1.6	-.9	-1.8	-.4	2.0	3.1	2.6	3.4	2.3	2.9	....	....
1955	.4	-.4	-.3	-.9	-.7	-1.4	2.0	2.0	3.2	2.6	3.3	2.2	....	....
1956	3.0	1.5	2.6	1.0	2.9	.7	3.4	2.5	3.8	3.8	3.2	3.8	....	....
1957	2.9	3.3	2.8	3.2	2.8	3.2	4.2	4.3	4.8	4.3	4.7	4.2	....	....
1958	1.8	2.8	1.2	2.1	2.4	4.5	2.7	3.7	4.6	5.3	4.5	4.6	-0.9	0.0
1959	1.7	.7	.6	.0	-1.0	-1.7	3.9	3.1	4.9	4.5	3.8	4.4	4.7	1.9
1960	1.4	1.7	1.2	.9	3.1	1.0	2.5	3.4	3.7	4.3	3.2	3.7	1.3	2.3
1961	.7	1.0	.0	.6	-.7	1.3	2.1	1.7	3.5	3.6	3.1	2.7	-1.3	.4
1962	1.3	1.0	.9	.9	1.3	.7	1.6	2.0	2.9	3.5	2.2	2.6	2.2	.4
1963	1.6	1.3	1.5	.9	2.0	1.6	2.4	2.0	2.8	2.9	2.5	2.6	-.9	.0
1964	1.0	1.3	.9	1.2	1.3	1.3	1.6	2.0	2.3	2.3	2.1	2.1	.0	-.4
1965	1.9	1.6	1.4	1.1	3.5	2.2	2.7	2.3	3.6	3.2	2.8	2.4	1.8	1.8
1966	3.5	2.9	2.5	2.6	4.0	5.0	4.8	3.8	8.3	5.3	6.7	4.4	1.7	1.7
1967	3.0	3.1	2.5	1.9	1.2	.9	4.3	4.3	8.0	8.8	6.3	7.2	1.7	2.1
1968	4.7	4.2	4.0	3.5	4.4	3.5	5.8	5.2	7.1	7.3	6.2	6.0	1.7	1.7
1969	6.2	5.5	5.4	4.7	7.0	5.1	7.7	6.9	7.3	8.2	6.2	6.7	2.9	2.5
1970	5.6	5.7	3.9	4.5	2.3	5.7	8.1	8.0	8.1	7.0	7.4	6.6	4.8	2.8
1971	3.3	4.4	2.8	3.6	4.3	3.1	4.1	5.7	5.4	7.4	4.6	6.2	3.1	3.9
1972	3.4	3.2	3.4	3.0	4.6	4.2	3.4	3.8	3.7	3.5	3.3	3.3	2.6	2.6
1973	8.7	6.2	10.4	7.4	20.3	14.5	6.2	4.4	6.0	4.5	5.3	4.0	17.0	8.1
1974	12.3	11.0	12.8	11.9	12.0	14.3	11.4	9.2	13.2	10.4	12.6	9.3	21.6	29.6
1975	6.9	9.1	6.2	8.8	6.6	8.5	8.2	9.6	10.3	12.6	9.8	12.0	11.4	10.5
1976	4.9	5.8	3.3	4.3	.5	3.0	7.2	8.3	10.8	10.1	10.0	9.5	7.1	7.1
1977	6.7	6.5	6.1	5.8	8.1	6.3	8.0	7.7	9.0	9.9	8.9	9.6	7.2	9.5
1978	9.0	7.6	8.8	7.2	11.8	9.9	9.3	8.6	9.3	8.5	8.8	8.4	7.9	6.3
1979	13.3	11.3	13.0	11.3	10.2	11.0	13.6	11.0	10.5	9.8	10.1	9.2	37.5	25.1
1980	12.5	13.5	11.0	12.3	10.2	8.6	14.2	15.4	10.1	11.3	9.9	11.0	18.0	30.9
1981	8.9	10.3	6.0	8.4	4.3	7.8	13.0	13.1	12.6	10.7	12.5	10.7	11.9	13.6
1982	3.8	6.2	3.6	4.1	3.1	4.1	4.3	9.0	11.2	11.8	11.0	11.6	1.3	1.5
1983	3.8	3.2	2.9	2.9	2.7	2.1	4.8	3.5	6.2	8.7	6.4	8.8	-.5	.7
1984	3.9	4.3	2.7	3.4	3.8	3.8	5.4	5.2	5.8	6.0	6.1	6.2	.2	1.0
1985	3.8	3.6	2.5	2.1	2.6	2.3	5.1	5.1	6.8	6.1	6.8	6.3	1.8	.7
1986	1.1	1.9	-2.0	-.9	3.8	3.2	4.5	5.0	7.9	7.7	7.7	7.5	-19.7	-13.2
1987	4.4	3.6	4.6	3.2	3.5	4.1	4.3	4.2	5.6	6.6	5.8	6.6	8.2	.5
1988	4.4	4.1	3.8	3.5	5.2	4.1	4.8	4.6	6.9	6.4	6.9	6.5	.5	.8
1989	4.6	4.8	4.1	4.7	5.6	5.8	5.1	4.9	8.6	7.7	8.5	7.7	5.1	5.6
1990	6.1	5.4	6.6	5.2	5.3	5.8	5.7	5.5	9.9	9.3	9.6	9.0	18.1	8.3
1991	3.1	4.2	1.2	3.1	1.9	2.9	4.6	5.1	8.0	8.9	7.9	8.7	-7.4	.4
1992	2.9	3.0	2.0	2.0	1.5	1.2	3.6	3.9	7.0	7.6	6.6	7.4	2.0	.5
1993	2.7	3.0	1.5	1.9	2.9	2.2	3.8	3.9	5.9	6.5	5.4	5.9	-1.4	1.2
1994	2.7	2.6	2.3	1.7	2.9	2.4	2.9	3.3	5.4	5.2	4.9	4.8	2.2	.4
1995	2.5	2.8	1.4	1.9	2.1	2.8	3.5	3.4	4.4	5.1	3.9	4.5	-1.3	.6
1996	3.3	3.0	3.2	2.6	4.3	3.3	3.3	3.2	3.2	3.7	3.0	3.5	8.6	4.7
1997	1.7	2.3	.2	1.4	1.5	2.6	2.8	3.0	2.9	2.9	2.8	2.8	-3.4	1.3
1998	1.6	1.6	.4	.1	2.3	2.2	2.6	2.7	3.2	3.2	3.4	3.2	-8.8	-7.7
1999	2.7	2.2	2.7	1.8	1.9	2.1	2.6	2.5	3.6	3.4	3.7	3.5	13.4	3.6
2000	3.4	3.4	2.7	3.3	2.8	2.3	3.9	3.4	4.6	4.3	4.2	4.1	14.2	16.9
2001	1.6	2.8	-1.4	1.0	2.8	3.2	3.7	4.1	4.8	4.8	4.7	4.6	-13.0	3.8
2002	2.4	1.6	1.2	-.7	1.5	1.8	3.2	3.1	5.6	5.1	5.0	4.7	10.7	-5.9
2003	1.9	2.3	.5	1.0	3.6	2.2	2.8	3.2	4.2	4.5	3.7	4.0	6.9	12.2
2004	3.3	2.7	3.6	2.3	2.7	3.4	3.1	2.9	4.9	5.0	4.2	4.4	16.6	10.9
2005	3.4	3.4	2.7	3.6	2.3	2.4	3.8	3.3	4.5	4.8	4.3	4.2	17.1	17.0
2006	2.5	3.2	1.3	2.4	2.1	2.4	3.4	3.8	4.1	4.1	3.6	4.0	2.9	11.2
2007	4.1	2.8	5.2	2.1	4.9	4.0	3.3	3.3	5.9	5.3	5.2	4.4	17.4	5.5
2008	.1	3.8	-4.1	4.3	5.9	5.5	3.0	3.5	3.0	4.2	2.6	3.7	-21.3	13.9
2009	2.7	-.4	5.5	-2.9	-.5	1.8	.9	1.4	3.4	3.2	3.4	3.2	18.2	-18.4
2010	1.5	1.6	2.0	2.9	1.5	.8	1.2	.8	3.4	3.5	3.3	3.4	7.7	9.5
2011	3.0	3.2	4.2	5.3	4.7	3.7	2.2	1.7	3.6	3.1	3.5	3.0	6.6	15.4
2012	1.7	2.1	1.0	2.0	1.8	2.6	2.2	2.1	3.7	3.9	3.2	3.7	.5	.9

[1] Changes from December to December are based on unadjusted indexes.
[2] Commodities and services.
[3] Household energy—gas (piped), electricity, fuel oil, etc.—and motor fuel. Motor oil, coolant, etc. also included through 1982.

Source: Department of Labor (Bureau of Labor Statistics).

TABLE B–65. Producer price indexes by stage of processing, 1966–2012

[1982=100]

Year or month	Total finished goods	Consumer foods			Finished goods excluding consumer foods					Total finished consumer goods
		Total	Crude	Processed	Total	Consumer goods			Capital equipment	
						Total	Durable	Nondurable		
1966	35.2	39.2	41.5	39.2		34.1	43.4	29.3	34.6	35.4
1967	35.6	38.5	39.6	38.8	35.0	34.7	44.1	30.0	35.8	35.6
1968	36.6	40.0	42.5	40.0	35.9	35.5	45.1	30.6	37.0	36.5
1969	38.0	42.4	45.9	42.3	36.9	36.3	45.9	31.5	38.3	37.9
1970	39.3	43.8	46.0	43.9	38.2	37.4	47.2	32.5	40.1	39.1
1971	40.5	44.5	45.8	44.7	39.6	38.7	48.9	33.5	41.7	40.2
1972	41.8	46.9	48.0	47.2	40.4	39.4	50.0	34.1	42.8	41.5
1973	45.6	56.5	63.6	55.8	42.0	41.2	50.9	36.1	44.2	46.0
1974	52.6	64.4	71.6	63.9	48.8	48.2	55.5	44.0	50.5	53.1
1975	58.2	69.8	71.7	70.3	54.7	53.2	61.0	48.9	58.2	58.2
1976	60.8	69.6	76.7	69.0	58.1	56.5	63.7	52.4	62.1	60.4
1977	64.7	73.3	79.5	72.7	62.2	60.6	67.4	56.8	66.1	64.3
1978	69.8	79.9	85.8	79.4	66.7	64.9	73.6	60.0	71.3	69.4
1979	77.6	87.3	92.3	86.8	74.6	73.5	80.8	69.3	77.5	77.5
1980	88.0	92.4	93.9	92.3	86.7	87.1	91.0	85.1	85.8	88.6
1981	96.1	97.8	104.4	97.2	95.6	96.1	96.4	95.8	94.6	96.6
1982	100.0	100.0	100.0	100.0	100.0	100.0	100.0	100.0	100.0	100.0
1983	101.6	101.0	102.4	100.9	101.8	101.2	102.8	100.5	102.8	101.3
1984	103.7	105.4	111.4	104.9	103.2	102.2	104.5	101.1	105.2	103.3
1985	104.7	104.6	102.9	104.8	104.6	103.3	106.5	101.7	107.5	103.8
1986	103.2	107.3	105.6	107.4	101.9	98.5	108.9	93.3	109.7	101.4
1987	105.4	109.5	107.1	109.6	104.0	100.7	111.5	94.9	111.7	103.6
1988	108.0	112.6	109.8	112.7	106.5	103.1	113.8	97.3	114.3	106.2
1989	113.6	118.7	119.6	118.6	111.8	108.9	117.6	103.8	118.8	112.1
1990	119.2	124.4	123.0	124.4	117.4	115.3	120.4	111.5	122.9	118.2
1991	121.7	124.1	119.3	124.4	120.9	118.7	123.9	115.0	126.7	120.5
1992	123.2	123.3	107.6	124.4	123.1	120.8	125.7	117.3	129.1	121.7
1993	124.7	125.7	114.4	126.5	124.4	121.7	128.0	117.6	131.4	123.0
1994	125.5	126.8	111.3	127.9	125.1	121.6	130.9	116.2	134.1	123.3
1995	127.9	129.0	118.8	129.8	127.5	124.0	132.7	118.8	136.7	125.6
1996	131.3	133.6	129.2	133.8	130.5	127.6	134.2	123.3	138.3	129.5
1997	131.8	134.5	126.6	135.1	130.9	128.2	133.7	124.3	138.2	130.2
1998	130.7	134.3	127.2	134.8	129.5	126.4	132.9	122.2	137.6	128.9
1999	133.0	135.1	125.5	135.9	132.3	130.5	133.0	127.9	137.6	132.0
2000	138.0	137.2	123.5	138.3	138.1	138.4	133.9	138.7	138.8	138.2
2001	140.7	141.3	127.7	142.4	140.4	141.4	134.0	142.8	139.7	141.5
2002	138.9	140.1	128.5	141.0	138.3	138.8	133.0	139.8	139.1	139.4
2003	143.3	145.9	130.0	147.2	142.4	144.7	133.1	148.4	139.5	145.3
2004	148.5	152.7	138.2	153.9	147.2	150.9	135.0	156.6	141.4	151.7
2005	155.7	155.7	140.2	156.9	155.5	161.9	136.6	172.0	144.6	160.4
2006	160.4	156.7	151.3	157.1	161.0	169.2	136.9	182.6	146.9	166.0
2007	166.6	167.0	170.2	166.7	166.2	175.6	138.3	191.7	149.5	173.5
2008	177.1	178.3	175.5	178.6	176.6	189.1	141.2	210.5	153.8	186.3
2009	172.5	175.5	157.8	177.3	171.1	179.4	144.3	194.1	156.7	179.1
2010	179.8	182.4	172.6	183.3	178.3	190.4	144.9	210.1	157.3	189.1
2011	190.5	193.9	182.3	195.0	188.9	205.5	147.4	231.5	159.7	203.3
2012 ᵖ	194.2	199.0	167.8	202.0	192.2	209.1	151.0	235.1	162.8	207.3
2011: Jan	184.4	186.9	190.5	186.3	183.0	197.0	145.7	219.7	158.4	195.2
Feb	186.6	193.4	230.7	188.9	184.2	198.7	146.0	222.1	158.7	198.2
Mar	189.1	192.9	198.9	191.9	187.4	203.7	146.2	229.5	158.8	201.8
Apr	191.4	193.0	182.6	194.0	190.1	207.8	146.8	235.2	159.2	204.8
May	192.5	191.0	160.0	194.3	191.9	210.5	146.6	239.4	159.2	206.3
June	191.4	192.4	170.8	194.7	190.3	207.8	146.9	235.2	159.5	204.7
July	192.2	193.5	165.8	196.5	191.0	208.8	147.2	236.6	159.7	205.7
Aug	191.7	195.7	169.1	198.5	189.8	207.0	147.3	233.8	159.7	204.9
Sept	192.6	197.0	175.9	199.2	190.7	208.3	147.3	235.7	159.8	206.2
Oct	191.8	195.9	174.9	198.1	189.9	206.3	149.7	231.6	161.2	204.5
Nov	191.7	197.9	187.1	198.9	189.4	205.5	149.7	230.4	161.3	204.4
Dec	191.1	197.2	180.9	198.9	188.8	204.4	149.5	228.8	161.4	203.4
2012: Jan	192.0	197.0	166.1	199.9	190.0	206.0	150.2	230.8	162.1	204.5
Feb	192.9	196.7	159.2	200.2	191.1	207.6	150.3	233.2	162.3	205.6
Mar	194.4	197.3	167.3	200.2	192.8	210.4	150.3	237.3	162.3	207.8
Apr	194.9	197.5	165.6	200.5	193.4	211.2	150.5	238.4	162.5	208.5
May	193.7	197.2	158.2	200.9	192.0	208.9	150.2	235.1	162.4	206.7
June	192.8	198.1	165.6	201.2	190.7	206.9	150.4	232.1	162.5	205.5
July	193.2	198.1	162.9	201.4	191.2	207.4	151.0	232.5	162.8	205.8
Aug	195.4	200.0	175.1	202.4	193.5	211.1	150.9	238.1	162.8	209.1
Sept [1]	196.7	200.8	174.9	203.3	194.9	213.6	150.4	242.1	162.5	211.2
Oct [1]	196.3	200.5	164.7	203.8	194.4	212.2	152.5	238.9	163.5	210.0
Nov [1]	194.5	203.1	178.4	205.5	191.7	207.6	152.7	232.0	163.8	207.3
Dec [1]	193.6	201.8	176.0	204.3	190.8	206.4	152.4	230.3	163.6	206.1

[1] Data have been revised through August 2012; data are subject to revision four months after date of original publication.

See next page for continuation of table.

[1982=100]

Year or month	Intermediate materials, supplies, and components								Crude materials for further processing				
	Total	Foods and feeds [2]	Other	Materials and components		Processed fuels and lubricants	Containers	Supplies	Total	Foodstuffs and feedstuffs	Nonfood materials		
				For manufacturing	For construction						Total	Fuel	Other
1966	32.0		31.3	34.3	33.6	16.8	34.5	36.5	33.1	42.7		10.9	28.3
1967	32.2	41.8	31.7	34.5	34.0	16.9	35.0	36.8	31.3	40.3	21.1	11.3	26.5
1968	33.0	41.5	32.5	35.3	35.7	16.5	35.9	37.1	31.8	40.9	21.6	11.5	27.1
1969	34.1	42.9	33.6	36.5	37.7	16.6	37.2	37.8	33.9	44.1	22.5	12.0	28.4
1970	35.4	45.6	34.8	38.0	38.3	17.7	39.0	39.7	35.2	45.2	23.8	13.8	29.1
1971	36.8	46.7	36.2	38.9	40.8	19.5	40.8	40.8	36.0	46.1	24.7	15.7	29.4
1972	38.2	49.5	37.7	40.4	43.0	20.1	42.7	42.5	39.9	51.5	27.0	16.8	32.3
1973	42.4	70.3	40.6	44.1	46.5	22.2	45.2	51.7	54.5	72.6	34.3	18.6	42.9
1974	52.5	83.6	50.5	56.0	55.0	33.6	53.3	56.8	61.4	76.4	44.1	24.8	54.5
1975	58.0	81.6	56.6	61.7	60.1	39.4	60.0	61.8	61.6	77.4	43.7	30.6	50.0
1976	60.9	77.4	60.0	64.0	64.1	42.3	63.1	65.8	63.4	76.8	48.2	34.5	54.9
1977	64.9	79.6	64.1	67.4	69.3	47.7	65.9	69.3	65.5	77.5	51.7	42.0	56.3
1978	69.5	84.8	68.6	72.0	76.5	49.9	71.0	72.9	73.4	87.3	57.5	48.2	61.9
1979	78.4	94.5	77.4	80.9	84.2	61.6	79.4	80.2	85.9	100.0	69.6	57.3	75.5
1980	90.3	105.5	89.4	91.7	91.3	85.0	89.1	89.9	95.3	104.6	84.6	69.4	91.8
1981	98.6	104.6	98.2	98.7	97.9	100.6	96.7	96.9	103.0	103.9	101.8	84.8	109.8
1982	100.0	100.0	100.0	100.0	100.0	100.0	100.0	100.0	100.0	100.0	100.0	100.0	100.0
1983	100.6	103.6	100.5	101.2	102.8	95.4	100.4	101.8	101.3	101.8	100.7	105.1	98.8
1984	103.1	105.7	103.0	104.1	105.6	95.7	105.9	104.1	103.5	104.7	102.2	105.1	101.0
1985	102.7	97.3	103.0	103.3	107.3	92.8	109.0	104.4	95.8	94.8	96.9	102.7	94.3
1986	99.1	96.2	99.3	102.2	108.1	72.7	110.3	105.6	87.7	93.2	81.6	92.2	76.0
1987	101.5	99.2	101.7	105.3	109.8	73.3	114.5	107.7	93.7	96.2	87.9	84.1	88.5
1988	107.1	109.5	106.9	113.2	116.1	71.2	120.1	113.7	96.0	106.1	85.5	82.1	85.9
1989	112.0	113.8	111.9	118.1	121.3	76.4	125.4	118.1	103.1	111.2	93.4	85.3	95.8
1990	114.5	113.3	114.5	118.7	122.9	85.9	127.7	119.4	108.9	113.1	101.5	84.8	107.3
1991	114.4	111.1	114.6	118.1	124.5	85.3	128.1	121.4	101.2	105.5	94.6	82.9	97.5
1992	114.7	110.7	114.9	117.9	126.5	84.5	127.7	122.7	100.4	105.1	93.5	84.0	94.2
1993	116.2	112.7	116.4	118.9	132.0	84.7	126.4	125.0	102.4	108.4	94.7	87.1	94.1
1994	118.5	114.8	118.7	122.1	136.6	83.1	129.7	127.0	101.8	106.5	94.8	82.4	97.0
1995	124.9	114.8	125.5	130.4	142.1	84.2	148.8	132.1	102.7	105.8	96.8	72.1	105.8
1996	125.7	128.1	125.6	128.6	143.6	90.0	141.1	135.9	113.8	121.5	104.5	92.6	105.7
1997	125.6	125.4	125.7	128.3	146.5	89.3	136.0	135.9	111.1	112.2	106.4	101.3	103.5
1998	123.0	116.2	123.4	126.1	146.8	81.1	140.8	134.8	96.8	103.9	88.4	86.7	84.5
1999	123.2	111.1	123.9	124.6	148.9	84.6	142.5	134.2	98.2	98.7	94.3	91.2	91.1
2000	129.2	111.7	130.1	128.1	150.7	102.0	151.6	136.9	120.6	100.2	130.4	136.9	118.0
2001	129.7	115.9	130.5	127.4	150.6	104.5	153.1	138.7	121.0	106.1	126.8	151.4	101.5
2002	127.8	115.5	128.5	126.1	151.3	96.3	152.1	138.9	108.1	99.5	111.4	117.3	101.0
2003	133.7	125.9	134.2	129.7	153.6	112.6	153.7	141.5	135.3	113.5	148.2	185.7	116.9
2004	142.6	137.1	143.0	137.9	166.4	124.3	159.3	146.7	159.0	127.0	179.2	211.4	149.2
2005	154.0	133.8	155.1	146.0	176.6	150.0	167.1	151.9	182.2	122.7	223.4	279.7	176.7
2006	164.0	135.2	165.4	155.9	188.4	162.8	175.0	157.0	184.8	119.3	230.6	241.5	210.0
2007	170.7	154.4	171.5	162.4	192.5	173.9	180.3	161.7	207.1	146.7	246.3	236.8	238.7
2008	188.3	181.6	188.7	177.2	205.4	206.2	191.8	173.8	251.8	163.4	313.9	298.3	308.5
2009	172.5	166.0	173.0	162.7	202.9	161.9	195.8	172.2	175.2	134.5	197.5	166.3	211.1
2010	183.4	171.7	184.4	174.0	205.7	185.2	201.2	175.0	212.2	152.4	249.3	188.0	280.8
2011	199.8	192.3	200.4	189.8	212.8	215.0	205.4	184.2	249.4	188.4	284.0	181.5	342.0
2012 p	200.7	201.5	200.6	189.0	218.4	213.1	207.0	188.9	241.4	196.2	263.2	144.4	332.4
2011: Jan	190.6	180.2	191.4	181.5	208.3	196.2	203.4	179.6	235.9	171.6	274.9	186.5	323.8
Feb	193.7	185.0	194.4	185.2	209.5	200.9	203.9	180.9	242.8	184.4	275.5	190.0	322.2
Mar	197.6	189.1	198.2	187.7	210.9	212.0	204.4	182.3	248.2	185.7	284.4	176.9	345.7
Apr	201.0	192.5	201.7	191.1	212.1	218.6	204.9	183.9	261.3	193.1	301.7	187.3	367.0
May	203.2	192.9	204.0	192.6	212.8	224.3	206.4	184.5	255.5	190.3	293.6	189.7	352.1
June	203.3	194.1	204.0	192.4	213.7	224.2	206.8	185.2	256.8	195.3	291.3	190.8	347.5
July	204.1	195.3	204.8	193.3	214.7	225.1	207.1	185.7	256.9	192.6	293.9	191.0	351.7
Aug	202.8	197.9	203.1	192.7	214.6	219.5	205.9	186.1	251.2	196.3	279.7	190.1	329.2
Sept	203.2	198.7	203.5	192.8	214.5	221.0	206.0	186.7	251.1	192.4	283.4	178.8	342.8
Oct	200.2	194.9	200.5	190.6	214.4	212.2	205.4	185.8	242.8	186.3	273.8	171.7	331.8
Nov	199.9	194.6	200.2	189.5	214.2	213.9	205.3	185.4	248.5	188.6	282.2	164.0	350.8
Dec	198.5	192.9	198.9	187.7	214.2	211.9	205.4	184.9	242.0	184.5	274.0	160.9	339.5
2012: Jan	198.8	193.3	199.1	188.6	215.3	209.8	205.5	185.5	246.0	188.8	277.6	154.4	349.1
Feb	200.0	193.4	200.4	190.5	216.8	210.1	206.7	186.0	245.2	190.9	274.4	142.3	351.4
Mar	203.3	194.9	203.9	192.6	217.4	220.0	206.7	187.1	248.7	195.8	276.4	135.2	359.1
Apr	203.0	196.2	203.4	192.7	218.3	216.9	207.0	187.7	242.0	190.6	269.0	126.9	352.3
May	201.5	197.6	201.7	191.4	219.1	211.4	207.0	188.4	234.9	189.9	257.0	125.2	334.2
June	199.7	198.9	199.6	187.9	219.1	210.7	206.7	188.4	227.1	188.9	244.2	133.8	308.5
July	198.8	201.7	198.4	186.6	218.5	208.8	206.2	189.1	232.9	196.2	248.4	141.5	310.4
Aug	200.7	207.4	200.1	186.8	218.7	216.2	206.1	190.6	242.7	201.4	261.4	147.5	327.5
Sept [1]	202.9	209.7	202.2	188.3	219.1	222.5	206.3	191.2	244.5	201.7	264.3	141.3	335.9
Oct [1]	201.8	209.4	201.0	188.0	219.2	217.7	206.5	191.1	242.3	202.4	259.7	149.3	323.9
Nov [1]	199.4	208.6	198.5	187.3	219.4	207.8	209.2	190.6	244.1	204.3	261.4	163.9	317.6
Dec [1]	199.1	206.6	198.4	187.5	220.0	205.6	210.0	190.5	245.9	204.0	264.8	171.0	318.6

[2] Intermediate materials for food manufacturing and feeds.

Source: Department of Labor (Bureau of Labor Statistics).

Table B-66. Producer price indexes by stage of processing, special groups, 1974–2012

[1982=100]

Year or month	Finished goods						Intermediate materials, supplies, and components				Crude materials for further processing			
				Excluding foods and energy										
	Total	Foods	Energy	Total	Capital equipment	Consumer goods excluding foods and energy	Total	Foods and feeds[1]	Energy	Other	Total	Foodstuffs and feedstuffs	Energy	Other
1974	52.6	64.4	26.2	53.6	50.5	55.5	52.5	83.6	33.1	54.0	61.4	76.4	27.8	83.3
1975	58.2	69.8	30.7	59.7	58.2	60.6	58.0	81.6	38.7	60.2	61.6	77.4	33.3	69.3
1976	60.8	69.6	34.3	63.1	62.1	63.7	60.9	77.4	41.5	63.8	63.4	76.8	35.3	80.2
1977	64.7	73.3	39.7	66.9	66.1	67.3	64.9	79.6	46.8	67.6	65.5	77.5	40.4	79.8
1978	69.8	79.9	42.3	71.9	71.3	72.2	69.5	84.8	49.1	72.5	73.4	87.3	45.2	87.8
1979	77.6	87.3	57.1	78.3	77.5	78.8	78.4	94.5	61.1	80.7	85.9	100.0	54.9	106.2
1980	88.0	92.4	85.2	87.1	85.8	87.8	90.3	105.5	84.9	90.3	95.3	104.6	73.1	113.1
1981	96.1	97.8	101.5	94.6	94.6	94.6	98.6	104.6	100.5	97.7	103.0	103.9	97.7	111.7
1982	100.0	100.0	100.0	100.0	100.0	100.0	100.0	100.0	100.0	100.0	100.0	100.0	100.0	100.0
1983	101.6	101.0	95.2	103.0	102.8	103.1	100.6	103.6	95.3	101.6	101.3	101.8	98.7	105.3
1984	103.7	105.4	91.2	105.5	105.2	105.7	103.1	105.7	95.5	104.7	103.5	104.7	98.0	111.7
1985	104.7	104.6	87.6	108.1	107.5	108.4	102.7	97.3	92.6	105.2	95.8	94.8	93.3	104.9
1986	103.2	107.3	63.0	110.6	109.7	111.1	99.1	96.2	72.6	104.9	87.7	93.2	71.8	103.1
1987	105.4	109.5	61.8	113.3	111.7	114.2	101.5	99.2	73.0	107.8	93.7	96.2	75.0	115.7
1988	108.0	112.6	59.8	117.0	114.3	118.5	107.1	109.5	70.9	115.2	96.0	106.1	67.7	133.0
1989	113.6	118.7	65.7	122.1	118.8	124.0	112.0	113.8	76.1	120.2	103.1	111.2	75.9	137.9
1990	119.2	124.4	75.0	126.6	122.9	128.8	114.5	113.3	85.5	120.9	108.9	113.1	85.9	136.3
1991	121.7	124.1	78.1	131.1	126.7	133.7	114.4	111.1	85.1	121.4	101.2	105.5	80.4	128.2
1992	123.2	123.3	77.8	134.2	129.1	137.3	114.7	110.7	84.3	122.0	100.4	105.1	78.8	128.4
1993	124.7	125.7	78.0	135.8	131.4	138.5	116.2	112.7	84.6	123.8	102.4	108.4	76.7	140.2
1994	125.5	126.8	77.0	137.1	134.1	139.0	118.5	114.8	83.0	127.1	101.8	106.5	72.1	156.2
1995	127.9	129.0	78.1	140.0	136.7	141.9	124.9	114.8	84.1	135.2	102.7	105.8	69.4	173.6
1996	131.3	133.6	83.2	142.0	138.3	144.3	125.7	128.1	89.8	134.0	113.8	121.5	85.0	155.8
1997	131.8	134.5	83.4	142.4	138.2	145.1	125.6	125.4	89.0	134.2	111.1	112.2	87.3	156.5
1998	130.7	134.3	75.1	143.7	137.6	147.7	123.0	116.2	80.8	133.5	96.8	103.9	68.6	142.1
1999	133.0	135.1	78.8	146.1	137.6	151.7	123.2	111.1	84.3	133.1	98.2	98.7	78.5	135.2
2000	138.0	137.2	94.1	148.0	138.8	154.0	129.2	111.7	101.7	136.6	120.6	100.2	122.1	145.2
2001	140.7	141.3	96.7	150.0	139.7	156.9	129.7	115.9	104.1	136.4	121.0	106.1	123.3	130.7
2002	138.9	140.1	88.8	150.2	139.1	157.6	127.8	115.5	95.9	135.8	108.1	99.5	102.0	135.7
2003	143.3	145.9	102.0	150.5	139.5	157.9	133.7	125.9	111.9	138.5	135.3	113.5	147.2	152.5
2004	148.5	152.7	113.0	152.7	141.4	160.3	142.6	137.1	123.2	146.5	159.0	127.0	174.6	193.0
2005	155.7	155.7	132.6	156.4	144.6	164.3	154.0	133.8	149.2	154.6	182.2	122.7	234.0	202.4
2006	160.4	156.7	145.9	158.7	146.9	166.7	164.0	135.2	162.8	163.8	184.8	119.3	226.9	244.5
2007	166.6	167.0	156.3	161.7	149.5	170.0	170.7	154.4	174.6	168.4	207.1	146.7	232.8	282.6
2008	177.1	178.3	178.7	167.2	153.8	176.4	188.3	181.6	208.1	180.9	251.8	163.4	309.4	324.4
2009	172.5	175.5	146.9	171.5	156.7	181.6	172.5	166.0	162.5	173.4	175.2	134.5	176.8	248.4
2010	179.8	182.4	166.9	173.6	157.3	185.1	183.4	171.7	187.8	180.8	212.2	152.4	216.7	329.1
2011	190.5	193.9	193.0	177.8	159.7	190.8	199.8	192.3	219.8	192.0	249.4	188.4	240.4	390.4
2012 p	194.2	199.0	192.5	182.4	162.8	196.8	200.7	201.5	218.2	192.6	241.4	196.2	218.7	369.7
2011: Jan	184.4	186.9	177.4	175.8	158.4	188.2	190.6	180.2	199.5	186.4	235.9	171.6	232.0	381.1
Feb	186.6	193.4	180.6	176.1	158.7	188.7	193.7	185.0	204.7	188.7	242.8	184.4	229.1	391.6
Mar	189.1	192.9	191.6	176.4	158.8	189.0	197.6	189.1	216.6	190.2	248.2	185.7	241.5	387.8
Apr	191.4	193.0	200.0	176.9	159.2	189.5	201.0	192.5	223.6	192.5	261.3	193.1	260.6	399.1
May	192.5	191.0	206.1	176.9	159.2	189.7	203.2	192.9	229.4	193.8	255.5	190.3	251.9	393.8
June	191.4	192.4	199.5	177.2	159.5	189.9	203.3	194.1	229.1	193.9	256.8	195.3	246.9	399.6
July	192.2	193.5	200.3	177.9	159.7	191.0	204.1	195.3	230.8	194.4	256.9	192.6	249.9	401.0
Aug	191.7	195.7	195.6	178.1	159.7	191.4	202.8	197.9	224.1	194.2	251.2	196.3	231.0	402.2
Sept	192.6	197.0	197.9	178.3	159.8	191.8	203.2	198.7	226.0	194.1	251.1	192.4	235.6	401.4
Oct	191.8	195.9	191.2	179.8	161.2	193.4	200.2	194.9	217.4	192.8	242.8	186.3	229.8	381.2
Nov	191.7	197.9	189.3	179.9	161.3	193.4	199.9	194.6	219.0	192.0	248.5	188.6	243.2	373.5
Dec	191.1	197.2	186.3	180.1	161.4	193.7	198.5	192.9	216.9	190.9	242.0	184.5	232.7	372.7
2012: Jan	192.0	197.0	187.6	181.3	162.1	195.4	198.8	193.3	215.1	191.7	246.0	188.8	233.1	383.3
Feb	192.9	196.7	190.9	181.5	162.3	195.5	200.0	193.4	215.9	193.2	245.2	190.9	228.1	383.5
Mar	194.4	197.3	196.8	181.6	162.3	195.6	203.3	194.9	226.2	194.6	248.7	195.8	228.9	387.6
Apr	194.9	197.5	198.5	181.7	162.5	195.7	203.0	196.2	222.9	194.9	242.0	190.6	220.5	382.7
May	193.7	197.2	193.4	181.7	162.4	195.8	201.5	197.6	217.1	194.4	234.9	189.9	207.7	374.4
June	192.8	198.1	188.8	181.8	162.5	195.9	199.7	198.9	215.5	192.2	227.1	188.9	197.4	357.7
July	193.2	198.1	188.2	182.2	162.8	197.1	198.8	201.7	213.0	191.4	232.9	196.2	204.7	354.2
Aug	195.4	200.0	196.1	182.7	162.8	197.4	200.7	207.4	220.9	191.2	242.7	201.4	219.4	361.4
Sept[2]	196.7	203.8	201.9	182.4	162.5	197.2	202.9	209.7	227.5	192.0	244.5	201.7	221.7	364.9
Oct[2]	196.3	200.5	197.1	183.6	163.5	198.4	201.8	209.4	222.6	191.9	242.3	202.4	218.8	357.7
Nov[2]	194.5	203.1	186.7	183.8	163.8	198.6	199.4	208.6	212.3	191.8	244.1	204.3	220.3	361.9
Dec[2]	193.6	201.8	183.8	183.7	163.6	198.7	199.1	206.6	210.0	192.2	245.9	204.0	223.1	367.4

[1] Intermediate materials for food manufacturing and feeds.

[2] Data have been revised through August 2012; data are subject to revision four months after date of original publication.

Source: Department of Labor (Bureau of Labor Statistics).

TABLE B–67. Producer price indexes for major commodity groups, 1966–2012

[1982=100]

Year or month	Farm products and processed foods and feeds			Industrial commodities				
	Total	Farm products	Processed foods and feeds	Total	Textile products and apparel	Hides, skins, leather, and related products	Fuels and related products and power	Chemicals and allied products
1966	41.6	43.7	40.2	31.5	48.9	39.4	14.1	34.0
1967	40.2	41.3	39.8	32.0	48.9	38.1	14.4	34.2
1968	41.1	42.3	40.6	32.8	50.7	39.3	14.3	34.1
1969	43.4	45.0	42.7	33.9	51.8	41.5	14.6	34.2
1970	44.9	45.8	44.6	35.2	52.4	42.0	15.3	35.0
1971	45.8	46.6	45.5	36.5	53.3	43.4	16.6	35.6
1972	49.2	51.6	48.0	37.8	55.5	50.0	17.1	35.6
1973	63.9	72.7	58.9	40.3	60.5	54.5	19.4	37.6
1974	71.3	77.4	68.0	49.2	68.0	55.2	30.1	50.2
1975	74.0	77.0	72.6	54.9	67.4	56.5	35.4	62.0
1976	73.6	78.8	70.8	58.4	72.4	63.9	38.3	64.0
1977	75.9	79.4	74.0	62.5	75.3	68.3	43.6	65.9
1978	83.0	87.7	80.6	67.0	78.1	76.1	46.5	68.0
1979	92.3	99.6	88.5	75.7	82.5	96.1	58.9	76.0
1980	98.3	102.9	95.9	88.0	89.7	94.7	82.8	89.0
1981	101.1	105.2	98.9	97.4	97.6	99.3	100.2	98.4
1982	100.0	100.0	100.0	100.0	100.0	100.0	100.0	100.0
1983	102.0	102.4	101.8	101.1	100.3	103.2	95.9	100.3
1984	105.5	105.5	105.4	103.3	102.7	109.0	94.8	102.9
1985	100.7	95.1	103.5	103.7	102.9	108.9	91.4	103.7
1986	101.2	92.9	105.4	100.0	103.2	113.0	69.8	102.6
1987	103.7	95.5	107.9	102.6	105.1	120.4	70.2	106.4
1988	110.0	104.9	112.7	106.3	109.2	131.4	66.7	116.3
1989	115.4	110.9	117.8	111.6	112.3	136.3	72.9	123.0
1990	118.6	112.2	121.9	115.8	115.0	141.7	82.3	123.6
1991	116.4	105.7	121.9	116.5	116.3	138.9	81.2	125.6
1992	115.9	103.6	122.1	117.4	117.8	140.4	80.4	125.9
1993	118.4	107.1	124.0	119.0	118.0	143.7	80.0	128.2
1994	119.1	106.3	125.5	120.7	118.3	148.5	77.8	132.1
1995	120.5	107.4	127.0	125.5	120.8	153.7	78.0	142.5
1996	129.7	122.4	133.3	127.3	122.4	150.5	85.8	142.1
1997	127.0	112.9	134.0	127.7	122.6	154.2	86.1	143.6
1998	122.7	104.6	131.6	124.8	122.9	148.0	75.3	143.9
1999	120.3	98.4	131.1	126.5	121.1	146.0	80.5	144.2
2000	122.0	99.5	133.1	134.8	121.4	151.5	103.5	151.0
2001	126.2	103.8	137.3	135.7	121.3	158.4	105.3	151.8
2002	123.9	99.0	136.2	132.4	119.9	157.6	93.2	151.9
2003	132.8	111.5	143.4	139.1	119.8	162.3	112.9	161.8
2004	142.0	123.3	151.2	147.6	121.0	164.5	126.9	174.4
2005	141.3	118.5	153.1	160.2	122.8	165.4	156.4	192.0
2006	141.2	117.0	153.8	168.8	124.5	168.4	166.7	205.8
2007	157.8	143.4	165.1	175.1	125.8	173.6	177.6	214.8
2008	173.8	161.3	180.5	192.3	128.9	173.1	214.6	245.5
2009	161.4	134.6	176.2	174.8	129.5	157.0	158.7	229.4
2010	171.2	151.0	182.3	187.0	131.7	181.4	185.8	246.6
2011	193.9	186.7	197.5	202.0	141.7	199.9	215.9	275.1
2012 p	200.6	192.4	205.2	202.1	142.2	202.0	212.1	276.8
2011: Jan	182.9	173.3	187.9	194.2	136.1	192.8	198.4	262.2
Feb	191.0	189.8	191.3	196.4	137.7	196.3	201.9	267.3
Mar	191.4	185.1	194.5	200.4	139.7	198.3	214.2	270.3
Apr	195.2	191.1	197.1	204.2	141.1	202.9	223.9	276.4
May	193.5	186.0	197.3	205.7	143.0	203.6	227.6	280.6
June	196.2	192.6	197.8	205.0	143.3	203.0	224.0	279.7
July	195.7	188.4	199.4	205.9	143.3	203.4	225.5	280.5
Aug	198.4	192.2	201.6	203.7	143.6	202.9	217.4	280.1
Sept	198.3	190.3	202.4	204.4	143.8	203.5	219.9	280.9
Oct	194.5	183.5	200.3	201.9	143.3	200.8	212.4	277.2
Nov	195.8	186.7	200.6	202.1	143.0	196.6	215.1	274.9
Dec	193.5	181.3	200.0	200.6	142.1	195.0	210.9	271.1
2012: Jan	195.1	184.7	200.7	201.4	141.9	194.7	210.9	275.3
Feb	195.5	185.7	200.9	202.4	142.2	192.7	212.1	278.1
Mar	197.7	191.1	201.6	205.1	142.6	201.9	219.6	283.0
Apr	196.9	187.0	202.3	204.7	142.5	203.4	217.3	283.9
May	196.6	185.1	202.8	202.6	142.8	204.8	210.4	281.5
June	197.1	184.7	203.7	200.0	142.1	203.6	205.5	273.9
July	200.9	193.9	205.0	199.6	141.9	202.9	205.1	273.0
Aug	204.5	199.4	207.8	202.1	141.8	202.3	214.6	273.6
Sept [1]	205.7	199.7	209.3	203.9	142.0	203.2	220.7	275.4
Oct [1]	205.2	198.0	209.4	202.9	141.7	202.6	216.2	275.2
Nov [1]	206.2	199.9	209.9	200.6	142.4	202.6	207.2	274.0
Dec [1]	205.2	200.0	208.4	200.4	142.1	209.1	205.3	274.9

[1] Data have been revised through August 2012; data are subject to revision four months after date of original publication.

See next page for continuation of table.

[1982=100]

Year or month	Rubber and plastic products	Lumber and wood products	Pulp, paper, and allied products	Metals and metal products	Machinery and equipment	Furniture and household durables	Non-metallic mineral products	Transportation equipment Total	Transportation equipment Motor vehicles and equipment	Miscellaneous products
1966	40.5	35.2	34.2	32.8	34.7	47.4	30.7		39.2	35.3
1967	41.4	35.1	34.6	33.2	35.9	48.3	31.2		39.8	36.2
1968	42.8	39.8	35.0	34.0	37.0	49.7	32.4		40.9	37.0
1969	43.6	44.0	36.0	36.0	38.2	50.7	33.6	40.4	41.7	38.1
1970	44.9	39.9	37.5	38.7	40.0	51.9	35.3	41.9	43.3	39.8
1971	45.2	44.7	38.1	39.4	41.4	53.1	38.2	44.2	45.7	40.8
1972	45.3	50.7	39.3	40.9	42.3	53.8	39.4	45.5	47.0	41.5
1973	46.6	62.2	42.3	44.0	43.7	55.7	40.7	46.1	47.4	43.3
1974	56.4	64.5	52.5	57.0	50.0	61.8	47.8	50.3	51.4	48.1
1975	62.2	62.1	59.0	61.5	57.9	67.5	54.4	56.7	57.6	53.4
1976	66.0	72.2	62.1	65.0	61.3	70.3	58.2	60.5	61.2	55.6
1977	69.4	83.0	64.6	69.3	65.2	73.2	62.6	64.6	65.2	59.4
1978	72.4	96.9	67.7	75.3	70.3	77.5	69.6	69.5	70.0	66.7
1979	80.5	105.5	75.9	86.0	76.7	82.8	77.6	75.3	75.8	75.5
1980	90.1	101.5	86.3	95.0	86.0	90.7	88.4	82.9	83.1	93.6
1981	96.4	102.8	94.8	99.6	94.4	95.9	96.7	94.3	94.6	96.1
1982	100.0	100.0	100.0	100.0	100.0	100.0	100.0	100.0	100.0	100.0
1983	100.8	107.9	103.3	101.8	102.7	103.4	101.6	102.8	102.2	104.8
1984	102.3	108.0	110.3	104.8	105.1	105.7	105.4	105.2	104.1	107.0
1985	101.9	106.6	113.3	104.4	107.2	107.1	108.6	107.9	106.4	109.4
1986	101.9	107.2	116.1	103.2	108.8	108.2	110.0	110.5	109.1	111.6
1987	103.0	112.8	121.8	107.1	110.4	109.9	110.0	112.5	111.7	114.9
1988	109.3	118.9	130.4	118.7	113.2	113.1	111.2	114.3	113.1	120.2
1989	112.6	126.7	137.8	124.1	117.4	116.9	112.6	117.7	116.2	126.5
1990	113.6	129.7	141.2	122.9	120.7	119.2	114.7	121.5	118.2	134.2
1991	115.1	132.1	142.9	120.2	123.0	121.2	117.2	126.4	122.1	140.8
1992	115.1	146.6	145.2	119.2	123.4	122.2	117.3	130.4	124.9	145.3
1993	116.0	174.0	147.3	119.2	124.0	123.7	120.0	133.7	128.0	145.4
1994	117.6	180.0	152.5	124.8	125.1	126.1	124.2	137.2	131.4	141.9
1995	124.3	178.1	172.2	134.5	126.6	128.2	129.0	139.7	133.0	145.4
1996	123.8	176.1	168.7	131.0	126.5	130.4	131.0	141.7	134.1	147.7
1997	123.2	183.8	167.9	131.8	125.9	130.8	133.2	141.6	132.7	150.9
1998	122.6	179.1	171.7	127.8	124.9	131.3	135.4	141.2	131.4	156.0
1999	122.5	183.6	174.1	124.6	124.3	131.7	138.9	141.8	131.7	166.6
2000	125.5	178.2	183.7	128.1	124.0	132.6	142.5	143.8	132.3	170.8
2001	127.2	174.4	184.8	125.4	123.7	133.2	144.3	145.2	131.5	181.3
2002	126.8	173.3	185.9	125.9	122.9	133.5	146.2	144.6	129.9	182.4
2003	130.1	177.4	190.0	129.2	121.9	133.9	148.2	145.7	129.6	179.6
2004	133.8	195.6	195.7	149.6	122.1	135.1	153.2	148.6	131.0	183.2
2005	143.8	196.5	202.6	160.8	123.7	139.4	164.2	151.0	131.5	195.1
2006	153.8	194.4	209.8	181.6	126.2	142.6	179.9	152.6	131.0	205.6
2007	155.0	192.4	216.9	193.5	127.3	144.7	186.2	155.0	132.2	210.3
2008	165.9	191.3	226.8	213.0	129.7	148.9	197.1	158.6	134.1	216.6
2009	165.2	182.8	225.6	186.8	131.3	153.1	202.4	162.2	137.0	217.5
2010	170.7	192.7	236.9	207.6	131.1	153.2	201.8	163.4	137.6	221.5
2011	182.7	194.7	245.1	225.9	132.7	156.4	205.0	166.1	139.4	229.2
2012 *p*	186.8	201.7	244.1	219.9	134.3	160.5	210.9	169.7	142.2	235.5
2011: Jan	175.2	193.4	243.0	219.8	131.6	153.7	202.3	164.7	138.4	225.7
Feb	176.5	194.7	243.2	224.2	132.0	154.4	202.6	164.9	138.5	226.6
Mar	178.2	195.8	244.3	225.7	132.2	155.1	202.9	165.0	138.5	227.1
Apr	180.3	195.6	245.0	229.2	132.5	155.5	203.5	165.5	139.0	227.4
May	182.5	194.3	245.6	228.3	132.6	155.7	204.9	165.3	138.7	227.5
June	185.2	193.4	246.2	228.4	132.9	156.2	205.7	165.6	138.9	228.0
July	186.2	193.6	247.1	230.0	133.0	157.0	206.6	165.8	139.0	229.9
Aug	186.2	194.7	247.2	229.0	133.1	157.1	206.6	166.1	139.1	230.0
Sept	186.3	194.3	247.5	228.1	133.1	157.7	206.5	165.7	138.5	232.0
Oct	186.4	195.8	246.2	223.8	133.2	158.3	206.1	168.3	141.4	232.0
Nov	185.2	195.3	243.2	222.5	133.3	158.3	206.0	168.4	141.4	232.1
Dec	184.5	195.8	242.9	222.3	133.4	158.3	206.6	168.3	141.2	232.6
2012: Jan	184.8	196.3	242.7	223.6	133.8	159.4	208.3	169.0	141.8	233.5
Feb	185.9	197.8	243.8	225.2	134.1	160.0	209.0	168.8	141.5	234.4
Mar	187.5	199.8	244.3	225.3	134.1	160.1	209.4	168.9	141.6	235.2
Apr	189.0	200.4	244.2	224.3	134.2	160.7	210.4	169.1	141.7	234.9
May	189.2	202.3	244.3	222.7	134.4	161.0	210.8	168.9	141.3	234.8
June	188.3	202.3	244.2	218.5	134.3	160.9	211.4	169.1	141.5	234.7
July	187.3	201.1	243.7	215.6	134.4	160.9	212.0	169.8	142.1	235.9
Aug	186.1	202.7	243.4	215.7	134.3	160.5	212.1	169.9	142.0	236.1
Sept [1]	186.1	203.9	242.7	217.4	134.4	160.9	211.9	169.3	141.4	236.1
Oct [1]	185.9	203.0	243.7	216.4	134.2	161.3	211.9	171.2	143.7	236.3
Nov [1]	186.0	204.3	245.3	216.4	134.4	160.7	211.8	171.5	144.0	236.7
Dec [1]	185.8	206.1	246.6	217.6	134.3	160.2	212.0	171.4	143.7	238.0

Source: Department of Labor (Bureau of Labor Statistics).

[Percent change]

Year or month	Total finished goods Dec. to Dec.[1]	Total finished goods Year to year	Finished consumer foods Dec. to Dec.[1]	Finished consumer foods Year to year	Finished goods excluding consumer foods — Total Dec. to Dec.[1]	Total Year to year	Consumer goods Dec. to Dec.[1]	Consumer goods Year to year	Capital equipment Dec. to Dec.[1]	Capital equipment Year to year	Finished energy goods Dec. to Dec.[1]	Finished energy goods Year to year	Finished goods excluding foods and energy Dec. to Dec.[1]	Finished goods excluding foods and energy Year to year
1973	11.7	9.1	22.7	20.5	6.6	4.0	7.5	4.6	5.1	3.3				
1974	18.3	15.4	12.8	14.0	21.1	16.2	20.3	17.0	22.7	14.3			17.7	11.4
1975	6.6	10.6	5.6	8.4	7.2	12.1	6.8	10.4	8.1	15.2	16.3	17.2	6.0	11.4
1976	3.8	4.5	-2.5	-.3	6.2	6.2	6.0	6.2	6.5	6.7	11.6	11.7	5.7	5.7
1977	6.7	6.4	6.9	5.3	6.8	7.1	6.7	7.3	7.2	6.4	12.0	15.7	6.2	6.0
1978	9.3	7.9	11.7	9.0	8.3	7.2	8.5	7.1	8.0	7.9	8.5	6.5	8.4	7.5
1979	12.8	11.2	7.4	9.3	14.8	11.8	17.6	13.3	8.8	8.7	58.1	35.0	9.4	8.9
1980	11.8	13.4	7.5	5.8	13.4	16.2	14.1	18.5	11.4	10.7	27.9	49.2	10.8	11.2
1981	7.1	9.2	1.5	5.8	8.7	10.3	8.6	10.3	9.2	10.3	14.1	19.1	7.7	8.6
1982	3.6	4.1	2.0	2.2	4.2	4.6	4.2	4.1	3.9	5.7	-.1	-1.5	4.9	5.7
1983	.6	1.6	2.3	1.0	.0	1.8	-.9	1.2	2.0	2.8	-9.2	-4.8	1.9	3.0
1984	1.7	2.1	3.5	4.4	1.1	1.4	.8	1.0	1.8	2.3	-4.2	-4.2	2.0	2.4
1985	1.8	1.0	.6	-.8	2.2	1.4	2.1	1.1	2.7	2.2	-.2	-3.9	2.7	2.5
1986	-2.3	-1.4	2.8	2.6	-4.0	-2.6	-6.6	-4.6	2.1	2.0	-38.1	-28.1	2.7	2.3
1987	2.2	2.1	-.2	2.1	3.2	2.1	4.1	2.2	1.3	1.8	11.2	-1.9	2.1	2.4
1988	4.0	2.5	5.7	2.8	3.2	2.4	3.1	2.4	3.6	2.3	-3.6	-3.2	4.3	3.3
1989	4.9	5.2	5.2	5.4	4.8	5.0	5.3	5.6	3.8	3.9	9.5	9.9	4.2	4.4
1990	5.7	4.9	2.6	4.8	6.9	5.0	8.7	5.9	3.4	3.5	30.7	14.2	3.5	3.7
1991	-.1	2.1	-1.5	-.2	.3	3.0	-.7	2.9	2.5	3.1	-9.6	4.1	3.1	3.6
1992	1.6	1.2	1.6	-.6	1.6	1.8	1.6	1.8	1.7	1.9	-.3	-.4	2.0	2.4
1993	.2	1.2	2.4	1.9	-.4	1.1	-1.4	.7	1.8	1.8	-4.1	.3	.4	1.2
1994	1.7	.6	1.1	.9	1.9	.6	2.0	-.1	2.0	2.1	3.5	-1.3	1.6	1.0
1995	2.3	1.9	1.9	1.7	2.3	1.9	2.3	2.0	2.2	1.9	1.1	1.4	2.6	2.1
1996	2.8	2.7	3.4	3.6	2.6	2.4	3.7	2.9	.4	1.2	11.7	6.5	.6	1.4
1997	-1.2	.4	-.8	.7	-1.2	.3	-1.5	.5	-.6	-.1	-6.4	.2	.0	.3
1998	.0	-.8	.1	-.1	-.1	-1.1	-.1	-1.4	.0	-.4	-11.7	-10.0	2.5	.9
1999	2.9	1.8	.8	.6	3.5	2.2	5.1	3.2	.3	.0	18.1	4.9	.9	1.7
2000	3.6	3.8	1.7	1.6	4.1	4.4	5.5	6.1	1.2	.9	16.6	19.4	1.3	1.3
2001	-1.6	2.0	1.8	3.0	-2.6	1.7	-3.9	2.2	.0	.6	-17.1	2.8	.9	1.4
2002	1.2	-1.3	-.6	-.8	1.7	-1.5	2.9	-1.8	-.6	-.4	12.3	-8.2	-.5	.1
2003	4.0	3.2	7.7	4.1	3.0	3.0	4.1	4.3	.8	.3	11.4	14.9	1.0	.2
2004	4.2	3.6	3.1	4.7	4.5	3.4	5.5	4.3	2.4	1.4	13.4	10.8	2.3	1.5
2005	5.4	4.8	1.7	2.0	6.4	5.6	8.8	7.3	1.2	2.3	23.9	17.3	1.4	2.4
2006	1.1	3.0	1.7	.6	1.0	3.5	.4	4.5	2.3	1.6	-2.0	10.0	2.0	1.5
2007	6.2	3.9	7.6	6.6	5.8	3.2	7.7	3.8	1.4	1.8	17.8	7.1	2.0	1.9
2008	-.9	6.3	3.2	6.8	-2.1	6.3	-4.8	7.7	4.3	2.9	-20.3	14.3	4.5	3.4
2009	4.3	-2.6	1.2	-1.6	4.9	-3.1	7.4	-5.1	-.1	1.9	19.4	-17.8	.9	2.6
2010	3.8	4.2	3.4	3.9	3.8	4.2	5.4	6.1	.4	.4	10.8	13.6	1.4	1.2
2011	4.7	6.0	6.0	6.3	4.3	5.9	5.3	7.9	2.3	1.5	7.8	15.6	3.0	2.4
2012 [p]	1.3	1.9	2.3	2.6	1.1	1.7	1.0	1.8	1.4	1.9	-1.3	-.3	2.0	2.6

Percent change from preceding month

	Total finished goods Unadjusted	Seasonally adjusted	Finished consumer foods Unadjusted	Seasonally adjusted	Total Unadjusted	Seasonally adjusted	Consumer goods Unadjusted	Seasonally adjusted	Capital equipment Unadjusted	Seasonally adjusted	Finished energy goods Unadjusted	Seasonally adjusted	Finished goods excl foods and energy Unadjusted	Seasonally adjusted
2011: Jan	1.0	0.8	0.5	0.4	1.1	0.8	1.4	1.1	0.4	0.3	2.6	1.7	0.6	0.5
Feb	1.2	1.1	3.5	3.5	.7	.7	.9	.8	.2	.3	1.8	1.8	.2	.2
Mar	1.3	.5	-.3	-.5	1.7	.8	2.5	1.0	.1	.3	6.1	2.0	.2	.3
Apr	1.2	.7	.1	.1	1.4	.8	2.0	1.0	.3	.3	4.4	2.0	.3	.3
May	.6	.1	-1.0	-1.2	.9	.4	1.3	.4	.0	.1	3.1	.9	.0	.2
June	-.6	.1	.7	.8	-.8	-.1	-1.3	-.3	.2	.4	-3.2	-1.2	.2	.3
July	.4	.5	.6	1.0	.4	.4	.5	.5	.1	.3	.4	.2	.4	.5
Aug	-.3	.2	1.1	1.0	-.6	.0	-.9	.0	.0	.0	-2.3	-.4	.1	.2
Sept	.5	.9	.7	.5	.5	1.1	.6	1.4	.1	.2	1.2	3.0	.1	.3
Oct	-.4	-.3	-.6	.1	-.4	-.4	-1.0	-.6	.9	-.1	-3.4	-1.5	.8	.0
Nov	-.1	.1	1.0	1.0	-.3	-.1	-.4	-.1	.1	.0	-1.0	-.3	.1	.1
Dec	-.3	-.1	-.4	-.7	-.3	.1	-.5	.0	.1	.2	-1.6	-.3	.1	.2
2012: Jan	.5	.3	-.1	-.1	.6	.3	.8	.3	.4	.3	.7	-.2	.7	.6
Feb	.5	.4	-.2	-.2	.6	.6	.8	.8	.1	.2	1.8	1.8	.1	.1
Mar	.8	-.2	.3	.1	.9	-.2	1.3	-.4	.0	.1	3.1	-1.2	.1	.2
Apr	.3	-.3	.1	-.1	.3	-.3	.4	-.6	.1	.1	.9	-1.4	.1	.1
May	-.6	-1.0	-.2	-.4	-.7	-1.2	-1.1	-1.8	-.1	-.1	-2.6	-4.4	.0	.1
June	-.5	.2	.5	.6	-.7	.0	-1.0	.0	.1	.2	-2.4	-.6	.1	.2
July	.2	.3	.0	.4	.3	.3	.2	.2	.2	.4	-.3	-.5	.4	.6
Aug	1.1	1.6	1.0	.9	1.2	1.8	1.8	2.7	.0	.0	4.2	6.3	.1	.1
Sept[2]	.7	1.2	.4	.3	.7	1.3	1.2	2.1	-.2	.0	3.0	4.9	-.2	.0
Oct[2]	-.2	-.2	-.1	.4	-.3	-.3	-.7	-.3	.6	-.3	-2.4	-.5	.7	-.2
Nov[2]	-.9	-.8	1.3	1.3	-1.4	-1.2	-2.2	-2.0	.2	.2	-5.3	-4.6	.1	.1
Dec[2]	-.5	-.2	-.4	-.9	-.5	-.1	-.6	.0	-.1	-.1	-1.6	-.3	-.1	.1

[1] Changes from December to December are based on unadjusted indexes.
[2] Data have been revised through August 2012; data are subject to revision four months after date of original publication.

Source: Department of Labor (Bureau of Labor Statistics).

Money Stock, Credit, and Finance

Table B-69. Money stock and debt measures, 1973-2012

[Averages of daily figures, except debt end-of-period basis; billions of dollars, seasonally adjusted]

Year and month	M1 — Sum of currency, demand deposits, travelers checks, and other checkable deposits (OCDs)	M2 — M1 plus retail MMMF balances, savings deposits (including MMDAs), and small time deposits [2]	Debt [1] — Debt of domestic nonfinancial sectors	Percent change — From year or 6 months earlier [3] M1	Percent change — From year or 6 months earlier [3] M2	Percent change — From previous period [4] Debt
December:						
1973	262.9	855.5	1,895.5	5.5	6.6	10.7
1974	274.2	902.1	2,069.1	4.3	5.4	9.2
1975	287.1	1,016.2	2,259.8	4.7	12.6	9.3
1976	306.2	1,152.0	2,503.0	6.7	13.4	10.8
1977	330.9	1,270.3	2,824.0	8.1	10.3	12.8
1978	357.3	1,366.0	3,207.9	8.0	7.5	13.8
1979	381.8	1,473.7	3,596.3	6.9	7.9	12.1
1980	408.5	1,599.8	3,944.3	7.0	8.6	9.5
1981	436.7	1,755.5	4,351.9	6.9	9.7	10.3
1982	474.8	1,907.1	4,773.1	8.7	8.6	10.4
1983	521.4	2,124.2	5,348.6	9.8	11.4	12.0
1984	551.6	2,307.3	6,134.8	5.8	8.6	14.8
1985	619.8	2,493.0	7,110.6	12.4	8.0	15.6
1986	724.7	2,729.6	7,953.0	16.9	9.5	11.9
1987	750.2	2,829.4	8,656.1	3.5	3.7	9.1
1988	786.7	2,991.1	9,437.0	4.9	5.7	9.1
1989	792.9	3,154.9	10,139.3	.8	5.5	7.3
1990	824.7	3,272.9	10,825.1	4.0	3.7	6.5
1991	897.0	3,371.9	11,295.2	8.8	3.0	4.4
1992	1,024.9	3,423.4	11,812.7	14.3	1.5	4.6
1993	1,129.8	3,472.8	12,494.8	10.2	1.4	5.6
1994	1,150.8	3,485.7	13,141.1	1.9	.4	5.1
1995	1,127.5	3,628.2	13,810.3	-2.0	4.1	5.0
1996	1,081.3	3,806.8	14,515.9	-4.1	4.9	5.1
1997	1,072.8	4,020.1	15,306.5	-.8	5.6	5.5
1998	1,096.1	4,360.1	16,304.6	2.2	8.5	6.5
1999	1,122.9	4,617.8	17,351.4	2.4	5.9	6.2
2000	1,087.9	4,898.0	18,225.2	-3.1	6.1	5.0
2001	1,182.9	5,400.7	19,366.4	8.7	10.3	6.4
2002	1,220.4	5,739.4	20,789.1	3.2	6.3	7.3
2003	1,306.6	6,036.8	22,502.7	7.1	5.2	8.0
2004	1,375.9	6,388.5	25,321.9	5.3	5.8	9.3
2005	1,374.7	6,654.6	27,647.6	-.1	4.2	9.2
2006	1,366.3	7,038.4	30,013.7	-.6	5.8	8.6
2007	1,374.1	7,448.4	32,549.8	.6	5.8	8.4
2008	1,604.7	8,183.2	34,441.1	16.8	9.9	5.8
2009	1,695.4	8,486.6	35,372.5	5.7	3.7	3.1
2010	1,836.3	8,781.8	36,790.7	8.3	3.5	4.1
2011	2,160.4	9,637.1	38,120.7	17.6	9.7	3.6
2012	2,440.2	10,402.4		13.0	7.9	
2011: Jan	1,854.4	8,800.6		15.5	5.1	
Feb	1,876.0	8,856.8		14.8	5.4	
Mar	1,890.0	8,899.4	37,017.1	14.3	5.4	2.5
Apr	1,902.1	8,947.6		13.7	5.4	
May	1,940.2	8,999.7		12.6	5.7	
June	1,951.9	9,080.1	37,258.4	12.6	6.8	2.5
July	1,998.3	9,266.3		15.5	10.6	
Aug	2,112.0	9,489.6		25.2	14.3	
Sept	2,123.2	9,519.4	37,657.7	24.7	13.9	4.3
Oct	2,141.8	9,549.0		25.2	13.4	
Nov	2,159.5	9,601.2		22.6	13.4	
Dec	2,160.4	9,637.1	38,120.7	21.4	12.3	4.9
2012: Jan	2,200.1	9,710.6		20.2	9.6	
Feb	2,215.0	9,745.9		9.8	5.4	
Mar	2,221.9	9,782.1	38,558.4	9.3	5.5	4.6
Apr	2,250.8	9,825.5		10.2	5.8	
May	2,260.7	9,867.5		9.4	5.5	
June	2,265.4	9,918.6	39,046.2	9.7	5.8	5.1
July	2,310.8	10,010.0		10.1	6.2	
Aug	2,339.0	10,082.4		11.2	6.9	
Sept	2,373.8	10,158.8	39,284.3	13.7	7.7	2.4
Oct	2,419.5	10,242.7		15.0	8.5	
Nov	2,403.5	10,293.6		12.6	8.6	
Dec	2,440.2	10,402.4		15.4	9.8	

[1] Consists of outstanding credit market debt of the U.S. Government, State and local governments, and private nonfinancial sectors.
[2] Money market mutual fund (MMMF). Money market deposit account (MMDA).
[3] Annual changes are from December to December; monthly changes are from six months earlier at a simple annual rate.
[4] Annual changes are from fourth quarter to fourth quarter. Quarterly changes are from previous quarter at annual rate.

Note: For further information on the composition of M1 and M2, see the H6 release of the Federal Reserve Board. The Federal Reserve no longer publishes the M3 monetary aggregate and most of its components. Institutional money market mutual funds is published as a memorandum item in the H.6 release, and the component on large-denomination time deposits is published in other Federal Reserve Board releases. For details, see H.6 release of March 23, 2006.

Source: Board of Governors of the Federal Reserve System.

TABLE B–70. Components of money stock measures, 1973–2012

[Averages of daily figures; billions of dollars, seasonally adjusted]

Year and month	Currency	Nonbank travelers checks	Demand deposits	Other checkable deposits (OCDs)		
				Total	At commercial banks	At thrift institutions
December:						
1973	60.8	1.4	200.3	0.3	0.0	0.3
1974	67.0	1.7	205.1	.4	.2	.4
1975	72.8	2.1	211.3	.9	.4	.5
1976	79.5	2.6	221.5	2.7	1.3	1.4
1977	87.4	2.9	236.4	4.2	1.8	2.3
1978	96.0	3.3	249.5	8.5	5.3	3.1
1979	104.8	3.5	256.6	16.8	12.7	4.2
1980	115.3	3.9	261.2	28.1	20.8	7.3
1981	122.5	4.1	231.4	78.7	63.0	15.6
1982	132.5	4.1	234.1	104.1	80.5	23.6
1983	146.2	4.7	238.5	132.1	97.3	34.8
1984	156.1	5.0	243.4	147.1	104.7	42.4
1985	167.7	5.6	266.9	179.5	124.7	54.9
1986	180.4	6.1	302.9	235.2	161.0	74.2
1987	196.7	6.6	287.7	259.2	178.2	81.0
1988	212.0	7.0	287.1	280.6	192.5	88.1
1989	222.3	6.9	278.6	285.1	197.4	87.7
1990	246.5	7.7	276.8	293.7	208.7	85.0
1991	267.1	7.7	289.6	332.5	241.6	90.9
1992	292.1	8.2	340.0	384.6	280.8	103.8
1993	321.7	8.0	385.4	414.6	302.6	112.0
1994	354.7	8.6	383.6	404.0	297.4	106.6
1995	372.8	9.0	389.0	356.6	249.0	107.6
1996	394.5	8.8	402.2	275.8	172.1	103.7
1997	425.2	8.4	393.9	245.2	148.3	96.9
1998	460.4	8.5	377.1	250.0	143.8	106.2
1999	517.9	8.6	353.3	243.2	139.7	103.5
2000	531.3	8.3	310.0	238.2	133.2	105.1
2001	581.3	8.0	336.0	257.5	142.1	115.4
2002	626.3	7.8	307.0	279.3	154.3	125.1
2003	662.5	7.7	326.3	310.0	175.2	134.8
2004	697.6	7.6	343.0	327.8	187.0	140.8
2005	724.0	7.2	324.7	318.8	180.7	138.1
2006	749.6	6.7	305.0	304.9	176.7	128.2
2007	760.1	6.3	302.4	305.4	172.8	132.6
2008	816.1	5.5	471.9	311.1	178.5	132.6
2009	863.7	5.1	443.4	383.2	234.0	149.2
2010	918.7	4.7	512.8	400.1	239.0	161.1
2011	1,001.5	4.3	742.2	412.4	237.1	175.3
2012	1,090.9	3.8	901.7	443.7	248.1	195.6
2011: Jan	923.3	4.7	525.1	401.3	236.1	165.3
Feb	929.5	4.6	539.4	402.5	236.3	166.2
Mar	937.3	4.6	544.9	403.1	236.5	166.7
Apr	946.5	4.6	552.6	398.4	229.6	168.9
May	956.1	4.6	577.8	401.7	234.4	167.3
June	963.1	4.5	583.5	400.8	235.6	165.2
July	969.6	4.5	621.1	403.1	235.7	167.4
Aug	976.5	4.4	718.6	412.5	239.8	172.7
Sept	982.1	4.4	724.8	411.9	238.3	173.5
Oct	986.3	4.4	740.8	410.3	235.6	174.7
Nov	994.3	4.3	747.3	413.6	238.7	174.8
Dec	1,001.5	4.3	742.2	412.4	237.1	175.3
2012: Jan	1,010.2	4.2	767.9	417.7	238.1	179.6
Feb	1,018.7	4.2	770.6	421.6	239.6	182.0
Mar	1,026.9	4.1	767.8	423.1	239.8	183.2
Apr	1,033.3	4.1	787.8	425.6	240.4	185.2
May	1,039.1	4.0	791.3	426.3	240.9	185.4
June	1,045.4	4.0	795.1	420.9	236.0	184.9
July	1,052.3	4.0	822.9	431.7	243.4	188.3
Aug	1,059.5	3.9	842.3	433.2	243.8	189.4
Sept	1,068.6	3.9	867.2	434.0	242.3	191.8
Oct	1,077.6	3.9	899.9	438.1	246.2	191.9
Nov	1,083.1	3.9	884.5	432.1	240.5	191.6
Dec	1,090.9	3.8	901.7	443.7	248.1	195.6

See next page for continuation of table.

Table B–70. Components of money stock measures, 1973–2012—*Continued*

[Averages of daily figures; billions of dollars, seasonally adjusted]

Year and month	Savings deposits [1]			Small-denomination time deposits [2]			Retail money funds	Institutional money funds [3]
	Total	At commercial banks	At thrift institutions	Total	At commercial banks	At thrift institutions		
December:								
1973	326.8	128.0	198.7	265.8	116.8	149.0	0.1	
1974	338.6	136.8	201.8	287.9	123.1	164.8	1.4	0.2
1975	388.9	161.2	227.6	337.9	142.3	195.5	2.4	.5
1976	453.2	201.8	251.4	390.7	155.5	235.2	1.8	.6
1977	492.2	218.8	273.4	445.5	167.5	278.0	1.8	1.0
1978	481.9	216.5	265.4	521.0	185.1	335.8	5.8	3.5
1979	423.8	195.0	228.8	634.3	235.5	398.7	33.9	10.4
1980	400.3	185.7	214.5	728.5	286.2	442.3	62.5	16.0
1981	343.9	159.0	184.9	823.1	347.7	475.4	151.7	38.2
1982	400.1	190.1	210.0	850.9	379.9	471.0	181.3	48.8
1983	684.9	363.2	321.7	784.1	350.9	433.1	133.8	40.9
1984	704.7	389.3	315.4	888.8	387.9	500.9	162.2	65.1
1985	815.3	456.6	358.6	885.7	386.4	499.3	172.2	68.2
1986	940.9	533.5	407.4	858.4	369.4	489.0	205.7	89.2
1987	937.4	534.8	402.6	921.0	391.7	529.3	220.7	96.0
1988	926.4	542.4	383.9	1,037.1	451.2	585.9	241.0	97.4
1989	893.7	541.1	352.6	1,151.3	533.8	617.6	316.9	115.9
1990	922.9	581.3	341.6	1,173.3	610.7	562.6	352.0	145.2
1991	1,044.5	664.8	379.6	1,065.3	602.2	463.1	365.2	195.8
1992	1,187.2	754.2	433.1	867.7	508.1	359.7	343.6	222.1
1993	1,219.3	785.3	434.0	781.5	467.9	313.6	342.3	228.3
1994	1,151.3	752.8	398.5	817.5	503.6	313.9	366.1	225.5
1995	1,135.9	774.8	361.0	932.4	575.8	356.5	432.4	279.9
1996	1,274.8	906.1	368.8	947.9	594.2	353.7	502.7	341.8
1997	1,401.8	1,022.9	378.8	967.6	625.5	342.2	577.9	416.8
1998	1,605.1	1,188.6	416.5	951.3	626.4	324.9	707.6	572.3
1999	1,739.8	1,288.7	451.1	955.2	636.9	318.3	799.9	678.3
2000	1,877.4	1,423.7	453.8	1,046.0	700.8	345.3	886.7	833.8
2001	2,309.6	1,738.8	570.8	974.6	636.0	338.5	933.7	1,252.9
2002	2,772.1	2,058.7	713.4	894.7	591.3	303.5	852.1	1,314.6
2003	3,162.0	2,337.3	824.7	818.1	541.9	276.2	750.1	1,163.7
2004	3,508.8	2,632.6	876.2	828.4	551.9	276.5	675.5	1,107.8
2005	3,606.5	2,776.9	829.6	993.7	646.7	347.0	679.8	1,178.2
2006	3,693.7	2,910.4	783.3	1,205.9	780.6	425.3	772.6	1,394.3
2007	3,870.1	3,042.5	827.5	1,275.8	858.7	417.1	928.5	1,962.5
2008	4,100.6	3,330.0	770.6	1,457.1	1,078.0	379.1	1,020.9	2,459.1
2009	4,830.0	3,991.6	838.4	1,182.3	862.5	319.8	779.0	2,254.2
2010	5,345.0	4,426.1	918.8	927.2	656.3	270.9	673.3	1,893.7
2011	6,050.1	5,047.9	1,002.2	765.5	536.7	228.8	661.1	1,763.1
2012	6,694.5	5,731.5	963.0	632.6	455.3	177.4	635.1	1,742.7
2011: Jan	5,366.9	4,436.7	930.2	909.1	643.5	265.6	670.3	1,846.4
Feb	5,419.5	4,476.0	943.4	896.7	634.2	262.5	664.7	1,824.8
Mar	5,464.1	4,507.7	956.4	883.8	623.6	260.1	661.6	1,846.0
Apr	5,516.4	4,559.4	957.0	871.9	614.7	257.2	657.2	1,875.3
May	5,545.1	4,576.5	968.6	858.8	604.4	254.5	655.7	1,895.5
June	5,626.7	4,657.6	969.1	843.8	593.0	250.8	657.7	1,872.9
July	5,780.5	4,802.9	977.6	829.0	581.9	247.1	658.5	1,838.4
Aug	5,892.3	4,909.0	983.3	812.7	569.9	242.8	672.6	1,746.6
Sept	5,930.7	4,945.4	985.3	798.0	559.0	239.0	667.5	1,768.3
Oct	5,950.3	4,961.6	988.7	785.0	549.9	235.2	671.9	1,765.3
Nov	6,003.1	5,006.0	997.0	772.8	541.5	231.3	665.9	1,758.1
Dec	6,050.1	5,047.9	1,002.2	765.5	536.7	228.8	661.1	1,763.1
2012: Jan	6,098.3	5,097.1	1,001.1	756.0	533.7	222.3	656.3	1,759.9
Feb	6,140.1	5,158.5	981.6	745.5	532.7	212.9	645.3	1,746.8
Mar	6,188.5	5,197.4	991.1	732.9	524.9	208.0	638.8	1,751.1
Apr	6,217.5	5,221.4	996.1	721.0	515.4	205.7	636.2	1,739.2
May	6,264.7	5,256.5	1,008.2	709.4	506.4	203.0	632.7	1,735.2
June	6,325.0	5,312.5	1,012.5	699.3	498.7	200.5	628.9	1,727.4
July	6,385.2	5,360.1	1,025.0	688.1	491.7	196.4	625.9	1,730.3
Aug	6,442.1	5,411.6	1,030.5	677.8	484.8	193.0	623.5	1,741.8
Sept	6,494.6	5,462.9	1,031.7	667.4	478.0	189.4	623.0	1,750.7
Oct	6,543.9	5,506.7	1,037.2	656.2	470.0	186.2	623.1	1,741.8
Nov	6,620.1	5,664.5	955.6	643.7	463.9	179.8	626.2	1,734.7
Dec	6,694.5	5,731.5	963.0	632.6	455.3	177.4	635.1	1,742.7

[1] Savings deposits including money market deposit accounts (MMDAs); data prior to 1982 are savings deposits only.
[2] Small-denomination deposits are those issued in amounts of less than $100,000.
[3] Institutional money funds are not part of non-M1 M2.

Note: See also Table B–69.

Source: Board of Governors of the Federal Reserve System.

TABLE B–71. Aggregate reserves of depository institutions and the monetary base, 1982–2012

[Averages of daily figures [1]; millions of dollars; seasonally adjusted, except as noted]

| Year and month | Adjusted for changes in reserve requirements [2] | | | | | Borrowings from the Federal Reserve (NSA) [3] | | Other borrowings from the Federal Reserve [5] | | | | |
| | Reserves of depository institutions | | | | Monetary base (NSA) [3] | Total [4] | Term auction credit | Primary | Primary dealer and other broker-dealer credit [6] | Asset-backed commercial paper money market mutual fund liquidity facility | Credit extended to American International Group, Inc., net [7] | Term asset-backed securities loan facility, net [8] |
	Total	Non-borrowed	Required	Excess (NSA) [3]								
December:												
1982	23,600	22,966	23,100	500	160,127	634						
1983	25,367	24,593	24,806	561	175,467	774						
1984	26,913	23,727	26,078	835	187,253	3,186						
1985	31,569	30,251	30,505	1,064	203,556	1,318						
1986	38,841	38,014	37,667	1,174	223,417	827						
1987	38,913	38,136	37,893	1,020	239,830	777						
1988	40,454	38,738	39,392	1,062	256,897	1,716						
1989	40,487	40,222	39,545	942	267,761	265						
1990	41,767	41,441	40,101	1,665	293,339	326						
1991	45,516	45,324	44,526	990	317,523	192						
1992	54,422	54,298	53,267	1,155	350,885	124						
1993	60,567	60,485	59,497	1,070	386,720	82						
1994	59,466	59,257	58,295	1,171	418,474	209						
1995	56,484	56,226	55,193	1,291	434,645	257						
1996	50,185	50,030	48,766	1,419	451,935	155						
1997	46,876	46,551	45,189	1,687	479,798	324						
1998	45,174	45,058	43,662	1,513	513,821	117						
1999	42,149	41,829	40,855	1,295	593,383	[9] 320						
2000	38,685	38,475	37,359	1,326	584,928	210						
2001	41,384	41,317	39,740	1,643	635,575	67						
2002	40,275	40,195	38,267	2,008	681,486	80						
2003	42,542	42,496	41,495	1,047	720,115	46		17				
2004	46,425	46,362	44,517	1,908	759,085	63		11				
2005	44,963	44,795	43,063	1,900	787,348	169		97				
2006	43,124	42,933	41,261	1,863	812,353	191		111				
2007	43,133	27,702	41,348	1,785	824,795	15,430	11,613	3,787				
2008	820,187	166,621	52,868	767,318	1,654,966	653,565	438,327	88,245	47,631	32,102	47,206	
2009	1,138,682	968,755	63,483	1,075,199	2,019,207	169,927	82,014	19,025	0	0	22,023	46,310
2010	1,077,359	1,031,871	70,723	1,006,636	2,011,056	45,488	0	41			20,394	25,025
2011	1,597,100	1,587,574	94,894	1,502,206	2,612,059	9,526	0	103				9,400
2012	1,569,019	1,568,224	110,270	1,458,750	2,672,629	795	0	12				760
2011: Jan	1,106,871	1,074,624	70,404	1,036,466	2,045,212	32,246	0	51			8,368	23,818
Feb	1,262,561	1,240,628	72,559	1,190,001	2,206,970	21,933	0	28				21,902
Mar	1,436,155	1,416,273	74,008	1,362,146	2,388,590	19,882	0	11				19,864
Apr	1,526,629	1,508,786	74,682	1,451,947	2,488,261	17,842	0	14				17,820
May	1,587,841	1,572,695	75,353	1,512,488	2,559,360	15,146	0	10				15,115
June	1,666,615	1,653,372	77,890	1,588,726	2,644,882	13,243	0	24				13,178
July	1,696,633	1,684,238	78,516	1,618,117	2,681,175	12,395	0	7				12,315
Aug	1,666,698	1,654,864	83,354	1,583,344	2,657,711	11,834	0	5				11,737
Sept	1,642,237	1,630,662	91,260	1,550,977	2,638,155	11,575	0	19				11,474
Oct	1,638,130	1,626,919	92,993	1,545,136	2,638,317	11,210	0	19				11,140
Nov	1,591,703	1,581,362	93,934	1,497,769	2,599,444	10,341	0	20				10,301
Dec	1,597,100	1,587,574	94,894	1,502,206	2,612,059	9,526	0	103				9,400
2012: Jan	1,614,301	1,605,687	94,850	1,519,451	2,638,085	8,614	0	27				8,580
Feb	1,657,931	1,649,998	97,811	1,560,121	2,690,186	7,933	0	13				7,920
Mar	1,607,819	1,600,490	98,226	1,509,593	2,648,073	7,330	0	12				7,314
Apr	1,584,770	1,577,905	98,593	1,486,176	2,631,505	6,865	0	21				6,834
May	1,556,689	1,550,503	99,230	1,457,460	2,609,160	6,187	0	16				6,143
June	1,557,175	1,551,961	99,699	1,457,475	2,615,667	5,214	0	19				5,139
July	1,584,049	1,579,791	101,000	1,483,049	2,649,394	4,258	0	26				4,135
Aug	1,582,288	1,579,017	104,538	1,477,750	2,654,466	3,271	0	39				3,094
Sept	1,515,888	1,513,923	106,447	1,409,441	2,597,253	1,965	0	62				1,781
Oct	1,525,144	1,523,678	106,870	1,418,274	2,615,619	1,466	0	17				1,383
Nov	1,546,809	1,545,757	111,505	1,435,303	2,643,310	1,051	0	9				1,006
Dec	1,569,019	1,568,224	110,270	1,458,750	2,672,629	795	0	12				760

[1] Data are prorated averages of biweekly (maintenance period) averages of daily figures.

[2] Aggregate reserves incorporate adjustments for discontinuities associated with regulatory changes to reserve requirements. For details on aggregate reserves series see Federal Reserve Bulletin.

[3] Not seasonally adjusted (NSA).

[4] Includes secondary, seasonal, other credit extensions, adjustment credit, and extended credit not shown separately.

[5] Does not include credit extensions made by the Federal Reserve Bank of New York to Maiden Lane LLC, Maiden Lane II LLC, Maiden Lane III LLC, and Commercial Paper Funding Facility LLC.

[6] Includes credit extended through the Primary Dealer Credit Facility and credit extended to certain other broker-dealers.

[7] Includes outstanding principal and capitalized interest net of unamortized deferred commitment fees and allowance for loan restructuring. Excludes credit extended to consolidated LLCs as described in footnote 5.

[8] Includes credit extended by Federal Reserve Bank of New York to eligible borrowers through the Term Asset-Backed Securities Loan Facility.

[9] Total includes borrowing under the terms and conditions established for the Century Date Change Special Liquidity Facility in effect from October 1, 1999 through April 7, 2000.

Source: Board of Governors of the Federal Reserve System.

TABLE B–72. Bank credit at all commercial banks, 1975–2012

[Monthly average; billions of dollars, seasonally adjusted [1]]

Year and month	Total bank credit	Securities in bank credit [2]			Loans and leases in bank credit						
		Total securities	U.S. Treasury and agency securities	Other securities	Total loans and leases [3]	Commercial and industrial loans	Real estate loans			Consumer loans [6]	Other loans and leases [7]
							Total [4]	Revolving home equity loans	Commercial loans [5]		
December:											
1975	737.8	204.9	118.1	86.8	532.9	183.4	134.1			104.3	111.1
1976	798.6	226.7	137.5	89.1	571.9	185.2	148.5			115.8	122.3
1977	885.6	234.3	137.5	96.8	651.3	204.7	175.1			138.0	133.5
1978	1,003.7	240.2	138.4	101.9	763.5	237.2	210.5			164.4	151.3
1979	1,118.1	257.8	146.1	111.7	860.3	279.7	241.7			183.8	155.1
1980	1,216.9	293.4	171.5	121.9	923.5	312.0	262.3			178.7	170.5
1981	1,297.7	306.8	179.8	127.0	990.9	350.3	283.6			182.1	174.8
1982	1,397.6	333.8	202.4	131.4	1,063.8	392.0	299.7			187.9	184.2
1983	1,549.6	398.1	260.4	137.8	1,151.5	413.9	330.4			212.9	194.3
1984	1,715.9	401.1	260.0	141.1	1,314.8	473.4	376.2			253.8	211.3
1985	1,883.5	440.5	264.2	176.3	1,443.0	499.1	422.1			291.1	230.8
1986	2,077.6	498.9	310.3	188.6	1,578.6	539.2	490.6			314.8	234.0
1987	2,226.4	526.1	336.3	189.8	1,700.3	565.1	585.8	30.6		327.1	222.3
1988	2,399.8	549.7	360.5	189.2	1,850.1	604.7	663.2	41.2		355.2	226.9
1989	2,562.9	571.1	401.6	169.5	1,991.8	637.1	760.6	51.5		373.4	220.7
1990	2,700.0	619.2	460.2	159.1	2,080.8	640.1	842.5	63.5		375.2	222.9
1991	2,807.5	727.5	564.3	163.2	2,080.0	617.9	868.6	71.9		363.3	230.2
1992	2,907.2	824.1	664.7	159.5	2,083.0	596.8	887.7	75.0		354.5	244.1
1993	3,059.9	894.5	730.0	164.5	2,165.4	583.8	928.6	74.2		385.9	267.1
1994	3,233.6	891.6	721.9	169.7	2,342.0	644.0	987.6	76.0		443.3	267.1
1995	3,461.2	893.0	703.3	189.7	2,568.2	715.2	1,061.8	79.8		484.0	307.3
1996	3,634.9	893.4	698.6	194.8	2,741.5	778.7	1,122.2	86.3		506.9	333.7
1997	3,956.5	985.6	750.2	235.4	2,970.9	845.6	1,220.2	98.8		500.0	405.1
1998	4,368.5	1,096.9	795.3	301.6	3,271.6	939.0	1,311.1	97.2		497.7	524.0
1999	4,628.2	1,144.5	811.1	333.4	3,483.7	1,001.7	1,460.8	101.2		506.7	514.4
2000	5,023.8	1,174.2	787.7	386.5	3,849.6	1,087.1	1,639.6	129.3		556.3	566.6
2001	5,208.9	1,307.4	838.8	468.5	3,901.5	1,024.0	1,759.7	153.8		574.4	543.4
2002	5,642.8	1,490.4	1,004.2	486.2	4,152.4	962.5	2,011.6	212.4		610.4	567.9
2003	6,003.0	1,622.1	1,088.7	533.3	4,380.9	889.6	2,209.9	278.7		664.8	616.6
2004	6,586.3	1,741.4	1,145.8	595.6	4,844.9	913.4	2,555.8	395.4	1,081.6	690.8	684.9
2005	7,305.0	1,852.9	1,135.7	717.1	5,452.2	1,043.6	2,926.0	443.2	1,271.9	702.5	780.1
2006	8,091.9	1,985.7	1,188.1	797.7	6,106.1	1,191.4	3,367.9	467.8	1,459.6	736.5	810.2
2007	8,895.2	2,103.6	1,109.9	993.8	6,791.6	1,430.8	3,593.6	484.6	1,583.5	798.1	969.1
2008	9,344.9	2,096.6	1,238.0	858.6	7,248.4	1,572.7	3,816.1	588.0	1,726.7	875.3	984.3
2009	8,985.8	2,326.7	1,448.9	877.8	6,659.1	1,278.9	3,773.6	603.0	1,638.9	835.6	771.0
2010	9,184.1	2,429.6	1,640.4	789.2	6,754.5	1,208.7	3,609.6	581.9	1,498.0	1,114.4	821.8
2011	9,404.9	2,498.1	1,700.7	797.4	6,906.8	1,331.8	3,489.5	548.6	1,415.8	1,091.1	994.3
2012	9,949.1	2,742.8	1,881.1	861.7	7,206.3	1,503.2	3,541.9	514.6	1,422.8	1,116.7	1,044.6
2011: Jan	9,162.1	2,426.1	1,642.4	783.7	6,736.0	1,212.6	3,599.8	576.8	1,488.4	1,080.7	842.9
Feb	9,121.6	2,415.6	1,633.2	782.4	6,705.9	1,216.8	3,567.6	574.3	1,480.7	1,076.4	845.1
Mar	9,120.8	2,428.5	1,644.6	783.9	6,692.3	1,226.3	3,537.8	571.6	1,469.8	1,075.3	852.8
Apr	9,154.9	2,444.1	1,670.0	774.1	6,710.9	1,236.9	3,516.5	568.4	1,460.9	1,079.4	878.1
May	9,155.7	2,439.4	1,668.2	771.2	6,716.3	1,249.9	3,505.6	565.6	1,456.6	1,079.2	881.7
June	9,159.3	2,432.9	1,659.0	774.0	6,726.4	1,256.9	3,500.2	562.8	1,449.7	1,083.1	886.2
July	9,202.5	2,432.8	1,651.6	781.2	6,769.7	1,269.4	3,495.5	559.8	1,440.3	1,087.8	917.0
Aug	9,244.4	2,447.5	1,658.9	788.6	6,796.9	1,289.8	3,487.8	557.2	1,431.9	1,085.4	933.9
Sept	9,261.9	2,456.6	1,668.3	788.3	6,805.3	1,295.2	3,484.1	555.5	1,425.9	1,084.8	941.1
Oct	9,322.9	2,463.7	1,679.4	784.3	6,859.2	1,309.1	3,493.5	553.2	1,419.3	1,086.3	970.3
Nov	9,379.6	2,477.2	1,687.8	789.3	6,902.5	1,317.7	3,495.4	550.9	1,417.8	1,087.9	1,001.5
Dec	9,404.9	2,498.1	1,700.7	797.4	6,906.8	1,331.8	3,489.5	548.6	1,415.8	1,091.1	994.3
2012: Jan	9,474.7	2,529.3	1,725.6	803.7	6,945.4	1,350.5	3,509.1	548.3	1,416.3	1,089.4	996.4
Feb	9,565.0	2,563.7	1,753.5	810.1	7,001.3	1,373.7	3,539.7	549.7	1,427.5	1,090.1	997.9
Mar	9,591.4	2,576.4	1,775.6	800.8	7,015.0	1,384.0	3,545.0	546.0	1,425.6	1,093.9	992.1
Apr	9,636.2	2,595.2	1,796.1	799.1	7,041.0	1,403.9	3,540.2	543.4	1,424.2	1,096.9	1,000.0
May	9,678.6	2,604.6	1,806.4	798.2	7,074.1	1,411.6	3,539.5	540.2	1,419.7	1,106.7	1,016.3
June	9,706.7	2,609.2	1,806.5	802.7	7,097.5	1,433.0	3,529.9	536.9	1,417.8	1,106.8	1,027.8
July	9,755.9	2,641.5	1,828.8	812.7	7,114.4	1,451.2	3,526.7	532.9	1,417.3	1,106.6	1,029.8
Aug	9,779.5	2,647.1	1,834.0	813.1	7,132.3	1,462.8	3,525.4	529.7	1,415.4	1,107.7	1,036.5
Sept	9,801.9	2,658.9	1,837.4	821.5	7,143.0	1,465.1	3,528.2	525.9	1,414.3	1,108.8	1,040.9
Oct	9,818.7	2,669.4	1,838.5	830.8	7,149.3	1,478.5	3,519.8	521.2	1,413.1	1,110.2	1,040.8
Nov	9,860.5	2,692.2	1,852.4	839.8	7,168.4	1,481.4	3,542.6	518.7	1,415.3	1,113.2	1,031.2
Dec	9,949.1	2,742.8	1,881.1	861.7	7,206.3	1,503.2	3,541.9	514.6	1,422.8	1,116.7	1,044.6

[1] Data are prorated averages of Wednesday values for domestically chartered commercial banks, branches and agencies of foreign banks, New York State investment companies (through September 1996), and Edge Act and agreement corporations.
[2] Includes securities held in trading accounts, held-to-maturity, and available for sale. Excludes all non-security trading assets, such as derivatives with a positive fair value or loans held in trading accounts.
[3] Excludes unearned income. Includes the allowance for loan and lease losses. Excludes Federal funds sold to, reverse repurchase agreements (RPs) with, and loans to commercial banks. Includes all loans held in trading accounts under a fair value option.
[4] Includes closed-end residential loans, not shown separately.
[5] Includes construction, land development, and other land loans, and loans secured by farmland, multifamily (5 or more) residential properties, and nonfarm nonresidential properties.
[6] Includes credit cards and other consumer loans.
[7] Includes other items, not shown separately.
Note: Data in this table are shown as of January 25, 2013.
Source: Board of Governors of the Federal Reserve System.

Table B–73. Bond yields and interest rates, 1941–2012

[Percent per annum]

| Year and month | U.S. Treasury securities | | | | | Corporate bonds (Moody's) | | High-grade municipal bonds (Standard & Poor's) | New-home mortgage yields[4] | Prime rate charged by banks[5] | Discount window (Federal Reserve Bank of New York)[5,6] | | Federal funds rate[7] |
| | Bills (at auction)[1] | | Constant maturities[2] | | | | | | | | | | |
	3-month	6-month	3-year	10-year	30-year	Aaa[3]	Baa				Primary credit	Adjustment credit	
1941	0.103					2.77	4.33	2.10		1.50		1.00	
1942	.326					2.83	4.28	2.36		1.50		[8]1.00	
1943	.373					2.73	3.91	2.06		1.50		[8]1.00	
1944	.375					2.72	3.61	1.86		1.50		[8]1.00	
1945	.375					2.62	3.29	1.67		1.50		[8]1.00	
1946	.375					2.53	3.05	1.64		1.50		[8]1.00	
1947	.594					2.61	3.24	2.01		1.50–1.75		1.00	
1948	1.040					2.82	3.47	2.40		1.75–2.00		1.34	
1949	1.102					2.66	3.42	2.21		2.00		1.50	
1950	1.218					2.62	3.24	1.98		2.07		1.59	
1951	1.552					2.86	3.41	2.00		2.56		1.75	
1952	1.766					2.96	3.52	2.19		3.00		1.75	
1953	1.931		2.47	2.85		3.20	3.74	2.72		3.17		1.99	
1954	.953		1.63	2.40		2.90	3.51	2.37		3.05		1.60	
1955	1.753		2.47	2.82		3.06	3.53	2.53		3.16		1.89	1.79
1956	2.658		3.19	3.18		3.36	3.88	2.93		3.77		2.77	2.73
1957	3.267		3.98	3.65		3.89	4.71	3.60		4.20		3.12	3.11
1958	1.839		2.84	3.32		3.79	4.73	3.56		3.83		2.15	1.57
1959	3.405	3.832	4.46	4.33		4.38	5.05	3.95		4.48		3.36	3.31
1960	2.93	3.25	3.98	4.12		4.41	5.19	3.73		4.82		3.53	3.21
1961	2.38	2.61	3.54	3.88		4.35	5.08	3.46		4.50		3.00	1.95
1962	2.78	2.91	3.47	3.95		4.33	5.02	3.18		4.50		3.00	2.71
1963	3.16	3.25	3.67	4.00		4.26	4.86	3.23	5.89	4.50		3.23	3.18
1964	3.56	3.69	4.03	4.19		4.40	4.83	3.22	5.83	4.50		3.55	3.50
1965	3.95	4.05	4.22	4.28		4.49	4.87	3.27	5.81	4.54		4.04	4.07
1966	4.88	5.08	5.23	4.93		5.13	5.67	3.82	6.25	5.63		4.50	5.11
1967	4.32	4.63	5.03	5.07		5.51	6.23	3.98	6.46	5.63		4.19	4.22
1968	5.34	5.47	5.68	5.64		6.18	6.94	4.51	6.97	6.31		5.17	5.66
1969	6.68	6.85	7.02	6.67		7.03	7.81	5.81	7.81	7.96		5.87	8.21
1970	6.43	6.53	7.29	7.35		8.04	9.11	6.51	8.45	7.91		5.95	7.17
1971	4.35	4.51	5.66	6.16		7.39	8.56	5.70	7.74	5.73		4.88	4.67
1972	4.07	4.47	5.72	6.21		7.21	8.16	5.27	7.60	5.25		4.50	4.44
1973	7.04	7.18	6.96	6.85		7.44	8.24	5.18	7.96	8.03		6.45	8.74
1974	7.89	7.93	7.84	7.56		8.57	9.50	6.09	8.92	10.81		7.83	10.51
1975	5.84	6.12	7.50	7.99		8.83	10.61	6.89	9.00	7.86		6.25	5.82
1976	4.99	5.27	6.77	7.61		8.43	9.75	6.49	9.00	6.84		5.50	5.05
1977	5.27	5.52	6.68	7.42	7.75	8.02	8.97	5.56	9.02	6.83		5.46	5.54
1978	7.22	7.58	8.29	8.41	8.49	8.73	9.49	5.90	9.56	9.06		7.46	7.94
1979	10.05	10.02	9.70	9.43	9.28	9.63	10.69	6.39	10.78	12.67		10.29	11.20
1980	11.51	11.37	11.51	11.43	11.27	11.94	13.67	8.51	12.66	15.26		11.77	13.35
1981	14.03	13.78	14.46	13.92	13.45	14.17	16.04	11.23	14.70	18.87		13.42	16.39
1982	10.69	11.08	12.93	13.01	12.76	13.79	16.11	11.57	15.14	14.85		11.01	12.24
1983	8.63	8.75	10.45	11.10	11.18	12.04	13.55	9.47	12.57	10.79		8.50	9.09
1984	9.53	9.77	11.92	12.46	12.41	12.71	14.19	10.15	12.38	12.04		8.80	10.23
1985	7.47	7.64	9.64	10.62	10.79	11.37	12.72	9.18	11.55	9.93		7.69	8.10
1986	5.98	6.03	7.06	7.67	7.78	9.02	10.39	7.38	10.17	8.33		6.32	6.80
1987	5.82	6.05	7.68	8.39	8.59	9.38	10.58	7.73	9.31	8.21		5.66	6.66
1988	6.69	6.92	8.26	8.85	8.96	9.71	10.83	7.76	9.19	9.32		6.20	7.57
1989	8.12	8.04	8.55	8.49	8.45	9.26	10.18	7.24	10.13	10.87		6.93	9.21
1990	7.51	7.47	8.26	8.55	8.61	9.32	10.36	7.25	10.05	10.01		6.98	8.10
1991	5.42	5.49	6.82	7.86	8.14	8.77	9.80	6.89	9.32	8.46		5.45	5.69
1992	3.45	3.57	5.30	7.01	7.67	8.14	8.98	6.41	8.24	6.25		3.25	3.52
1993	3.02	3.14	4.44	5.87	6.59	7.22	7.93	5.63	7.20	6.00		3.00	3.02
1994	4.29	4.66	6.27	7.09	7.37	7.96	8.62	6.19	7.49	7.15		3.60	4.21
1995	5.51	5.59	6.25	6.57	6.88	7.59	8.20	5.95	7.87	8.83		5.21	5.83
1996	5.02	5.09	5.99	6.44	6.71	7.37	8.05	5.75	7.80	8.27		5.02	5.30
1997	5.07	5.18	6.10	6.35	6.61	7.26	7.86	5.55	7.71	8.44		5.00	5.46
1998	4.81	4.85	5.14	5.26	5.58	6.53	7.22	5.12	7.07	8.35		4.92	5.35
1999	4.66	4.76	5.49	5.65	5.87	7.04	7.87	5.43	7.04	8.00		4.62	4.97
2000	5.85	5.92	6.22	6.03	5.94	7.62	8.36	5.77	7.52	9.23		5.73	6.24
2001	3.44	3.39	4.09	5.02	5.49	7.08	7.95	5.19	7.00	6.91		3.40	3.88
2002	1.62	1.69	3.10	4.61	5.43	6.49	7.80	5.05	6.43	4.67		1.17	1.67
2003	1.01	1.06	2.10	4.01		5.67	6.77	4.73	5.80	4.12	2.12		1.13
2004	1.38	1.57	2.78	4.27		5.63	6.39	4.63	5.77	4.34	2.34		1.35
2005	3.16	3.40	3.93	4.29		5.24	6.06	4.29	5.94	6.19	4.19		3.22
2006	4.73	4.80	4.77	4.80	4.91	5.59	6.48	4.42	6.63	7.96	5.96		4.97
2007	4.41	4.48	4.35	4.63	4.84	5.56	6.48	4.42	6.41	8.05	5.86		5.02
2008	1.48	1.71	2.24	3.66	4.28	5.63	7.45	4.80	6.05	5.09	2.39		1.92
2009	.16	.29	1.43	3.26	4.08	5.31	7.30	4.64	5.14	3.25	.50		.16
2010	.14	.20	1.11	3.22	4.25	4.94	6.04	4.16	4.80	3.25	.72		.18
2011	.06	.10	.75	2.78	3.91	4.64	5.66	4.29	4.56	3.25	.75		.10
2012	.09	.13	.38	1.80	2.92	3.67	4.94	3.14	3.69	3.25	.75		.14

[1] High bill rate at auction, issue date within period, bank-discount basis. On or after October 28, 1998, data are stop yields from uniform-price auctions. Before that date, they are weighted average yields from multiple-price auctions.

See next page for continuation of table.

TABLE B–73. Bond yields and interest rates, 1941–2012—*Continued*

[Percent per annum]

Year and month	U.S. Treasury securities					Corporate bonds (Moody's)		High-grade municipal bonds (Standard & Poor's)	New-home mortgage yields [4]	Prime rate charged by banks [5]	Discount window (Federal Reserve Bank of New York) [5,6]			Federal funds rate [7]
	Bills (at auction) [1]		Constant maturities [2]			Aaa [3]	Baa				Primary credit	Adjustment credit		
	3-month	6-month	3-year	10-year	30-year									
											High-low	High-low	High-low	
2008: Jan	2.86	2.84	2.51	3.74	4.33	5.33	6.54	4.00	6.02	7.25–6.00	4.75–3.50	....		3.94
Feb	2.21	2.09	2.19	3.74	4.52	5.53	6.82	4.35	5.96	6.00–6.00	3.50–3.50	....		2.98
Mar	1.38	1.53	1.80	3.51	4.39	5.51	6.89	4.67	5.92	6.00–5.25	3.50–2.50	....		2.61
Apr	1.32	1.54	2.23	3.68	4.44	5.55	6.97	4.43	5.98	5.25–5.00	2.50–2.25	....		2.28
May	1.71	1.82	2.69	3.88	4.60	5.57	6.93	4.34	6.01	5.00–5.00	2.25–2.25	....		1.98
June	1.89	2.15	3.08	4.10	4.69	5.68	7.07	4.48	6.13	5.00–5.00	2.25–2.25	....		2.00
July	1.72	1.99	2.87	4.01	4.57	5.67	7.16	4.88	6.29	5.00–5.00	2.25–2.25	....		2.01
Aug	1.79	1.96	2.70	3.89	4.50	5.64	7.15	4.90	6.33	5.00–5.00	2.25–2.25	....		2.00
Sept	1.46	1.78	2.32	3.69	4.27	5.65	7.31	5.03	6.09	5.00–5.00	2.25–2.25	....		1.81
Oct	.84	1.39	1.86	3.81	4.17	6.28	8.88	5.68	6.10	5.00–4.00	2.25–1.25	....		.97
Nov	.30	.86	1.51	3.53	4.00	6.12	9.21	5.28	6.16	4.00–4.00	1.25–1.25	....		.39
Dec	.04	.32	1.07	2.42	2.87	5.05	8.43	5.53	5.67	4.00–3.25	1.25–0.50	....		.16
2009: Jan	.12	.31	1.13	2.52	3.13	5.05	8.14	5.13	5.11	3.25–3.25	0.50–0.50	....		.15
Feb	.31	.46	1.37	2.87	3.59	5.27	8.08	5.00	5.09	3.25–3.25	0.50–0.50	....		.22
Mar	.25	.43	1.31	2.82	3.64	5.50	8.42	5.15	5.10	3.25–3.25	0.50–0.50	....		.18
Apr	.17	.37	1.32	2.93	3.76	5.39	8.39	4.88	4.96	3.25–3.25	0.50–0.50	....		.15
May	.19	.31	1.39	3.29	4.23	5.54	8.06	4.60	4.92	3.25–3.25	0.50–0.50	....		.18
June	.17	.32	1.76	3.72	4.52	5.61	7.50	4.84	5.17	3.25–3.25	0.50–0.50	....		.21
July	.19	.29	1.55	3.56	4.41	5.41	7.09	4.69	5.40	3.25–3.25	0.50–0.50	....		.16
Aug	.18	.27	1.65	3.59	4.37	5.26	6.58	4.58	5.32	3.25–3.25	0.50–0.50	....		.16
Sept	.13	.22	1.48	3.40	4.19	5.13	6.31	4.13	5.26	3.25–3.25	0.50–0.50	....		.15
Oct	.08	.17	1.46	3.39	4.19	5.15	6.29	4.20	5.14	3.25–3.25	0.50–0.50	....		.12
Nov	.06	.16	1.32	3.40	4.31	5.19	6.32	4.35	5.08	3.25–3.25	0.50–0.50	....		.12
Dec	.07	.17	1.38	3.59	4.49	5.26	6.37	4.16	5.01	3.25–3.25	0.50–0.50	....		.12
2010: Jan	.06	.15	1.49	3.73	4.60	5.26	6.25	4.22	5.04	3.25–3.25	0.50–0.50	....		.11
Feb	.10	.18	1.40	3.69	4.62	5.35	6.34	4.23	5.08	3.25–3.25	0.75–0.50	....		.13
Mar	.15	.22	1.51	3.73	4.64	5.27	6.27	4.22	5.09	3.25–3.25	0.75–0.75	....		.16
Apr	.15	.24	1.64	3.85	4.69	5.29	6.25	4.24	5.21	3.25–3.25	0.75–0.75	....		.20
May	.16	.23	1.32	3.42	4.29	4.96	6.05	4.15	5.12	3.25–3.25	0.75–0.75	....		.20
June	.12	.19	1.17	3.20	4.13	4.88	6.23	4.18	5.00	3.25–3.25	0.75–0.75	....		.18
July	.16	.20	.98	3.01	3.99	4.72	6.01	4.11	4.87	3.25–3.25	0.75–0.75	....		.18
Aug	.15	.19	.78	2.70	3.80	4.49	5.66	3.91	4.67	3.25–3.25	0.75–0.75	....		.19
Sept	.15	.19	.74	2.65	3.77	4.53	5.66	3.76	4.52	3.25–3.25	0.75–0.75	....		.19
Oct	.13	.17	.57	2.54	3.87	4.68	5.72	3.83	4.40	3.25–3.25	0.75–0.75	....		.19
Nov	.13	.17	.67	2.76	4.19	4.87	5.92	4.30	4.26	3.25–3.25	0.75–0.75	....		.19
Dec	.15	.20	.99	3.29	4.42	5.02	6.10	4.72	4.44	3.25–3.25	0.75–0.75	....		.18
2011: Jan	.15	.18	1.03	3.39	4.52	5.04	6.09	5.02	4.75	3.25–3.25	0.75–0.75	....		.17
Feb	.14	.17	1.28	3.58	4.65	5.22	6.15	4.92	4.94	3.25–3.25	0.75–0.75	....		.16
Mar	.11	.16	1.17	3.41	4.51	5.13	6.03	4.70	4.98	3.25–3.25	0.75–0.75	....		.14
Apr	.06	.12	1.21	3.46	4.50	5.16	6.02	4.71	4.91	3.25–3.25	0.75–0.75	....		.10
May	.04	.08	.94	3.17	4.29	4.96	5.78	4.34	4.86	3.25–3.25	0.75–0.75	....		.09
June	.04	.10	.71	3.00	4.23	4.99	5.75	4.22	4.61	3.25–3.25	0.75–0.75	....		.09
July	.03	.08	.68	3.00	4.27	4.93	5.76	4.24	4.55	3.25–3.25	0.75–0.75	....		.07
Aug	.05	.09	.38	2.30	3.65	4.37	5.36	3.92	4.29	3.25–3.25	0.75–0.75	....		.10
Sept	.02	.05	.35	1.98	3.18	4.09	5.27	3.79	4.36	3.25–3.25	0.75–0.75	....		.08
Oct	.02	.06	.47	2.15	3.13	3.98	5.37	3.94	4.19	3.25–3.25	0.75–0.75	....		.07
Nov	.01	.05	.39	2.01	3.02	3.87	5.14	3.95	4.26	3.25–3.25	0.75–0.75	....		.08
Dec	.02	.05	.39	1.98	2.98	3.93	5.25	3.76	4.18	3.25–3.25	0.75–0.75	....		.07
2012: Jan	.02	.06	.36	1.97	3.03	3.85	5.23	3.43	4.09	3.25–3.25	0.75–0.75	....		.08
Feb	.08	.11	.38	1.97	3.11	3.85	5.14	3.25	4.01	3.25–3.25	0.75–0.75	....		.10
Mar	.09	.14	.51	2.17	3.28	3.99	5.23	3.51	3.72	3.25–3.25	0.75–0.75	....		.13
Apr	.08	.14	.43	2.05	3.18	3.96	5.19	3.47	3.93	3.25–3.25	0.75–0.75	....		.14
May	.09	.14	.39	1.80	2.93	3.80	5.07	3.21	3.88	3.25–3.25	0.75–0.75	....		.16
June	.09	.14	.39	1.62	2.70	3.64	5.02	3.30	3.80	3.25–3.25	0.75–0.75	....		.16
July	.10	.14	.33	1.53	2.59	3.40	4.87	3.14	3.76	3.25–3.25	0.75–0.75	....		.16
Aug	.11	.14	.37	1.68	2.77	3.48	4.91	3.07	3.67	3.25–3.25	0.75–0.75	....		.13
Sept	.10	.13	.34	1.72	2.88	3.49	4.84	3.02	3.62	3.25–3.25	0.75–0.75	....		.14
Oct	.10	.15	.37	1.75	2.90	3.47	4.58	2.89	3.58	3.25–3.25	0.75–0.75	....		.16
Nov	.11	.15	.36	1.65	2.80	3.50	4.51	2.68	3.46	3.25–3.25	0.75–0.75	....		.16
Dec	.08	.12	.35	1.72	2.88	3.65	4.63	2.73	3.40	3.25–3.25	0.75–0.75	....		.16

[2] Yields on the more actively traded issues adjusted to constant maturities by the Department of the Treasury. The 30-year Treasury constant maturity series was discontinued on February 18, 2002, and reintroduced on February 9, 2006.

[3] Beginning with December 7, 2001, data for corporate Aaa series are industrial bonds only.

[4] Effective rate (in the primary market) on conventional mortgages, reflecting fees and charges as well as contract rate and assuming, on the average, repayment at end of 10 years. Rates beginning with January 1973 not strictly comparable with prior rates.

[5] For monthly data, high and low for the period. Prime rate for 1947–1948 are ranges of the rate in effect during the period.

[6] Primary credit replaced adjustment credit as the Federal Reserve's principal discount window lending program effective January 9, 2003.

[7] Since July 19, 1975, the daily effective rate is an average of the rates on a given day weighted by the volume of transactions at these rates. Prior to that date, the daily effective rate was the rate considered most representative of the day's transactions, usually the one at which most transactions occurred.

[8] From October 30, 1942 to April 24, 1946, a preferential rate of 0.50 percent was in effect for advances secured by Government securities maturing in one year or less.

Sources: Department of the Treasury, Board of Governors of the Federal Reserve System, Federal Housing Finance Agency, Moody's Investors Service, and Standard & Poor's.

TABLE B–74. Credit market borrowing, 2004–2012

[Billions of dollars; quarterly data at seasonally adjusted annual rates]

Item	2004	2005	2006	2007	2008	2009	2010	2011
NONFINANCIAL SECTORS								
Domestic	2,087.2	2,325.7	2,383.9	2,527.0	1,891.4	1,059.0	1,437.7	1,324.6
By instrument	2,087.2	2,325.7	2,383.9	2,527.0	1,891.4	1,059.0	1,437.7	1,324.6
Commercial paper	15.3	−7.7	22.4	11.3	7.7	−73.1	24.5	33.4
Treasury securities	362.5	307.3	183.7	237.5	1,239.0	1,443.7	1,579.6	1,066.8
Agency- and GSE-backed securities [1]	−0.6	−.4	−.3	−.4	.2	.1	.7	1.1
Municipal securities	203.7	198.1	170.0	235.5	92.4	155.3	99.7	−52.8
Corporate bonds	87.7	54.2	208.3	311.1	205.5	387.6	422.8	384.6
Depository institution loans n.e.c.	17.3	139.0	149.3	228.0	188.4	−303.1	−51.5	71.7
Other loans and advances	52.9	117.2	150.1	305.5	67.8	−145.7	−84.3	71.1
Mortgages	1,231.2	1,417.6	1,385.1	1,057.3	70.4	−290.1	−523.4	−337.6
Home	1,021.4	1,113.9	1,081.2	710.9	−120.4	−202.1	−354.6	−255.1
Multifamily residential	47.0	60.9	37.4	86.9	42.5	5.8	−13.7	−5.1
Commercial	150.2	233.7	263.2	254.8	126.3	−90.3	−165.0	−82.2
Farm	12.5	9.1	3.3	4.6	22.0	−3.4	9.9	4.8
Consumer credit	117.2	100.4	115.2	141.3	20.1	−115.9	−30.5	86.2
By sector	2,087.2	2,325.7	2,383.9	2,527.0	1,891.4	1,059.0	1,437.7	1,324.6
Household sector	1,051.5	1,170.3	1,165.0	843.8	−26.1	−231.6	−296.0	−209.2
Nonfinancial business	495.0	706.8	934.5	1,299.5	660.3	−266.3	83.9	518.6
Corporate	240.3	365.2	519.3	837.9	341.5	−146.4	279.0	533.9
Noncorporate	254.7	341.6	415.2	461.6	318.8	−120.0	−195.1	−15.3
State and local governments	178.8	141.7	100.9	146.7	17.9	113.0	69.5	−52.7
Federal Government	361.9	306.9	183.4	237.1	1,239.2	1,443.9	1,580.2	1,067.9
Foreign borrowing in the United States	155.3	113.0	332.6	170.3	−226.2	211.8	75.3	34.8
Commercial paper	69.2	38.6	98.4	−69.3	−71.0	59.4	−2.7	−53.5
Bonds	85.8	64.5	227.8	218.7	−158.8	163.3	59.9	57.8
Depository institution loans n.e.c.	3.8	14.5	13.8	24.1	5.1	−11.2	17.9	29.2
Other loans and advances	−3.6	−4.6	−7.4	−3.2	−1.5	.3	.2	1.4
Nonfinancial domestic and foreign borrowing	2,242.5	2,438.7	2,716.4	2,697.3	1,665.1	1,270.8	1,513.0	1,359.4
FINANCIAL SECTORS								
By instrument	938.9	1,113.1	1,340.2	1,815.2	899.1	−1,810.6	−939.3	−430.8
Open market paper	21.7	214.2	196.3	−111.4	−125.6	−448.2	−101.7	−68.1
GSE issues [1]	75.0	−84.0	35.6	282.4	271.7	−475.3	−233.8	−187.2
Agency- and GSE-backed mortgage pool securities [1]	40.8	164.5	292.6	623.3	497.0	415.3	186.9	165.3
Corporate bonds	668.5	744.6	799.3	710.4	−280.5	−587.7	−583.2	−321.5
Depository institution loans n.e.c.	33.4	15.5	−11.5	80.1	496.4	−435.4	−62.9	31.6
Other loans and advances	74.1	44.4	21.2	225.8	33.3	−282.6	−144.7	−60.0
Mortgages	25.5	14.1	6.6	4.7	6.8	3.4	.2	9.1
By sector	938.9	1,113.1	1,340.2	1,815.2	899.1	−1,810.6	−939.3	−430.8
U.S.-chartered depository institutions	81.2	54.1	43.8	222.6	−1.1	−292.3	−161.2	−73.8
Foreign banking offices in the United States	0.1	.0	−.3	.0	−.2	.0	.0	.0
Credit unions	2.3	3.3	4.2	13.4	8.3	−14.1	−.4	−2.0
Life insurance companies	3.0	.4	2.7	14.5	26.2	−6.6	−3.2	1.8
Government-sponsored enterprises	75.0	−84.0	35.6	282.4	271.7	−475.3	−233.8	−187.2
Agency- and GSE-backed mortgage pools [1]	40.8	164.5	292.6	623.3	497.0	415.3	186.9	165.3
Asset-backed securities issuers	439.6	731.0	800.5	351.5	−411.1	−738.8	−505.6	−255.4
Finance companies	134.3	33.5	34.8	34.9	−79.4	−156.2	−174.9	11.4
REITs [2]	94.6	55.4	15.5	10.2	−53.8	−50.0	−2.1	28.2
Brokers and dealers	15.2	.1	6.4	−4.0	77.7	−49.7	36.9	−37.9
Holding companies	55.7	50.1	75.0	151.9	97.3	−8.0	−16.5	−16.5
Funding corporations	−2.9	104.7	29.1	114.5	466.4	−434.8	−65.3	−64.6
ALL SECTORS, BY INSTRUMENT								
Total	3,181.4	3,551.9	4,056.6	4,512.5	2,564.3	−539.8	573.7	928.6
Open market paper	106.2	245.1	317.1	−169.4	−189.0	−461.9	−79.9	−88.2
Treasury securities	362.5	307.3	183.7	237.5	1,239.0	1,443.7	1,579.6	1,066.8
Agency- and GSE-backed securities [1]	115.2	80.0	327.9	905.3	768.9	−59.9	−46.2	−20.8
Municipal securities	203.7	198.1	170.0	235.5	92.4	155.3	99.7	−52.8
Corporate and foreign bonds	842.0	863.4	1,235.4	1,240.3	−233.8	−36.8	−100.5	120.9
Depository institution loans n.e.c.	54.5	169.0	151.7	332.1	689.9	−749.7	−96.5	132.5
Other loans and advances	123.4	156.9	163.9	528.1	99.6	−428.0	−228.8	12.5
Mortgages	1,256.7	1,431.8	1,391.7	1,062.0	77.2	−286.7	−523.1	−328.5
Consumer credit	117.2	100.4	115.2	141.3	20.1	−115.9	−30.5	86.2

[1] Government-sponsored enterprises (GSE).
[2] Real estate investment trusts (REITs).

See next page for continuation of table.

TABLE B–74. Credit market borrowing, 2004–2012—*Continued*

[Billions of dollars; quarterly data at seasonally adjusted annual rates]

Item	2011				2012		
	I	II	III	IV	I	II	III
NONFINANCIAL SECTORS							
Domestic	905.3	943.7	1,597.5	1,851.7	1,768.8	1,971.3	952.1
By instrument	905.3	943.7	1,597.5	1,851.7	1,768.8	1,971.3	952.1
Commercial paper	25.8	49.5	29.7	28.5	−2.4	34.5	−30.0
Treasury securities	849.7	791.7	1,337.1	1,288.8	1,431.5	1,182.8	690.5
Agency- and GSE-backed securities [1]	1.2	.2	1.9	1.1	−3.3	.1	−.3
Municipal securities	−70.1	−75.4	−15.1	−50.5	2.8	109.7	−6.8
Corporate bonds	404.3	461.2	322.4	350.4	470.1	370.2	514.8
Depository institution loans n.e.c.	25.1	−91.2	96.5	256.4	286.6	393.4	34.3
Other loans and advances	−12.9	121.8	80.9	94.7	−119.5	−16.3	−38.6
Mortgages	−384.5	−392.2	−304.0	−269.6	−446.0	−276.0	−329.0
Home	−290.9	−269.2	−199.6	−260.8	−342.9	−214.4	−297.8
Multifamily residential	−40.6	−2.9	3.3	19.9	1.0	26.7	43.5
Commercial	−57.2	−125.0	−112.7	−33.7	−109.0	−93.3	−79.6
Farm	4.2	4.9	5.0	5.0	5.0	5.0	5.0
Consumer credit	66.7	78.1	48.2	151.9	149.0	172.9	117.2
By sector	905.3	943.7	1,597.5	1,851.7	1,768.8	1,971.3	952.1
Household sector	−267.2	−355.9	−223.5	9.8	−120.7	160.9	−261.7
Nonfinancial business	407.3	591.1	486.6	589.3	462.4	534.4	526.4
Corporate	463.0	634.6	514.0	524.0	440.4	510.6	510.3
Noncorporate	−55.7	−43.5	−27.4	65.3	22.1	23.8	16.2
State and local governments	−85.6	−83.3	−4.5	−37.4	−1.0	93.0	−2.8
Federal Government	850.9	791.8	1,339.0	1,290.0	1,428.1	1,182.9	690.2
Foreign borrowing in the United States	319.5	80.5	−144.8	−115.9	−1.1	−108.6	98.2
Commercial paper	120.2	−51.9	−256.4	−25.9	35.8	−51.3	80.2
Bonds	151.0	120.2	69.2	−109.4	−73.6	−106.0	3.6
Depository institution loans n.e.c.	47.9	13.7	41.7	13.4	29.0	44.8	9.7
Other loans and advances	0.5	−1.5	.6	6.0	7.7	3.9	4.8
Nonfinancial domestic and foreign borrowing	1,224.9	1,024.2	1,452.7	1,735.9	1,767.7	1,862.6	1,050.4
FINANCIAL SECTORS							
By instrument	−115.1	−701.5	−402.6	−503.8	−352.7	−696.2	−163.2
Open market paper	82.9	−79.9	−51.8	−223.6	−6.2	−34.7	−31.9
GSE issues [1]	11.1	−479.9	−138.3	−141.7	−274.9	−155.0	−113.2
Agency- and GSE-backed mortgage pool securities [1]	243.6	153.0	135.8	128.9	159.6	136.2	94.9
Corporate bonds	−351.3	−376.2	−324.4	−234.0	−61.6	−431.4	−138.9
Depository institution loans n.e.c.	−51.2	158.1	56.1	−36.4	−150.8	−301.2	64.2
Other loans and advances	−57.3	−95.0	−84.4	−3.4	−29.2	65.0	−52.9
Mortgages	7.1	18.4	4.2	6.5	10.4	24.9	14.6
By sector	−115.1	−701.5	−402.6	−503.8	−352.7	−696.2	−163.2
U.S.-chartered depository institutions	−78.0	−99.1	−99.2	−18.8	−41.2	−10.1	−97.8
Foreign banking offices in the United States	0.0	.0	.0	.0	.0	.0	.0
Credit unions	−9.6	−3.5	3.7	1.6	−5.1	3.3	2.6
Life insurance companies	1.8	2.4	.9	1.9	6.6	15.7	−.2
Government-sponsored enterprises	11.1	−479.9	−138.3	−141.7	−274.9	−155.0	−113.2
Agency- and GSE-backed mortgage pools [1]	243.6	153.0	135.8	128.9	159.6	136.2	94.9
Asset-backed securities issuers	−306.3	−229.2	−284.6	−201.6	−239.6	−260.2	−163.3
Finance companies	21.2	−94.6	129.1	−10.3	−25.2	−123.1	80.5
REITs [2]	44.5	16.9	13.9	37.3	26.6	57.3	23.4
Brokers and dealers	−5.9	−72.7	−43.4	−29.7	24.9	16.5	−65.2
Holding companies	83.6	46.4	−83.6	−112.2	12.3	−360.2	57.8
Funding corporations	−121.0	58.9	−37.0	−159.2	3.3	−16.7	17.3
ALL SECTORS, BY INSTRUMENT							
Total	1,109.8	322.7	1,050.1	1,232.0	1,415.0	1,166.4	887.2
Open market paper	228.9	−82.3	−278.5	−221.0	27.2	−51.4	18.3
Treasury securities	849.7	791.7	1,337.1	1,288.8	1,431.5	1,182.8	690.5
Agency- and GSE-backed securities [1]	255.9	−326.7	−.5	−11.7	−118.7	−18.7	−18.6
Municipal securities	−70.1	−75.4	−15.1	−50.5	2.8	109.7	−6.8
Corporate and foreign bonds	204.0	205.2	67.2	7.0	334.9	−167.3	379.5
Depository institution loans n.e.c.	21.8	80.6	194.4	233.3	164.9	137.0	108.2
Other loans and advances	−69.6	25.2	−2.9	97.3	−141.0	52.7	−86.7
Mortgages	−377.4	−373.8	−299.8	−263.1	−435.5	−251.1	−314.4
Consumer credit	66.7	78.1	48.2	151.9	149.0	172.9	117.2

Source: Board of Governors of the Federal Reserve System.

TABLE B–75. Mortgage debt outstanding by type of property and of financing, 1955–2012

[Billions of dollars]

End of year or quarter	All proper-ties	Farm proper-ties	Nonfarm properties				Nonfarm properties by type of mortgage					
							Government underwritten				Conventional[2]	
			Total	1- to 4- family houses	Multi-family proper-ties	Com-mercial proper-ties	Total[1]	1- to 4-family houses			Total	1- to 4-family houses
								Total	FHA-insured	VA-guar-anteed		
1955	129.9	9.0	120.9	88.2	14.3	18.3	42.9	38.9	14.3	24.6	78.0	49.3
1956	144.5	9.8	134.6	99.0	14.9	20.7	47.8	43.9	15.5	28.4	86.8	55.1
1957	156.5	10.4	146.1	107.6	15.3	23.2	51.6	47.2	16.5	30.7	94.6	60.4
1958	171.8	11.1	160.7	117.7	16.8	26.1	55.2	50.1	19.7	30.4	105.5	67.6
1959	191.6	12.1	179.5	131.6	18.7	29.2	59.3	53.8	23.8	30.0	120.2	77.7
1960	208.3	12.8	195.4	142.7	20.3	32.4	62.3	56.4	26.7	29.7	133.1	86.3
1961	229.1	13.9	215.1	155.8	23.0	36.4	65.6	59.1	29.5	29.6	149.5	96.7
1962	252.7	15.2	237.5	170.5	25.8	41.1	69.4	62.2	32.3	29.9	168.1	108.3
1963	280.0	16.8	263.1	187.9	29.0	46.2	73.4	65.9	35.0	30.9	189.7	122.0
1964	307.4	18.9	288.4	204.8	33.6	50.0	77.2	69.2	38.3	30.9	211.3	135.6
1965	334.7	21.2	313.5	221.9	37.2	54.5	81.2	73.1	42.0	31.1	232.4	148.8
1966	357.9	23.1	334.8	234.4	40.3	60.1	84.1	76.1	44.8	31.3	250.7	158.3
1967	382.5	25.0	357.4	248.7	43.9	64.8	88.2	79.9	47.4	32.5	269.3	168.8
1968	412.1	27.3	384.8	266.1	47.3	71.4	93.4	84.4	50.6	33.8	291.4	181.6
1969	442.5	29.2	413.3	283.9	52.3	77.1	100.2	90.2	54.5	35.7	313.1	193.7
1970	474.5	30.5	444.0	298.0	60.1	85.8	109.2	97.3	59.9	37.3	334.7	200.8
1971	525.0	32.4	492.7	326.4	70.1	96.2	120.7	105.2	65.7	39.5	371.9	221.2
1972	598.2	35.4	562.9	367.0	82.8	113.1	131.1	113.0	68.2	44.7	431.7	254.1
1973	673.9	39.8	634.1	408.7	93.2	132.3	135.0	116.2	66.2	50.0	499.1	292.4
1974	734.0	44.9	689.1	441.5	100.0	147.5	140.2	121.3	65.1	56.2	548.8	320.2
1975	793.9	49.9	744.0	483.2	100.7	160.1	147.0	127.7	66.1	61.6	597.0	355.5
1976	881.1	55.4	825.7	546.4	105.9	173.4	154.0	133.5	66.5	67.0	671.6	412.9
1977	1,013.0	63.8	949.2	642.5	114.3	192.3	161.7	141.6	68.0	73.6	787.4	500.9
1978	1,165.5	72.8	1,092.8	753.7	125.2	213.9	176.4	153.4	71.4	82.0	916.4	600.3
1979	1,331.5	86.8	1,244.7	870.8	135.0	238.8	199.0	172.9	81.0	92.0	1,045.7	697.9
1980	1,467.6	97.5	1,370.1	969.7	141.1	259.3	225.1	195.2	93.6	101.6	1,145.1	774.5
1981	1,591.5	107.2	1,484.3	1,046.5	139.2	298.6	238.9	207.6	101.3	106.2	1,245.4	838.9
1982	1,676.1	111.3	1,564.8	1,091.1	141.1	332.6	248.9	217.9	108.0	109.9	1,315.9	873.3
1983	1,871.7	113.7	1,757.9	1,214.9	154.3	388.6	279.8	248.8	127.4	121.4	1,478.1	966.1
1984	2,120.6	112.4	2,008.2	1,358.9	177.4	471.9	294.8	265.9	136.7	129.1	1,713.4	1,093.0
1985	2,370.3	94.1	2,276.2	1,528.8	205.9	541.5	328.3	288.8	153.0	135.8	1,947.8	1,240.0
1986	2,657.9	84.0	2,573.9	1,732.8	239.2	601.9	370.5	328.6	185.5	143.1	2,203.4	1,404.2
1987	2,996.2	75.8	2,920.4	1,960.9	261.6	697.9	431.4	387.9	235.5	152.4	2,489.0	1,573.0
1988	3,313.1	70.8	3,242.3	2,194.7	278.1	769.6	459.7	414.2	258.8	155.4	2,782.6	1,780.5
1989	3,585.4	68.8	3,516.6	2,428.1	288.9	799.6	486.8	440.1	282.8	157.3	3,029.8	1,988.0
1990	3,788.2	67.6	3,720.6	2,613.6	287.4	819.6	517.9	470.9	310.9	160.0	3,202.7	2,142.7
1991	3,929.8	67.5	3,862.4	2,771.9	280.4	810.1	537.2	493.3	330.6	162.7	3,325.2	2,278.6
1992	4,043.4	67.9	3,975.5	2,942.0	264.4	769.1	533.3	489.8	326.0	163.8	3,442.2	2,452.2
1993	4,174.8	68.4	4,106.4	3,100.9	259.4	746.0	513.4	469.5	303.2	166.2	3,592.9	2,631.4
1994	4,339.0	69.9	4,269.1	3,278.2	258.7	732.2	559.3	514.2	336.8	177.3	3,709.8	2,764.0
1995	4,524.8	71.7	4,453.0	3,445.4	264.7	743.0	584.3	537.1	352.3	184.7	3,868.8	2,908.3
1996	4,792.4	74.4	4,718.0	3,668.4	277.5	772.0	620.3	571.2	379.2	192.0	4,097.7	3,097.3
1997	5,104.8	78.5	5,026.3	3,902.5	290.9	832.9	656.7	605.7	405.7	200.0	4,369.6	3,296.8
1998	5,589.5	83.1	5,506.4	4,259.0	325.1	922.4	674.1	623.8	417.9	205.9	4,832.4	3,635.2
1999	6,195.1	87.2	6,107.9	4,683.1	366.5	1,058.4	731.5	678.8	462.3	216.5	5,376.4	4,004.3
2000	6,752.6	84.7	6,667.9	5,106.6	396.2	1,165.2	773.1	720.0	499.9	220.1	5,894.8	4,386.6
2001	7,460.4	88.5	7,371.9	5,658.5	437.9	1,275.4	772.7	718.5	497.4	221.2	6,599.2	4,940.0
2002	8,361.2	95.4	8,265.8	6,413.3	477.5	1,375.1	759.3	704.0	486.2	217.7	7,506.5	5,709.3
2003	9,376.2	83.2	9,293.1	7,240.1	550.1	1,502.9	709.2	653.3	438.7	214.6	8,583.9	6,586.8
2004	10,650.7	95.7	10,555.0	8,279.3	600.2	1,675.6	661.5	605.4	398.1	207.3	9,893.5	7,674.0
2005	12,097.1	104.8	11,992.9	9,408.5	657.4	1,927.1	606.6	550.4	348.4	202.0	11,386.3	8,858.0
2006	13,481.9	108.0	13,373.9	10,484.3	694.4	2,195.1	600.2	543.5	336.9	206.6	12,773.7	9,940.9
2007	14,566.0	112.7	14,453.3	11,217.0	776.4	2,459.9	609.2	552.6	342.6	210.0	13,844.2	10,664.4
2008	14,661.3	133.0	14,528.3	11,127.5	828.1	2,572.7	807.2	750.7	534.0	216.7	13,721.0	10,376.8
2009	14,370.0	132.0	14,238.0	10,918.3	836.5	2,483.3	1,005.0	944.3	752.6	191.7	13,233.0	9,974.0
2010	13,712.3	140.6	13,571.7	10,413.6	825.5	2,332.5	1,227.7	1,156.2	934.4	221.8	12,344.0	9,257.4
2011	13,383.8	145.9	13,237.9	10,158.0	830.2	2,249.7	1,368.6	1,291.3	1,036.0	255.3	11,869.3	8,866.7
2011: I	13,617.0	141.5	13,475.4	10,339.0	824.8	2,311.7	1,269.2	1,196.6	966.4	230.2	12,206.2	9,142.3
II	13,525.3	143.4	13,381.9	10,272.3	824.0	2,285.6	1,307.7	1,233.3	994.6	238.7	12,074.2	9,039.0
III	13,443.8	144.7	13,299.1	10,214.2	825.1	2,259.8	1,360.0	1,283.5	1,035.2	248.2	11,939.1	8,930.8
IV	13,383.8	145.9	13,237.9	10,158.0	830.2	2,249.7	1,368.6	1,291.3	1,036.0	255.3	11,869.3	8,866.7
2012: I	13,276.2	147.2	13,129.0	10,071.5	829.9	2,227.7	1,462.6	1,384.0	1,120.6	263.4	11,666.5	8,687.5
II	13,209.2	148.4	13,060.8	10,013.2	836.0	2,211.5	3,269.3	3,188.1	2,912.5	275.6	9,791.5	6,825.1
III p	13,119.2	149.7	12,969.5	9,926.0	846.6	2,196.9	1,529.5	1,445.1	1,158.4	286.6	11,440.0	8,480.9

[1] Includes Federal Housing Administration (FHA)–insured multi-family properties, not shown separately.
[2] Derived figures. Total includes multi-family and commercial properties with conventional mortgages, not shown separately.

Source: Board of Governors of the Federal Reserve System, based on data from various Government and private organizations.

TABLE B-76. Mortgage debt outstanding by holder, 1955–2012

[Billions of dollars]

End of year or quarter	Total	Major financial institutions				Other holders		
		Total	Savings institutions [1]	Commercial banks [2]	Life insurance companies	Federal and related agencies [3]	Mortgage pools or trusts [4]	Individuals and others
1955	129.9	99.3	48.9	21.0	29.4	5.2	0.1	25.3
1956	144.5	111.2	55.5	22.7	33.0	6.0	.1	27.1
1957	156.5	119.7	61.2	23.3	35.2	7.5	.2	29.1
1958	171.8	131.5	68.9	25.5	37.1	7.8	.2	32.3
1959	191.6	145.5	78.1	28.1	39.2	10.0	.2	35.9
1960	208.3	157.5	86.9	28.8	41.8	11.3	.2	39.3
1961	229.1	172.6	98.0	30.4	44.2	11.9	.3	44.2
1962	252.7	192.5	111.1	34.5	46.9	12.2	.4	47.6
1963	280.0	217.1	127.2	39.4	50.5	11.3	.5	51.0
1964	307.4	241.0	141.9	44.0	55.2	11.6	.6	54.1
1965	334.7	264.6	154.9	49.7	60.0	12.7	.9	56.6
1966	357.9	280.7	161.8	54.4	64.6	16.2	1.3	59.7
1967	382.5	298.7	172.3	58.9	67.5	19.0	2.0	62.8
1968	412.1	319.7	184.3	65.5	70.0	22.6	2.5	67.3
1969	442.5	338.9	196.4	70.5	72.0	27.9	3.2	72.4
1970	474.5	355.9	208.3	73.3	74.4	33.6	4.8	80.2
1971	525.0	394.2	236.2	82.5	75.5	36.8	9.5	84.5
1972	598.2	449.9	273.6	99.3	76.9	40.1	14.4	93.8
1973	673.9	505.4	305.0	119.1	81.4	46.6	18.0	103.9
1974	734.0	542.6	324.2	132.1	86.2	58.4	23.8	109.2
1975	793.9	581.2	355.8	136.2	89.2	67.0	34.1	111.5
1976	881.1	647.5	404.6	151.3	91.6	66.9	49.8	116.9
1977	1,013.0	745.2	469.4	179.0	96.8	70.2	70.3	127.3
1978	1,165.5	848.2	528.0	214.0	106.2	81.9	88.6	146.8
1979	1,331.5	938.2	574.6	245.2	118.4	97.3	118.7	177.3
1980	1,467.6	996.8	603.1	262.7	131.1	114.6	145.9	210.4
1981	1,591.5	1,040.5	618.5	284.2	137.7	126.4	168.0	256.6
1982	1,676.1	1,021.3	578.1	301.3	142.0	138.7	224.4	291.6
1983	1,871.7	1,108.1	626.6	330.5	151.0	148.3	297.3	317.9
1984	2,120.6	1,247.8	709.7	381.4	156.7	158.5	350.7	363.7
1985	2,370.3	1,363.5	760.5	431.2	171.8	166.9	438.6	401.2
1986	2,657.9	1,476.5	778.0	504.7	193.8	202.1	549.5	429.8
1987	2,996.2	1,667.6	860.5	594.8	212.4	188.5	700.8	439.2
1988	3,313.1	1,834.3	924.5	676.9	232.9	192.5	785.7	500.7
1989	3,585.4	1,935.2	910.3	770.7	254.2	197.8	922.2	530.2
1990	3,788.2	1,918.8	801.6	849.3	267.9	239.0	1,085.9	544.5
1991	3,929.8	1,846.2	705.4	881.3	259.5	266.0	1,269.6	548.1
1992	4,043.4	1,770.4	627.9	900.5	242.0	286.1	1,440.0	547.0
1993	4,174.8	1,770.1	598.4	947.8	223.9	326.0	1,561.1	517.5
1994	4,339.0	1,824.7	596.2	1,012.7	215.8	315.6	1,696.9	501.9
1995	4,524.8	1,900.1	596.8	1,090.2	213.1	307.9	1,812.1	504.7
1996	4,792.4	1,981.9	628.3	1,145.4	208.2	294.4	1,989.2	527.0
1997	5,104.8	2,084.0	631.8	1,245.3	206.8	285.2	2,165.9	569.7
1998	5,589.5	2,194.6	644.0	1,337.0	213.6	291.9	2,486.7	616.4
1999	6,195.1	2,394.3	668.1	1,495.4	230.8	319.8	2,831.8	649.2
2000	6,752.6	2,619.0	723.0	1,660.1	235.9	339.9	3,097.3	696.4
2001	7,460.4	2,790.9	758.0	1,789.8	243.0	372.0	3,556.7	740.8
2002	8,361.2	3,089.3	781.0	2,058.3	250.0	432.3	3,994.5	845.1
2003	9,376.2	3,387.3	870.6	2,255.8	260.9	694.1	4,353.4	941.5
2004	10,650.7	3,926.3	1,057.4	2,595.6	273.3	703.2	4,834.3	1,186.9
2005	12,097.7	4,396.2	1,152.7	2,958.0	285.5	665.4	5,700.7	1,335.4
2006	13,481.9	4,783.6	1,076.8	3,403.1	303.8	687.5	6,622.5	1,388.3
2007	14,566.0	5,064.6	1,094.0	3,644.4	326.2	725.5	7,422.3	1,353.7
2008	14,661.3	5,044.4	860.6	3,841.3	342.4	801.2	7,564.7	1,251.1
2009	14,370.0	4,778.1	633.3	3,818.6	326.1	816.1	7,612.1	1,163.8
2010	13,712.3	4,583.5	614.8	3,651.2	317.5	5,127.5	3,047.3	953.9
2011	13,383.8	4,448.2	586.2	3,529.5	332.5	5,034.6	2,994.7	906.3
2011: I	13,617.0	4,469.6	600.2	3,550.9	318.4	5,162.4	3,041.5	943.6
II	13,525.3	4,435.6	590.9	3,521.9	322.8	5,127.8	3,029.2	932.8
III	13,443.8	4,433.8	589.4	3,515.8	328.6	5,073.9	3,020.6	915.4
IV	13,383.8	4,448.2	586.2	3,529.5	332.5	5,034.6	2,994.7	906.3
2012: I	13,276.2	4,385.3	502.0	3,546.6	336.7	5,034.5	2,960.7	895.7
II	13,209.2	4,390.4	498.2	3,551.8	340.5	4,982.3	2,955.3	881.1
III *p*	13,119.2	4,351.4	456.9	3,551.0	343.5	4,956.5	2,931.3	879.9

[1] Includes savings banks and savings and loan associations. Data reported by Federal Savings and Loan Insurance Corporation–insured institutions include loans in process for 1987 and exclude loans in process beginning with 1988.

[2] Includes loans held by nondeposit trust companies but not loans held by bank trust departments.

[3] Includes Government National Mortgage Association (GNMA or Ginnie Mae), Federal Housing Administration, Veterans Administration, Farmers Home Administration (FmHA), Federal Deposit Insurance Corporation, Resolution Trust Corporation (through 1995), and in earlier years Reconstruction Finance Corporation, Homeowners Loan Corporation, Federal Farm Mortgage Corporation, and Public Housing Administration. Also includes U.S.-sponsored agencies such as Federal National Mortgage Association (FNMA or Fannie Mae), Federal Land Banks, Federal Home Loan Mortgage Corporation (FHLMC or Freddie Mac), Federal Agricultural Mortgage Corporation (Farmer Mac, beginning 1994), Federal Home Loan Banks (beginning 1997), and mortgage pass-through securities issued or guaranteed by GNMA, FHLMC, FNMA, FmHA, or Farmer Mac. Other U.S. agencies (amounts small or current separate data not readily available) included with "individuals and others."

[4] Includes private mortgage pools.

Source: Board of Governors of the Federal Reserve System, based on data from various Government and private organizations.

TABLE B–77. Consumer credit outstanding, 1961–2012

[Amount outstanding (end of month); millions of dollars, seasonally adjusted]

Year and month	Total consumer credit [1]	Revolving	Nonrevolving [2]
December:			
1961	62,248.53		62,248.53
1962	68,126.72		68,126.72
1963	76,581.45		76,581.45
1964	85,959.57		85,959.57
1965	95,954.72		95,954.72
1966	101,788.22		101,788.22
1967	106,842.64		106,842.64
1968	117,399.09		115,357.55
1969	127,156.18	3,604.84	123,551.35
1970	131,551.55	4,961.46	126,590.09
1971	146,930.18	8,245.33	138,684.84
1972	166,189.10	9,379.24	156,809.86
1973	190,086.31	11,342.22	178,744.09
1974	198,917.84	13,241.26	185,676.58
1975	204,002.00	14,495.27	189,506.73
1976	225,721.59	16,489.05	209,232.54
1977	260,562.70	37,414.82	223,147.88
1978	306,100.39	45,690.95	260,409.43
1979	348,589.11	53,596.43	294,992.67
1980	351,920.05	54,970.05	296,950.00
1981	371,301.44	60,928.00	310,373.44
1982	389,848.74	66,348.30	323,500.44
1983	437,068.86	79,027.25	358,041.61
1984	517,278.98	100,385.63	416,893.35
1985	599,711.23	124,465.80	475,245.43
1986	654,750.24	141,068.15	513,682.08
1987	686,318.77	160,853.91	525,464.86
1988 [3]	731,917.76	184,593.12	547,324.64
1989	794,612.18	211,229.83	583,382.34
1990	808,230.57	238,642.62	569,587.95
1991	798,028.97	263,768.55	534,260.42
1992	806,118.69	278,449.67	527,669.02
1993	865,650.58	309,908.02	555,742.56
1994	997,301.74	365,569.56	631,732.19
1995	1,140,744.36	443,920.09	696,824.27
1996	1,253,437.09	507,516.57	745,920.52
1997	1,324,757.33	540,005.56	784,751.77
1998	1,420,996.44	581,414.78	839,581.66
1999	1,531,105.96	610,696.47	920,409.49
2000	1,716,969.72	682,646.37	1,034,323.35
2001	1,867,852.87	714,840.73	1,153,012.14
2002	1,972,112.21	750,947.45	1,221,164.76
2003	2,077,360.69	768,258.31	1,309,102.38
2004	2,192,246.17	799,552.18	1,392,693.99
2005	2,290,928.13	829,518.36	1,461,409.78
2006	2,384,965.33	929,429.78	1,455,535.55
2007	2,528,775.42	1,008,127.28	1,520,648.14
2008	2,548,862.43	1,010,282.04	1,538,580.39
2009	2,438,736.82	921,861.60	1,516,875.22
2010	2,545,282.88	850,151.66	1,695,131.22
2011	2,631,510.34	851,448.52	1,780,061.81
2011: Jan	2,544,892.95	845,469.23	1,699,423.73
Feb	2,553,773.09	843,296.86	1,710,476.23
Mar	2,561,958.28	848,420.57	1,713,537.71
Apr	2,564,359.03	842,765.04	1,721,593.99
May	2,572,348.56	848,895.93	1,723,452.63
June	2,581,495.29	850,225.36	1,731,269.93
July	2,591,348.89	847,065.37	1,744,283.52
Aug	2,583,147.01	847,261.30	1,735,885.71
Sept	2,593,538.51	847,694.65	1,745,843.85
Oct	2,597,148.26	848,668.24	1,748,480.03
Nov	2,615,280.16	852,390.05	1,762,890.11
Dec	2,631,510.34	851,448.52	1,780,061.81
2012: Jan	2,646,312.10	848,502.46	1,797,809.63
Feb	2,655,344.21	848,995.39	1,806,348.82
Mar	2,668,764.36	852,798.89	1,815,965.46
Apr	2,679,362.86	849,042.02	1,830,320.84
May	2,698,795.72	858,753.82	1,840,041.90
June	2,709,149.21	855,543.63	1,853,605.58
July	2,707,369.33	851,320.80	1,856,048.53
Aug	2,726,375.25	856,350.47	1,870,024.78
Sept	2,738,361.55	854,138.08	1,884,223.46
Oct	2,752,437.33	857,574.19	1,894,863.14
Nov p	2,768,482.45	858,391.10	1,910,091.35

[1] Covers most short- and intermediate-term credit extended to individuals. Credit secured by real estate is excluded.
[2] Includes automobile loans and all other loans not included in revolving credit, such as loans for mobile homes, education, boats, trailers, or vacations. These loans may be secured or unsecured. Beginning with 1977, includes student loans extended by the Federal Government and by SLM Holding Corporation.
[3] Data newly available in January 1989 result in breaks in these series between December 1988 and subsequent months.

Source: Board of Governors of the Federal Reserve System.

TABLE B–78. Federal receipts, outlays, surplus or deficit, and debt, fiscal years, 1946–2013

[Billions of dollars; fiscal years]

Fiscal year or period	Total			On-budget			Off-budget			Federal debt (end of period)		Addendum: Gross domestic product
	Receipts	Outlays	Surplus or deficit (–)	Receipts	Outlays	Surplus or deficit (–)	Receipts	Outlays	Surplus or deficit (–)	Gross Federal	Held by the public	
1946	39.3	55.2	–15.9	38.1	55.0	–17.0	1.2	0.2	1.0	271.0	241.9	222.6
1947	38.5	34.5	4.0	37.1	34.2	2.9	1.5	.3	1.2	257.1	224.3	233.2
1948	41.6	29.8	11.8	39.9	29.4	10.5	1.6	.4	1.2	252.0	216.3	256.6
1949	39.4	38.8	.6	37.7	38.4	–.7	1.7	.4	1.3	252.6	214.3	271.3
1950	39.4	42.6	–3.1	37.3	42.0	–4.7	2.1	.5	1.6	256.9	219.0	273.1
1951	51.6	45.5	6.1	48.5	44.2	4.3	3.1	1.3	1.8	255.3	214.3	320.2
1952	66.2	67.7	–1.5	62.6	66.0	–3.4	3.6	1.7	1.9	259.1	214.8	348.7
1953	69.6	76.1	–6.5	65.5	73.8	–8.3	4.1	2.3	1.8	266.0	218.4	372.5
1954	69.7	70.9	–1.2	65.1	67.9	–2.8	4.6	2.9	1.7	270.8	224.5	377.0
1955	65.5	68.4	–3.0	60.4	64.5	–4.1	5.1	4.0	1.1	274.4	226.6	395.9
1956	74.6	70.6	3.9	68.2	65.7	2.5	6.4	5.0	1.5	272.7	222.2	427.0
1957	80.0	76.6	3.4	73.2	70.6	2.6	6.8	6.0	.8	272.3	219.3	450.9
1958	79.6	82.4	–2.8	71.6	74.9	–3.3	8.0	7.5	.5	279.7	226.3	460.0
1959	79.2	92.1	–12.8	71.0	83.1	–12.1	8.3	9.0	–.7	287.5	234.7	490.2
1960	92.5	92.2	.3	81.9	81.3	.5	10.6	10.9	–.2	290.5	236.8	518.9
1961	94.4	97.7	–3.3	82.3	86.0	–3.8	12.1	11.7	.4	292.6	238.4	529.9
1962	99.7	106.8	–7.1	87.4	93.3	–5.9	12.3	13.5	–1.3	302.9	248.0	567.8
1963	106.6	111.3	–4.8	92.4	96.4	–4.0	14.2	15.0	–.8	310.3	254.0	599.2
1964	112.6	118.5	–5.9	96.2	102.8	–6.5	16.4	15.7	.6	316.1	256.8	641.5
1965	116.8	118.2	–1.4	100.1	101.7	–1.6	16.7	16.5	.2	322.3	260.8	687.5
1966	130.8	134.5	–3.7	111.7	114.8	–3.1	19.1	19.7	–.6	328.5	263.7	755.8
1967	148.8	157.5	–8.6	124.4	137.0	–12.6	24.4	20.4	4.0	340.4	266.6	810.0
1968	153.0	178.1	–25.2	128.1	155.8	–27.7	24.9	22.3	2.6	368.7	289.5	868.4
1969	186.9	183.6	3.2	157.9	158.4	–.5	29.0	25.2	3.7	365.8	278.1	948.1
1970	192.8	195.6	–2.8	159.3	168.0	–8.7	33.5	27.6	5.9	380.9	283.2	1,012.7
1971	187.1	210.2	–23.0	151.3	177.3	–26.1	35.8	32.8	3.0	408.2	303.0	1,080.0
1972	207.3	230.7	–23.4	167.4	193.5	–26.1	39.9	37.2	2.7	435.9	322.4	1,176.5
1973	230.8	245.7	–14.9	184.7	200.0	–15.2	46.1	45.7	.3	466.3	340.9	1,310.6
1974	263.2	269.4	–6.1	209.3	216.5	–7.2	53.9	52.9	1.1	483.9	343.7	1,438.5
1975	279.1	332.3	–53.2	216.6	270.8	–54.1	62.5	61.6	.9	541.9	394.7	1,560.2
1976	298.1	371.8	–73.7	231.7	301.1	–69.4	66.4	70.7	–4.3	629.0	477.4	1,738.1
Transition quarter ..	81.2	96.0	–14.7	63.2	77.3	–14.1	18.0	18.7	–.7	643.6	495.5	459.4
1977	355.6	409.2	–53.7	278.7	328.7	–49.9	76.8	80.5	–3.7	706.4	549.1	1,973.5
1978	399.6	458.7	–59.2	314.2	369.6	–55.4	85.4	89.2	–3.8	776.6	607.1	2,217.5
1979	463.3	504.0	–40.7	365.3	404.9	–39.6	98.0	99.1	–1.1	829.5	640.3	2,501.4
1980	517.1	590.9	–73.8	403.9	477.0	–73.1	113.2	113.9	–.7	909.0	711.9	2,724.2
1981	599.3	678.2	–79.0	469.1	543.0	–73.9	130.2	135.3	–5.1	994.8	789.4	3,057.0
1982	617.8	745.7	–128.0	474.3	594.9	–120.6	143.5	150.9	–7.4	1,137.3	924.6	3,223.7
1983	600.6	808.4	–207.8	453.2	660.9	–207.7	147.3	147.4	–.1	1,371.7	1,137.3	3,440.7
1984	666.4	851.8	–185.4	500.4	685.6	–185.3	166.1	166.2	–.1	1,564.6	1,307.0	3,844.4
1985	734.0	946.3	–212.3	547.9	769.4	–221.5	186.2	176.9	9.2	1,817.4	1,507.3	4,146.3
1986	769.2	990.4	–221.2	568.9	806.8	–237.9	200.2	183.5	16.7	2,120.5	1,740.6	4,403.9
1987	854.3	1,004.0	–149.7	640.9	809.2	–168.4	213.4	194.8	18.6	2,346.0	1,889.8	4,651.4
1988	909.2	1,064.4	–155.2	667.7	860.0	–192.3	241.5	204.4	37.1	2,601.1	2,051.6	5,008.5
1989	991.1	1,143.7	–152.6	727.4	932.8	–205.4	263.7	210.9	52.8	2,867.8	2,190.7	5,399.5
1990	1,032.0	1,253.0	–221.0	750.3	1,027.9	–277.6	281.7	225.1	56.6	3,206.3	2,411.6	5,734.5
1991	1,055.0	1,324.2	–269.2	761.1	1,082.5	–321.4	293.9	241.7	52.2	3,598.2	2,689.0	5,930.5
1992	1,091.2	1,381.5	–290.3	788.8	1,129.2	–340.4	302.4	252.3	50.1	4,001.8	2,999.7	6,242.0
1993	1,154.3	1,409.4	–255.1	842.4	1,142.8	–300.4	311.9	266.6	45.3	4,351.0	3,248.4	6,587.3
1994	1,258.6	1,461.8	–203.2	923.5	1,182.4	–258.8	335.0	279.4	55.7	4,643.3	3,433.1	6,976.6
1995	1,351.8	1,515.7	–164.0	1,000.7	1,227.1	–226.4	351.1	288.7	62.4	4,920.6	3,604.4	7,341.1
1996	1,453.1	1,560.5	–107.4	1,085.6	1,259.6	–174.0	367.5	300.9	66.6	5,181.5	3,734.1	7,718.3
1997	1,579.2	1,601.1	–21.9	1,187.2	1,290.5	–103.2	392.0	310.6	81.4	5,369.2	3,772.3	8,211.7
1998	1,721.7	1,652.5	69.3	1,305.9	1,335.9	–29.9	415.8	316.6	99.2	5,478.2	3,721.1	8,663.0
1999	1,827.5	1,701.8	125.6	1,383.0	1,381.1	1.9	444.5	320.8	123.7	5,605.5	3,632.4	9,208.4
2000	2,025.2	1,789.0	236.2	1,544.6	1,458.2	86.4	480.6	330.8	149.8	5,628.7	3,409.8	9,821.0
2001	1,991.1	1,862.8	128.2	1,483.6	1,516.0	–32.4	507.5	346.8	160.7	5,769.9	3,319.6	10,225.3
2002	1,853.1	2,010.9	–157.8	1,337.8	1,655.2	–317.4	515.3	355.7	159.7	6,198.4	3,540.4	10,543.9
2003	1,782.3	2,159.9	–377.6	1,258.5	1,796.9	–538.4	523.8	363.0	160.8	6,760.0	3,913.4	10,980.2
2004	1,880.1	2,292.8	–412.7	1,345.4	1,913.3	–568.0	534.7	379.5	155.2	7,354.7	4,295.5	11,676.0
2005	2,153.6	2,472.0	–318.3	1,576.1	2,069.7	–493.6	577.5	402.2	175.3	7,905.3	4,592.2	12,428.6
2006	2,406.9	2,655.1	–248.2	1,798.5	2,233.0	–434.5	608.4	422.1	186.3	8,451.4	4,829.0	13,206.5
2007	2,568.0	2,728.7	–160.7	1,932.9	2,275.0	–342.2	635.1	453.6	181.5	8,950.7	5,035.1	13,861.4
2008	2,524.0	2,982.5	–458.6	1,865.9	2,507.8	–641.8	658.0	474.8	183.3	9,986.1	5,803.1	14,334.4
2009	2,105.0	3,517.7	–1,412.7	1,451.0	3,000.7	–1,549.7	654.0	517.0	137.0	11,875.9	7,544.7	13,960.7
2010	2,162.7	3,457.1	–1,294.4	1,531.0	2,902.4	–1,371.4	631.7	554.7	77.0	13,528.8	9,018.9	14,348.4
2011	2,303.5	3,603.1	–1,299.6	1,737.7	3,104.5	–1,366.8	565.8	498.6	67.2	14,764.2	10,128.2	14,929.4
2012 (estimates) [1]..	2,441.9	3,652.6	–1,210.7	1,870.3	3,147.3	–1,277.0	571.6	505.3	66.3	16,207.0	11,413.7	15,538.1
2013 (estimates) [1]..	2,763.6	3,754.2	–990.6	2,090.5	3,122.3	–1,031.8	673.1	631.9	41.2	17,482.7	12,571.9	16,225.6

[1] Estimates from *Mid-Session Review*, Budget of the U.S. Government, Fiscal Year 2013, issued July 2012.

Note: Fiscal years through 1976 were on a July 1–June 30 basis; beginning with October 1976 (fiscal year 1977), the fiscal year is on an October 1–September 30 basis. The transition quarter is the three-month period from July 1, 1976 through September 30, 1976.

See *Budget of the United States Government, Fiscal Year 2013*, for additional information.

Sources: Department of Commerce (Bureau of Economic Analysis), Department of the Treasury, and Office of Management and Budget.

TABLE B–79. Federal receipts, outlays, surplus or deficit, and debt, as percent of gross domestic product, fiscal years 1940–2013

[Percent; fiscal years]

Fiscal year or period	Receipts	Outlays		Surplus or deficit (−)	Federal debt (end of period)	
		Total	National defense		Gross Federal	Held by public
1940	6.8	9.8	1.7	−3.0	52.4	44.2
1941	7.6	12.0	5.6	−4.3	50.4	42.3
1942	10.1	24.3	17.8	−14.2	54.9	47.0
1943	13.3	43.6	37.0	−30.3	79.1	70.9
1944	20.9	43.6	37.8	−22.7	97.6	88.3
1945	20.4	41.9	37.5	−21.5	117.5	106.2
1946	17.7	24.8	19.2	−7.2	121.7	108.7
1947	16.5	14.8	5.5	1.7	110.3	96.2
1948	16.2	11.6	3.5	4.6	98.2	84.3
1949	14.5	14.3	4.8	.2	93.1	79.0
1950	14.4	15.6	5.0	−1.1	94.1	80.2
1951	16.1	14.2	7.4	1.9	79.7	66.9
1952	19.0	19.4	13.2	−.4	74.3	61.6
1953	18.7	20.4	14.2	−1.7	71.4	58.6
1954	18.5	18.8	13.1	−.3	71.8	59.5
1955	16.5	17.3	10.8	−.8	69.3	57.2
1956	17.5	16.5	10.0	.9	63.9	52.0
1957	17.7	17.0	10.1	.8	60.4	48.6
1958	17.3	17.9	10.2	−.6	60.8	49.2
1959	16.2	18.8	10.0	−2.6	58.6	47.9
1960	17.8	17.8	9.3	.1	56.0	45.6
1961	17.8	18.4	9.4	−.6	55.2	45.0
1962	17.6	18.8	9.2	−1.3	53.4	43.7
1963	17.8	18.6	8.9	−.8	51.8	42.4
1964	17.6	18.5	8.5	−.9	49.3	40.0
1965	17.0	17.2	7.4	−.2	46.9	37.9
1966	17.3	17.8	7.7	−.5	43.5	34.9
1967	18.4	19.4	8.8	−1.1	42.0	32.9
1968	17.6	20.5	9.4	−2.9	42.5	33.3
1969	19.7	19.4	8.7	.3	38.6	29.3
1970	19.0	19.3	8.1	−.3	37.6	28.0
1971	17.3	19.5	7.3	−2.1	37.8	28.1
1972	17.6	19.6	6.7	−2.0	37.1	27.4
1973	17.6	18.7	5.9	−1.1	35.6	26.0
1974	18.3	18.7	5.5	−.4	33.6	23.9
1975	17.9	21.3	5.5	−3.4	34.7	25.3
1976	17.1	21.4	5.2	−4.2	36.2	27.5
Transition quarter	17.7	20.9	4.8	−3.2	35.0	27.0
1977	18.0	20.7	4.9	−2.7	35.8	27.8
1978	18.0	20.7	4.7	−2.7	35.0	27.4
1979	18.5	20.1	4.7	−1.6	33.2	25.6
1980	19.0	21.7	4.9	−2.7	33.4	26.1
1981	19.6	22.2	5.2	−2.6	32.5	25.8
1982	19.2	23.1	5.7	−4.0	35.3	28.7
1983	17.5	23.5	6.1	−6.0	39.9	33.1
1984	17.3	22.2	5.9	−4.8	40.7	34.0
1985	17.7	22.8	6.1	−5.1	43.8	36.4
1986	17.5	22.5	6.2	−5.0	48.2	39.5
1987	18.4	21.6	6.1	−3.2	50.4	40.6
1988	18.2	21.3	5.8	−3.1	51.9	41.0
1989	18.4	21.2	5.6	−2.8	53.1	40.6
1990	18.0	21.9	5.2	−3.9	55.9	42.1
1991	17.8	22.3	4.6	−4.5	60.7	45.3
1992	17.5	22.1	4.8	−4.7	64.1	48.1
1993	17.5	21.4	4.4	−3.9	66.1	49.3
1994	18.0	21.0	4.0	−2.9	66.6	49.2
1995	18.4	20.6	3.7	−2.2	67.0	49.1
1996	18.8	20.2	3.4	−1.4	67.1	48.4
1997	19.2	19.5	3.3	−.3	65.4	45.9
1998	19.9	19.1	3.1	.8	63.2	43.0
1999	19.8	18.5	3.0	1.4	60.9	39.4
2000	20.6	18.2	3.0	2.4	57.3	34.7
2001	19.5	18.2	3.0	1.3	56.4	32.5
2002	17.6	19.1	3.3	−1.5	58.8	33.6
2003	16.2	19.7	3.7	−3.4	61.6	35.6
2004	16.1	19.6	3.9	−3.5	63.0	36.8
2005	17.3	19.9	4.0	−2.6	63.6	36.9
2006	18.2	20.1	4.0	−1.9	64.0	36.6
2007	18.5	19.7	4.0	−1.2	64.6	36.3
2008	17.6	20.8	4.3	−3.2	69.7	40.5
2009	15.1	25.2	4.7	−10.1	85.1	54.0
2010	15.1	24.1	4.8	−9.0	94.3	62.9
2011	15.4	24.1	4.7	−8.7	98.9	67.8
2012 (estimates)	15.7	23.5	4.4	−7.8	104.3	73.5
2013 (estimates)	17.0	23.1	4.2	−6.1	107.7	77.5

Note: See footnote 1 and Note, Table B–78.

Sources: Department of the Treasury and Office of Management and Budget.

TABLE B–80. Federal receipts and outlays, by major category, and surplus or deficit, fiscal years 1946–2013

[Billions of dollars; fiscal years]

Fiscal year or period	Receipts (on-budget and off-budget)					Outlays (on-budget and off-budget)										Surplus or deficit (−) (on-budget and off-budget)
	Total	Individual income taxes	Corporation income taxes	Social insurance and retirement receipts	Other	Total	National defense		International affairs	Health	Medicare	Income security	Social security	Net interest	Other	
							Total	Department of Defense, military								
1946	39.3	16.1	11.9	3.1	8.2	55.2	42.7	....	1.9	0.2	....	2.4	0.4	4.1	3.6	−15.9
1947	38.5	17.9	8.6	3.4	8.5	34.5	12.8	....	5.8	.2	....	2.8	.5	4.2	8.2	4.0
1948	41.6	19.3	9.7	3.8	8.8	29.8	9.1	....	4.6	.2	....	2.5	.6	4.3	8.5	11.8
1949	39.4	15.6	11.2	3.8	8.9	38.8	13.2	....	6.1	.2	....	3.2	.7	4.5	11.1	.6
1950	39.4	15.8	10.4	4.3	8.9	42.6	13.7	....	4.7	.3	....	4.1	.8	4.8	14.2	−3.1
1951	51.6	21.6	14.1	5.7	10.2	45.5	23.6	....	3.6	.3	....	3.4	1.6	4.7	8.4	6.1
1952	66.2	27.9	21.2	6.4	10.6	67.7	46.1	....	2.7	.3	....	3.7	2.1	4.7	8.1	−1.5
1953	69.6	29.8	21.2	6.8	11.7	76.1	52.8	....	2.1	.3	....	3.8	2.7	5.2	9.1	−6.5
1954	69.7	29.5	21.1	7.2	11.9	70.9	49.3	....	1.6	.3	....	4.4	3.4	4.8	7.1	−1.2
1955	65.5	28.7	17.9	7.9	11.0	68.4	42.7	....	2.2	.3	....	5.1	4.4	4.9	8.9	−3.0
1956	74.6	32.2	20.9	9.3	12.2	70.6	42.5	....	2.4	.4	....	4.7	5.5	5.1	10.1	3.9
1957	80.0	35.6	21.2	10.0	13.2	76.6	45.4	....	3.1	.5	....	5.4	6.7	5.4	10.1	3.4
1958	79.6	34.7	20.1	11.2	13.6	82.4	46.8	....	3.4	.5	....	7.5	8.2	5.6	10.3	−2.8
1959	79.2	36.7	17.3	11.7	13.5	92.1	49.0	....	3.1	.7	....	8.2	9.7	5.8	15.5	−12.8
1960	92.5	40.7	21.5	14.7	15.6	92.2	48.1	....	3.0	.8	....	7.4	11.6	6.9	14.4	.3
1961	94.4	41.3	21.0	16.4	15.7	97.7	49.6	....	3.2	.9	....	9.7	12.5	6.7	15.2	−3.3
1962	99.7	45.6	20.5	17.0	16.5	106.8	52.3	50.1	5.6	1.2	....	9.2	14.4	6.9	17.2	−7.1
1963	106.6	47.6	21.6	19.8	17.6	111.3	53.4	51.1	5.3	1.5	....	9.3	15.8	7.7	18.3	−4.8
1964	112.6	48.7	23.5	22.0	18.5	118.5	54.8	52.6	4.9	1.8	....	9.7	16.6	8.2	22.6	−5.9
1965	116.8	48.8	25.5	22.2	20.3	118.2	50.6	48.8	5.3	1.8	....	9.5	17.5	8.6	25.0	−1.4
1966	130.8	55.4	30.1	25.5	19.8	134.5	58.1	56.6	5.6	2.5	0.1	9.7	20.7	9.4	28.5	−3.7
1967	148.8	61.5	34.0	32.6	20.7	157.5	71.4	70.1	5.6	3.4	2.7	10.3	21.7	10.3	32.1	−8.6
1968	153.0	68.7	28.7	33.9	21.7	178.1	81.9	80.4	5.3	4.4	4.6	11.8	23.9	11.1	35.1	−25.2
1969	186.9	87.2	36.7	39.0	23.9	183.6	82.5	80.8	4.6	5.2	5.7	13.1	27.3	12.7	32.6	3.2
1970	192.8	90.4	32.8	44.4	25.2	195.6	81.7	80.1	4.3	5.9	6.2	15.7	30.3	14.4	37.2	−2.8
1971	187.1	86.2	26.8	47.3	26.8	210.2	78.9	77.5	4.2	6.8	6.6	22.9	35.9	14.8	40.0	−23.0
1972	207.3	94.7	32.2	52.6	27.8	230.7	79.2	77.6	4.8	8.7	7.5	27.7	40.2	15.5	47.3	−23.4
1973	230.8	103.2	36.2	63.1	28.3	245.7	76.7	75.0	4.1	9.4	8.1	28.3	49.1	17.3	52.8	−14.9
1974	263.2	119.0	38.6	75.1	30.6	269.4	79.3	77.9	5.7	10.7	9.6	33.7	55.9	21.4	52.9	−6.1
1975	279.1	122.4	40.6	84.5	31.5	332.3	86.5	84.9	7.1	12.9	12.9	50.2	64.7	23.2	74.8	−53.2
1976	298.1	131.6	41.4	90.8	34.3	371.8	89.6	87.9	6.4	15.7	15.8	60.8	73.9	26.7	82.7	−73.7
Transition quarter	81.2	38.8	8.5	25.2	8.8	96.0	22.3	21.8	2.5	3.9	4.3	15.0	19.8	6.9	21.4	−14.7
1977	355.6	157.6	54.9	106.5	36.6	409.2	97.2	95.1	6.4	17.3	19.3	61.1	85.1	29.9	93.0	−53.7
1978	399.6	181.0	60.0	121.0	37.7	458.7	104.5	102.3	7.5	18.5	22.8	61.5	93.9	35.5	114.7	−59.2
1979	463.3	217.8	65.7	138.9	40.8	504.0	116.3	113.6	7.5	20.5	26.5	66.4	104.1	42.6	120.2	−40.7
1980	517.1	244.1	64.6	157.8	50.6	590.9	134.0	130.9	12.7	23.2	32.1	86.6	118.5	52.5	131.3	−73.8
1981	599.3	285.9	61.1	182.7	69.5	678.2	157.5	153.9	13.1	26.9	39.1	100.3	139.6	68.8	133.0	−79.0
1982	617.8	297.7	49.2	201.5	69.3	745.7	185.3	180.7	12.3	27.4	46.6	108.2	156.0	85.0	125.0	−128.0
1983	600.6	288.9	37.0	209.0	65.6	808.4	209.9	204.4	11.8	28.6	52.6	123.0	170.7	89.8	121.8	−207.8
1984	666.4	298.4	56.9	239.4	71.8	851.8	227.4	220.9	15.9	30.4	57.5	113.4	178.2	111.1	117.9	−185.4
1985	734.0	334.5	61.3	265.2	73.0	946.3	252.7	245.1	16.2	33.5	65.8	129.0	188.6	129.5	131.0	−212.3
1986	769.2	349.0	63.1	283.9	73.2	990.4	273.4	265.4	14.1	35.9	70.2	120.6	198.8	136.0	141.4	−221.2
1987	854.3	392.6	83.9	303.3	74.5	1,004.0	282.0	273.9	11.6	40.0	75.1	124.1	207.4	138.6	125.2	−149.7
1988	909.2	401.2	94.5	334.3	79.2	1,064.4	290.4	281.9	10.5	44.5	78.9	130.4	219.3	151.8	138.7	−155.2
1989	991.1	445.7	103.3	359.4	82.7	1,143.7	303.6	294.8	9.6	48.4	85.0	137.4	232.5	169.0	158.3	−152.6
1990	1,032.0	466.9	93.5	380.0	91.5	1,253.0	299.3	289.7	13.8	57.7	98.1	148.7	248.6	184.3	202.5	−221.0
1991	1,055.0	467.8	98.1	396.0	93.1	1,324.2	273.3	262.3	15.8	71.2	104.5	172.5	269.0	194.4	223.5	−269.2
1992	1,091.2	476.0	100.3	413.7	101.3	1,381.5	298.3	286.8	16.1	89.5	119.0	199.6	287.6	199.3	172.1	−290.3
1993	1,154.3	509.7	117.5	428.3	98.8	1,409.4	291.1	278.5	17.2	99.4	130.6	210.0	304.6	198.7	170.9	−255.1
1994	1,258.6	543.1	140.4	461.5	113.7	1,461.8	281.6	268.6	17.1	107.1	144.7	217.2	319.6	202.9	171.5	−203.2
1995	1,351.8	590.2	157.0	484.5	120.1	1,515.7	272.1	259.4	16.4	115.4	159.9	223.8	335.8	232.1	160.2	−164.0
1996	1,453.1	656.4	171.8	509.4	115.4	1,560.5	265.7	253.1	13.5	119.4	174.2	229.7	349.7	241.1	167.2	−107.4
1997	1,579.2	737.5	182.3	539.4	120.1	1,601.1	270.5	258.3	15.2	123.8	190.0	235.0	365.3	244.0	157.3	−21.9
1998	1,721.7	828.6	188.7	571.8	132.6	1,652.5	268.2	255.8	13.1	131.4	192.8	237.8	379.2	241.1	188.9	69.3
1999	1,827.5	879.5	184.7	611.8	151.5	1,701.8	274.8	261.2	15.2	141.0	190.4	242.5	390.0	229.8	218.1	125.6
2000	2,025.2	1,004.5	207.3	652.9	160.6	1,789.0	294.4	281.0	17.2	154.5	197.1	253.7	409.4	222.9	239.7	236.2
2001	1,991.1	994.3	151.1	694.0	151.7	1,862.8	304.7	290.2	16.5	172.2	217.4	269.8	433.0	206.2	243.1	128.2
2002	1,853.1	858.3	148.0	700.8	146.0	2,010.9	348.5	331.8	22.3	196.5	230.9	312.7	456.0	170.9	273.1	−157.8
2003	1,782.3	793.7	131.8	713.0	143.9	2,159.9	404.7	387.1	21.2	219.5	249.4	334.6	474.7	153.1	302.6	−377.6
2004	1,880.1	809.0	189.4	733.4	148.4	2,292.8	455.8	436.4	26.9	240.1	269.4	333.1	495.5	160.2	311.8	−412.7
2005	2,153.6	927.2	278.3	794.1	154.0	2,472.0	495.3	474.1	34.6	250.5	298.6	345.8	523.3	184.0	339.8	−318.3
2006	2,406.9	1,043.9	353.9	837.8	171.2	2,655.1	521.8	499.3	29.5	252.7	329.9	352.5	548.5	226.6	393.5	−248.2
2007	2,568.0	1,163.5	370.2	869.6	164.7	2,728.7	551.3	528.5	28.5	266.4	375.4	366.0	586.2	237.1	317.9	−160.7
2008	2,524.0	1,145.7	304.3	900.2	173.7	2,982.5	616.1	594.6	28.9	280.6	390.8	431.3	617.0	252.8	365.2	−458.6
2009	2,105.0	915.3	138.2	890.9	160.5	3,517.7	661.0	636.7	37.5	334.3	430.1	533.2	683.0	186.9	651.6	−1,412.7
2010	2,162.7	898.5	191.4	864.8	207.9	3,457.1	693.5	666.7	45.2	369.1	451.6	622.2	706.7	196.2	372.5	−1,294.4
2011	2,303.5	1,091.5	181.1	818.8	212.1	3,603.1	705.6	678.1	45.7	372.5	485.7	597.4	730.8	230.0	435.5	−1,299.6
2012 (estimates)[1]	2,449.1	1,132.2	242.3	845.3	229.3	3,538.4	680.4	650.9	47.2	346.7	471.8	542.2	773.3	222.5	454.3	−1,089.4
2013 (estimates)[2]	2,763.6	1,291.8	294.1	947.1	230.6	3,754.2	675.5	647.3	57.9	380.3	515.2	544.1	818.9	228.6	533.7	−990.6

[1] Estimates from Final Monthly Treasury Statement, issued October 2012.
[2] Estimates from Mid-Session Review, Budget of the U.S. Government, Fiscal Year 2013, issued July 2012.

Note: See Note, Table B–78.

Sources: Department of the Treasury and Office of Management and Budget.

TABLE B–81. Federal receipts, outlays, surplus or deficit, and debt, fiscal years 2007–2012

[Millions of dollars; fiscal years]

Description	Actual					Estimates [1]
	2007	2008	2009	2010	2011	2012
RECEIPTS, OUTLAYS, AND SURPLUS OR DEFICIT						
Total:						
Receipts	2,567,985	2,523,991	2,104,989	2,162,706	2,303,466	2,449,093
Outlays	2,728,686	2,982,544	3,517,677	3,457,079	3,603,059	3,538,446
Surplus or deficit (–)	−160,701	−458,553	−1,412,688	−1,294,373	−1,299,593	−1,089,353
On-budget:						
Receipts	1,932,896	1,865,945	1,450,980	1,531,019	1,737,678	1,879,592
Outlays	2,275,049	2,507,793	3,000,661	2,902,397	3,104,453	3,030,856
Surplus or deficit (–)	−342,153	−641,848	−1,549,681	−1,371,378	−1,366,775	−1,151,264
Off-budget:						
Receipts	635,089	658,046	654,009	631,687	565,788	569,501
Outlays	453,637	474,751	517,016	554,682	498,606	507,590
Surplus or deficit (–)	181,452	183,295	136,993	77,005	67,182	61,911
OUTSTANDING DEBT, END OF PERIOD						
Gross Federal debt	8,950,744	9,986,082	11,875,851	13,528,807	14,764,222	16,048,111
Held by Federal Government accounts	3,915,615	4,183,032	4,331,144	4,509,926	4,636,016	4,768,258
Held by the public	5,035,129	5,803,050	7,544,707	9,018,882	10,128,206	11,279,854
Federal Reserve System	779,632	491,127	769,160	811,669	1,664,660	....
Other	4,255,497	5,311,923	6,775,547	8,207,213	8,463,546	....
RECEIPTS BY SOURCE						
Total: On-budget and off-budget	2,567,985	2,523,991	2,104,989	2,162,706	2,303,466	2,449,093
Individual income taxes	1,163,472	1,145,747	915,308	898,549	1,091,473	1,132,206
Corporation income taxes	370,243	304,346	138,229	191,437	181,085	242,289
Social insurance and retirement receipts	869,607	900,155	890,917	864,814	818,792	845,313
On-budget	234,518	242,109	236,908	233,127	253,004	....
Off-budget	635,089	658,046	654,009	631,687	565,788	....
Excise taxes	65,069	67,334	62,483	66,909	72,381	79,061
Estate and gift taxes	26,044	28,844	23,482	18,885	7,399	13,973
Customs duties and fees	26,010	27,568	22,453	25,298	29,519	30,307
Miscellaneous receipts	47,540	49,997	52,117	96,814	102,817	105,943
Deposits of earnings by Federal Reserve System	32,043	33,598	34,318	75,845	82,546	....
All other	15,497	16,399	17,799	20,969	20,271	....
OUTLAYS BY FUNCTION						
Total: On-budget and off-budget	2,728,686	2,982,544	3,517,677	3,457,079	3,603,059	3,538,446
National defense	551,271	616,072	661,023	693,498	705,557	680,413
International affairs	28,482	28,857	37,529	45,195	45,685	47,236
General science, space, and technology	25,525	26,773	28,417	30,100	29,466	29,226
Energy	−860	628	4,749	11,611	12,174	14,760
Natural resources and environment	31,716	31,817	35,568	43,661	45,470	41,843
Agriculture	17,662	18,387	22,237	21,356	20,662	19,711
Commerce and housing credit	487	27,870	291,535	−82,316	−12,573	40,333
On-budget	−4,606	25,453	291,231	−87,016	−13,381	....
Off-budget	5,093	2,417	304	4,700	808	....
Transportation	72,905	77,616	84,289	91,972	92,966	91,206
Community and regional development	29,567	23,952	27,676	23,894	23,883	26,113
Education, training, employment, and social services	91,656	91,287	79,749	128,598	101,233	89,063
Health	266,382	280,599	334,335	369,068	372,504	346,707
Medicare	375,407	390,758	430,093	451,636	485,653	471,789
Income security	365,975	431,313	533,224	622,210	597,352	542,227
Social security	586,153	617,027	682,963	706,737	730,811	773,288
On-budget	19,307	17,830	34,071	23,317	101,933	....
Off-budget	566,846	599,197	648,892	683,420	628,878	....
Veterans benefits and services	72,818	84,653	95,429	108,384	127,189	124,603
Administration of justice	41,244	48,097	52,581	54,383	56,056	57,557
General government	17,425	20,323	22,017	23,014	27,476	23,436
Net interest	237,109	252,757	186,902	196,194	229,962	222,470
On-budget	343,112	366,475	304,856	314,696	345,943	....
Off-budget	−106,003	−113,718	−117,954	−118,502	−115,981	....
Allowances	....	....	....	....	....	−103,535
Undistributed offsetting receipts	−82,238	−86,242	−92,639	−82,116	−88,467	....
On-budget	−69,939	−73,097	−78,413	−67,180	−73,368	....
Off-budget	−12,299	−13,145	−14,226	−14,936	−15,099	....

[1] Estimates from *Final Monthly Treasury Statement*, issued October 2012.

Note: See Note, Table B–78.

Sources: Department of the Treasury and Office of Management and Budget.

TABLE B–82. Federal and State and local government current receipts and expenditures, national income and product accounts (NIPA), 1964–2012

[Billions of dollars; quarterly data at seasonally adjusted annual rates]

Year or quarter	Total government			Federal Government			State and local government			Addendum: Grants-in-aid to State and local governments
	Current receipts	Current expenditures	Net government saving (NIPA)	Current receipts	Current expenditures	Net Federal Government saving (NIPA)	Current receipts	Current expenditures	Net State and local government saving (NIPA)	
1964	166.6	159.3	7.3	111.8	110.9	0.9	61.3	54.9	6.4	6.5
1965	180.3	170.6	9.8	121.0	117.7	3.2	66.5	60.0	6.5	7.2
1966	202.8	192.8	10.0	138.0	135.7	2.3	74.9	67.2	7.8	10.1
1967	217.7	220.0	–2.3	146.9	156.2	–9.3	82.5	75.5	7.0	11.7
1968	252.1	247.0	5.1	171.3	173.7	–2.4	93.5	86.0	7.5	12.7
1969	283.5	267.0	16.5	192.7	184.1	8.6	105.5	97.5	8.0	14.6
1970	286.9	295.2	–8.4	186.1	201.6	–15.5	120.1	113.0	7.1	19.3
1971	303.6	325.8	–22.2	191.9	220.6	–28.7	134.9	128.5	6.5	23.2
1972	347.0	356.3	–9.3	220.3	245.2	–24.9	158.4	142.8	15.6	31.7
1973	390.4	386.5	3.9	250.8	262.6	–11.8	174.3	158.6	15.7	34.8
1974	431.8	436.9	–5.2	280.0	294.5	–14.5	188.1	178.7	9.3	36.3
1975	442.1	510.2	–68.2	277.6	348.3	–70.6	209.6	207.1	2.5	45.1
1976	505.9	552.2	–46.3	323.0	376.7	–53.7	233.7	226.3	7.4	50.7
1977	567.3	600.3	–33.0	364.0	410.1	–46.1	259.9	246.8	13.1	56.6
1978	646.1	656.3	–10.2	424.0	452.9	–28.9	287.6	268.9	18.7	65.5
1979	728.9	729.9	–1.0	486.9	500.9	–14.0	308.4	295.4	13.0	66.3
1980	798.7	846.5	–47.8	532.8	589.5	–56.6	338.2	329.4	8.8	72.3
1981	917.7	966.9	–49.2	619.9	676.7	–56.8	370.2	362.7	7.6	72.5
1982	939.3	1,076.8	–137.5	617.4	752.6	–135.3	391.4	393.6	–2.2	69.5
1983	1,000.3	1,171.7	–171.4	643.3	819.5	–176.2	428.6	423.7	4.9	71.6
1984	1,113.5	1,261.0	–147.5	710.0	881.5	–171.5	480.2	456.2	23.9	76.7
1985	1,214.6	1,370.9	–156.3	774.4	953.0	–178.6	521.1	498.7	22.4	80.9
1986	1,290.1	1,464.0	–173.9	816.0	1,010.7	–194.6	561.6	540.9	20.7	87.6
1987	1,403.2	1,540.5	–137.4	896.5	1,045.9	–149.3	590.6	578.6	12.0	83.9
1988	1,502.4	1,623.6	–121.2	958.5	1,096.9	–138.4	635.5	618.3	17.2	91.6
1989	1,627.2	1,741.0	–113.8	1,038.0	1,172.0	–133.9	687.5	667.4	20.1	98.3
1990	1,709.3	1,879.5	–170.3	1,082.8	1,259.2	–176.4	738.0	731.8	6.2	111.4
1991	1,759.7	1,984.0	–224.2	1,101.9	1,320.3	–218.4	789.4	795.2	–5.8	131.6
1992	1,845.1	2,149.0	–303.9	1,148.0	1,450.5	–302.5	846.2	847.6	–1.4	149.1
1993	1,948.2	2,229.4	–281.2	1,224.1	1,504.3	–280.2	888.2	889.1	–.9	164.0
1994	2,091.9	2,304.0	–212.2	1,322.1	1,542.5	–220.4	944.8	936.6	8.2	175.1
1995	2,215.5	2,412.5	–197.0	1,407.8	1,614.0	–206.2	991.9	982.7	9.2	184.2
1996	2,380.4	2,505.7	–125.3	1,526.4	1,674.7	–148.2	1,045.1	1,022.1	23.0	191.1
1997	2,557.2	2,581.1	–23.8	1,656.2	1,716.3	–60.1	1,099.5	1,063.2	36.3	198.4
1998	2,729.8	2,649.3	80.5	1,777.9	1,744.3	33.6	1,164.5	1,117.6	46.9	212.6
1999	2,902.5	2,761.9	140.6	1,895.0	1,796.2	98.8	1,240.4	1,198.6	41.8	232.9
2000	3,132.4	2,906.0	226.5	2,057.1	1,871.9	185.2	1,322.6	1,281.3	41.3	247.3
2001	3,118.2	3,093.6	24.6	2,020.3	1,979.8	40.5	1,374.0	1,389.9	–15.9	276.1
2002	2,967.9	3,274.7	–306.9	1,859.3	2,112.1	–252.8	1,412.7	1,466.8	–54.1	304.2
2003	3,043.4	3,458.6	–415.2	1,885.1	2,261.5	–376.4	1,496.3	1,535.1	–38.8	338.0
2004	3,265.7	3,653.5	–387.8	2,013.9	2,393.4	–379.5	1,601.0	1,609.3	–8.4	349.2
2005	3,659.3	3,916.4	–257.1	2,290.1	2,573.1	–283.0	1,730.4	1,704.5	25.9	361.2
2006	3,995.2	4,147.9	–152.7	2,524.5	2,728.3	–203.8	1,829.7	1,778.6	51.0	359.0
2007	4,197.0	4,430.0	–233.0	2,654.7	2,900.0	–245.2	1,923.1	1,910.8	12.2	380.8
2008	4,051.6	4,737.3	–685.7	2,502.2	3,115.7	–613.5	1,944.8	2,017.0	–72.2	395.5
2009	3,705.3	5,047.9	–1,342.6	2,226.5	3,455.8	–1,229.3	1,961.4	2,074.6	–113.2	482.6
2010	3,906.8	5,304.4	–1,397.7	2,395.4	3,703.4	–1,308.0	2,042.4	2,132.1	–89.7	531.1
2011	4,086.1	5,425.5	–1,339.4	2,519.6	3,757.0	–1,237.4	2,064.4	2,166.3	–102.0	497.8
2012 ^p		5,488.6			3,757.8			2,198.8		468.0
2009: I	3,689.9	4,817.4	–1,127.4	2,218.7	3,230.6	–1,011.8	1,909.9	2,025.5	–115.6	438.7
II	3,661.8	5,085.2	–1,423.4	2,207.4	3,520.9	–1,313.5	1,955.3	2,065.2	–109.9	500.8
III	3,694.9	5,139.0	–1,444.1	2,206.5	3,525.1	–1,318.6	1,975.9	2,101.5	–125.5	487.6
IV	3,774.7	5,150.0	–1,375.3	2,273.4	3,546.8	–1,273.5	2,004.4	2,106.3	–101.8	503.1
2010: I	3,824.3	5,250.6	–1,426.3	2,326.6	3,641.8	–1,315.2	2,011.8	2,122.9	–111.1	514.2
II	3,856.9	5,284.8	–1,427.9	2,365.8	3,685.3	–1,319.5	2,010.5	2,118.9	–108.4	519.4
III	3,946.0	5,321.4	–1,375.4	2,427.2	3,730.2	–1,303.1	2,061.9	2,134.3	–72.4	543.1
IV	3,999.8	5,360.9	–1,361.0	2,461.9	3,756.3	–1,294.4	2,085.6	2,152.3	–66.7	547.7
2011: I	4,065.7	5,391.7	–1,326.0	2,509.8	3,737.1	–1,227.3	2,073.9	2,172.6	–98.7	517.9
II	4,093.2	5,475.6	–1,382.3	2,522.9	3,830.6	–1,307.7	2,098.0	2,172.6	–74.6	527.6
III	4,076.4	5,426.4	–1,350.0	2,511.3	3,743.3	–1,232.0	2,045.2	2,163.2	–118.0	480.1
IV	4,109.2	5,408.3	–1,299.1	2,534.3	3,716.8	–1,182.6	2,040.5	2,157.0	–116.5	465.6
2012: I	4,260.1	5,446.5	–1,186.4	2,664.9	3,723.6	–1,058.7	2,050.4	2,178.1	–127.6	455.3
II	4,259.3	5,498.3	–1,239.0	2,659.5	3,774.8	–1,115.4	2,066.7	2,190.3	–123.7	466.9
III	4,272.0	5,499.2	–1,227.2	2,673.4	3,760.6	–1,087.2	2,069.2	2,209.2	–140.0	470.6
IV ^p		5,510.4			3,772.1			2,217.6		479.4

Note: Federal grants-in-aid to State and local governments are reflected in Federal current expenditures and State and local current receipts. Total government current receipts and expenditures have been adjusted to eliminate this duplication.

Source: Department of Commerce (Bureau of Economic Analysis).

TABLE B–83. Federal and State and local government current receipts and expenditures, national income and product accounts (NIPA), by major type, 1964–2012

[Billions of dollars; quarterly data at seasonally adjusted annual rates]

Year or quarter	Current receipts									Current expenditures					Net government saving
		Current tax receipts				Contributions for government social insurance	Income receipts on assets	Current transfer receipts	Current surplus of government enterprises		Consumption expenditures	Current transfer payments	Interest payments	Subsidies	
	Total	Total[1]	Personal current taxes	Taxes on production and imports	Taxes on corporate income					Total[2]					
1964	166.6	137.5	52.1	57.3	28.0	22.5	3.7	1.6	1.3	159.3	108.6	35.1	12.9	2.7	7.3
1965	180.3	149.5	57.7	60.7	30.9	23.5	4.1	1.9	1.3	170.6	115.9	38.0	13.7	3.0	9.8
1966	202.8	163.5	66.4	63.2	33.7	31.4	4.7	2.2	1.0	192.8	131.8	42.0	15.1	3.9	10.0
1967	217.7	173.8	73.0	67.9	32.7	35.0	5.5	2.5	.9	220.0	149.5	50.3	16.4	3.8	-2.3
1968	252.1	203.1	87.0	76.4	39.4	38.8	6.4	2.6	1.2	247.0	165.7	58.4	18.8	4.2	5.1
1969	283.5	228.4	104.5	83.9	39.7	44.3	7.0	2.7	1.0	267.0	178.2	64.1	20.2	4.5	16.5
1970	286.9	229.2	103.1	91.4	34.4	46.6	8.2	2.9	.0	295.2	190.1	77.3	23.1	4.8	-8.4
1971	303.6	240.3	101.7	100.5	37.7	51.5	9.0	3.1	-.2	325.8	204.7	92.2	24.5	4.7	-22.2
1972	347.0	273.8	123.6	107.9	41.9	59.6	9.5	3.6	.5	356.3	220.8	103.0	26.3	6.6	-9.3
1973	390.4	299.3	132.4	117.2	49.3	76.0	11.6	3.9	-.4	386.5	234.8	115.2	31.3	5.2	3.9
1974	431.8	328.1	151.0	124.9	51.8	85.8	14.4	4.5	-.9	436.9	261.7	135.9	35.6	3.3	-5.2
1975	442.1	334.3	147.6	135.3	50.9	89.9	16.1	5.1	-3.2	510.2	294.6	171.3	40.0	4.5	-68.2
1976	505.9	383.6	172.3	146.4	64.2	102.0	16.3	5.8	-1.8	552.2	316.6	184.3	46.3	5.1	-46.3
1977	567.3	431.0	197.5	159.7	73.0	113.9	18.4	6.8	-2.7	600.3	346.6	195.9	50.8	7.1	-33.0
1978	646.1	484.8	229.4	170.9	83.5	132.1	23.2	8.2	-2.2	656.3	376.5	210.9	60.2	8.9	-10.2
1979	728.9	537.9	268.7	180.1	88.0	153.7	30.8	9.4	-2.9	729.9	412.3	236.0	72.9	8.5	-1.0
1980	798.7	585.6	298.9	200.3	84.8	167.2	39.9	11.1	-5.1	846.5	465.9	281.7	89.1	9.8	-47.8
1981	917.7	663.5	345.2	235.6	81.1	196.9	50.2	12.7	-5.6	966.9	520.6	318.1	116.7	11.5	-49.2
1982	939.3	659.5	354.1	240.9	63.1	210.1	58.9	15.3	-4.5	1,076.8	568.1	354.7	138.9	15.0	-137.5
1983	1,000.3	694.1	352.3	263.3	77.2	227.2	65.3	16.9	-3.2	1,171.7	610.5	382.5	156.9	21.3	-171.4
1984	1,113.5	762.5	377.4	289.8	94.0	258.8	74.3	19.7	-1.9	1,261.0	657.6	395.3	187.3	21.1	-147.5
1985	1,214.6	823.9	417.3	308.1	96.5	282.8	84.0	23.4	.6	1,370.9	720.1	420.4	208.8	21.4	-156.3
1986	1,290.1	868.8	437.2	323.4	106.5	304.9	89.7	25.9	.9	1,464.0	776.1	446.6	216.3	24.9	-173.9
1987	1,403.2	965.7	489.1	347.5	127.1	324.6	85.6	27.0	.2	1,540.5	815.1	464.4	230.8	30.3	-137.4
1988	1,502.4	1,018.9	504.9	374.5	137.2	363.2	89.9	27.9	2.6	1,623.6	852.8	493.6	247.7	29.5	-121.2
1989	1,627.2	1,109.2	566.1	398.9	141.5	386.9	93.7	32.5	4.9	1,741.0	902.9	538.1	272.5	27.4	-113.8
1990	1,709.3	1,161.3	592.7	425.0	140.6	412.1	98.0	36.3	1.6	1,879.5	966.0	592.4	294.2	27.0	-170.3
1991	1,759.7	1,179.9	586.6	457.1	133.6	432.2	97.0	44.9	5.7	1,984.0	1,015.8	628.9	311.7	27.5	-224.2
1992	1,845.1	1,239.7	610.5	483.4	143.1	457.1	89.6	50.5	8.2	2,149.0	1,050.4	756.3	312.3	30.1	-303.9
1993	1,948.2	1,317.8	646.5	503.1	165.4	479.6	86.8	55.3	8.7	2,229.4	1,075.4	804.6	312.7	36.7	-281.2
1994	2,091.9	1,425.6	690.5	545.2	186.7	510.7	86.0	60.0	9.6	2,304.0	1,108.9	839.9	322.7	32.5	-212.2
1995	2,215.5	1,516.7	743.9	557.9	211.0	535.5	91.8	58.4	13.1	2,412.5	1,141.4	882.4	353.9	34.8	-197.0
1996	2,380.4	1,641.5	832.0	580.8	223.6	557.9	99.9	66.8	14.4	2,505.7	1,176.7	929.2	364.6	35.2	-125.3
1997	2,557.2	1,780.0	926.2	611.6	237.1	590.3	103.6	69.3	14.1	2,581.1	1,222.1	954.6	370.6	33.8	-23.8
1998	2,729.8	1,910.8	1,026.4	639.5	239.2	627.8	102.7	75.3	13.3	2,649.3	1,263.2	978.1	371.6	36.4	80.5
1999	2,902.5	2,035.8	1,107.5	673.6	248.8	664.6	106.4	81.7	14.1	2,761.9	1,343.9	1,014.9	357.9	45.2	140.6
2000	3,132.4	2,202.8	1,232.3	708.6	254.7	709.4	118.8	92.3	9.1	2,906.0	1,426.6	1,071.5	362.0	45.8	226.5
2001	3,118.2	2,163.7	1,234.8	727.7	193.5	736.9	114.6	98.9	4.0	3,093.6	1,524.4	1,169.0	341.5	58.7	24.6
2002	2,967.9	2,002.1	1,050.4	762.8	181.3	755.2	99.9	104.3	6.3	3,274.7	1,639.9	1,280.9	312.6	41.4	-306.9
2003	3,043.4	2,047.9	1,000.3	806.8	231.8	782.8	96.8	108.9	7.0	3,458.6	1,756.8	1,354.8	298.0	49.1	-415.2
2004	3,265.7	2,213.2	1,047.8	863.4	292.0	831.7	100.3	119.3	1.2	3,653.5	1,860.4	1,440.1	306.6	46.4	-387.8
2005	3,659.3	2,546.8	1,208.6	930.2	395.9	877.4	111.9	126.7	-3.5	3,916.4	1,977.9	1,534.9	342.7	60.9	-257.1
2006	3,995.2	2,807.4	1,352.4	986.8	454.2	926.4	129.6	136.0	-4.2	4,147.9	2,093.3	1,631.0	372.2	51.4	-152.7
2007	4,197.0	2,951.2	1,488.7	1,027.2	420.6	964.2	144.2	149.2	-11.8	4,430.0	2,217.8	1,743.4	414.3	54.6	-233.0
2008	4,051.6	2,774.1	1,435.7	1,038.6	281.0	992.1	137.5	163.9	-16.0	4,737.3	2,381.0	1,903.1	400.2	52.9	-685.7
2009	3,705.3	2,428.5	1,144.6	1,023.2	245.9	968.1	143.1	181.2	-15.6	5,047.9	2,460.3	2,170.0	357.9	59.7	-1,342.6
2010	3,906.8	2,614.4	1,194.8	1,055.0	349.5	988.2	141.8	181.9	-19.5	5,304.4	2,552.0	2,308.0	387.4	57.0	-1,397.7
2011	4,086.1	2,863.5	1,398.0	1,097.9	351.8	923.8	141.7	183.7	-26.5	5,425.5	2,579.5	2,350.1	434.2	61.6	-1,339.4
2012 p	....	....	1,474.7	1,130.4	....	952.9	138.7	176.1	-34.0	5,488.6	2,590.4	2,406.0	431.3	60.9	....
2009: I	3,689.9	2,417.1	1,199.7	1,010.1	191.4	970.3	137.9	181.1	-16.6	4,817.4	2,390.7	2,057.0	313.3	56.4	-1,127.4
II	3,661.8	2,370.8	1,121.3	1,016.5	217.5	970.8	145.2	190.5	-15.4	5,085.2	2,445.3	2,206.7	376.4	56.8	-1,423.4
III	3,694.9	2,429.1	1,125.6	1,027.7	262.5	965.8	142.2	172.2	-14.5	5,139.0	2,486.5	2,208.6	375.4	68.5	-1,444.1
IV	3,774.7	2,496.8	1,131.7	1,038.4	312.3	965.4	147.1	181.1	-15.8	5,150.0	2,518.6	2,207.8	366.6	57.0	-1,375.3
2010: I	3,824.3	2,541.8	1,156.9	1,043.3	327.7	979.6	140.7	179.1	-16.8	5,250.6	2,539.3	2,286.6	368.5	56.2	-1,426.3
II	3,856.9	2,565.3	1,173.0	1,050.5	326.8	987.9	141.8	180.5	-18.5	5,284.8	2,551.2	2,285.0	392.2	56.4	-1,427.9
III	3,946.0	2,646.8	1,211.8	1,058.6	361.9	992.1	142.8	184.5	-20.1	5,321.4	2,556.9	2,320.7	387.1	56.7	-1,375.4
IV	3,999.8	2,703.9	1,237.5	1,067.5	381.8	993.1	141.8	183.5	-22.5	5,360.9	2,560.5	2,339.9	401.9	58.6	-1,361.0
2011: I	4,065.7	2,844.2	1,372.5	1,084.5	373.1	918.9	142.4	183.4	-23.1	5,391.7	2,565.5	2,348.9	417.7	59.6	-1,326.0
II	4,093.2	2,868.6	1,396.6	1,099.0	358.1	923.6	142.0	183.6	-24.4	5,475.6	2,591.3	2,357.1	465.5	61.9	-1,382.3
III	4,076.4	2,853.1	1,403.8	1,098.2	334.2	925.3	142.1	183.4	-27.5	5,426.4	2,591.0	2,343.6	429.5	62.4	-1,350.0
IV	4,109.2	2,888.1	1,419.1	1,109.8	341.8	927.3	140.5	184.4	-31.1	5,408.3	2,570.4	2,350.9	424.4	62.7	-1,299.1
2012: I	4,260.1	3,020.5	1,450.8	1,128.5	425.9	947.1	140.3	184.2	-32.0	5,446.5	2,586.9	2,380.1	418.6	60.8	-1,186.4
II	4,259.3	3,027.3	1,465.2	1,130.9	414.4	949.0	139.0	178.1	-34.1	5,498.3	2,580.3	2,395.5	461.5	61.0	-1,239.0
III	4,272.0	3,045.8	1,476.5	1,128.4	423.9	953.3	138.0	170.4	-35.5	5,499.2	2,618.7	2,419.2	400.7	60.6	-1,227.2
IV p	....	....	1,506.2	1,133.7	....	962.3	137.5	171.7	-34.4	5,510.4	2,575.6	2,429.2	444.5	61.0	....

[1] Includes taxes from the rest of the world, not shown separately.
[2] Includes an item for the difference between wage accruals and disbursements, not shown separately.

Source: Department of Commerce (Bureau of Economic Analysis).

TABLE B–84. Federal Government current receipts and expenditures, national income and product accounts (NIPA), 1964–2012

[Billions of dollars; quarterly data at seasonally adjusted annual rates]

Year or quarter	Current receipts									Current expenditures					Net Federal Government saving
	Total	Current tax receipts				Contributions for government social insurance	Income receipts on assets	Current transfer receipts	Current surplus of government enterprises	Total [2]	Consumption expenditures	Current transfer payments [3]	Interest payments	Subsidies	
		Total [1]	Personal current taxes	Taxes on production and imports	Taxes on corporate income										
1964	111.8	87.7	46.0	15.4	26.1	21.8	1.8	0.7	−0.3	110.9	62.8	35.4	10.0	2.7	0.9
1965	121.0	95.6	51.1	15.4	28.9	22.7	1.9	1.1	−.3	117.7	65.7	38.5	10.6	3.0	3.2
1966	138.0	104.7	58.6	14.4	31.4	30.6	2.1	1.2	−.6	135.7	75.7	44.4	11.6	3.9	2.3
1967	146.9	109.8	64.4	15.2	30.0	34.1	2.5	1.1	−.6	156.2	87.0	52.8	12.7	3.8	−9.3
1968	171.3	129.7	76.4	16.9	36.1	37.9	2.9	1.1	−.3	173.7	95.3	59.7	14.6	4.1	−2.4
1969	192.7	146.0	91.7	17.8	36.1	43.3	2.7	1.1	−.4	184.1	98.3	65.5	15.8	4.5	8.6
1970	186.1	137.9	88.9	18.1	30.6	45.5	3.1	1.1	−1.5	201.6	98.6	80.5	17.7	4.8	−15.5
1971	191.9	138.6	85.8	19.0	33.5	50.3	3.5	1.1	−1.6	220.6	101.9	96.1	17.9	4.6	−28.7
1972	220.3	158.2	102.8	18.5	36.6	58.3	3.6	1.3	−1.1	245.2	107.6	112.7	18.8	6.6	−24.9
1973	250.8	173.0	109.6	19.8	43.3	74.5	3.8	1.3	−1.8	262.6	108.8	125.9	22.8	5.1	−11.8
1974	280.0	192.1	126.5	20.1	45.1	84.1	4.2	1.4	−1.8	294.5	117.9	146.9	26.0	3.2	−14.5
1975	277.6	186.8	120.7	22.1	43.6	88.1	4.9	1.5	−3.6	348.3	129.5	185.6	28.9	4.3	−70.6
1976	323.0	217.9	141.2	21.4	54.6	99.8	5.9	1.6	−2.2	376.7	137.1	200.9	33.8	4.9	−53.7
1977	364.0	247.2	162.2	22.7	61.6	111.1	6.7	2.0	−3.0	410.1	150.7	215.5	37.1	6.9	−46.1
1978	424.0	286.6	188.9	25.3	71.4	128.7	8.5	2.7	−2.5	452.9	163.3	235.7	45.3	8.7	−28.9
1979	486.9	325.9	224.6	25.7	74.4	149.8	10.7	3.1	−2.6	500.9	178.9	258.0	55.7	8.2	−14.0
1980	532.8	355.5	250.0	33.7	70.3	163.6	13.7	3.9	−3.9	589.5	207.4	302.9	69.7	9.4	−56.6
1981	619.9	407.7	290.6	49.9	65.7	193.0	18.3	4.1	−3.2	676.7	238.3	333.5	93.9	11.1	−56.8
1982	617.4	386.3	295.0	41.0	49.0	206.0	22.2	5.7	−2.9	752.6	263.3	363.0	111.8	14.6	−135.3
1983	643.3	393.2	286.2	44.4	41.3	223.1	23.8	6.1	−3.0	819.5	286.4	387.2	124.6	20.9	−176.2
1984	710.0	425.2	301.4	47.3	75.2	254.1	26.6	7.4	−3.4	881.5	309.9	400.8	150.3	20.7	−171.5
1985	774.4	460.2	336.0	46.1	76.3	277.9	29.1	9.7	−2.6	953.0	338.3	424.0	169.4	21.0	−178.6
1986	816.0	479.2	350.0	43.7	83.8	298.9	31.3	8.5	−1.9	1,010.7	358.0	449.9	178.2	24.6	−194.6
1987	896.5	543.6	392.5	45.9	103.2	317.4	27.5	11.0	−3.0	1,045.9	373.7	457.6	184.6	30.0	−149.3
1988	958.5	566.2	402.8	49.8	111.1	354.8	29.4	10.5	−2.3	1,096.9	381.7	486.8	199.3	29.2	−138.4
1989	1,038.0	621.2	451.5	49.7	117.2	378.0	28.0	12.7	−1.7	1,172.0	398.5	527.1	219.3	27.1	−133.9
1990	1,082.8	642.2	470.1	50.9	118.1	402.0	29.6	14.2	−5.3	1,259.2	419.0	576.2	237.5	26.6	−176.4
1991	1,101.9	635.6	461.3	61.8	109.9	420.6	29.1	18.2	−1.6	1,320.3	438.3	604.0	250.9	27.1	−218.4
1992	1,148.0	659.9	475.2	63.3	118.8	444.0	24.8	19.4	−.0	1,450.5	444.1	725.4	251.3	29.7	−302.5
1993	1,224.1	713.0	505.5	66.4	138.5	465.5	25.5	21.3	−1.3	1,504.3	441.2	773.4	253.4	36.3	−280.2
1994	1,322.1	781.4	542.5	79.0	156.7	496.2	22.7	22.8	−.9	1,542.5	440.7	808.3	261.3	32.2	−220.4
1995	1,407.8	844.6	585.8	75.6	179.3	521.9	23.3	18.4	−.3	1,614.0	440.1	849.0	290.4	34.5	−206.2
1996	1,526.4	931.9	663.3	72.9	190.6	545.4	26.5	23.8	−1.2	1,674.7	446.5	896.0	297.3	34.9	−148.2
1997	1,652.2	1,030.1	744.2	77.8	203.0	579.4	25.4	21.3	−.1	1,716.3	457.5	925.4	300.0	33.4	−60.1
1998	1,777.9	1,115.8	825.2	80.7	204.2	617.4	21.2	22.6	.8	1,744.3	454.6	954.9	298.8	35.9	33.6
1999	1,895.0	1,195.4	893.0	83.4	213.0	654.8	20.6	23.4	.8	1,796.2	473.3	995.4	282.7	44.8	98.8
2000	2,057.1	1,309.6	995.6	87.3	219.4	698.6	24.5	25.7	−1.2	1,871.9	496.0	1,047.4	283.3	45.3	185.2
2001	2,020.3	1,249.4	991.8	85.3	164.7	723.3	24.5	27.0	−4.0	1,979.8	530.2	1,140.0	258.6	51.1	40.5
2002	1,859.3	1,073.5	828.6	86.8	150.5	739.3	20.3	26.1	.2	2,112.1	590.5	1,252.1	229.1	40.5	−252.8
2003	1,885.1	1,070.2	774.2	89.3	197.8	762.8	22.8	25.6	3.7	2,261.5	660.3	1,339.4	212.9	49.0	−376.4
2004	2,013.9	1,153.8	799.2	94.3	250.3	807.6	23.2	29.0	.3	2,393.4	721.4	1,405.0	221.0	46.0	−379.5
2005	2,290.1	1,383.7	931.9	98.8	341.0	852.6	23.7	33.6	−3.5	2,573.1	765.8	1,491.3	255.4	60.5	−283.0
2006	2,524.5	1,558.3	1,049.9	99.4	395.0	904.6	26.1	38.3	−2.9	2,728.3	811.0	1,587.1	279.2	51.0	−203.8
2007	2,654.7	1,637.6	1,165.6	94.5	362.8	945.3	29.8	44.8	−2.7	2,900.0	848.9	1,690.4	313.2	47.4	−245.2
2008	2,502.2	1,447.7	1,101.3	94.0	233.7	973.1	30.7	54.4	−3.7	3,115.7	931.7	1,841.9	292.1	49.9	−613.5
2009	2,226.5	1,163.6	857.0	91.4	200.4	949.1	48.1	70.2	−4.5	3,455.8	987.0	2,157.5	253.1	58.3	−1,229.3
2010	2,395.4	1,309.8	894.2	95.5	305.1	969.8	53.0	69.8	−7.0	3,703.4	1,055.8	2,310.8	281.4	55.4	−1,308.0
2011	2,519.6	1,502.7	1,075.2	107.4	304.2	905.5	55.3	68.8	−12.7	3,757.0	1,061.5	2,309.4	325.0	61.1	−1,237.4
2012 p			1,139.9	116.0		935.5	53.4	59.2	−17.7	3,757.8	1,059.4	2,319.4	318.5	60.4	
2009: I	2,218.7	1,162.3	915.8	86.8	144.3	951.0	39.6	70.5	−4.8	3,230.6	954.6	2,015.7	205.9	54.4	−1,011.8
II	2,207.4	1,130.7	846.4	94.2	174.5	951.7	49.6	79.7	−4.4	3,520.9	979.5	2,214.0	271.6	55.6	−1,313.5
III	2,206.5	1,154.0	832.0	91.8	216.9	947.0	48.3	61.1	−3.9	3,525.1	998.7	2,187.6	271.5	67.3	−1,318.6
IV	2,273.4	1,207.2	834.2	92.7	265.9	946.8	54.7	69.6	−5.0	3,546.8	1,015.1	2,212.5	263.4	55.7	−1,273.5
2010: I	2,326.6	1,252.3	860.3	92.4	285.7	961.1	49.8	68.6	−5.1	3,641.8	1,034.2	2,289.1	264.0	54.6	−1,315.2
II	2,365.8	1,282.0	887.4	95.3	284.3	969.5	52.2	68.3	−6.2	3,685.3	1,057.0	2,287.8	286.2	54.3	−1,319.5
III	2,427.2	1,333.9	908.2	97.2	314.1	973.8	55.0	71.7	−7.2	3,730.2	1,068.3	2,325.8	281.0	55.1	−1,303.1
IV	2,461.9	1,371.3	921.0	97.1	336.1	974.8	54.8	70.4	−9.4	3,756.3	1,063.6	2,340.6	294.5	57.7	−1,294.4
2011: I	2,509.8	1,494.0	1,052.6	102.4	324.8	900.5	55.7	69.7	−10.0	3,737.1	1,054.2	2,314.8	309.3	58.8	−1,227.3
II	2,522.9	1,504.1	1,068.5	108.3	312.4	905.1	55.6	69.0	−11.0	3,830.6	1,071.0	2,341.8	356.4	61.4	−1,307.7
III	2,511.3	1,494.2	1,082.0	108.1	287.1	907.0	55.5	68.1	−13.4	3,743.3	1,069.0	2,292.3	320.1	62.0	−1,232.0
IV	2,534.3	1,518.5	1,097.7	110.9	292.5	909.2	54.5	68.3	−16.4	3,716.8	1,052.0	2,288.6	314.0	62.2	−1,182.6
2012: I	2,664.9	1,629.2	1,124.9	113.3	375.7	929.3	54.7	68.3	−16.7	3,723.6	1,055.6	2,301.0	306.7	60.4	−1,058.7
II	2,659.5	1,631.2	1,131.0	115.2	368.1	931.5	53.2	61.6	−18.0	3,774.8	1,054.8	2,310.8	348.7	60.6	−1,115.4
III	2,673.4	1,650.1	1,141.4	116.1	375.5	936.0	53.0	53.1	−18.8	3,760.6	1,086.3	2,326.1	288.1	60.1	−1,087.2
IV p			1,162.4	119.5		945.1	52.7	53.6	−17.4	3,772.1	1,041.1	2,339.8	330.6	60.6	

[1] Includes taxes from the rest of the world, not shown separately.
[2] Includes an item for the difference between wage accruals and disbursements, not shown separately.
[3] Includes Federal grants-in-aid to State and local governments. See Table B–82 for data on Federal grants-in-aid.

Source: Department of Commerce (Bureau of Economic Analysis).

TABLE B–85. State and local government current receipts and expenditures, national income and product accounts (NIPA), 1964–2012

[Billions of dollars; quarterly data at seasonally adjusted annual rates]

Year or quarter	Current receipts									Current expenditures					Net State and local government saving
	Total	Current tax receipts				Contributions for government social insurance	Income receipts on assets	Current transfer receipts [1]	Current surplus of government enterprises	Total [2]	Consumption expenditures	Government social benefit payments to persons	Interest payments	Subsidies	
		Total	Personal current taxes	Taxes on production and imports	Taxes on corporate income										
1964	61.3	49.8	6.1	41.8	1.8	0.7	1.9	7.3	1.6	54.9	45.8	6.2	2.9	0.0	6.4
1965	66.5	53.9	6.6	45.3	2.0	.8	2.2	8.0	1.7	60.0	50.2	6.7	3.1	.0	6.5
1966	74.9	58.8	7.8	48.8	2.2	.8	2.6	11.1	1.6	67.2	56.1	7.6	3.4	.0	7.8
1967	82.5	64.0	8.6	52.8	2.6	.9	3.0	13.1	1.5	75.5	62.6	9.2	3.7	.0	7.0
1968	93.5	73.4	10.6	59.5	3.3	.9	3.5	14.2	1.5	86.0	70.4	11.4	4.2	.0	7.5
1969	105.5	82.5	12.8	66.0	3.6	1.0	4.3	16.2	1.5	97.5	79.8	13.2	4.4	.0	8.0
1970	120.1	91.3	14.2	73.3	3.7	1.1	5.2	21.1	1.5	113.0	91.5	16.1	5.3	.0	7.1
1971	134.9	101.7	15.9	81.5	4.3	1.2	5.5	25.2	1.4	128.5	102.7	19.3	6.5	.0	6.5
1972	158.4	115.6	20.9	89.4	5.3	1.3	5.9	34.0	1.6	142.8	113.2	22.0	7.5	.1	15.6
1973	174.3	126.3	22.8	97.4	6.0	1.5	7.8	37.3	1.5	158.6	126.0	24.1	8.5	.1	15.7
1974	188.1	136.0	24.5	104.8	6.7	1.7	10.2	39.3	.9	178.7	143.7	25.3	9.6	.1	9.3
1975	209.6	147.4	26.9	113.2	7.3	1.8	11.2	48.7	.4	207.1	165.1	30.8	11.1	.2	2.5
1976	233.7	165.7	31.1	125.0	9.6	2.2	10.4	55.0	.4	226.3	179.5	34.1	12.5	.2	7.4
1977	259.9	183.7	35.4	136.9	11.4	2.8	11.7	61.4	.3	246.8	195.9	37.0	13.7	.2	13.1
1978	287.6	198.2	40.5	145.6	12.1	3.4	14.7	71.1	.3	268.9	213.2	40.8	14.9	.2	18.7
1979	308.4	212.0	44.0	154.4	13.6	3.9	20.1	72.7	-.3	295.4	233.3	44.3	17.2	.3	13.0
1980	338.2	230.0	48.9	166.7	14.5	3.6	26.3	79.5	-1.2	329.4	258.4	51.2	19.4	.4	8.8
1981	370.2	255.8	54.6	185.7	15.4	3.9	32.0	81.0	-2.4	362.7	282.3	57.1	22.8	.4	7.6
1982	391.4	273.2	59.1	200.0	14.0	4.0	36.7	79.1	-1.6	393.6	304.9	61.2	27.1	.5	-2.2
1983	428.6	300.9	66.1	218.9	15.9	4.1	41.4	82.4	-.2	423.7	324.1	66.9	32.3	.4	4.9
1984	480.2	337.3	76.0	242.5	18.8	4.7	47.7	89.0	1.5	456.2	347.7	71.2	37.0	.4	23.9
1985	521.1	363.7	81.4	262.1	20.2	4.9	54.8	94.5	3.2	498.7	381.8	77.3	39.4	.3	22.4
1986	561.6	389.5	87.2	279.7	22.7	6.0	58.4	105.0	2.8	540.9	418.1	84.3	38.2	.3	20.7
1987	590.6	422.1	96.6	301.6	23.9	7.2	58.2	100.0	3.1	578.6	441.4	90.7	46.2	.3	12.0
1988	635.5	452.8	102.1	324.6	26.0	8.4	60.5	109.0	4.8	618.3	471.0	98.5	48.4	.4	17.2
1989	687.5	488.0	114.6	349.1	24.2	9.0	65.7	118.1	6.7	667.4	504.5	109.3	53.2	.4	20.1
1990	738.0	519.1	122.6	374.1	22.5	10.0	68.5	133.5	6.9	731.8	547.0	127.7	56.8	.4	6.2
1991	789.4	544.3	125.3	395.3	23.6	11.6	68.0	158.2	7.3	795.2	577.5	156.5	60.8	.4	-5.8
1992	846.2	579.8	135.3	420.1	24.4	13.1	64.8	180.3	8.3	847.6	606.2	180.0	61.0	.4	-1.4
1993	888.2	604.7	141.1	436.8	26.9	14.1	61.3	198.1	9.9	889.1	634.2	195.2	59.4	.4	-.9
1994	944.8	644.2	148.0	466.3	30.0	14.5	63.3	212.3	10.5	936.6	668.2	206.7	61.4	.3	8.2
1995	991.9	672.1	158.1	482.4	31.7	13.6	68.5	224.2	13.5	982.7	701.3	217.6	63.5	.3	9.2
1996	1,045.1	709.6	168.7	507.9	33.0	12.5	73.4	234.0	15.6	1,022.1	730.2	224.3	67.3	.3	23.0
1997	1,099.5	749.9	182.0	533.8	34.1	10.8	78.2	246.4	14.2	1,063.2	764.5	227.6	70.6	.4	36.3
1998	1,164.5	794.9	201.2	558.8	34.9	10.4	81.5	265.3	12.5	1,117.6	808.6	235.8	72.8	.4	46.9
1999	1,240.4	840.4	214.5	590.2	35.8	9.8	85.8	291.1	13.3	1,198.6	870.6	252.3	75.2	.4	41.8
2000	1,322.6	893.2	236.7	621.3	35.2	10.8	94.3	313.9	10.4	1,281.3	930.6	271.4	78.8	.5	41.3
2001	1,374.0	914.3	243.0	642.4	28.9	13.7	90.0	348.0	8.0	1,389.9	994.2	305.1	83.0	7.7	-15.9
2002	1,412.7	928.7	221.8	676.0	30.9	15.9	79.6	382.3	6.1	1,466.8	1,049.4	333.0	83.5	.9	-54.1
2003	1,496.3	977.7	226.2	717.5	34.0	20.1	74.0	421.3	3.3	1,535.1	1,096.5	353.4	85.1	.1	-38.8
2004	1,601.0	1,059.4	248.6	769.1	41.7	24.1	77.1	439.4	1.0	1,609.3	1,139.1	384.3	85.6	.4	-8.4
2005	1,730.4	1,163.1	276.7	831.4	54.9	24.8	88.3	454.3	.1	1,704.5	1,212.0	404.8	87.3	.4	25.9
2006	1,829.7	1,249.0	302.5	887.4	59.2	21.8	103.5	456.7	-1.3	1,778.6	1,282.3	402.9	93.0	.4	51.0
2007	1,923.1	1,313.6	323.1	932.7	57.8	18.9	114.5	485.1	-9.1	1,910.8	1,368.9	433.7	101.1	7.1	12.2
2008	1,944.8	1,326.4	334.4	944.6	47.4	19.0	106.8	505.0	-12.3	2,017.0	1,449.2	456.7	108.1	3.0	-72.2
2009	1,961.4	1,264.9	287.6	931.8	45.5	19.0	95.0	593.6	-11.1	2,074.6	1,473.3	495.1	104.8	1.4	-113.2
2010	2,042.4	1,304.6	300.6	959.5	44.5	18.4	88.8	643.2	-12.5	2,132.1	1,496.2	528.3	106.0	1.6	-89.7
2011	2,064.4	1,360.8	322.8	990.4	47.6	18.3	86.4	612.7	-13.8	2,166.3	1,518.0	538.5	109.2	.5	-102.0
2012 p			334.7	1,014.3		17.5	85.3	584.9	-16.3	2,198.8	1,530.9	554.6	112.8	.5	
2009: I	1,909.9	1,254.8	284.4	923.3	47.1	19.3	98.3	549.3	-11.8	2,025.5	1,436.1	480.0	107.4	2.0	-115.6
II	1,955.3	1,240.1	274.9	922.3	42.9	19.1	95.6	611.6	-11.0	2,065.2	1,465.8	493.5	104.7	1.2	-109.9
III	1,975.9	1,275.2	293.6	935.9	45.6	18.8	93.9	598.7	-10.6	2,101.5	1,487.9	508.6	103.8	1.2	-125.5
IV	2,004.4	1,289.6	297.4	945.7	46.4	18.6	92.4	614.6	-10.8	2,106.3	1,503.5	498.4	103.1	1.2	-101.8
2010: I	2,011.8	1,289.4	296.6	950.9	41.9	18.5	90.9	624.7	-11.7	2,122.9	1,505.2	511.7	104.5	1.6	-111.1
II	2,010.5	1,283.3	285.6	955.2	42.5	18.4	89.6	631.5	-12.4	2,118.9	1,494.2	516.6	106.0	2.1	-108.4
III	2,061.9	1,312.9	303.6	961.4	47.8	18.3	87.7	655.9	-12.9	2,134.3	1,488.6	538.0	106.1	1.6	-72.4
IV	2,085.6	1,332.6	316.5	970.4	45.7	18.4	86.9	660.8	-13.1	2,152.3	1,496.9	546.9	107.5	1.0	-66.7
2011: I	2,073.9	1,350.2	319.9	982.1	48.3	18.4	86.7	631.7	-13.1	2,172.6	1,511.4	552.0	108.3	.9	-98.7
II	2,098.0	1,364.5	328.1	990.7	45.7	18.4	86.4	642.2	-13.5	2,172.6	1,520.3	542.9	109.0	.4	-74.6
III	2,045.2	1,358.9	321.7	990.1	47.1	18.3	86.6	595.4	-14.1	2,163.2	1,522.0	531.4	109.3	.4	-118.0
IV	2,040.5	1,369.6	321.4	998.8	49.3	18.1	86.0	581.6	-14.7	2,157.0	1,518.4	527.9	110.3	.4	-116.5
2012: I	2,050.4	1,391.2	325.9	1,015.2	50.1	17.8	85.7	571.1	-15.4	2,178.1	1,531.4	534.4	111.9	.5	-127.6
II	2,066.7	1,396.1	334.2	1,015.7	46.2	17.5	85.8	583.4	-16.1	2,190.3	1,525.5	551.6	112.8	.5	-123.7
III	2,069.2	1,395.7	335.0	1,012.3	48.4	17.3	85.0	587.8	-16.7	2,209.2	1,532.4	563.7	112.6	.5	-140.0
IV p			343.8	1,014.2		17.2	84.8	597.5	-17.0	2,217.6	1,534.4	568.8	113.9	.5	

[1] Includes Federal grants-in-aid. See Table B–82 for data on Federal grants-in-aid.
[2] Includes an item for the difference between wage accruals and disbursements, not shown separately.

Source: Department of Commerce (Bureau of Economic Analysis).

TABLE B–86. State and local government revenues and expenditures, selected fiscal years, 1948–2010

[Millions of dollars]

Fiscal year [1]	General revenues by source [2]							General expenditures by function [2]				
	Total	Property taxes	Sales and gross receipts taxes	Individual income taxes	Corpora- tion net income taxes	Revenue from Federal Govern- ment	All other [3]	Total [4]	Edu- cation	High- ways	Public welfare [4]	All other [4, 5]
1948	17,250	6,126	4,442	543	592	1,861	3,686	17,684	5,379	3,036	2,099	7,170
1950	20,911	7,349	5,154	788	593	2,486	4,541	22,787	7,177	3,803	2,940	8,867
1952	25,181	8,652	6,357	998	846	2,566	5,762	26,098	8,318	4,650	2,386	10,744
1953	27,307	9,375	6,927	1,065	817	2,870	6,253	27,910	9,390	4,987	2,914	10,619
1954	29,012	9,967	7,276	1,127	778	2,966	6,898	30,701	10,557	5,527	3,060	11,557
1955	31,073	10,735	7,643	1,237	744	3,131	7,583	33,724	11,907	6,452	3,168	12,197
1956	34,670	11,749	8,691	1,538	890	3,335	8,467	36,715	13,224	6,953	3,139	13,399
1957	38,164	12,864	9,467	1,754	984	3,843	9,252	40,375	14,134	7,816	3,485	14,940
1958	41,219	14,047	9,829	1,759	1,018	4,865	9,701	44,851	15,919	8,567	3,818	16,547
1959	45,306	14,983	10,437	1,994	1,001	6,377	10,514	48,887	17,283	9,592	4,136	17,876
1960	50,505	16,405	11,849	2,463	1,180	6,974	11,634	51,876	18,719	9,428	4,404	19,325
1961	54,037	18,002	12,463	2,613	1,266	7,131	12,562	56,201	20,574	9,844	4,720	21,063
1962	58,252	19,054	13,494	3,037	1,308	7,871	13,488	60,206	22,216	10,357	5,084	22,549
1963	62,891	20,089	14,456	3,269	1,505	8,722	14,850	64,815	23,776	11,135	5,481	24,423
1963–64	68,443	21,241	15,762	3,791	1,695	10,002	15,952	69,302	26,286	11,664	5,766	25,586
1964–65	74,000	22,583	17,118	4,090	1,929	11,029	17,251	74,678	28,563	12,221	6,315	27,579
1965–66	83,036	24,670	19,085	4,760	2,038	13,214	19,269	82,843	33,287	12,770	6,757	30,029
1966–67	91,197	26,047	20,530	5,825	2,227	15,370	21,198	93,350	37,919	13,932	8,218	33,281
1967–68	101,264	27,747	22,911	7,308	2,518	17,181	23,599	102,411	41,158	14,481	9,857	36,915
1968–69	114,550	30,673	26,519	8,908	3,180	19,153	26,117	116,728	47,238	15,417	12,110	41,963
1969–70	130,756	34,054	30,322	10,812	3,738	21,857	29,973	131,332	52,718	16,427	14,679	47,508
1970–71	144,927	37,852	33,233	11,900	3,424	26,146	32,372	150,674	59,413	18,095	18,226	54,940
1971–72	167,535	42,877	37,518	15,227	4,416	31,342	36,156	168,549	65,813	19,021	21,117	62,598
1972–73	190,222	45,283	42,047	17,994	5,425	39,264	40,210	181,357	69,713	18,615	23,582	69,447
1973–74	207,670	47,705	46,098	19,491	6,015	41,820	46,542	199,222	75,833	19,946	25,085	78,358
1974–75	228,171	51,491	49,815	21,454	6,642	47,034	51,735	230,722	87,858	22,528	28,156	92,180
1975–76	256,176	57,001	54,547	24,575	7,273	55,589	57,191	256,731	97,216	23,907	32,604	103,004
1976–77	285,157	62,527	60,641	29,246	9,174	62,444	61,125	274,215	102,780	23,058	35,906	112,472
1977–78	315,960	66,422	67,596	33,176	10,738	69,592	68,435	296,984	110,758	24,609	39,140	122,478
1978–79	343,236	64,944	74,247	36,932	12,128	75,164	79,822	327,517	119,448	28,440	41,898	137,731
1979–80	382,322	68,499	79,927	42,080	13,321	83,029	95,467	369,086	133,211	33,311	47,288	155,276
1980–81	423,404	74,969	85,971	46,426	14,143	90,294	111,599	407,449	145,784	34,603	54,105	172,957
1981–82	457,654	82,067	93,613	50,738	15,028	87,282	128,925	436,733	154,282	34,520	57,996	189,935
1982–83	486,753	89,105	100,247	55,129	14,258	90,007	138,008	466,516	163,876	36,655	60,906	205,080
1983–84	542,730	96,457	114,097	64,871	16,798	96,935	153,571	505,008	176,108	39,419	66,414	223,068
1984–85	598,121	103,757	126,376	70,361	19,152	106,158	172,317	553,899	192,686	44,989	71,479	244,745
1985–86	641,486	111,709	135,005	74,365	19,994	113,099	187,314	605,623	210,819	49,368	75,868	269,568
1986–87	686,860	121,203	144,091	83,935	22,425	114,857	200,350	657,134	226,619	52,355	82,650	295,510
1987–88	726,762	132,212	156,452	88,350	23,663	117,602	208,482	704,921	242,683	55,621	89,090	317,527
1988–89	786,129	142,400	166,336	97,806	25,926	125,824	227,838	762,360	263,898	58,105	97,879	342,479
1989–90	849,502	155,613	177,885	105,640	23,566	136,802	249,996	834,818	288,148	61,057	110,518	375,094
1990–91	902,207	167,999	185,570	109,341	22,242	154,099	262,955	908,108	309,302	64,937	130,402	403,467
1991–92	979,137	180,337	197,731	115,638	23,880	179,174	282,376	981,253	324,652	67,351	158,723	430,526
1992–93	1,041,643	189,744	209,649	123,235	26,417	198,663	293,935	1,030,434	342,287	68,370	170,705	449,072
1993–94	1,100,490	197,141	223,628	128,810	28,320	215,492	307,099	1,077,665	353,287	72,067	183,394	468,916
1994–95	1,169,505	203,451	237,268	137,931	31,406	228,771	330,677	1,149,863	378,273	77,109	196,703	497,779
1995–96	1,222,821	209,440	248,993	146,844	32,009	234,891	350,645	1,193,276	398,859	79,092	197,354	517,971
1996–97	1,289,237	218,877	261,418	159,042	33,820	244,847	371,233	1,249,984	418,416	82,062	203,779	545,727
1997–98	1,365,762	230,150	274,883	175,630	34,412	255,048	395,639	1,318,042	450,365	87,214	208,120	572,343
1998–99	1,434,029	239,672	290,993	189,309	33,922	270,628	409,505	1,402,369	483,259	93,018	218,957	607,134
1999–2000	1,541,322	249,178	309,290	211,661	36,059	291,950	443,186	1,506,797	521,612	101,336	237,336	646,512
2000–01	1,647,161	263,689	320,217	226,334	35,296	324,033	477,592	1,626,066	563,575	107,235	261,622	693,634
2001–02	1,684,879	279,191	324,123	202,832	28,152	360,546	490,035	1,736,866	594,694	115,295	285,464	741,413
2002–03	1,763,212	296,683	337,787	199,407	31,369	389,264	508,702	1,821,917	621,335	117,696	310,783	772,102
2003–04	1,887,397	317,941	361,027	215,215	33,716	423,112	536,386	1,908,543	655,182	117,215	340,523	795,622
2004–05	2,026,034	335,779	384,266	242,273	43,256	438,558	581,902	2,012,110	688,314	126,350	365,295	832,151
2005–06	2,197,475	364,559	417,735	268,667	53,081	452,975	640,458	2,123,663	728,917	136,502	373,846	884,398
2006–07	2,329,356	388,701	440,331	290,278	60,626	464,585	684,834	2,259,899	773,676	144,714	388,277	953,232
2007–08	2,421,977	409,540	449,945	304,902	57,231	477,441	722,919	2,406,183	826,061	153,831	408,920	1,017,372
2008–09	2,425,812	431,896	433,373	270,894	46,281	537,174	706,193	2,501,260	852,172	154,172	436,698	1,058,219
2009–10	2,502,055	441,661	431,176	260,338	42,860	623,732	702,288	2,542,453	859,965	155,870	460,739	1,065,879

[1] Fiscal years not the same for all governments. See Note.
[2] Excludes revenues or expenditures of publicly owned utilities and liquor stores and of insurance-trust activities. Intergovernmental receipts and payments between State and local governments are also excluded.
[3] Includes motor vehicle license taxes, other taxes, and charges and miscellaneous revenues.
[4] Includes intergovernmental payments to the Federal Government.
[5] Includes expenditures for libraries, hospitals, health, employment security administration, veterans' services, air transportation, sea and inland port facilities, parking facilities, transit subsidies, police protection, fire protection, correction, protective inspection and regulation, sewerage, natural resources, parks and recreation, housing and community development, solid waste management, financial administration, judicial and legal, general public buildings, other government administration, interest on general debt, and other general expenditures, not elsewhere classified.

Note: Except for States listed, data for fiscal years listed from 1963–64 to 2009–10 are the aggregation of data for government fiscal years that ended in the 12-month period from July 1 to June 30 of those years; Texas used August and Alabama and Michigan used September as end dates. Data for 1963 and earlier years include data for government fiscal years ending during that particular calendar year.
Data prior to 1952 are not available for intervening years.
Source: Department of Commerce (Bureau of the Census).

TABLE B–87. U.S. Treasury securities outstanding by kind of obligation, 1974–2012

[Billions of dollars]

End of year or month	Total Treasury securities outstanding [1]	Marketable Total [2]	Treasury bills	Treasury notes	Treasury bonds	Treasury inflation-protected securities Total	Notes	Bonds	Nonmarketable Total	U.S. savings securities [3]	Foreign series [4]	Government account series	Other [5]
Fiscal year:													
1974	473.2	266.6	105.0	128.4	33.1	....	....		206.7	61.9	25.0	115.4	4.3
1975	532.1	315.6	128.6	150.3	36.8	....	....		216.5	65.5	23.2	124.2	3.6
1976	619.3	392.6	161.2	191.8	39.6	....	....		226.7	69.7	21.5	130.6	4.9
1977	697.6	443.5	156.1	241.7	45.7	....	....		254.1	75.4	21.8	140.1	16.8
1978	767.0	485.2	160.9	267.9	56.4	....	....		281.8	79.8	21.7	153.3	27.1
1979	819.0	506.7	161.4	274.2	71.1	....	....		312.3	80.4	28.1	176.4	27.4
1980	906.4	594.5	199.8	310.9	83.8	....	....		311.9	72.7	25.2	189.8	24.2
1981	996.5	683.2	223.4	363.6	96.2	....	....		313.3	68.0	20.5	201.1	23.7
1982	1,140.9	824.4	277.9	442.9	103.6	....	....		316.5	67.3	14.6	210.5	24.1
1983	1,375.8	1,024.0	340.7	557.5	125.7	....	....		351.8	70.0	11.5	234.7	35.6
1984	1,559.6	1,176.6	356.8	661.7	158.1	....	....		383.0	72.8	8.8	259.5	41.8
1985	1,821.0	1,360.2	384.2	776.4	199.5	....	....		460.8	77.0	6.6	313.9	63.3
1986	2,122.7	1,564.3	410.7	896.9	241.7	....	....		558.4	85.6	4.1	365.9	102.8
1987	2,347.8	1,676.0	378.3	1,005.1	277.6	....	....		671.8	97.0	4.4	440.7	129.8
1988	2,599.9	1,802.9	398.5	1,089.6	299.9	....	....		797.0	106.2	6.3	536.5	148.0
1989	2,836.3	1,892.8	406.6	1,133.2	338.0	....	....		943.5	114.0	6.8	663.7	159.0
1990	3,210.9	2,092.8	482.5	1,218.1	377.2	....	....		1,118.2	122.2	36.0	779.4	180.6
1991	3,662.8	2,390.7	564.6	1,387.7	423.4	....	....		1,272.1	133.5	41.6	908.4	188.5
1992	4,061.8	2,677.5	634.3	1,566.3	461.8	....	....		1,384.3	148.3	37.0	1,011.0	188.0
1993	4,408.6	2,904.9	658.4	1,734.2	497.4	....	....		1,503.7	167.0	42.5	1,114.3	179.9
1994	4,689.5	3,091.6	697.3	1,867.5	511.8	....	....		1,597.9	176.4	42.0	1,211.7	167.8
1995	4,950.6	3,260.4	742.5	1,980.3	522.6	....	....		1,690.2	181.2	41.0	1,324.3	143.8
1996	5,220.8	3,418.4	761.2	2,098.7	543.5	....	....		1,802.4	184.1	37.5	1,454.7	126.1
1997	5,407.5	3,439.6	701.9	2,122.2	576.2	24.4	24.4		1,967.9	182.7	34.9	1,608.5	141.9
1998	5,518.7	3,331.0	637.6	2,009.1	610.4	58.8	41.9	17.0	2,187.7	180.8	35.1	1,777.3	194.4
1999	5,647.2	3,233.0	653.2	1,828.8	643.7	92.4	67.6	24.8	2,414.2	180.0	31.0	2,005.2	198.1
2000	5,622.1	2,992.8	616.2	1,611.3	635.3	115.0	81.6	33.4	2,629.3	177.7	25.4	2,242.9	183.3
2001 [1]	5,807.5	2,930.7	734.9	1,433.0	613.0	134.9	95.1	39.7	2,876.7	186.5	18.3	2,492.1	179.9
2002	6,228.2	3,136.7	868.3	1,521.6	593.0	138.9	93.7	45.1	3,091.5	193.3	12.5	2,707.3	178.4
2003	6,783.2	3,460.7	918.2	1,799.5	576.9	166.1	120.0	46.1	3,322.5	201.6	11.0	2,912.2	197.7
2004	7,379.1	3,846.1	961.5	2,109.6	552.0	223.0	....		3,533.0	204.2	5.9	3,130.0	192.9
2005	7,932.7	4,084.9	914.3	2,328.8	520.7	307.1	....		3,847.8	203.6	3.1	3,380.6	260.5
2006	8,507.0	4,303.0	911.5	2,447.2	534.7	395.6	....		4,203.9	203.7	3.0	3,722.7	274.5
2007	9,007.7	4,448.1	958.1	2,458.0	561.1	456.9	....		4,559.5	197.1	3.0	4,026.8	332.6
2008	10,024.7	5,236.0	1,489.8	2,624.8	582.9	524.5	....		4,788.7	194.3	3.0	4,297.7	293.8
2009	11,909.8	7,009.7	1,992.5	3,773.8	679.8	551.7	....		4,900.1	192.5	4.9	4,454.3	248.4
2010	13,561.6	8,498.3	1,788.5	5,255.9	849.9	593.8	....		5,063.3	188.8	4.2	4,645.3	225.0
2011	14,790.3	9,624.5	1,477.5	6,412.5	1,020.4	705.7	....		5,165.8	185.2	3.0	4,793.9	183.7
2012	16,066.2	10,749.8	1,616.0	7,120.7	1,198.2	807.8	....		5,316.5	183.7	3.0	4,939.5	190.4
2011: Jan	14,131.1	8,964.7	1,760.5	5,672.2	905.9	615.8	....		5,166.3	187.5	4.0	4,755.8	219.0
Feb	14,194.8	9,048.2	1,738.5	5,750.8	922.3	626.3	....		5,146.6	187.3	3.8	4,741.3	214.1
Mar	14,270.1	9,132.7	1,698.5	5,847.9	935.3	640.8	....		5,137.4	186.9	3.8	4,733.0	213.7
Apr	14,287.6	9,136.6	1,638.5	5,903.5	948.9	635.4	....		5,151.1	186.6	3.8	4,748.0	212.7
May	14,344.7	9,262.2	1,578.5	6,054.7	964.9	653.8	....		5,082.4	186.4	3.7	4,684.8	207.5
June	14,343.1	9,334.6	1,531.5	6,151.3	977.9	665.5	....		5,008.4	186.1	3.7	4,620.4	198.3
July	14,342.4	9,377.6	1,492.5	6,204.3	990.9	681.5	....		4,964.7	185.8	3.1	4,588.2	187.7
Aug	14,684.3	9,521.8	1,493.5	6,318.7	1,007.4	693.8	....		5,162.5	185.4	3.0	4,791.3	182.8
Sept	14,790.3	9,624.5	1,477.5	6,412.5	1,020.4	705.7	....		5,165.8	185.2	3.0	4,793.9	183.7
Oct	14,993.7	9,746.5	1,482.5	6,507.0	1,033.4	715.2	....		5,247.2	185.6	3.0	4,872.2	186.4
Nov	15,110.5	9,878.3	1,512.5	6,579.0	1,050.6	727.8	....		5,232.2	185.5	3.0	4,857.2	186.5
Dec	15,222.9	9,936.9	1,520.5	6,605.1	1,064.1	738.8	....		5,286.1	185.3	3.0	4,913.9	183.9
2012: Jan	15,356.1	10,068.9	1,525.4	6,711.3	1,078.0	745.7	....		5,287.2	185.2	3.8	4,922.0	176.2
Feb	15,488.9	10,222.3	1,610.4	6,754.4	1,096.0	753.0	....		5,266.6	185.0	3.8	4,902.1	175.7
Mar	15,582.1	10,338.3	1,674.4	6,776.5	1,109.9	769.0	....		5,243.8	184.8	3.6	4,870.8	184.6
Apr	15,692.4	10,400.1	1,613.4	6,883.3	1,125.3	769.6	....		5,292.3	184.9	3.4	4,923.6	191.5
May	15,770.7	10,486.2	1,605.4	6,941.5	1,142.3	788.5	....		5,284.5	184.7	3.2	4,901.7	195.0
June	15,855.0	10,520.7	1,596.4	6,962.9	1,156.2	798.1	....		5,334.4	184.4	3.0	4,953.1	193.8
July	15,933.2	10,607.3	1,581.0	7,067.2	1,169.2	782.9	....		5,325.9	184.2	3.0	4,952.9	185.8
Aug	16,015.8	10,757.0	1,663.0	7,105.8	1,185.2	795.9	....		5,258.7	183.9	3.0	4,885.5	186.4
Sept	16,066.2	10,749.8	1,616.0	7,120.7	1,198.2	807.8	....		5,316.5	183.7	3.0	4,939.5	190.4
Oct	16,261.5	10,887.5	1,622.0	7,228.2	1,211.2	819.0	....		5,374.0	183.5	3.0	4,992.1	195.4
Nov	16,369.5	11,032.8	1,695.0	7,267.7	1,227.2	835.8	....		5,336.8	183.2	3.0	4,959.9	190.7
Dec	16,432.7	11,053.2	1,629.0	7,327.1	1,240.2	849.8	....		5,379.5	182.5	3.0	4,999.6	194.4

[1] Data beginning with January 2001 are interest-bearing and non-interest-bearing securities; prior data are interest-bearing securities only.
[2] Data from 1986 to 2002 and 2005 to 2012 include Federal Financing Bank securities, not shown separately.
[3] Through 1996, series is U.S. savings bonds. Beginning 1997, includes U.S. retirement plan bonds, U.S. individual retirement bonds, and U.S. savings notes previously included in "other" nonmarketable securities.
[4] Nonmarketable certificates of indebtedness, notes, bonds, and bills in the Treasury foreign series of dollar-denominated and foreign-currency-denominated issues.
[5] Includes depository bonds; retirement plan bonds; Rural Electrification Administration bonds; State and local bonds; special issues held only by U.S. Government agencies and trust funds and the Federal home loan banks; for the period July 2003 through February 2004, depositary compensation securities; and beginning August 2008, Hope bonds for the HOPE For Homeowners Program.

Note: Through fiscal year 1976, the fiscal year was on a July 1–June 30 basis; beginning with October 1976 (fiscal year 1977), the fiscal year is on an October 1–September 30 basis.

Source: Department of the Treasury.

TABLE B–88. Maturity distribution and average length of marketable interest-bearing public debt securities held by private investors, 1974–2012

End of year or month	Amount outstanding, privately held	Maturity class					Average length[1]
		Within 1 year	1 to 5 years	5 to 10 years	10 to 20 years	20 years and over	
		Millions of dollars					Months
Fiscal year:							
1974	164,862	87,150	50,103	14,197	9,930	3,481	35
1975	210,382	115,677	65,852	15,385	8,857	4,611	32
1976	279,782	150,296	90,578	24,169	8,087	6,652	31
1977	326,674	161,329	113,319	33,067	8,428	10,531	35
1978	356,501	163,819	132,993	33,500	11,383	14,805	39
1979	380,530	181,883	127,574	32,279	18,489	20,304	43
1980	463,717	220,084	156,244	38,809	25,901	22,679	41
1981	549,863	256,187	182,237	48,743	32,569	30,127	43
1982	682,043	314,436	221,783	75,749	33,017	37,058	43
1983	862,631	379,579	294,955	99,174	40,826	48,097	44
1984	1,017,488	437,941	332,808	130,417	49,664	66,658	49
1985	1,185,675	472,661	402,766	159,383	62,853	88,012	54
1986	1,354,275	506,903	467,348	189,995	70,664	119,365	59
1987	1,445,366	483,582	526,746	209,160	72,862	153,016	65
1988	1,555,208	524,201	552,993	232,453	74,186	171,375	66
1989	1,654,660	546,751	578,333	247,428	80,616	201,532	70
1990	1,841,903	626,297	630,144	267,573	82,713	235,176	70
1991	2,113,799	713,778	761,243	280,574	84,900	273,304	70
1992	2,363,802	808,705	866,329	295,921	84,706	308,141	69
1993	2,562,336	858,135	978,714	306,663	94,345	324,479	69
1994	2,719,861	877,932	1,128,322	289,998	88,208	335,401	66
1995	2,870,781	1,002,875	1,157,492	290,111	87,297	333,006	63
1996	3,011,185	1,058,558	1,212,258	306,643	111,360	322,366	62
1997	2,998,846	1,017,913	1,206,993	321,622	154,205	298,113	64
1998	2,856,637	940,572	1,105,175	319,331	157,347	334,212	68
1999	2,728,011	915,145	962,644	378,163	149,703	322,356	72
2000	2,469,152	858,903	791,540	355,382	167,082	296,246	75
2001	2,328,302	900,178	650,522	329,247	174,653	273,702	73
2002	2,492,821	939,986	802,032	311,176	203,816	235,811	66
2003	2,804,092	1,057,049	955,239	351,552	243,755	196,497	61
2004	3,145,244	1,127,850	1,150,979	414,728	243,036	208,652	59
2005	3,334,411	1,100,783	1,279,646	499,386	281,229	173,367	58
2006	3,496,359	1,140,553	1,295,589	589,748	290,733	179,736	59
2007	3,634,666	1,176,510	1,309,871	677,905	291,963	178,417	58
2008	4,745,256	2,042,003	1,468,455	719,347	352,430	163,022	49
2009	6,228,565	2,604,676	2,074,723	994,688	350,550	203,928	49
2010	7,676,335	2,479,518	2,955,561	1,529,283	340,861	371,112	57
2011	7,951,366	2,503,926	3,084,882	1,543,847	309,151	509,559	60
2012	9,039,954	2,896,780	3,851,873	1,487,726	270,921	532,654	55
2011: Jan	7,825,784	2,559,917	2,968,708	1,552,207	328,998	415,954	57
Feb	7,810,240	2,568,072	2,962,896	1,527,039	329,050	423,183	57
Mar	7,781,983	2,555,954	2,937,225	1,528,474	329,019	431,311	58
Apr	7,653,649	2,522,043	2,870,226	1,496,984	324,243	440,152	58
May	7,721,626	2,499,253	2,953,201	1,499,893	317,188	452,090	59
June	7,706,588	2,474,344	2,961,638	1,486,856	315,369	468,382	59
July	7,674,300	2,481,706	2,924,762	1,471,149	315,618	481,063	60
Aug	7,861,156	2,495,843	3,048,014	1,510,394	310,042	496,863	60
Sept	7,951,366	2,503,926	3,084,882	1,543,847	309,151	509,559	60
Oct	8,074,439	2,546,549	3,164,655	1,539,649	307,001	516,584	60
Nov	8,196,987	2,615,920	3,234,816	1,535,457	292,136	518,658	59
Dec	8,205,749	2,641,533	3,251,453	1,505,074	289,711	517,978	59
2012: Jan	8,399,585	2,652,591	3,412,176	1,527,281	287,847	519,690	58
Feb	8,551,311	2,743,327	3,479,479	1,513,140	285,554	529,809	58
Mar	8,608,508	2,820,573	3,477,460	1,498,189	283,948	528,338	57
Apr	8,729,683	2,776,665	3,614,220	1,528,759	288,053	521,987	57
May	8,815,377	2,795,764	3,682,506	1,524,989	287,006	525,113	57
June	8,792,599	2,808,138	3,667,577	1,501,719	285,192	529,973	56
July	8,950,594	2,818,970	3,790,401	1,528,840	282,782	529,601	56
Aug	9,102,348	2,934,717	3,855,400	1,507,576	273,162	531,493	55
Sept	9,039,954	2,896,780	3,851,873	1,487,726	270,921	532,654	55
Oct	9,228,648	2,906,732	3,997,210	1,516,348	269,465	538,893	55
Nov	9,361,541	2,992,450	4,051,300	1,513,173	263,682	540,956	54
Dec	9,373,556	2,932,843	4,124,101	1,516,995	261,723	537,895	54

[1] Average length calculations are to call date. Treasury inflation-protected securities—notes, first offered in 1997, and bonds, first offered in 1998—are included in the average length calculation from 1997 forward.

Note: Through fiscal year 1976, the fiscal year was on a July 1–June 30 basis; beginning with October 1976 (fiscal year 1977), the fiscal year is on an October 1–September 30 basis.

Data shown in this table are as of January 23, 2013.

Source: Department of the Treasury.

TABLE B–89. Estimated ownership of U.S. Treasury securities, 1999–2012

[Billions of dollars]

End of month	Total public debt [1]	Federal Reserve and Intragovernmental holdings [2]	Total privately held	Depository institutions [3]	U.S. savings bonds [4]	Pension funds Private [5]	Pension funds State and local governments	Insurance companies	Mutual funds [6]	State and local governments	Foreign and international [7]	Other investors [8]
1999: Mar	5,651.6	2,324.1	3,327.5	247.4	180.6	135.5	211.5	137.5	245.0	288.4	1,272.3	609.4
June	5,638.8	2,439.6	3,199.2	240.6	180.0	142.9	213.8	133.6	228.1	298.6	1,258.8	502.7
Sept	5,656.3	2,480.9	3,175.4	241.2	180.0	150.9	204.8	128.0	222.5	299.2	1,281.4	467.3
Dec	5,776.1	2,542.2	3,233.9	248.7	179.3	153.0	198.8	123.4	228.7	304.5	1,268.7	528.8
2000: Mar	5,773.4	2,590.6	3,182.8	237.7	178.6	150.2	196.9	120.0	222.3	306.3	1,085.0	685.7
June	5,685.9	2,698.6	2,987.3	222.2	177.7	149.0	194.9	116.5	205.4	309.3	1,060.7	551.7
Sept	5,674.2	2,737.9	2,936.3	220.5	177.7	147.9	185.5	113.7	207.8	307.9	1,038.8	536.5
Dec	5,662.2	2,781.8	2,880.4	201.5	176.9	145.0	179.1	110.2	225.7	310.0	1,015.2	516.9
2001: Mar	5,773.7	2,880.9	2,892.8	188.0	184.8	153.4	177.3	109.1	225.3	316.9	1,012.5	525.4
June	5,726.8	3,004.2	2,722.6	188.1	185.5	148.5	183.1	108.1	221.0	324.8	983.3	380.2
Sept	5,807.5	3,027.8	2,779.7	189.1	186.5	149.9	166.8	106.8	234.1	321.2	992.2	433.1
Dec	5,943.4	3,123.9	2,819.5	181.5	190.4	145.8	155.1	105.7	261.9	328.4	1,040.1	410.6
2002: Mar	6,006.0	3,156.8	2,849.2	187.6	192.0	152.7	163.3	114.0	266.1	327.6	1,057.2	388.8
June	6,126.5	3,276.7	2,849.8	204.7	192.8	152.1	153.9	122.0	253.8	333.6	1,123.1	313.7
Sept	6,228.2	3,303.5	2,924.7	209.3	193.3	154.5	156.3	130.4	256.8	338.6	1,188.6	296.9
Dec	6,405.7	3,387.2	3,018.5	222.6	194.9	153.8	158.9	139.7	281.0	354.7	1,235.6	277.4
2003: Mar	6,460.8	3,390.8	3,070.0	153.6	196.9	165.8	162.1	139.5	296.6	350.0	1,275.2	330.2
June	6,670.1	3,505.4	3,164.7	145.4	199.2	170.2	161.3	138.7	302.3	347.9	1,371.9	327.8
Sept	6,783.2	3,515.3	3,267.9	146.8	201.6	167.7	155.5	137.4	287.1	357.7	1,443.3	371.0
Dec	6,998.0	3,620.1	3,377.9	153.1	203.9	172.2	148.6	136.5	280.9	364.2	1,523.1	395.4
2004: Mar	7,131.1	3,628.3	3,502.8	162.8	204.5	169.8	143.6	172.4	280.8	374.1	1,670.0	324.8
June	7,274.3	3,742.8	3,531.5	158.6	204.6	173.3	134.9	174.6	258.7	381.2	1,735.4	310.1
Sept	7,379.6	3,772.0	3,607.1	138.5	204.2	174.0	140.8	182.9	255.0	381.7	1,794.5	335.5
Dec	7,596.1	3,905.6	3,690.5	125.0	204.5	173.7	151.0	188.5	254.1	389.1	1,849.3	355.4
2005: Mar	7,776.9	3,921.6	3,855.3	141.8	204.2	177.3	158.0	193.3	261.1	412.0	1,952.2	355.5
June	7,836.5	4,033.5	3,803.0	126.9	204.2	181.0	171.3	195.0	248.7	444.0	1,877.5	354.4
Sept	7,932.7	4,067.8	3,864.9	125.3	203.6	184.2	164.8	200.7	244.7	463.7	1,929.6	348.2
Dec	8,170.4	4,199.8	3,970.6	117.1	205.2	184.9	153.8	202.3	251.3	475.0	2,033.9	347.0
2006: Mar	8,371.2	4,257.2	4,114.0	113.0	206.0	186.7	153.0	200.3	248.7	473.2	2,082.1	450.9
June	8,420.0	4,389.2	4,030.8	119.5	205.2	191.6	150.9	196.1	244.2	524.9	1,977.8	420.5
Sept	8,507.0	4,432.8	4,074.2	113.6	203.7	201.7	154.7	196.8	235.7	526.2	2,025.3	416.5
Dec	8,680.2	4,558.1	4,122.1	114.8	202.4	207.2	156.2	197.9	250.7	551.7	2,103.1	338.1
2007: Mar	8,849.7	4,576.6	4,273.1	119.8	200.3	221.3	158.3	185.4	264.5	582.0	2,194.8	346.8
June	8,867.7	4,715.1	4,152.6	110.4	198.6	232.0	159.3	168.9	267.7	608.9	2,192.0	214.7
Sept	9,007.7	4,738.0	4,269.7	119.7	197.1	246.1	138.9	155.1	306.3	586.0	2,235.3	285.1
Dec	9,229.2	4,833.5	4,395.7	129.8	196.5	257.2	141.6	141.9	362.9	588.1	2,353.2	224.5
2008: Mar	9,437.6	4,694.7	4,742.9	125.0	195.4	270.3	142.0	152.1	484.4	582.4	2,506.3	285.0
June	9,492.0	4,685.8	4,806.2	112.7	195.0	276.7	141.8	159.4	477.2	574.3	2,587.4	281.7
Sept	10,024.7	4,692.7	5,332.0	130.0	194.3	292.3	143.9	163.4	656.1	544.8	2,802.4	404.8
Dec	10,699.8	4,806.4	5,893.4	105.0	194.1	297.3	146.4	171.4	768.8	526.7	3,077.2	606.6
2009: Mar	11,126.9	4,785.2	6,341.7	125.6	194.0	331.3	150.2	191.0	716.0	556.0	3,265.7	812.0
June	11,545.3	5,026.8	6,518.5	140.8	193.6	354.0	159.9	200.0	695.6	554.3	3,460.8	759.5
Sept	11,909.8	5,127.1	6,782.7	198.1	192.5	398.8	167.3	210.2	644.9	543.8	3,570.6	856.4
Dec	12,311.3	5,276.9	7,034.4	202.4	191.3	430.5	174.5	222.0	666.3	547.2	3,685.1	915.2
2010: Mar	12,773.1	5,259.8	7,513.3	269.4	190.2	462.8	179.1	225.7	646.4	545.4	3,877.9	1,116.4
June	13,201.8	5,345.1	7,856.7	266.1	189.6	485.2	182.0	231.8	632.1	537.1	4,070.0	1,262.8
Sept	13,561.6	5,350.5	8,211.1	322.9	188.7	502.1	185.5	240.6	607.4	531.3	4,324.2	1,308.4
Dec	14,025.2	5,656.2	8,368.9	319.1	187.9	520.8	185.6	248.4	638.0	538.7	4,435.6	1,294.9
2011: Mar	14,270.0	5,958.9	8,311.1	321.2	186.7	532.5	187.9	251.4	641.0	526.0	4,481.4	1,183.1
June	14,343.1	6,220.4	8,122.7	279.3	186.0	542.5	186.9	250.6	653.0	508.7	4,690.6	825.1
Sept	14,790.3	6,328.0	8,462.4	293.7	185.1	569.0	189.0	253.4	719.4	487.9	4,912.2	852.7
Dec	15,222.8	6,439.6	8,783.3	279.7	185.2	583.9	188.9	260.7	827.9	485.2	5,007.4	964.3
2012: Mar	15,582.3	6,397.2	9,185.1	320.2	184.8	596.4	189.3	260.5	882.2	483.4	5,148.3	1,120.1
June	15,855.5	6,475.8	9,379.7	304.4	184.7	605.2	189.6	259.1	864.5	489.6	5,312.4	1,170.3
Sept	16,066.2	6,446.8	9,619.4	337.4	183.8	615.6	190.3	263.8	889.1	492.2	5,475.4	1,171.8
Dec	16,432.7	6,523.7	9,909.1	....	182.5	....	....	....	....	....	....	....

[1] Face value.
[2] Federal Reserve holdings exclude Treasury securities held under repurchase agreements.
[3] Includes U.S. chartered depository institutions, foreign banking offices in U.S., banks in U.S. affiliated areas, credit unions, and bank holding companies.
[4] Current accrual value.
[5] Includes Treasury securities held by the Federal Employees Retirement System Thrift Savings Plan "G Fund."
[6] Includes money market mutual funds, mutual funds, and closed-end investment companies.
[7] Includes nonmarketable foreign series, Treasury securities, and Treasury deposit funds. Excludes Treasury securities held under repurchase agreements in custody accounts at the Federal Reserve Bank of New York. Estimates reflect benchmarks to this series at differing intervals; for further detail, see *Treasury Bulletin* and http://www.treas.gov/tic/ticsec2.shtml.
[8] Includes individuals, Government-sponsored enterprises, brokers and dealers, bank personal trusts and estates, corporate and noncorporate businesses, and other investors.

Note: Data shown in this table is as of January 23, 2013.

Source: Department of the Treasury.

TABLE B–90. Corporate profits with inventory valuation and capital consumption adjustments, 1964–2012

[Billions of dollars; quarterly data at seasonally adjusted annual rates]

Year or quarter	Corporate profits with inventory valuation and capital consumption adjustments	Taxes on corporate income	Corporate profits after tax with inventory valuation and capital consumption adjustments		
			Total	Net dividends	Undistributed profits with inventory valuation and capital consumption adjustments
1964	75.5	28.2	47.4	18.2	29.2
1965	86.5	31.1	55.5	20.2	35.3
1966	92.5	33.9	58.7	20.7	38.0
1967	90.2	32.9	57.3	21.5	35.8
1968	97.3	39.6	57.6	23.5	34.1
1969	94.5	40.0	54.5	24.2	30.3
1970	82.5	34.8	47.7	24.3	23.4
1971	96.1	38.2	57.9	25.0	32.9
1972	111.4	42.3	69.1	26.8	42.2
1973	124.5	50.0	74.5	29.9	44.6
1974	115.1	52.8	62.3	33.2	29.1
1975	133.3	51.6	81.7	33.0	48.7
1976	161.6	65.3	96.3	39.0	57.3
1977	191.8	74.4	117.4	44.8	72.6
1978	218.4	84.9	133.6	50.8	82.8
1979	225.4	90.0	135.3	57.5	77.8
1980	201.4	87.2	114.2	64.1	50.2
1981	223.3	84.3	138.9	73.8	65.2
1982	205.7	66.5	139.2	77.7	61.5
1983	259.8	80.6	179.2	83.5	95.7
1984	318.6	97.5	221.1	90.8	130.3
1985	332.5	99.4	233.1	97.6	135.6
1986	314.1	109.7	204.5	106.2	98.3
1987	367.8	130.4	237.4	112.3	125.1
1988	426.6	141.6	285.0	129.9	155.1
1989	425.6	146.1	279.5	158.0	121.5
1990	434.4	145.4	289.0	169.1	120.0
1991	457.3	138.6	318.7	180.7	138.0
1992	496.2	148.7	347.5	188.0	159.5
1993	543.7	171.0	372.7	202.9	169.7
1994	628.2	193.1	435.1	235.7	199.4
1995	716.2	217.8	498.3	254.4	243.9
1996	801.5	231.5	570.0	297.7	272.3
1997	884.8	245.4	639.4	331.2	308.2
1998	812.4	248.4	564.1	351.5	212.6
1999	856.3	258.8	597.5	337.4	260.1
2000	819.2	265.1	554.1	377.9	176.3
2001	784.2	203.3	580.9	370.9	210.0
2002	872.2	192.3	679.9	399.3	280.6
2003	977.8	243.8	734.0	424.9	309.2
2004	1,246.9	306.1	940.8	550.3	390.5
2005	1,456.1	412.4	1,043.7	557.3	486.4
2006	1,608.3	473.3	1,135.0	704.8	430.3
2007	1,510.6	445.5	1,065.2	794.5	270.7
2008	1,248.4	309.0	939.4	786.9	152.5
2009	1,342.3	269.4	1,073.0	554.1	518.8
2010	1,702.4	373.3	1,329.1	600.9	728.2
2011	1,827.0	379.0	1,447.9	697.2	750.7
2012 ᵖ	....	....	....	779.2	....
2009: I	1,198.4	214.9	983.5	652.4	331.1
II	1,243.3	240.5	1,002.8	548.4	454.3
III	1,403.2	285.0	1,118.2	502.4	615.9
IV	1,524.5	337.0	1,187.4	513.3	674.1
2010: I	1,648.0	351.1	1,297.0	554.9	742.1
II	1,625.4	350.2	1,275.2	585.8	689.4
III	1,747.5	385.5	1,362.1	618.1	744.0
IV	1,788.8	406.6	1,382.3	645.0	737.3
2011: I	1,723.3	398.7	1,324.6	677.6	647.0
II	1,800.9	385.1	1,415.8	687.5	728.4
III	1,830.5	362.0	1,468.5	705.9	762.6
IV	1,953.1	370.4	1,582.8	717.9	864.9
2012: I	1,900.1	453.6	1,446.6	727.1	719.4
II	1,921.9	443.3	1,478.5	747.5	731.0
III	1,967.6	452.4	1,515.2	760.3	754.8
IV ᵖ	....	....	....	881.8	....

Source: Department of Commerce (Bureau of Economic Analysis).

TABLE B–91. Corporate profits by industry, 1964–2012

[Billions of dollars; quarterly data at seasonally adjusted annual rates]

		Corporate profits with inventory valuation adjustment and without capital consumption adjustment												
		Domestic industries												Rest of the world
Year or quarter	Total	Total	Financial			Nonfinancial								
			Total	Federal Reserve banks	Other	Total	Manu-factur-ing[1]	Trans-porta-tion[2]	Utilities	Whole-sale trade	Retail trade	Infor-mation	Other	
SIC:[3]														
1964	68.6	64.1	8.8	1.1	7.6	55.4	32.6	10.2	....	3.4	4.5	....	4.7	4.5
1965	78.9	74.2	9.3	1.3	8.0	64.9	39.8	11.0	....	3.8	4.9	....	5.4	4.7
1966	84.6	80.1	10.7	1.7	9.1	69.3	42.6	12.0	....	4.0	4.9	....	5.9	4.5
1967	82.0	77.2	11.2	2.0	9.2	66.0	39.2	10.9	....	4.1	5.7	....	6.1	4.8
1968	88.8	83.2	12.8	2.5	10.3	70.4	41.9	11.0	....	4.6	6.4	....	6.6	5.6
1969	85.5	78.9	13.6	3.1	10.5	65.3	37.3	10.7	....	4.9	6.4	....	6.1	6.6
1970	74.4	67.3	15.4	3.5	11.9	52.0	27.5	8.3	....	4.4	6.0	....	5.8	7.1
1971	88.3	80.4	17.6	3.3	14.3	62.8	35.1	8.9	....	5.2	7.2	....	6.4	7.9
1972	101.6	92.1	19.2	3.3	15.8	72.9	42.2	9.5	....	6.9	7.4	....	7.0	9.5
1973	115.4	100.5	20.5	4.5	16.1	80.0	47.2	9.1	....	8.2	6.7	....	8.8	14.9
1974	109.6	92.1	20.2	5.7	14.5	71.9	41.4	7.6	....	11.5	2.3	....	9.1	17.5
1975	135.0	120.4	20.2	5.6	14.6	100.2	55.2	11.0	....	13.8	8.2	....	12.0	14.6
1976	165.6	149.1	25.0	5.9	19.1	124.1	71.4	15.3	....	12.9	10.5	....	14.0	16.5
1977	194.8	175.7	31.9	6.1	25.8	143.8	79.4	18.6	....	15.6	12.4	....	17.8	19.1
1978	222.4	199.6	39.5	7.6	31.9	160.0	90.5	21.8	....	15.6	12.3	....	19.8	22.9
1979	232.0	197.4	40.4	9.4	30.9	157.0	89.8	17.0	....	18.8	9.9	....	21.6	34.6
1980	211.4	175.9	34.0	11.8	22.2	142.0	78.3	18.4	....	17.2	6.2	....	21.8	35.5
1981	219.1	189.4	29.1	14.4	14.7	160.3	91.1	20.3	....	22.4	9.9	....	16.7	29.7
1982	191.1	158.5	26.0	15.2	10.8	132.5	67.1	23.1	....	19.6	13.5	....	9.3	32.6
1983	226.6	191.5	35.5	14.6	21.0	156.0	76.2	29.5	....	21.0	18.8	....	10.4	35.1
1984	264.6	228.1	34.4	16.4	18.0	193.7	91.8	40.1	....	29.5	21.1	....	11.1	36.6
1985	257.5	219.4	45.9	16.3	29.5	173.5	84.3	33.8	....	23.9	22.2	....	9.2	38.1
1986	253.0	213.5	56.8	15.5	41.2	156.7	57.9	35.8	....	24.1	23.5	....	15.5	39.5
1987	306.9	258.8	61.6	16.2	45.3	197.3	87.5	42.4	....	19.0	24.0	....	24.4	48.0
1988	367.7	310.8	68.8	18.1	50.7	242.0	122.5	48.9	....	20.4	21.0	....	29.3	57.0
1989	374.1	307.0	80.2	20.6	59.5	226.8	112.1	43.8	....	22.1	22.1	....	26.7	67.1
1990	398.8	322.7	92.3	21.8	70.5	230.4	114.4	44.7	....	19.6	21.6	....	30.1	76.1
1991	430.3	353.8	122.1	20.7	101.4	231.7	99.4	53.8	....	22.2	27.7	....	28.7	76.5
1992	471.6	398.5	142.7	18.3	124.4	255.8	100.8	59.2	....	25.5	29.2	....	41.1	73.1
1993	515.0	438.1	133.4	16.7	116.7	304.7	116.8	70.2	....	26.7	40.6	....	50.4	76.9
1994	586.6	508.6	129.2	18.5	110.7	379.5	150.1	85.2	....	31.8	47.2	....	65.2	78.0
1995	666.0	573.1	160.1	22.9	137.2	413.0	176.7	87.9	....	28.0	44.8	....	75.5	92.9
1996	743.8	641.8	167.5	22.5	144.9	474.4	192.0	93.7	....	40.6	53.7	....	94.5	102.0
1997	815.9	708.3	187.4	24.3	163.2	520.9	212.2	86.5	....	48.2	65.9	....	108.1	107.6
1998	738.6	635.9	159.6	25.6	134.0	476.2	173.4	81.1	....	51.7	74.7	....	95.5	102.8
1999	776.6	655.0	190.4	26.7	163.8	464.6	174.6	59.1	....	51.7	75.6	....	103.6	121.5
2000	755.7	610.0	194.4	31.2	163.2	415.7	166.5	45.8	....	55.6	71.4	....	76.4	145.6
NAICS:[3]														
1998	738.6	635.9	159.5	25.6	133.9	476.4	155.8	21.3	33.5	52.8	67.3	21.9	123.7	102.8
1999	776.6	655.0	189.3	26.7	162.6	465.7	148.8	16.5	33.7	54.8	65.7	12.5	133.6	121.5
2000	755.7	610.0	189.6	31.2	158.4	420.4	143.9	15.2	25.6	58.7	60.7	–15.5	131.8	145.6
2001	720.8	551.1	228.0	28.9	199.1	323.1	49.7	1.2	25.2	51.3	72.6	–24.4	147.4	169.7
2002	762.8	604.9	265.2	23.5	241.7	339.7	47.7	–.1	12.3	49.1	81.6	–3.8	153.0	157.9
2003	892.2	726.4	311.8	20.1	291.8	414.6	69.4	7.4	12.4	54.8	88.9	4.9	176.7	165.8
2004	1,195.1	990.1	362.3	20.0	342.3	627.8	154.1	14.4	19.4	75.6	93.4	45.6	225.2	205.0
2005	1,609.5	1,370.0	443.6	26.6	417.0	926.4	247.2	29.0	29.8	92.2	122.6	81.3	324.3	239.4
2006	1,784.7	1,527.8	448.0	33.8	414.1	1,079.9	304.5	42.1	54.4	103.7	133.2	92.4	349.6	256.8
2007	1,691.1	1,340.2	345.5	36.0	309.5	994.7	271.3	27.7	50.3	99.9	117.8	93.6	334.2	350.9
2008	1,315.5	908.9	122.2	35.1	87.1	786.7	195.5	31.9	30.7	86.3	81.6	75.1	285.7	406.6
2009	1,443.6	1,090.8	374.8	47.3	327.5	716.0	131.0	24.8	23.1	86.6	108.0	72.8	269.7	352.8
2010	1,777.7	1,376.1	424.3	71.6	352.7	951.8	233.5	48.1	27.9	98.2	122.6	86.0	335.4	401.6
2011	1,791.6	1,352.7	408.3	75.9	332.3	944.4	244.9	45.5	17.7	96.3	108.9	85.5	345.7	438.9
2010: I	1,758.0	1,369.3	416.0	71.6	344.3	953.3	210.5	39.6	43.2	99.5	125.7	87.3	347.4	388.8
II	1,741.0	1,332.7	372.9	74.0	298.9	959.8	235.2	51.3	11.1	114.3	124.2	84.9	338.7	408.3
III	1,824.6	1,420.2	425.8	71.4	354.4	994.4	252.1	57.5	31.7	103.9	121.0	91.5	336.7	404.4
IV	1,787.0	1,382.2	482.4	69.2	413.2	899.8	236.2	44.2	25.5	75.1	119.5	80.4	318.8	404.8
2011: I	1,679.4	1,258.8	417.6	72.1	345.4	841.2	215.5	41.1	8.9	79.1	109.1	78.7	308.9	420.6
II	1,764.6	1,328.4	365.6	79.8	285.8	962.8	229.2	45.8	36.5	94.7	101.9	90.2	364.5	436.3
III	1,798.8	1,351.0	380.8	76.6	304.1	970.2	248.9	45.6	10.2	105.3	103.8	87.5	368.9	447.8
IV	1,923.5	1,472.5	469.1	75.2	393.9	1,003.4	285.9	49.5	15.1	106.0	120.9	85.4	340.6	450.9
2012: I	2,100.8	1,697.9	481.2	74.5	406.6	1,216.8	363.5	56.7	38.3	134.6	138.6	109.8	375.3	402.9
II	2,124.3	1,687.7	441.9	74.2	367.6	1,245.8	372.8	55.0	41.3	149.6	136.4	118.6	372.2	436.5
III	2,167.5	1,739.2	509.6	69.4	440.1	1,229.6	367.6	54.6	42.0	130.2	138.3	118.1	378.7	428.3

[1] See Table B–92 for industry detail.
[2] Data on Standard Industrial Classification (SIC) basis include transportation and public utilities. Those on North American Industry Classification System (NAICS) basis include transporation and warehousing. Utilities classified separately in NAICS (as shown beginning 1998).
[3] SIC-based industry data use the 1987 SIC for data beginning in 1987 and the 1972 SIC for prior data. NAICS-based data use 2002 NAICS.

Note: Industry data on SIC basis and NAICS basis are not necessarily the same and are not strictly comparable.

Source: Department of Commerce (Bureau of Economic Analysis).

Table B–92. Corporate profits of manufacturing industries, 1964–2012

[Billions of dollars; quarterly data at seasonally adjusted annual rates]

Year or quarter	Total manufacturing	Corporate profits with inventory valuation adjustment and without capital consumption adjustment										
		Durable goods [2]						Nondurable goods [2]				
		Total [1]	Fabricated metal products	Machinery	Computer and electronic products	Electrical equipment, appliances, and components	Motor vehicles, bodies and trailers, and parts	Other	Total	Food and beverage and tobacco products	Chemical products	Petroleum and coal products	Other
SIC: [3]												
1964	32.6	18.1	1.5	3.3	....	1.7	4.6	4.4	14.5	2.7	4.1	2.4	5.3
1965	39.8	23.3	2.1	4.0	....	2.7	6.2	5.2	16.5	2.9	4.6	2.9	6.1
1966	42.6	24.1	2.4	4.6	....	3.0	5.2	5.2	18.6	3.3	4.9	3.4	6.9
1967	39.2	21.3	2.5	4.2	....	3.0	4.0	4.9	18.0	3.3	4.3	4.0	6.4
1968	41.9	22.5	2.3	4.2	....	2.9	5.5	5.6	19.4	3.2	5.3	3.8	7.1
1969	37.3	19.2	2.0	3.8	....	2.3	4.8	4.9	18.1	3.1	4.6	3.4	7.0
1970	27.5	10.5	1.1	3.1	....	1.3	1.3	2.9	17.0	3.2	3.9	3.7	6.1
1971	35.1	16.6	1.5	3.1	....	2.0	5.2	4.1	18.5	3.6	4.5	3.8	6.6
1972	42.2	22.9	2.2	4.6	....	2.9	6.0	5.6	19.3	3.0	5.3	3.4	7.7
1973	47.2	25.2	2.7	4.9	....	3.2	5.9	6.2	22.1	2.5	6.2	5.4	7.9
1974	41.4	15.3	1.8	3.3	....	.6	.7	4.0	26.1	2.6	5.3	10.9	7.3
1975	55.2	20.6	3.3	5.1	....	2.6	2.3	4.7	34.5	8.6	6.4	10.1	9.5
1976	71.4	31.4	3.9	6.9	....	3.8	7.4	7.3	39.9	7.1	8.2	13.5	11.1
1977	79.4	38.0	4.5	8.6	....	5.9	9.4	8.5	41.4	6.9	7.8	13.1	13.6
1978	90.5	45.4	5.0	10.7	....	6.7	9.0	10.5	45.1	6.2	8.3	15.8	14.8
1979	89.8	37.2	5.3	9.5	....	5.6	4.7	8.5	52.6	5.8	7.2	24.8	14.7
1980	78.3	18.9	4.4	8.0	....	5.2	–4.3	2.7	59.5	6.1	5.7	34.7	13.1
1981	91.1	19.5	4.5	9.0	....	5.2	.3	–2.6	71.6	9.2	8.0	40.0	14.5
1982	67.1	5.0	2.7	3.1	....	1.7	.0	2.1	62.1	7.3	5.1	34.7	15.0
1983	76.2	19.5	3.1	4.0	....	3.5	5.3	8.4	56.7	6.3	7.4	23.9	19.1
1984	91.8	39.3	4.7	6.0	....	5.1	9.2	14.6	52.6	6.8	8.2	17.6	20.1
1985	84.3	29.7	4.9	5.7	....	2.6	7.4	10.1	54.6	8.8	6.6	18.7	20.5
1986	57.9	26.3	5.2	.8	....	2.7	4.6	12.1	31.7	7.5	7.5	–4.7	21.3
1987	87.5	41.3	5.5	5.6	....	6.1	3.8	17.7	46.2	11.2	14.6	–1.4	21.9
1988	122.5	54.8	6.6	11.3	....	7.8	6.3	16.7	67.7	9.7	18.8	12.9	26.4
1989	112.1	51.8	6.4	12.4	....	9.5	2.8	14.3	60.3	11.2	18.3	6.6	24.2
1990	114.4	44.5	6.1	12.0	....	8.7	–1.8	16.1	69.9	14.4	17.0	16.5	22.0
1991	99.4	35.1	5.3	5.8	....	10.2	–5.3	17.5	64.3	18.3	16.3	7.4	22.3
1992	100.8	41.2	6.3	7.6	....	10.6	–.9	17.6	59.6	18.4	16.1	–.8	25.9
1993	116.8	56.5	7.4	7.6	....	15.4	6.1	19.6	60.4	16.5	16.0	2.8	25.0
1994	150.1	75.8	11.2	9.3	....	23.2	8.0	21.7	74.3	20.4	23.6	1.5	28.9
1995	176.7	82.3	11.9	14.9	....	22.0	.2	26.1	94.4	27.6	28.2	7.4	31.2
1996	192.0	92.0	14.6	17.0	....	20.7	4.5	29.5	99.9	22.7	26.6	15.3	35.3
1997	212.2	104.8	17.1	16.9	....	26.0	5.2	33.3	107.4	25.2	32.4	17.6	32.3
1998	173.4	86.7	16.1	19.6	....	9.1	5.9	29.8	86.6	22.0	26.2	7.1	31.4
1999	174.6	77.9	16.1	12.0	....	5.3	7.5	34.8	96.6	28.1	24.8	4.6	39.2
2000	166.5	64.6	15.5	16.2	....	5.1	–1.4	28.1	101.9	26.0	15.3	29.7	30.9
NAICS: [3]												
1998	155.8	82.7	16.4	15.3	4.2	6.2	6.4	34.2	73.1	22.1	25.0	5.3	20.7
1999	148.8	71.2	16.4	11.7	–6.8	6.4	7.7	35.9	77.6	30.9	22.8	2.2	21.7
2000	143.9	60.0	15.8	7.7	4.2	5.9	–.7	27.1	83.9	26.0	13.8	27.6	16.5
2001	49.7	–26.9	9.8	2.0	–48.6	1.9	–8.9	16.8	76.6	28.2	11.6	29.7	7.1
2002	47.7	–7.7	9.1	1.4	–34.4	.0	–4.5	20.7	55.4	25.3	17.8	1.3	11.0
2003	69.4	–4.3	8.0	1.0	–14.7	2.2	–11.7	10.8	73.8	24.0	18.9	23.5	7.4
2004	154.1	40.7	12.2	7.1	–4.3	.6	–6.8	31.9	113.4	24.3	24.7	49.1	15.3
2005	247.2	95.6	18.1	14.5	9.0	–1.4	1.1	54.2	151.7	27.3	25.7	79.4	19.3
2006	304.5	118.9	18.7	19.2	17.4	11.5	–6.8	58.9	185.7	32.5	52.5	76.6	24.0
2007	271.3	96.1	20.5	22.1	11.0	–1.2	–16.4	60.2	175.2	30.7	48.3	73.5	22.7
2008	195.5	56.8	15.8	16.6	12.2	4.6	–33.1	40.7	138.6	29.9	23.9	77.8	7.1
2009	131.0	21.1	11.3	7.3	19.1	9.1	–49.7	24.0	109.9	43.3	38.5	11.9	16.2
2010	233.5	103.1	15.0	17.5	35.2	7.7	–11.7	39.3	130.4	41.2	45.9	23.5	19.8
2011	244.9	100.3	16.4	21.5	27.6	5.1	–12.7	42.4	144.6	34.6	50.1	40.8	19.1
2010: I	210.5	95.6	13.4	14.2	37.6	7.6	–19.6	42.4	114.9	42.0	35.0	19.6	18.3
II	235.2	99.8	12.6	16.3	31.2	8.7	–9.2	40.2	135.4	41.9	40.4	34.1	19.1
III	252.1	110.2	16.5	19.6	34.3	8.0	–4.3	36.0	141.9	46.3	56.6	17.1	21.9
IV	236.2	106.7	17.7	19.9	37.8	6.5	–13.8	38.7	129.5	34.7	51.6	23.4	19.8
2011: I	215.5	82.1	14.9	18.7	22.1	6.2	–15.1	35.3	133.4	36.0	46.8	30.4	20.2
II	229.2	87.1	15.3	19.4	25.3	4.4	–14.5	37.2	142.1	34.8	42.7	48.8	15.8
III	248.9	98.6	16.1	22.1	26.4	4.5	–16.4	45.9	150.3	29.4	51.7	51.8	17.3
IV	285.9	133.2	19.4	25.6	36.4	5.4	–4.8	51.2	152.7	38.3	59.1	32.2	23.0
2012: I	363.5	174.9	23.6	30.2	42.2	10.2	3.3	65.4	188.6	47.5	63.3	45.4	32.4
II	372.8	185.7	24.4	33.3	46.2	7.6	5.0	69.2	187.1	44.8	65.0	46.2	31.1
III	367.6	181.0	23.9	34.1	43.9	9.0	3.7	66.4	186.6	45.0	57.5	48.5	35.6

[1] For Standard Industrial Classification (SIC) data, includes primary metal industries, not shown separately.
[2] Industry groups shown in column headings reflect North American Industry Classification System (NAICS) classification for data beginning 1998. For data on SIC basis, the industry groups would be industrial machinery and equipment (now machinery), electronic and other electric equipment (now electrical equipment, appliances, and components), motor vehicles and equipment (now motor vehicles, bodies and trailers, and parts), food and kindred products (now food and beverage and tobacco products), and chemicals and allied products (now chemical products).
[3] See footnote 3 and Note, Table B–91.

Source: Department of Commerce (Bureau of Economic Analysis).

Table B–93. Sales, profits, and stockholders' equity, all manufacturing corporations, 1971–2012

[Billions of dollars]

Year or quarter	All manufacturing corporations				Durable goods industries				Nondurable goods industries			
	Sales (net)	Before income taxes [1]	After income taxes	Stock-holders' equity [2]	Sales (net)	Before income taxes [1]	After income taxes	Stock-holders' equity [2]	Sales (net)	Before income taxes [1]	After income taxes	Stock-holders' equity [2]
1971	751.1	52.9	31.0	320.8	381.8	26.5	14.5	160.4	369.3	26.5	16.5	160.5
1972	849.5	63.2	36.5	343.4	435.8	33.6	18.4	171.4	413.7	29.6	18.0	172.0
1973	1,017.2	81.4	48.1	374.1	527.3	43.6	24.8	188.7	489.9	37.8	23.3	185.4
1973: IV	275.1	21.4	13.0	386.4	140.1	10.8	6.3	194.7	135.0	10.6	6.7	191.7
New series:												
1973: IV	236.6	20.6	13.2	368.0	122.7	10.1	6.2	185.8	113.9	10.5	7.0	182.1
1974	1,060.6	92.1	58.7	395.0	529.0	41.1	24.7	196.0	531.6	51.0	34.1	199.0
1975	1,065.2	79.9	49.1	423.4	521.1	35.3	21.4	208.1	544.1	44.6	27.7	215.3
1976	1,203.2	104.9	64.5	462.7	589.6	50.7	30.8	224.3	613.7	54.3	33.7	238.4
1977	1,328.1	115.1	70.4	496.7	657.3	57.9	34.8	239.9	670.8	57.2	35.5	256.8
1978	1,496.4	132.5	81.1	540.5	760.7	69.6	41.8	262.6	735.7	62.9	39.3	277.9
1979	1,741.8	154.2	98.7	600.5	865.7	72.4	45.2	292.5	876.1	81.8	53.5	308.0
1980	1,912.8	145.8	92.6	668.1	889.1	57.4	35.6	317.7	1,023.7	88.4	56.9	350.4
1981	2,144.7	158.6	101.3	743.4	979.5	67.2	41.6	350.4	1,165.2	91.3	59.6	393.0
1982	2,039.4	108.2	70.9	770.2	913.1	34.7	21.7	355.5	1,126.4	73.6	49.3	414.7
1983	2,114.3	133.1	85.8	812.8	973.5	48.7	30.0	372.4	1,140.8	84.4	55.8	440.4
1984	2,335.0	165.6	107.6	864.2	1,107.6	75.5	48.9	395.6	1,227.5	90.0	58.8	468.5
1985	2,331.4	137.0	87.6	866.2	1,142.6	61.5	38.6	420.9	1,188.8	75.6	49.1	445.3
1986	2,220.9	129.3	83.1	874.7	1,125.5	52.1	32.6	436.3	1,095.4	77.2	50.5	438.4
1987	2,378.2	173.0	115.6	900.9	1,178.0	78.0	53.0	444.3	1,200.3	95.1	62.6	456.6
1988 [3]	2,596.2	215.3	153.8	957.6	1,284.7	91.6	66.9	468.7	1,311.5	123.7	86.8	488.9
1989	2,745.1	187.6	135.1	999.0	1,356.6	75.1	55.5	501.3	1,388.5	112.6	79.6	497.7
1990	2,810.7	158.1	110.1	1,043.8	1,357.2	57.3	40.7	515.0	1,453.5	100.8	69.4	528.9
1991	2,761.1	98.7	66.4	1,064.1	1,304.0	13.9	7.2	506.8	1,457.1	84.8	59.3	557.4
1992 [4]	2,890.2	31.4	22.1	1,034.7	1,389.8	−33.7	−24.0	473.9	1,500.4	65.1	46.0	560.8
1993	3,015.1	117.9	83.2	1,039.7	1,490.2	38.9	27.4	482.7	1,524.9	79.0	55.7	557.1
1994	3,255.8	243.5	174.9	1,110.1	1,657.6	121.0	87.1	533.3	1,598.2	122.5	87.8	576.8
1995	3,528.3	274.5	198.2	1,242.6	1,807.7	130.6	94.3	613.7	1,720.6	143.9	103.9	627.0
1996	3,757.6	306.6	224.9	1,348.0	1,941.6	146.6	106.1	673.9	1,816.0	160.0	118.8	674.2
1997	3,920.0	331.4	244.5	1,462.7	2,075.8	167.0	121.4	743.4	1,844.2	164.4	123.1	719.3
1998	3,949.4	314.7	234.4	1,482.9	2,168.8	175.1	127.8	779.9	1,780.7	139.6	106.5	703.0
1999	4,148.9	355.3	257.8	1,569.3	2,314.2	198.8	140.3	869.6	1,834.6	156.5	117.5	699.7
2000	4,548.2	381.1	275.3	1,823.1	2,457.4	190.7	131.8	1,054.3	2,090.8	190.5	143.5	768.7
2000: IV	1,163.6	69.2	46.8	1,892.4	620.4	31.2	19.3	1,101.5	543.2	38.0	27.4	790.9
NAICS: [5]												
2000: IV	1,128.8	62.1	41.7	1,833.8	623.0	26.9	15.4	1,100.0	505.8	35.2	26.3	733.8
2001	4,295.0	83.2	36.2	1,843.0	2,321.2	−69.0	−76.1	1,080.5	1,973.8	152.2	112.3	762.5
2002	4,216.4	195.5	134.7	1,804.0	2,260.6	45.9	21.6	1,024.8	1,955.8	149.6	113.1	779.2
2003	4,397.2	305.7	237.0	1,952.2	2,282.7	117.6	88.2	1,040.8	2,114.5	188.1	148.9	911.5
2004	4,934.1	447.5	348.2	2,206.3	2,537.3	200.0	156.5	1,212.9	2,396.7	247.5	191.6	993.5
2005	5,411.5	524.2	401.3	2,410.4	2,730.5	211.3	161.2	1,304.0	2,681.0	312.9	240.2	1,106.5
2006	5,782.7	604.6	470.3	2,678.6	2,910.2	249.1	192.8	1,384.0	2,872.5	355.5	277.5	1,294.6
2007	6,060.0	602.8	442.7	2,921.8	3,015.7	246.8	159.4	1,493.1	3,044.4	356.1	283.3	1,428.7
2008	6,374.1	388.1	266.3	2,980.4	2,969.5	97.7	43.3	1,480.6	3,404.6	290.4	223.1	1,499.8
2009	5,109.8	360.6	286.5	2,781.1	2,426.9	84.5	54.9	1,342.5	2,683.0	276.1	231.6	1,438.5
2010	5,756.0	584.3	477.9	3,176.5	2,707.7	287.3	232.5	1,559.5	3,048.3	297.1	245.4	1,617.0
2011	6,485.4	721.7	593.9	3,502.7	2,927.8	335.3	284.1	1,741.3	3,557.6	386.4	309.8	1,761.4
2010: I	1,349.2	138.7	108.3	3,043.5	625.2	59.3	45.7	1,489.4	724.0	79.4	62.6	1,554.1
II	1,461.7	141.8	117.2	3,117.5	688.8	81.5	65.8	1,528.1	772.9	60.3	51.4	1,589.4
III	1,463.5	155.6	127.5	3,219.3	696.3	74.9	60.6	1,578.2	767.2	80.7	66.9	1,641.1
IV	1,481.5	148.2	125.0	3,325.9	697.3	71.6	60.4	1,642.3	784.2	76.6	64.5	1,683.6
2011: I	1,532.5	179.0	143.8	3,441.2	694.9	82.7	65.9	1,700.1	837.6	96.3	77.9	1,741.1
II	1,657.4	202.1	164.0	3,551.2	732.7	91.4	75.5	1,760.6	924.7	110.7	88.5	1,790.6
III	1,650.6	184.7	150.5	3,542.7	743.4	86.0	70.8	1,762.4	907.2	98.7	79.7	1,780.4
IV	1,644.9	155.9	135.6	3,475.6	756.7	75.1	71.9	1,742.1	888.2	80.8	63.7	1,733.5
2012: I	1,649.1	181.2	145.3	3,580.5	756.5	86.2	68.6	1,801.1	892.6	95.0	76.6	1,779.4
II	1,692.4	196.9	158.9	3,584.7	794.9	94.9	75.1	1,833.0	897.5	102.0	83.8	1,751.7
III	1,652.5	167.6	134.9	3,655.9	770.5	78.1	61.2	1,860.6	881.9	89.5	73.7	1,795.3

[1] In the old series, "income taxes" refers to Federal income taxes only, as State and local income taxes had already been deducted. In the new series, no income taxes have been deducted.

[2] Annual data are average equity for the year (using four end-of-quarter figures).

[3] Beginning with 1988, profits before and after income taxes reflect inclusion of minority stockholders' interest in net income before and after income taxes.

[4] Data for 1992 (most significantly 1992:I) reflect the early adoption of Financial Accounting Standards Board Statement 106 (Employer's Accounting for Post-Retirement Benefits Other Than Pensions) by a large number of companies during the fourth quarter of 1992. Data for 1993 (1993:I) also reflect adoption of Statement 106. Corporations must show the cumulative effect of a change in accounting principle in the first quarter of the year in which the change is adopted.

[5] Data based on the North American Industry Classification System (NAICS). Other data shown are based on the Standard Industrial Classification (SIC).

Note: Data are not necessarily comparable from one period to another due to changes in accounting principles, industry classifications, sampling procedures, etc. For explanatory notes concerning compilation of the series, see *Quarterly Financial Report for Manufacturing, Mining, Trade, and Selected Service Industries*, Department of Commerce, Bureau of the Census.

Source: Department of Commerce (Bureau of the Census).

TABLE B–94. Relation of profits after taxes to stockholders' equity and to sales, all manufacturing corporations, 1963–2012

Year or quarter	Ratio of profits after income taxes (annual rate) to stockholders' equity—percent [1]			Profits after income taxes per dollar of sales—cents		
	All manufacturing corporations	Durable goods industries	Nondurable goods industries	All manufacturing corporations	Durable goods industries	Nondurable goods industries
1963	10.3	10.1	10.4	4.7	4.5	4.9
1964	11.6	11.7	11.5	5.2	5.1	5.4
1965	13.0	13.8	12.2	5.6	5.7	5.5
1966	13.4	14.2	12.7	5.6	5.6	5.6
1967	11.7	11.7	11.8	5.0	4.8	5.3
1968	12.1	12.2	11.9	5.1	4.9	5.2
1969	11.5	11.4	11.5	4.8	4.6	5.0
1970	9.3	8.3	10.3	4.0	3.5	4.5
1971	9.7	9.0	10.3	4.1	3.8	4.5
1972	10.6	10.8	10.5	4.3	4.2	4.4
1973	12.8	13.1	12.6	4.7	4.7	4.8
1973: IV	13.4	12.9	14.0	4.7	4.5	5.0
New series:						
1973: IV	14.3	13.3	15.3	5.6	5.0	6.1
1974	14.9	12.6	17.1	5.5	4.7	6.4
1975	11.6	10.3	12.9	4.6	4.1	5.1
1976	13.9	13.7	14.2	5.4	5.2	5.5
1977	14.2	14.5	13.8	5.3	5.3	5.3
1978	15.0	16.0	14.2	5.4	5.5	5.3
1979	16.4	15.4	17.4	5.7	5.2	6.1
1980	13.9	11.2	16.3	4.8	4.0	5.6
1981	13.6	11.9	15.2	4.7	4.2	5.1
1982	9.2	6.1	11.9	3.5	2.4	4.4
1983	10.6	8.1	12.7	4.1	3.1	4.9
1984	12.5	12.4	12.5	4.6	4.4	4.8
1985	10.1	9.2	11.0	3.8	3.4	4.1
1986	9.5	7.5	11.5	3.7	2.9	4.6
1987	12.8	11.9	13.7	4.9	4.5	5.2
1988 [2]	16.1	14.3	17.8	5.9	5.2	6.6
1989	13.5	11.1	16.0	4.9	4.1	5.7
1990	10.6	7.9	13.1	3.9	3.0	4.8
1991	6.2	1.4	10.6	2.4	.5	4.1
1992 [3]	2.1	-5.1	8.2	.8	-1.7	3.1
1993	8.0	5.7	10.0	2.8	1.8	3.7
1994	15.8	16.3	15.2	5.4	5.3	5.5
1995	16.0	15.4	16.6	5.6	5.2	6.0
1996	16.7	15.7	17.6	6.0	5.5	6.5
1997	16.7	16.3	17.1	6.2	5.8	6.7
1998	15.8	16.4	15.2	5.9	5.9	6.0
1999	16.4	16.1	16.8	6.2	6.1	6.4
2000	15.1	12.5	18.7	6.1	5.4	6.9
2000: IV	9.9	7.0	13.9	4.0	3.1	5.1
NAICS: [4]						
2000: IV	9.1	5.6	14.3	3.7	2.5	5.2
2001	2.0	-7.0	14.7	.8	-3.3	5.7
2002	7.5	2.1	14.5	3.2	1.0	5.8
2003	12.1	8.5	16.3	5.4	3.9	7.0
2004	15.8	12.9	19.3	7.1	6.2	8.0
2005	16.7	12.4	21.7	7.4	5.9	9.0
2006	17.6	13.9	21.4	8.1	6.6	9.7
2007	15.2	10.7	19.8	7.3	5.3	9.3
2008	8.9	2.9	14.9	4.2	1.5	6.6
2009	10.3	4.1	16.1	5.6	2.3	8.6
2010	15.0	14.9	15.2	8.3	8.6	8.1
2011	17.0	16.3	17.6	9.2	9.7	8.7
2010: I	14.2	12.3	16.1	8.0	7.3	8.6
II	15.0	17.2	12.9	8.0	9.6	6.6
III	15.8	15.3	16.3	8.7	8.7	8.7
IV	15.0	14.7	15.3	8.4	8.7	8.2
2011: I	16.7	15.5	17.9	9.4	9.5	9.3
II	18.5	17.2	19.8	9.9	10.3	9.6
III	17.0	16.1	17.9	9.1	9.5	8.8
IV	15.6	16.5	14.7	8.2	9.5	7.2
2012: I	16.2	15.2	17.2	8.8	9.1	8.6
II	17.7	16.4	19.1	9.4	9.5	9.3
III	14.8	13.2	16.4	8.2	7.9	8.4

[1] Annual ratios based on average equity for the year (using four end-of-quarter figures). Quarterly ratios based on equity at end of quarter.
[2] See footnote 3, Table B–93.
[3] See footnote 4, Table B–93.
[4] See footnote 5, Table B–93.
Note: Based on data in millions of dollars.
See Note, Table B–93.
Source: Department of Commerce (Bureau of the Census).

TABLE B-95. Historical stock prices and yields, 1949-2003

Year	Common stock prices [1]									Common stock yields (Standard & Poor's) (percent) [5]	
	Composite (Dec. 31, 2002= 5,000) [3]	New York Stock Exchange (NYSE) indexes [2]					Dow Jones industrial average [2]	Standard & Poor's composite index (1941–43=10) [2]	Nasdaq composite index (Feb. 5, 1971=100) [2]	Dividend- price ratio [6]	Earnings- price ratio [7]
		December 31, 1965=50									
		Com- posite	Industrial	Transpor- tation	Utility [4]	Finance					
1949		9.02					179.48	15.23		6.59	15.48
1950		10.87					216.31	18.40		6.57	13.99
1951		13.08					257.64	22.34		6.13	11.82
1952		13.81					270.76	24.50		5.80	9.47
1953		13.67					275.97	24.73		5.80	10.26
1954		16.19					333.94	29.69		4.95	8.57
1955		21.54					442.72	40.49		4.08	7.95
1956		24.40					493.01	46.62		4.09	7.55
1957		23.67					475.71	44.38		4.35	7.89
1958		24.56					491.66	46.24		3.97	6.23
1959		30.73					632.12	57.38		3.23	5.78
1960		30.01					618.04	55.85		3.47	5.90
1961		35.37					691.55	66.27		2.98	4.62
1962		33.49					639.76	62.38		3.37	5.82
1963		37.51					714.81	69.87		3.17	5.50
1964		43.76					834.05	81.37		3.01	5.32
1965		47.39					910.88	88.17		3.00	5.59
1966	487.92	46.15	46.18	50.26	90.81	44.45	873.60	85.26		3.40	6.63
1967	536.84	50.77	51.97	53.51	90.86	49.82	879.12	91.93		3.20	5.73
1968	585.47	55.37	58.00	50.58	88.38	65.85	906.00	98.70		3.07	5.67
1969	578.01	54.67	57.44	46.96	85.60	70.49	876.72	97.84		3.24	6.08
1970	483.39	45.72	48.03	32.14	74.47	60.00	753.19	83.22		3.83	6.45
1971	573.33	54.22	57.92	44.35	79.05	70.38	884.76	98.29	107.44	3.14	5.41
1972	637.52	60.29	65.73	50.17	76.95	78.35	950.71	109.20	128.52	2.84	5.50
1973	607.11	57.42	63.08	37.74	75.38	70.12	923.88	107.43	109.90	3.06	7.12
1974	463.54	43.84	48.08	31.89	59.58	49.67	759.37	82.85	76.29	4.47	11.59
1975	483.55	45.73	50.52	31.10	63.00	47.14	802.49	86.16	77.20	4.31	9.15
1976	575.85	54.46	60.44	39.57	73.94	52.94	974.92	102.01	89.90	3.77	8.90
1977	567.66	53.69	57.86	41.09	81.84	55.25	894.63	98.20	98.71	4.62	10.79
1978	567.81	53.70	58.23	43.50	78.44	56.65	820.23	96.02	117.53	5.28	12.03
1979	616.68	58.32	64.76	47.34	76.41	61.42	844.40	103.01	136.57	5.47	13.46
1980	720.15	68.10	78.70	60.61	74.69	64.25	891.41	118.78	168.61	5.26	12.66
1981	782.62	74.02	85.44	72.61	77.81	73.52	932.92	128.05	203.18	5.20	11.96
1982	728.84	68.93	78.18	60.41	79.49	71.99	884.36	119.71	188.97	5.81	11.60
1983	979.52	92.63	107.45	89.36	93.99	95.34	1,190.34	160.41	285.43	4.40	8.03
1984	977.33	92.46	108.01	85.63	92.89	89.28	1,178.48	160.46	248.88	4.64	10.02
1985	1,142.97	108.09	123.79	104.11	113.49	114.21	1,328.23	186.84	290.19	4.25	8.12
1986	1,438.02	136.00	155.85	119.87	142.72	147.20	1,792.76	236.34	366.96	3.49	6.09
1987	1,709.79	161.70	195.31	140.39	148.59	146.48	2,275.99	286.83	402.57	3.08	5.48
1988	1,585.14	149.91	180.95	134.12	143.53	127.26	2,060.82	265.79	374.43	3.64	8.01
1989	1,903.36	180.02	216.23	175.28	174.87	151.88	2,508.91	322.84	437.81	3.45	7.42
1990	1,939.47	183.46	225.78	158.62	181.20	133.26	2,678.94	334.59	409.17	3.61	6.47
1991	2,181.72	206.33	258.14	173.99	185.32	150.82	2,929.33	376.18	491.69	3.24	4.79
1992	2,421.51	229.01	284.62	201.09	198.91	179.26	3,284.29	415.74	599.26	2.99	4.22
1993	2,638.96	249.58	299.99	242.49	228.90	216.42	3,522.06	451.41	715.16	2.78	4.46
1994	2,687.02	254.12	315.25	247.29	209.06	209.73	3,793.77	460.42	751.65	2.82	5.83
1995	3,078.56	291.15	367.34	269.41	220.30	238.45	4,493.76	541.72	925.19	2.56	6.09
1996	3,787.20	358.17	453.98	327.33	249.77	303.89	5,742.89	670.50	1,164.96	2.19	5.24
1997	4,827.35	456.54	574.52	414.60	283.82	424.48	7,441.15	873.43	1,469.49	1.77	4.57
1998	5,818.26	550.26	681.57	468.69	378.12	516.35	8,625.52	1,085.50	1,794.91	1.49	3.46
1999	6,546.81	619.16	774.78	491.60	473.73	530.86	10,464.88	1,327.33	2,728.15	1.25	3.17
2000	6,805.89	643.66	810.63	413.60	477.65	553.13	10,734.90	1,427.22	3,783.67	1.15	3.63
2001	6,397.85	605.07	748.26	443.59	377.30	595.61	10,189.13	1,194.18	2,035.00	1.32	2.95
2002	5,578.89	527.62	657.37	431.10	260.85	555.27	9,226.43	993.94	1,539.73	1.61	2.92
2003 [3]	5,447.46		633.18	436.51	237.77	565.75	8,993.59	965.23	1,647.17	1.77	3.84

[1] Averages of daily closing prices.
[2] Includes stocks as follows: for NYSE, all stocks listed; for Dow Jones industrial average, 30 stocks; for Standard & Poor's (S&P) composite index, 500 stocks; and for Nasdaq composite index, over 5,000.
[3] The NYSE relaunched the composite index on January 9, 2003, incorporating new definitions, methodology, and base value. (The composite index based on December 31, 1965=50 was discontinued.) Subset indexes on financial, energy, and health care were released by the NYSE on January 8, 2004 (see Table B–96). NYSE indexes shown in this table for industrials, utilities, transportation, and finance were discontinued.
[4] Effective April 1993, the NYSE doubled the value of the utility index to facilitate trading of options and futures on the index. Annual indexes prior to 1993 reflect the doubling.
[5] Based on 500 stocks in the S&P composite index.
[6] Aggregate cash dividends (based on latest known annual rate) divided by aggregate market value based on Wednesday closing prices. Monthly data are averages of weekly figures; annual data are averages of monthly figures.
[7] Quarterly data are ratio of earnings (after taxes) for four quarters ending with particular quarter-to-price index for last day of that quarter. Annual data are averages of quarterly ratios.

Sources: New York Stock Exchange, Dow Jones & Co., Inc., Standard & Poor's, and Nasdaq Stock Market.

TABLE B–96. Common stock prices and yields, 2000–2012

Year or month	Common stock prices [1]							Common stock yields (Standard & Poor's) (percent) [4]	
	New York Stock Exchange (NYSE) indexes (December 31, 2002=5,000) [2,3]				Dow Jones industrial average [2]	Standard & Poor's composite index (1941–43=10) [2]	Nasdaq composite index (Feb. 5, 1971=100) [2]	Dividend-price ratio [5]	Earnings-price ratio [6]
	Composite	Financial	Energy	Health care					
2000	6,805.89	....	....	....	10,734.90	1,427.22	3,783.67	1.15	3.63
2001	6,397.85	....	....	....	10,189.13	1,194.18	2,035.00	1.32	2.95
2002	5,578.89	....	....	....	9,226.43	993.94	1,539.73	1.61	2.92
2003	5,447.46	5,583.00	5,273.90	5,288.67	8,993.59	965.23	1,647.17	1.77	3.84
2004	6,612.62	6,822.18	6,952.36	5,924.80	10,317.39	1,130.65	1,986.53	1.72	4.89
2005	7,349.00	7,383.70	9,377.84	6,283.96	10,547.67	1,207.23	2,099.32	1.83	5.36
2006	8,357.99	8,654.40	11,206.94	6,685.06	11,408.67	1,310.46	2,263.41	1.87	5.78
2007	9,648.82	9,321.39	13,339.99	7,191.79	13,169.98	1,477.19	2,578.47	1.86	5.29
2008	8,036.88	6,278.38	13,258.42	6,171.19	11,252.62	1,220.04	2,161.65	2.37	3.54
2009	6,091.02	3,987.04	10,020.30	5,456.63	8,876.15	948.05	1,845.38	2.40	1.86
2010	7,230.43	4,744.05	10,943.85	6,230.62	10,662.80	1,139.97	2,349.89	1.98	6.04
2011	7,871.41	4,641.01	12,880.35	6,847.80	11,966.36	1,267.64	2,677.44	2.05	6.77
2012	8,011.65	4,616.63	12,512.32	7,503.05	12,967.08	1,379.35	2,965.56	2.24	
2009: Jan	5,477.14	3,337.14	9,295.97	5,256.13	8,396.20	865.58	1,537.20	3.01	
Feb	5,051.42	2,823.74	8,785.04	5,106.78	7,690.50	805.23	1,485.98	3.07	
Mar	4,739.72	2,633.65	8,266.81	4,596.81	7,235.47	757.13	1,432.23	2.92	.86
Apr	5,338.39	3,313.47	8,839.95	4,771.71	7,992.12	848.15	1,641.15	2.60	
May	5,823.10	3,819.95	9,848.66	5,051.78	8,398.37	902.41	1,726.08	2.41	
June	5,985.64	3,924.19	10,189.64	5,224.16	8,593.00	926.12	1,826.99	2.35	.82
July	6,026.55	4,000.66	9,765.09	5,410.22	8,679.75	935.82	1,873.84	2.31	
Aug	6,577.18	4,646.60	10,295.91	5,706.96	9,375.06	1,009.72	1,997.16	2.12	
Sept	6,839.88	4,844.93	10,791.73	5,838.22	9,634.97	1,044.55	2,084.75	2.06	1.19
Oct	6,986.35	4,918.07	11,342.57	5,931.28	9,857.34	1,067.66	2,122.85	2.02	
Nov	7,079.38	4,848.04	11,486.95	6,155.21	10,227.55	1,088.07	2,143.53	1.99	
Dec	7,167.51	4,734.07	11,335.23	6,430.25	10,433.44	1,110.38	2,220.60	1.95	4.57
2010: Jan	7,257.37	4,795.75	11,548.08	6,523.83	10,471.24	1,123.58	2,267.77	1.92	
Feb	6,958.36	4,567.29	10,840.96	6,320.43	10,214.51	1,089.16	2,194.44	2.00	
Mar	7,349.86	4,942.17	11,194.52	6,453.81	10,677.52	1,152.05	2,362.24	1.90	5.21
Apr	7,607.49	5,187.03	11,690.25	6,391.99	11,052.15	1,197.32	2,475.72	1.84	
May	7,010.08	4,689.81	10,491.24	5,929.68	10,500.19	1,125.06	2,319.24	1.98	
June	6,767.75	4,484.05	9,960.54	5,838.56	10,159.27	1,083.36	2,235.23	2.09	6.51
July	6,814.61	4,553.76	10,007.16	5,867.77	10,222.24	1,079.80	2,210.27	2.10	
Aug	6,922.30	4,588.87	10,186.03	5,939.69	10,350.40	1,087.28	2,205.28	2.10	
Sept	7,149.32	4,694.66	10,423.43	6,208.29	10,598.07	1,122.08	2,298.35	2.06	6.30
Oct	7,482.15	4,778.71	11,164.11	6,456.56	11,044.49	1,171.58	2,441.30	1.97	
Nov	7,608.40	4,770.65	11,639.37	6,389.44	11,198.31	1,198.89	2,530.99	1.94	
Dec	7,837.43	4,875.84	12,180.49	6,447.34	11,465.26	1,241.53	2,631.56	1.90	6.15
2011: Jan	8,093.40	5,097.71	12,861.65	6,570.59	11,802.37	1,282.62	2,717.21	1.84	
Feb	8,361.70	5,292.98	13,680.69	6,658.62	12,190.00	1,321.12	2,783.54	1.80	
Mar	8,274.78	5,157.33	13,896.16	6,696.08	12,081.48	1,304.49	2,722.29	1.90	6.13
Apr	8,470.07	5,177.21	14,197.31	6,989.18	12,434.88	1,331.51	2,797.07	1.92	
May	8,414.33	5,067.79	13,534.36	7,345.34	12,579.99	1,338.31	2,815.08	1.95	
June	8,108.71	4,814.06	13,118.75	7,214.22	12,097.31	1,287.29	2,687.76	2.04	6.35
July	8,286.83	4,846.73	13,678.27	7,290.81	12,512.33	1,325.18	2,810.58	1.99	
Aug	7,342.37	4,215.95	11,964.10	6,587.04	11,326.62	1,185.31	2,504.62	2.20	
Sept	7,099.58	3,958.64	11,370.24	6,578.35	11,175.45	1,173.88	2,524.14	2.25	7.69
Oct	7,255.05	4,048.81	11,760.87	6,666.64	11,515.93	1,207.22	2,594.78	2.28	
Nov	7,348.85	3,991.61	12,243.52	6,696.20	11,804.33	1,226.41	2,606.29	2.22	
Dec	7,401.26	4,023.34	12,258.25	6,880.58	12,075.68	1,243.32	2,601.67	2.24	6.91
2012: Jan	7,737.68	4,295.28	12,782.96	7,122.69	12,550.89	1,300.58	2,743.80	2.17	
Feb	8,071.44	4,593.42	13,318.47	7,208.35	12,889.05	1,352.49	2,928.98	2.11	
Mar	8,166.75	4,740.40	13,196.85	7,305.10	13,079.47	1,389.24	3,035.92	2.09	6.29
Apr	8,043.14	4,664.43	12,499.31	7,363.86	13,030.75	1,386.43	3,035.10	2.20	
May	7,713.74	4,393.13	11,789.32	7,200.82	12,721.08	1,341.27	2,900.41	2.31	
June	7,555.41	4,290.69	11,377.92	7,204.25	12,544.90	1,323.48	2,850.35	2.38	6.45
July	7,766.83	4,409.41	11,945.87	7,493.65	12,814.10	1,359.78	2,920.11	2.33	
Aug	8,011.67	4,545.72	12,575.01	7,617.84	13,134.90	1,403.44	3,032.67	2.26	
Sept	8,279.78	4,794.62	12,954.45	7,830.79	13,418.50	1,443.42	3,136.80	2.21	6.00
Oct	8,295.68	4,855.25	12,812.78	7,988.93	13,380.65	1,437.82	3,060.26	2.24	
Nov	8,129.90	4,804.71	12,343.98	7,757.04	12,896.44	1,394.51	2,941.02	2.33	
Dec	8,367.74	5,012.50	12,550.75	7,943.33	13,144.18	1,422.29	3,003.79	2.28	

[1] Averages of daily closing prices.
[2] Includes stocks as follows: for NYSE, all stocks listed (in 2012, over 2,900); for Dow Jones industrial average, 30 stocks; for Standard & Poor's (S&P) composite index, 500 stocks; and for Nasdaq composite index, in 2012, over 2,400.
[3] The NYSE relaunched the composite index on January 9, 2003, incorporating new definitions, methodology, and base value. Subset indexes on financial, energy, and health care were released by the NYSE on January 8, 2004.
[4] Based on 500 stocks in the S&P composite index.
[5] Aggregate cash dividends (based on latest known annual rate) divided by aggregate market value based on Wednesday closing prices. Monthly data are averages of weekly figures, annual data are averages of monthly figures.
[6] Quarterly data are ratio of earnings (after taxes) for four quarters ending with particular quarter-to-price index for last day of that quarter. Annual data are averages of quarterly ratios.

Sources: New York Stock Exchange, Dow Jones & Co., Inc., Standard & Poor's, and Nasdaq Stock Market.

AGRICULTURE
TABLE B–97. Real farm income, 1950–2012
[Billions of chained (2005) dollars]

Year	Income of farm operators from farming [1]						Production expenses	Net farm income
	Gross farm income							
		Value of farm sector production				Direct Government payments		
	Total [2]	Total	Crops [3,4]	Livestock [4]	Forestry and services			
1950	226.3	224.4	90.2	124.0	10.1	1.9	133.0	93.2
1951	244.8	243.0	89.7	142.7	10.6	1.8	142.9	101.8
1952	236.3	234.6	95.9	127.3	11.3	1.7	142.6	93.5
1953	212.9	211.6	87.5	112.7	11.4	1.3	132.7	80.1
1954	209.2	207.6	88.3	108.2	11.1	1.6	133.5	75.7
1955	202.0	200.6	86.0	103.3	11.2	1.4	133.8	68.0
1956	198.0	194.8	84.2	99.7	10.9	3.2	132.4	65.6
1957	196.0	190.3	76.9	102.3	11.0	5.7	133.5	62.3
1958	214.6	208.6	82.7	114.4	11.5	6.0	142.0	72.6
1959	206.3	202.6	80.4	109.9	12.3	3.7	148.0	58.3
1960	207.2	203.5	84.2	106.7	12.6	3.8	147.0	60.2
1961	215.3	207.4	84.0	110.4	13.0	7.9	151.8	63.5
1962	221.8	212.7	87.3	112.2	13.2	9.2	158.6	63.2
1963	224.8	216.0	93.0	109.3	13.7	8.8	163.8	61.0
1964	216.0	204.8	86.1	104.5	14.2	11.1	162.4	53.6
1965	233.4	221.0	95.4	111.3	14.4	12.3	168.7	64.7
1966	246.1	230.1	89.3	126.1	14.7	16.0	178.0	68.1
1967	239.0	224.4	90.9	118.2	15.3	14.6	180.6	58.4
1968	235.2	219.5	85.9	118.4	15.2	15.7	179.3	55.9
1969	243.9	227.5	85.1	126.8	15.6	16.4	182.1	61.8
1970	241.6	226.3	84.3	126.4	15.6	15.3	182.6	59.0
1971	243.0	230.7	91.6	123.1	16.0	12.3	184.2	58.7
1972	266.8	251.9	97.3	138.4	16.2	14.9	193.8	72.9
1973	351.4	342.1	152.9	171.8	17.4	9.3	229.3	122.1
1974	320.1	318.3	160.1	139.5	18.7	1.7	231.2	88.8
1975	299.2	296.8	150.0	127.9	18.9	2.4	223.3	75.9
1976	289.6	287.6	136.1	131.2	20.2	2.1	232.8	56.8
1977	287.8	283.0	135.3	125.2	22.4	4.8	235.2	52.6
1978	317.6	310.1	140.0	145.5	24.6	7.5	255.3	62.3
1979	344.0	340.9	152.1	162.5	26.2	3.1	281.4	62.6
1980	312.2	309.5	134.6	147.1	27.9	2.7	278.4	33.8
1981	317.9	314.2	150.8	134.6	28.8	3.7	266.5	51.4
1982	295.7	289.4	129.4	127.0	33.0	6.3	252.7	42.9
1983	266.6	250.5	98.6	121.4	30.6	16.1	241.9	24.7
1984	280.6	266.5	129.8	120.3	16.3	14.1	237.2	43.4
1985	261.1	248.6	119.4	111.8	17.4	12.5	214.9	46.2
1986	247.6	228.9	100.4	112.2	16.3	18.7	198.2	49.3
1987	259.8	234.0	99.5	116.9	17.7	25.8	201.2	58.6
1988	265.4	243.8	103.3	117.3	23.2	21.6	206.2	59.1
1989	275.4	259.7	117.1	119.9	22.7	15.6	208.6	66.8
1990	273.7	260.8	115.1	124.6	21.1	12.9	209.7	64.0
1991	256.7	245.7	108.5	116.6	20.6	11.0	202.9	53.8
1992	261.8	249.8	116.3	113.8	19.8	12.0	196.3	65.5
1993	261.9	244.8	105.6	117.5	21.7	17.1	202.2	59.7
1994	270.4	260.5	125.7	112.3	22.5	9.9	204.6	65.8
1995	258.4	249.4	117.5	107.5	24.4	8.9	209.6	48.7
1996	283.6	274.8	139.1	110.7	24.9	8.8	212.7	70.9
1997	281.3	272.4	132.9	113.8	25.7	8.9	220.6	60.6
1998	271.8	257.3	119.3	110.0	28.0	14.5	216.7	55.1
1999	270.5	245.8	106.8	109.6	29.3	24.8	215.6	54.9
2000	272.4	246.2	107.0	111.7	27.5	26.2	215.3	57.1
2001	275.4	250.7	104.7	117.2	28.7	24.7	214.9	60.5
2002	250.1	236.6	106.2	101.4	29.1	13.5	207.6	42.5
2003	274.8	257.3	115.3	111.5	30.4	17.6	210.1	64.8
2004	304.7	291.3	129.3	128.4	33.6	13.4	214.3	90.3
2005	298.5	274.1	114.4	126.5	33.2	24.4	219.7	78.8
2006	281.1	265.8	115.0	115.6	35.2	15.3	225.4	55.6
2007	319.6	308.4	142.2	130.3	35.9	11.2	253.7	65.9
2008	347.9	336.6	168.6	129.3	38.7	11.3	269.5	78.4
2009	313.5	302.3	153.9	109.4	39.0	11.1	255.9	57.5
2010	329.4	318.2	155.7	127.0	35.6	11.2	257.0	72.4
2011	377.9	368.8	180.7	145.2	42.9	9.2	273.9	104.0
2012 p	392.2	382.6	188.7	142.9	50.9	9.6	286.0	106.2

[1] The GDP chain-type price index is used to convert the current-dollar statistics to 2005=100 equivalents.
[2] Value of production, Government payments, other farm-related cash income, and nonmoney income produced by farms including imputed rent of farm dwellings.
[3] Crop receipts include proceeds received from commodities placed under Commodity Credit Corporation loans.
[4] The value of production equates to the sum of cash receipts, home consumption, and the value of the change in inventories.

Note: Data for 2012 are forecasts.

Source: Department of Agriculture (Economic Research Service).

TABLE B–98. Farm business balance sheet, 1960–2012

[Billions of chained (2005) dollars]

End of year	Total assets	Real estate	Livestock and poultry [1]	Machinery and motor vehicles	Crops stored [2]	Purchased inputs [3]	Financial assets	Total claims	Real estate debt [4]	Non–real estate debt [5]	Farm equity
1960	936.4	662.1	83.8	102.4	34.2		53.9	936.4	60.7	59.8	815.8
1961	964.6	685.6	87.2	102.3	34.4		55.0	964.6	65.4	62.8	836.4
1962	989.5	705.3	90.7	104.3	34.2		55.1	989.5	70.7	69.0	849.8
1963	1,019.7	738.0	82.2	105.6	38.4		55.4	1,019.7	77.7	75.6	866.4
1964	1,042.6	768.2	73.9	108.5	35.8		56.3	1,042.6	86.0	78.1	878.5
1965	1,107.1	809.9	88.2	112.5	39.6		57.1	1,107.1	94.8	84.7	927.6
1966	1,141.0	834.8	92.5	117.3	39.5		56.8	1,141.0	100.9	90.3	949.7
1967	1,163.9	855.8	89.1	124.4	37.9		56.6	1,163.9	107.0	92.7	964.3
1968	1,166.8	859.3	91.9	125.9	33.5		56.2	1,166.8	112.2	87.1	967.5
1969	1,157.9	844.4	98.7	123.8	35.8		55.2	1,157.9	114.2	86.5	957.2
1970	1,145.1	831.3	97.4	124.7	35.7		56.0	1,145.1	111.9	87.3	945.9
1971	1,180.3	850.9	106.6	126.9	38.9		56.9	1,180.3	112.7	93.9	973.7
1972	1,274.6	911.1	126.3	129.9	48.6		58.7	1,274.6	117.7	100.2	1,056.7
1973	1,486.8	1,059.8	150.5	140.9	76.0		59.6	1,486.8	125.0	112.2	1,249.6
1974 [6]	1,463.4	1,093.2	80.0	157.9	73.4		58.9	1,463.4	128.9	114.4	1,220.1
1975	1,519.9	1,141.3	87.4	170.9	61.1		59.3	1,519.9	130.2	118.3	1,271.4
1976	1,662.4	1,284.8	81.7	178.1	57.9		59.9	1,662.4	136.4	128.5	1,397.4
1977	1,723.7	1,347.5	84.5	183.4	54.1		54.3	1,723.7	147.7	139.1	1,436.9
1978	1,922.9	1,487.8	123.9	194.9	58.8		57.4	1,922.9	156.8	149.4	1,616.6
1979	2,087.8	1,611.6	140.1	209.8	68.2		58.0	2,087.8	173.0	163.8	1,751.1
1980	2,092.2	1,637.1	126.8	203.8	68.7		55.8	2,092.2	178.3	161.4	1,752.5
1981	1,907.1	1,501.3	102.3	193.3	56.4		53.8	1,907.1	179.5	160.1	1,567.5
1982	1,733.8	1,351.1	95.5	187.1	46.6		53.6	1,733.8	174.3	157.1	1,402.4
1983	1,662.4	1,305.6	85.9	176.3	41.2		53.5	1,662.4	170.0	152.7	1,339.8
1984	1,499.5	1,105.2	82.7	210.2	43.6	3.3	54.4	1,499.5	169.3	146.0	1,184.1
1985	1,257.8	950.3	75.0	139.5	37.1	2.0	53.9	1,257.8	152.5	126.6	978.8
1986	1,145.0	860.2	75.7	125.3	25.8	3.3	54.7	1,145.0	133.4	106.6	905.1
1987	1,167.1	869.6	89.4	121.4	27.5	4.9	54.2	1,167.1	117.0	96.7	953.4
1988	1,176.1	868.5	92.8	120.8	35.3	5.2	53.6	1,176.1	105.6	92.9	977.5
1989	1,169.5	862.5	95.2	120.9	34.4	3.7	52.9	1,169.5	98.8	89.5	981.2
1990	1,163.1	856.7	98.0	119.4	32.1	3.9	53.0	1,163.1	93.6	87.8	981.7
1991	1,128.2	835.0	91.0	114.8	29.7	3.5	54.2	1,128.2	90.1	86.1	951.9
1992	1,132.8	836.5	92.6	110.7	31.6	5.2	56.2	1,132.8	88.6	83.1	961.1
1993	1,161.3	865.5	93.0	109.1	29.8	4.8	59.2	1,161.3	87.4	84.1	989.8
1994	1,169.4	880.9	85.0	108.5	29.1	6.3	59.5	1,169.4	87.5	86.3	995.6
1995	1,183.5	907.4	70.8	107.3	33.6	4.1	60.1	1,183.5	87.9	87.3	1,008.3
1996	1,206.1	925.4	72.5	105.9	38.1	5.2	58.9	1,206.1	89.5	89.2	1,027.4
1997	1,242.3	955.0	79.3	104.9	38.6	5.8	58.7	1,242.3	92.8	92.6	1,056.8
1998	1,265.9	982.0	74.1	105.0	35.0	5.9	64.0	1,265.9	97.1	95.3	1,073.5
1999	1,311.4	1,021.4	84.3	103.5	32.6	4.6	65.1	1,311.4	100.4	92.7	1,118.3
2000	1,356.1	1,066.7	86.5	101.6	31.5	5.5	64.3	1,356.1	95.5	89.3	1,171.4
2001	1,384.2	1,098.0	86.6	102.3	27.8	4.6	64.9	1,384.2	97.6	90.5	1,196.1
2002	1,366.4	1,083.3	82.0	104.3	25.1	6.1	65.6	1,366.4	103.5	88.7	1,174.2
2003	1,469.6	1,181.4	83.4	106.5	26.0	6.0	66.3	1,469.6	88.4	86.1	1,295.2
2004	1,640.8	1,348.6	82.1	111.4	25.2	5.9	67.7	1,640.8	98.8	89.1	1,452.8
2005	1,779.4	1,487.0	81.1	113.1	24.3	6.5	67.5	1,779.4	104.8	91.6	1,583.0
2006	1,863.3	1,574.9	78.2	110.6	22.0	6.3	71.3	1,863.3	104.7	92.5	1,666.1
2007	1,934.7	1,648.7	75.9	108.0	21.4	6.6	74.2	1,934.7	106.1	95.4	1,733.2
2008	1,863.7	1,568.6	74.2	113.6	25.4	6.6	75.1	1,863.7	124.0	98.5	1,641.1
2009	1,875.6	1,574.3	72.8	115.0	30.0	6.6	76.8	1,875.6	119.9	100.9	1,654.8
2010	1,973.7	1,670.0	73.3	115.3	32.1	6.6	76.5	1,973.7	127.2	99.6	1,837.1
2011	2,102.8	1,794.7	71.6	117.8	31.1	6.7	80.9	2,102.8	128.9	95.3	1,878.7
2012 [p]	2,216.9	1,906.0	70.4	120.5	30.2	6.9	82.9	2,216.9	126.1	100.7	1,990.1

[1] Excludes commercial broilers; excludes horses and mules; excludes turkeys beginning with 1986 data.
[2] Non–Commodity Credit Corporation (CCC) crops held on farms plus value above loan rate for crops held under CCC.
[3] Includes fertilizer, chemicals, fuels, parts, feed, seed, and other supplies.
[4] Includes CCC storage and drying facilities loans.
[5] Does not include CCC crop loans.
[6] Beginning with 1974 data, farms are defined as places with sales of $1,000 or more annually.

Note: Data exclude operator and other dwellings.
Data for 2012 are forecasts.

Source: Department of Agriculture (Economic Research Service).

TABLE B–99. Farm output and productivity indexes, 1950–2009

[2005=100]

Year	Farm output				Productivity indicators	
	Total	Livestock and products	Crops	Farm-related output	Farm output per unit of total input	Farm output per unit of labor input
1950	39	47	35	25	39	10
1951	40	49	36	24	40	11
1952	41	50	38	24	41	11
1953	42	50	38	23	42	12
1954	42	52	37	23	43	12
1955	43	54	38	25	43	13
1956	44	56	38	25	43	14
1957	43	55	38	27	43	15
1958	46	56	41	30	45	17
1959	47	58	42	37	46	17
1960	49	59	44	39	48	19
1961	50	62	44	38	49	20
1962	50	62	45	37	49	20
1963	52	64	46	38	50	21
1964	51	65	45	34	51	22
1965	53	64	47	33	52	23
1966	53	65	46	30	51	25
1967	54	67	49	30	53	28
1968	55	67	50	29	54	28
1969	56	67	52	27	55	29
1970	55	69	49	24	54	30
1971	60	72	55	25	58	33
1972	60	73	55	25	58	34
1973	62	73	59	27	60	35
1974	58	70	53	28	56	33
1975	62	68	61	29	61	36
1976	63	71	61	28	60	37
1977	67	72	66	28	63	40
1978	68	72	68	30	60	41
1979	71	73	74	31	62	43
1980	69	75	67	31	60	42
1981	74	75	77	27	67	45
1982	75	75	78	56	69	50
1983	65	76	60	57	60	44
1984	74	75	75	52	71	51
1985	77	77	79	66	75	58
1986	75	78	74	64	74	55
1987	76	79	74	65	75	55
1988	72	80	66	77	72	52
1989	77	80	75	80	78	57
1990	80	82	80	76	81	64
1991	81	84	79	81	82	64
1992	86	86	87	76	88	69
1993	82	87	78	76	83	69
1994	91	91	93	74	89	66
1995	86	93	82	84	82	63
1996	89	91	89	79	89	70
1997	94	94	94	91	91	74
1998	94	95	93	105	90	79
1999	96	98	94	113	90	81
2000	97	98	95	103	94	90
2001	97	97	95	110	95	90
2002	95	99	91	106	94	88
2003	97	100	95	99	97	93
2004	101	98	104	104	102	101
2005	100	100	100	100	100	100
2006	99	102	95	106	101	105
2007	102	103	102	92	99	106
2008	103	103	104	88	104	110
2009	106	102	110	84	106	119

Note: Farm output includes primary agricultural activities and certain secondary activities that are closely linked to agricultural production for which information on production and input use cannot be separately observed. Secondary output (alternatively, farm-related output) includes recreation activities, the imputed value of employer-provided housing, land rentals under the Conservation Reserve, and services such as custom machine work and custom livestock feeding

See Table B–100 for farm inputs

Source: Department of Agriculture (Economic Research Service).

TABLE B–100. Farm input use, selected inputs, 1950–2012

Year	Farm employment (thousands) [1] Total	Self-employed and unpaid family workers [2]	Hired workers [3]	Crops harvested (millions of acres) [4]	Total farm input	Capital input Total [5]	Durable equipment	Labor input Total	Hired labor	Self-employed and unpaid family labor	Intermediate input Total	Farm Origin [6]	Energy and lubricants [7]	Agricultural chemicals	Purchased services
1950	9,283	6,965	2,318	345	99	120	84	388	310	435	50	52	81	30	51
1951	8,653	6,464	2,189	344	100	122	94	373	299	417	52	54	84	28	56
1952	8,441	6,301	2,140	349	100	124	102	365	292	408	52	53	88	28	59
1953	7,904	5,817	2,087	348	100	125	107	350	284	389	52	54	90	26	56
1954	7,893	5,782	2,111	346	98	126	113	343	268	388	50	52	89	26	55
1955	7,719	5,675	2,044	340	101	126	115	335	263	378	54	57	92	27	57
1956	7,367	5,451	1,916	324	101	126	116	314	240	358	56	60	92	29	59
1957	6,966	5,046	1,920	324	101	125	115	291	230	327	58	63	90	27	61
1958	6,667	4,705	1,962	324	102	123	113	278	232	304	61	67	88	28	63
1959	6,565	4,621	1,944	324	104	123	114	276	227	305	64	68	89	32	74
1960	6,155	4,260	1,895	324	102	123	115	260	227	280	63	68	90	33	71
1961	5,994	4,135	1,859	302	101	123	113	254	226	270	63	67	93	35	70
1962	5,841	3,997	1,844	295	103	122	111	255	225	272	65	70	94	33	70
1963	5,500	3,700	1,800	298	103	123	111	244	225	255	67	72	95	36	69
1964	5,206	3,585	1,621	298	101	123	113	229	203	245	66	70	97	39	67
1965	4,964	3,465	1,499	298	101	123	115	224	191	243	66	70	98	41	68
1966	4,574	3,224	1,350	294	102	124	118	208	172	229	70	76	100	46	69
1967	4,303	3,036	1,267	306	102	124	122	195	160	216	71	76	99	49	72
1968	4,207	2,974	1,233	300	101	125	128	195	155	218	70	77	100	39	69
1969	4,050	2,843	1,207	290	102	125	130	191	156	212	72	81	101	42	67
1970	3,951	2,727	1,224	293	102	124	131	183	157	198	74	82	101	49	64
1971	3,868	2,665	1,203	305	102	124	132	180	155	195	75	83	99	51	64
1972	3,870	2,664	1,206	294	104	123	133	179	155	194	78	87	98	54	64
1973	3,947	2,702	1,245	321	104	123	135	178	157	190	78	86	99	58	68
1974	3,919	2,588	1,331	328	103	124	143	177	167	183	77	83	95	61	66
1975	3,818	2,481	1,337	336	102	125	149	174	170	176	75	80	112	55	70
1976	3,741	2,369	1,372	337	106	127	153	171	172	171	80	83	126	64	73
1977	3,660	2,347	1,313	345	105	129	158	167	167	166	79	83	132	60	73
1978	3,682	2,410	1,272	338	112	130	162	164	157	168	89	93	139	64	87
1979	3,549	2,320	1,229	348	115	131	168	167	163	169	92	96	127	71	91
1980	3,605	2,302	1,303	352	115	133	174	162	162	163	92	96	124	79	82
1981	3,497	2,241	1,256	366	111	132	175	162	161	163	87	91	119	75	78
1982	3,335	2,142	1,193	362	109	130	172	151	145	154	87	94	112	63	84
1983	3,282	1,991	1,291	306	108	128	165	149	160	142	87	94	108	60	83
1984	3,091	1,930	1,161	348	105	124	157	144	149	141	84	87	112	68	81
1985	2,760	1,753	1,007	342	103	122	149	133	135	132	83	88	101	66	84
1986	2,693	1,740	953	325	101	118	139	135	130	139	83	89	93	71	76
1987	2,681	1,717	964	302	101	114	129	138	133	141	83	88	104	69	79
1988	2,727	1,725	1,002	297	100	112	122	140	137	141	82	87	104	60	79
1989	2,637	1,709	928	318	98	110	116	135	128	139	81	84	103	63	85
1990	2,568	1,649	919	322	99	108	113	126	128	125	86	90	103	70	81
1991	2,591	1,682	909	318	99	108	110	127	127	127	86	89	103	70	85
1992	2,505	1,640	865	319	97	106	107	124	121	126	84	89	102	64	81
1993	2,367	1,510	857	308	98	105	103	119	120	118	88	91	102	66	91
1994	2,613	1,774	839	321	102	104	99	137	117	149	90	92	105	69	95
1995	2,597	1,730	867	314	105	104	96	137	121	148	95	96	110	72	100
1996	2,433	1,602	831	326	100	102	94	127	116	134	91	89	110	77	95
1997	2,432	1,557	875	333	103	102	92	126	122	129	96	93	113	82	102
1998	2,284	1,405	879	326	105	102	91	120	124	117	100	98	114	86	107
1999	2,239	1,326	913	327	107	101	92	119	129	112	105	103	115	91	110
2000	2,126	1,249	877	325	102	101	92	107	109	106	101	101	113	93	103
2001	2,084	1,211	873	321	102	100	91	107	110	105	100	98	110	93	105
2002	2,115	1,243	872	316	101	100	93	108	111	106	98	97	120	85	99
2003	2,066	1,181	885	324	100	99	94	104	109	102	99	101	100	99	96
2004	2,012	1,188	824	321	99	99	96	101	100	101	98	99	108	97	95
2005	1,988	1,208	780	321	100	100	100	100	100	100	100	100	100	100	100
2006	1,900	1,148	752	312	98	100	102	94	96	93	99	101	95	88	102
2007	1,832	1,082	750	322	103	99	102	96	104	91	108	105	108	103	112
2008	1,786	1,054	732	327	99	101	104	94	99	90	101	97	98	104	105
2009	1,757	1,018	739	319	100	101	107	89	98	84	103	98	119	106	101
2010	1,756	991	765	322	....										
2011	1,764	1,013	751	311	....										
2012 p	....	....	....	326	....										

[1] Persons involved in farmwork.

[2] Data from Current Population Survey (CPS) conducted by the Department of Commerce, Census Bureau, for the Department of Labor, Bureau of Labor Statistics.

[3] Data from national income and product accounts from Department of Commerce, Bureau of Economic Analysis.

[4] Acreage harvested plus acreages in fruits, tree nuts, and vegetables and minor crops. Includes double-cropping.

[5] Consists of durable equipment, service buildings, land, and inventories.

[6] Consists of seed, feed, and purchased livestock.

[7] Consists of petroleum fuels, natural gas, electricity, hydraulic fluids, and lubricants.

Source: Department of Agriculture (Economic Research Service).

TABLE B-101. Agricultural price indexes and farm real estate value, 1975–2012

[1990-92=100, except as noted]

Year or month	Prices received by farmers			Prices paid by farmers											Adden-dum: Average farm real estate value per acre (dollars)[4]
	All farm products	Crops	Live-stock and products	All commodities, services, interest, taxes, and wage rates[1]	Production items									Wage rates	
					Total[2]	Feed	Live-stock and poultry[3]	Fertil-izer	Agri-cultural chemicals	Fuels	Farm machinery	Farm services	Rent		
1975	73	88	62	47	55	83	39	87	72	40	38	48		44	340
1976	75	87	64	50	59	83	47	74	78	43	43	52		48	397
1977	73	83	64	53	61	82	48	72	71	46	47	57		51	474
1978	83	89	78	58	67	80	65	72	66	48	51	60		55	531
1979	94	98	90	66	76	89	88	77	67	61	56	66		60	628
1980	98	107	89	75	85	98	85	96	71	86	63	81		65	737
1981	100	111	89	82	92	110	80	104	77	98	70	89		70	819
1982	94	98	90	86	94	99	78	105	83	97	76	96		74	823
1983	98	108	88	86	92	107	76	100	87	94	81	82		76	788
1984	101	111	91	89	94	112	73	103	90	93	85	86		77	801
1985	91	98	86	86	91	95	74	98	90	93	85	85		78	713
1986	87	87	88	85	86	88	73	90	89	76	83	83		81	640
1987	89	86	91	87	87	83	85	86	87	76	85	84		85	599
1988	99	104	93	91	90	104	91	94	89	77	89	85		87	632
1989	104	109	100	96	95	110	93	99	93	83	94	91		95	668
1990	104	103	105	99	99	103	102	97	95	100	96	96	96	96	683
1991	100	101	99	100	100	98	102	103	101	104	100	98	100	100	703
1992	98	101	97	101	101	99	96	100	103	96	104	103	104	105	713
1993	101	102	100	104	104	102	104	96	109	93	107	110	100	108	736
1994	100	105	95	106	106	106	94	105	112	89	113	110	108	111	798
1995	102	112	92	109	108	103	82	121	116	89	120	115	117	114	844
1996	112	127	99	115	115	129	75	125	119	102	125	116	128	117	887
1997	107	115	98	118	119	125	94	121	121	106	128	116	136	123	926
1998	102	107	97	115	113	111	88	112	122	84	132	115	120	129	974
1999	96	97	95	115	111	100	95	105	121	94	135	114	113	135	1,030
2000	96	96	97	119	115	102	110	110	120	129	139	118	110	140	1,090
2001	102	99	106	123	120	109	111	123	121	121	144	120	117	146	1,150
2002	98	105	90	124	119	112	102	108	119	115	148	120	120	153	1,210
2003	106	110	103	128	124	114	109	124	121	140	151	125	123	157	1,270
2004	118	115	122	134	132	121	128	140	121	165	162	127	126	160	1,340
2005	114	110	119	142	140	117	138	164	123	216	173	133	129	165	1,610
2006	115	120	111	150	148	124	144	176	128	239	182	139	141	171	1,830
2007	136	142	130	161	160	149	131	216	129	264	191	146	147	177	2,010
2008	149	169	130	183	190	194	124	392	139	344	209	146	165	183	2,170
2009	131	151	112	178	182	186	115	275	149	229	222	156	184	188	2,110
2010	141	154	130	183	188	180	133	252	144	284	230	161	190	189	2,200
2011	178	204	152	203	215	226	155	328	145	362	244	164	205	192	2,390
2012	190	220	157	215	229	261	168	336	153	358	256	168	212	199	2,650
2011: Jan	166	189	137	195	204	204	151	305	144	320	237	163	205	195	....
Feb	171	200	144	197	207	212	155	304	145	335	238	163	205	195	....
Mar	173	198	152	201	212	212	159	318	145	363	239	164	205	195	....
Apr	176	201	156	203	215	223	160	326	144	380	240	163	205	189	....
May	178	209	152	204	216	230	149	327	144	383	242	164	205	189	....
June	180	210	153	203	215	232	146	328	143	373	242	165	205	189	....
July	183	212	155	204	217	233	152	333	144	371	243	165	205	189	....
Aug	184	211	158	205	217	239	147	331	145	368	245	165	205	189	....
Sept	180	204	152	205	218	241	146	332	146	368	247	165	205	189	....
Oct	185	204	154	205	217	231	156	342	148	360	249	164	205	193	....
Nov	184	206	157	206	219	227	165	349	147	369	250	164	205	193	....
Dec	179	198	157	206	218	225	168	346	148	359	251	164	205	193	....
2012: Jan	189	212	156	210	222	226	178	347	149	356	251	167	212	199	....
Feb	181	206	158	211	223	229	186	333	152	364	252	167	212	199	....
Mar	184	210	160	213	227	235	184	333	152	382	252	167	212	199	....
Apr	178	208	152	215	228	246	176	339	150	380	257	167	212	197	....
May	178	209	151	215	229	253	145	345	151	359	257	168	212	197	....
June	182	214	152	214	228	253	169	348	152	335	258	169	212	197	....
July	190	228	150	214	227	268	148	345	152	334	258	169	212	196	....
Aug	193	231	155	216	231	287	151	324	154	357	258	169	212	196	....
Sept	193	224	156	218	233	290	156	328	154	368	258	169	212	196	....
Oct	209	237	163	218	233	286	163	329	153	367	258	168	212	203	....
Nov	206	236	168	218	232	281	166	331	155	353	259	168	212	203	....
Dec	201	228	168	217	231	276	170	332	157	345	259	167	212	203	....

[1] Includes items used for family living, not shown separately.
[2] Includes other production items, not shown separately.
[3] Includes cattle, hogs, dairy, and poultry.
[4] Average for 48 States. Annual data are: March 1 for 1975, February 1 for 1976–81, April 1 for 1982–85, February 1 for 1986–89, January 1 for 1990–2009, and annual average for 2010-2012.

Source: Department of Agriculture (National Agricultural Statistics Service).

[Billions of dollars]

Year	Exports							Imports					Agri-cultural trade balance
	Total [1]	Feed grains	Food grains [2]	Oilseeds and products	Cotton	Tobacco	Animals and products	Total [1]	Fruits, nuts, and vegetables [3]	Animals and products	Coffee	Cocoa beans and products	
1951	4.0	0.3	1.1	0.3	1.1	0.3	0.5	5.2	0.2	1.1	1.4	0.2	–1.1
1952	3.4	.3	1.1	.2	.9	.2	.3	4.5	.2	.7	1.4	.2	–1.1
1953	2.8	.3	.7	.2	.5	.3	.4	4.2	.2	.6	1.5	.2	–1.3
1954	3.1	.2	.5	.3	.8	.3	.5	4.0	.2	.5	1.5	.3	–.9
1955	3.2	.3	.6	.4	.5	.4	.6	4.0	.2	.5	1.4	.2	–.8
1956	4.2	.4	1.0	.5	.7	.3	.7	4.0	.2	.4	1.4	.2	.2
1957	4.5	.3	1.0	.5	1.0	.4	.7	4.0	.2	.5	1.4	.2	.6
1958	3.9	.5	.8	.4	.7	.4	.5	3.9	.2	.7	1.2	.2	*
1959	4.0	.6	.9	.6	.4	.3	.6	4.1	.2	.8	1.1	.2	–.1
1960	4.8	.5	1.2	.6	1.0	.4	.6	3.8	.2	.6	1.0	.2	1.0
1961	5.0	.5	1.4	.6	.9	.4	.6	3.7	.2	.7	1.0	.2	1.3
1962	5.0	.8	1.3	.7	.5	.4	.6	3.9	.2	.9	1.0	.2	1.2
1963	5.6	.8	1.5	.8	.6	.4	.7	4.0	.3	.9	1.0	.2	1.6
1964	6.3	.9	1.7	1.0	.7	.4	.8	4.1	.3	.8	1.2	.2	2.3
1965	6.2	1.1	1.4	1.2	.5	.4	.8	4.1	.3	.9	1.1	.1	2.1
1966	6.9	1.3	1.8	1.2	.4	.5	.7	4.5	.4	1.2	1.1	.1	2.4
1967	6.4	1.1	1.5	1.3	.5	.5	.7	4.4	.5	1.1	1.0	.2	1.9
1968	6.2	.9	1.3	1.3	.5	.5	.7	5.0	.6	1.3	1.2	.2	1.2
1969	5.9	.9	1.2	1.3	.3	.6	.8	5.0	.7	1.4	.9	.2	1.0
1970	7.2	1.1	1.4	1.9	.4	.5	.9	5.7	.7	1.6	1.2	.3	1.5
1971	7.7	1.0	1.3	2.2	.6	.5	1.0	5.8	.7	1.6	1.2	.2	1.9
1972	9.4	1.5	1.8	2.5	.5	.7	1.1	6.4	.8	1.9	1.3	.2	2.9
1973	17.6	3.6	4.7	4.4	.9	.7	1.6	8.4	1.0	2.6	1.7	.3	9.3
1974	21.9	4.7	5.4	5.8	1.4	.8	1.8	10.2	1.0	2.2	1.6	.5	11.7
1975	21.9	5.2	6.1	4.6	1.0	.9	1.7	9.3	1.0	1.8	1.7	.5	12.6
1976	23.0	6.0	4.7	5.2	1.1	.9	2.4	11.0	1.2	2.4	2.9	.6	12.0
1977	23.6	4.9	3.6	6.8	1.5	1.1	2.7	13.4	1.5	2.4	4.3	1.0	10.2
1978	29.4	5.9	5.5	8.4	1.7	1.4	3.1	14.8	1.8	3.1	4.1	1.4	14.6
1979	34.7	7.7	6.3	9.4	2.2	1.2	3.8	16.7	2.0	3.9	4.2	1.2	18.0
1980	41.2	9.8	7.9	10.0	2.9	1.3	3.8	17.4	2.0	3.8	4.2	.9	23.9
1981	43.3	9.4	9.6	10.1	2.3	1.5	4.3	16.8	2.5	3.5	2.9	.9	26.6
1982	36.6	6.4	7.9	9.8	2.0	1.5	4.0	15.2	2.8	3.7	2.9	.7	21.4
1983	36.1	7.3	7.4	9.4	1.8	1.5	3.8	16.6	2.9	3.8	2.8	.8	19.5
1984	37.8	8.1	7.5	9.1	2.4	1.5	4.3	19.3	3.7	4.0	3.3	1.1	18.5
1985	29.0	6.0	4.5	6.4	1.6	1.5	4.2	20.0	4.1	4.2	3.3	1.4	9.1
1986	26.2	3.1	3.9	7.3	.8	1.2	4.6	21.4	4.2	4.4	4.6	1.1	4.8
1987	28.7	3.8	3.8	7.2	1.6	1.1	5.2	20.4	4.3	4.8	2.9	1.2	8.3
1988	37.1	5.9	5.9	8.5	2.0	1.3	6.5	20.9	4.4	5.1	2.5	1.0	16.2
1989 [4]	40.0	7.7	7.1	6.4	2.2	1.3	6.4	21.9	4.8	5.1	2.4	1.0	18.2
1990	39.5	7.0	4.8	5.7	2.8	1.4	6.6	22.9	5.5	5.7	1.9	1.1	16.6
1991	39.4	5.7	4.2	6.4	2.5	1.4	7.0	22.9	5.4	5.5	1.9	1.1	16.5
1992	43.2	5.8	5.4	7.3	2.0	1.6	7.9	24.8	5.5	5.7	1.7	1.1	18.5
1993	43.0	5.0	5.7	7.3	1.6	1.3	8.0	25.1	5.6	5.9	1.5	1.0	17.9
1994	46.2	4.7	5.3	7.2	2.6	1.3	9.2	27.0	6.0	5.8	2.5	1.0	19.1
1995	56.2	8.1	6.7	8.9	3.7	1.4	10.9	30.3	6.5	6.0	3.3	1.1	26.0
1996	60.4	9.4	7.4	10.8	2.7	1.4	11.1	33.5	7.5	6.1	2.8	1.4	26.9
1997	57.1	6.0	5.3	12.1	2.7	1.5	11.3	36.1	7.8	6.5	3.9	1.5	21.0
1998	51.8	5.0	5.0	9.5	2.6	1.5	10.6	36.9	8.4	6.9	3.4	1.7	14.9
1999	48.4	5.5	4.7	8.1	1.0	1.3	10.4	37.7	9.3	7.3	2.9	1.5	10.7
2000	51.3	5.2	4.3	8.6	1.9	1.2	11.6	39.0	9.3	8.4	2.7	1.4	12.3
2001	53.7	5.2	4.2	9.2	2.2	1.3	12.4	39.4	9.7	9.2	1.7	1.5	14.3
2002	53.1	5.5	4.5	9.6	2.0	1.0	11.1	41.9	10.4	9.0	1.7	1.8	11.2
2003	59.4	5.4	5.0	11.7	3.4	1.0	12.2	47.4	11.6	8.9	2.0	2.4	12.0
2004	61.4	6.4	6.3	10.4	4.2	1.0	10.4	54.0	13.1	10.6	2.3	2.5	7.4
2005	63.2	5.4	5.7	10.2	3.9	1.0	12.2	59.3	14.4	11.5	3.0	2.8	3.9
2006	71.0	7.7	5.5	11.3	4.5	1.1	13.5	65.3	15.8	11.5	3.3	2.7	5.6
2007	90.0	10.9	9.9	15.6	4.6	1.2	17.2	71.9	18.1	12.4	3.8	2.7	18.1
2008	114.8	14.9	13.6	23.7	4.8	1.2	21.3	80.5	19.5	12.0	4.4	3.3	34.3
2009	98.5	9.4	7.7	24.1	3.3	1.2	18.0	71.7	18.9	10.1	4.1	3.5	26.8
2010	115.8	10.6	9.2	27.2	5.7	1.2	22.3	81.9	21.3	11.2	4.9	4.3	34.0
2011	136.4	14.7	13.4	26.1	8.4	1.1	27.8	98.9	24.0	12.3	8.1	4.7	37.4
Jan-Nov:													
2011	124.6	13.4	12.6	23.6	7.8	1.0	25.4	90.5	21.9	11.2	7.3	4.3	34.1
2012	128.3	9.4	9.5	30.9	5.8	1.0	26.6	94.6	22.6	12.4	6.5	3.7	33.7

* Less than $50 million.

[1] Total includes items not shown separately.

[2] Rice, wheat, and wheat flour.

[3] Includes fruit, nut, and vegetable preparations and fruit juices.

[4] In 1989, the World Customs Organization established new trade codes that harmonized reporting of commodity trade around the world. Significant changes were made in individual commodity groupings. Those changes are reflected in the data from 1989 forward.

Note: Data derived from official estimates released by the Department of Commerce, Census Bureau. Agricultural commodities are defined as (1) nonmarine food products and (2) other products of agriculture that have not passed through complex processes of manufacture. Export value, at U.S. port of exportation, is based on the selling price and includes inland freight, insurance, and other charges to the port. Import value, defined generally as the market value in the foreign country, excludes import duties, ocean freight, and marine insurance.

Source: Department of Agriculture (Economic Research Service).

TABLE B–103. U.S. international transactions, 1953–2012

[Millions of dollars; quarterly data seasonally adjusted. Credits (+), debits (–)]

Year or quarter	Goods [1] Exports	Goods [1] Imports	Goods [1] Balance on goods	Services Net military trans-actions [2]	Services Net travel and trans-por-tation	Services Other services, net	Balance on goods and services	Income receipts and payments Receipts	Income receipts and payments Payments	Income receipts and payments Balance on income	Unilateral current transfers, net [2]	Balance on current account
1953	12,412	−10,975	1,437	1,753	−238	307	3,259	2,736	−624	2,112	−6,657	−1,286
1954	12,929	−10,353	2,576	902	−269	305	3,514	2,929	−582	2,347	−5,642	219
1955	14,424	−11,527	2,897	−113	−297	299	2,786	3,406	−676	2,730	−5,086	430
1956	17,556	−12,803	4,753	−221	−361	447	4,618	3,837	−735	3,102	−4,990	2,730
1957	19,562	−13,291	6,271	−423	−189	482	6,141	4,180	−796	3,384	−4,763	4,762
1958	16,414	−12,952	3,462	−849	−633	486	2,466	3,790	−825	2,965	−4,647	784
1959	16,458	−15,310	1,148	−831	−821	573	69	4,132	−1,061	3,071	−4,422	−1,282
1960	19,650	−14,758	4,892	−1,057	−964	639	3,508	4,616	−1,238	3,379	−4,062	2,824
1961	20,108	−14,537	5,571	−1,131	−978	732	4,195	4,999	−1,245	3,755	−4,127	3,822
1962	20,781	−16,260	4,521	−912	−1,152	912	3,370	5,618	−1,324	4,294	−4,277	3,387
1963	22,272	−17,048	5,224	−742	−1,309	1,036	4,210	6,157	−1,560	4,596	−4,392	4,414
1964	25,501	−18,700	6,801	−794	−1,146	1,161	6,022	6,824	−1,783	5,041	−4,240	6,823
1965	26,461	−21,510	4,951	−487	−1,280	1,480	4,664	7,437	−2,088	5,350	−4,583	5,431
1966	29,310	−25,493	3,817	−1,043	−1,331	1,497	2,940	7,528	−2,481	5,047	−4,955	3,031
1967	30,666	−26,866	3,800	−1,187	−1,750	1,742	2,604	8,021	−2,747	5,274	−5,294	2,583
1968	33,626	−32,991	635	−596	−1,548	1,759	250	9,367	−3,378	5,990	−5,629	611
1969	36,414	−35,807	607	−718	−1,763	1,964	91	10,913	−4,869	6,044	−5,735	399
1970	42,469	−39,866	2,603	−641	−2,038	2,330	2,254	11,748	−5,515	6,233	−6,156	2,331
1971	43,319	−45,579	−2,260	653	−2,345	2,649	−1,303	12,707	−5,435	7,272	−7,402	−1,433
1972	49,381	−55,797	−6,416	1,072	−3,063	2,965	−5,443	14,765	−6,572	8,192	−8,544	−5,795
1973	71,410	−70,499	911	740	−3,158	3,406	1,900	21,808	−9,655	12,153	−6,913	7,140
1974	98,306	−103,811	−5,505	165	−3,184	4,231	−4,292	27,587	−12,084	15,503	−9,249	1,962
1975	107,088	−98,185	8,903	1,461	−2,812	4,854	12,404	25,351	−12,564	12,787	−7,075	18,116
1976	114,745	−124,228	−9,483	931	−2,558	5,027	−6,082	29,375	−13,311	16,063	−5,686	4,295
1977	120,816	−151,907	−31,091	1,731	−3,565	5,680	−27,246	32,354	−14,217	18,137	−5,226	−14,335
1978	142,075	−176,002	−33,927	857	−3,573	6,879	−29,763	42,088	−21,680	20,408	−5,788	−15,143
1979	184,439	−212,007	−27,568	−1,313	−2,935	7,251	−24,565	63,834	−32,961	30,873	−6,593	−285
1980	224,250	−249,750	−25,500	−1,822	−997	8,912	−19,407	72,606	−42,532	30,073	−8,349	2,317
1981	237,044	−265,067	−28,023	−844	144	12,552	−16,172	86,529	−53,626	32,903	−11,702	5,030
1982	211,157	−247,642	−36,485	112	−992	13,209	−24,156	91,747	−56,583	35,164	−16,544	−5,536
1983	201,799	−268,901	−67,102	−563	−4,227	14,124	−57,767	90,000	−53,614	36,386	−17,310	−38,691
1984	219,926	−332,418	−112,492	−2,547	−8,438	14,404	−109,073	108,819	−73,756	35,063	−20,335	−94,344
1985	215,915	−338,088	−122,173	−4,390	−9,798	14,483	−121,880	98,542	−72,819	25,723	−21,998	−118,155
1986	223,344	−368,425	−145,081	−5,181	−8,779	20,502	−138,538	97,064	−81,571	15,494	−24,132	−147,177
1987	250,208	−409,765	−159,557	−3,844	−8,010	19,728	−151,684	108,184	−93,891	14,293	−23,265	−160,655
1988	320,230	−447,189	−126,959	−6,320	−3,013	21,725	−114,566	136,713	−118,026	18,687	−25,274	−121,153
1989	359,916	−477,665	−117,749	−6,749	3,551	27,805	−93,142	161,287	−141,463	19,824	−26,169	−99,486
1990	387,401	−498,438	−111,037	−7,599	7,501	30,270	−80,864	171,742	−143,192	28,550	−26,654	−78,968
1991	414,083	−491,020	−76,937	−5,274	16,561	34,516	−31,135	149,214	−125,084	24,130	9,904	2,898
1992	439,631	−536,528	−96,897	−1,448	19,969	39,164	−39,212	133,766	−109,531	24,234	−36,636	−51,613
1993	456,943	−589,394	−132,451	1,385	19,714	41,041	−70,310	136,057	−110,741	25,316	−39,812	−84,806
1994	502,859	−668,690	−165,831	2,570	16,305	48,463	−98,493	166,521	−149,375	17,146	−40,265	−121,612
1995	575,204	−749,374	−174,170	4,600	21,772	51,414	−96,384	210,244	−189,353	20,891	−38,074	−113,567
1996	612,113	−803,113	−191,000	5,385	25,015	56,535	−104,065	226,129	−203,811	22,318	−43,017	−124,764
1997	678,366	−876,794	−198,428	4,968	22,152	63,035	−108,273	256,804	−244,195	12,609	−45,062	−140,726
1998	670,416	−918,637	−248,221	5,220	10,210	66,651	−166,140	261,819	−257,554	4,265	−53,187	−215,062
1999	698,218	−1,034,389	−336,171	−7,245	6,606	73,649	−263,159	295,423	−283,492	11,931	−50,428	−301,656
2000	784,781	−1,230,568	−445,787	−6,488	2,462	73,065	−376,749	352,478	−333,300	19,178	−58,767	−416,338
2001	731,181	−1,152,464	−421,276	−8,324	−3,389	71,219	−361,771	292,430	−262,702	29,728	−64,561	−396,603
2002	697,439	−1,171,930	−474,491	−12,719	−4,465	74,242	−417,432	282,701	−257,526	25,175	−64,990	−457,248
2003	729,816	−1,270,225	−540,409	−17,060	−12,451	78,934	−490,984	322,411	−278,721	43,691	−71,796	−519,089
2004	821,986	−1,485,492	−663,507	−17,359	−16,225	91,734	−605,356	415,793	−350,712	65,081	−88,243	−628,519
2005	911,686	−1,692,416	−780,730	−15,594	−14,549	102,249	−708,624	537,339	−468,748	68,591	−105,741	−745,774
2006	1,039,406	−1,875,095	−835,689	−11,743	−11,276	105,420	−753,288	684,620	−640,438	44,182	−91,515	−800,621
2007	1,163,957	−1,982,843	−818,886	−10,826	2,599	130,386	−696,728	833,834	−732,349	101,485	−115,061	−710,303
2008	1,307,499	−2,137,608	−830,109	−13,600	16,365	129,006	−698,338	813,903	−666,814	147,089	−125,885	−677,135
2009	1,069,733	−1,575,491	−505,758	−14,461	14,527	126,538	−379,154	601,609	−481,891	119,717	−122,459	−381,896
2010	1,288,882	−1,934,006	−645,124	−15,639	21,257	144,769	−494,737	676,282	−492,423	183,859	−131,074	−441,951
2011	1,497,406	−2,235,819	−738,413	−11,564	31,339	158,758	−559,880	744,621	−517,614	227,007	−133,053	−465,926
2011: I	360,917	−542,276	−181,358	−3,448	6,063	41,518	−137,225	180,781	−128,330	52,451	−35,223	−119,997
II	372,160	−559,344	−187,184	−3,000	8,038	40,598	−141,549	189,499	−133,290	56,209	−33,777	−119,117
III	382,161	−562,778	−180,617	−2,679	9,431	39,044	−134,822	187,449	−128,971	58,478	−31,815	−108,158
IV	382,167	−571,421	−189,254	−2,437	7,805	37,600	−146,286	186,891	−127,022	59,869	−32,240	−118,656
2012: I	388,523	−582,821	−194,298	−2,432	7,617	40,749	−148,364	184,708	−137,277	47,431	−32,692	−133,624
II	394,114	−579,850	−185,736	−2,459	9,403	41,370	−137,423	184,002	−131,949	52,054	−32,743	−118,112
III p	393,395	−567,294	−173,899	−1,864	10,306	40,970	−124,488	184,416	−133,596	50,820	−33,839	−107,507

[1] Adjusted from Census data to align with concepts and definitions used to prepare the international and national economic accounts. The adjustments are necessary to supplement coverage of Census data, to eliminate duplication of transactions recorded elsewhere in the international accounts, to value transactions according to a standard definition, and for earlier years, to record transactions in the appropriate period.
[2] Includes transfers of goods and services under U.S. military grant programs.
[3] Consists of gold, special drawing rights, foreign currencies, and the U.S. reserve position in the International Monetary Fund (IMF).

See next page for continuation of table.

[Millions of dollars; quarterly data seasonally adjusted. Credits (+), debits (−)]

| Year or quarter | Capital account transactions, net | U.S.-owned assets abroad, excluding financial derivatives [increase/financial outflow (−)] | | | | Foreign-owned assets in the U.S., excluding financial derivatives [increase/financial inflow (+)] | | | Financial derivatives, net | Statistical discrepancy | |
		Total	U.S. official reserve assets [3]	Other U.S. Government assets	U.S. private assets	Total	Foreign official assets	Other foreign assets		Total (sum of the items with sign reversed)	Of which: Seasonal adjustment discrepancy
1953		1,256									
1954		480									
1955		182									
1956		−869									
1957		−1,165									
1958		2,292									
1959		1,035									
1960		−4,099	2,145	−1,100	−5,144	2,294	1,473	821		−1,019	
1961		−5,538	607	−910	−5,235	2,705	765	1,939		−989	
1962		−4,174	1,535	−1,085	−4,623	1,911	1,270	641		−1,124	
1963		−7,270	378	−1,662	−5,986	3,217	1,986	1,231		−360	
1964		−9,560	171	−1,680	−8,050	3,643	1,660	1,983		−907	
1965		−5,716	1,225	−1,605	−5,336	742	134	607		−457	
1966		−7,321	570	−1,543	−6,347	3,661	−672	4,333		629	
1967		−9,757	53	−2,423	−7,386	7,379	3,451	3,928		−205	
1968		−10,977	−870	−2,274	−7,833	9,928	−774	10,703		438	
1969		−11,585	−1,179	−2,200	−8,206	12,702	−1,301	14,002		−1,516	
1970		−9,337	2,481	−1,589	−10,229	7,226	7,775	−550		−219	
1971		−12,475	2,349	−1,884	−12,940	23,687	27,596	−3,909		−9,779	
1972		−14,497	−4	−1,568	−12,925	22,171	11,185	10,986		−1,879	
1973		−22,874	158	−2,644	−20,388	18,388	6,026	12,362		−2,654	
1974		−34,745	−1,467	366	−33,643	35,227	10,546	24,682		−2,444	
1975		−39,703	−849	−3,474	−35,380	16,870	7,027	9,843		4,717	
1976		−51,269	−2,558	−4,214	−44,498	37,839	17,693	20,147		9,134	
1977		−34,785	−375	−3,693	−30,717	52,770	36,816	15,954		−3,650	
1978		−61,130	732	−4,660	−57,202	66,275	33,678	32,597		9,997	
1979		−66,054	−1,133	−3,746	−61,176	40,693	−12,526	53,218		25,647	
1980		−86,967	−8,155	−5,162	−73,651	62,037	16,649	45,388		22,613	
1981		−114,147	−5,175	−5,097	−103,875	85,684	6,053	79,631		23,433	
1982		−127,882	−4,965	−6,131	−116,786	95,056	3,593	91,464		38,362	
1983		−66,373	−1,196	−5,006	−60,172	87,399	5,845	81,554		17,666	
1984		−40,376	−3,131	−5,489	−31,757	116,048	3,140	112,908		18,672	
1985		−44,752	−3,858	−2,821	−38,074	144,231	−1,119	145,349		18,677	
1986		−111,723	312	−2,022	−110,014	228,330	35,648	192,681		30,570	
1987		−79,296	9,149	1,006	−89,450	247,100	45,387	201,713		−7,149	
1988		−106,573	−3,912	2,967	−105,628	244,833	39,758	205,075		−17,107	
1989	−207	−175,383	−25,293	1,233	−151,323	222,777	8,503	214,274		52,299	
1990	−7,220	−81,234	−2,158	2,317	−81,393	139,357	33,910	105,447		28,066	
1991	−5,130	−64,388	5,763	2,924	−73,075	108,221	17,389	90,833		−41,601	
1992	1,449	−74,410	3,901	−1,667	−76,644	168,349	40,477	127,872		−43,775	
1993	−714	−200,552	−1,379	−351	−198,822	279,758	71,753	208,005		6,314	
1994	−1,111	−178,937	5,346	−390	−183,893	303,174	39,583	263,591		−1,514	
1995	−222	−352,264	−9,742	−984	−341,538	435,102	109,880	325,222		30,951	
1996	−7	−413,409	6,668	−989	−419,088	547,885	126,724	421,161		−9,705	
1997	−256	−485,475	−1,010	68	−484,533	704,452	19,036	685,416		−77,995	
1998	−8	−353,829	−6,783	−422	−346,624	420,794	−19,903	440,697		148,105	
1999	−4,176	−504,062	8,747	2,750	−515,559	742,210	43,543	698,667		67,684	
2000	−1	−560,523	−290	−941	−559,292	1,038,224	42,758	995,466		−61,361	
2001	13,198	−382,616	−4,911	−486	−377,219	782,870	28,059	754,811		−16,849	
2002	−141	−294,646	−3,681	345	−291,310	795,161	115,945	679,216		−43,126	
2003	−1,821	−325,424	1,523	537	−327,484	858,303	278,069	580,234		−11,969	
2004	3,049	−1,000,870	2,805	1,710	−1,005,385	1,533,201	397,755	1,135,446		93,138	
2005	13,116	−546,631	14,096	5,539	−566,266	1,247,347	259,268	988,079		31,942	
2006	−1,788	−1,285,729	2,374	5,346	−1,293,449	2,065,169	487,939	1,577,230	29,710	−6,742	
2007	384	−1,453,604	−122	−22,273	−1,431,209	2,064,642	481,043	1,583,599	6,222	92,660	
2008	6,010	332,109	−4,848	−529,615	866,571	431,406	554,634	−123,228	−32,947	−59,443	
2009	−140	−119,535	−52,256	541,342	−608,622	314,390	480,286	−165,896	44,816	142,365	
2010	−157	−939,484	−1,834	7,540	−945,189	1,308,279	398,188	910,091	14,076	59,237	
2011	−1,212	−483,653	−15,877	−103,666	−364,110	1,000,990	211,826	789,164	39,010	−89,208	
2011: I	−29	−372,944	−3,619	−547	−368,778	578,972	72,974	505,998	2,927	−88,930	17,684
II	−829	7,418	−6,267	−1,358	15,042	98,554	121,822	−23,268	7,419	6,555	−11,134
III	−300	−91,896	−4,079	−1,137	−86,679	266,397	19,889	246,508	−3,949	−62,094	−26,771
IV	−55	−26,231	−1,912	−100,624	76,305	57,067	−2,859	59,926	32,613	55,263	20,223
2012: I	−1	106,549	−1,233	51,076	56,706	59,564	69,711	−10,147	−1,396	−31,092	19,501
II	−291	248,186	−3,289	16,650	234,826	−143,607	79,772	−223,379	464	13,360	−11,580
III p		−229,774	−833	14,151	−243,092	281,960	130,281	151,679	−6,406	61,727	−27,070

Note: Data are on a balance of payments basis. Beginning with data for 1999, exports of goods under the U.S. Foreign Military Sales program and imports of petroleum abroad by U.S. military agencies are included in goods and excluded from net military transactions. Beginning with data for 1999, fuel purchases by air and ocean carriers in foreign ports are included in goods exports and imports and excluded from net travel and transportation.

Source: Department of Commerce (Bureau of Economic Analysis).

TABLE B–104. U.S. international trade in goods by principal end-use category, 1965–2012

[Billions of dollars; quarterly data seasonally adjusted]

Year or quarter	Exports							Imports						
	Total	Agricultural products	Nonagricultural products					Total	Petroleum and products	Nonpetroleum products				
			Total	Industrial supplies and materials	Capital goods except automotive	Automotive	Other			Total	Industrial supplies and materials	Capital goods except automotive	Automotive	Other
1965	26.5	6.3	20.2	7.6	8.1	1.9	2.6	21.5	2.0	19.5	9.1	1.5	0.9	8.0
1966	29.3	6.9	22.4	8.2	8.9	2.4	2.9	25.5	2.1	23.4	10.2	2.2	1.8	9.2
1967	30.7	6.5	24.2	8.5	9.9	2.8	3.0	26.9	2.1	24.8	10.0	2.5	2.4	9.9
1968	33.6	6.3	27.3	9.6	11.1	3.5	3.2	33.0	2.4	30.6	12.0	2.8	4.0	11.8
1969	36.4	6.1	30.3	10.3	12.4	3.9	3.7	35.8	2.6	33.2	11.8	3.4	4.9	13.0
1970	42.5	7.4	35.1	12.3	14.7	3.9	4.3	39.9	2.9	36.9	12.4	4.0	5.5	15.0
1971	43.3	7.8	35.5	10.9	15.4	4.7	4.5	45.6	3.7	41.9	13.8	4.3	7.4	16.4
1972	49.4	9.5	39.9	11.9	16.9	5.5	5.6	55.8	4.7	51.1	16.3	5.9	8.7	20.2
1973	71.4	18.0	53.4	17.0	22.0	6.9	7.6	70.5	8.4	62.1	19.6	8.3	10.3	23.9
1974	98.3	22.4	75.9	26.3	30.9	8.6	10.0	103.8	26.6	77.2	27.8	9.8	12.0	27.5
1975	107.1	22.2	84.8	26.8	36.6	10.6	10.8	98.2	27.0	71.2	24.0	10.2	11.7	25.3
1976	114.7	23.4	91.4	28.4	39.1	12.1	11.7	124.2	34.6	89.7	29.8	12.3	16.2	31.4
1977	120.8	24.3	96.5	29.8	39.8	13.4	13.5	151.9	45.0	106.9	35.7	14.0	18.6	38.6
1978 [1]	142.1	29.9	112.2	34.2	47.5	15.2	15.3	176.0	42.6	133.4	40.7	19.3	25.0	48.4
1979	184.4	35.5	149.0	52.2	60.2	17.9	18.7	212.0	60.4	151.6	47.5	24.6	26.6	52.8
1980	224.3	42.0	182.2	65.1	76.3	17.4	23.4	249.8	79.5	170.2	53.0	31.6	28.3	57.4
1981	237.0	44.1	193.0	63.6	84.2	19.7	25.5	265.1	78.4	186.7	56.1	37.1	31.0	62.4
1982	211.2	37.3	173.9	57.7	76.5	17.2	22.4	247.6	62.0	185.7	48.6	38.4	34.3	64.3
1983	201.8	37.1	164.7	52.7	71.7	18.5	21.8	268.9	55.1	213.8	53.7	43.7	43.0	73.3
1984	219.9	38.4	181.5	56.8	77.0	22.4	25.3	332.4	58.1	274.4	66.1	60.4	56.5	91.4
1985	215.9	29.6	186.3	54.8	79.3	24.9	27.2	338.1	51.4	286.7	62.6	61.3	64.9	97.9
1986	223.3	27.2	196.2	59.4	82.8	25.1	28.9	368.4	34.3	334.1	69.9	72.0	78.1	114.2
1987	250.2	29.8	220.4	63.7	92.7	27.6	36.4	409.8	42.9	366.8	70.8	85.1	85.2	125.7
1988	320.2	38.8	281.4	82.6	119.1	33.4	46.3	447.2	39.6	407.6	83.1	102.2	87.9	134.4
1989 [1]	359.9	41.1	318.8	90.5	136.9	35.1	56.3	477.7	50.9	426.8	84.6	112.3	87.4	142.5
1990	387.4	40.2	347.2	97.0	153.0	36.2	61.0	498.4	62.3	436.1	83.0	116.4	88.2	148.5
1991	414.1	40.1	374.0	101.6	166.6	39.9	65.9	491.0	51.7	439.3	81.3	121.1	85.5	151.4
1992	439.6	44.1	395.6	101.7	176.4	46.9	70.6	536.5	51.6	484.9	89.1	134.8	91.5	169.6
1993	456.9	43.6	413.3	105.1	182.7	51.6	74.0	589.4	51.5	537.9	100.8	153.2	102.1	182.0
1994	502.9	47.1	455.8	112.7	205.7	57.5	79.9	668.7	51.3	617.4	113.6	185.0	118.1	200.6
1995	575.2	57.2	518.0	135.6	234.4	61.4	86.5	749.4	56.0	693.3	128.5	222.1	123.7	219.0
1996	612.1	61.5	550.6	138.7	254.0	64.4	93.6	803.1	72.7	730.4	136.1	228.4	128.7	237.1
1997	678.4	58.5	619.9	148.6	295.8	73.4	102.0	876.8	71.8	805.0	144.9	253.6	139.4	267.1
1998	670.4	53.2	617.3	139.4	299.8	72.5	105.5	918.6	50.9	867.7	151.6	269.8	148.6	297.7
1999	698.2	49.7	648.6	143.7	311.2	75.3	118.4	1,034.4	72.1	962.3	157.8	296.1	178.2	330.1
2000	784.8	52.8	732.0	168.4	357.0	80.4	126.3	1,230.6	126.1	1,104.4	183.5	347.7	195.0	378.3
2001	731.2	54.9	676.3	154.6	321.7	75.4	124.5	1,152.5	109.4	1,043.0	174.1	299.2	188.7	381.1
2002	697.4	54.5	642.9	151.4	290.4	78.9	122.1	1,171.9	109.3	1,062.7	166.3	284.9	202.8	408.6
2003	729.8	60.9	668.9	167.5	293.7	80.6	127.1	1,270.2	140.4	1,129.8	183.2	297.6	209.2	439.8
2004	822.0	62.9	759.0	199.1	327.5	89.2	143.2	1,485.5	189.9	1,295.6	234.5	346.1	227.3	487.6
2005	911.7	64.9	846.8	230.8	358.4	98.4	159.2	1,692.4	263.2	1,429.2	274.9	382.8	238.7	532.8
2006	1,039.4	72.9	966.5	275.0	404.0	107.3	180.2	1,875.1	316.7	1,558.4	302.5	422.6	256.0	577.3
2007	1,164.0	92.1	1,071.8	315.5	433.0	121.3	202.1	1,982.8	346.7	1,636.2	310.8	449.1	258.5	617.8
2008	1,307.5	118.0	1,189.5	389.5	457.7	121.5	220.9	2,137.6	476.1	1,661.5	335.5	458.7	233.2	634.1
2009	1,069.7	101.0	968.8	294.3	391.5	81.7	201.3	1,575.5	267.7	1,307.8	210.8	374.1	159.2	563.8
2010	1,288.9	119.0	1,169.9	387.8	447.8	112.0	222.3	1,934.0	353.8	1,580.3	269.2	450.3	225.6	635.1
2011	1,497.4	140.0	1,357.4	496.4	493.2	133.1	234.6	2,235.8	462.3	1,773.5	319.8	513.4	255.2	685.1
2009: I	254.1	23.1	231.0	66.1	98.6	17.1	49.2	376.6	55.7	321.0	55.3	93.1	32.5	140.2
II	253.9	25.5	228.4	68.1	94.3	17.0	49.0	364.9	59.9	305.0	47.1	88.0	32.3	137.6
III	270.1	25.3	244.8	77.2	95.9	22.1	49.7	399.0	72.3	326.7	50.5	92.8	43.6	139.8
IV	291.7	27.1	264.6	82.9	102.7	25.6	53.4	435.0	79.8	355.1	57.9	100.2	50.8	146.2
2010: I	304.0	28.4	275.6	89.4	106.0	26.5	53.7	456.6	88.7	367.9	63.4	102.7	51.0	150.8
II	315.5	26.9	288.6	95.8	110.7	27.9	54.2	480.1	88.7	391.5	67.2	111.2	56.4	156.6
III	325.2	29.4	295.8	97.5	114.0	28.3	56.0	492.1	86.3	405.8	67.4	116.4	58.8	163.2
IV	344.2	34.3	309.8	105.0	117.1	29.3	58.4	505.3	90.2	415.1	71.2	120.1	59.4	164.5
2011: I	360.9	36.5	324.4	117.2	118.3	31.8	57.1	542.3	111.4	430.8	76.6	123.2	62.9	168.1
II	372.2	35.6	336.6	122.8	122.5	32.5	58.7	559.3	119.4	440.0	81.1	127.6	58.2	173.0
III	382.2	33.9	348.2	129.1	125.5	34.4	59.3	562.8	114.2	448.6	82.4	129.5	66.3	170.4
IV	382.2	34.0	348.2	127.4	126.9	34.4	59.5	571.4	117.3	454.1	79.8	133.1	67.7	173.6
2012: I	388.5	33.8	354.7	127.1	131.2	36.5	59.9	582.8	119.4	463.4	79.6	137.7	73.5	172.7
II	394.1	36.7	357.4	126.7	131.3	37.5	61.9	579.9	111.3	468.5	79.8	139.8	74.7	174.2
III ᵖ	393.4	40.6	352.8	120.9	133.6	36.4	61.8	567.3	100.7	466.6	80.1	136.5	76.1	173.8

[1] End-use commodity classifications beginning 1978 and 1989 are not strictly comparable with data for earlier periods. See *Survey of Current Business*, June 1988 and July 2001.

Note: Data are on a balance of payments basis. Beginning with data for 1999, exports of goods under the U.S. Foreign Military Sales program are included in "other" exports and imports of petroleum abroad by U.S. military agencies are included in imports of petroleum and products; prior to 1999, these transactions are included in services. Beginning with data for 1978, re-exports are assigned to detailed end-use categories in the same manner as exports of domestic goods.

Source: Department of Commerce (Bureau of Economic Analysis).

[Millions of dollars]

Item	2004	2005	2006	2007	2008	2009	2010	2011	2012 first 3 quarters at annual rate [1]
EXPORTS									
Total, all countries	821,986	911,686	1,039,406	1,163,957	1,307,499	1,069,733	1,288,882	1,497,406	1,568,043
Europe	194,296	213,452	247,642	288,916	331,868	263,832	289,515	335,393	340,572
Euro area [2]	127,373	138,294	156,150	180,691	203,542	164,870	178,076	198,248	197,984
France	21,157	22,612	24,009	27,217	29,681	26,989	27,369	28,490	31,616
Germany	31,782	34,874	41,919	50,115	55,322	43,949	48,526	49,626	50,096
Italy	10,903	11,627	12,750	14,372	15,755	12,428	14,396	16,246	16,663
United Kingdom	36,158	38,870	45,673	51,104	54,873	46,827	49,038	57,036	57,543
Canada	190,042	212,340	231,346	249,819	262,282	205,457	250,132	282,277	296,644
Latin America and Other Western Hemisphere	172,629	193,679	223,288	243,863	289,785	239,374	302,901	368,416	399,693
Brazil	13,870	15,343	19,008	24,304	32,435	26,097	35,353	42,821	42,753
Mexico	110,837	120,444	133,998	136,166	151,610	129,214	163,532	198,711	216,967
Venezuela	4,788	6,439	9,017	10,218	12,638	9,348	10,648	12,338	17,364
Asia and Pacific	226,576	244,220	280,513	312,005	339,342	291,572	369,060	418,116	429,717
China	34,833	41,874	54,813	64,313	71,346	70,636	93,029	105,263	107,972
India	6,170	8,014	9,775	15,048	17,845	16,480	19,335	21,616	22,029
Japan	53,458	54,817	59,276	62,796	67,178	52,944	61,483	67,204	73,271
Korea, Republic of	26,835	28,639	33,515	35,874	36,746	29,703	39,794	45,150	45,863
Singapore	19,606	20,755	24,172	25,932	28,576	22,648	29,105	31,373	30,437
Taiwan	22,264	22,794	23,817	26,854	26,177	19,402	26,763	27,113	25,756
Middle East	24,357	32,151	37,754	45,533	55,755	44,920	48,881	59,397	67,232
Africa	14,086	15,844	18,863	23,817	28,468	24,578	28,393	33,808	34,184
Memorandum: Members of OPEC [3]	22,570	31,781	39,265	48,757	65,386	50,430	54,526	65,370	78,508
IMPORTS									
Total, all countries	1,485,492	1,692,416	1,875,095	1,982,843	2,137,608	1,575,491	1,934,006	2,235,819	2,306,620
Europe	323,567	358,581	386,870	414,509	446,750	333,100	385,359	453,605	459,049
Euro area [2]	211,259	231,450	248,580	270,765	281,395	213,884	244,345	289,108	296,687
France	31,830	34,210	37,431	41,865	44,556	34,390	38,719	40,676	42,005
Germany	77,556	85,321	89,613	94,792	98,299	71,688	82,866	99,425	107,557
Italy	28,239	31,226	32,869	35,268	36,567	26,691	28,771	34,327	37,095
United Kingdom	46,418	51,469	54,087	57,215	59,418	47,780	50,706	51,878	54,944
Canada	259,377	293,960	305,822	319,498	341,640	227,208	281,034	320,538	330,629
Latin America and Other Western Hemisphere	257,925	297,364	337,128	351,251	382,247	288,475	365,045	442,901	461,476
Brazil	21,250	24,571	26,547	25,831	30,719	20,208	24,203	31,549	33,611
Mexico	158,598	173,771	202,434	215,350	220,856	179,638	232,726	267,345	285,417
Venezuela	24,946	34,006	37,206	39,997	51,531	28,149	32,825	43,391	38,463
Asia and Pacific	546,224	614,121	691,217	725,995	738,752	603,702	741,047	818,921	866,705
China	197,456	244,699	289,246	322,975	339,580	297,872	366,125	400,642	418,485
India	15,625	18,896	21,969	24,233	25,888	21,336	29,682	36,338	42,017
Japan	131,500	140,380	150,847	148,271	142,393	97,783	122,925	131,836	150,569
Korea, Republic of	46,757	44,142	46,386	48,648	49,312	39,919	49,535	57,454	60,023
Singapore	15,713	15,556	18,381	18,919	16,873	16,323	18,454	20,081	20,621
Taiwan	35,193	35,350	38,699	38,814	36,857	28,731	35,974	41,526	39,087
Middle East	52,721	63,112	73,523	79,473	114,613	60,504	76,274	106,531	119,659
Africa	45,678	65,278	80,535	92,116	113,605	62,501	85,248	93,323	69,104
Memorandum: Members of OPEC [3]	95,215	125,501	146,507	176,145	245,143	113,100	151,467	193,947	185,176
BALANCE (excess of exports +)									
Total, all countries	−663,507	−780,730	−835,689	−818,886	−830,109	−505,758	−645,124	−738,413	−738,577
Europe	−129,271	−145,129	−139,228	−125,593	−114,882	−69,268	−95,844	−118,212	−118,477
Euro area [2]	−83,887	−93,156	−92,430	−90,074	−77,853	−49,014	−66,269	−90,860	−98,701
France	−10,674	−11,598	−13,422	−14,649	−14,875	−7,402	−11,350	−12,186	−10,391
Germany	−45,774	−50,447	−47,694	−44,677	−42,977	−27,739	−34,340	−49,799	−57,460
Italy	−17,336	−19,599	−20,119	−20,896	−20,812	−14,263	−14,375	−18,081	−20,432
United Kingdom	−10,260	−12,599	−8,414	−6,110	−4,545	−954	−1,668	5,158	2,599
Canada	−69,335	−81,620	−74,476	−69,679	−79,359	−21,751	−30,902	−38,261	−33,984
Latin America and Other Western Hemisphere	−85,297	−103,685	−113,839	−107,388	−92,462	−49,101	−62,144	−74,486	−61,780
Brazil	−7,380	−9,228	−7,539	−1,528	1,716	5,890	11,150	11,272	9,145
Mexico	−47,761	−53,327	−68,436	−79,184	−69,246	−50,424	−69,195	−68,634	−68,451
Venezuela	−20,157	−27,567	−28,189	−29,779	−38,893	−18,801	−22,177	−31,053	−21,097
Asia and Pacific	−319,648	−369,901	−410,705	−413,990	−399,410	−312,130	−371,987	−400,805	−436,989
China	−162,623	−202,825	−234,433	−258,662	−268,234	−227,236	−273,096	−295,378	−310,513
India	−9,455	−10,882	−12,194	−9,185	−8,043	−4,856	−10,347	−14,722	−19,988
Japan	−78,042	−85,562	−91,571	−85,475	−75,214	−44,840	−61,442	−64,632	−77,299
Korea, Republic of	−19,922	−15,503	−12,872	−12,774	−12,566	−10,216	−9,741	−12,304	−14,160
Singapore	3,893	5,199	5,791	7,013	11,703	6,326	10,652	11,292	9,815
Taiwan	−12,928	−12,555	−14,883	−11,959	−10,680	−9,329	−9,211	−14,413	−13,329
Middle East	−28,364	−30,961	−35,769	−33,940	−58,859	−15,585	−27,393	−47,134	−52,427
Africa	−31,593	−49,434	−61,672	−68,298	−85,137	−37,923	−56,855	−59,514	−34,920
Memorandum: Members of OPEC [3]	−72,645	−93,720	−107,242	−127,389	−179,757	−62,670	−96,941	−128,577	−106,667

[1] Preliminary; seasonally adjusted.

[2] Euro area consists of: Austria, Belgium, Cyprus (beginning in 2008), Estonia (beginning in 2011), Finland, France, Germany, Greece (beginning in 2001), Ireland, Italy, Luxembourg, Malta (beginning in 2008), Netherlands, Portugal, Slovakia (beginning in 2009), Slovenia (beginning in 2007), and Spain.

[3] Organization of Petroleum Exporting Countries, consisting of Algeria, Angola (beginning in 2007), Ecuador (beginning in 2007), Indonesia (ending in 2008), Iran, Iraq, Kuwait, Libya, Nigeria, Qatar, Saudi Arabia, United Arab Emirates, and Venezuela.

Note: Data are on a balance of payments basis. For further details, and additional data by country, see *Survey of Current Business*, January 2013.

Source: Department of Commerce (Bureau of Economic Analysis).

TABLE B–106. U.S. international trade in goods on balance of payments (BOP) and Census basis, and trade in services on BOP basis, 1985–2012

[Billions of dollars; monthly data seasonally adjusted]

Year or month	Goods: Exports (f.a.s. value) [1,2]							Goods: Imports (customs value) [6]							Services (BOP basis)	
	Total, BOP basis [3,4]	Census basis (by end-use category)						Total, BOP basis [4]	Census basis (by end-use category)						Exports [4]	Imports [4]
		Total, Census basis [3,5]	Foods, feeds, and beverages	Industrial supplies and materials	Capital goods except automotive	Automotive vehicles, parts, and engines	Consumer goods (nonfood) except automotive		Total, Census basis [5]	Foods, feeds, and beverages	Industrial supplies and materials	Capital goods except automotive	Automotive vehicles, parts, and engines	Consumer goods (nonfood) except automotive		
1985	215.9	[8] 218.8	24.0	58.5	73.9	22.9	12.6	338.1	[7] 336.5	21.9	113.9	65.1	66.8	68.3	73.2	72.9
1986	223.3	[8] 227.2	22.3	57.3	75.8	21.7	14.2	368.4	365.4	24.4	101.3	71.8	78.2	79.4	86.7	80.1
1987	250.2	254.1	24.3	66.7	86.2	24.6	17.7	409.8	406.2	24.8	111.0	84.5	85.2	88.7	98.7	90.8
1988	320.2	322.4	32.3	85.1	109.2	29.3	23.1	447.2	441.0	24.8	118.3	101.4	87.7	95.9	110.9	98.5
1989	359.9	363.8	37.2	99.3	138.8	34.8	36.4	477.7	473.2	25.1	132.3	113.3	86.1	102.9	127.1	102.5
1990	387.4	393.6	35.1	104.4	152.7	37.4	43.3	498.4	495.3	26.6	143.2	116.4	87.3	105.7	147.8	117.7
1991	414.1	421.7	35.7	109.7	166.7	40.0	45.9	491.0	488.5	26.5	131.6	120.7	85.7	108.0	164.3	118.5
1992	439.6	448.2	40.3	109.1	175.9	47.0	51.4	536.5	532.7	27.6	138.6	134.3	91.8	122.7	177.3	119.6
1993	456.9	465.1	40.6	111.8	181.7	52.4	54.7	589.4	580.7	27.9	145.6	152.4	102.4	134.0	185.9	123.8
1994	502.9	512.6	42.0	121.4	205.0	57.8	60.0	668.7	663.3	31.0	162.0	184.4	118.3	146.3	200.4	133.1
1995	575.2	584.7	50.5	146.2	233.0	61.8	64.4	749.4	743.5	33.2	181.8	221.4	123.8	159.9	219.2	141.4
1996	612.1	625.1	55.5	147.7	253.0	65.0	70.1	803.1	795.3	35.7	204.5	228.1	128.9	172.0	239.5	152.6
1997	678.4	689.2	51.5	158.2	294.5	74.0	77.4	876.8	869.7	39.7	213.8	253.3	139.8	193.8	256.1	165.9
1998	670.4	682.1	46.4	148.3	299.4	72.4	80.3	918.6	911.9	41.2	200.1	269.5	148.7	217.0	262.8	180.7
1999	698.2	695.8	46.0	147.5	310.8	75.3	80.9	1,034.4	1,024.6	43.6	221.4	295.7	179.0	241.9	268.8	195.8
2000	784.8	781.9	47.9	172.6	356.9	80.4	89.4	1,230.6	1,218.0	46.0	299.0	347.0	195.9	281.8	288.0	219.0
2001	731.2	729.1	49.4	160.1	321.7	75.4	88.3	1,152.5	1,141.0	46.6	273.9	298.0	189.8	284.3	276.5	217.0
2002	697.4	693.1	49.6	156.8	290.4	78.9	84.4	1,171.9	1,161.4	49.7	267.7	283.3	203.7	307.8	283.4	226.4
2003	729.8	724.8	55.0	173.0	293.7	80.6	89.9	1,270.2	1,257.1	55.8	313.8	295.9	210.1	333.9	293.7	244.3
2004	822.0	814.9	56.6	203.9	327.5	89.2	103.2	1,485.5	1,469.7	62.1	412.8	343.6	228.2	372.9	341.2	283.0
2005	911.7	901.1	59.0	233.0	358.4	98.4	115.3	1,692.4	1,673.5	68.1	523.8	379.3	239.4	407.2	375.8	303.6
2006	1,039.4	1,026.0	66.0	276.0	404.0	107.3	129.1	1,875.1	1,853.9	74.9	602.0	418.3	256.6	442.6	420.4	338.0
2007	1,164.0	1,148.2	84.3	316.4	433.0	121.3	146.0	1,982.8	1,957.0	81.7	634.7	444.5	256.7	474.6	490.6	368.4
2008	1,307.5	1,287.4	108.3	388.0	457.7	121.5	161.3	2,137.6	2,103.6	89.0	779.5	453.7	231.2	481.6	535.2	403.4
2009	1,069.7	1,056.0	93.9	296.5	391.2	81.7	149.5	1,575.5	1,559.6	81.6	462.4	370.5	157.7	427.3	509.2	382.6
2010	1,288.9	1,278.3	107.7	391.5	447.5	112.0	165.2	1,934.0	1,913.2	91.7	602.5	449.3	225.1	483.2	553.6	403.2
2011	1,497.4	1,480.4	126.2	500.3	493.0	133.1	175.0	2,235.8	2,207.8	107.5	755.8	510.7	254.6	514.1	606.0	427.4
2011: Jan	119.1	117.6	10.4	39.4	39.0	10.6	13.9	181.0	178.9	8.4	60.8	41.7	21.2	41.7	49.0	34.6
Feb	117.7	115.9	10.4	38.6	39.1	10.2	13.9	177.0	174.8	8.6	57.4	39.9	20.3	43.6	48.9	34.3
Mar	124.2	122.5	11.1	41.3	40.2	11.1	14.4	184.3	182.1	8.6	63.6	41.3	21.2	42.0	50.0	34.8
Apr	125.6	124.1	10.9	42.7	41.0	10.7	14.7	184.1	181.9	8.9	63.0	41.8	19.1	43.7	50.1	35.1
May	124.9	123.5	10.9	41.5	41.2	10.9	14.4	187.9	185.5	9.0	66.2	42.7	19.4	42.8	50.8	35.4
June	121.7	120.2	10.2	39.8	40.2	10.9	14.9	187.3	184.8	9.1	64.5	42.5	19.6	43.2	51.0	35.7
July	126.6	125.1	10.4	42.2	41.9	11.8	14.5	187.5	185.1	8.9	63.0	42.9	22.3	43.0	51.8	36.4
Aug	126.5	125.2	10.5	42.9	41.7	11.1	14.7	186.7	184.4	8.9	62.9	42.8	21.5	42.4	51.9	36.4
Sept	129.1	127.5	10.4	44.3	41.8	11.4	15.2	188.6	186.0	9.1	63.9	43.0	22.4	42.3	51.6	36.5
Oct	127.9	126.7	10.4	42.9	42.4	11.4	14.8	188.4	185.9	9.4	62.2	43.7	21.8	43.4	50.8	36.0
Nov	126.4	125.2	10.3	42.1	42.2	11.3	14.9	189.7	187.4	9.3	63.5	43.6	22.6	42.7	50.3	35.9
Dec	127.9	126.8	10.5	42.8	42.2	11.8	14.8	193.3	191.1	9.2	64.8	44.9	23.2	43.4	49.9	36.2
2012: Jan	128.0	126.5	10.4	41.8	43.2	12.5	14.4	194.8	192.5	9.6	65.4	44.5	24.2	43.1	50.8	36.2
Feb	128.4	126.9	9.8	42.1	43.3	12.1	14.8	188.4	186.4	9.0	62.0	44.6	24.6	40.3	51.9	36.4
Mar	132.2	130.8	10.2	43.9	44.6	11.9	14.9	199.6	197.5	9.2	65.7	47.8	24.6	43.8	52.7	36.9
Apr	130.6	129.0	10.9	42.9	43.2	12.3	15.1	195.8	193.8	9.2	65.2	45.8	24.3	43.5	52.1	36.5
May	130.8	129.6	11.8	42.0	43.9	12.2	14.9	193.9	191.9	9.1	61.5	47.2	24.8	43.2	52.5	36.3
June	132.8	131.5	11.0	42.6	44.2	12.9	15.8	190.2	188.2	9.0	59.1	46.0	25.5	42.4	52.9	36.4
July	130.7	129.3	12.9	40.2	44.1	12.3	15.3	188.4	186.6	9.1	57.2	45.4	26.2	42.9	52.8	36.7
Aug	128.7	127.2	11.8	39.0	44.5	12.2	14.9	187.6	185.6	9.2	58.7	44.9	25.3	41.6	53.0	36.7
Sept	133.9	132.5	12.9	42.4	44.9	11.9	15.4	191.3	189.2	9.3	59.7	45.5	24.4	44.2	53.4	36.3
Oct	127.7	126.3	11.5	39.6	43.0	11.6	15.3	186.8	184.6	8.9	60.1	45.1	24.0	40.7	53.1	36.1
Nov [p]	129.3	128.1	11.1	40.2	44.0	12.3	15.4	195.0	193.1	9.4	61.4	45.5	25.6	45.3	53.2	36.3

[1] Department of Defense shipments of grant-aid military supplies and equipment under the Military Assistance Program are excluded from total exports through 1985 and included beginning 1986.

[2] F.a.s. (free alongside ship) value basis at U.S. port of exportation for exports.

[3] Beginning with data for 1989, exports have been adjusted for undocumented exports to Canada and are included in the appropriate end-use categories. For prior years, only total exports include this adjustment.

[4] Beginning with data for 1999, exports of goods under the U.S. Foreign Military Sales program and fuel purchases by foreign air and ocean carriers in U.S. ports are included in goods exports (BOP basis) and excluded from services exports. Beginning with data for 1999, imports of petroleum abroad by U.S. military agencies and fuel purchases by U.S. air and ocean carriers in foreign ports are included in goods imports (BOP basis) and excluded from services imports.

[5] Total includes "other" exports or imports, not shown separately.

[6] Total arrivals of imported goods other than in-transit shipments.

[7] Total includes revisions not reflected in detail.

[8] Total exports are on a revised statistical month basis; end-use categories are on a statistical month basis.

Note: Goods on a Census basis are adjusted to a BOP basis by the Bureau of Economic Analysis, in line with concepts and definitions used to prepare international and national accounts. The adjustments are necessary to supplement coverage of Census data, to eliminate duplication of transactions recorded elsewhere in international accounts, to value transactions according to a standard definition, and for earlier years, to record transactions in the appropriate period.

Data include international trade of the U.S. Virgin Islands, Puerto Rico, and U.S. Foreign Trade Zones.

Source: Department of Commerce (Bureau of the Census and Bureau of Economic Analysis).

TABLE B–107. International investment position of the United States at year-end, 2005–2011

[Millions of dollars]

Type of investment	2005	2006	2007	2008	2009	2010	2011 ᵖ
NET INTERNATIONAL INVESTMENT POSITION OF THE UNITED STATES	-1,932,149	-2,191,653	-1,796,005	-3,260,158	-2,321,770	-2,473,599	-4,030,250
Financial derivatives, net	57,915	59,836	71,472	159,635	126,335	110,382	126,252
Net international investment position, excluding financial derivatives	-1,990,064	-2,251,489	-1,867,477	-3,419,793	-2,448,105	-2,583,981	-4,156,502
U.S.-OWNED ASSETS ABROAD	11,961,552	14,428,137	18,399,676	19,464,717	18,511,691	20,298,413	21,132,370
Financial derivatives, gross positive fair value	1,190,029	1,238,995	2,559,332	6,127,450	3,489,779	3,652,313	4,704,666
U.S.-owned assets abroad, excluding financial derivatives	10,771,523	13,189,142	15,840,344	13,337,267	15,021,912	16,646,100	16,427,704
U.S. official reserve assets	188,043	219,853	277,211	293,732	403,804	488,673	536,036
Gold [1]	134,175	165,267	218,025	227,439	284,380	367,537	400,355
Special drawing rights	8,210	8,870	9,476	9,340	57,814	56,824	54,956
Reserve position in the International Monetary Fund	8,036	5,040	4,244	7,683	11,385	12,492	30,080
Foreign currencies	37,622	40,676	45,466	49,270	50,225	51,820	50,645
U.S. Government assets, other than official reserve assets	77,523	72,189	94,471	624,099	82,774	75,235	178,901
U.S. credits and other long-term assets [2]	76,960	71,635	70,015	69,877	71,830	74,399	78,373
Repayable in dollars	76,687	71,362	69,742	69,604	71,557	74,126	78,100
Other [3]	273	273	273	273	273	273	273
U.S. foreign currency holdings and U.S. short-term assets [4]	563	554	24,456	554,222	10,944	836	100,528
U.S. private assets	10,505,957	12,897,100	15,468,662	12,419,436	14,535,334	16,082,192	15,712,767
Direct investment at current cost	2,651,721	2,948,172	3,553,095	3,748,512	4,029,457	4,306,843	4,681,569
Foreign securities	4,329,259	5,604,475	6,835,079	3,985,712	5,565,636	6,336,370	5,922,001
Bonds	1,011,554	1,275,515	1,587,089	1,237,284	1,570,341	1,689,462	1,763,754
Corporate stocks	3,317,705	4,328,960	5,247,990	2,748,428	3,995,295	4,646,908	4,158,247
U.S. claims on unaffiliated foreigners reported by U.S. nonbanking concerns	1,018,462	1,184,073	1,233,341	930,909	930,337	874,762	796,827
U.S. claims reported by U.S. banks and securities brokers, not included elsewhere	2,506,515	3,160,380	3,847,147	3,754,303	4,009,904	4,564,217	4,312,370
FOREIGN-OWNED ASSETS IN THE UNITED STATES	13,893,701	16,619,790	20,195,681	22,724,875	20,833,461	22,772,012	25,162,620
Financial derivatives, gross negative fair value	1,132,114	1,179,159	2,487,860	5,967,815	3,363,444	3,541,931	4,578,414
Foreign-owned assets in the United States, excluding financial derivatives	12,761,587	15,440,631	17,707,821	16,757,060	17,470,017	19,230,081	20,584,206
Foreign official assets in the United States	2,313,295	2,832,999	3,411,831	3,943,862	4,402,809	4,912,727	5,250,792
U.S. Government securities	1,725,193	2,167,112	2,540,062	3,264,139	3,588,575	3,993,275	4,277,348
U.S. Treasury securities	1,340,598	1,558,317	1,736,687	2,400,516	2,879,612	3,364,758	3,653,065
Other	384,595	608,795	803,375	863,623	708,963	628,517	624,283
Other U.S. Government liabilities [5]	22,869	26,053	31,860	40,694	99,119	110,464	119,359
U.S. liabilities reported by U.S. banks and securities brokers, not included elsewhere	296,647	297,012	406,031	256,355	187,507	179,540	209,550
Other foreign official assets	268,586	342,822	433,878	382,674	527,608	629,448	644,535
Other foreign assets	10,448,292	12,607,632	14,295,990	12,813,198	13,067,208	14,317,354	15,333,414
Direct investment at current cost	1,905,979	2,154,062	2,345,923	2,397,396	2,398,208	2,597,707	2,908,791
U.S. Treasury securities	643,793	567,861	639,755	852,458	790,985	1,101,828	1,418,050
U.S. securities other than U.S. Treasury securities	4,352,998	5,372,339	6,190,018	4,620,661	5,319,948	5,933,958	5,968,177
Corporate and other bonds	2,243,135	2,824,871	3,289,070	2,770,606	2,825,638	2,915,698	2,909,962
Corporate stocks	2,109,863	2,547,468	2,900,948	1,850,055	2,494,310	3,018,260	3,058,215
U.S. currency	280,400	282,627	271,952	301,139	313,771	342,090	397,086
U.S. liabilities to unaffiliated foreigners reported by U.S. nonbanking concerns	658,177	799,471	863,140	740,553	706,387	643,618	629,728
U.S. liabilities reported by U.S. banks and securities brokers, not included elsewhere	2,606,945	3,431,272	3,985,202	3,900,991	3,537,909	3,698,153	4,011,582
Memoranda:							
Direct investment abroad at market value	3,637,996	4,470,343	5,274,991	3,102,418	4,287,203	4,766,730	4,499,962
Direct investment in the United States at market value	2,817,970	3,293,053	3,551,307	2,486,446	2,995,459	3,397,411	3,509,359

[1] U.S. official gold stock is valued at market prices.

[2] Also includes paid-in capital subscriptions to international financial institutions and resources provided to foreigners under foreign assistance programs requiring repayment over several years. Excludes World War I debts that are not being serviced.

[3] Includes indebtedness that the borrower may contractually, or at its option, repay with its currency, with a third country's currency, or by delivery of materials or transfer of services.

[4] Beginning in 2007, includes foreign-currency-denominated assets obtained through temporary reciprocal currency arrangements between the Federal Reserve System and foreign central banks.

[5] Includes U.S. Government liabilities associated with military sales contracts and U.S. Government reserve-related liabilities from allocations of special drawing rights (SDRs).

Note: For details regarding these data, see Survey of Current Business, July 2012.

Source: Department of Commerce (Bureau of Economic Analysis).

TABLE B–108. Industrial production and consumer prices, major industrial countries, 1986–2012

Year or quarter	United States[1]	Canada	Japan	France	Germany[2]	Italy	United Kingdom
	Industrial production (Index, 2007=100)[3]						
1986	55.3	64.3	73.9	74.3	64.0	75.0	81.0
1987	58.1	67.0	76.5	75.8	64.3	77.3	84.2
1988	61.1	71.5	83.8	78.8	66.5	82.2	88.3
1989	61.7	71.2	88.7	81.7	69.7	85.2	90.1
1990	62.3	69.3	92.3	86.6	73.3	85.4	89.8
1991	61.3	66.8	93.9	86.2	78.2	84.6	86.8
1992	63.0	67.7	88.2	84.6	76.5	83.7	87.1
1993	65.1	70.9	84.9	81.1	70.7	81.7	89.0
1994	68.5	75.4	85.7	84.6	72.8	86.6	93.8
1995	71.8	78.8	88.3	86.8	73.6	91.8	95.5
1996	75.0	79.7	90.1	86.6	73.6	90.2	96.8
1997	80.4	84.3	93.8	90.0	75.8	93.7	98.1
1998	85.1	87.2	87.2	93.2	78.6	94.9	99.6
1999	88.7	92.3	87.6	94.7	79.4	94.6	100.7
2000	92.3	100.3	92.2	98.1	83.9	98.6	102.8
2001	89.1	96.3	86.2	98.9	84.1	97.4	101.2
2002	89.3	97.8	85.1	97.5	83.2	96.0	99.6
2003	90.4	97.9	87.6	96.5	83.7	95.4	99.3
2004	92.5	99.5	91.8	97.8	86.2	95.2	100.2
2005	95.5	101.4	93.2	97.9	89.2	94.7	99.4
2006	97.6	100.8	97.1	98.8	94.3	98.1	99.5
2007	100.0	100.0	100.0	100.0	100.0	100.0	100.0
2008	96.5	95.5	96.6	97.2	100.0	96.2	97.2
2009	85.4	84.5	75.5	84.9	83.6	78.3	88.4
2010	90.1	89.7	88.1	88.9	92.6	83.6	90.3
2011	93.7	92.8	86.0	90.4	99.7	83.8	89.6
2012 p	97.1		85.2				
2011: I	92.6	92.8	86.4	91.0	98.5	84.6	90.8
II	92.9	91.9	82.8	90.5	99.5	85.0	89.7
III	94.2	93.1	87.3	90.4	101.3	83.5	89.6
IV	95.3	93.5	87.6	89.8	99.6	82.1	88.4
2012: I	96.7	93.4	88.7	89.3	99.4	80.2	88.1
II	97.3	93.9	87.0	88.8	99.2	78.6	87.3
III	97.4	93.7	83.3	88.5	100.1	78.2	87.9
IV p	97.6		81.8				
	Consumer prices (Index, 1982–84=100)						
1986	109.6	113.5	104.8	117.2	104.7	128.9	114.9
1987	113.6	118.4	105.0	121.1	105.0	135.0	119.7
1988	118.3	123.2	105.7	124.3	106.3	141.9	125.6
1989	124.0	129.3	108.1	128.7	109.2	150.8	135.4
1990	130.7	135.5	111.4	133.1	112.2	160.4	148.2
1991	136.2	143.1	115.1	137.3	116.7	170.6	156.9
1992	140.3	145.2	117.0	140.6	122.7	179.4	162.7
1993	144.5	147.9	118.5	143.6	128.1	187.3	165.3
1994	148.2	148.2	119.3	146.0	131.6	194.9	169.4
1995	152.4	151.4	119.2	148.6	133.9	205.2	175.1
1996	156.9	153.8	119.3	151.5	135.8	213.2	179.4
1997	160.5	156.2	121.4	153.3	138.4	217.6	185.0
1998	163.0	157.8	122.2	154.3	139.7	221.9	191.4
1999	166.6	160.5	121.8	155.2	140.5	225.5	194.3
2000	172.2	164.9	121.0	157.8	142.5	231.2	200.0
2001	177.1	169.1	120.1	160.3	145.3	237.7	203.7
2002	179.9	172.9	119.0	163.4	147.4	243.5	207.0
2003	184.0	177.7	118.7	166.9	148.9	250.1	213.0
2004	188.9	181.0	118.7	170.4	151.4	255.6	219.3
2005	195.3	185.0	118.4	173.4	153.7	260.6	225.6
2006	201.6	188.7	118.6	176.3	156.2	266.1	232.8
2007	207.342	192.7	118.7	178.9	159.7	270.9	242.7
2008	215.303	197.3	120.3	184.0	163.9	280.0	252.4
2009	214.537	197.9	118.7	184.1	164.5	282.2	251.1
2010	218.056	201.4	117.9	186.9	166.3	286.5	262.7
2011	224.939	207.2	117.5	190.9	170.2	294.5	276.3
2012 p	229.594	210.4	117.5	194.6	173.5	303.4	285.2
2011: I	221.666	204.8	117.4	189.1	168.8	291.0	271.3
II	225.531	207.6	117.7	191.2	169.9	293.8	276.0
III	226.452	208.0	117.7	191.1	170.7	295.5	277.5
IV	226.108	208.6	117.4	192.3	171.2	297.7	280.4
2012: I	227.907	209.6	117.7	193.4	172.4	300.5	281.5
II	229.793	210.9	117.9	195.0	173.2	303.4	284.6
III	230.297	210.5	117.2	194.8	174.0	304.8	285.6
IV p	230.380	210.5	117.1	195.3	174.6	305.0	289.0

[1] See Note, Table B–51 for information on U.S. industrial production series.
[2] Prior to 1991 data are for West Germany only.
[3] All data exclude construction. Quarterly data are seasonally adjusted.
Note: National sources data have been rebased for industrial production and consumer prices.
Sources: As reported by each country, Board of Governors of the Federal Reserve System, and Department of Labor (Bureau of Labor Statistics).

TABLE B–109. Civilian unemployment rate, and hourly compensation, major industrial countries, 1986–2012

[Quarterly data seasonally adjusted]

Year or quarter	United States	Canada	Japan	France	Germany [1]	Italy	United Kingdom
	Civilian unemployment rate (Percent) [2]						
1986	7.0	9.2	2.7	9.0	6.6	7.5	11.4
1987	6.2	8.4	2.6	9.2	6.3	7.9	10.5
1988	5.5	7.4	2.4	8.9	6.3	7.9	8.6
1989	5.3	7.1	2.2	8.3	5.7	7.8	7.3
1990	[3]5.6	7.7	2.0	8.0	5.0	7.0	7.1
1991	6.8	9.8	2.0	8.2	[3]5.6	[3]6.9	8.9
1992	7.5	10.7	2.1	9.1	6.7	7.3	10.0
1993	6.9	10.8	2.4	10.2	8.0	[3]9.8	10.4
1994	[3]6.1	[3]9.6	2.6	10.8	8.5	10.8	9.5
1995	5.6	8.6	2.9	10.2	8.2	11.3	8.7
1996	5.4	8.8	3.1	10.7	9.0	11.3	8.1
1997	4.9	8.4	3.1	10.8	9.9	11.3	7.0
1998	4.5	7.7	3.8	10.4	9.3	11.4	6.3
1999	4.2	7.0	4.2	10.1	[3]8.5	11.0	6.0
2000	4.0	6.1	4.4	8.6	7.8	10.1	5.5
2001	4.7	6.5	4.5	7.8	7.9	9.1	5.1
2002	5.8	7.0	4.9	8.0	8.6	8.6	5.2
2003	6.0	6.9	4.6	8.6	9.3	8.5	5.0
2004	5.5	6.4	4.2	9.0	10.3	8.1	4.8
2005	5.1	6.0	3.8	9.0	[3]11.2	7.8	4.9
2006	4.6	5.5	3.6	8.9	10.3	6.9	5.5
2007	4.6	5.2	3.6	8.1	8.7	6.2	5.4
2008	5.8	5.3	3.7	7.5	7.6	6.8	5.7
2009	9.3	7.3	4.8	9.2	7.8	7.9	7.7
2010	9.6	7.1	4.8	9.5	7.1	8.5	7.9
2011	8.9	6.5	4.2	9.4	6.0	8.5	8.1
2012	8.1						
2011: I	9.0	6.7	4.4	9.2	6.2	8.1	7.8
II	9.1	6.5	4.3	9.2	6.0	8.1	7.9
III	9.0	6.3	4.0	9.3	5.9	8.6	8.3
IV	8.7	6.5	4.1	9.5	5.8	9.3	8.4
2012: I	8.2	6.4	4.2	9.7	5.7	10.1	8.2
II	8.2	6.4	4.0	9.9	5.7	10.6	8.1
III	8.0	6.3	3.8	10.0	5.8	10.7	7.9
IV	7.8						
	Manufacturing hourly compensation in U.S. dollars (Index, 2002=100) [4]						
1986	53.8	64.5	48.5	54.1	46.2	61.2	41.9
1987	55.6	69.2	58.2	64.7	58.3	75.9	51.5
1988	57.5	78.0	67.2	67.6	62.1	81.2	59.0
1989	59.3	84.9	66.1	66.7	61.0	85.0	57.5
1990	62.1	91.8	67.2	81.8	76.3	104.8	70.3
1991	65.8	100.0	77.1	83.5	78.9	110.0	79.0
1992	68.9	99.4	84.8	93.5	92.1	118.0	79.0
1993	70.5	94.2	99.5	91.1	92.3	96.3	69.4
1994	72.2	91.5	110.2	96.4	98.5	99.1	72.4
1995	73.4	93.3	123.8	110.6	117.7	103.6	76.1
1996	74.6	95.3	108.0	109.7	117.3	115.6	74.9
1997	76.5	95.3	100.3	99.5	103.5	109.6	82.5
1998	81.2	94.0	95.0	99.3	103.9	105.9	89.4
1999	84.8	96.1	109.3	98.4	101.8	103.4	93.1
2000	91.3	99.0	114.6	89.7	92.7	92.1	91.4
2001	94.8	97.6	102.9	89.3	92.7	92.1	90.2
2002	100.0	100.0	100.0	100.0	100.0	100.0	100.0
2003	108.0	115.8	105.7	122.8	122.2	124.3	115.2
2004	108.9	129.0	112.0	139.3	135.0	141.5	135.6
2005	112.5	145.3	108.3	144.4	136.7	145.8	141.9
2006	114.8	163.1	100.9	151.4	143.4	150.3	152.4
2007	118.5	177.4	99.4	168.5	157.9	168.5	170.8
2008	123.5	181.6	117.2	185.8	174.0	189.1	163.3
2009	128.6	171.9	129.8	183.6	171.7	184.8	142.2
2010	130.0	185.9	136.9	178.0	160.8	180.3	147.5
2011	133.5	198.1	154.0	191.7	172.6	193.5	156.4

[1] Prior to 1991 data are for West Germany only.

[2] Civilian unemployment rates, approximating U.S. concepts. Quarterly data for Germany should be viewed as less precise indicators of unemployment under U.S. concepts than the annual data.

[3] There are breaks in the series for Canada (1994), Germany (1991, 1999, and 2005), Italy (1991 and 1993), and the United States (1990 and 1994). For details, see *International Comparisons of Annual Labor Force Statistics, Adjusted to U.S. Concepts, 16 Countries, 1970–2011*, June 7, 2012, Appendix B, at http://www.bls.gov/ilc/flscomparelf/country_notes.htm.

[4] Hourly compensation in manufacturing, U.S. dollar basis; data relate to all employed persons (employees and self-employed workers). For details, see *International Comparisons of Manufacturing Productivity and Unit Labor Cost Trends, 2011*, December 6, 2012.

Source: Department of Labor (Bureau of Labor Statistics).

TABLE B–110. Foreign exchange rates, 1993–2012

[Foreign currency units per U.S. dollar, except as noted; certified noon buying rates in New York]

Period	Australia (dollar)[1]	Canada (dollar)	China, P.R. (yuan)	EMU Members (euro)[1,2]	Germany (mark)[2]	Japan (yen)	Mexico (peso)	South Korea (won)	Sweden (krona)	Switzer-land (franc)	United Kingdom (pound)[1]
March 1973	1.4129	0.9967	2.2401		2.8132	261.90	0.013	398.85	4.4294	3.2171	2.4724
1993	.6799	1.2902	5.7795		1.6545	111.08	3.116	805.75	7.7956	1.4781	1.5016
1994	.7316	1.3664	8.6397		1.6216	102.18	3.385	806.93	7.7161	1.3667	1.5319
1995	.7407	1.3725	8.3700		1.4321	93.96	6.447	772.69	7.1406	1.1812	1.5785
1996	.7828	1.3638	8.3389		1.5049	108.78	7.600	805.00	6.7082	1.2361	1.5607
1997	.7437	1.3849	8.3193		1.7348	121.06	7.918	953.19	7.6447	1.4514	1.6376
1998	.6291	1.4836	8.3008		1.7597	130.99	9.152	1,400.40	7.9522	1.4506	1.6573
1999	.6454	1.4858	8.2783	1.0653		113.73	9.553	1,189.84	8.2740	1.5045	1.6172
2000	.5815	1.4855	8.2784	.9232		107.80	9.459	1,130.90	9.1735	1.6904	1.5156
2001	.5169	1.5487	8.2770	.8952		121.57	9.337	1,292.01	10.3425	1.6891	1.4396
2002	.5437	1.5704	8.2771	.9454		125.22	9.663	1,250.31	9.7233	1.5567	1.5025
2003	.6524	1.4008	8.2772	1.1321		115.94	10.793	1,192.08	8.0787	1.3450	1.6347
2004	.7365	1.3017	8.2768	1.2438		108.15	11.290	1,145.24	7.3480	1.2428	1.8330
2005	.7627	1.2115	8.1936	1.2449		110.11	10.894	1,023.75	7.4710	1.2459	1.8204
2006	.7535	1.1340	7.9723	1.2563		116.31	10.906	954.32	7.3718	1.2532	1.8434
2007	.8391	1.0734	7.6058	1.3711		117.76	10.928	928.97	6.7550	1.1999	2.0020
2008	.8537	1.0660	6.9477	1.4726		103.39	11.143	1,098.71	6.5846	1.0816	1.8545
2009	.7927	1.1412	6.8307	1.3935		93.68	13.498	1,274.63	7.6539	1.0860	1.5661
2010	.9200	1.0298	6.7696	1.3261		87.78	12.624	1,155.74	7.2053	1.0432	1.5452
2011	1.0332	.9887	6.4630	1.3931		79.70	12.427	1,106.94	6.4878	.8862	1.6043
2012	1.0359	.9995	6.3093	1.2859		79.82	13.154	1,126.16	6.7721	.9377	1.5853
2011: I	1.0055	.9856	6.5783	1.3699		82.24	12.060	1,118.58	6.4779	.9404	1.6027
II	1.0626	.9677	6.4986	1.4399		81.56	11.723	1,082.63	6.2607	.8699	1.6309
III	1.0496	.9803	6.4155	1.4123		77.62	12.332	1,084.50	6.4783	.8247	1.6102
IV	1.0133	1.0227	6.3584	1.3476		77.34	13.638	1,144.16	6.7460	.9127	1.5718
2012: I	1.0557	1.0009	6.3099	1.3121		79.40	12.966	1,129.61	6.7462	.9206	1.5721
II	1.0103	1.0102	6.3305	1.2836		80.07	13.533	1,151.78	6.9474	.9365	1.5828
III	1.0396	.9954	6.3516	1.2508		78.60	13.164	1,132.62	6.7433	.9626	1.5801
IV	1.0386	.9912	6.2437	1.2977		81.21	12.941	1,089.71	6.6463	.9309	1.6065

Trade-weighted value of the U.S. dollar

	Nominal				Real[7]		
	G-10 index (March 1973=100)[3]	Broad index (January 1997=100)[4]	Major currencies index (March 1973=100)[5]	OITP index (January 1997=100)[6]	Broad index (March 1973=100)[4]	Major currencies index (March 1973=100)[5]	OITP index (March 1973=100)[6]
1993	93.2	83.78	89.90	63.37	89.13	85.46	102.33
1994	91.3	90.87	88.43	80.54	88.96	85.10	102.34
1995	84.2	92.65	83.41	92.51	86.51	81.24	102.40
1996	87.3	97.46	87.25	98.24	88.52	86.14	99.40
1997	96.4	104.43	93.93	104.64	93.23	93.41	100.45
1998	98.8	115.89	98.45	125.89	101.20	98.47	113.61
1999		116.16	97.06	129.20	100.34	98.14	112.19
2000		119.55	101.76	129.81	104.16	104.80	112.25
2001		126.06	107.87	135.92	110.16	112.23	116.81
2002		126.83	106.18	140.41	110.32	110.62	119.26
2003		119.27	93.15	143.57	103.66	97.60	120.87
2004		113.76	85.51	143.38	99.03	90.62	119.47
2005		110.84	83.86	138.86	97.37	90.37	115.80
2006		108.71	82.60	135.40	96.25	90.29	113.09
2007		103.58	77.95	130.23	91.66	86.13	107.51
2008		99.88	74.39	126.79	87.82	83.13	102.31
2009		105.66	77.65	135.89	91.40	86.21	106.78
2010		101.82	75.34	130.37	87.11	83.81	100.21
2011		97.15	70.82	125.76	82.61	79.51	95.01
2012		99.82	73.50	128.28	84.36	82.81	95.51
2011: I		97.75	71.79	125.84	83.16	80.23	95.46
II		95.28	69.51	123.32	81.16	78.00	93.45
III		95.90	69.71	124.46	81.67	78.55	93.96
IV		99.63	72.35	129.42	84.47	81.26	97.17
2012: I		98.87	72.84	126.97	83.82	81.96	95.19
II		100.64	73.91	129.57	85.02	83.16	96.54
III		100.64	74.07	129.35	84.96	83.52	96.09
IV		99.18	73.13	127.28	83.63	82.61	94.22

[1] U.S. dollars per foreign currency unit.
[2] European Economic and Monetary Union (EMU) members consists of Austria, Belgium, Cyprus (beginning in 2008), Estonia (beginning in 2011), Finland, France, Germany, Greece (beginning in 2001), Ireland, Italy, Luxembourg, Malta (beginning in 2008), Netherlands, Portugal, Slovakia (beginning in 2009), Slovenia (beginning in 2007), and Spain.
[3] G-10 index discontinued after December 1998.
[4] Weighted average of the foreign exchange value of the U.S. dollar against the currencies of a broad group of major U.S. trading partners.
[5] Subset of the broad index. Consists of currencies of the Euro area, Australia, Canada, Japan, Sweden, Switzerland, and the United Kingdom.
[6] Subset of the broad index. Consists of other important U.S. trading partners (OITP) whose currencies do not circulate widely outside the country of issue.
[7] Adjusted for changes in consumer price indexes for the United States and other countries.

Source: Board of Governors of the Federal Reserve System.

TABLE B-111. International reserves, selected years, 1992-2012

[Millions of special drawing rights (SDRs); end of period]

Area and country	1992	2002	2008	2009	2010	2011	2012 October	2012 November
World [1]	760,743	1,893,351	4,847,162	5,481,698	6,299,077	6,973,923	7,358,466	7,396,619
Advanced economies [1]	557,729	1,160,382	1,674,769	1,954,435	2,196,889	2,439,216	2,610,056	2,621,991
United States	52,995	59,160	52,396	85,519	87,977	98,331	100,799	100,522
Japan	52,937	340,088	656,178	652,926	690,127	820,373	800,455	801,186
United Kingdom	27,300	27,973	29,142	35,881	44,728	51,983	58,601	58,563
Canada	8,662	27,225	28,426	34,601	37,015	42,766	44,056	44,331
Euro area (incl. ECB) [1]		195,771	154,221	192,559	207,103	218,426	228,970	229,941
Austria	9,703	7,480	6,101	5,491	6,542	7,471	8,191	8,268
Belgium	10,914	9,010	6,306	10,403	10,970	11,927	12,433	12,322
Cyprus	764	2,239	416	524	350	344	314	313
Estonia	127	736	2,574	2,534	1,660	127	183	184
Finland	3,862	6,885	4,587	6,250	4,813	5,173	5,584	5,554
France	22,522	24,268	24,630	32,487	38,974	34,404	36,752	38,364
Germany	69,489	41,516	31,846	42,059	44,277	47,416	48,295	48,132
Greece	3,606	6,083	350	1,118	976	939	966	977
Ireland	2,514	3,989	572	1,245	1,203	918	914	913
Italy	22,438	23,798	26,838	31,955	33,722	34,796	36,123	35,809
Luxembourg	66	114	220	469	488	589	576	584
Malta	927	1,625	239	340	348	326	422	392
Netherlands	17,492	7,993	8,140	12,088	12,683	13,888	15,143	15,107
Portugal	14,474	8,889	1,281	1,996	2,802	1,717	1,873	1,900
Slovak Republic		6,519	11,631	477	503	592	569	568
Slovenia	520	5,143	567	620	605	545	505	496
Spain	33,640	25,992	8,376	11,930	12,749	21,709	23,501	23,544
Australia	8,429	15,307	20,015	24,935	25,193	27,957	30,503	28,597
China, P.R.: (Hong Kong)	25,589	82,308	118,468	163,152	174,446	185,830	195,786	198,784
Czech Republic		17,342	23,812	26,268	27,227	25,853	28,258	28,480
Denmark	8,090	19,924	26,347	47,464	47,803	53,277	56,222	56,132
Iceland	364	326	2,284	2,435	3,703	5,506	2,731	2,665
Israel	3,729	17,714	27,601	38,663	46,043	48,769	49,265	49,304
Korea	12,463	89,272	130,607	172,201	189,293	198,238	208,113	210,109
New Zealand	2,239	3,650	7,175	9,947	10,859	11,081	12,694	12,802
Norway	8,725	23,579	33,079	31,166	34,284	32,175	35,576	36,324
San Marino		135	459	504	292	223		
Singapore	29,048	60,322	112,955	119,661	146,428	154,714	164,878	166,507
Sweden	16,667	12,807	16,967	27,481	27,781	28,817	29,599	29,703
Switzerland	27,100	31,693	30,426	63,810	146,285	183,152	304,088	306,480
Taiwan Province of China	60,333	119,381	189,864	222,586	248,527	251,602	259,612	261,718
Emerging and developing economies ..	195,929	729,126	3,168,632	3,523,707	4,098,458	4,530,994	4,744,657	4,770,883
By area:								
Developing Asia	63,406	368,214	1,657,594	1,977,867	2,375,427	2,643,163	2,703,297	2,715,069
China, P.R. (Mainland)	15,441	214,815	1,266,206	1,542,335	1,862,240	2,087,326		
India	4,584	50,174	161,036	169,782	179,375	177,330	175,373	175,782
Europe	13,684	107,521	480,693	501,070	550,677	567,042	590,870	593,704
Russia		32,840	267,908	266,503	288,925	296,673	309,547	311,348
Middle East and North Africa	45,316	107,687	604,017	591,275	655,152	721,669	808,881	815,450
Sub-Saharan Africa	8,421	27,004	102,116	102,651	104,519	116,222	126,059	127,088
Western Hemisphere	65,102	118,700	324,212	350,844	412,682	482,898	515,550	519,572
Brazil	16,457	27,593	125,239	151,448	186,434	228,243	243,377	244,295
Mexico	13,800	37,223	61,766	63,536	78,101	93,908	104,318	105,278
Memoranda:								
Export earnings: Fuel	40,861	131,380	901,614	861,593	939,233	1,039,808	1,150,647	1,159,411
Export earnings: Nonfuel	155,068	597,746	2,267,018	2,662,114	3,159,225	3,491,186	3,594,010	3,611,472

[1] Includes data for European Central Bank (ECB) beginning 1999. Detail does not add to totals shown.

Note: International reserves consists of monetary authorities' holdings of gold (at SDR 35 per ounce), SDRs, reserve positions in the International Monetary Fund, and foreign exchange.

U.S. dollars per SDR (end of period) are: 1.37500 in 1992; 1.35952 in 2002; 1.54027 in 2008; 1.56769 in 2009; 1.54003 in 2010; 1.53527 in 2011; 1.54057 in October 2012; and 1.53481 in November 2012.

Source: International Monetary Fund, *International Financial Statistics.*

TABLE B–112. Growth rates in real gross domestic product, 1994–2013

[Percent change]

Area and country	1994–2003 annual average	2004	2005	2006	2007	2008	2009	2010	2011	2012[1]	2013[1]
World	3.4	4.9	4.6	5.3	5.4	2.8	−.6	5.1	3.9	3.2	3.5
Advanced economies	2.8	3.1	2.6	3.0	2.8	.1	−3.5	3.0	1.6	1.3	1.4
Of which:											
United States	3.3	3.5	3.1	2.7	1.9	−.3	−3.1	2.4	1.8	2.3	2.0
Euro area [2]	2.2	2.2	1.7	3.2	3.0	.4	−4.4	2.0	1.4	−.4	−.2
Germany	1.5	.7	.8	3.9	3.4	.8	−5.1	4.0	3.1	.9	.6
France	2.2	2.5	1.8	2.5	2.3	−.1	−3.1	1.7	1.7	.2	.3
Italy	1.7	1.7	.9	2.2	1.7	−1.2	−5.5	1.8	.4	−2.1	−1.0
Spain	3.6	3.3	3.6	4.1	3.5	.9	−3.7	−.3	.4	−1.4	−1.5
Japan	0.9	2.4	1.3	1.7	2.2	−1.0	−5.5	4.5	−.6	2.0	1.2
United Kingdom	3.5	2.9	2.8	2.6	3.6	−1.0	−4.0	1.8	.9	−.2	1.0
Canada	3.5	3.1	3.0	2.8	2.2	.7	−2.8	3.2	2.6	2.0	1.8
Memorandum:											
Newly industrialized Asian economies [3]	5.1	5.9	4.8	5.8	5.9	1.8	−.7	8.5	4.0	1.8	3.2
Emerging market and developing economies	4.4	7.5	7.3	8.2	8.7	6.1	2.7	7.4	6.3	5.1	5.5
Regional groups:											
Central and eastern Europe	3.4	7.3	5.9	6.4	5.4	3.2	−3.6	4.6	5.3	1.8	2.4
Commonwealth of Independent States [4]	0.6	8.2	6.7	8.8	9.0	5.4	−6.4	4.8	4.9	3.6	3.8
Russia	0.7	7.2	6.4	8.2	8.5	5.2	−7.8	4.3	4.3	3.6	3.7
Developing Asia	7.0	8.5	9.5	10.3	11.4	7.9	7.0	9.5	8.0	6.6	7.1
China	9.4	10.1	11.3	12.7	14.2	9.6	9.2	10.4	9.3	7.8	8.2
India	6.0	7.6	9.0	9.5	10.0	6.9	5.9	10.1	7.9	4.5	5.9
Latin America and the Caribbean	2.5	6.0	4.7	5.7	5.8	4.2	−1.5	6.2	4.5	3.0	3.6
Brazil	2.5	5.7	3.2	4.0	6.1	5.2	−.3	7.5	2.7	1.0	3.5
Mexico	2.6	4.0	3.2	5.1	3.2	1.2	−6.0	5.6	3.9	3.8	3.5
Middle East and North Africa	4.0	6.2	5.3	6.3	5.7	4.5	2.6	5.0	3.5	5.2	3.4
Sub-Saharan Africa	4.0	7.1	6.2	6.4	7.1	5.6	2.8	5.3	5.3	4.8	5.8

[1] All figures are forecasts as published by the International Monetary Fund. For the United States, the second estimate by the Department of Commerce shows that real GDP rose 2.2 percent in 2012.

[2] Euro area consists of: Austria, Belgium, Cyprus, Estonia, Finland, France, Germany, Greece, Ireland, Italy, Luxembourg, Malta, Netherlands, Portugal, Slovak Republic, Slovenia, and Spain.

[3] Consists of Hong Kong SAR (Special Administrative Region of China), Korea, Singapore, and Taiwan Province of China.

[4] Includes Georgia and Mongolia, which are not members of the Commonwealth of Independent States but are included for reasons of geography and similarities in economic structure.

Note: For details on data shown in this table, see *World Economic Outlook*, October 2012, and *World Economic Outlook Update*, January 2013, published by the International Monetary Fund.

Sources: Department of Commerce (Bureau of Economic Analysis) and International Monetary Fund.